WORKBOOK
Illustration / Spring 2014

Publisher & Owner / **Bill Daniels**

Advertising Sales Director / **Suzanne Semnacher**

Advertising Sales / **Linda Levy**
Bob Pastore
Mary Preussel

Design Director / **Anita Atencio**

Director of Production / **Paul Semnacher**

Online Portfolio Manager / **Kirsten Larson**

Social Media Manager / **Will Daniels**

Social Media Associate / **Jacqueline Lopez**

Directory Manager / **Angelica Vinther**

Directory Marketing Manager / **John Nixon**

Research / **Denise Gastelum**
Jacqueline Lopez
David Pavao
Scytorya Rhodes
Quardell Scott

Technology / **Jim Hudak**
Stephen Chiang

Finance / **Allan Gallant**
Eduardo Chevez

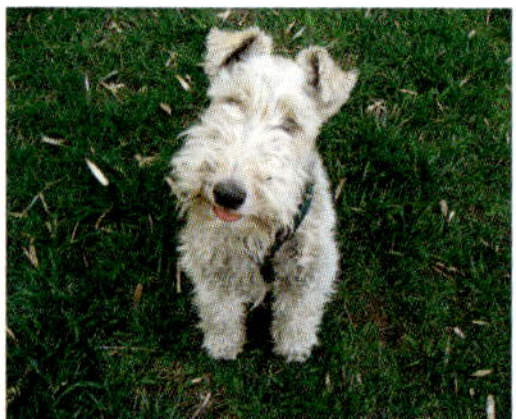

In Memory of our **Mr. "T"**

Meet our thin twin.

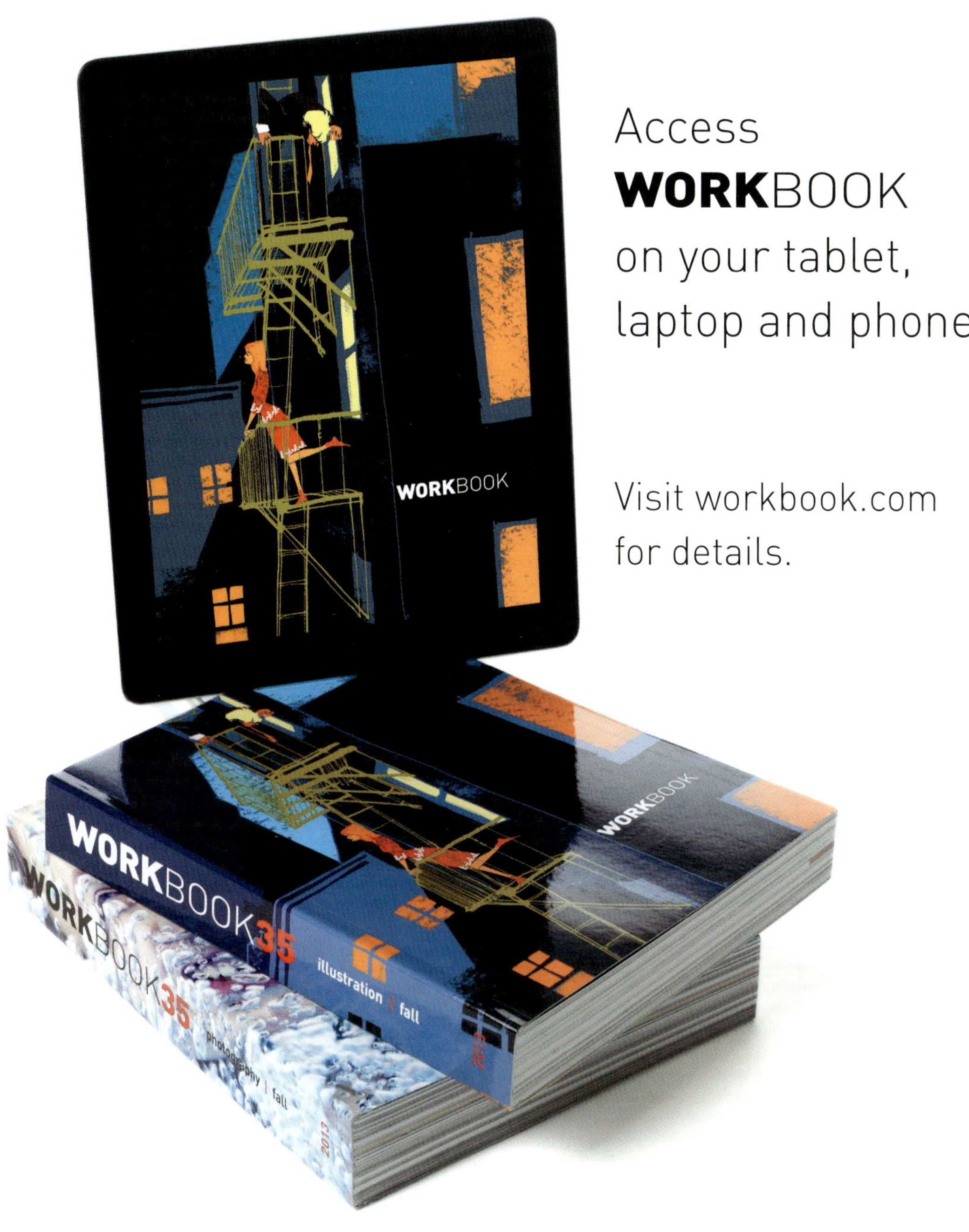

Access
WORKBOOK
on your tablet,
laptop and phone.

Visit workbook.com
for details.

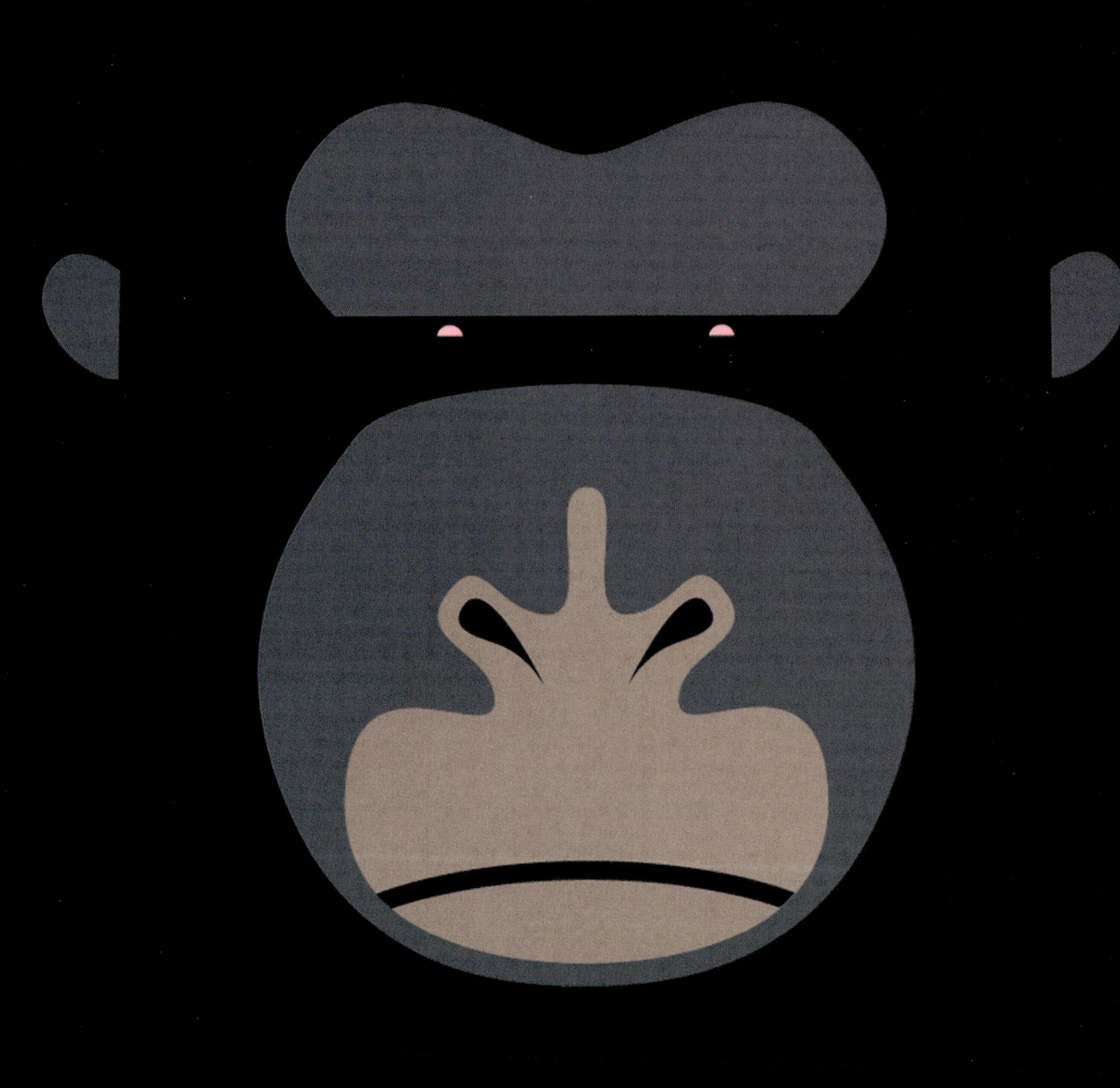

CONTENTS

C

D

*Artist's Representative

*Artist's Representative

*Artist's Representative

*Artist's Representative

/ LETTERING · LOGOS · DESIGN

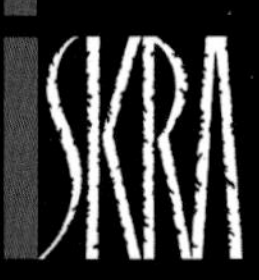

iSKRA

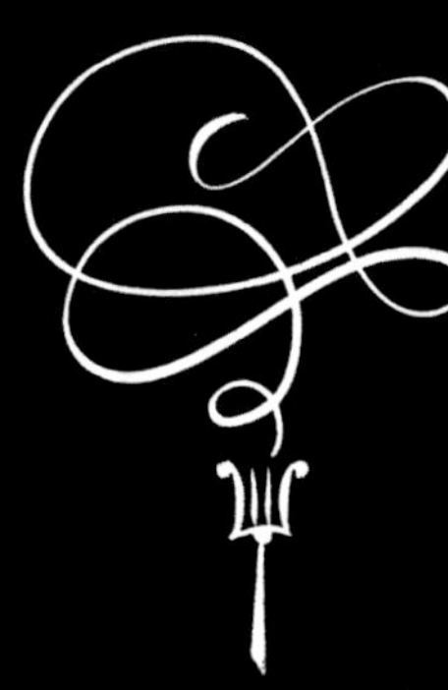

CONFESSIONS OF A WILD CHILD
Honey Springs
Costa Rican Blend
The Windflower
NO SLACK
SUNPOWER PRETZELS
Gold Quill Awards

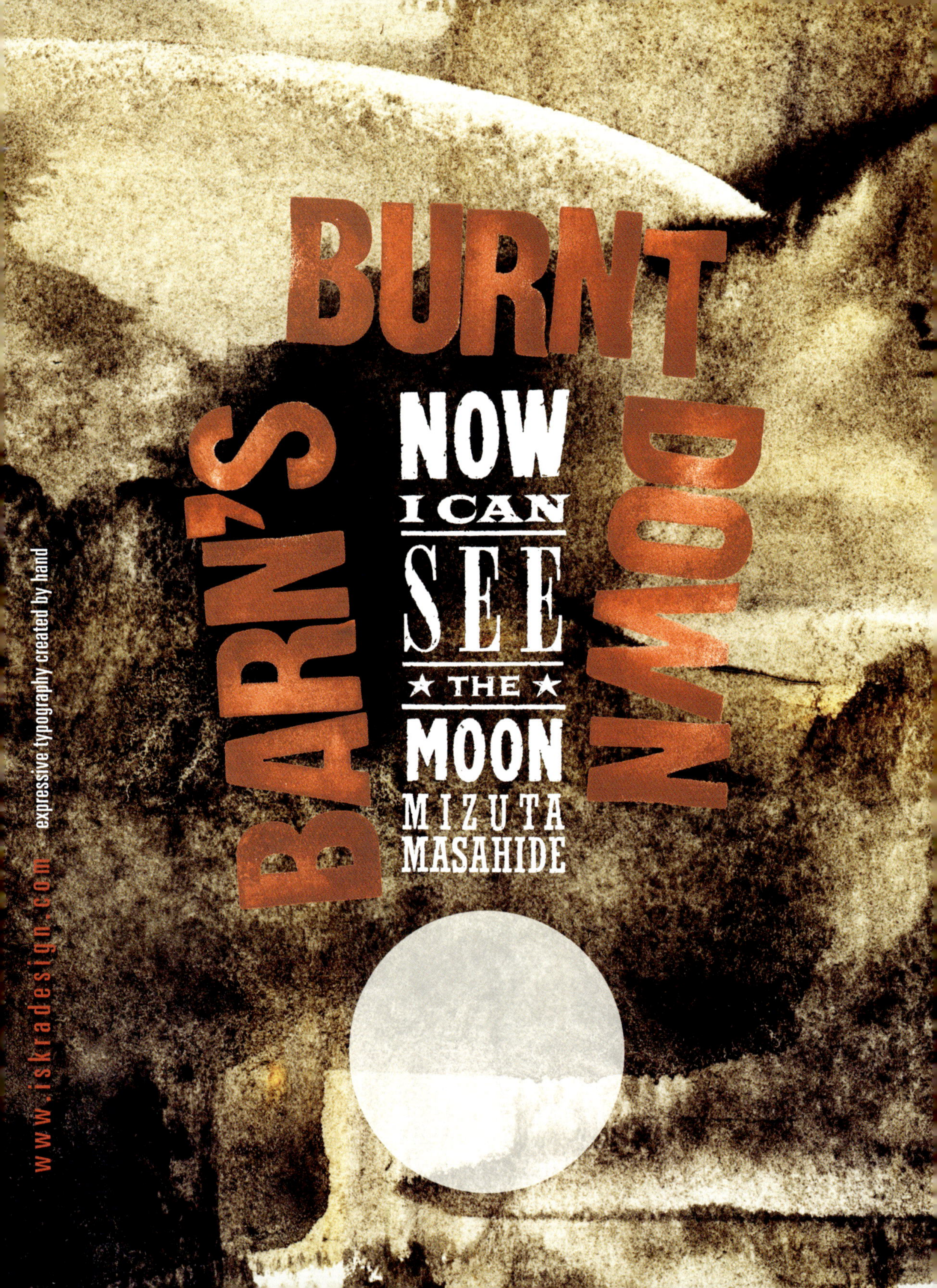

BURNT
DOWN
BARN'S
NOW
I CAN
SEE
★ THE ★
MOON
MIZUTA
MASAHIDE
www.iskradesign.com · expressive typography created by hand

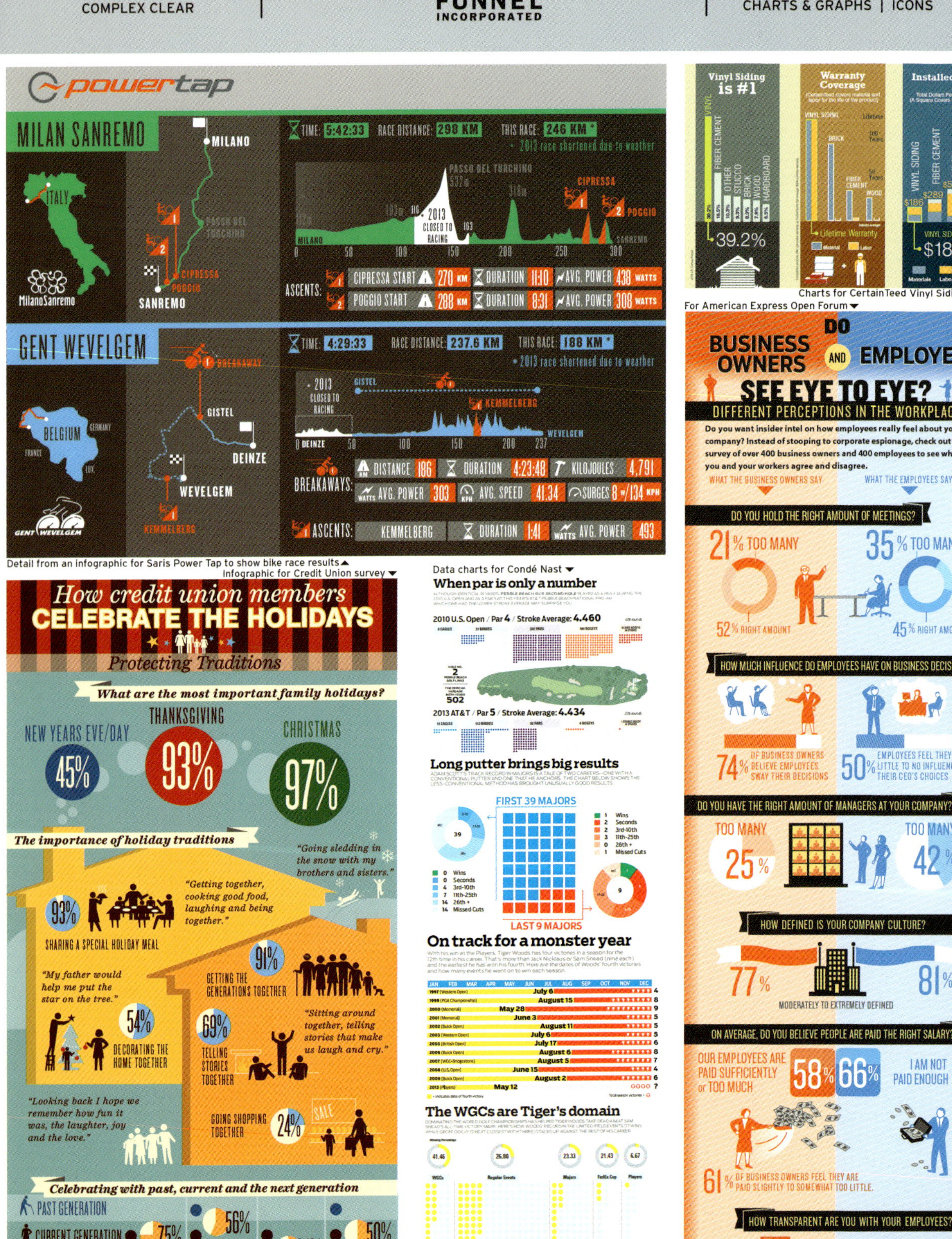

Detail from an infographic for Saris Power Tap to show bike race results ▲
Infographic for Credit Union survey ▼
For American Express Open Forum ▼

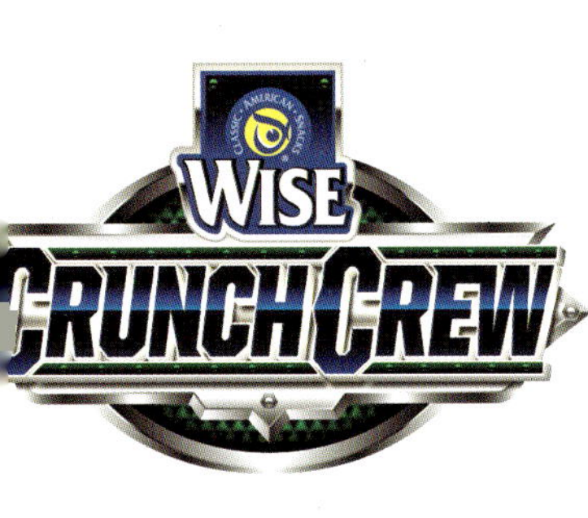
CLASSIC AMERICAN SNACKS
WISE
CRUNCH CREW

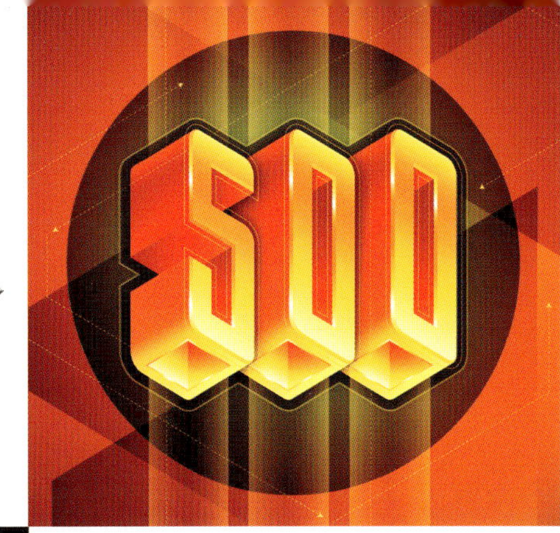
500

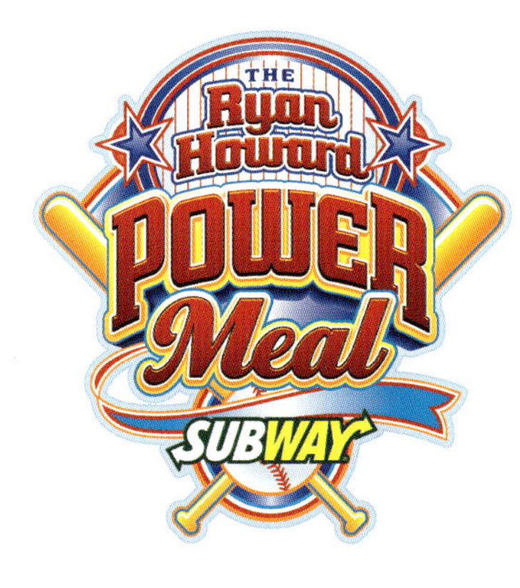
THE
Ryan Howard
POWER
Meal
SUBWAY

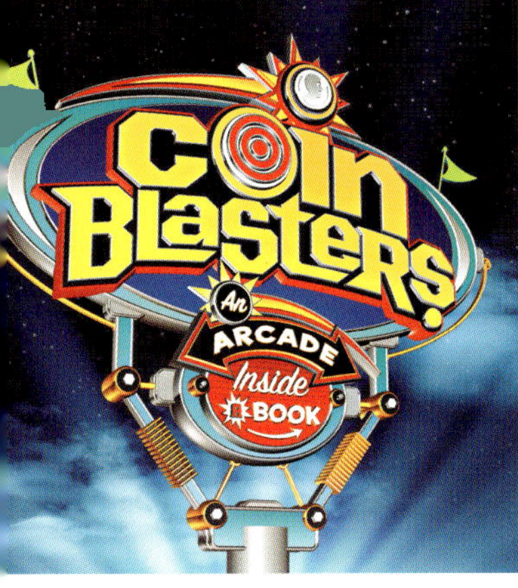
Coin Blasters!
An
ARCADE
Inside
BOOK

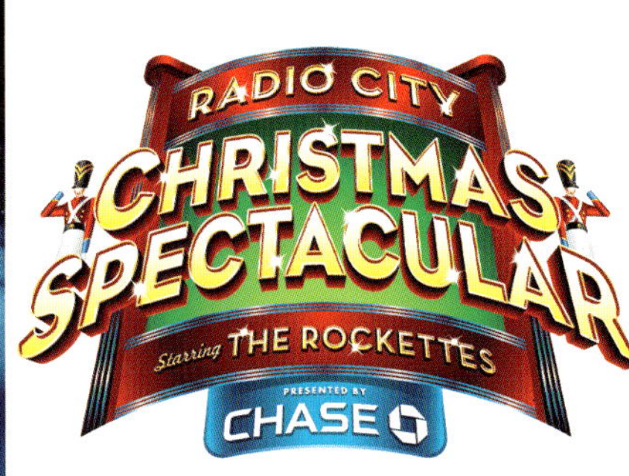
RADIO CITY
CHRISTMAS
SPECTACULAR
Starring THE ROCKETTES
PRESENTED BY
CHASE

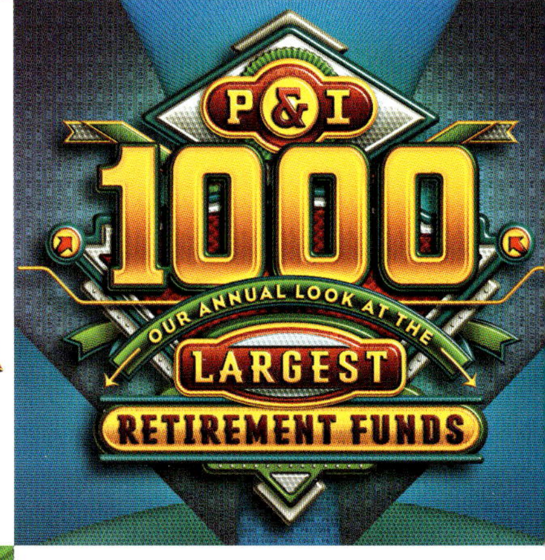
P&I
1000
OUR ANNUAL LOOK AT THE
LARGEST
RETIREMENT FUNDS

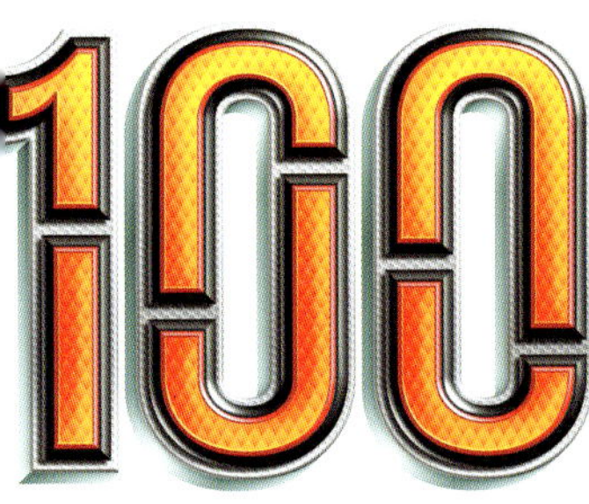
100

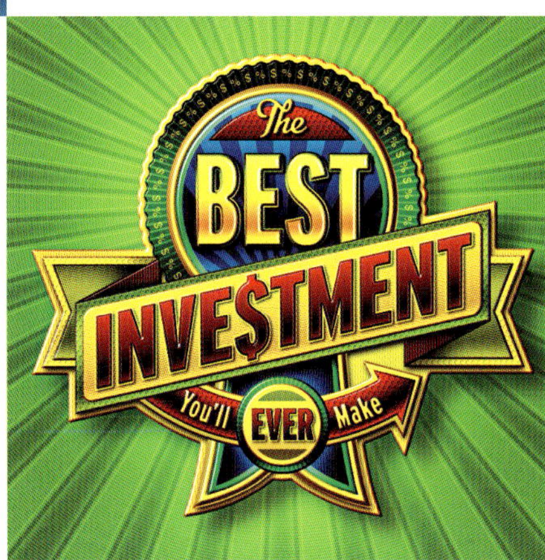
The
BEST
INVESTMENT
You'll EVER Make

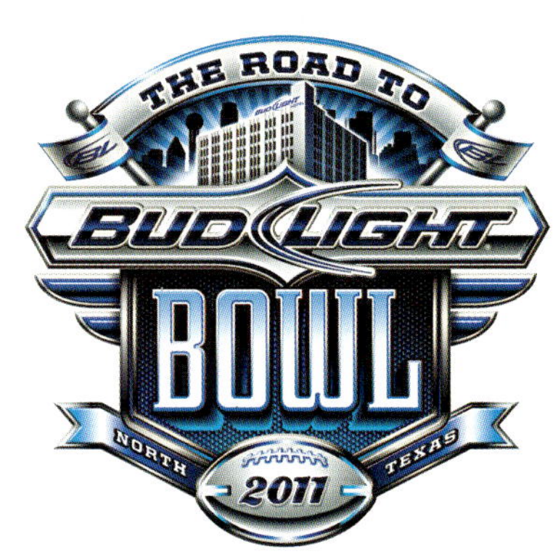
THE ROAD TO
BUD LIGHT
BOWL
NORTH   TEXAS
2011

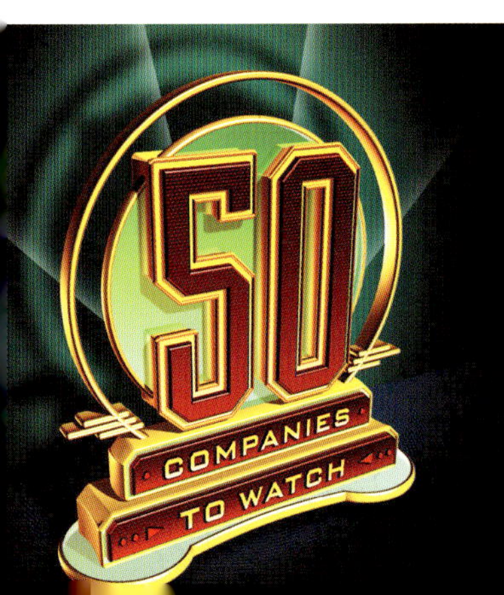
50
COMPANIES
TO WATCH

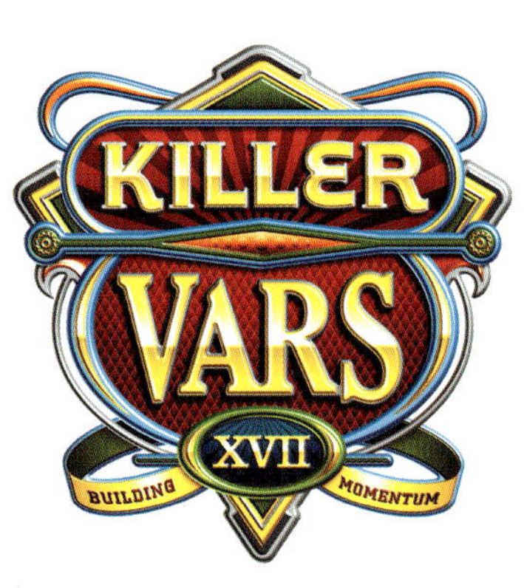
KILLER
VARS
XVII
BUILDING   MOMENTUM

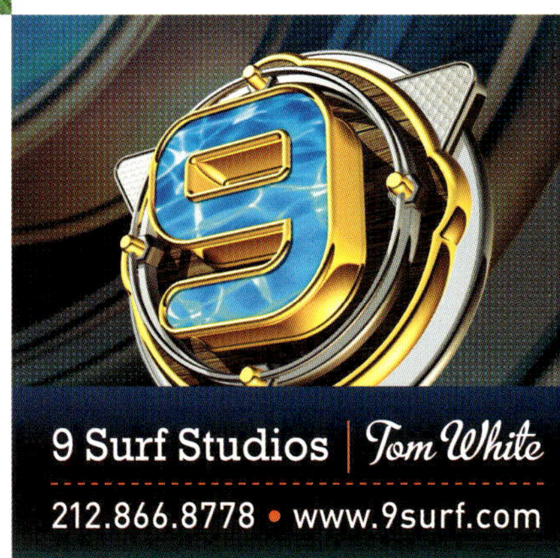
9
9 Surf Studios | Tom White
212.866.8778 • www.9surf.com

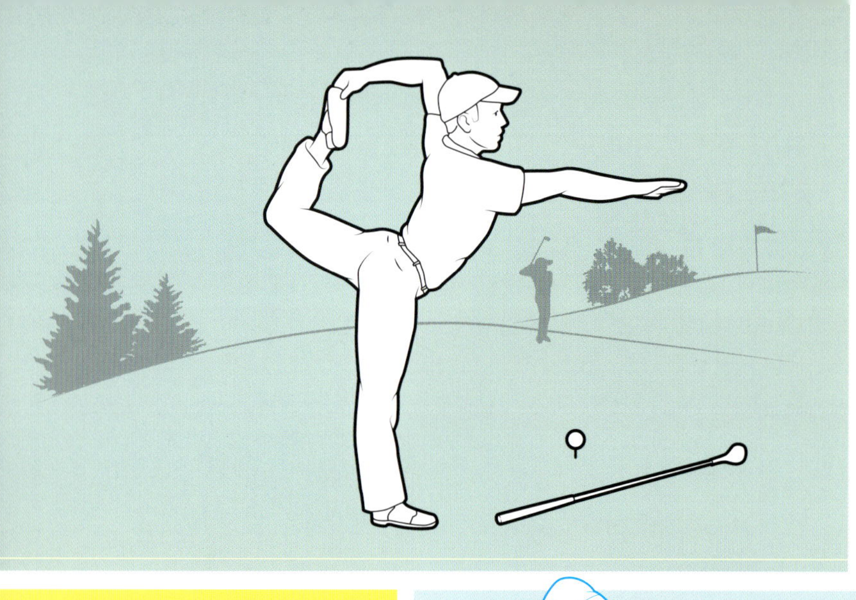

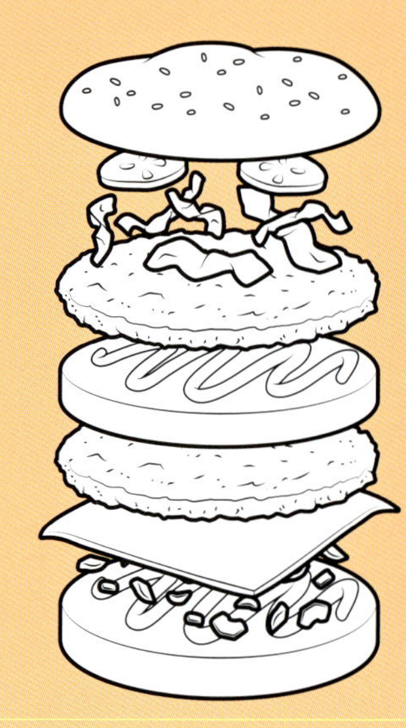

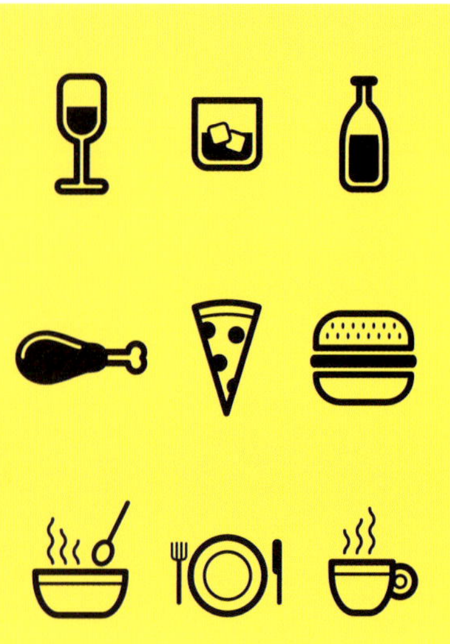

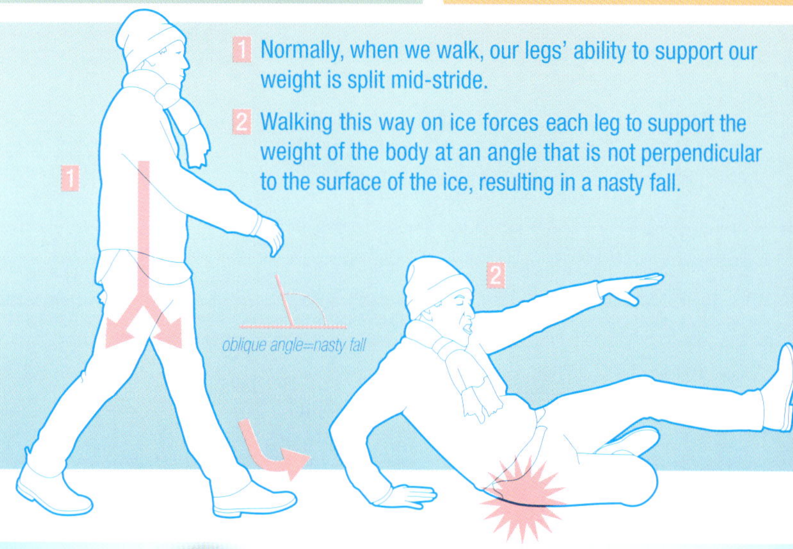

Normally, when we walk, our legs' ability to support our weight is split mid-stride.
Walking this way on ice forces each leg to support the weight of the body at an angle that is not perpendicular to the surface of the ice, resulting in a nasty fall.
oblique angle=nasty fall

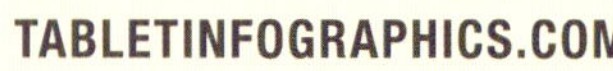

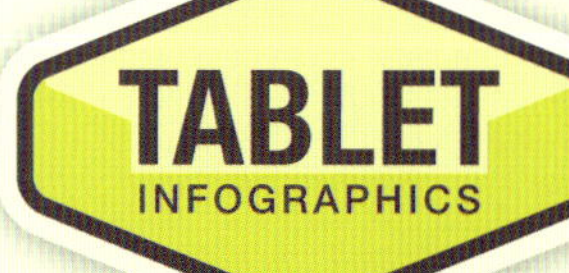

TABLET
INFOGRAPHICS

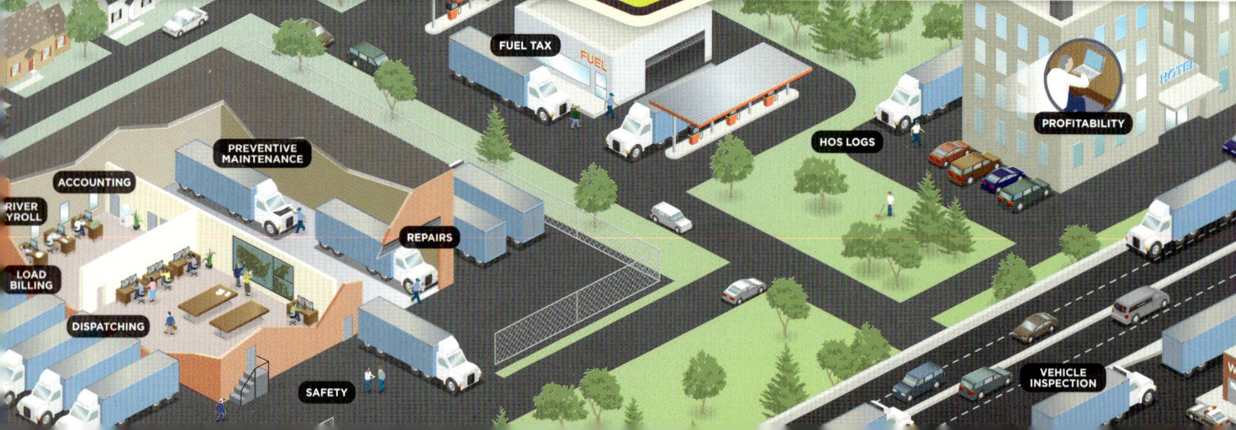

FUEL TAX
FUEL
PROFITABILITY
PREVENTIVE MAINTENANCE
HOS LOGS
ACCOUNTING
RIVER YROLL
REPAIRS
LOAD BILLING
DISPATCHING
SAFETY
VEHICLE INSPECTION

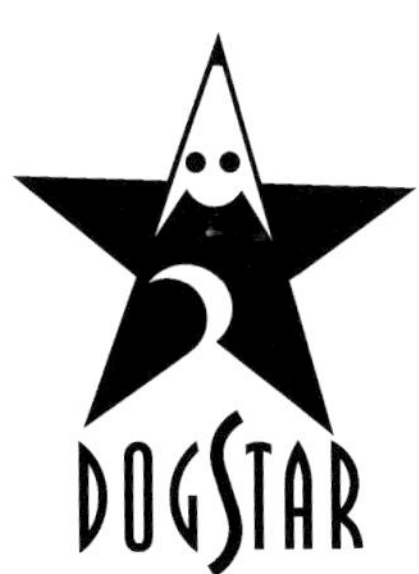

DESIGN & ILLUSTRATION
Rodney Davidson
205 591-2275
rodney@dogstardesign.com
www.dogstardesign.com

identity
iconography
character development
packaging
illustration

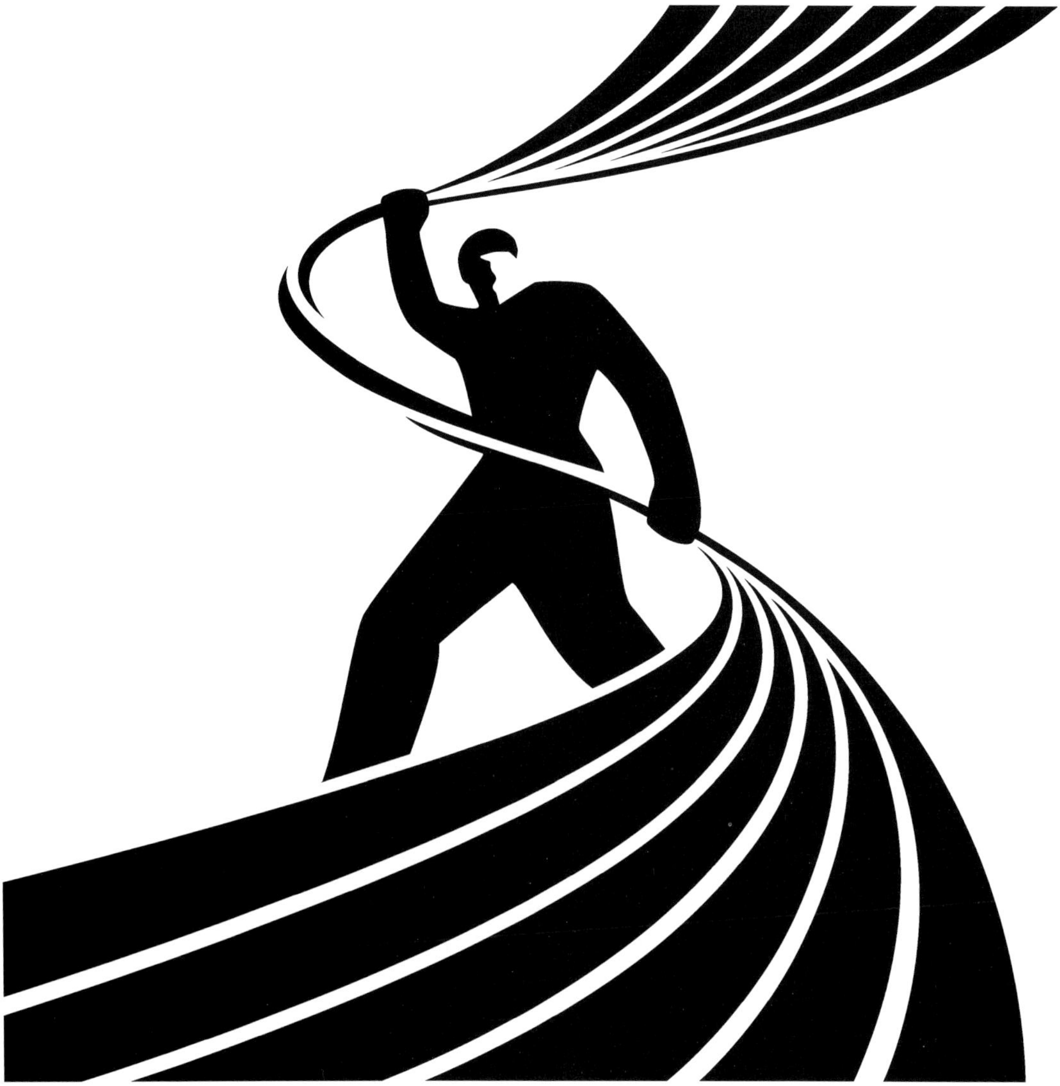

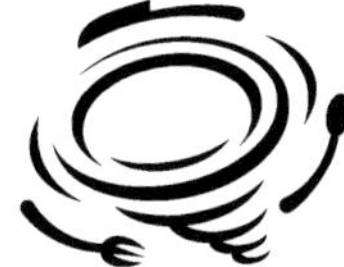

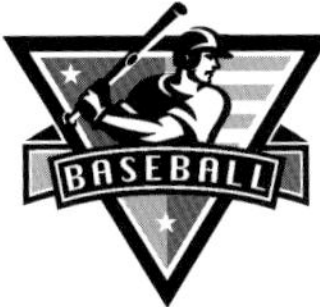

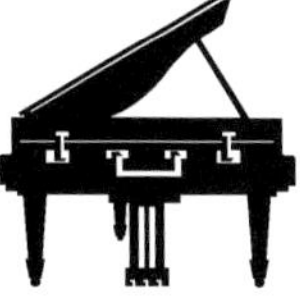

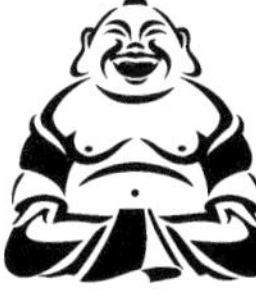

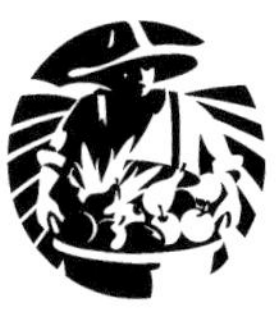

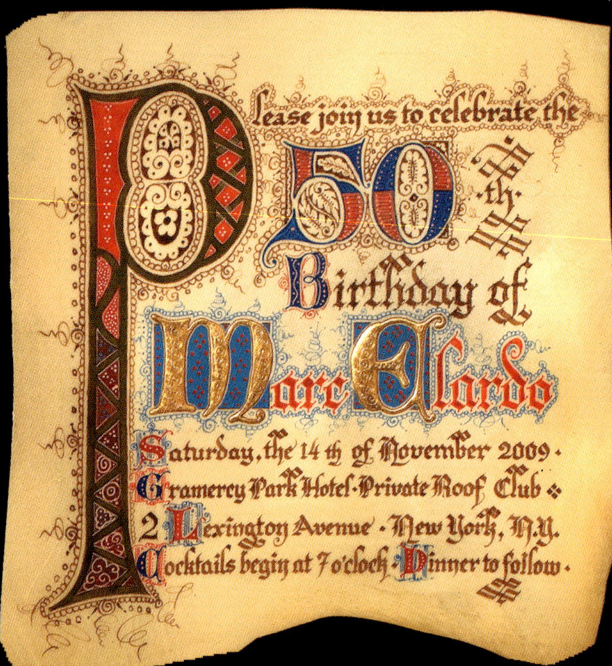

Please join us to celebrate the
50th
Birthday of
Marc Clardo
Saturday, the 14th of November 2009 ·
Gramercy Park Hotel · Private Roof Club ·
2 Lexington Avenue · New York, N.Y.
Cocktails begin at 7 o'clock · Dinner to follow ·

THE
TERROR
AND
THE
DREAM

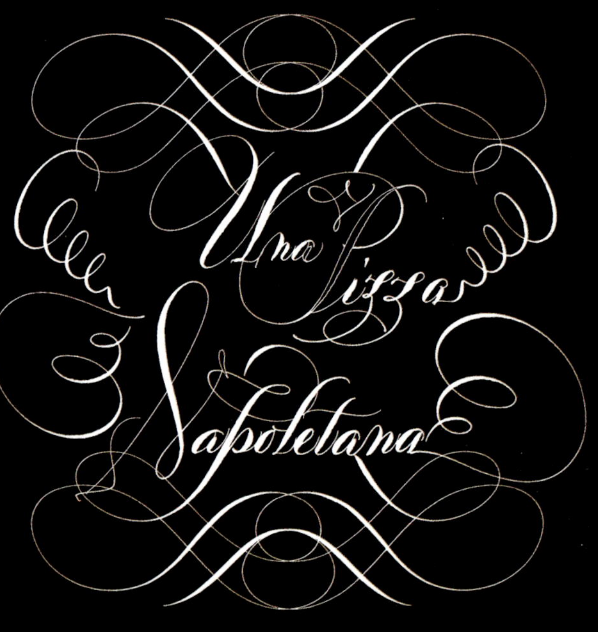

Una Pizza
Napoletana

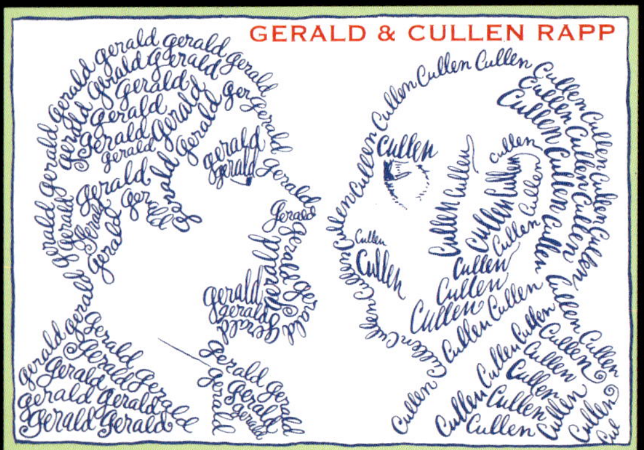

GERALD & CULLEN RAPP

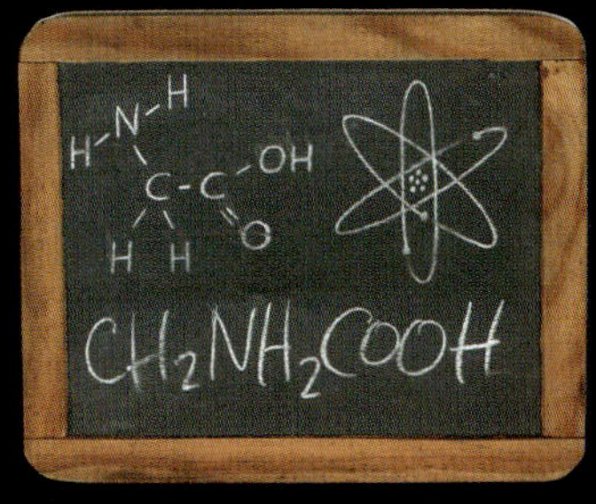

H–N–H
H–C–C–OH
H H O
CH_2NH_2COOH

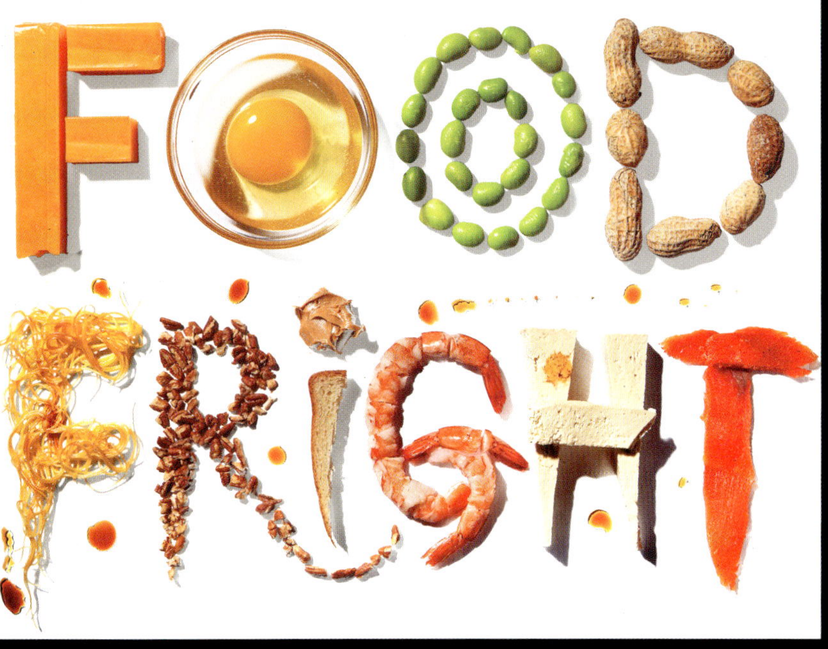

FOOD
FRIGHT

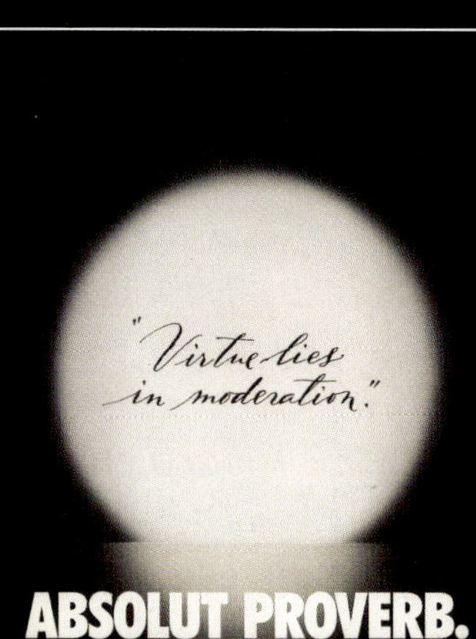

"Virtue lies in moderation."
ABSOLUT PROVERB.

IT'S THE SOFT WHITE, COMFORTING LIGHT YOU'RE FAMILIAR WITH. BUT IT'S A COMPACT FLUORESCENT. IT TURNS ON WITHOUT ANY DELAY. IT COMES IN A VERSATILE, COMPACT SIZE. IT'S INCREDIBLY ENERGY EFFICIENT. AND IT LASTS 10 TIMES LONGER THAN AN ORDINARY INCANDESCENT LIGHT BULB.* IT'S THE NEW SYLVANIA SOFT WHITE DULUX® EL.
SYLVANIA
BRILLIANT LIGHT

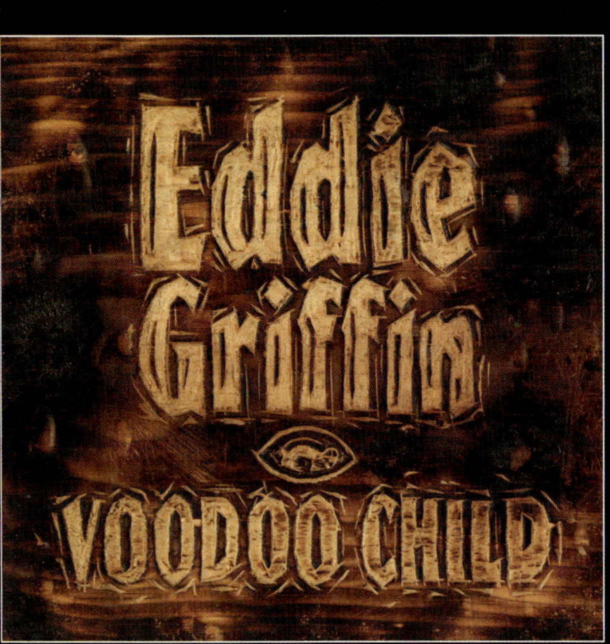

Eddie Griffin
VOODOO CHILD

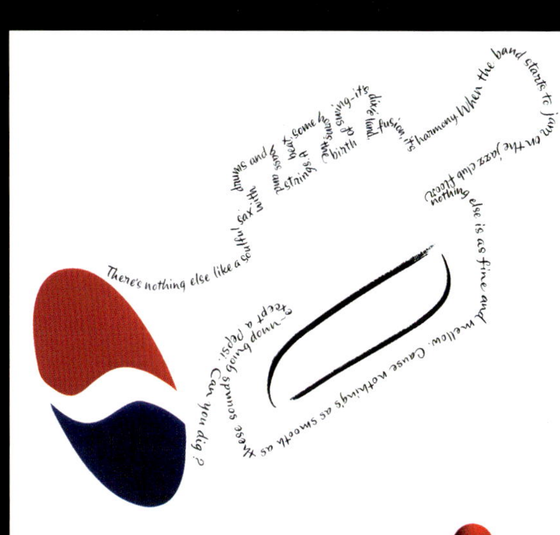

There's nothing else like a soulful sax with the drugs and you hear something, it's divine, it's divine loud, the birth, strings of a fusion. It's harmony when the band starts to jam at the jazz club floor. Nothing else is as fine and mellow. 'Cause nothing else is going down, except a Pepsi. How does these sounds as smooth as Can you dig?

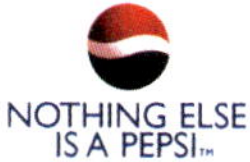

NOTHING ELSE IS A PEPSI™

/ ILLUSTRATION

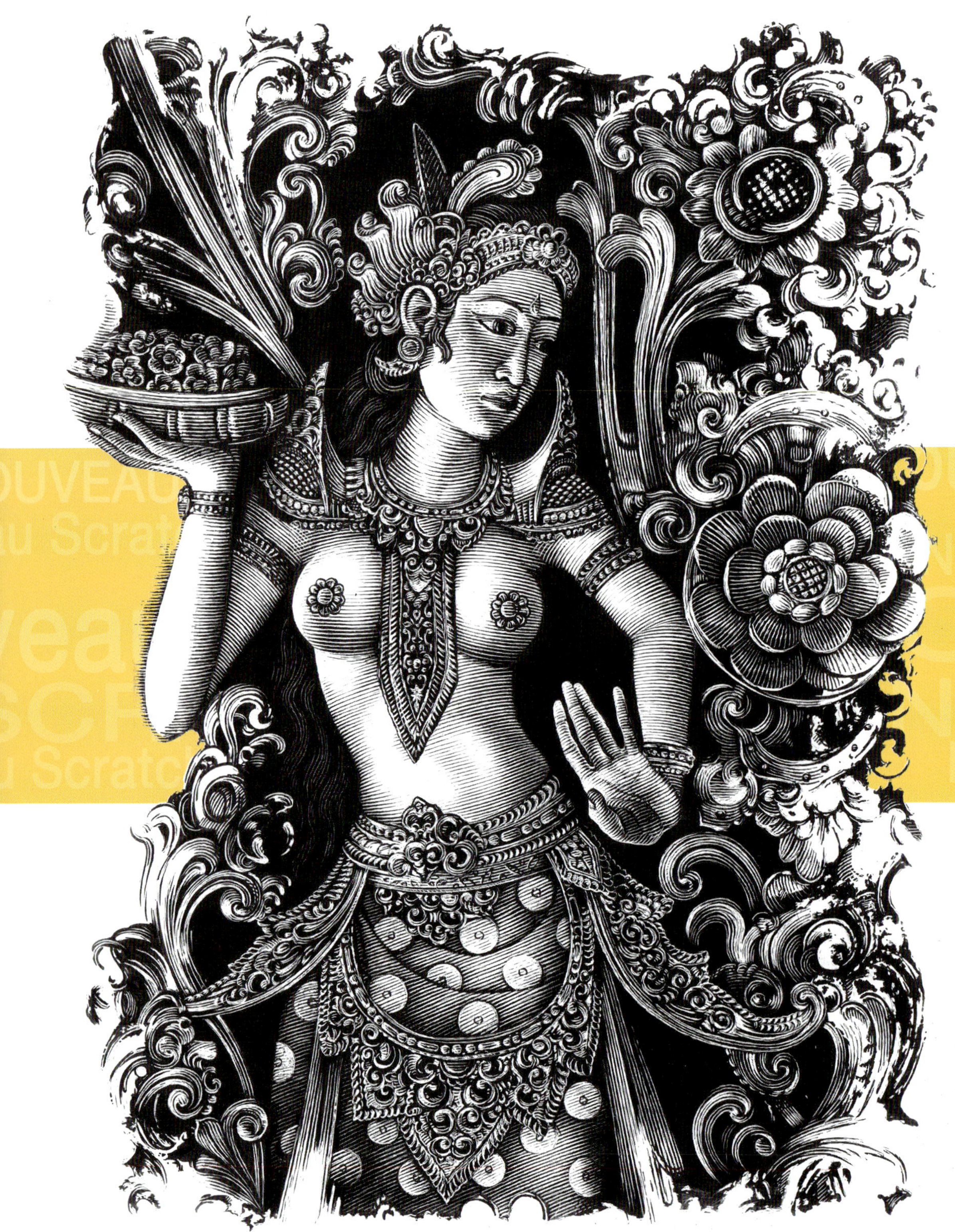

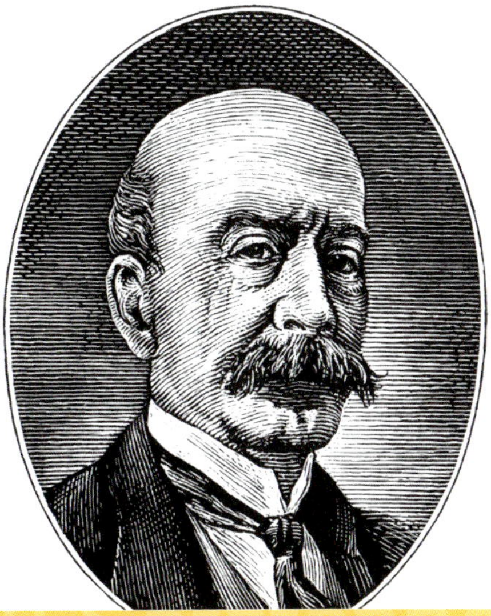

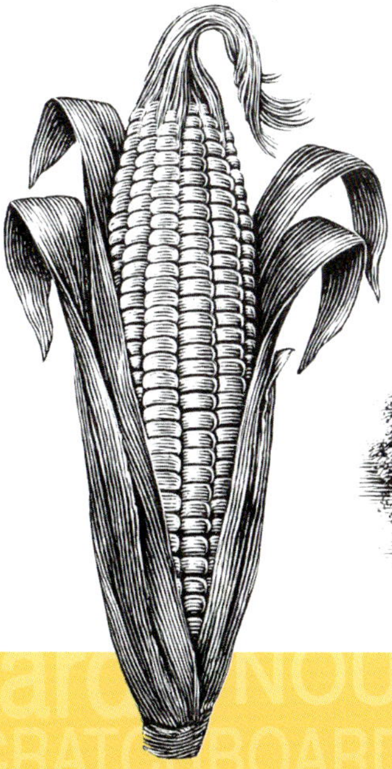

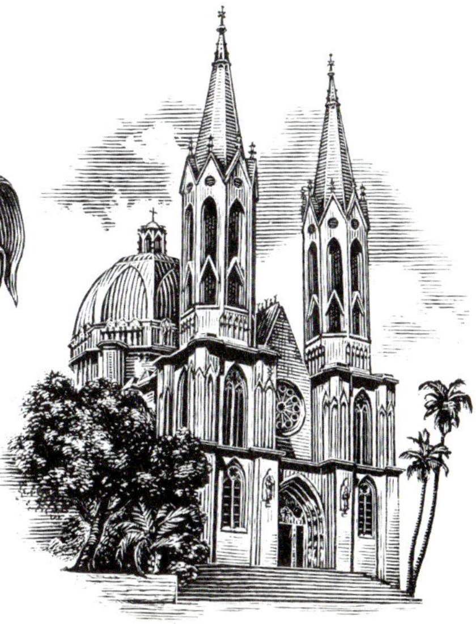

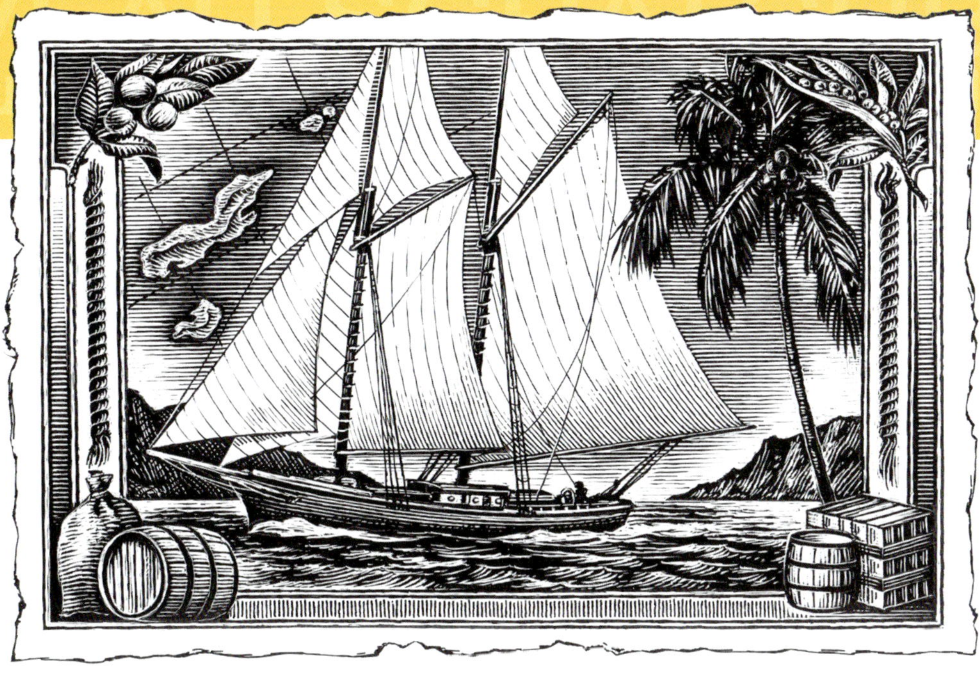

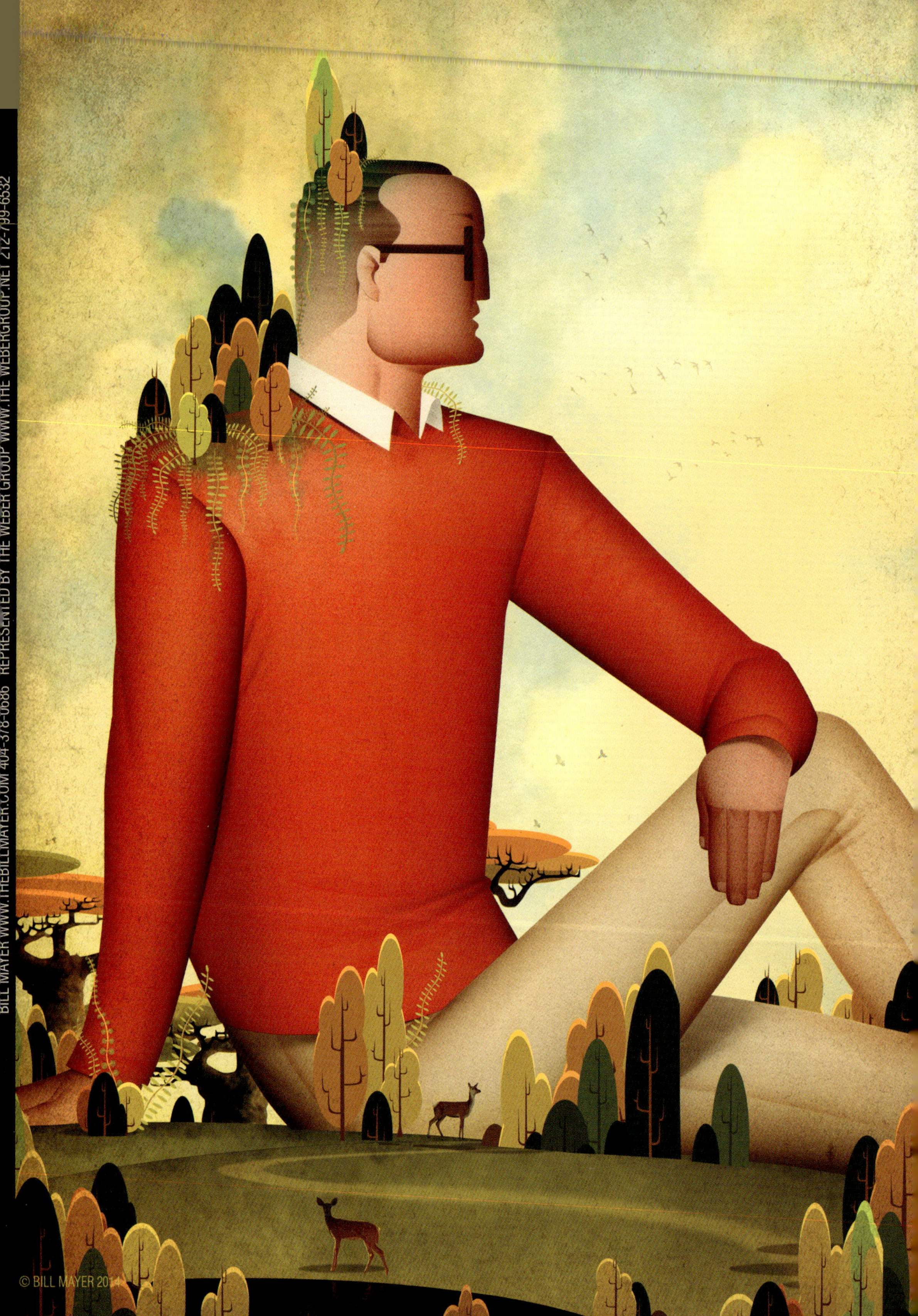
© BILL MAYER 2014

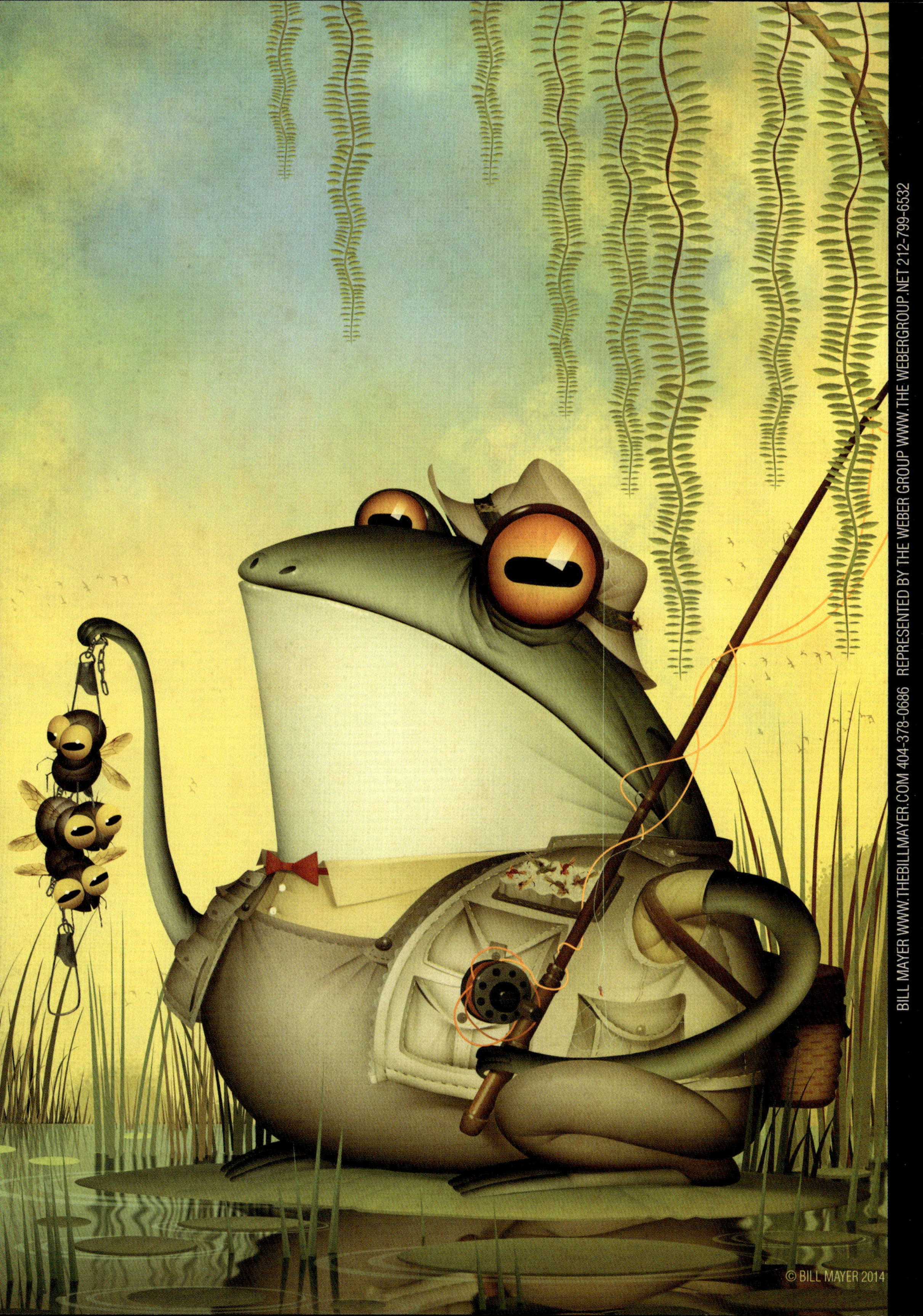
© BILL MAYER 2014

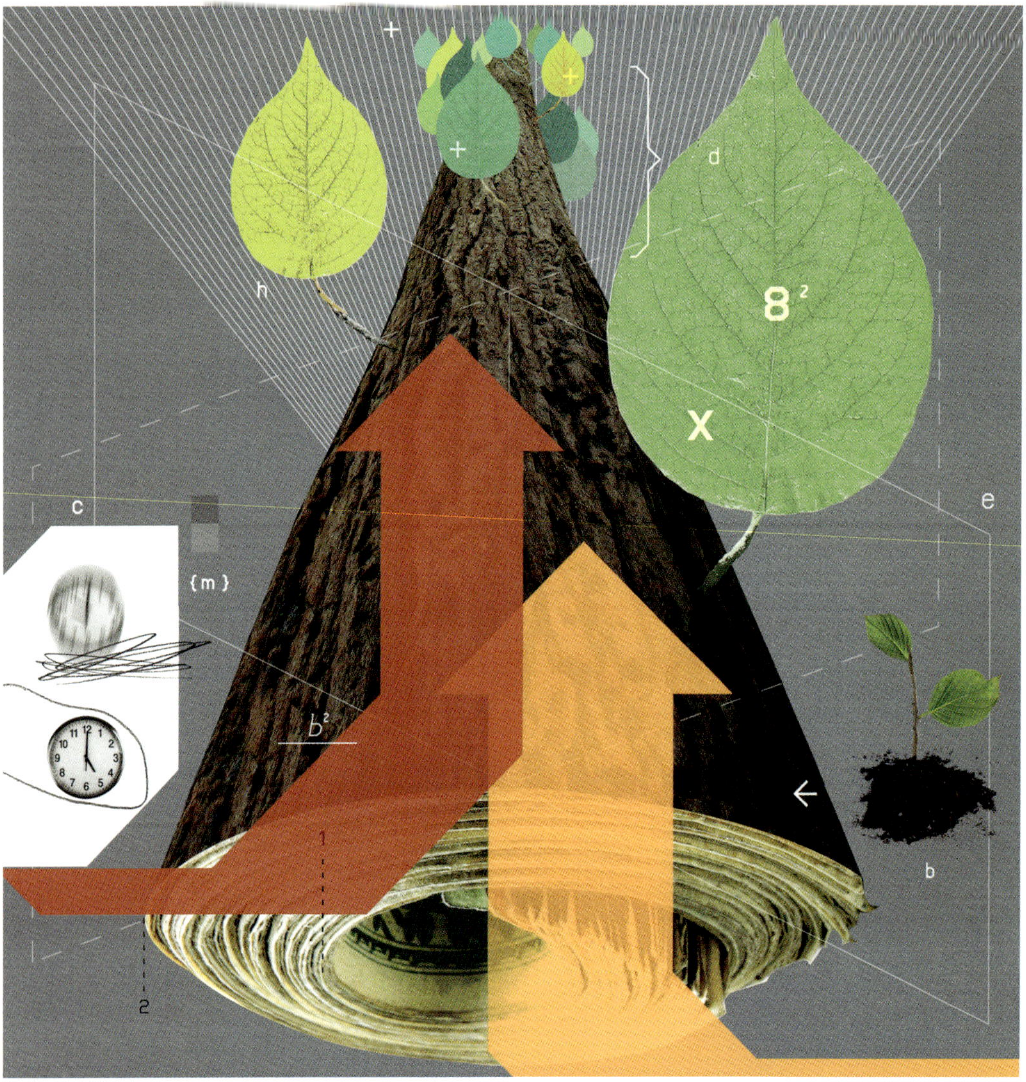

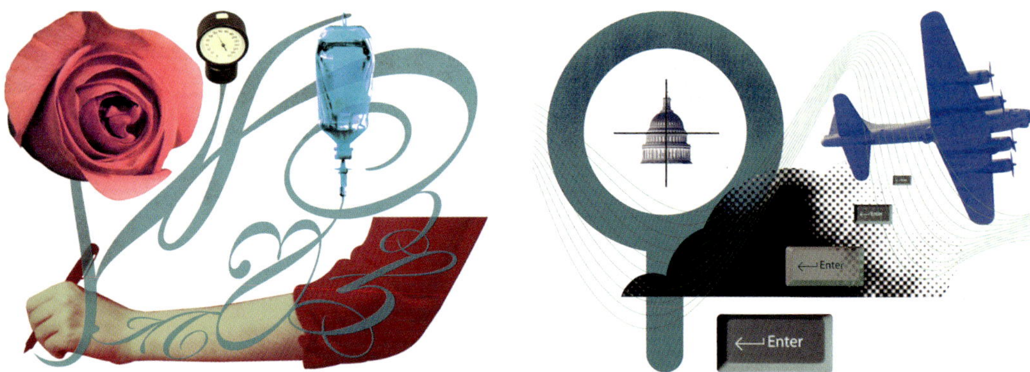

STUART BRADFORD ILLUSTRATION

415.485.6903 stuartbradfordart.com

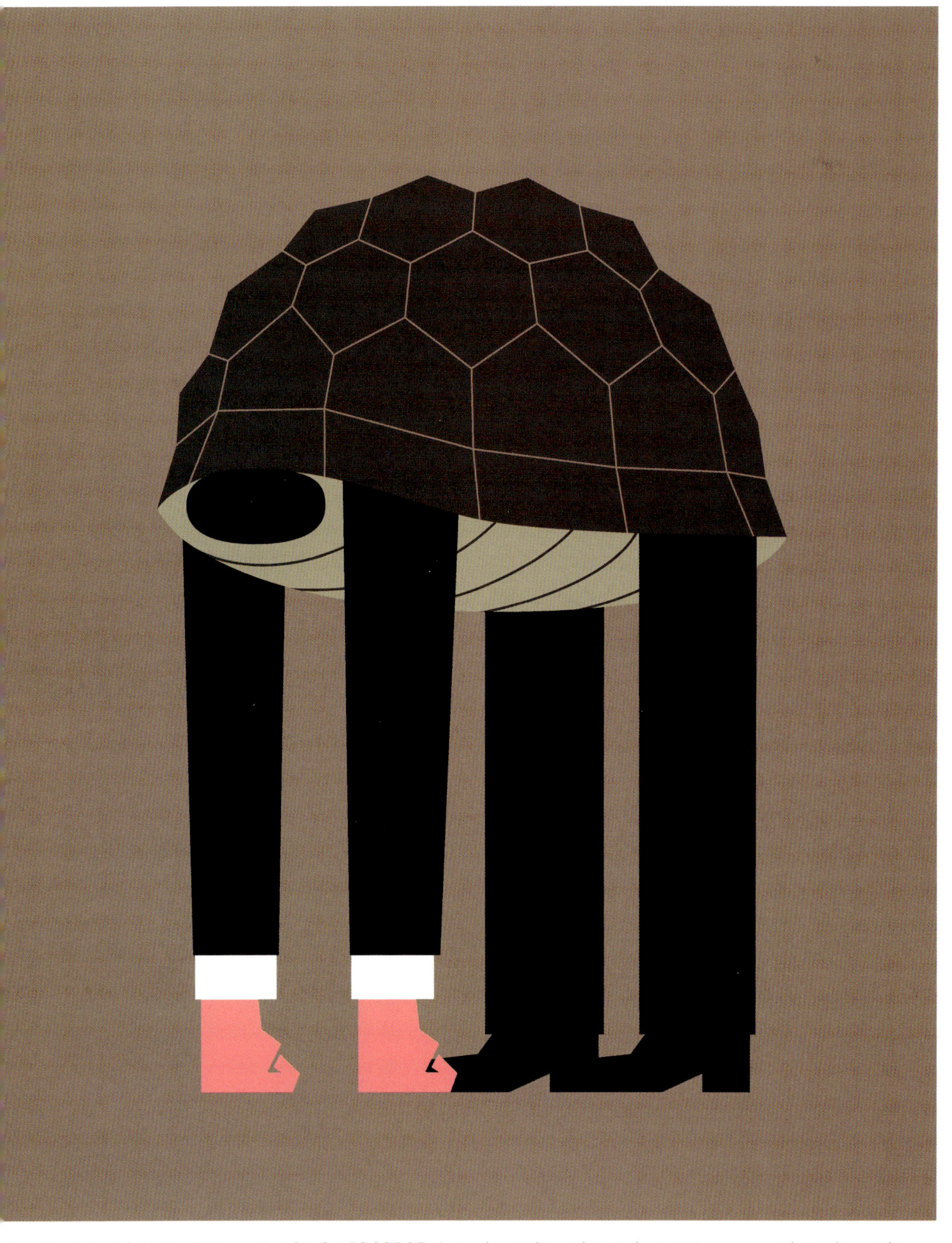

34

HEDGE

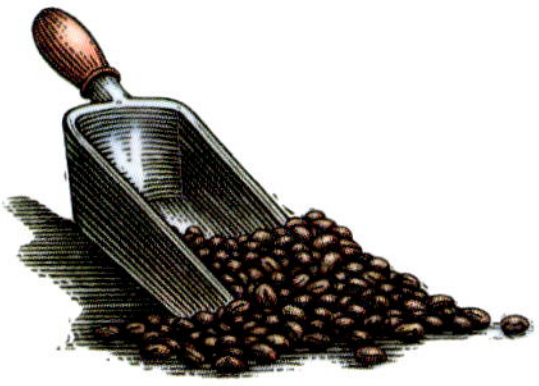

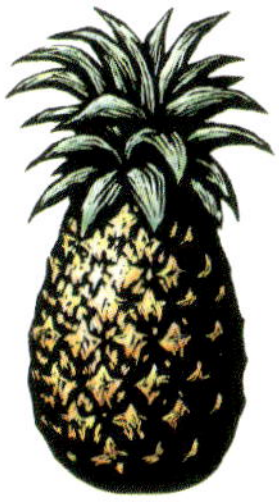

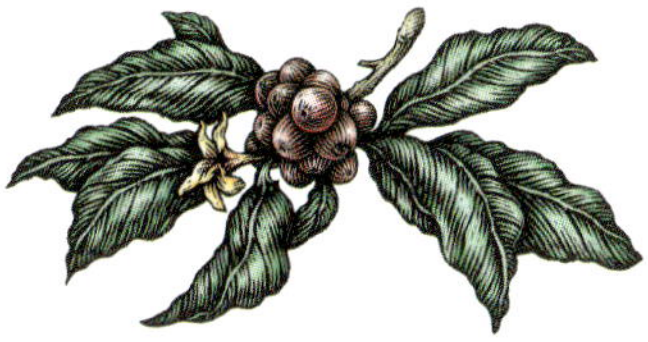

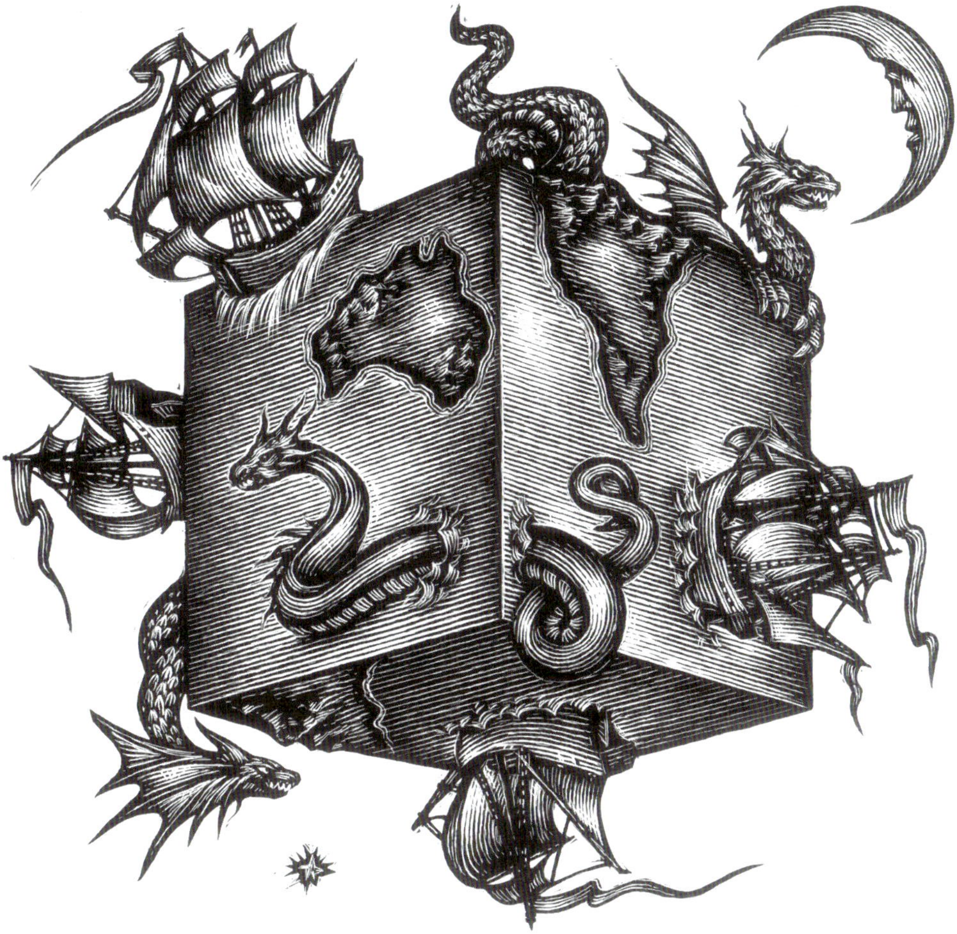

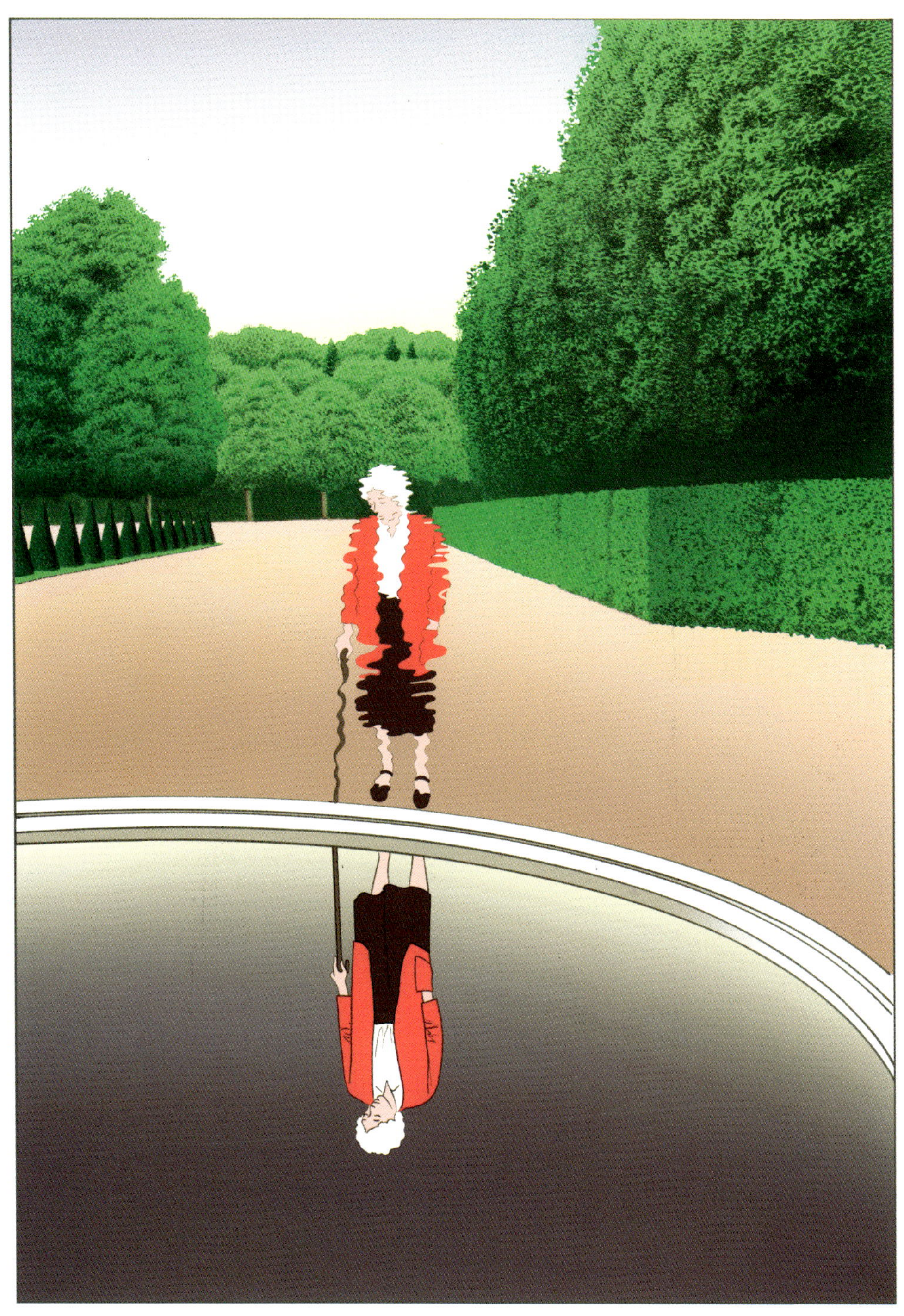

GUY BILLOUT

guy@guybillout.com   www.guybillout.com

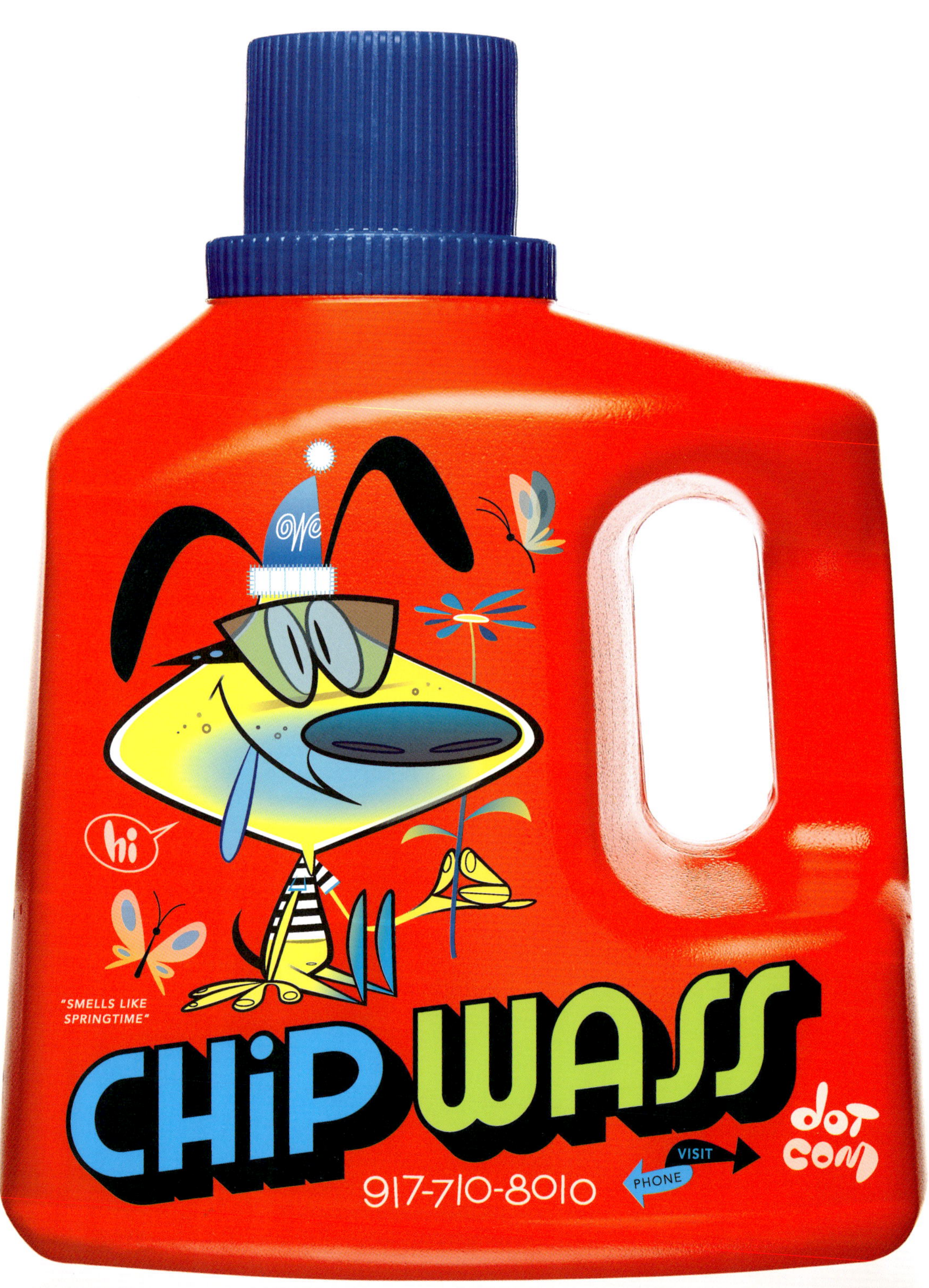
hi
"SMELLS LIKE SPRINGTIME"
CHIP WASS
dot com
917-710-8010
PHONE
VISIT

MUNROCAMPAGNA.COM
E. steve@munrocampagna.com   P. 312.335.8925
630 N State St #2109 Chicago, IL 60654

Anne Wertheim

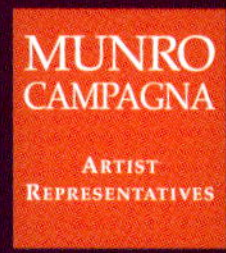

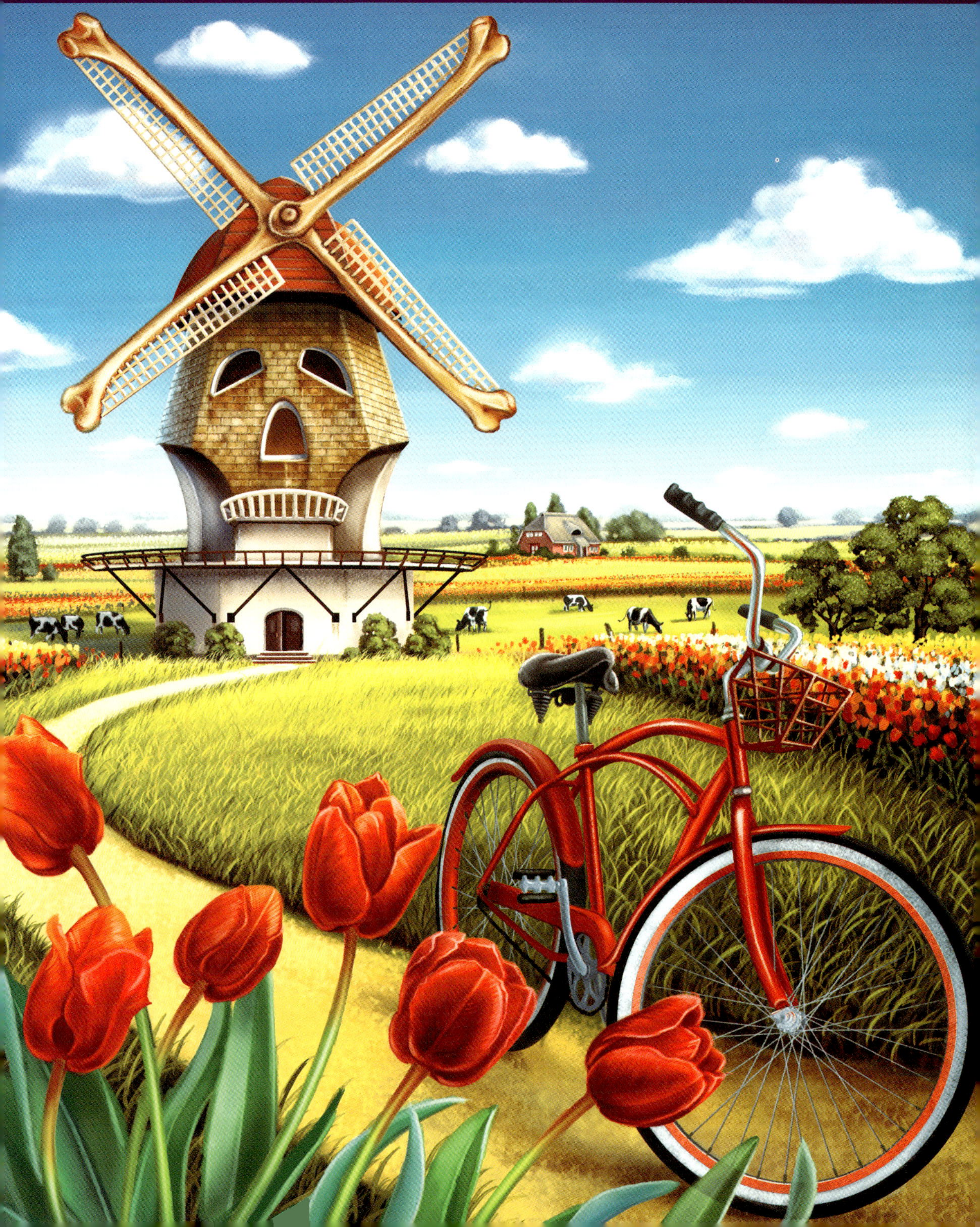

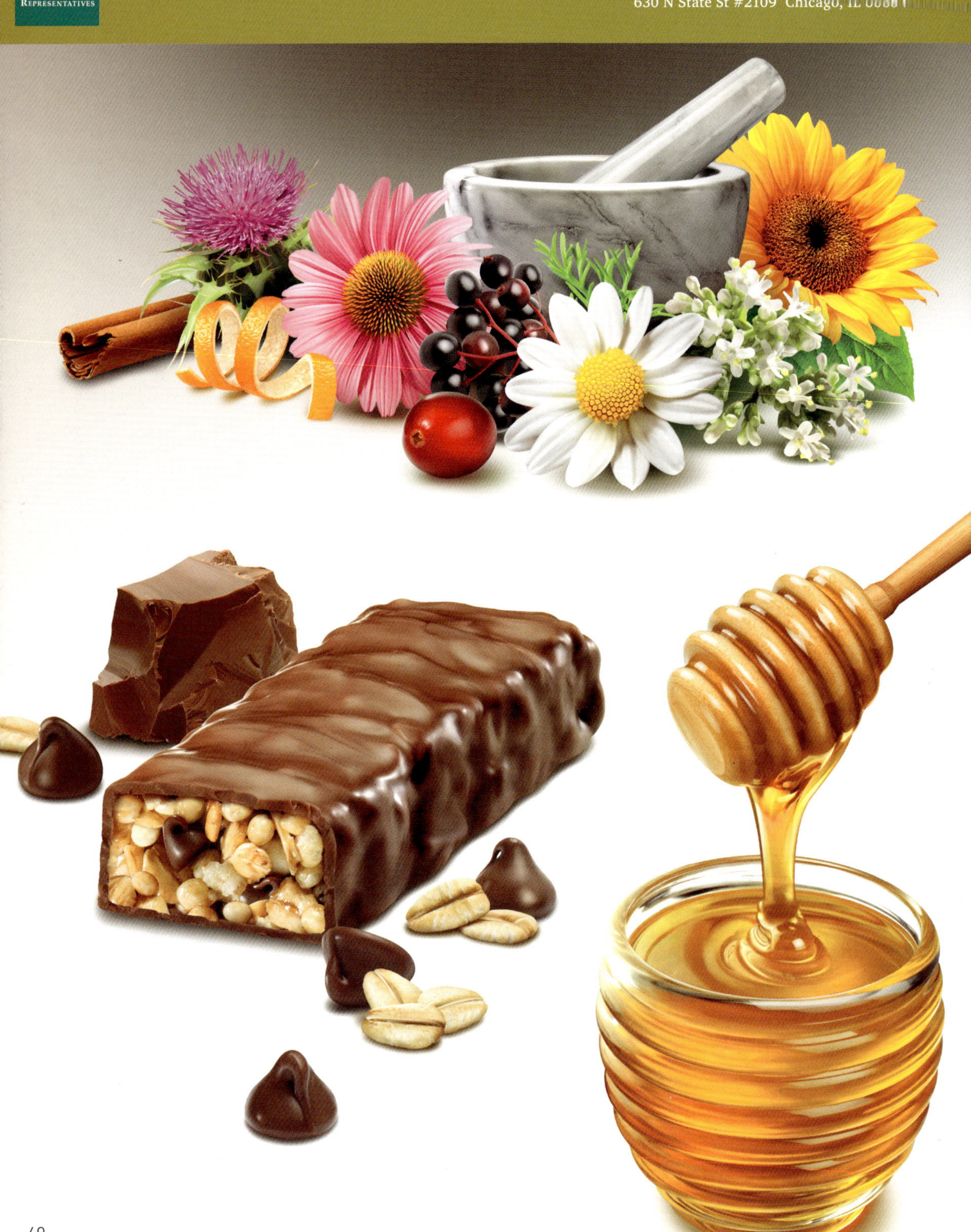

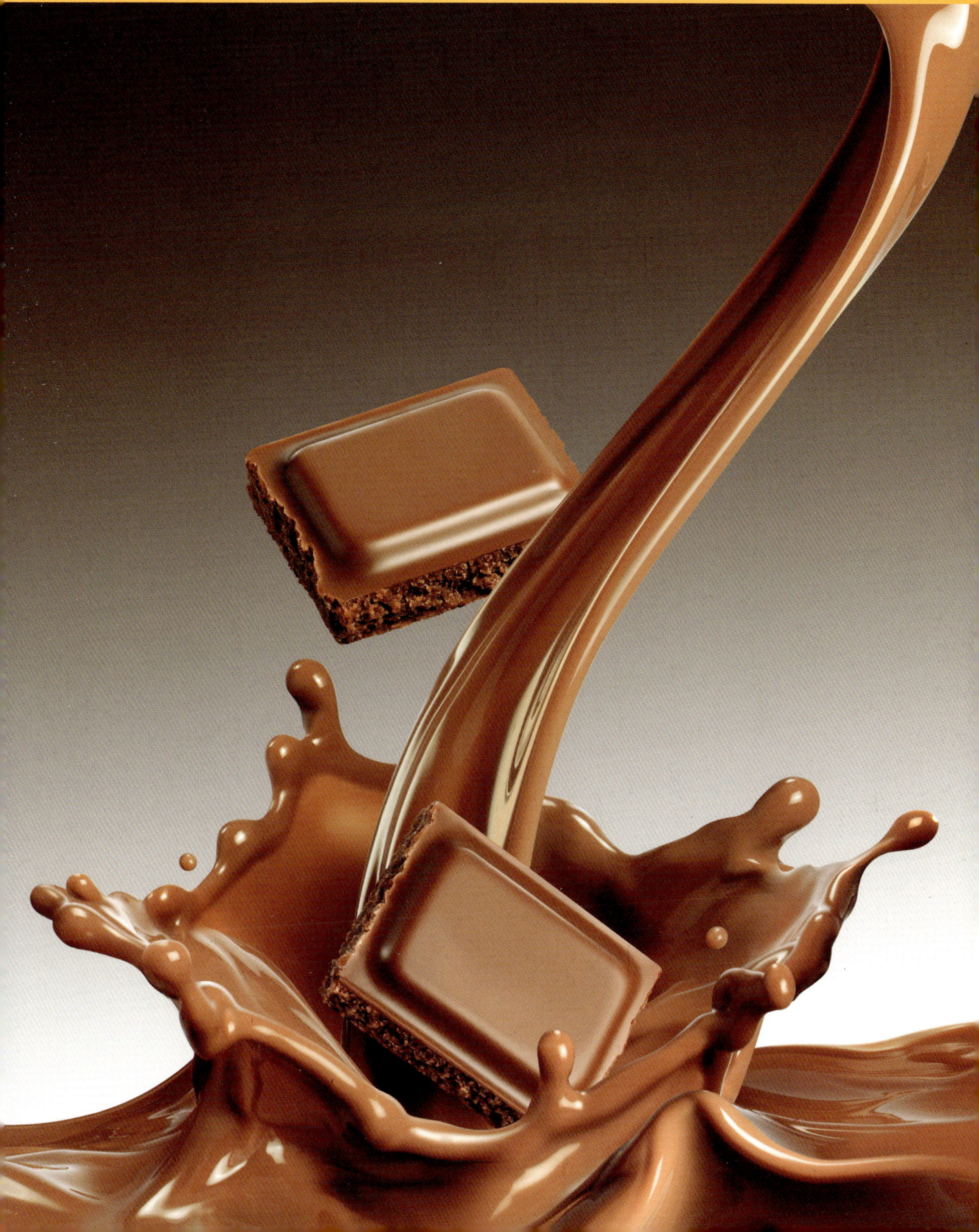

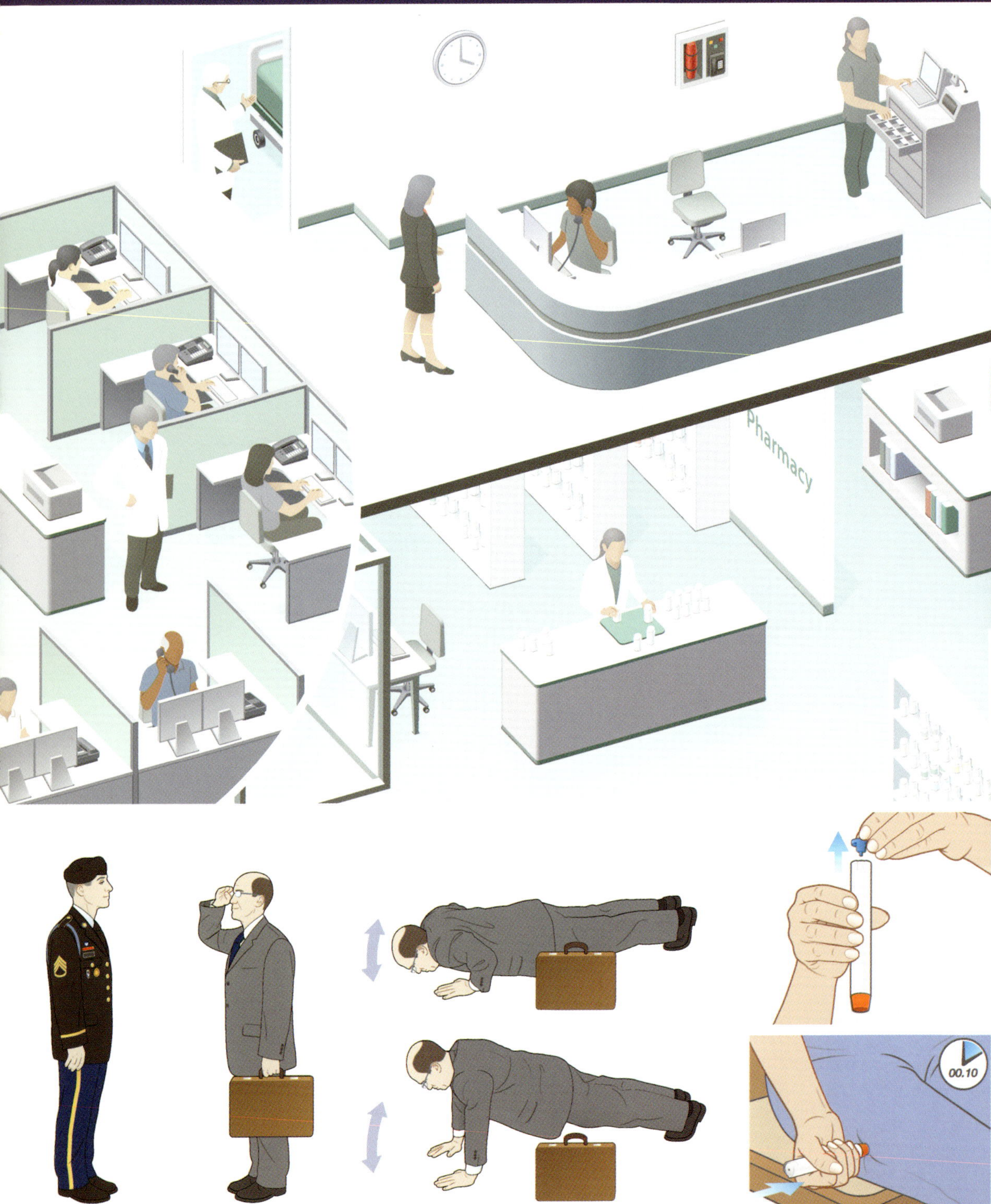

Pharmacy
00.10

MUNROCAMPAGNA.COM
E. steve@munrocampagna.com   P. 312.335.8925
630 N State St #2109 Chicago, IL 60654

Mike Right

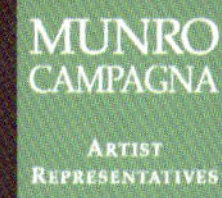

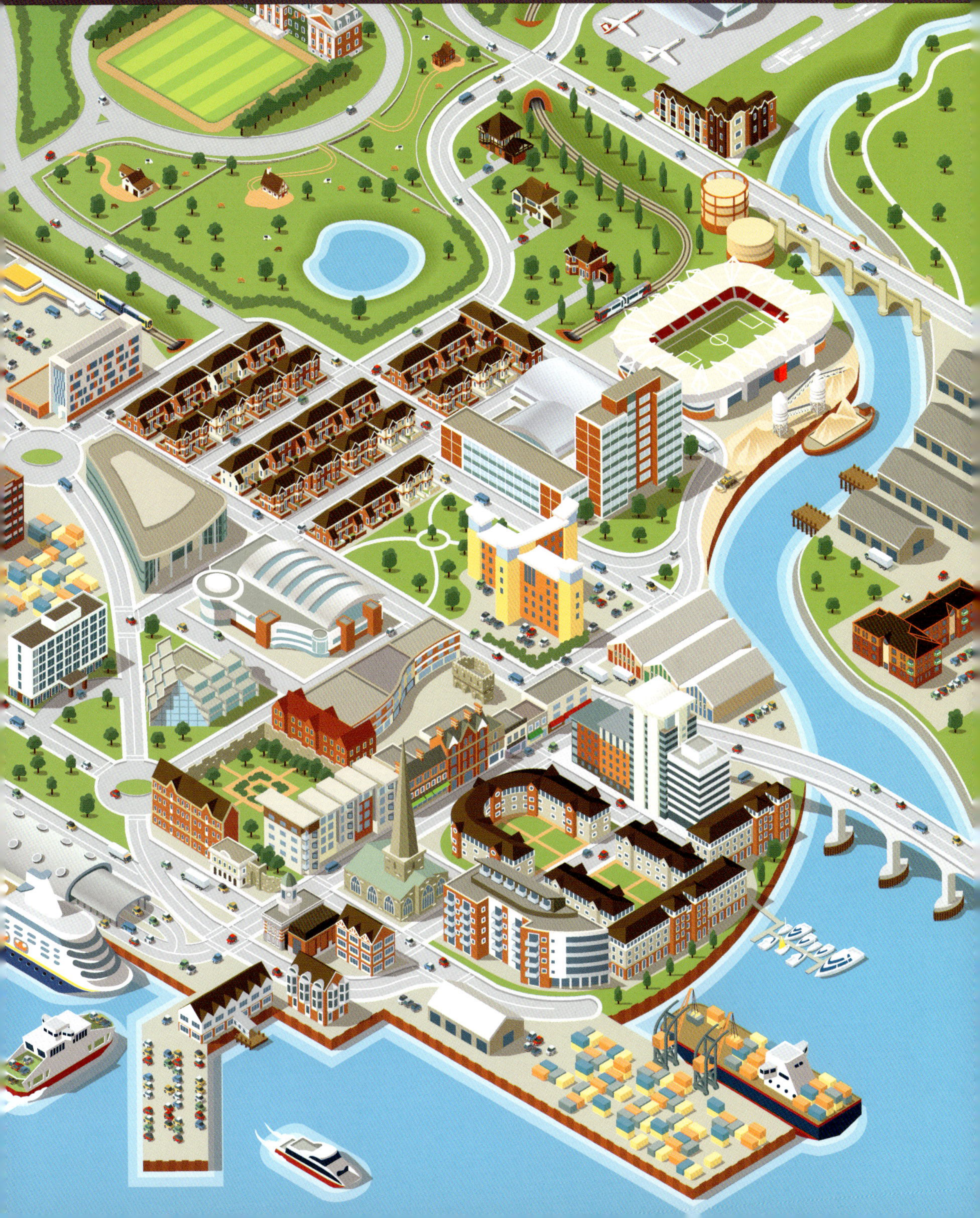

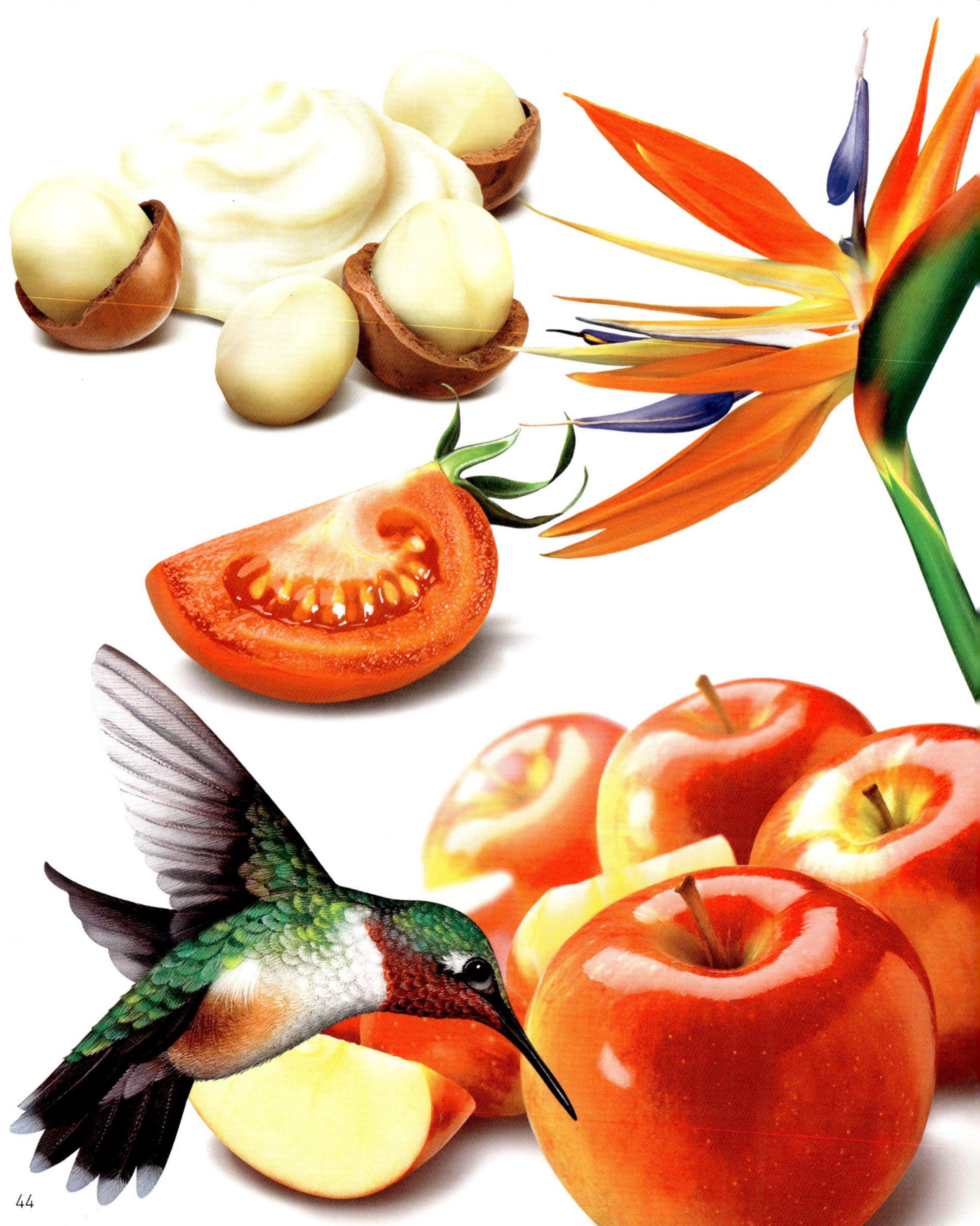

MUNROCAMPAGNA.COM
E. steve@munrocampagna.com   P. 312.335.8925
630 N State St #2109 Chicago, IL 60654

Mica Hendricks

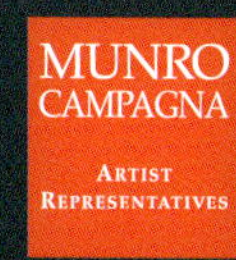

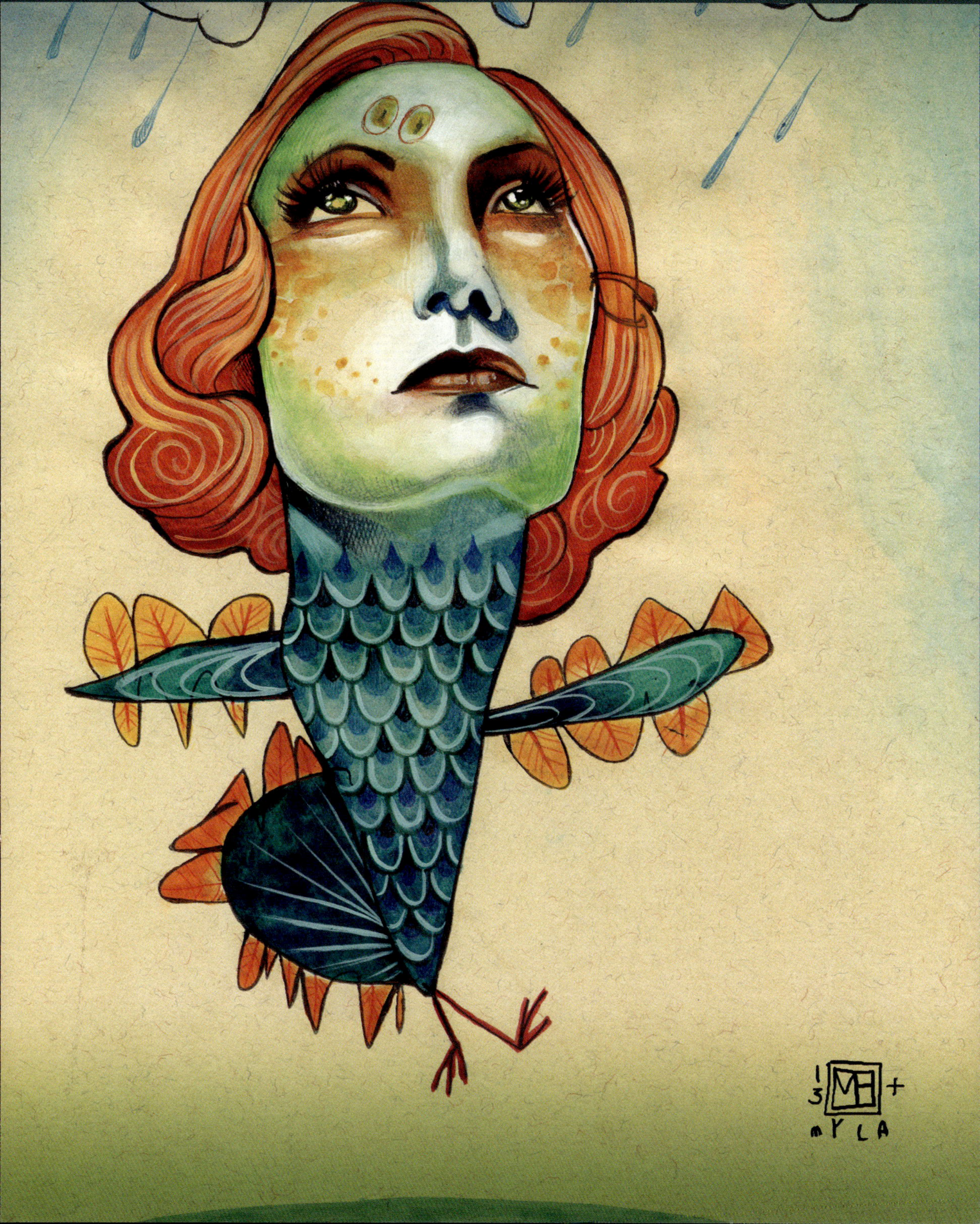

MUNRO
CAMPAGNA
ARTIST
REPRESENTATIVES

Tom Foty

MUNROCAMPAGNA.COM
E. steve@munrocampagna.com   P. 312.335.8925
630 N State St #2109 Chicago, IL 60654

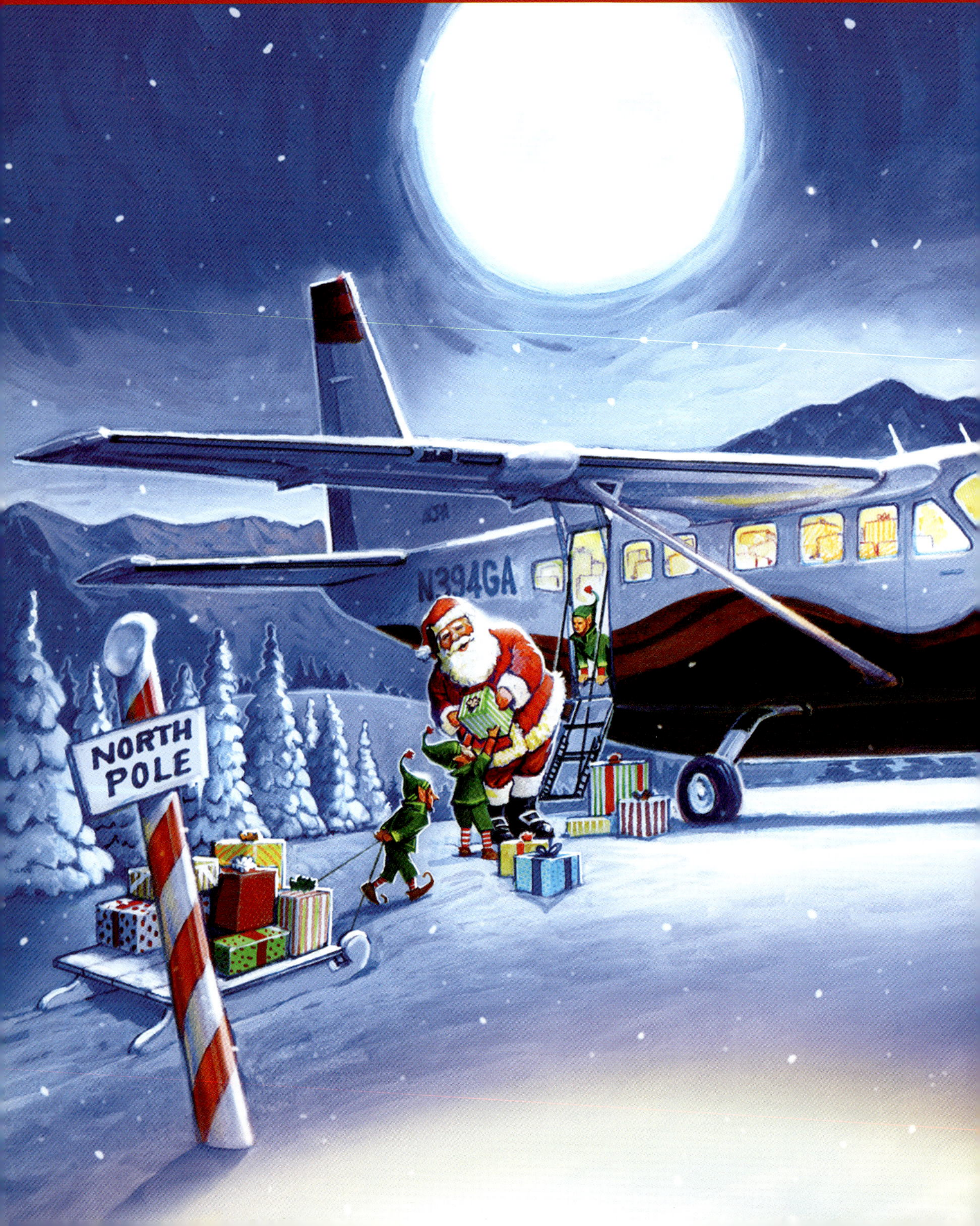

NORTH
POLE

N394GA

MUNROCAMPAGNA.COM
E. steve@munrocampagna.com   P. 312.335.8925
630 N State St #2109 Chicago, IL 60654

Mike Kasun

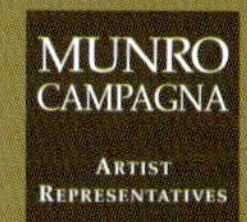

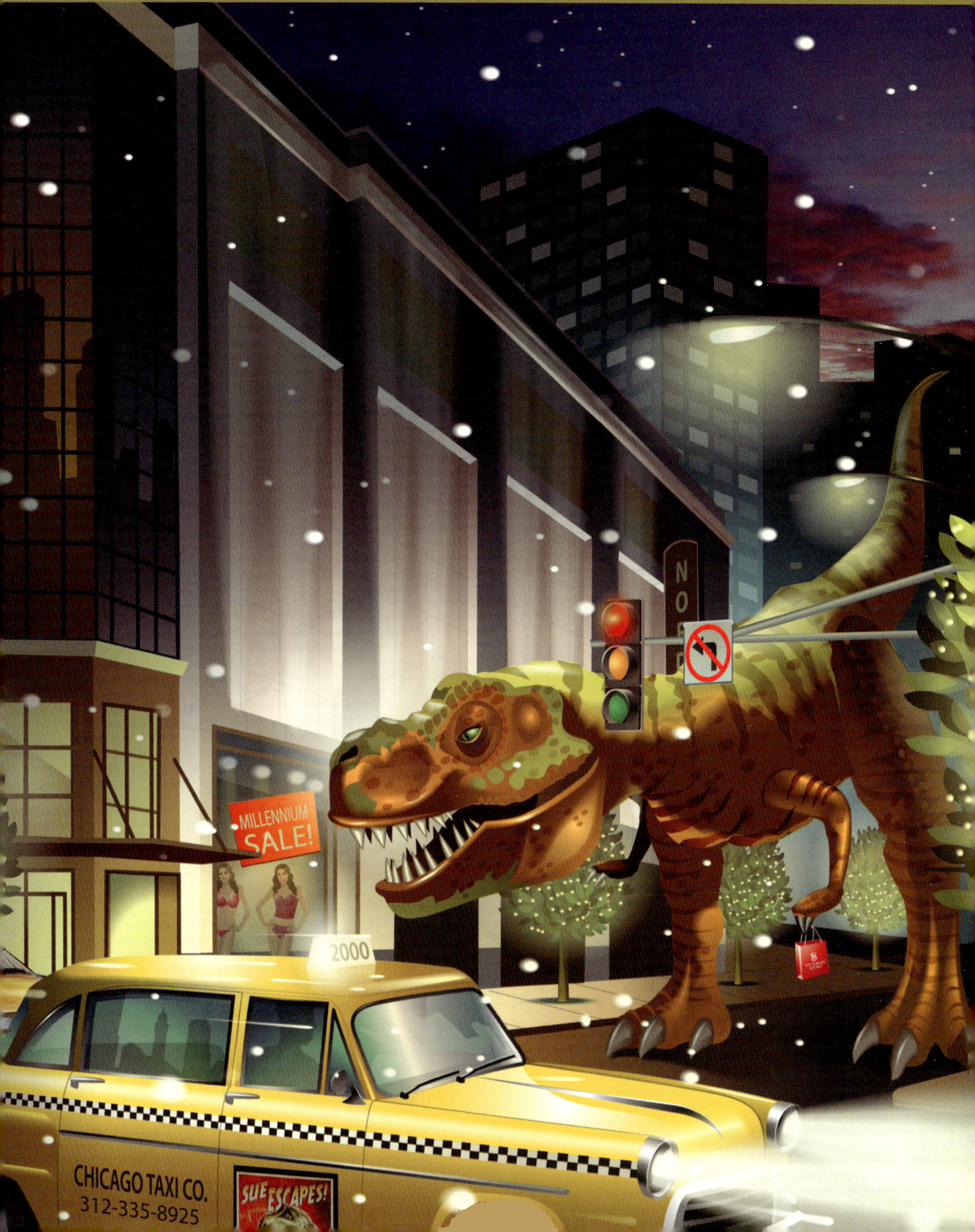

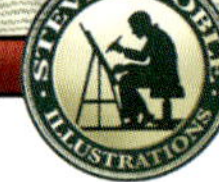

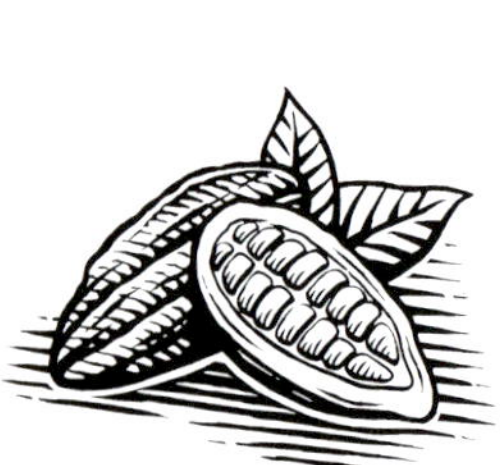

© Copyright 2013 - Rocky Mountain Chocolate

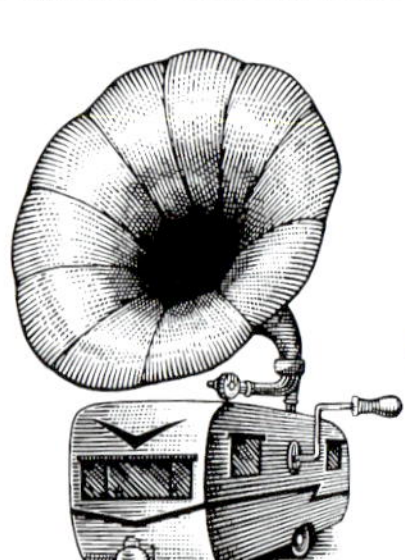

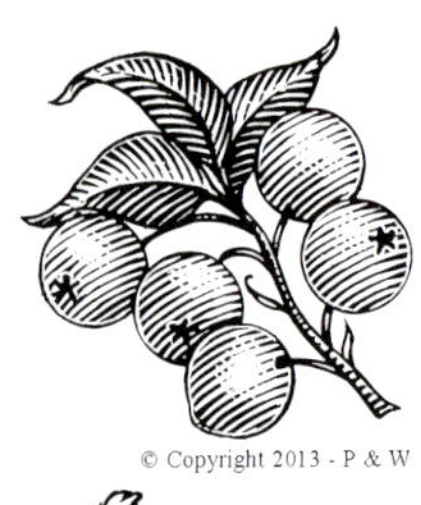

BANDWAGON

© Copyright 2013 - P & W

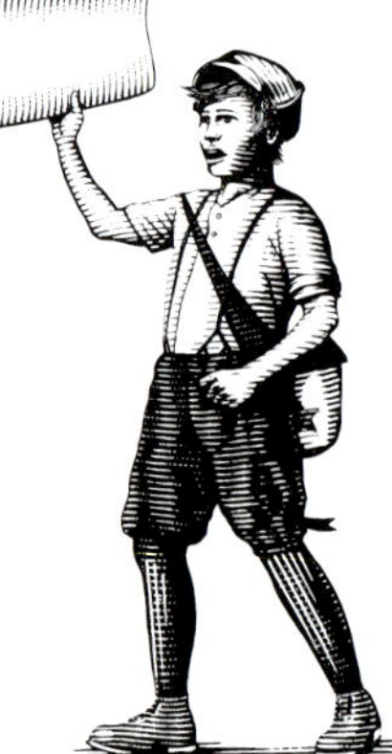

© Copyright 2013 - Paperboy

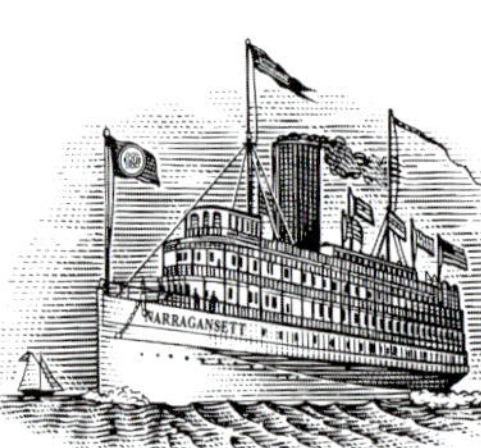

© Copyright 2013 - Naragansett

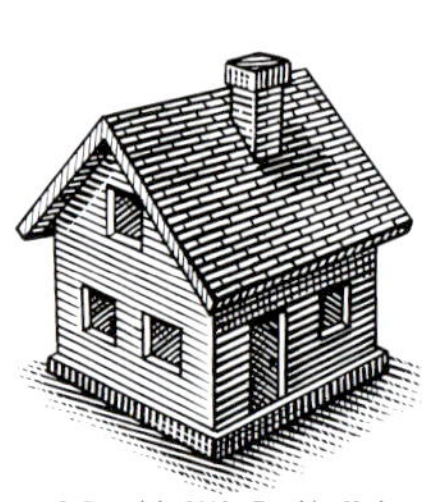

© Copyright 2013 - Bershire Hathaway

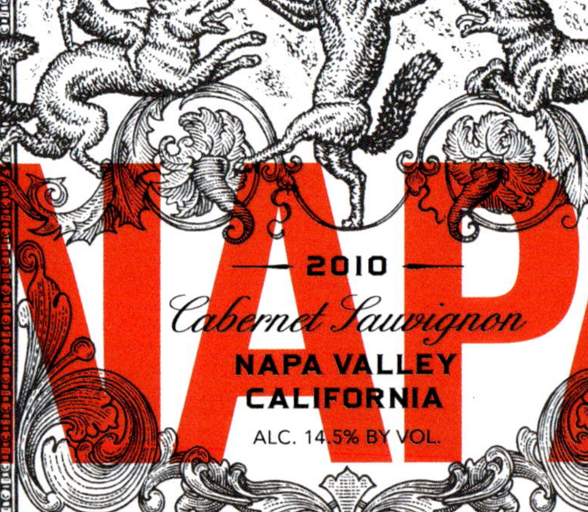

© Copyright 2013 - Mother Freedom

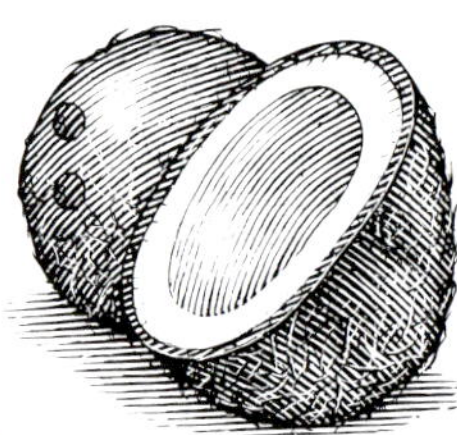

© Copyright 2013 - Burt's Bees

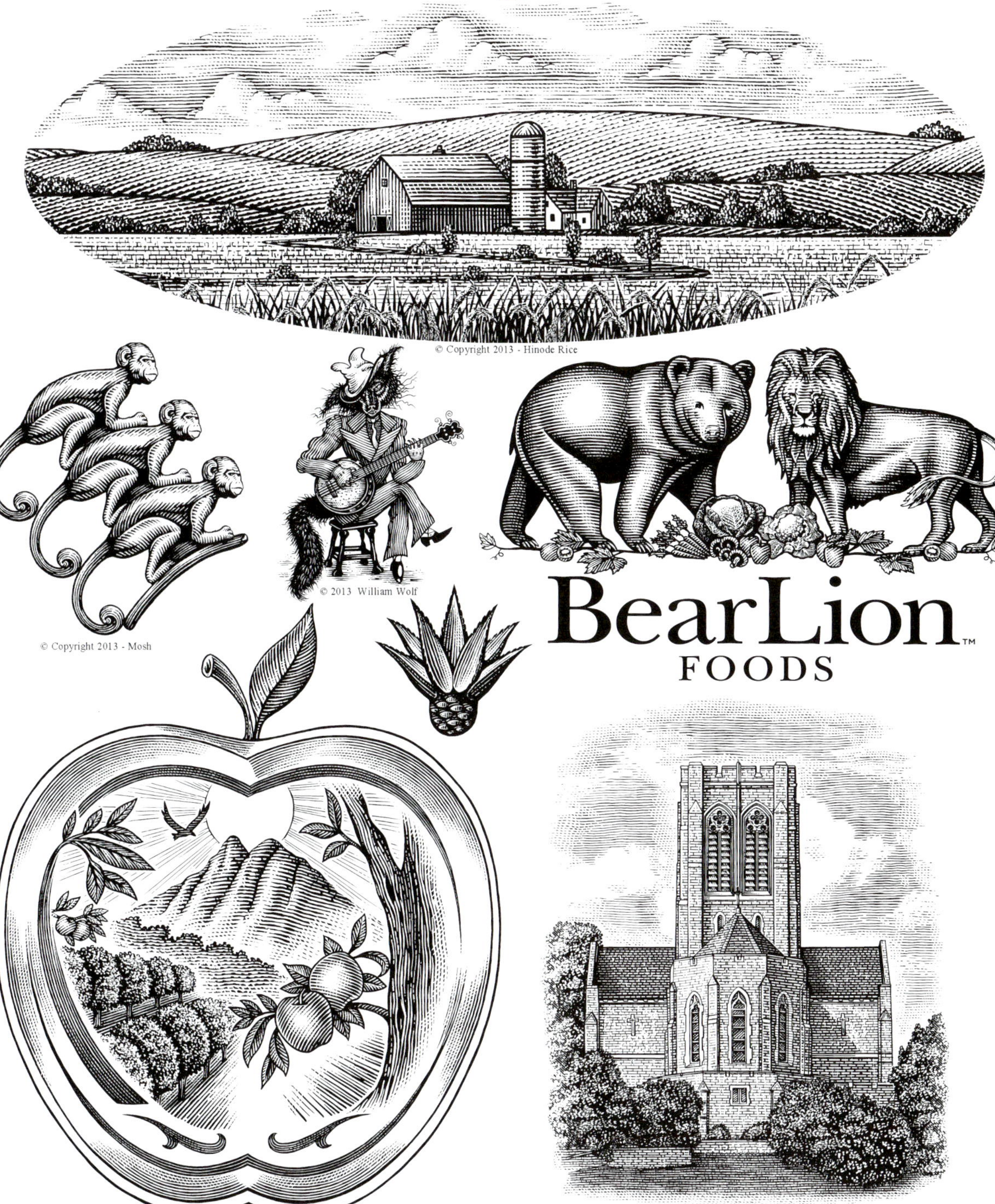

STEVEN NOBLE
CRATCHBOARD   LINE ART   ENGRAVINGS   WOODCUTS
ve@stevennoble.com   direct: 707-789-0166   mobile: 415-897-6961   www.stevennoble.com
© Copyright 2013 - Hinode Rice
© Copyright 2013 - Mosh
2013 William Wolf
BearLion
FOODS
© Copyright 2013 - Montano
• stock images: www.scratchboardstock.net •
World Class Illustrations from over 3,500 images and over 1,000 stock illustrations for clients from all over the world!
© Copyright 2013 - St. Phillips Cathedral
2006 Rosey Awards   •   Mead Show Award Winner 2001   •   Brand New 2009   •   Ad Pulp 2009   •   Communications Arts 1997   •   National Addy Awards 2010

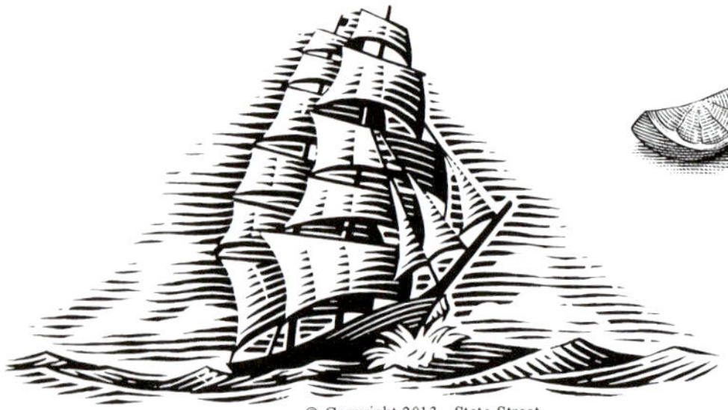

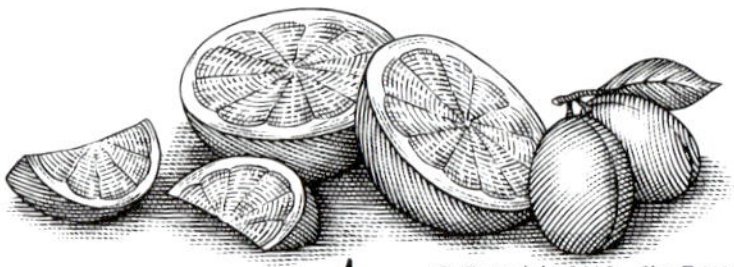

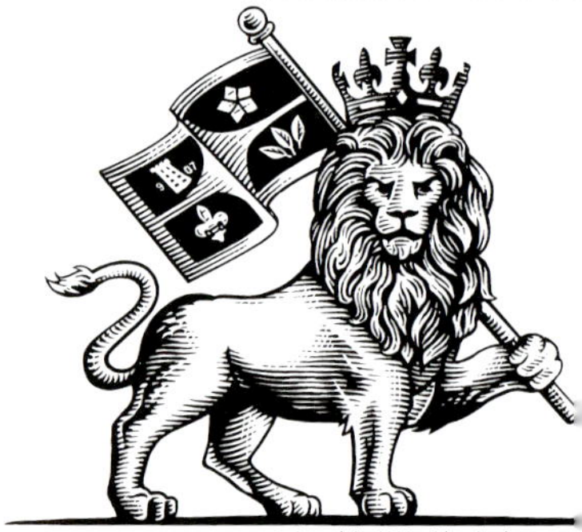

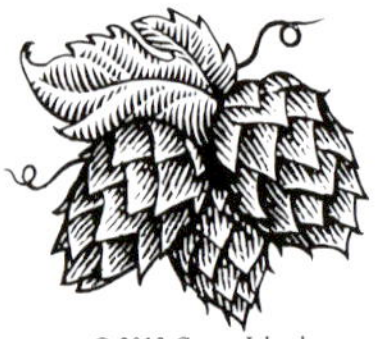

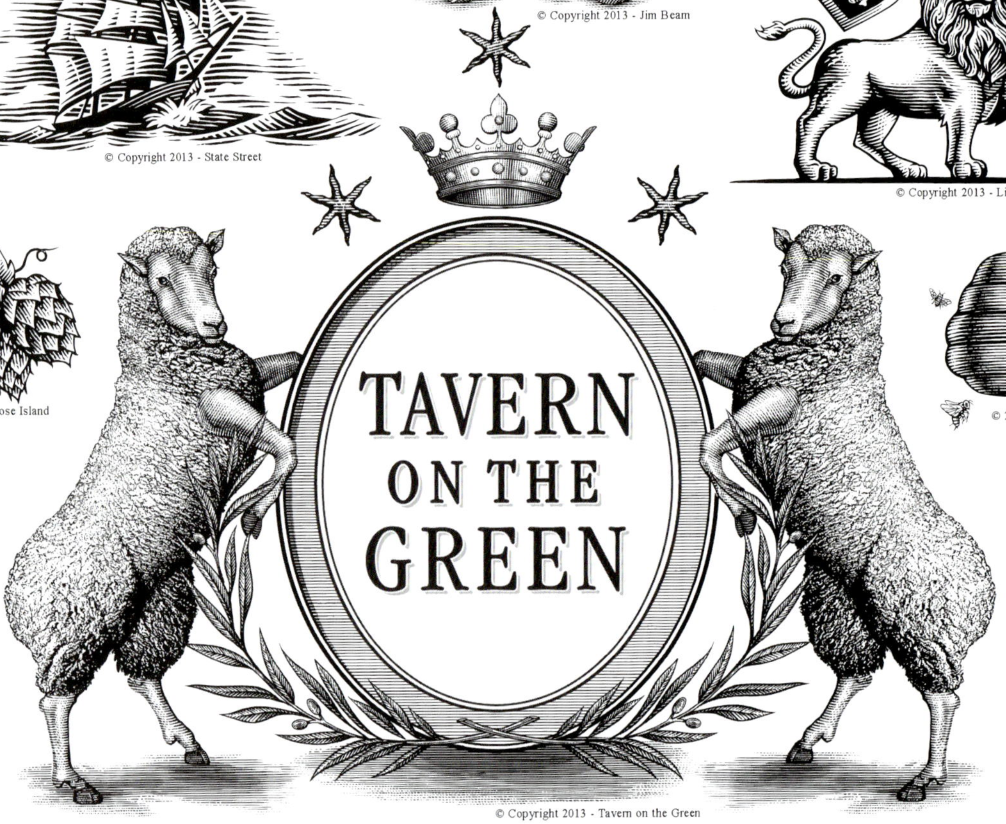

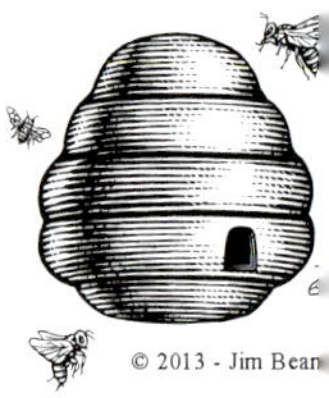

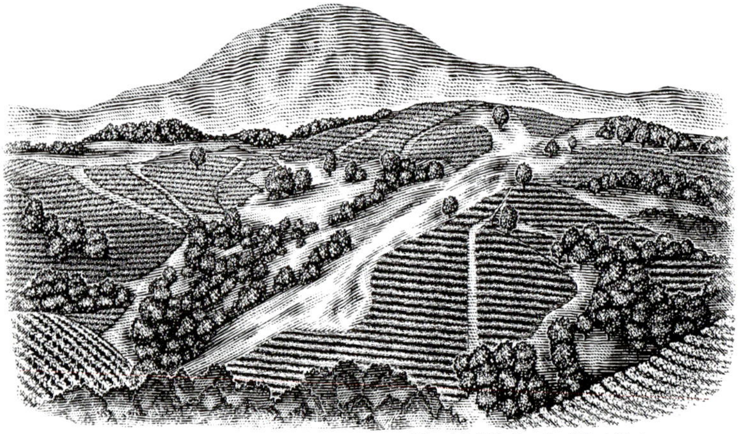

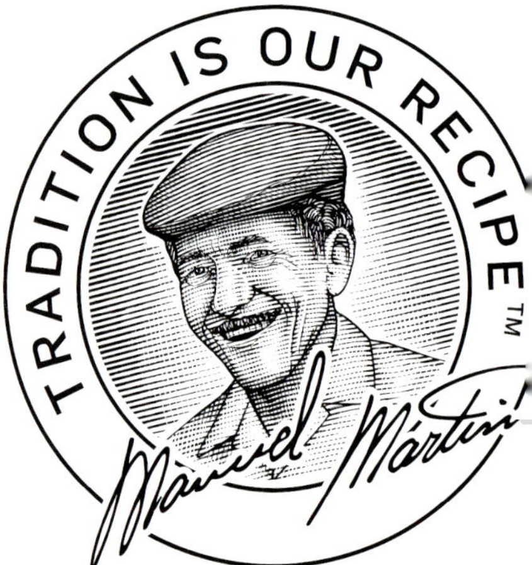

STEVEN NOBLE

eve@stevennoble.com   direct: 707-789-0166   mobile: 415-897-6961   www.stevennoble.com

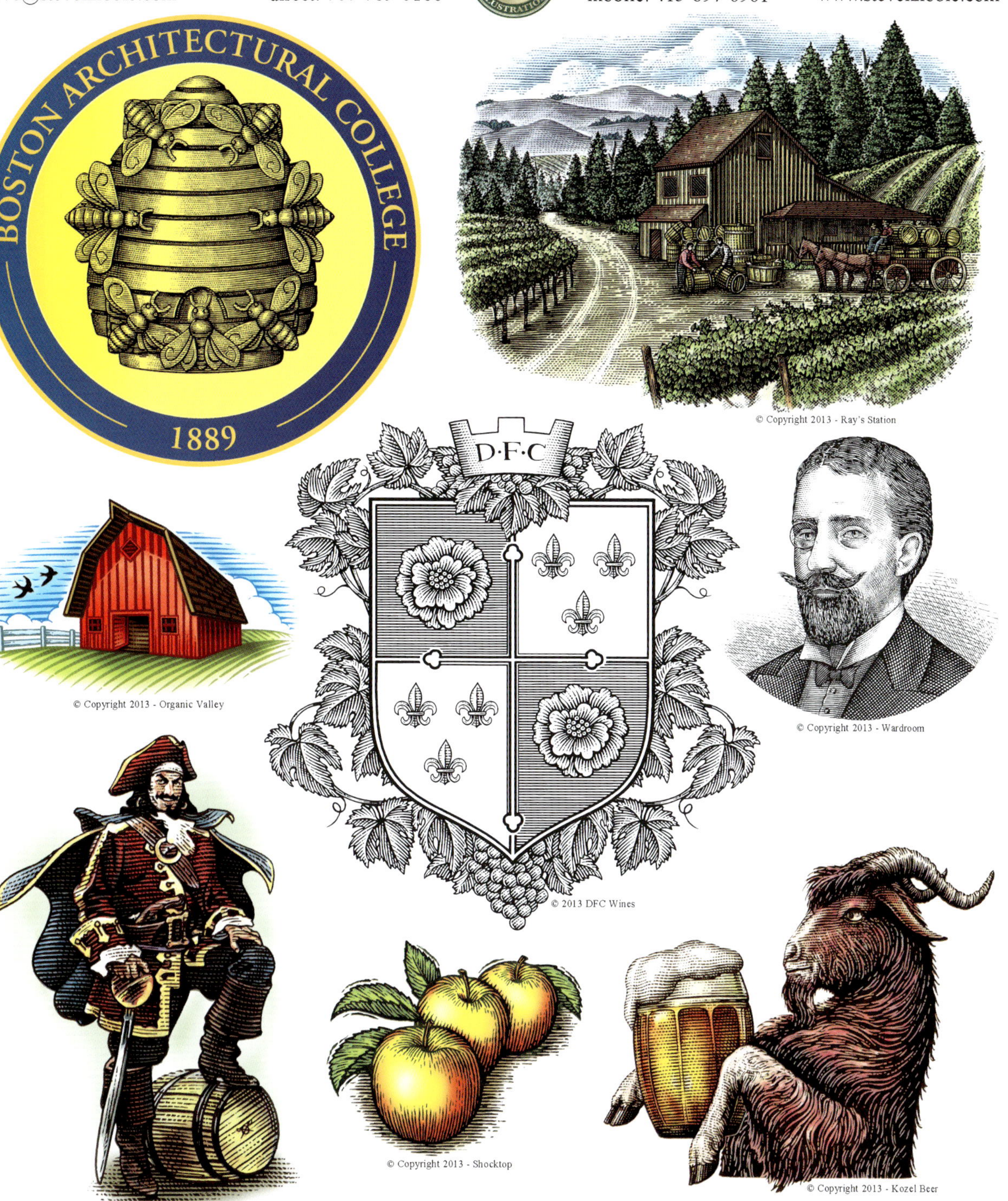

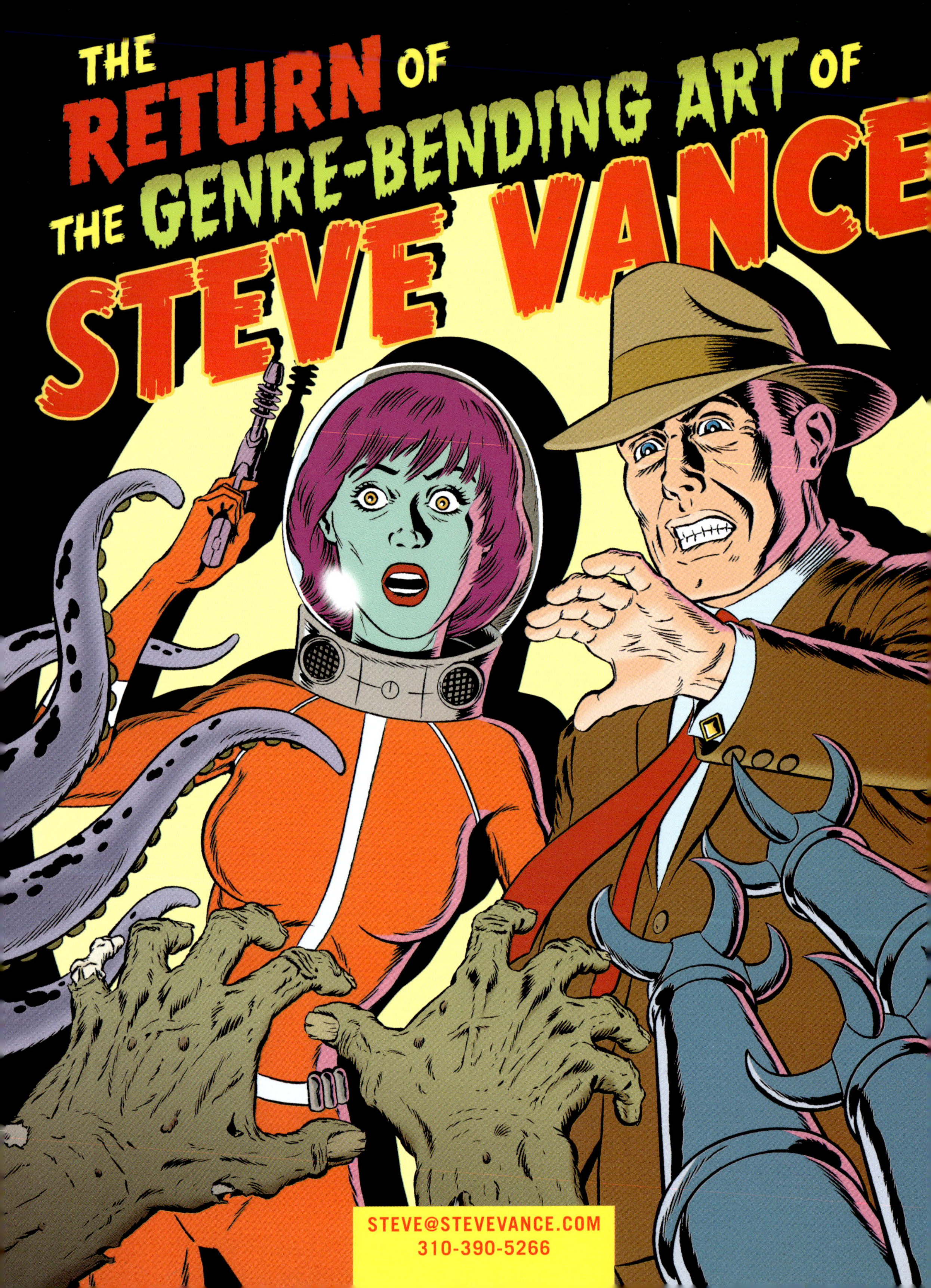
THE RETURN OF
THE GENRE-BENDING ART OF
STEVE VANCE
STEVE@STEVEVANCE.COM
310-390-5266

Andy Clarkson

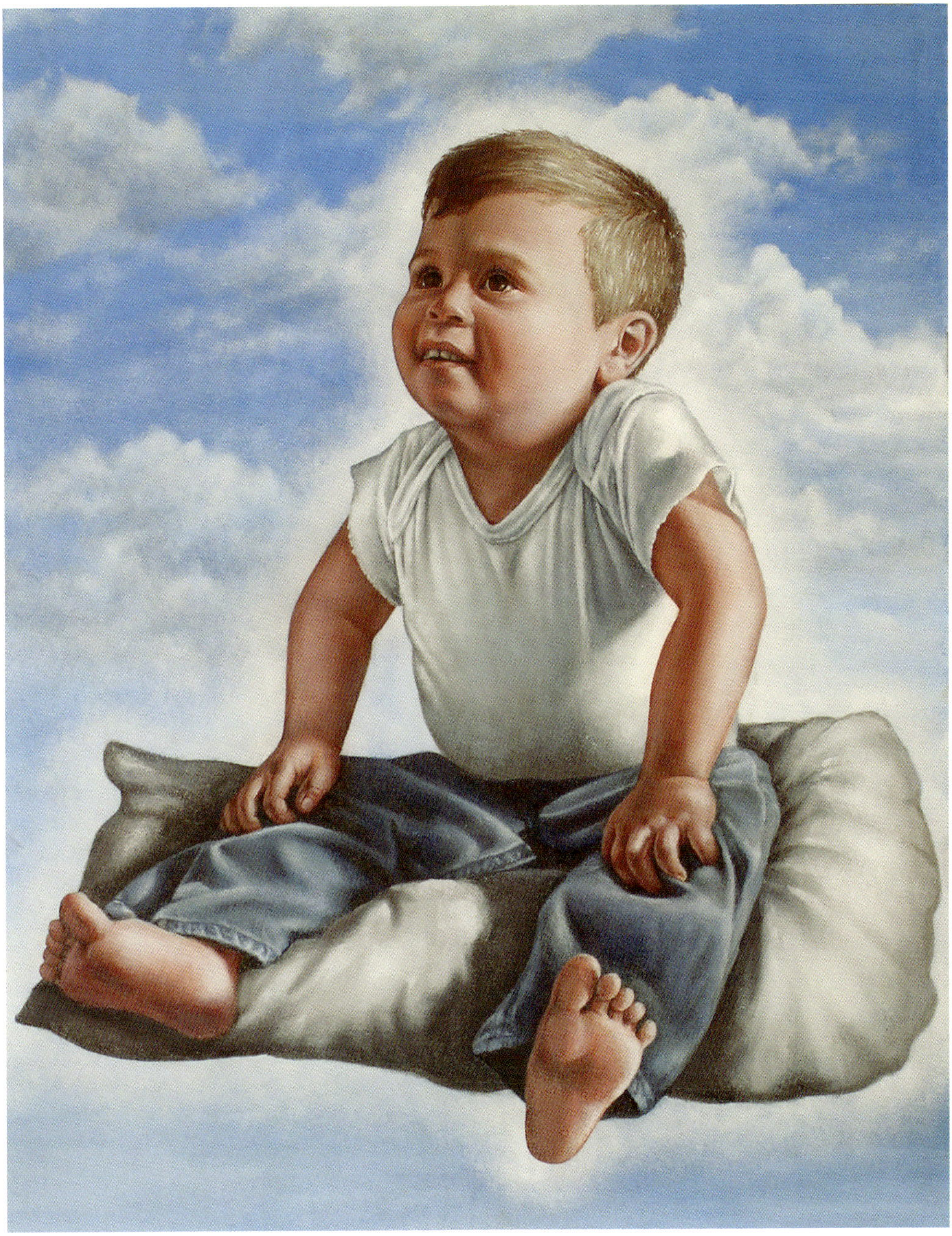

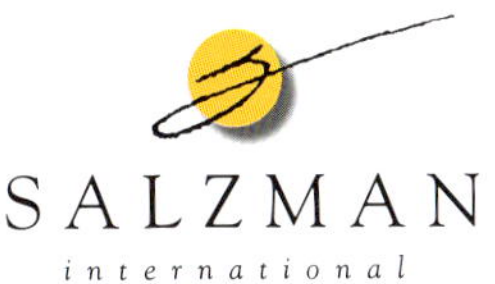

SALZMAN

international

415.285.8267   salzint.com   212.997.0115

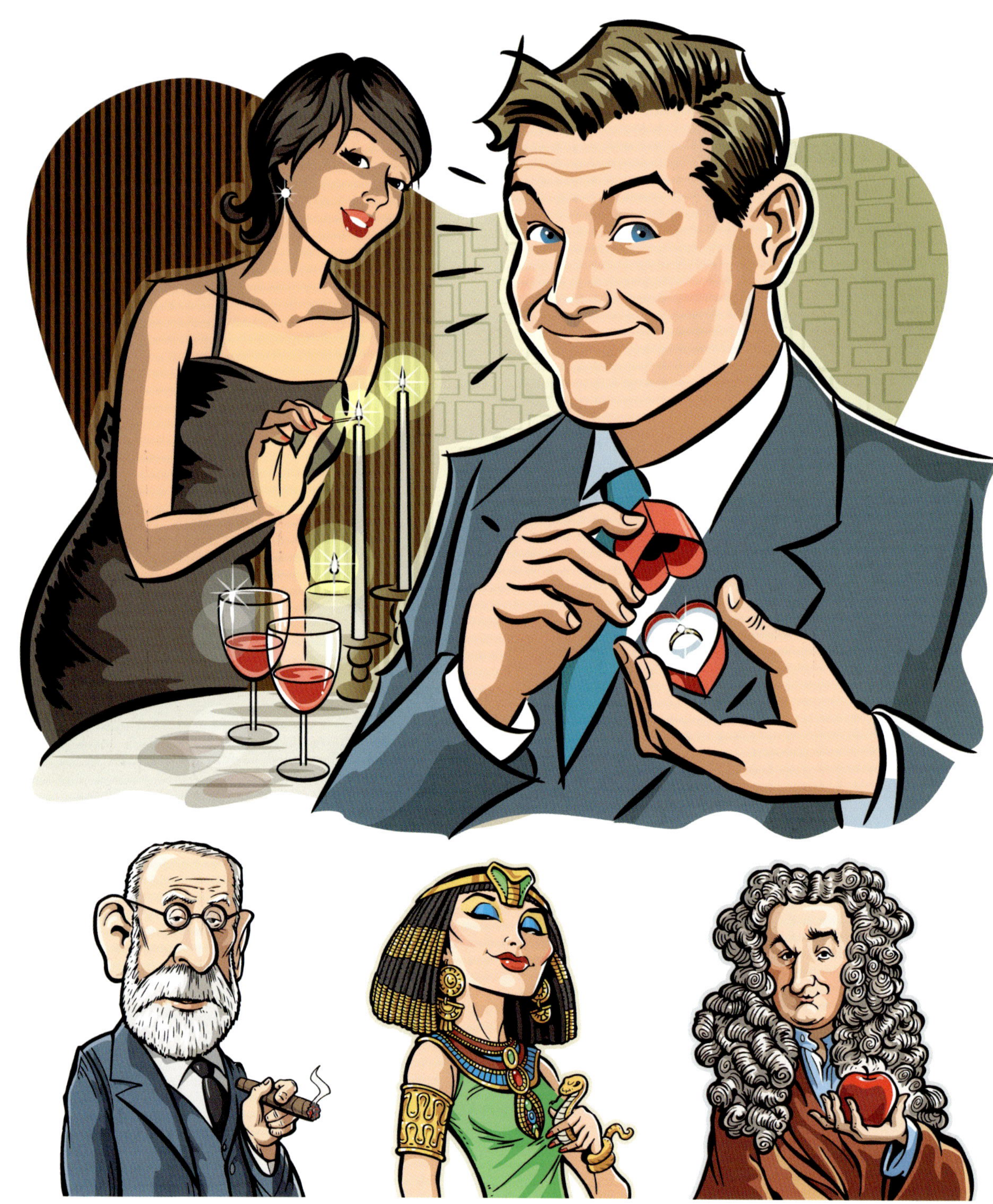

LARRY JONES ILLUSTRATION.COM

Denise Hilton Campbell

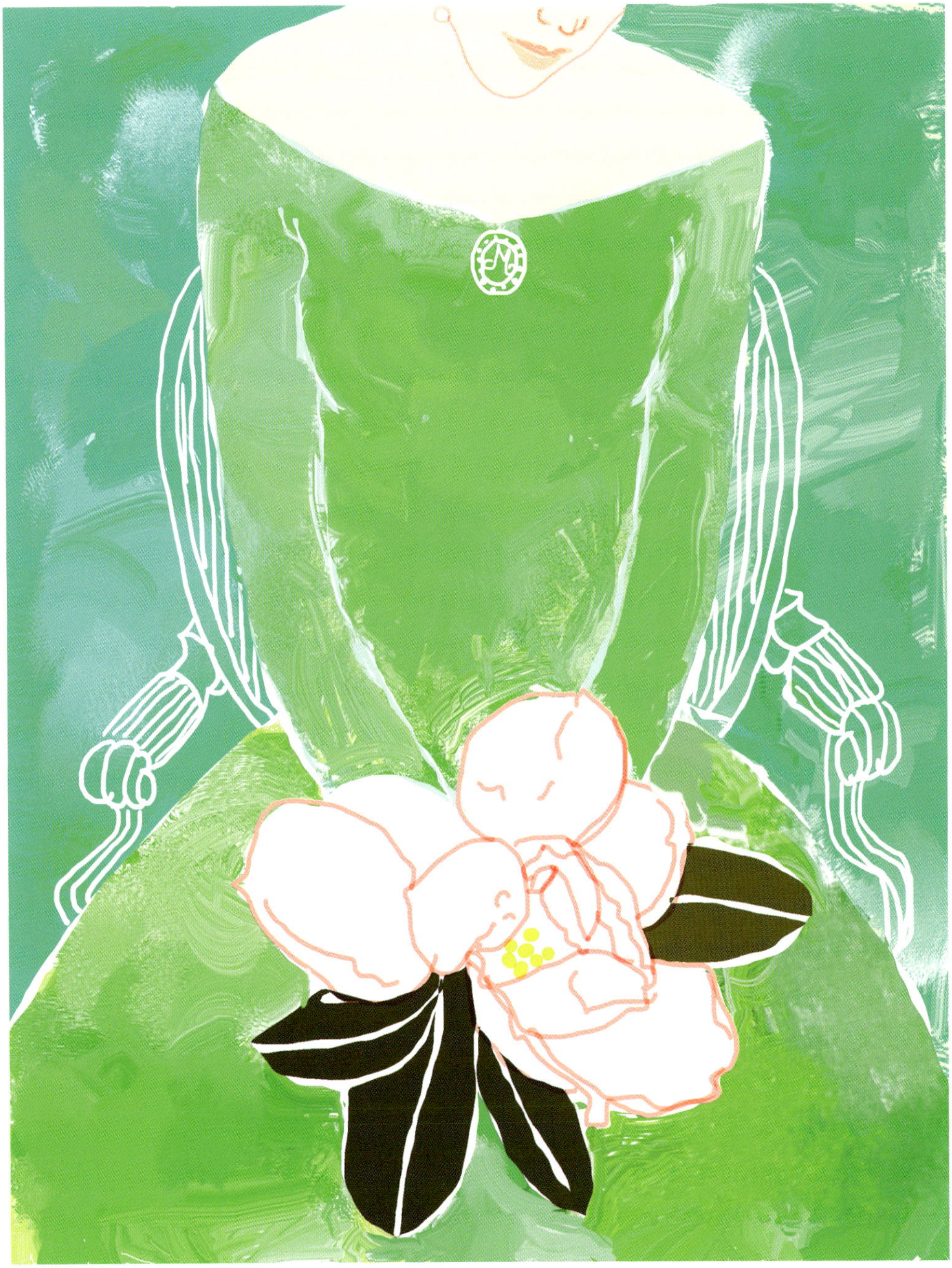

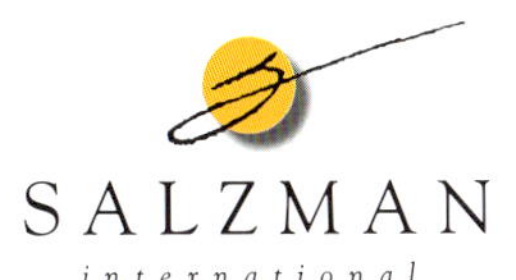

415.285.8267   salzint.com   212.997.0115

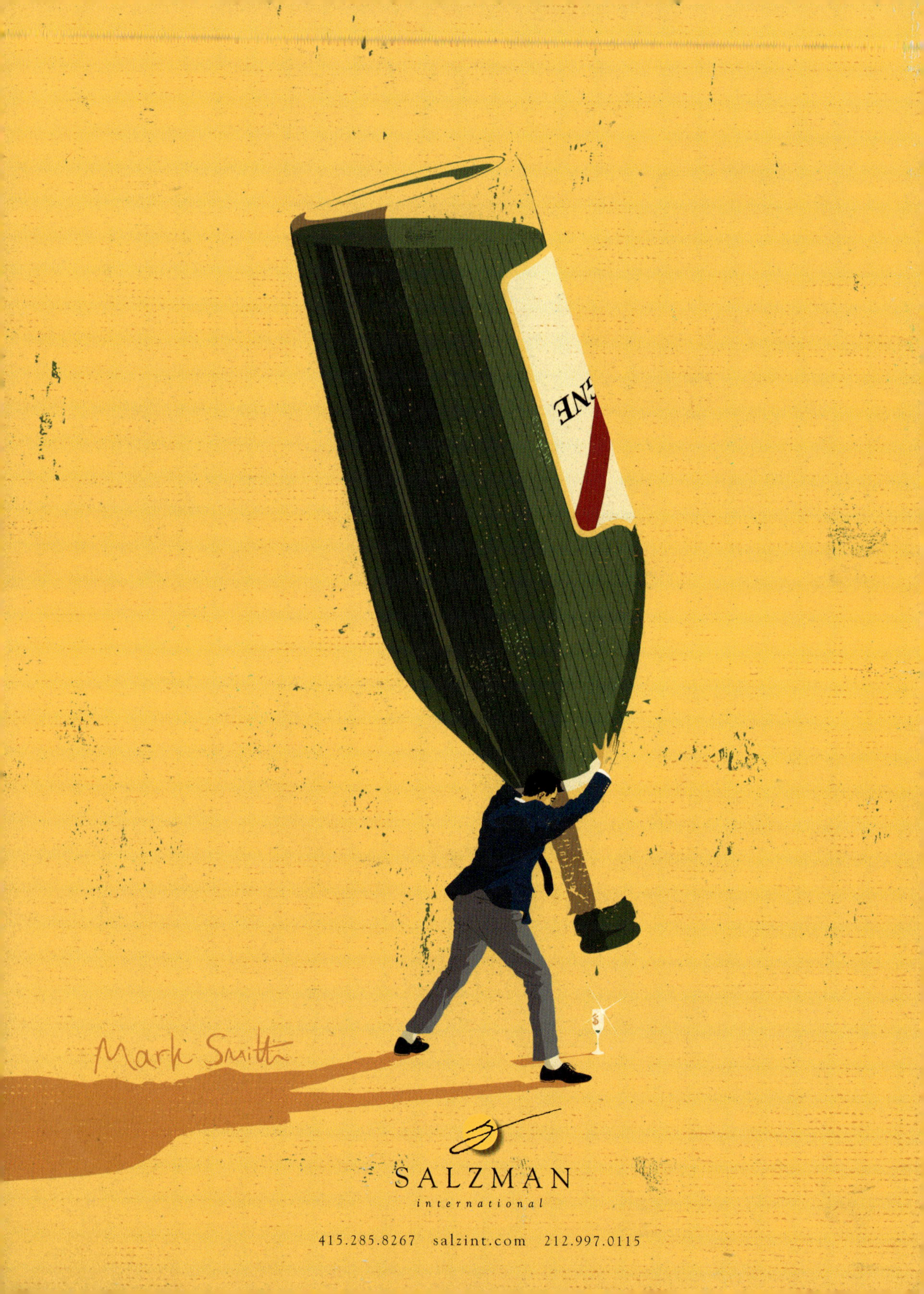

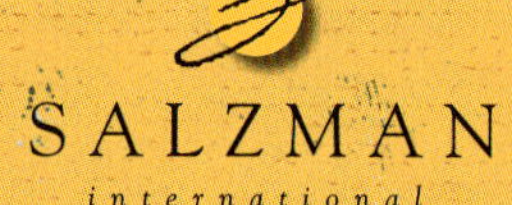
Mark Smith
SALZMAN
international
415.285.8267   salzint.com   212.997.0115

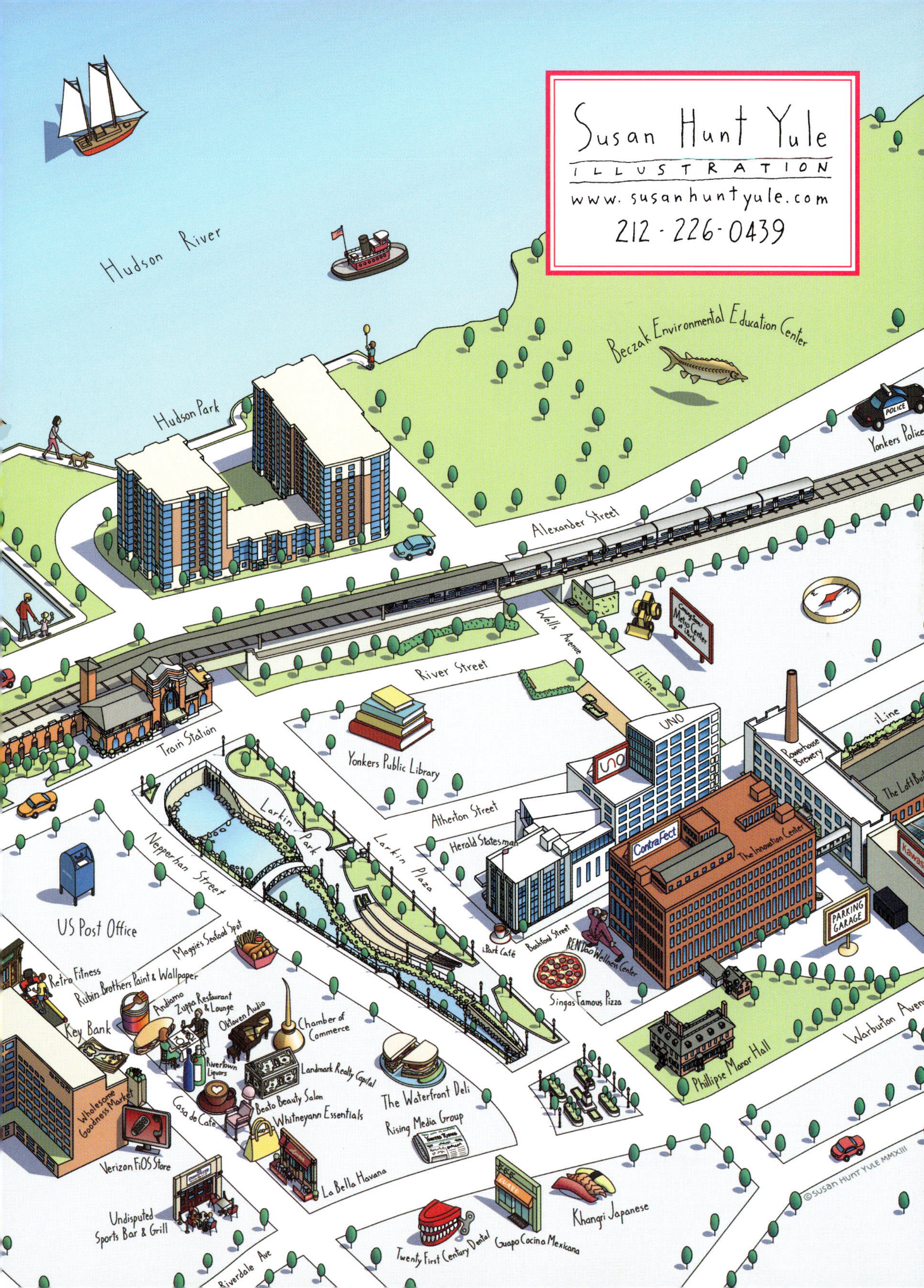

Susan Hunt Yule
ILLUSTRATION
www. susanhuntyule.com
212 · 226 · 0439
Hudson River
Beczak Environmental Education Center
Hudson Park
Yonkers Police
POLICE
Alexander Street
Wells Avenue
iLine
River Street
Metro Center
UNO
UNO
iLine
Powerhouse Brewery
The Loft Bu
Train Station
Yonkers Public Library
Larkin Park
Atherton Street
Larkin Plaza
Herald Statesman
ContraFect
The Innovation Center
Kawa
US Post Office
Nepperhan Street
PARKING GARAGE
Maggie's Seafood Spot
Retro Fitness
iPark Café
Bashford Street
REN Leo Wellness Center
Rubin Brothers Paint & Wallpaper
Andiamo
Zuppa Restaurant & Lounge
Oktaven Audio
Chamber of Commerce
Singas Famous Pizza
Key Bank
Rivertown Liquors
Landmark Realty Capital
The Waterfront Deli
Phillipse Manor Hall
Warburton Avenue
Casa de Café
Beato Beauty Salon
Whitneyann Essentials
Rising Media Group
Wholesome Goodness Market
Verizon FiOS Store
La Bella Havana
Undisputed Sports Bar & Grill
Twenty First Century Dental
Guapo Cocina Mexicana
Khangri Japanese
Riverdale Ave
©Susan Hunt Yule MMXIII

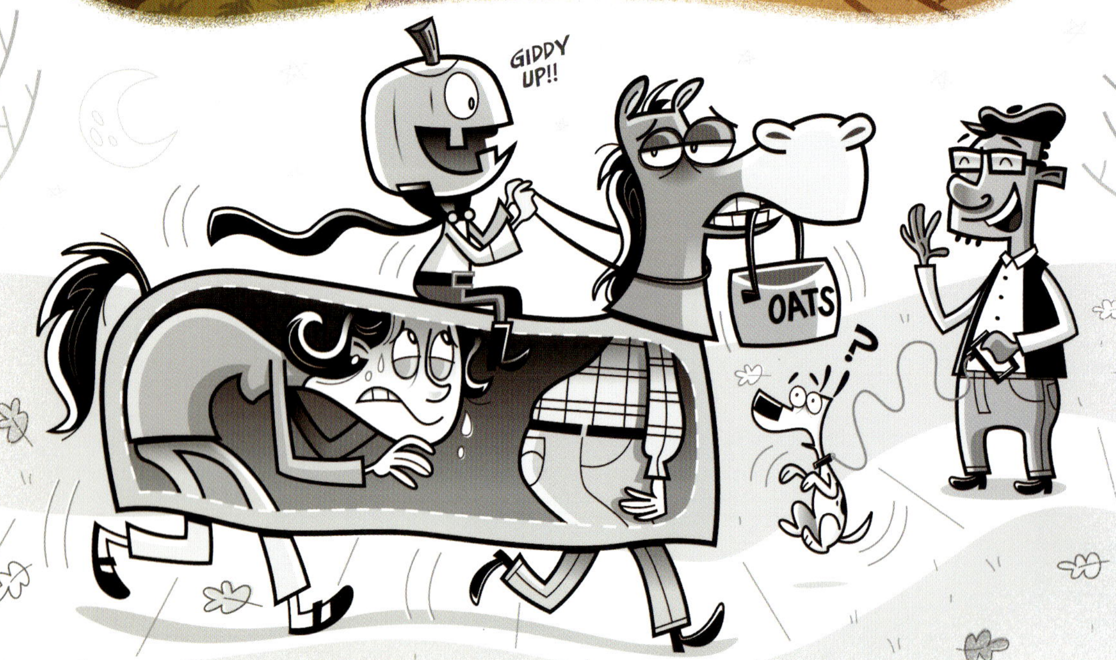

GIDDY UP!!
OATS

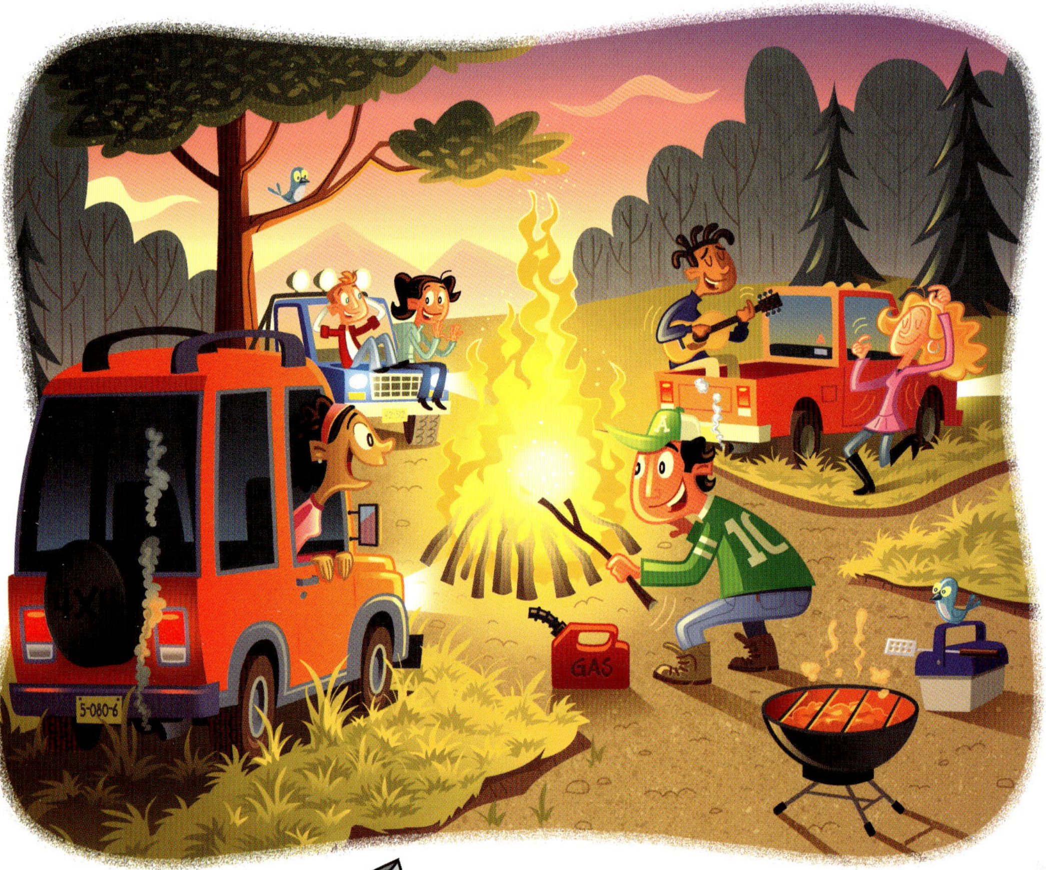

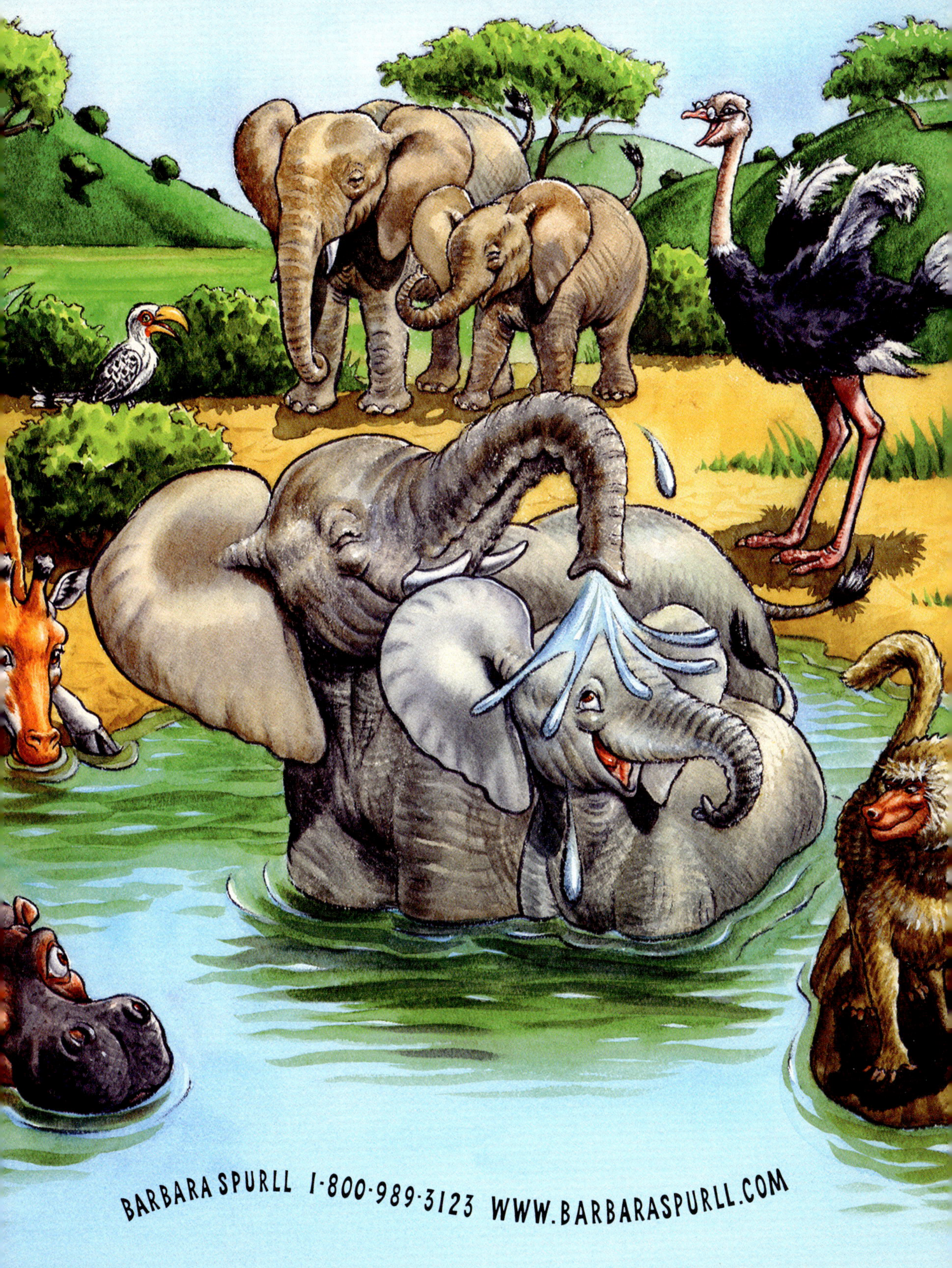BARBARA SPURLL 1·800·989·3123 WWW.BARBARASPURLL.COM

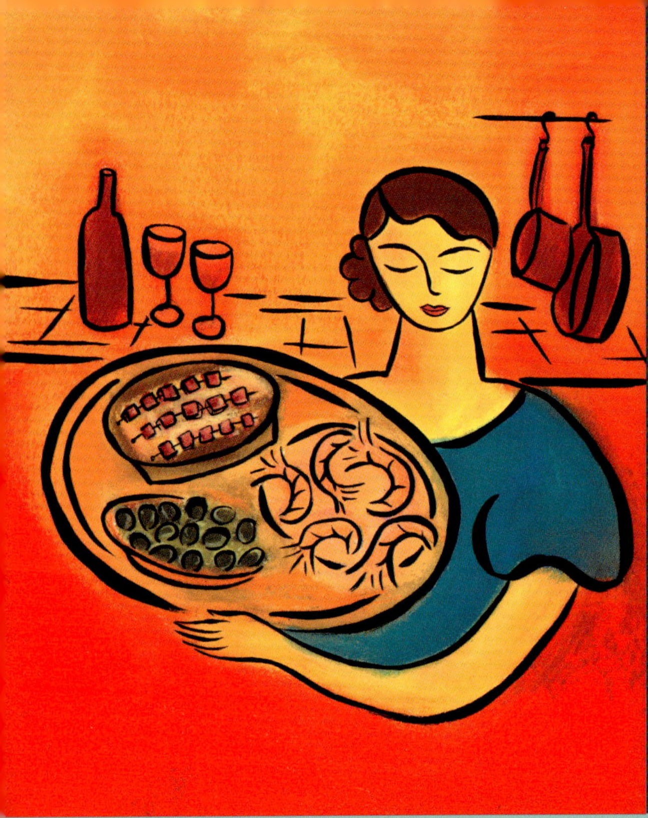

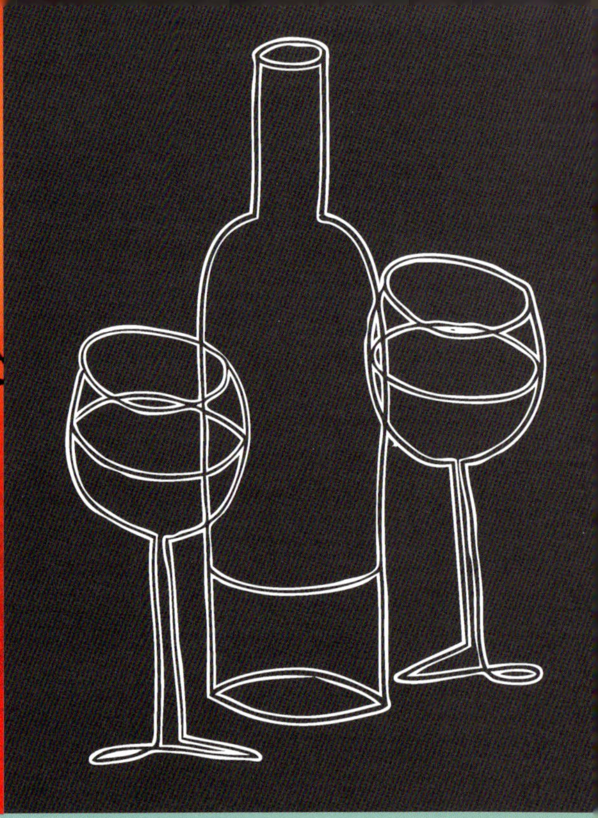

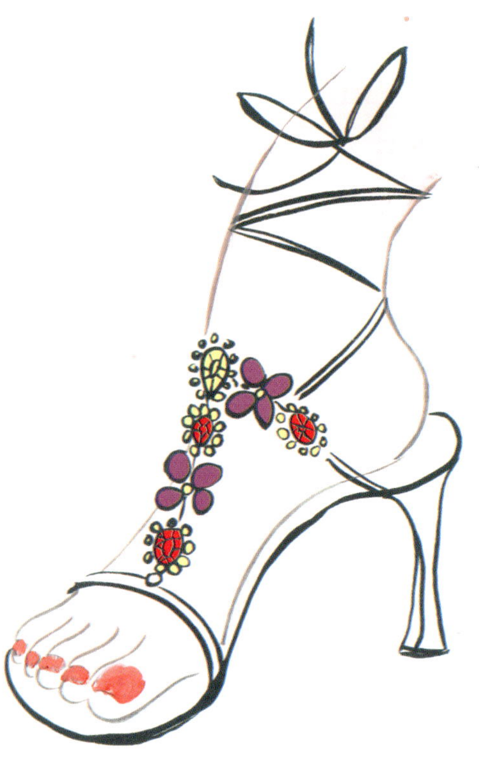

239 784 9321 { JANEDRAWS@ICLOUD.COM } WWW.JANEMJOLSNESS.COM

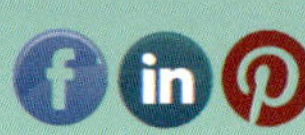

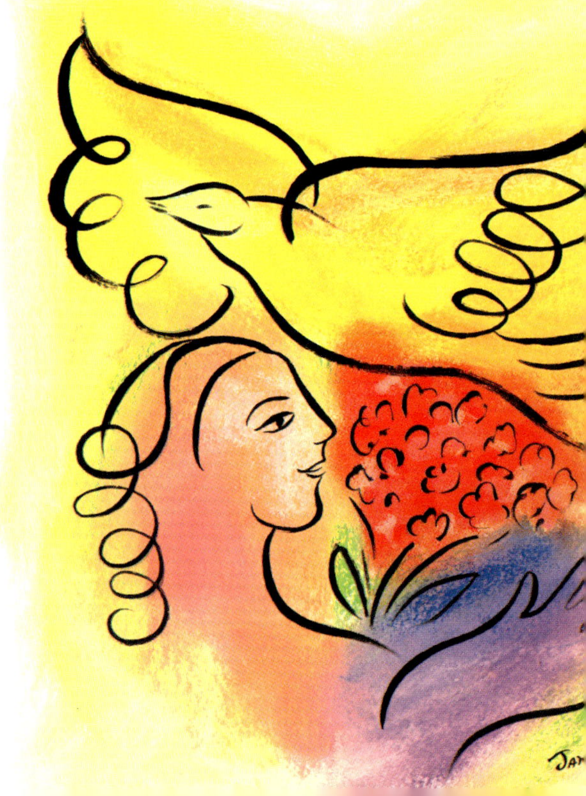

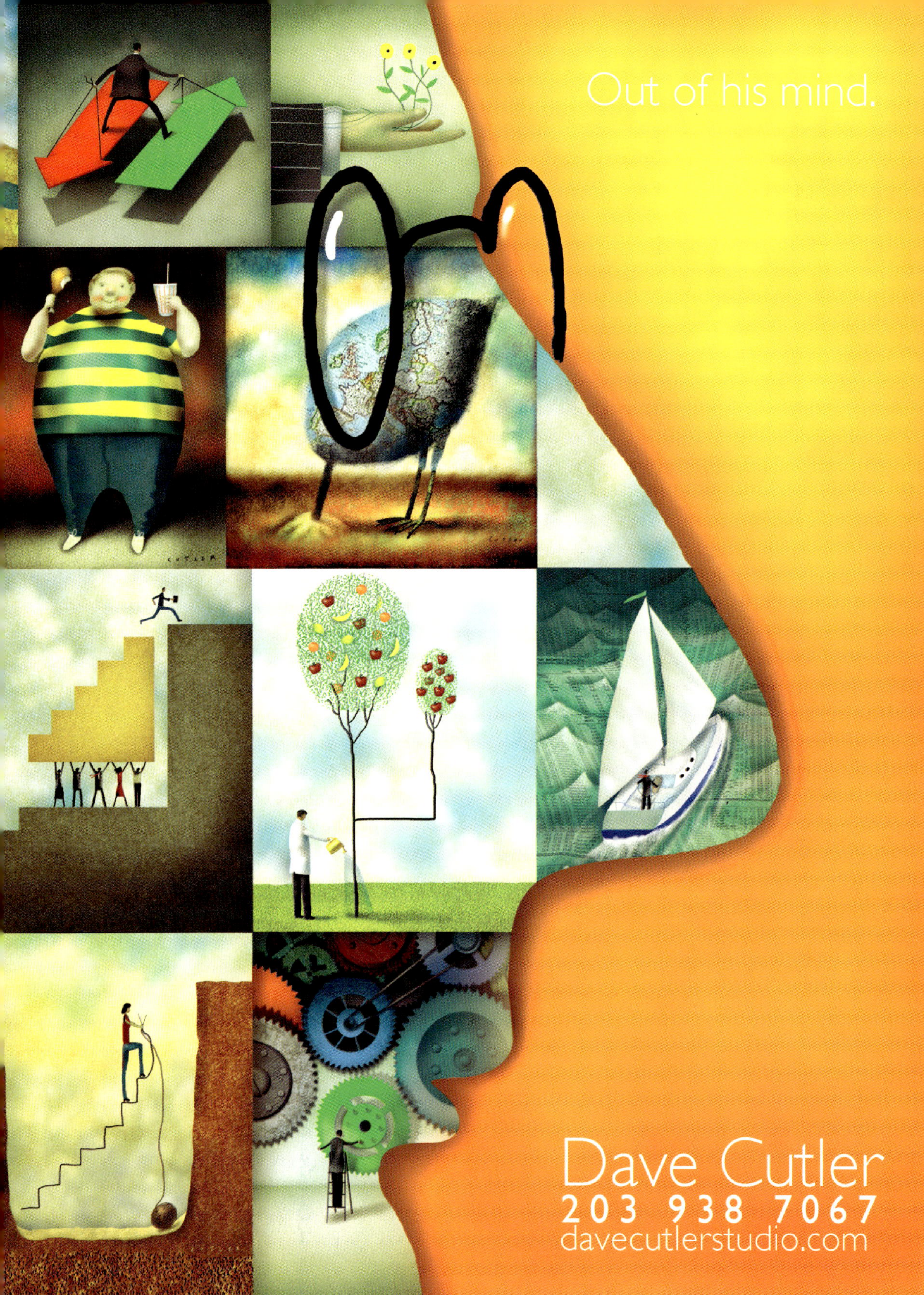

Out of his mind.

Dave Cutler
203 938 7067
davecutlerstudio.com

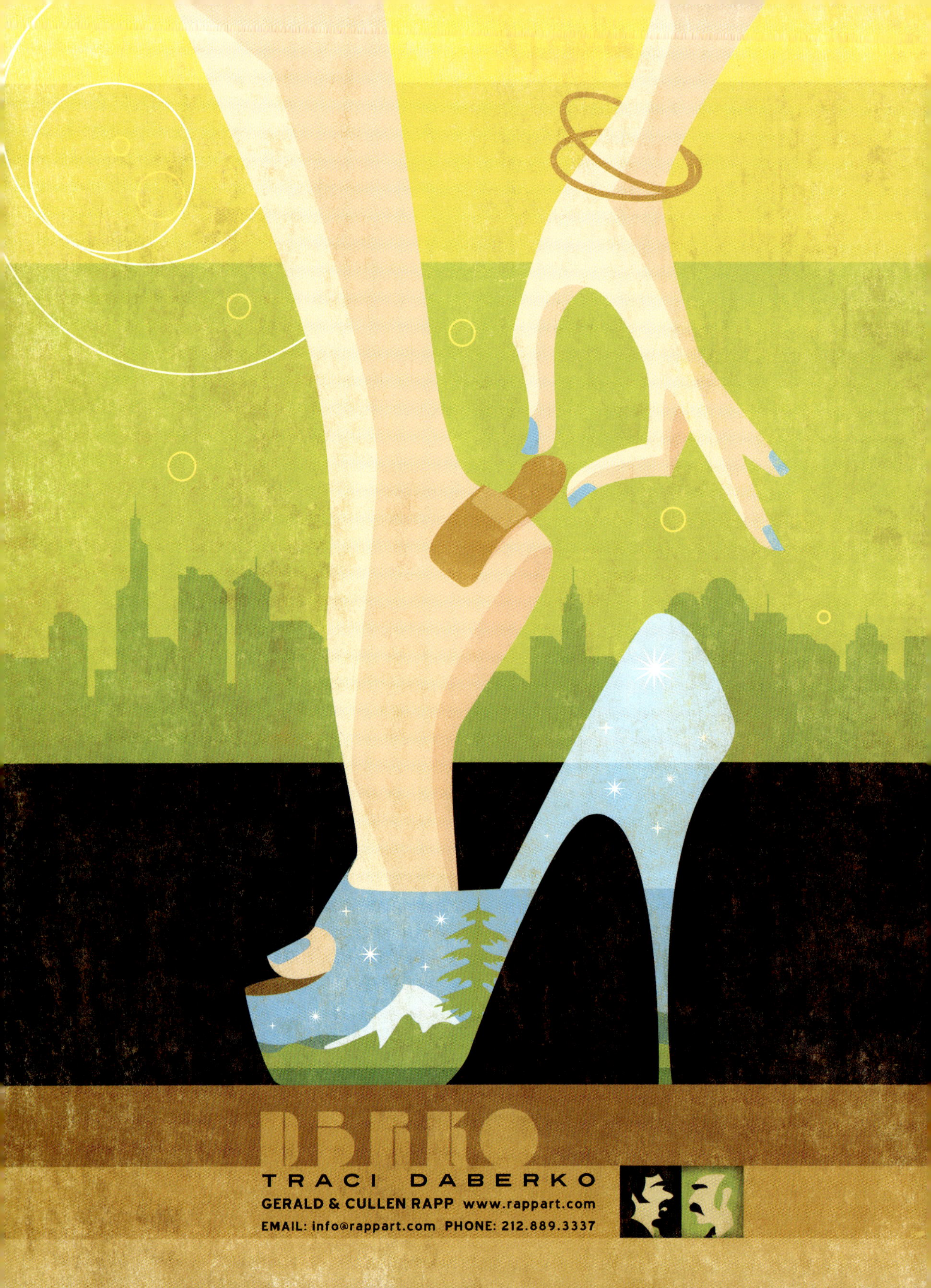
DABERKO
TRACI DABERKO
GERALD & CULLEN RAPP www.rappart.com
EMAIL: info@rappart.com PHONE: 212.889.3337

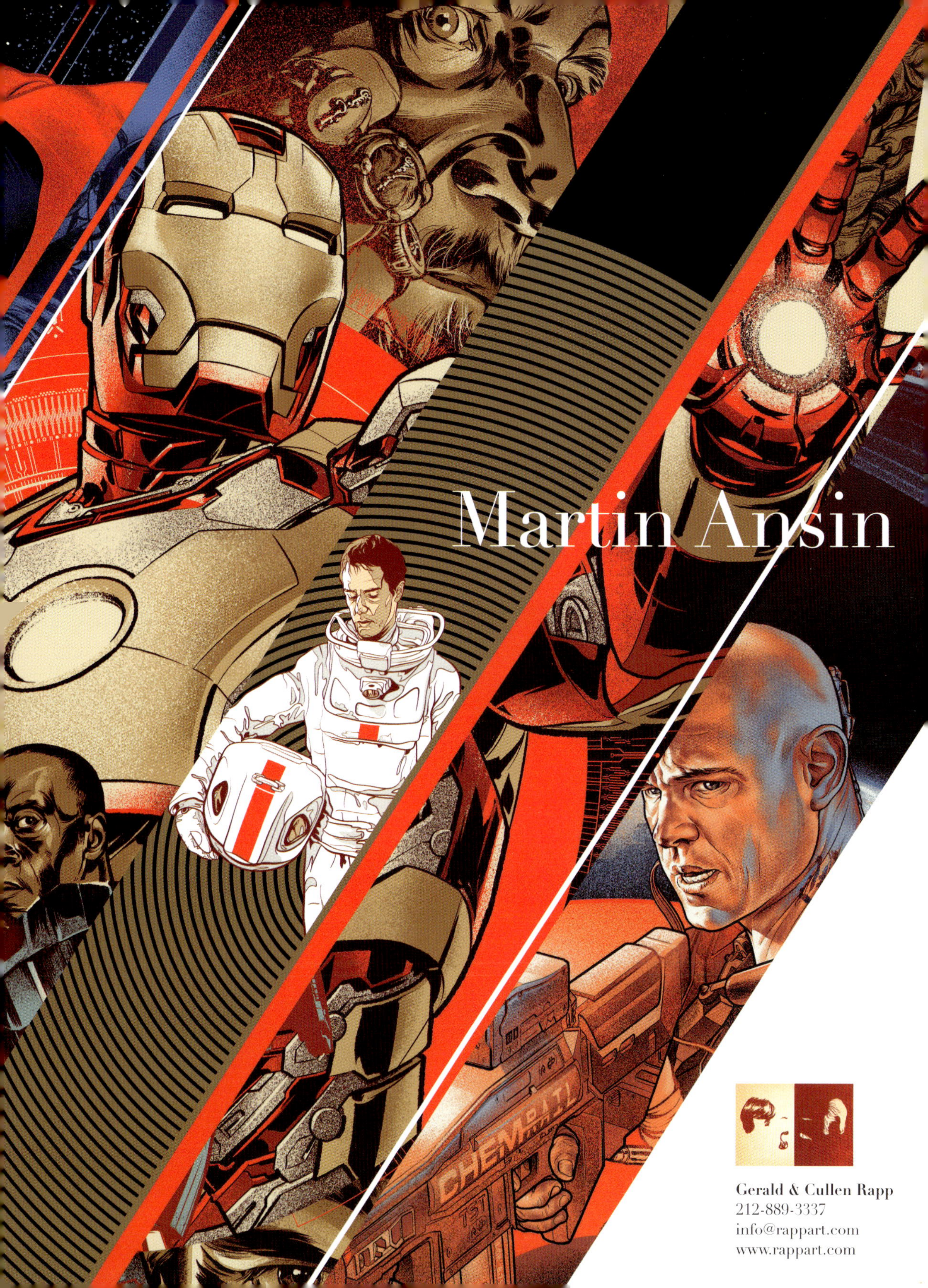

Martin Ansin
CHEMBITI

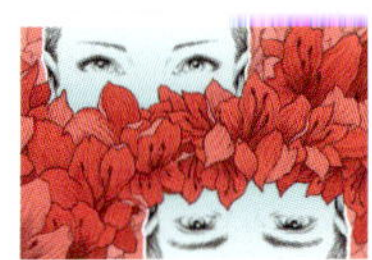

YUTA ONODA
www.yutaonoda.com

Gerald & Cullen Rapp | 212.889.3337
info@rappart.com | www.rappart.com

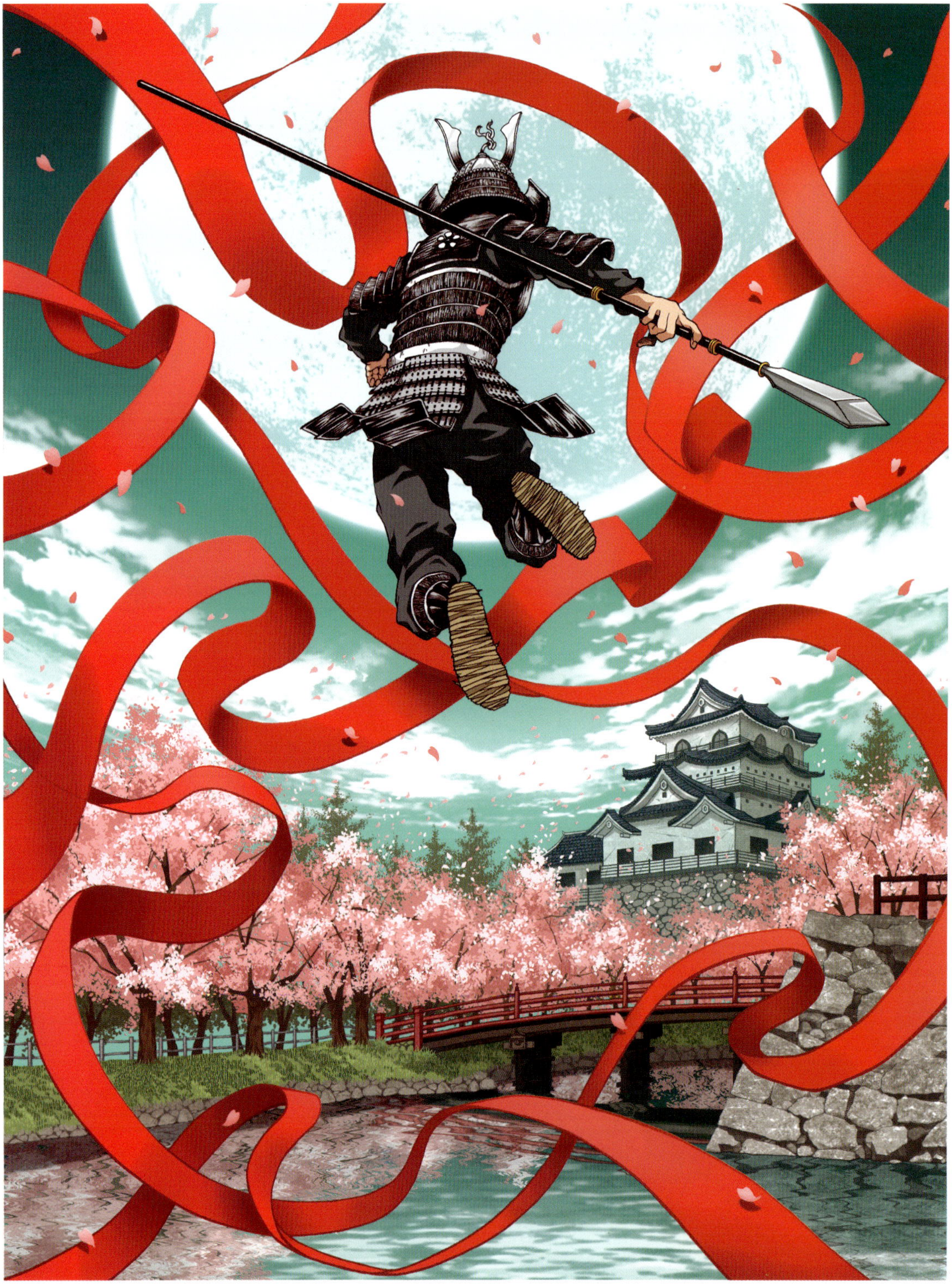

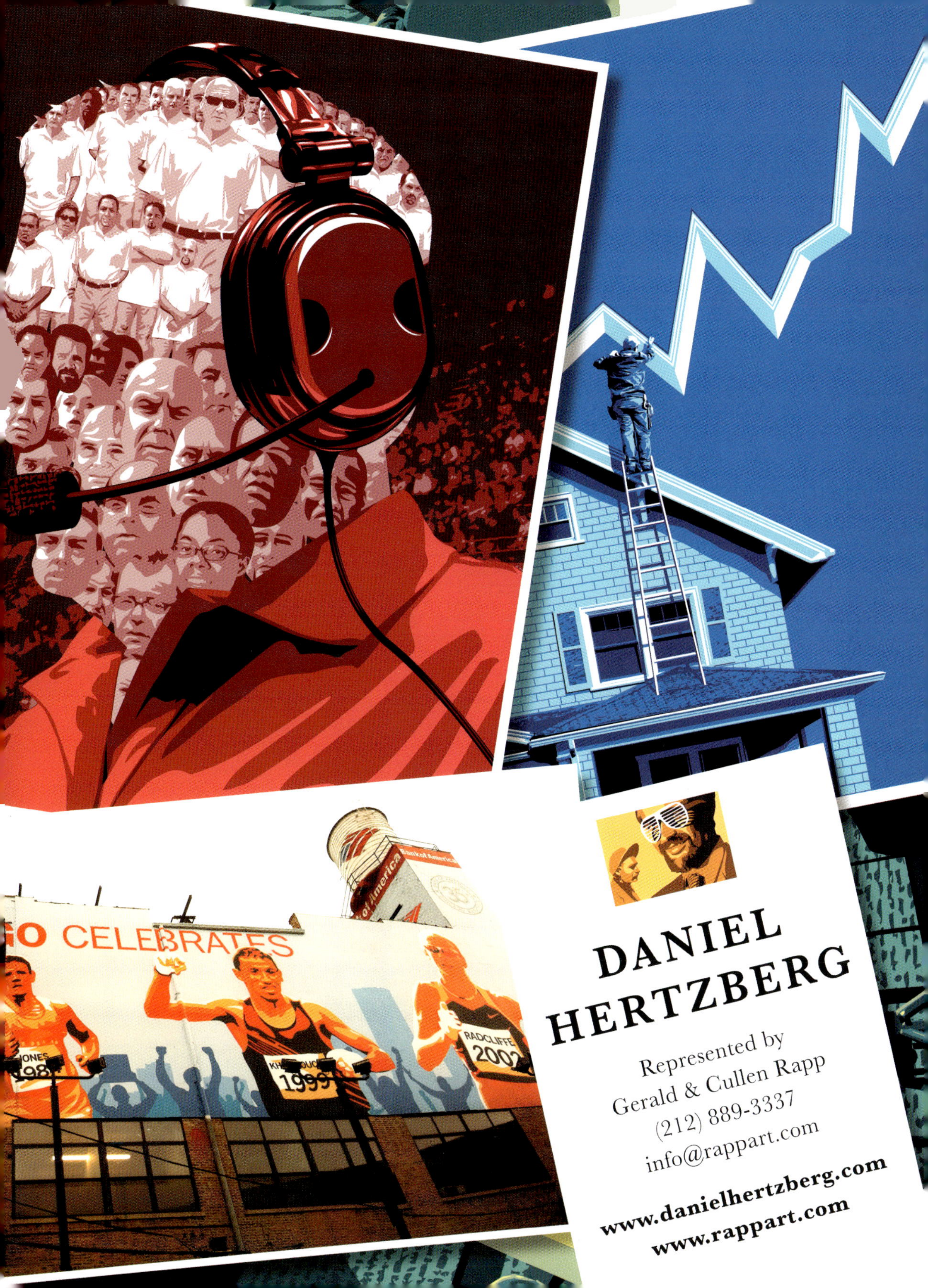
GO CELEBRATES
JONES 1981
1999
RADCLIFFE 2002
DANIEL
HERTZBERG
Represented by
Gerald & Cullen Rapp
(212) 889-3337
info@rappart.com
www.danielhertzberg.com
www.rappart.com

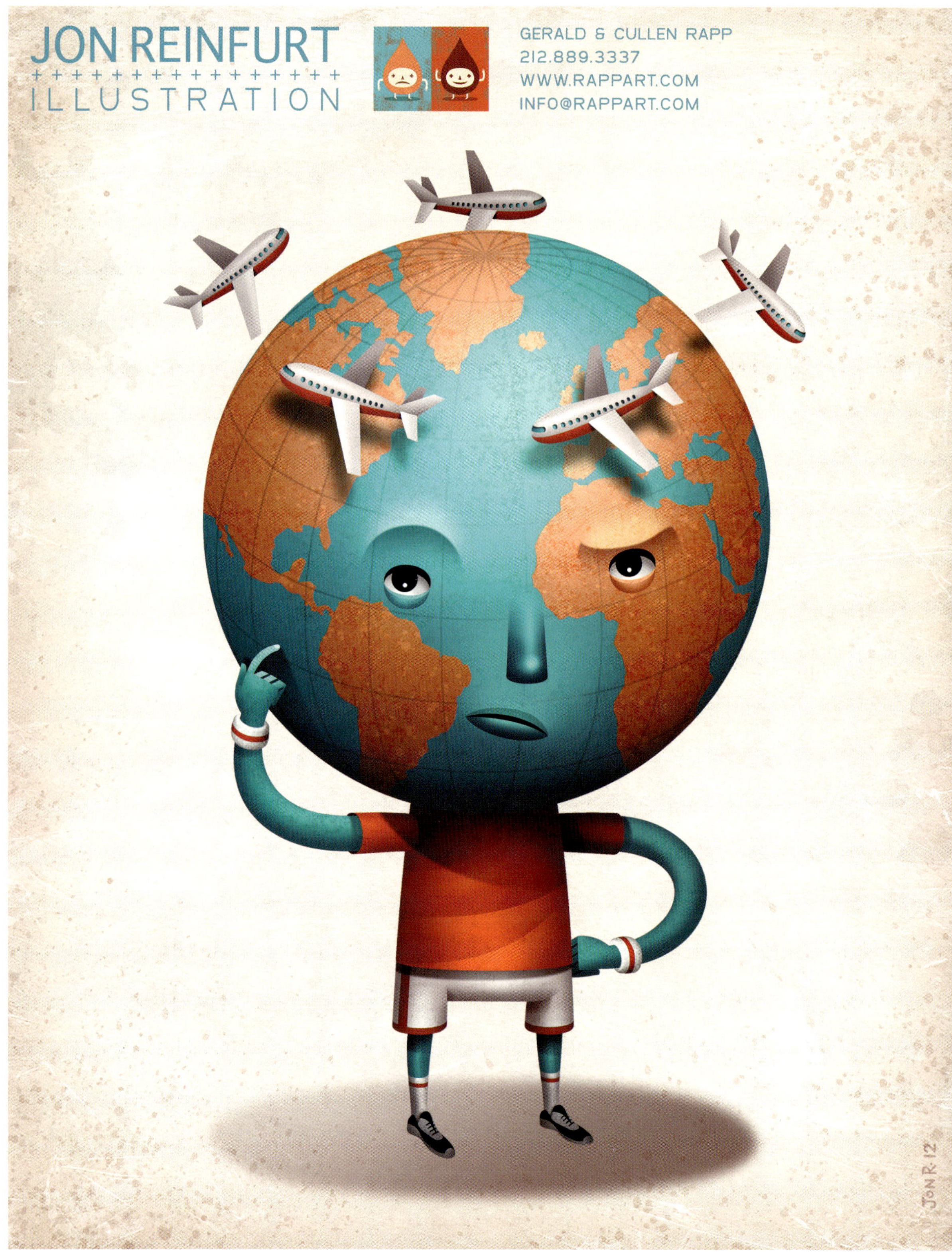
JON REINFURT
ILLUSTRATION
GERALD & CULLEN RAPP
212.889.3337
WWW.RAPPART.COM
INFO@RAPPART.COM

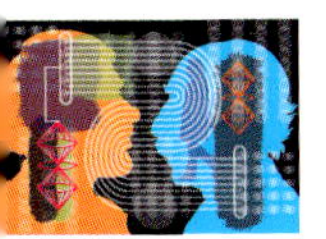

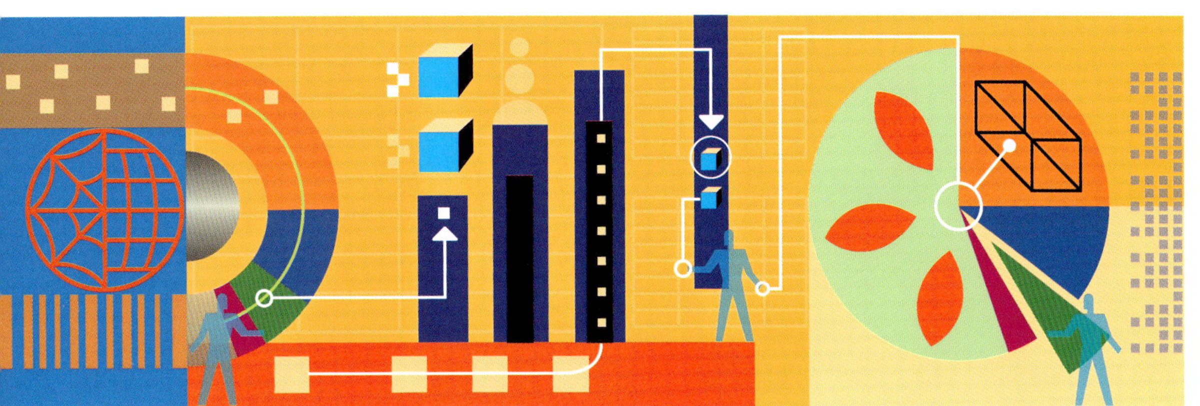

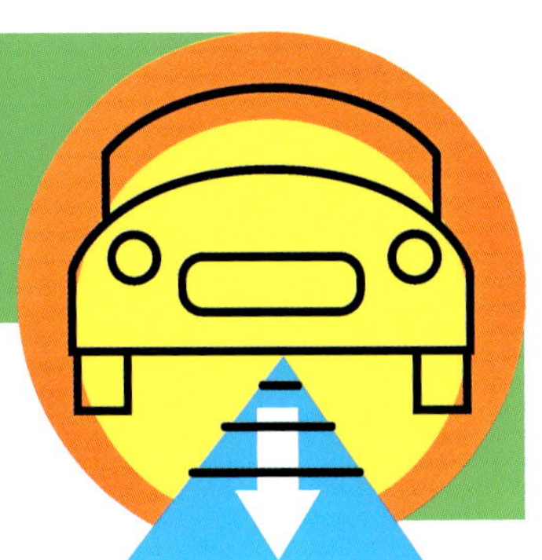

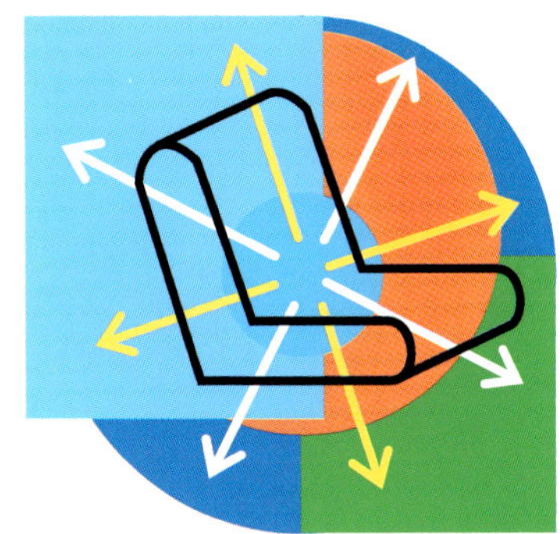

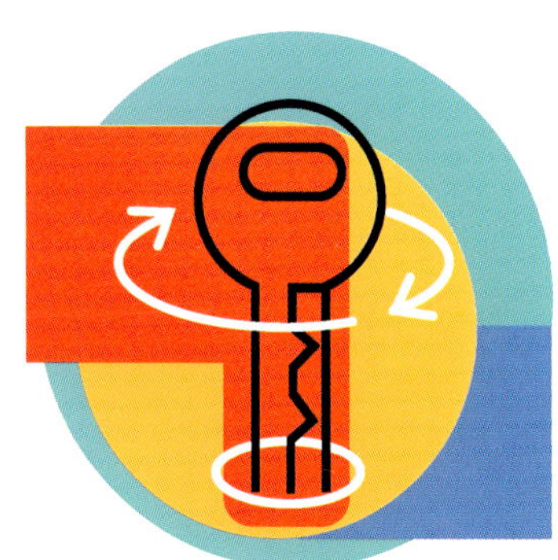

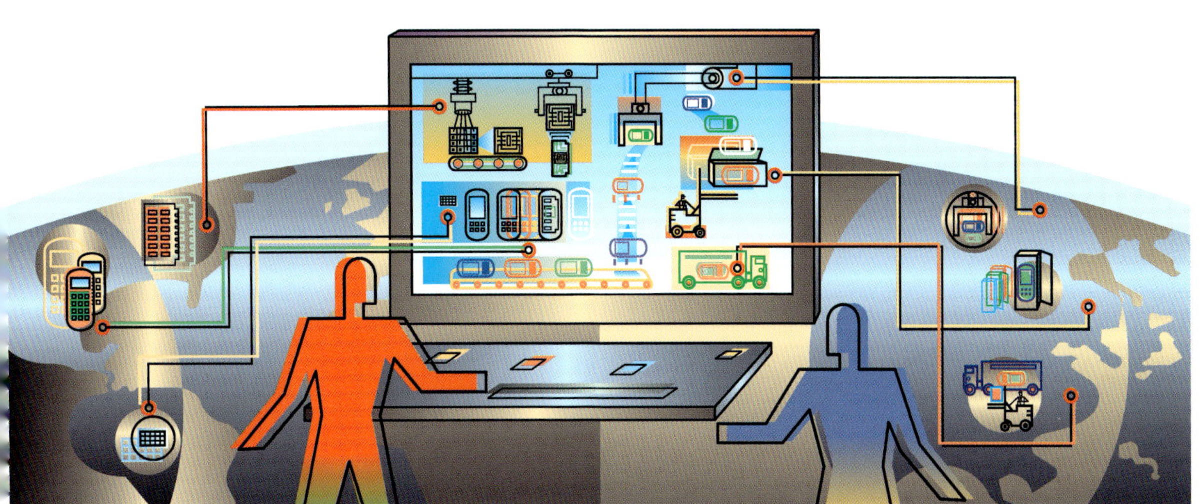

SCOTTY REIFSNYDER

Gerald & Cullen Rapp

212.889.3337

www.rappart.com

info@rappart.com

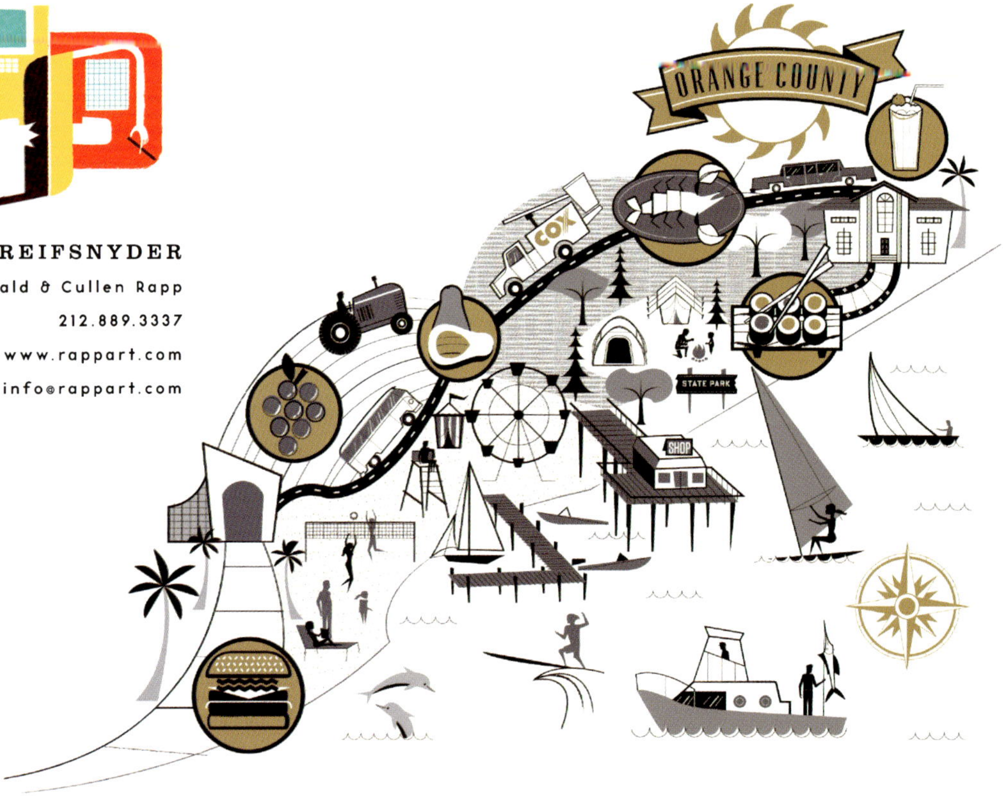

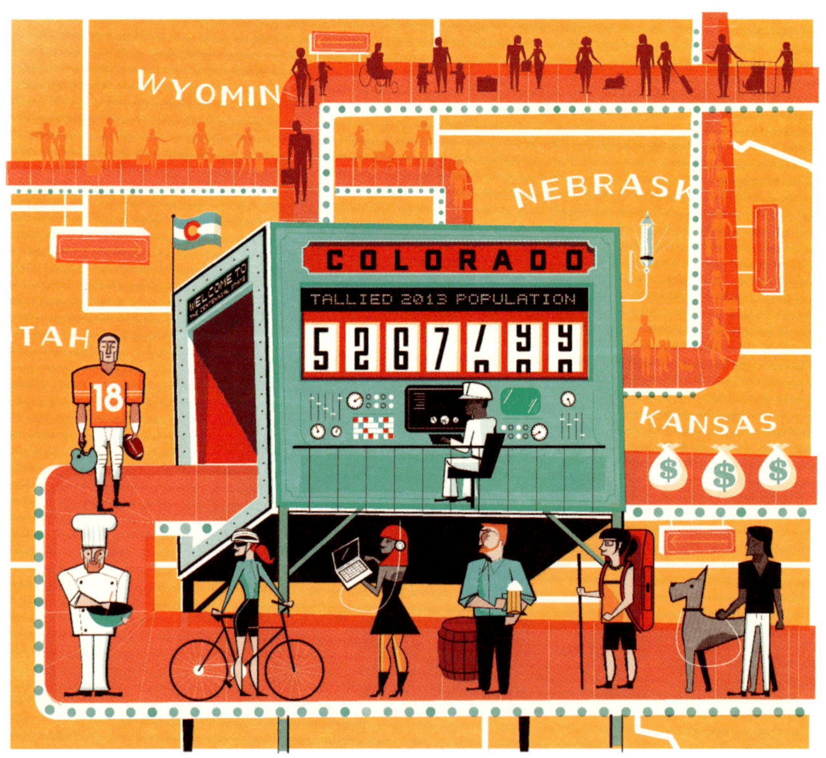

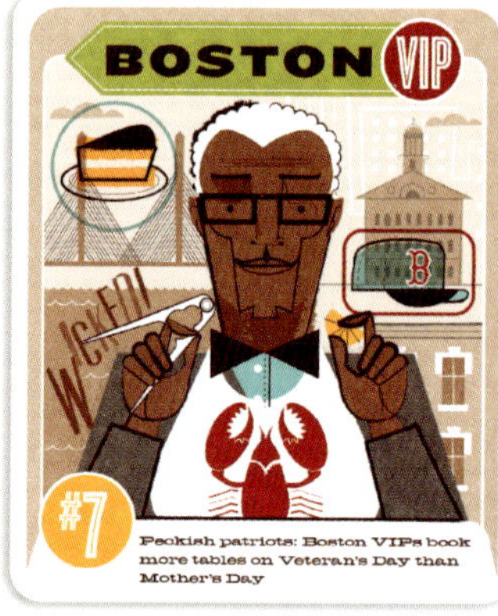

Peckish patriots: Boston VIPs book more tables on Veteran's Day than Mother's Day

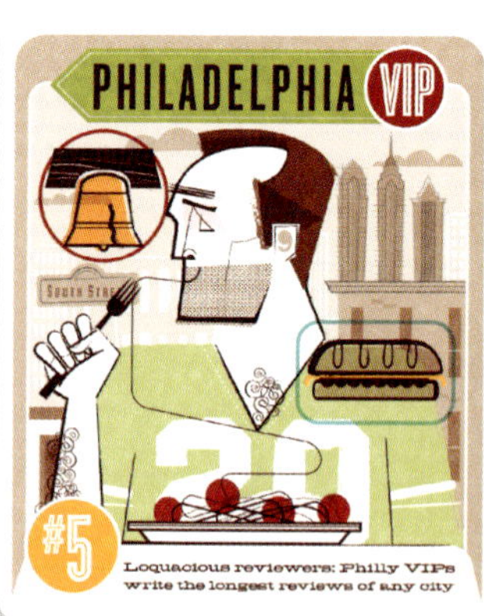

Loquacious reviewers: Philly VIPs write the longest reviews of any city

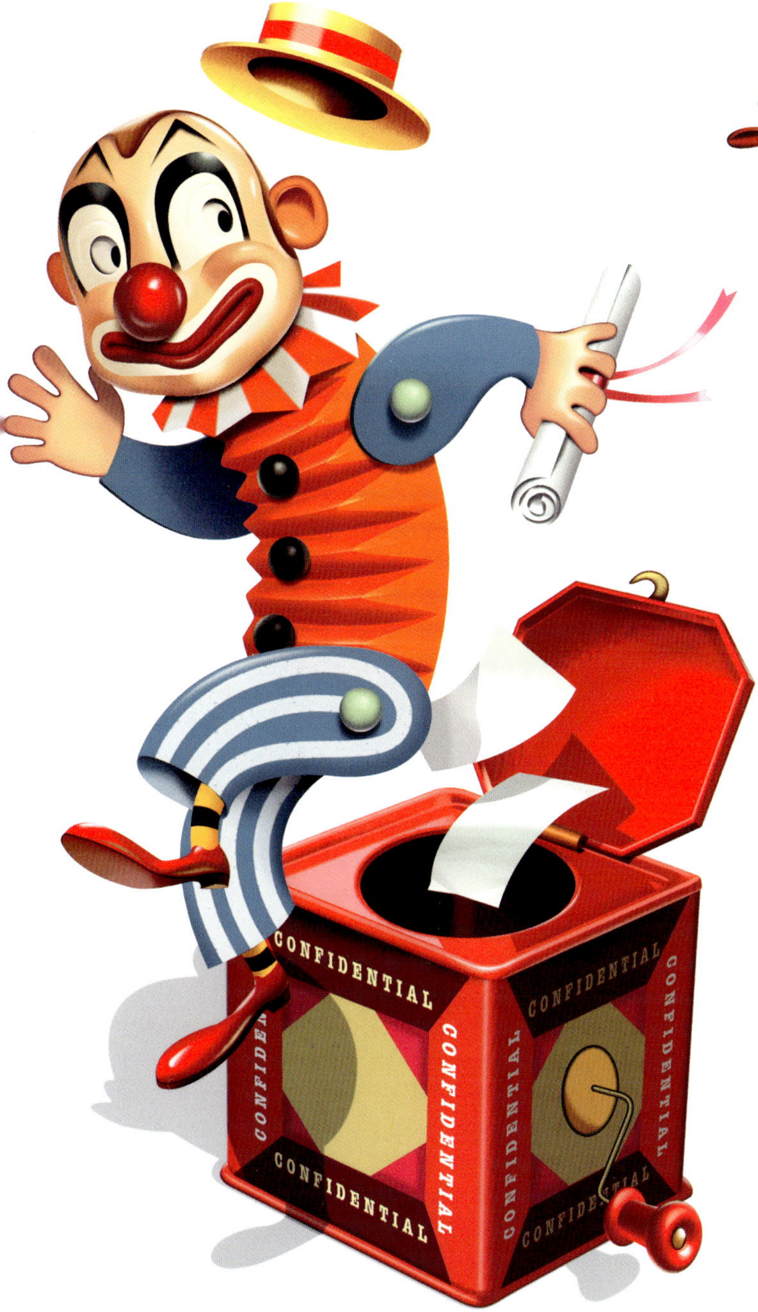

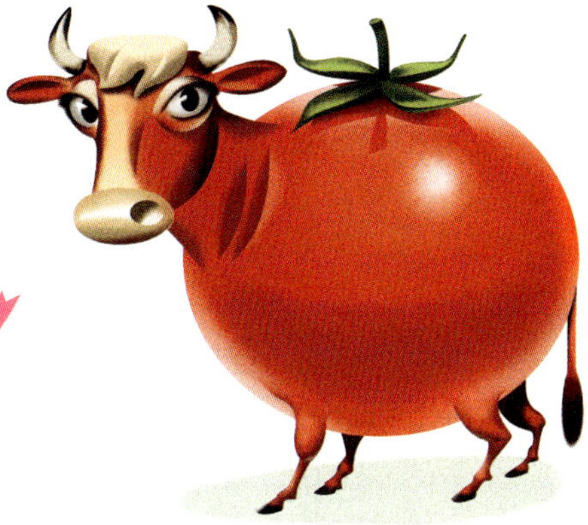

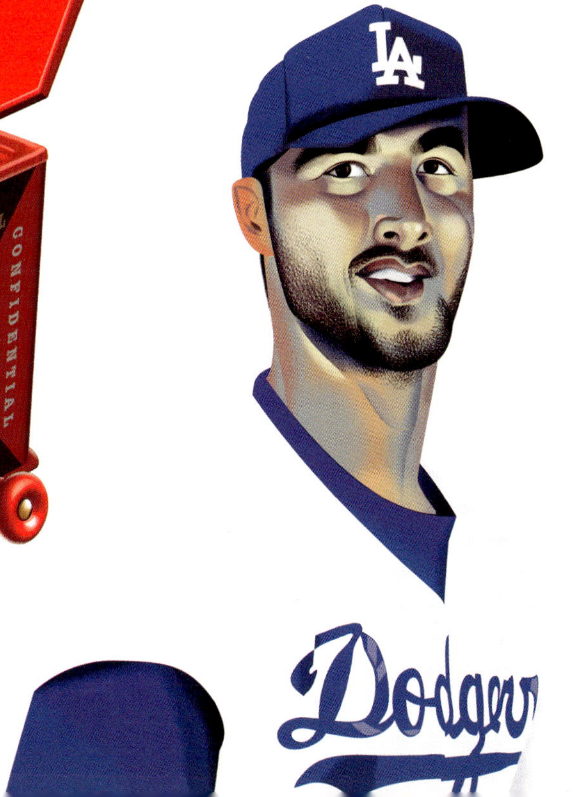

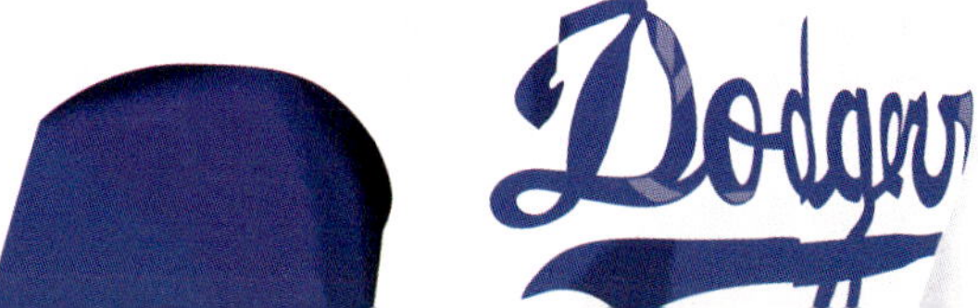

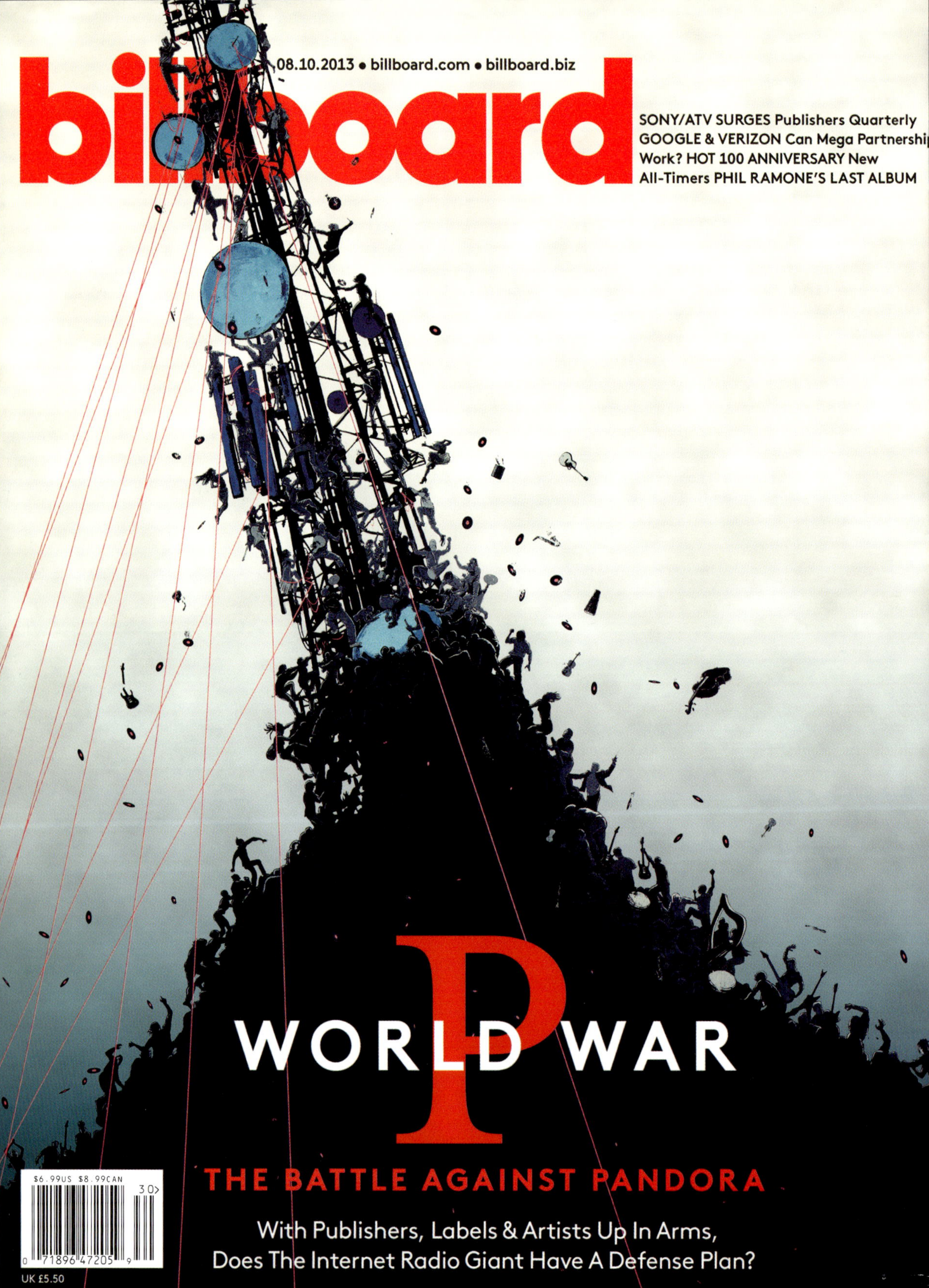

08.10.2013 ● billboard.com ● billboard.biz
billboard
SONY/ATV SURGES Publishers Quarterly
GOOGLE & VERIZON Can Mega Partnership
Work? HOT 100 ANNIVERSARY New
All-Timers PHIL RAMONE'S LAST ALBUM
WORLD WAR P
THE BATTLE AGAINST PANDORA
With Publishers, Labels & Artists Up In Arms,
Does The Internet Radio Giant Have A Defense Plan?
$6.99US $8.99CAN
UK £5.50

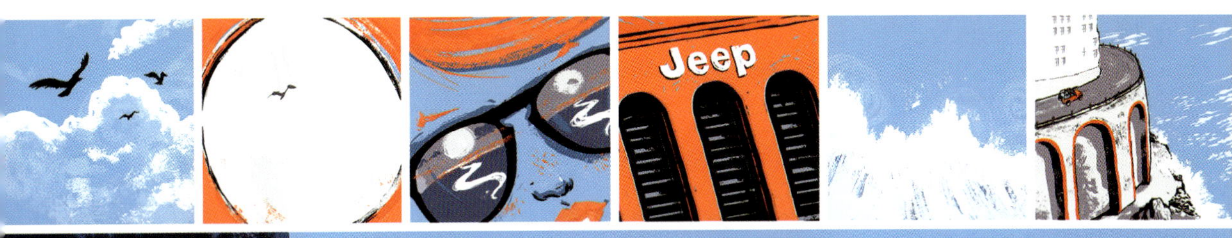
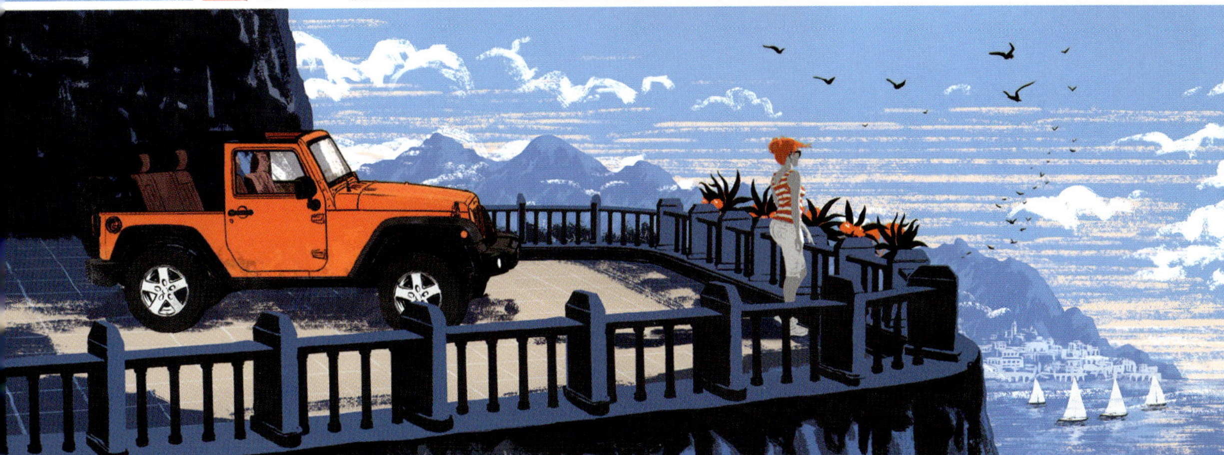
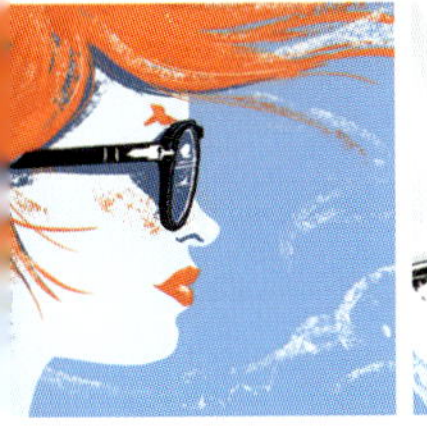
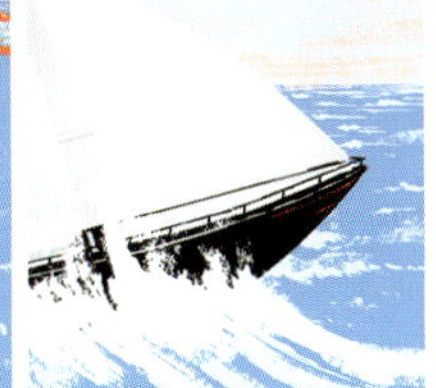
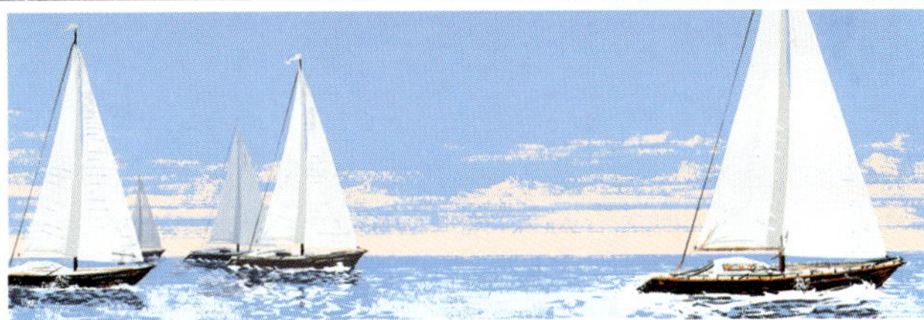
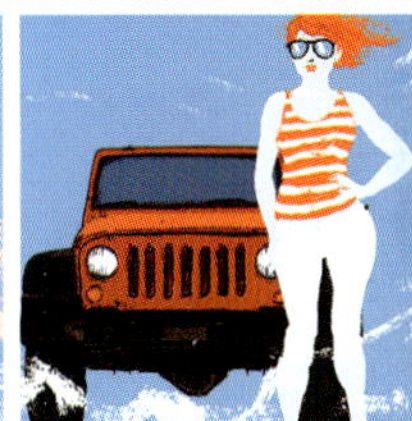
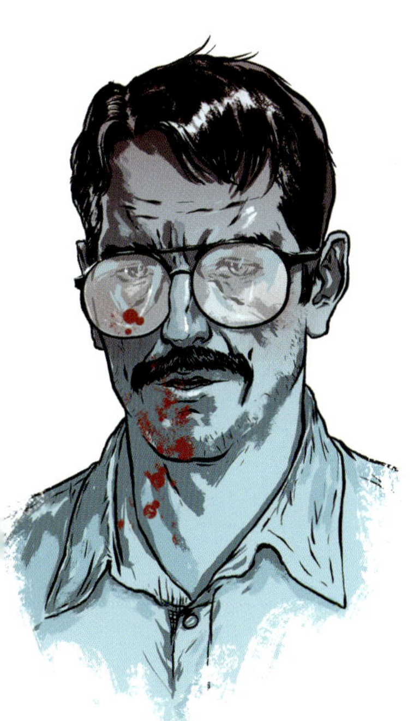
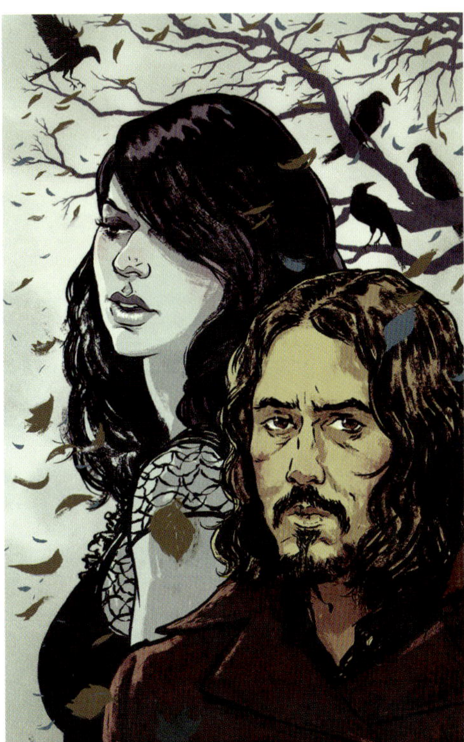
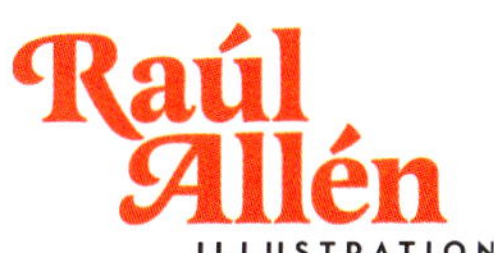

Raúl Allén
ILLUSTRATION
www.raulallen.com

Gerald & Cullen Rapp
INFO@RAPPART.COM
212 889 3337
www.rappart.com

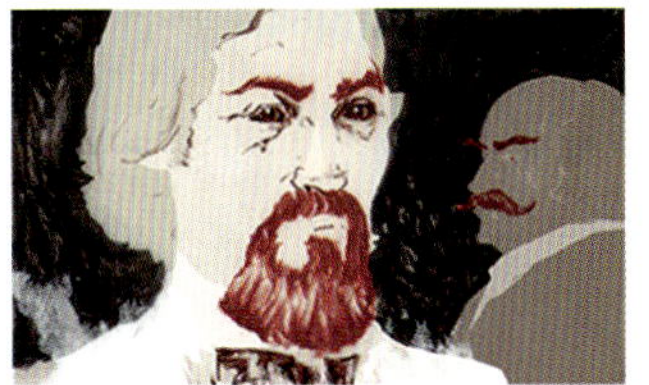

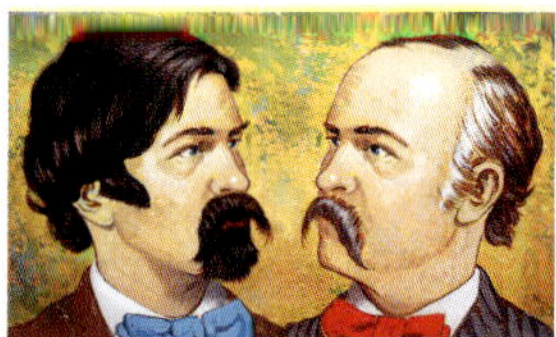

David M. Brinley

Gerald & Cullen Rapp
212.889.3337
info@rappart.com
www.rappart.com
www.davidbrinley.com

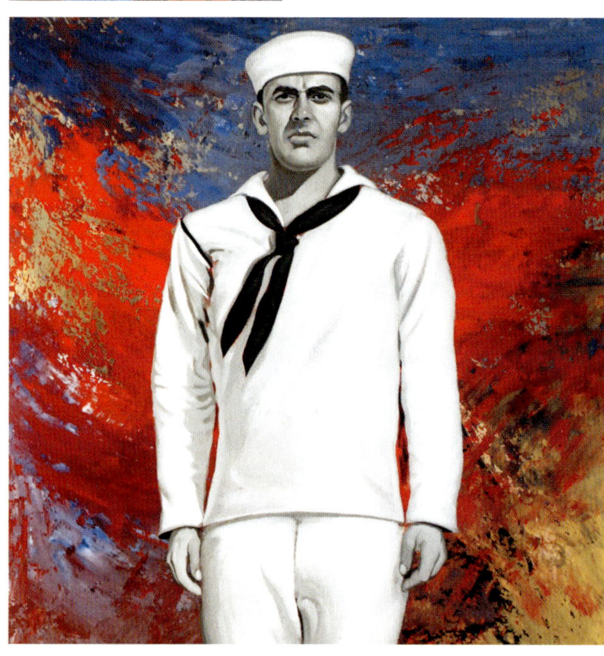

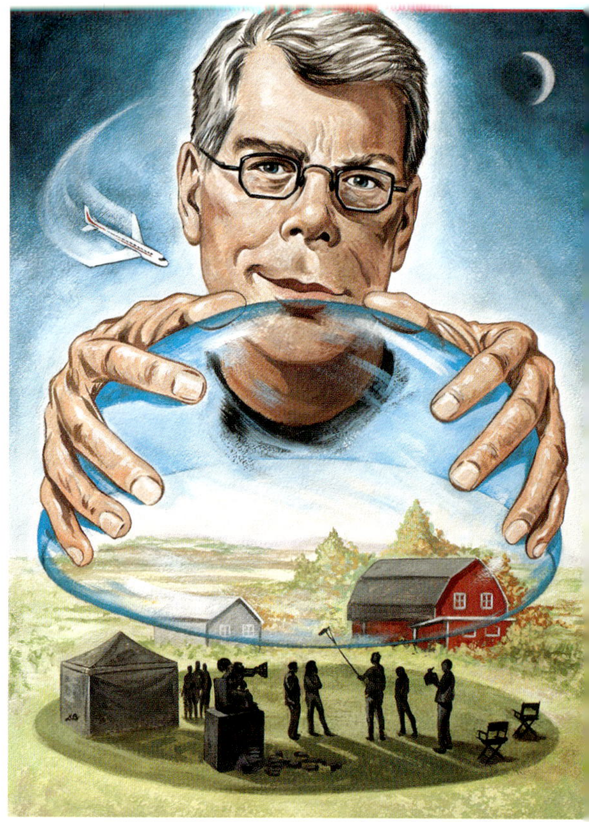

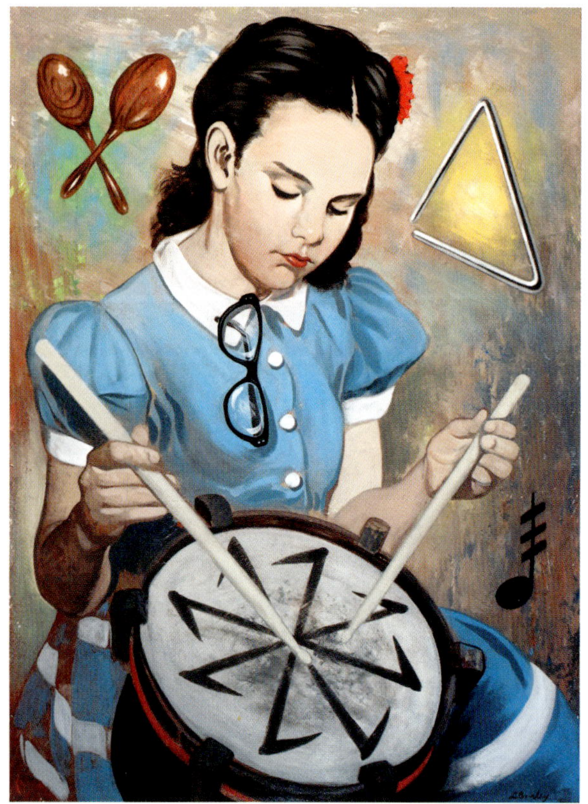

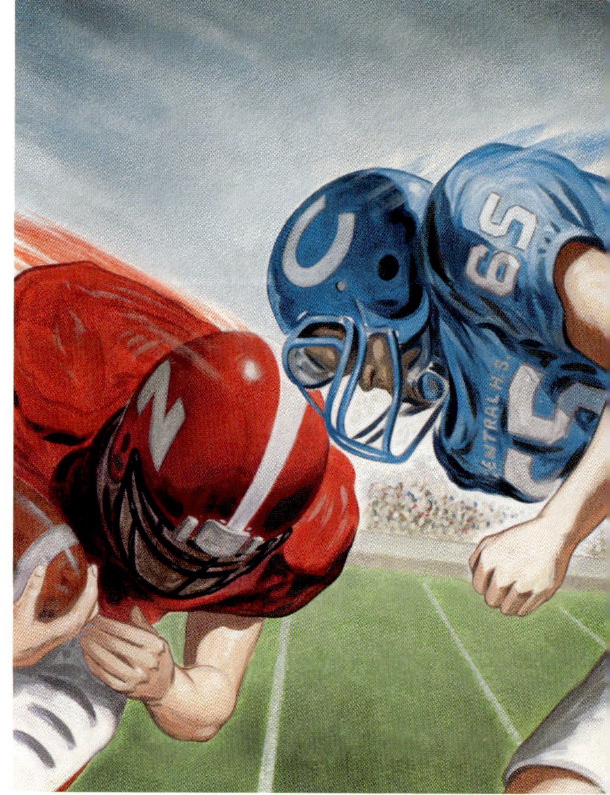

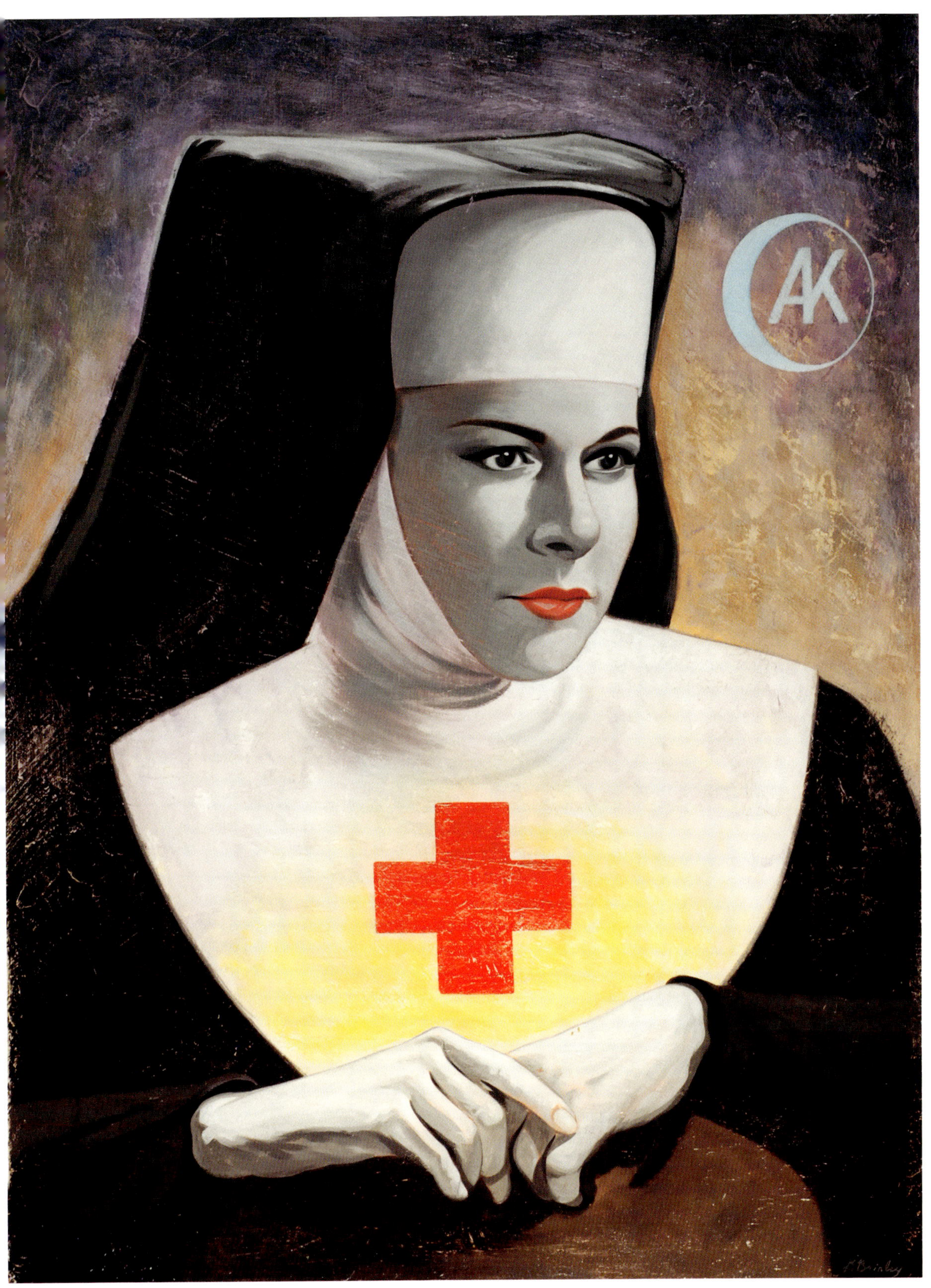
AK

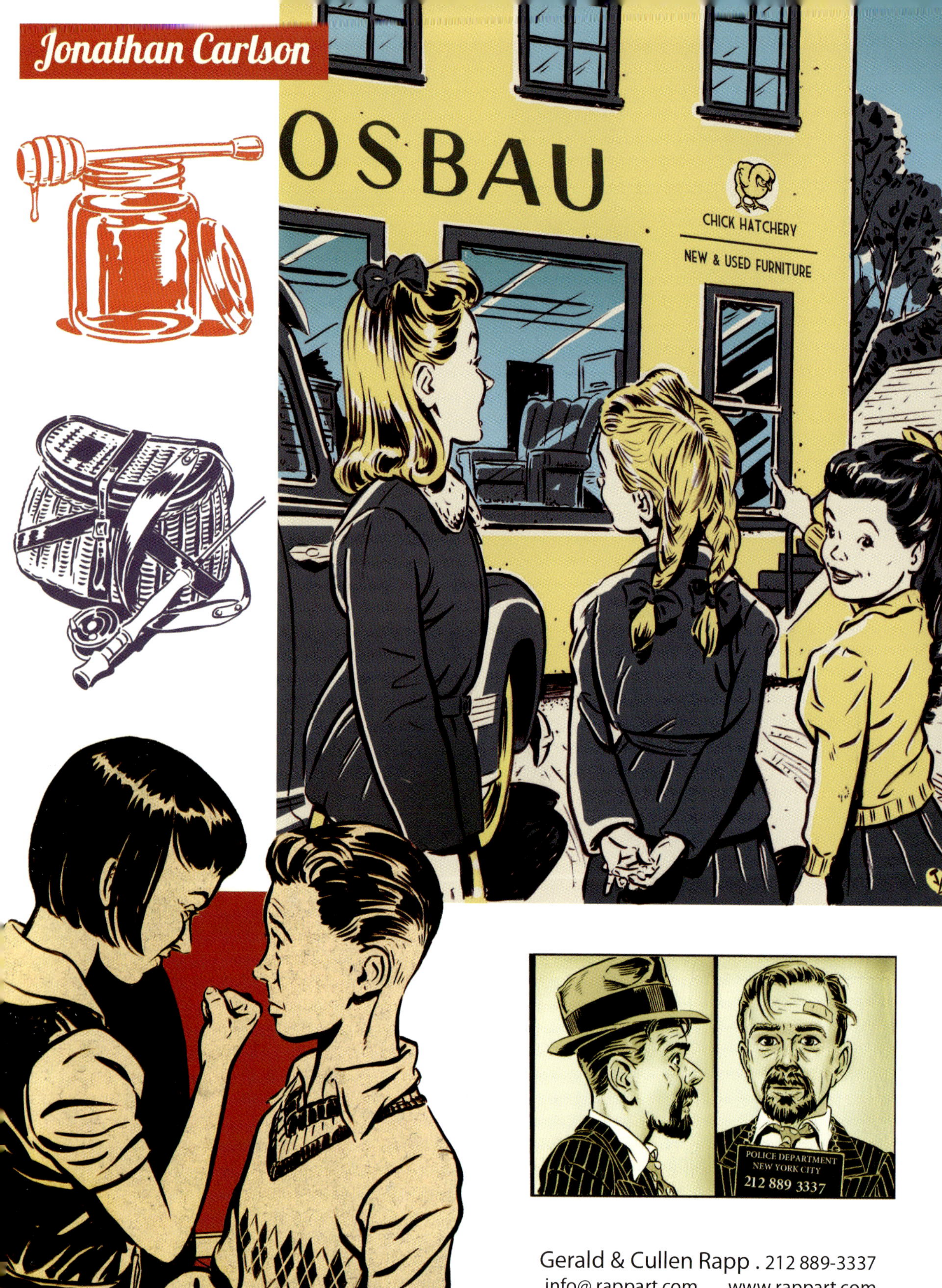

Jonathan Carlson
OSBAU
CHICK HATCHERY
NEW & USED FURNITURE
POLICE DEPARTMENT
NEW YORK CITY
212 889 3337
Gerald & Cullen Rapp . 212 889-3337
info@ rappart.com . www.rappart.com

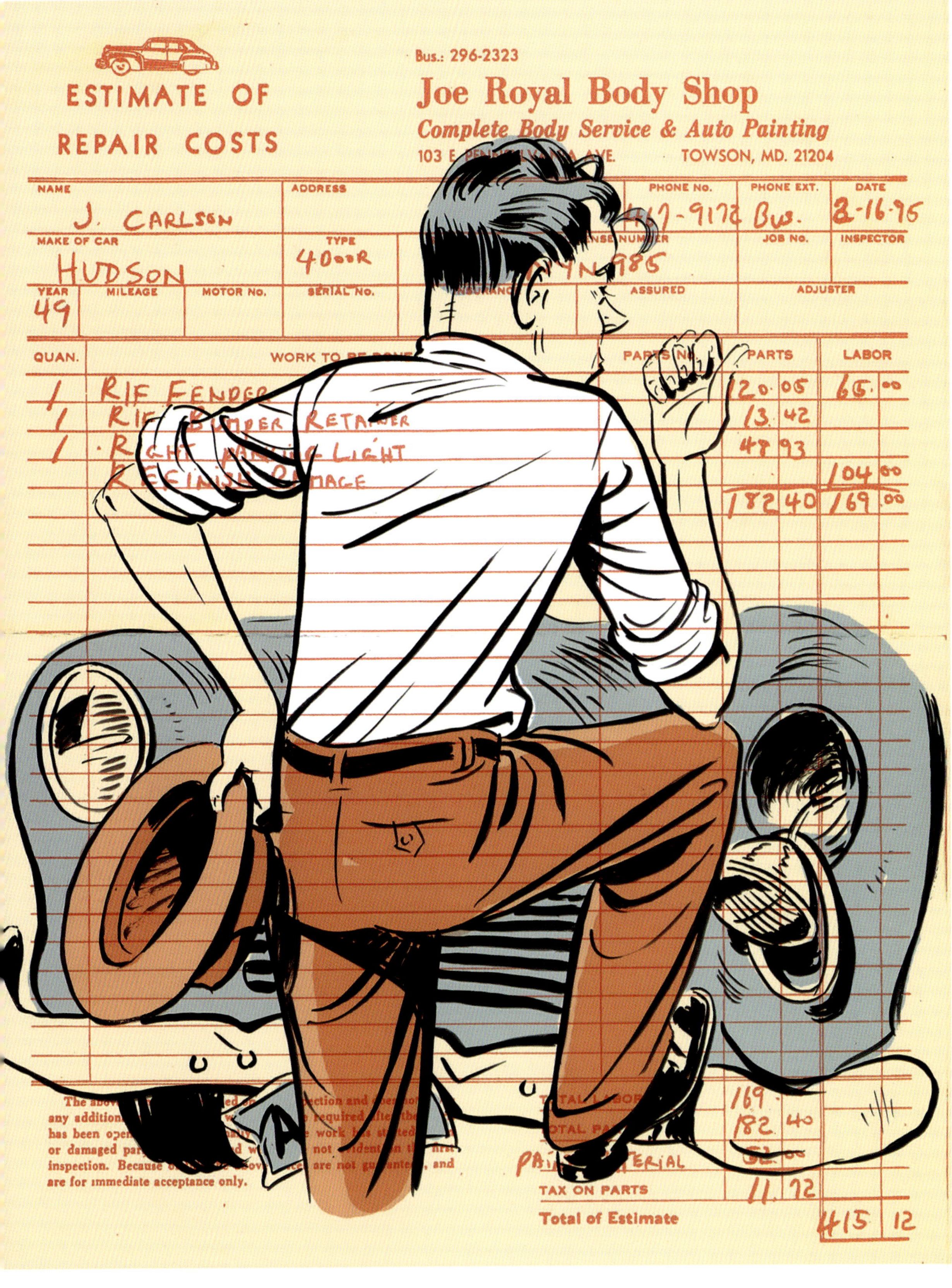

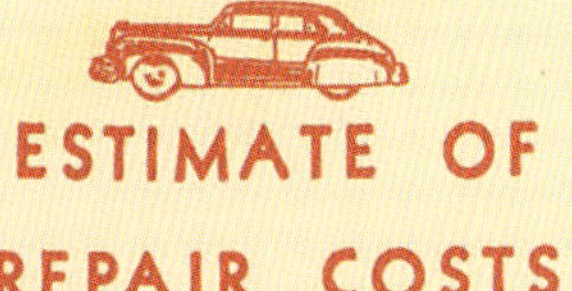

ESTIMATE OF REPAIR COSTS
Bus.: 296-2323
Joe Royal Body Shop
Complete Body Service & Auto Painting
103 E. PENNSYLVANIA AVE.   TOWSON, MD. 21204
NAME   J. CARLSON
ADDRESS
PHONE NO.   467-9172 Bus.
PHONE EXT.
DATE   3-16-95
MAKE OF CAR   HUDSON
TYPE   4 DooR
LICENSE NUMBER   YN 986
JOB NO.
INSPECTOR
YEAR   49
MILEAGE
MOTOR NO.
SERIAL NO.
INSURANCE
ASSURED
ADJUSTER
QUAN.   WORK TO BE DONE   PARTS NO.   PARTS   LABOR
1   RIF FENDER   20.05   65.00
1   RIF BUMPER RETAINER   13.42
1   RIGHT PARKING LIGHT   48.93
REFINISH DAMAGE   104.00
182.40   169.00
The above ... based on ... inspection and ... not
any additional ... required after the
has been open ... the work has started ...
or damaged parts ... and were not evident in the first
inspection. Because of the above price are not guaranteed, and
are for immediate acceptance only.
TOTAL LABOR   169.
TOTAL PARTS   182.40
PAINT MATERIAL   52.00
TAX ON PARTS   11.72
Total of Estimate   415   12

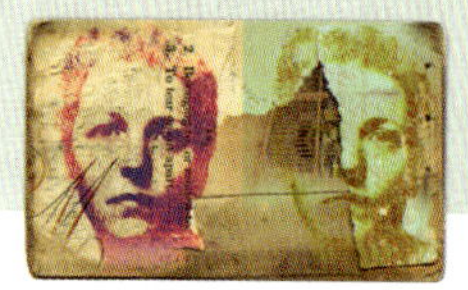

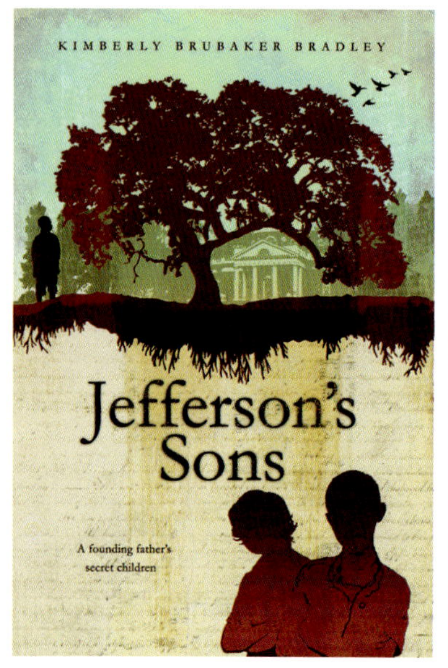

KIMBERLY BRUBAKER BRADLEY
Jefferson's Sons
A founding father's secret children

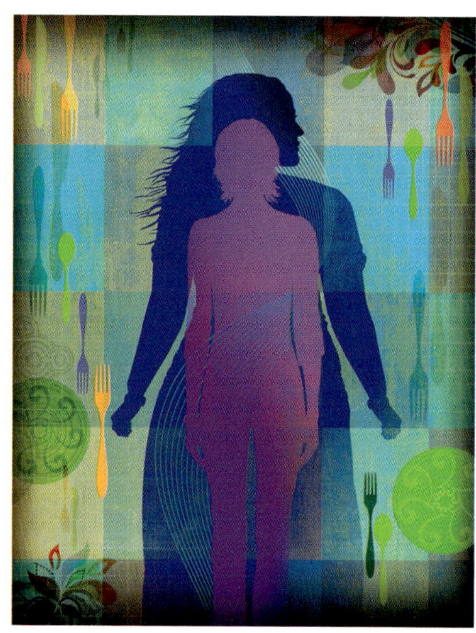

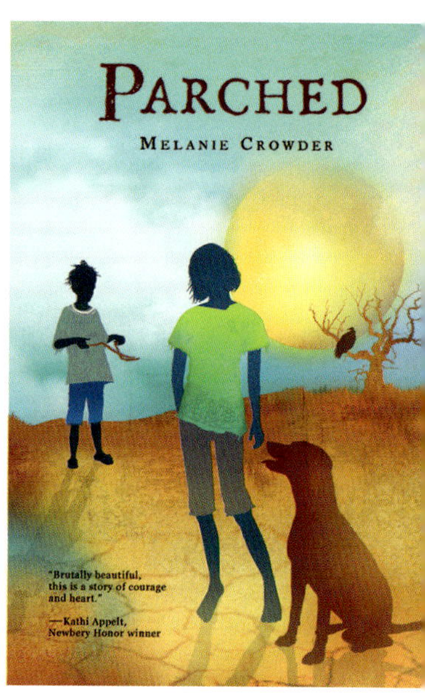

PARCHED
MELANIE CROWDER
"Brutally beautiful, this is a story of courage and heart."
—Kathi Appelt, Newbery Honor winner

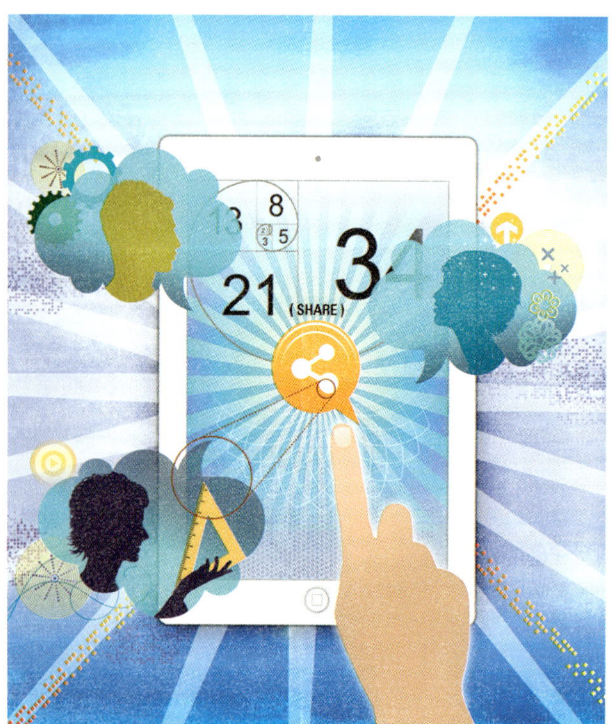

8
5
3
18
21 (SHARE) 34

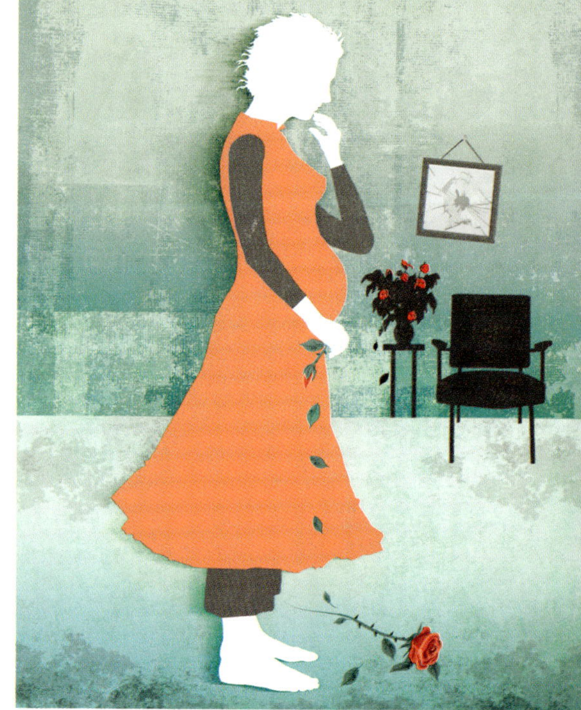

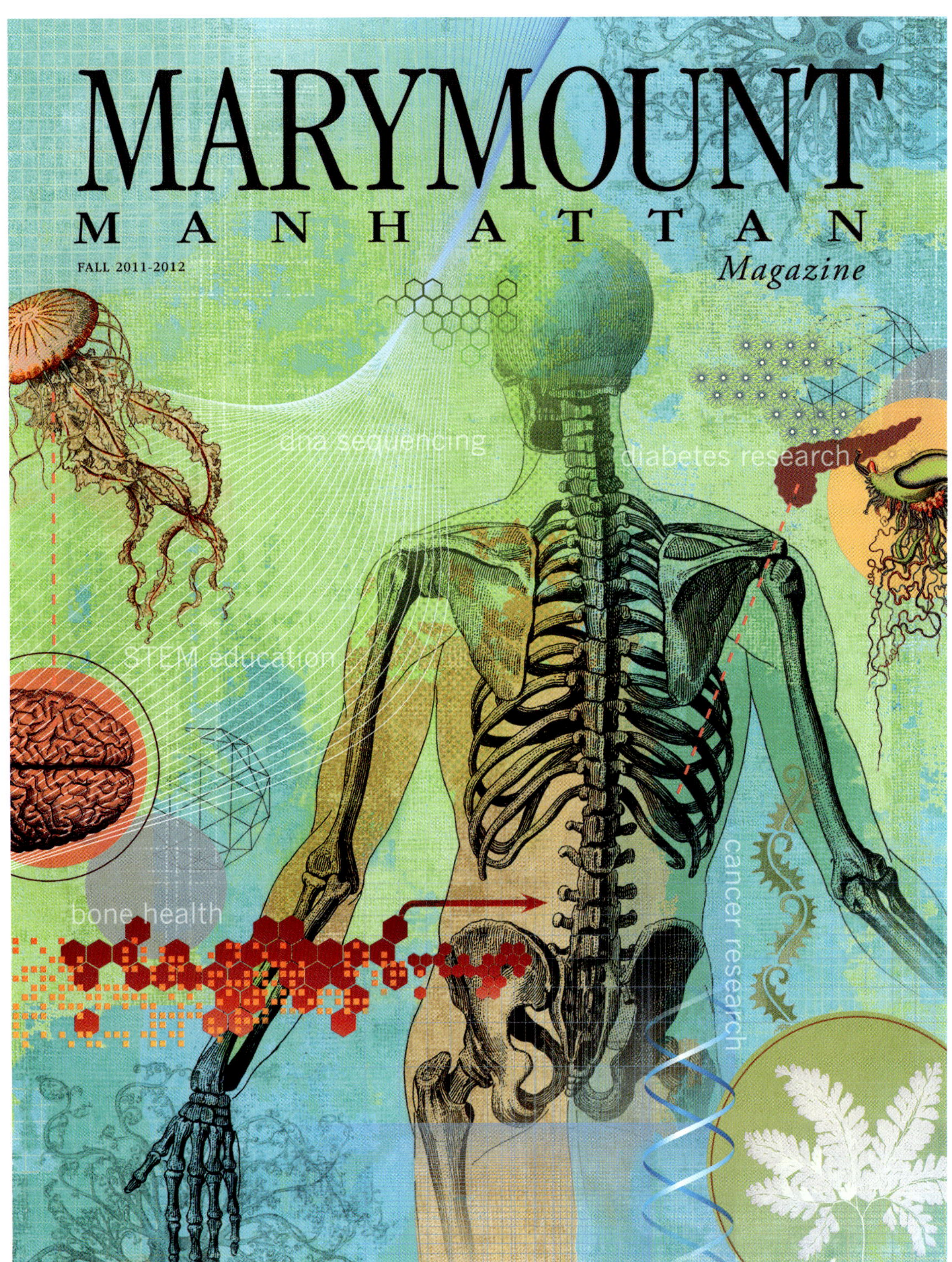
MARYMOUNT
MANHATTAN
Magazine
FALL 2011-2012
dna sequencing
diabetes research
STEM education
bone health
cancer research

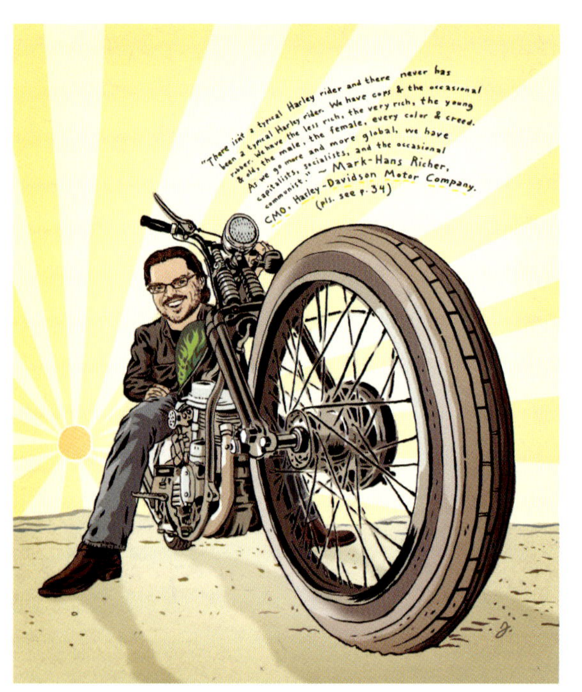

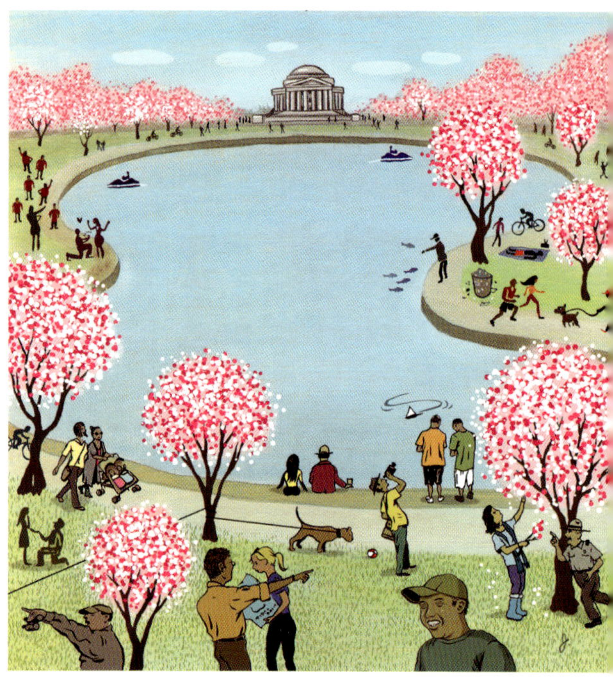

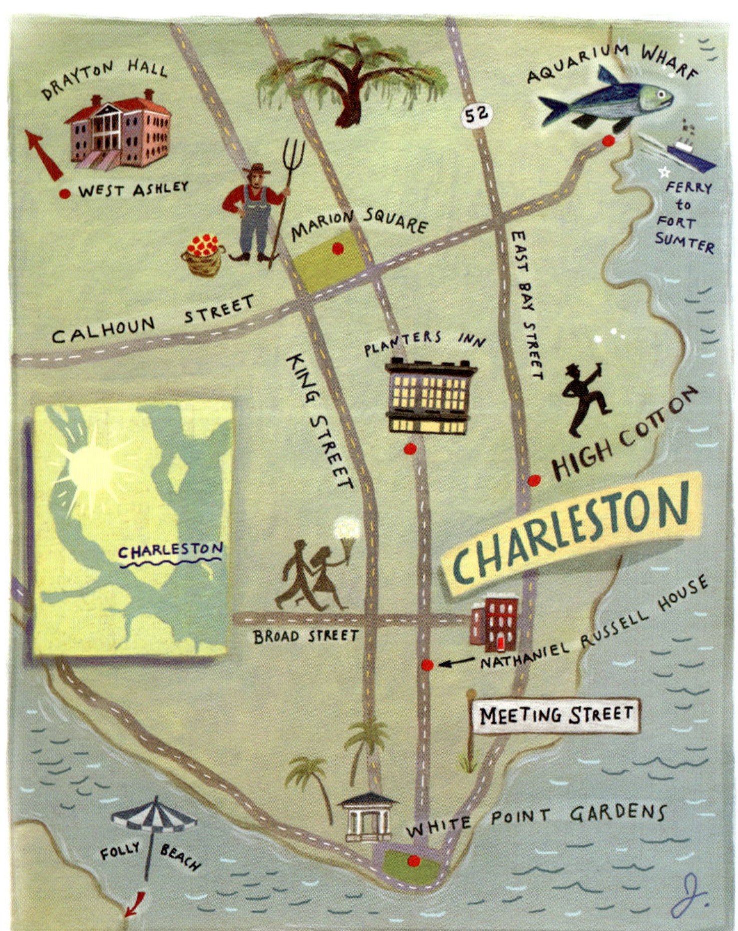

JOHN S. DYKES
ILLUSTRATION

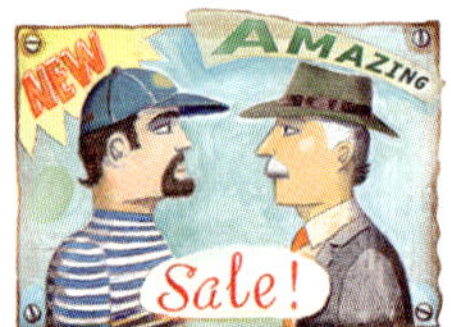

www.JSDYKES.com
www.RAPPART.com
info@RAPPART.com
212.889.3337

GERALD & CULLEN RAPP

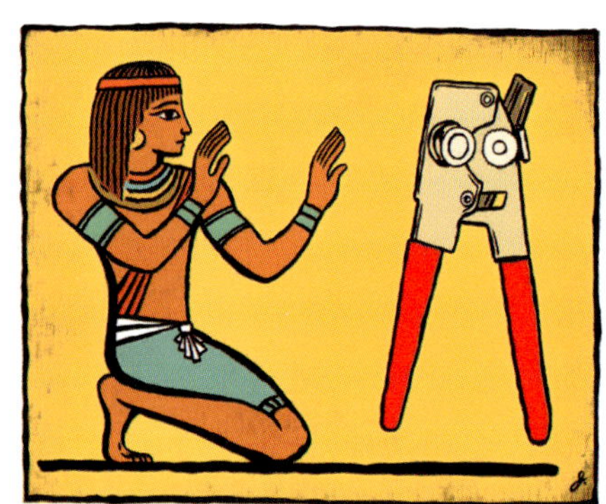

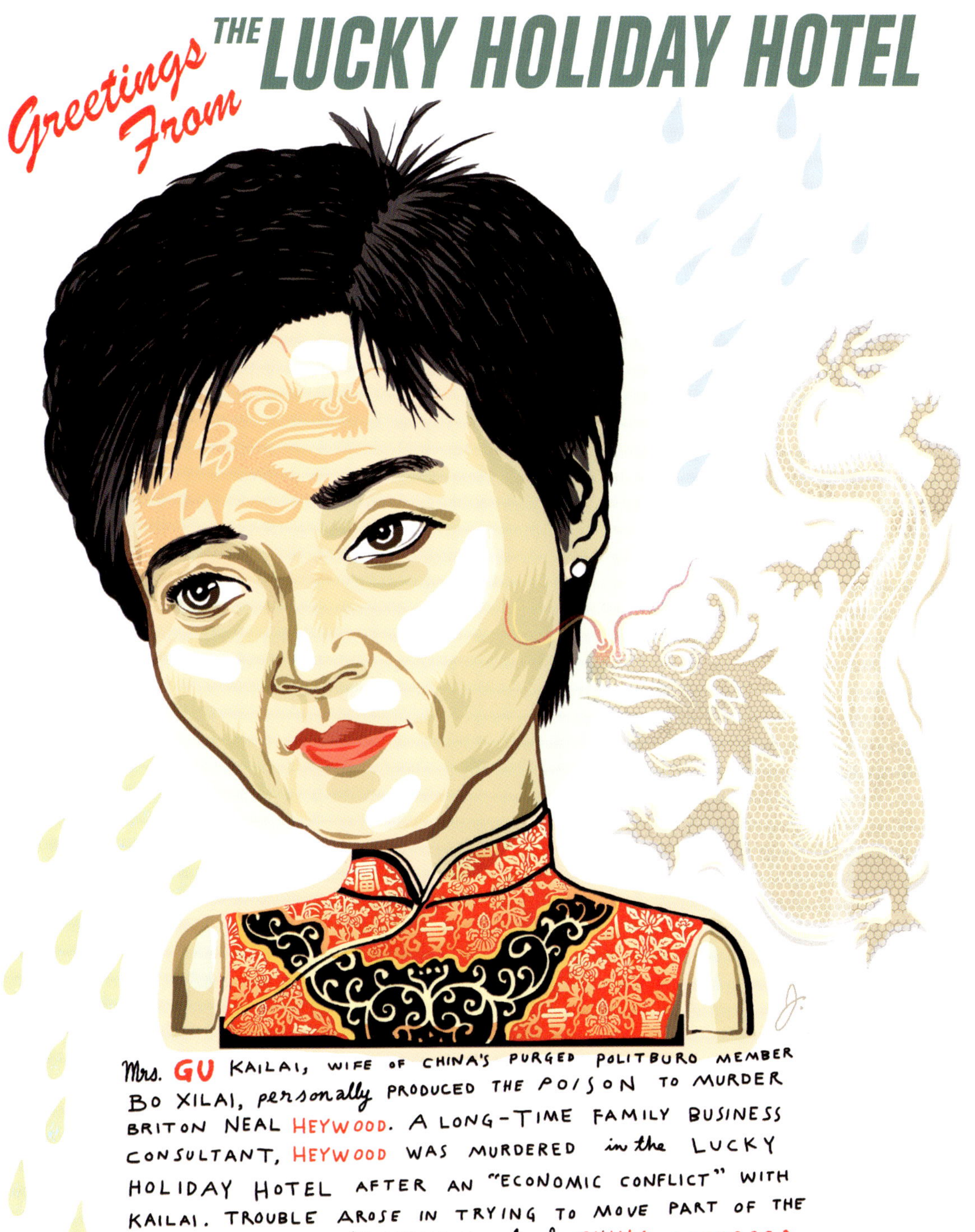

Greetings From THE LUCKY HOLIDAY HOTEL

Mrs. GU KAILAI, WIFE OF CHINA'S PURGED POLITBURO MEMBER BO XILAI, personally PRODUCED THE POISON TO MURDER BRITON NEAL HEYWOOD. A LONG-TIME FAMILY BUSINESS CONSULTANT, HEYWOOD WAS MURDERED in the LUCKY HOLIDAY HOTEL AFTER AN "ECONOMIC CONFLICT" WITH KAILAI. TROUBLE AROSE IN TRYING TO MOVE PART OF THE FAMILY'S $160 MILLION out of CHINA.

JOHN S. DYKES ILLUSTRATION   GERALD & CULLEN RAPP
www.JSDYKES.com • www.RAPPART.com • info@RAPPART.com • 212.889.3337

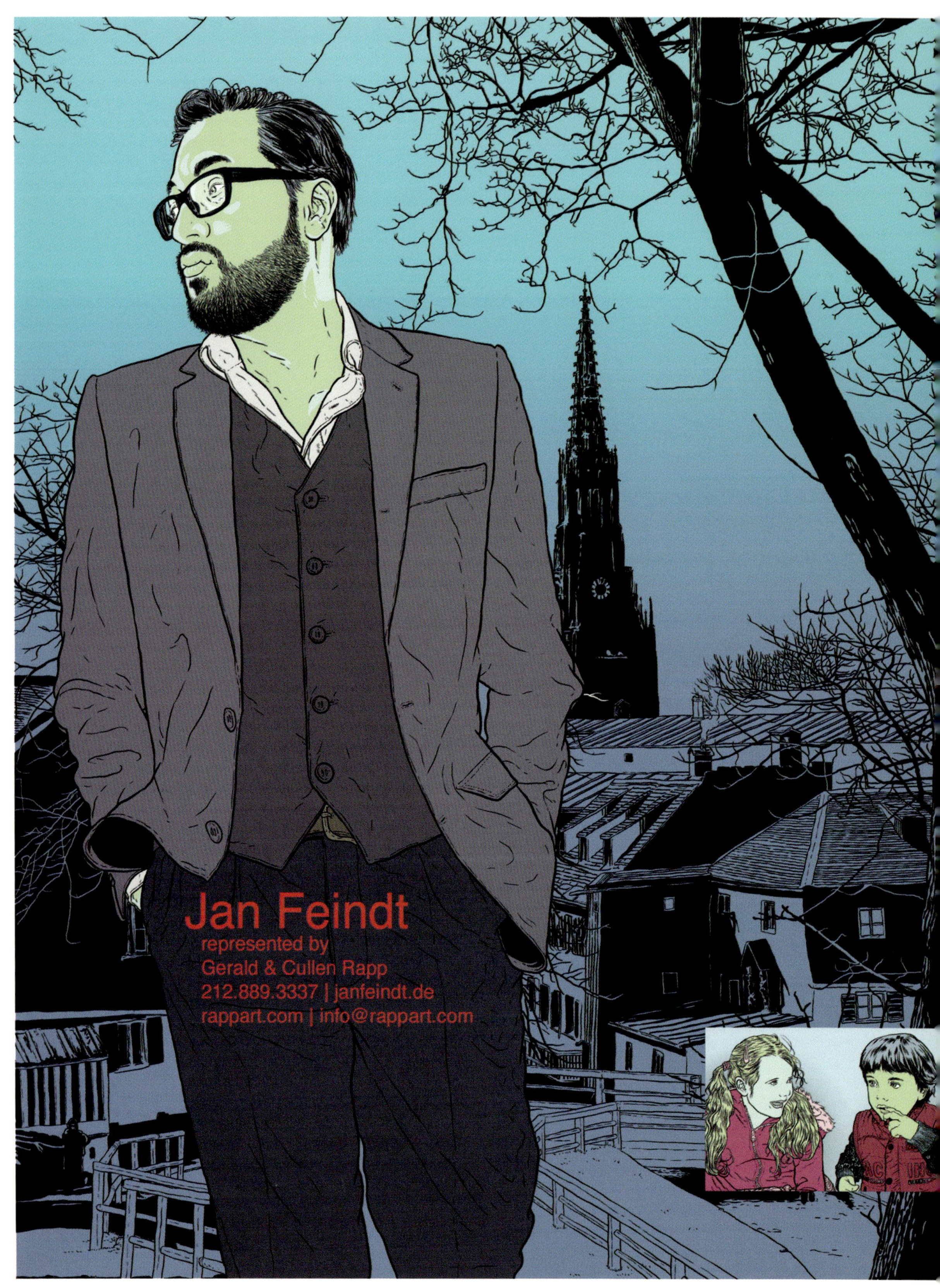

Jan Feindt
represented by
Gerald & Cullen Rapp
212.889.3337 | janfeindt.de
rappart.com | info@rappart.com

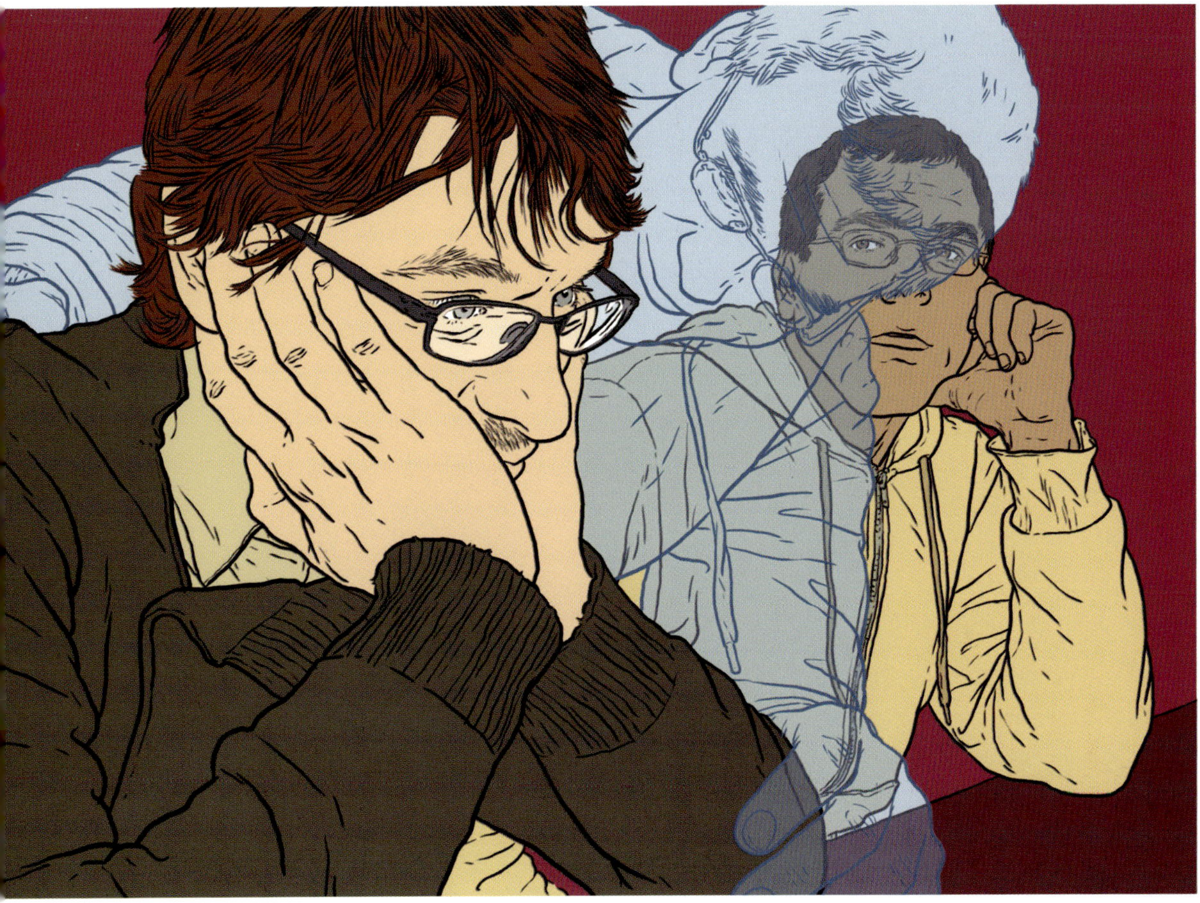

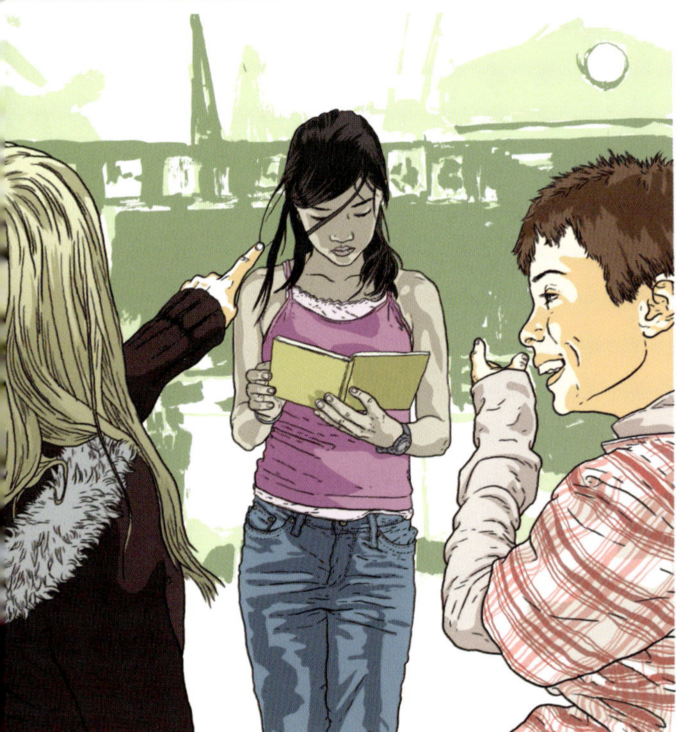
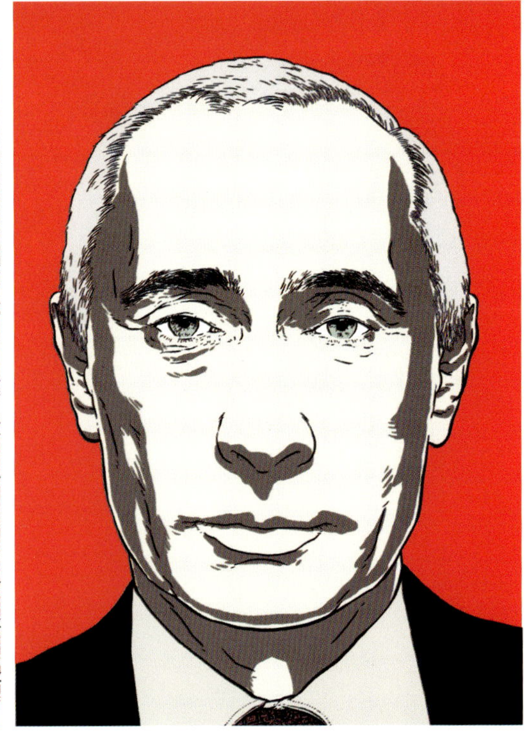

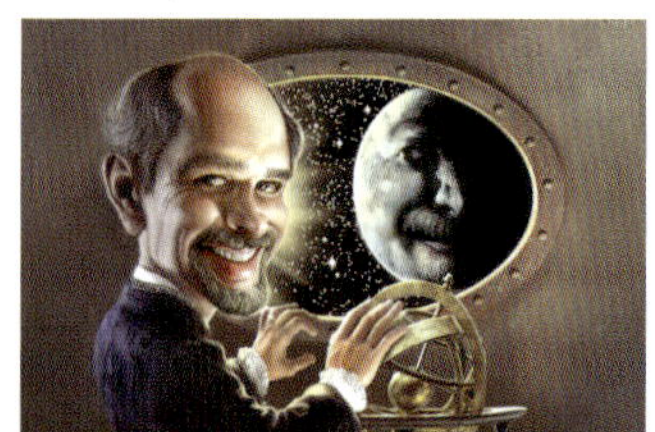

Mark Fredrickson

Gerald & Cullen Rapp

212-889-3337   www.rappart.com
info@rappart.com

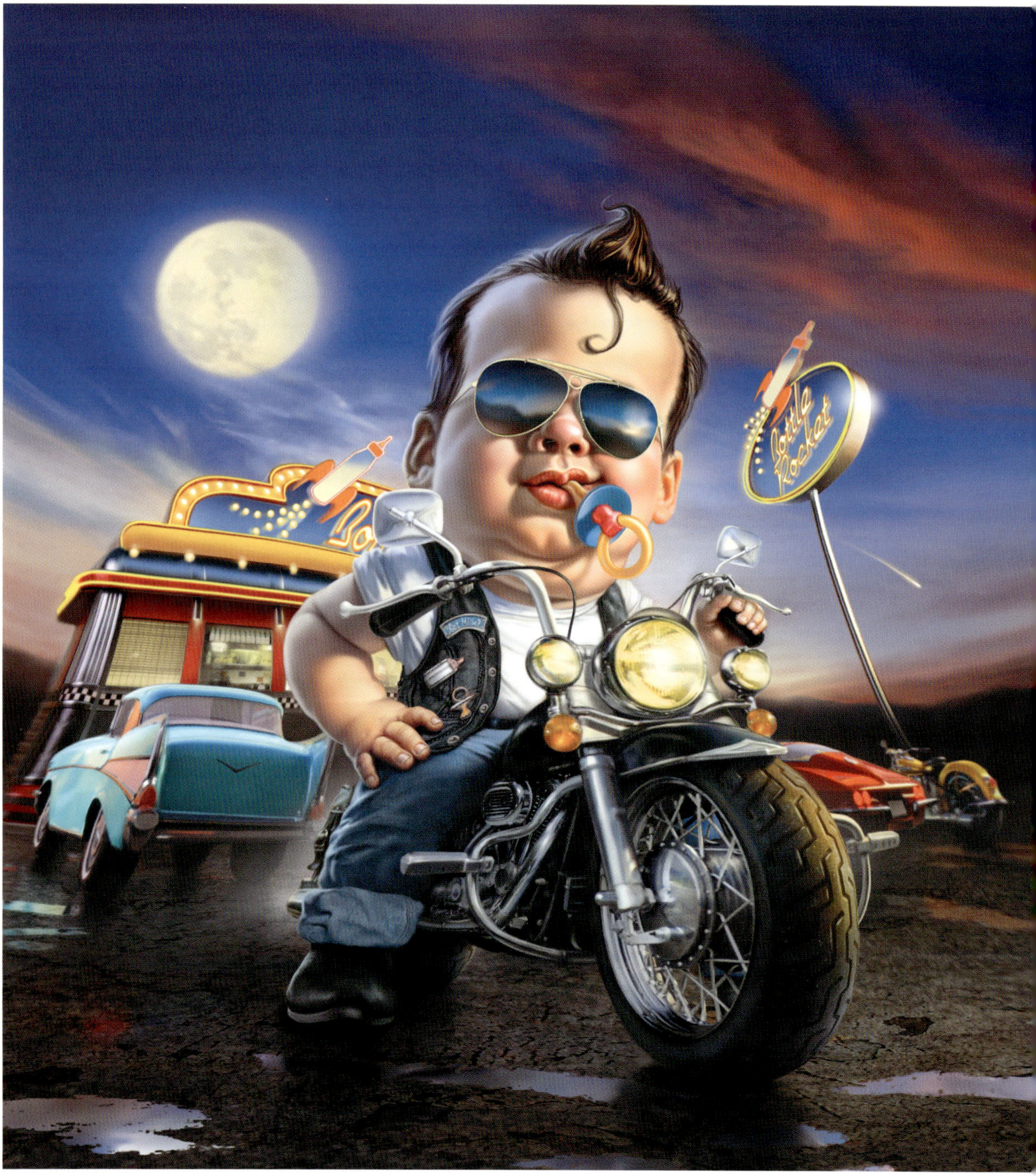

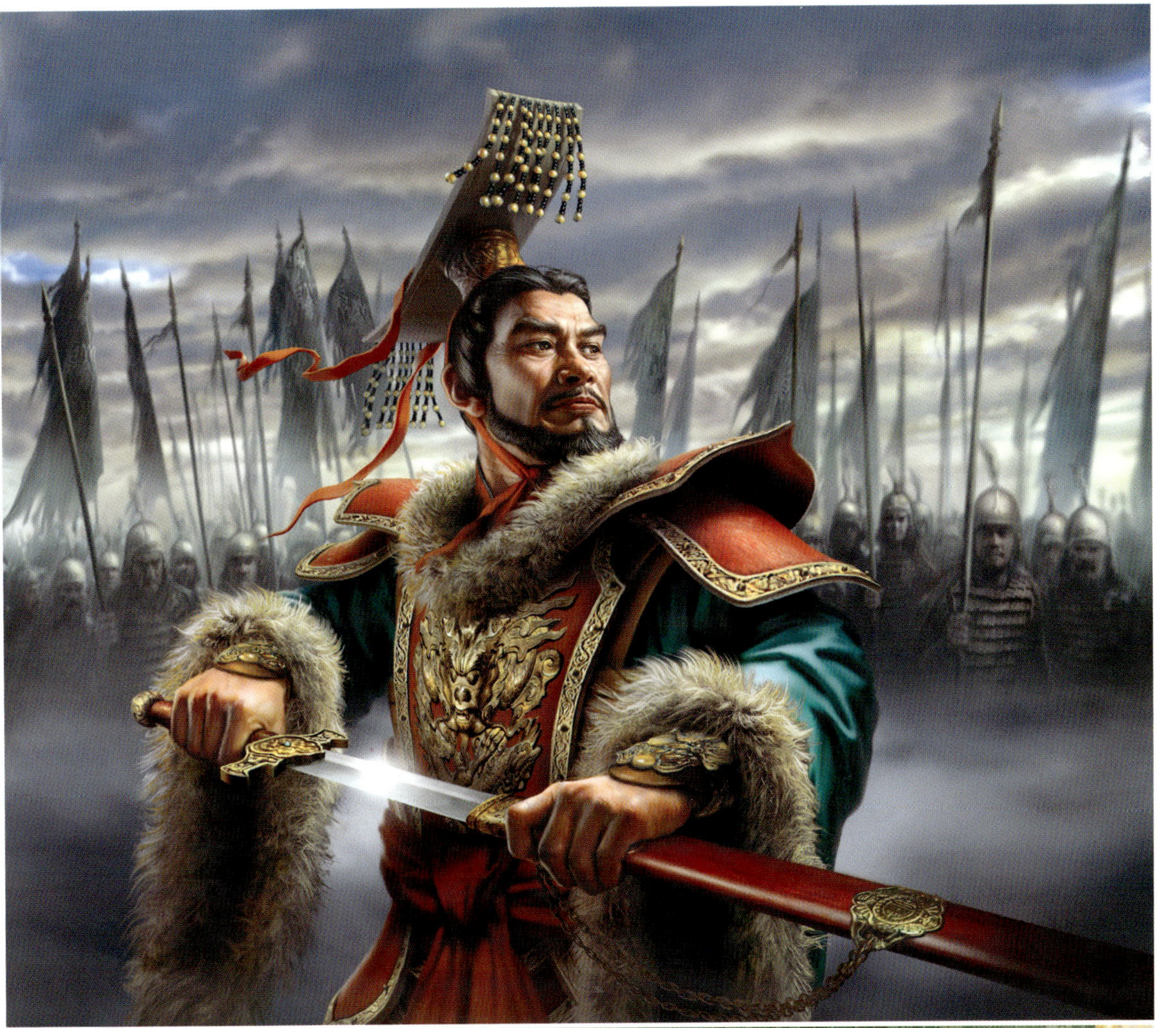

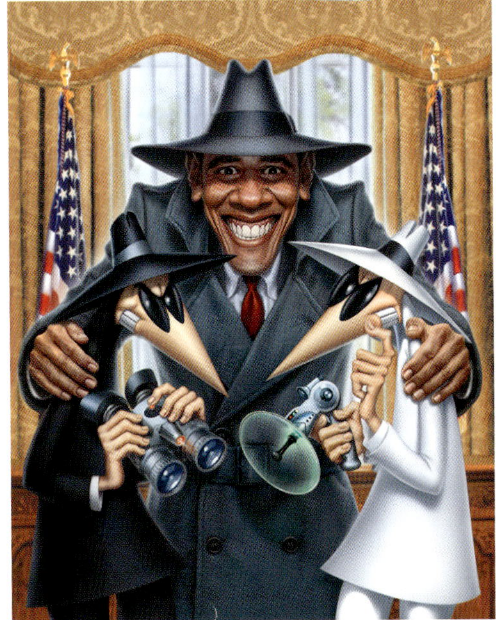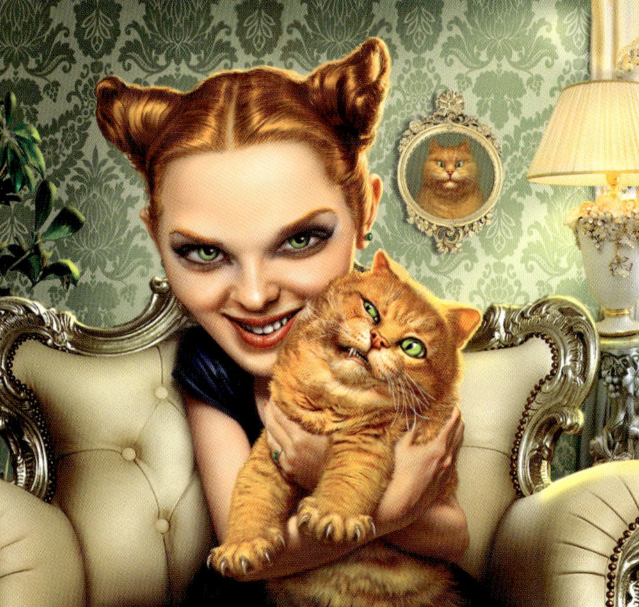

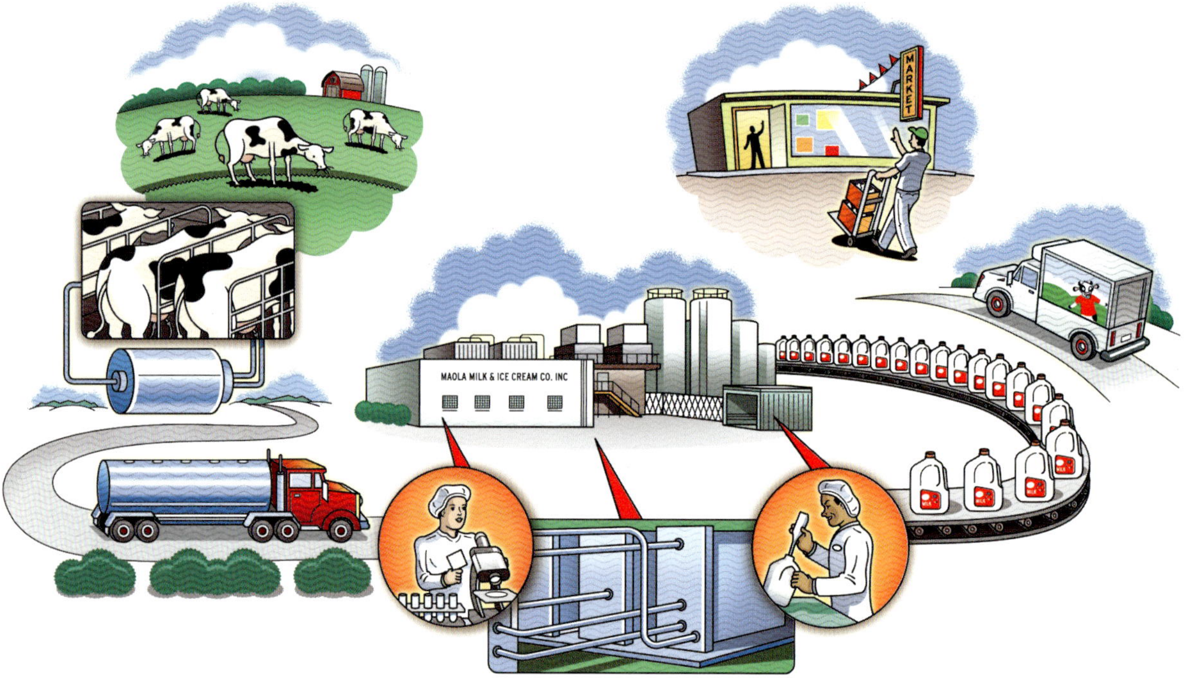

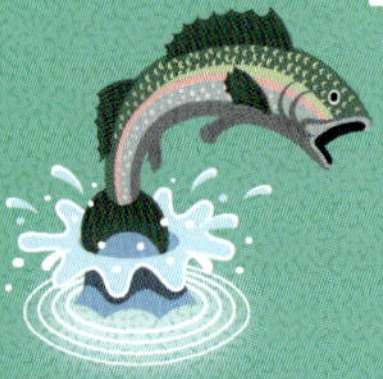

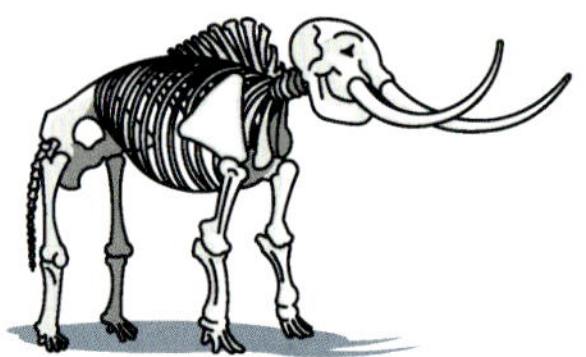
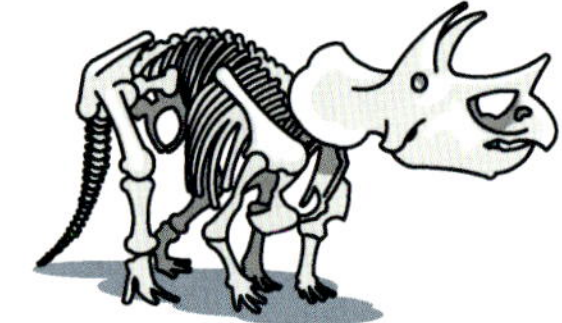
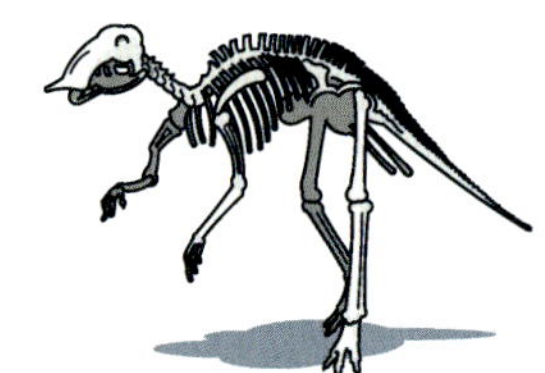

PETER+MARIA HOEY

are represented by:

GERALD *and* **CULLEN RAPP**

212.889.3337 INFO@RAPPART.COM PETERHOEY.COM

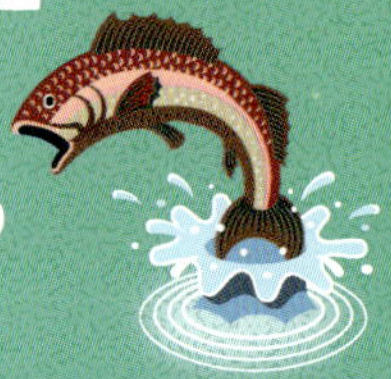

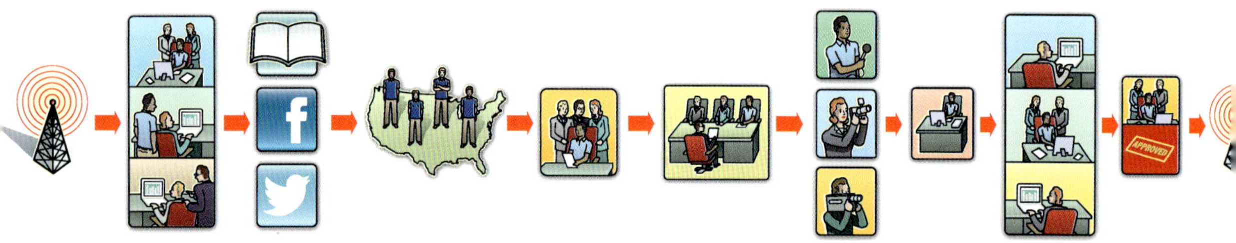

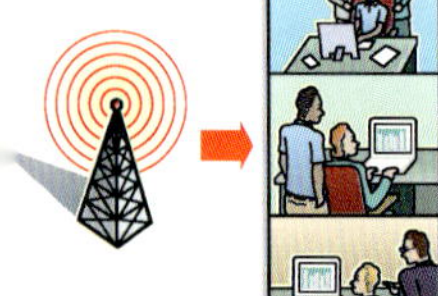
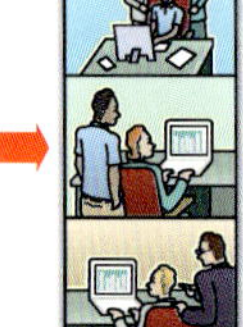
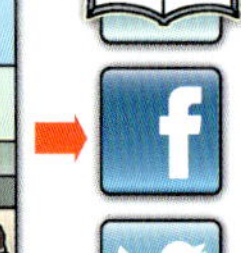
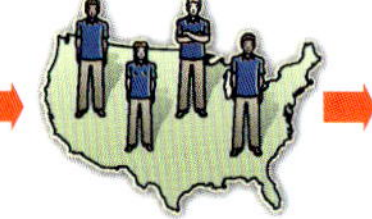
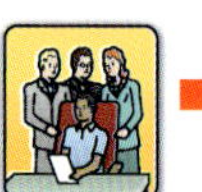
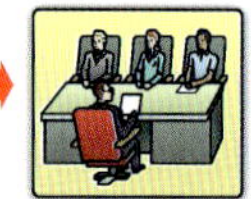
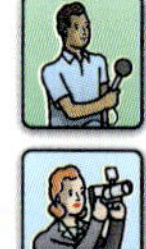
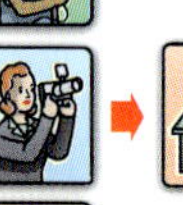

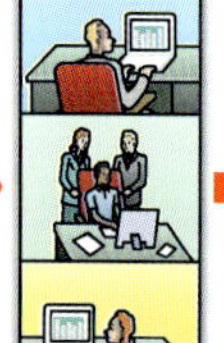
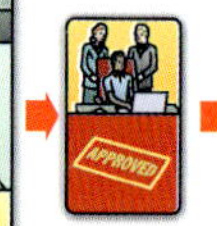
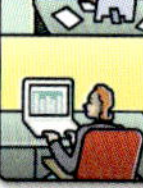

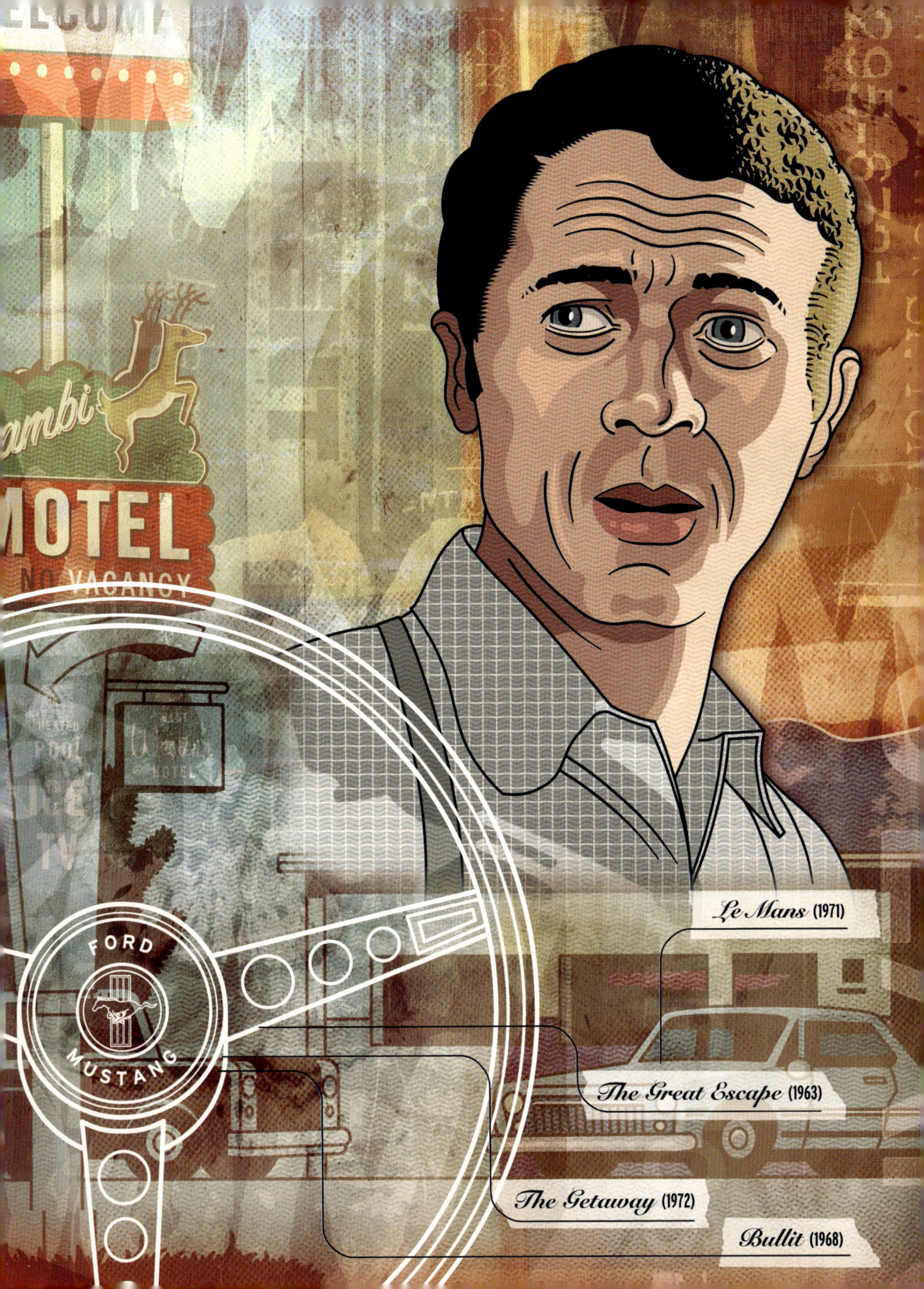

WELCOME
ambi
MOTEL
NO VACANCY
HEATED POOL
ICE
TV
FORD
MUSTANG
Le Mans (1971)
The Great Escape (1963)
The Getaway (1972)
Bullit (1968)

CELIA JOHNSON
GERALD & CULLEN RAPP

212 889 3337

info@rappart.com
www.rappart.com

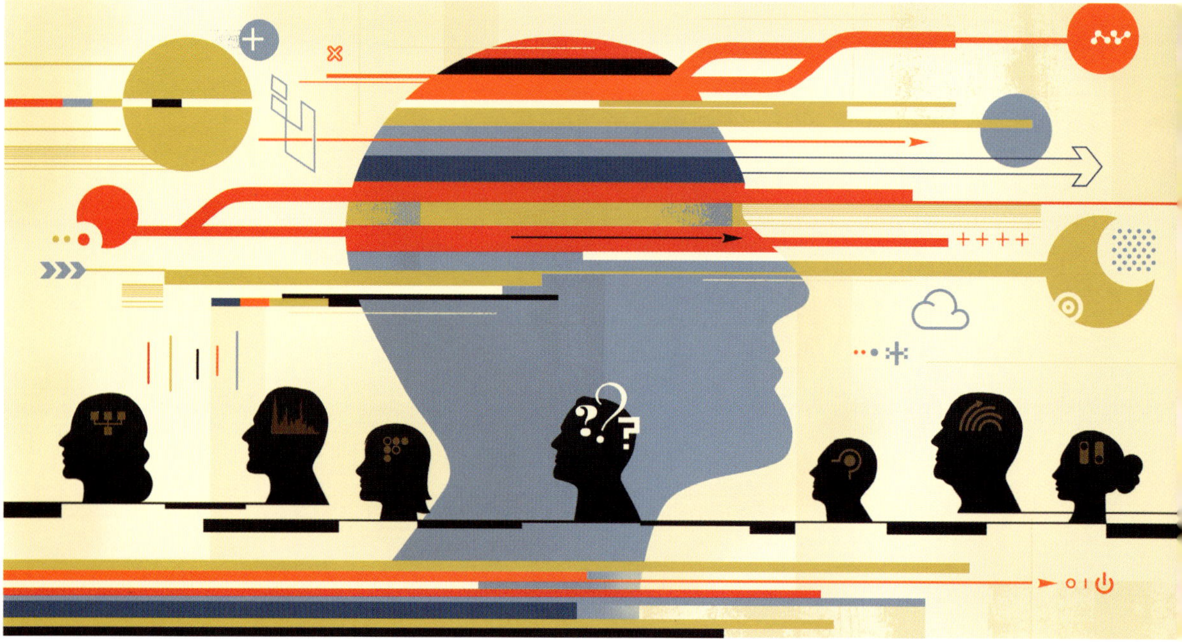

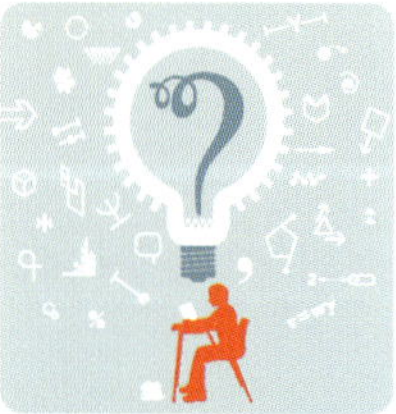

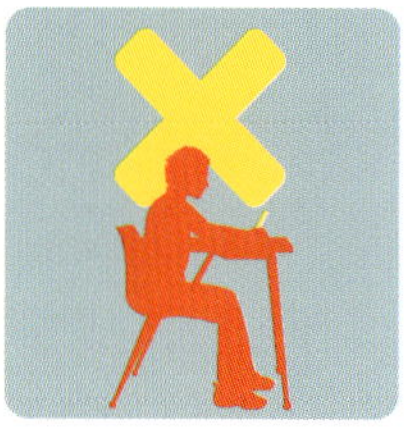

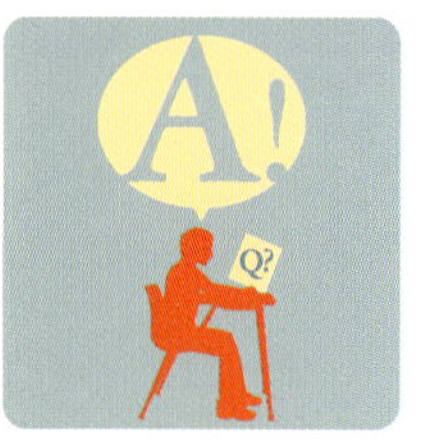
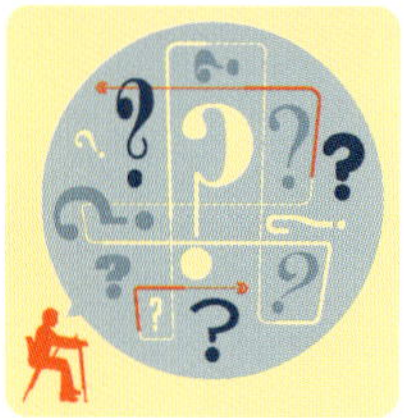
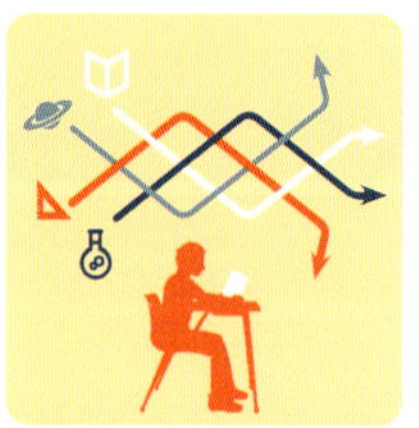

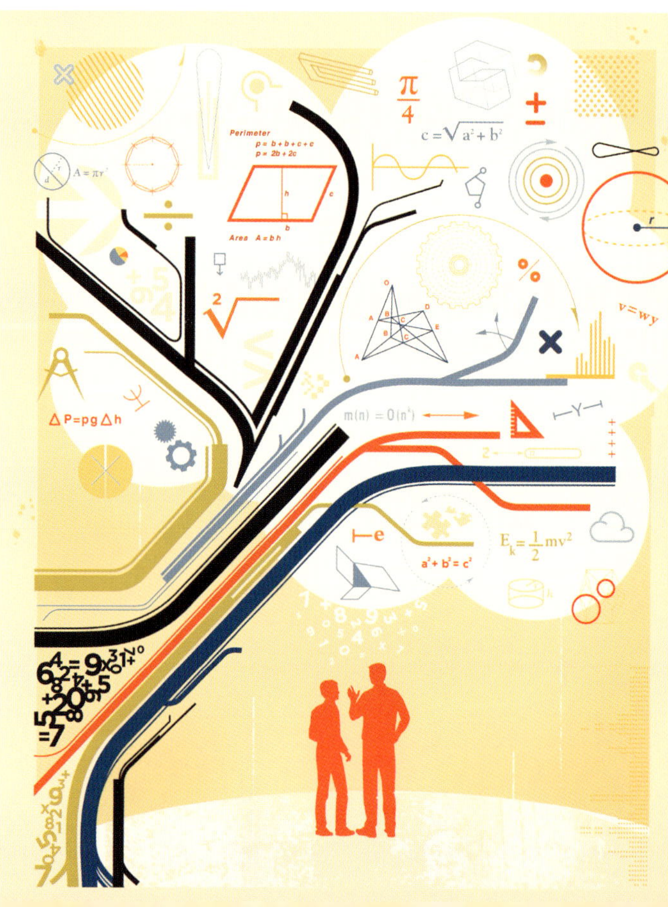

ABCDEFGHIJKLMNOPQRSTUVWXYZ

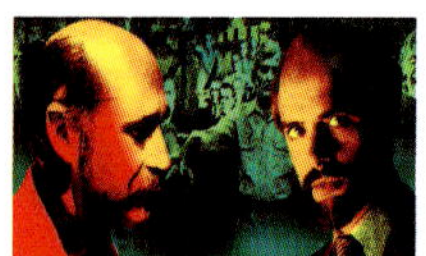

Sean McCabe

GERALD & CULLEN RAPP
212.889 3337 / info@rappart.com
www.rappart.com / www.wider-than-pictures.com

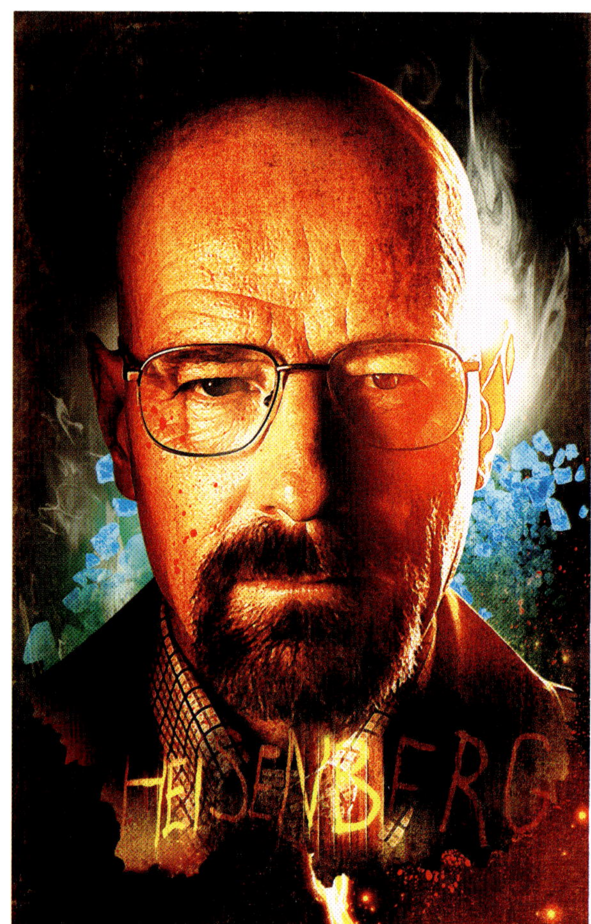

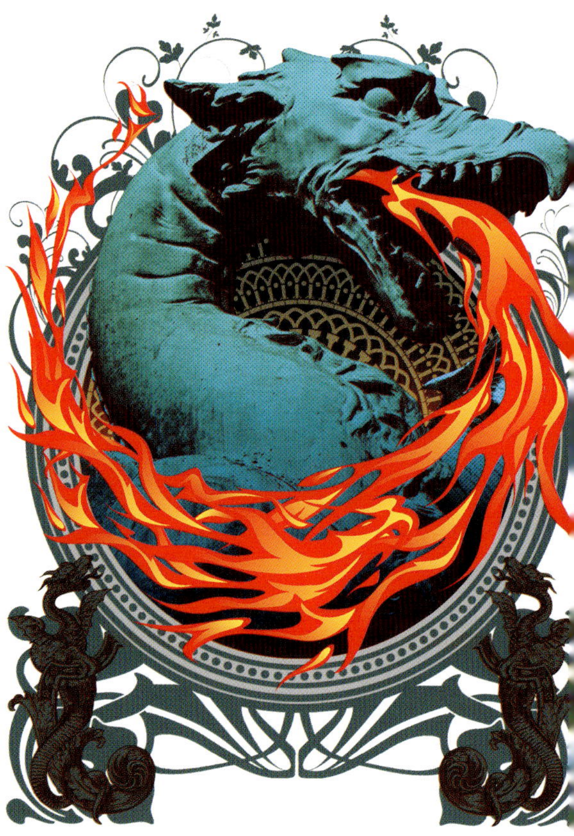

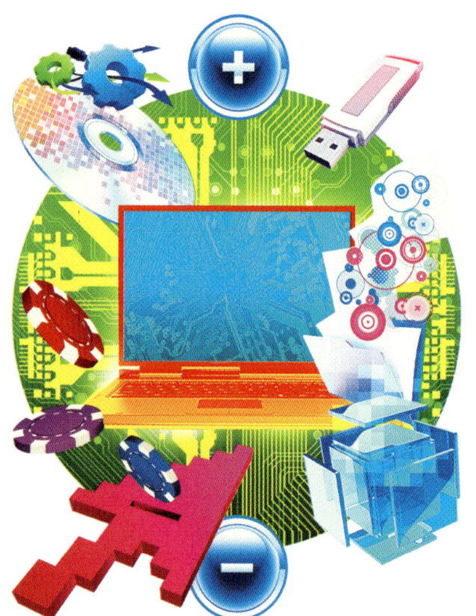

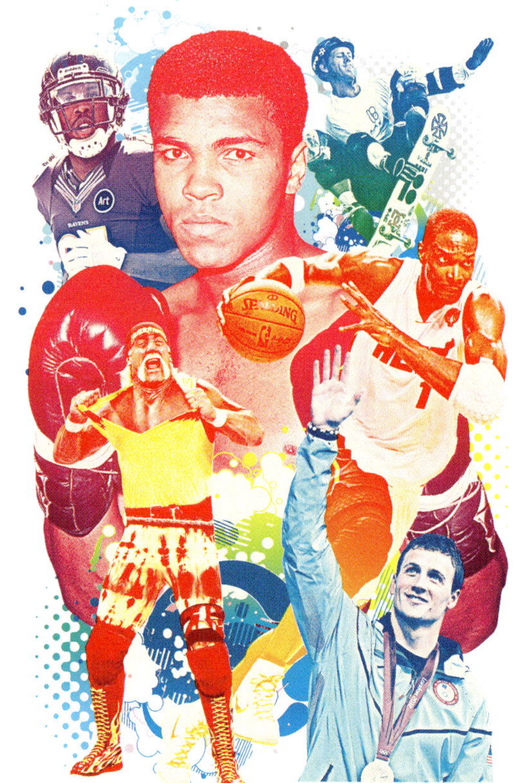

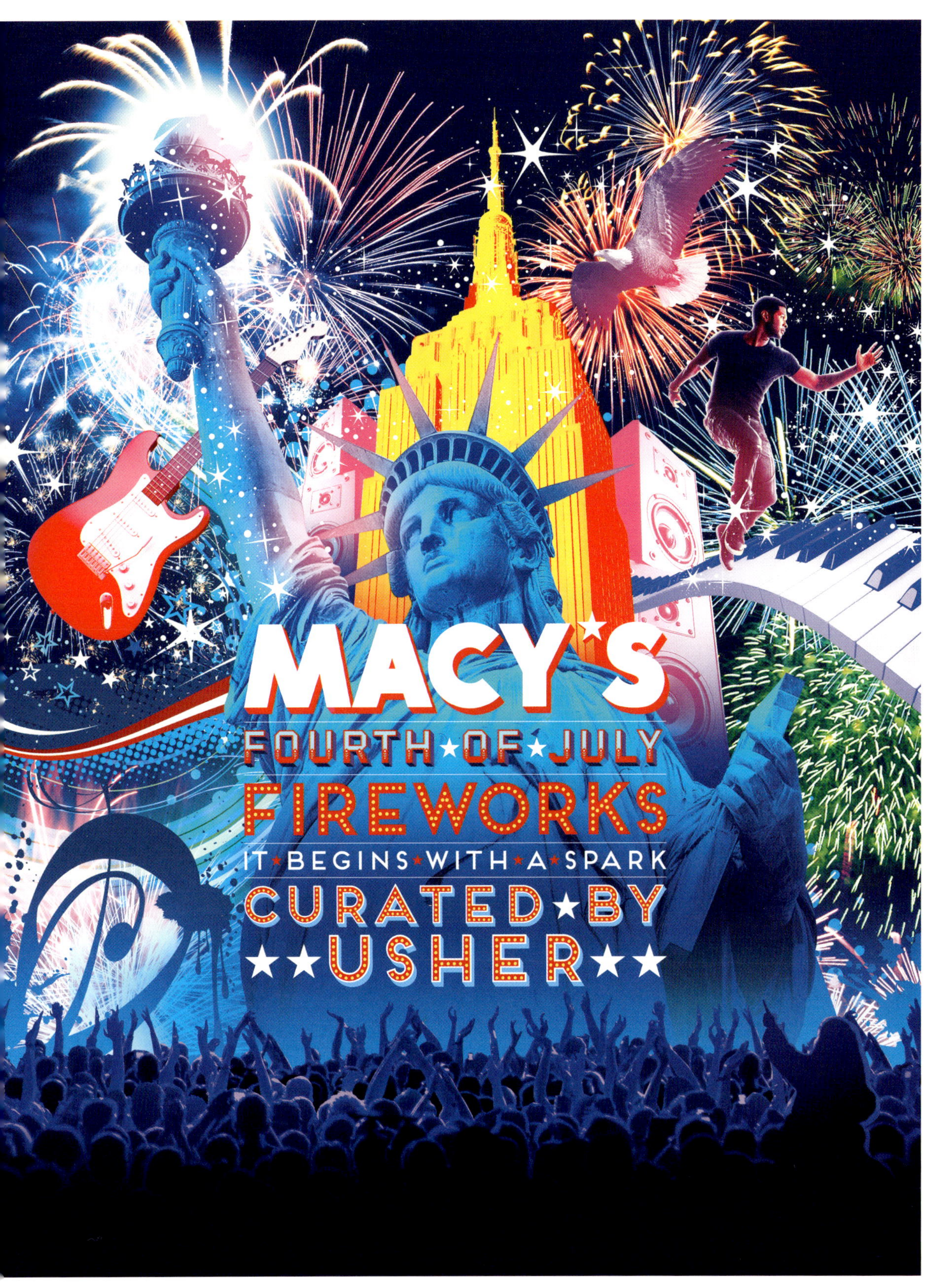
MACY'S
FOURTH OF JULY
FIREWORKS
IT BEGINS WITH A SPARK
CURATED BY
USHER

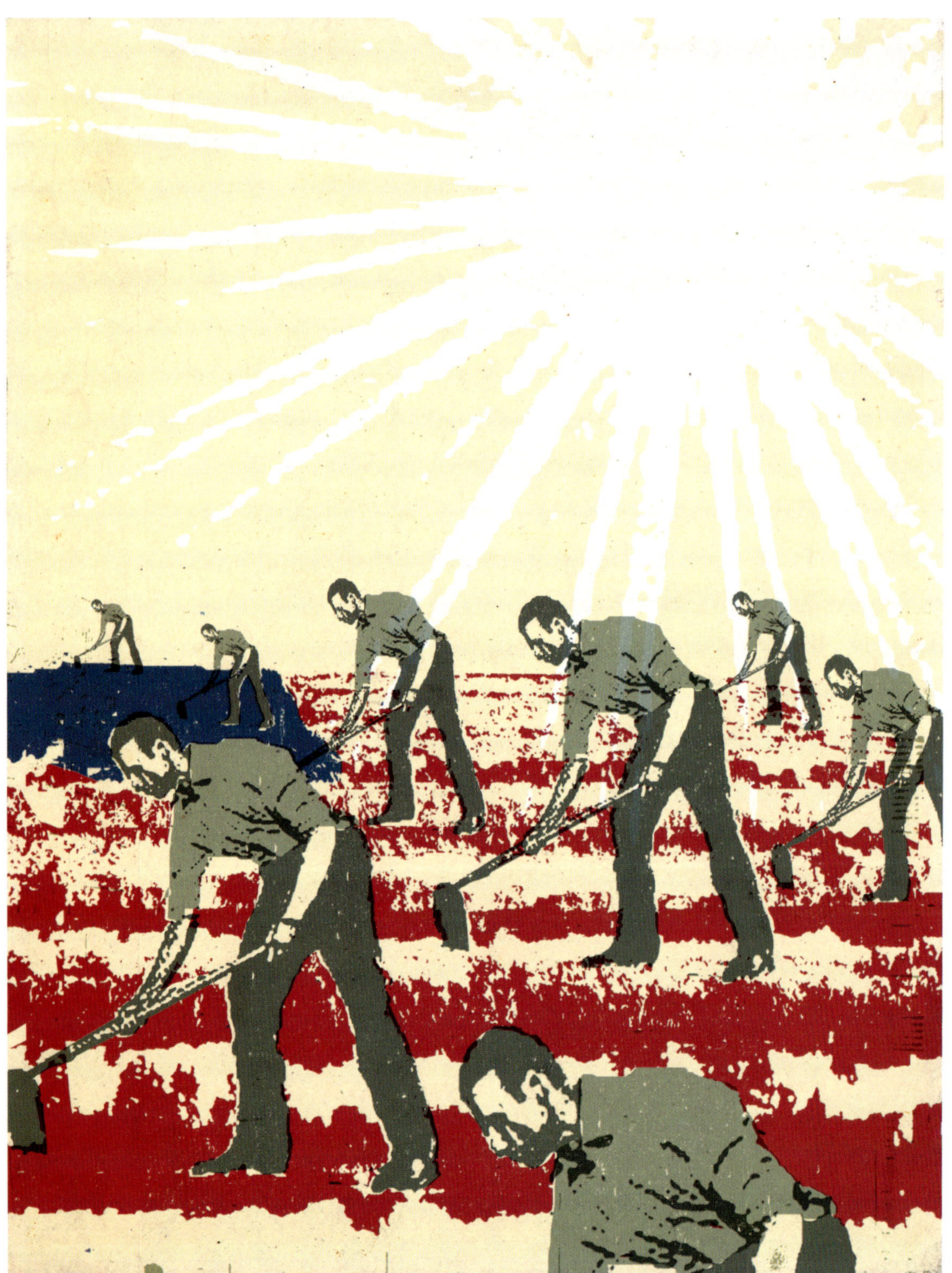

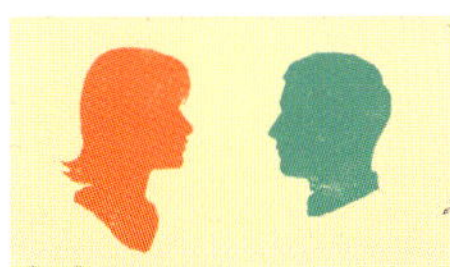

Richard Mia

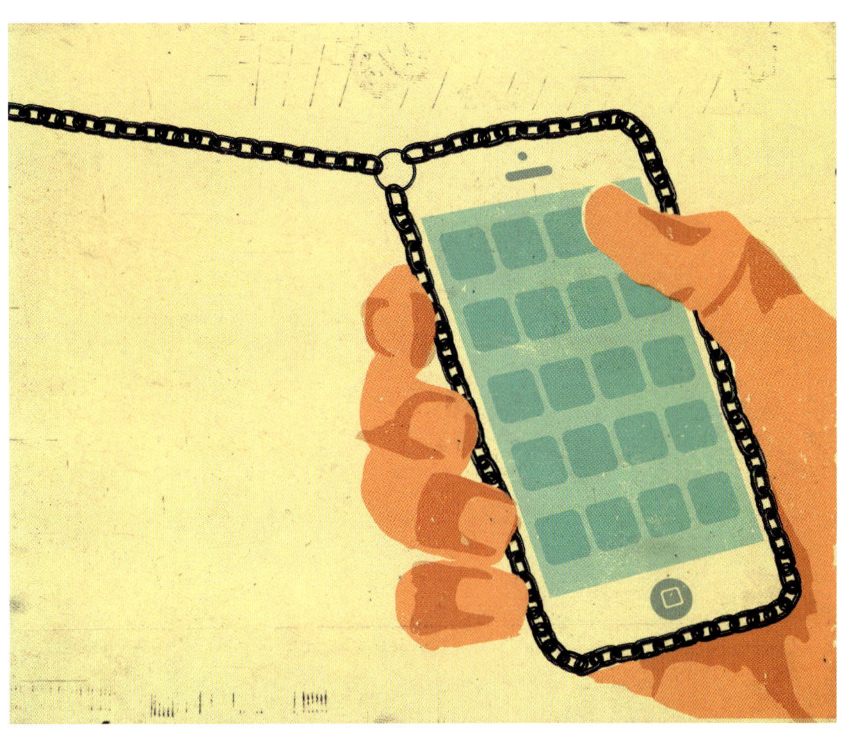

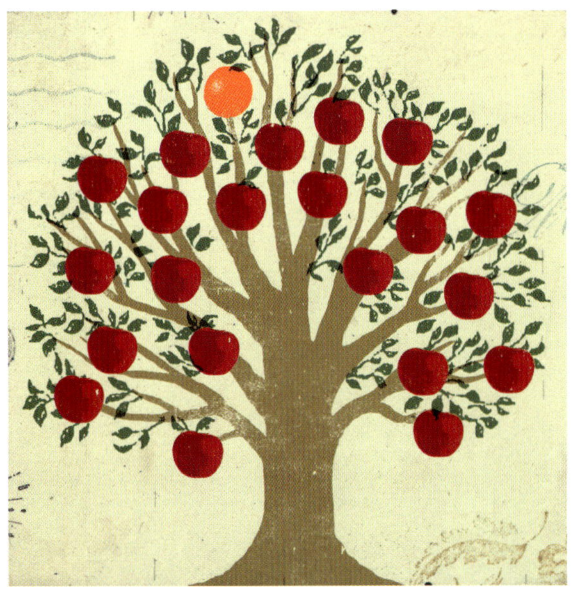

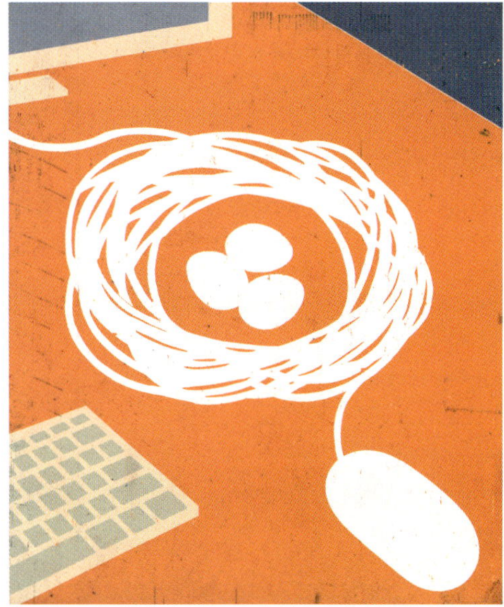

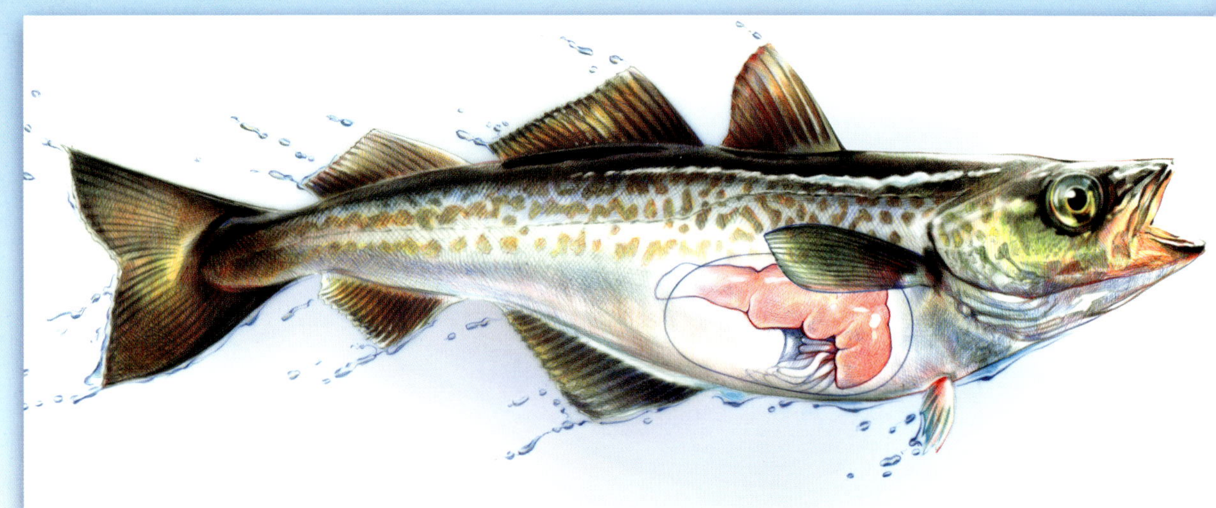

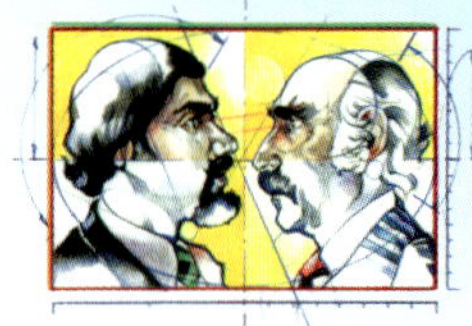

Bruce Morser

Gerald & Cullen Rapp
212 889 3337
info@rappart.com
www.rappart.com

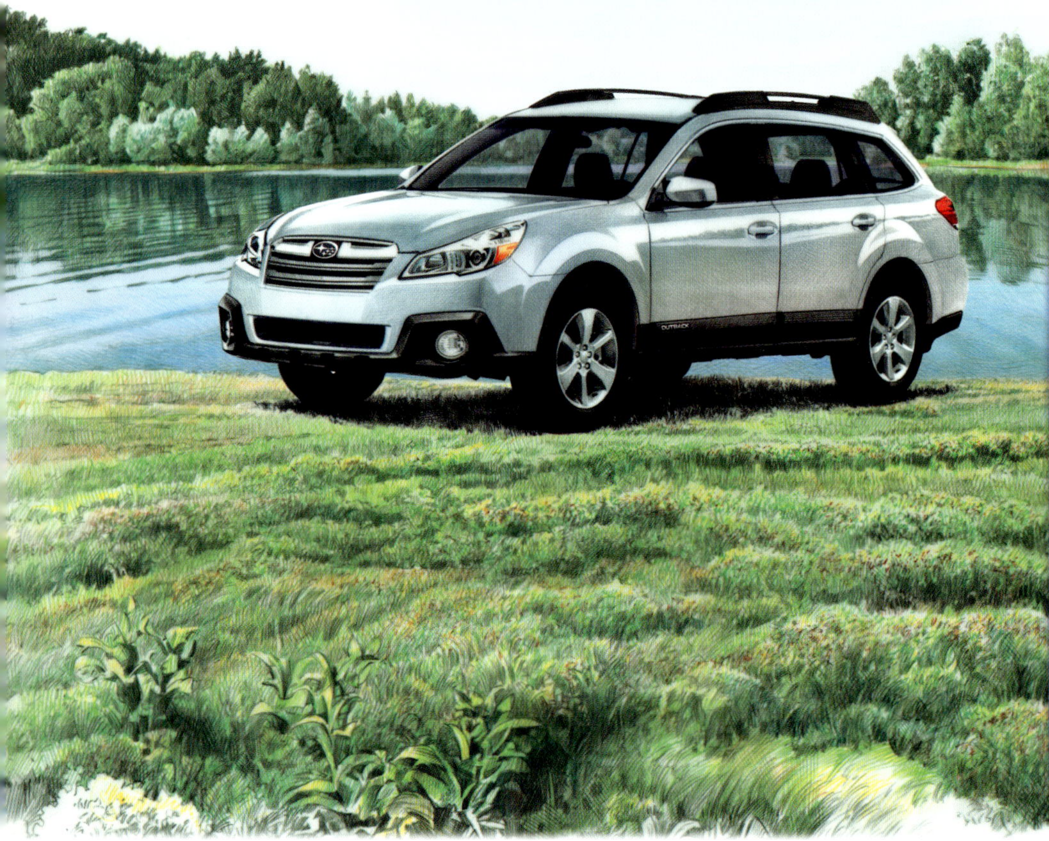

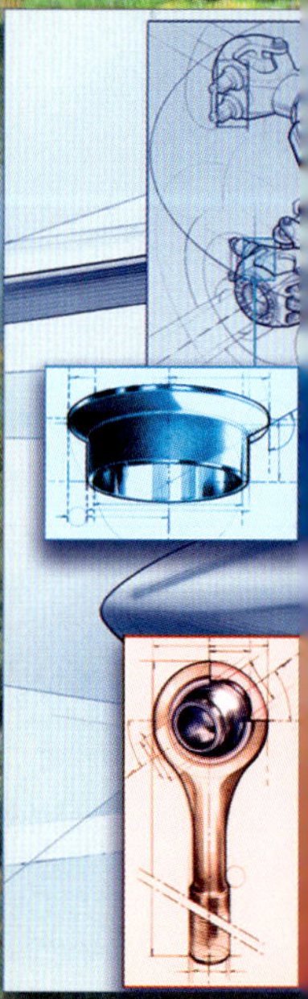

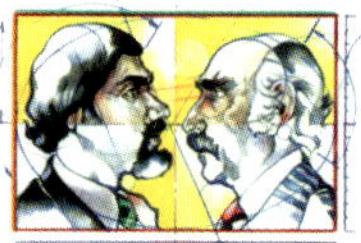

Bruce Morser

Gerald & Cullen Rapp
212 889 3337
info@rappart.com
www.rappart.com

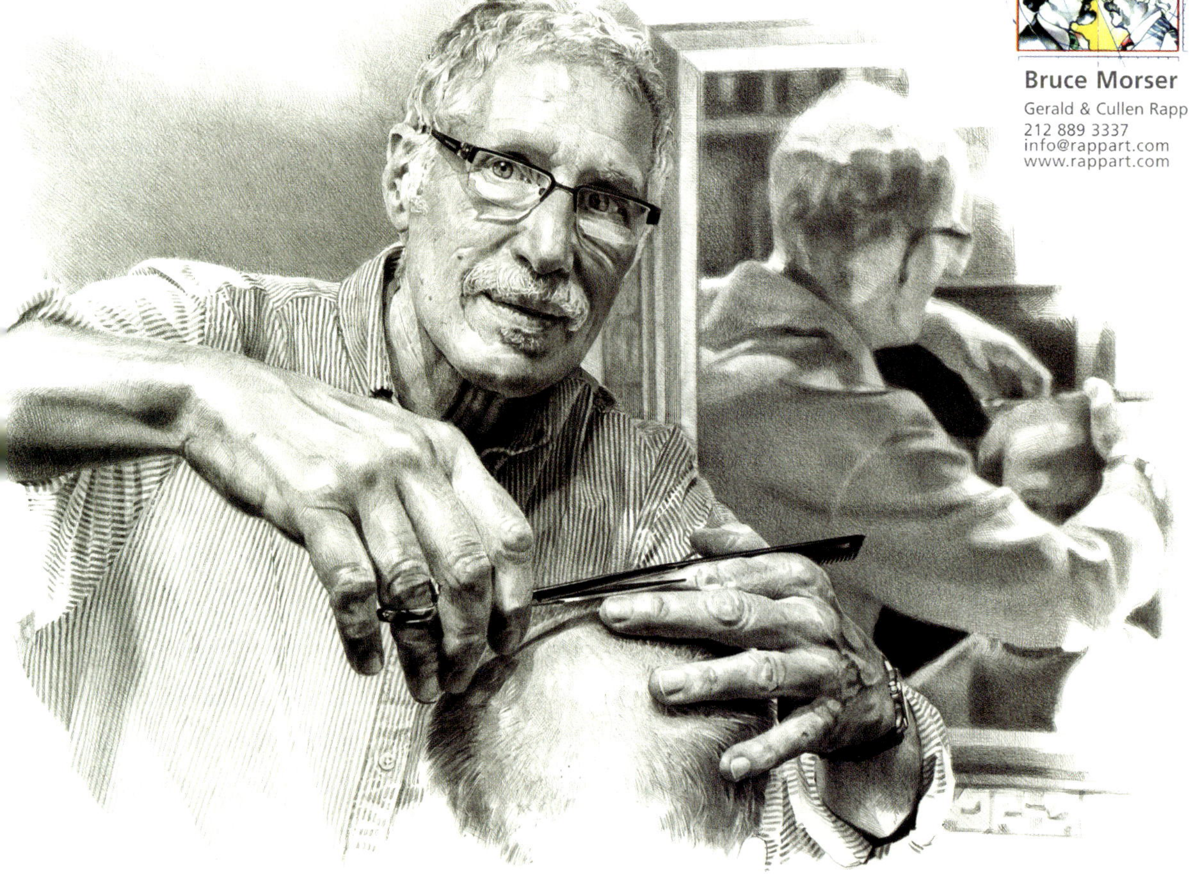

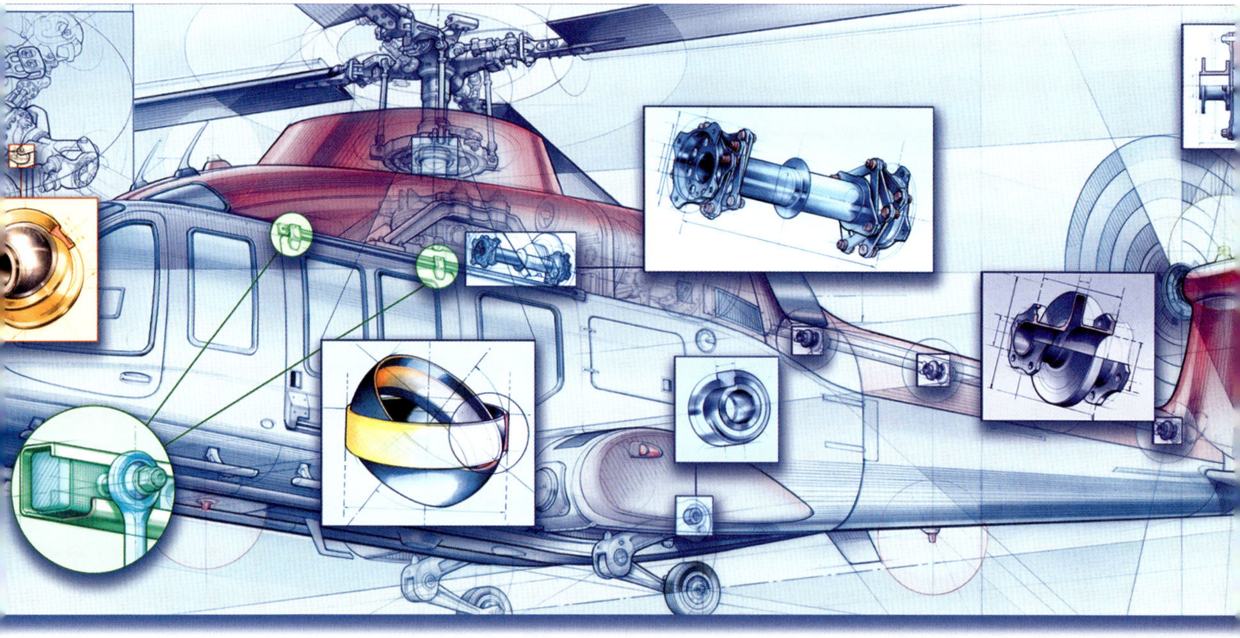

Robert Neubecker
Gerald & Cullen Rapp
212 889 3337
info@rappart.com
www.rappart.com/ neubecker.com

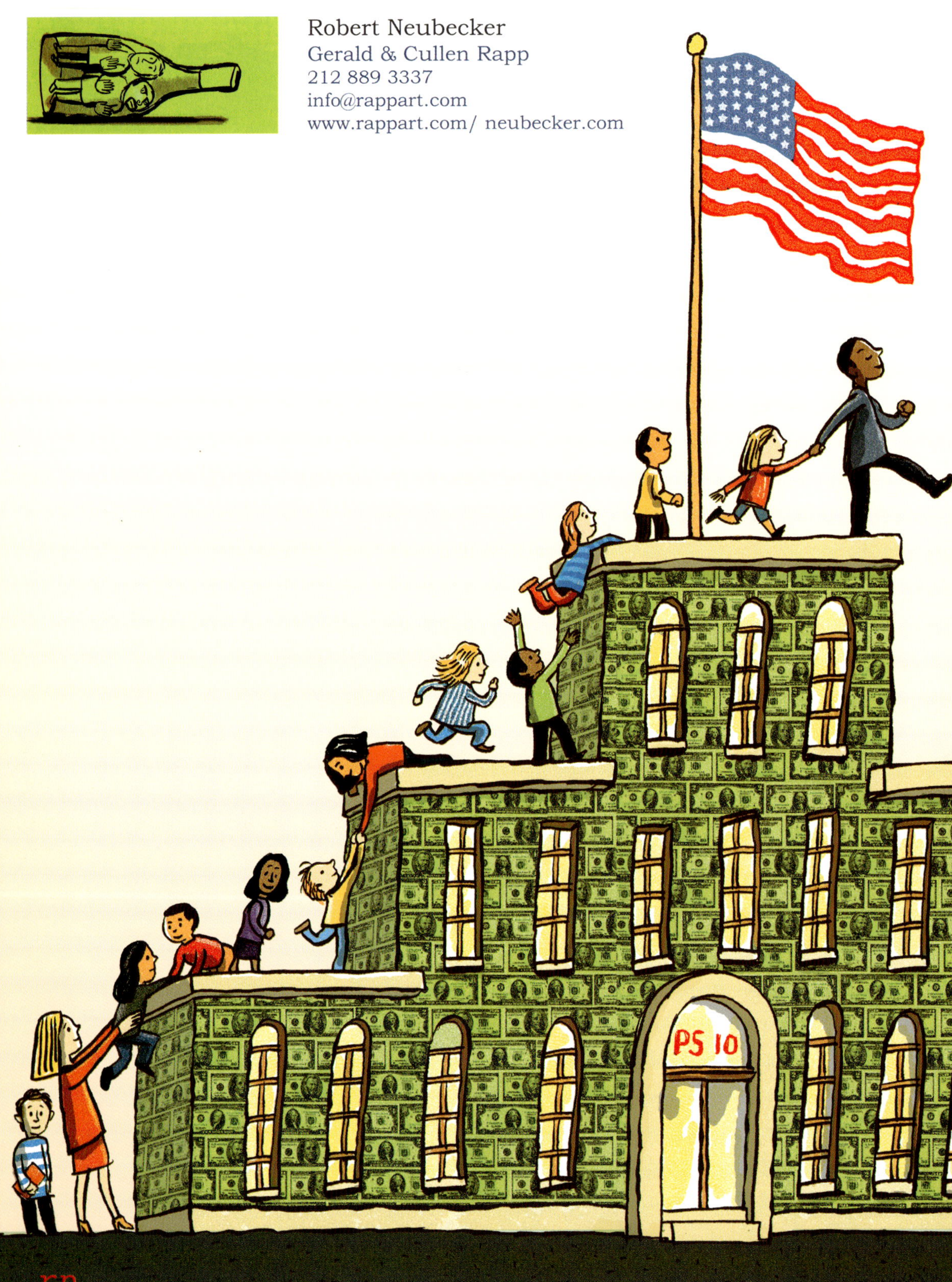

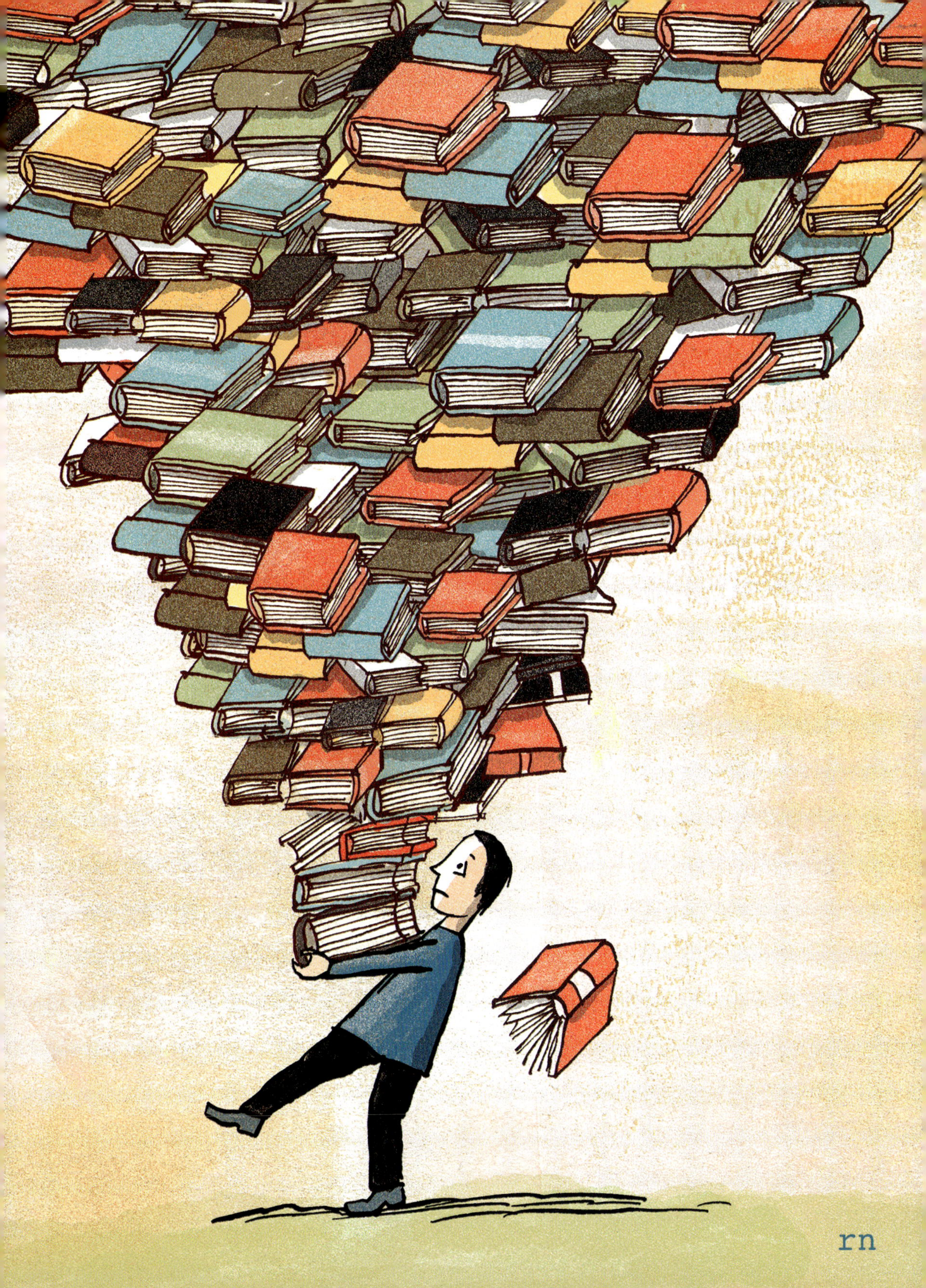

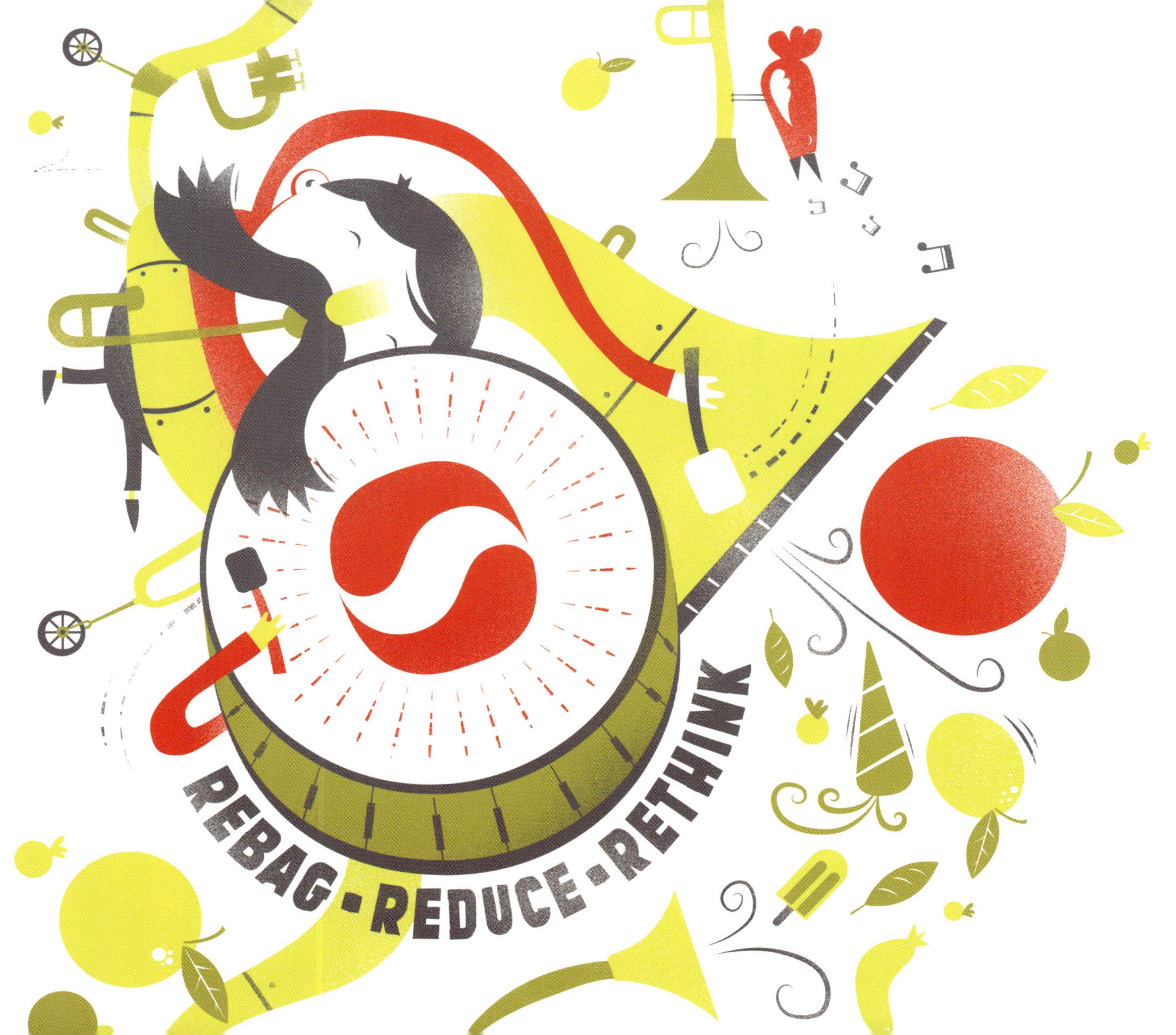

REBAG · REDUCE · RETHINK

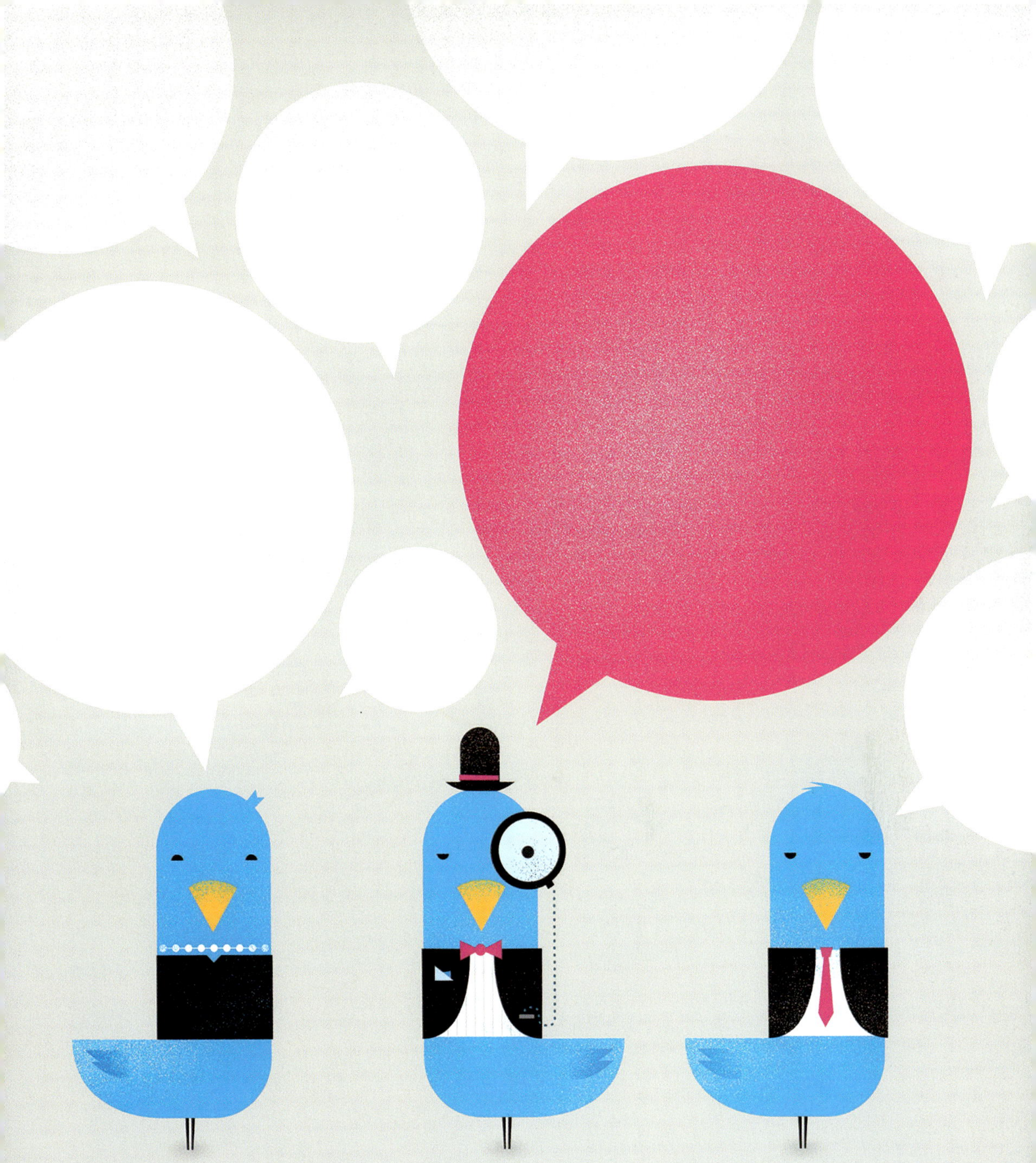

Shaw Nielsen
SHAWNIELSEN.COM

GERALD & CULLEN RAPP
WWW.RAPPART.COM
INFO@RAPPART.COM
212-889-3337

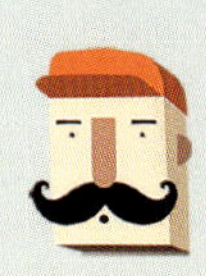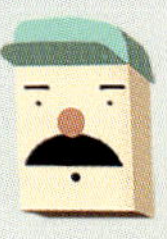

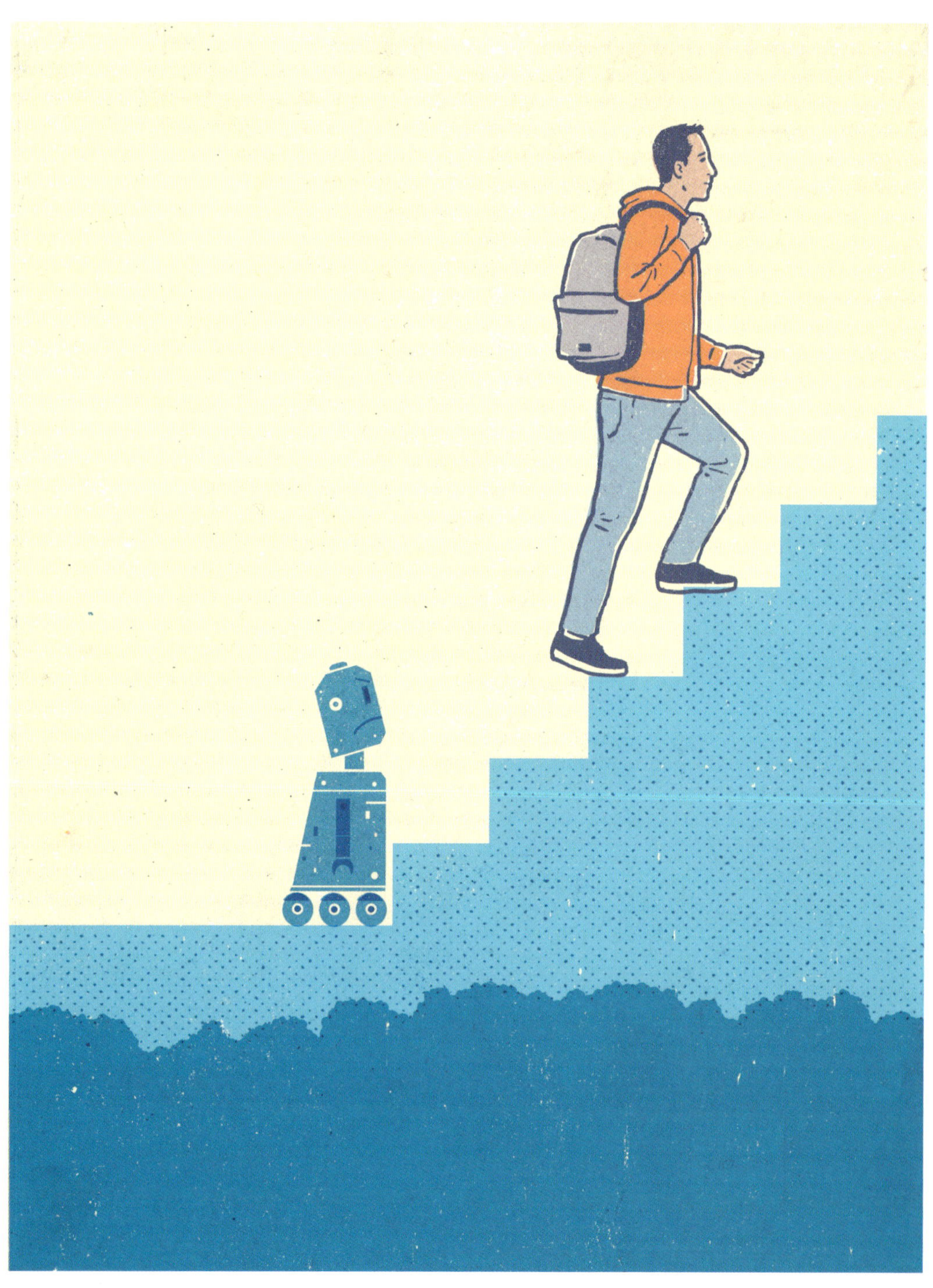

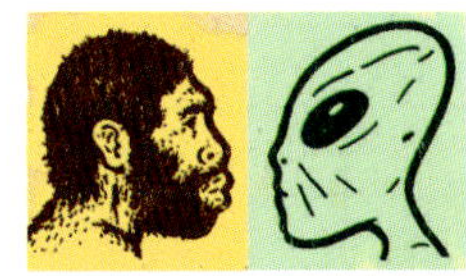

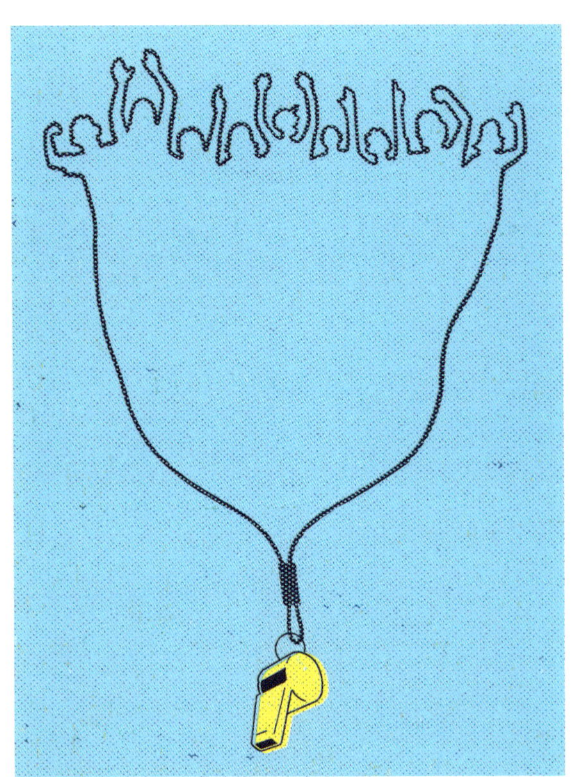

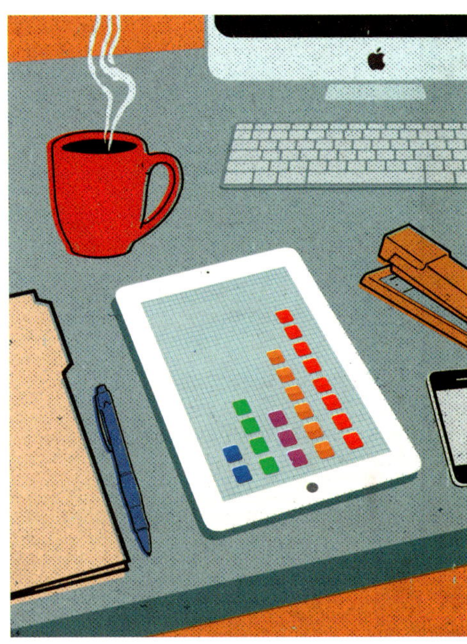

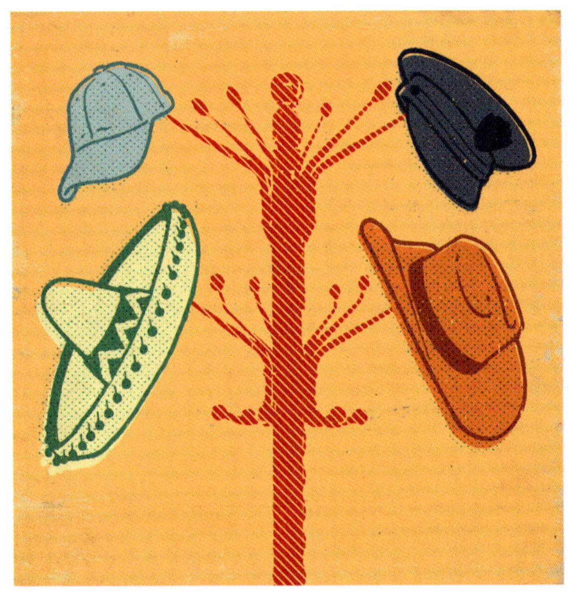

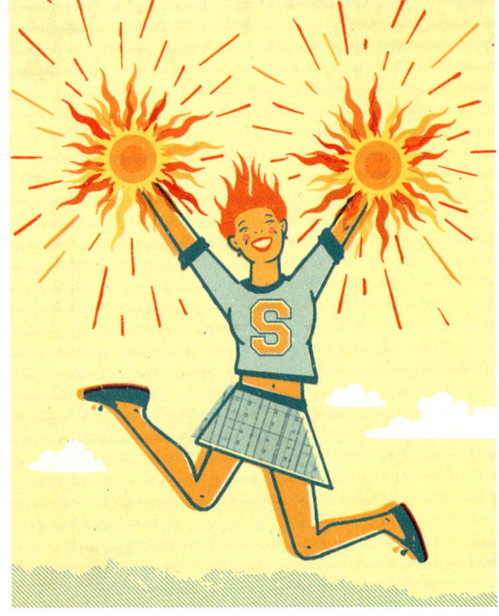

S

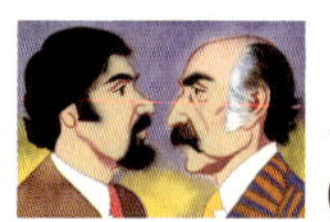

JEFFREY SMITH

Gerald & Cullen Rapp   212-889-3337   info@rappart.com   www.rappart.com

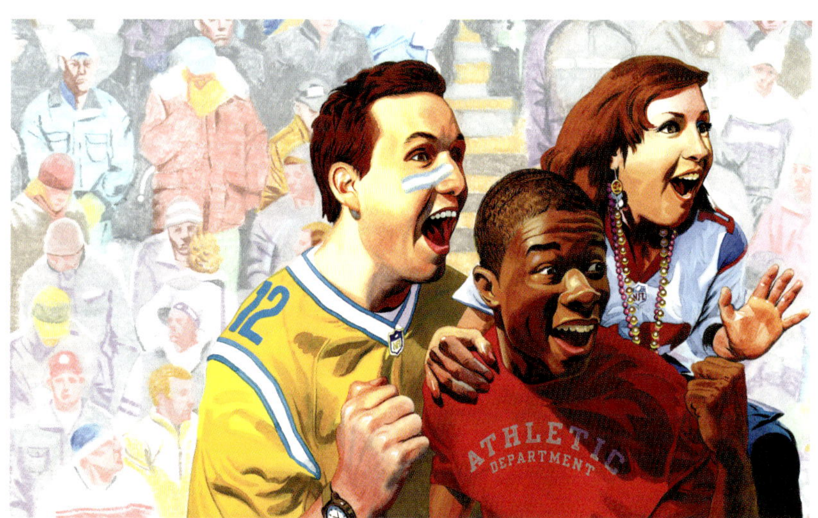

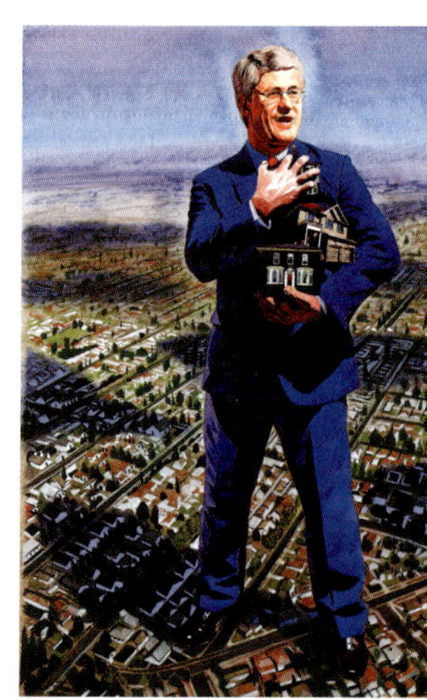

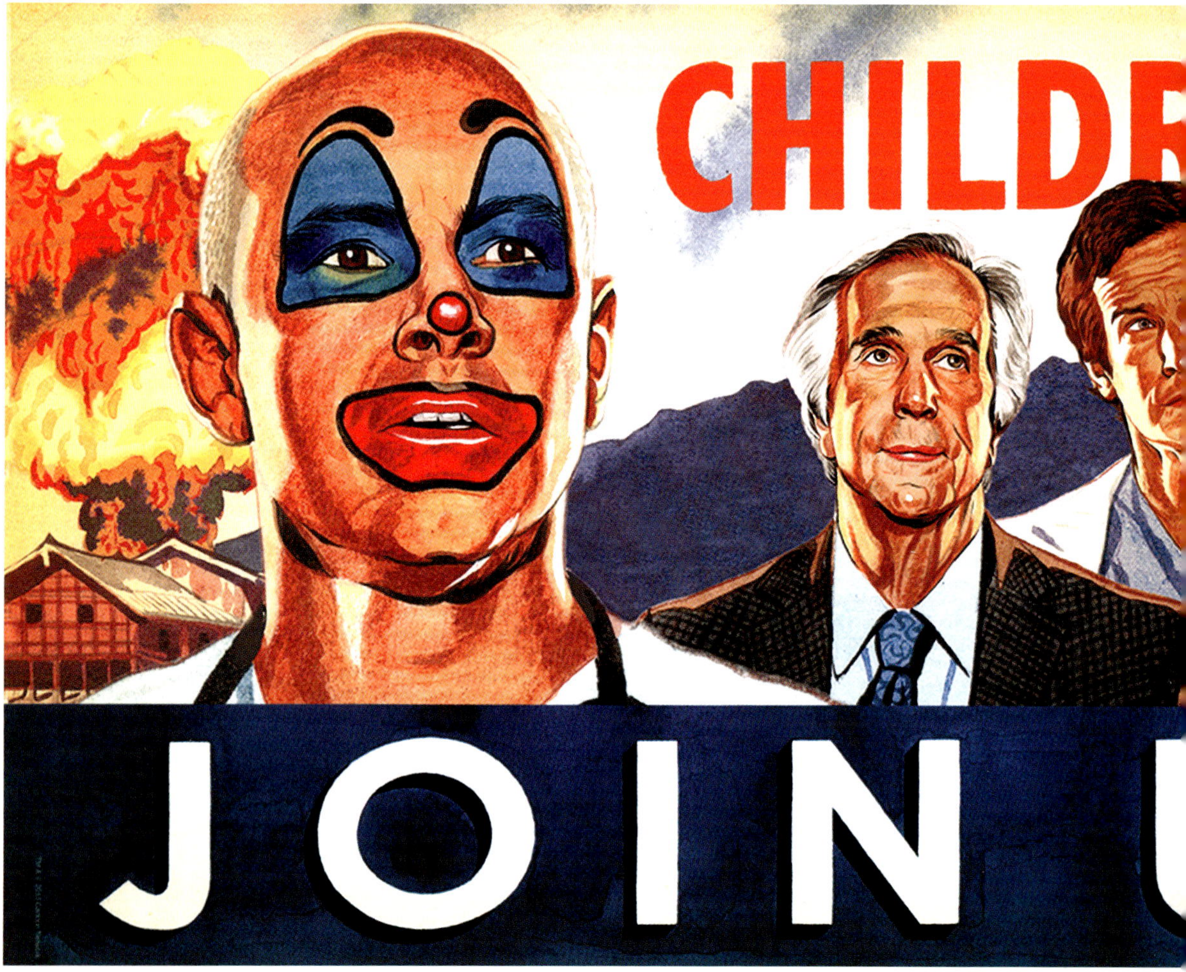

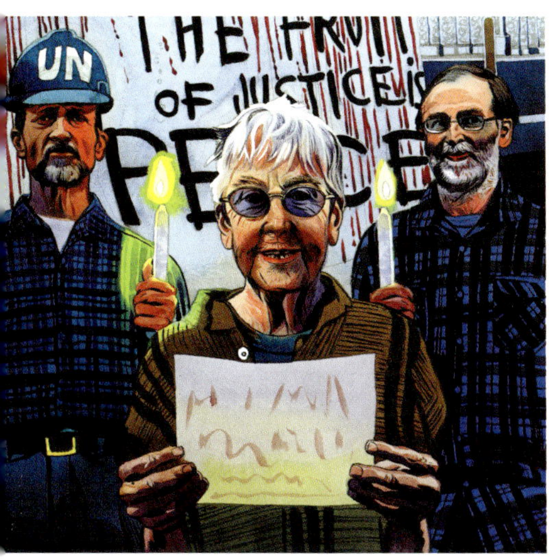

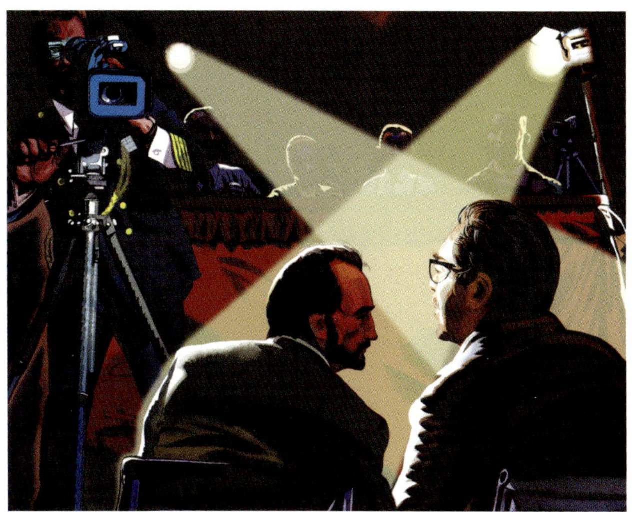

ENS HOSPITAL

THURSDAYS • MIDNIGHT

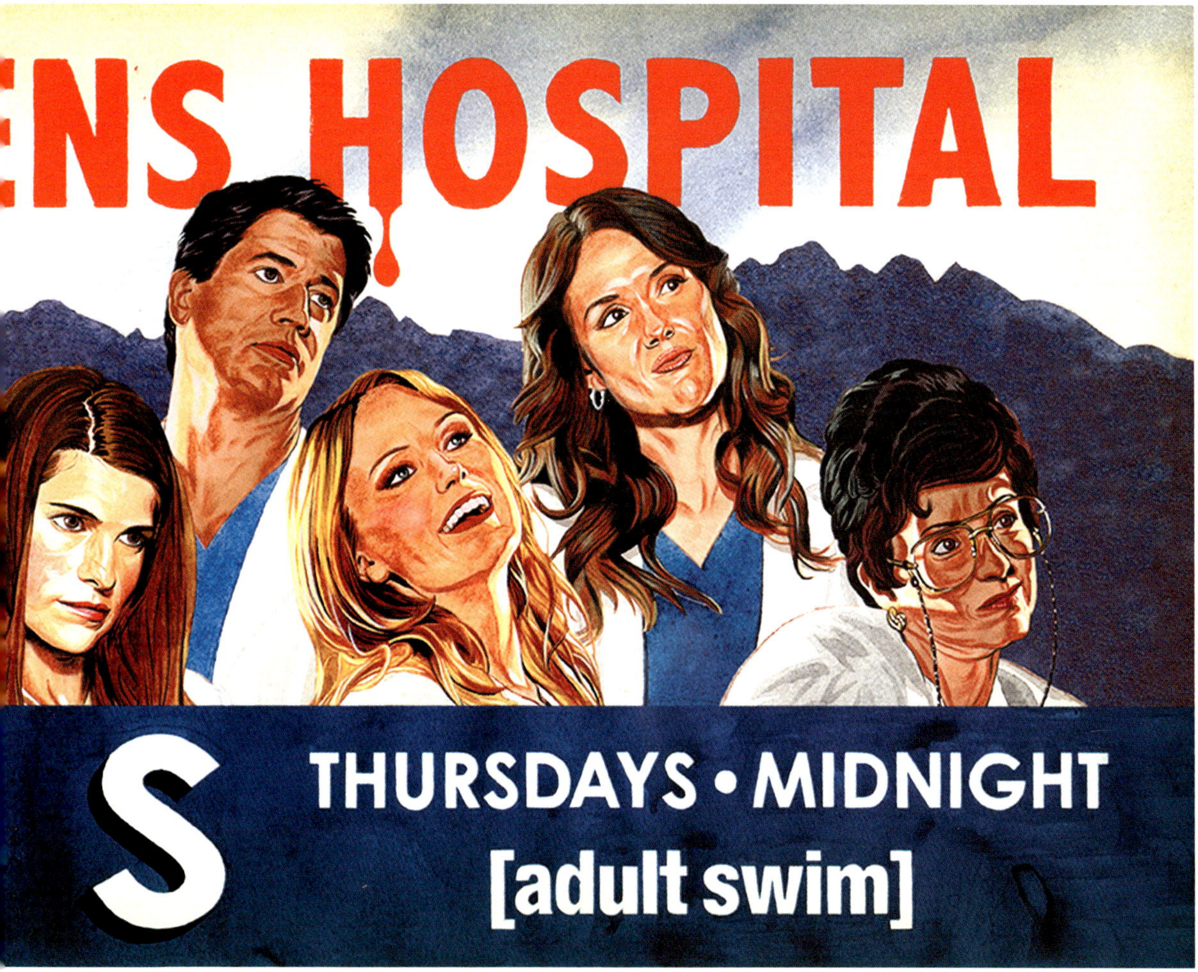

[adult swim]

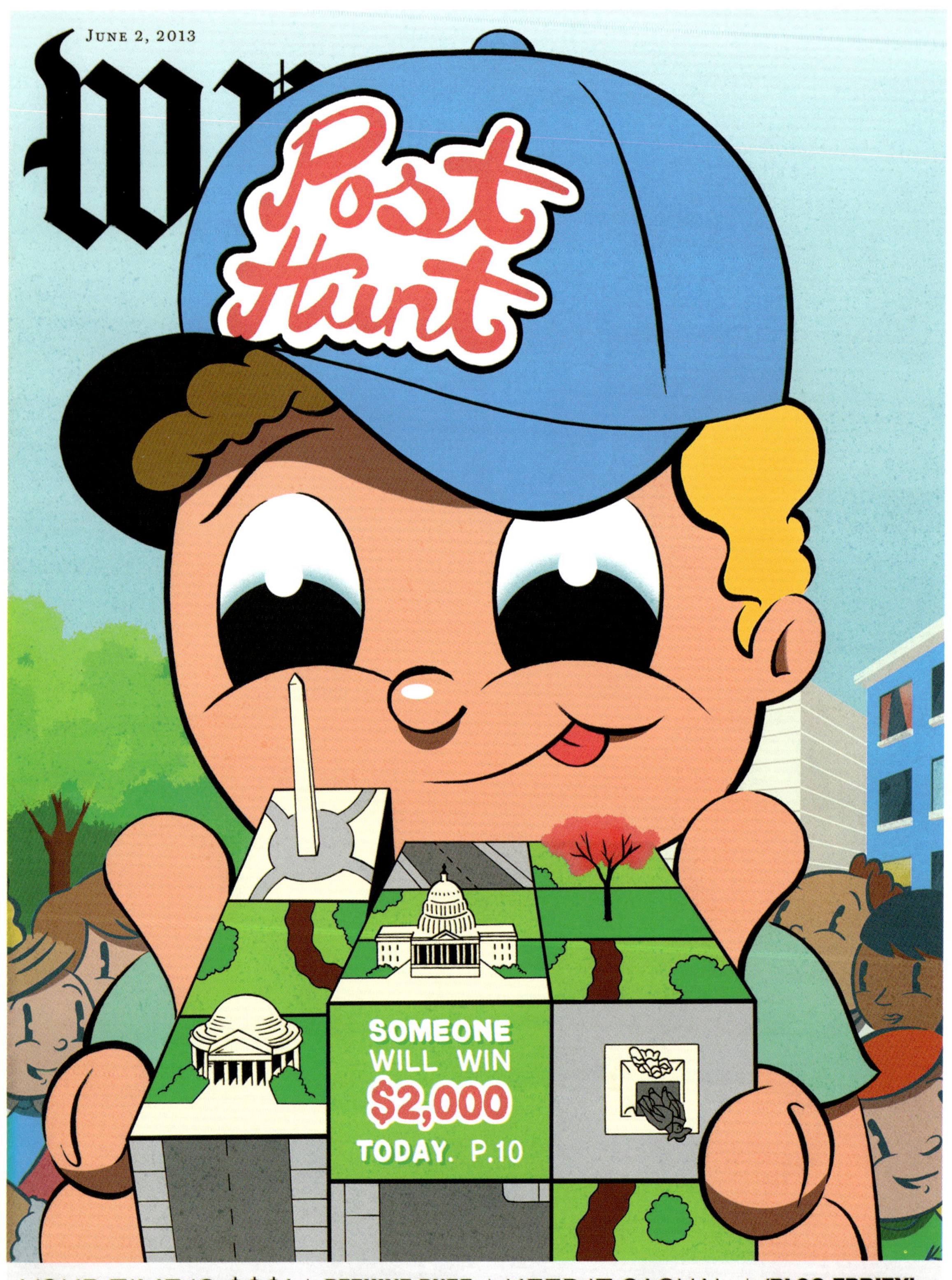

June 2, 2013
Post Hunt
SOMEONE WILL WIN $2,000 TODAY. P.10
YOUR TIME IS $$$!
@WORK ADVICE P.3
BEEHIVE BUZZ IN BALTIMORE, DO THE 'DO P.4
KEEP IT CASUAL IN DATE LAB P.8
'BLOG-EBRITY' D.C.'S MODERN SOCIALITES? P.18

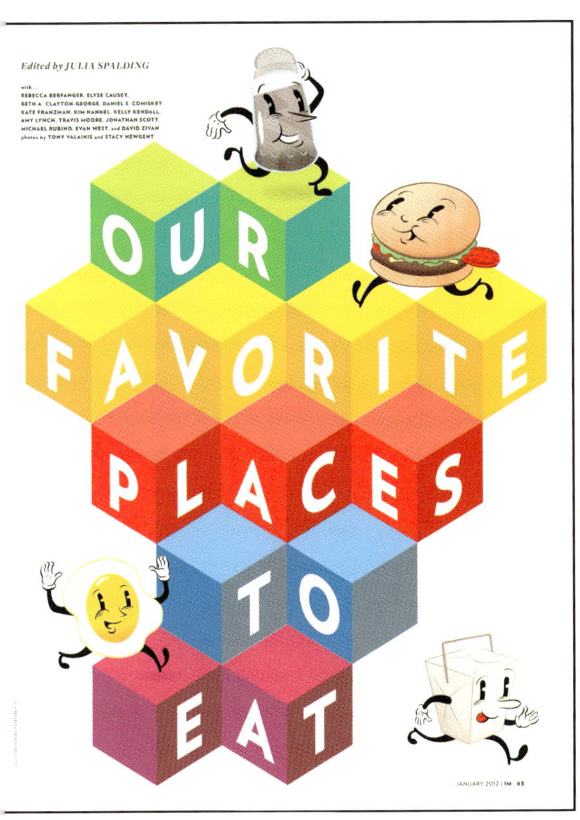

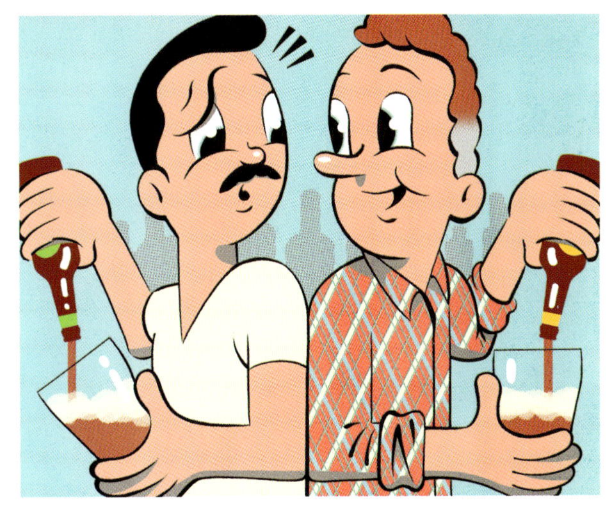

RYAN SNOOK

Represented by Gerald & Cullen Rapp

212 889 3337

info@rappart.com

www.rappart.com

www.ryansnook.com

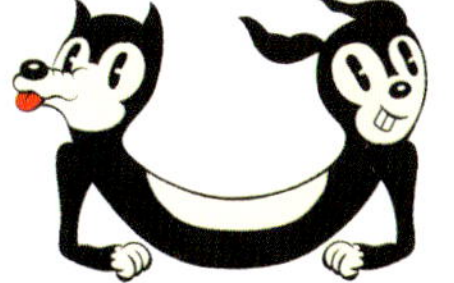

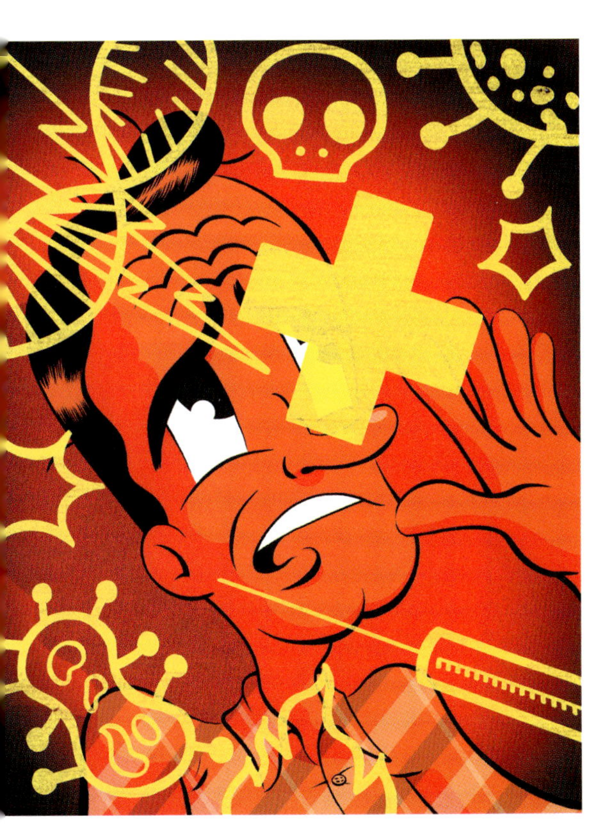

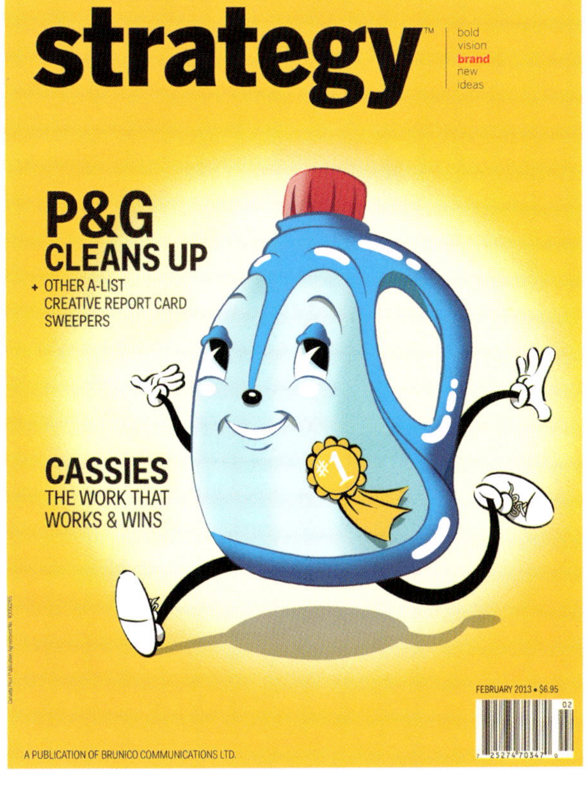

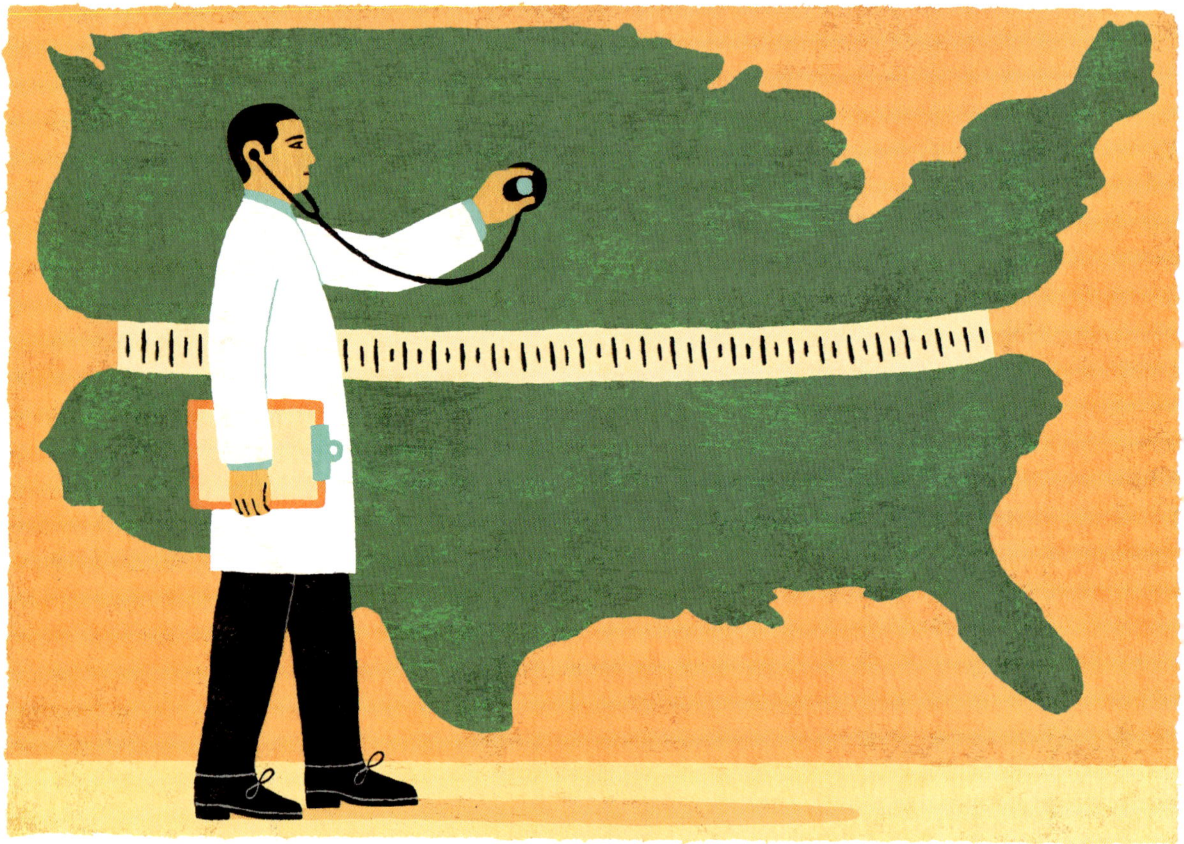

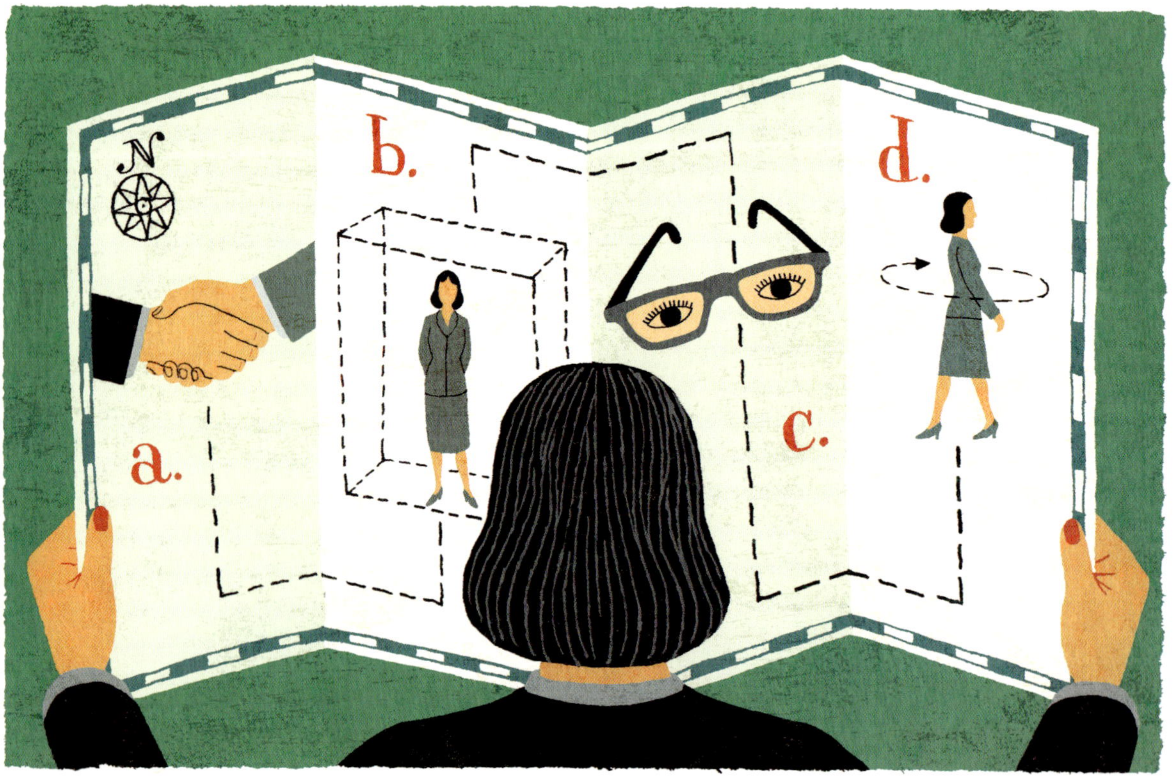

N
a.
b.
c.
d.

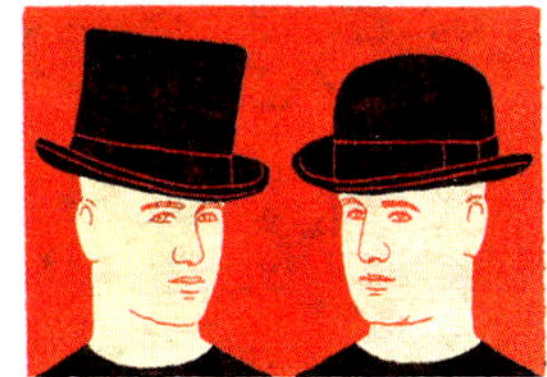

James Steinberg

Gerald & Cullen Rapp | 212-889-3337 | info@rappart.com
www.james-steinberg.com | www.rappart.com

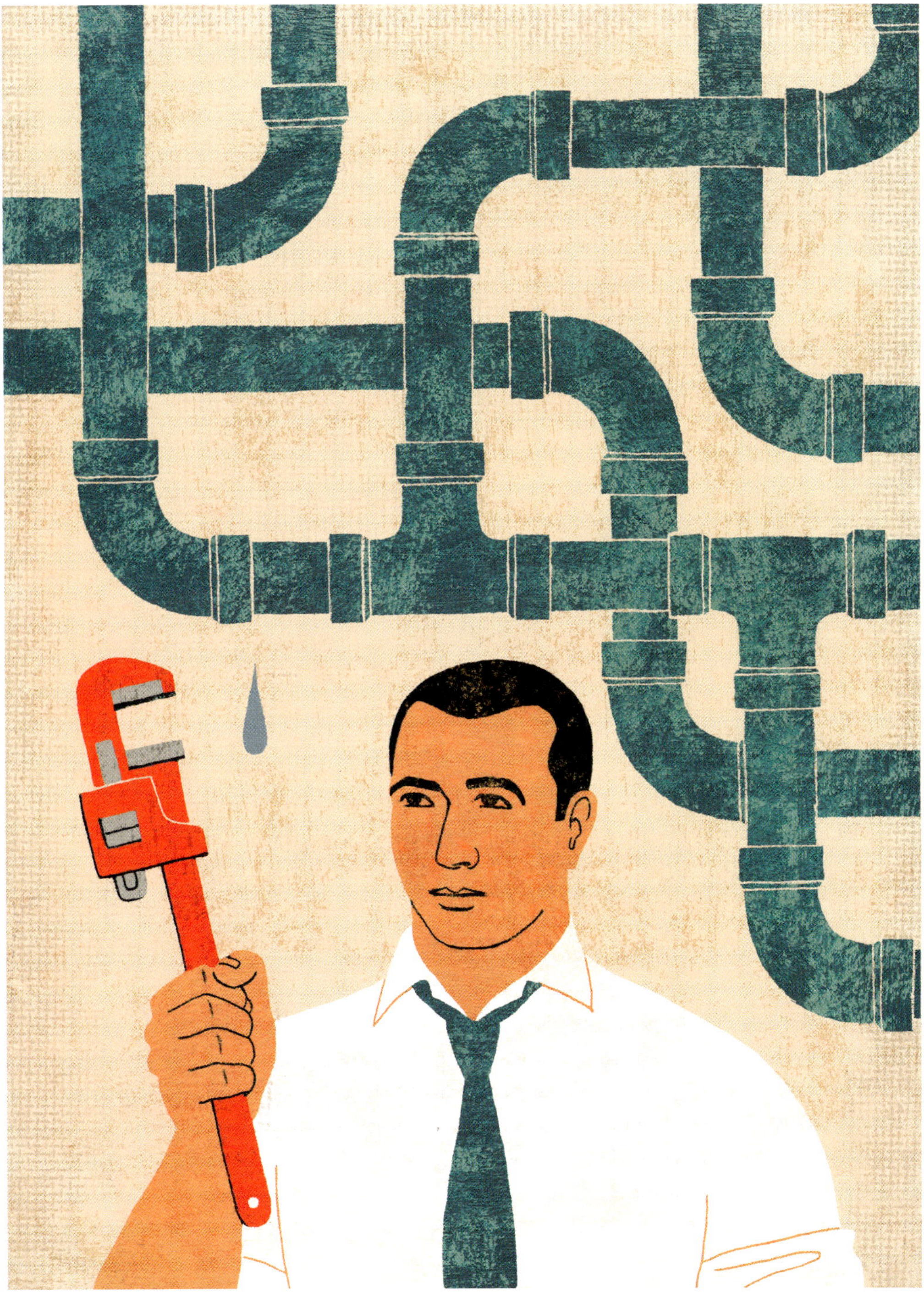

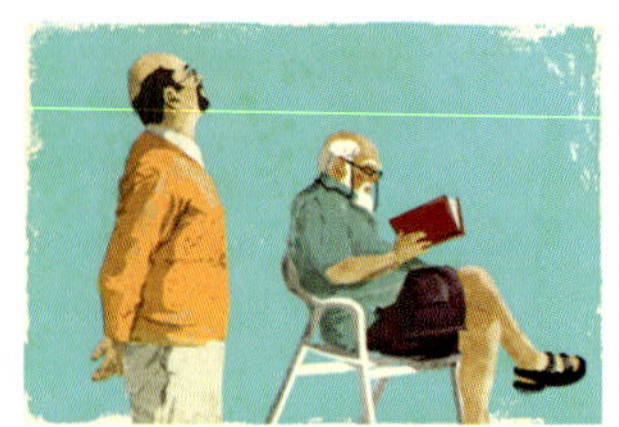

Gerald & Cullen Rapp

212-889-3337
info@rappart.com
www.rappart.com

EVA VÁZQUEZ   evavazquezdibujos.com

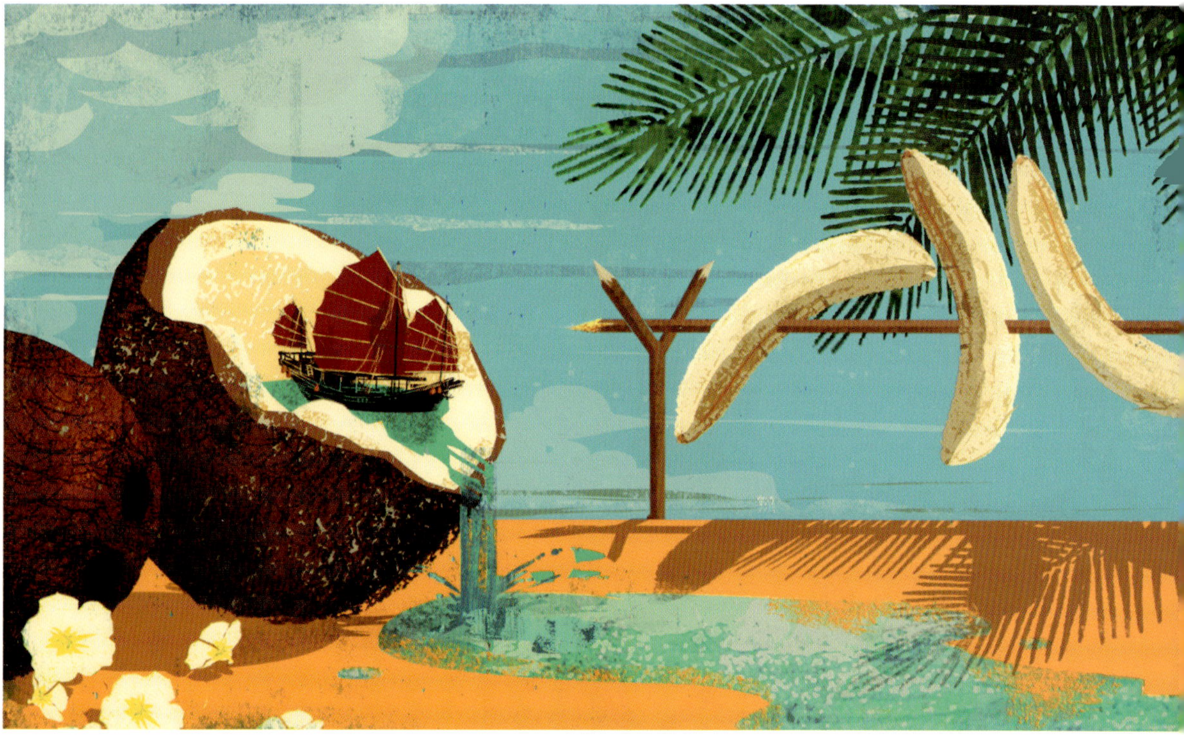

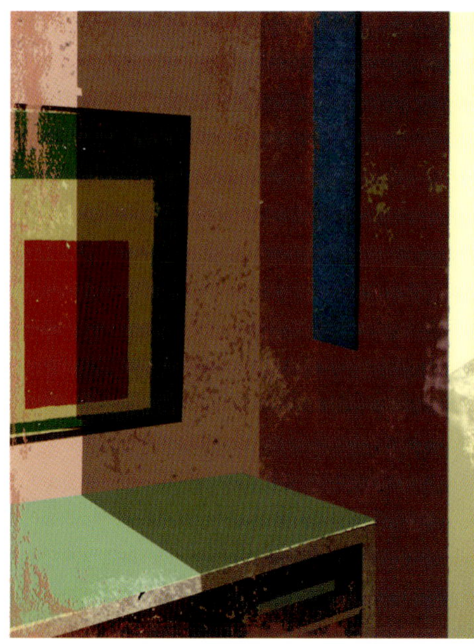

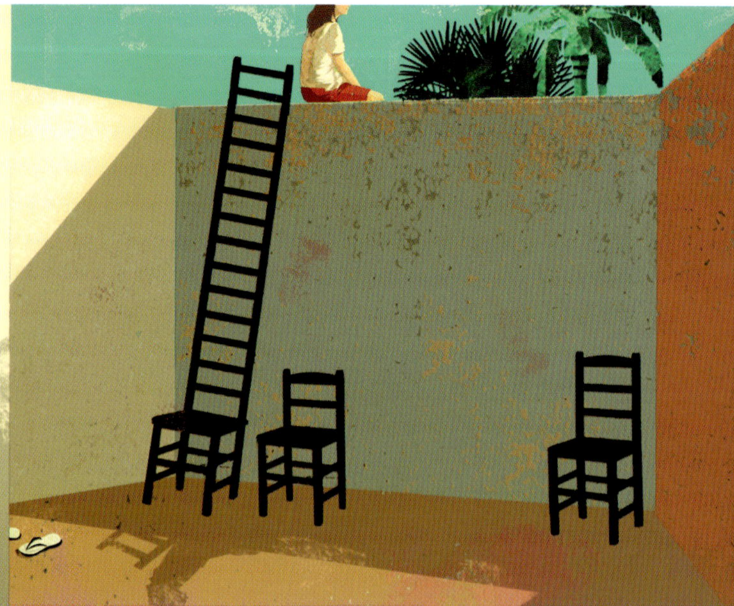

BRAD YEO

ww.bradyeo.com

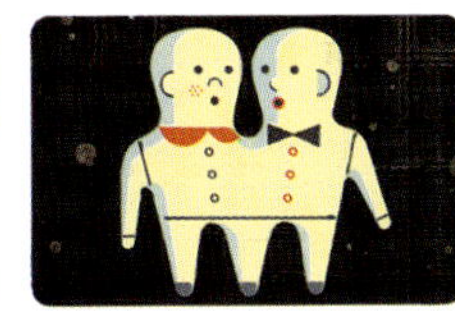

GERALD & CULLEN RAPP
www.rappart.com
info@rappart.com
(T) 212.889.3337

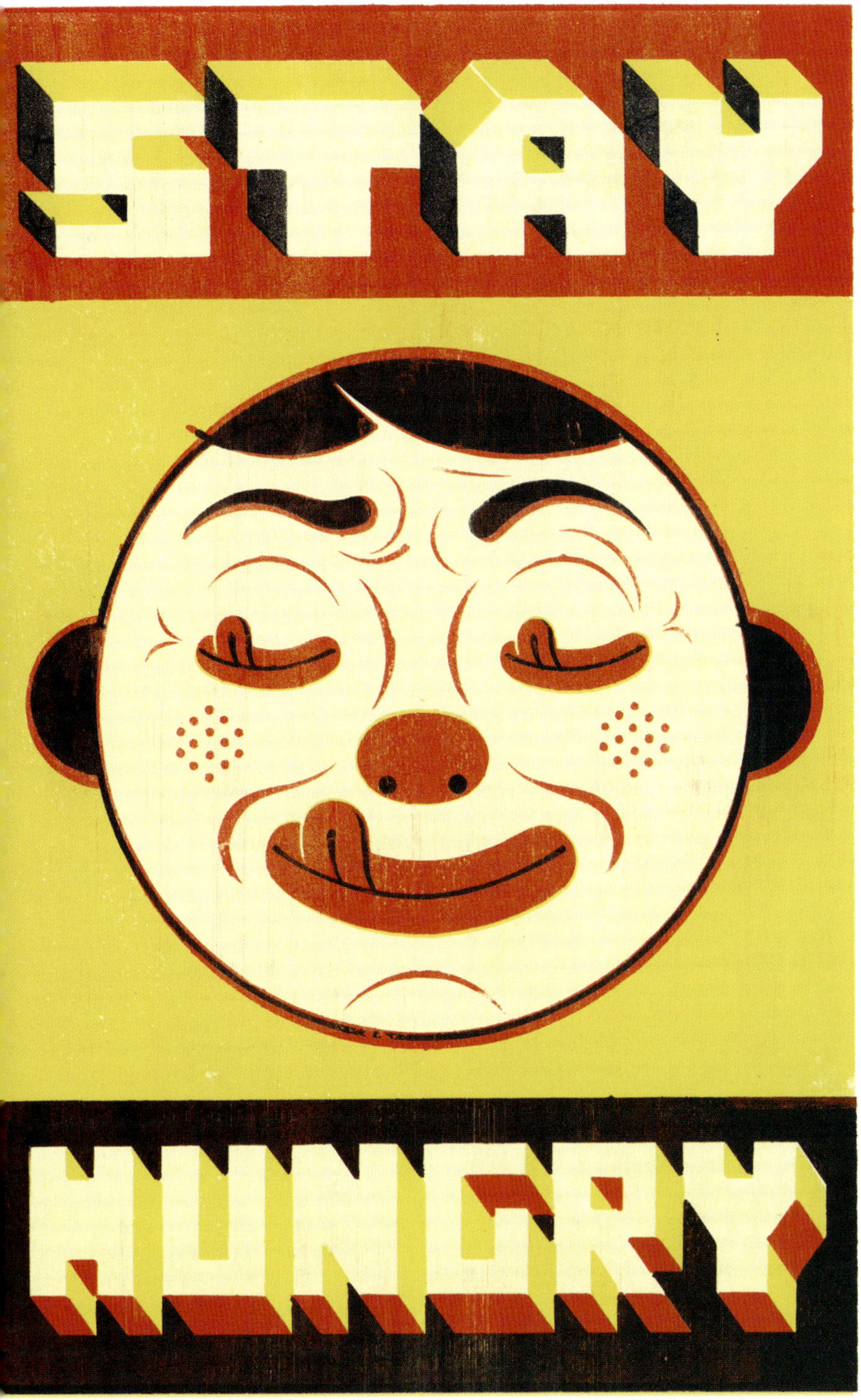

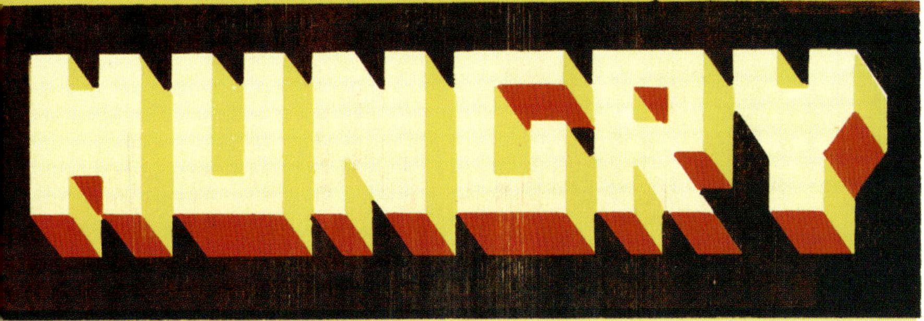

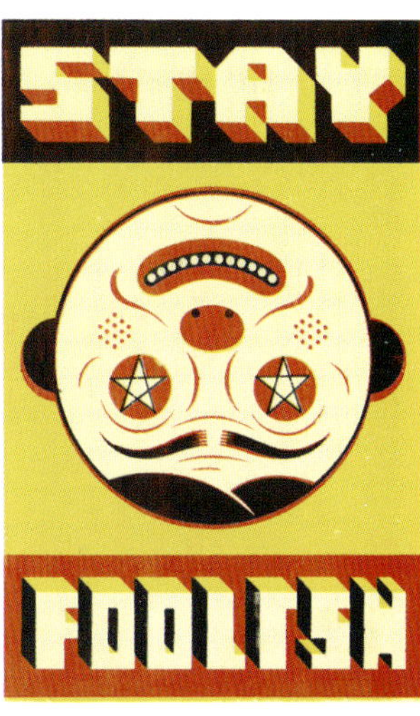

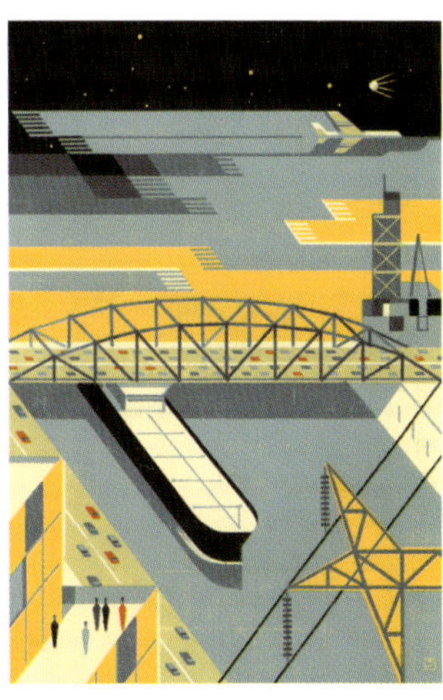

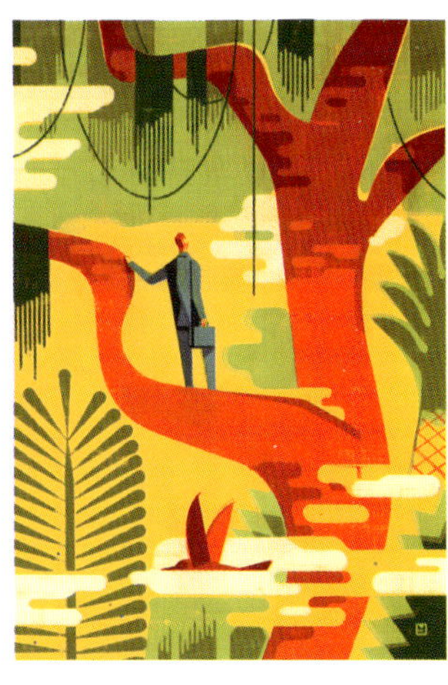

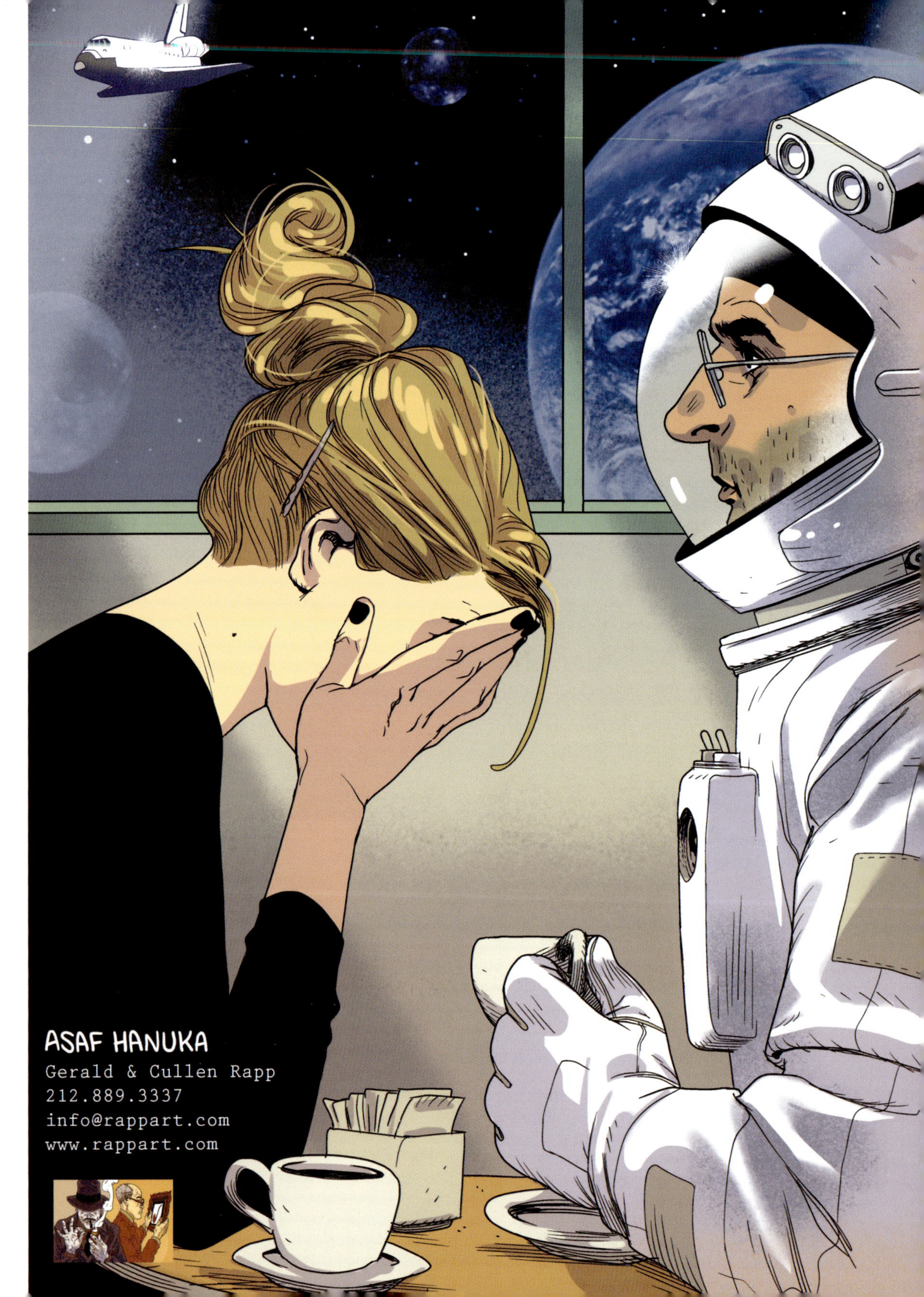
ASAF HANUKA
Gerald & Cullen Rapp
212.889.3337
info@rappart.com
www.rappart.com

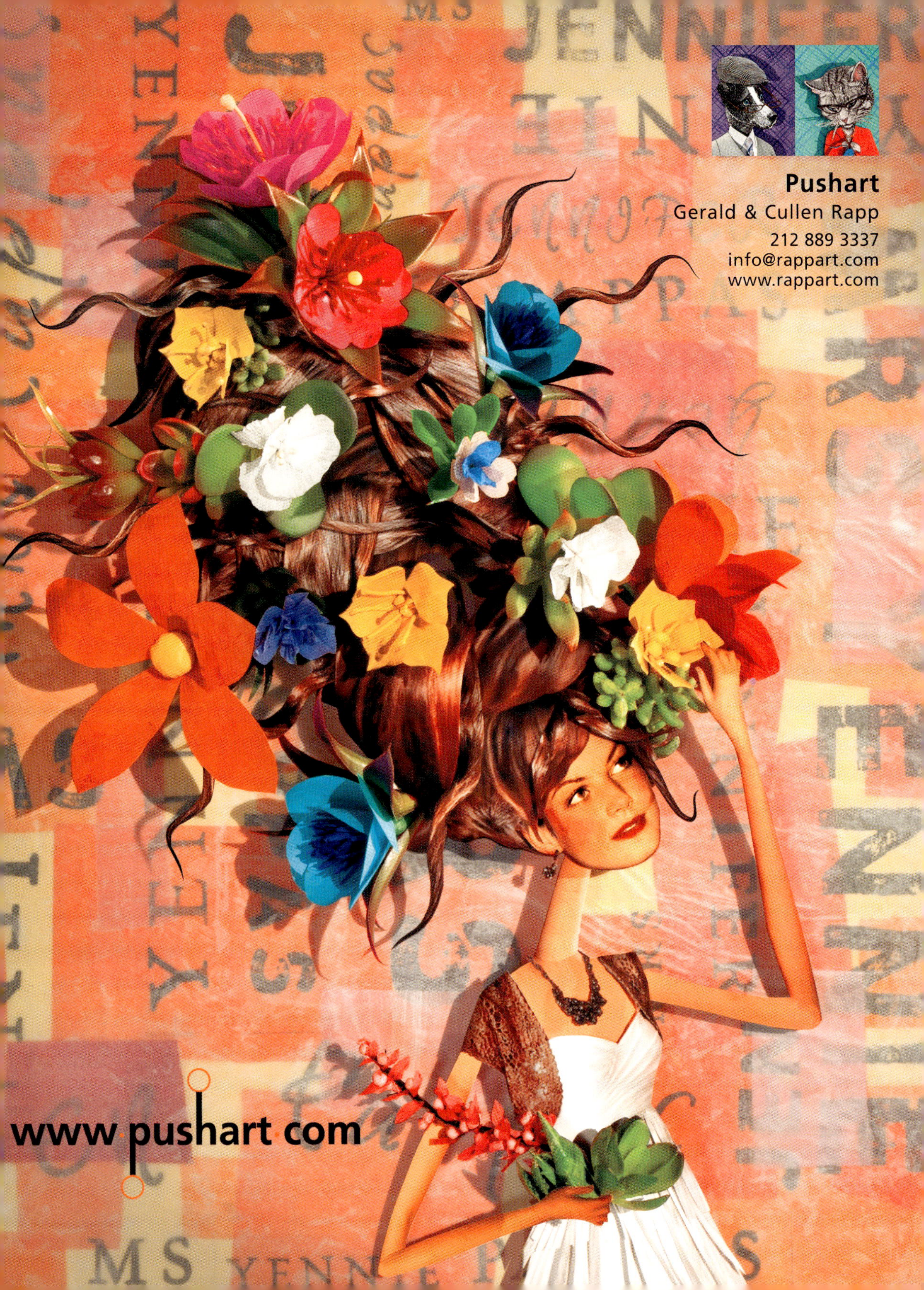
Pushart
Gerald & Cullen Rapp
212 889 3337
info@rappart.com
www.rappart.com

www.pushart com

*Douglas Jones
Gerald & Cullen Rapp Inc.
212.889.3337
www.rappart.com
www.douglasjones.com

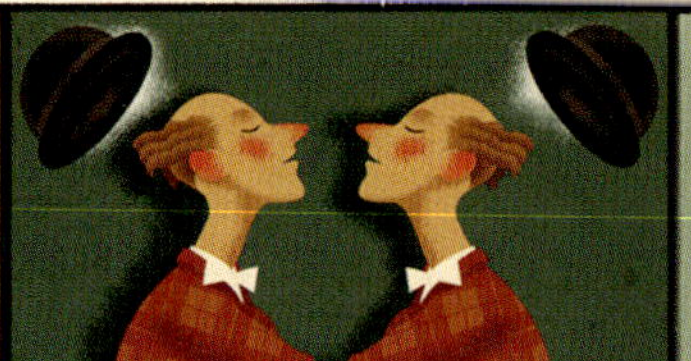

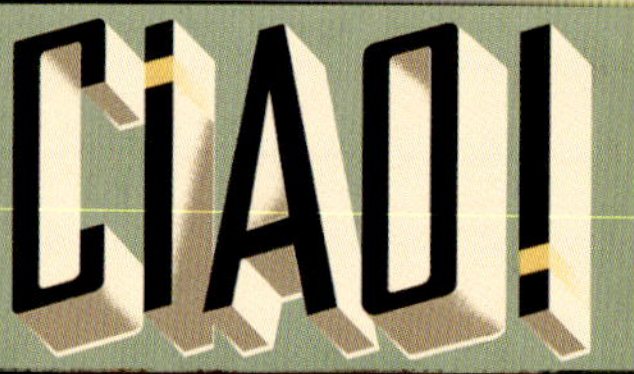

CIAO!

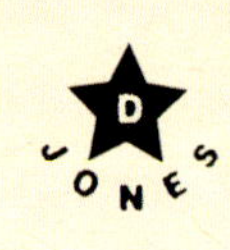

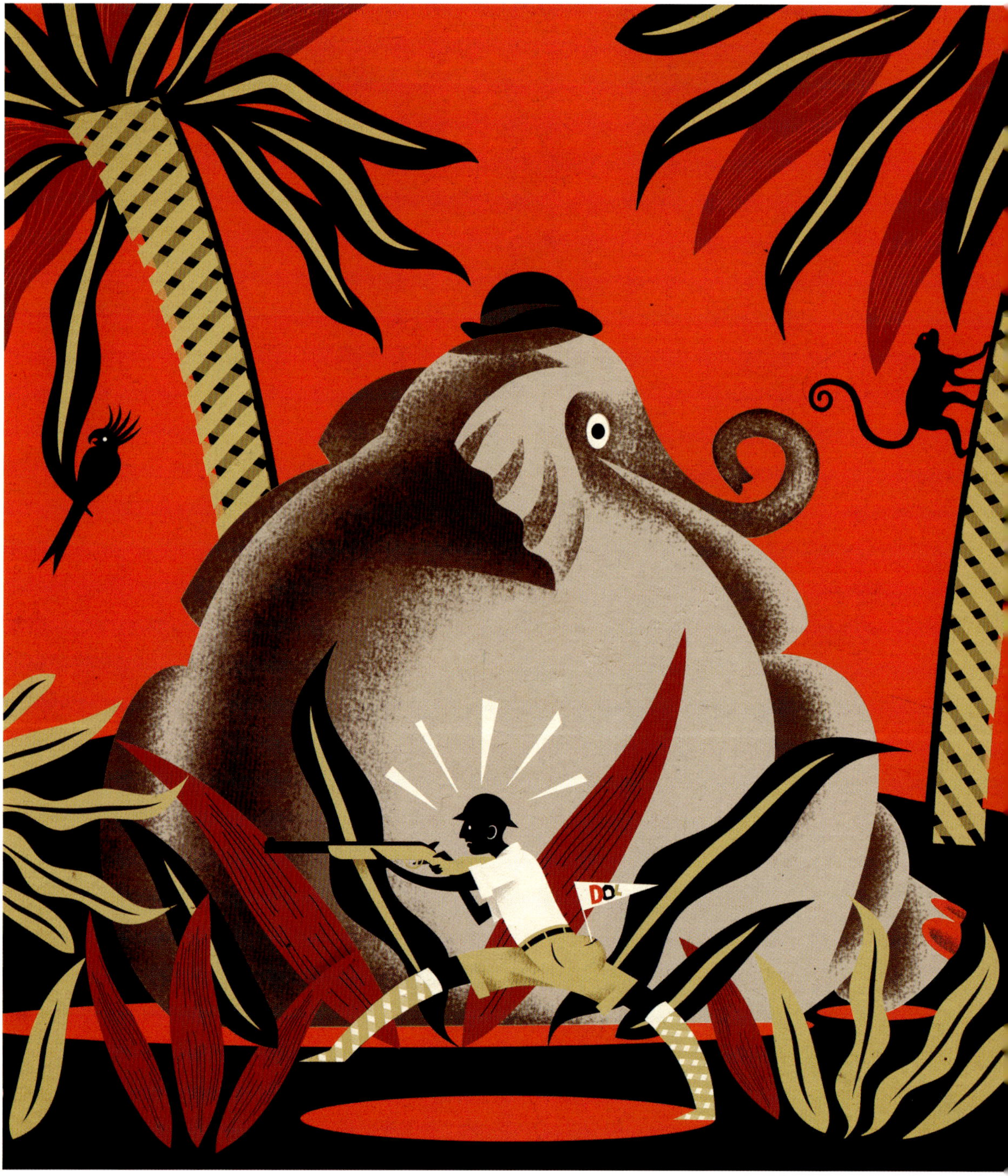

D
JONES

DOL

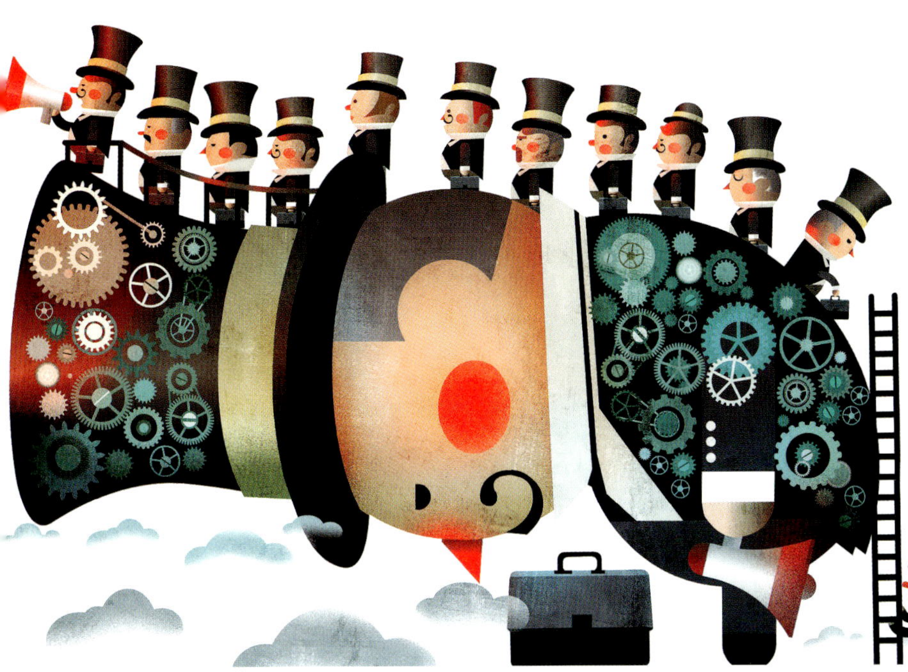

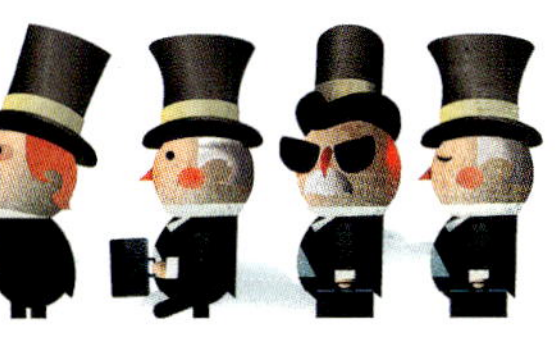

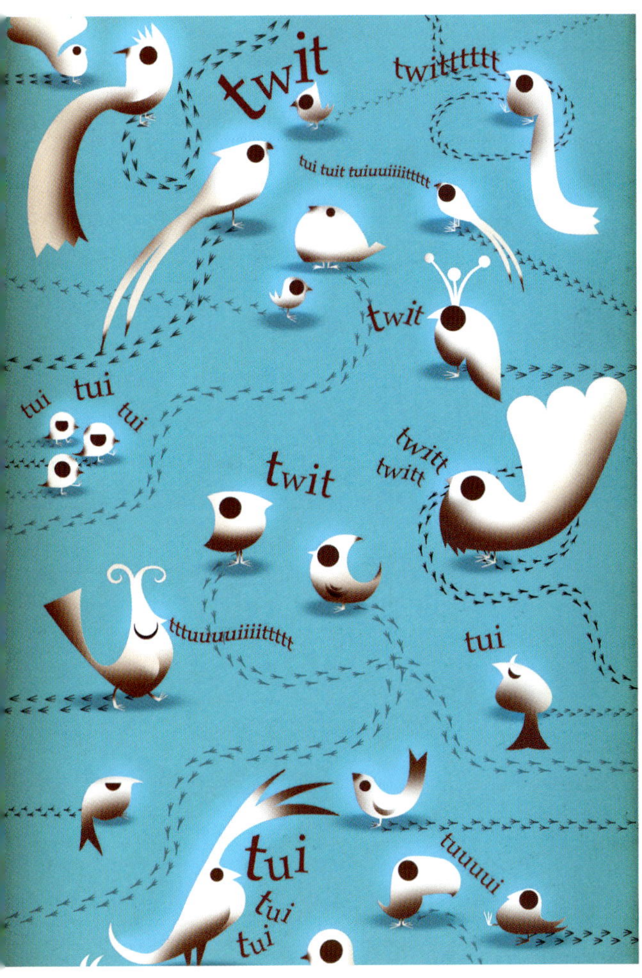

twit
twitttttt
tui tuit tuiuuiiiitttttt
twit
tui tui tui
twit
twitt
twitt
tttuuuuuiiiittttt
tui
tui
tui
tui
tuuuui

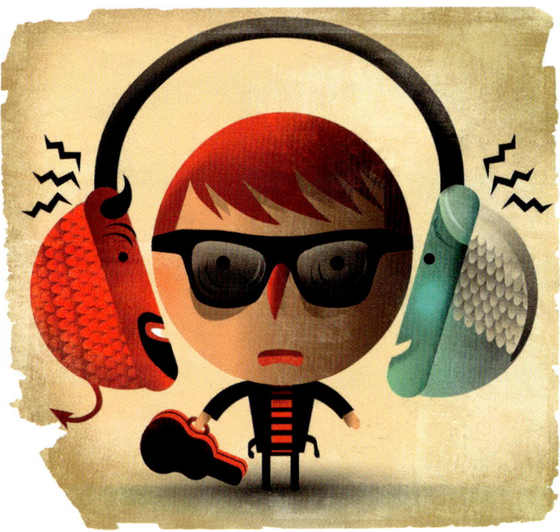

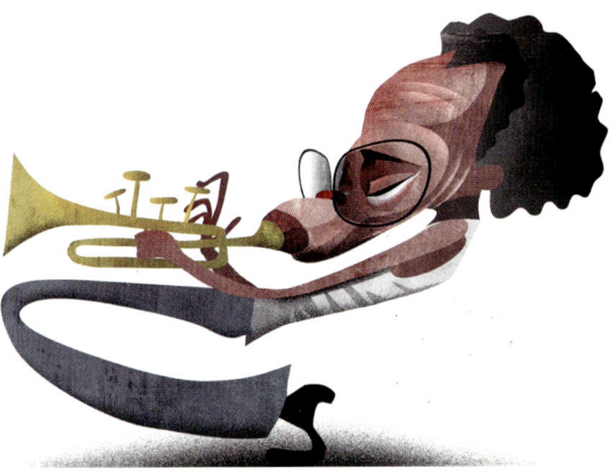

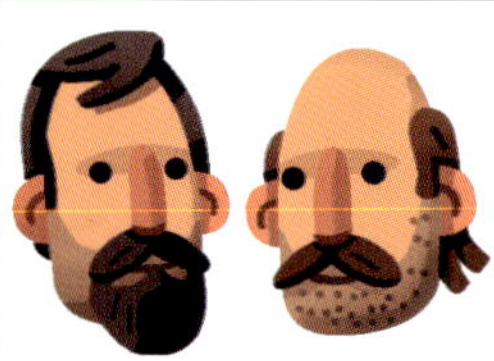
CHI BIRMINGHAM
represented by
GERALD & CULLEN RAPP
info@rappart.com
www.rappart.com
(T)   212.889.3337

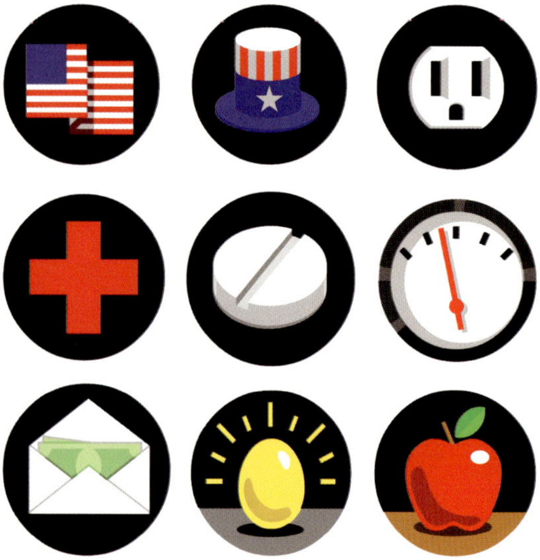

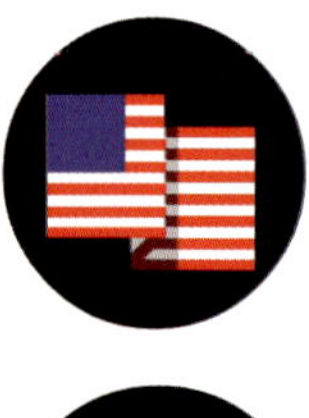

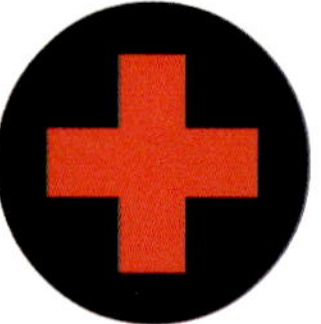
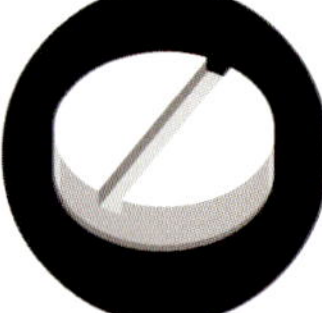
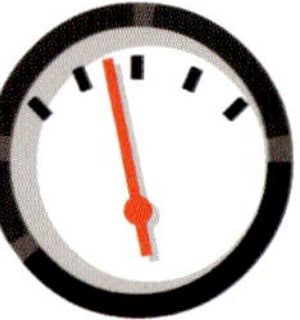

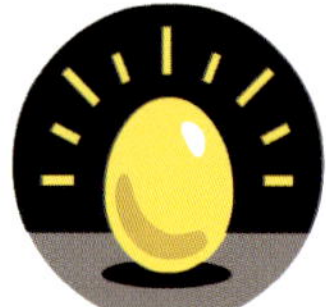
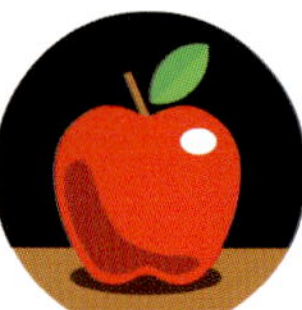
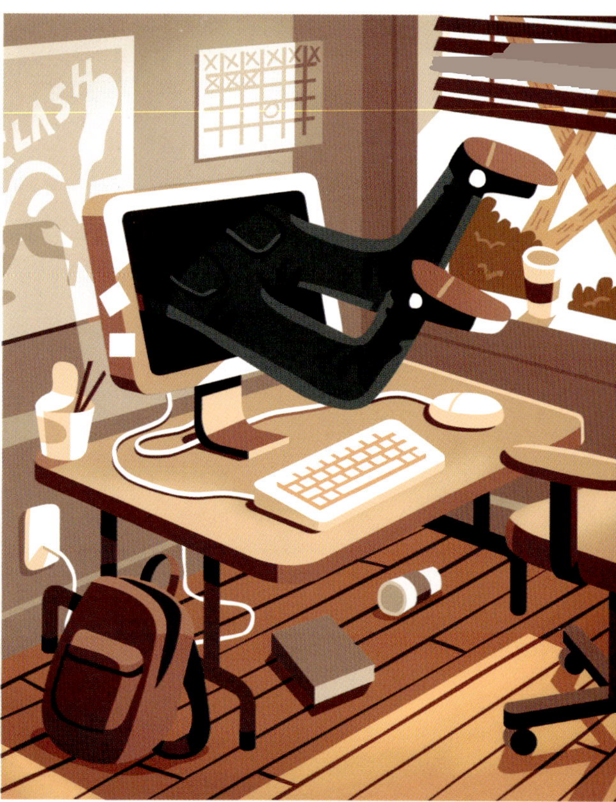

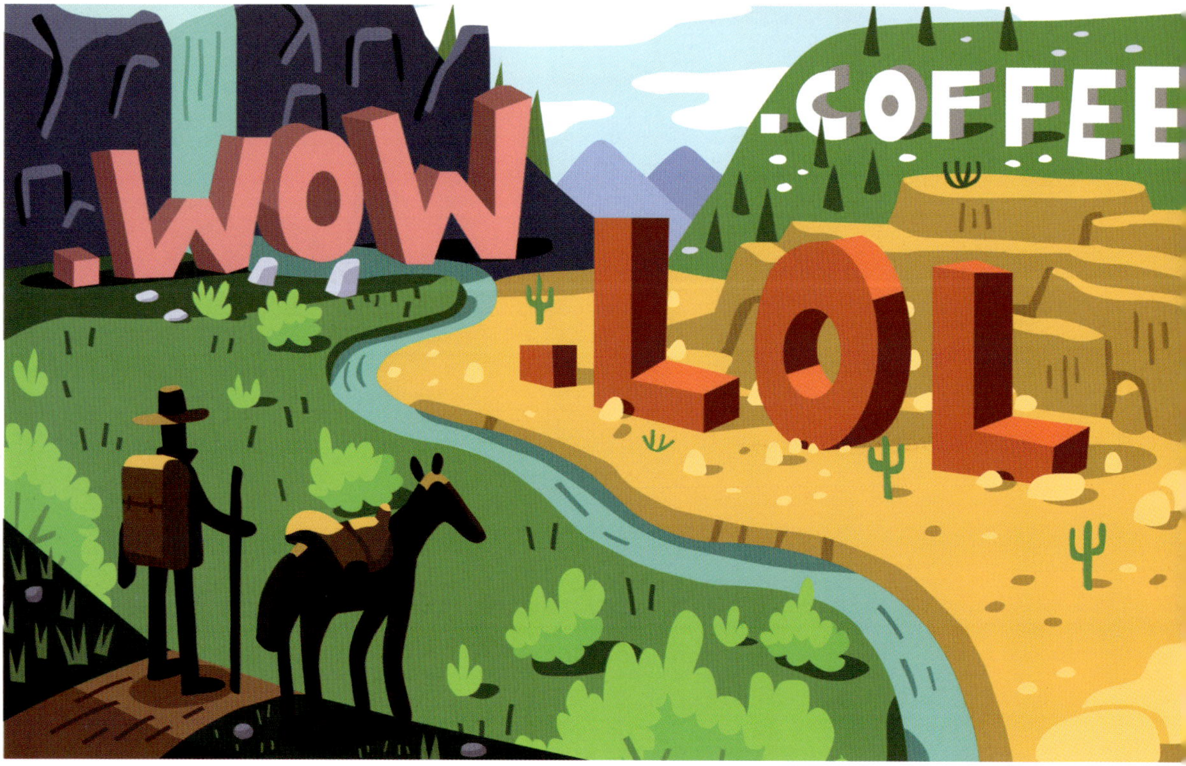

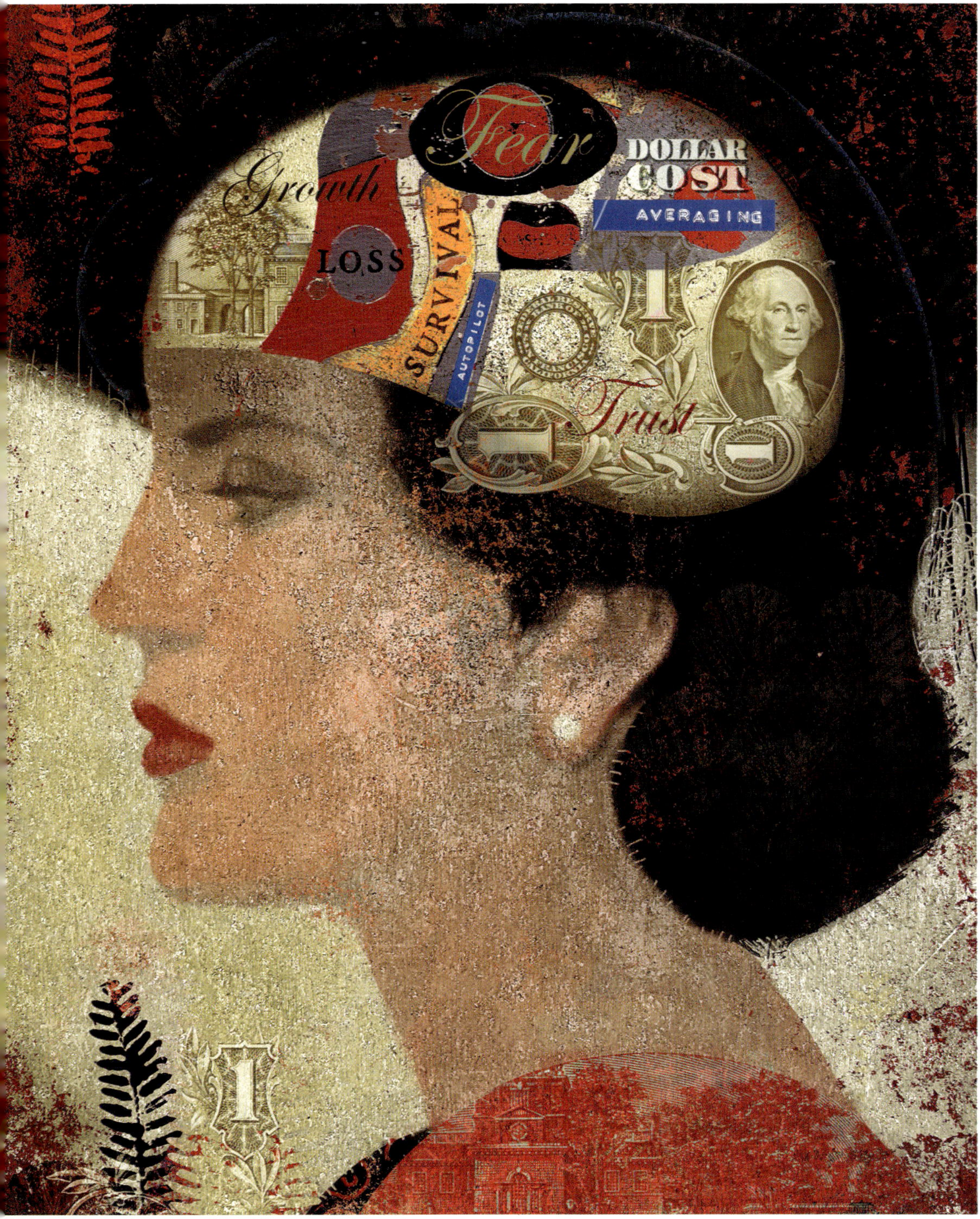

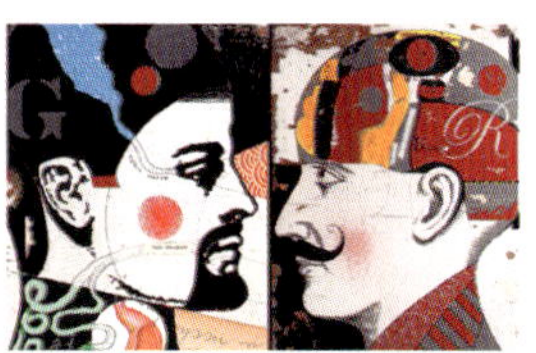

Fear
Growth
DOLLAR COST
AVERAGING
LOSS
SURVIVAL
AUTOPILOT
1
Trust
1

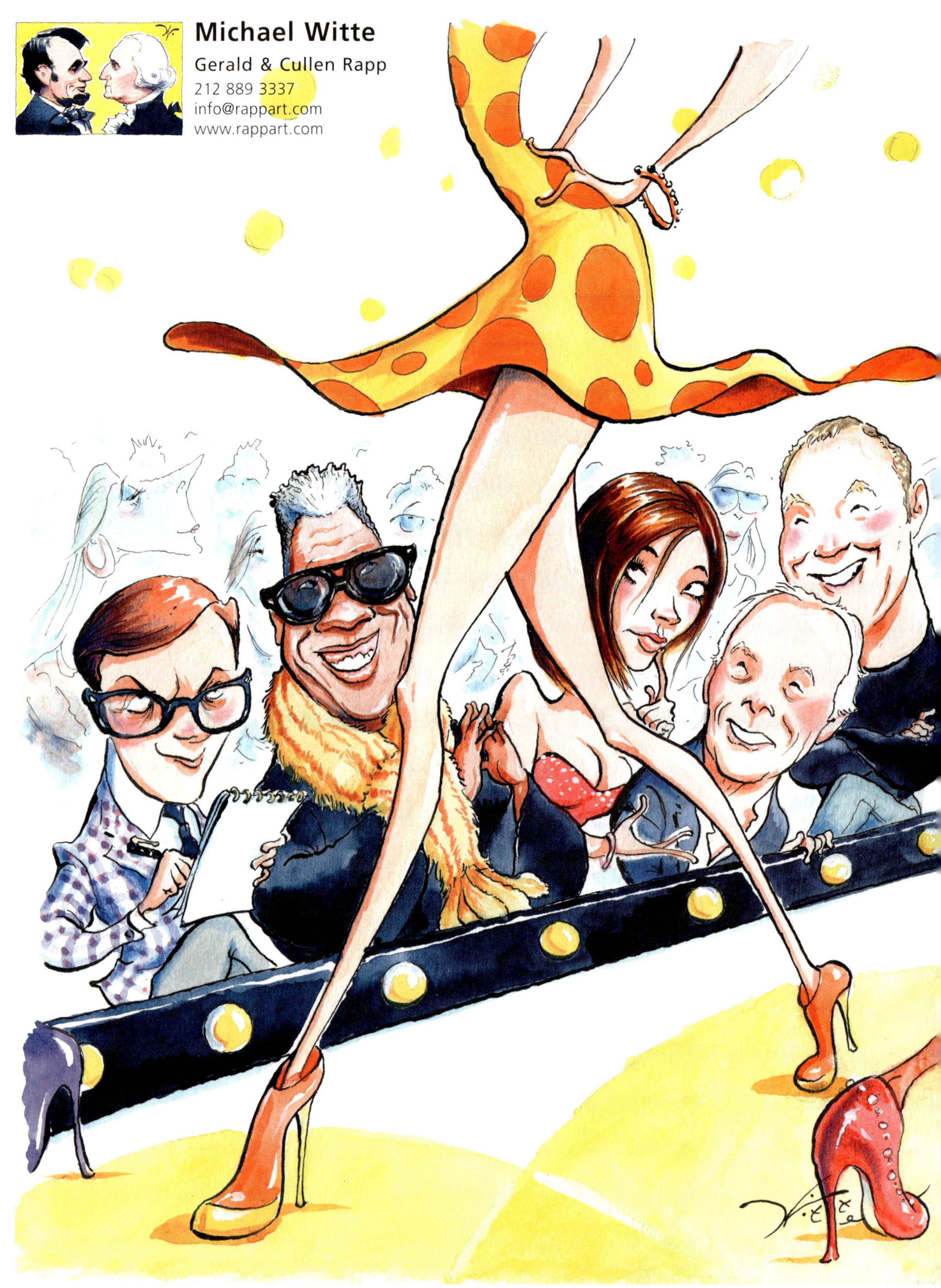

Michael Witte
Gerald & Cullen Rapp
212 889 3337
info@rappart.com
www.rappart.com

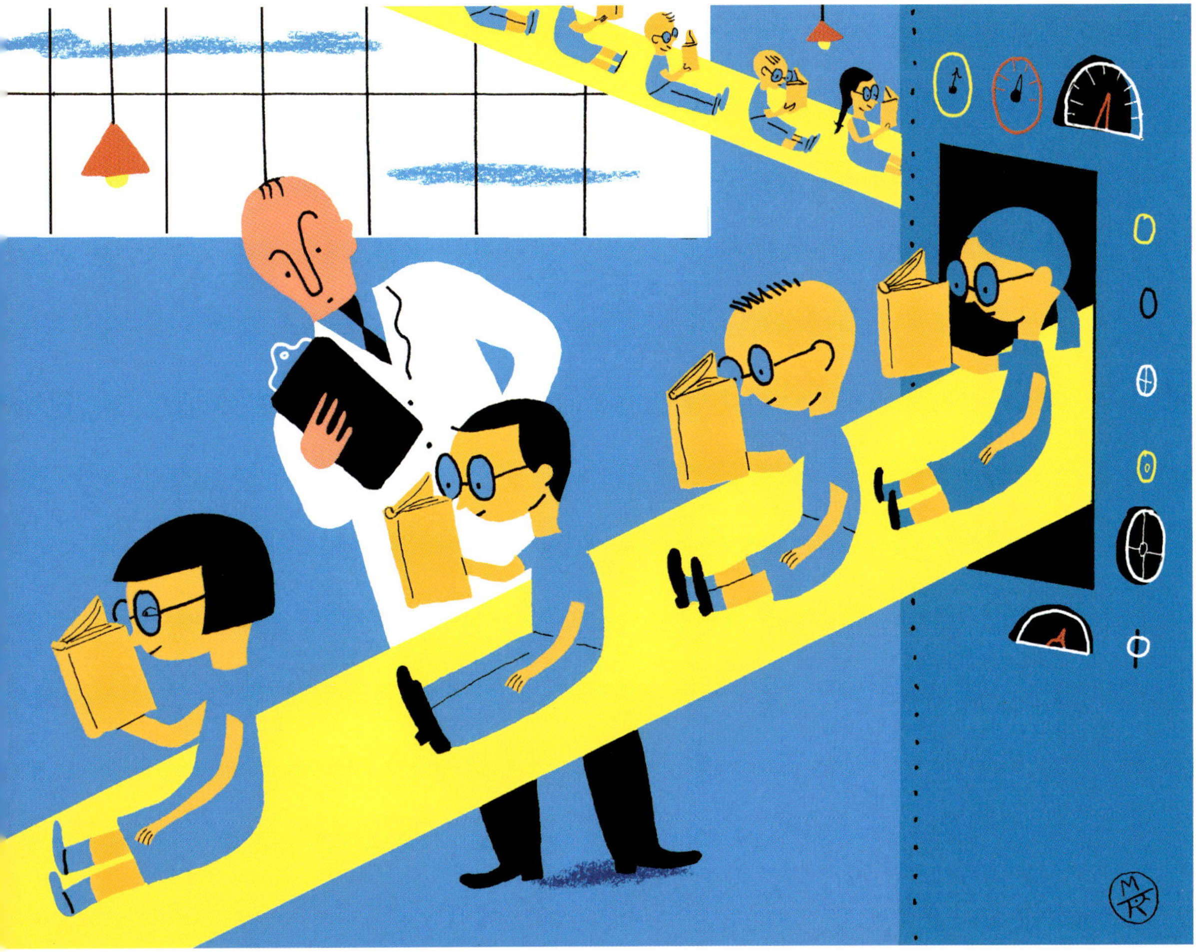

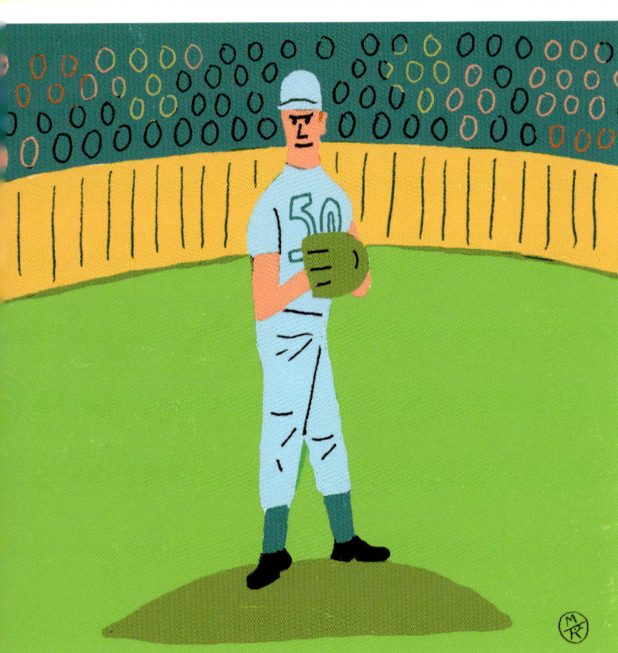

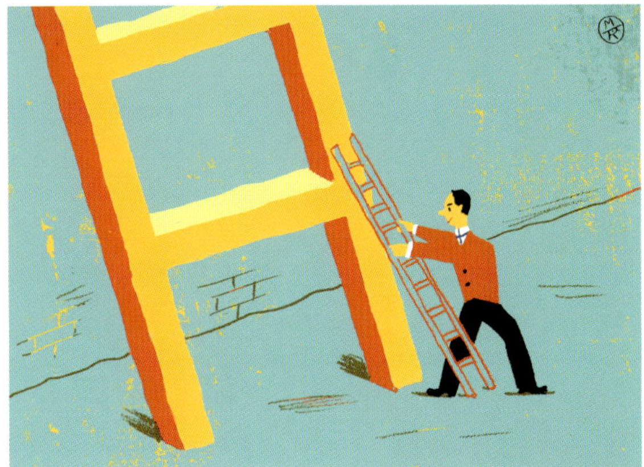

MARC ROSENTHAL

Represented by
Gerald & Cullen Rapp
212-889-3337
info@rappart.com
www.rappart.com
www.marc-rosenthal.com

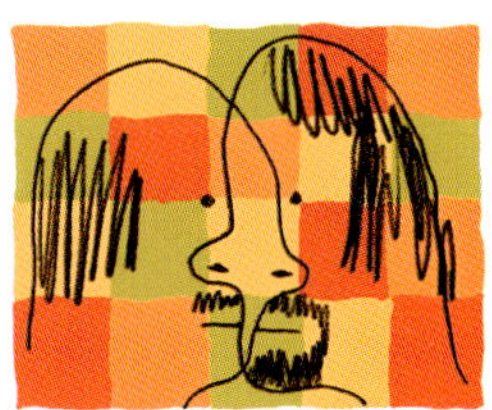

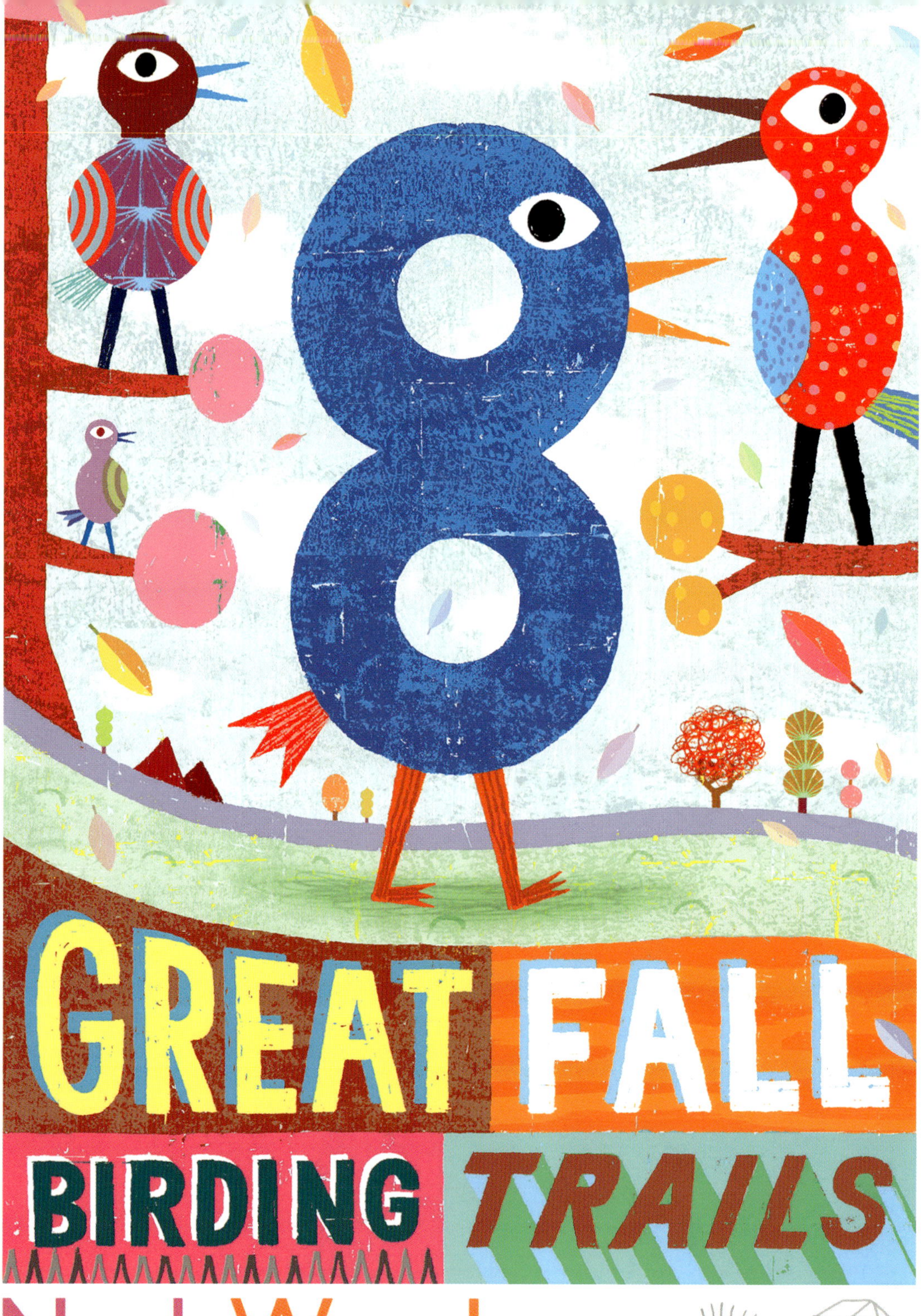

8

GREAT FALL BIRDING TRAILS

Noah Woods

Gerald & Cullen Rapp
212-889-3337

www.noahwoods.com
info@rappart.com
www.rappart.com

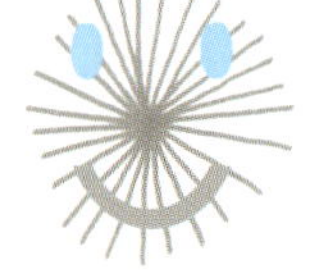
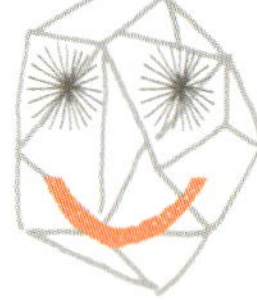

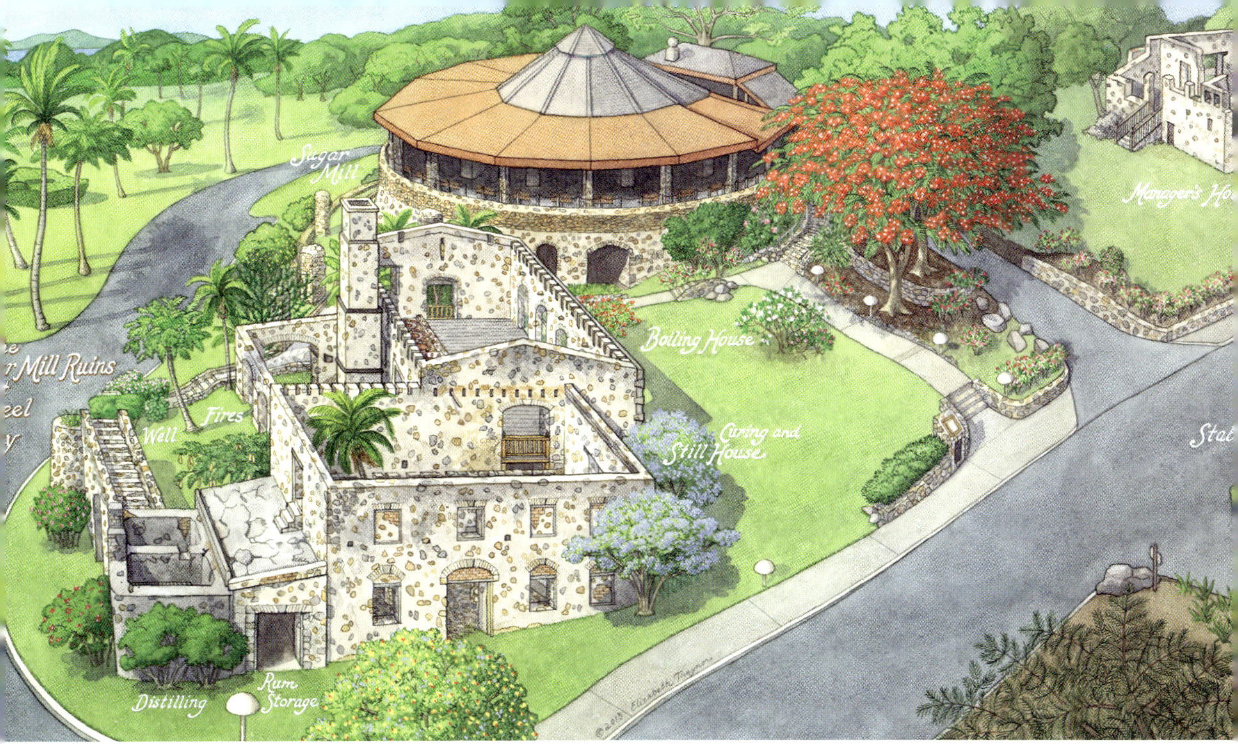

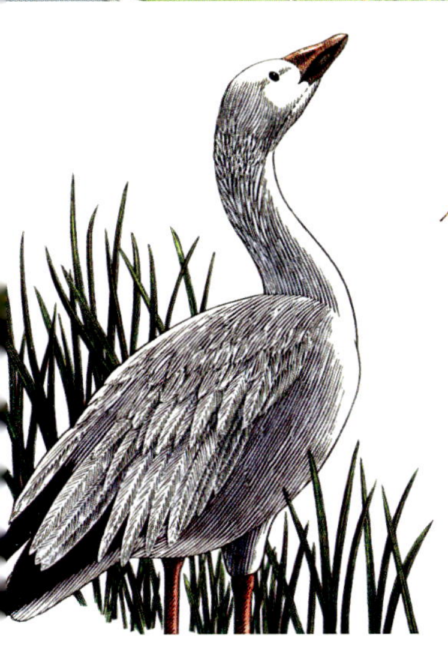
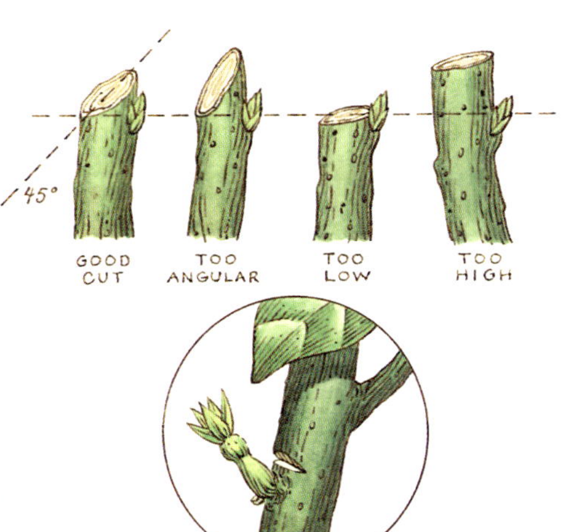

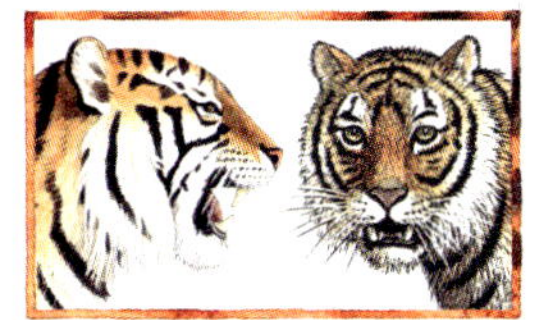

ELIZABETH TRAYNOR

Gerald & Cullen Rapp
212 889 3337
info@rappart.com
www.rappart.com
www.elizabethtraynor.com

Watercolor
Ink
Scratchboard

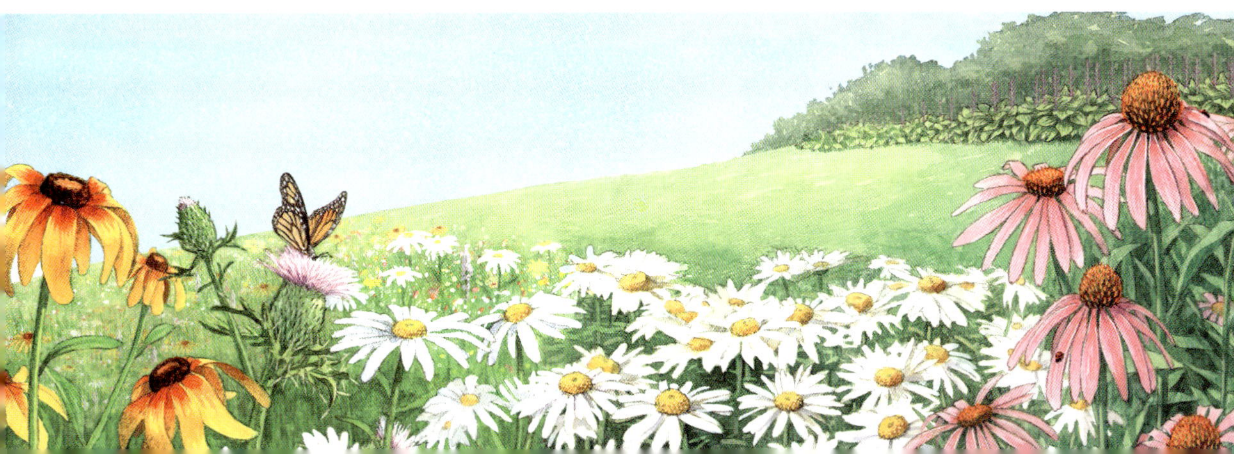

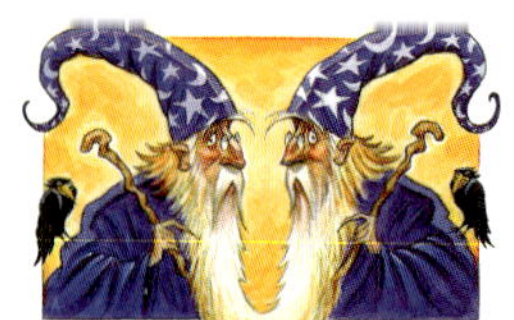

Brian Ajhar
Gerald & Cullen Rapp info@rappart.com   www.rappart.com
212.889.3337

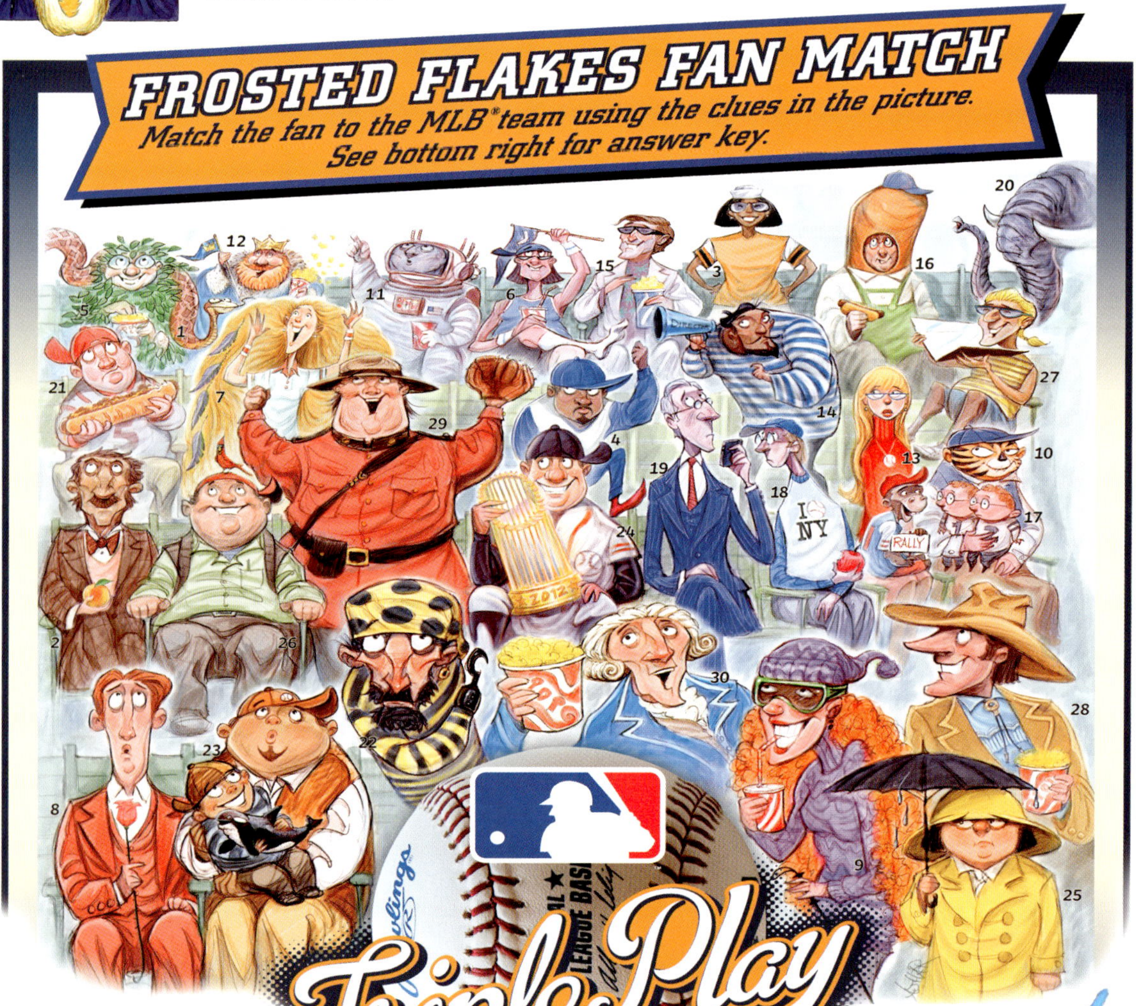

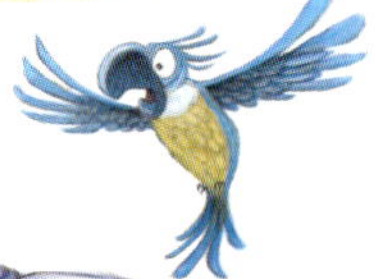

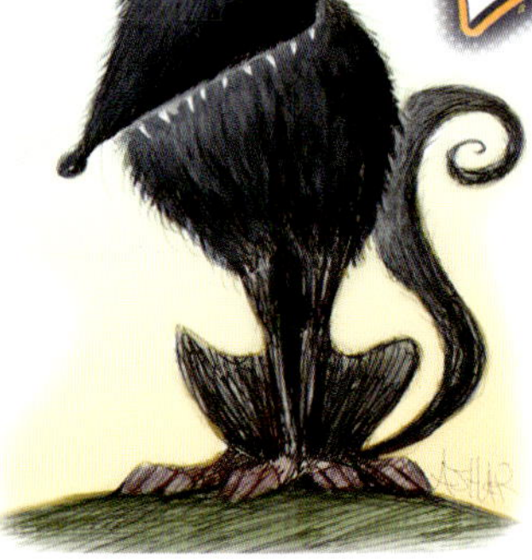

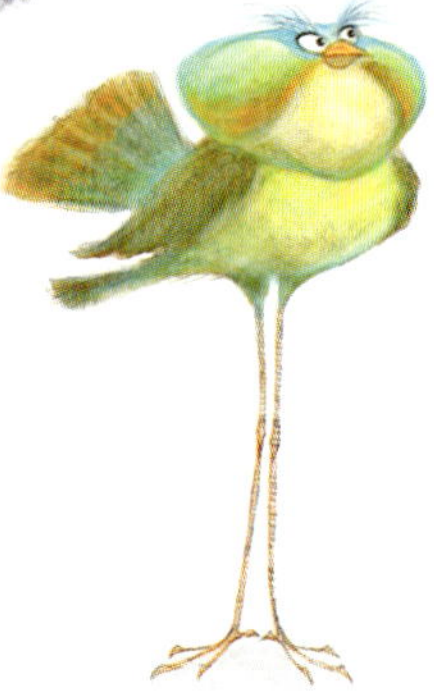

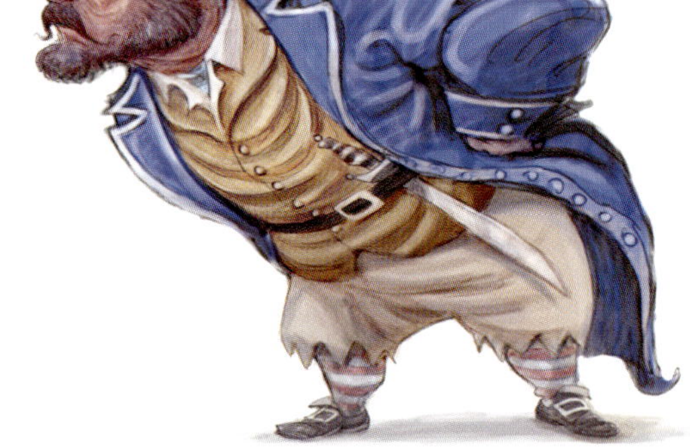

FROSTED FLAKES FAN MATCH

Match the fan to the MLB® team using the clues in the picture.
See bottom right for answer key.

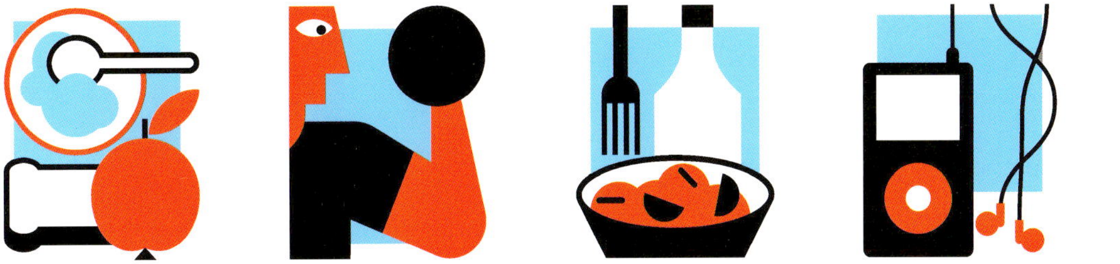

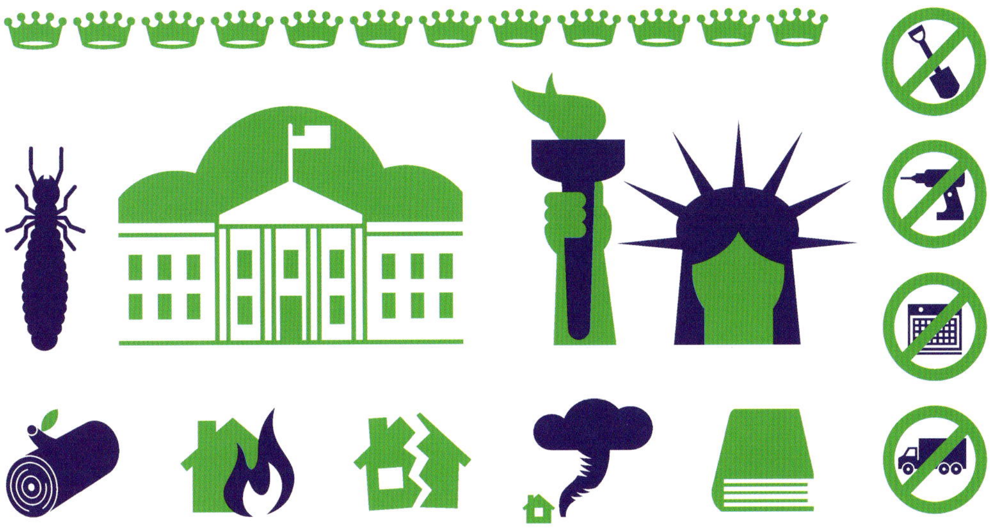

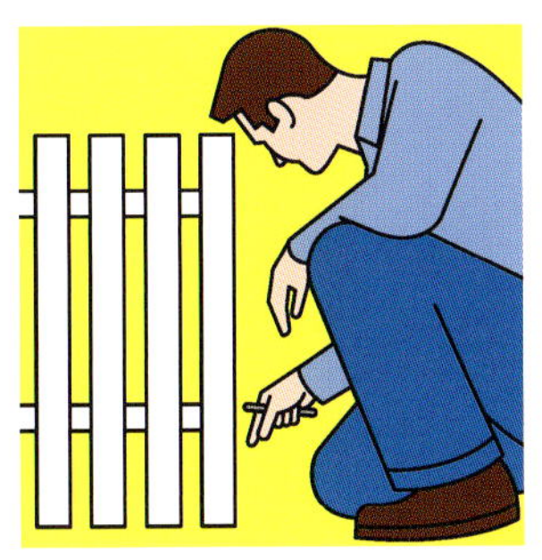
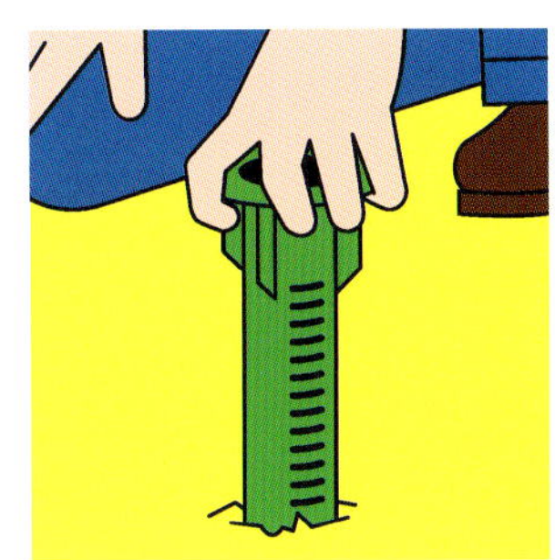
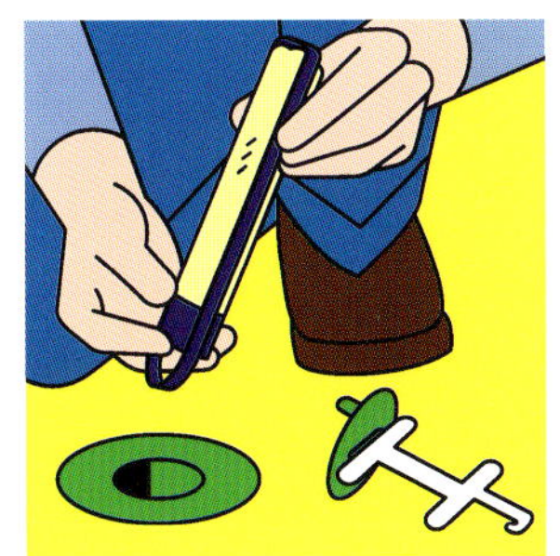
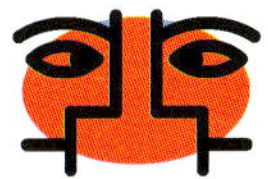

anders wenngren • gerald & cullen rapp • 212 889-3337 • info@rappart.com • www.rappart.com

joanie bernstein
ART rep
tele (239) 403-4393
JOANIE @ JOANIEBREP.COM
WWW.JOANIEBREP.COM

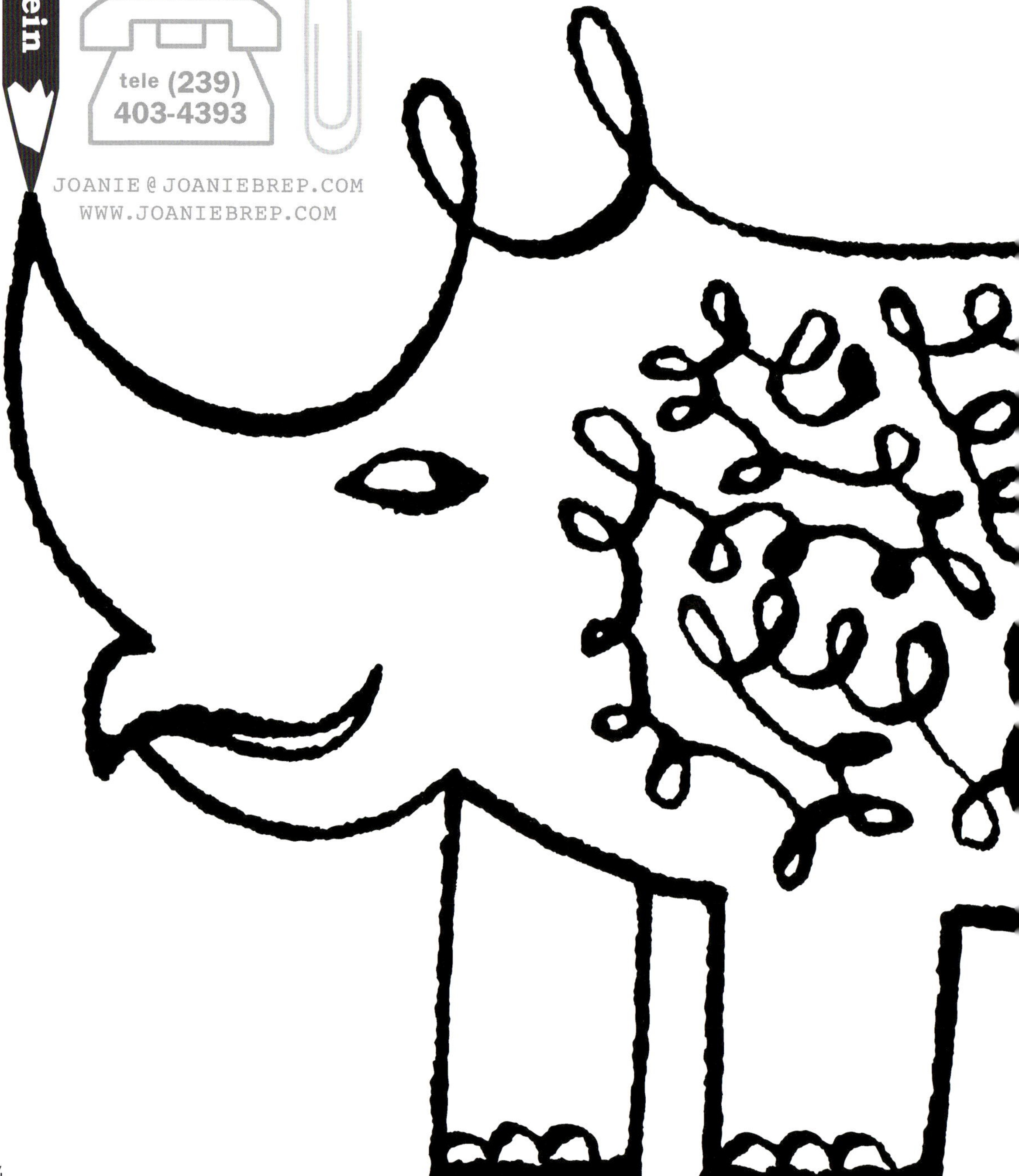

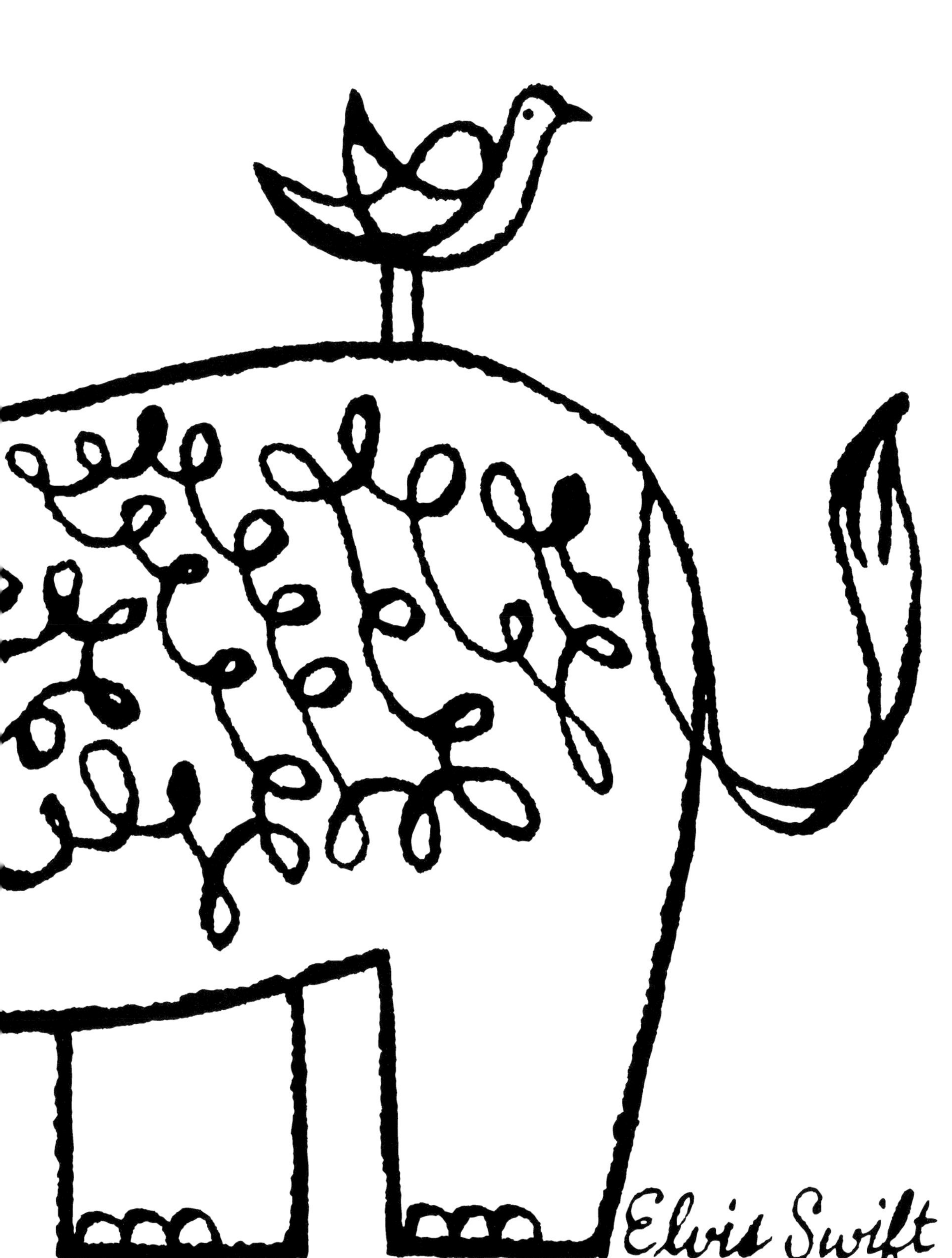
Elvis Swift

Neal Aspinall

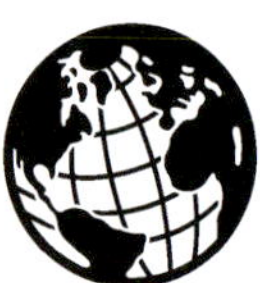 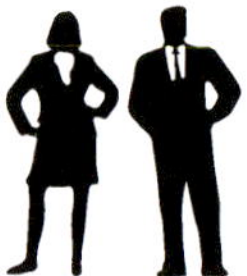 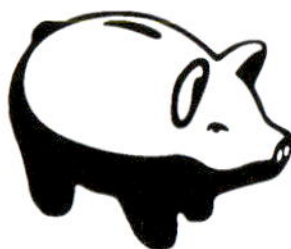 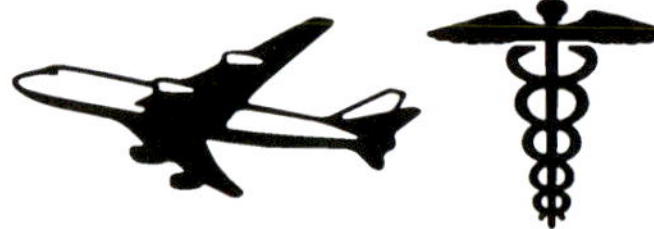 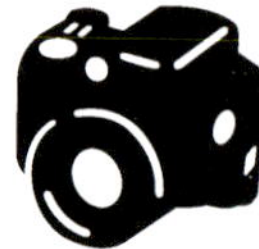

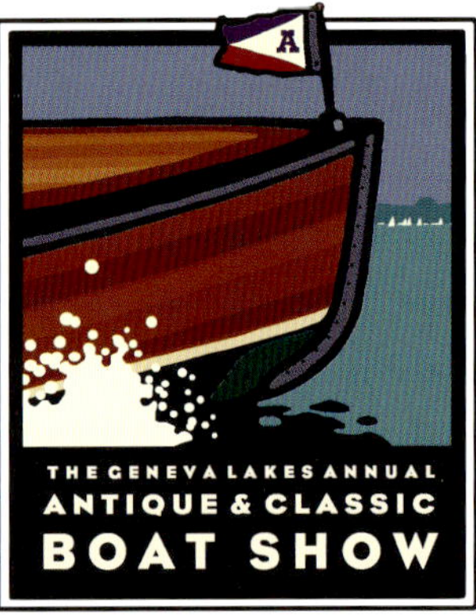

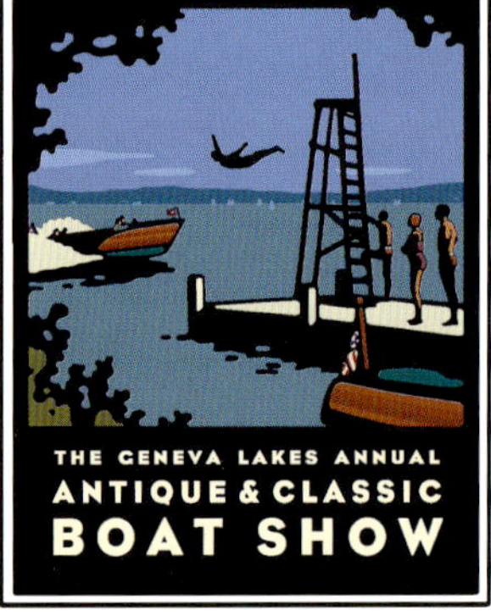

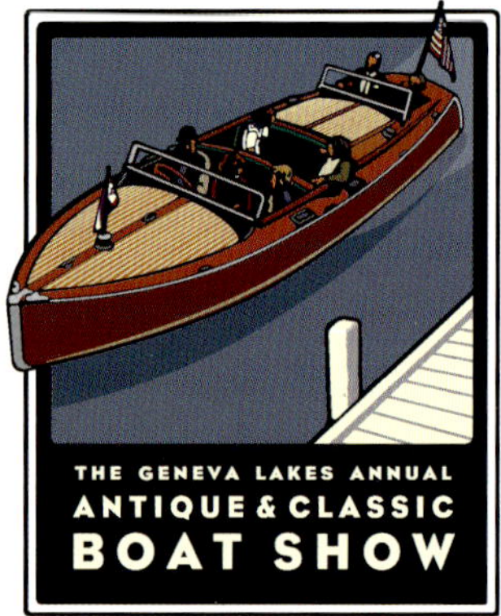

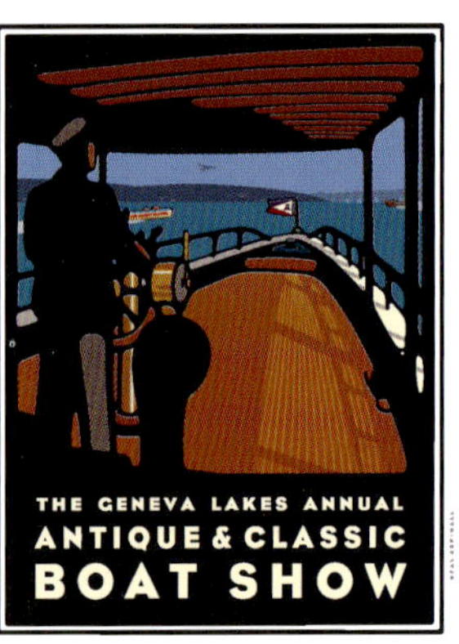

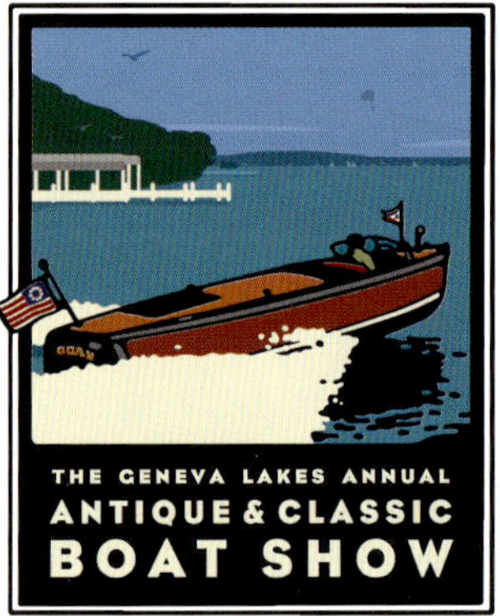

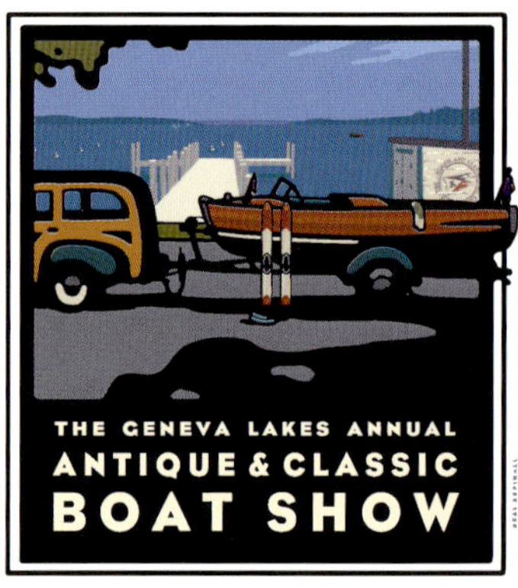

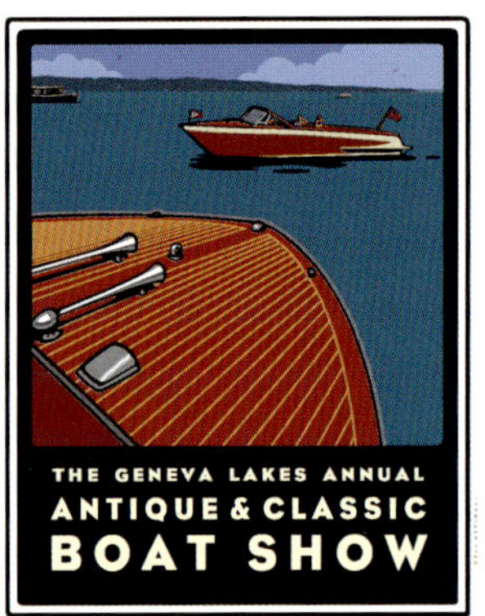

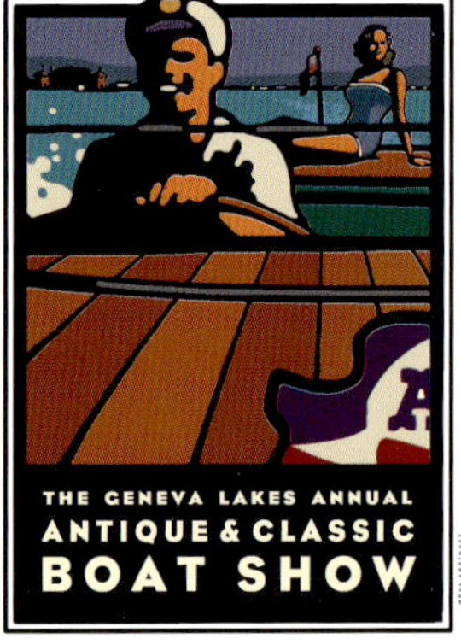

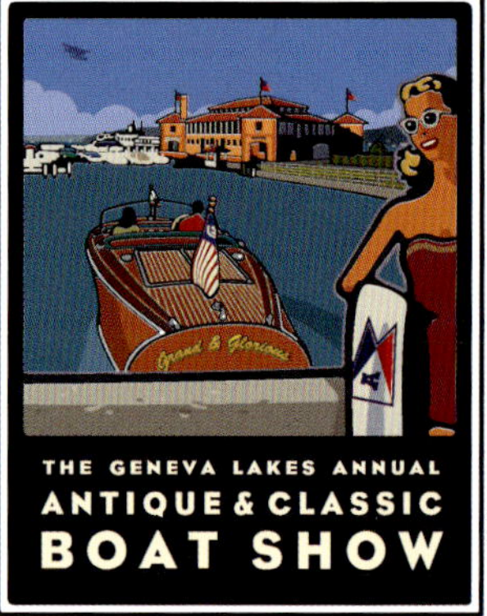

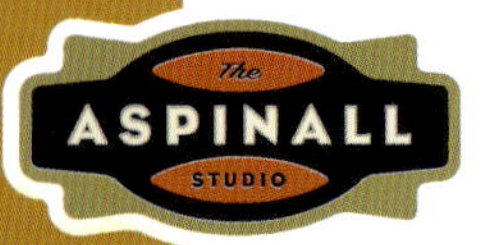

WWW.NEALASPINALL.COM

Shop the Aspinall Poster Store: www.nealaspinall.com/stock

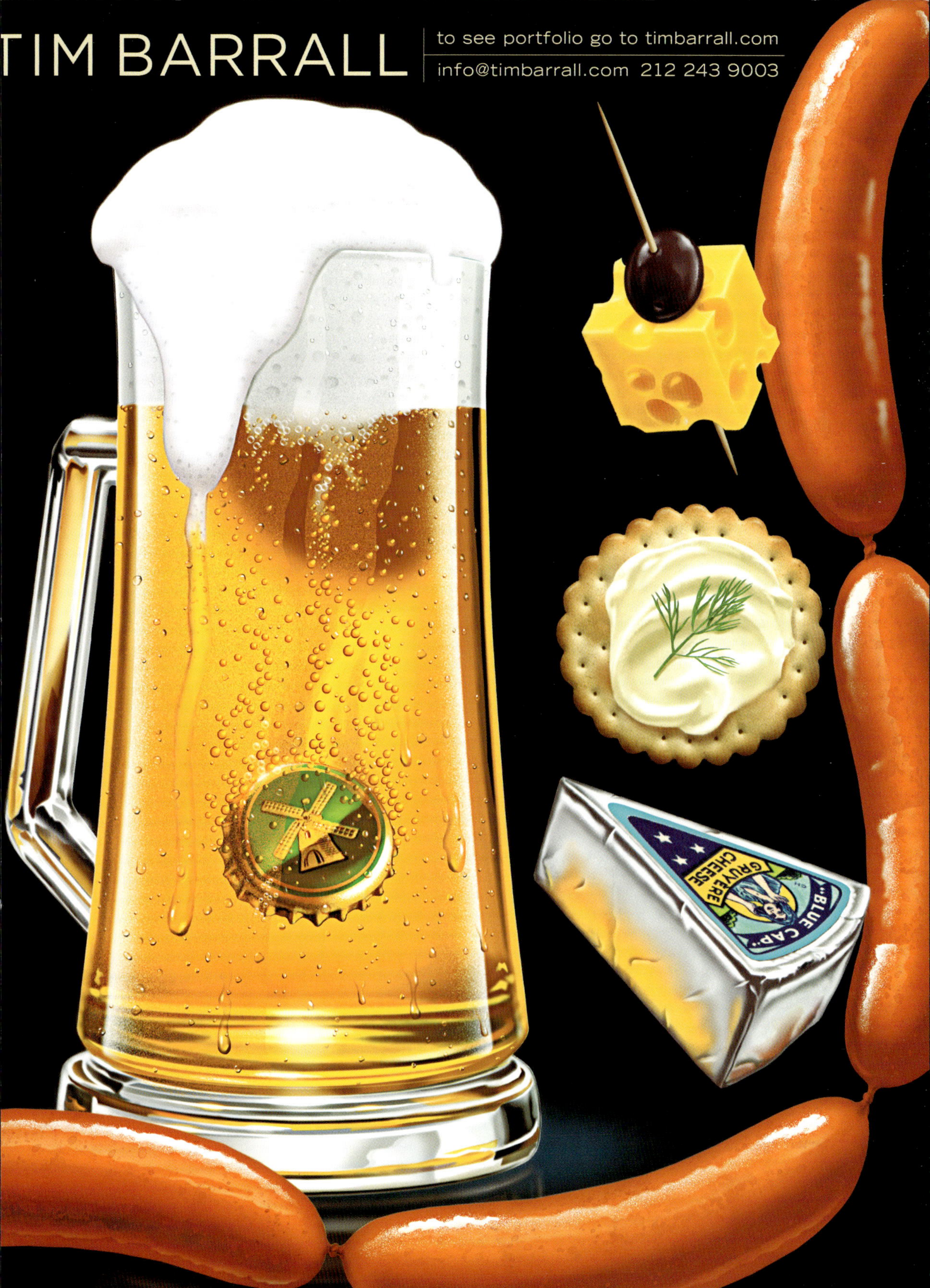

TIM BARRALL
to see portfolio go to timbarrall.com
info@timbarrall.com   212 243 9003
GRUYERE CHEESE
"BLUE CAP"

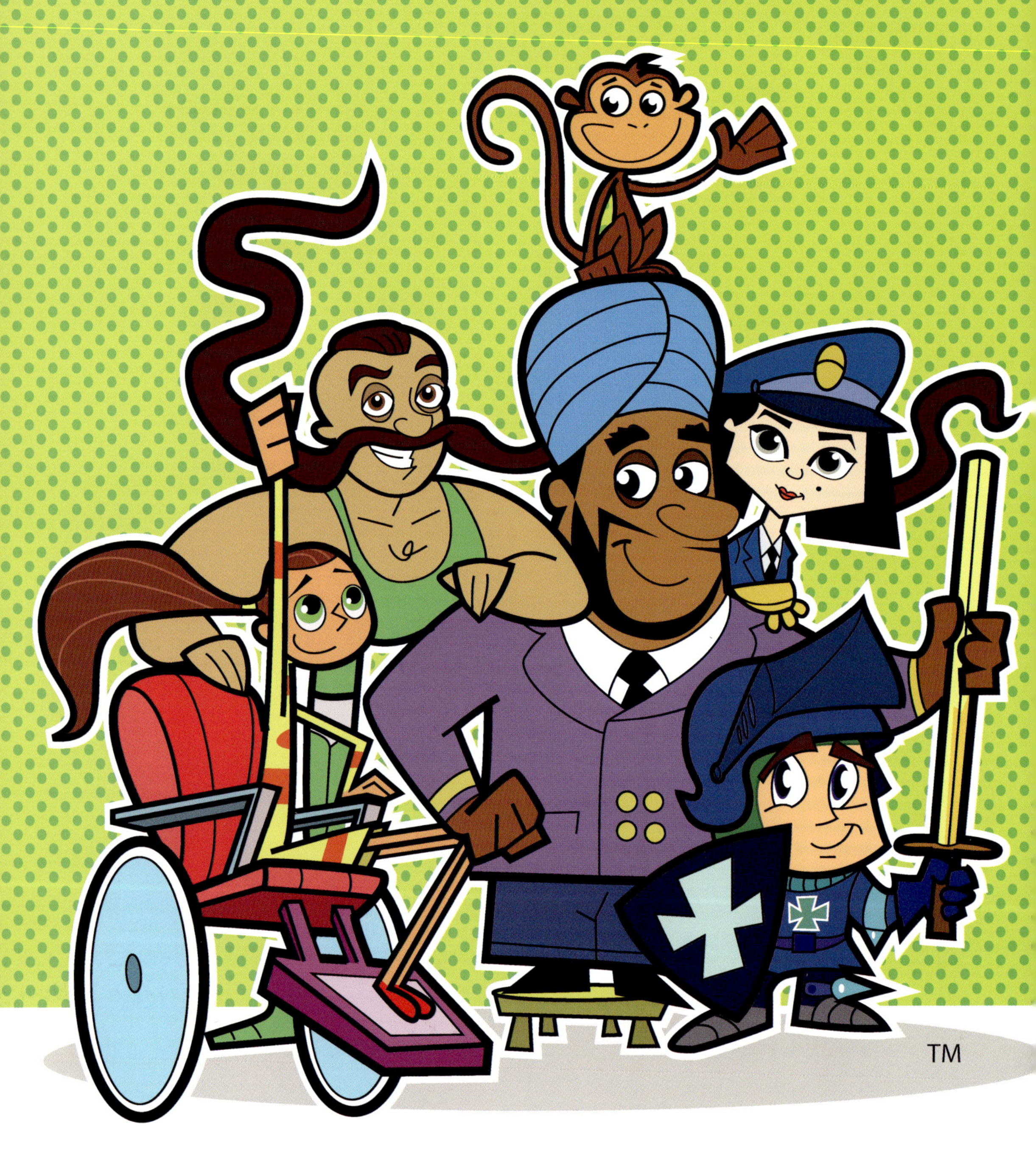

TM

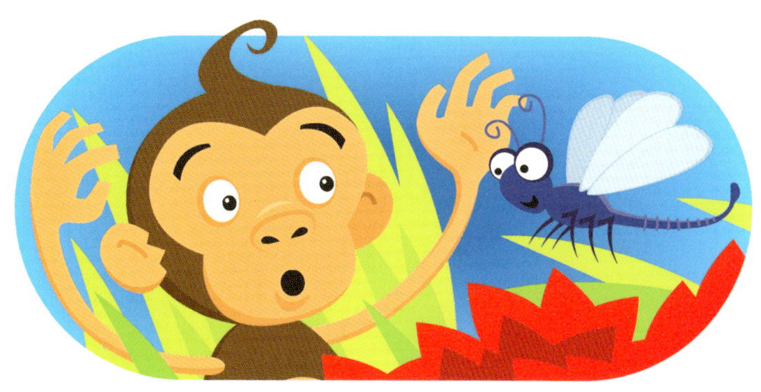

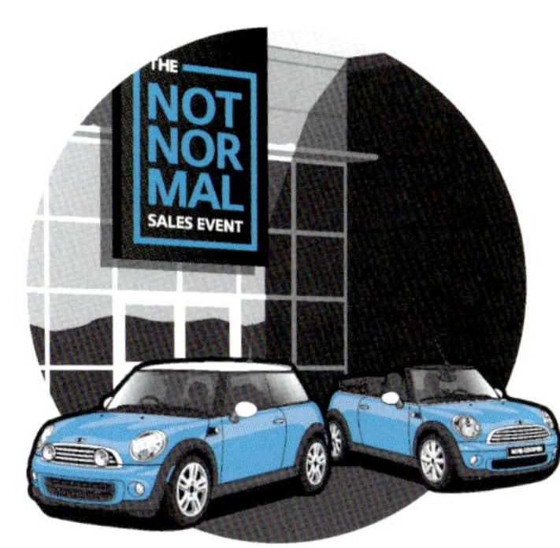
THE
NOT
NOR
MAL
SALES EVENT

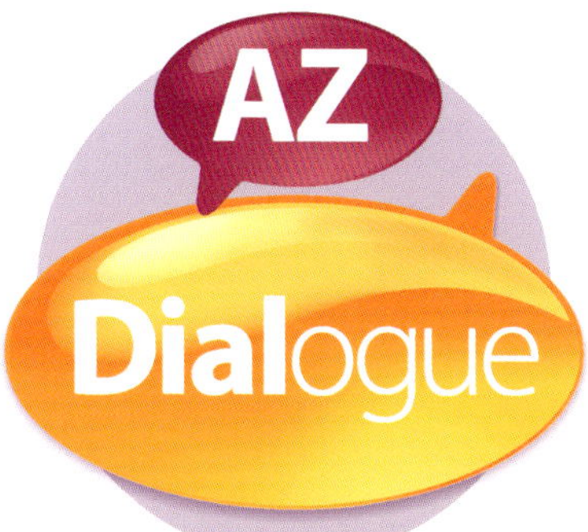
AZ
Dialogue

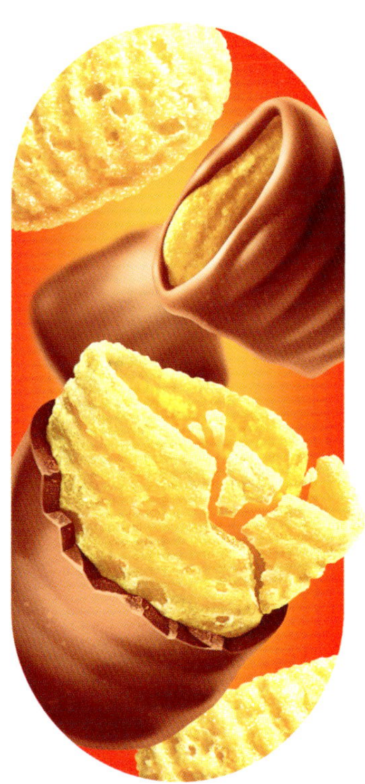

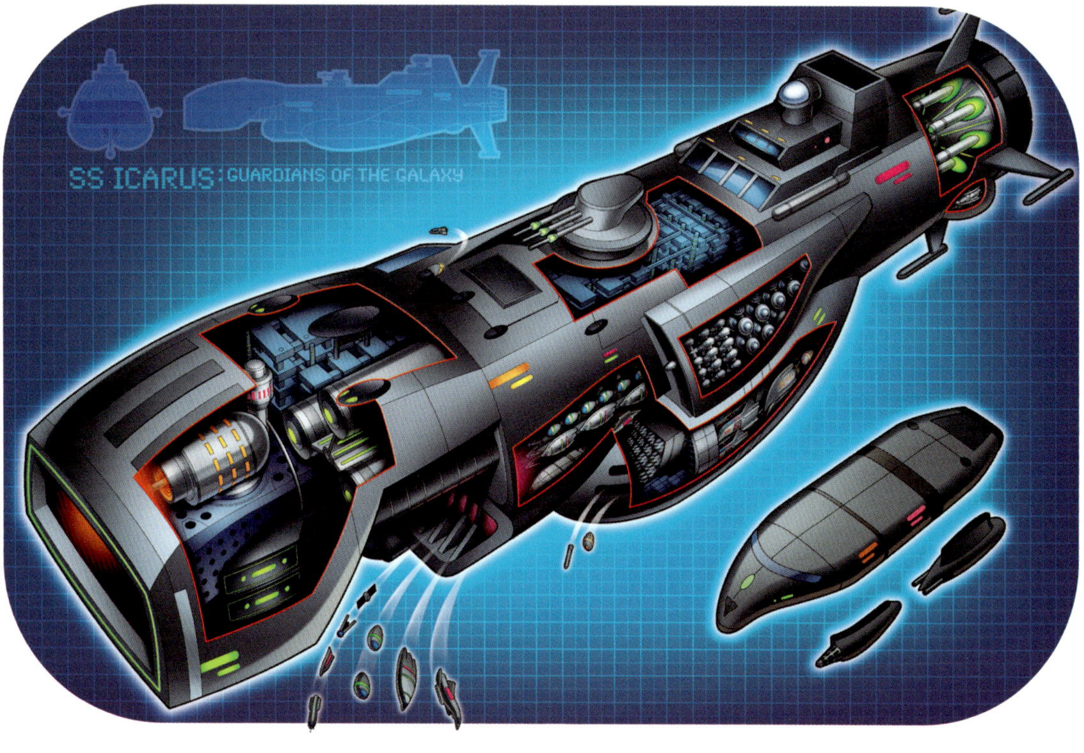

SS ICARUS: GUARDIANS OF THE GALAXY

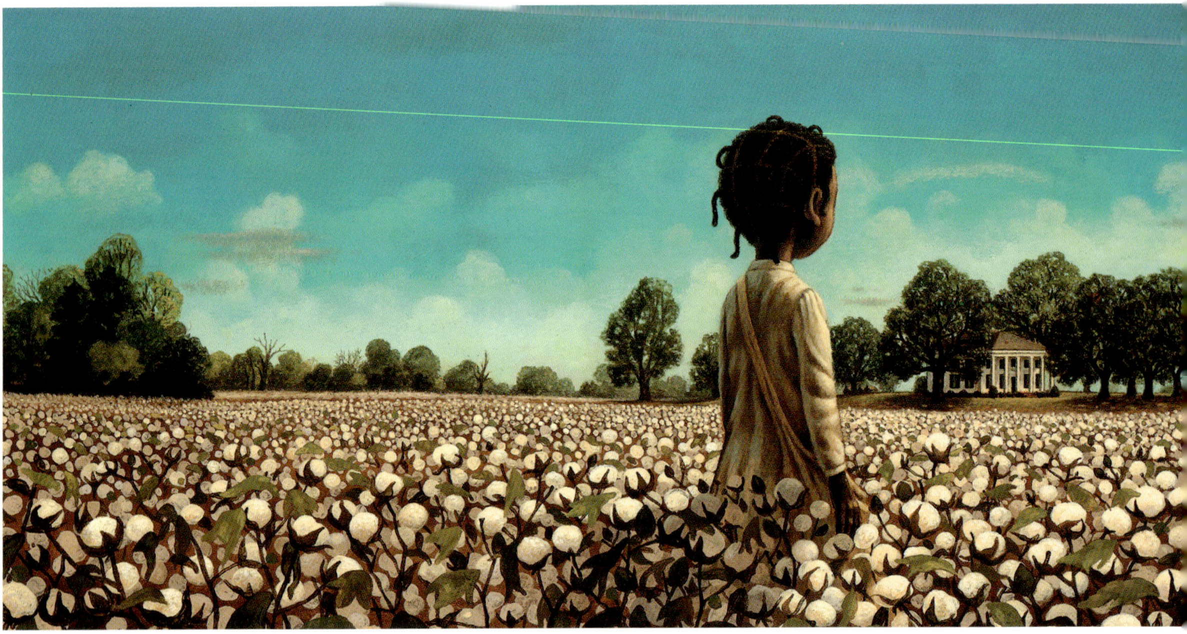

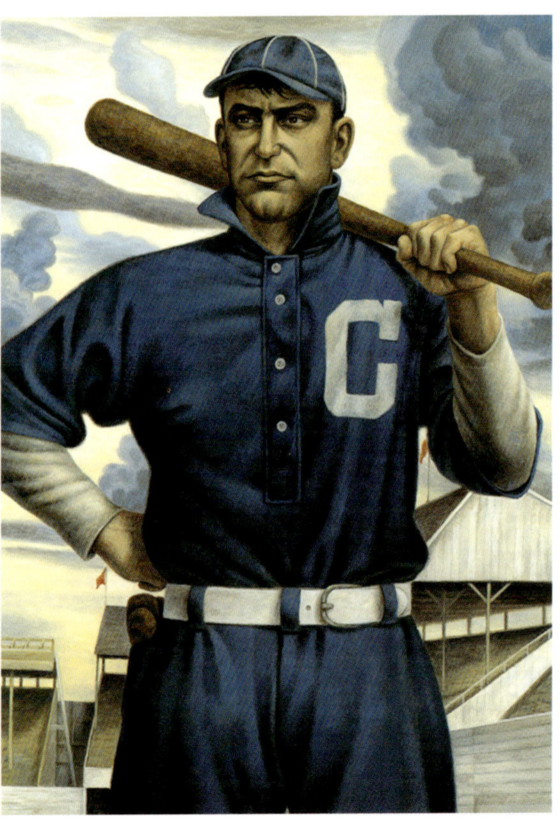

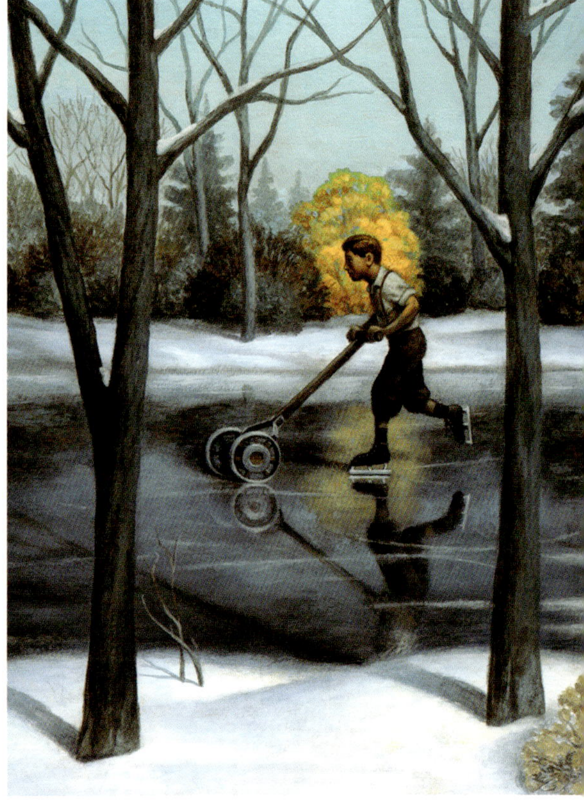

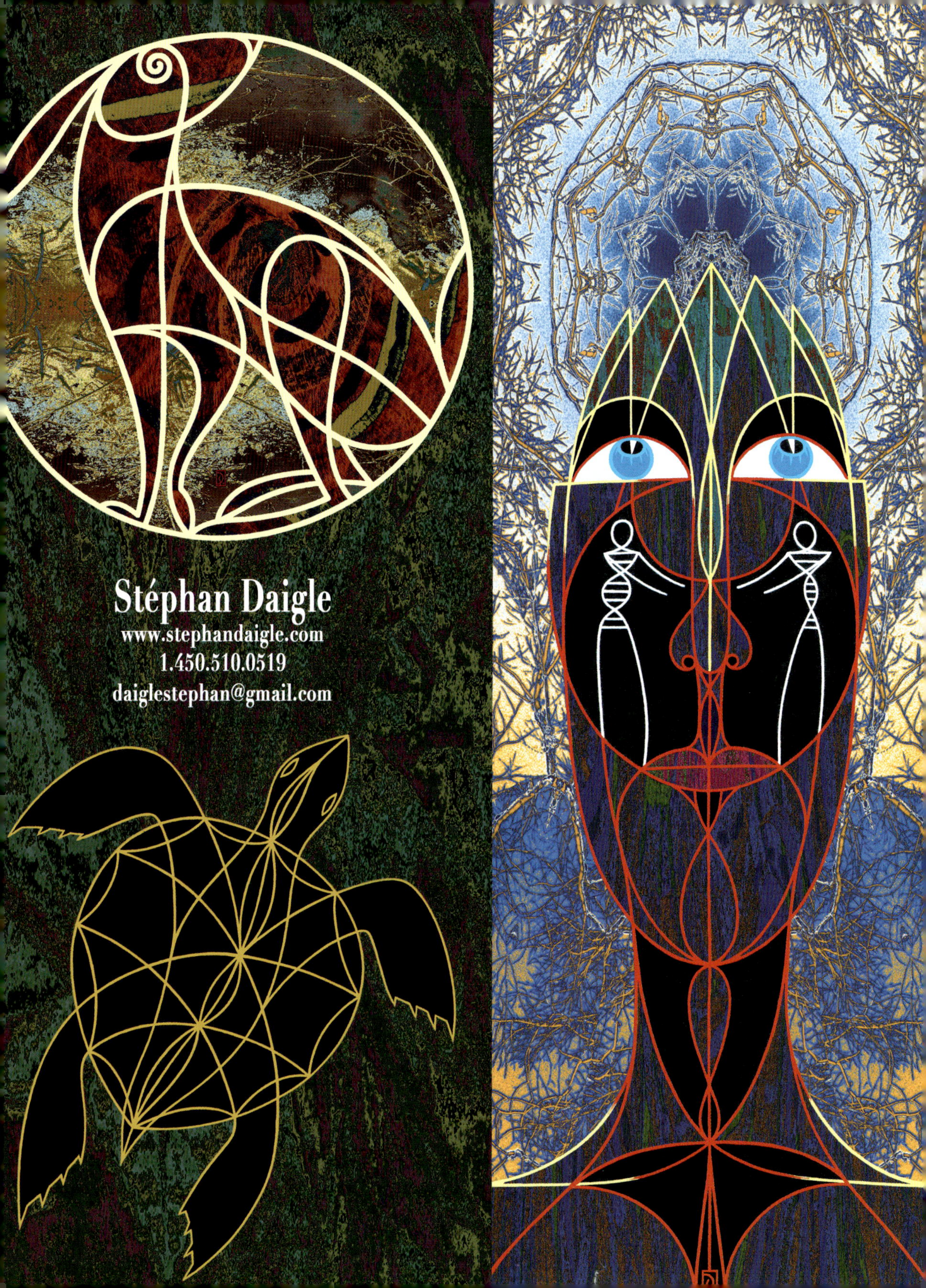

Stéphan Daigle
www.stephandaigle.com
1.450.510.0519
daiglestephan@gmail.com

PATRICK STEFANSKI
3D Design & Illustration

patrick@patrickstefanski.com
(201)855-6022

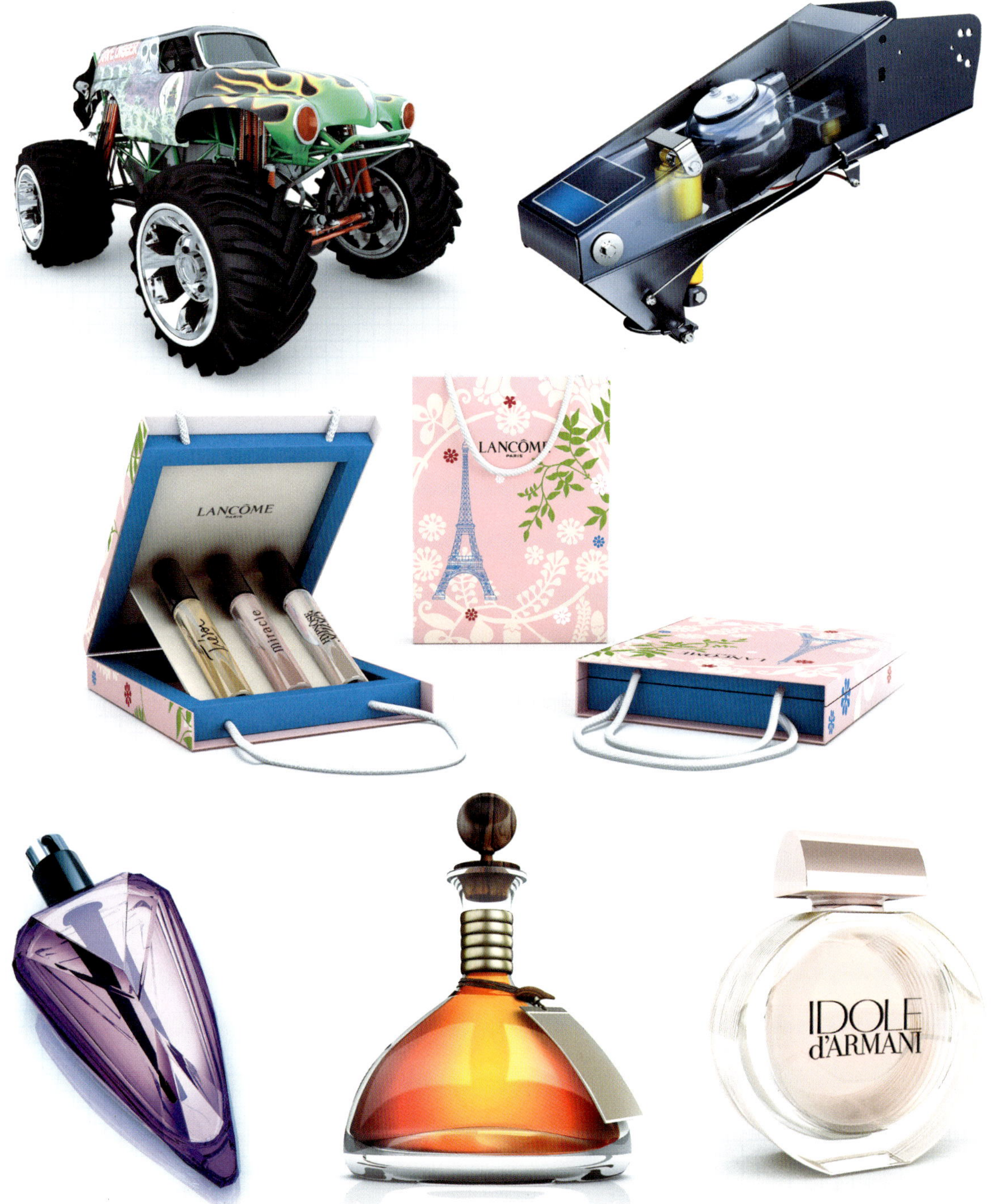

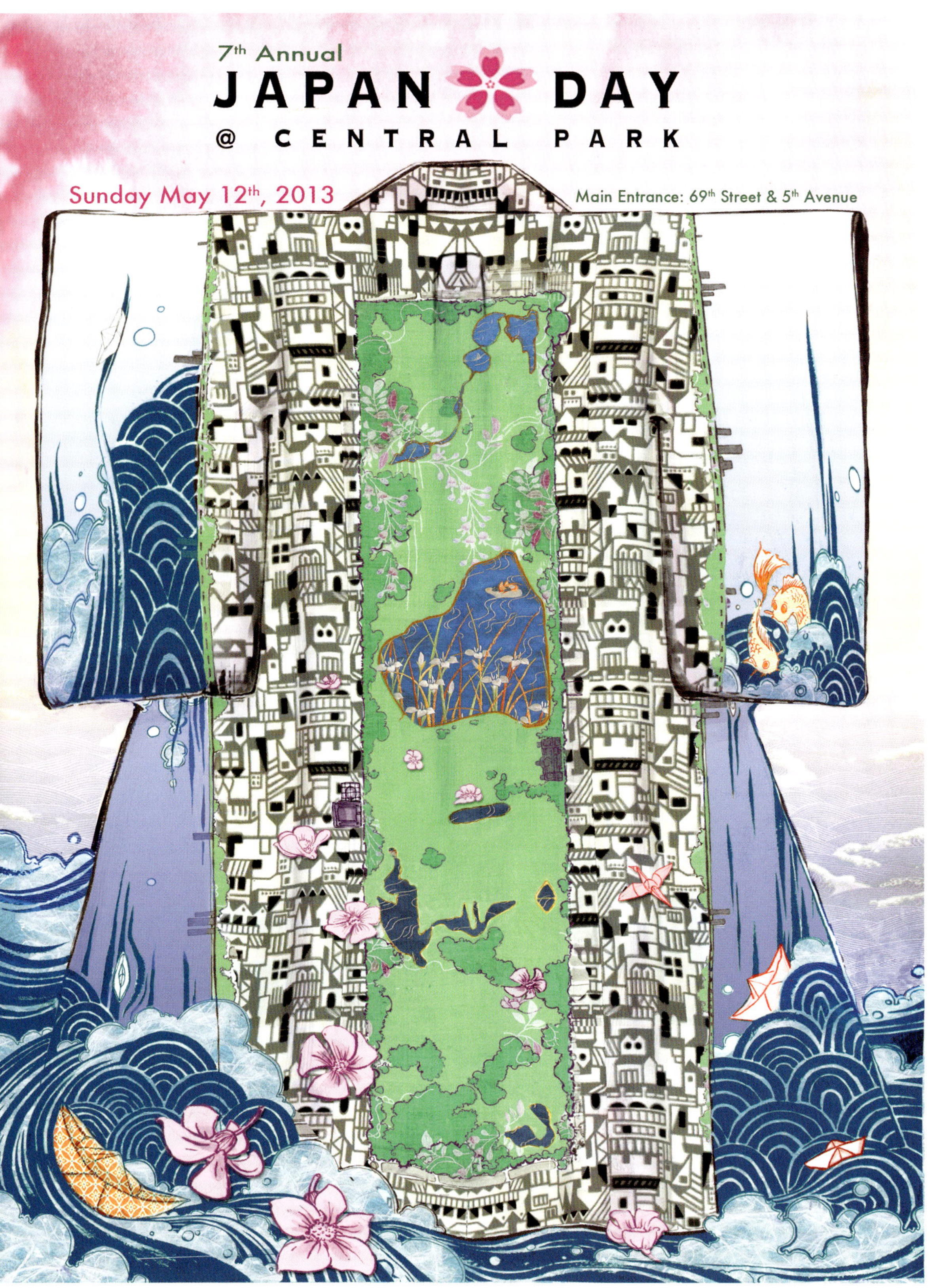

7th Annual
JAPAN DAY
@ CENTRAL PARK
Sunday May 12th, 2013
Main Entrance: 69th Street & 5th Avenue
COMM. BY GORGEOUS ENTERTAINMENT
WWW. SARAWOOLLEY.COM
917-982-1145

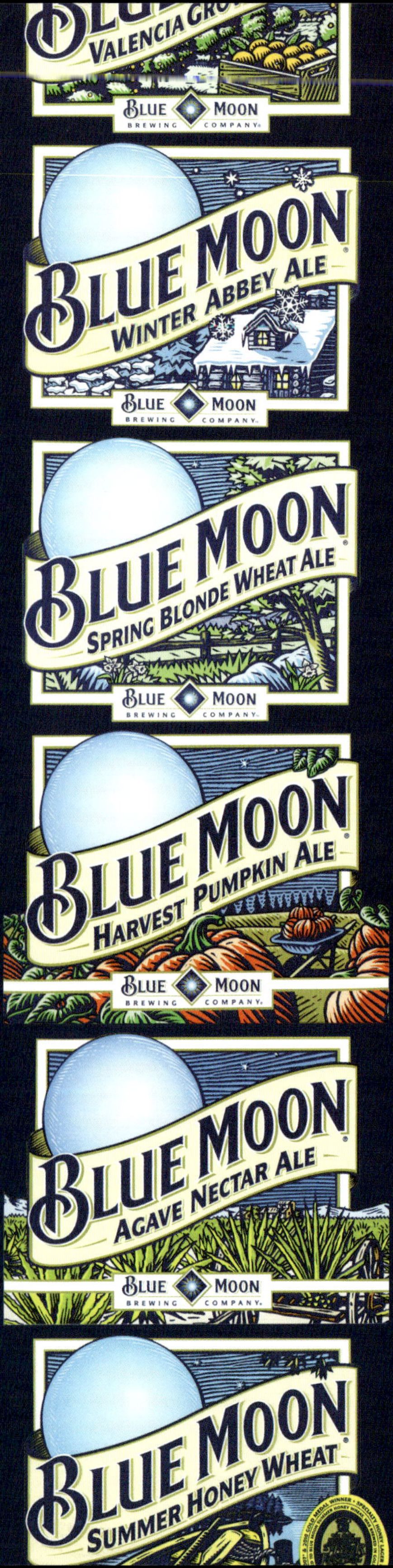

Ongoing label art for Blue Moon Seasonal and Year Round Beers ©2006-2013 Blue Moon Brewing Company

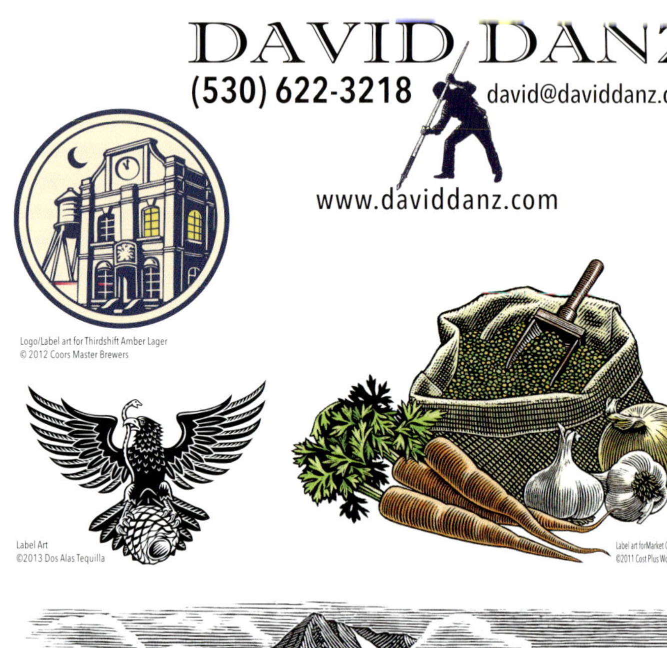

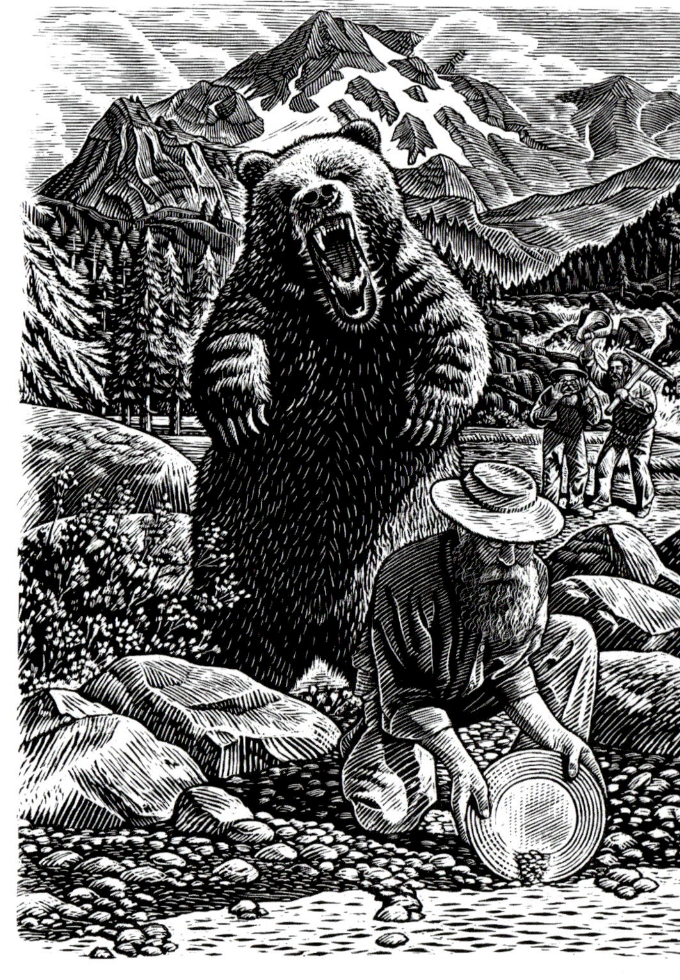

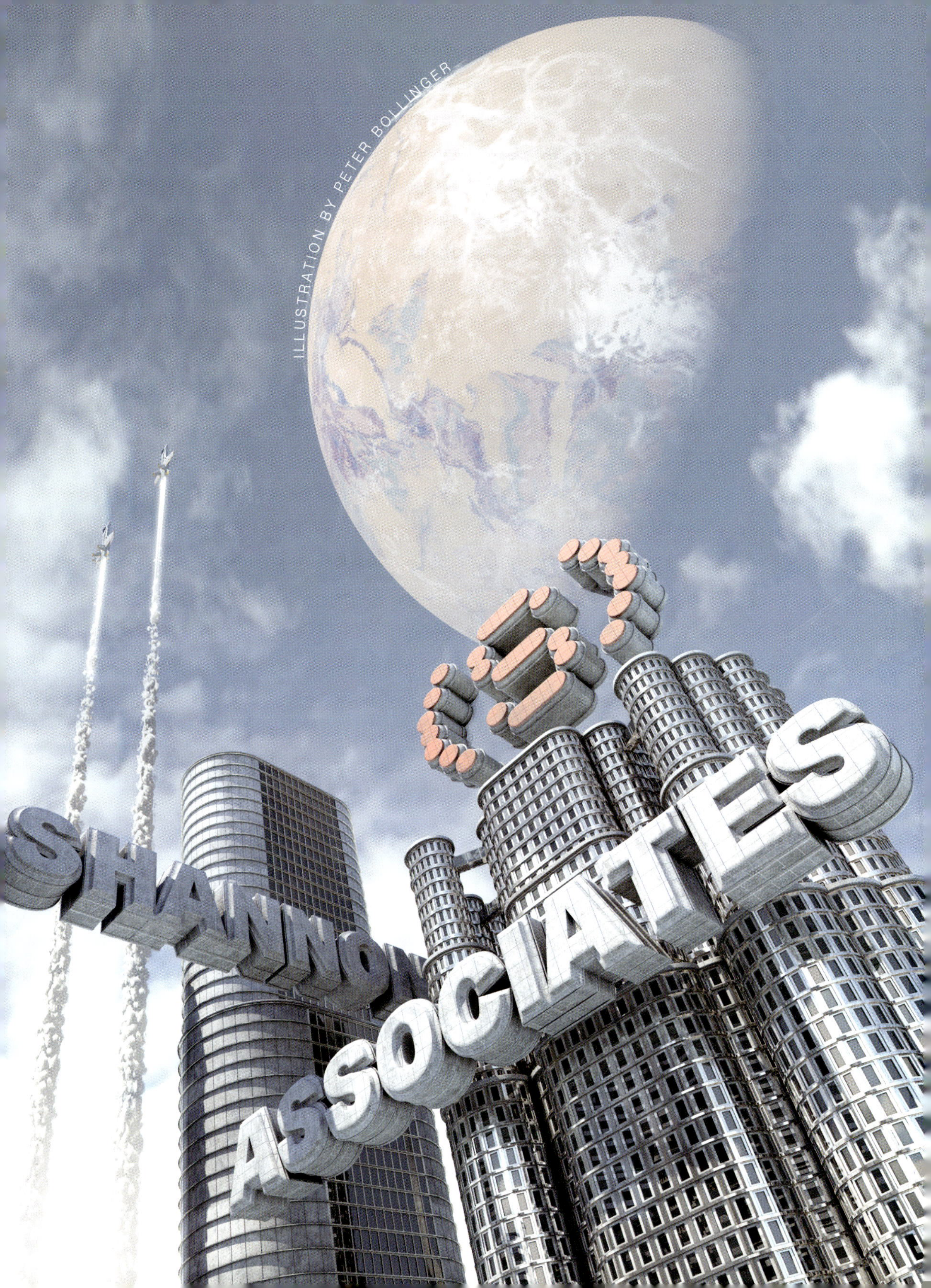

ILLUSTRATION BY PETER BOLLINGER
SHANNON ASSOCIATES

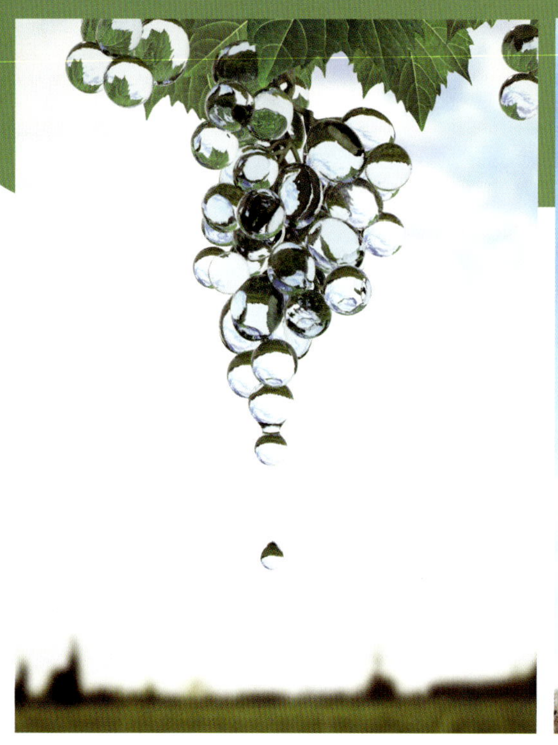
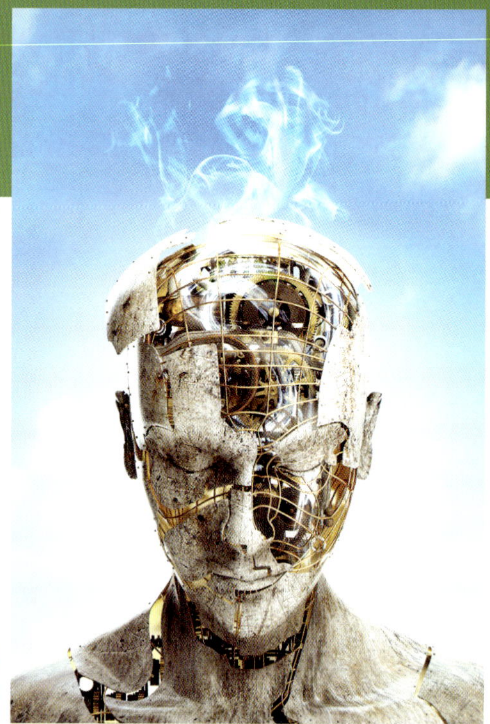
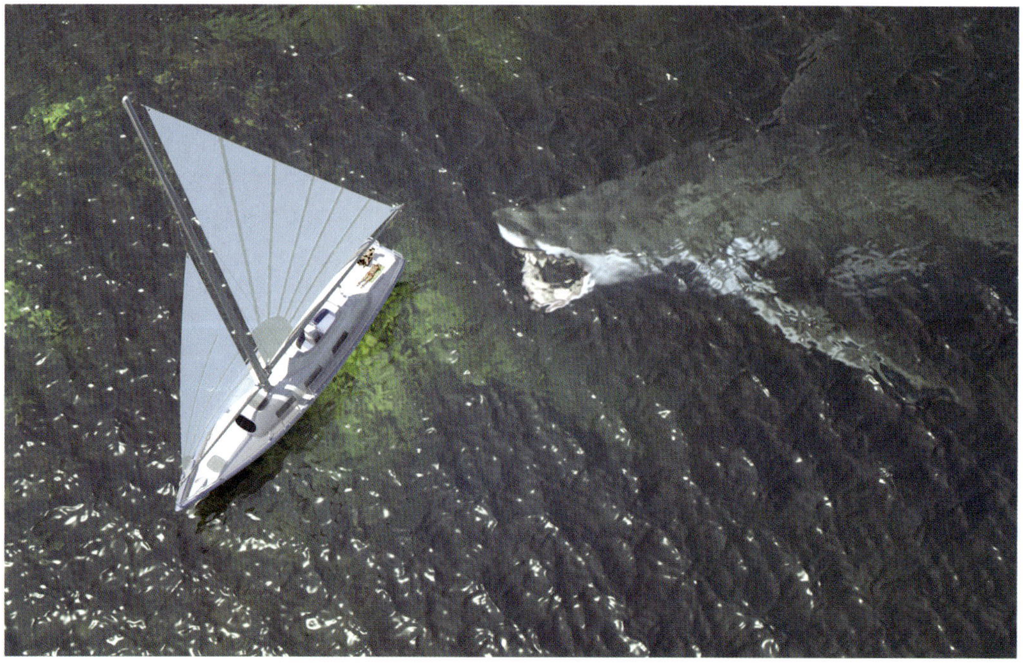

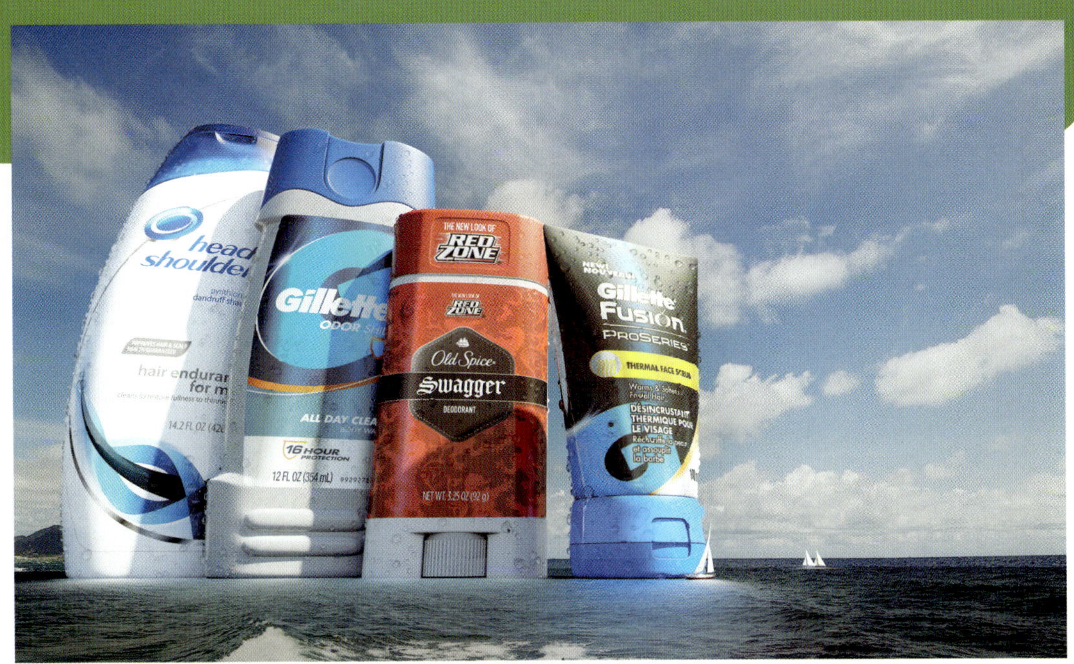
head
shoulders
pyrithione
dandruff sha
REPAIRS HAIR & SCALP
hair endurance
for m
14.2 FL OZ (42e
Gillette
ODOR SHI
ALL DAY CLEA
16 HOUR
PROTECTION
12 FL OZ (354 mL)
THE NEW LOOK OF
RED ZONE
RED ZONE
Old Spice
Swagger
DEODORANT
NET WT. 3.25 OZ (92 g)
NEW!
NOUVEAU!
Gillette
Fusion
PROSERIES
THERMAL FACE SCRUB
Warms & Softens
Facial Hair
DESINCRUSTAIT
THERMIQUE POUR
LE VISAGE
Réchauffe & ramollit
et assouplit
la barbe

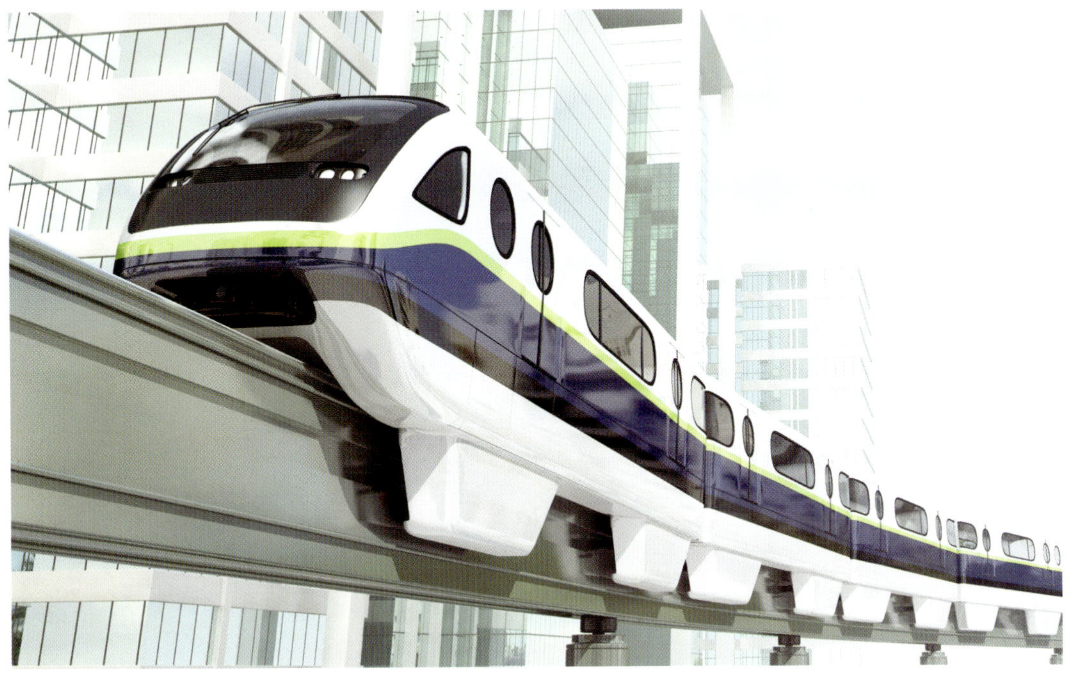

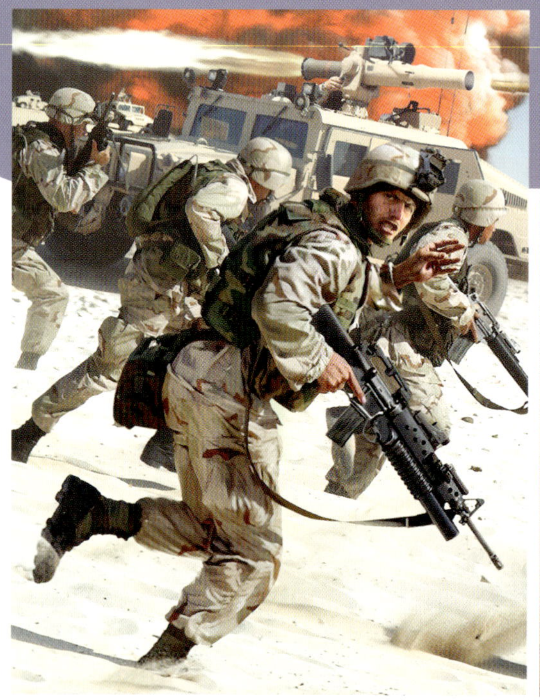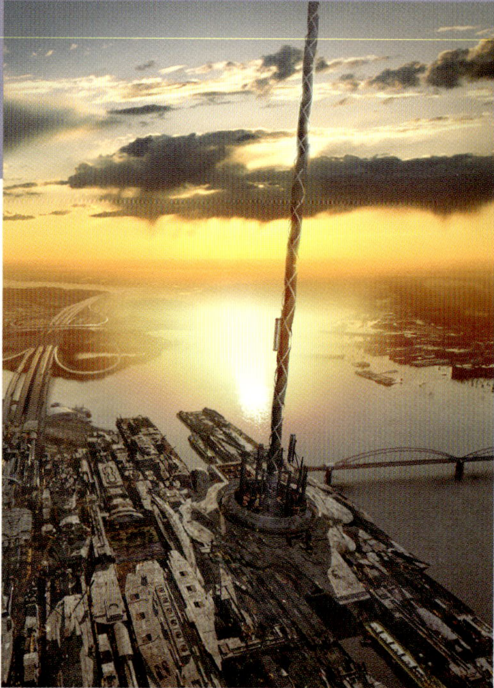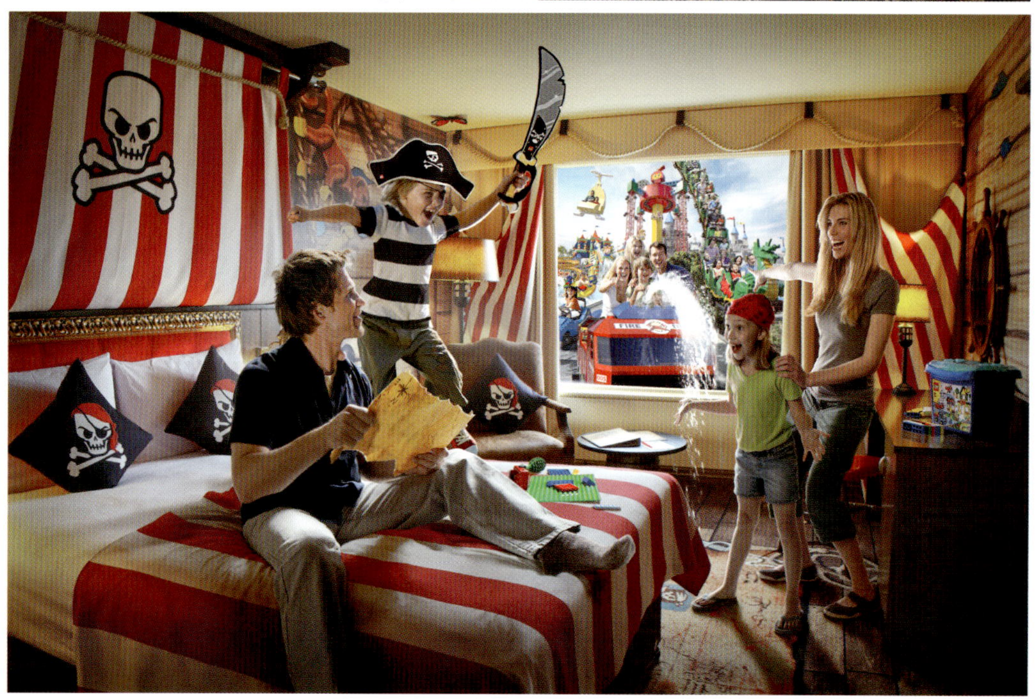

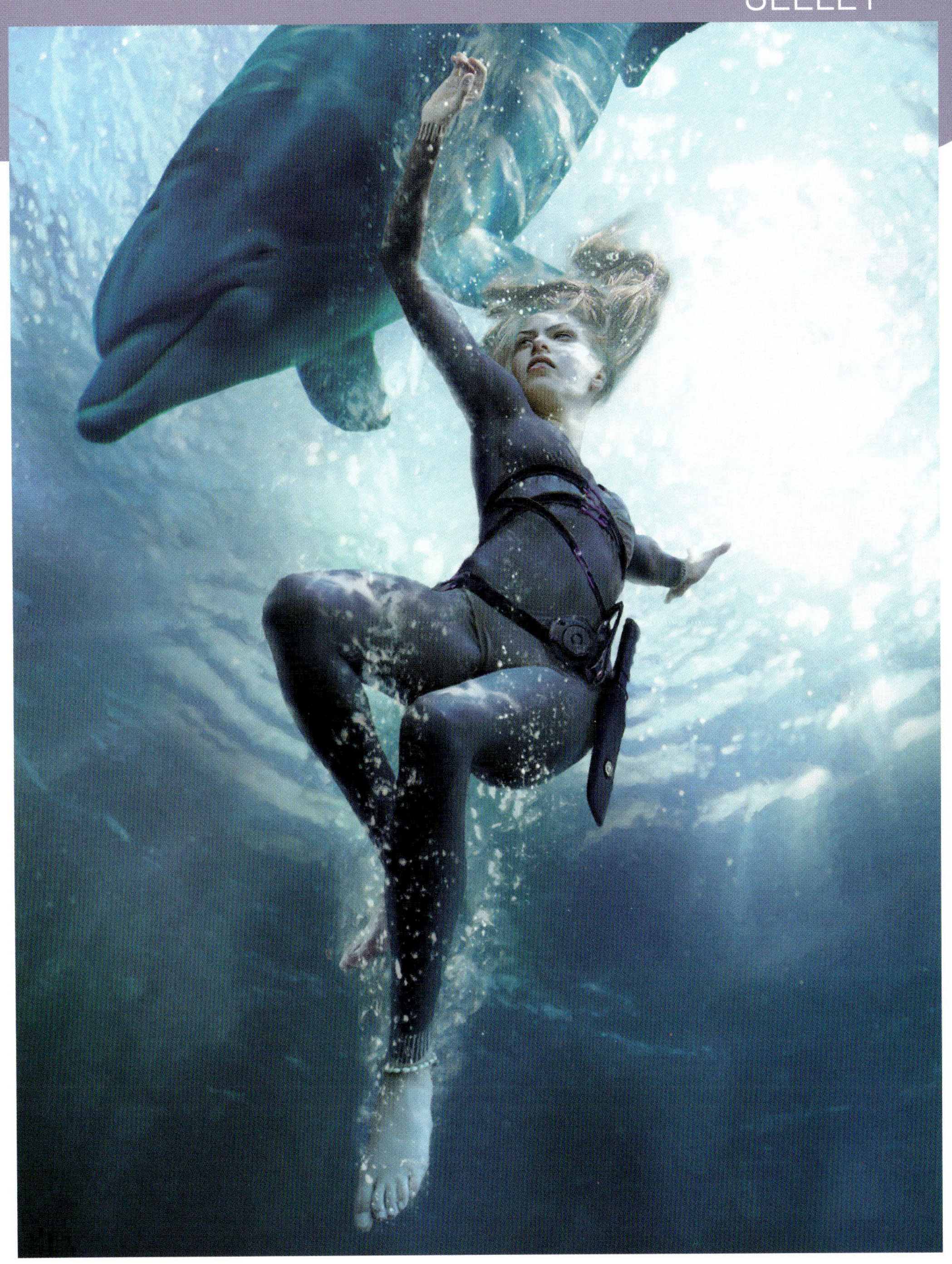
DAVE
SEELEY
SHANNON ASSOCIATES
212.333.2551

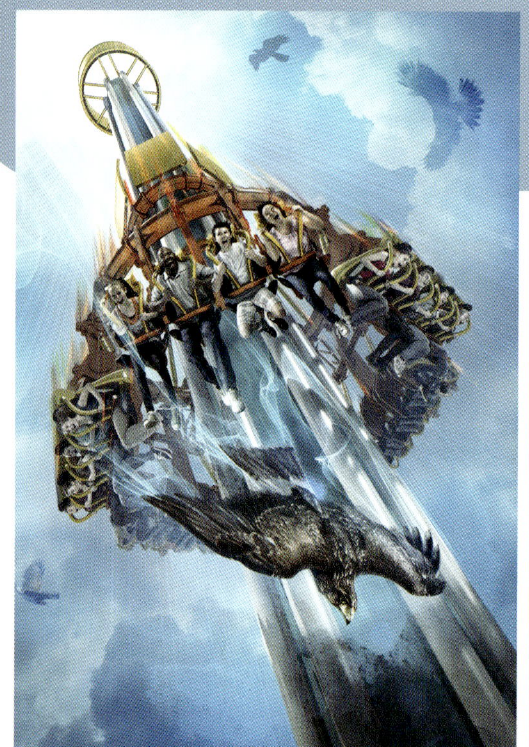

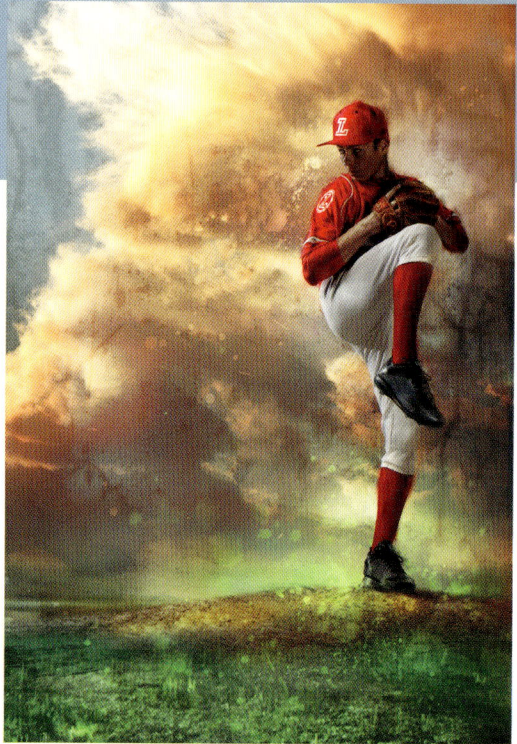

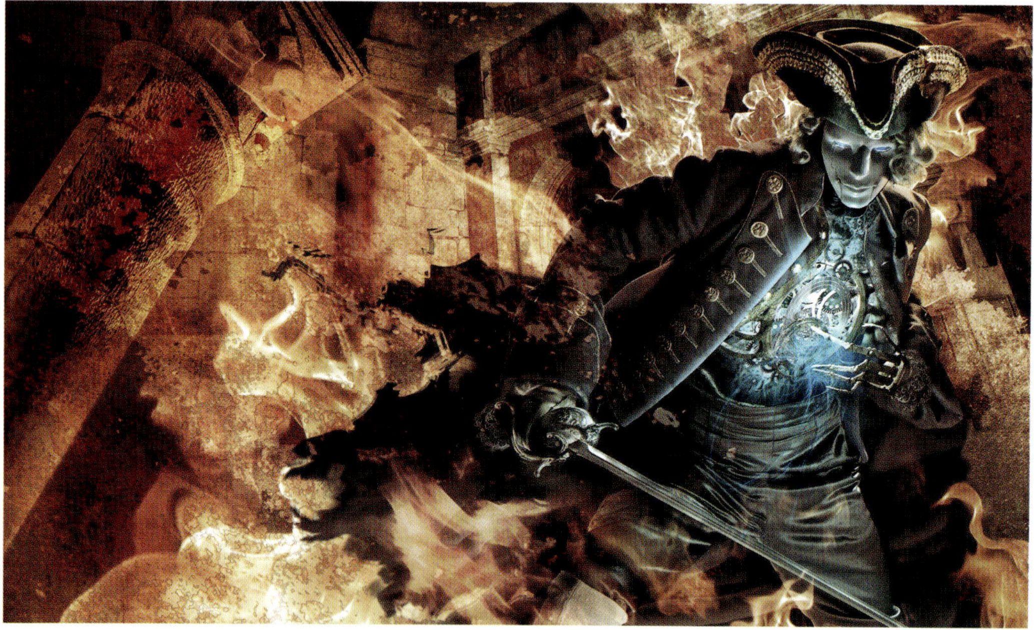

CLIFF
NIELSEN

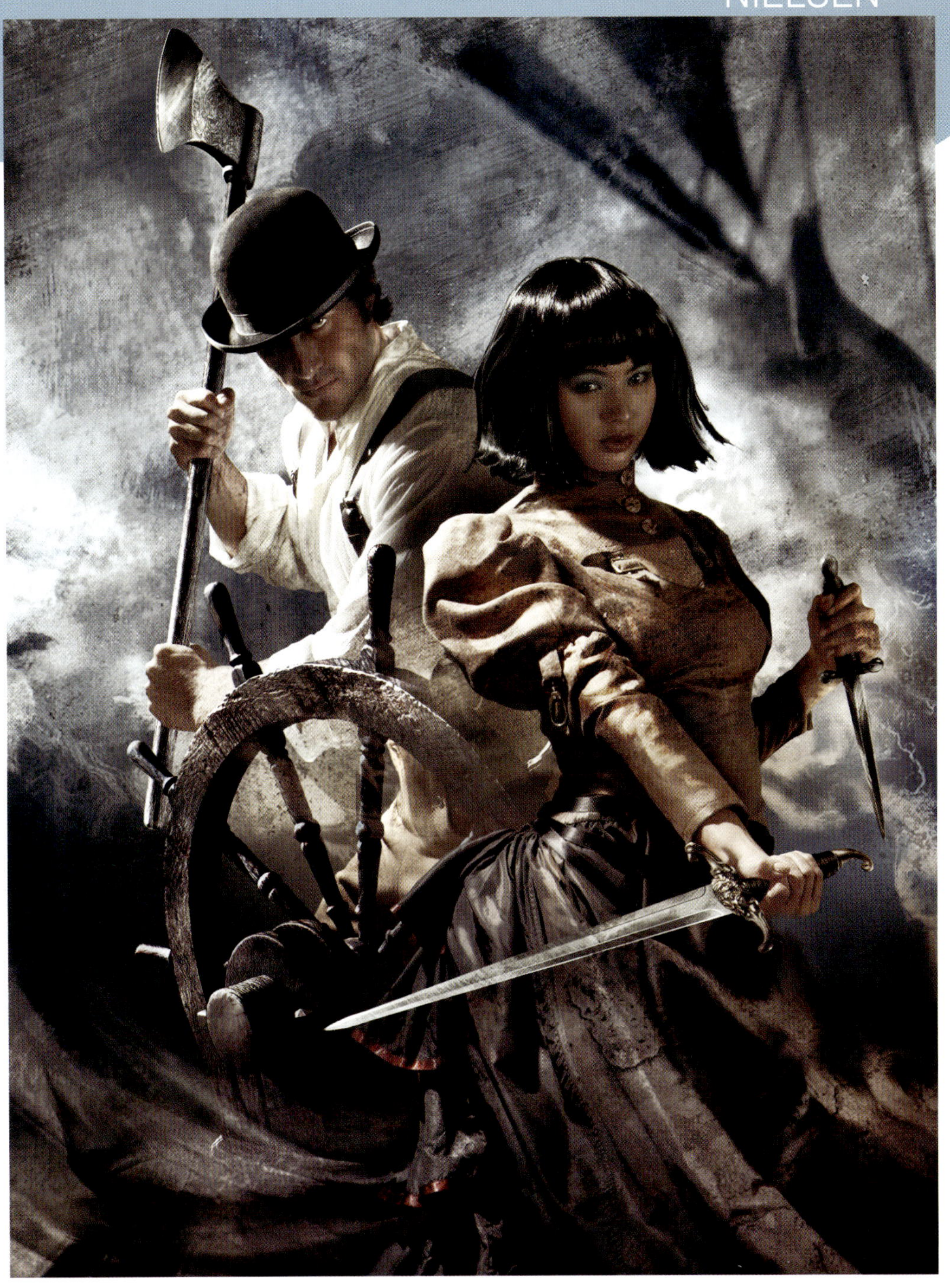

SHANNON ASSOCIATES
212.333.2551

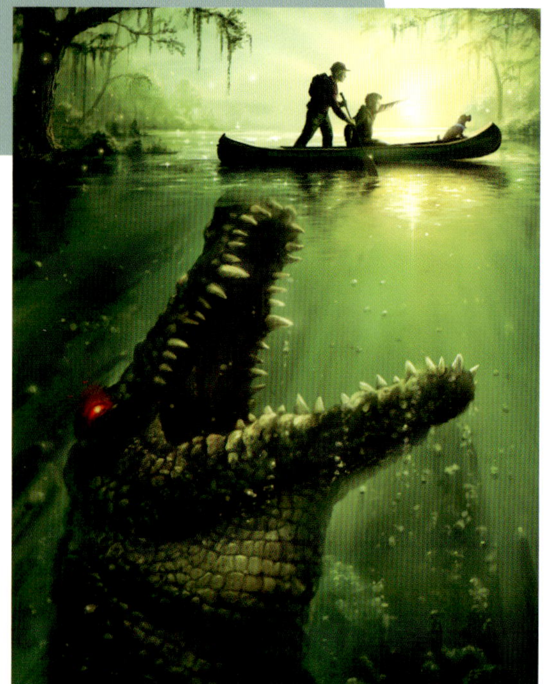

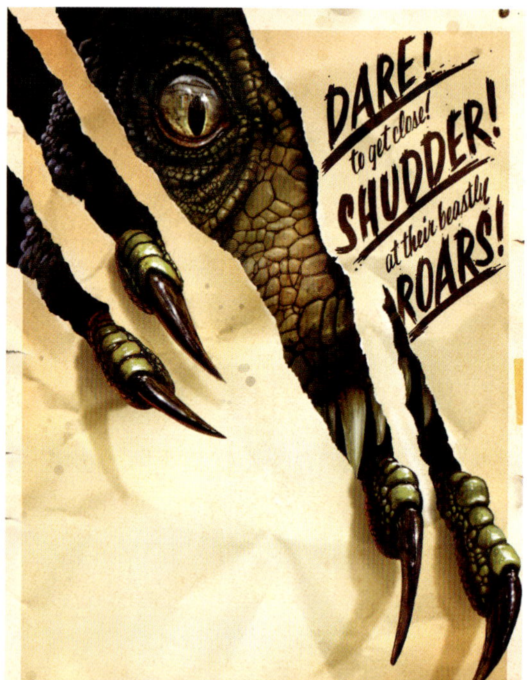
DARE!
to get close!
SHUDDER!
at their beastly
ROARS!

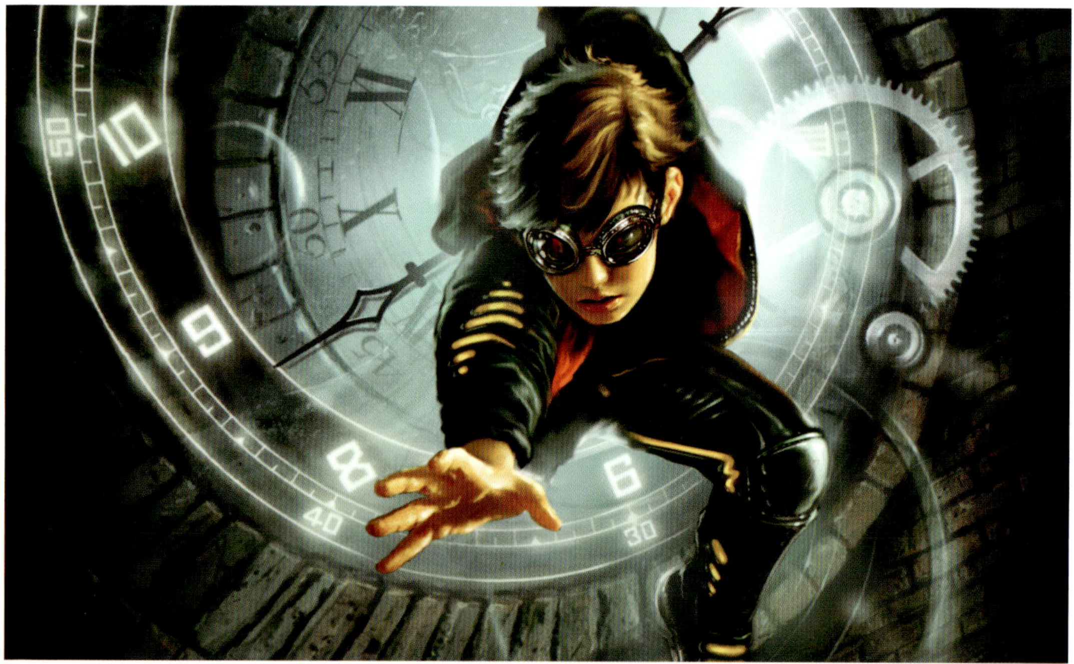

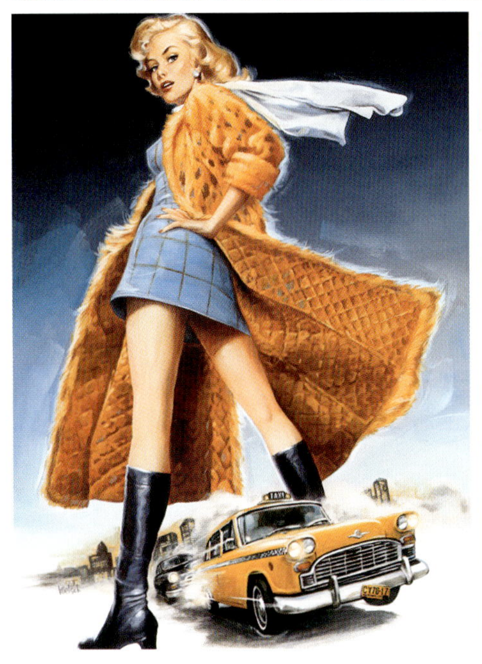
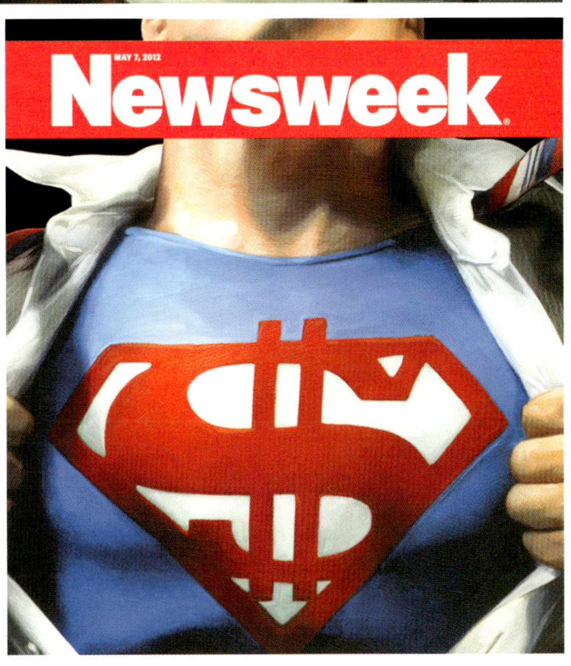
MAY 7, 2012
Newsweek.

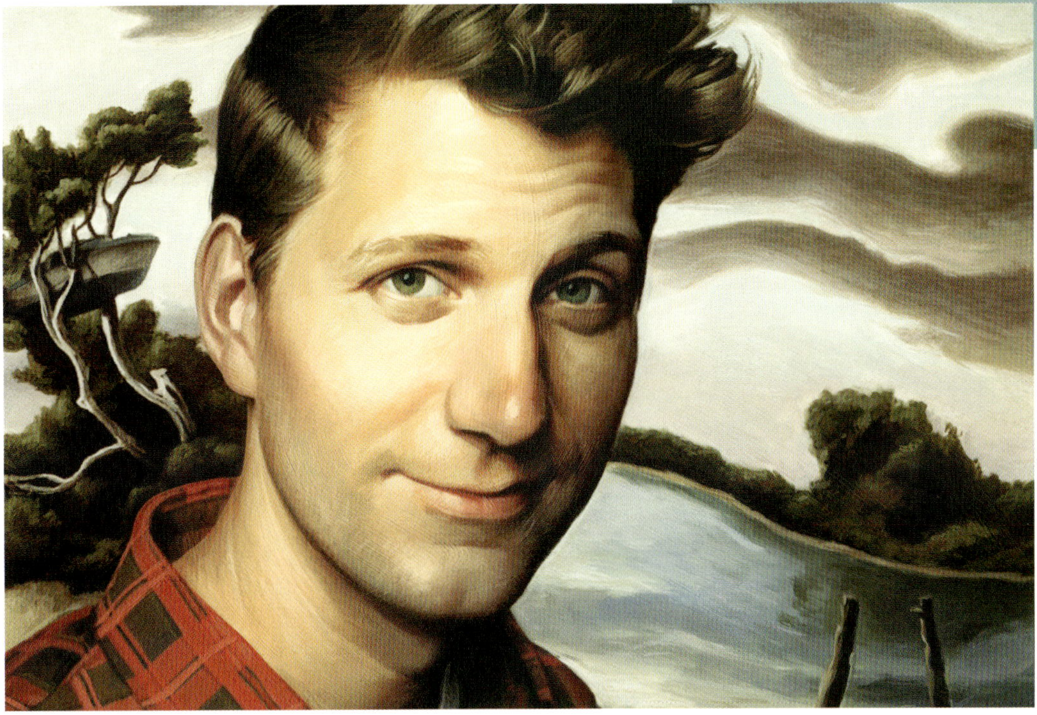

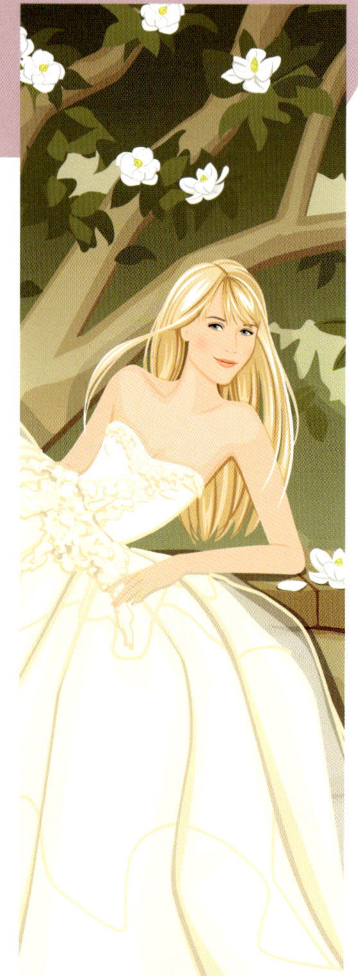

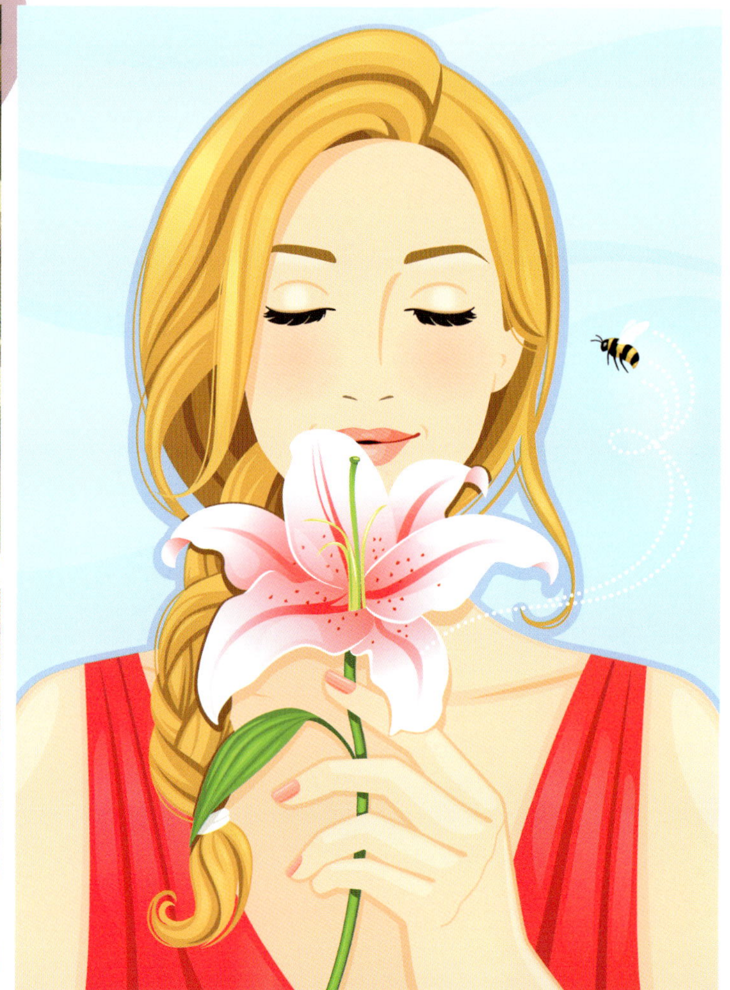

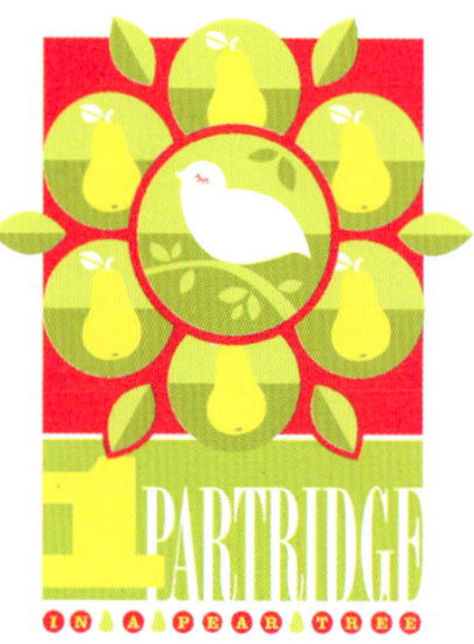
1 PARTRIDGE
IN A PEAR TREE

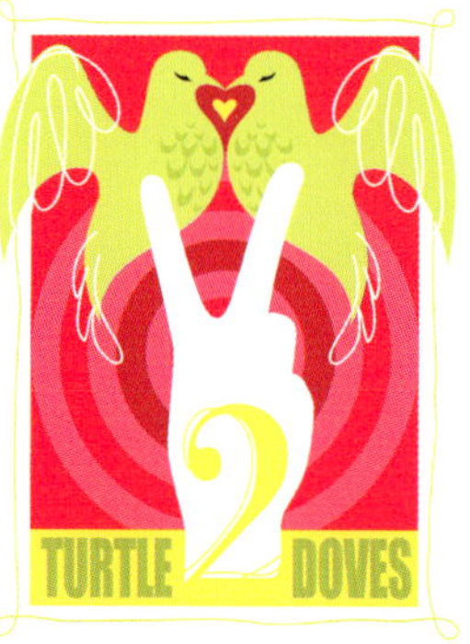
TURTLE 2 DOVES

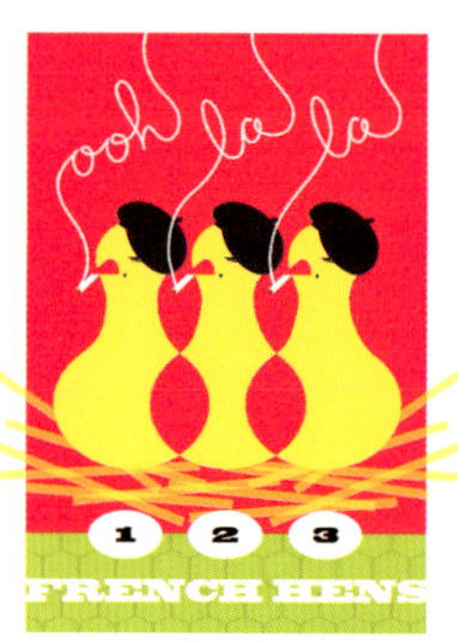
ooh la la
1 2 3
FRENCH HENS

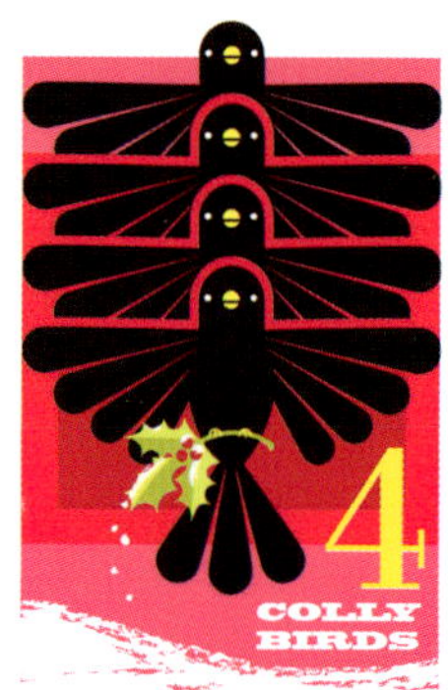
4 COLLY BIRDS

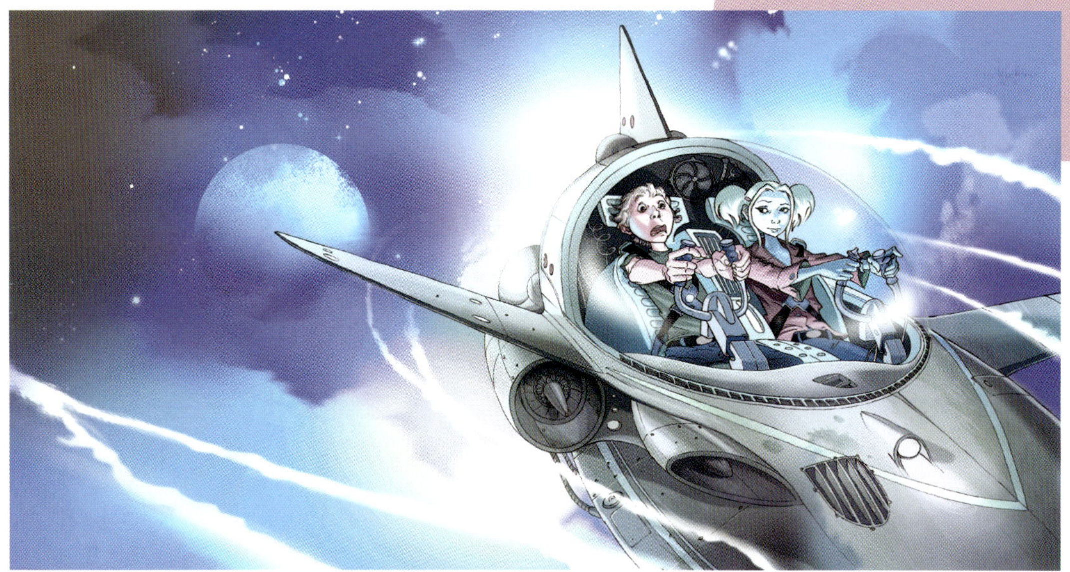

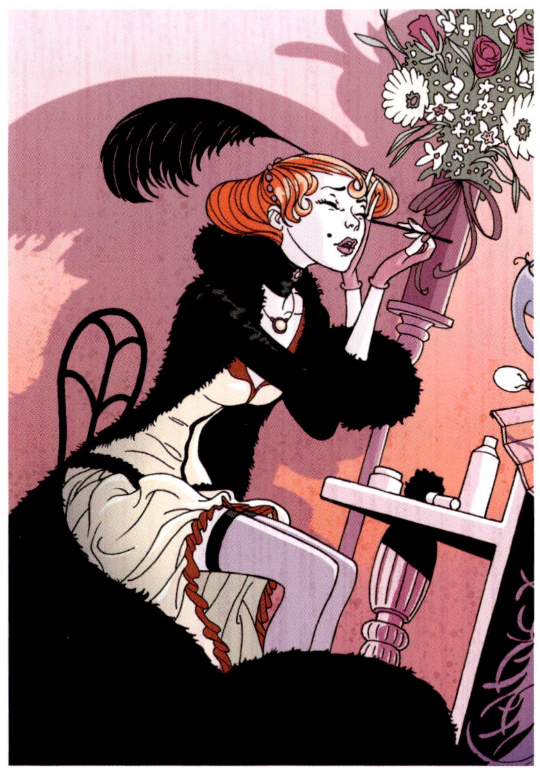

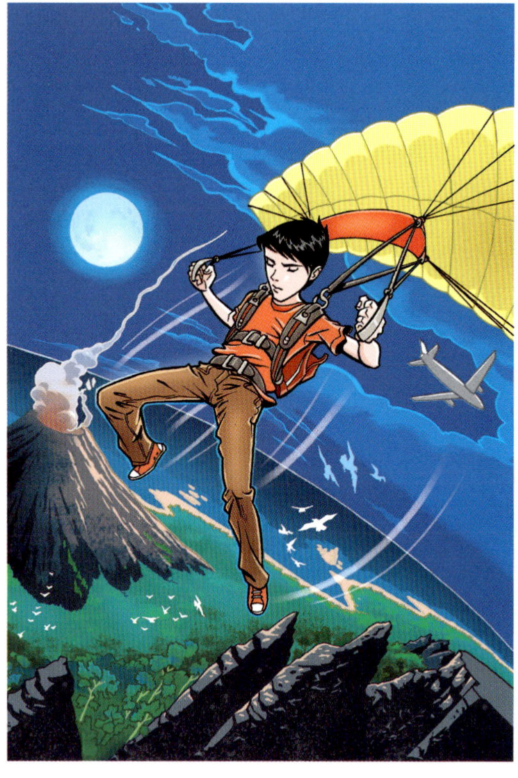

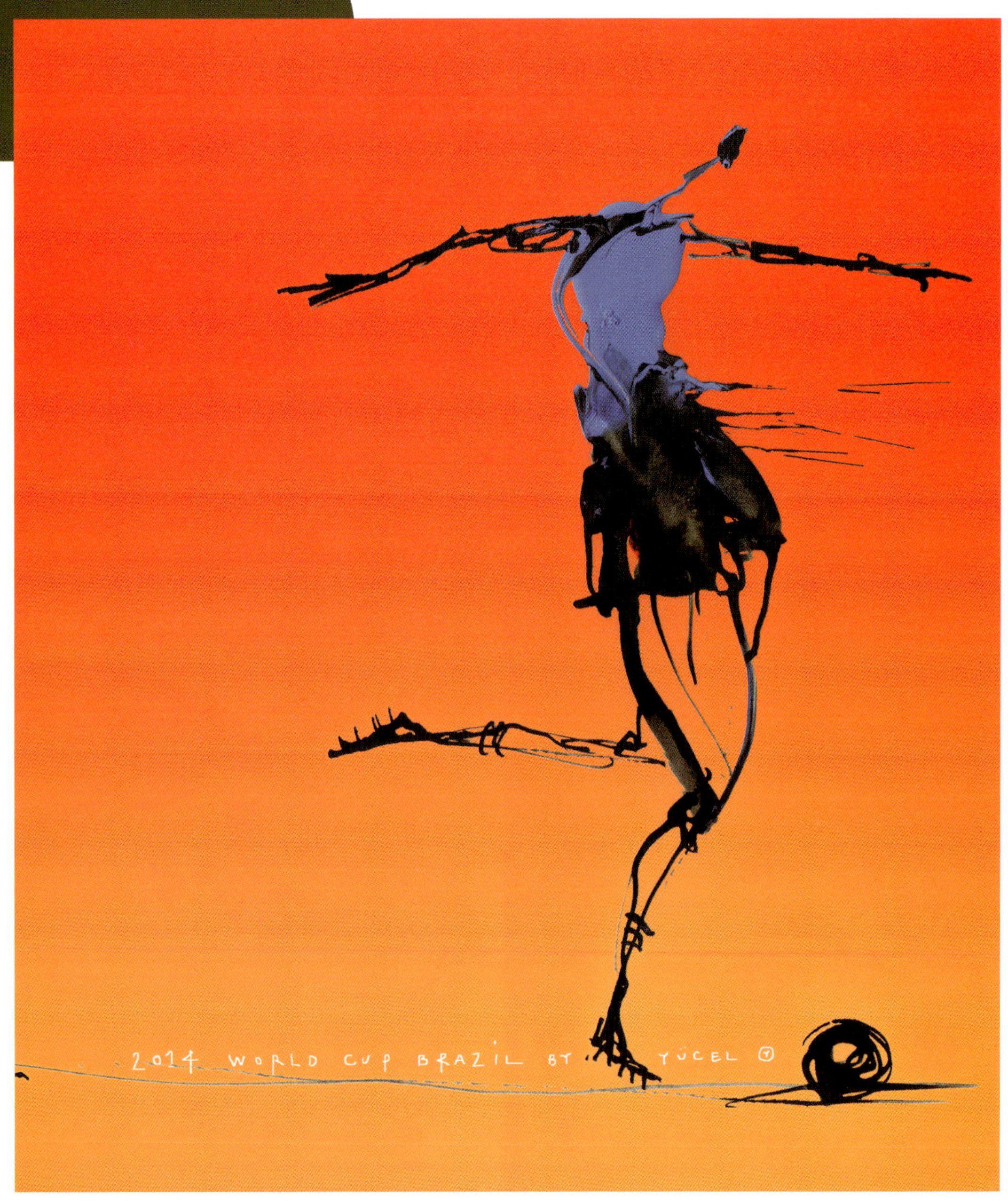
2014 WORLD CUP BRAZIL BY YUCEL

LIAM
PETERS

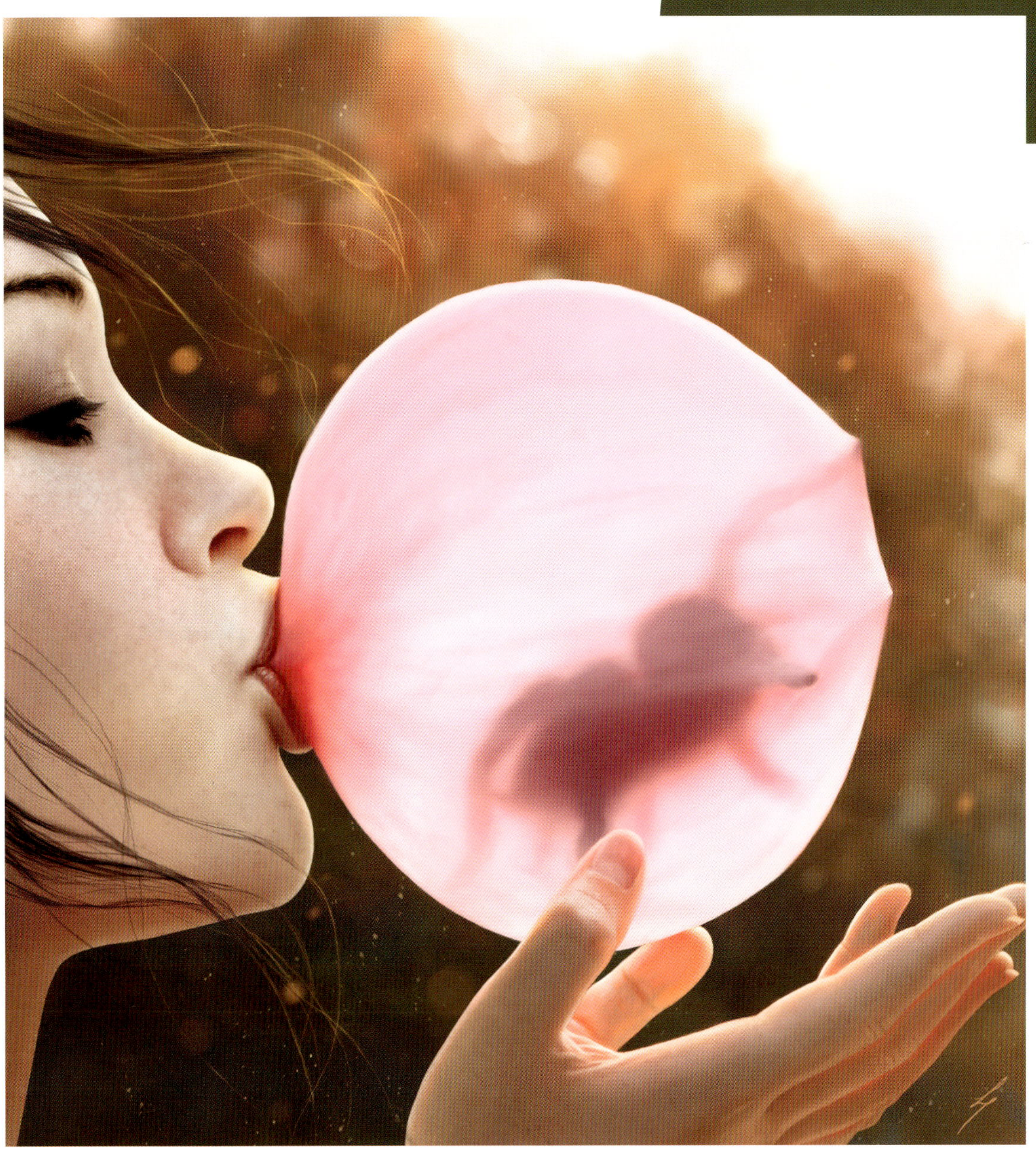

SHANNON ASSOCIATES
212.333.2551

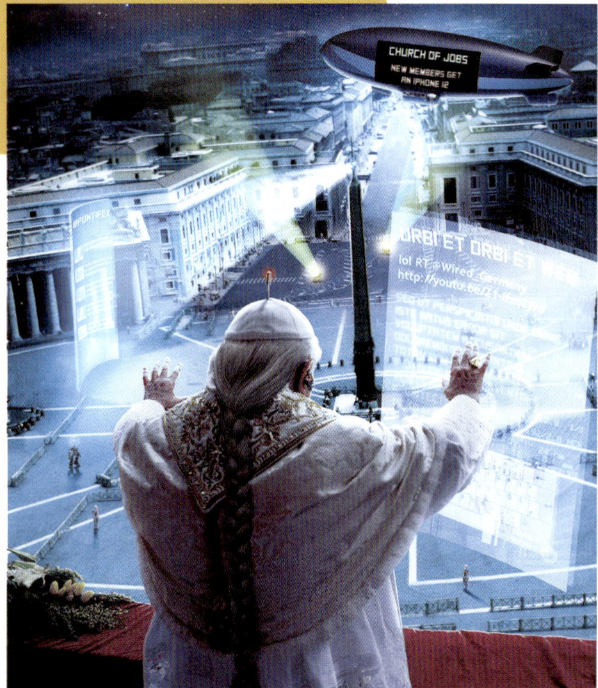

CHURCH OF JOBS
NEW MEMBERS GET
AN IPHONE 12
PONTIFEX
URBI ET ORBI ET WEB
lol RT @Wired_Germany
http://youtu.be/zs_z2zfvb9

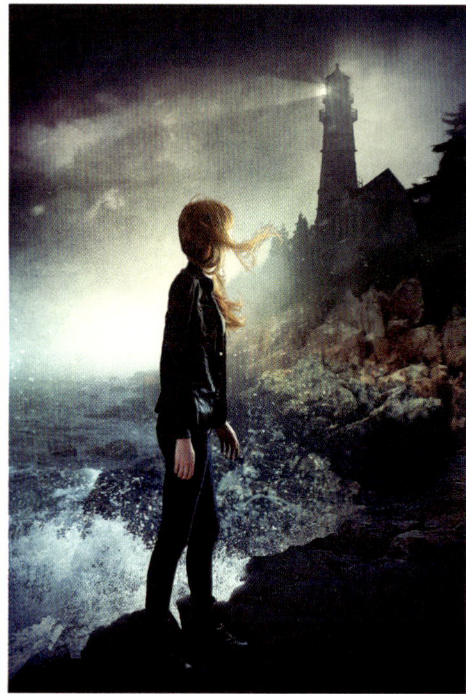

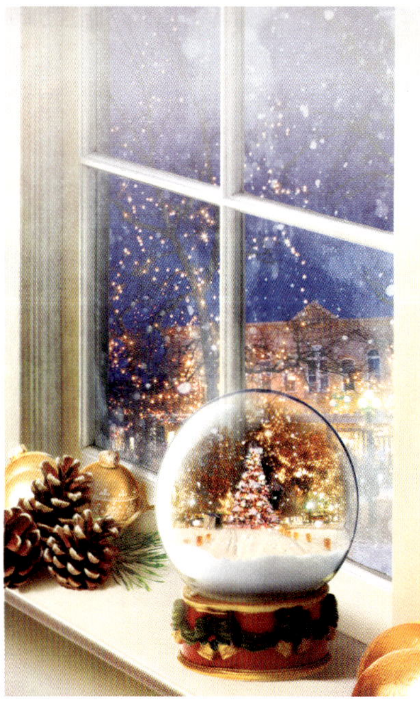

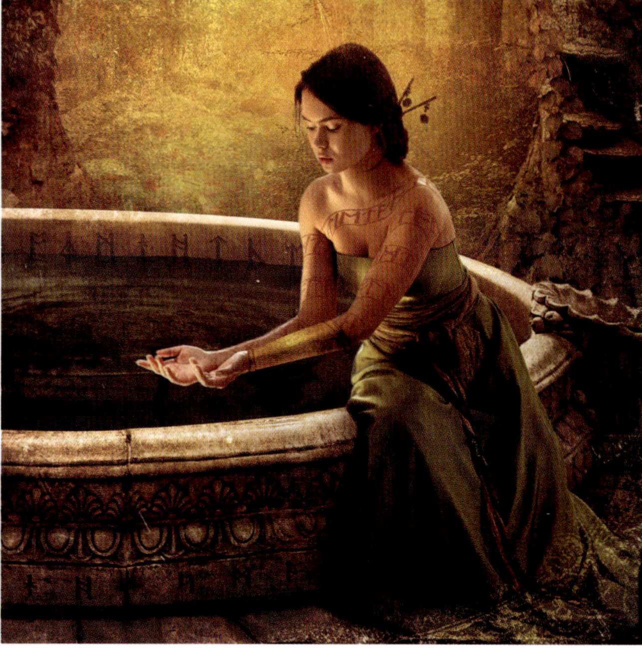

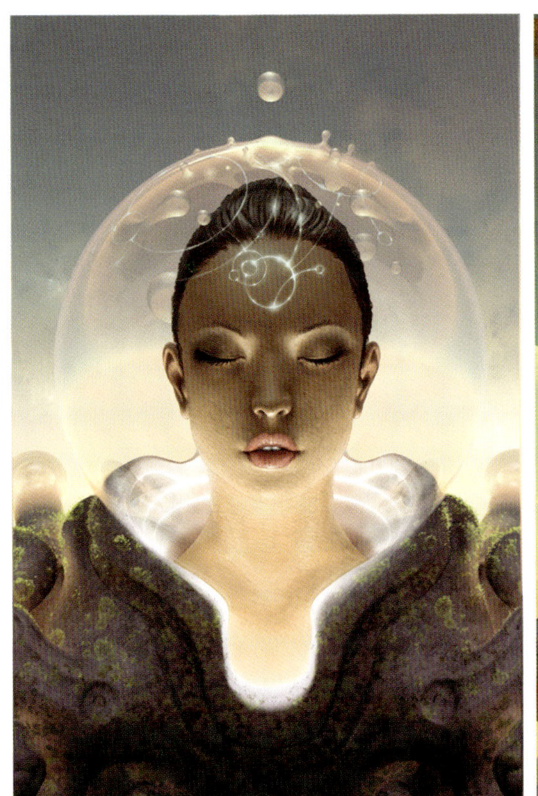

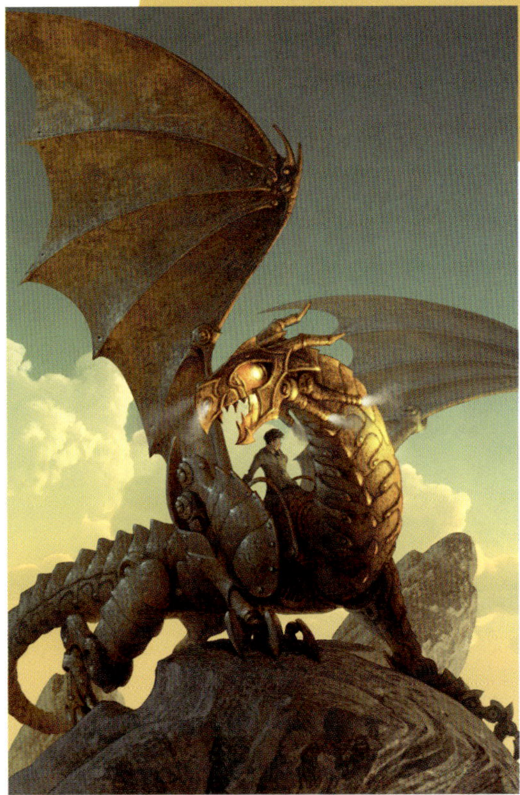

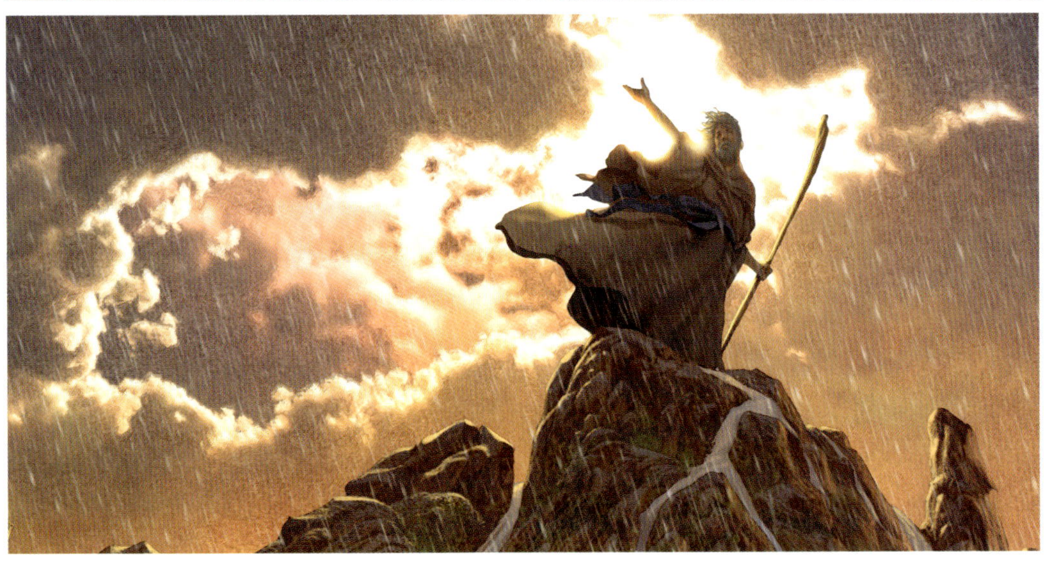

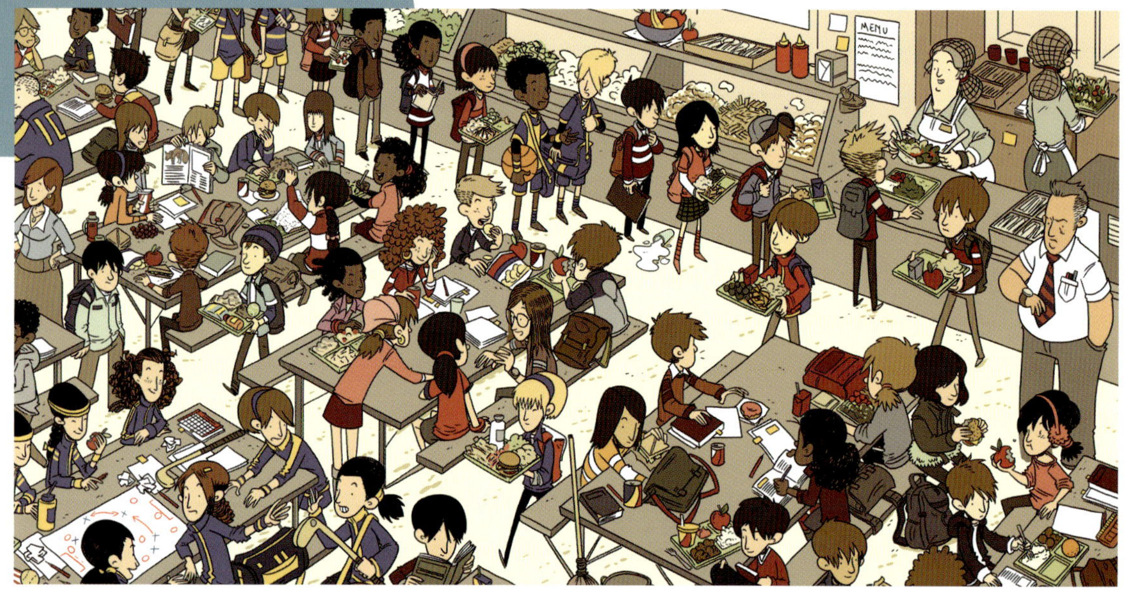

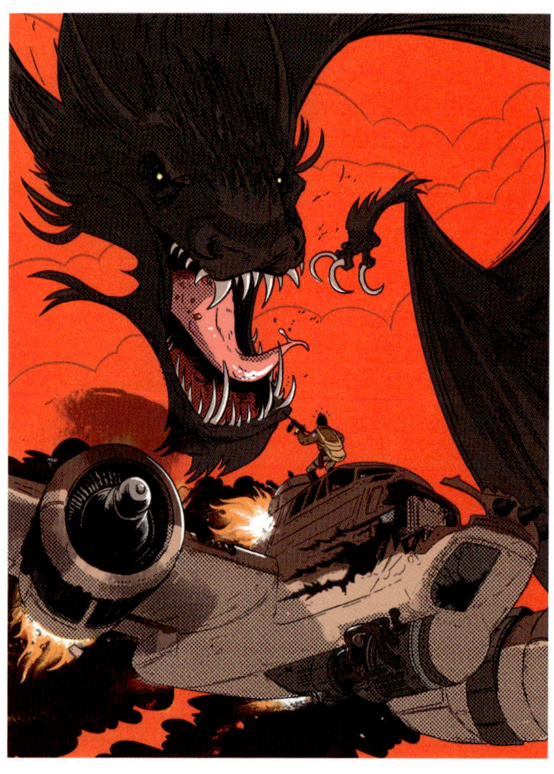

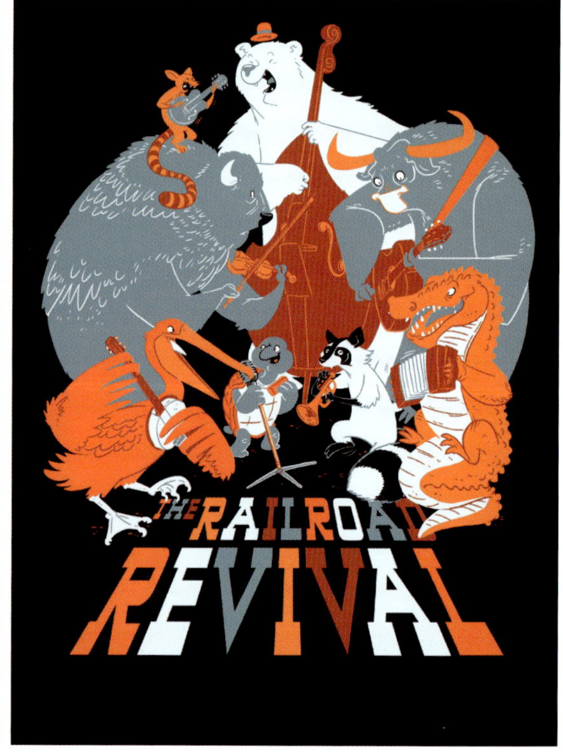
THE RAILROAD
REVIVAL

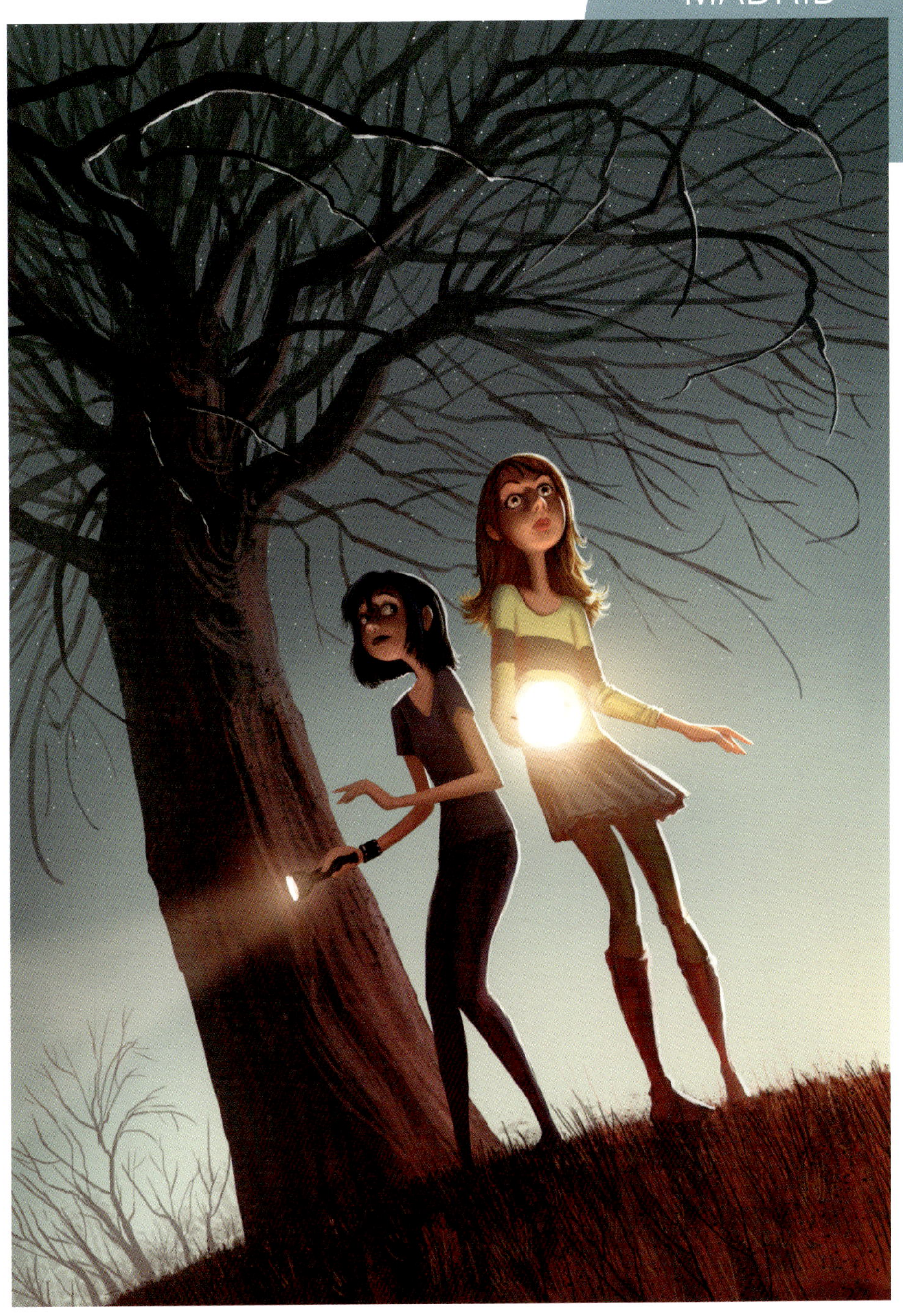

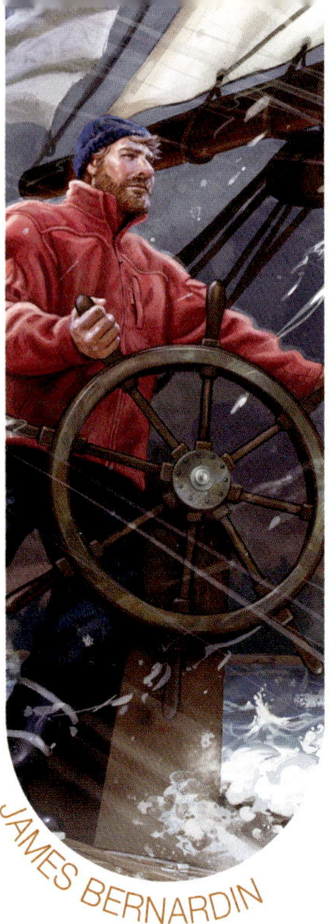

JAMES BERNARDIN

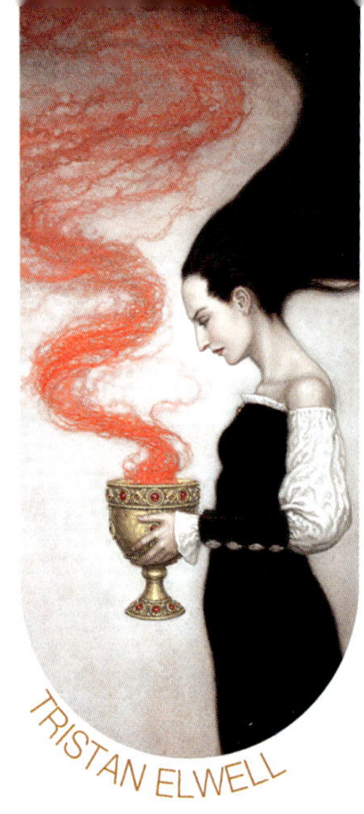

TRISTAN ELWELL

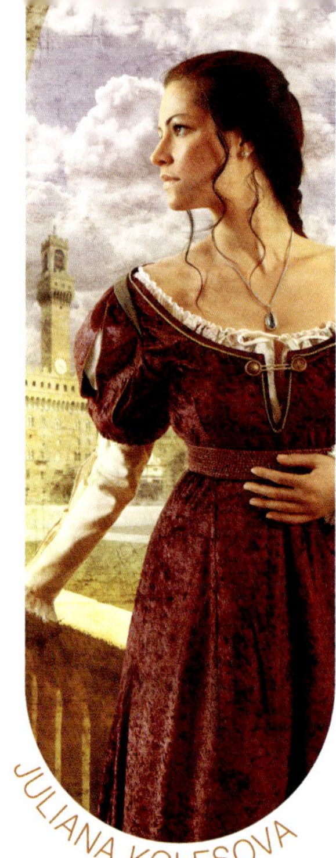

JULIANA KOLESOVA

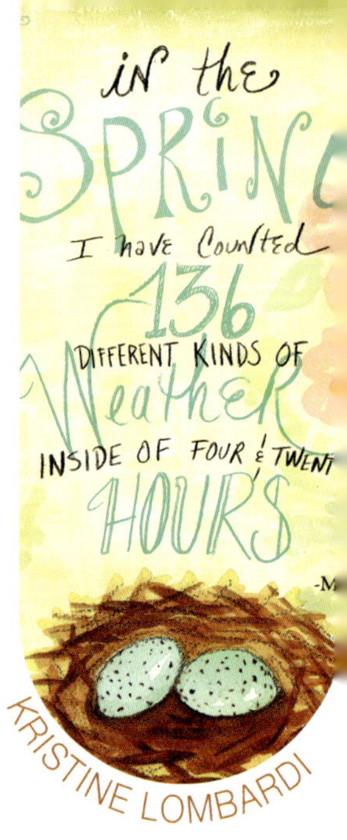

KRISTINE LOMBARDI

ROBERT HUNT

BLAKE MORROW

MORT DRUCKER

DAVID LEONARD

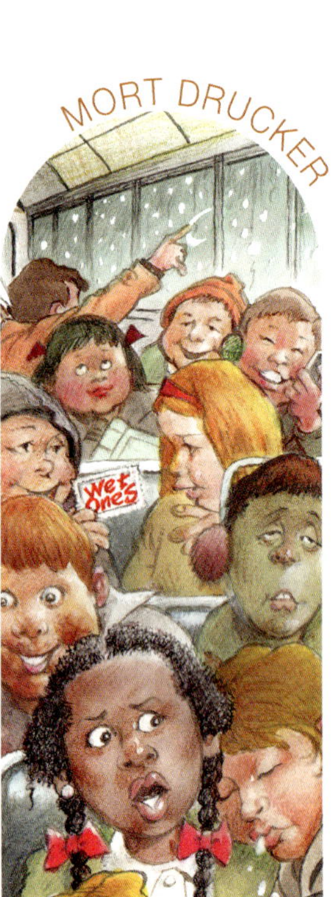

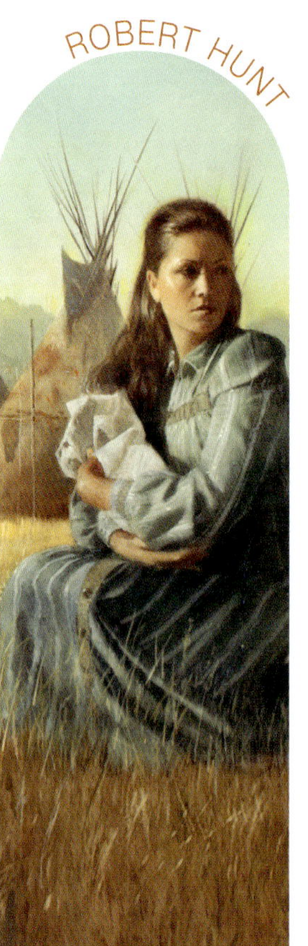

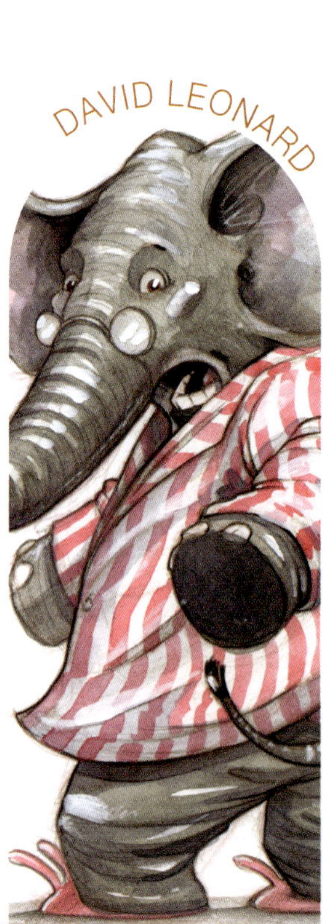

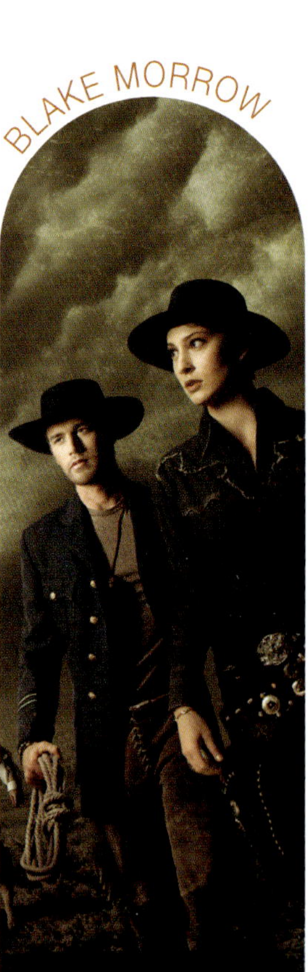

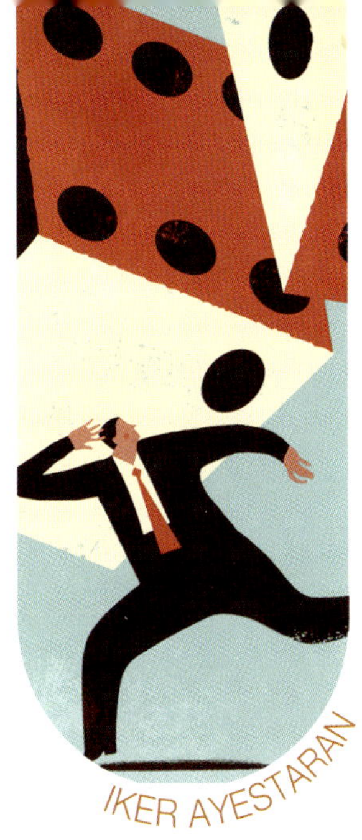

IKER AYESTARAN

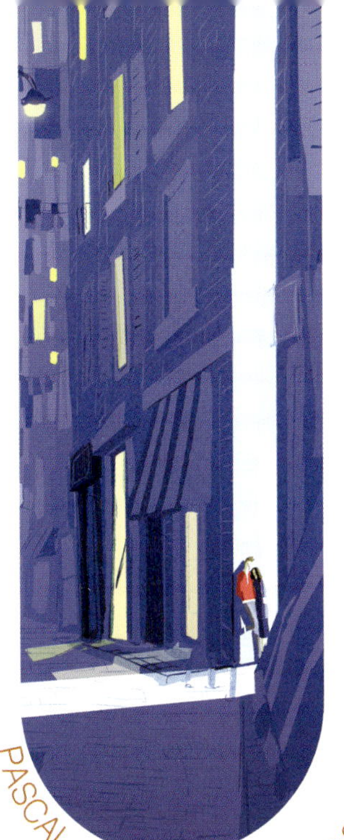

PASCAL CAMPION

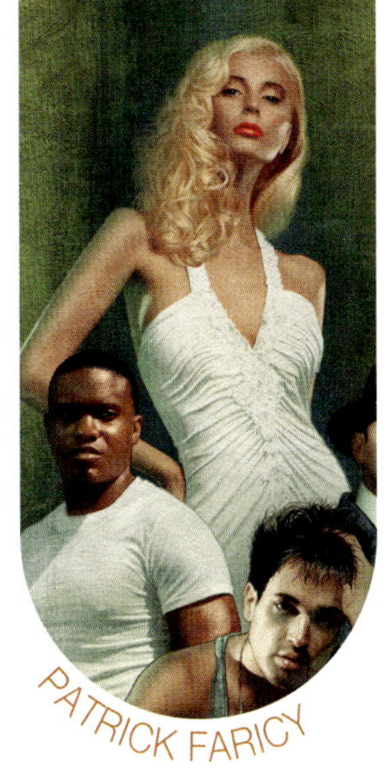

PATRICK FARICY

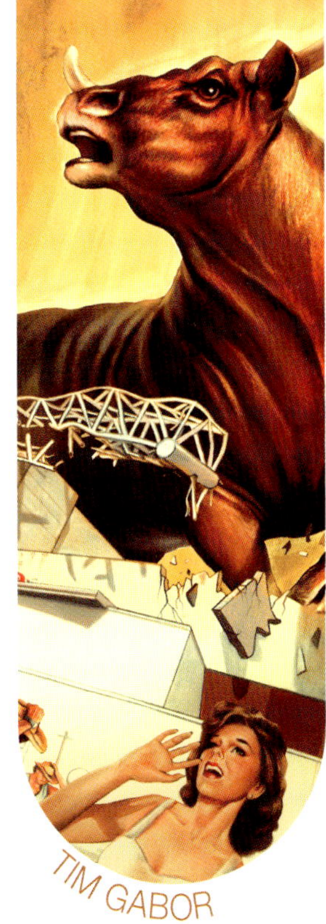

TIM GABOR

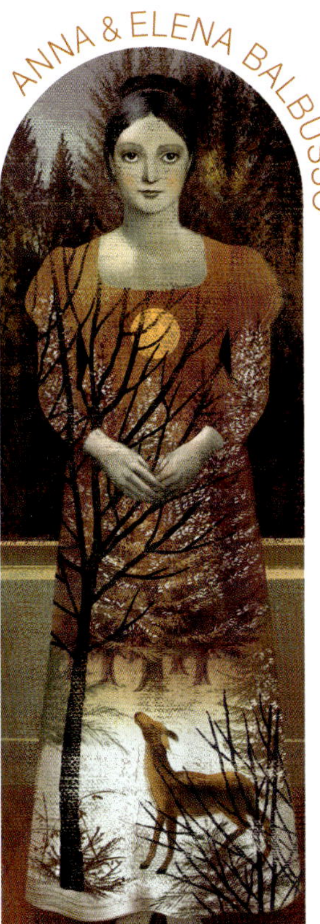

ANNA & ELENA BALBUSSO

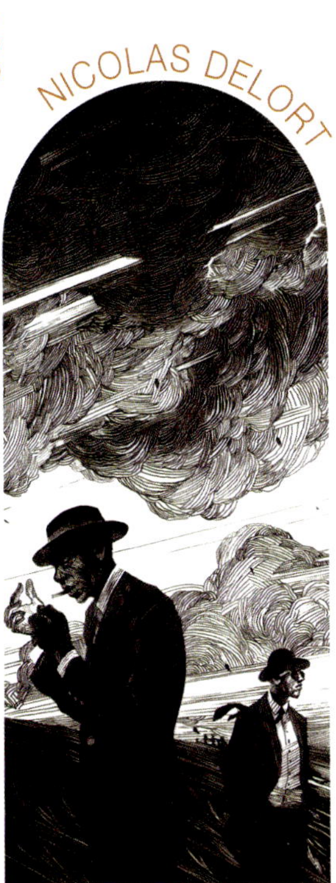

NICOLAS DELORT

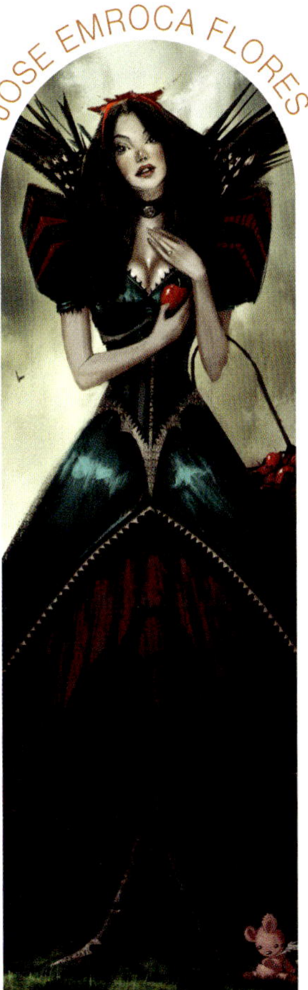

JOSE EMROCA FLORES

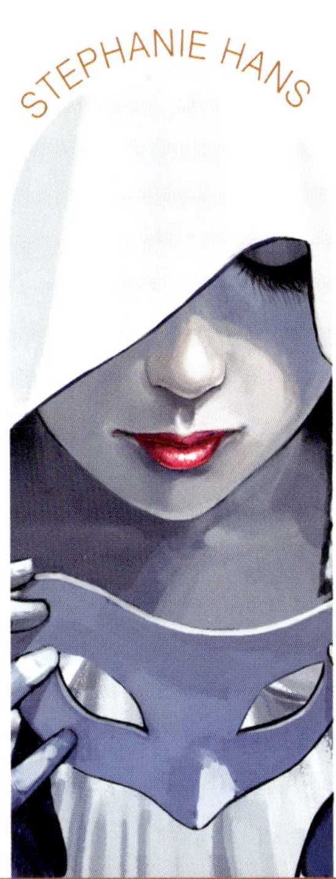

STEPHANIE HANS

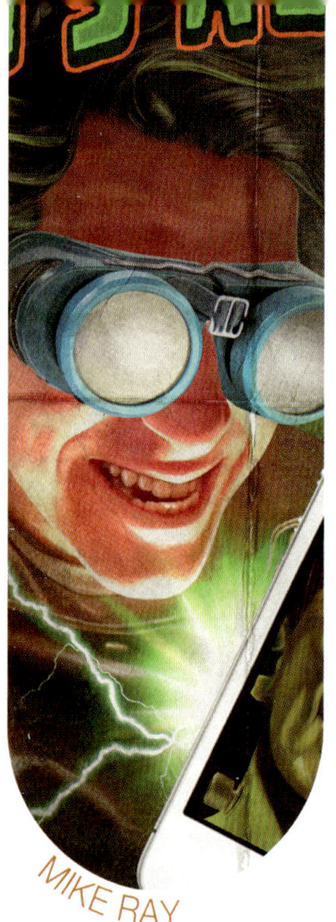

MIKE RAY

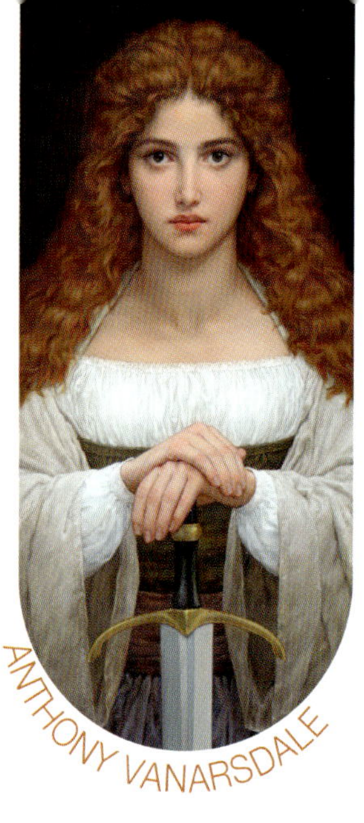

ANTHONY VANARSDALE

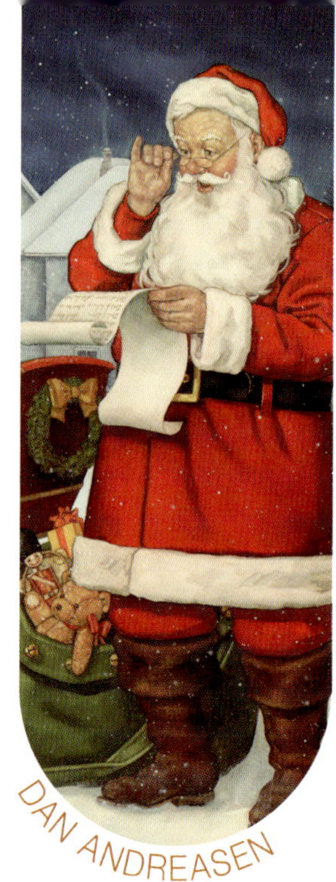

DAN ANDREASEN

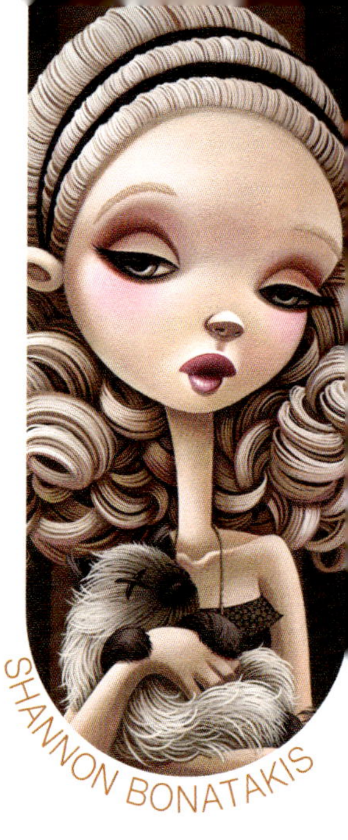

SHANNON BONATAKIS

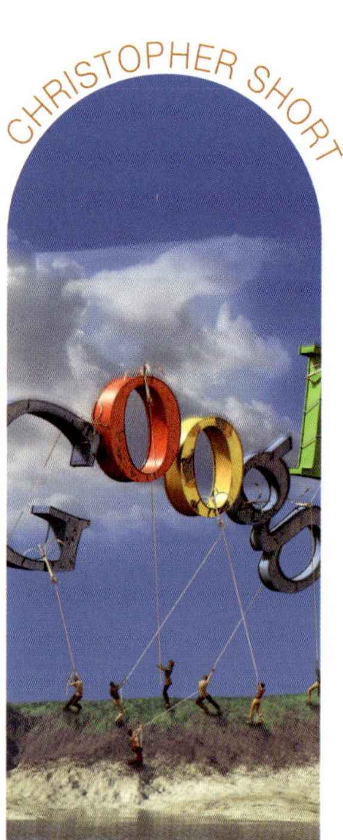

CHRISTOPHER SHORT

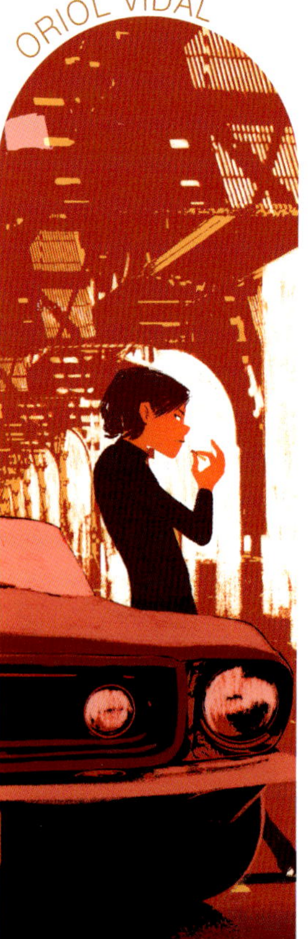

ORIOL VIDAL

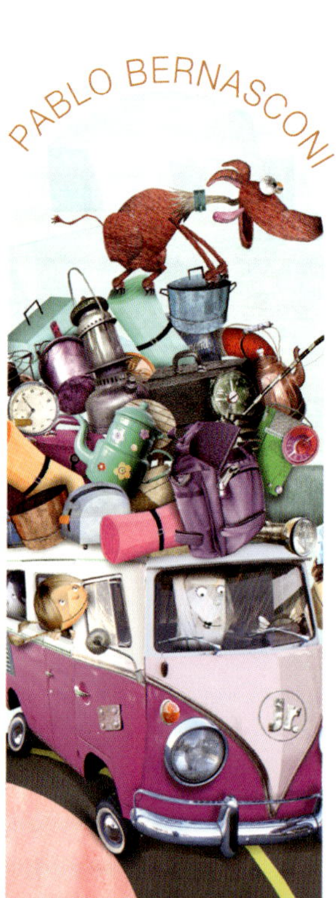

PABLO BERNASCONI

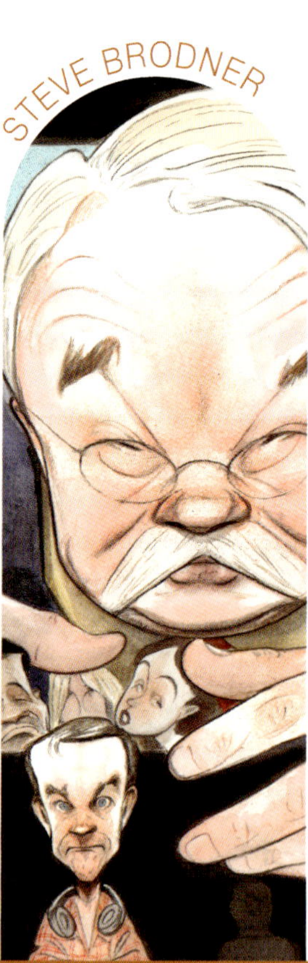

STEVE BRODNER

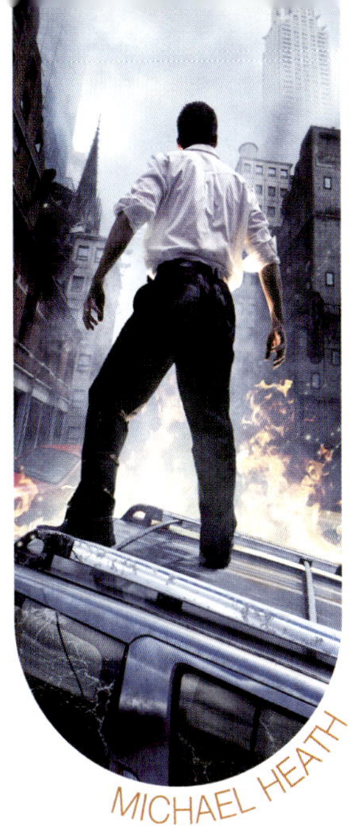

MICHAEL HEATH

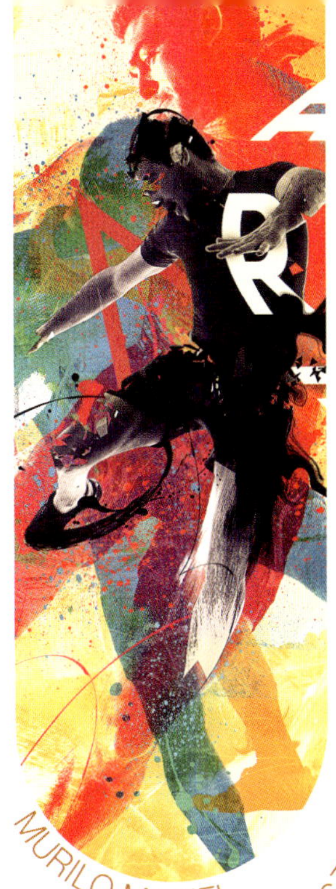

MURILO MACIEL

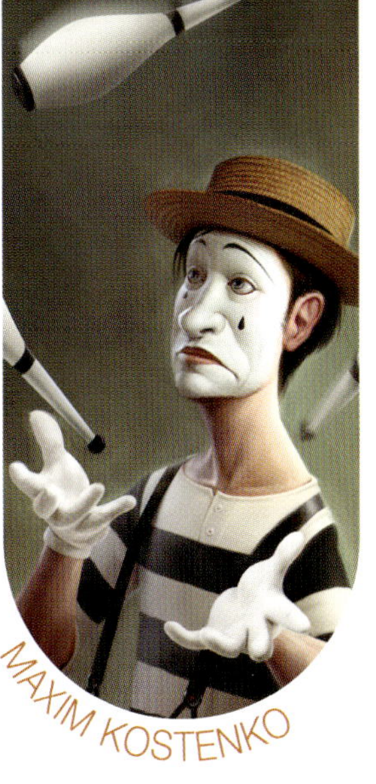

MAXIM KOSTENKO

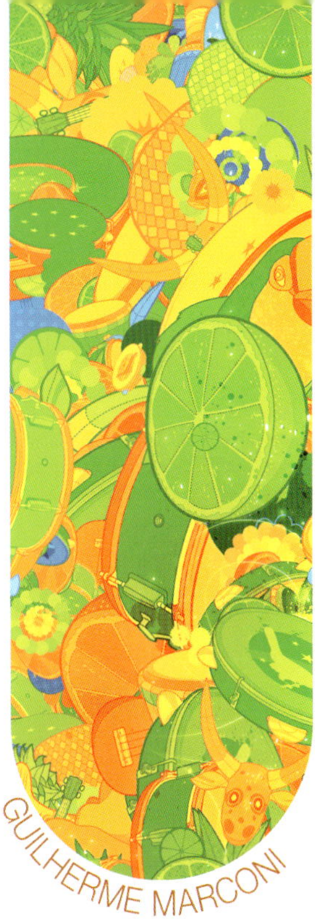

GUILHERME MARCONI

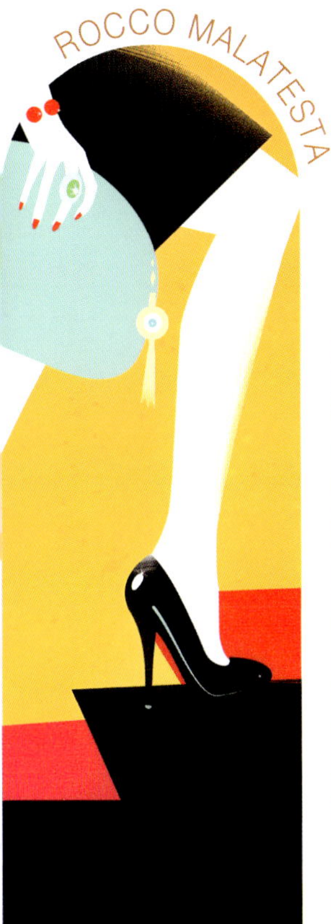

ROCCO MALATESTA

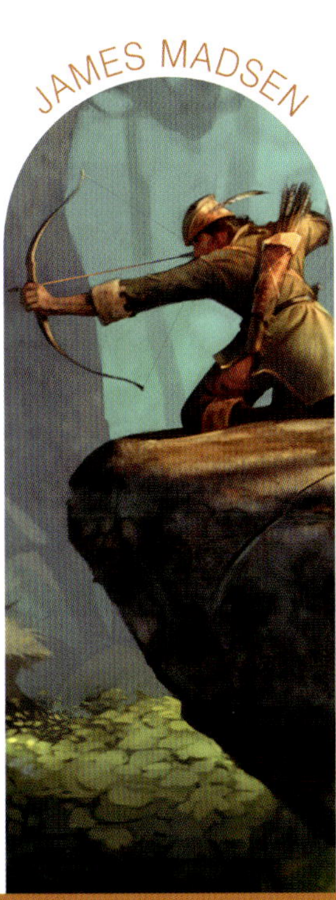

JAMES MADSEN

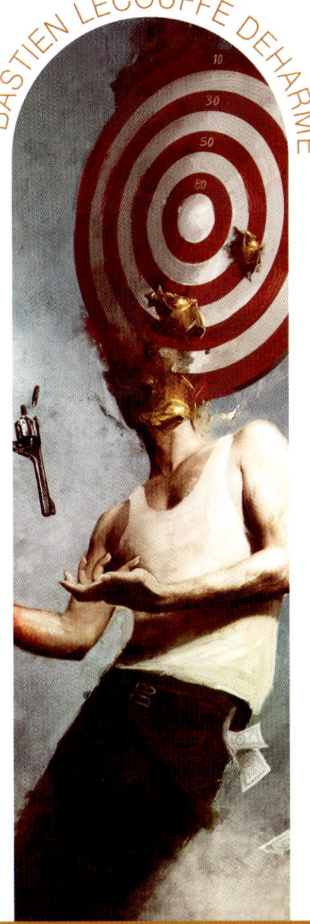

BASTIEN LECOUFFE DEHARME

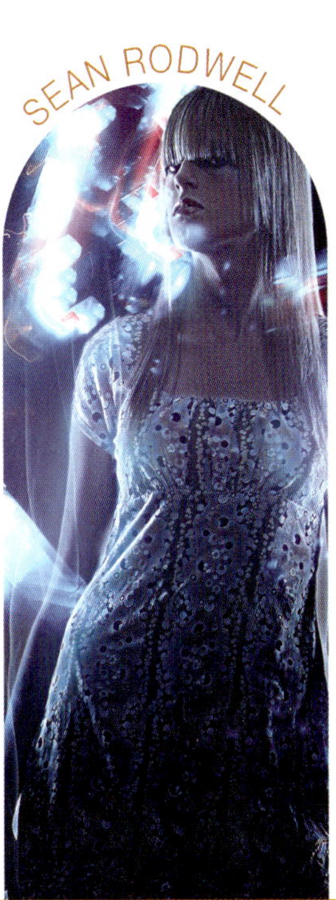

SEAN RODWELL

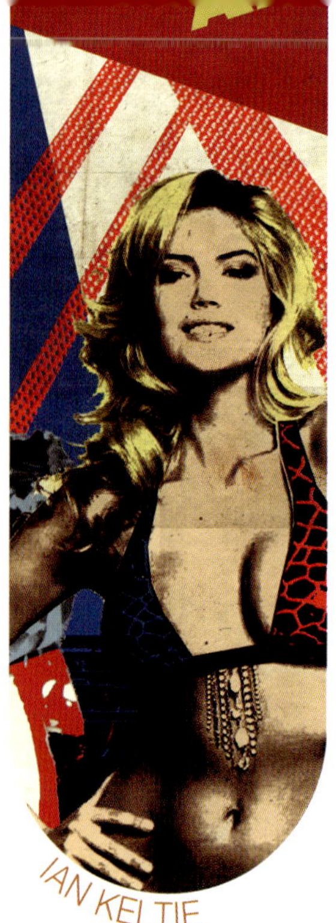

IAN KELTIE

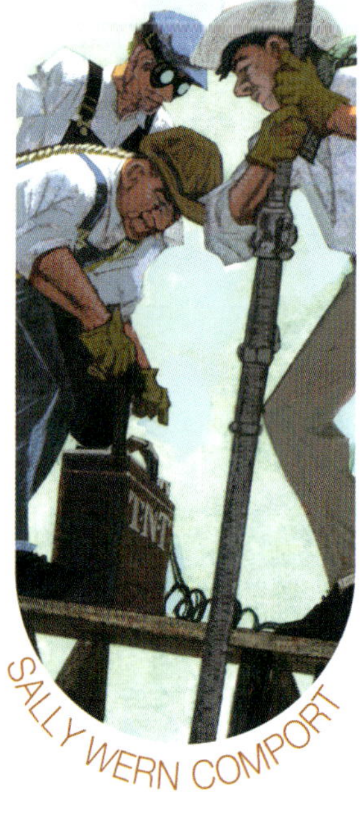

SALLY WERN COMPORT

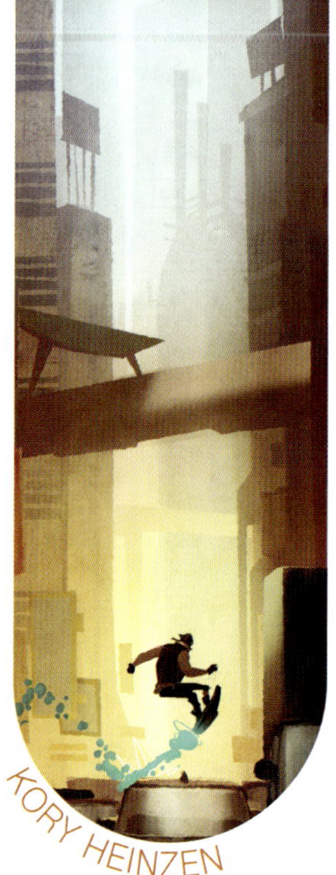

KORY HEINZEN

TORSTEIN NORDSTRAND

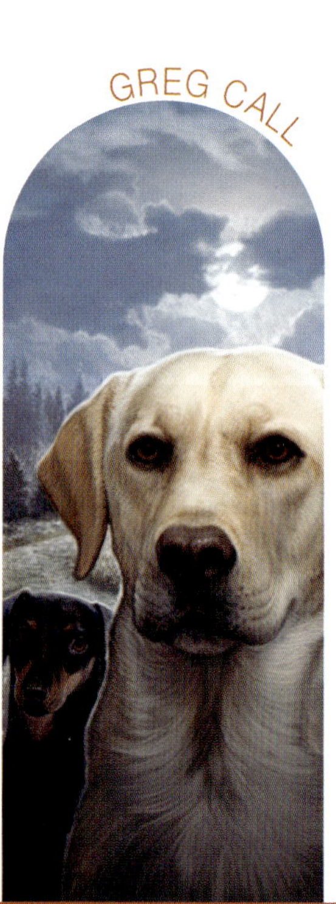

GREG CALL

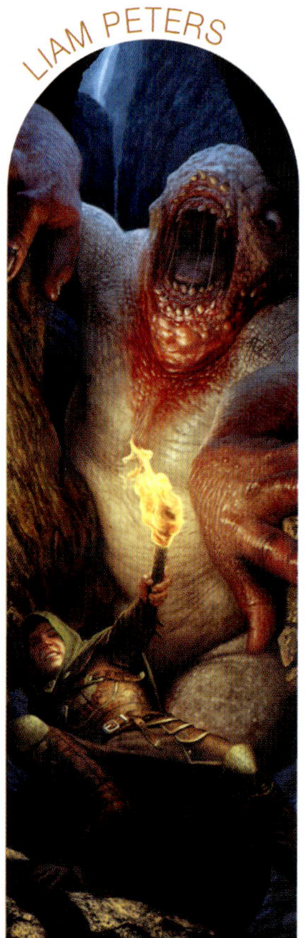

LIAM PETERS

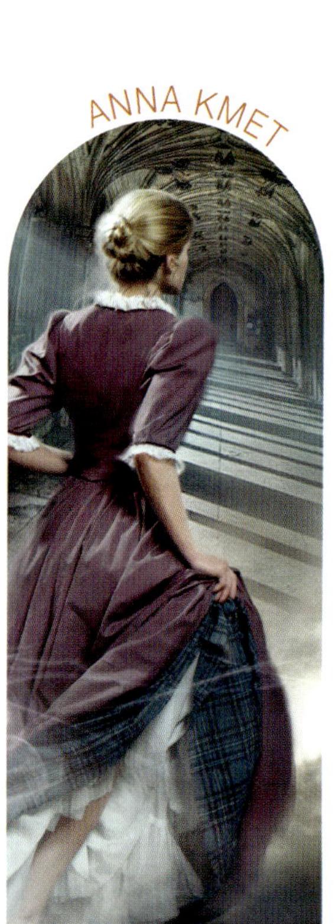

ANNA KMET

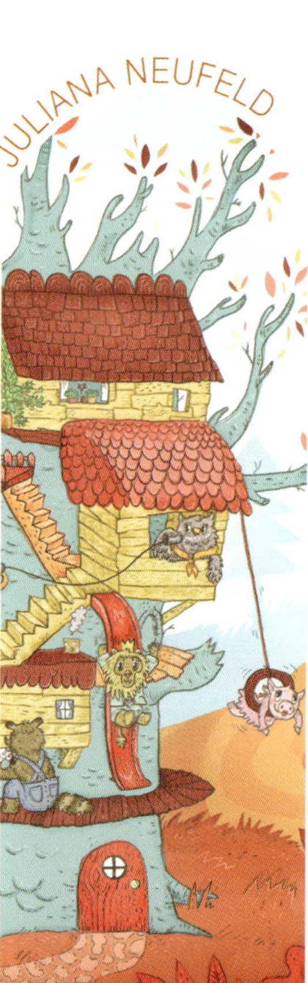

JULIANA NEUFELD

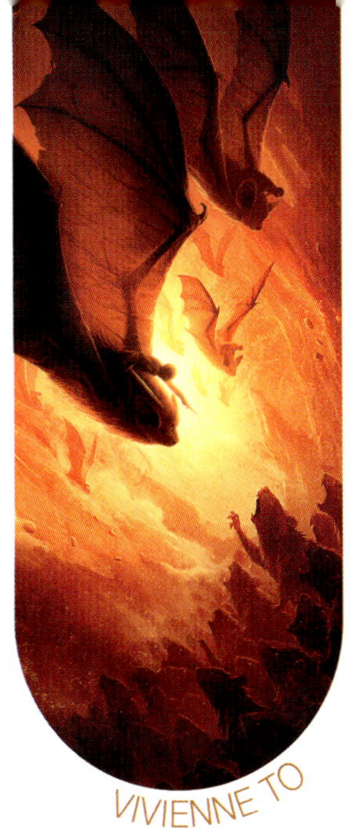

VIVIENNE TO

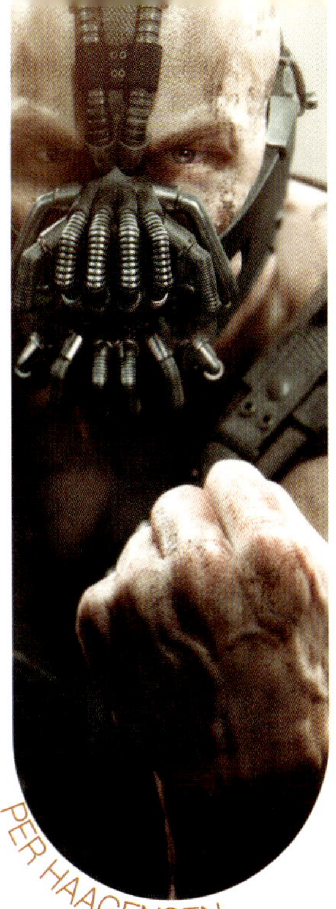

PER HAAGENSEN

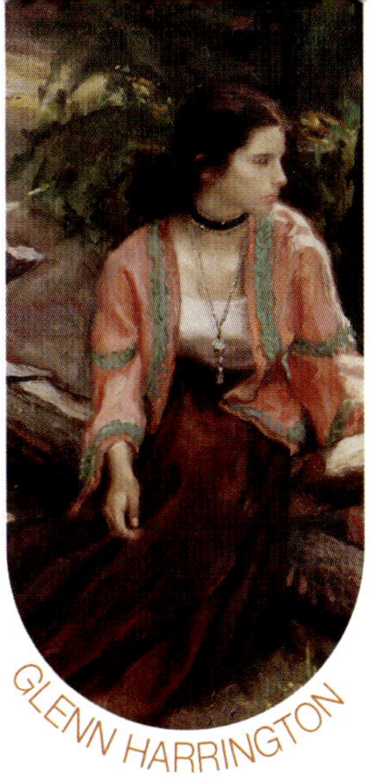

GLENN HARRINGTON

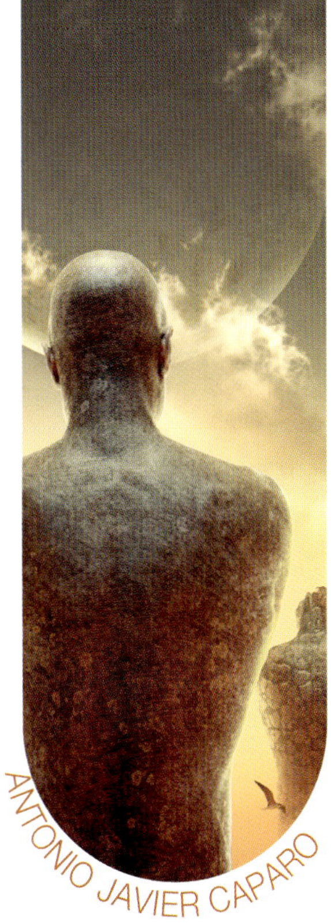

ANTONIO JAVIER CAPARO

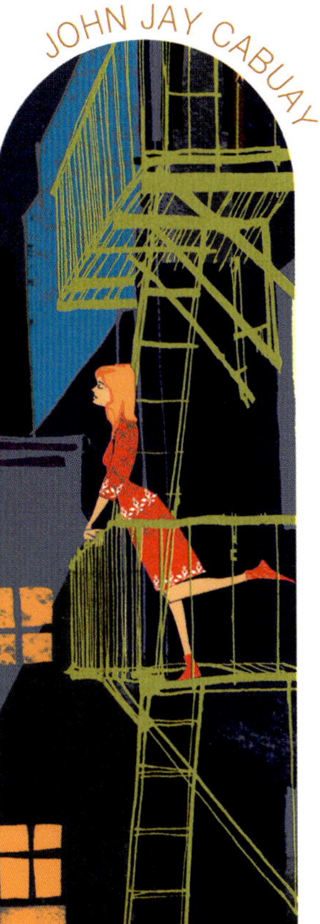

JOHN JAY CABUAY

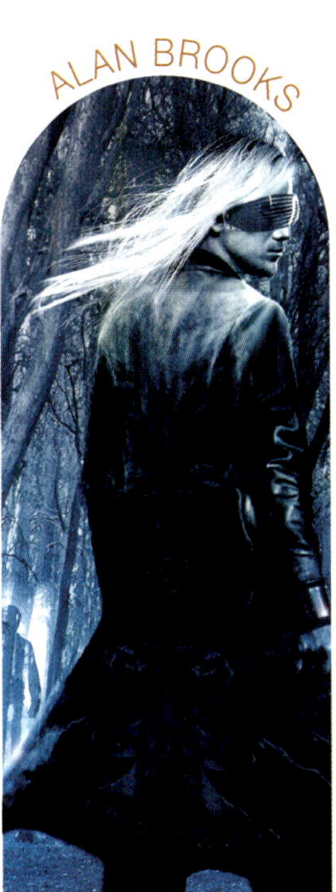

ALAN BROOKS

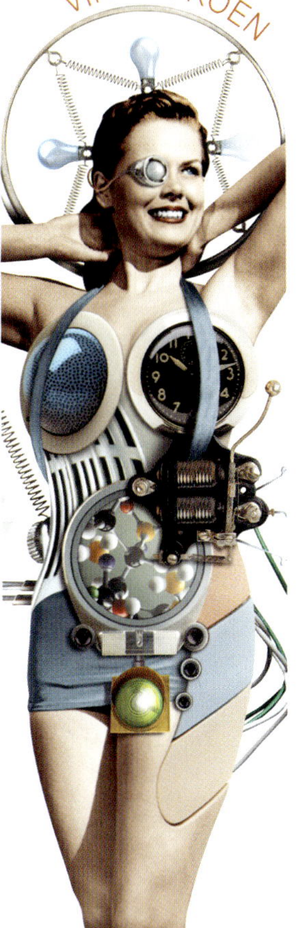

VIKTOR KOEN

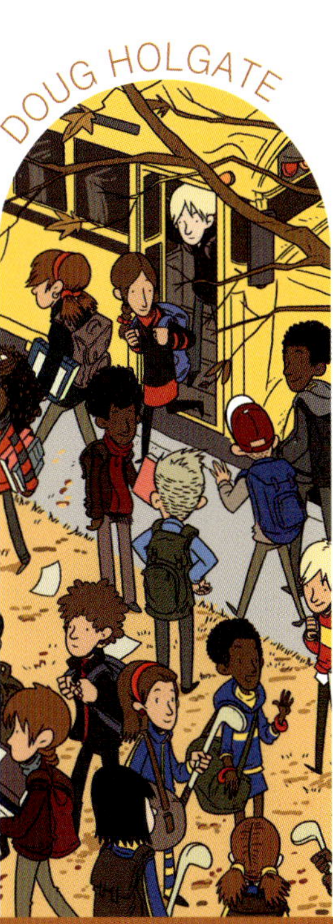

DOUG HOLGATE

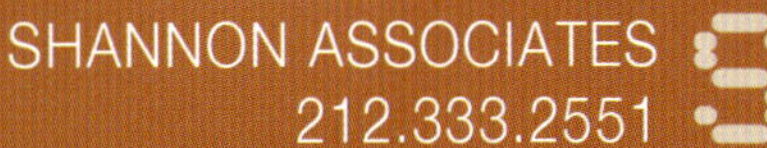

SHANNON ASSOCIATES
212.333.2551

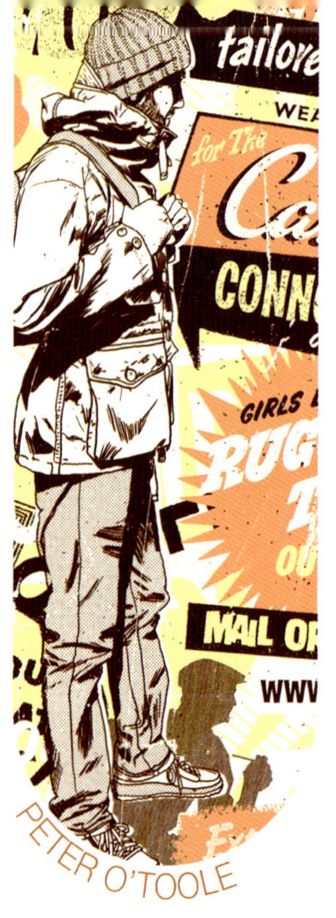

PETER O'TOOLE

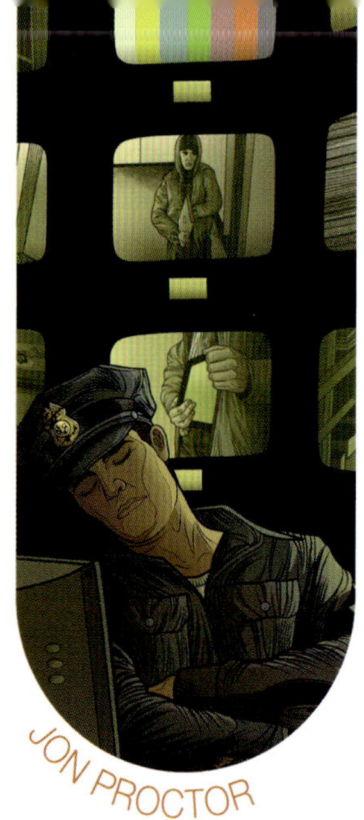

JON PROCTOR

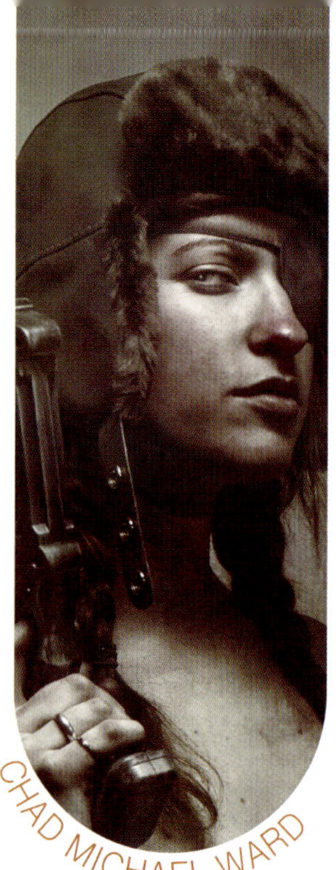

CHAD MICHAEL WARD

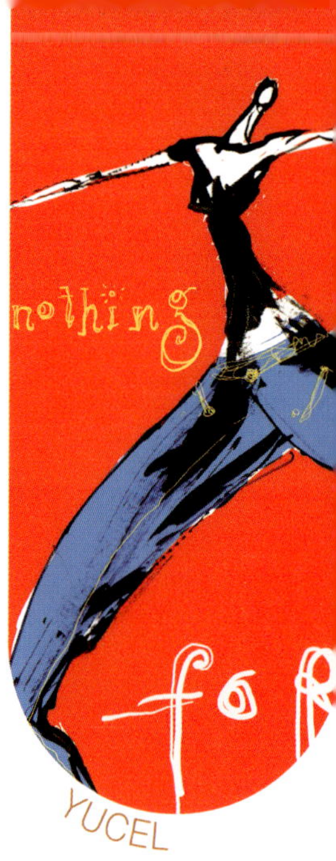

YUCEL

SHANE REBENSCHIED

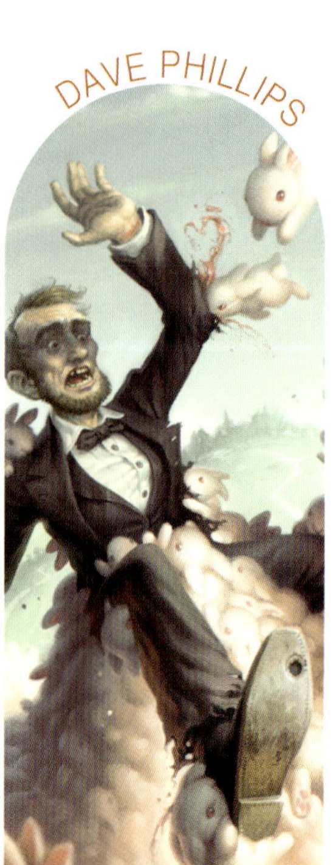

DAVE PHILLIPS

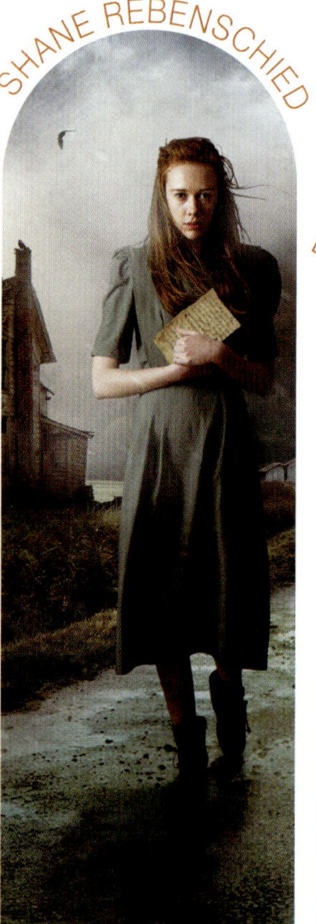

MARCELO BAEZ

RAFAEL SARMENTO

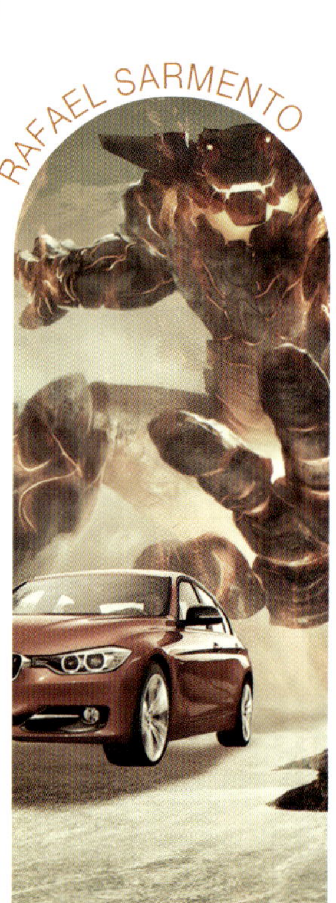

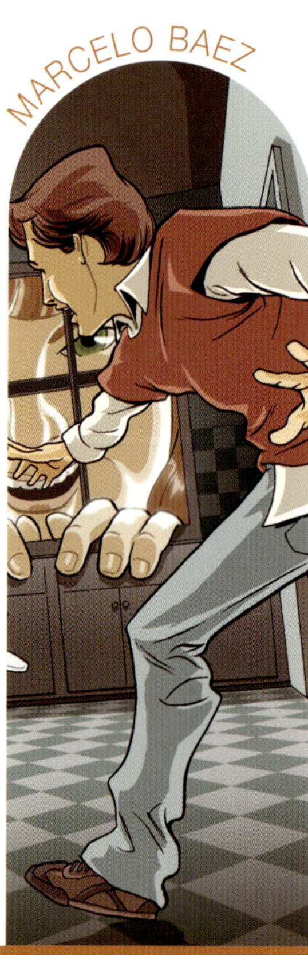

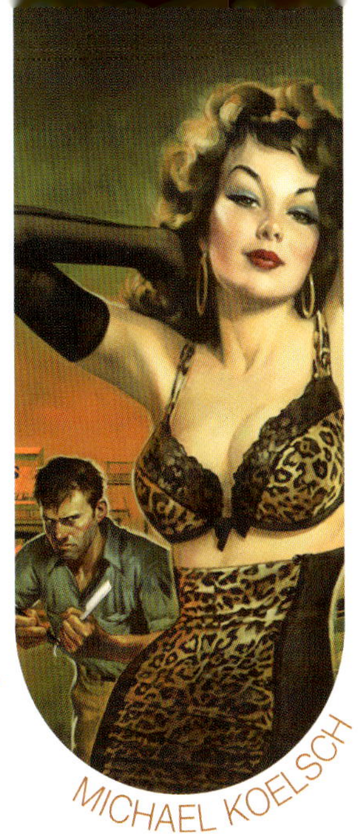

MICHAEL KOELSCH

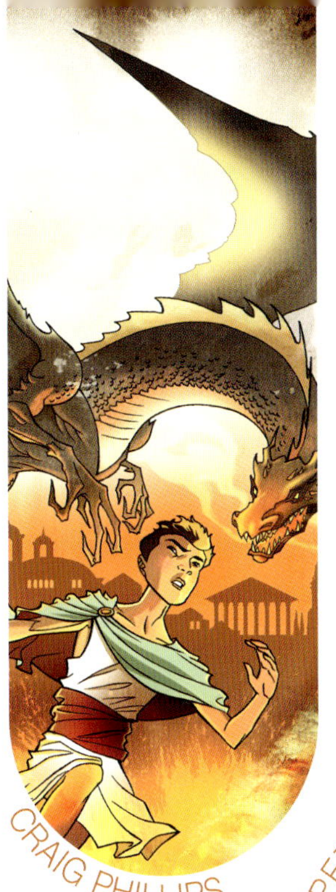

CRAIG PHILLIPS

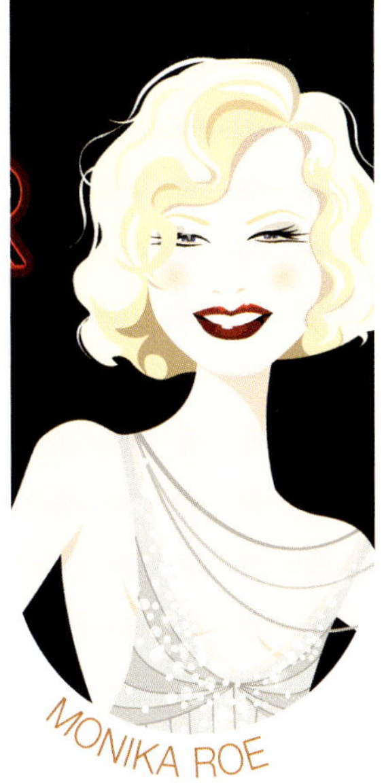

MONIKA ROE

PETER BOLLINGER

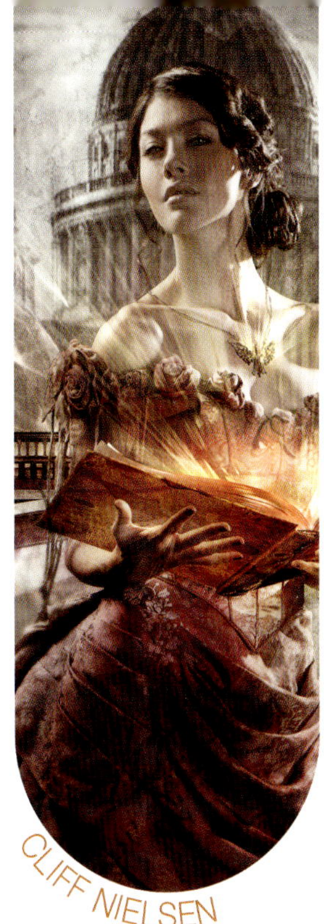

CLIFF NIELSEN

ERWIN MADRID

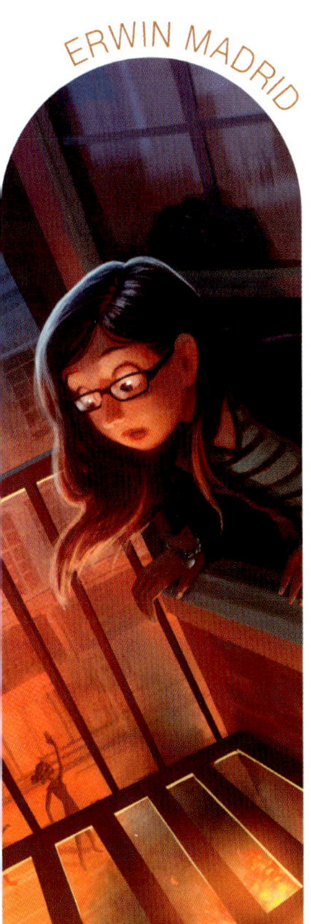

OWEN RICHARDSON

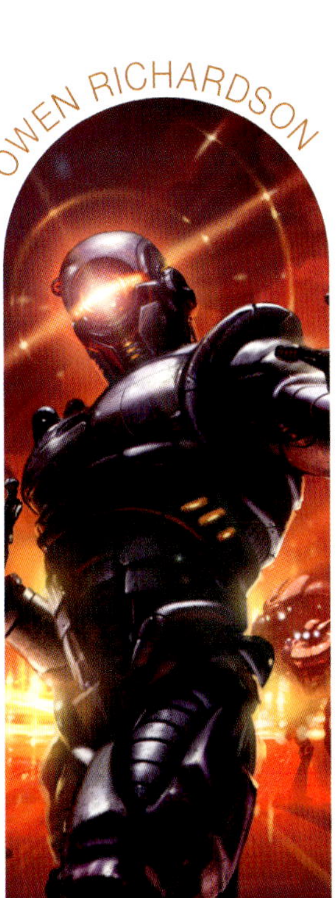

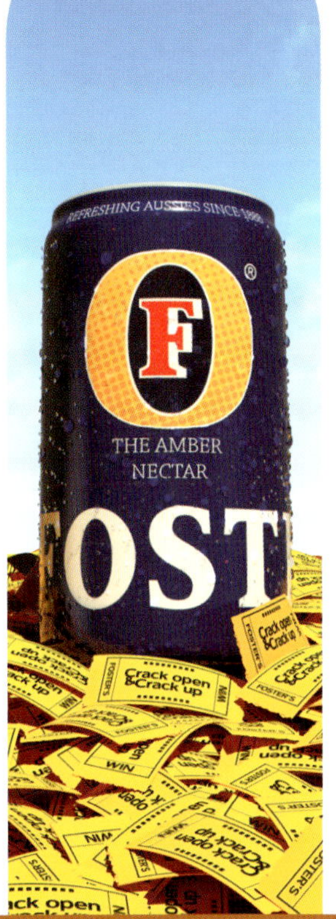

DAVE SEELEY

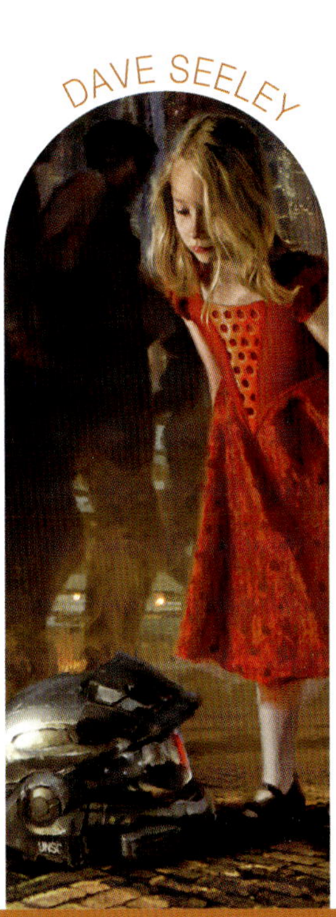

SHANNON ASSOCIATES
212.333.2551

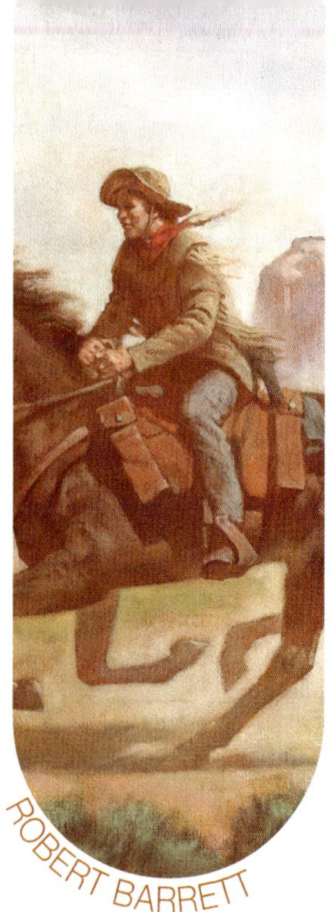

ROBERT BARRETT

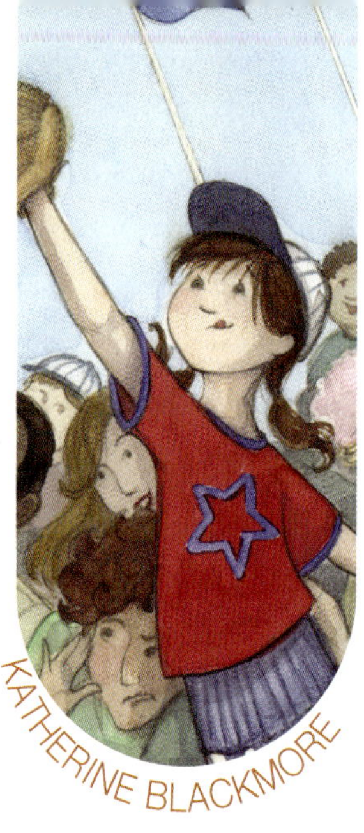

KATHERINE BLACKMORE

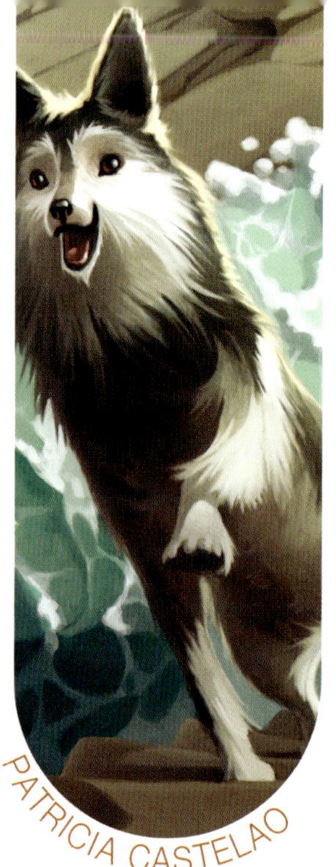

PATRICIA CASTELAO

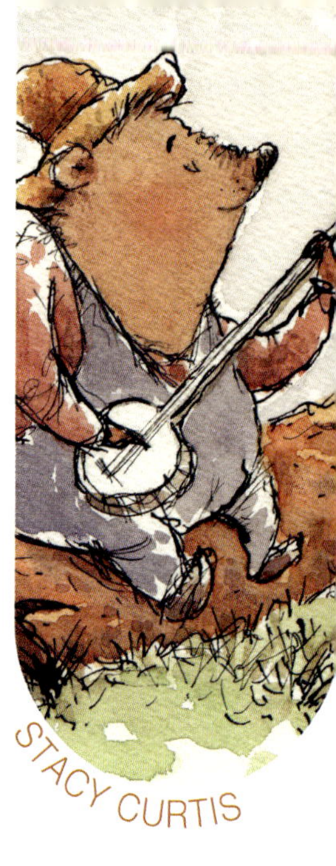

STACY CURTIS

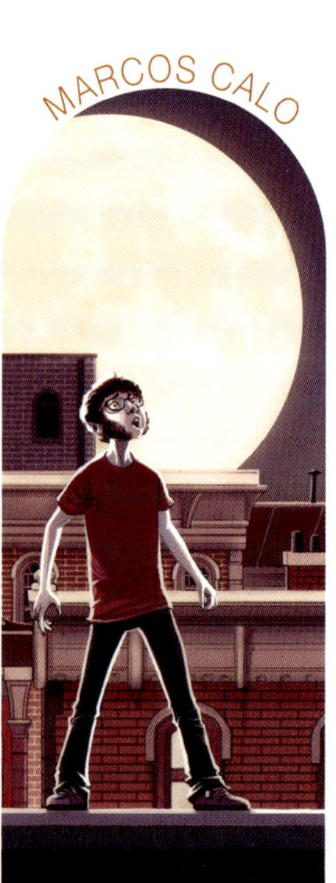

MARCOS CALO

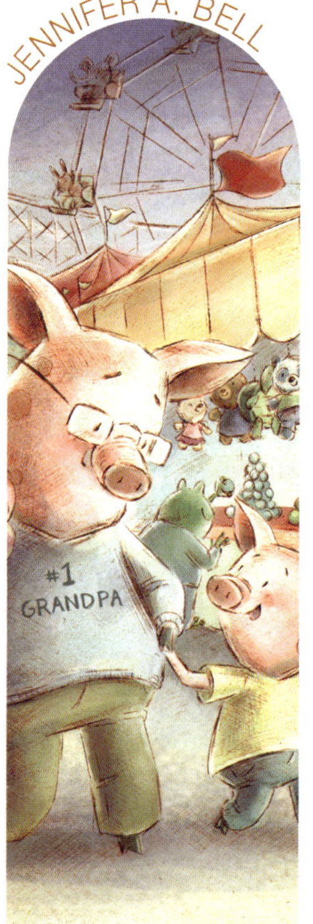

JENNIFER A. BELL

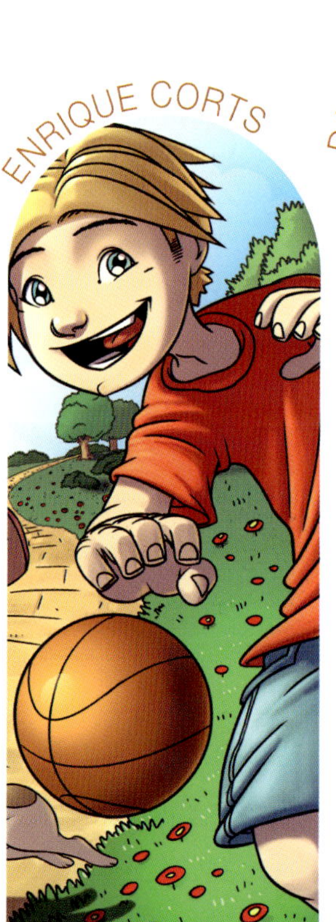

ENRIQUE CORTS

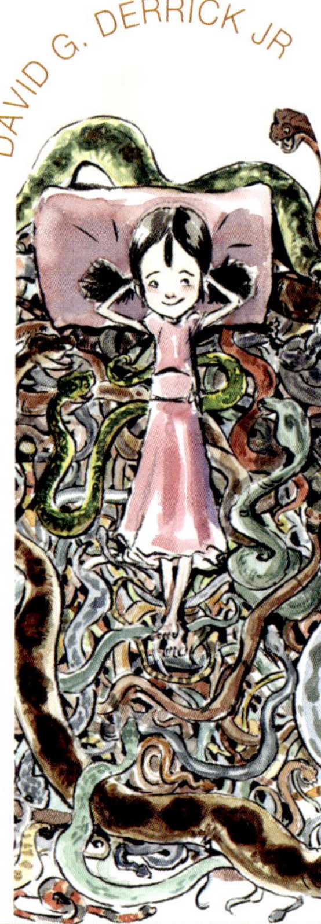

DAVID G. DERRICK JR

kidshannon.com

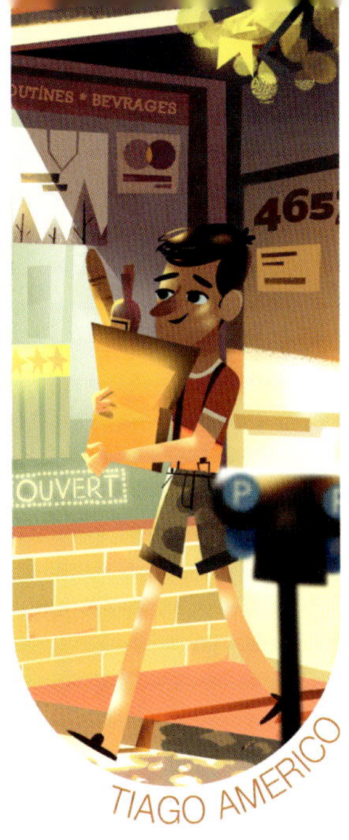

TIAGO AMERICO

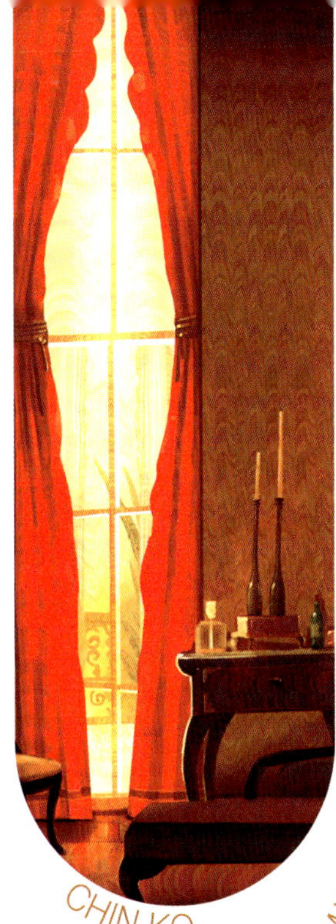

CHIN KO

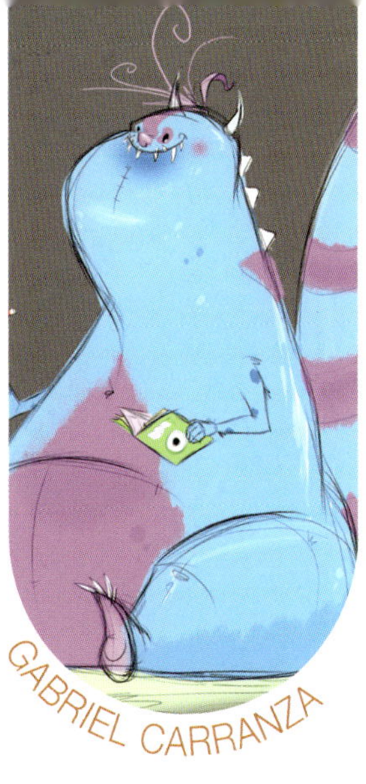

GABRIEL CARRANZA

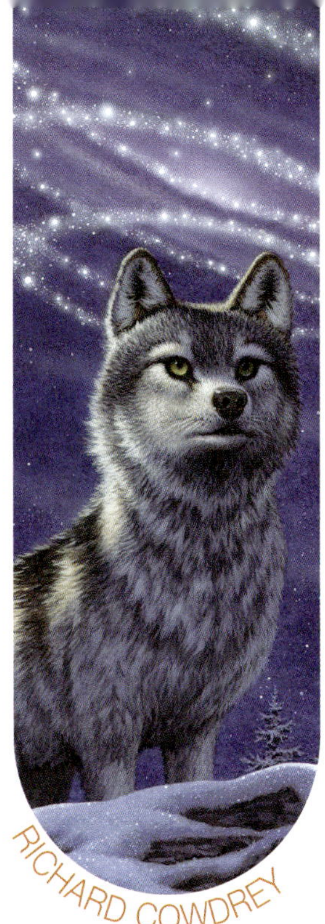

RICHARD COWDREY

STEPHEN GILPIN

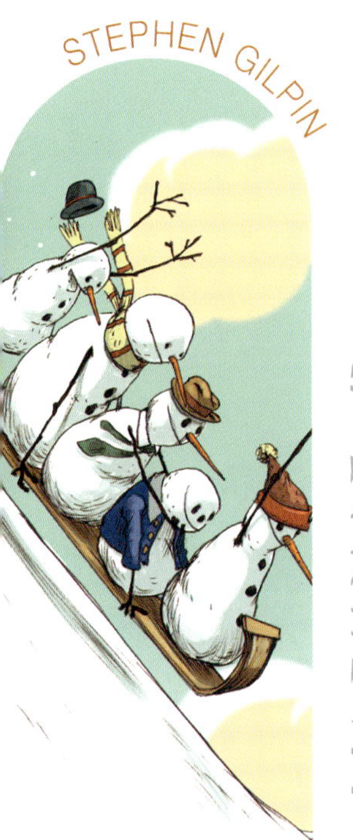

ERWIN HAYA

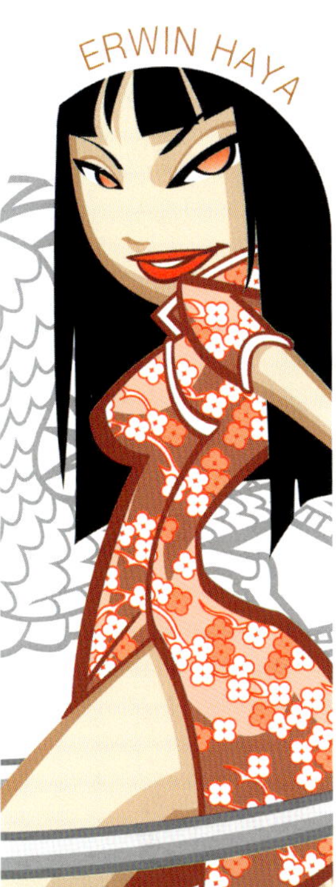

MICHELLE LAMOREAUX

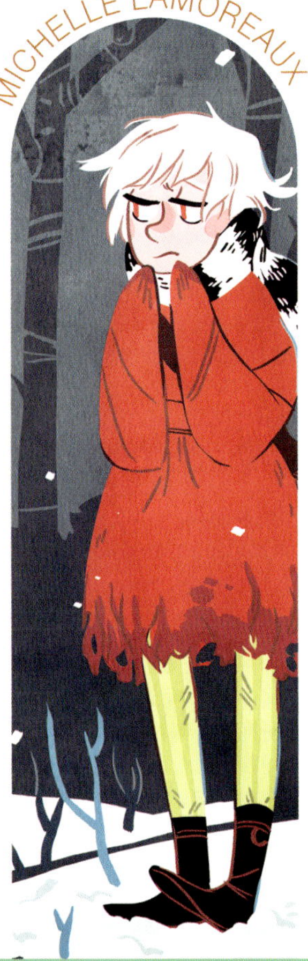

NATHAN HALE

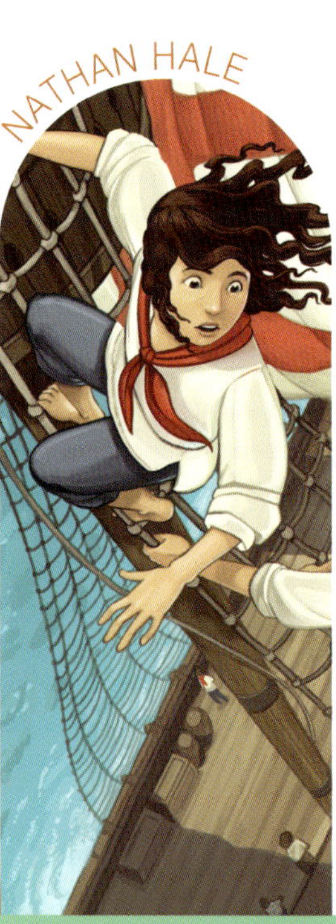

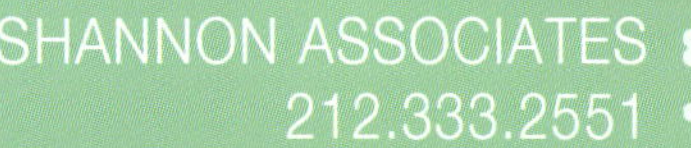

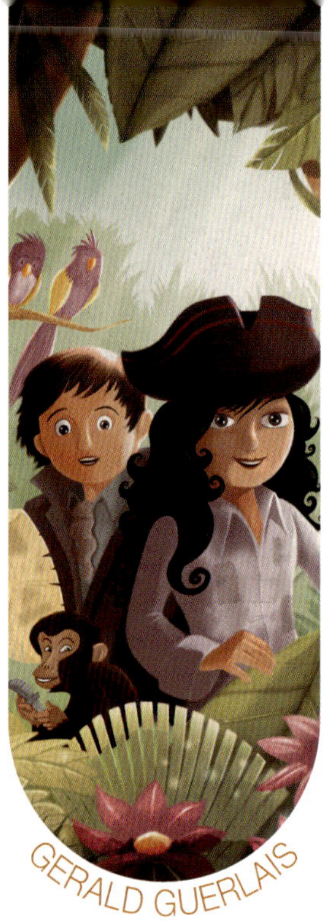

GERALD GUERLAIS

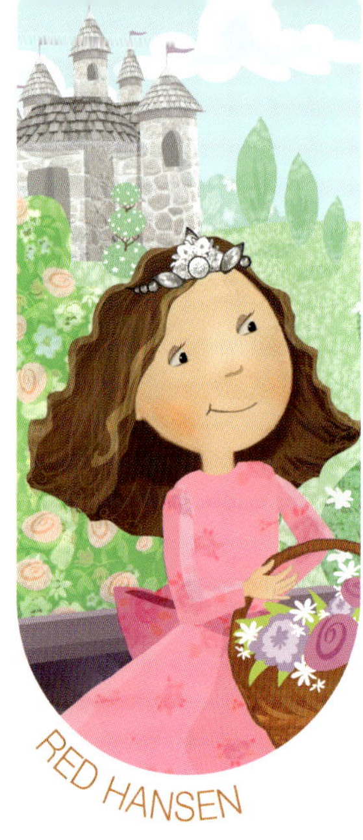

RED HANSEN

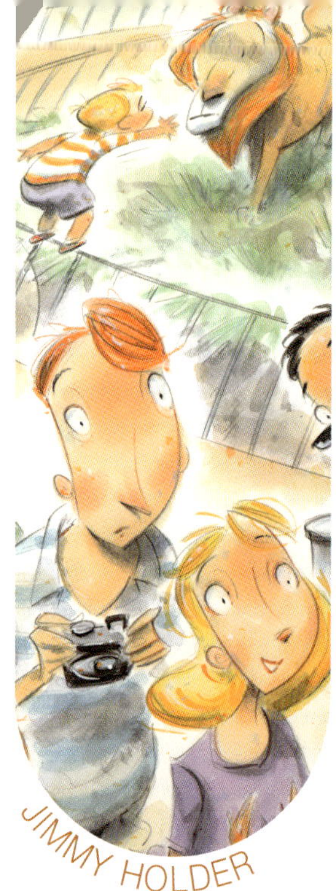

JIMMY HOLDER

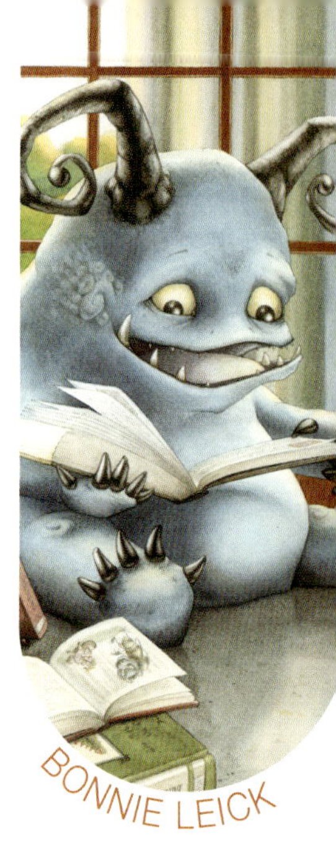

BONNIE LEICK

AMANDA HALEY

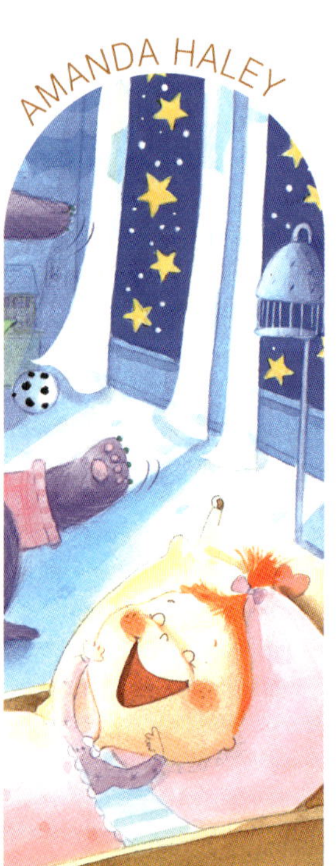

HOLLIE HIBBERT

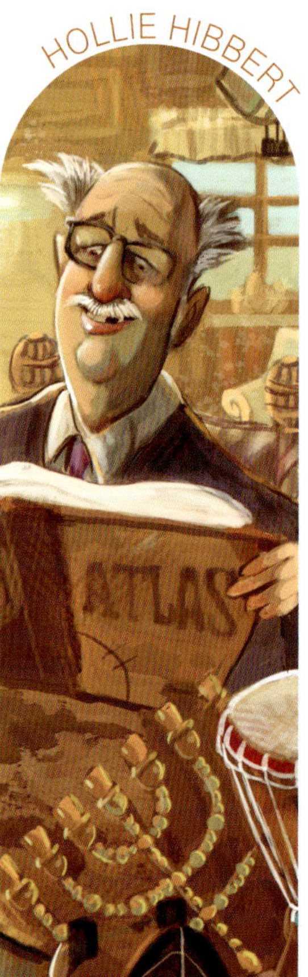

SHAHAR KOBER

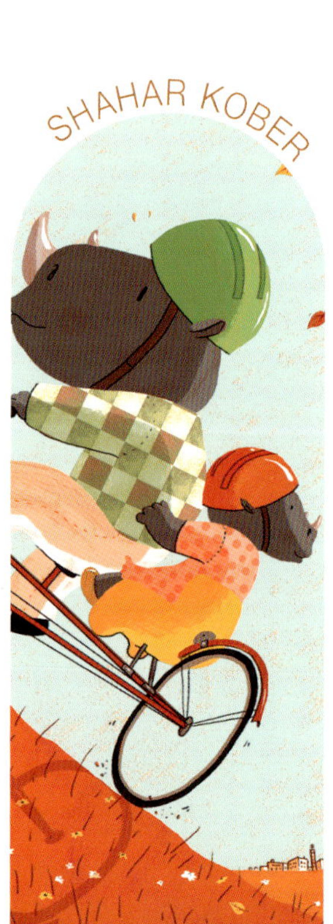

ARTHUR LIN

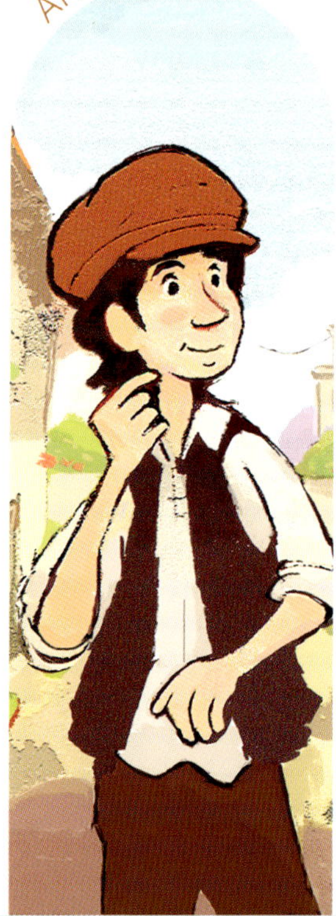

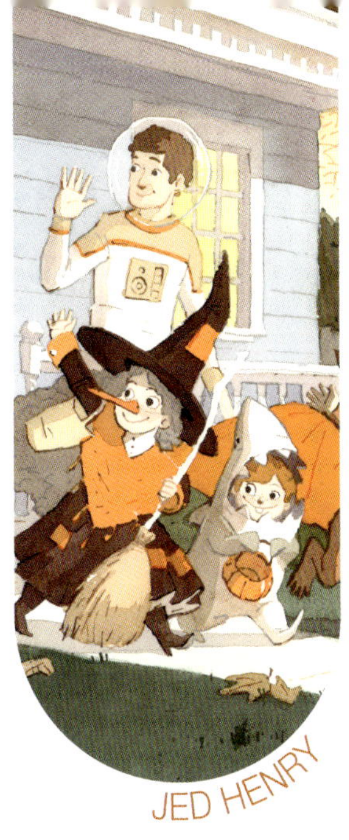

JED HENRY

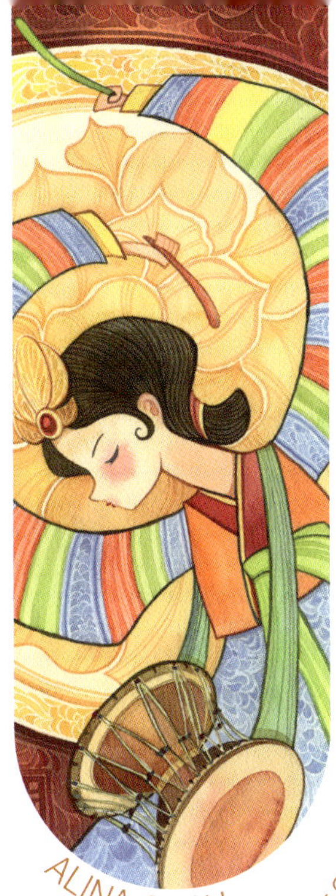

ALINA CHAU

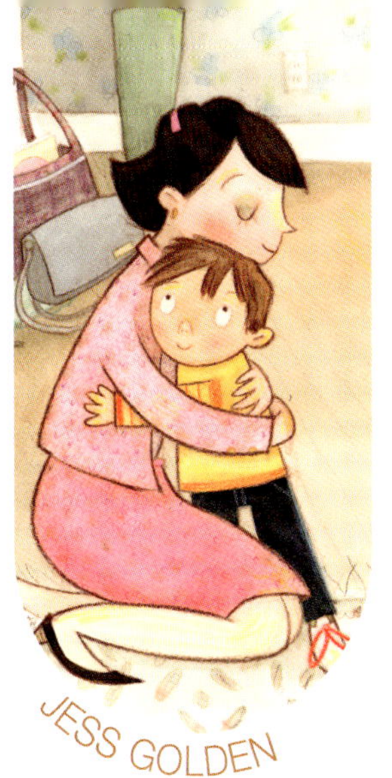

JESS GOLDEN

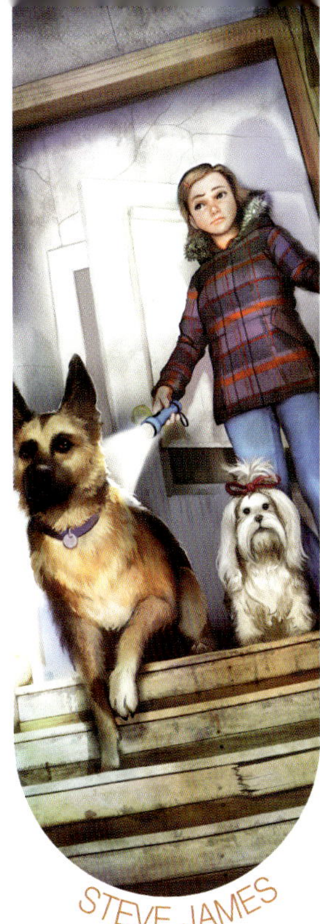

STEVE JAMES

AARON ZENZ

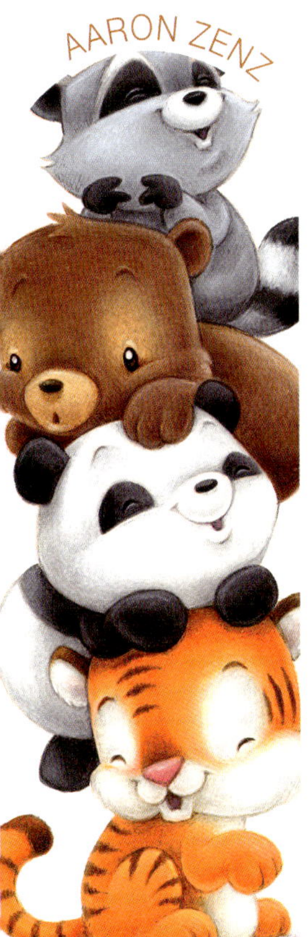

GUY FRANCIS

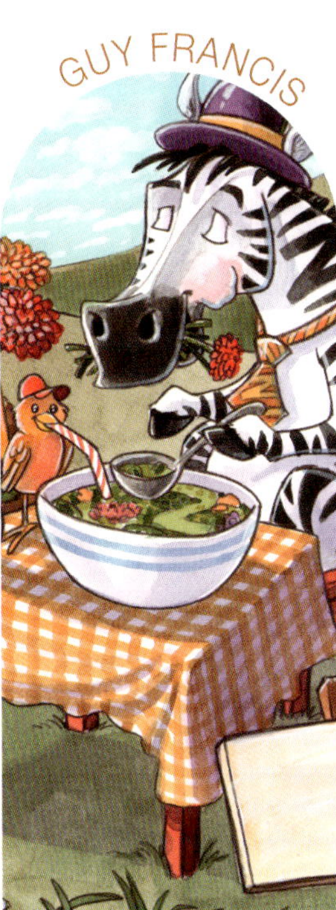

ALESSANDRA CIMATORIBUS

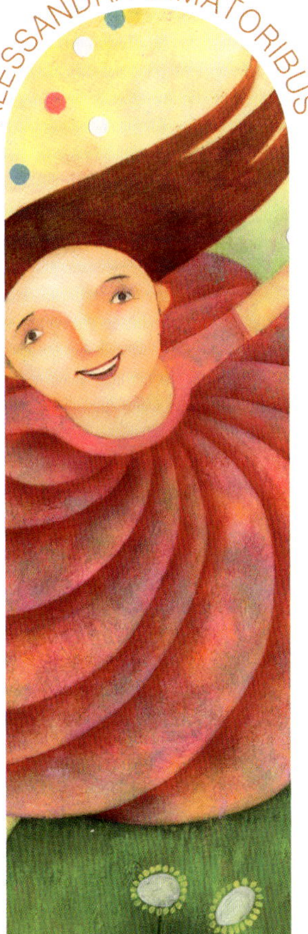

JENNIFER L. MEYER

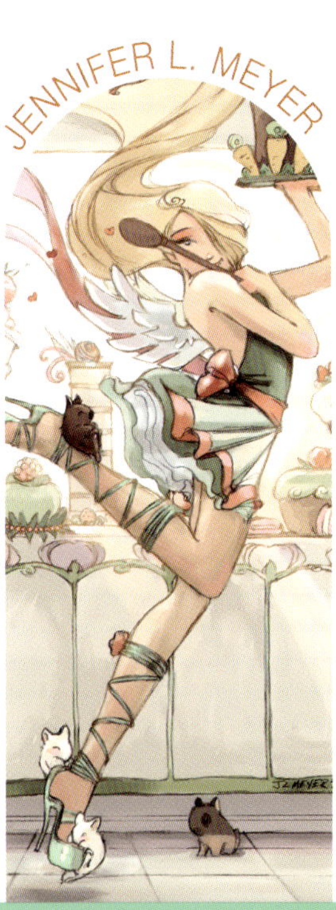

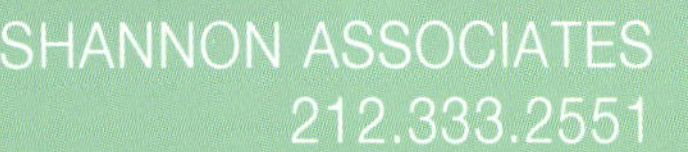

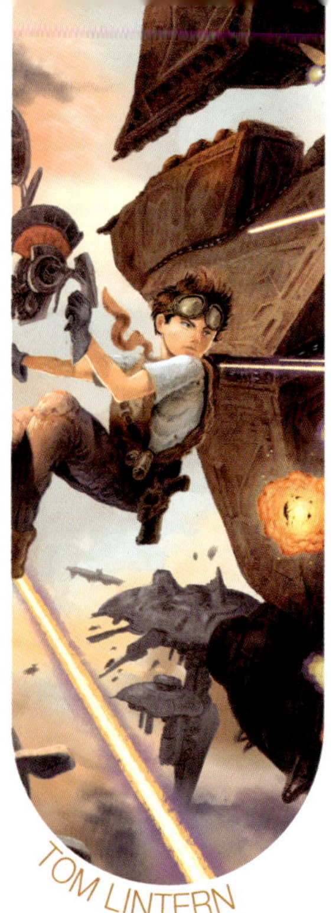

TOM LINTERN

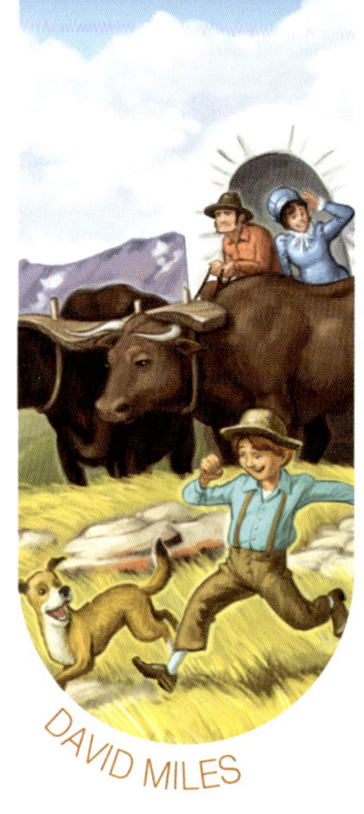

DAVID MILES

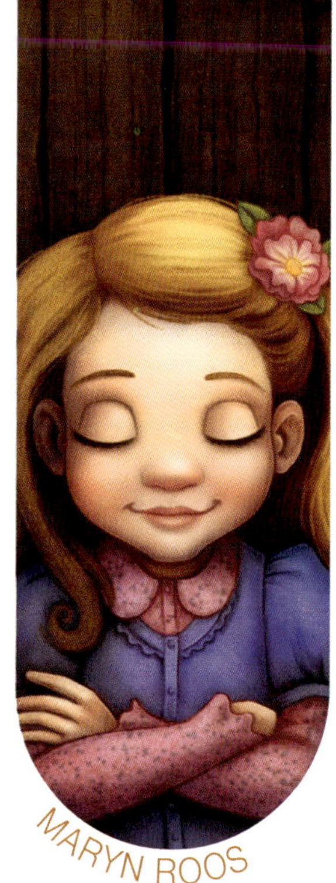

MARYN ROOS

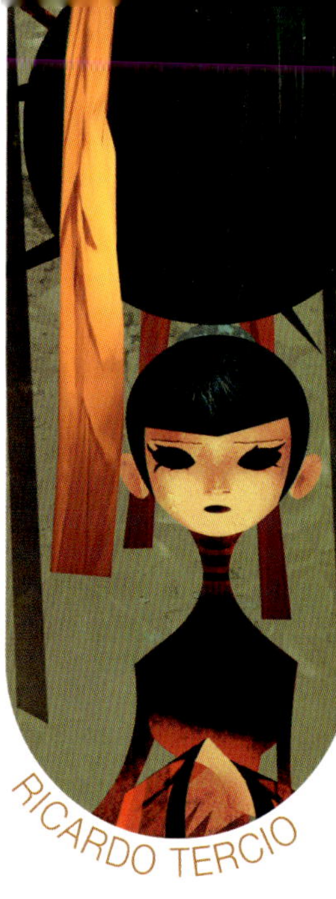

RICARDO TERCIO

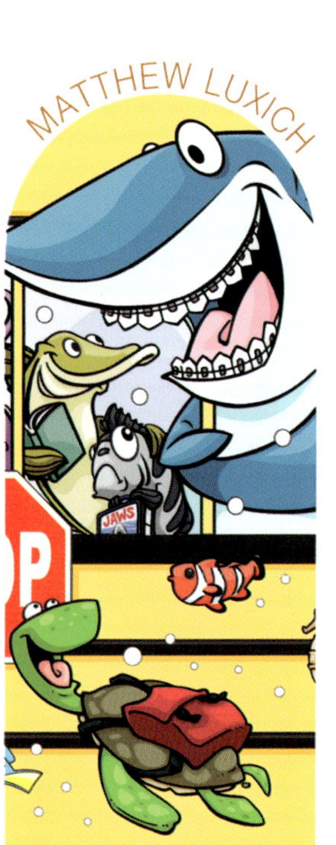

MATTHEW LUXICH

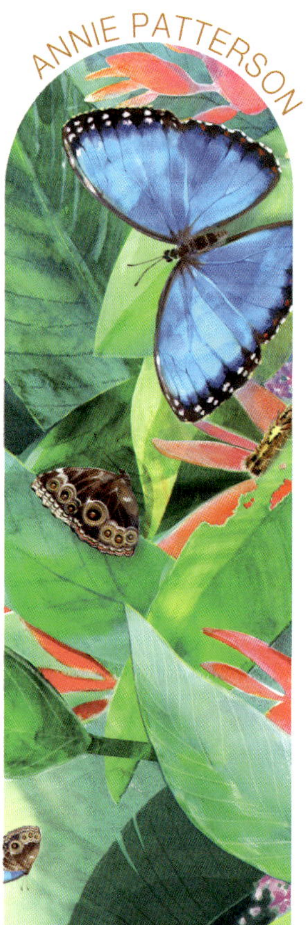

ANNIE PATTERSON

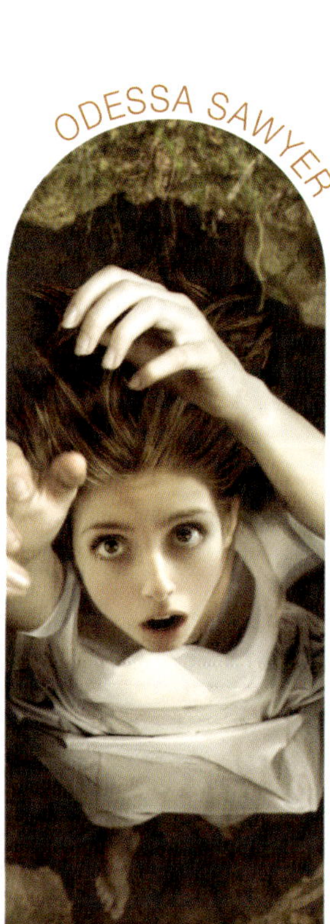

ODESSA SAWYER

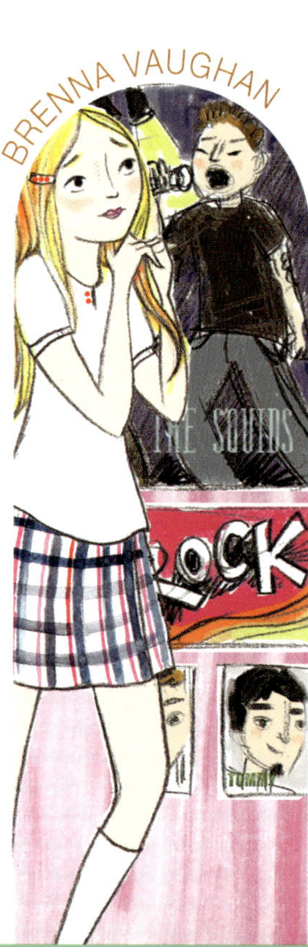

BRENNA VAUGHAN

kidshannon.com

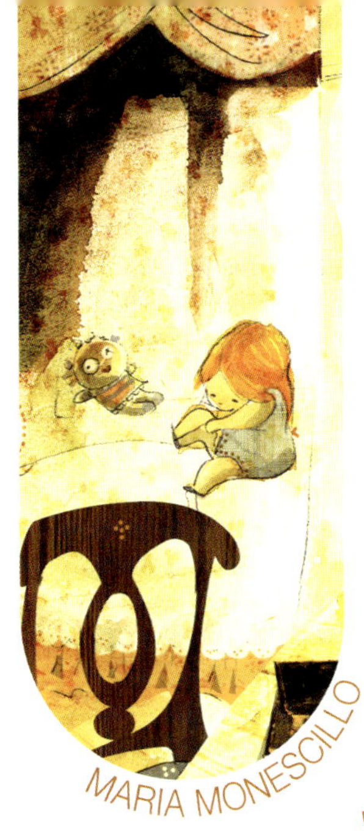

MARIA MONESCILLO

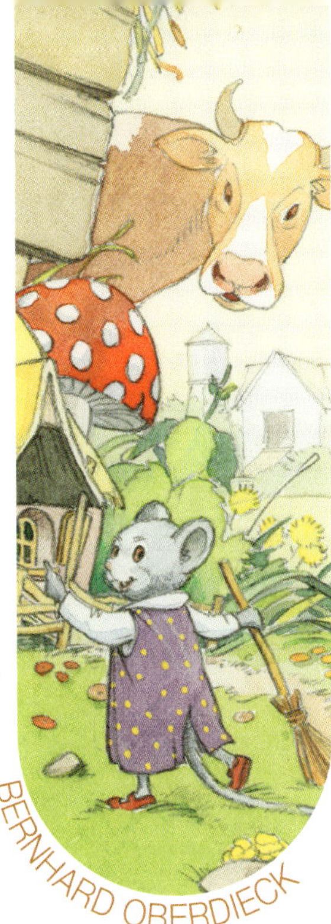

BERNHARD OBERDIECK

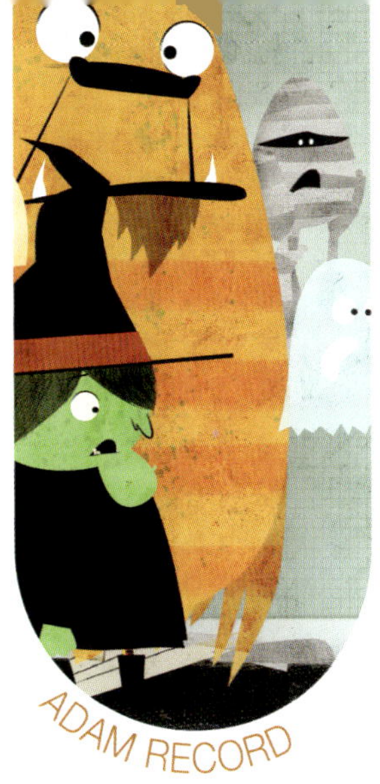

ADAM RECORD

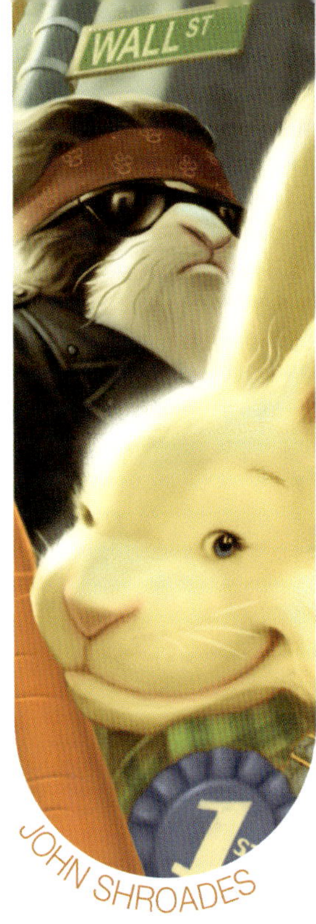

JOHN SHROADES

JULISSA MORA

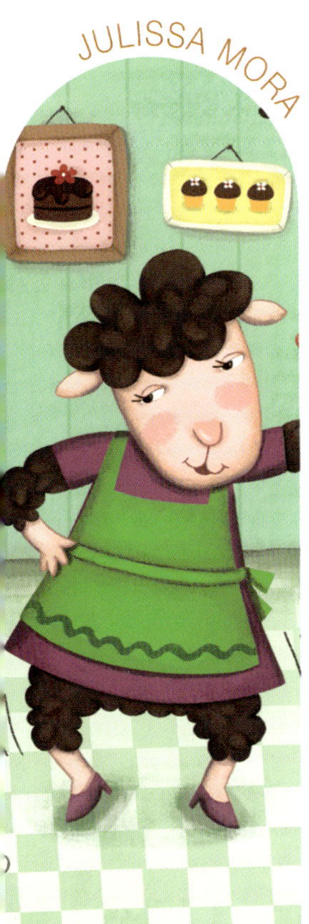

JIMMY PICKERING

VICTOR RIVAS

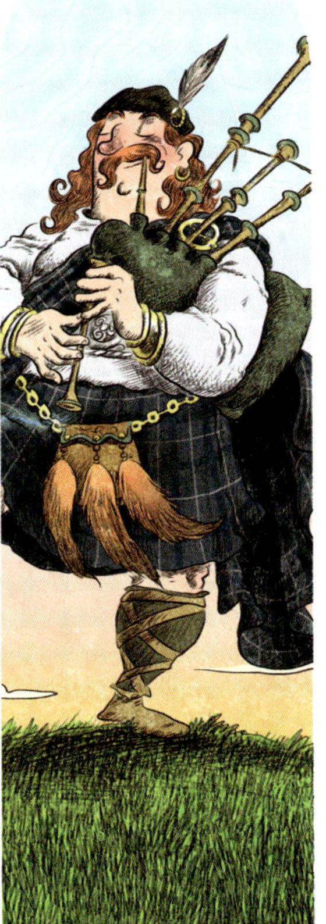

RYAN WOOD

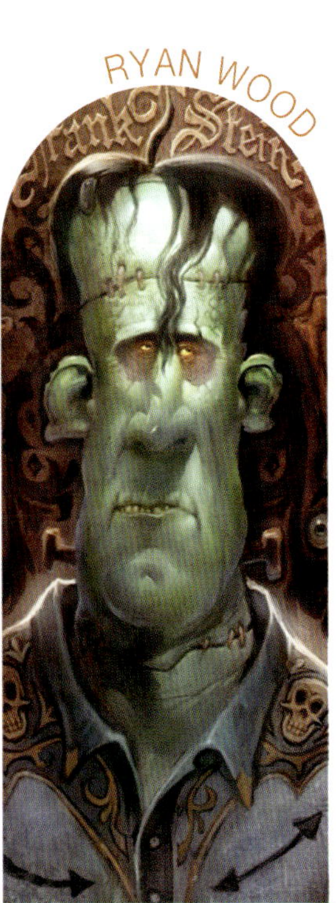

MICHAEL GLENWOOD

www.mglenwood.com   michael@mglenwood.com   **888.818.9811**

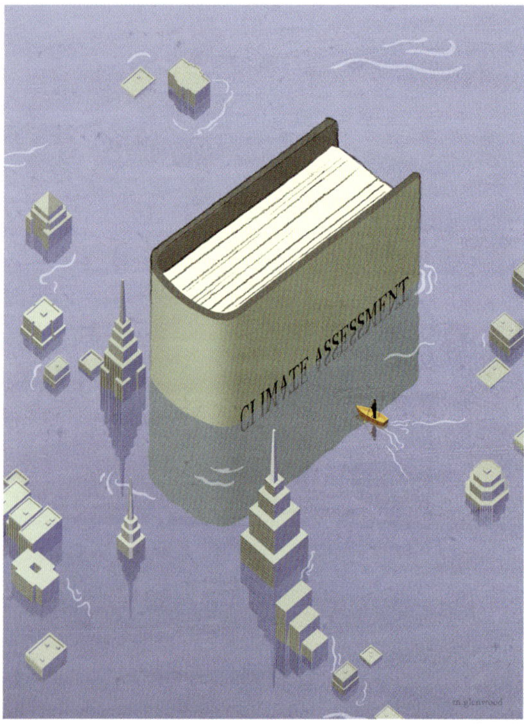

Federal Climate Assessment: Out of Date and a Little Too Late (Again)
Scientific American Magazine

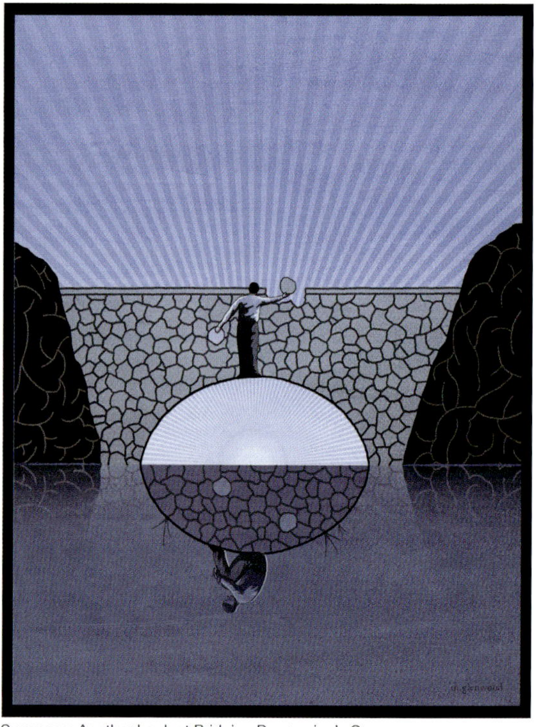

Synapses: Another Look at Bridging Depression's Gap
New Scientist Magazine

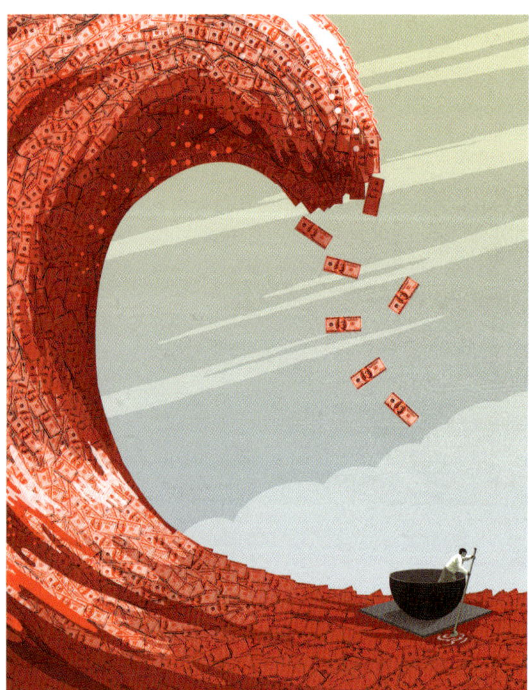

The Rising Tide of Student Debt
American Federation of Teachers

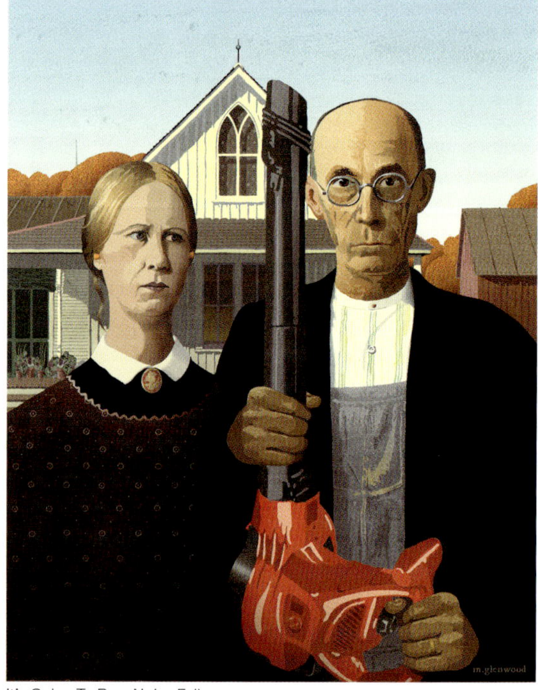

It's Going To Be a Noisy Fall
Blown Covers

AMY WUMMER

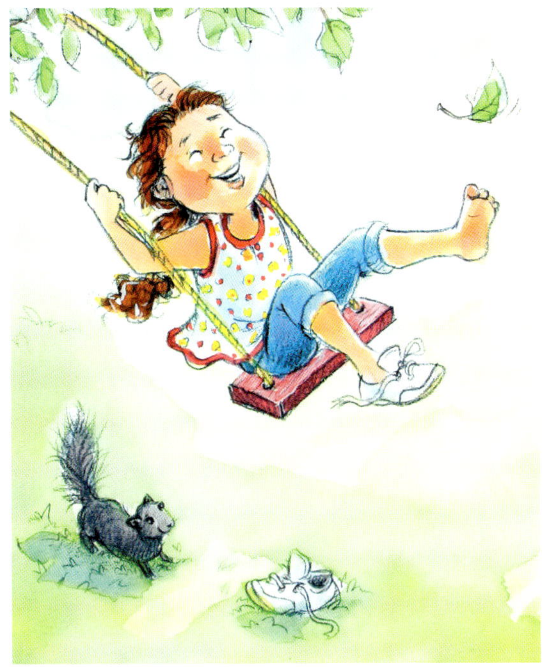

LAURA WATSON

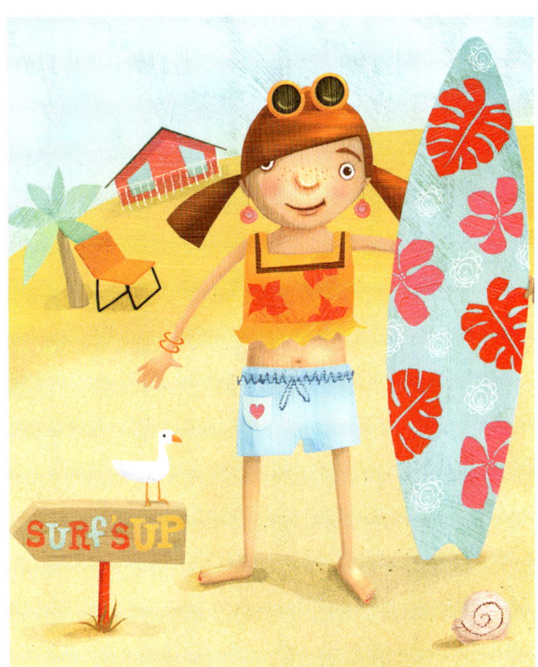

JESSE REISCH

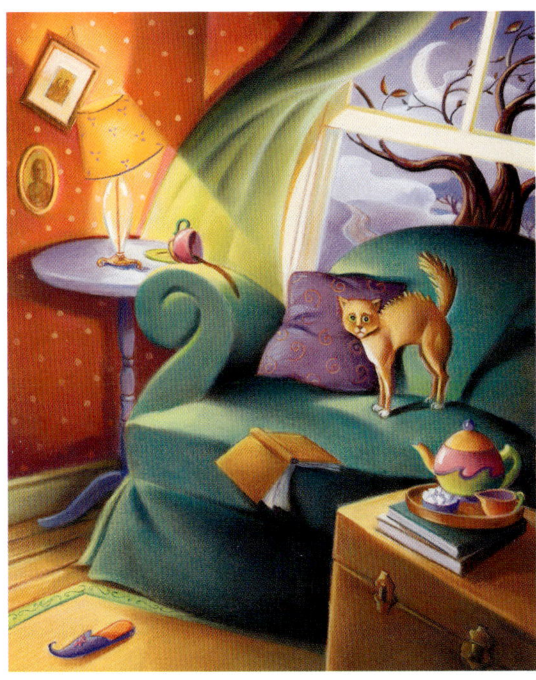

NATHALIE BEAUVOIS

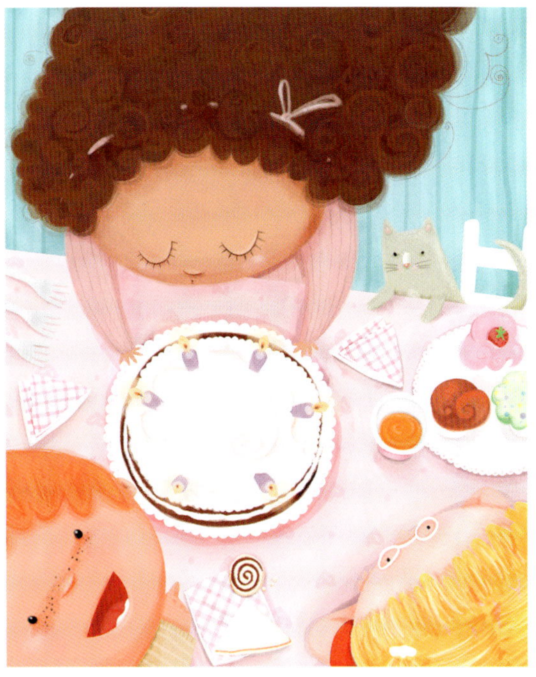

215.232.6666   **illustration**OnLine.com   DEBORAH WOLFE LTD

ROBIN BOYER

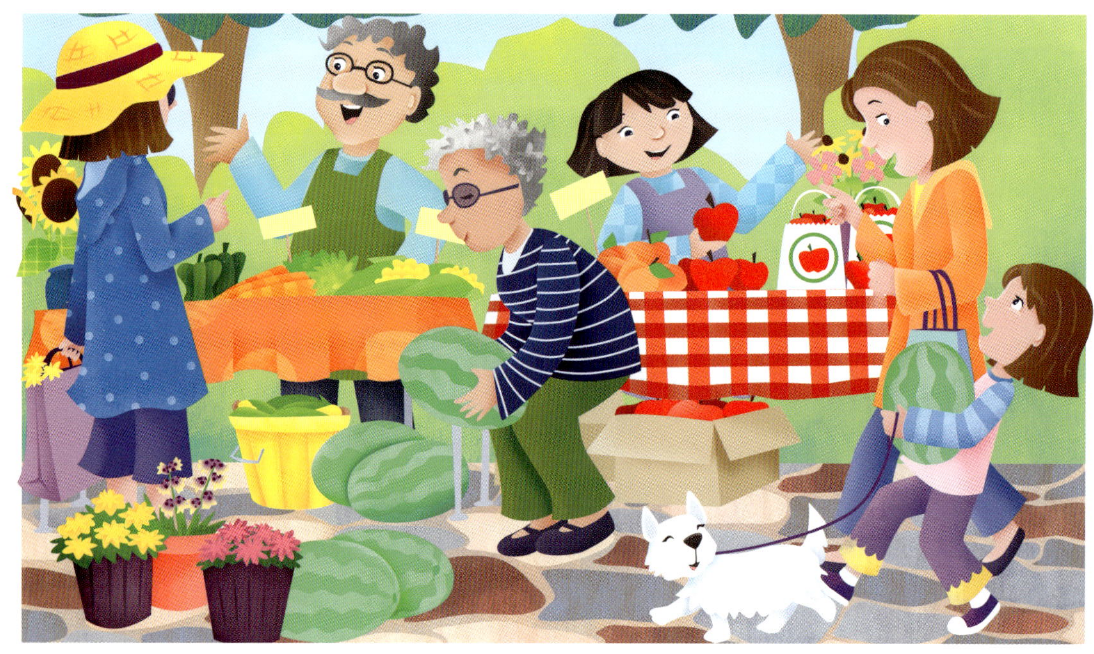

DAN MCGEEHAN

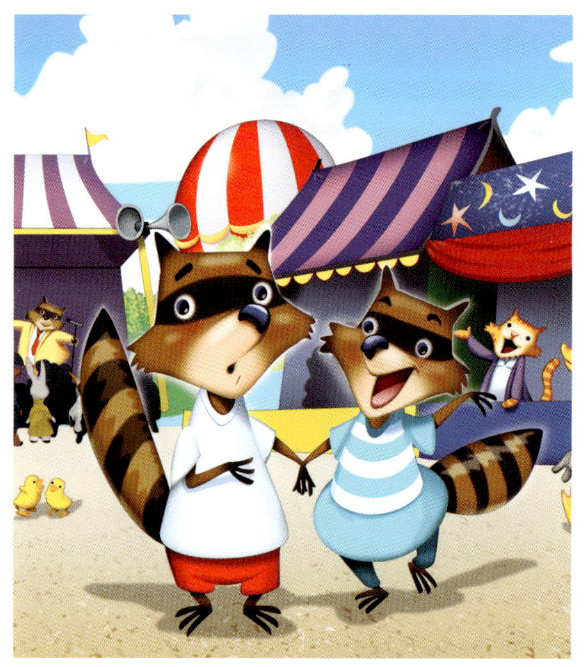

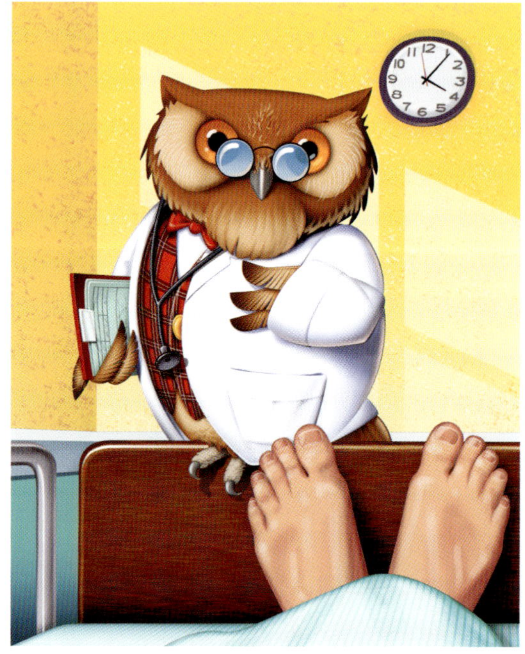

BOB KAYGANICH

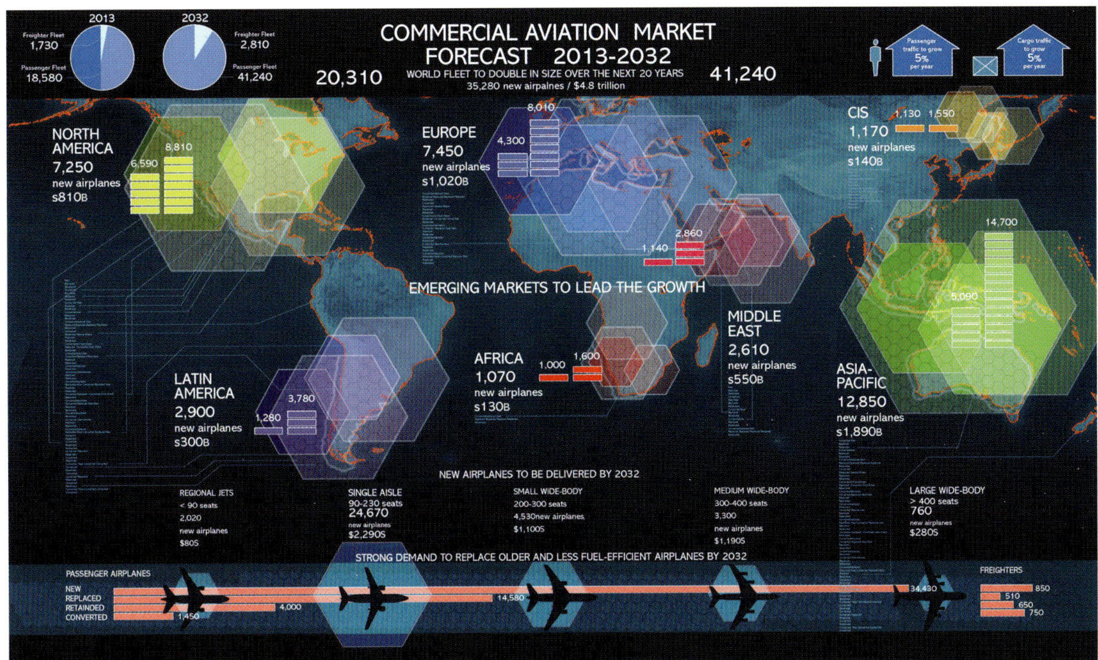

RALPH VOLTZ

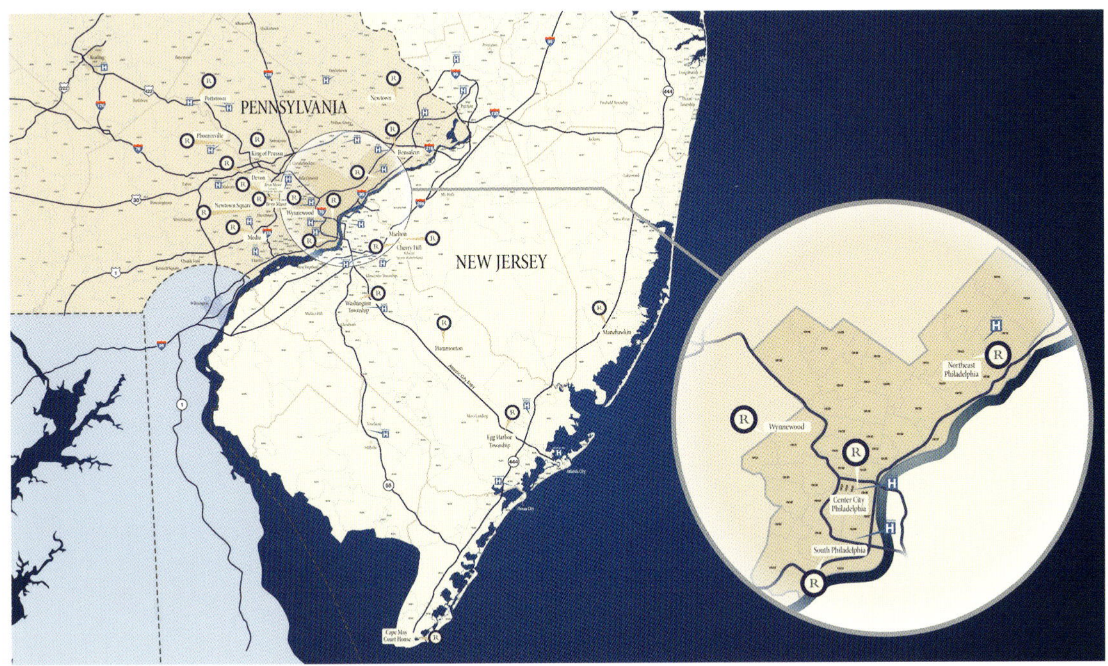

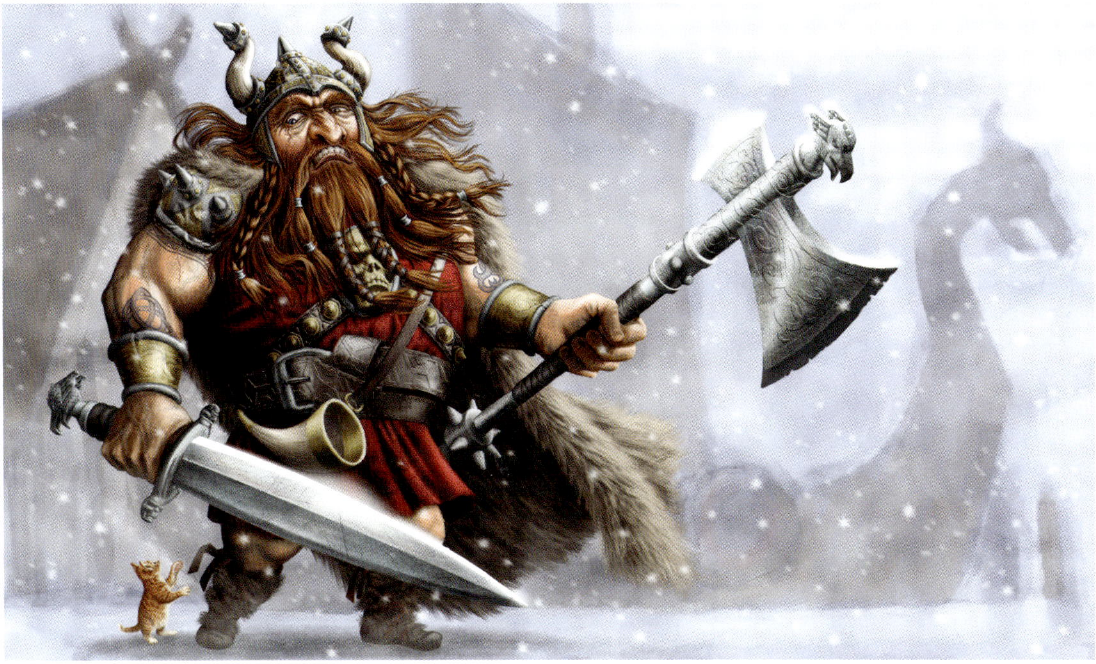

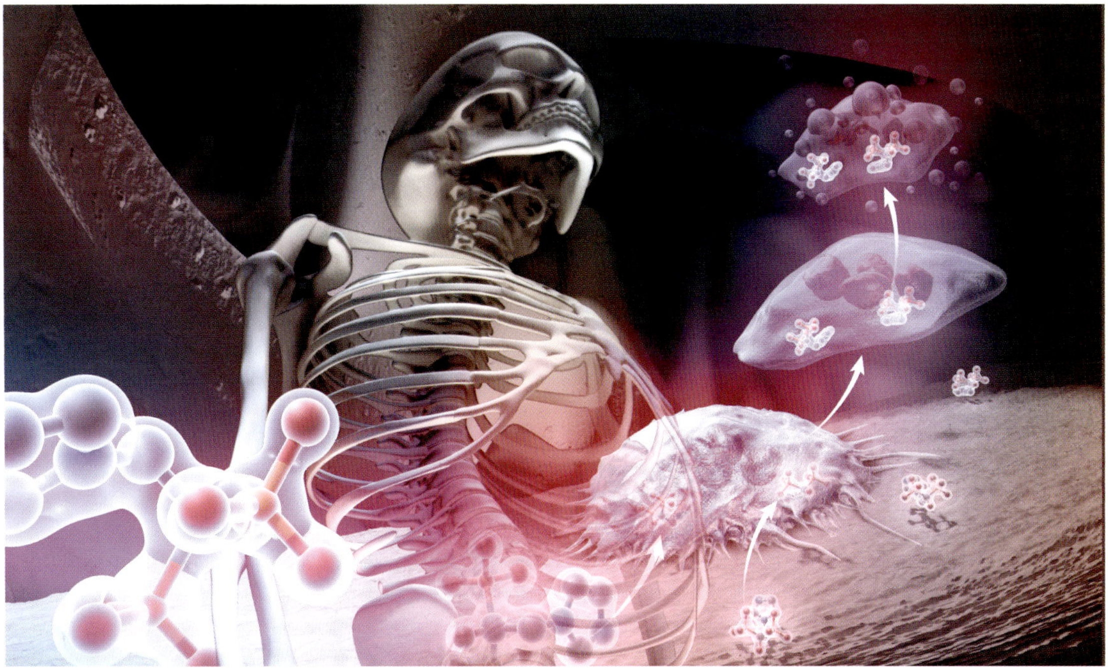

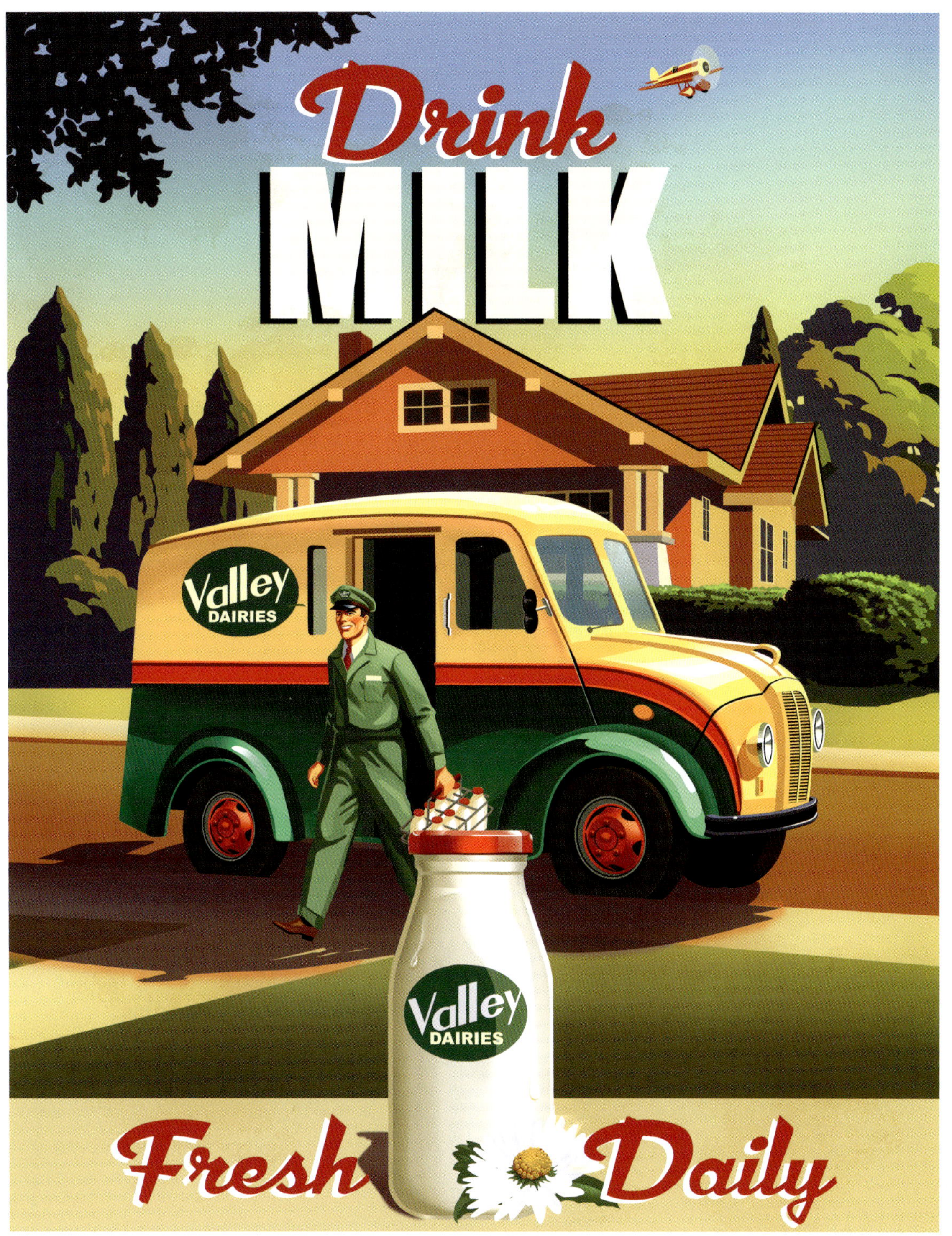

Drink
MILK
Valley
DAIRIES
Valley
DAIRIES
Fresh Daily
DAVID MOORE
215.232.6666
illustrationOnLine.com
DEBORAH WOLFE LTD

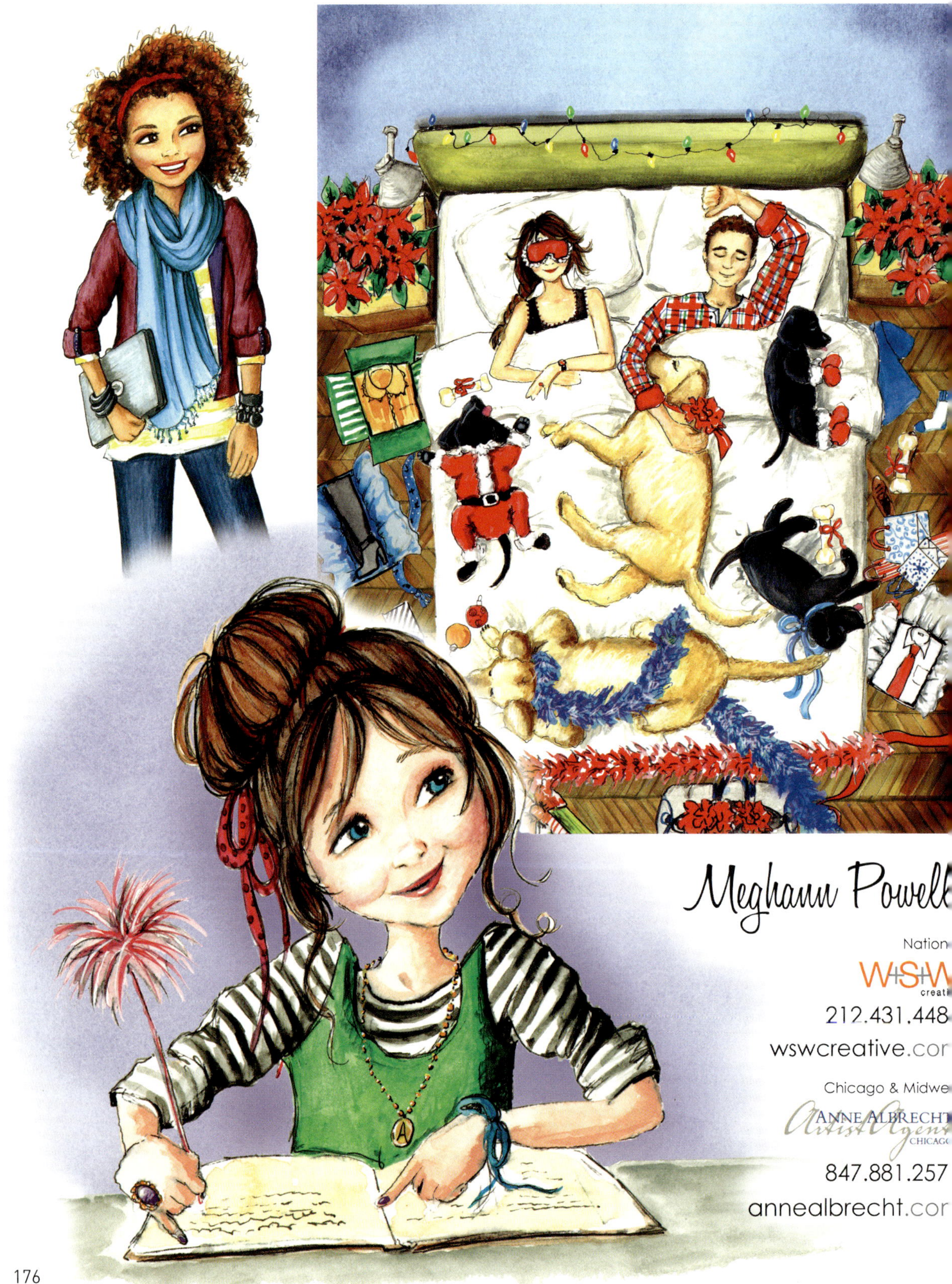

Meghann Powell
Nation
W+S+W
creati
212.431.448
wswcreative.cor
Chicago & Midwe
ANNE ALBRECHT
CHICAGO
847.881.257
annealbrecht.cor

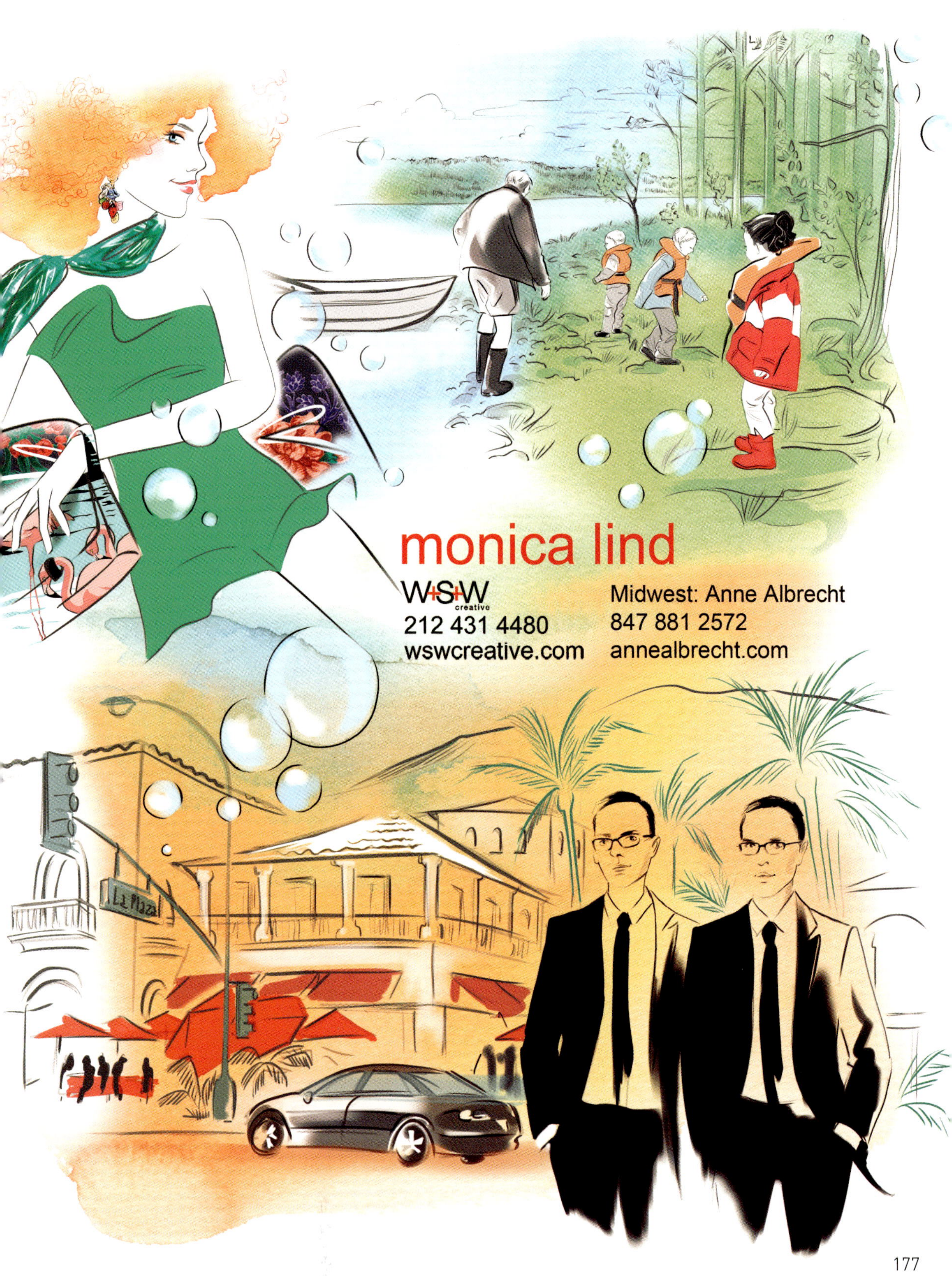
monica lind
W+S+W
creative
212 431 4480
wswcreative.com
Midwest: Anne Albrecht
847 881 2572
annealbrecht.com
La Plaza

LILLA ROGERS STUDIO

PHONE NO. **781.641.2787**

WEB **WWW.LILLAROGERS.COM**

Representing artists internationally

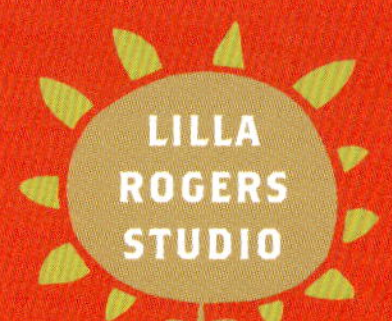

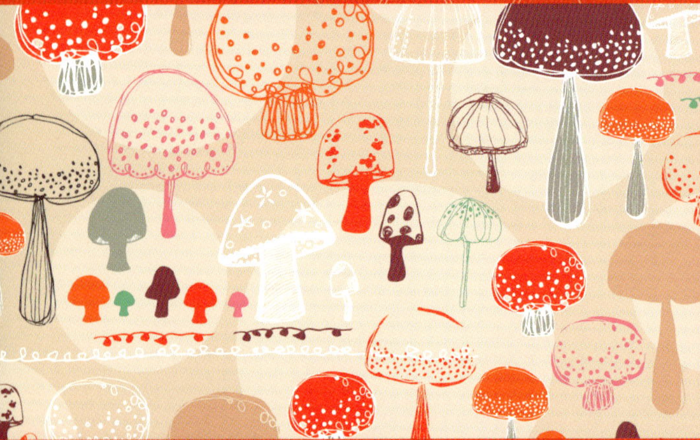

RACHAEL TAYLOR

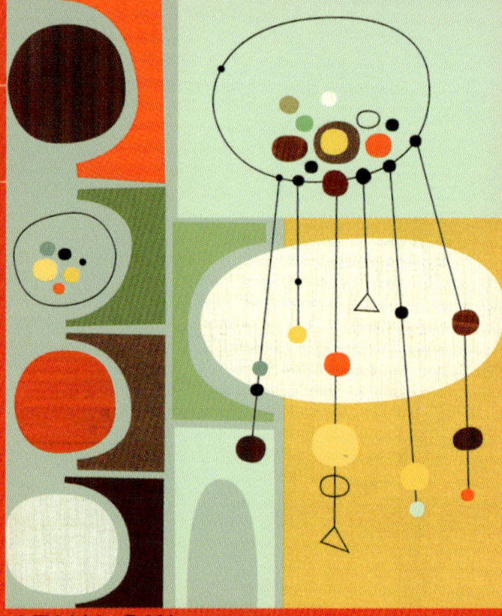

JENN SKI

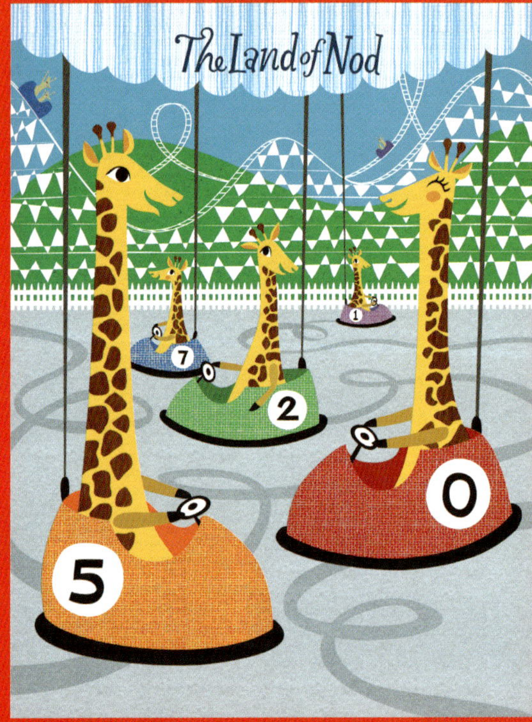

LISA DEJOHN

MIKE LOWERY

Land of Nod • Disney • Warner Bros. • Kellogg's • Always • Allure Magazine • Target • Chronicle • NY Public Library Children's Room Mural • Godiva • Nordstrom • Macy's •

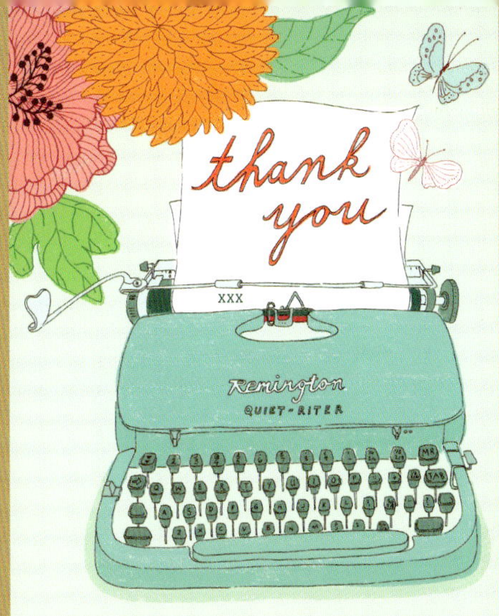

TRINA DALZIEL

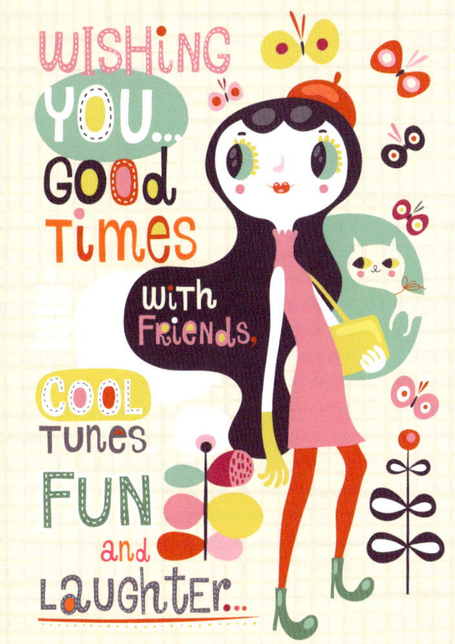

HELEN DARDIK

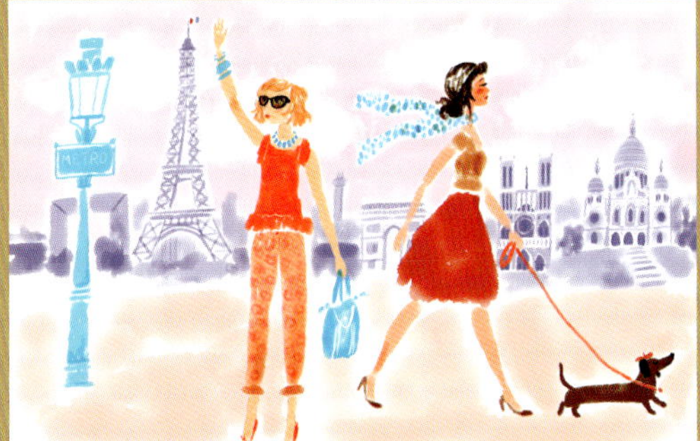

TALITHA SHIPMAN

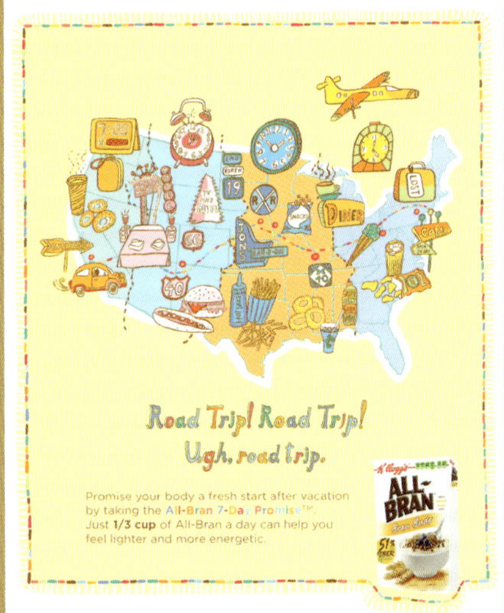

SARAJO FREIDEN

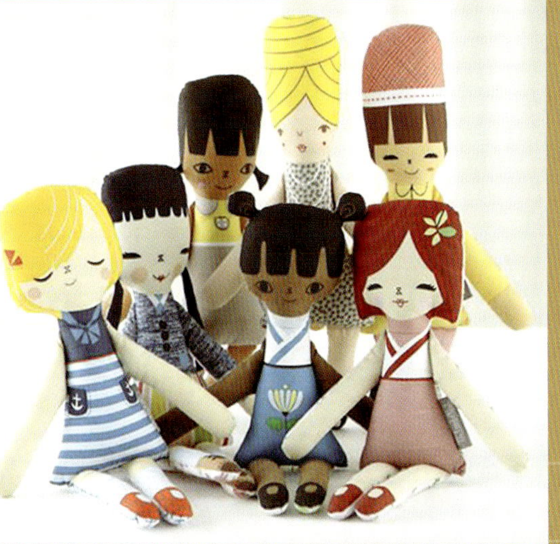

UZY ULTMAN

Barneys New York • Crate & Barrel • Blue Q • Conde Nast • Fisher Price • Urban Outfitters • IKEA • Hallmark • American Express • Bloomingdale's •

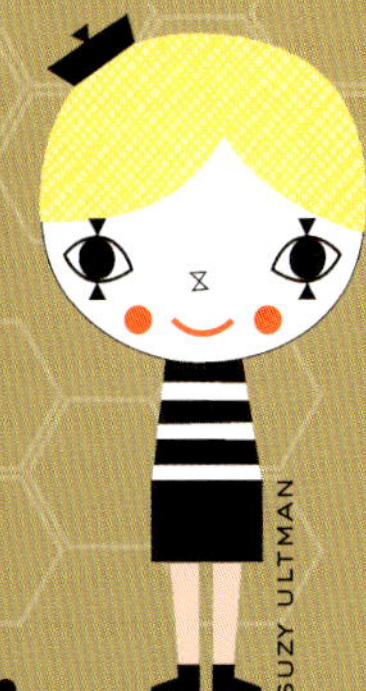

LILLA ROGERS STUDIO

PHONE NO. 781.641.2787

WEB WWW.LILLAROGERS.COM

Representing artists internationally

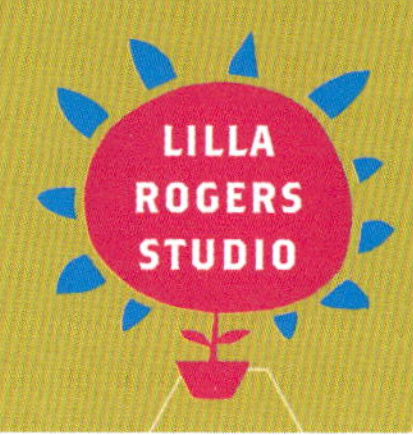

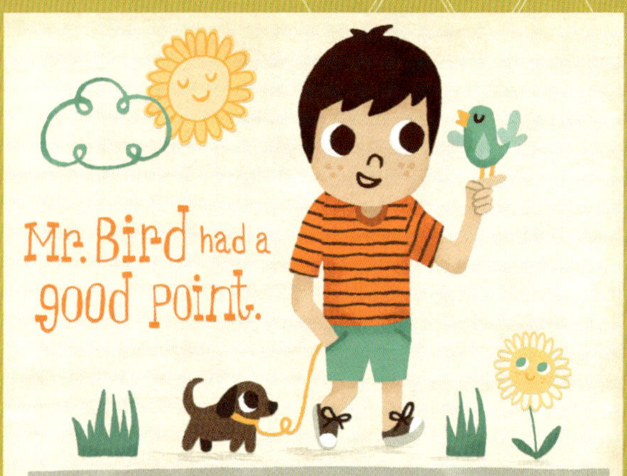

ALLISON COLE

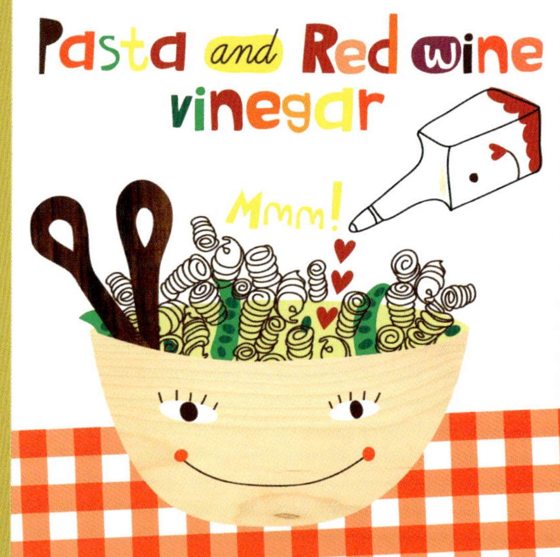

CAROLYN GAVIN

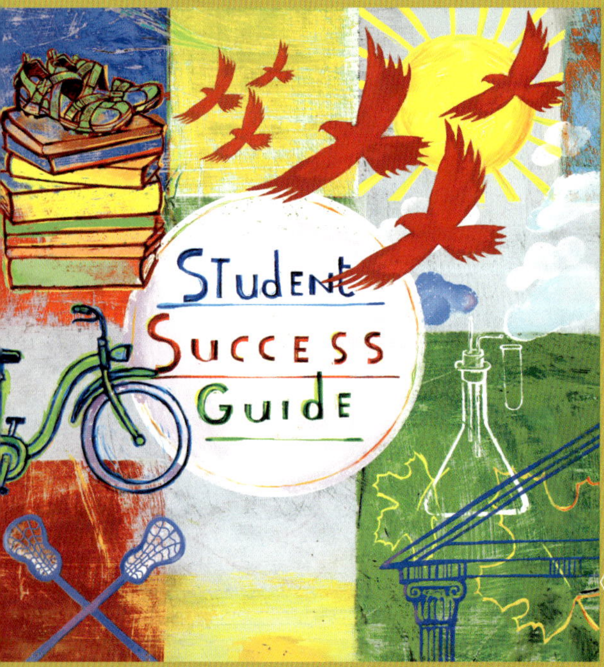

MARCO MARELLA

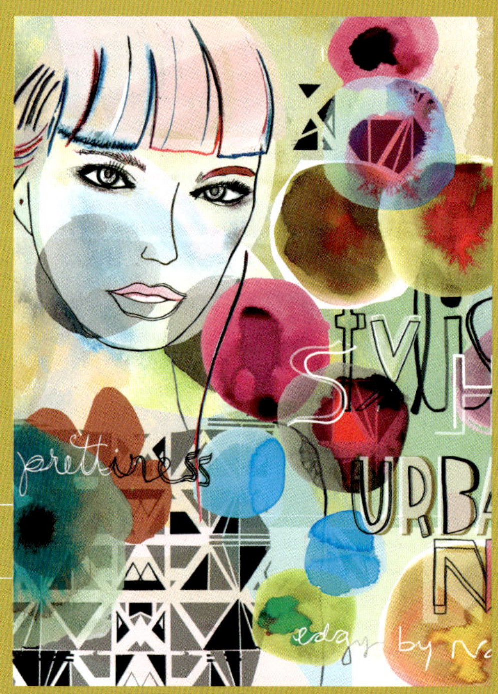

LINDA KETELHUT

Bergdorf Goodman • Cranium Games • German Elle • Mattel • Takashimaya • Suntory Japan •
Viacom • Klutz • Old Navy • SC Johnson • Young & Rubicam • Warner Bros. • Leo Burnett

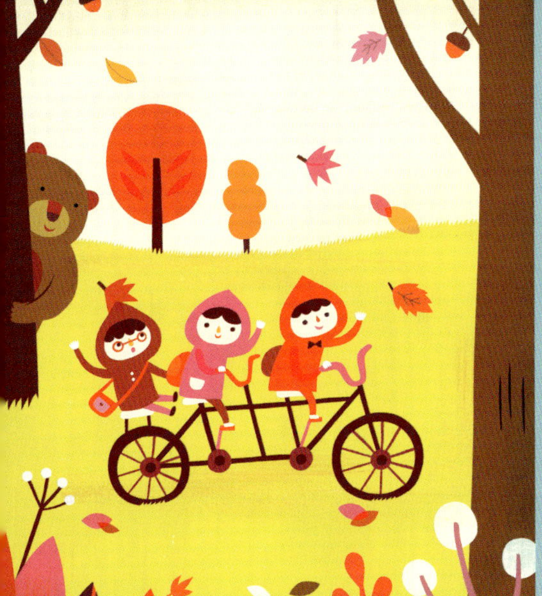

SINPING PAN

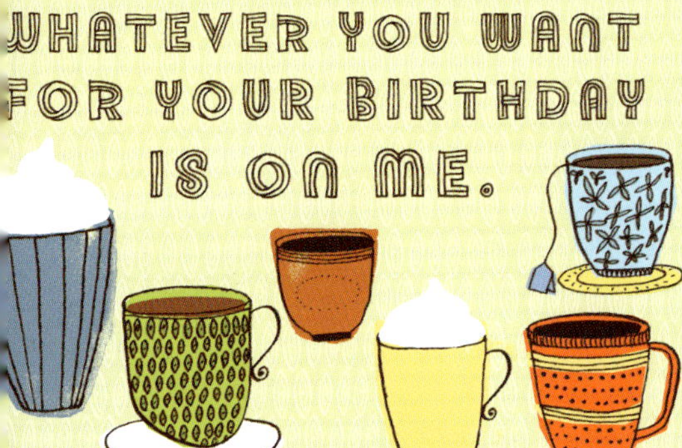

ON CANNELL

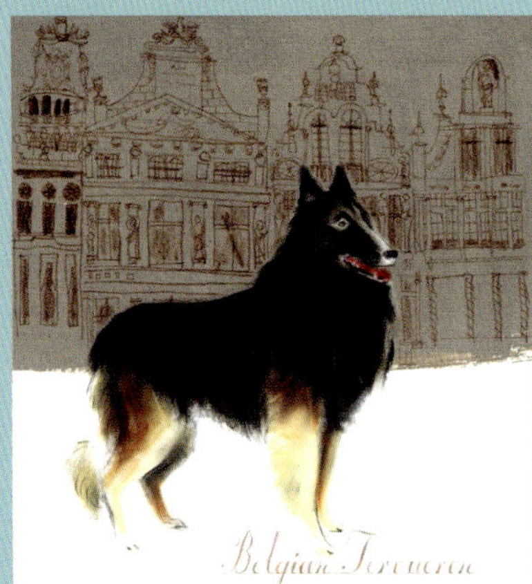

ANN BOYAJIAN

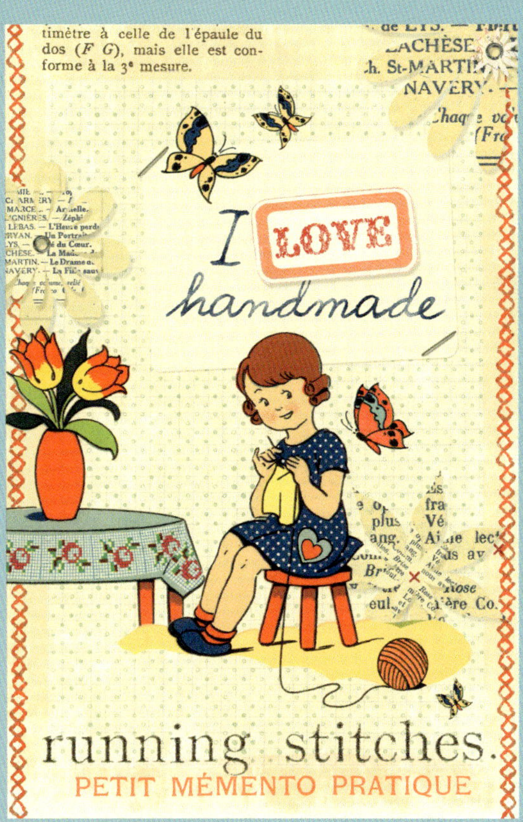

MACRINA BUSATO

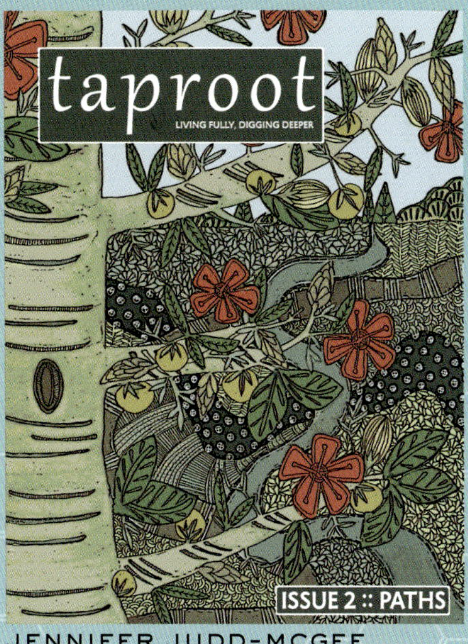

JENNIFER JUDD-MCGEE

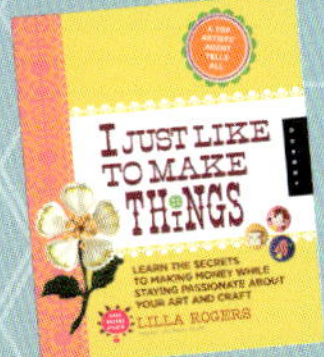

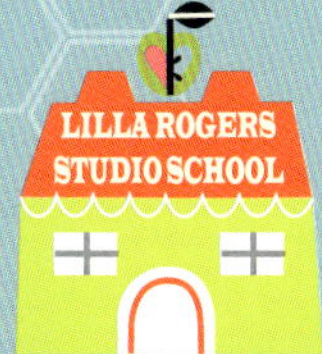

ashi Frozen Entrees • Art for a watertower in Albuquerque
All-Bran cereal print ads & packaging • Millions of products

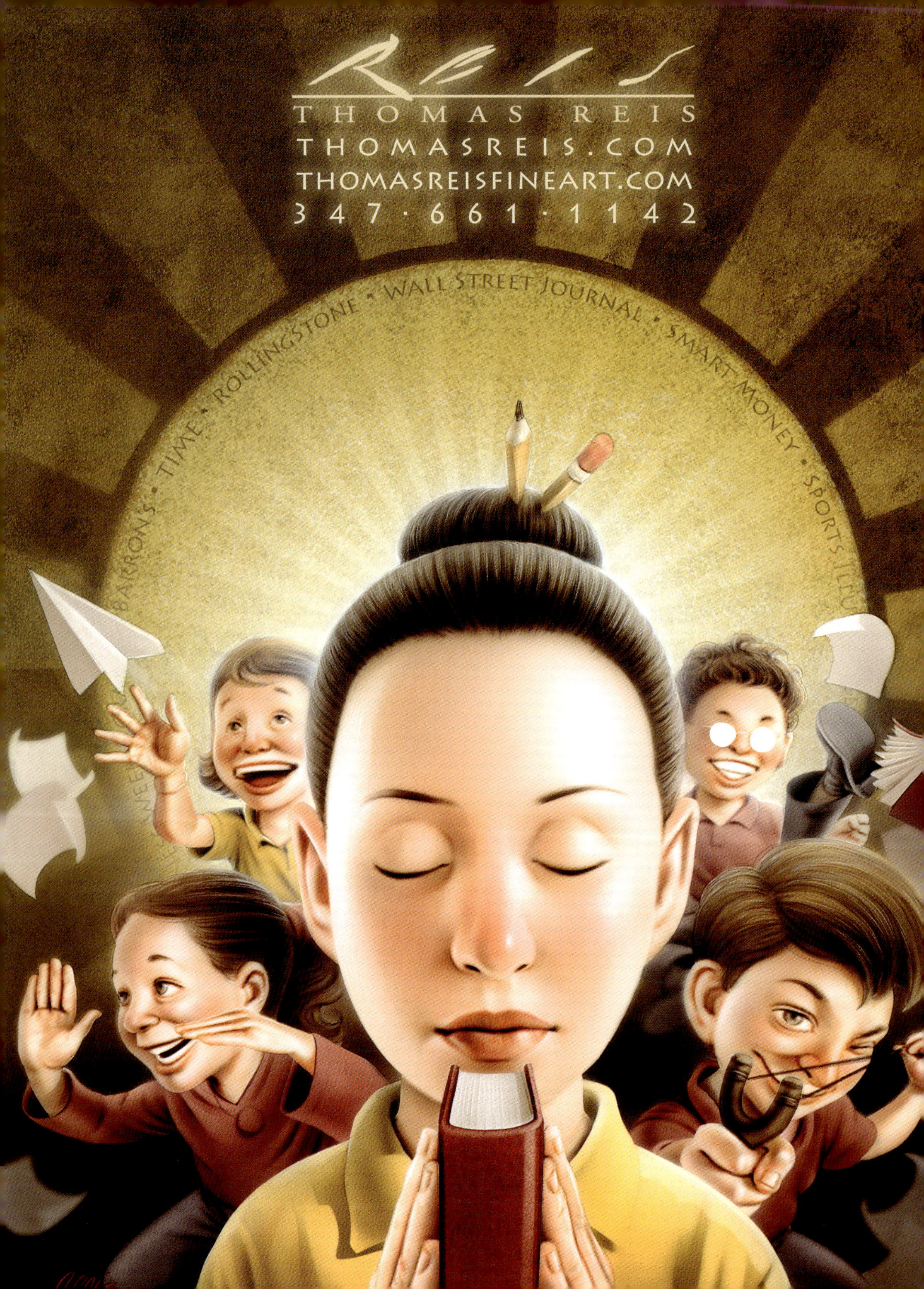
REIS
THOMAS REIS
THOMASREIS.COM
THOMASREISFINEART.COM
347·661·1142
ROLLINGSTONE · WALL STREET JOURNAL · SMART MONEY
BARRONS · TIME
SPORTS
NEWSWEEK

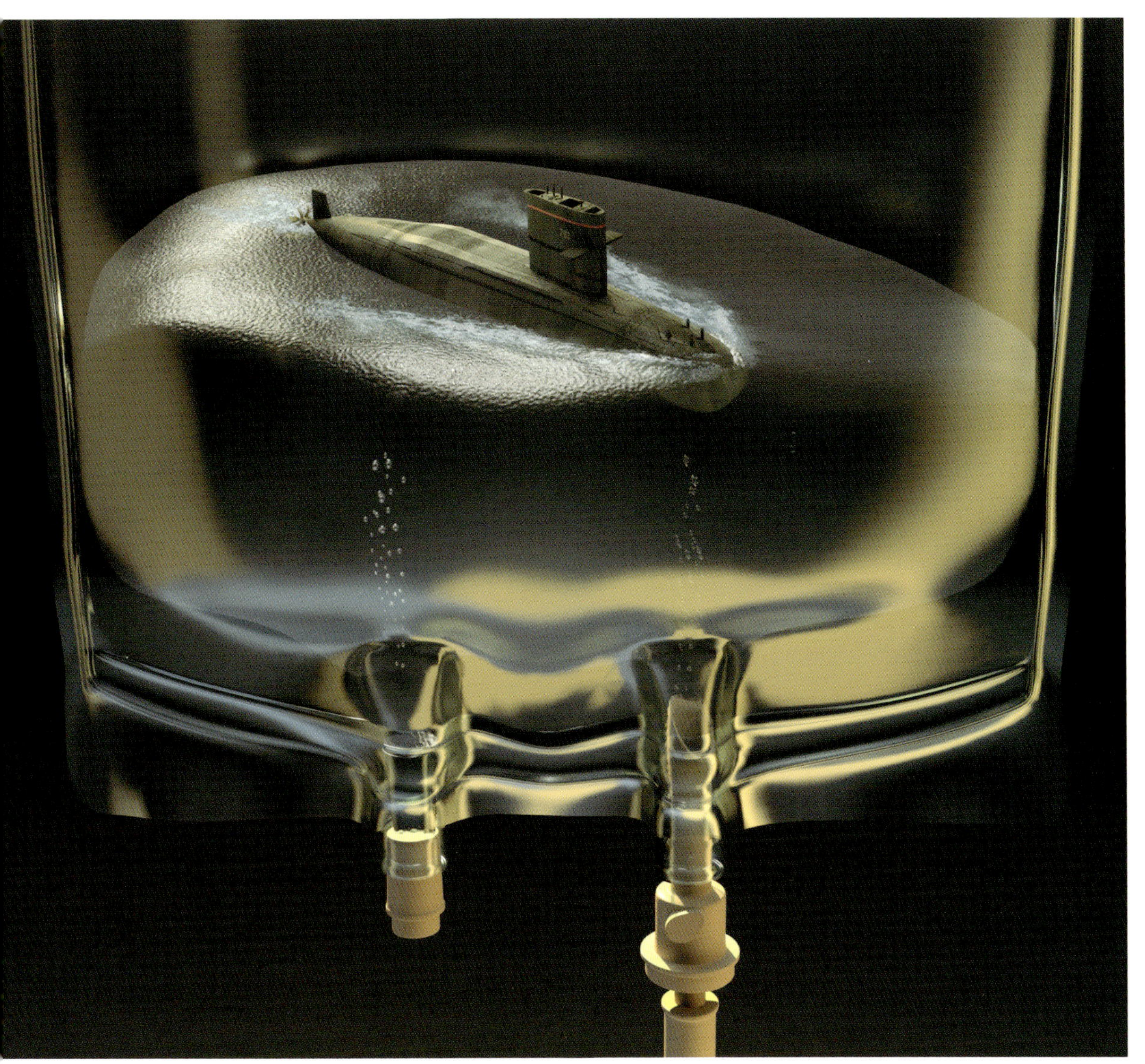

Durning 3D

Tel: 416.364.2594 · Cel:416.528.7980 · durning3d@rogers.com · www.durning3d.com

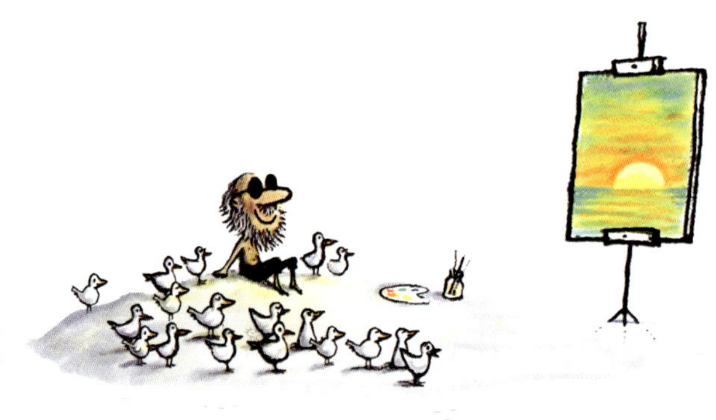

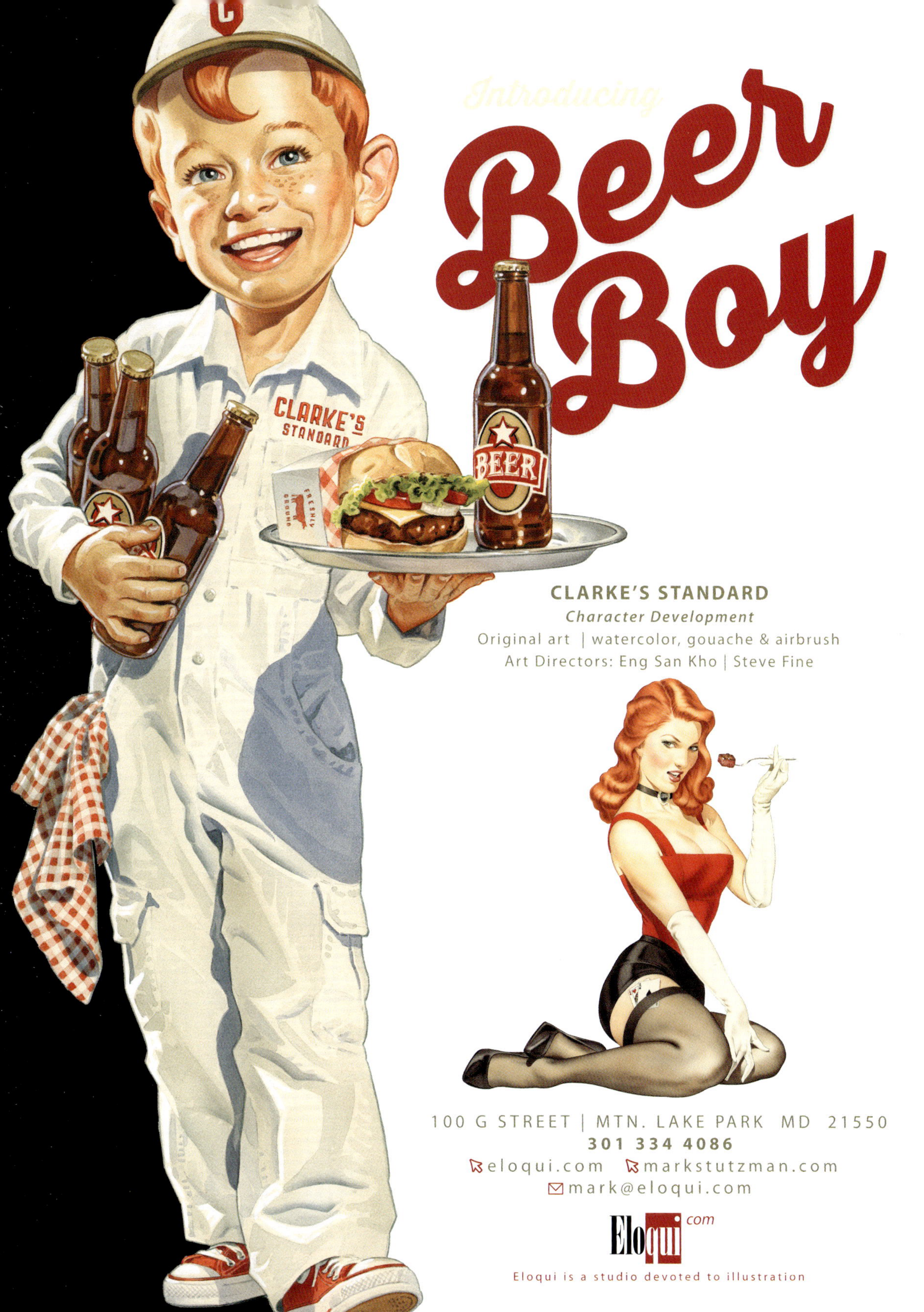

Introducing
Beer Boy
CLARKE'S STANDARD
CLARKE'S STANDARD
Character Development
Original art | watercolor, gouache & airbrush
Art Directors: Eng San Kho | Steve Fine
BEER
100 G STREET | MTN. LAKE PARK MD 21550
301 334 4086
eloqui.com   markstutzman.com
mark@eloqui.com
Eloqui com
Eloqui is a studio devoted to illustration

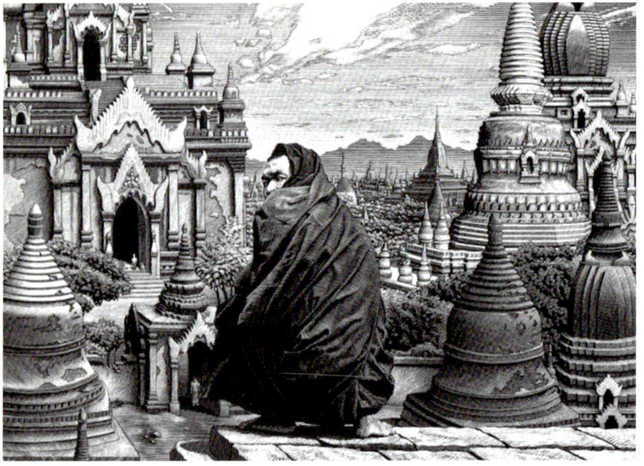

Patrick Arrasmith

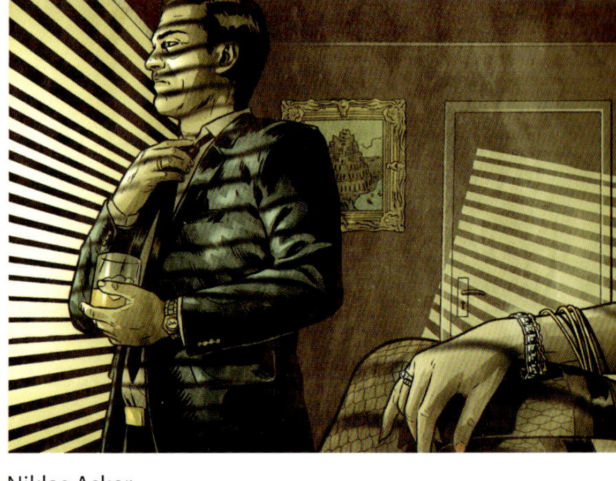

Niklas Asker

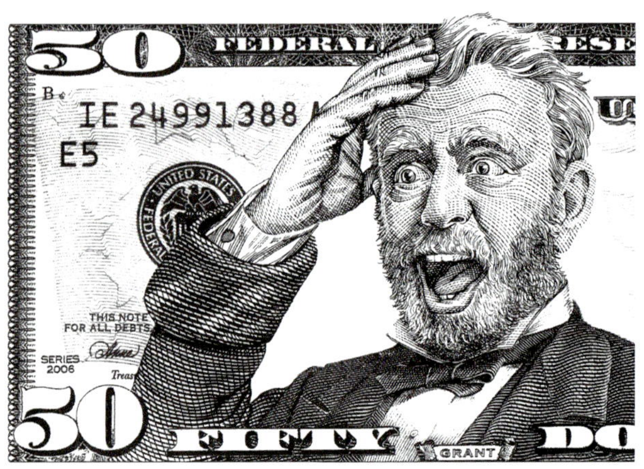

Kent Barton

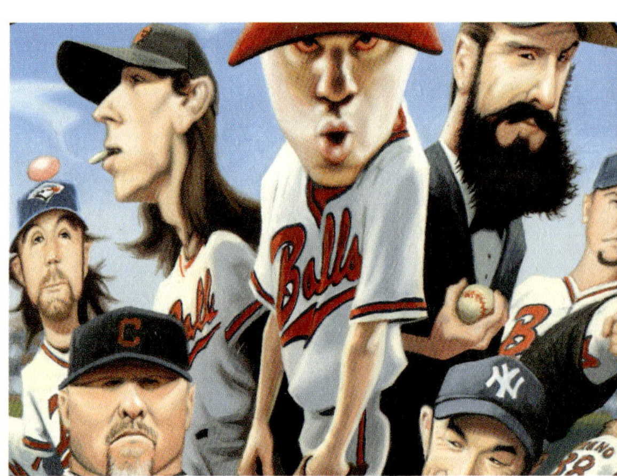

James Bennett

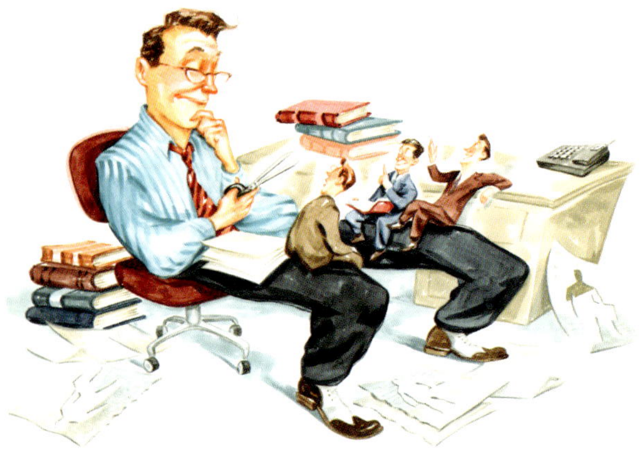

Tim Bower

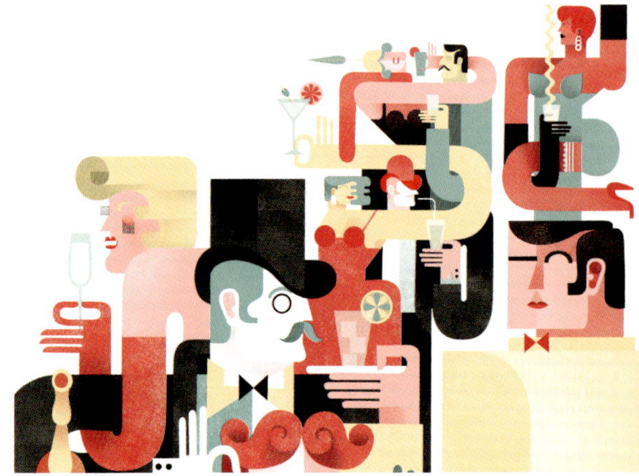

Maria Corte Maidagan

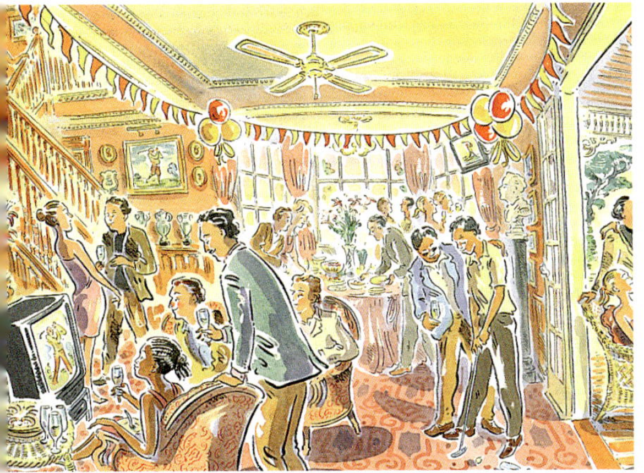

...ul Cox

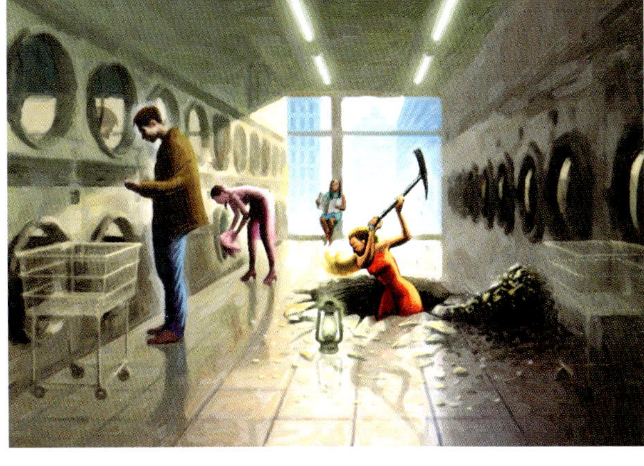

Eric Drooker

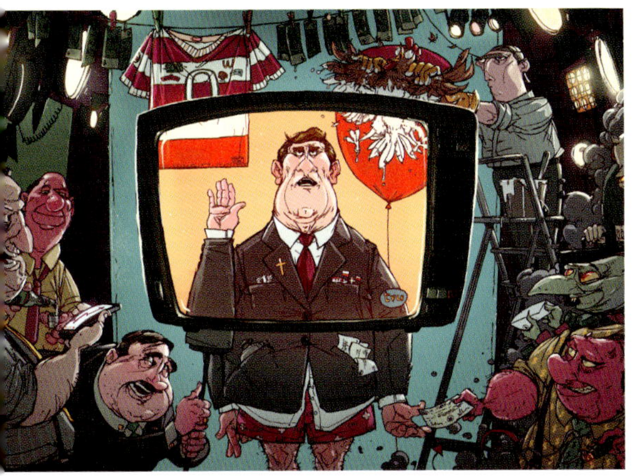

...chał Dziekan

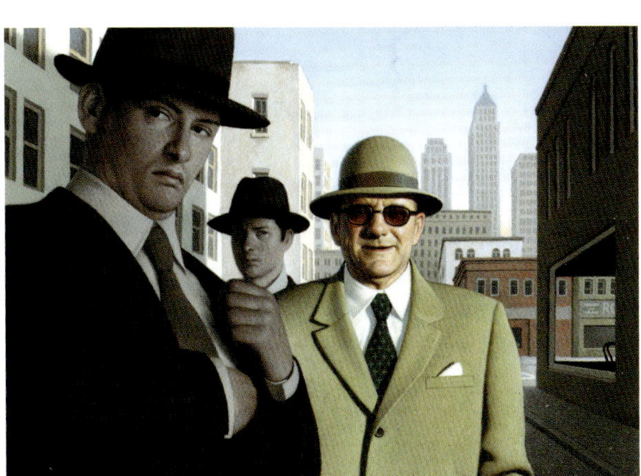

Thomas Ehretsmann

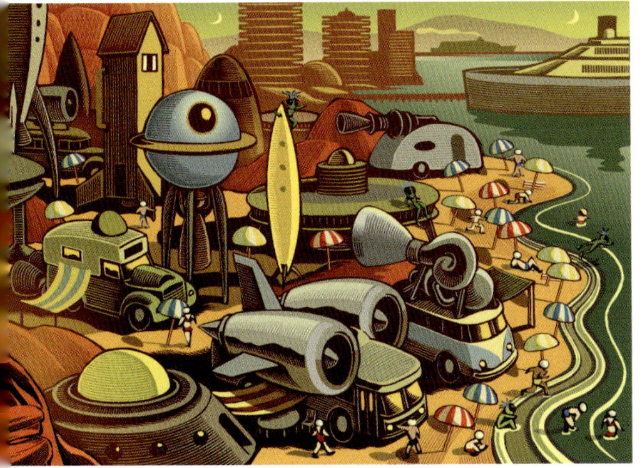

...hris Gall

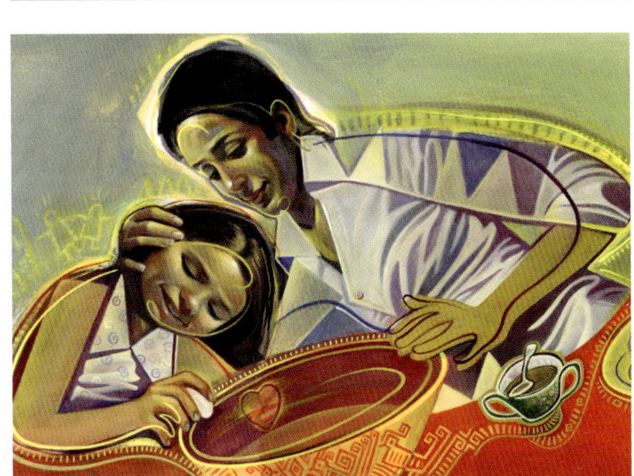

Rudy Gutierrez

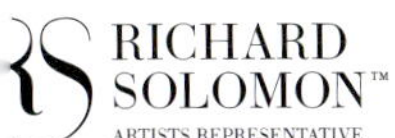

212 223 9545 · 917 841 1333
www.richardsolomon.com
richard@richardsolomon.com

110 E 30th St,
Ste. 501
New York, NY 10016

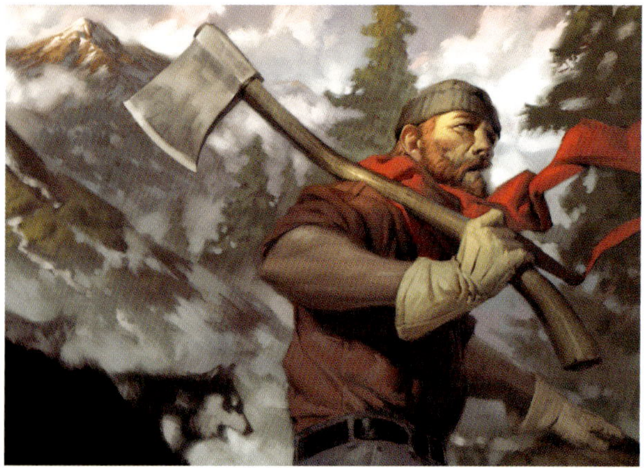

Tyler Jacobson

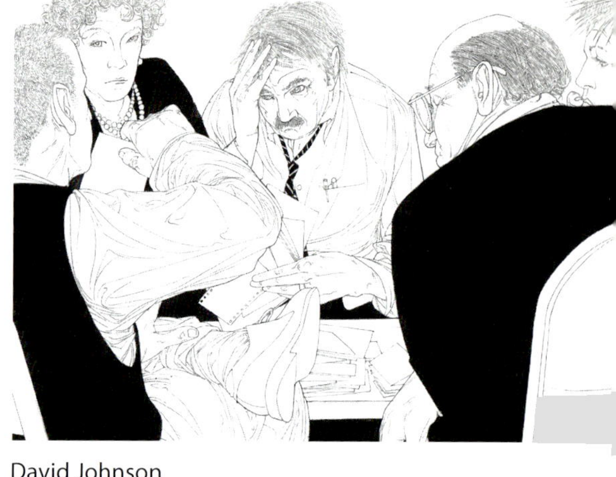

David Johnson

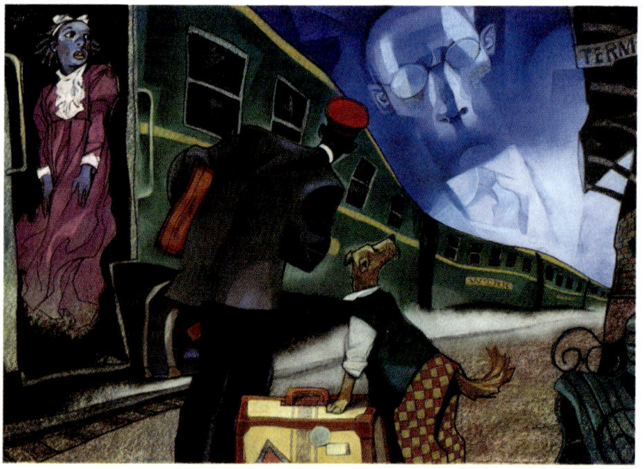

Gary Kelley

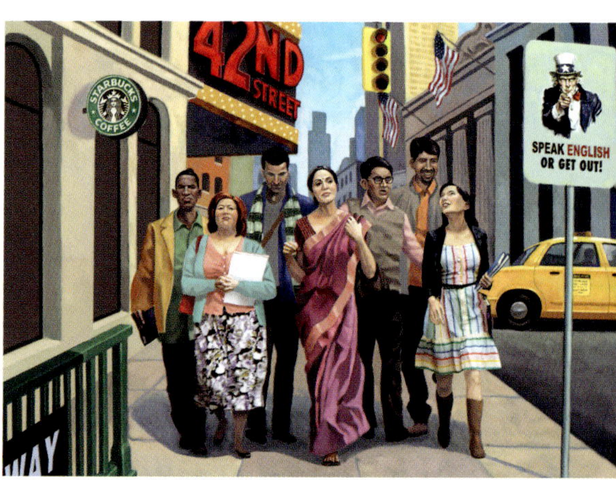

Murray Kimber

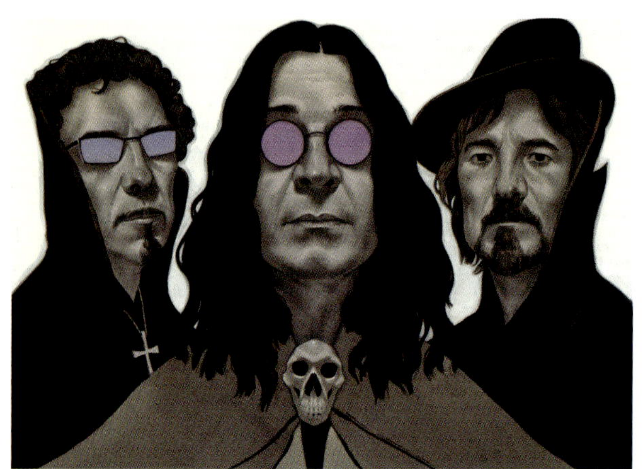

Edward Kinsella III

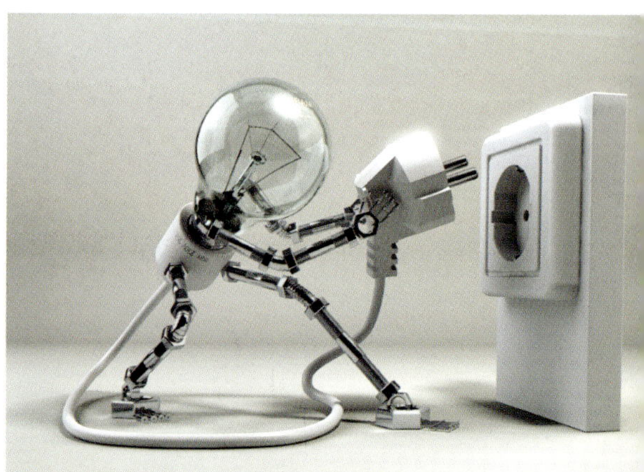

André Kutscherauer

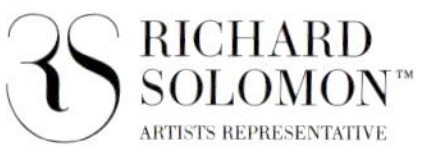

RICHARD
SOLOMON™
ARTISTS REPRESENTATIVE

212 223 9545 · 917 841 1333
www.richardsolomon.com
richard@richardsolomon.com

110 E 30th St,
Ste. 501
New York, NY 100

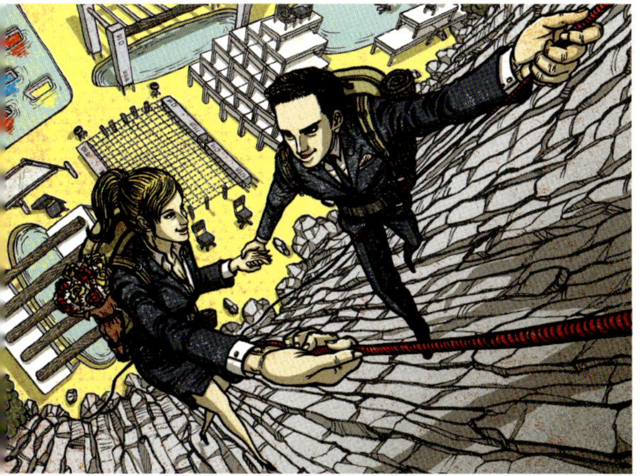

ngyun Lee

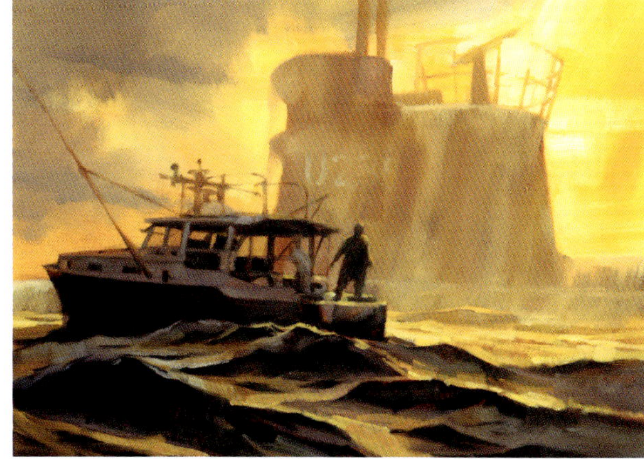

Gregory Manchess

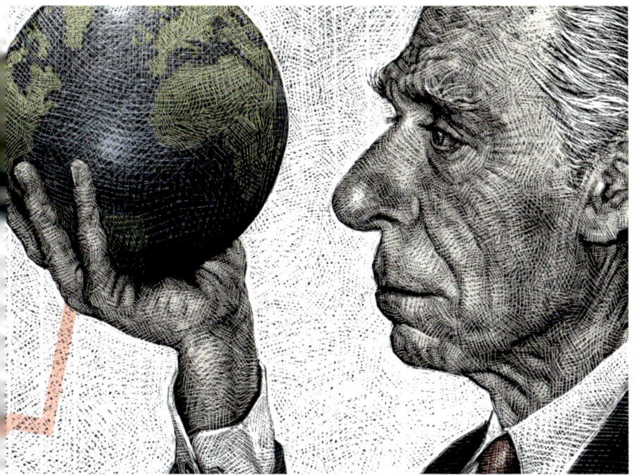

cardo Martínez

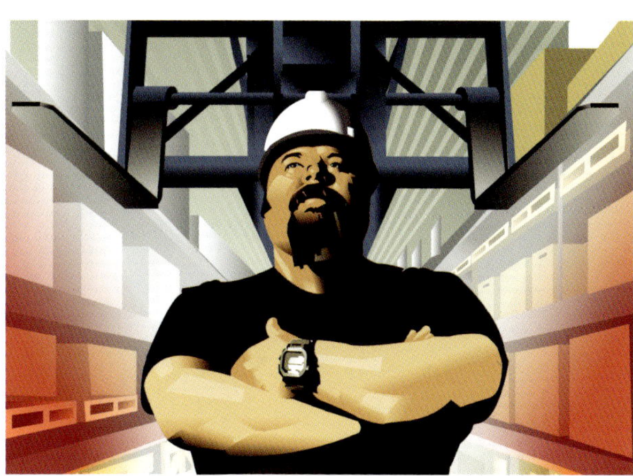

John Mattos

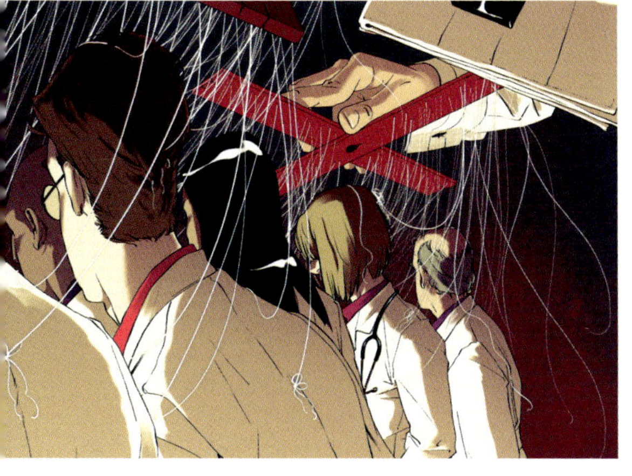

oñi Montes

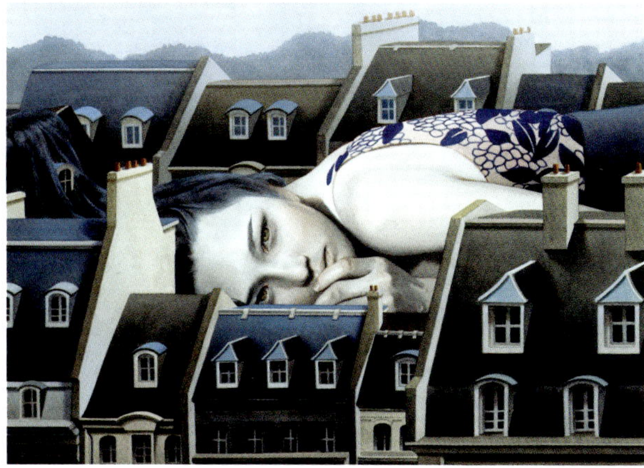

Tran Nguyen

RICHARD SOLOMON™
ARTISTS REPRESENTATIVE

212 223 9545 · 917 841 1333
www.richardsolomon.com
richard@richardsolomon.com

110 E 30th St,
Ste. 501
New York, NY 10016

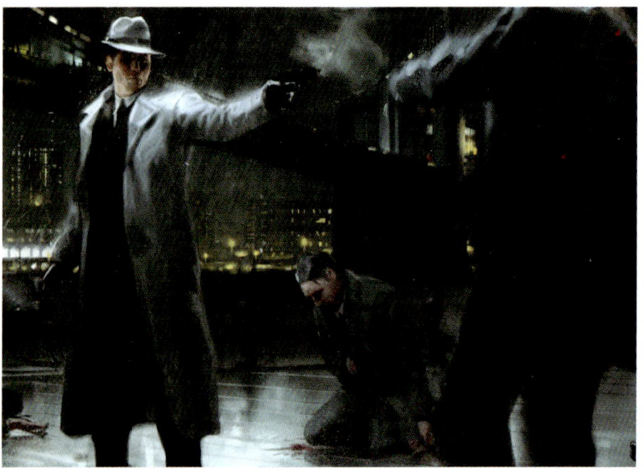

Karla Ortiz

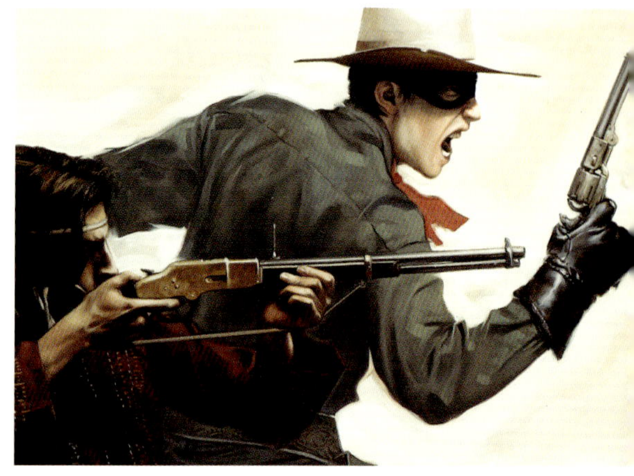

David Palumbo

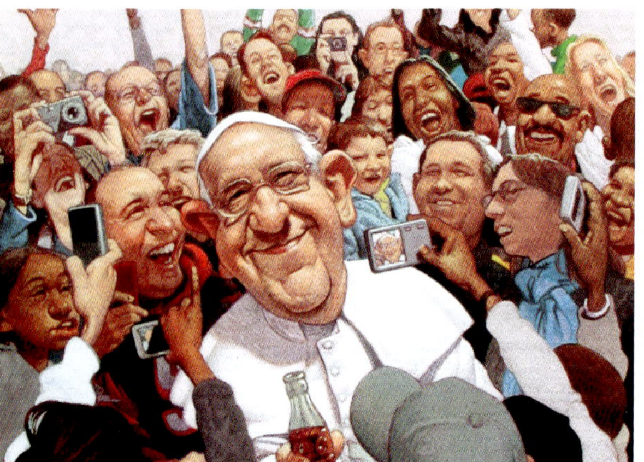

CF Payne

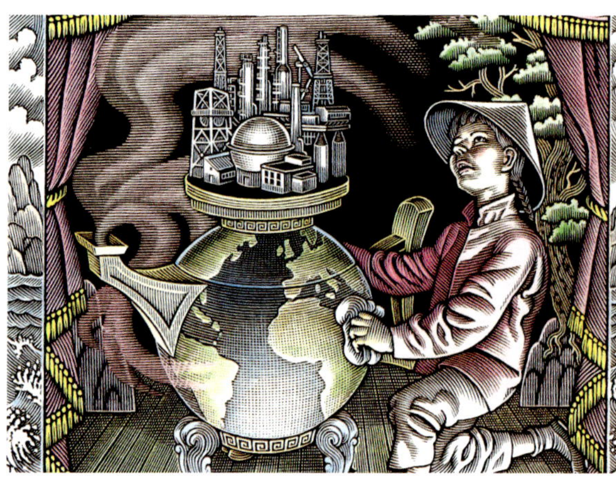

Bill Sanderson

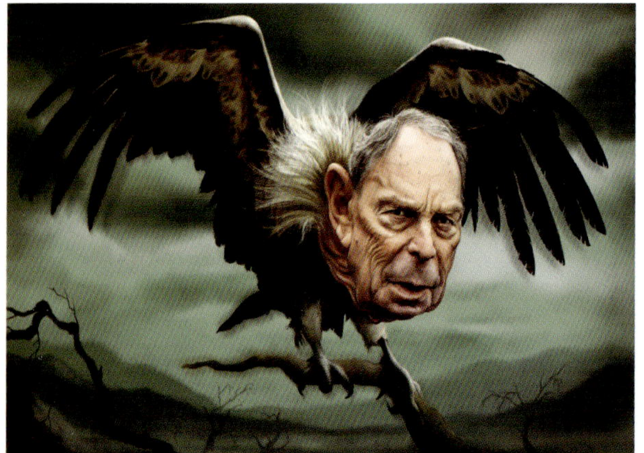

Jason Seiler

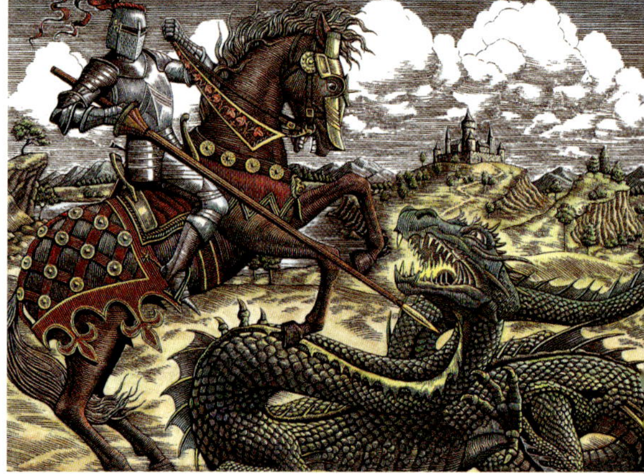

Douglas Smith

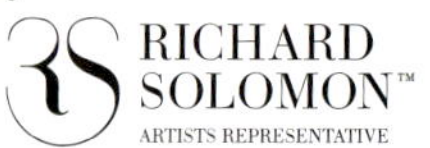

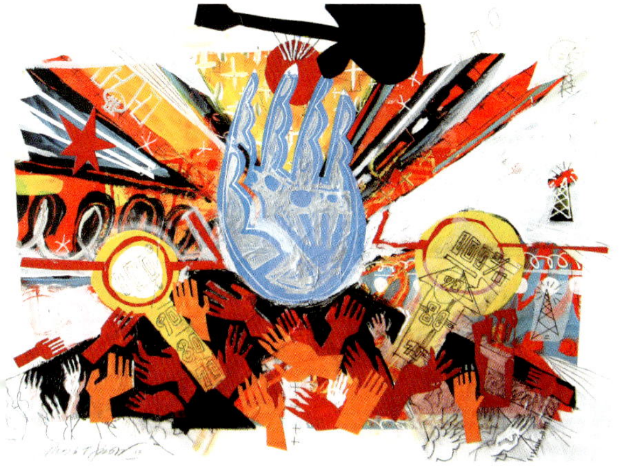

rk T Smith

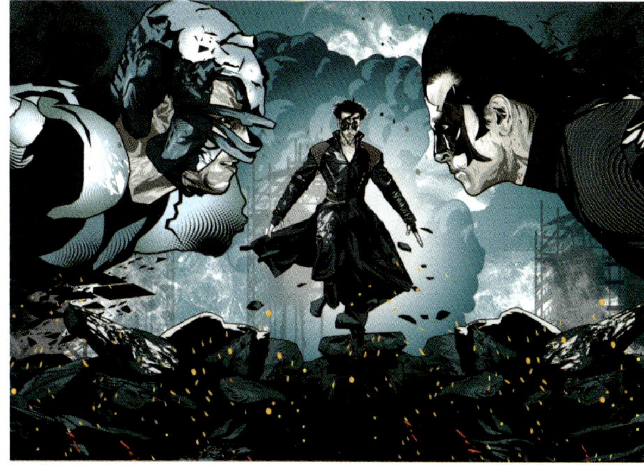

Guy Stauber

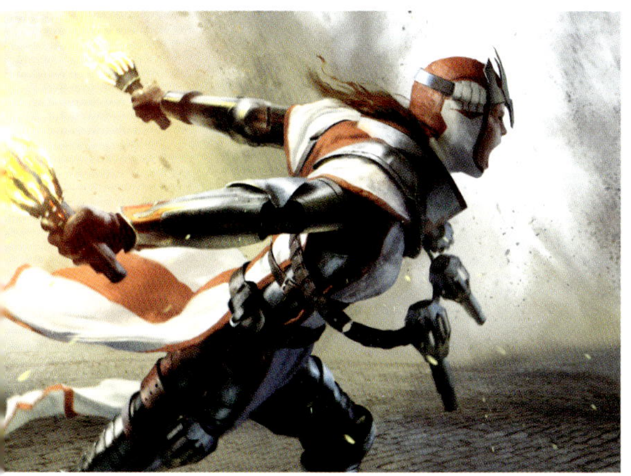

ase Stone

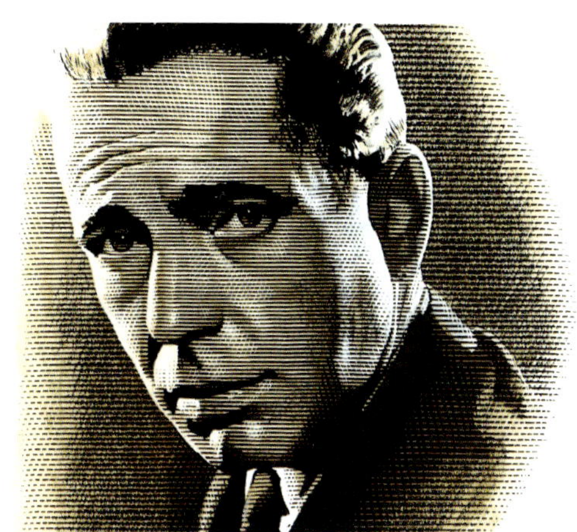

Mark Summers

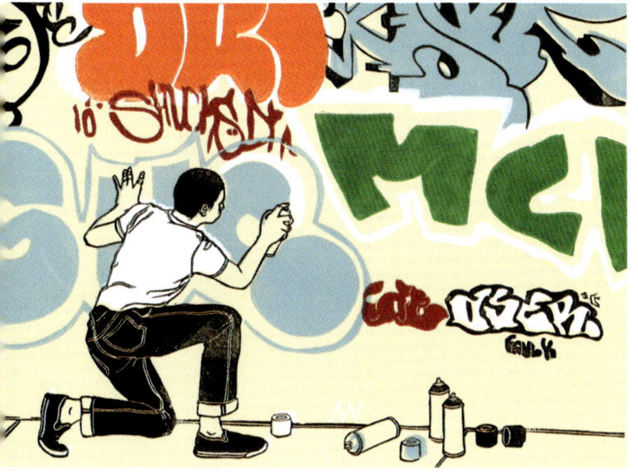

drew R Wright

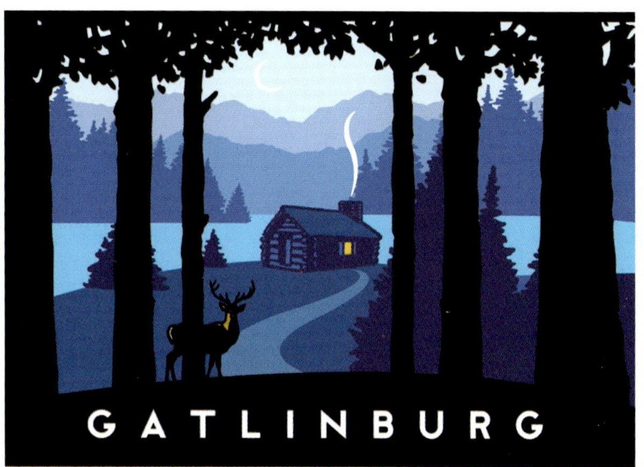

Ted Wright

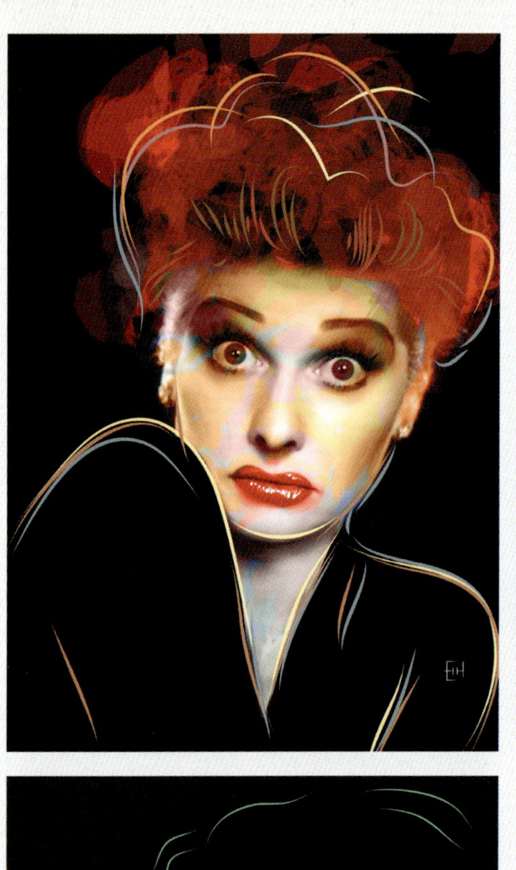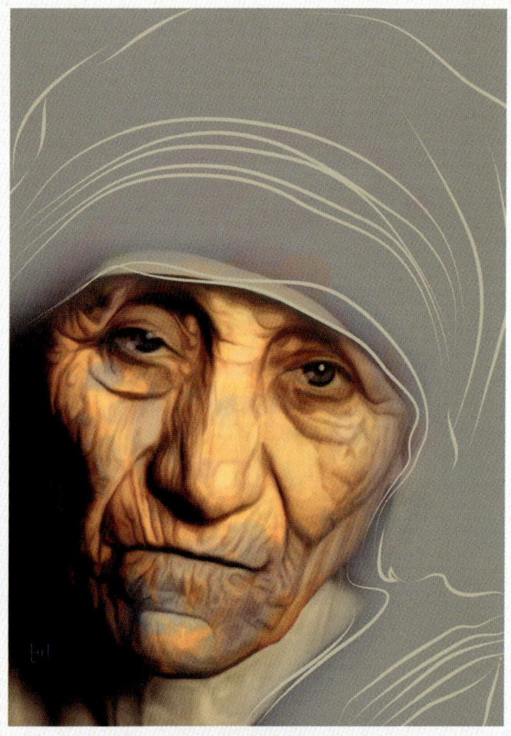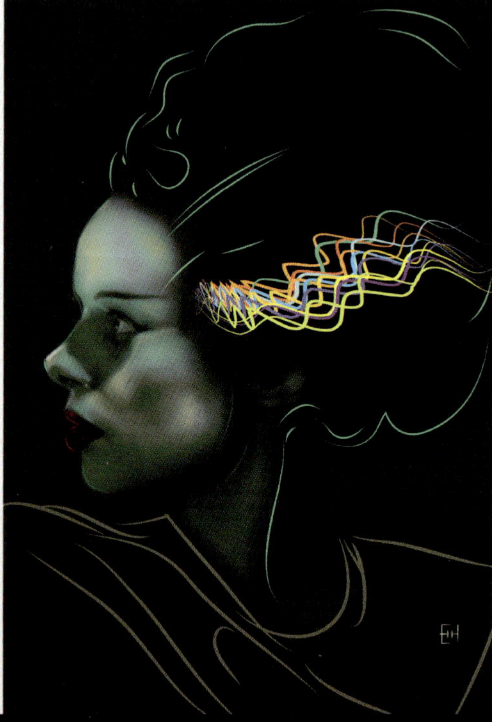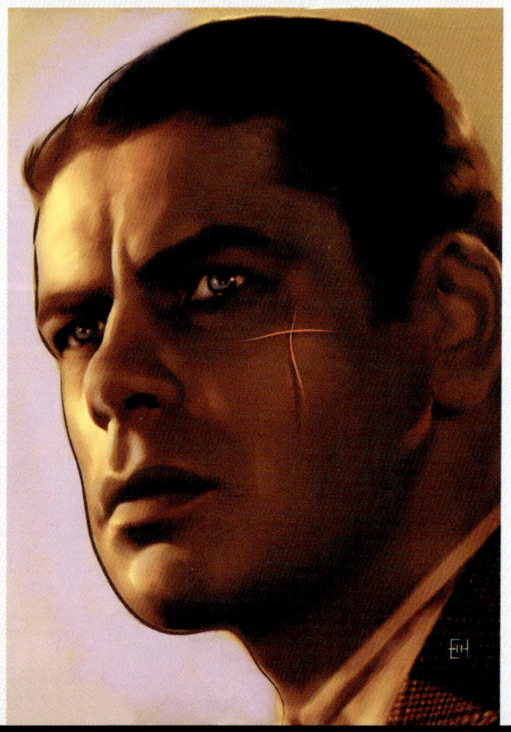

JACK HARRIS

302-290-0225
jackharris@me.com
www.jackharris.com

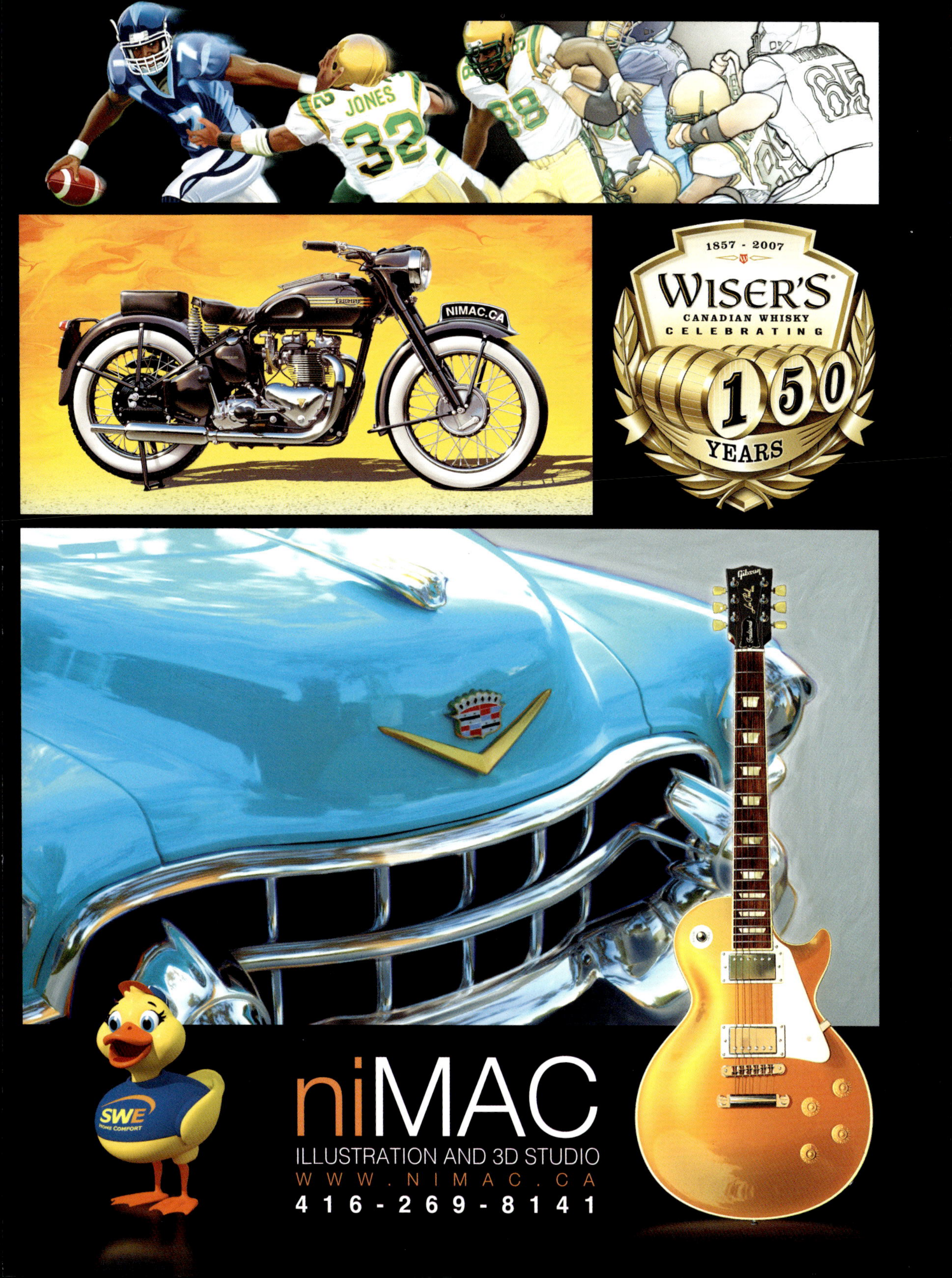

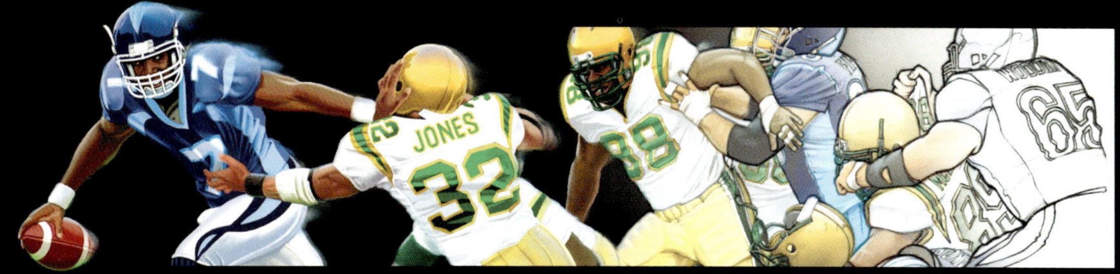

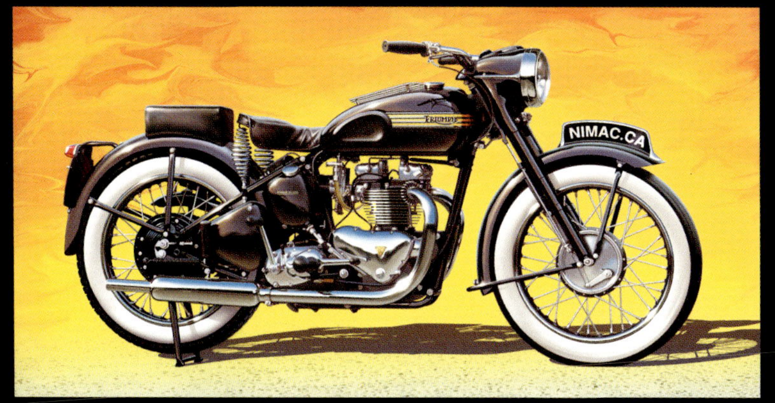

JONES
32
88
65
NIMAC.CA
TRIUMPH

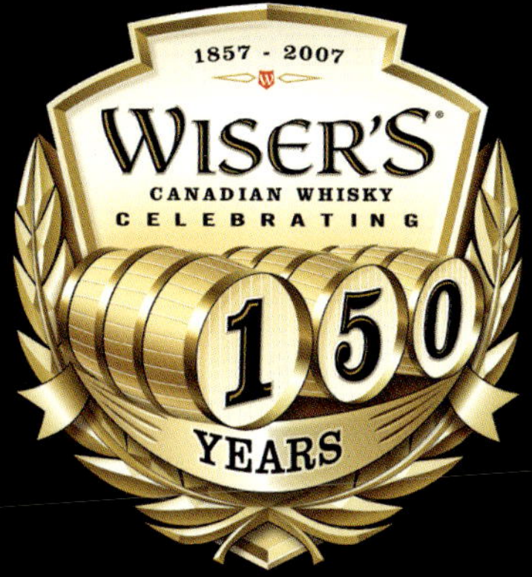

1857 - 2007
WISER'S
CANADIAN WHISKY
CELEBRATING
150
YEARS

SWE
HOME COMFORT
Gibson
niMAC
ILLUSTRATION AND 3D STUDIO
W W W . N I M A C . C A
4 1 6 - 2 6 9 - 8 1 4 1

Why so glum?

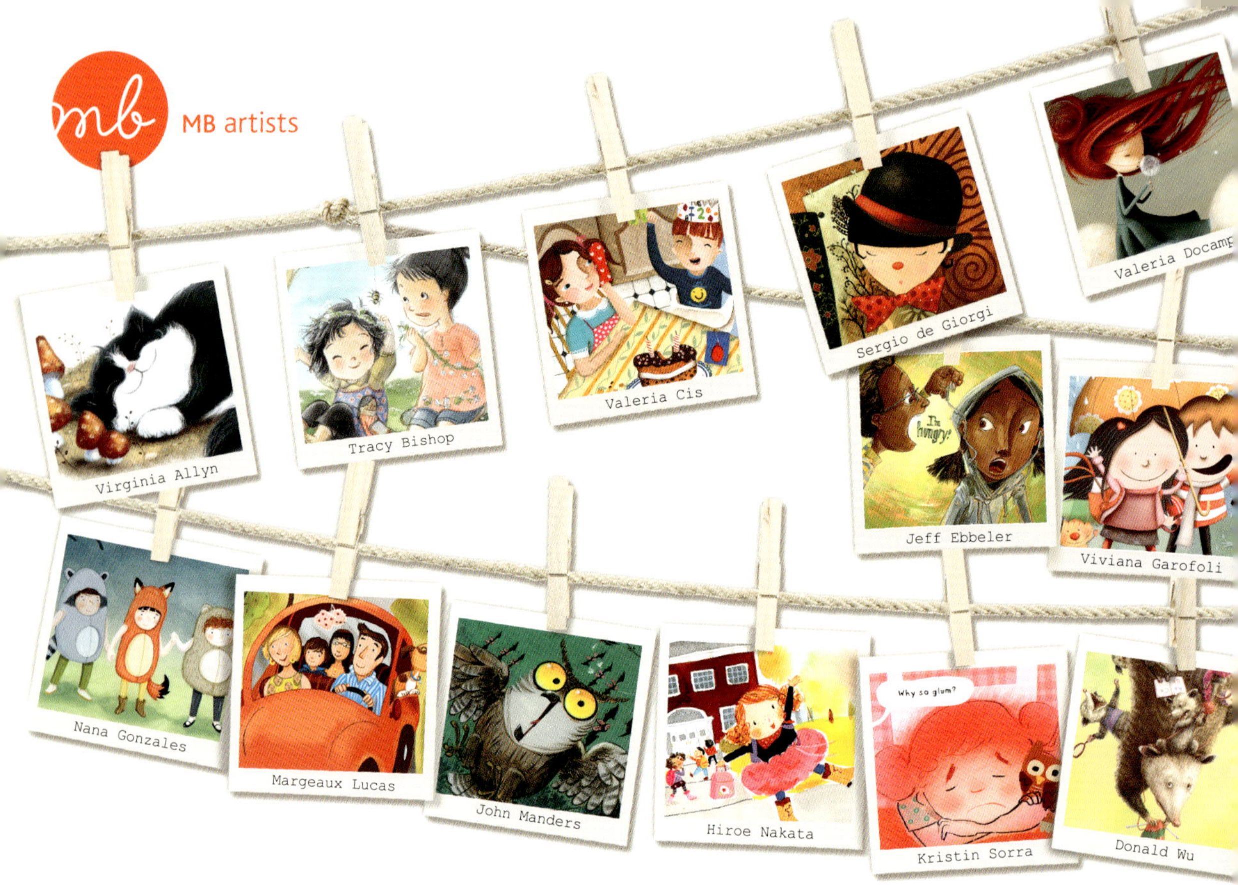

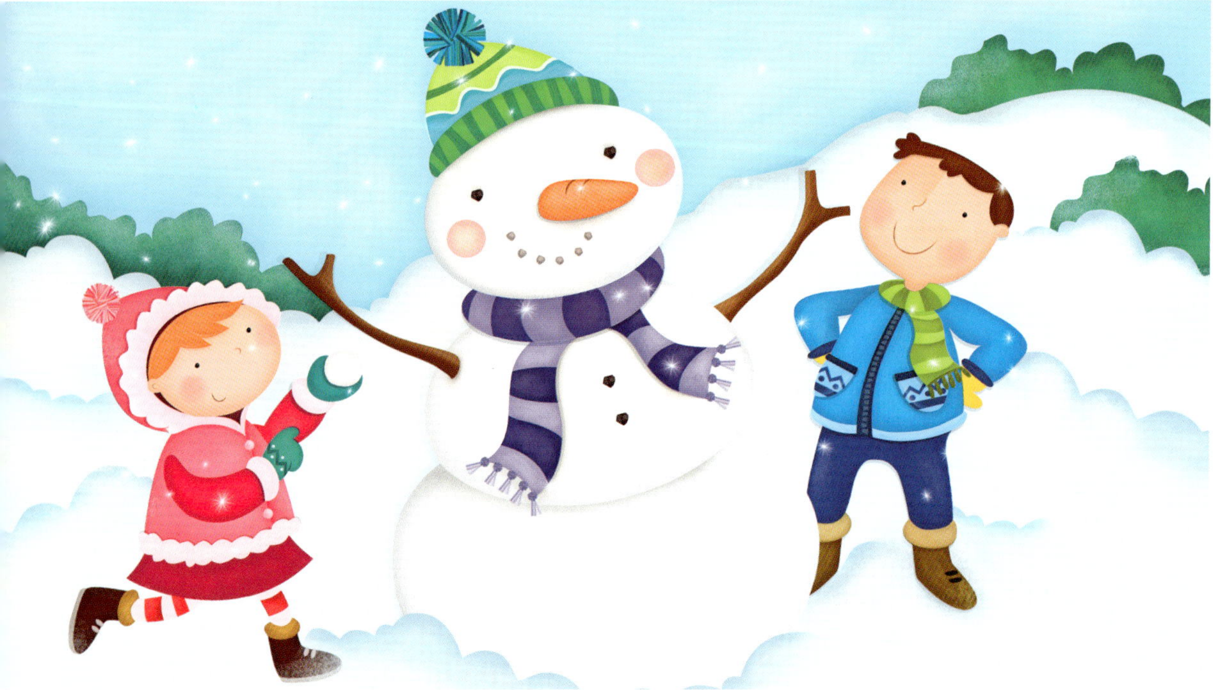

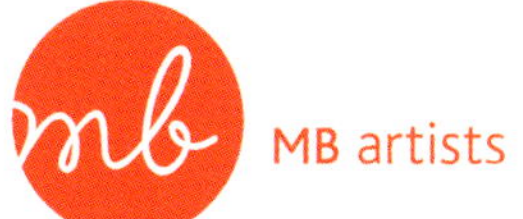

VALENTINA BELLONI

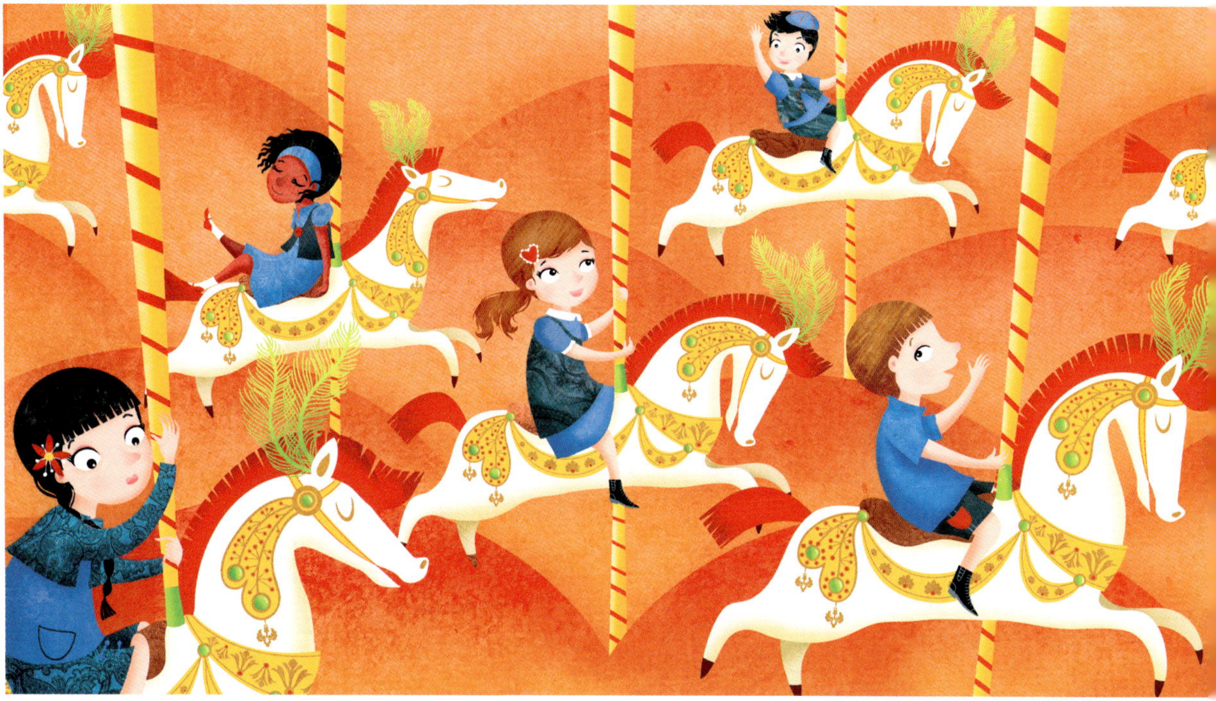

TRACY BISHOP

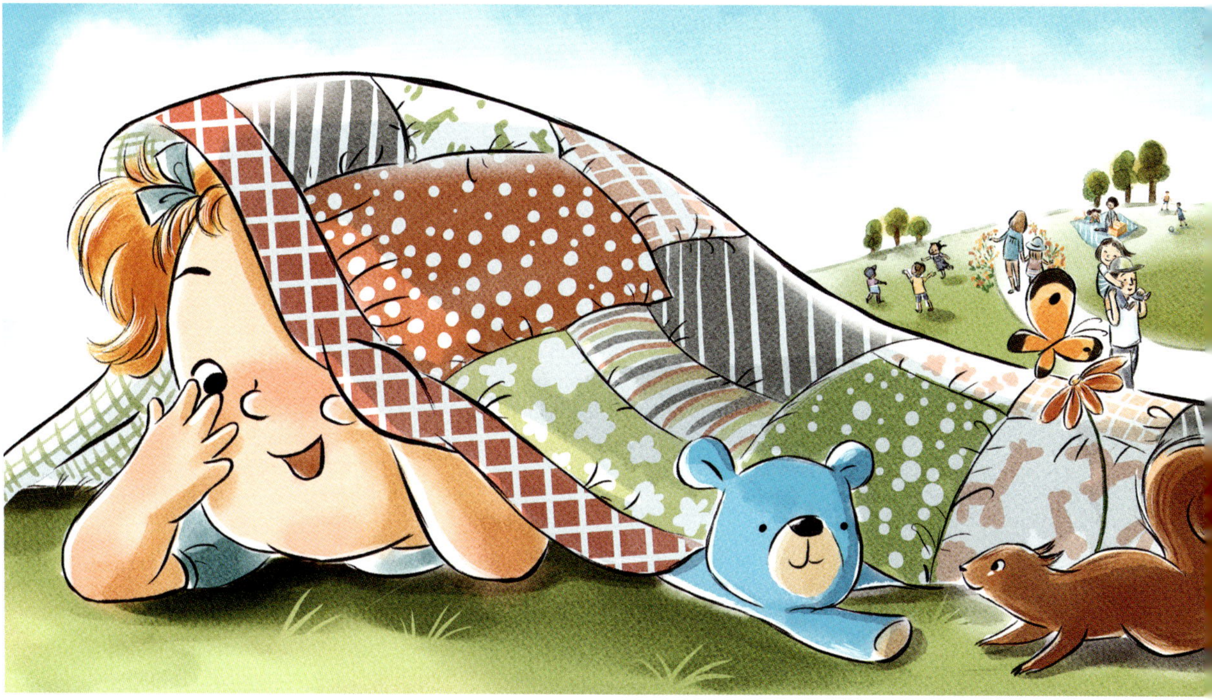

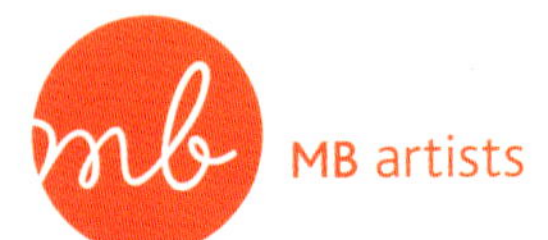

ABBY CARTER

MATTIA CERATO

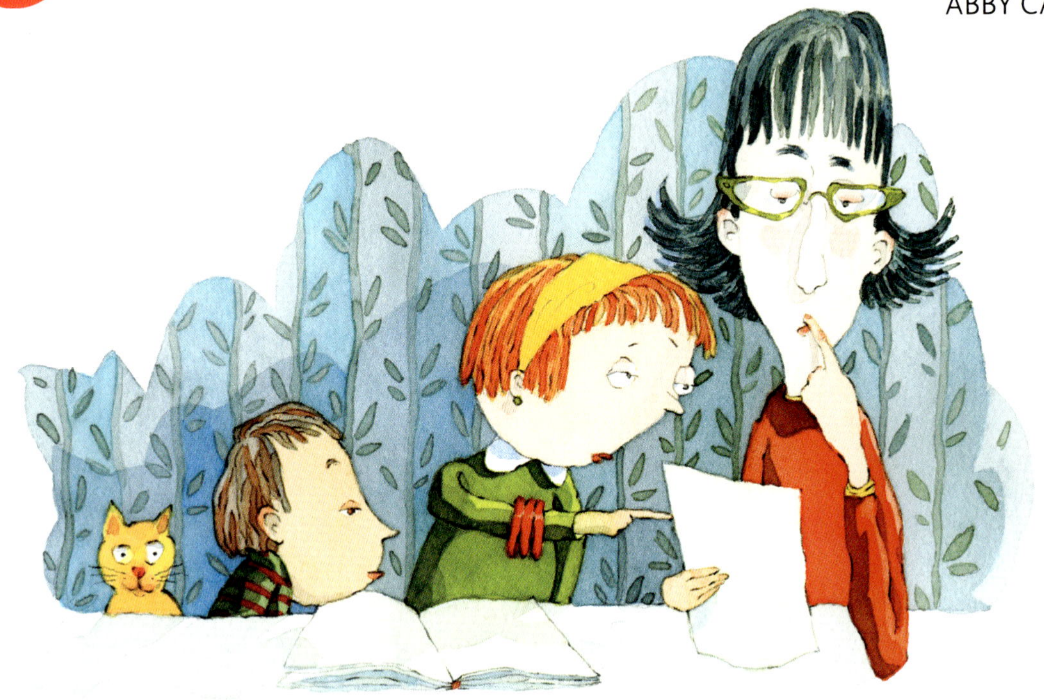

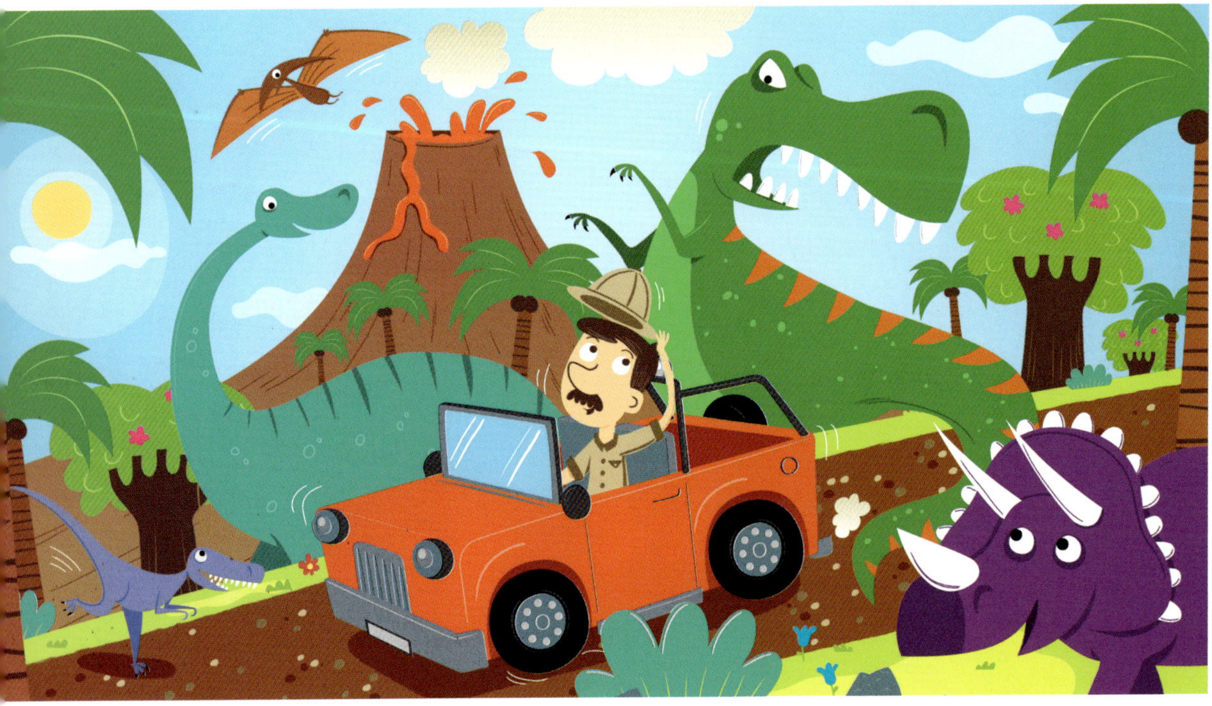

MELA BOLINAO **T** 212 689.7830 **F** 212 689.7829 www.mbartists.com

STEVE COX

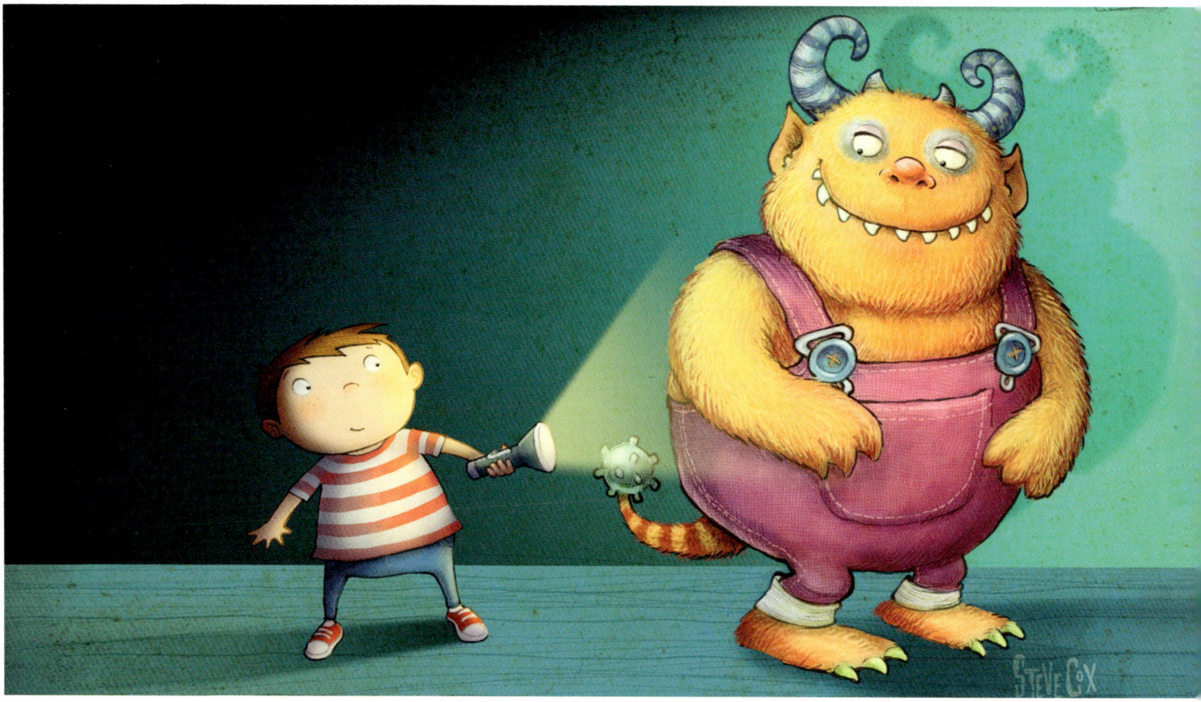

CAROLINA FARÍAS

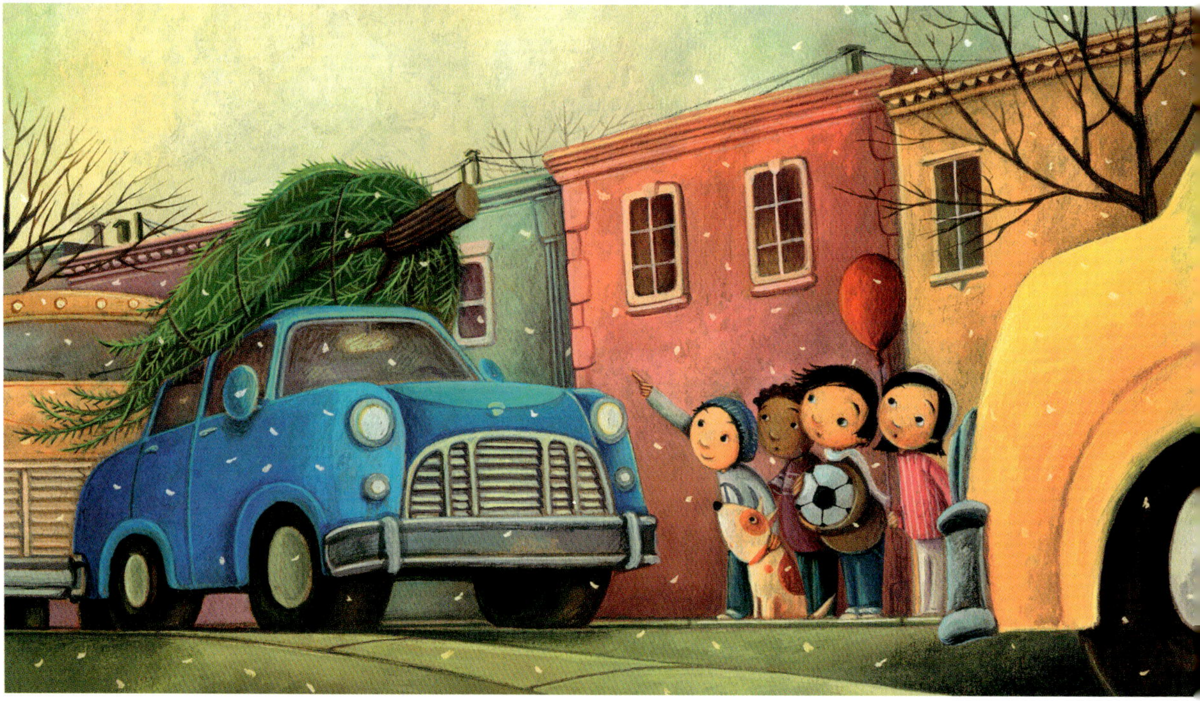

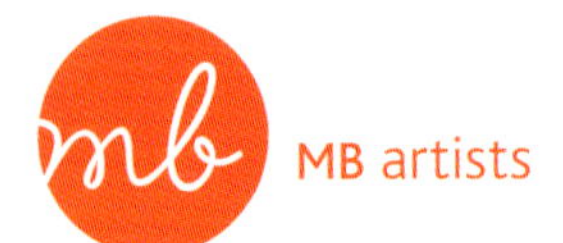

MB artists

PETER FRANCIS

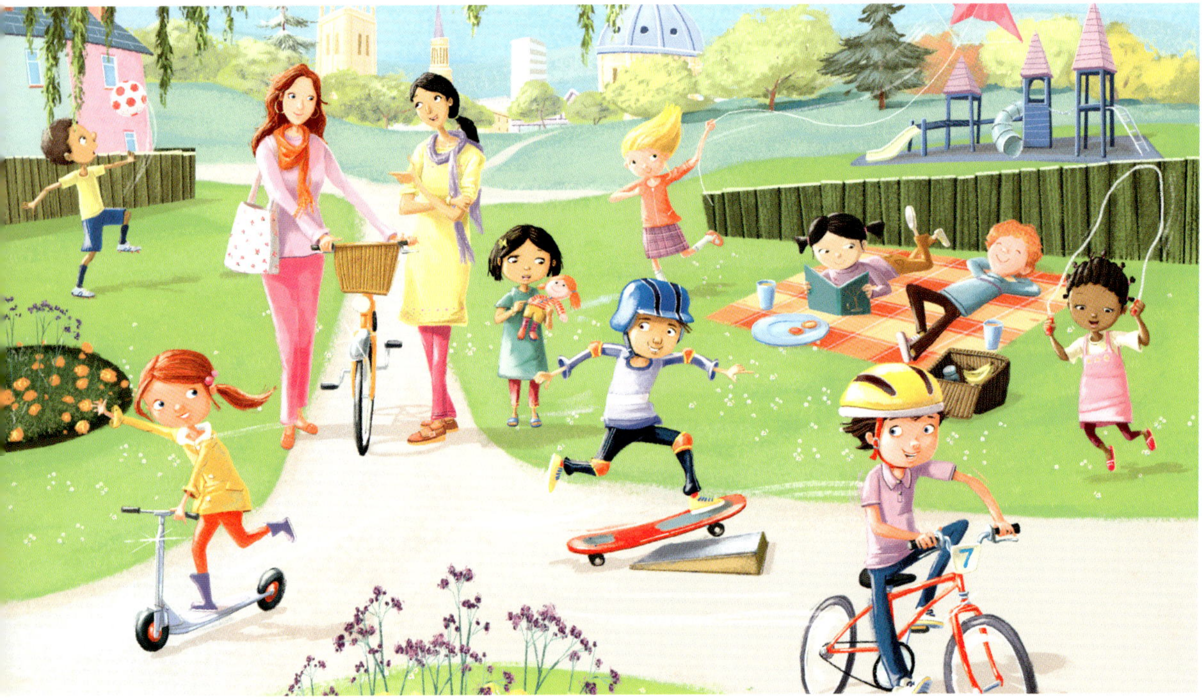

CLAUDINE GÉVRY

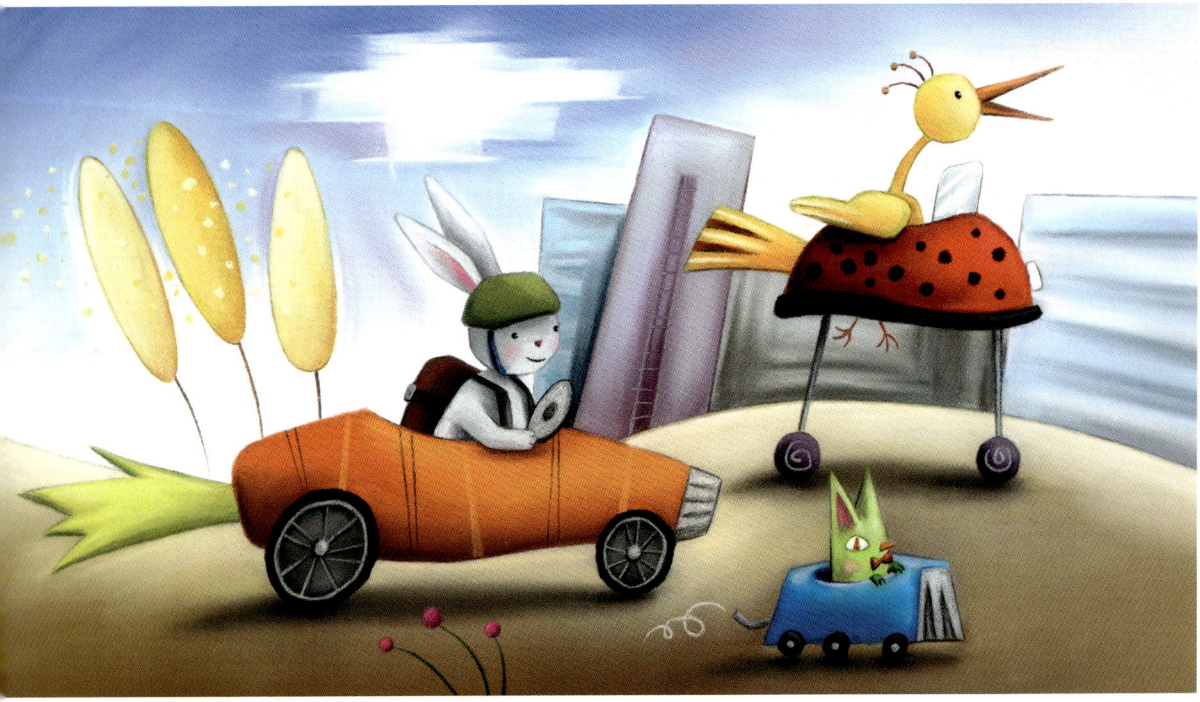

MELA BOLINAO T 212 689.7830 F 212 689.7829 www.mbartists.com

ALESSIA GIRASOLE

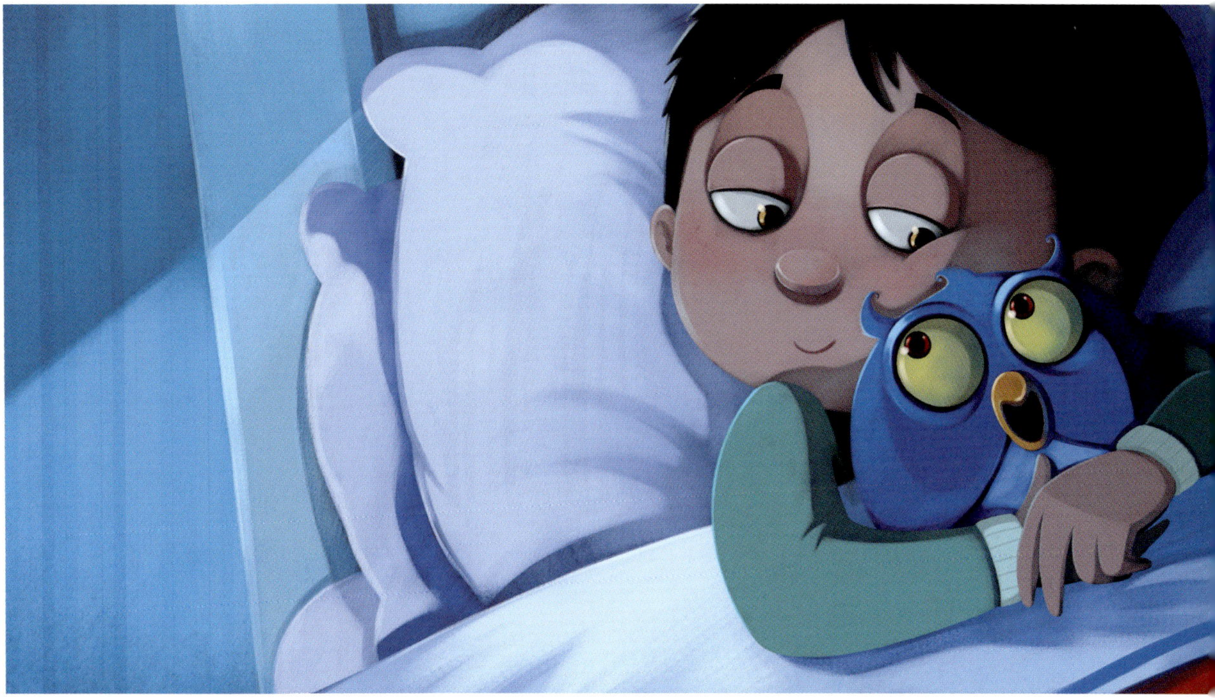

GYNUX

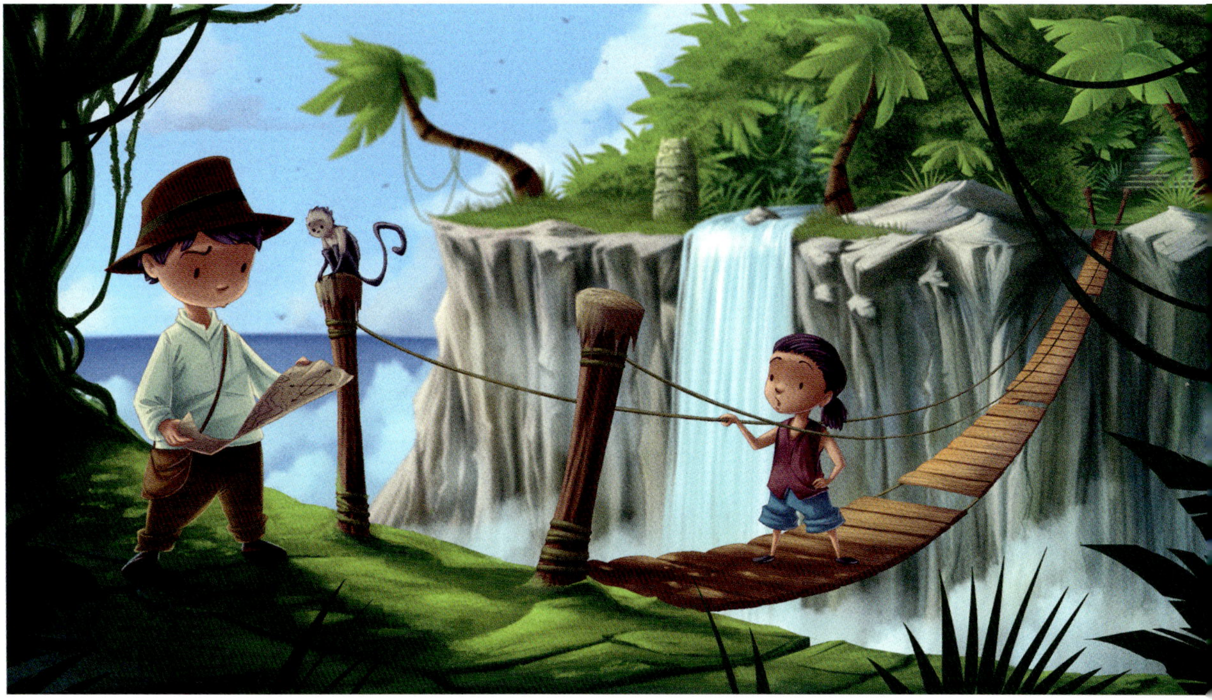

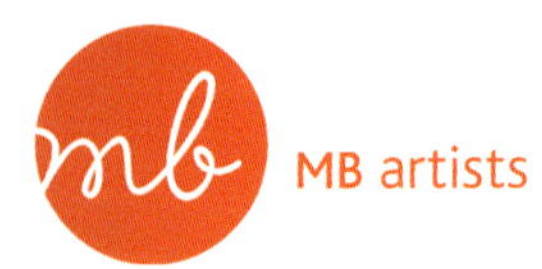

DANIEL GRIFFO

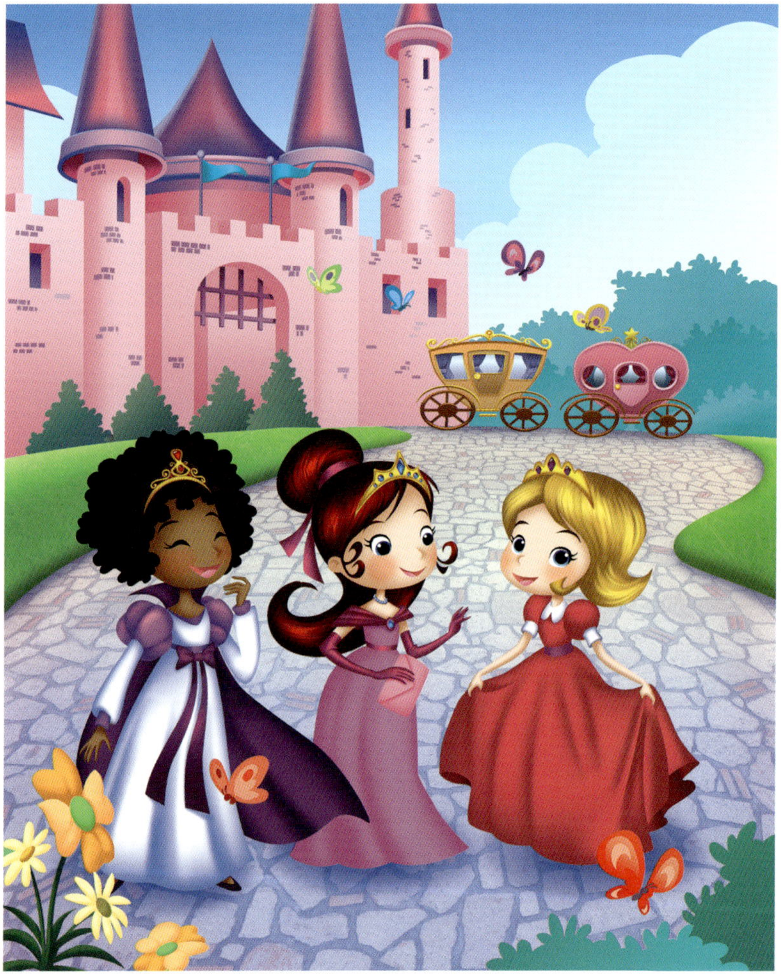

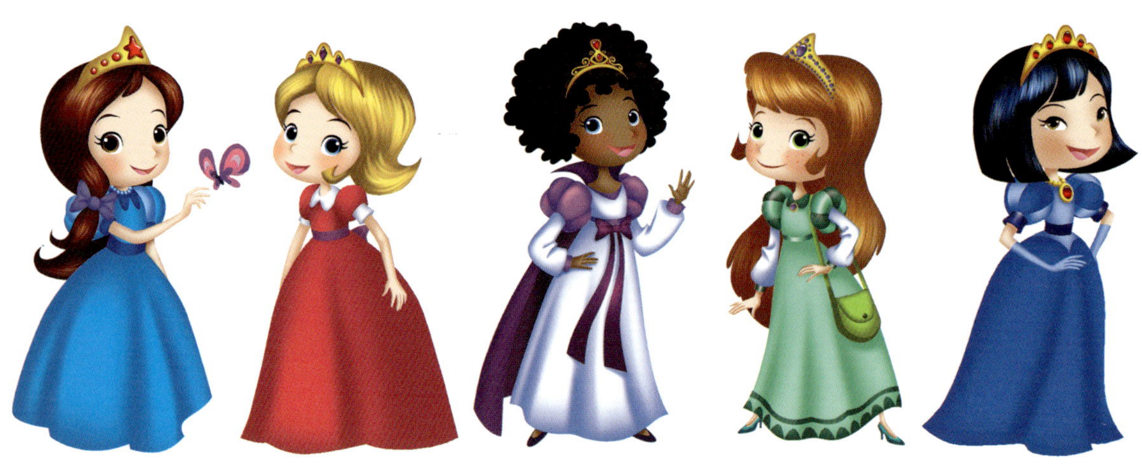

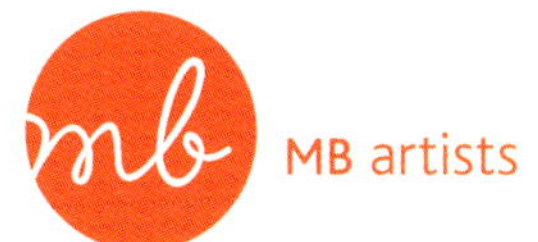

JANNIE HO

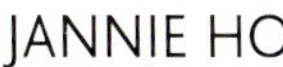

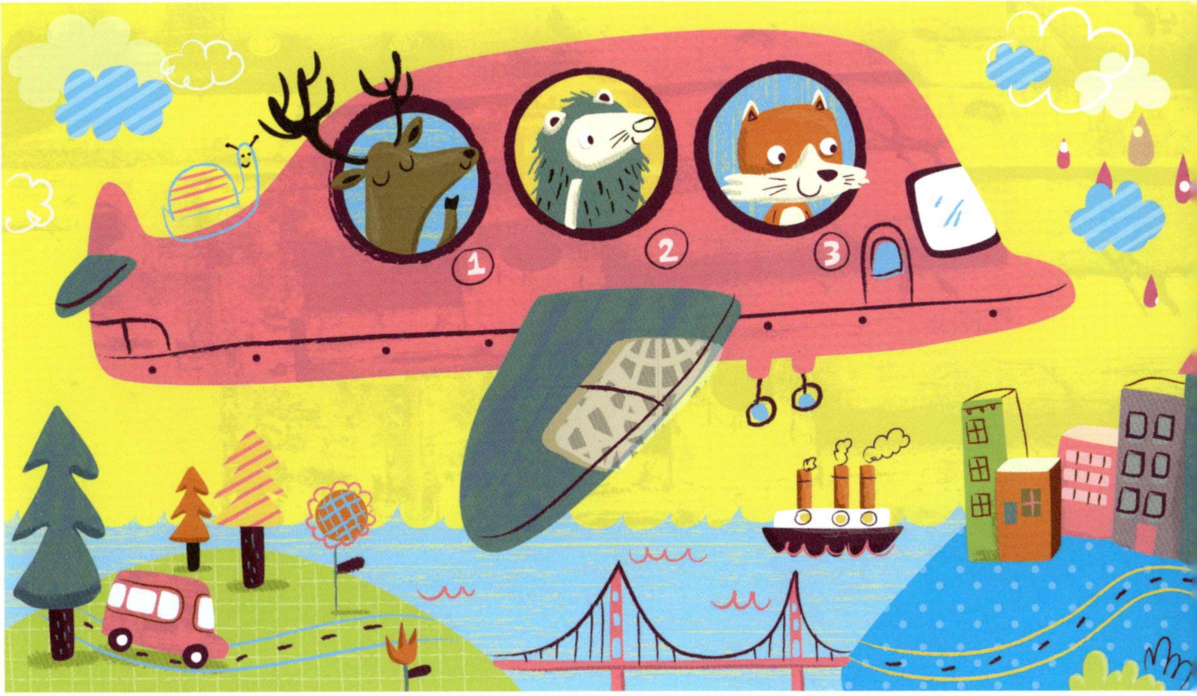

LAURA HULISKA-BEITH

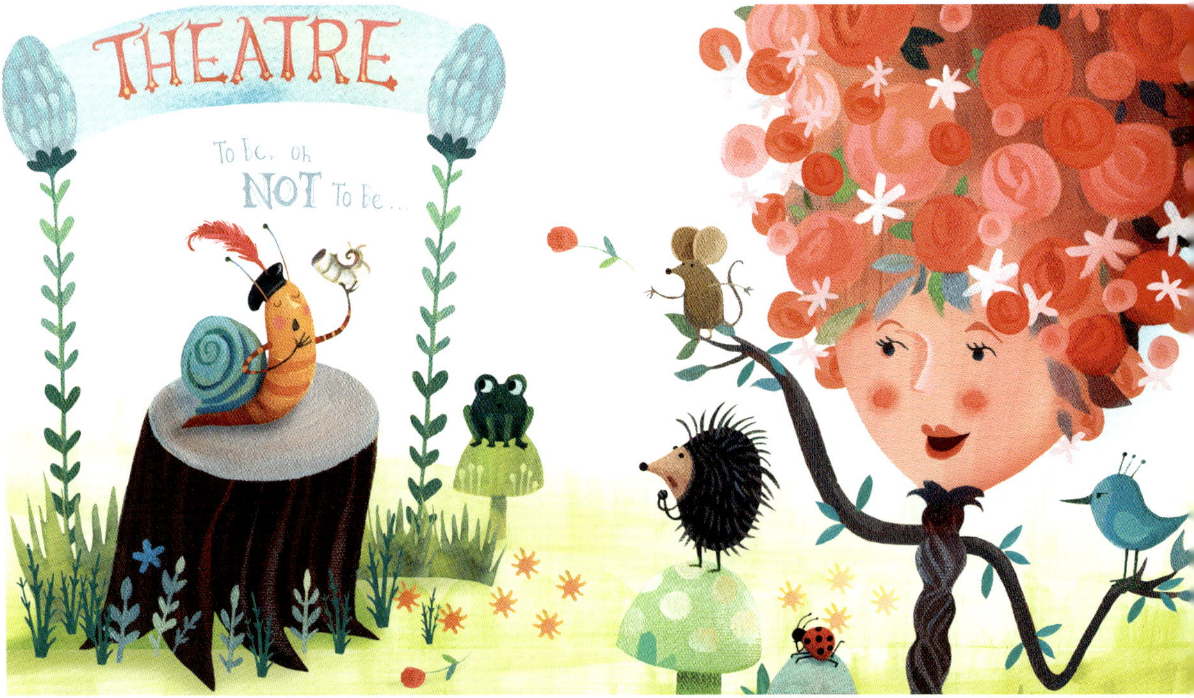

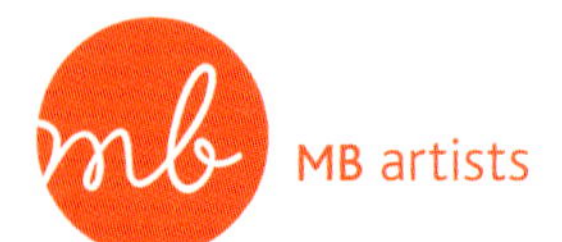
MB artists

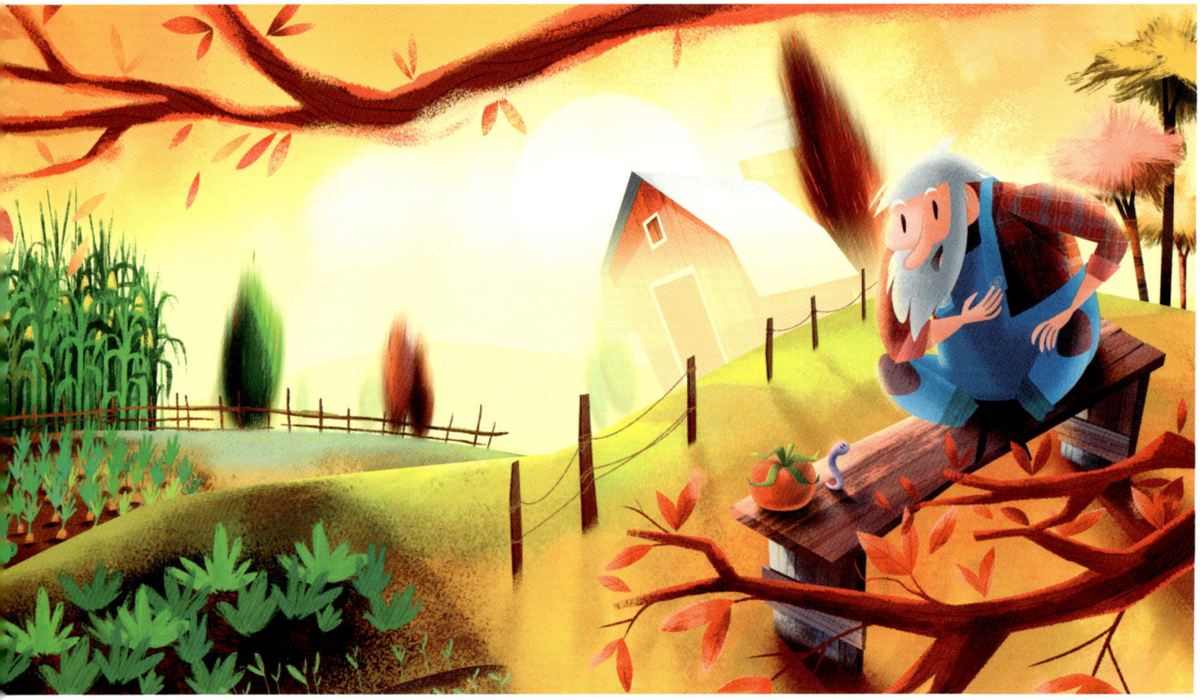

ANNE KENNEDY

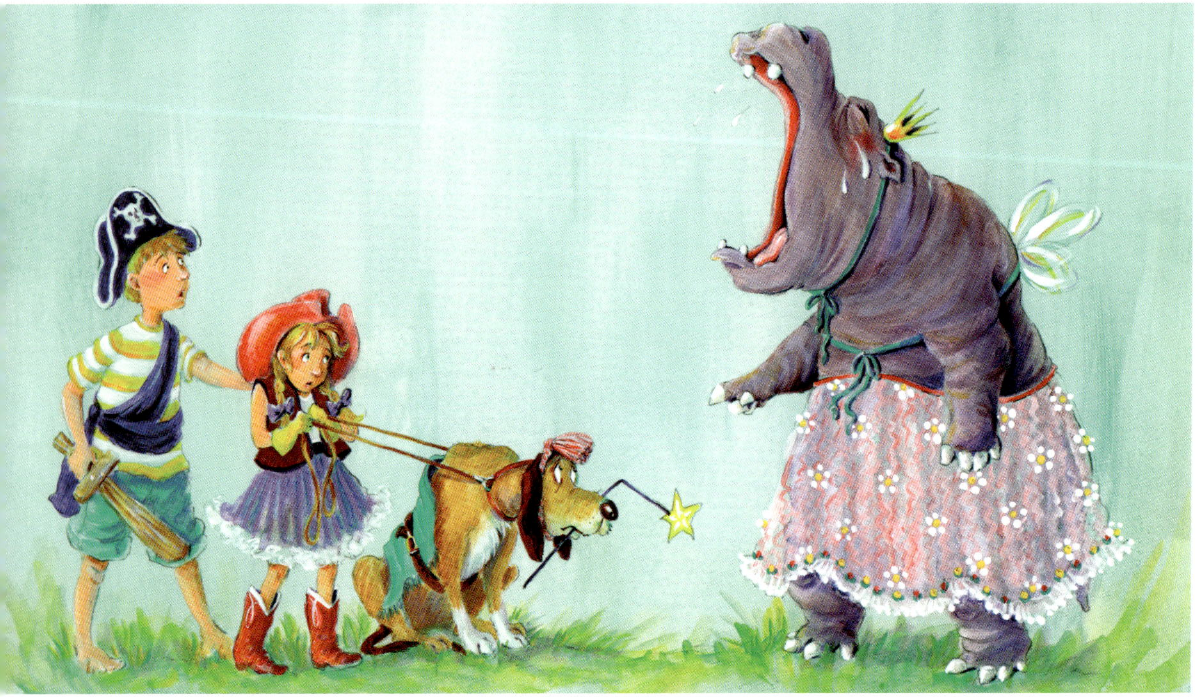

MELA BOLINAO **T** 212 689.7830 **F** 212 689.7829 www.mbartists.com

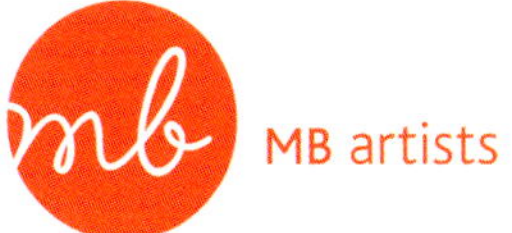

ANTHONY LEWIS

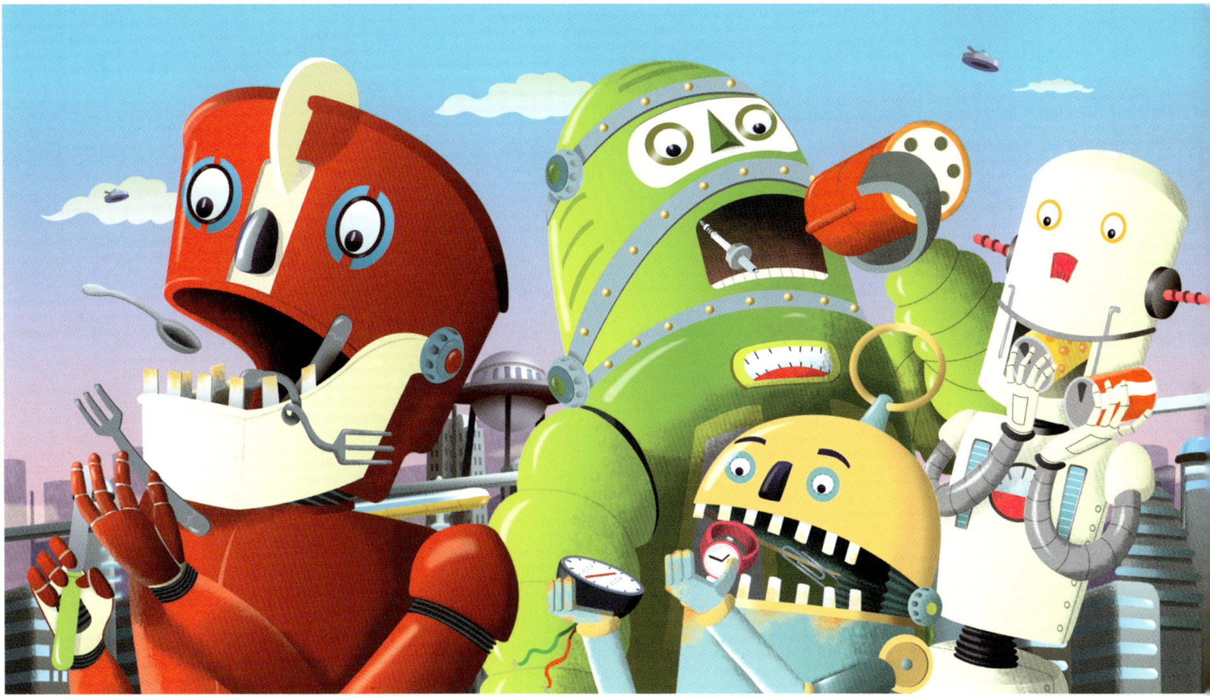

COLLEEN MADDEN

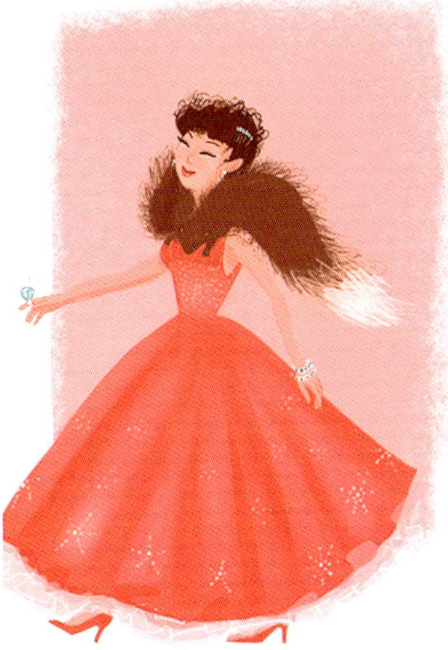

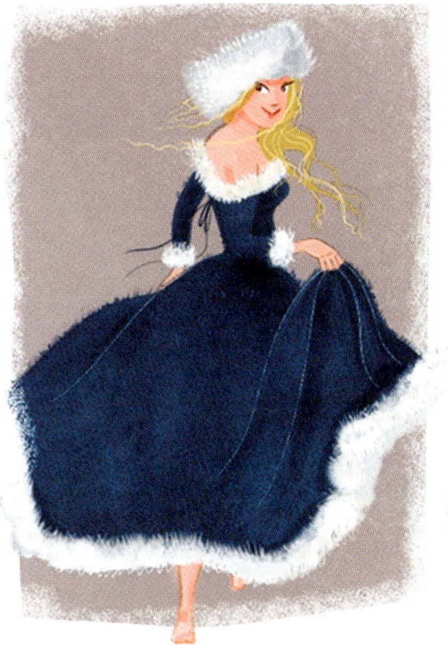

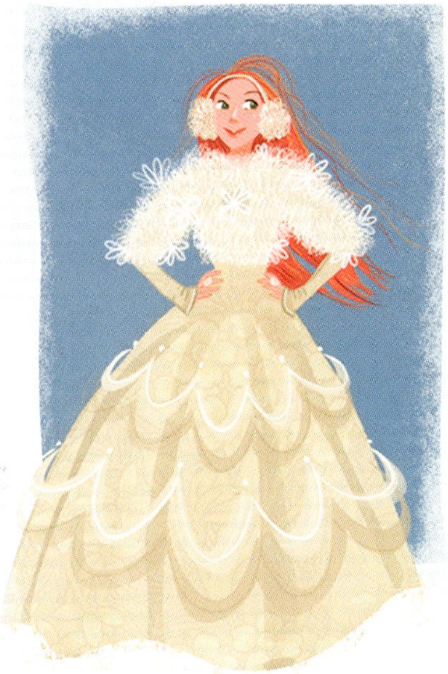

TAMMIE LYON

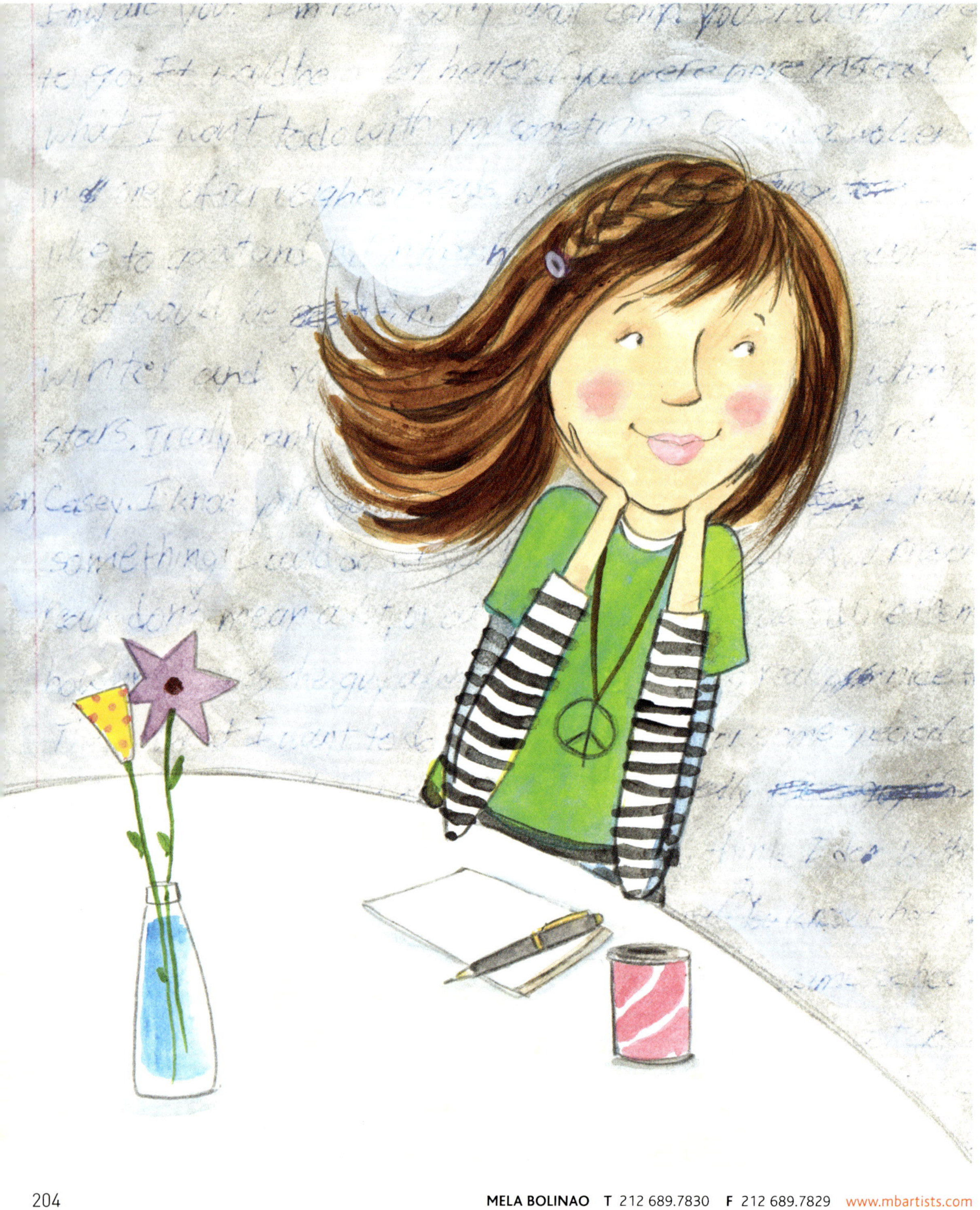

MELA BOLINAO T 212 689.7830 F 212 689.7829 www.mbartists.com

MACKY PAMINTUAN

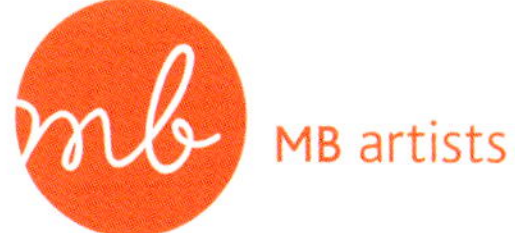

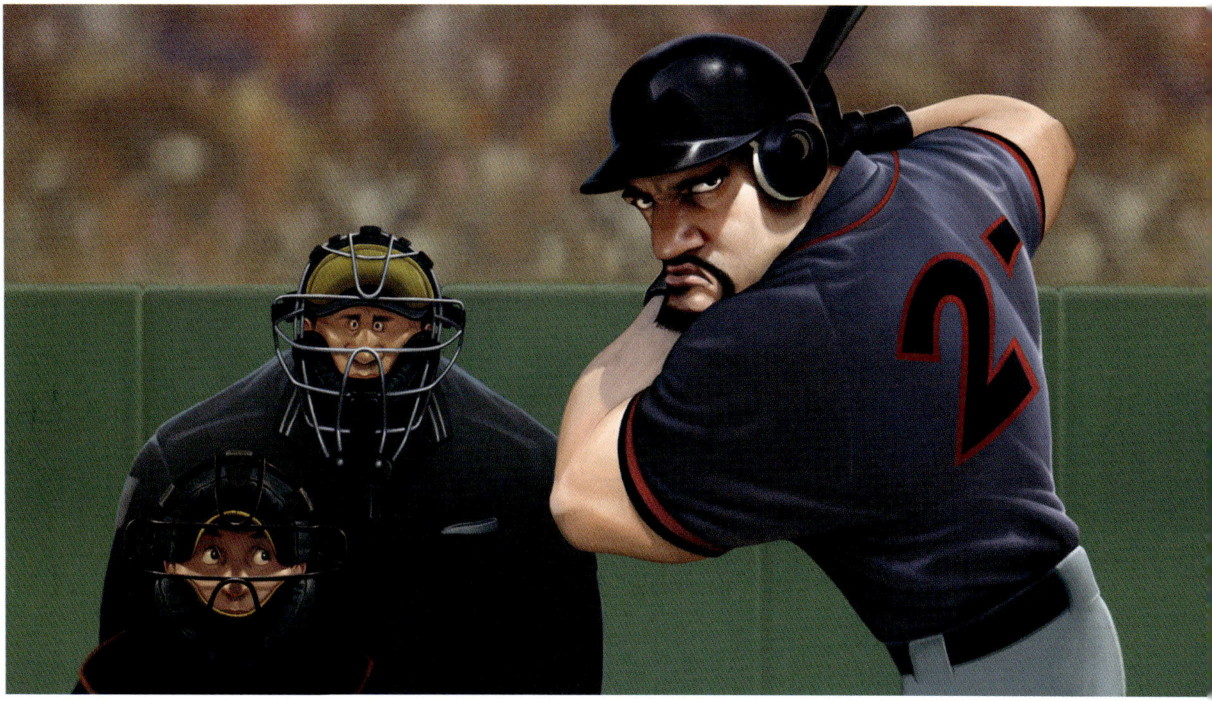

CECILIA RÉBORA

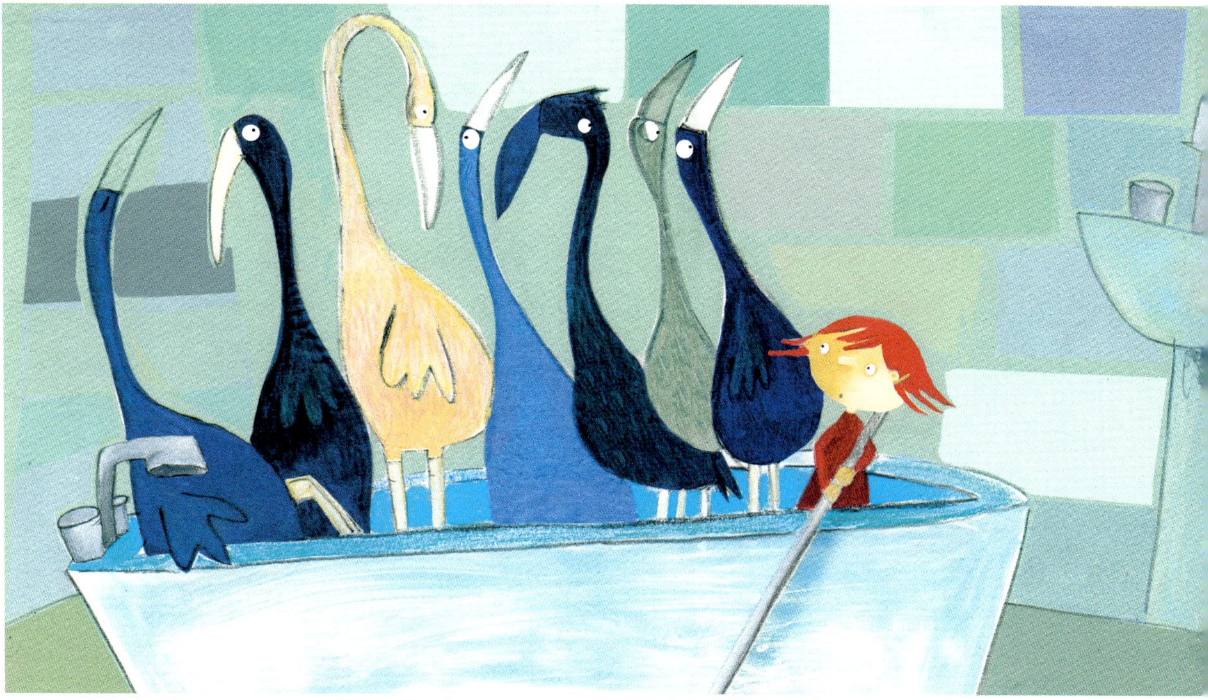

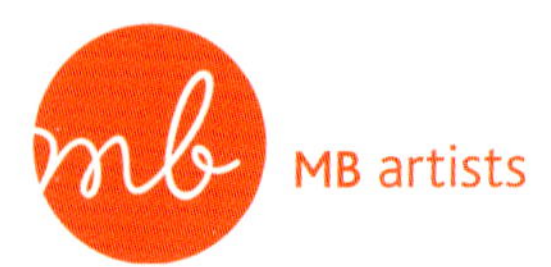

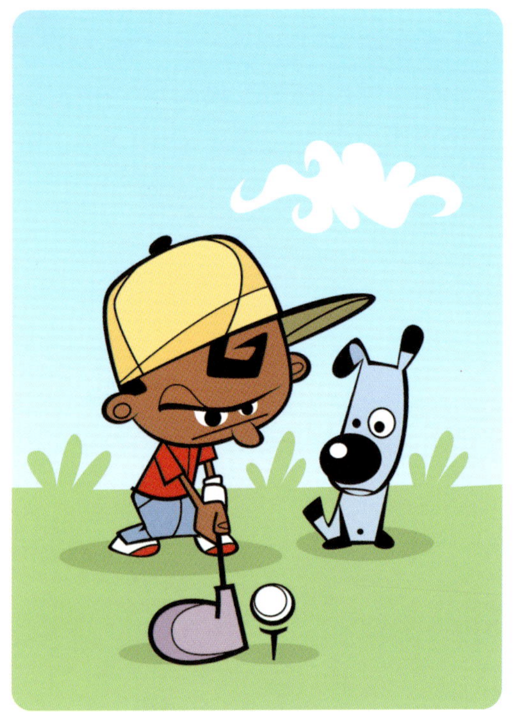

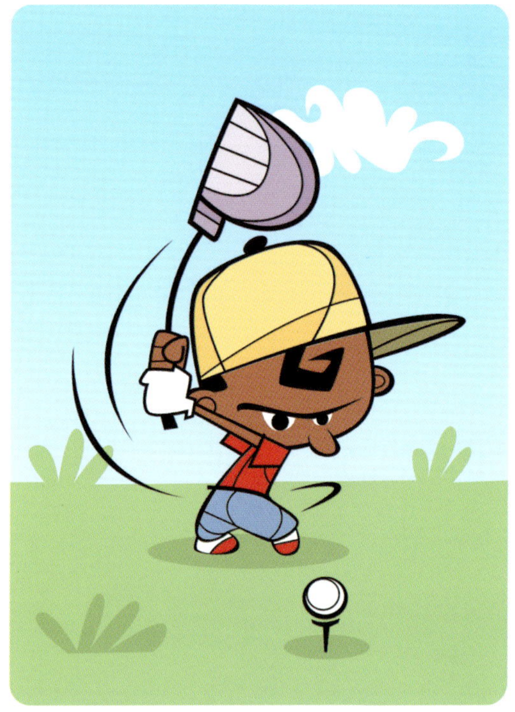

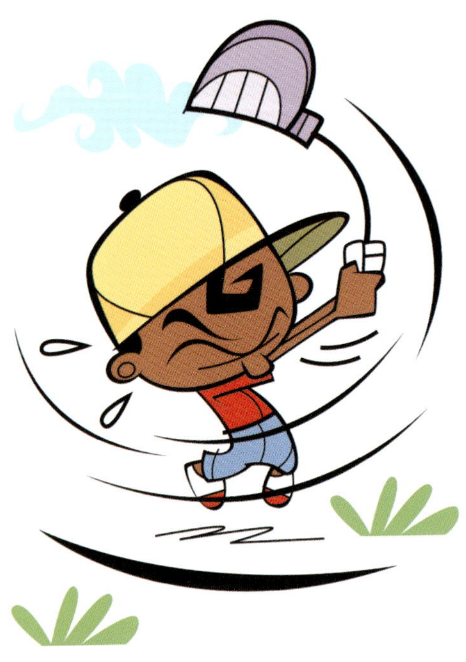

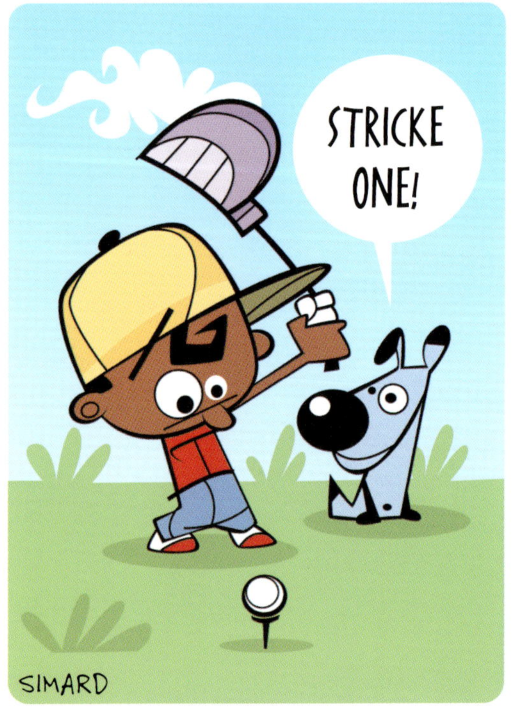

STRICKE ONE!
SIMARD

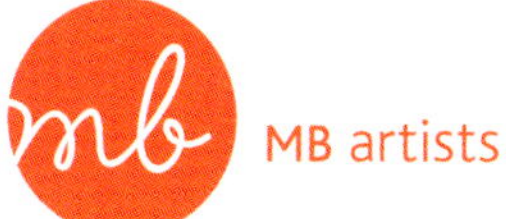

JOMIKE TEJIDO

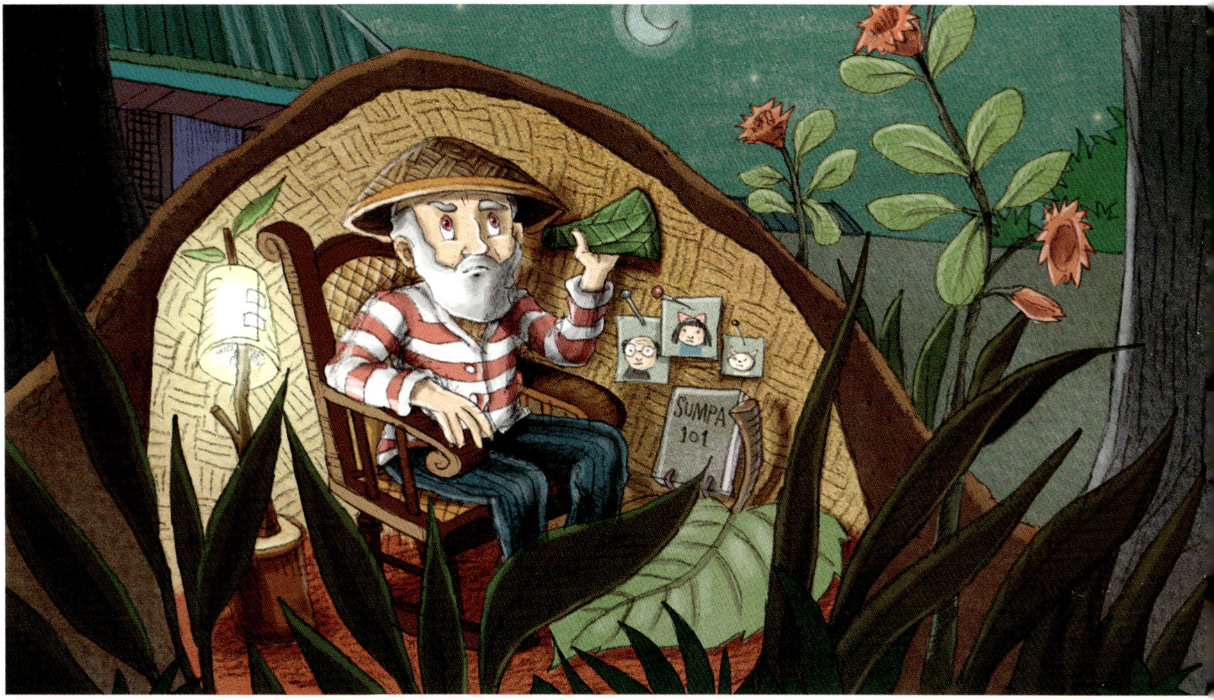

JENNIFER ZIVOIN

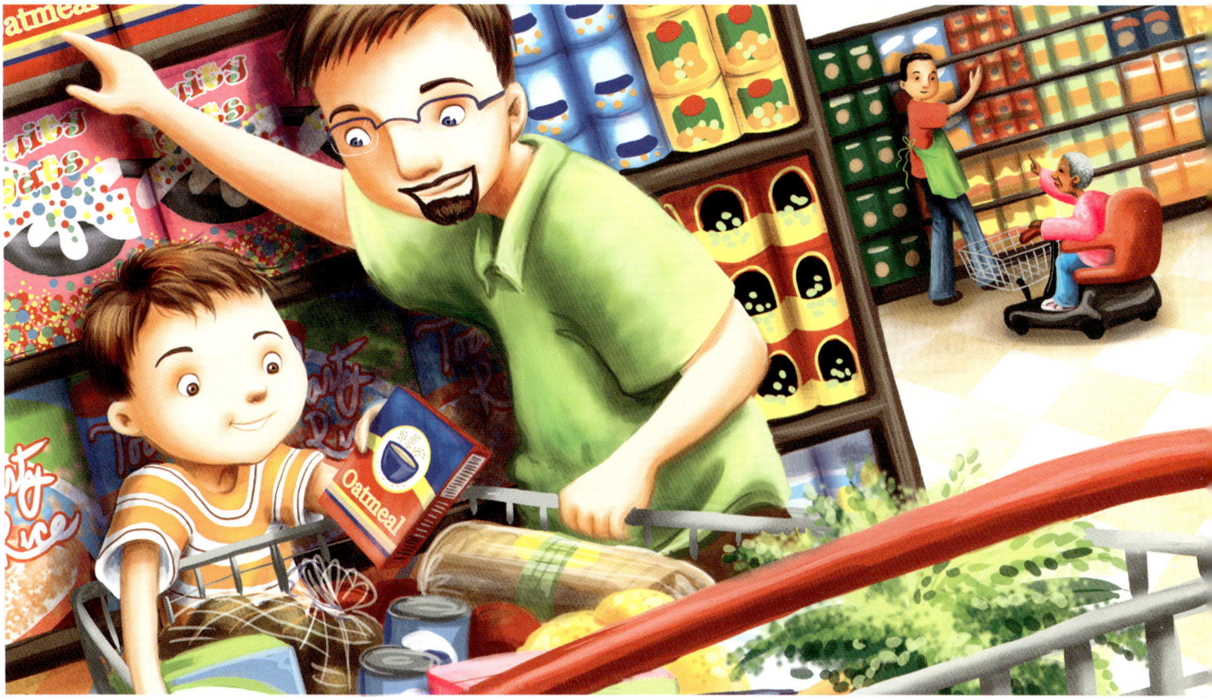

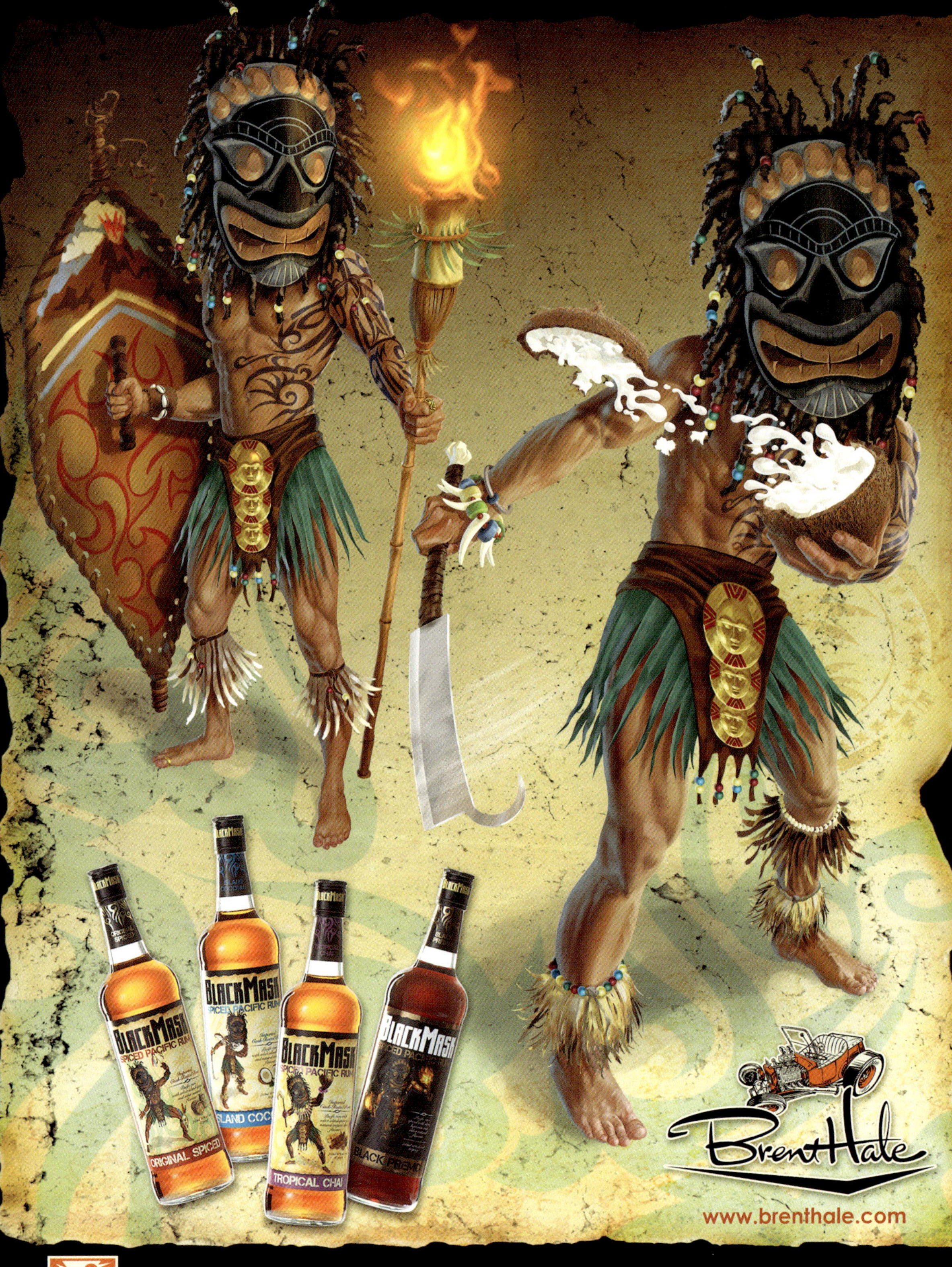

BLACKMASH
SPICED PACIFIC RUM
ORIGINAL SPICED

BLACKMASH
SPICED PACIFIC RUM
ISLAND COCO

BLACKMASH
SPICED PACIFIC RUM
TROPICAL CHAI

BLACKMASH
SPICED PACIFIC RUM
BLACK PREMO

BrentHale
www.brenthale.com

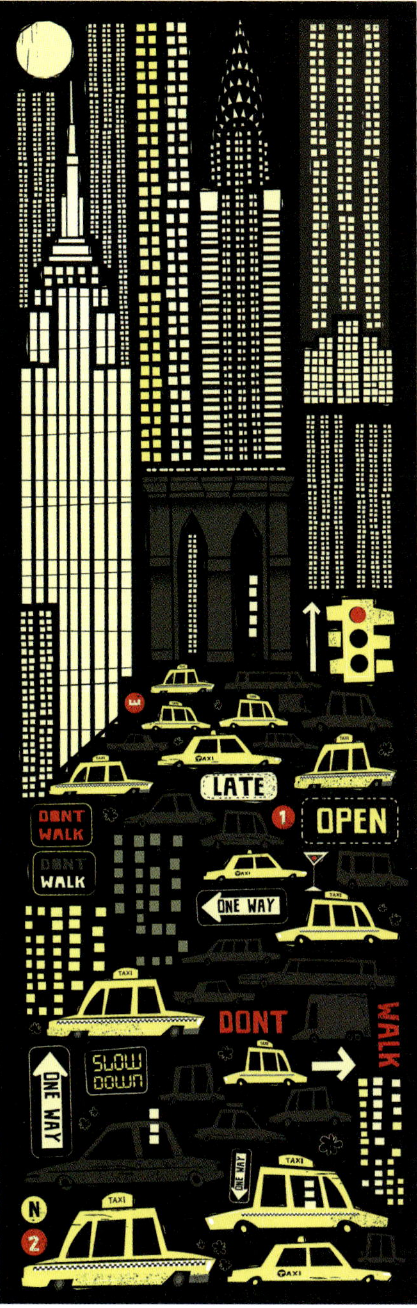

LATE
OPEN
DONT
WALK
DONT
WALK
ONE WAY
DONT
WALK
SLOW
DOWN
ONE WAY
TAXI
TAXI
TAXI
TAXI
TAXI
N
2

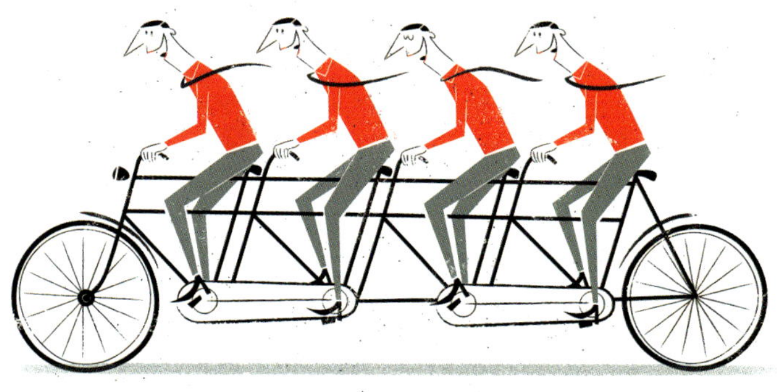

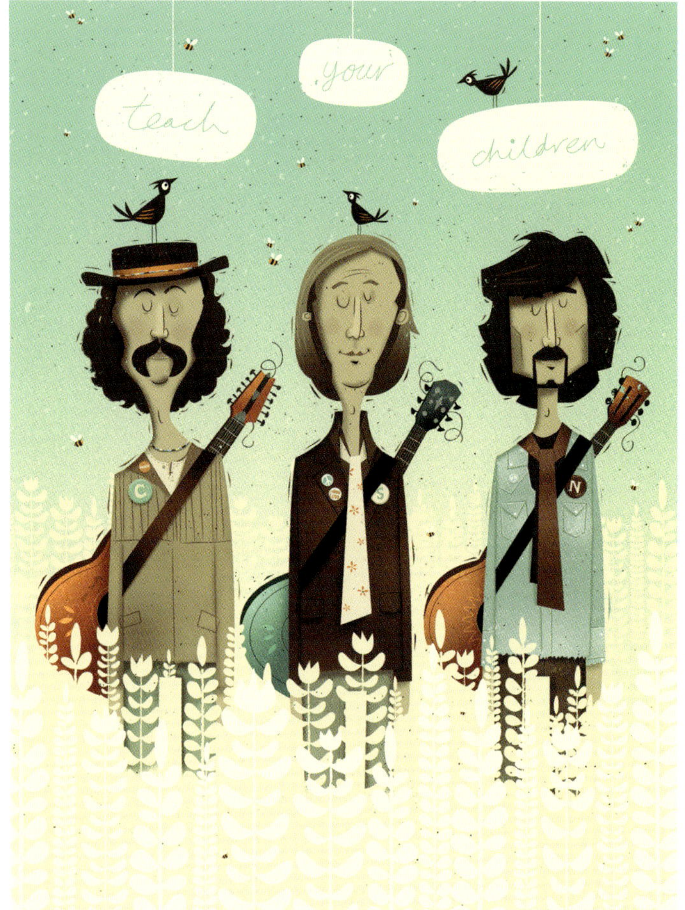

teach
your
children

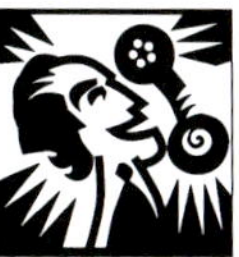

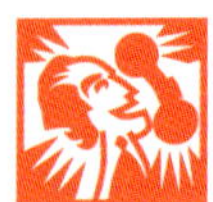

The art of
Genuine
CARTOON SUPERPOWER!
MARTY BAUMANN
WWW.MARTYBAUMANN.COM 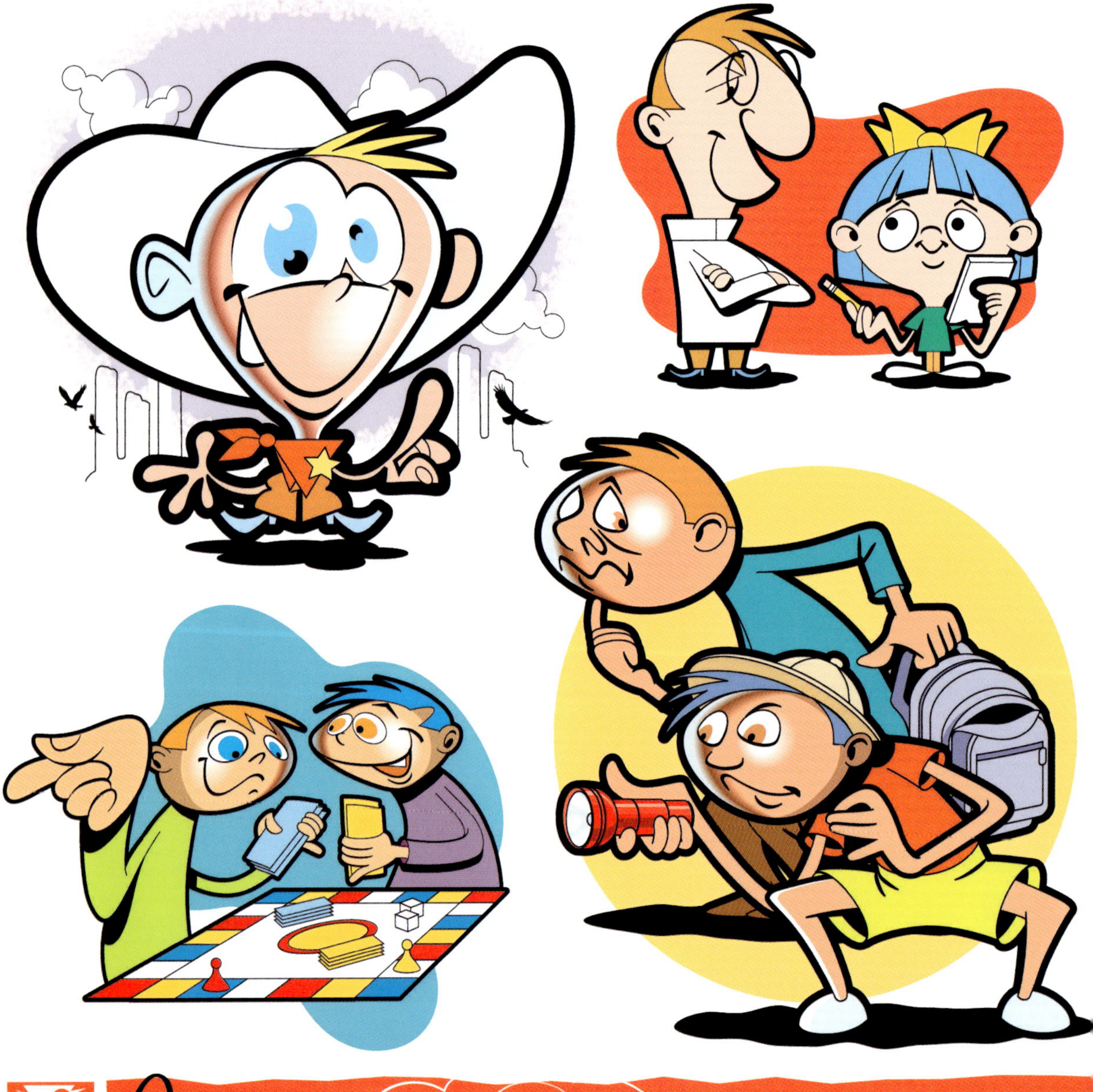
Contact JOHN BREWSTER · 203·226·4724

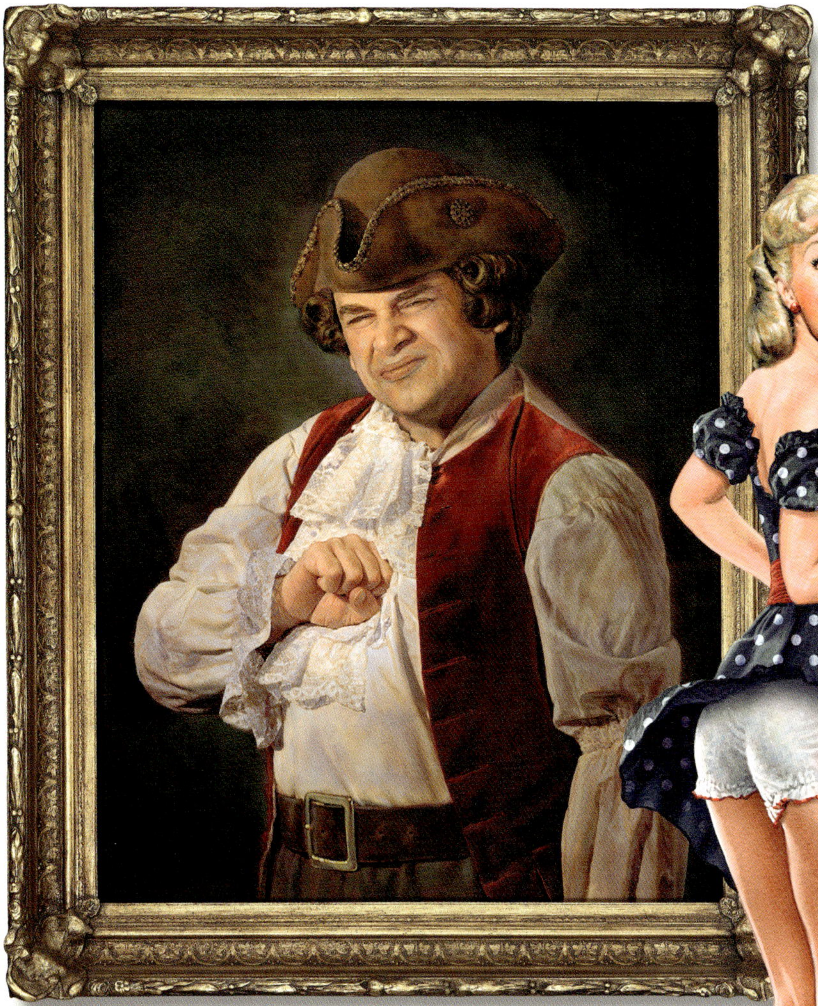

Client: Prilosec OTC/Larry "The Cable Guy"

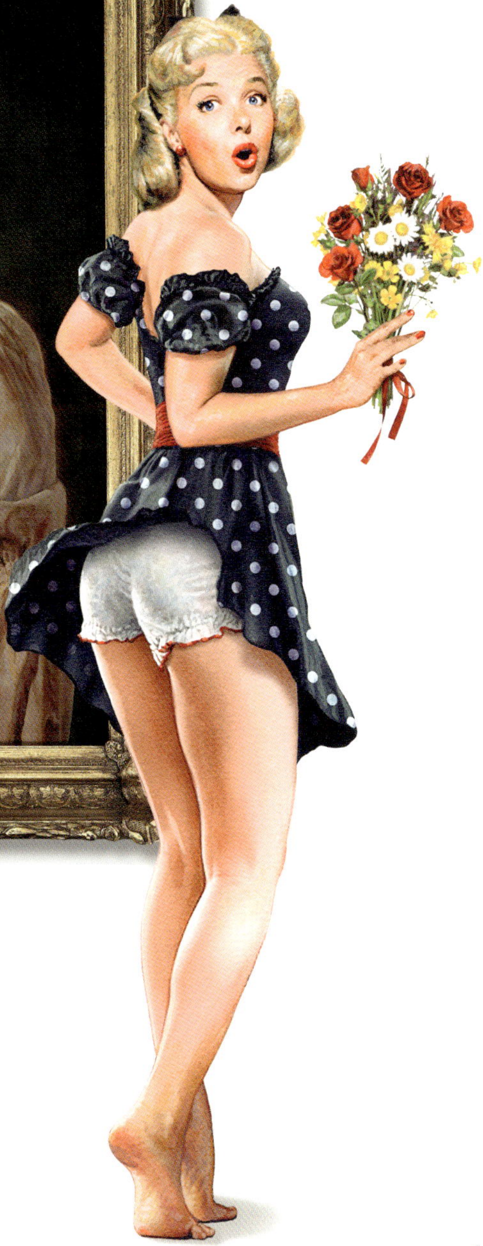

Sharif Tarabay

Client: Bloomers Flowers

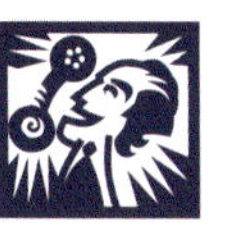

JOHN BREWSTER CREATIVE SERVICES
PHONE: 203.226.4724
FAX: 203.454.9904
E-MAIL: CREATIVE.SVCS@SNET.NET
WEB: BREWSTERCREATIVE.COM

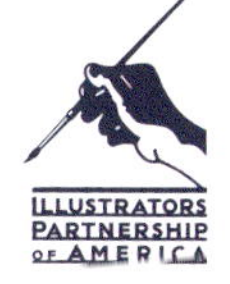

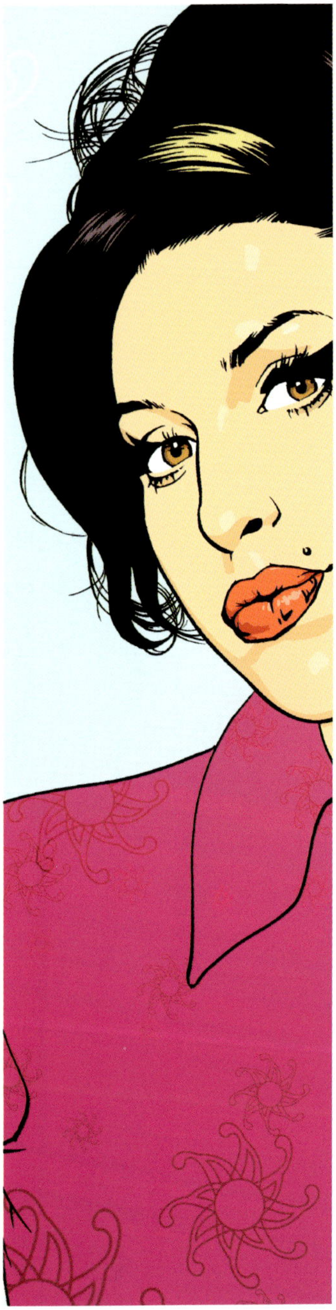

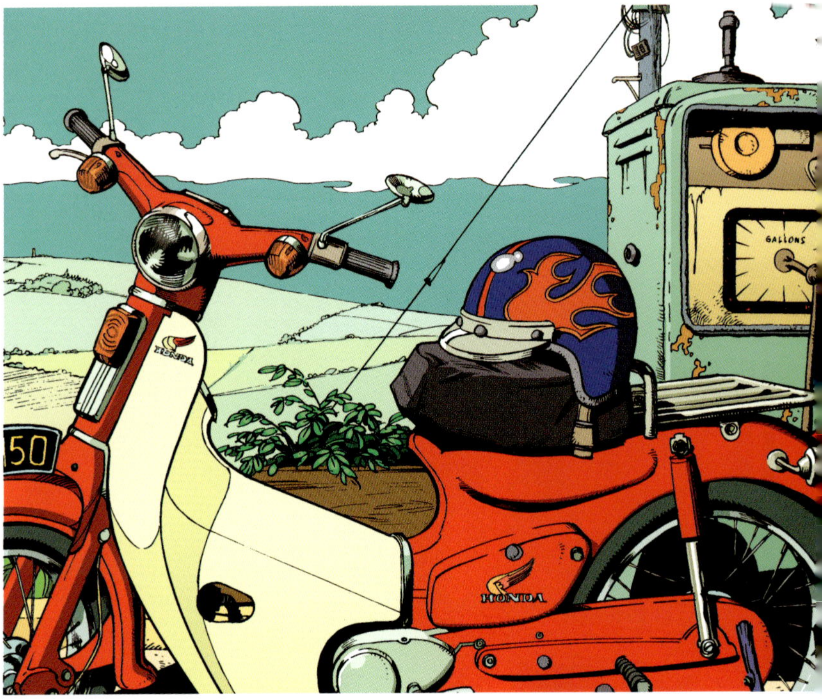

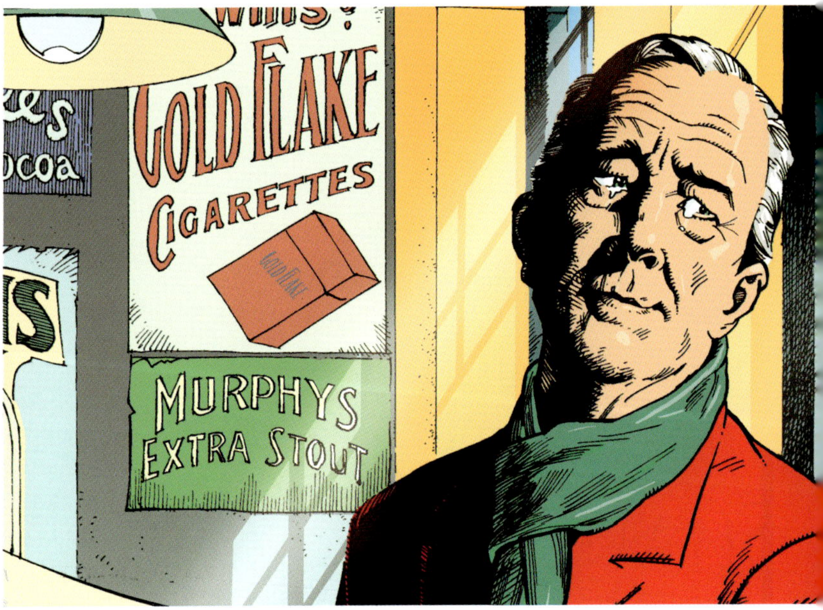

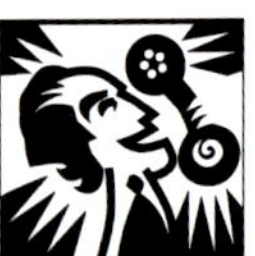

Glenn Gustafson

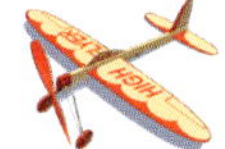
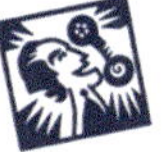

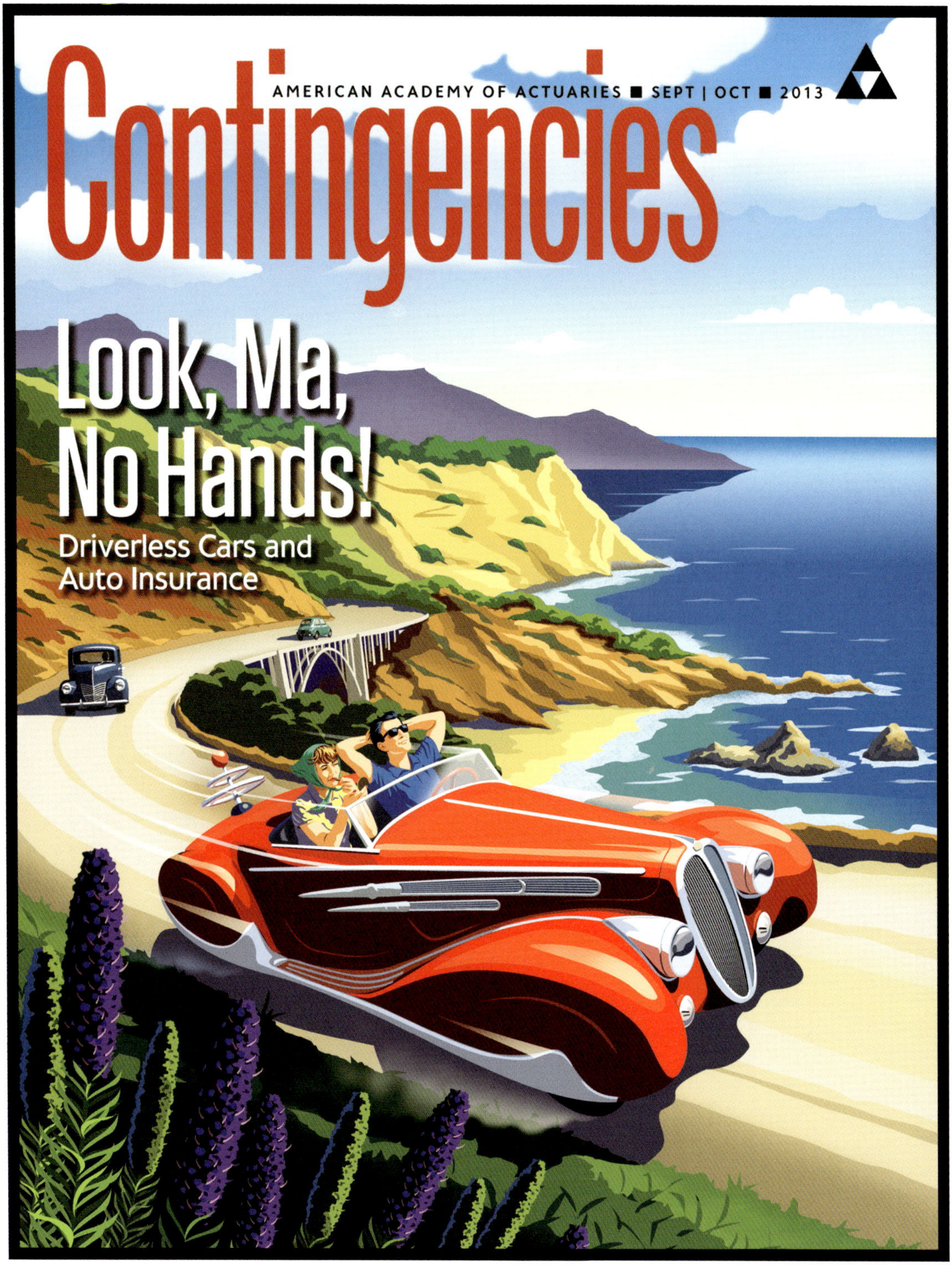

AMERICAN ACADEMY OF ACTUARIES ■ SEPT | OCT ■ 2013
Contingencies
Look, Ma, No Hands!
Driverless Cars and Auto Insurance
www.glenngustafson.com
Represented by: John Brewster ■ 203.226.4724

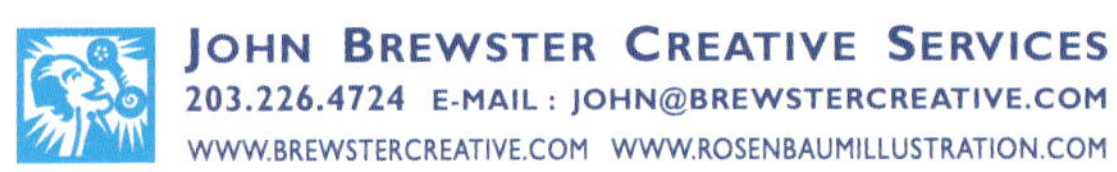

Jonathan & Georgina Rosenbaum

John Brewster Creative Services
203.226.4724 E-MAIL : JOHN@BREWSTERCREATIVE.COM
WWW.BREWSTERCREATIVE.COM   WWW.ROSENBAUMILLUSTRATION.COM

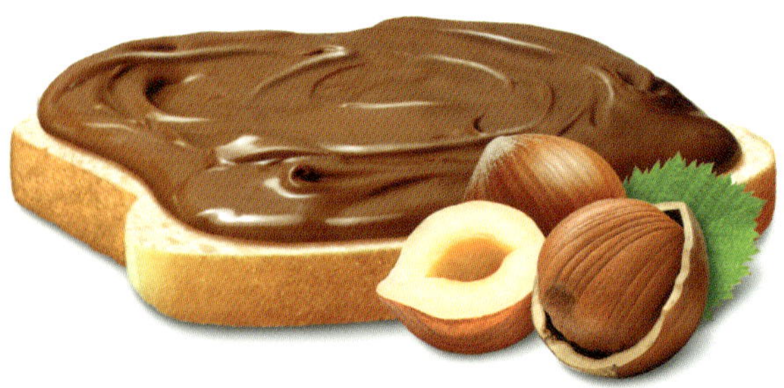

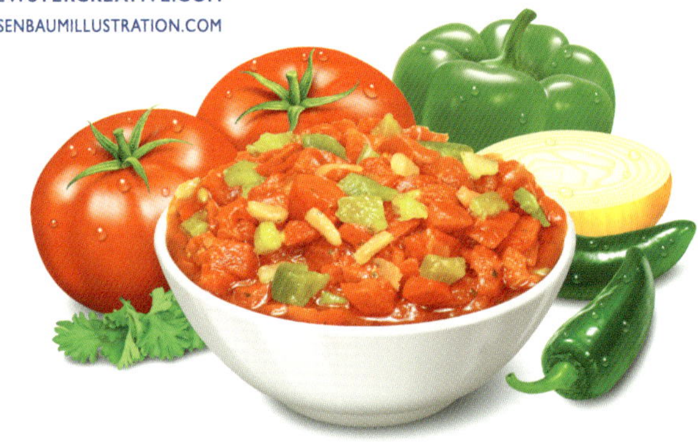

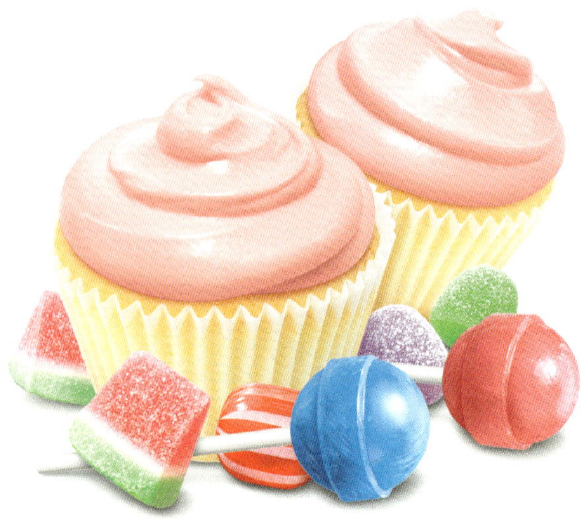

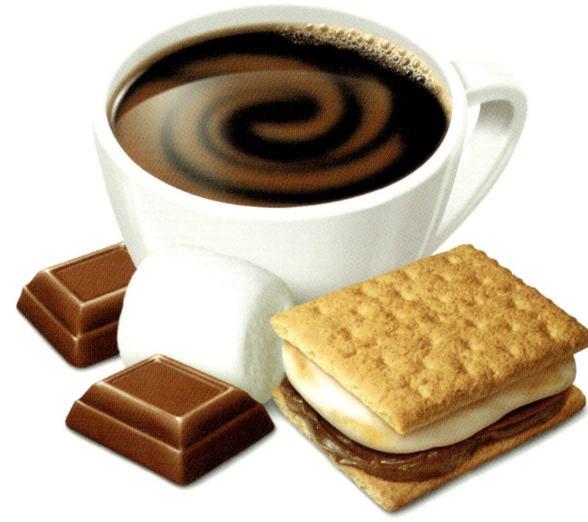

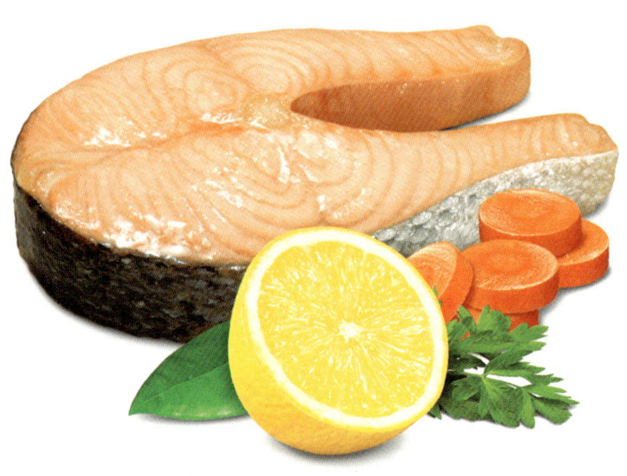

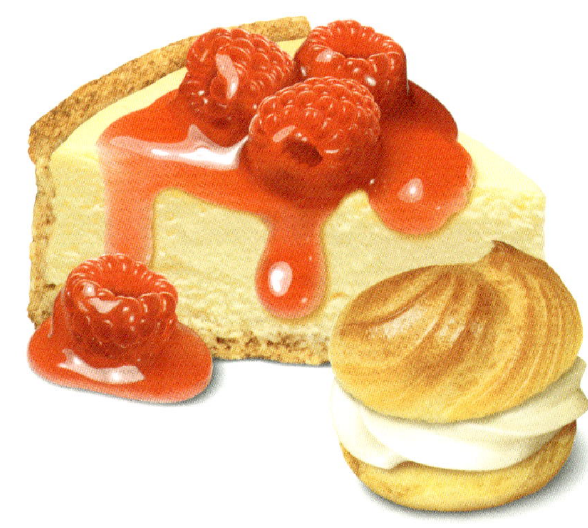

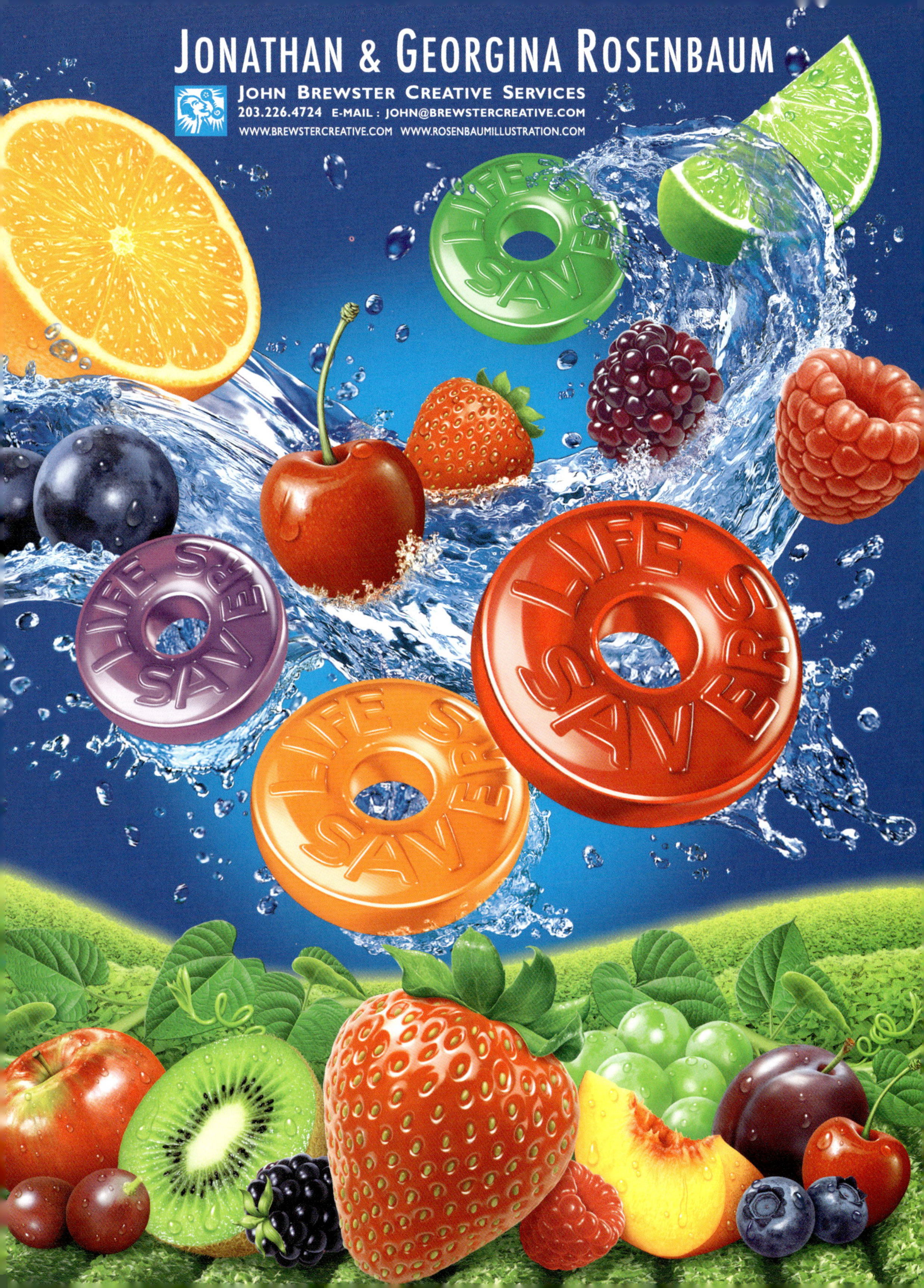

JONATHAN & GEORGINA ROSENBAUM
JOHN BREWSTER CREATIVE SERVICES
203.226.4724 E-MAIL : JOHN@BREWSTERCREATIVE.COM
WWW.BREWSTERCREATIVE.COM WWW.ROSENBAUMILLUSTRATION.COM
LIFE SAVERS

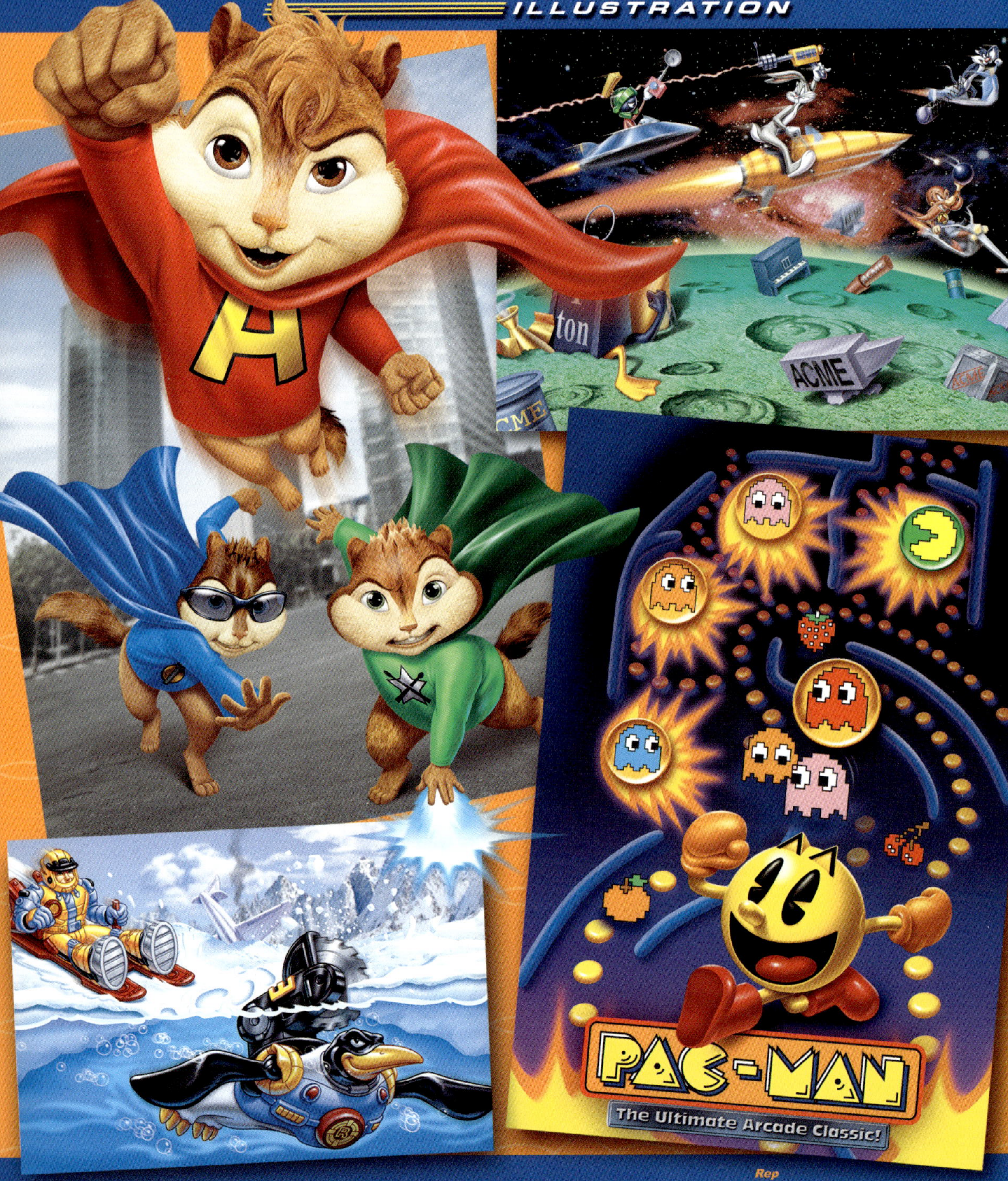

Phillip Hom
ILLUSTRATION
ACME
PAC-MAN
The Ultimate Arcade Classic!
studio
818.400.6395
studio@philliphom.com
www.philliphom.com
Rep
John Brewster
203.226.4724
john@brewstercreative.com
www.brewstercreative.com

LANE DU PONT

John Brewster Creative Services
Phone 203.226.4724
Fax 203.454.9904
John@brewstercreative.com
www.brewstercreative.com

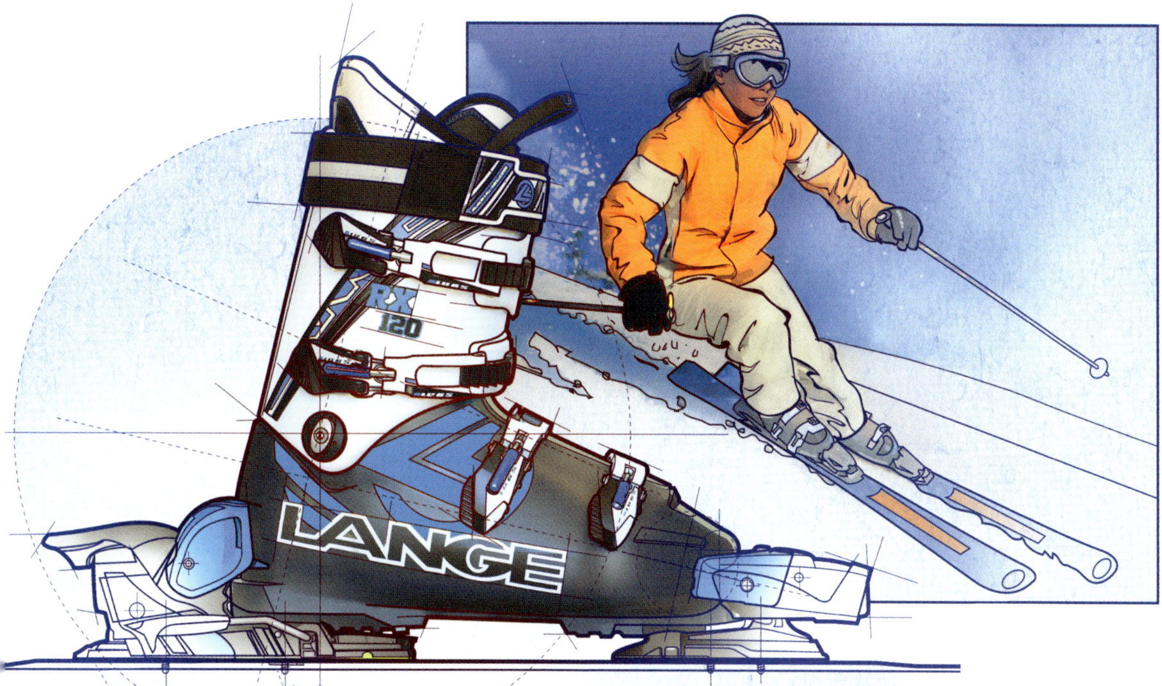

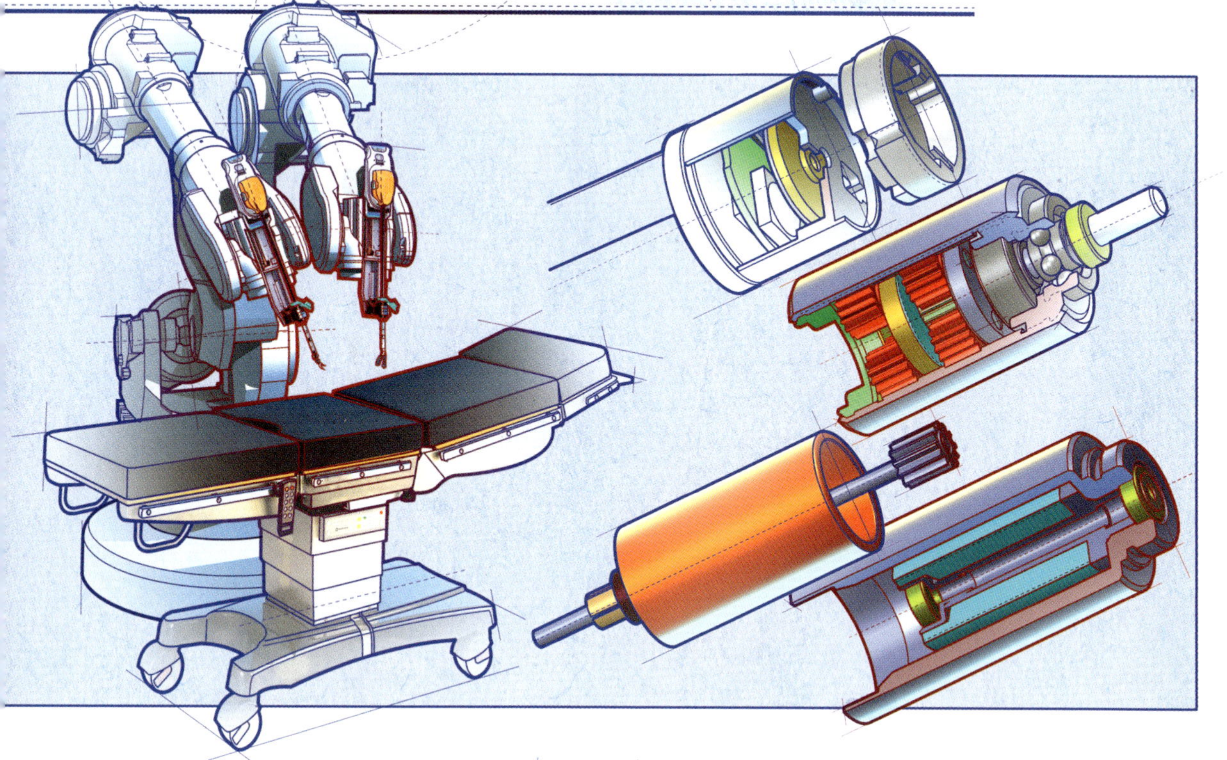

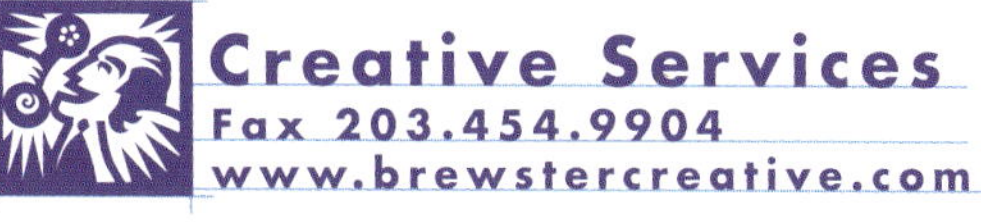

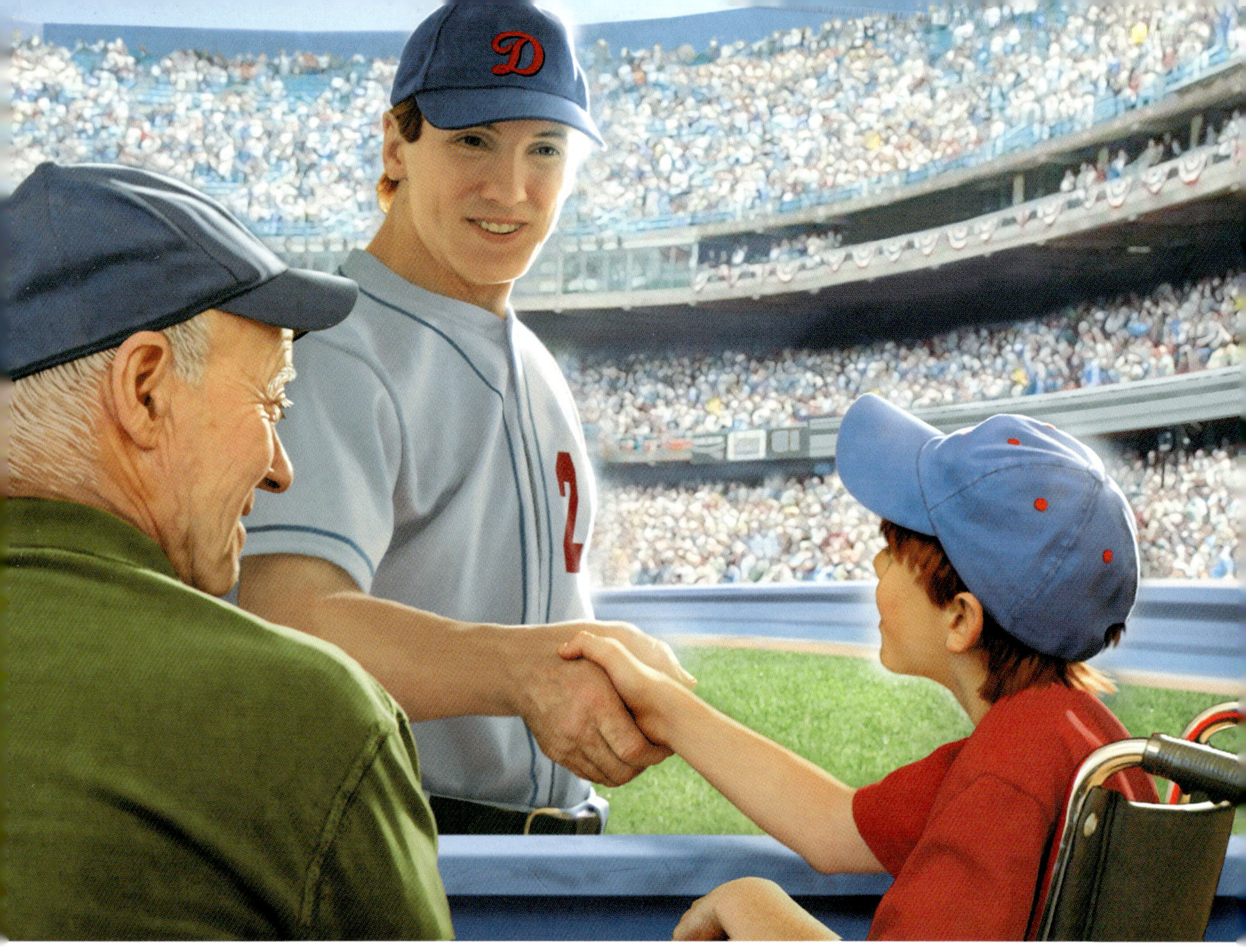

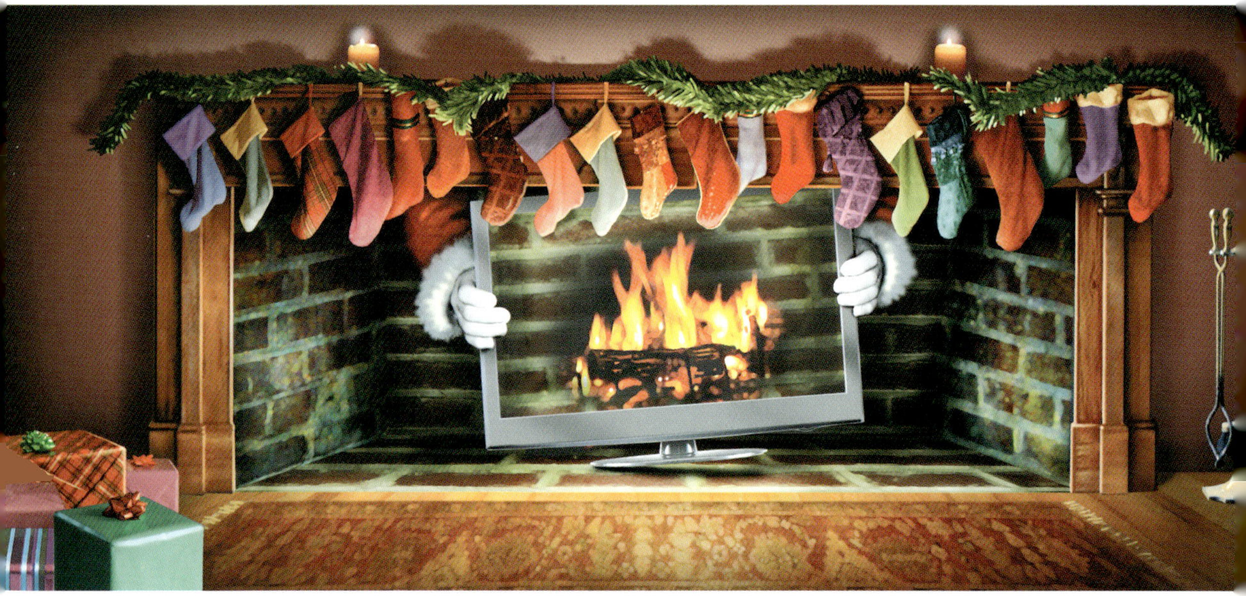

CHRISTOPHER PETERSON

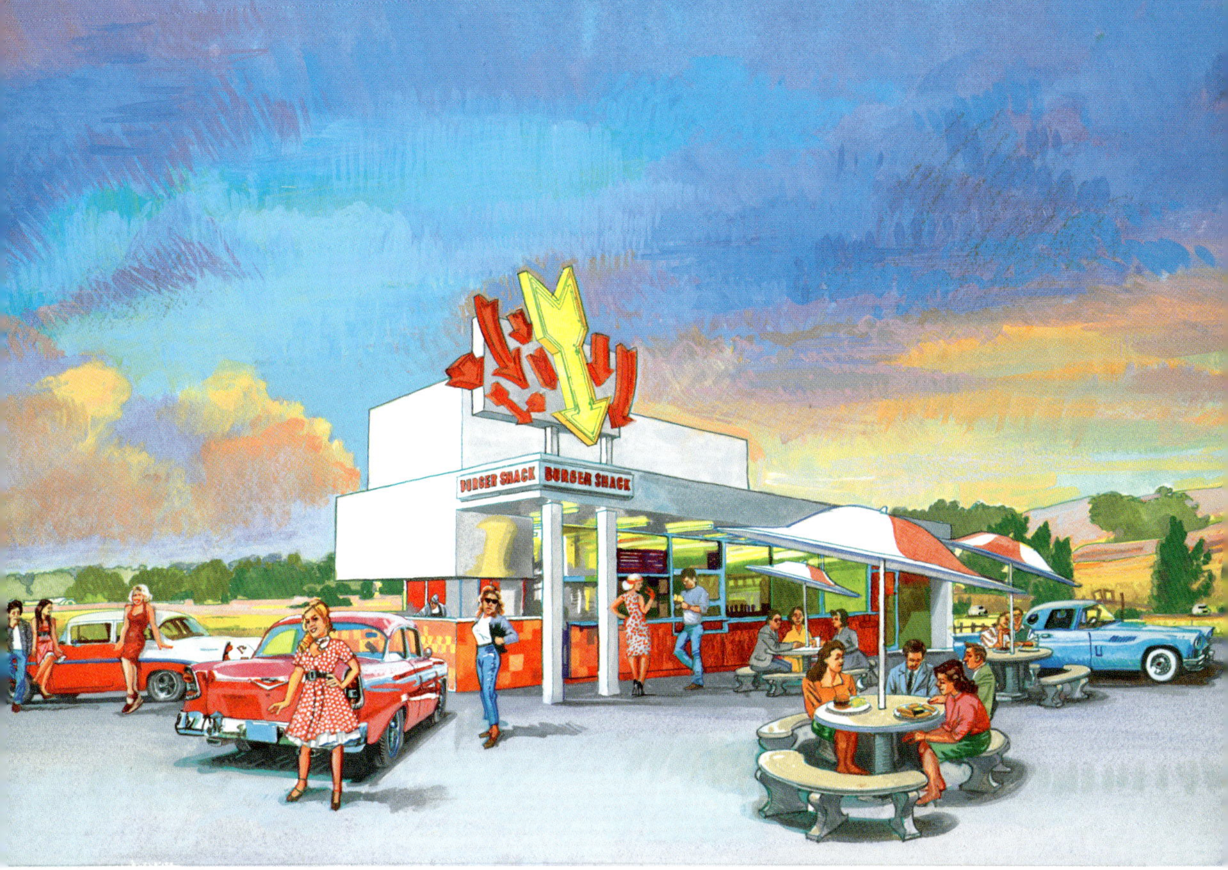

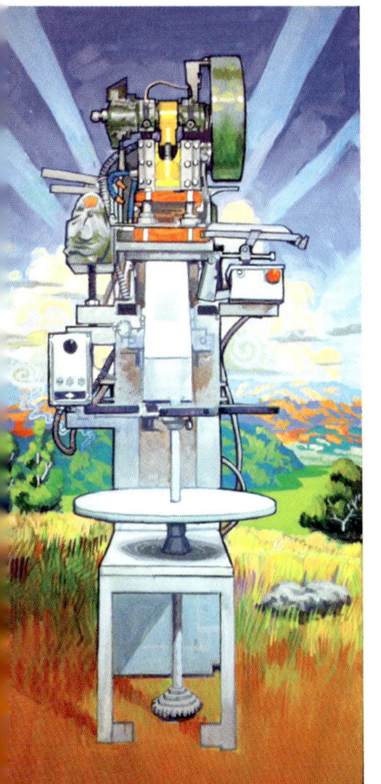

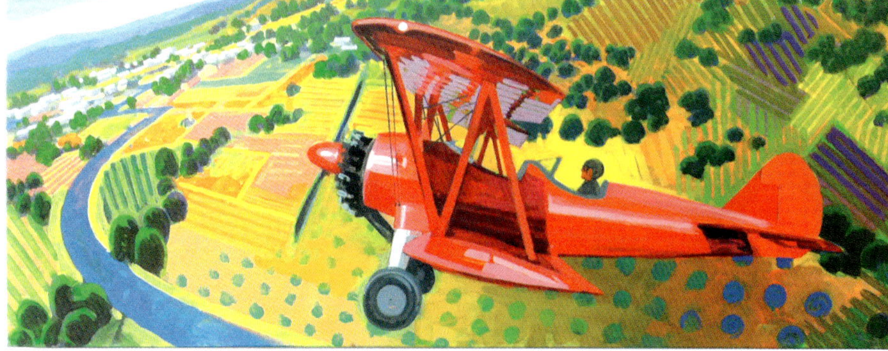

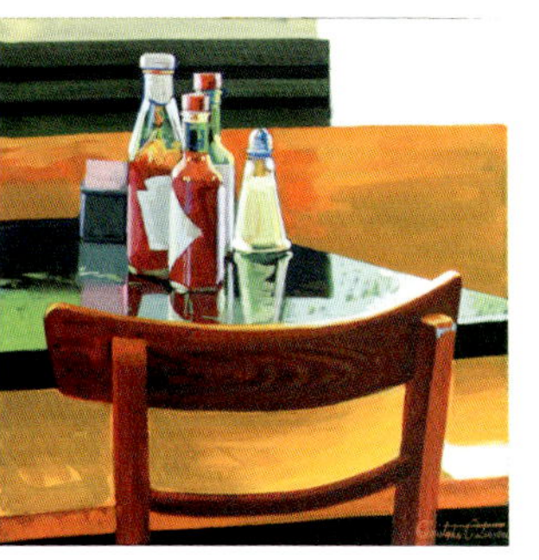

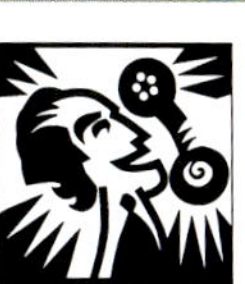

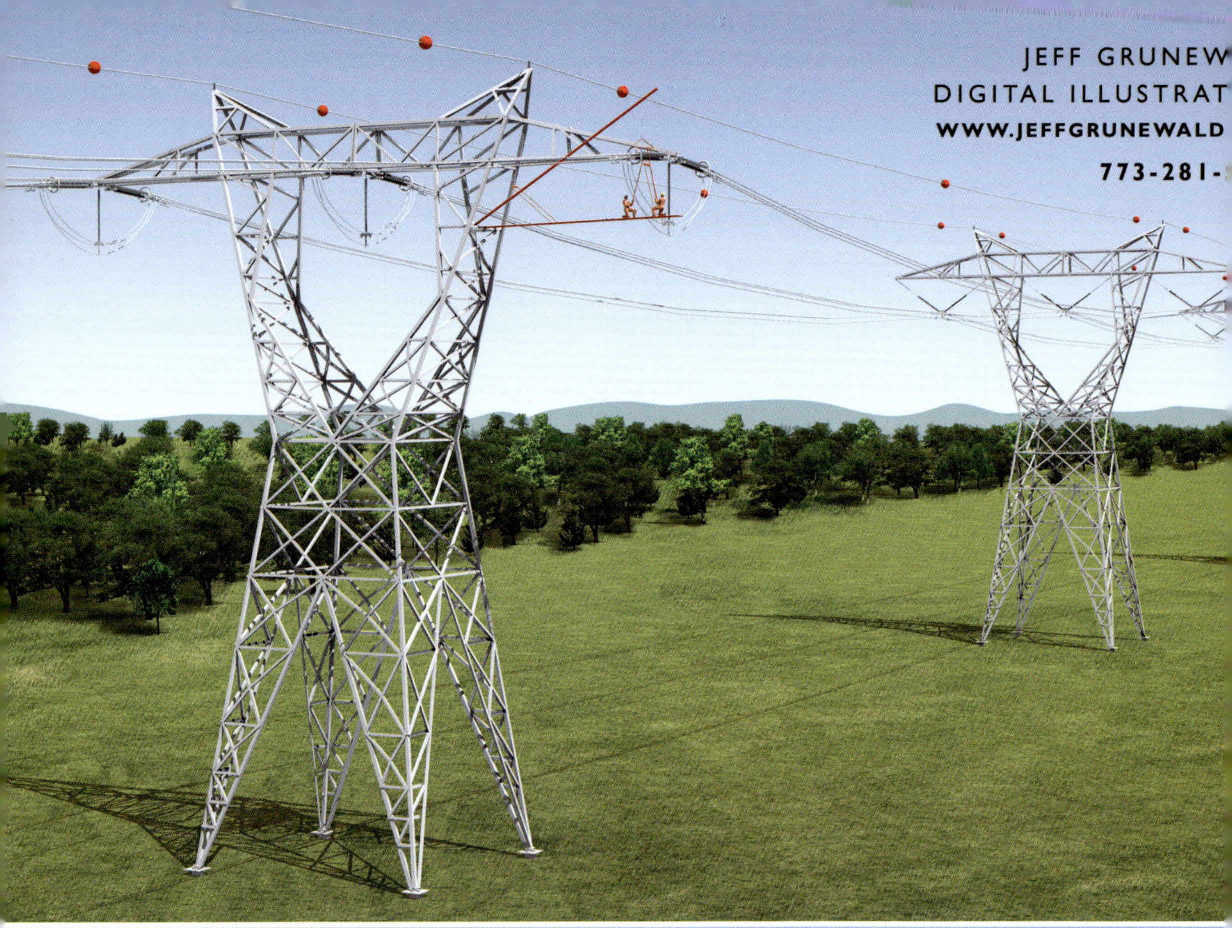

JEFF GRUNEW
DIGITAL ILLUSTRAT
WWW.JEFFGRUNEWALD
773-281-

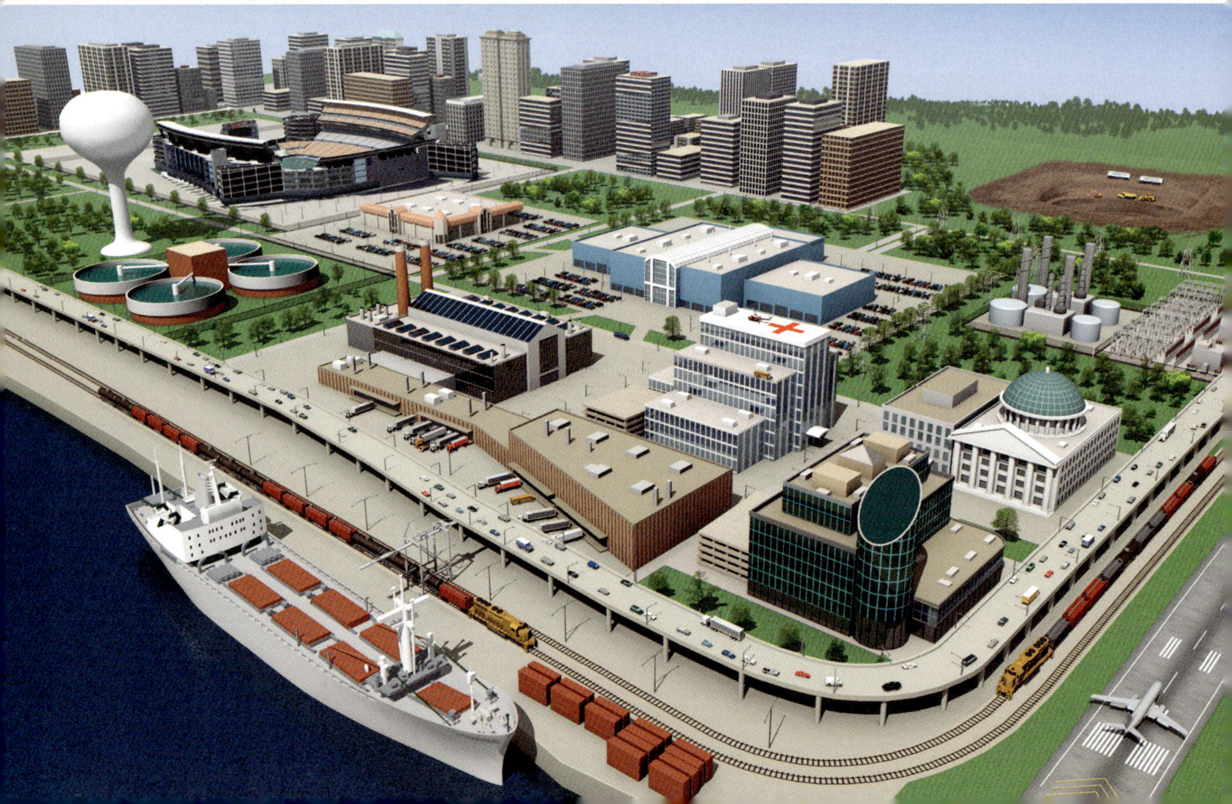

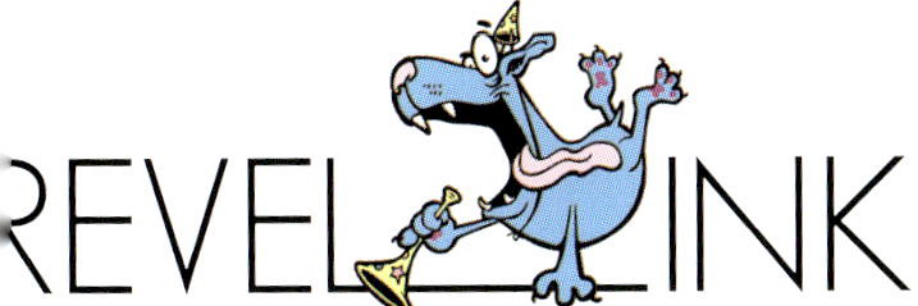

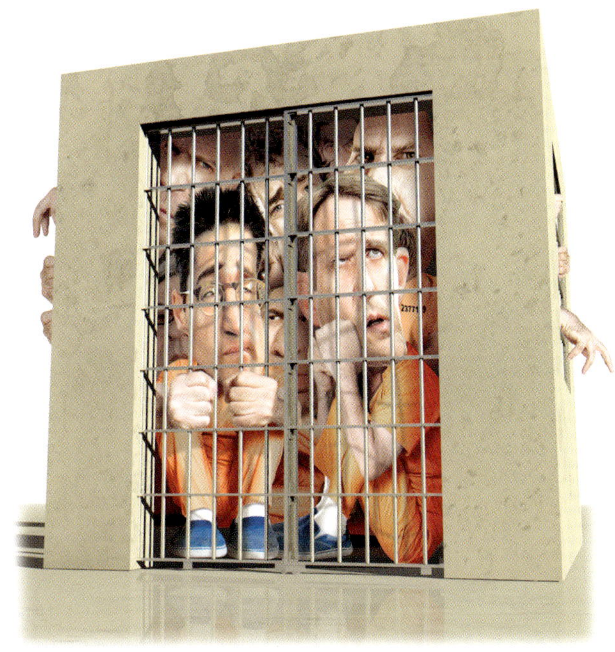

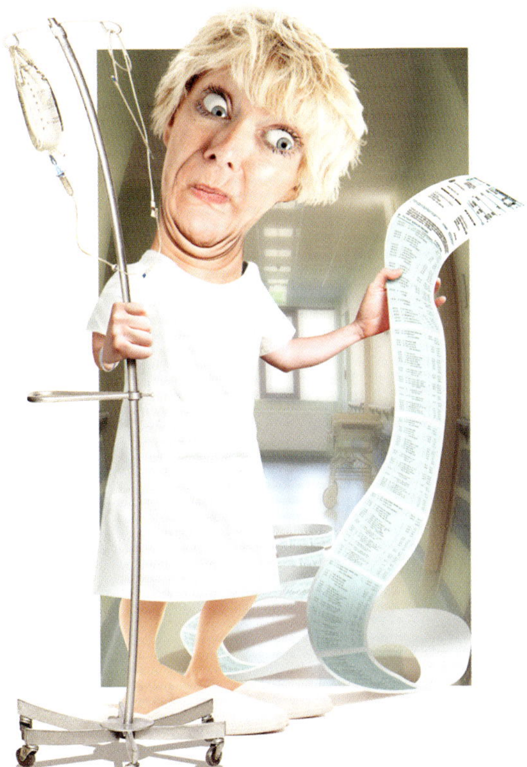

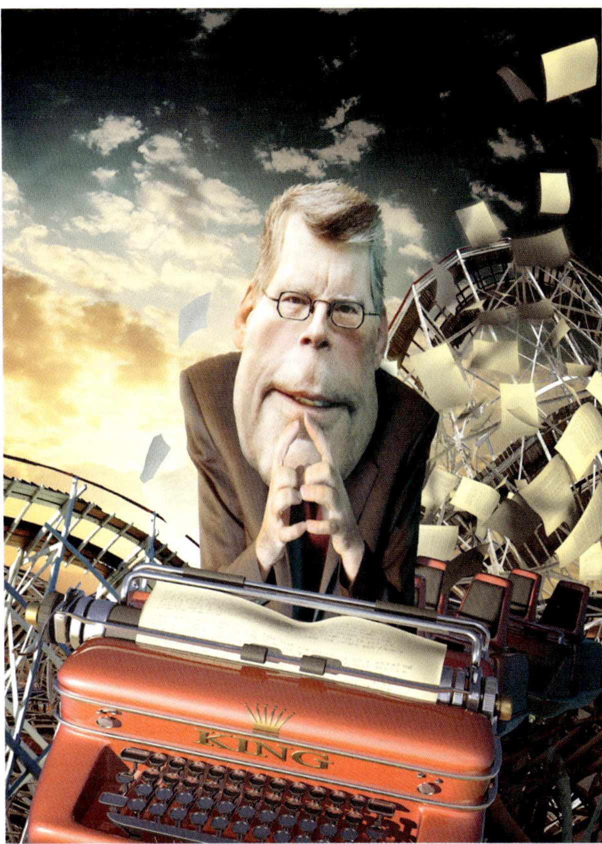

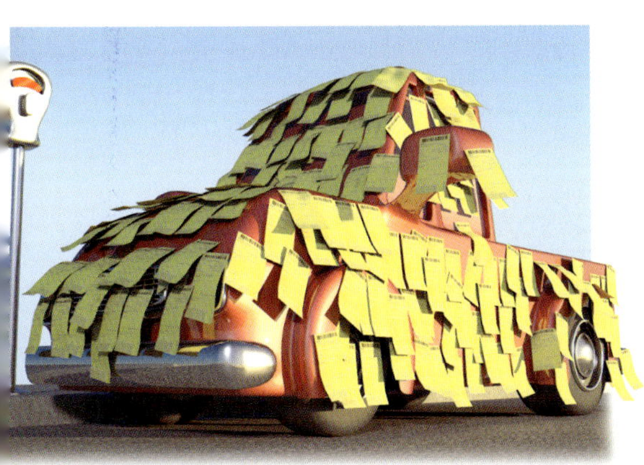

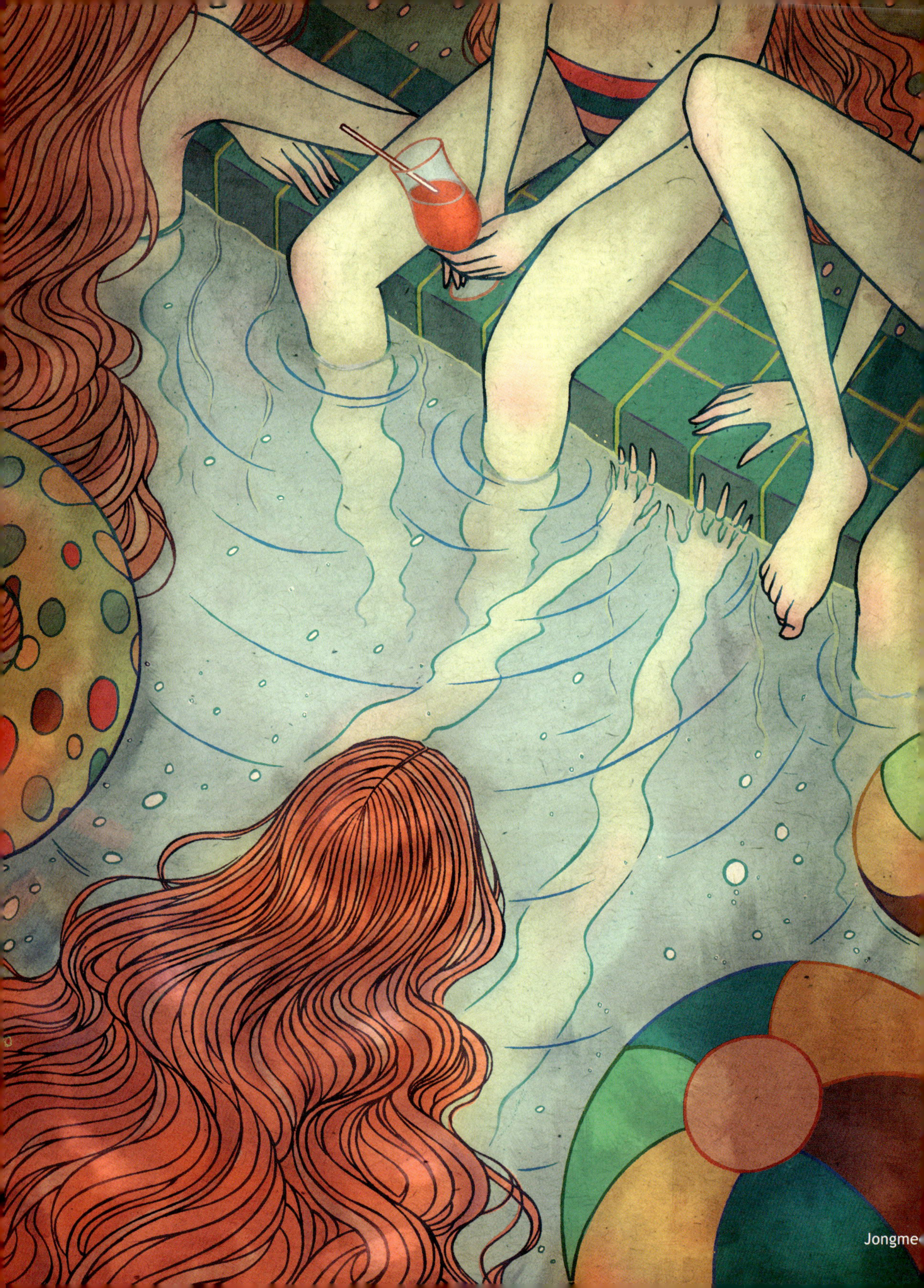
Jongme

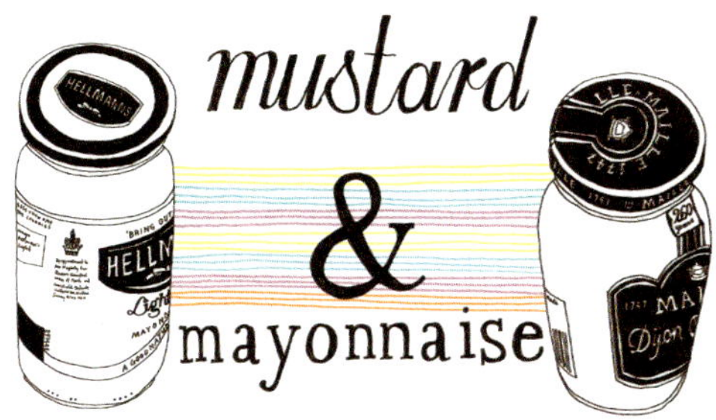

Zoe More O'Ferrall

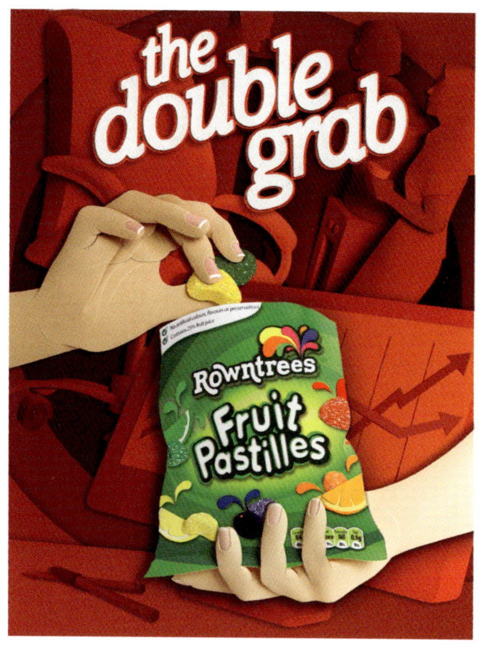

Gail Armstrong

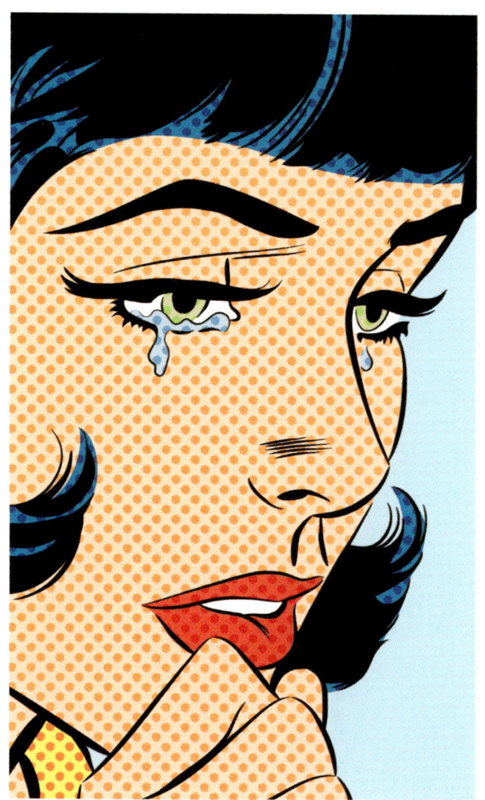

Joseph McDermott

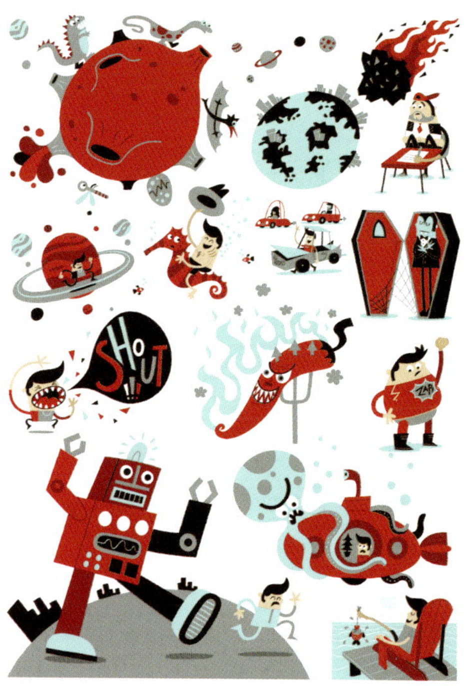

Tim Bradford

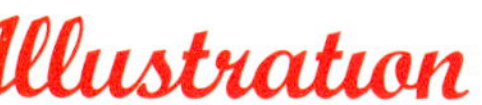
illustration

E howdy@illustrationweb.com
T 888.645.5878

70A Greenwich Ave #278
New York
NY 10011

illustrationweb.com

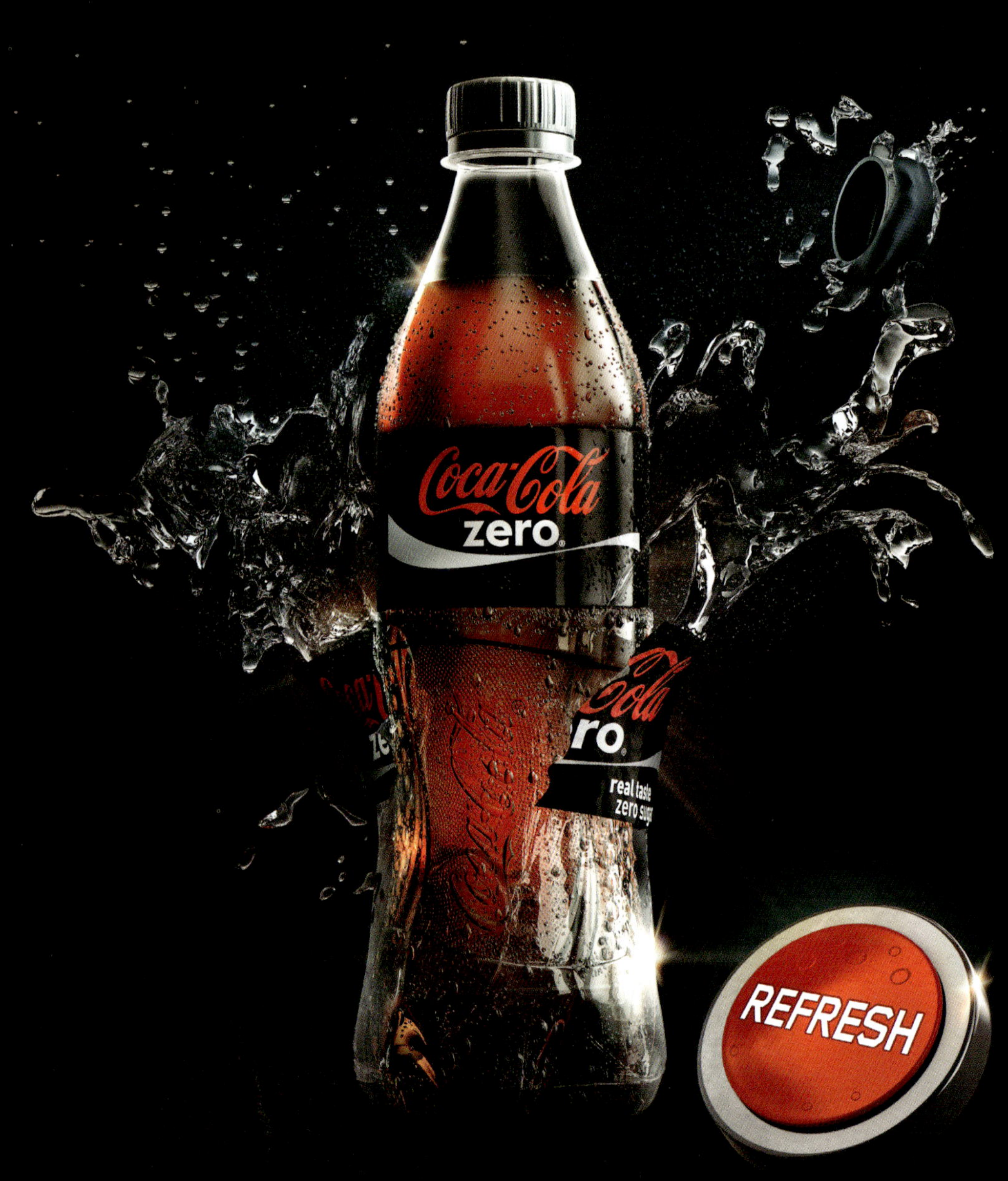
Coca-Cola
zero.
real taste
zero sugar
REFRESH
IGNIT

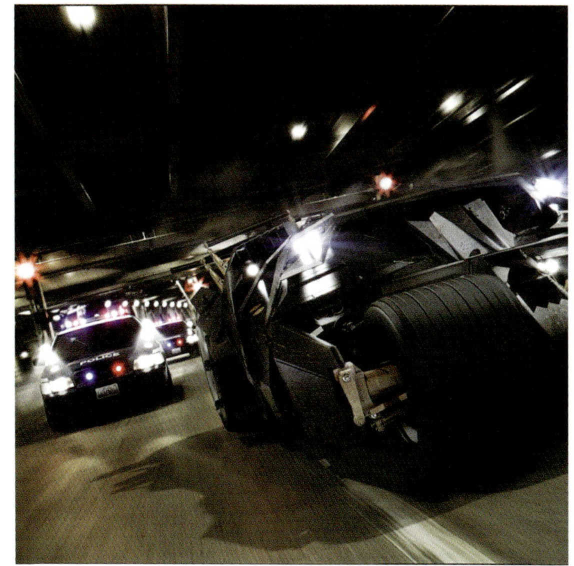
KLICK

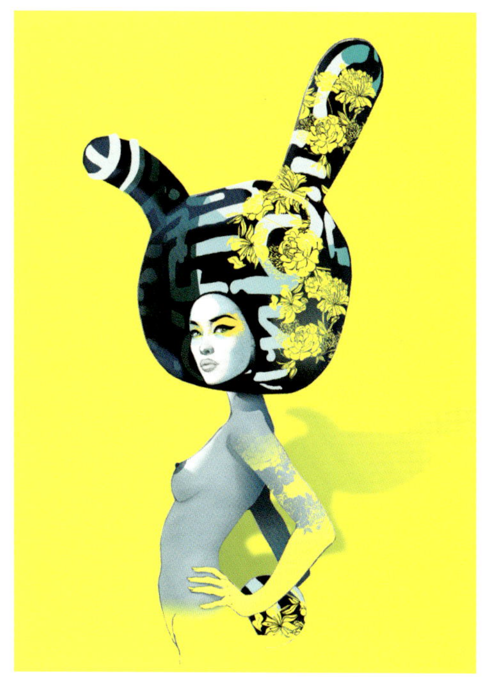
Gustabo

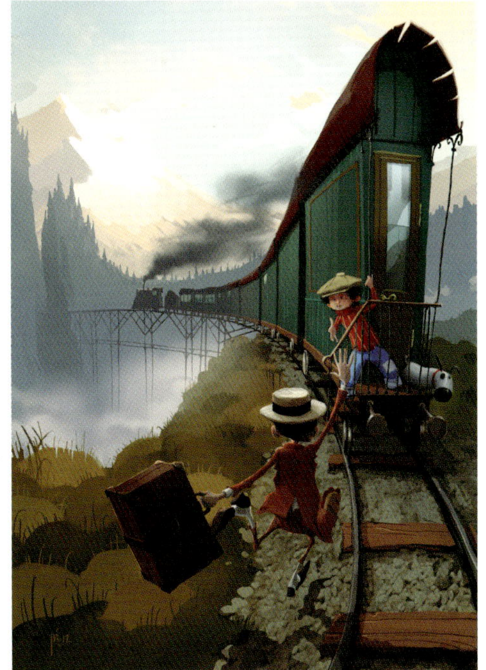
Fernando Juarez

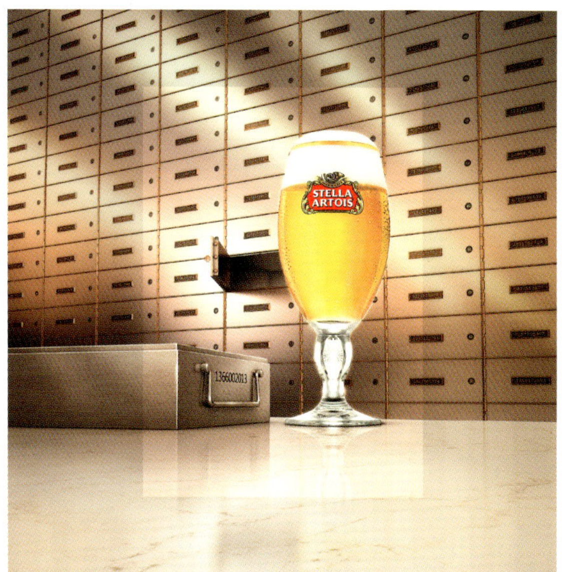

CUBE

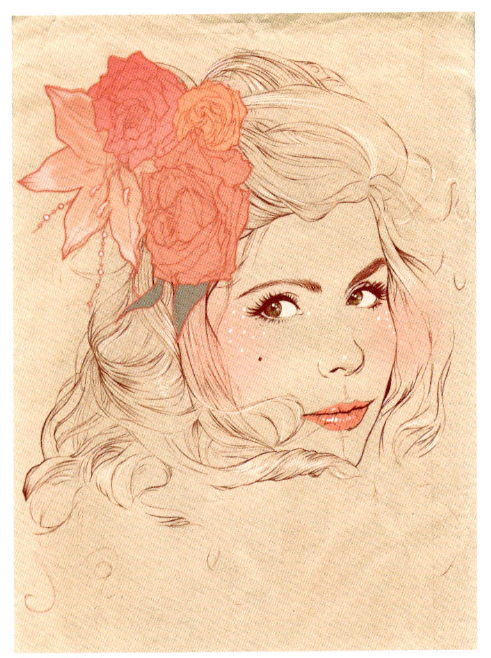

Miss Led

Jacqueline Bissett

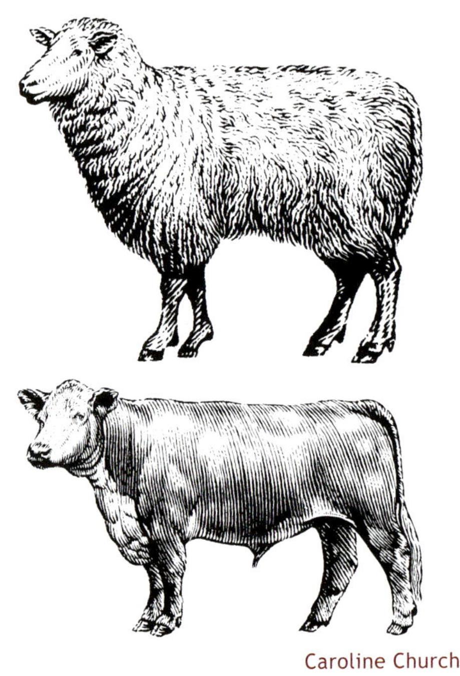

Caroline Church

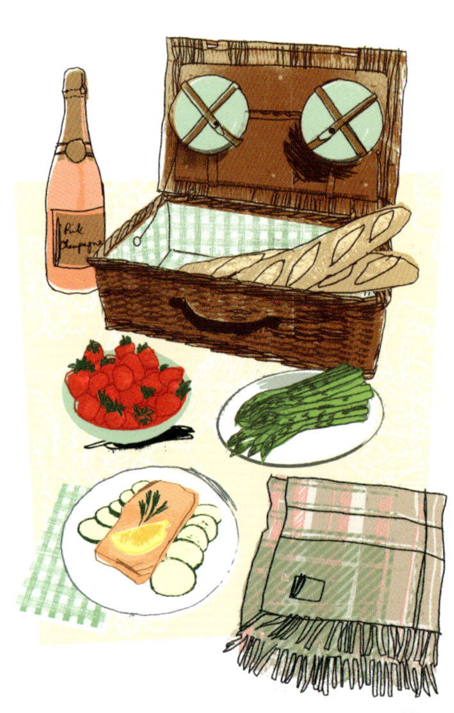

Kavel Rafferty

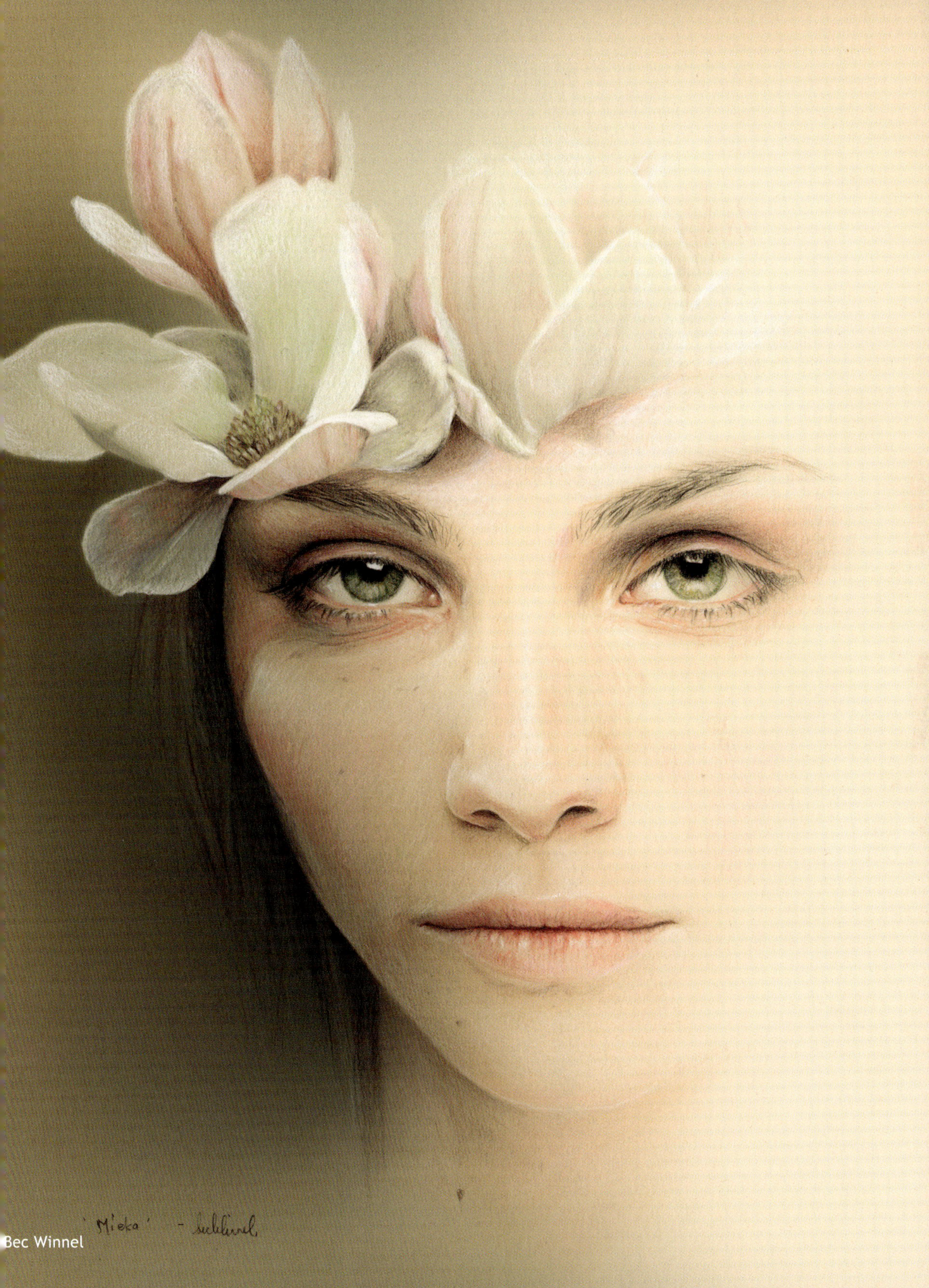

'Mieka' - becwinnel
Bec Winnel

Budweiser
AB
AB
KING OF BEERS
HYESU LEE

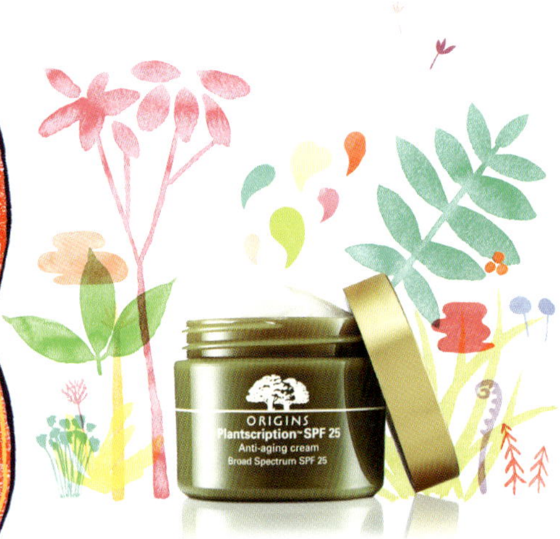

ORIGINS
Plantscription SPF 25
Anti-aging cream
Broad Spectrum SPF 25

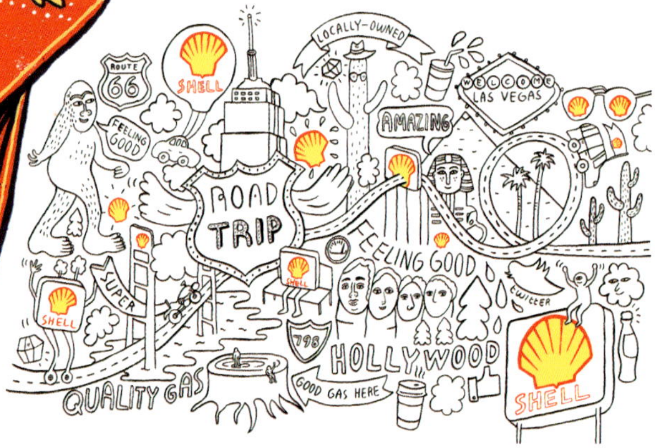

ROUTE 66
SHELL
LOCALLY-OWNED
WELCOME LAS VEGAS
FEELING GOOD
AMAZING
ROAD TRIP
SUPER
FEELING GOOD
TWITTER
SHELL
796
HOLLYWOOD
QUALITY GAS
GOOD GAS HERE
SHELL

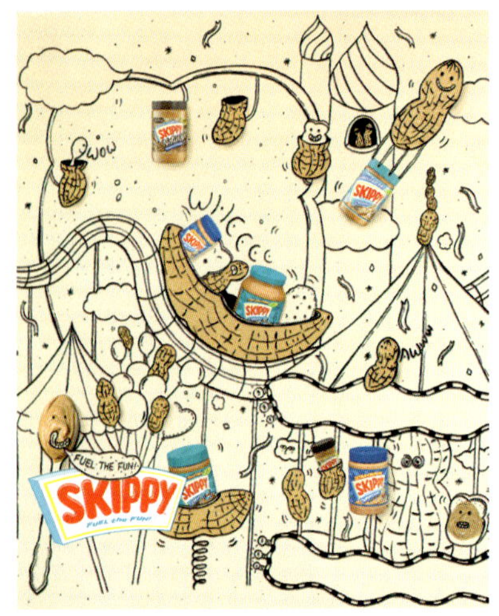

WOW
SKIPPY
FUEL THE FUN!
SKIPPY

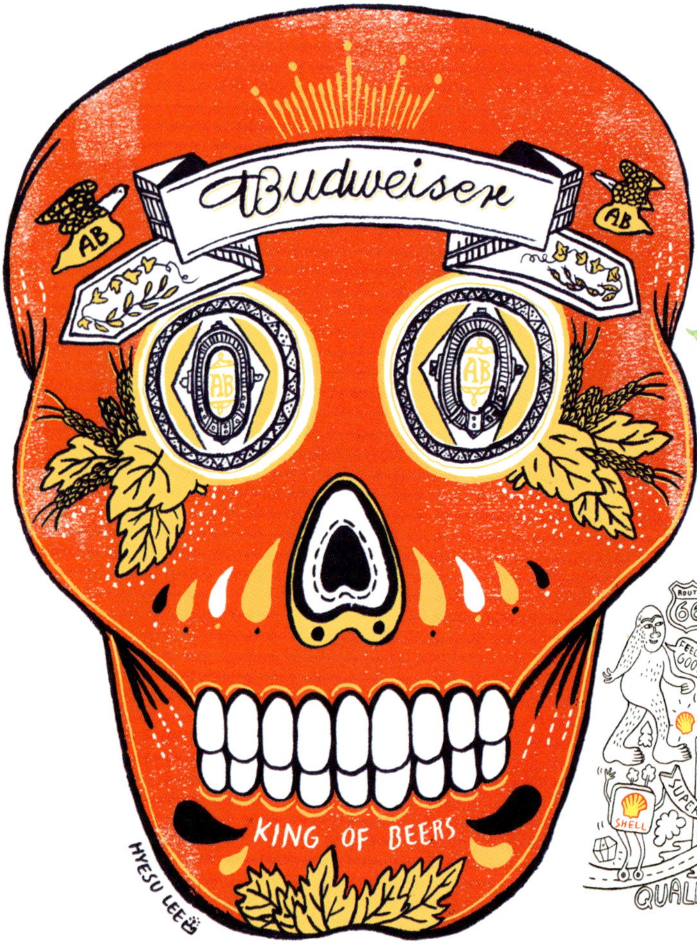

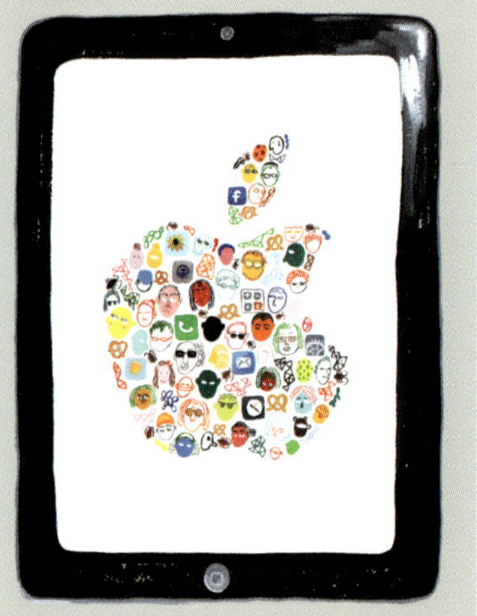

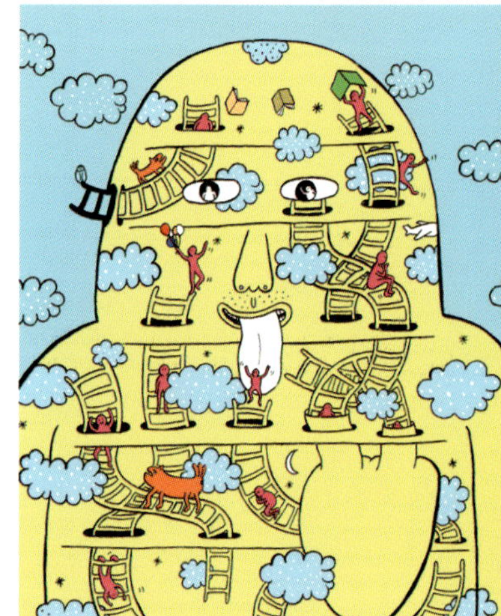

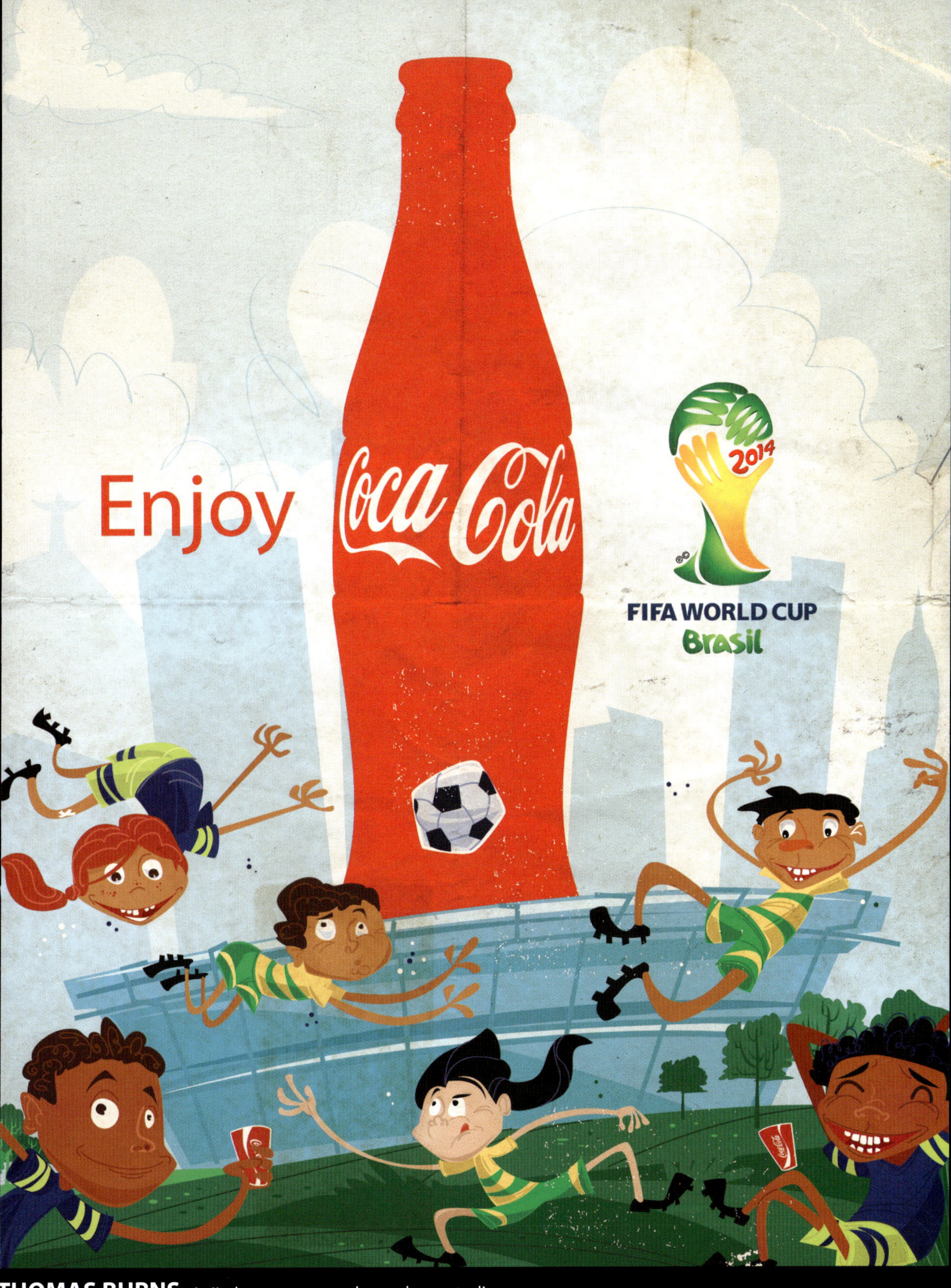

Enjoy
Coca-Cola
2014
FIFA WORLD CUP
Brasil

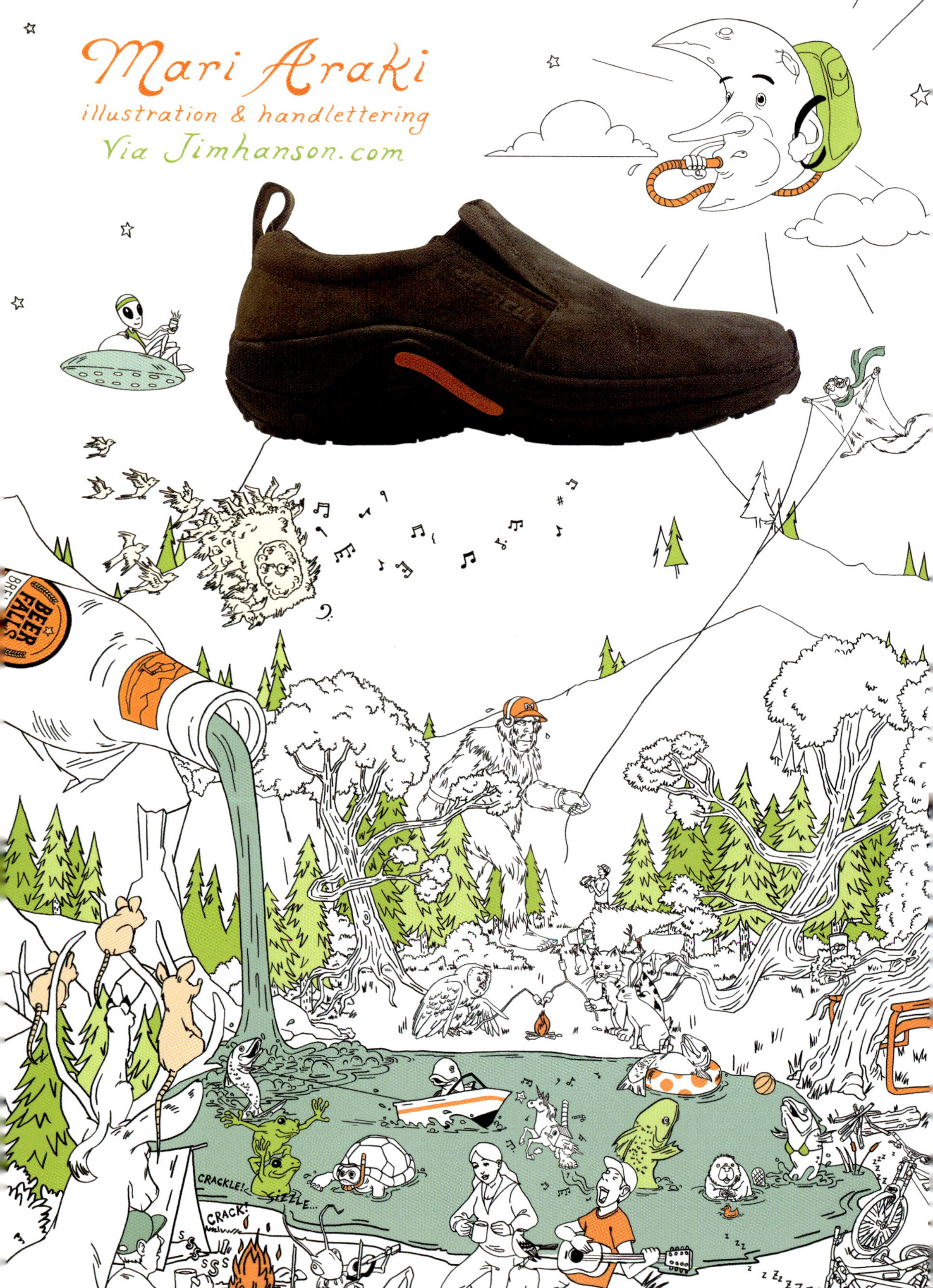

Mari Araki
illustration & handlettering
Via Jimhanson.com
BEER FALLS
BREL
CRACKLE!
SIZZLE...
CRACK!

ingo fast

EUSTON RD
HIGH ST
OLD ST
FENCHURCH ST
NEWHAM WAY
Regent's Park
BAKER ST
PICCADILLY
St James Park
River Thames
TOWER BRIDGE RD
Hyde Park
ingofast.com

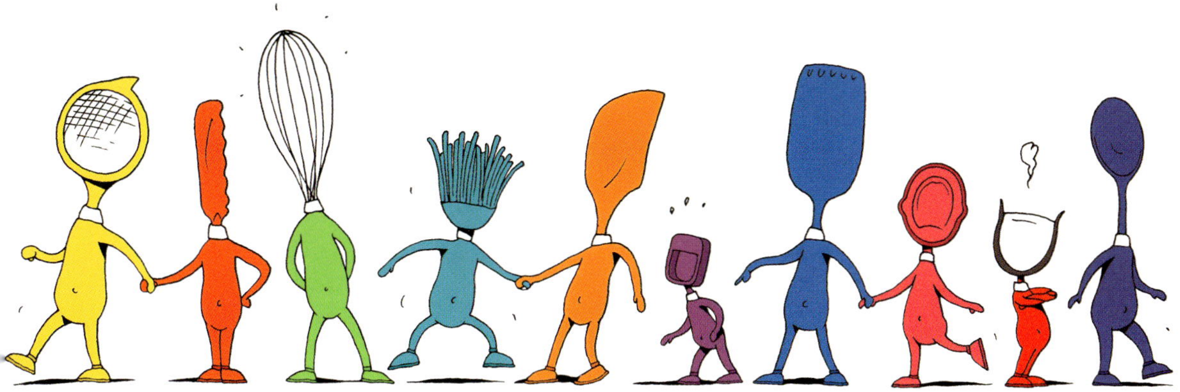

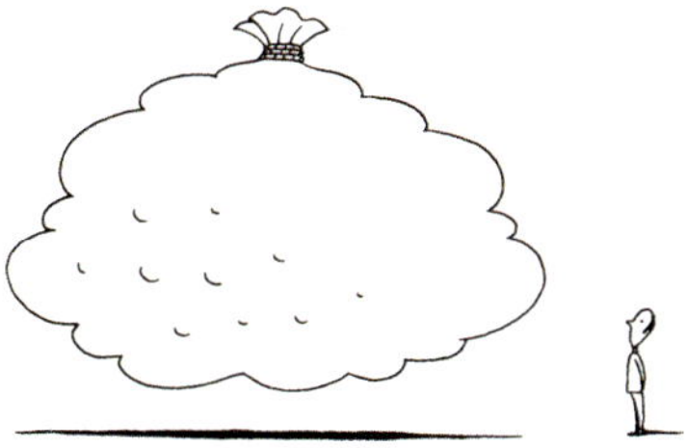

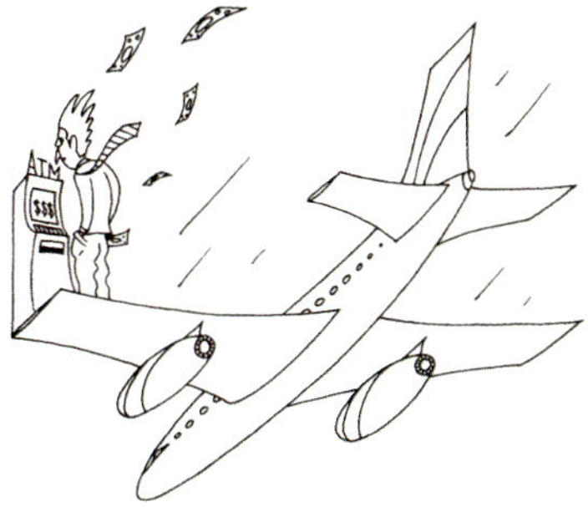

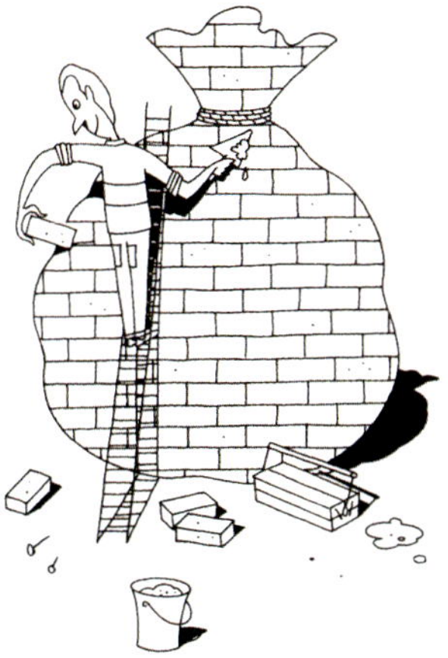

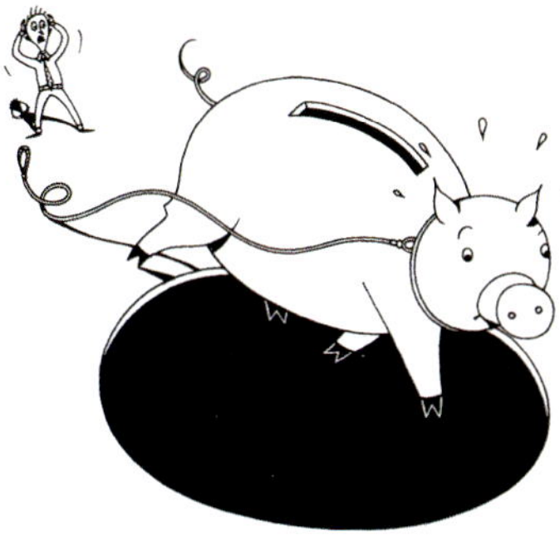

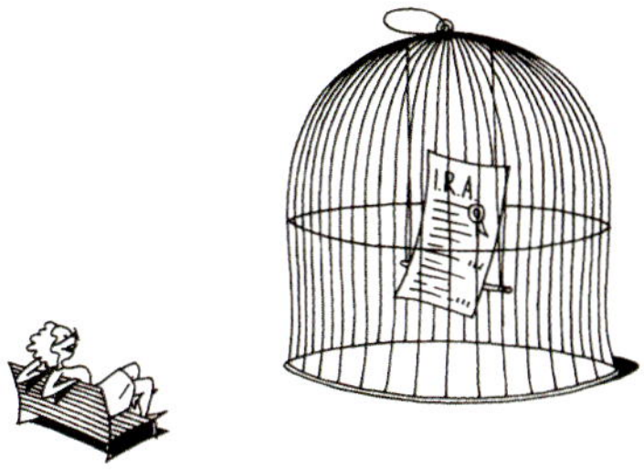

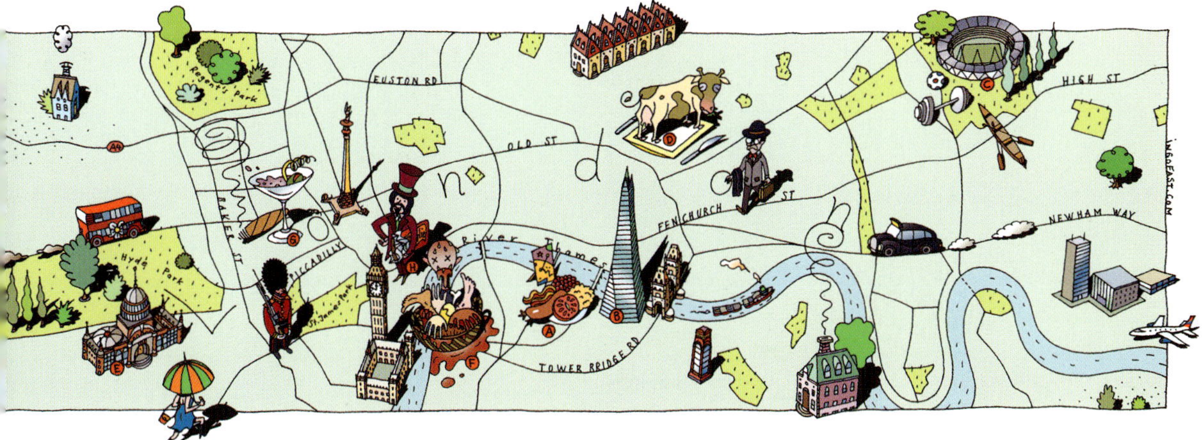

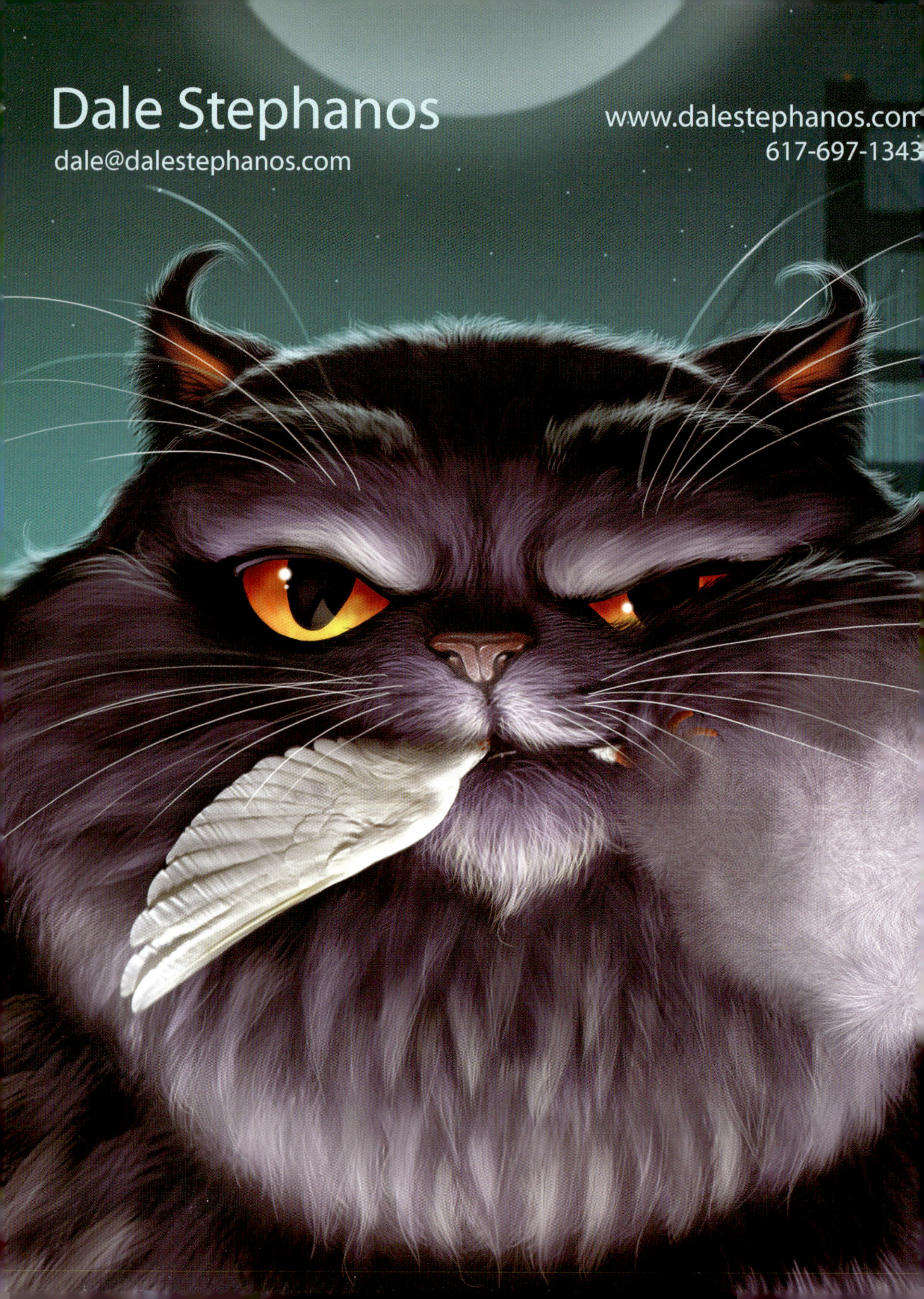

Dale Stephanos
dale@dalestephanos.com
www.dalestephanos.com
617-697-1343

cocotos.com

212.620.7556
tom@cocotos.com

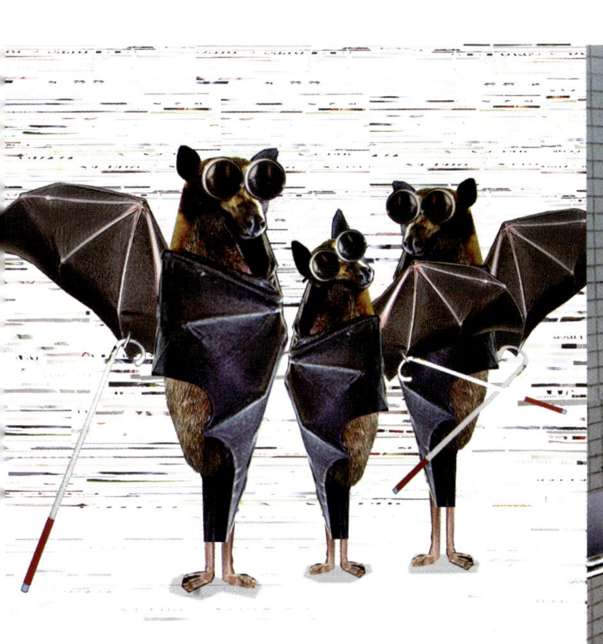

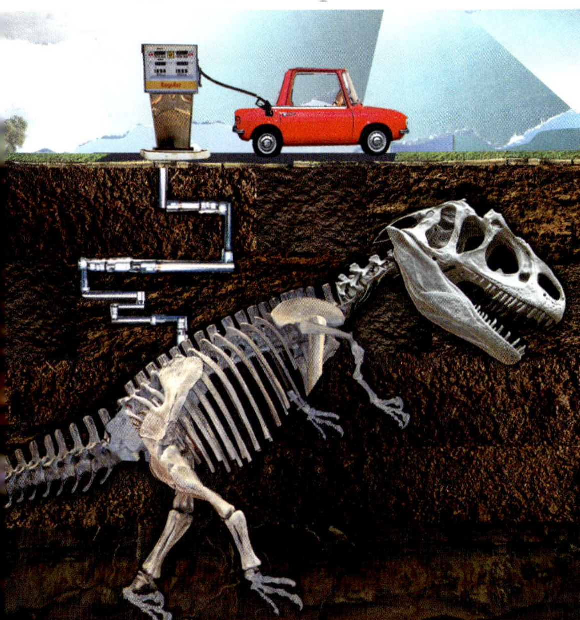

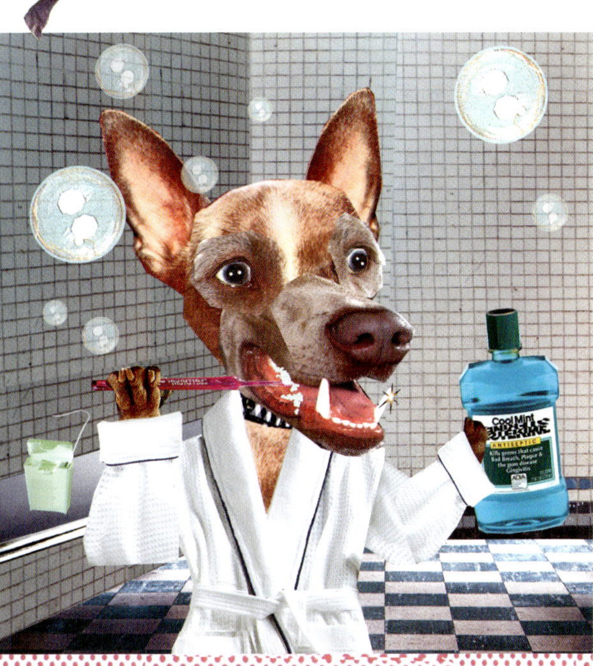

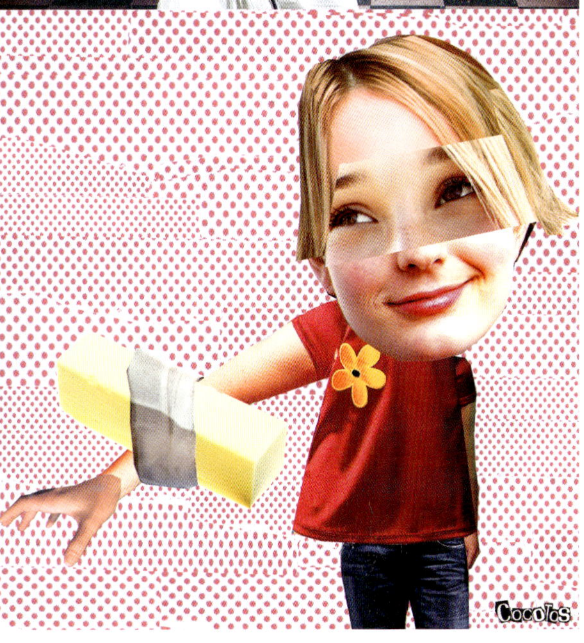

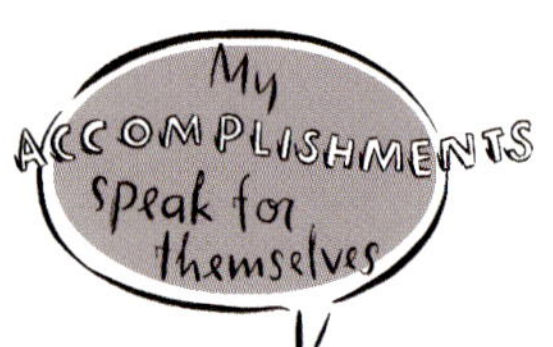
My ACCOMPLISHMENTS speak for themselves

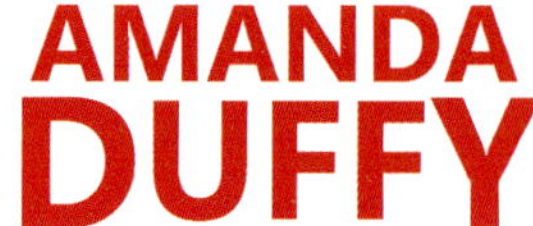
AMANDA
DUFFY
RATUNDERPAPER.COM
ratunderpaper@gmail.com
416-484-9922

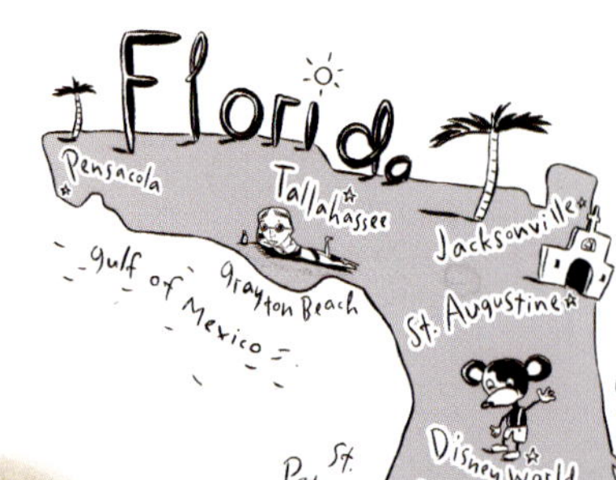
Florida
Pensacola
Tallahassee
Jacksonville
Grayton Beach
St. Augustine
Gulf of Mexico
Disney World
Canaveral
St. Petersburg
Tampa
Orlando
West Palm Beach
Sanibel Island
South Beach "SoBe"

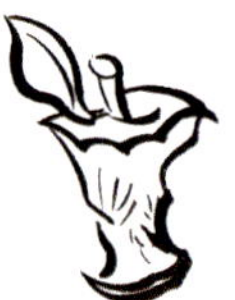

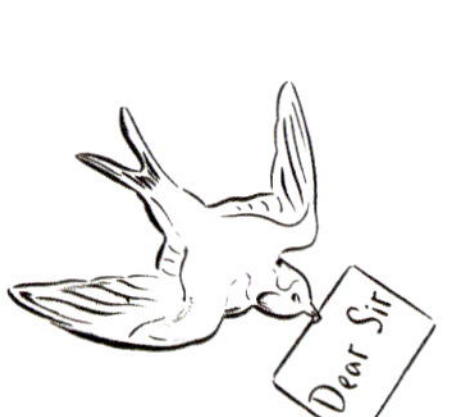
Dear Sir

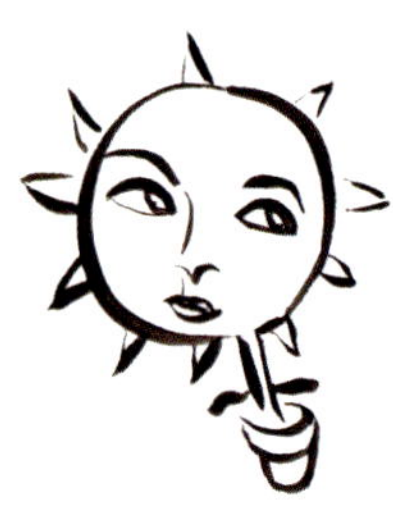

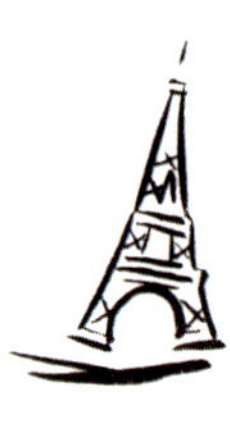

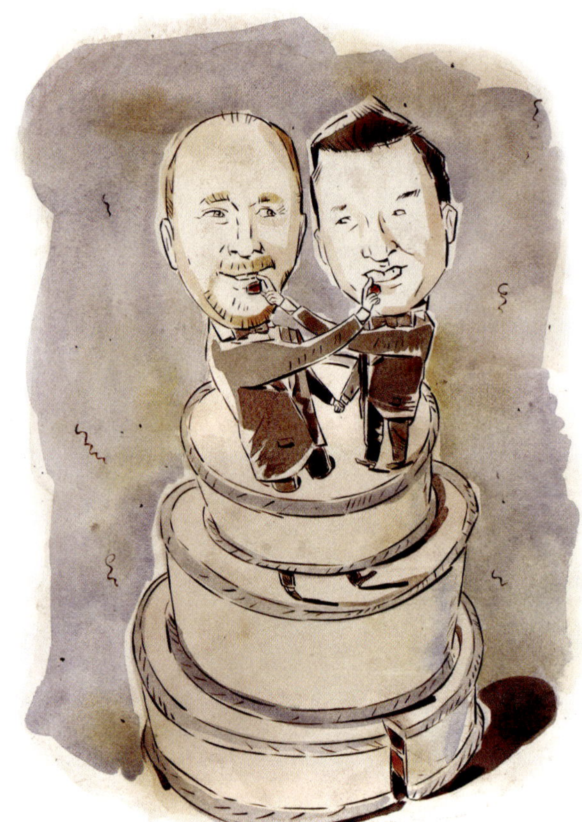

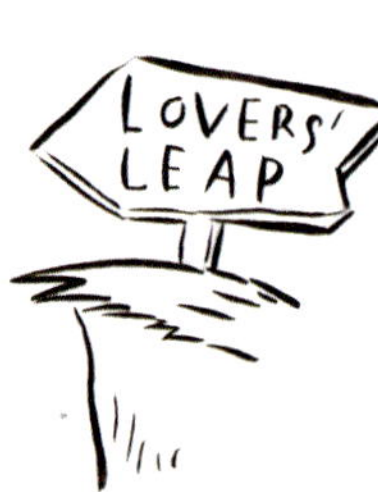
LOVERS' LEAP

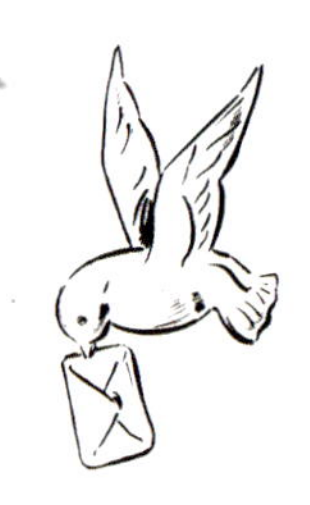

We need more FEEDBACK

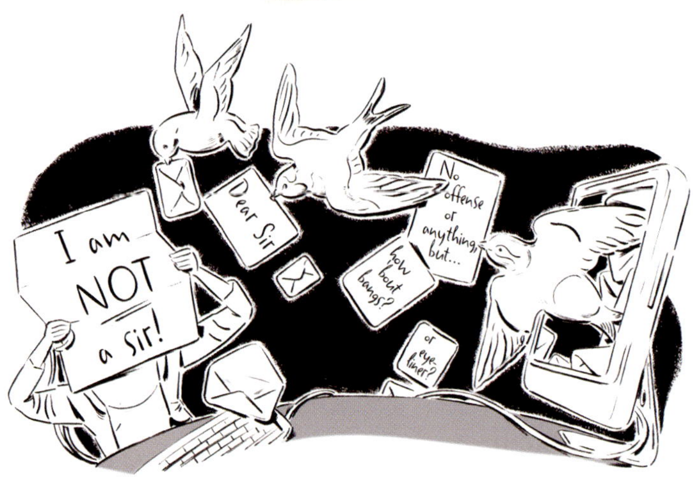
I am NOT a sir!
Dear Sir
No offense or anything, but...
how bout bangs?
or eye liner?

ANDRE JUNGET ILLUSTRATION

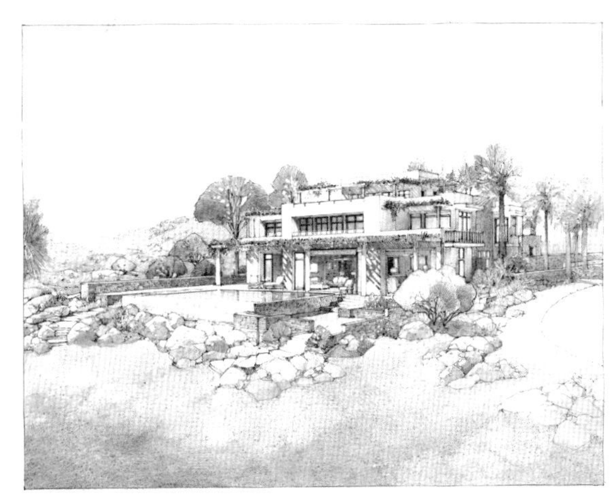

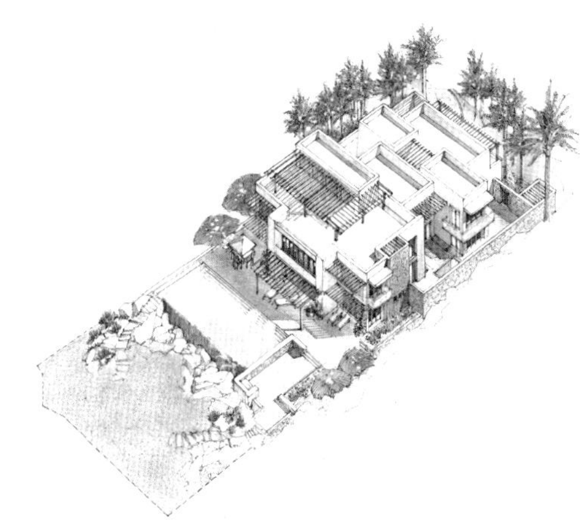

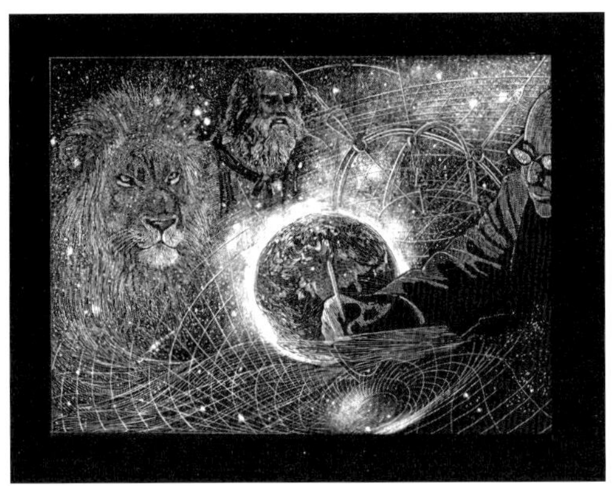

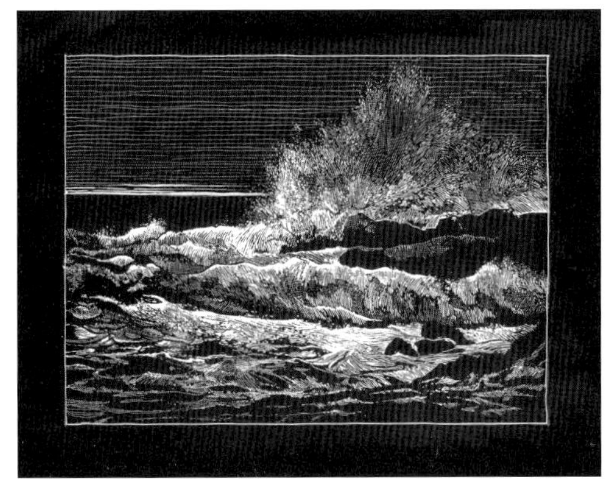

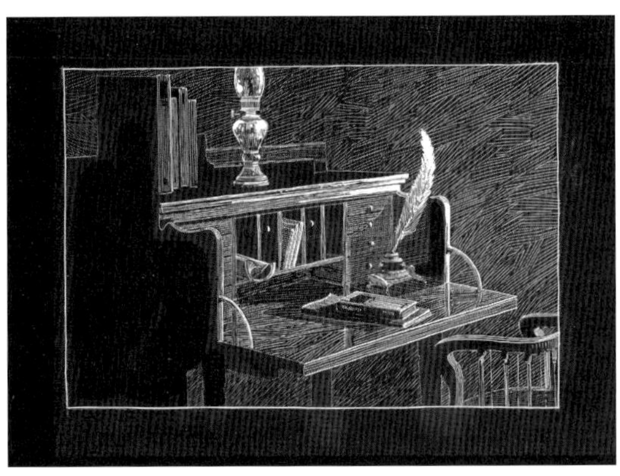

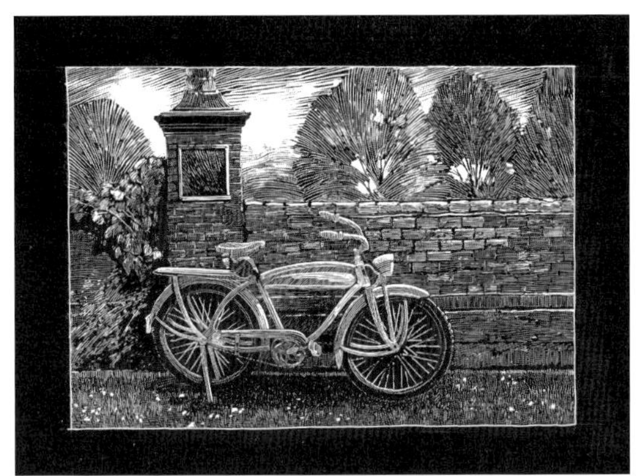

www.andrejunget.com   andre@andrejunget.com   347-743-1166

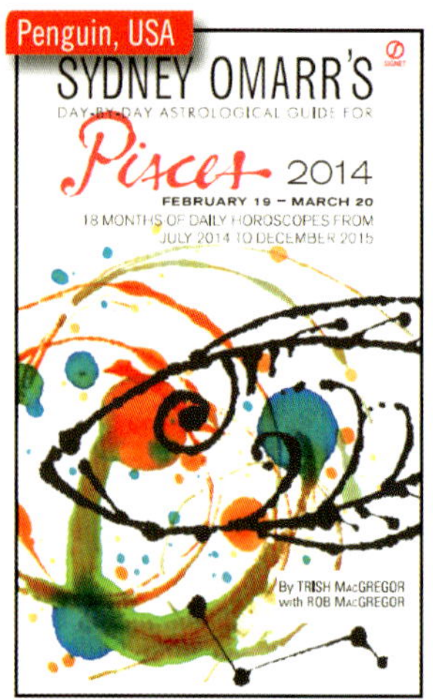

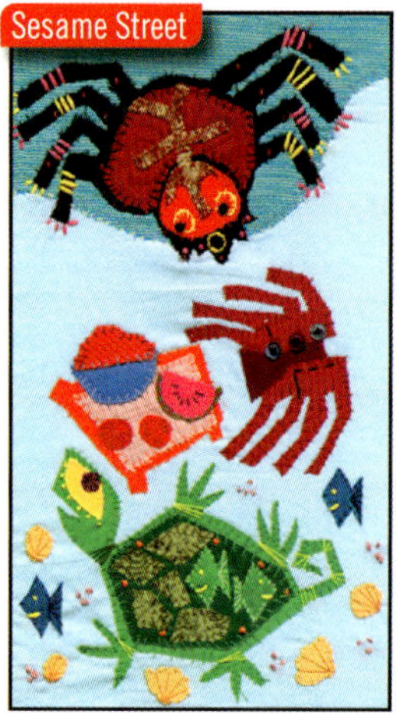

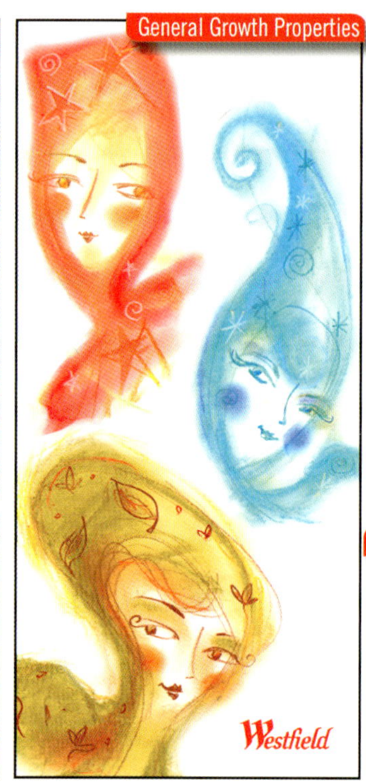

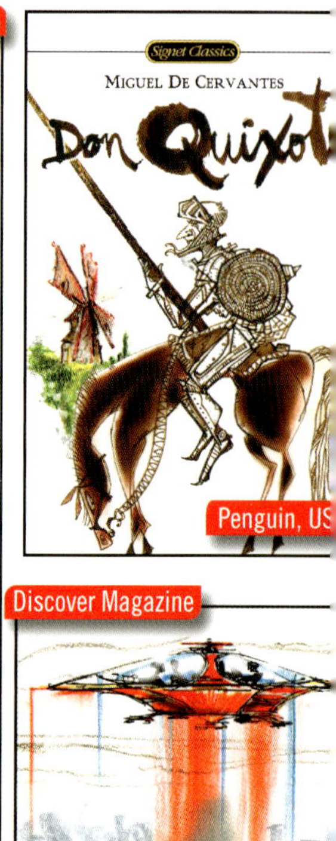

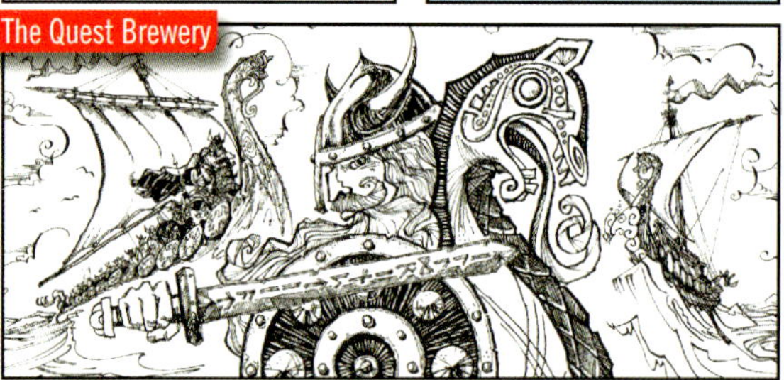

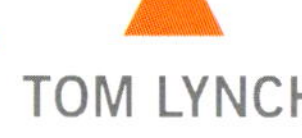

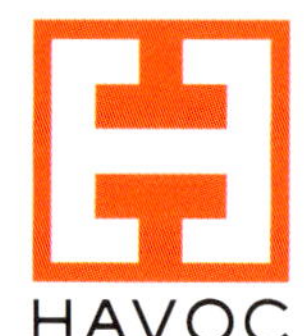

www.havocmedia.com / TOM LYNCH

HAVOC

TONY REONEGRO / 718.494.0118

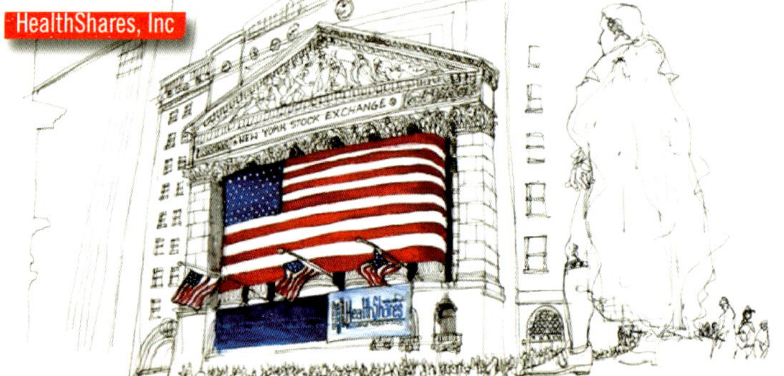

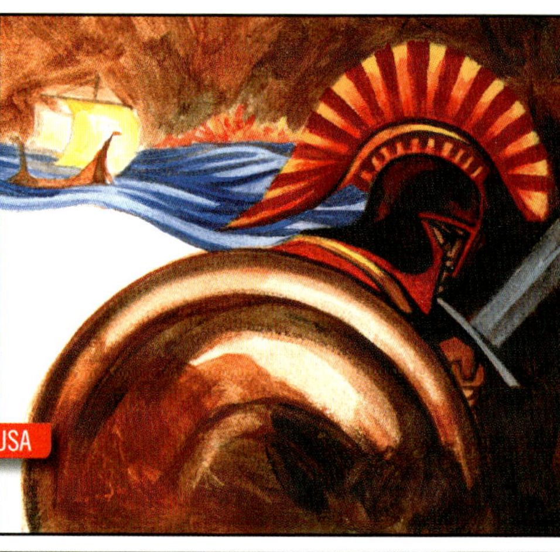

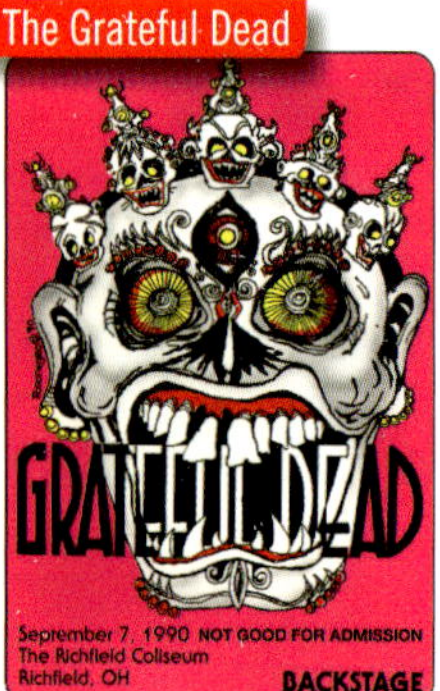

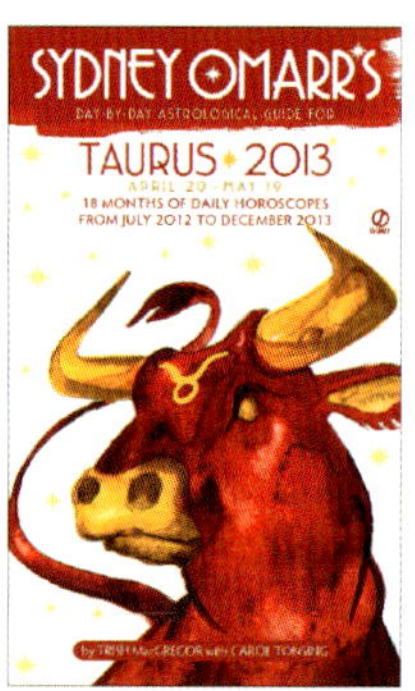

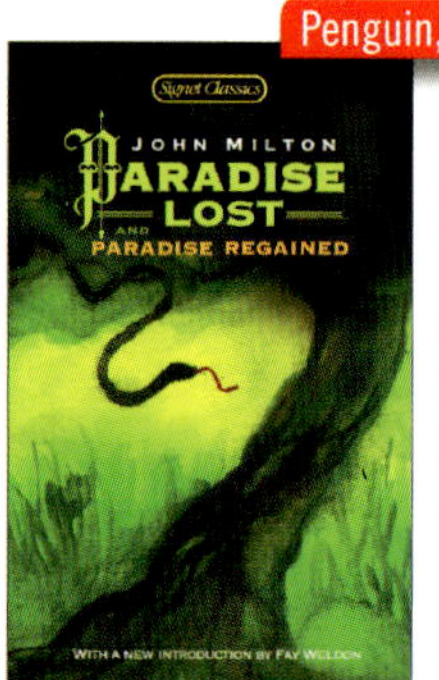

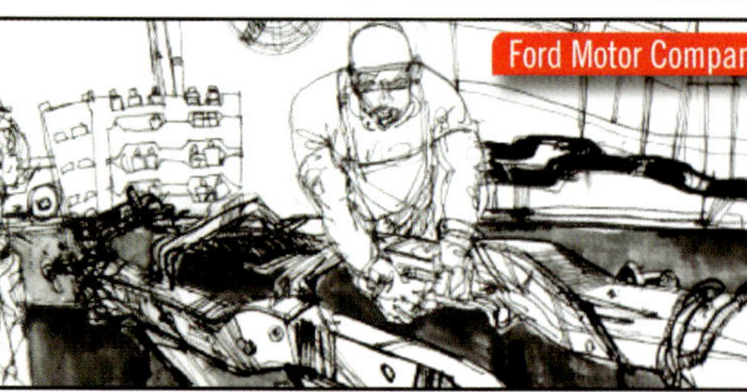

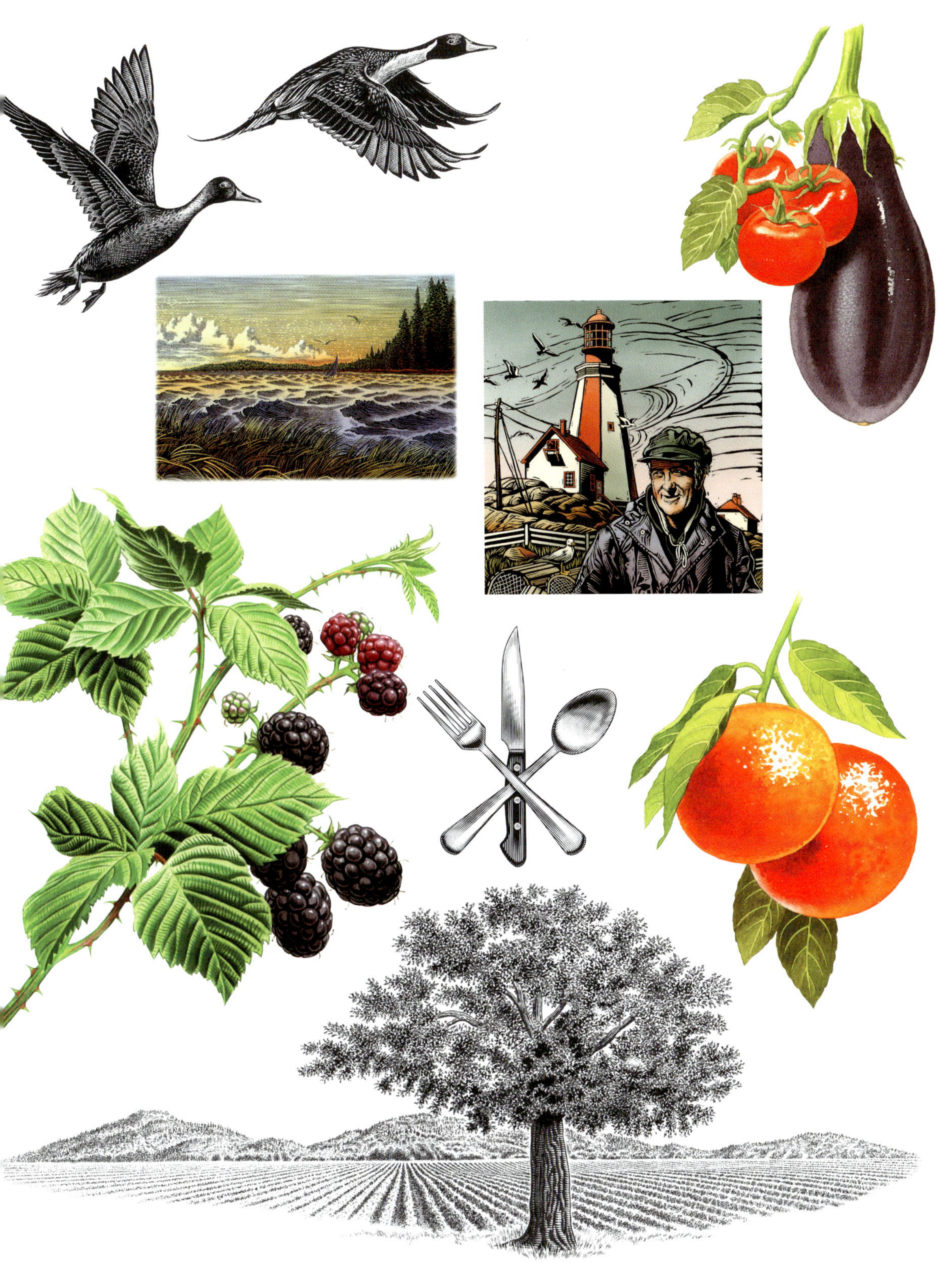

Raphael Montoliu www.montoliustudio.com raphaelmntl@gmail.com 707 263 6143

OTTOSTEININGER.COM

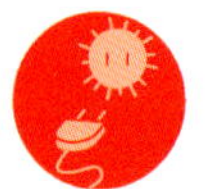
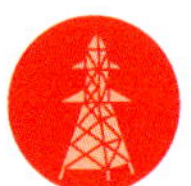
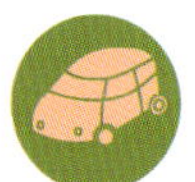

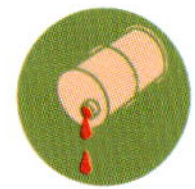
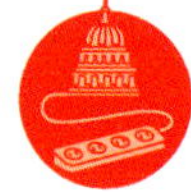
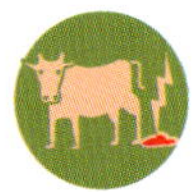
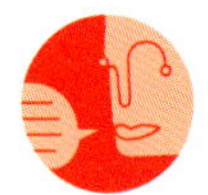

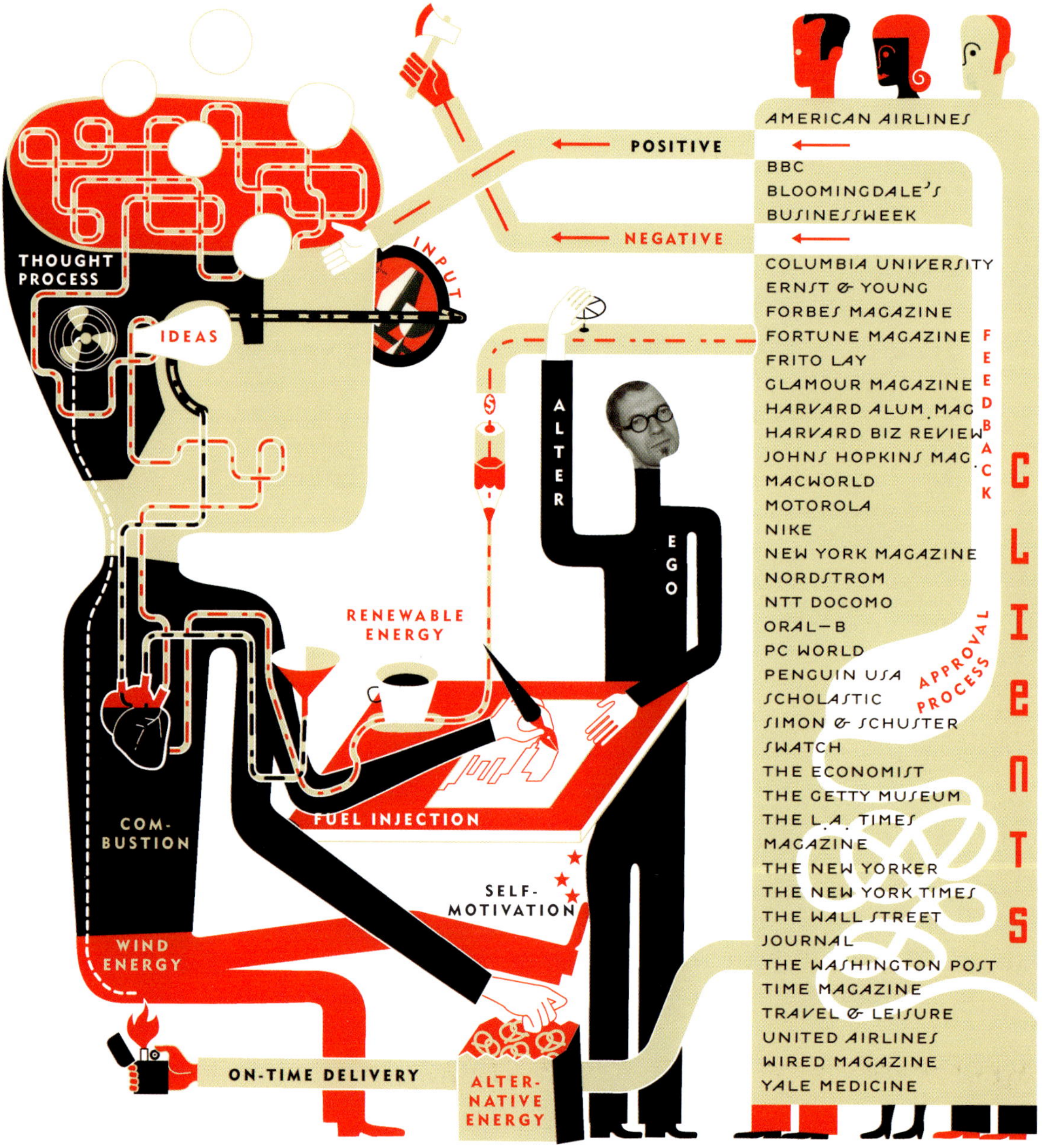

ILLUSTRATOR ANIMATOR ICON MAKER INFOGRAPHER

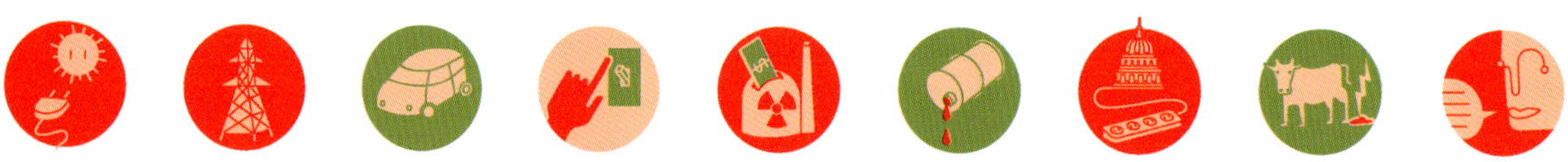

OTTO STEININGER.COM

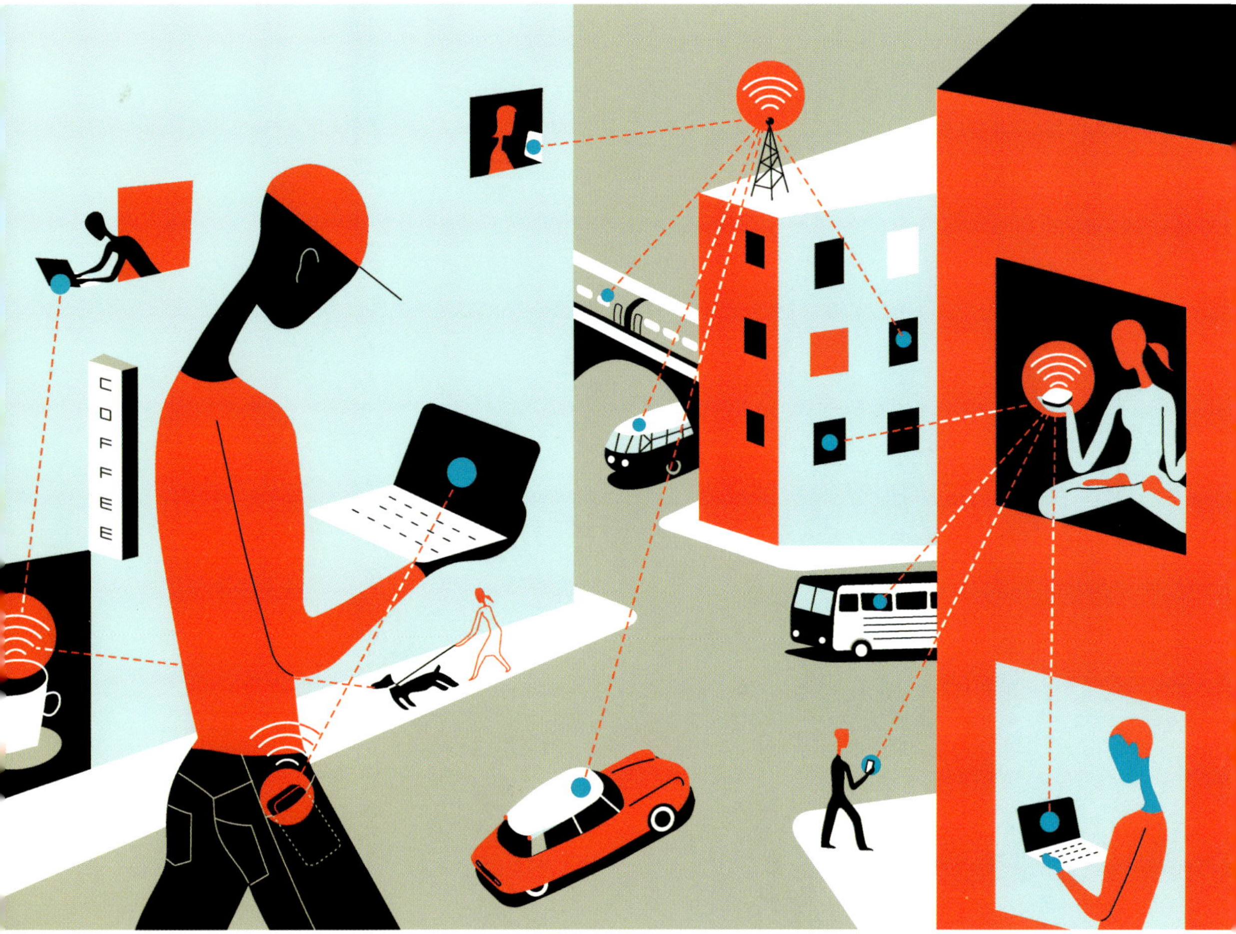

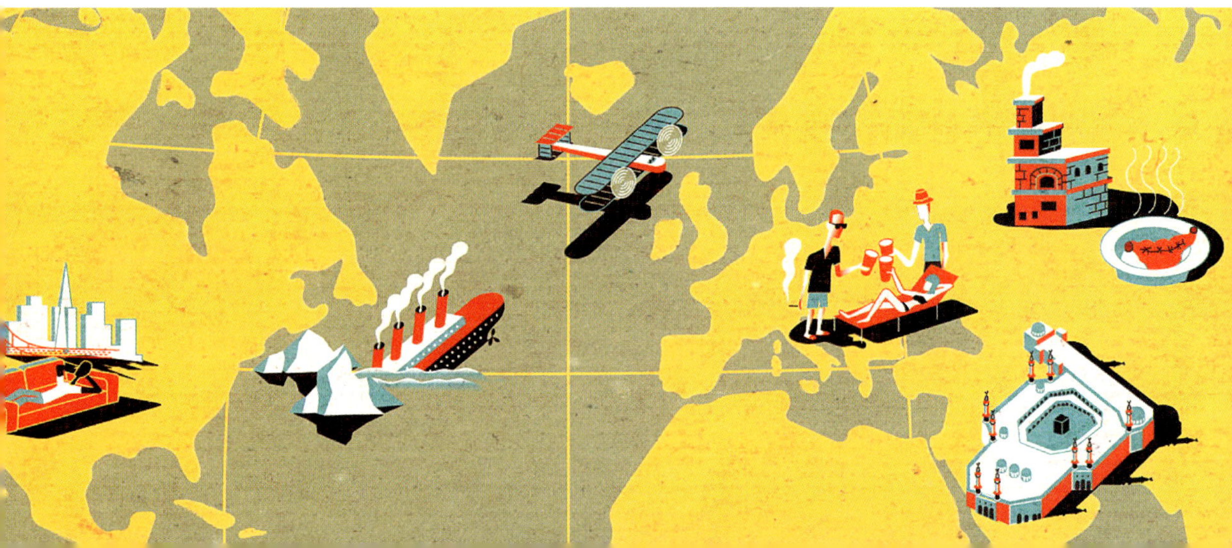

REPRESENTED BY THREE IN A BOX INC. WWW.THREEINABOX.COM
NEW YORK: 212-643-0896 | CHICAGO: 312-663-5506 | LOS ANGELES: 213-688-7428

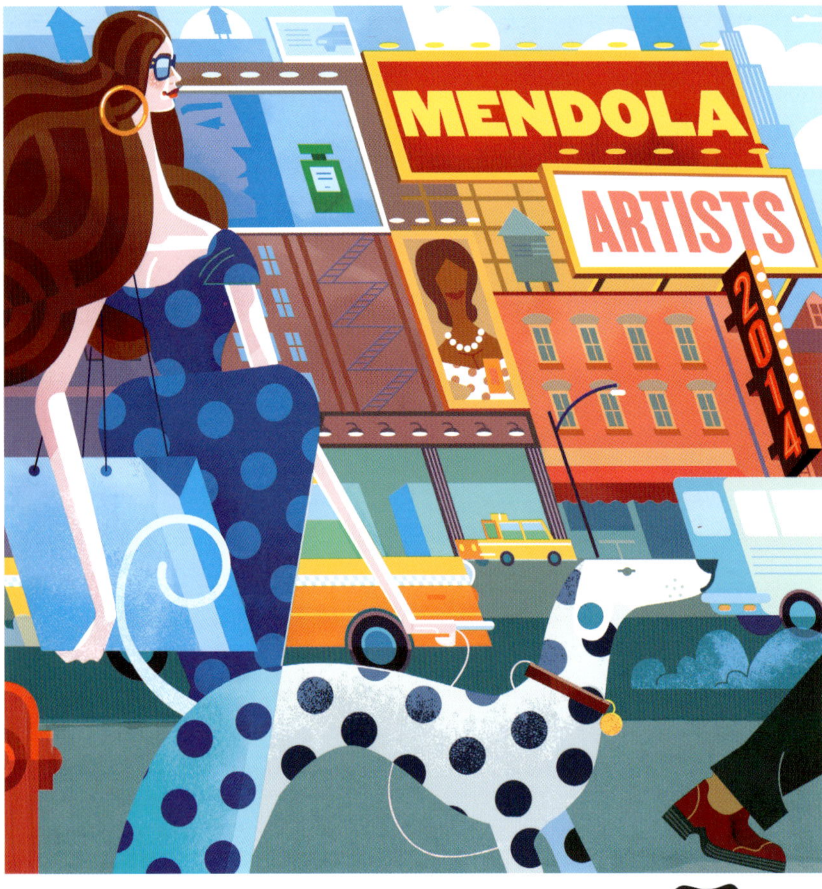

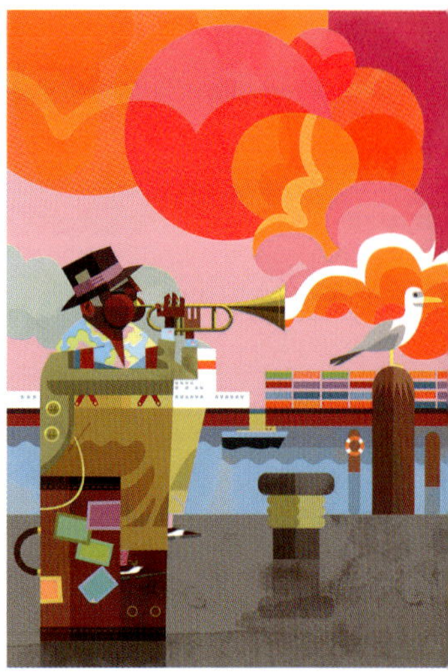

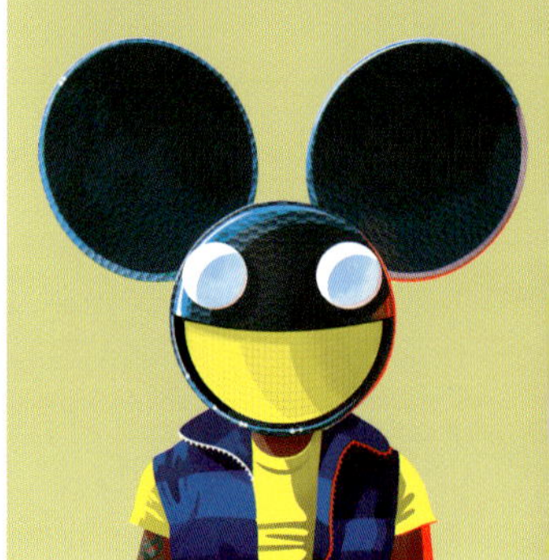

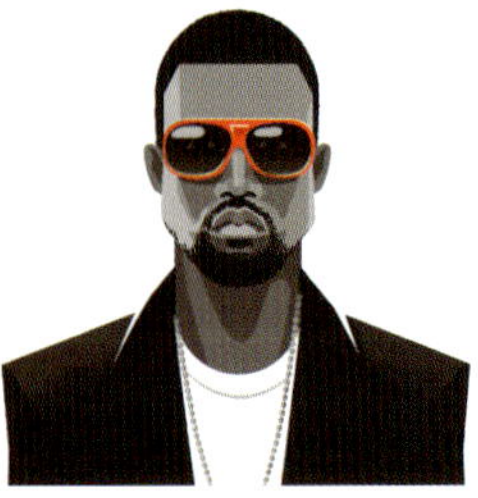

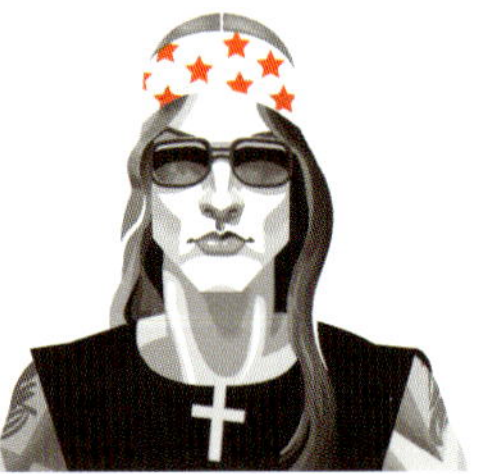

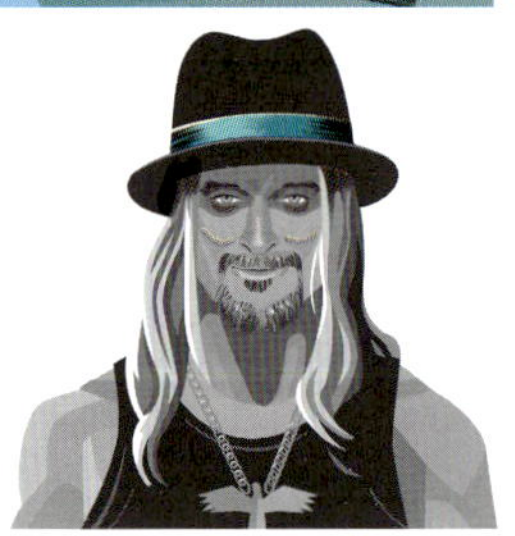

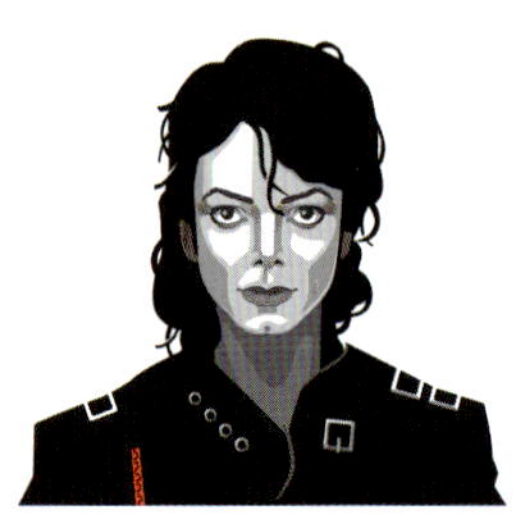

ESPN

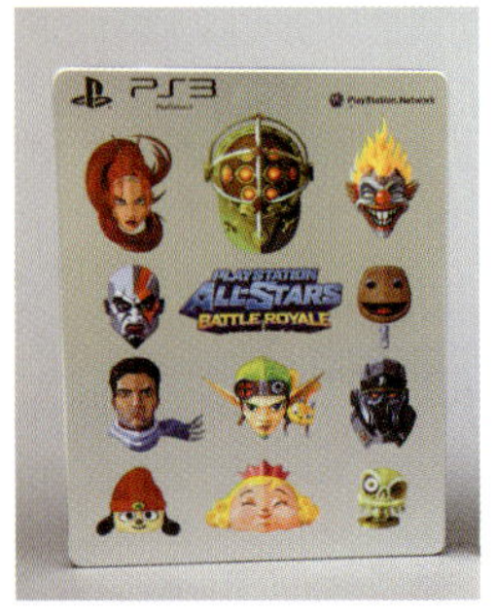

Sony Entertainment

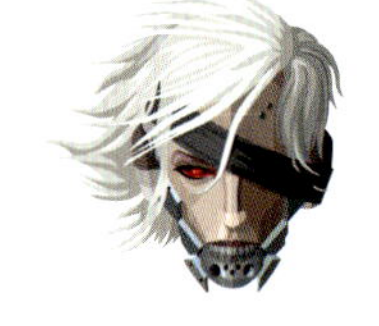

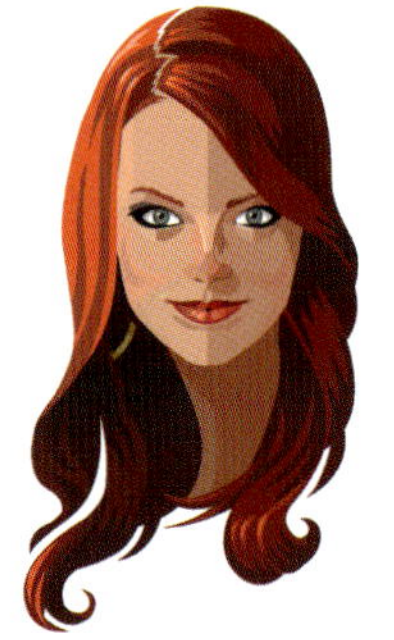

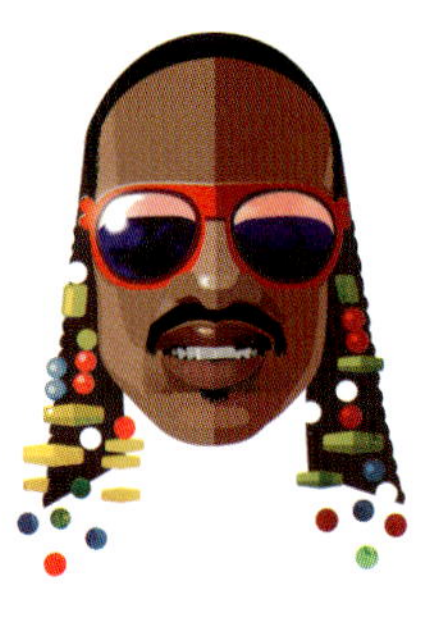

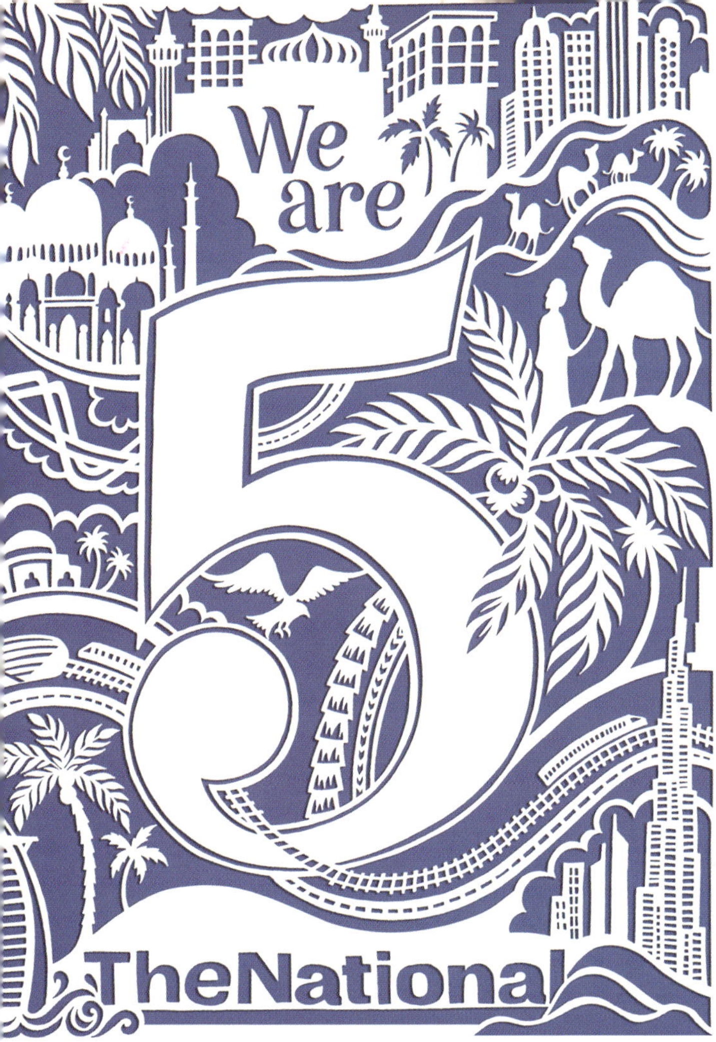

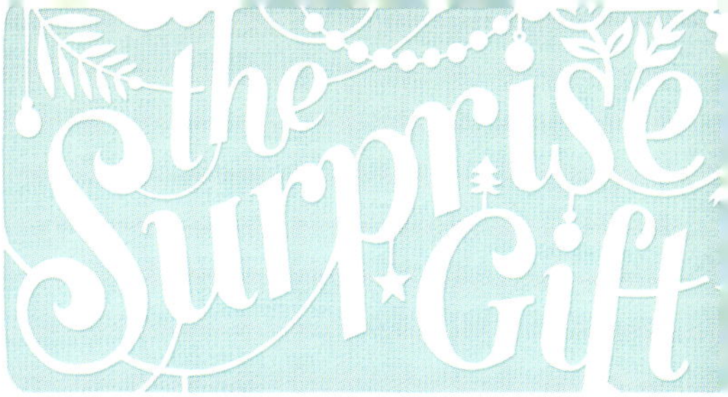

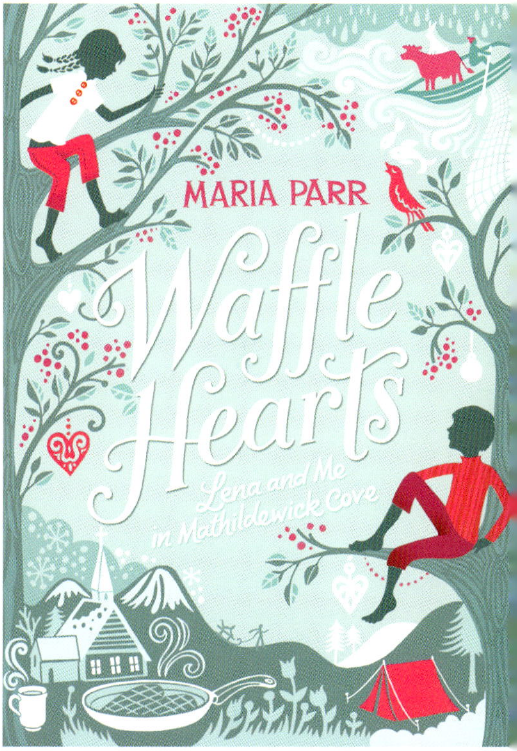

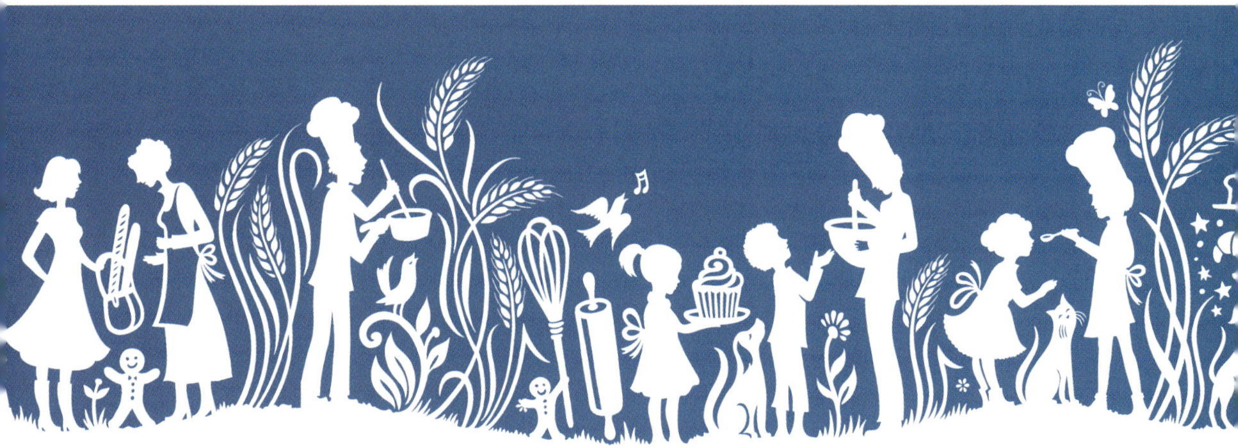

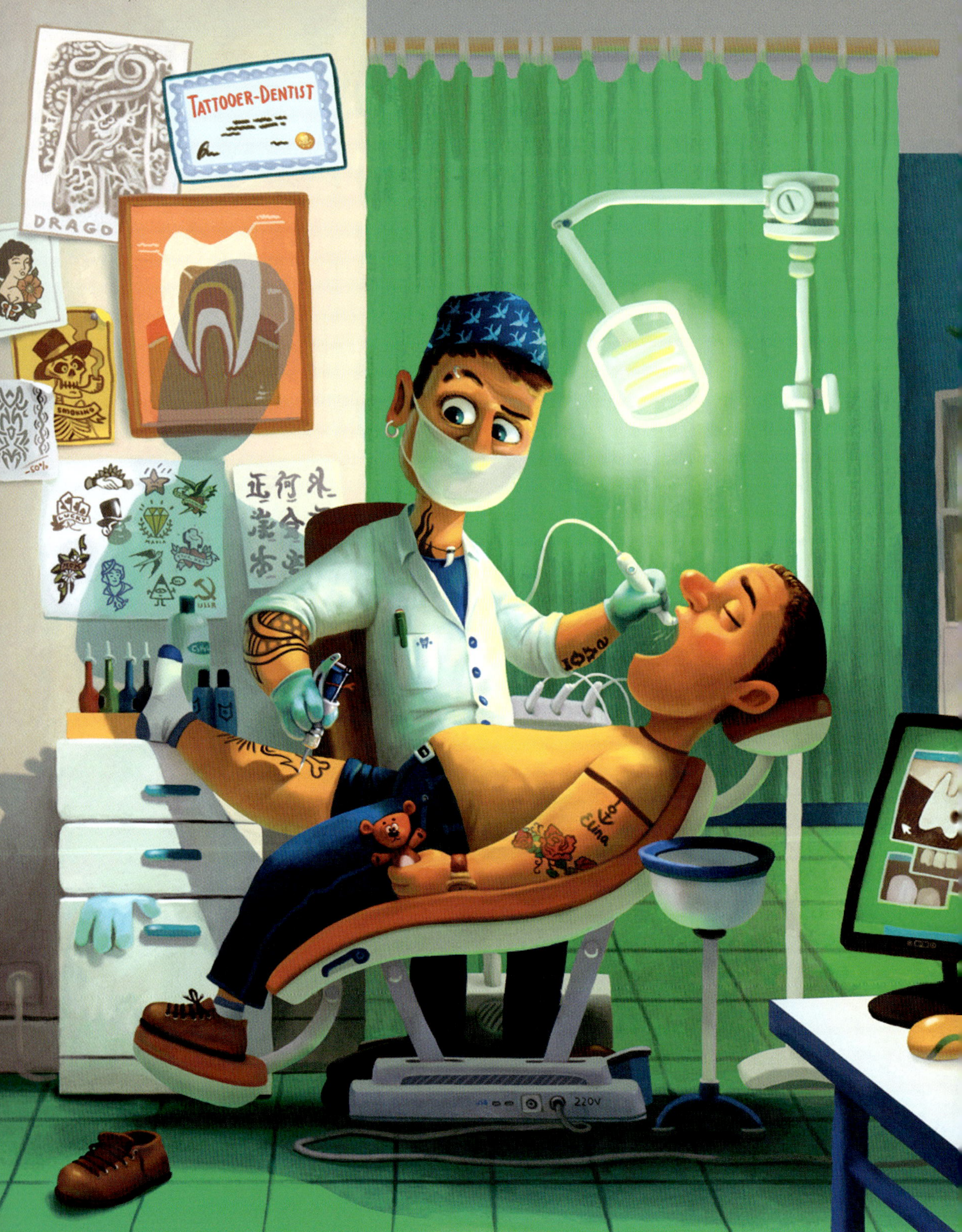

TATTOOER-DENTIST
DRAGO
220V

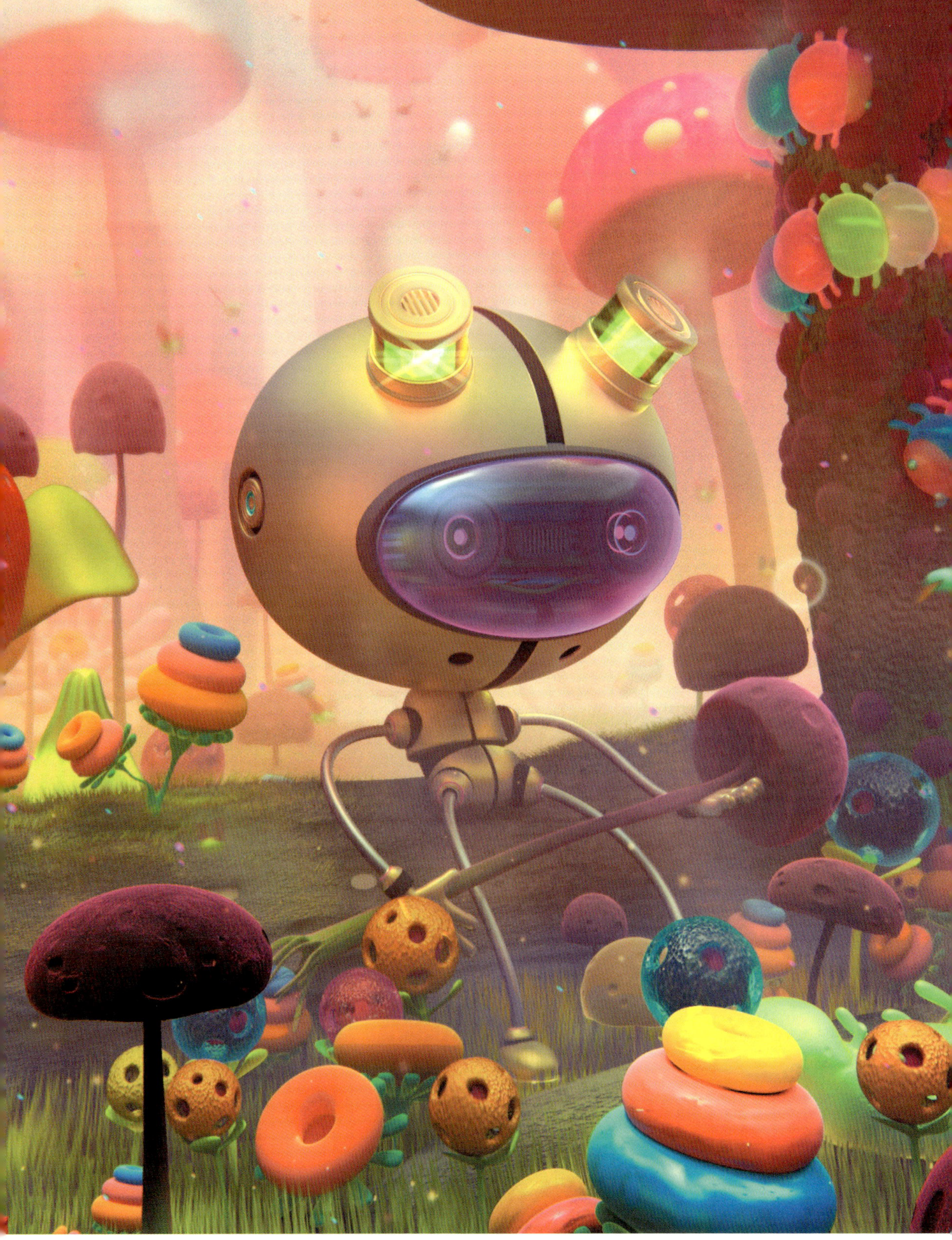

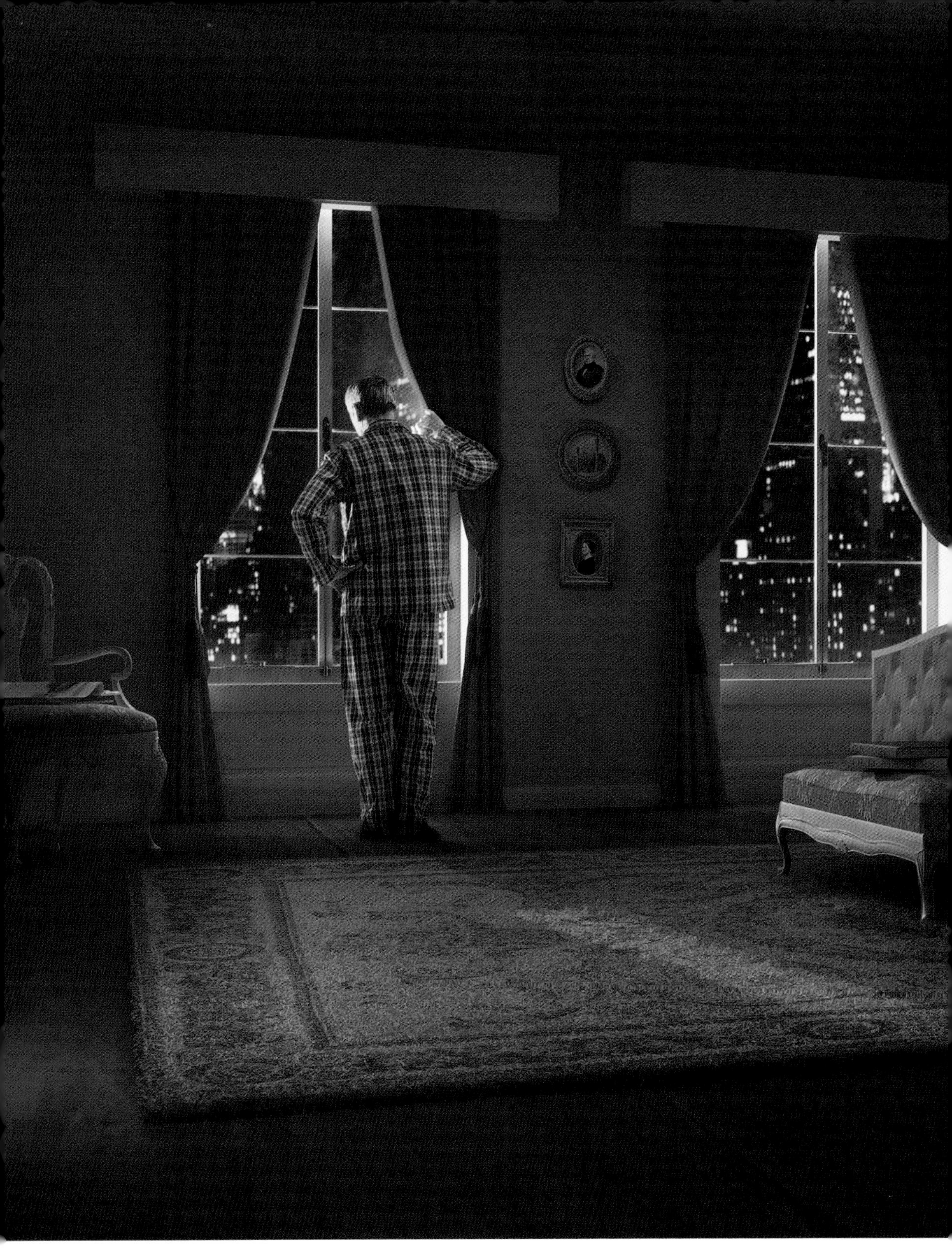
MENDOLA
portfolio
mendolaart.com
email
info@mendolaart.com
call
212.986.5680
represents
THE IMAGE FOUNDATION

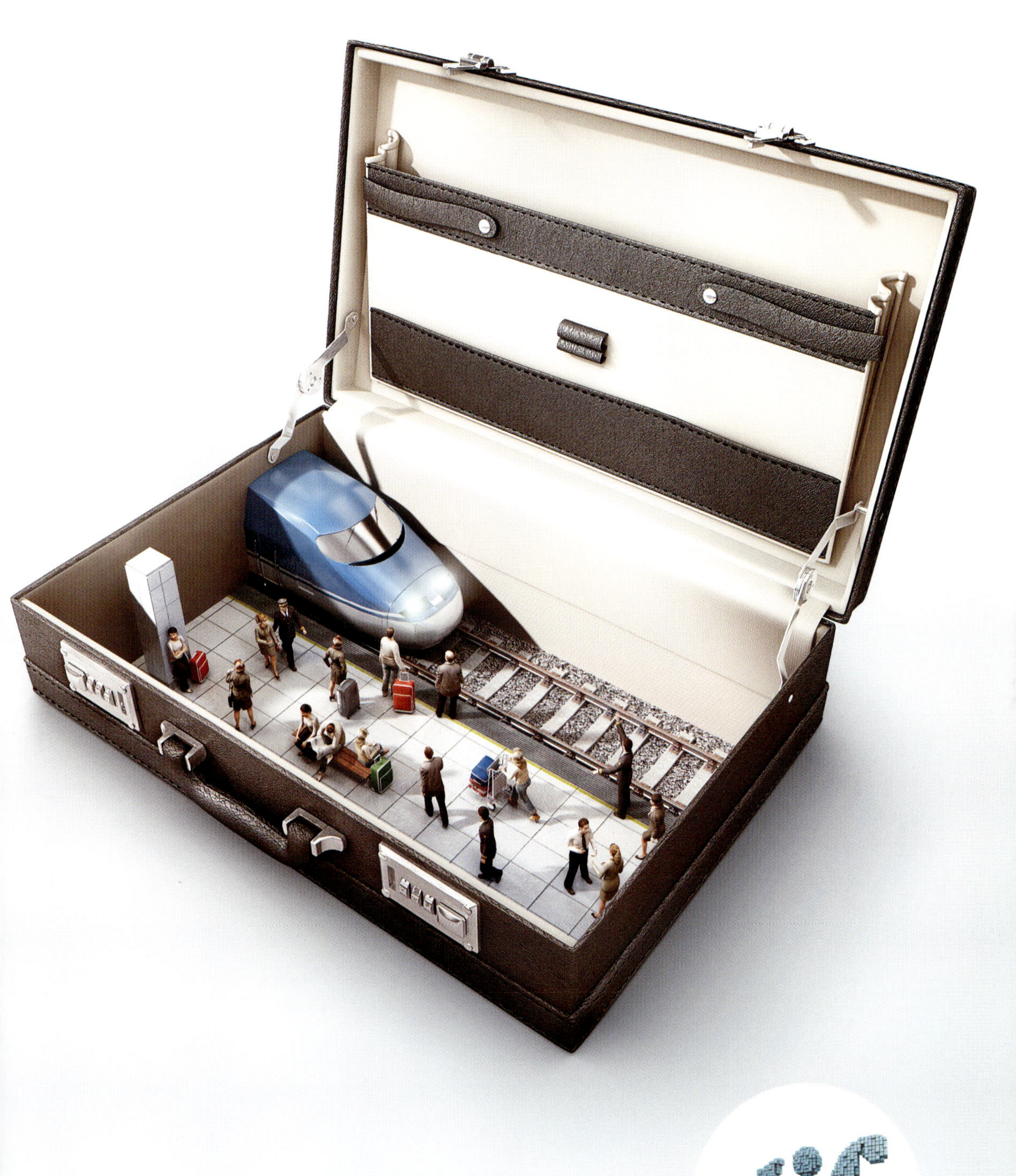

CGI, animation, creative photographic retouching

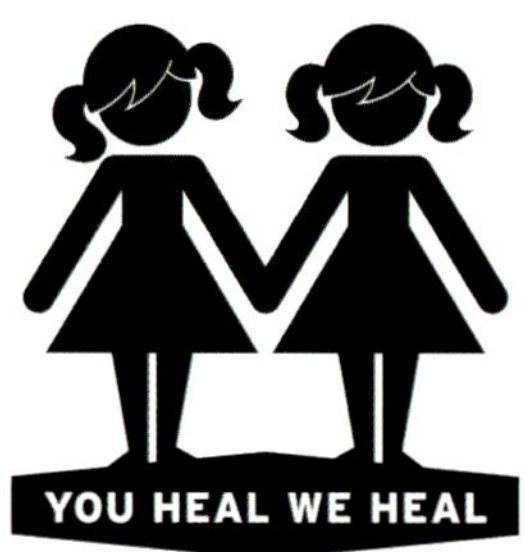

YOU HEAL WE HEAL

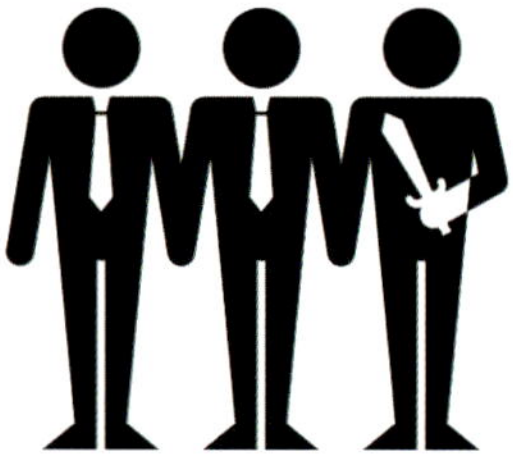

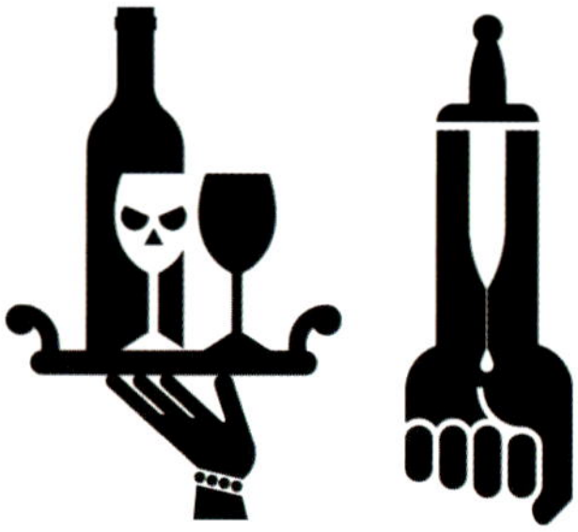

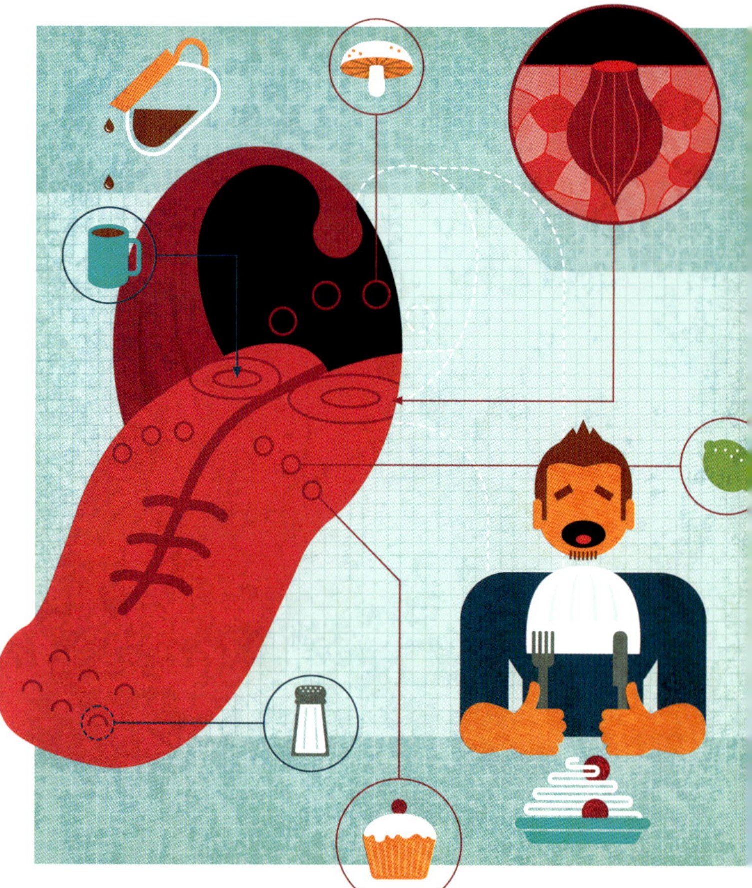

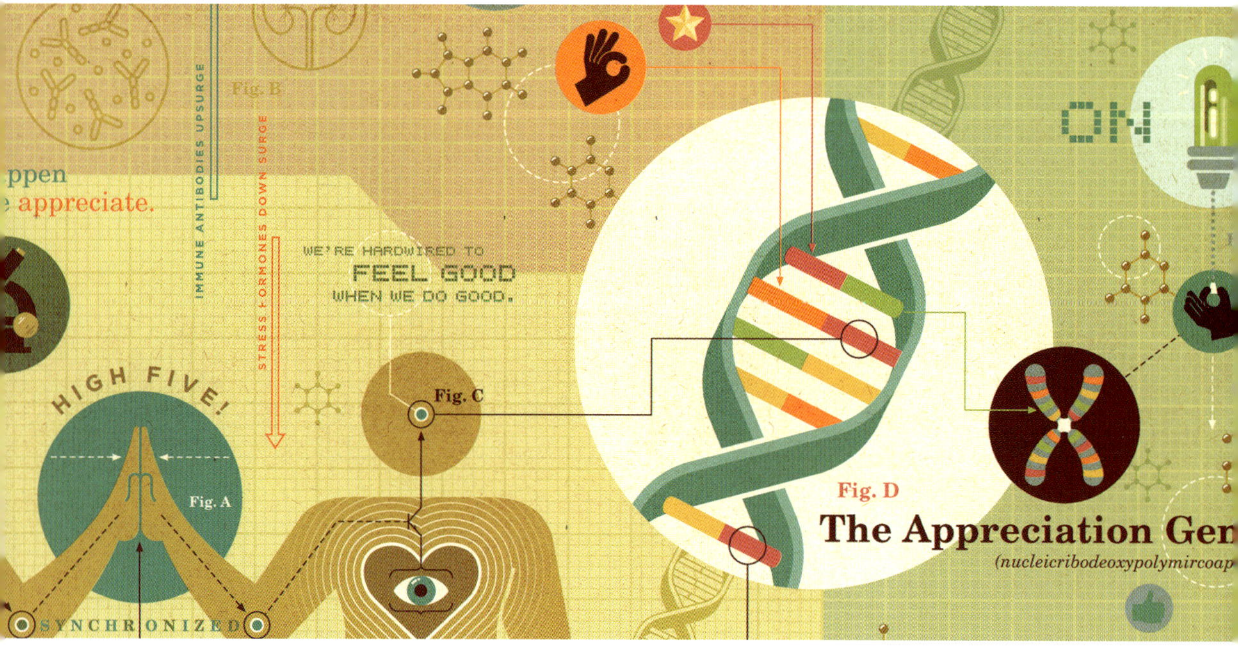

IMMUNE ANTIBODIES UPSURGE
Fig. B
STRESS HORMONES DOWN SURGE
ppen
appreciate.
WE'RE HARDWIRED TO
FEEL GOOD
WHEN WE DO GOOD.
HIGH FIVE!
Fig. C
Fig. A
SYNCHRONIZED
ON
Fig. D
The Appreciation Gen
(nucleicribodeoxypolymircoap

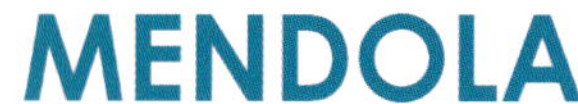

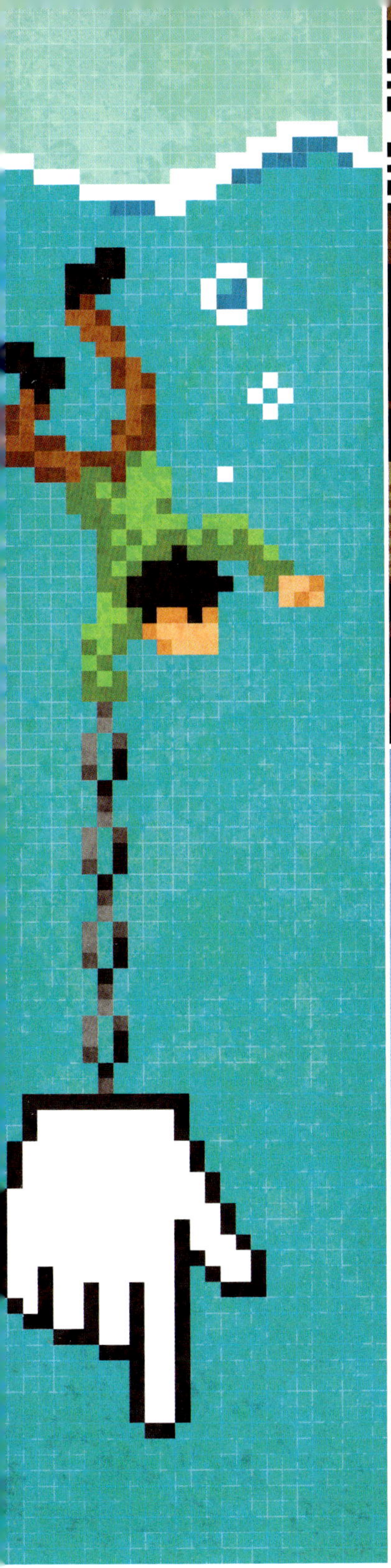

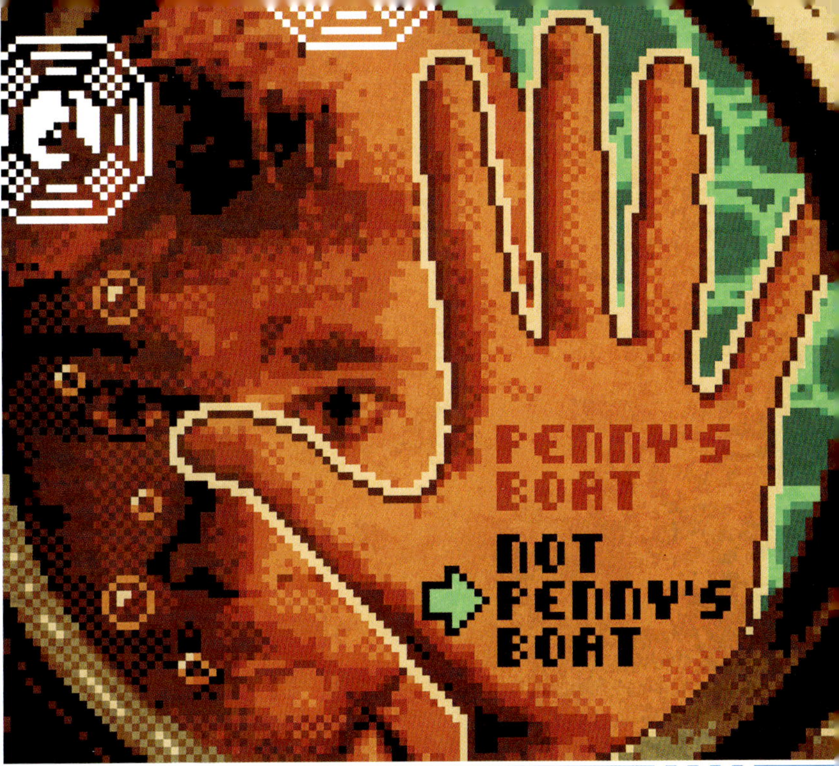

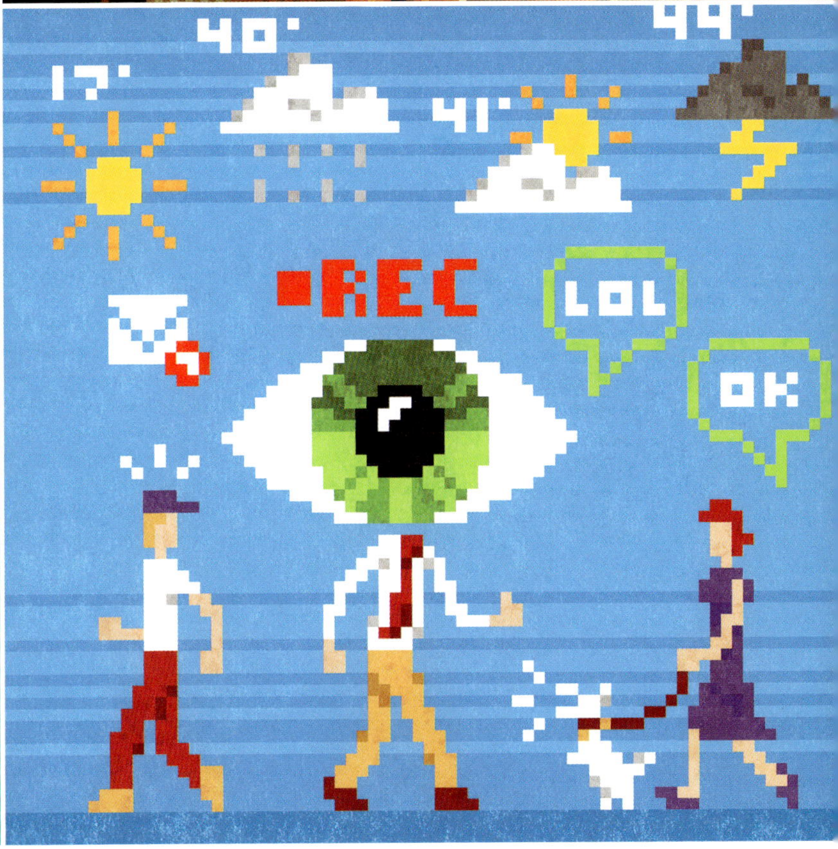

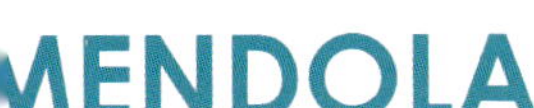

MENDOLA
portfolio
mendolaart.com
email
info@mendolaart.com
call
212.986.5680
represents - 8 Bit Pixel
JUDE BUFFUM

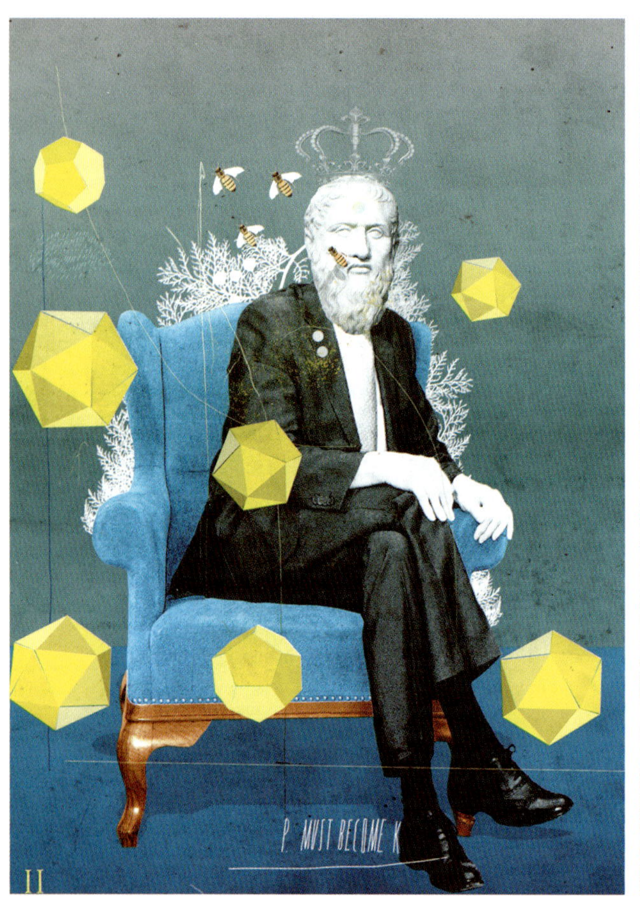

P. MUST BECOME K
II

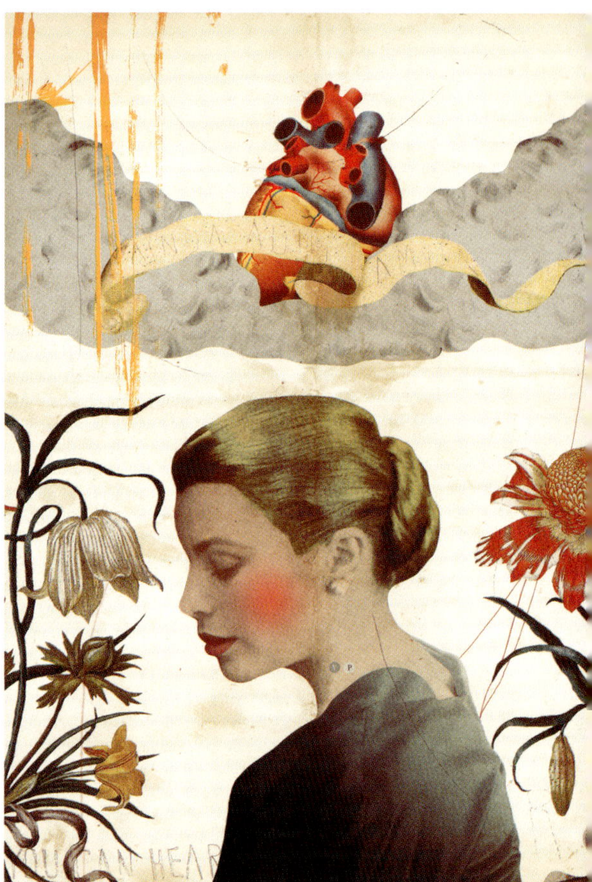

YOU CAN HEAR

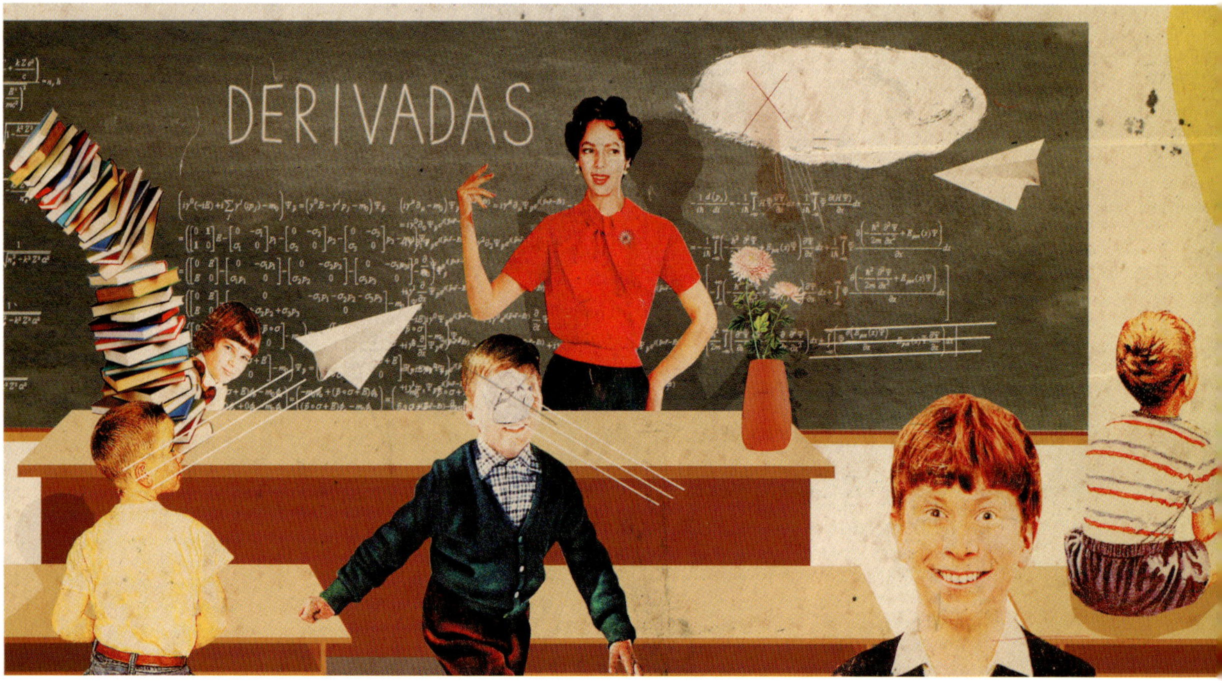

DERIVADAS

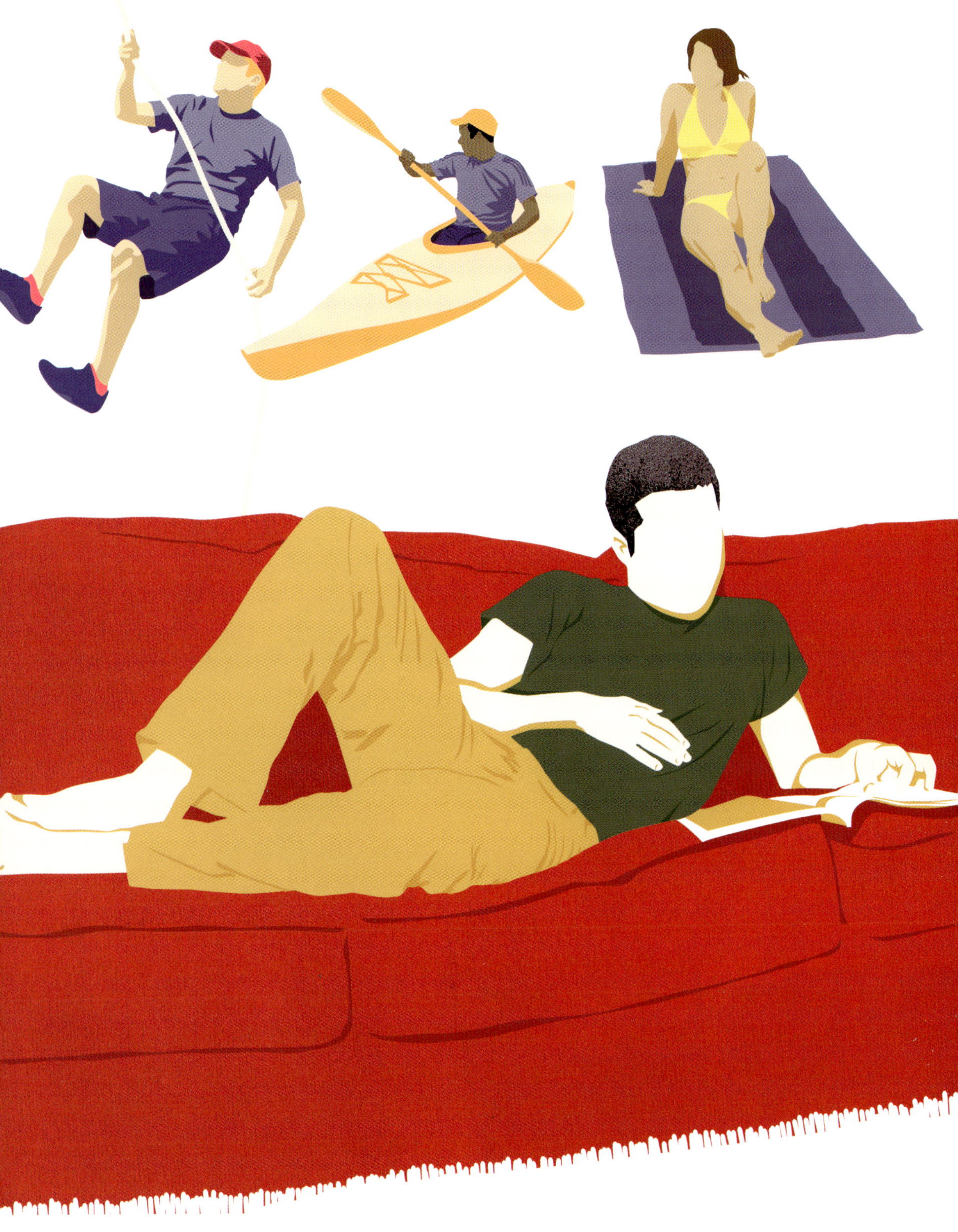
MENDOLA
portfolio
mendolaart.com
email
info@menolaart.com
call
212.986.5680
represents
AMY DeVOOGD

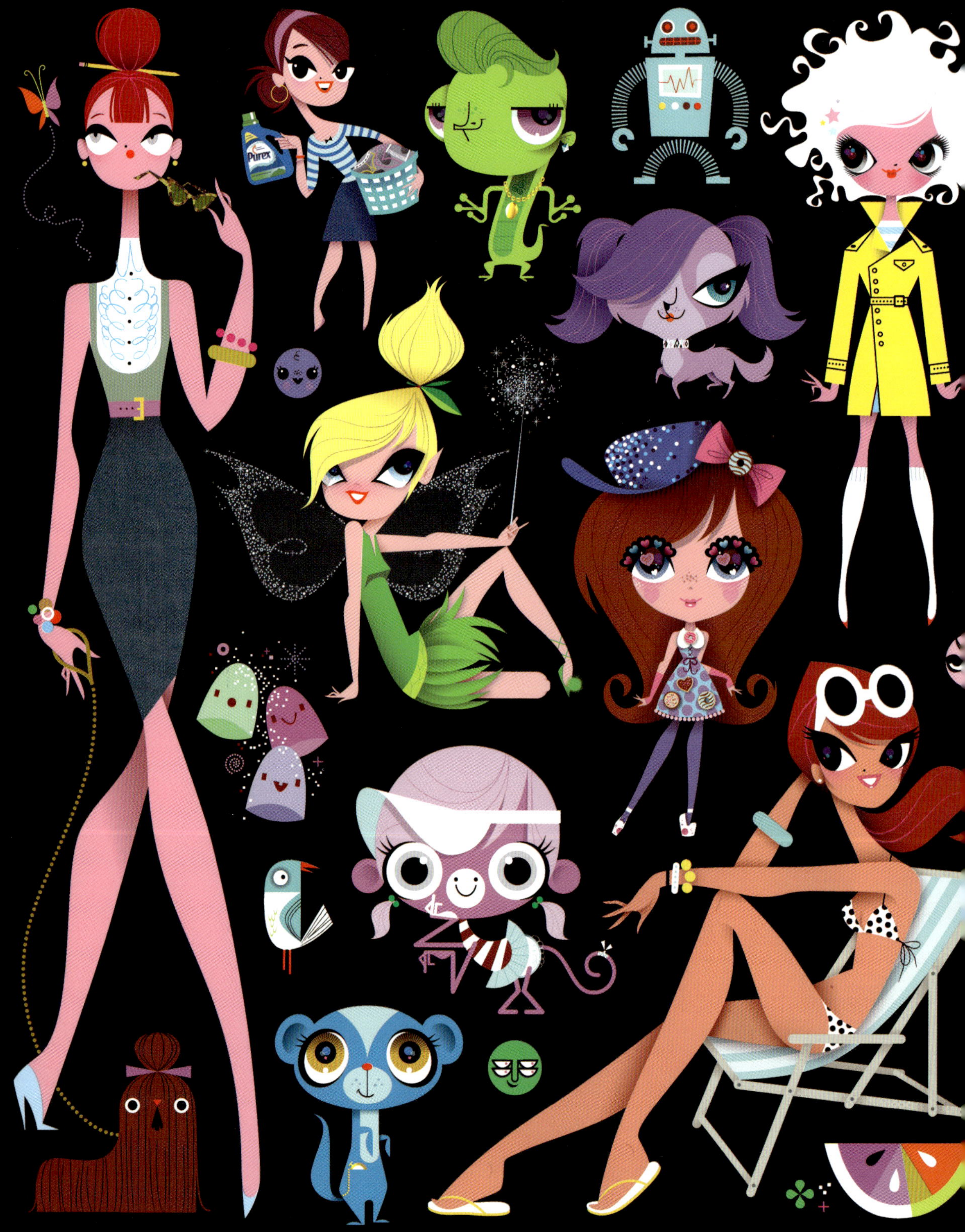
Purex

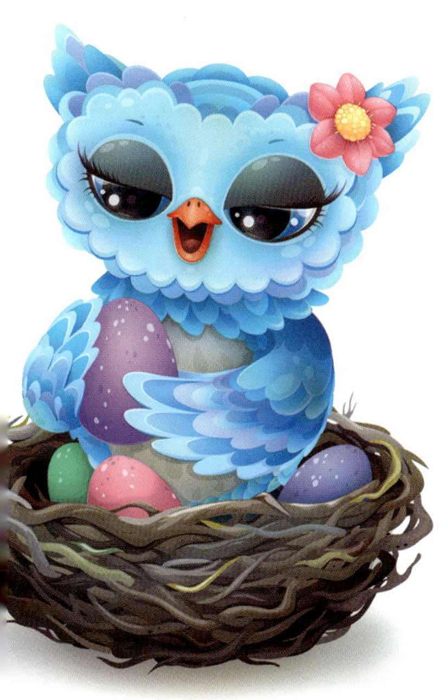
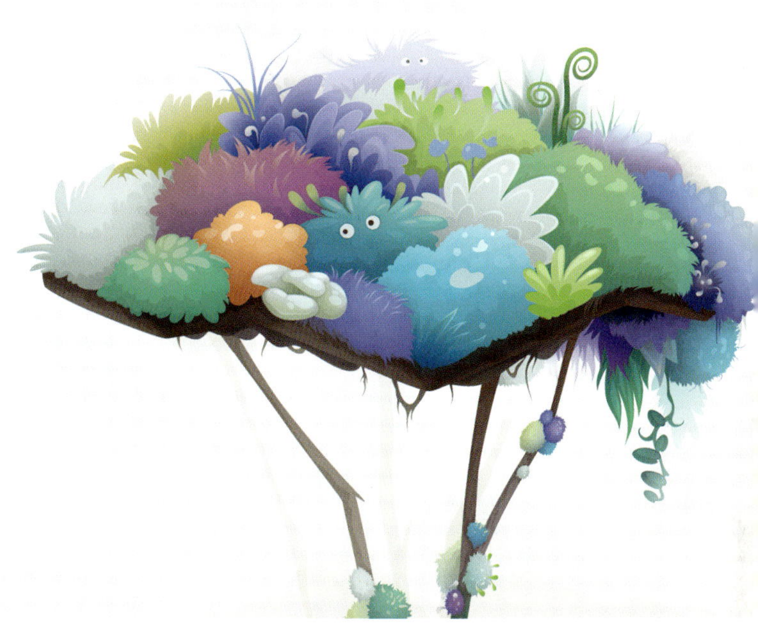
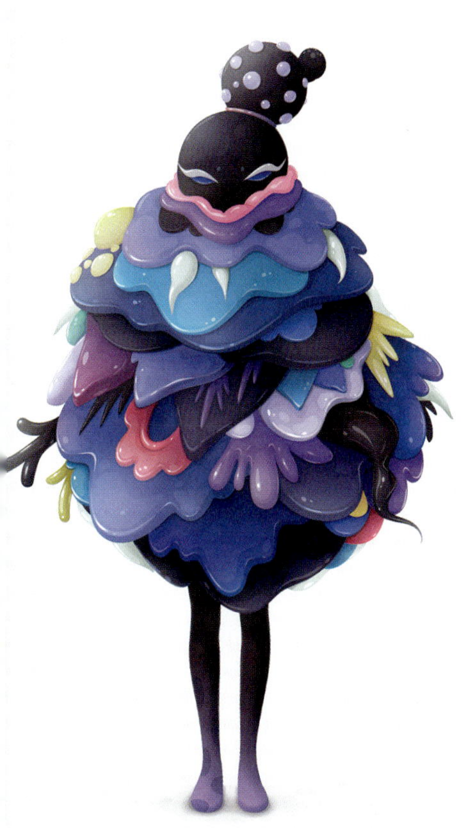
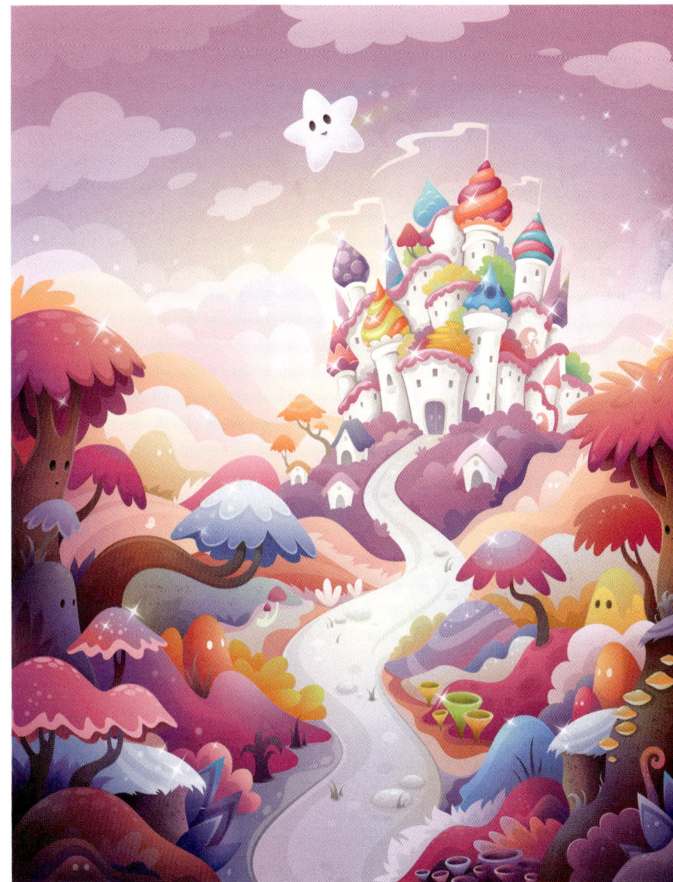

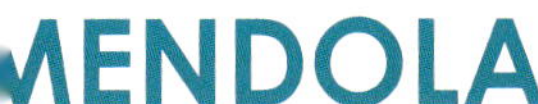

portfolio
mendolaart.com

email
info@menolaart.com

call
212.986.5680

represents
ZUTTO

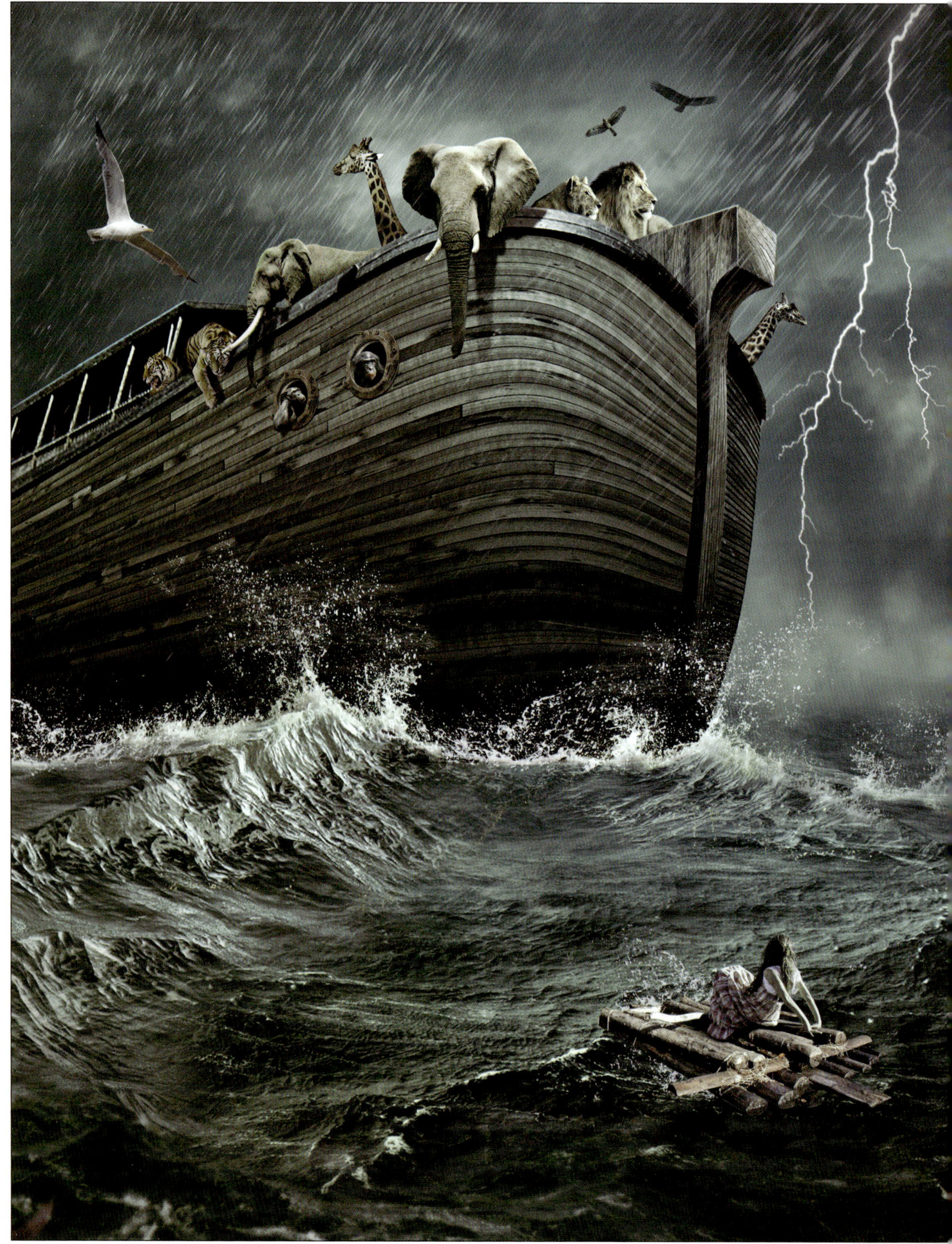

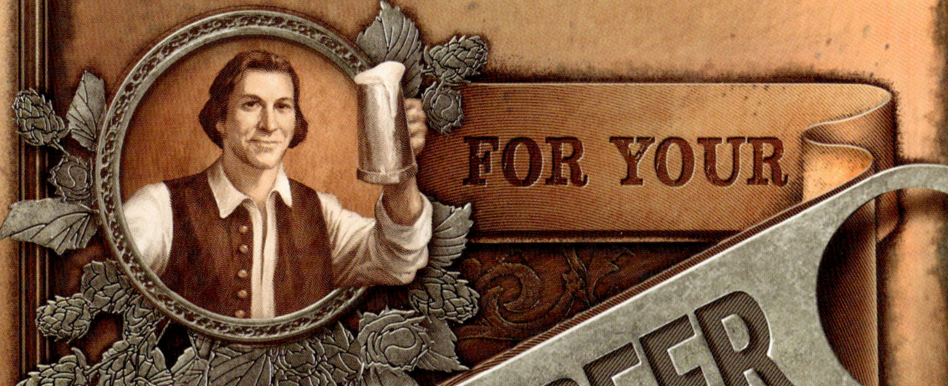

FOR YOUR
LOVE of BEER
2012 ANNUAL REPORT
SAMUEL ADAMS
PROUDLY BREWED AND BOTTLED BY
THE BOSTON BEER COMPANY INC.

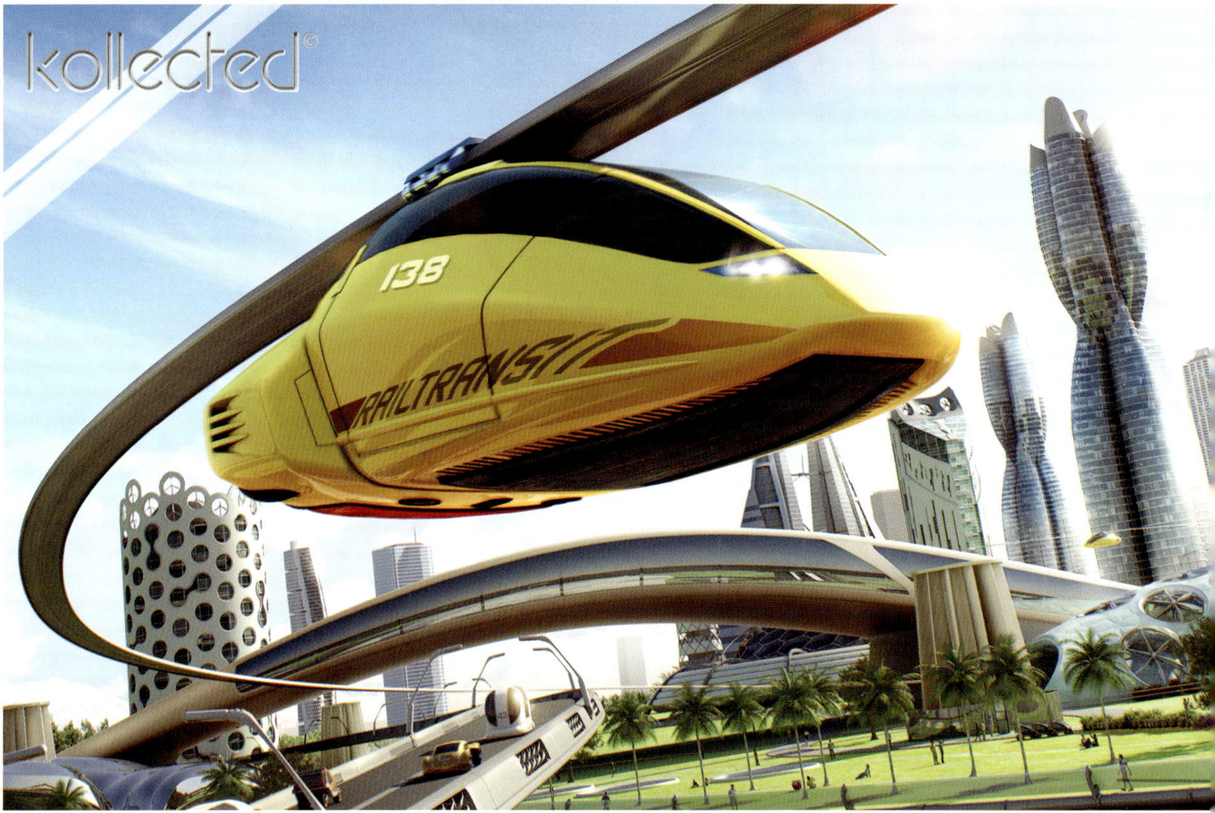

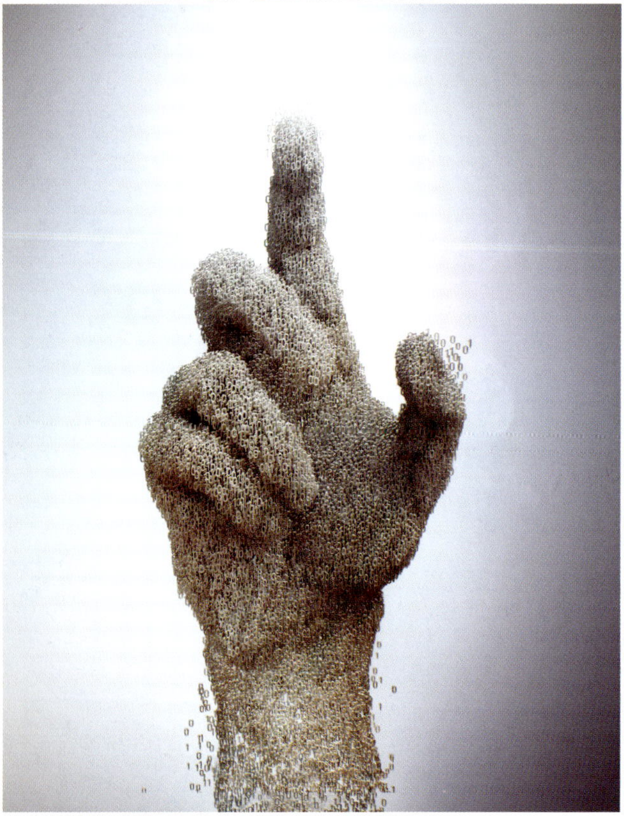

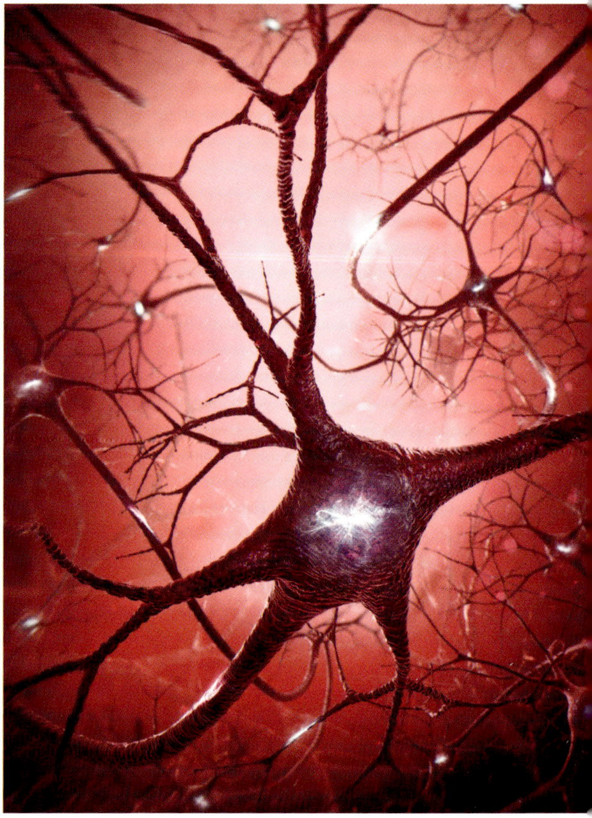

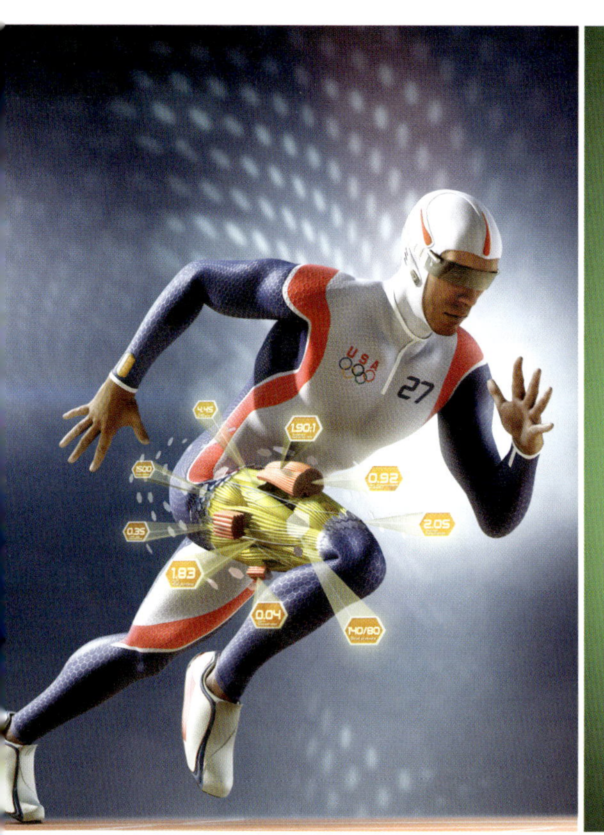

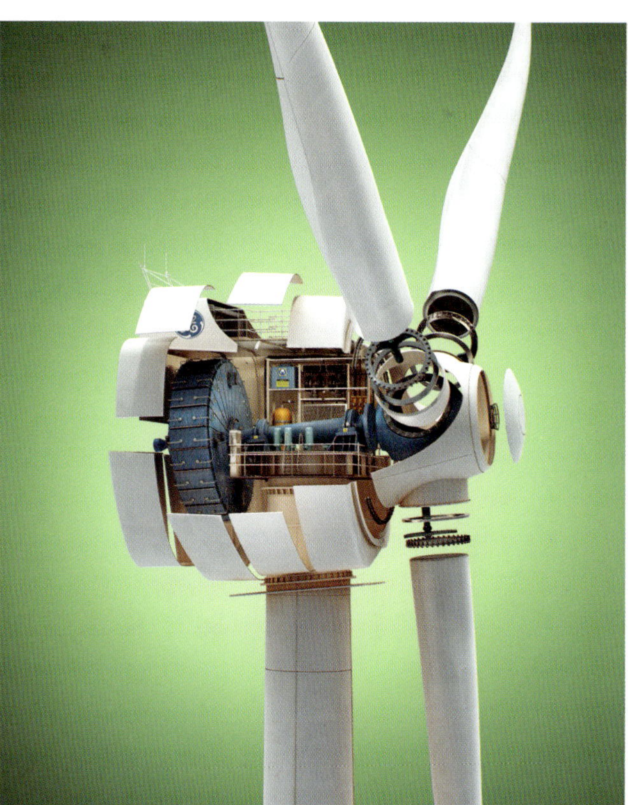

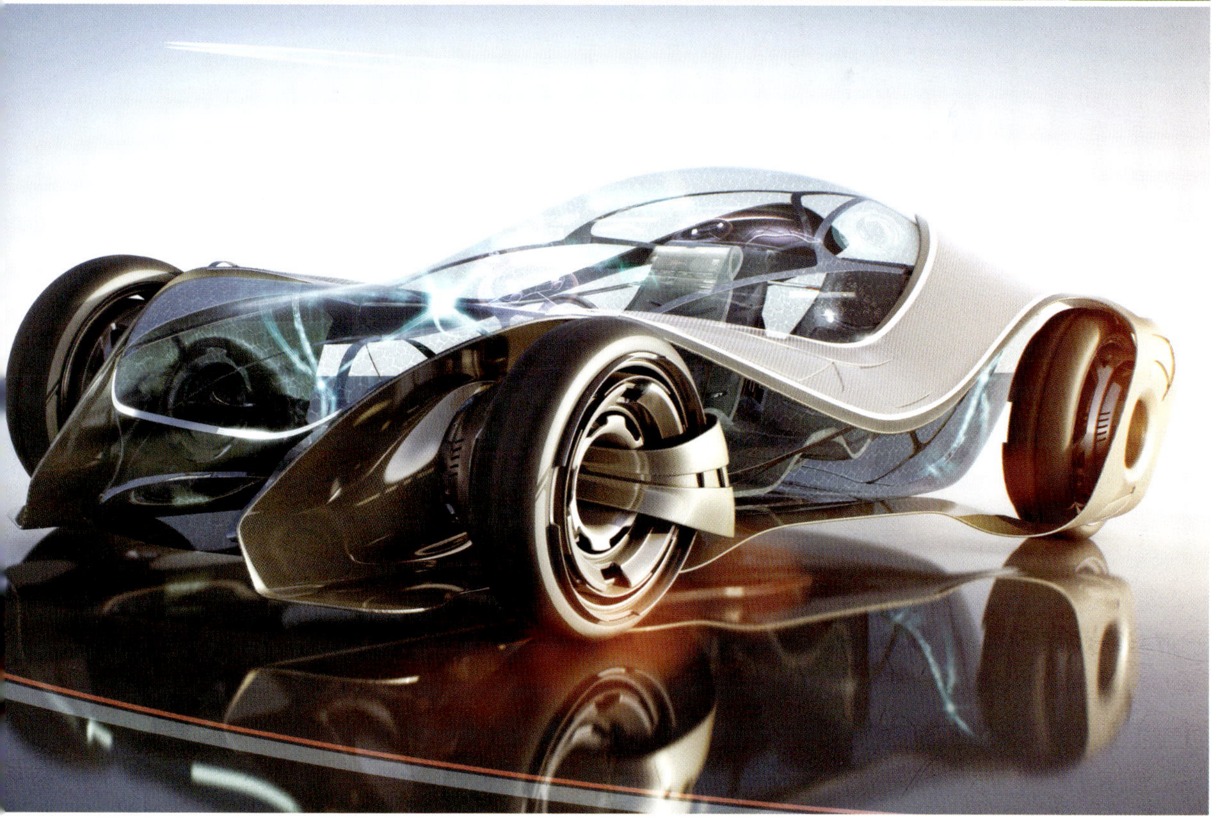

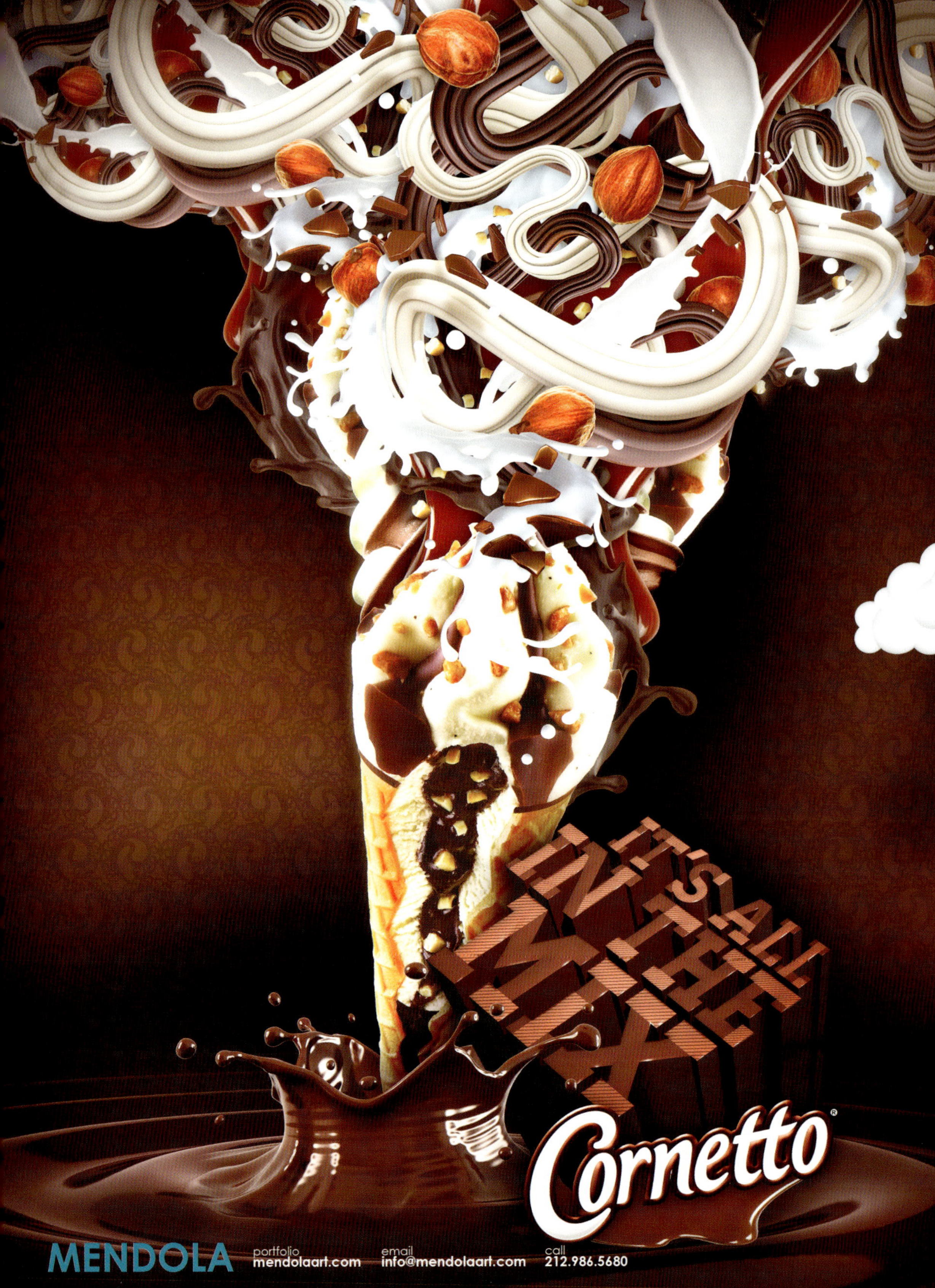

IT'S ALL IN THE MIX
Cornetto®
MENDOLA
portfolio
mendolaart.com
email
info@mendolaart.com
call
212.986.5680

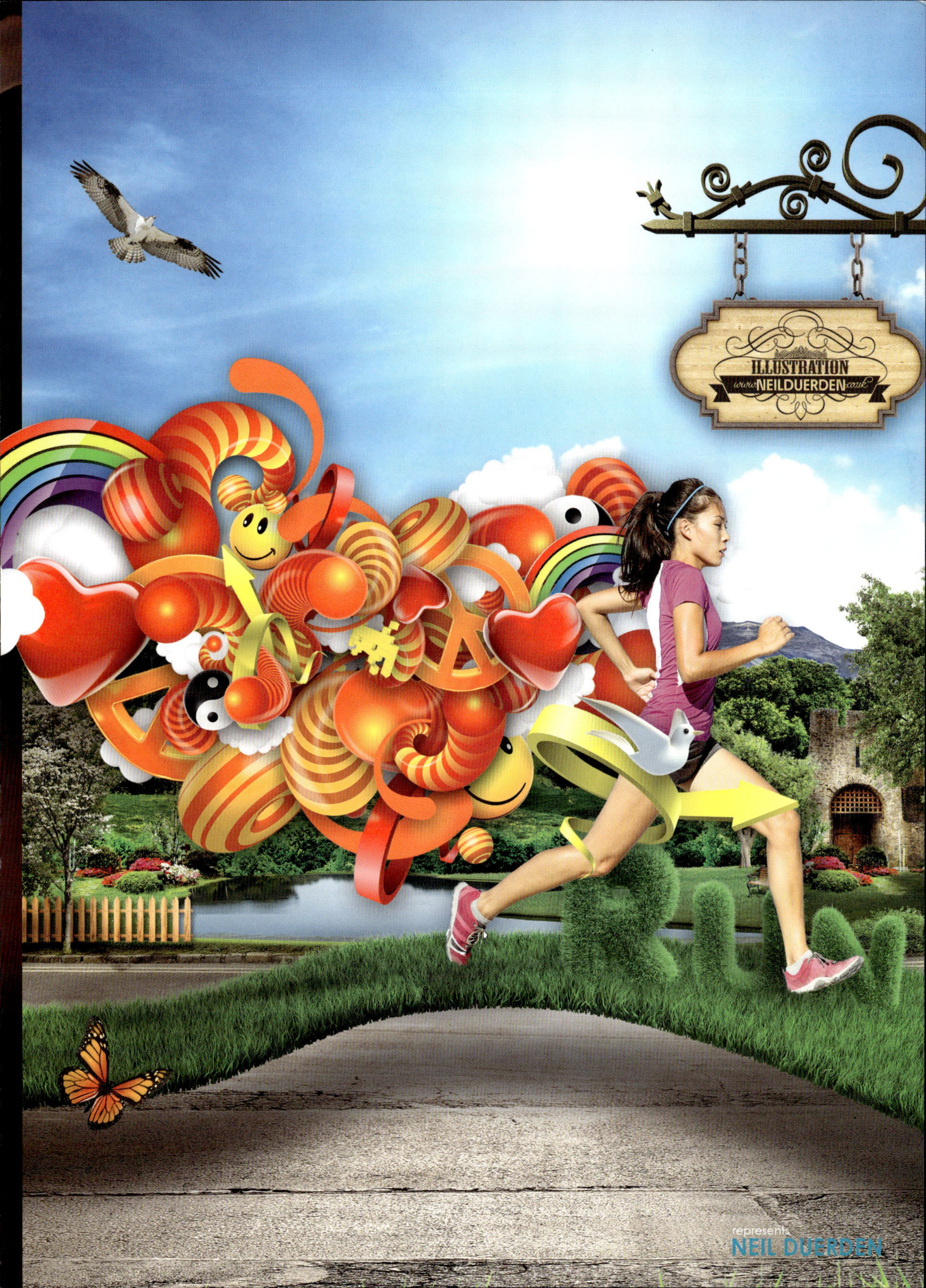

ILLUSTRATION
www.NEILDUERDEN.co.uk
represent.
NEIL DUERDEN

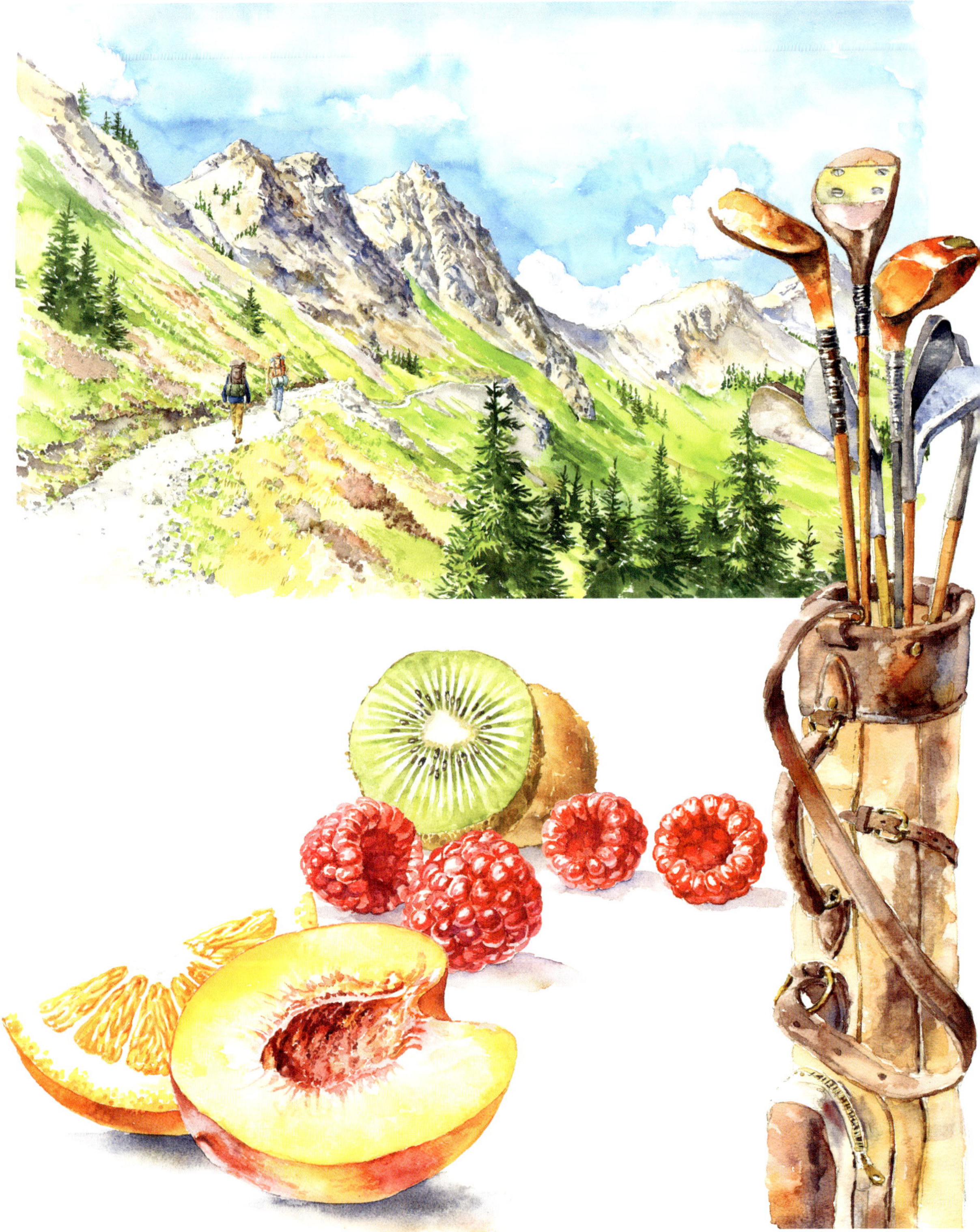

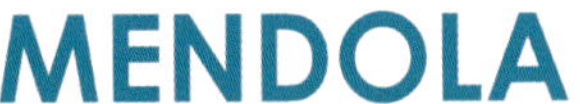

MENDOLA
portfolio
mendolaart.com
email
info@mendolaart.com
call
212.986.5680
represents
DAHL TAYLO

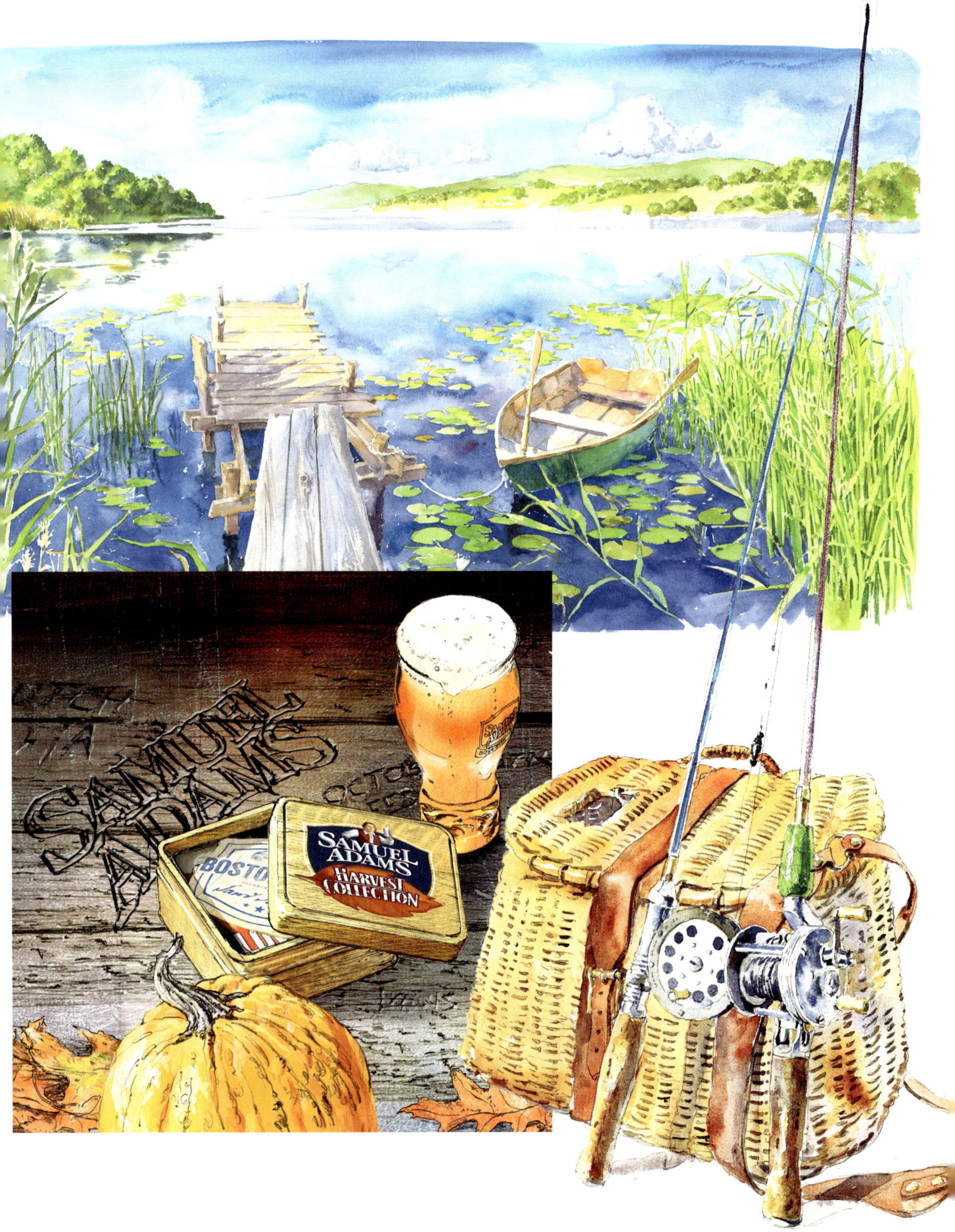

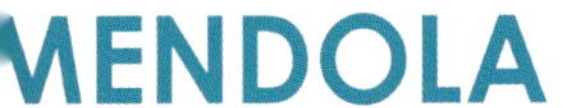

MENDOLA

portfolio
mendolaart.com

email
info@mendolaart.com

call
212.986.5680

represents
DAHL TAYLOR

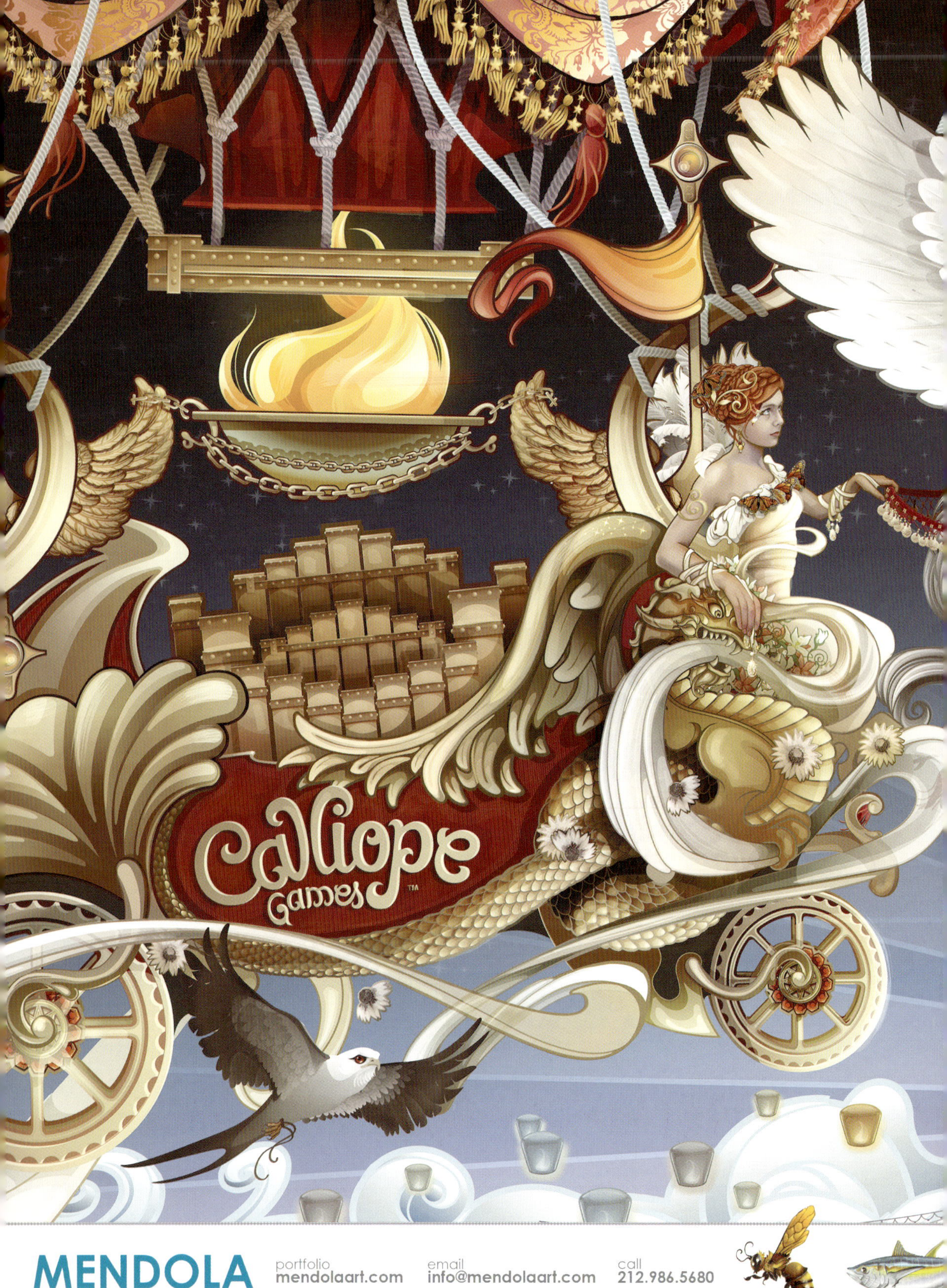
CALIOPE
Games ™
MENDOLA
portfolio
mendolaart.com
email
info@mendolaart.com
call
212.986.5680

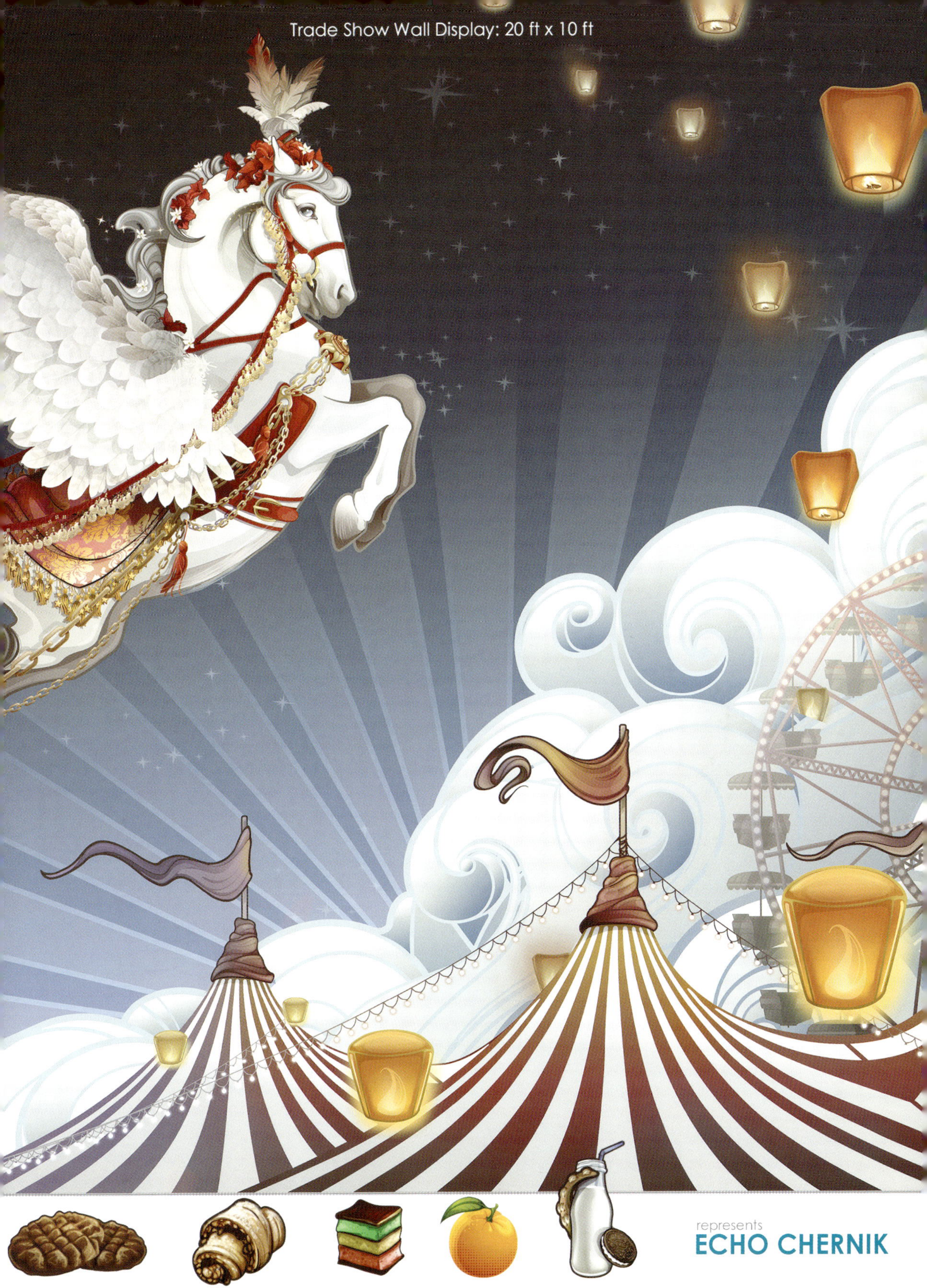

Trade Show Wall Display: 20 ft x 10 ft
represents
ECHO CHERNIK

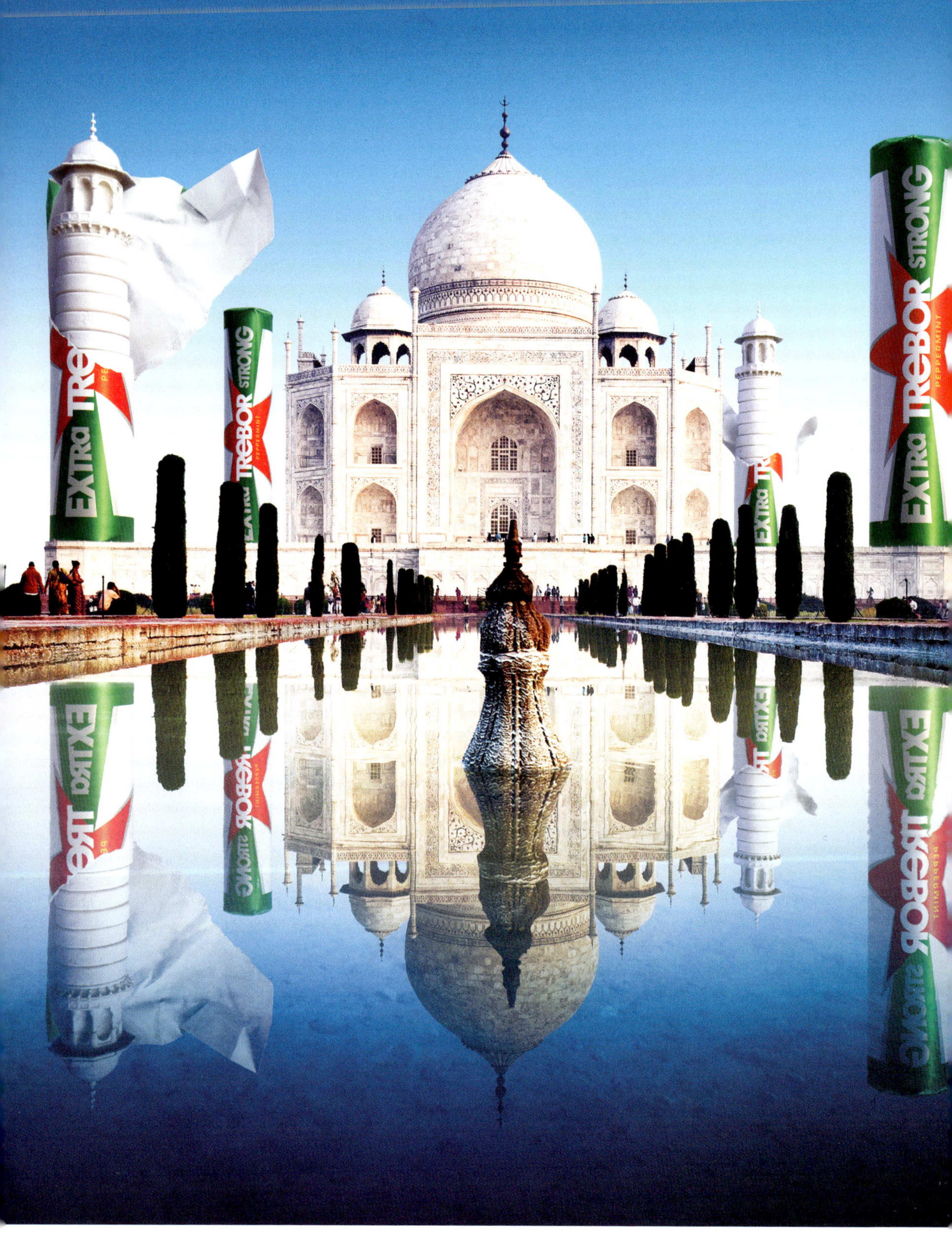

Extra TREBOR STRONG PEPPERMINT
TREBOR STRONG PEPPERMINT
EXTRA TREBOR STRONG PEPPERMINT

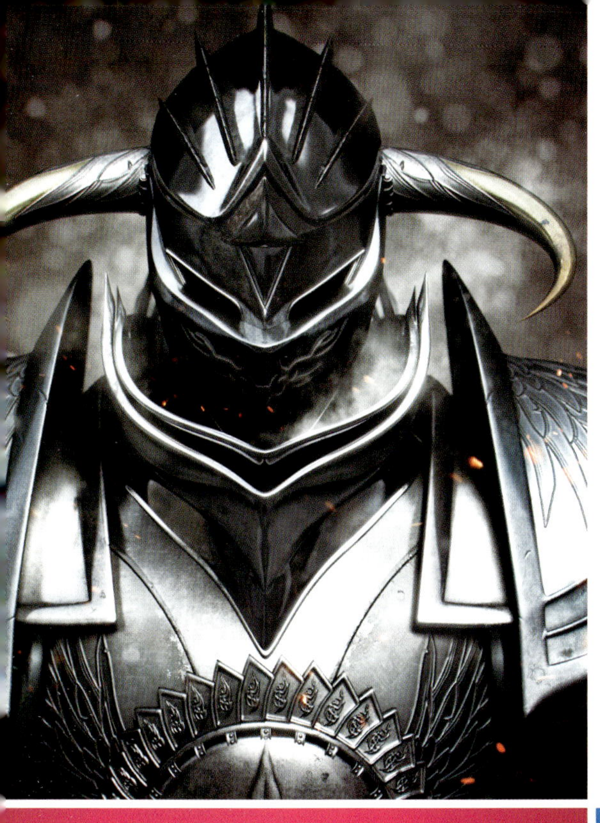

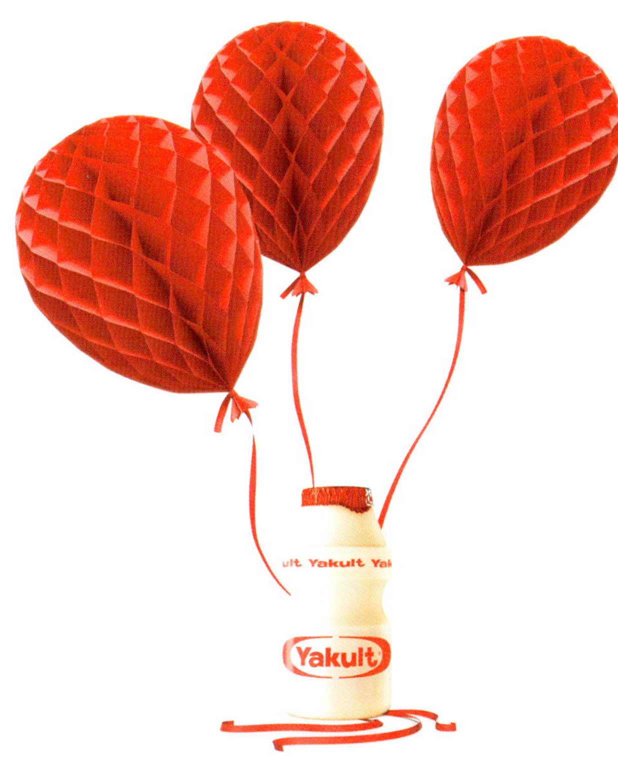

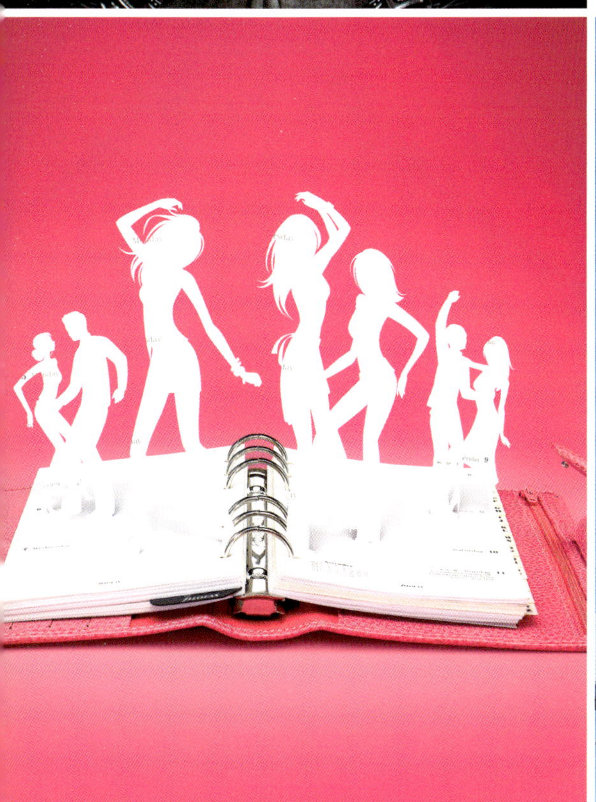

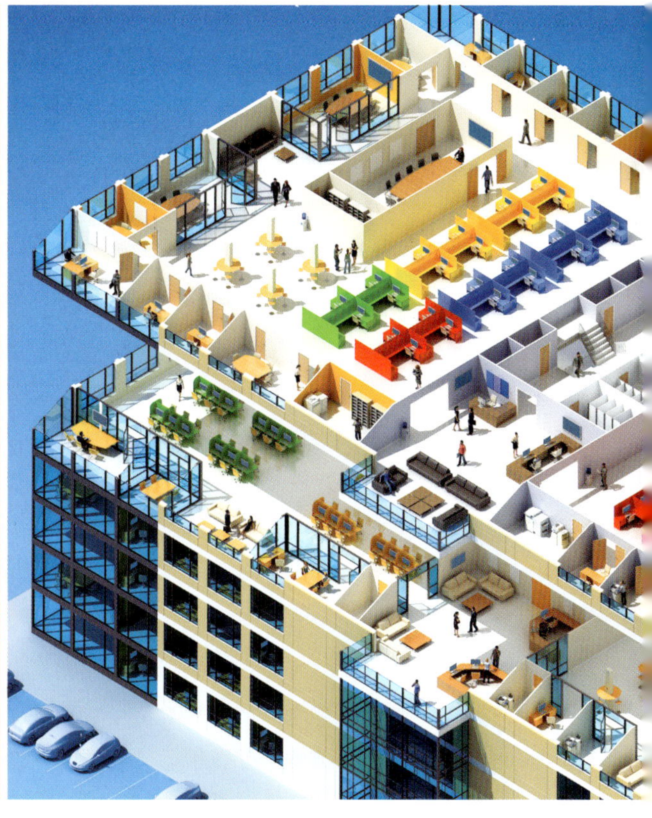

represents
DIGITAL PROGRESSION

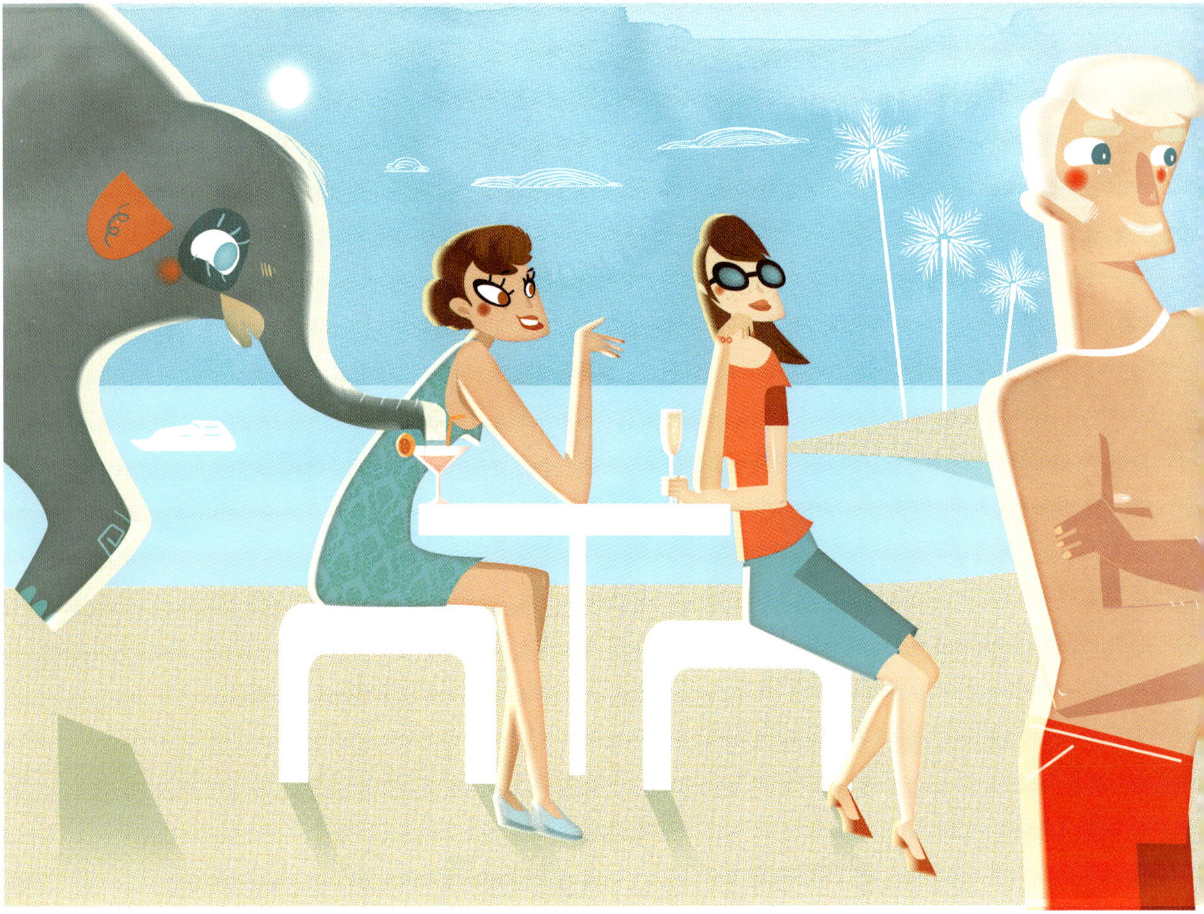

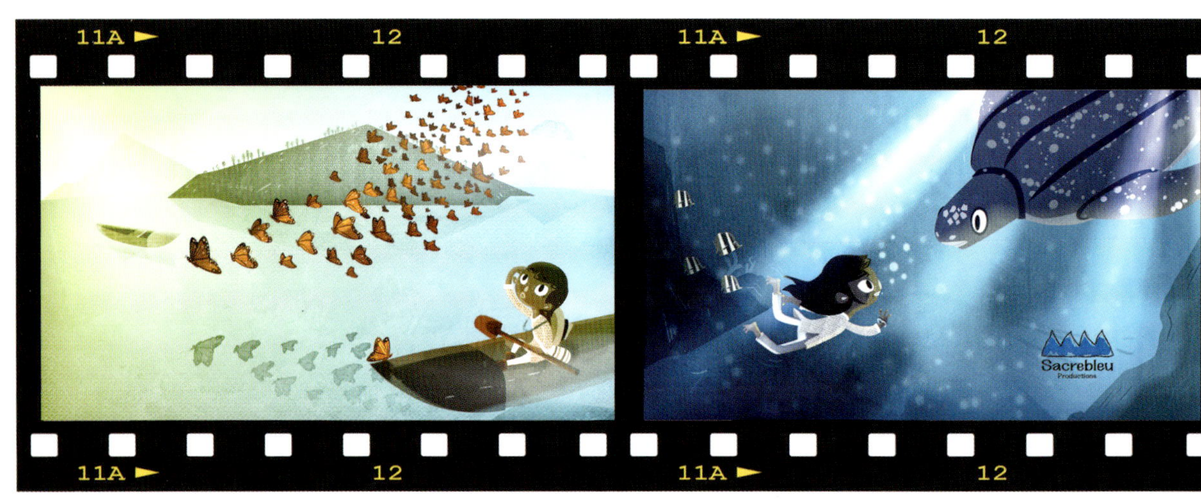
ILLUSTRATION, ANIMATION AND MOTION DESIGN
Sacrebleu
Productions

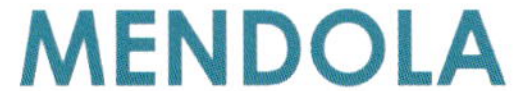
MENDOLA
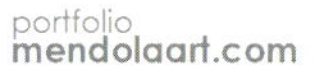
portfolio
mendolaart.com
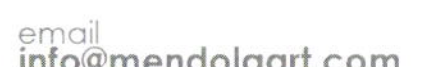
email
info@mendolaart.com
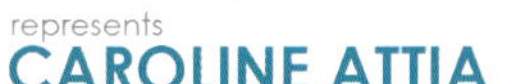
call
212.986.5680
represents
CAROLINE ATTIA

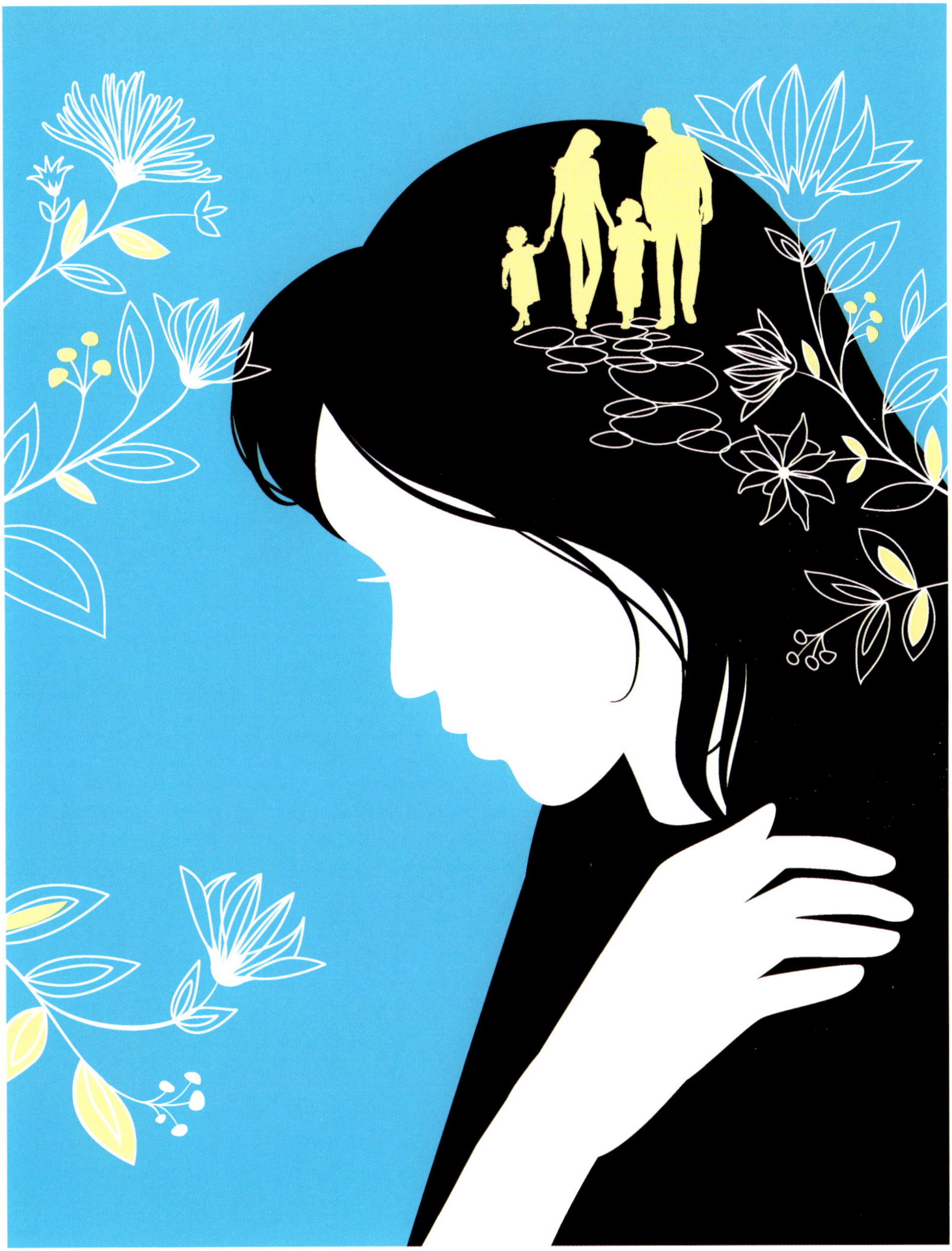

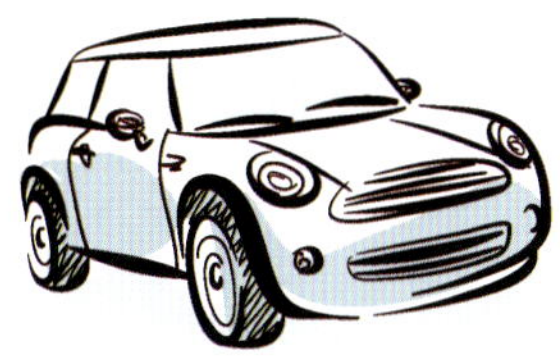
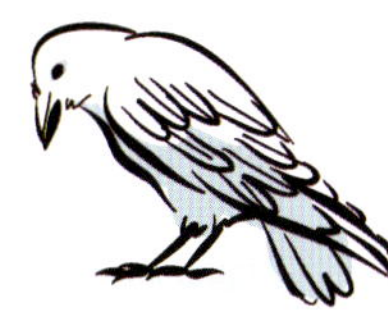
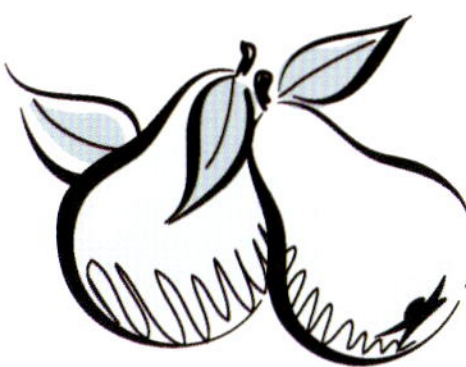
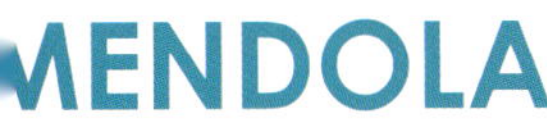

MENDOLA
portfolio
mendolaart.com
email
info@mendolaart.com
call
212.986.5680
represents
MONA DALY

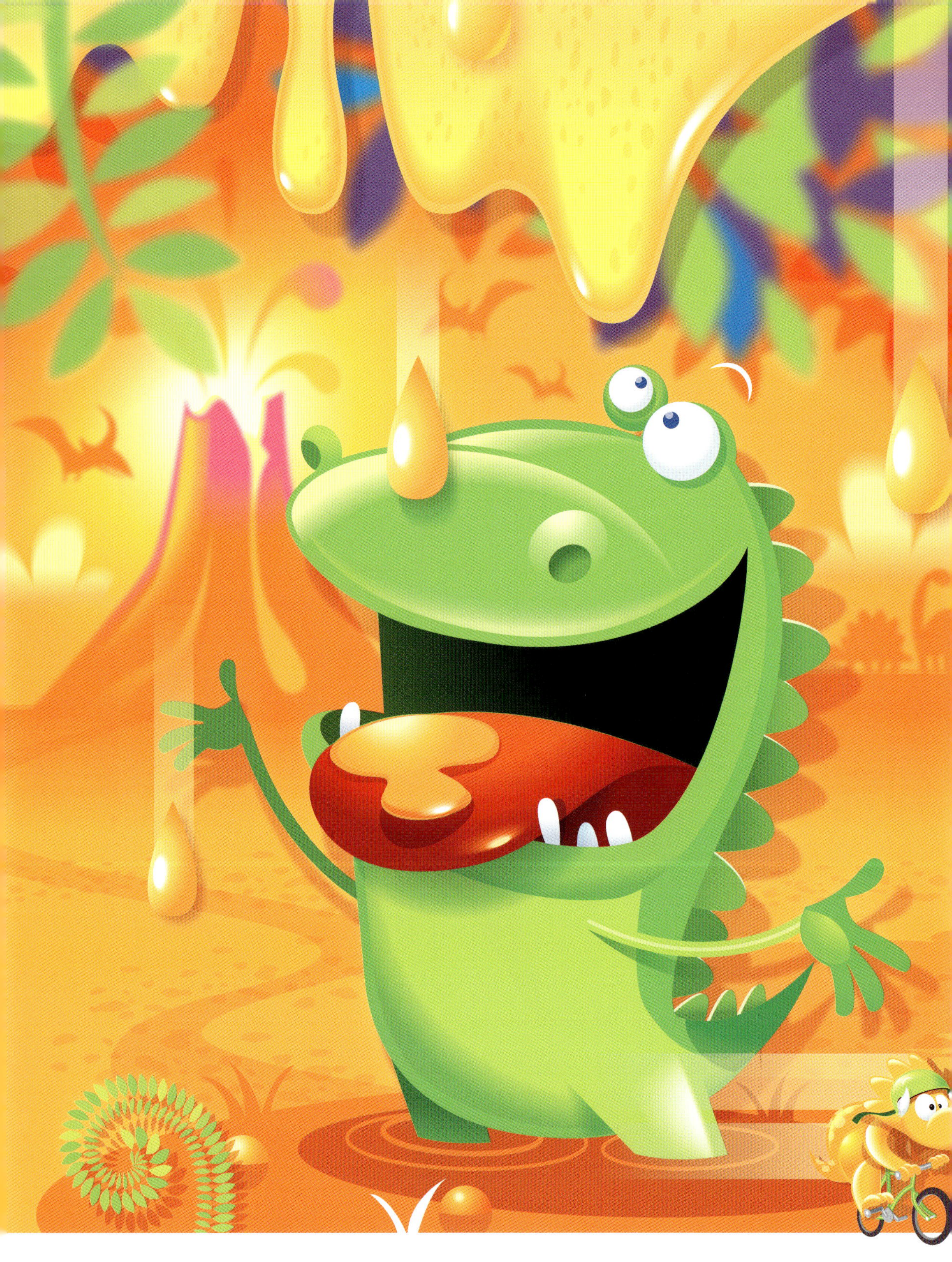

MENDOLA
portfolio
mendolaart.com
email
info@mendolaart.com
call
212.986.5680
represents
RUSSELL BENFAN

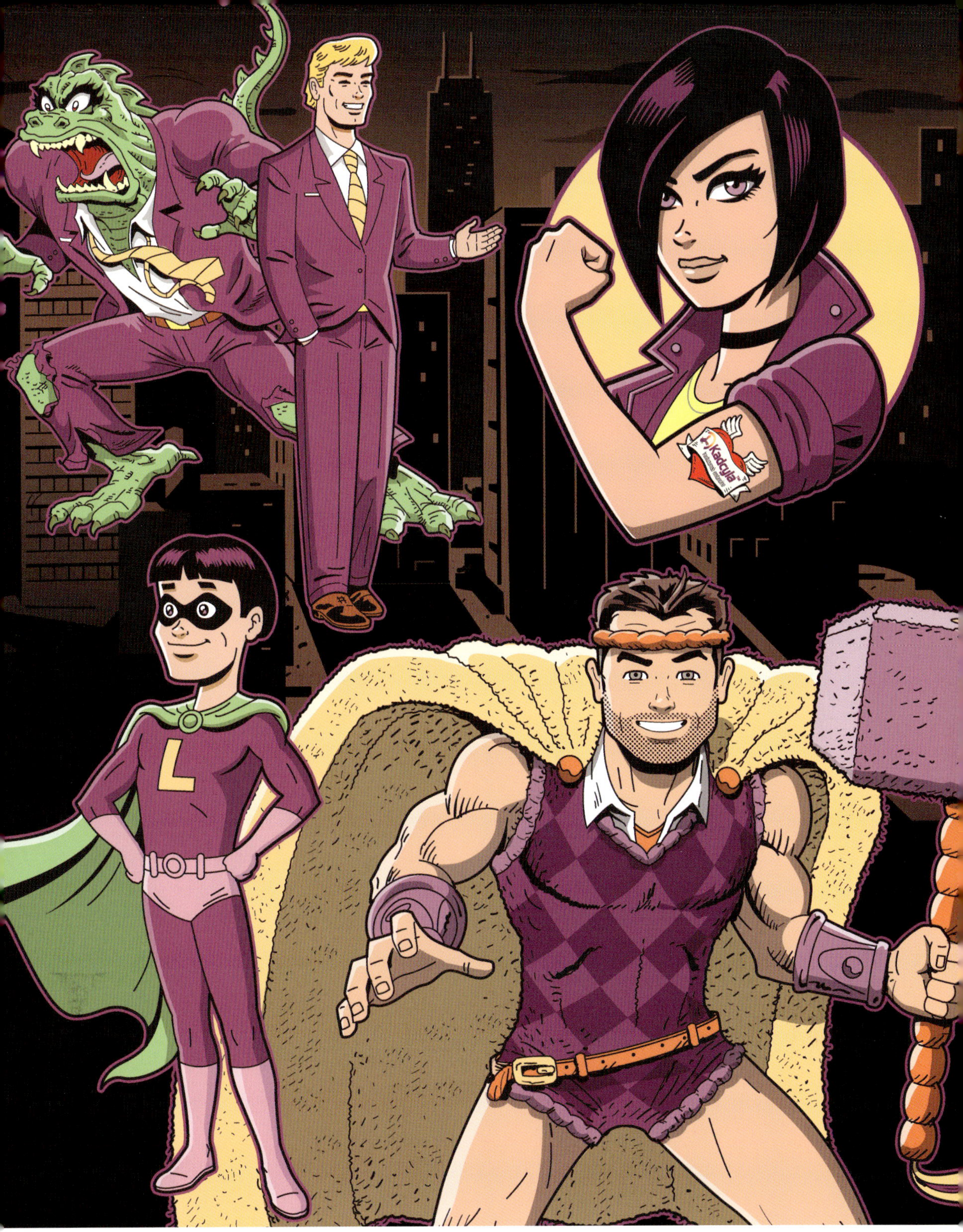

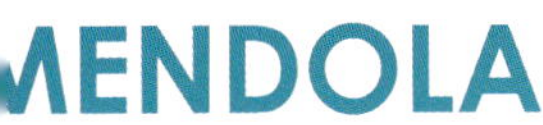

MENDOLA

portfolio
mendolaart.com

email
info@mendolaart.com

call
212.986.5680

represents
KENNY KIERNAN
KennyK.com

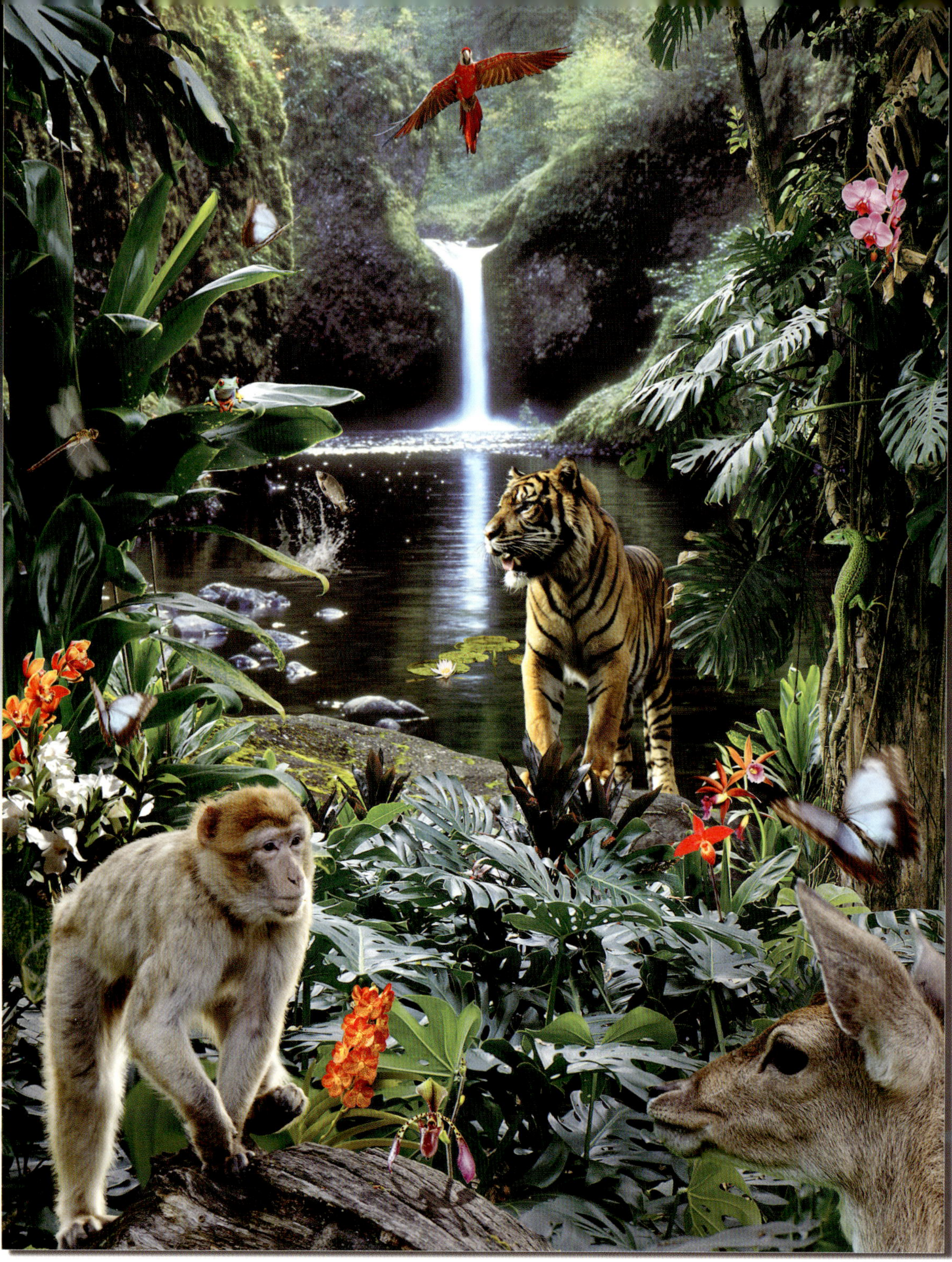

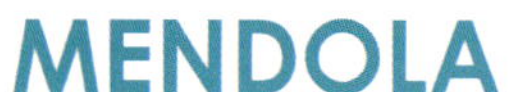

MENDOLA
portfolio
mendolaart.com
email
info@mendolaart.com
call
212.986.5680

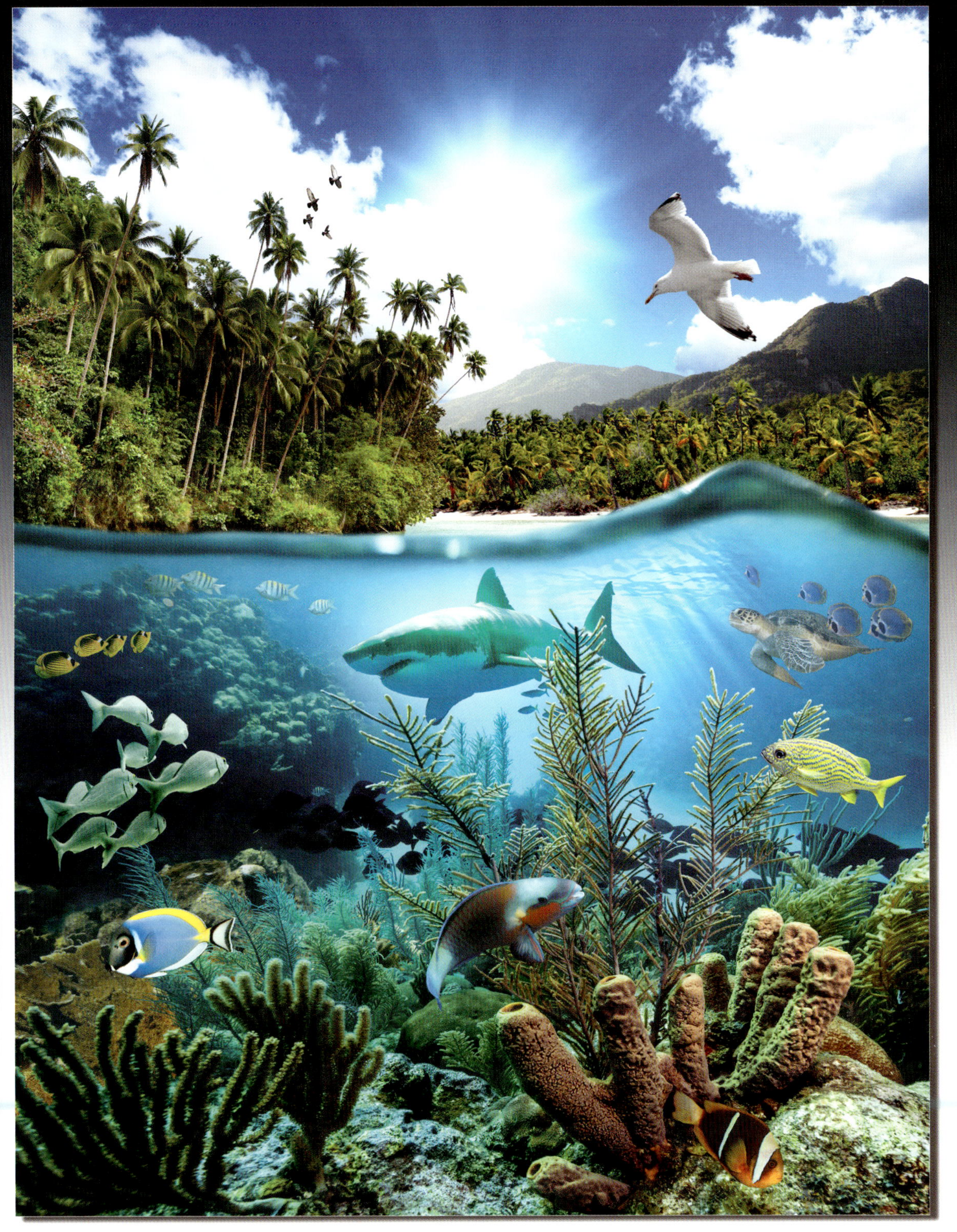

represents
JEFF MANGIAT

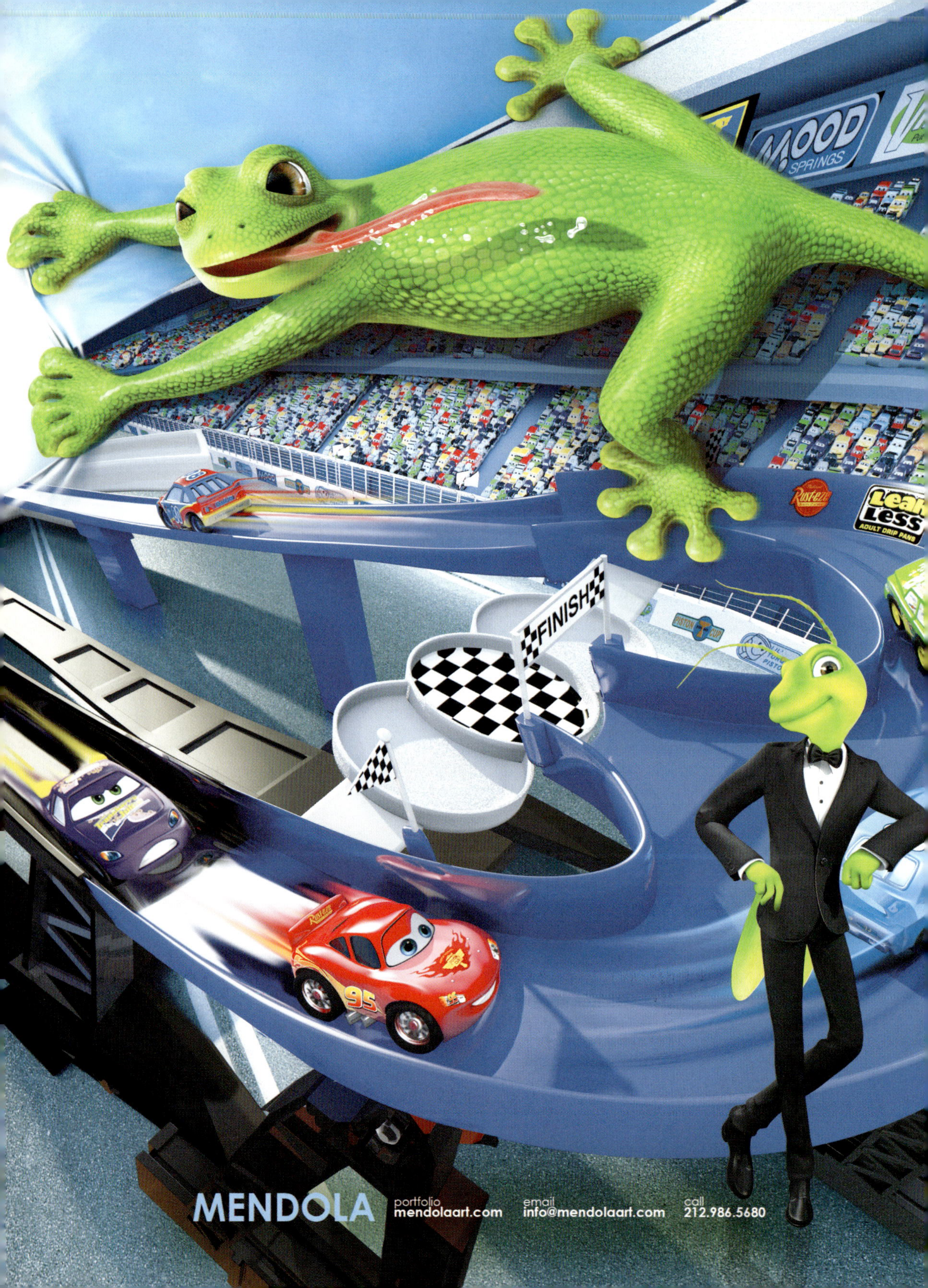

MOOD
SPRINGS
FINISH
95
MENDOLA
portfolio
mendolaart.com
email
info@mendolaart.com
call
212.986.5680

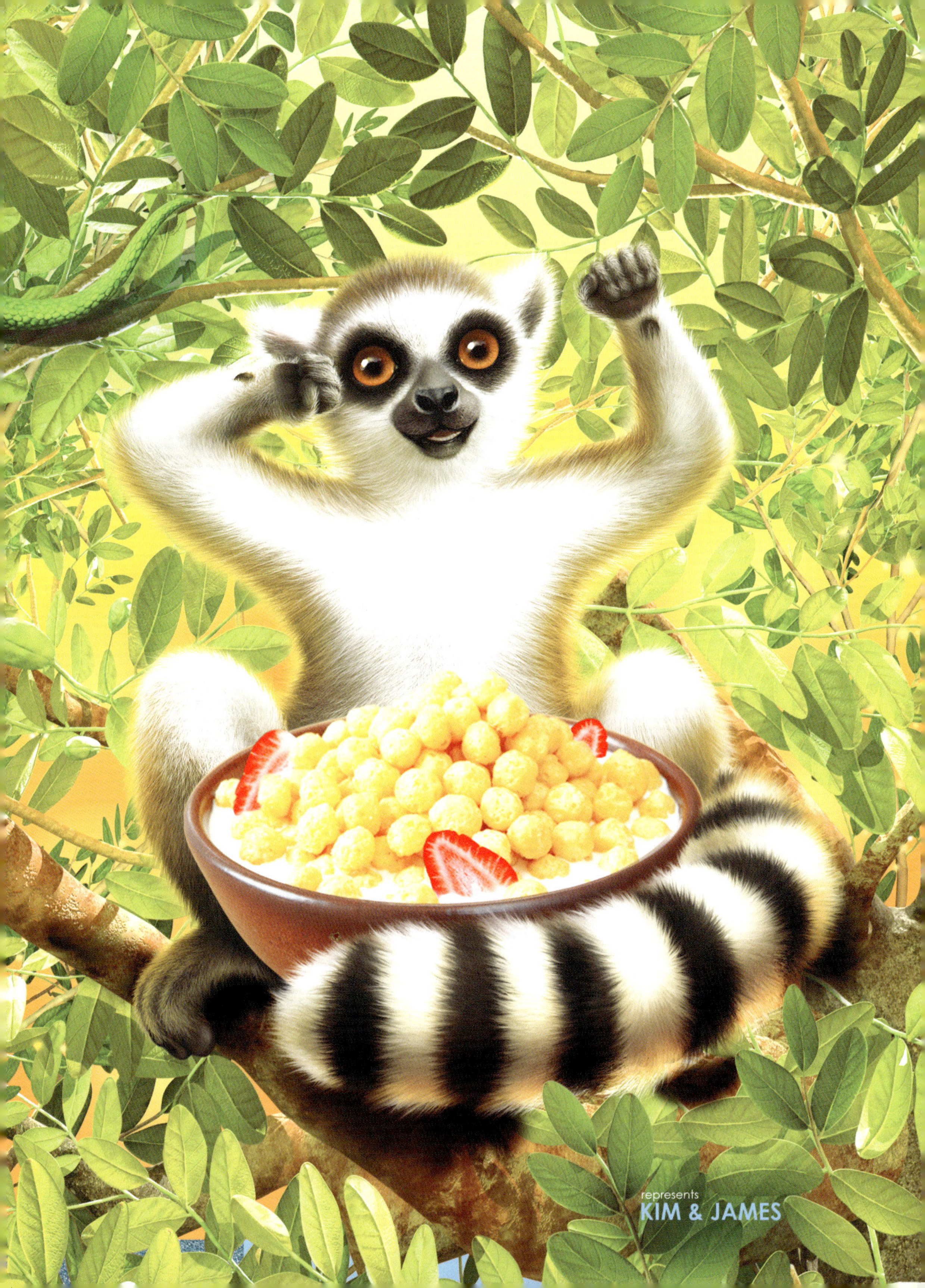
represents
KIM & JAMES

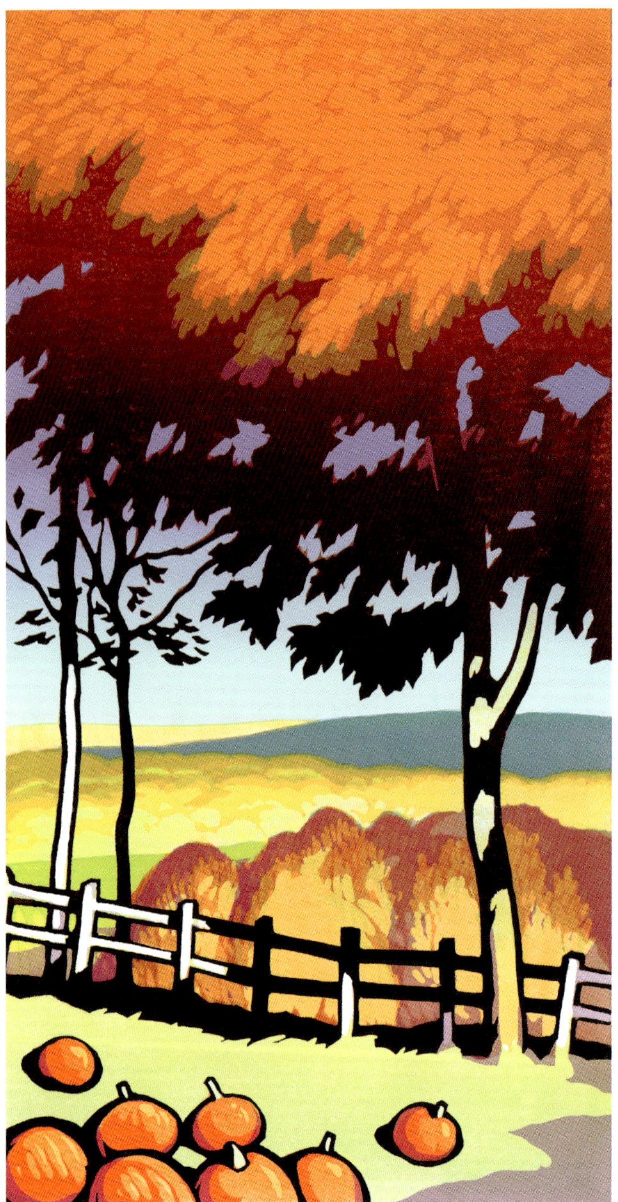

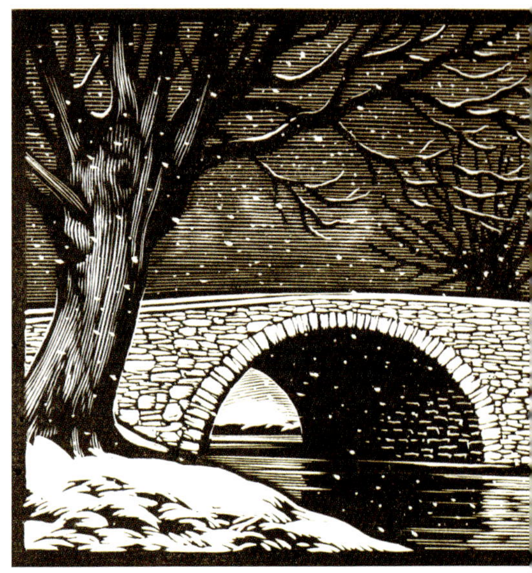

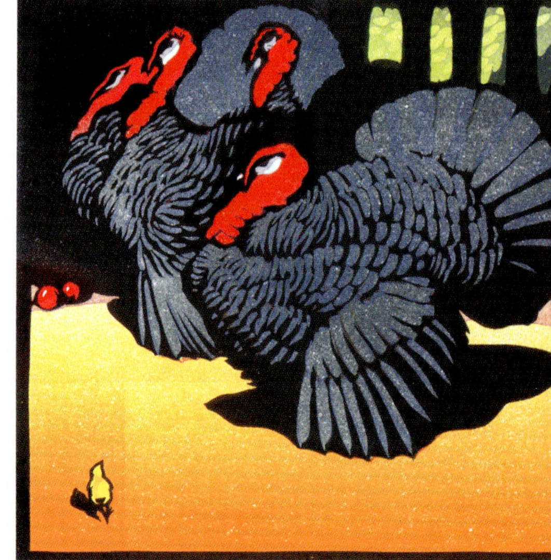

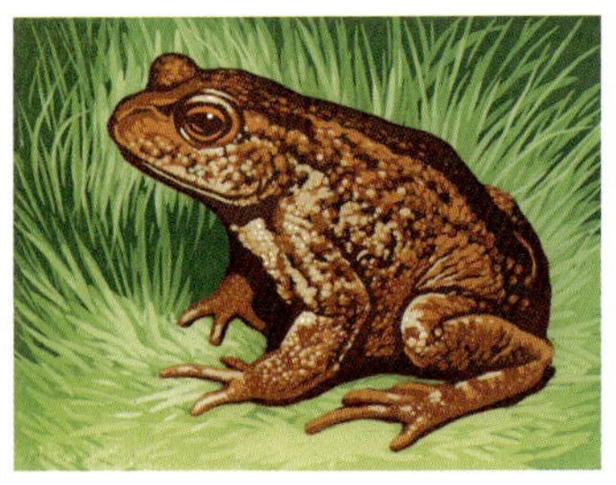

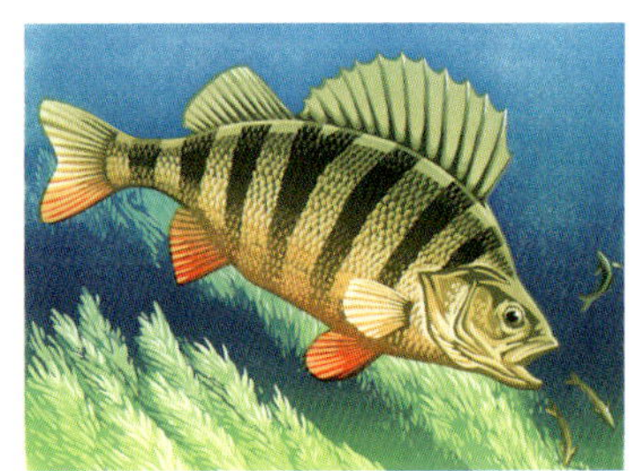

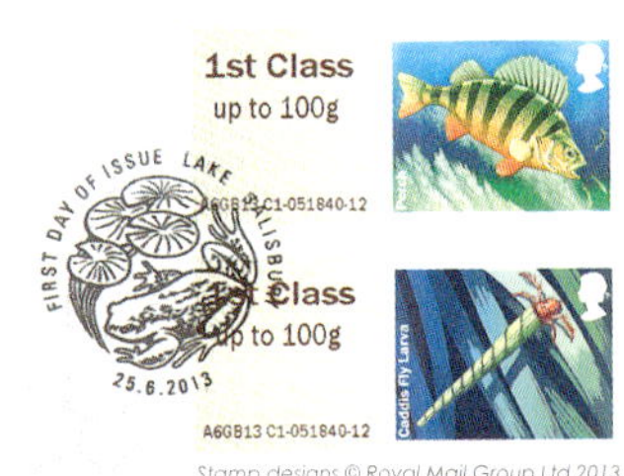

MENDOLA

portfolio
mendolaart.com

email
info@mendolaart.com

call
212.986.5680

represents
CHRIS WORMEL

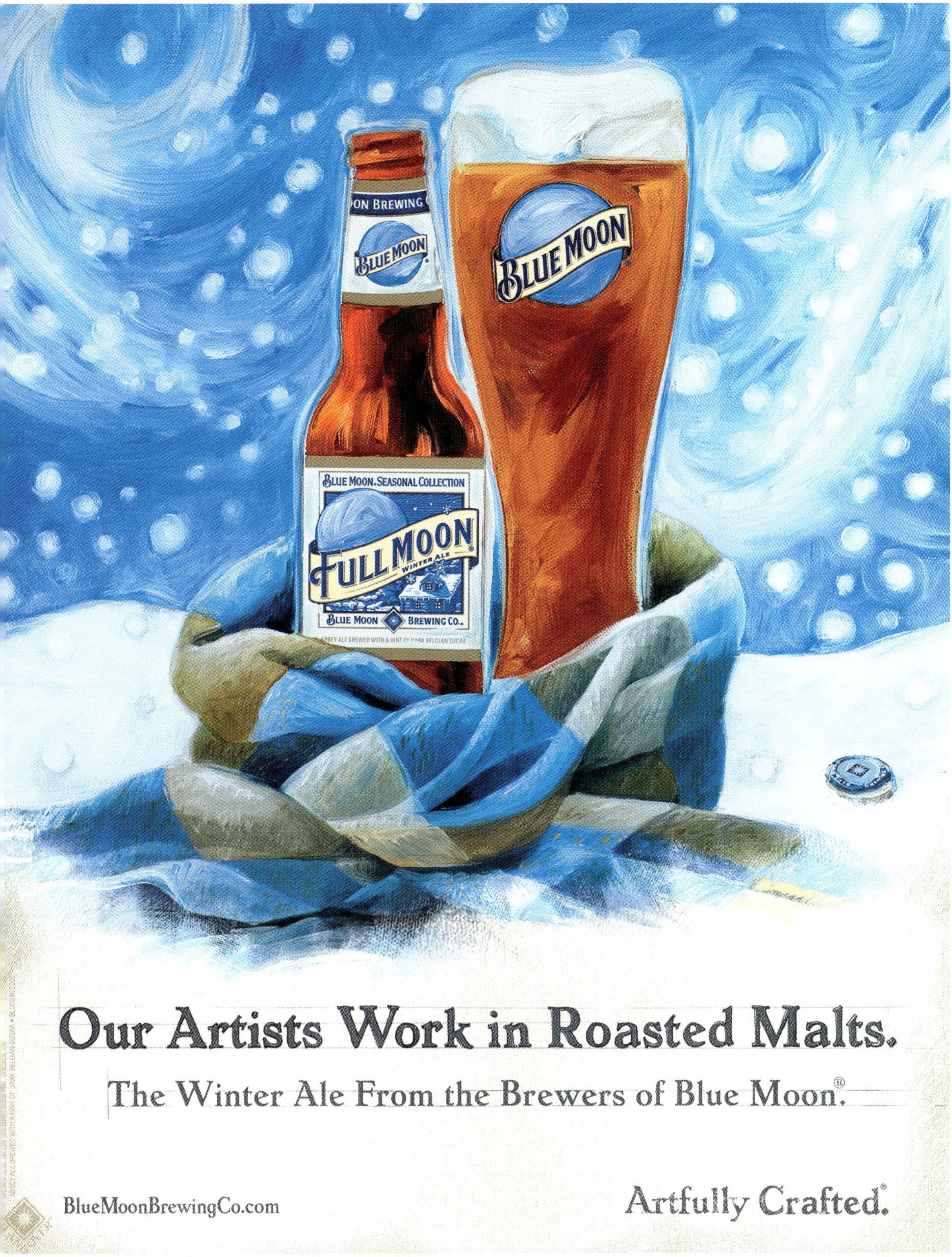

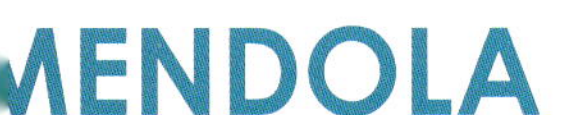

MENDOLA

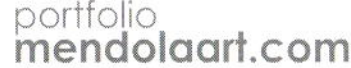

portfolio
mendolaart.com

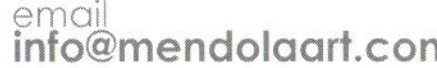

email
info@mendolaart.com

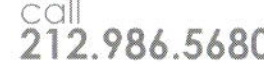

call
212.986.5680

ON BREWING
BLUE MOON
BLUE MOON
BLUE MOON · SEASONAL COLLECTION
FULL MOON
WINTER ALE
BLUE MOON BREWING CO.
ABBEY ALE BREWED WITH A HINT OF DARK BELGIAN SUGAR

Our Artists Work in Roasted Malts.
The Winter Ale From the Brewers of Blue Moon.

BlueMoonBrewingCo.com

Artfully Crafted.

represents
SHELLY BARTEK

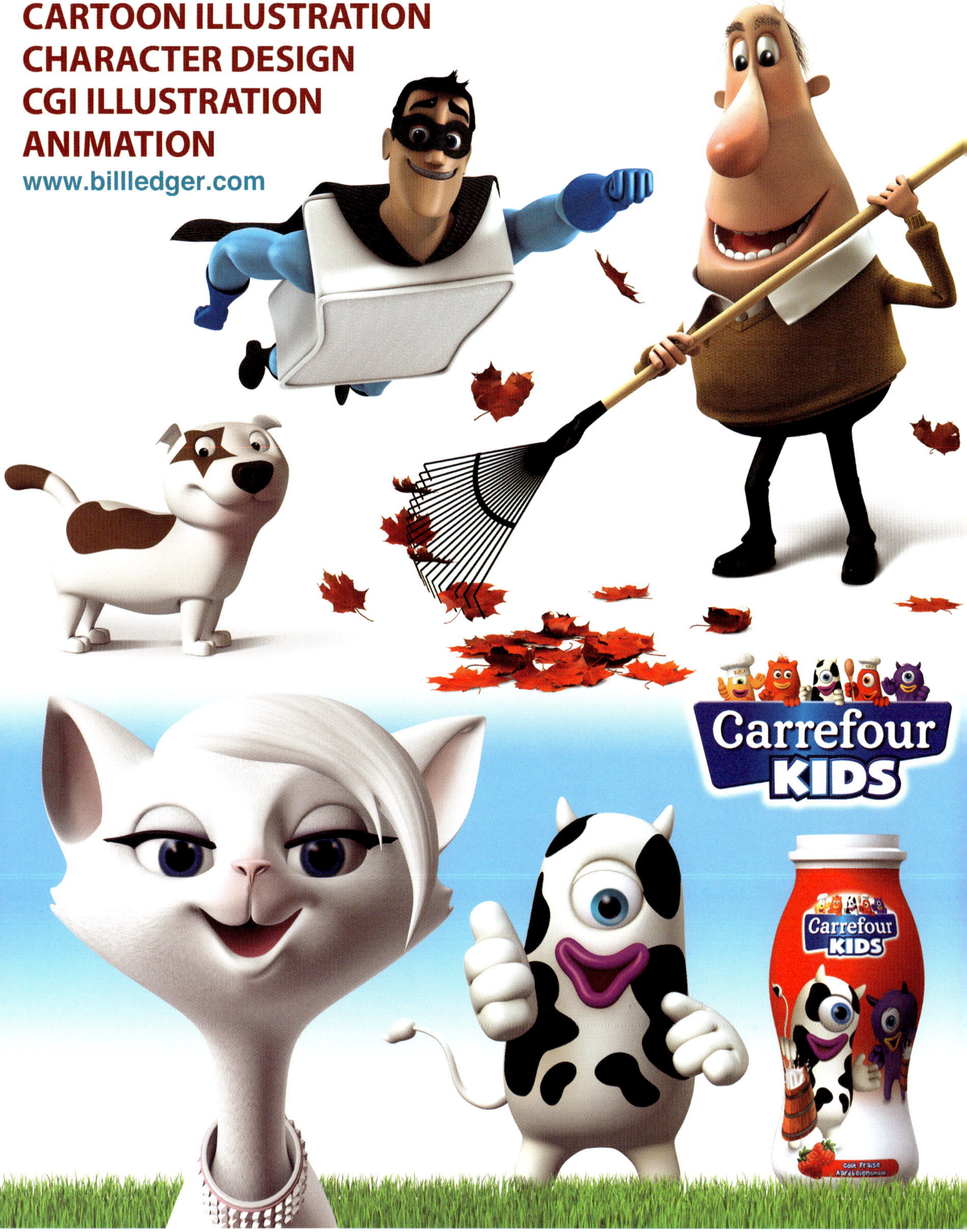

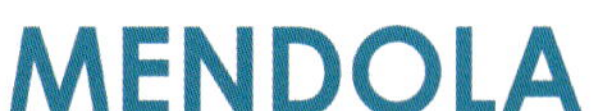

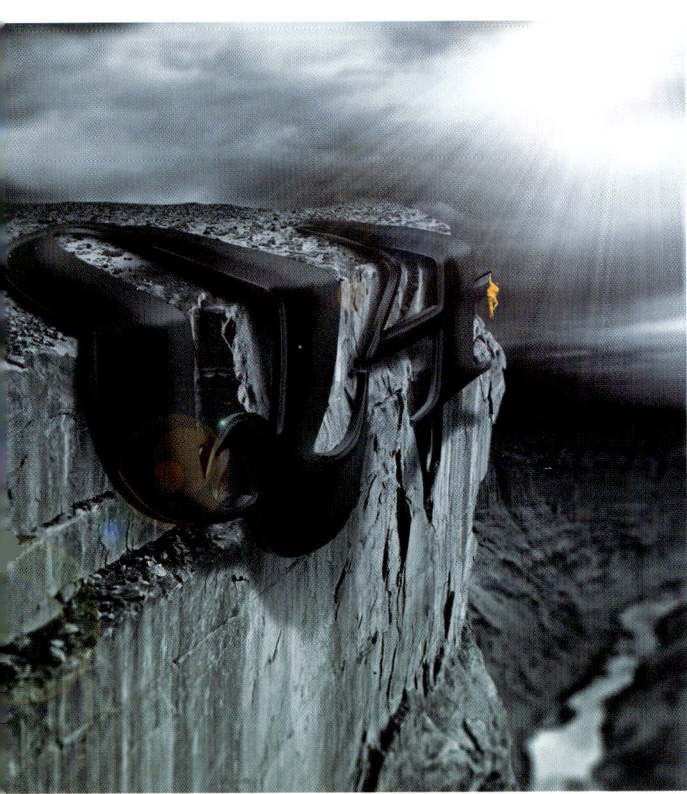

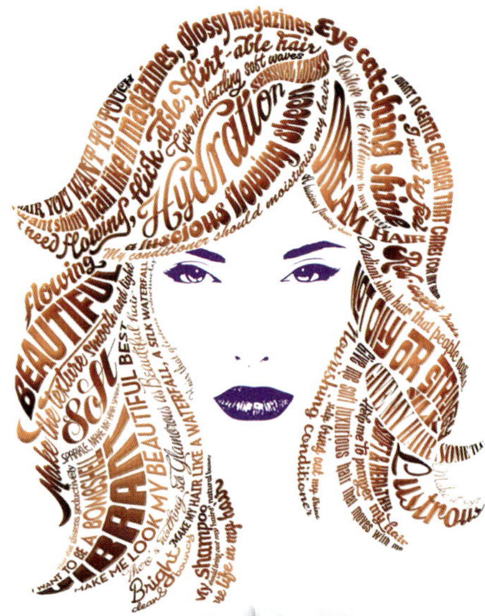

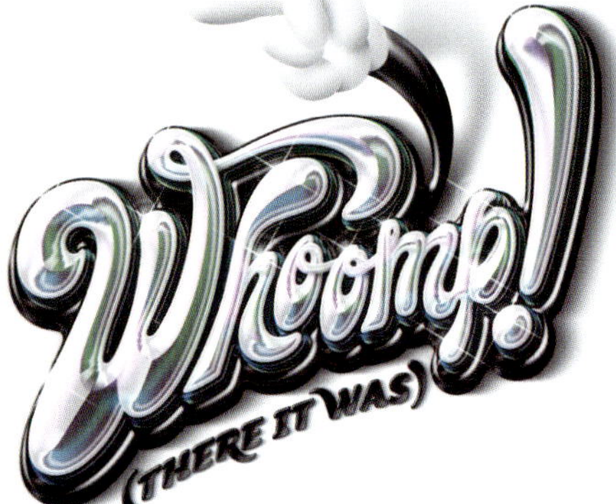
Whoomp!
(THERE IT WAS)

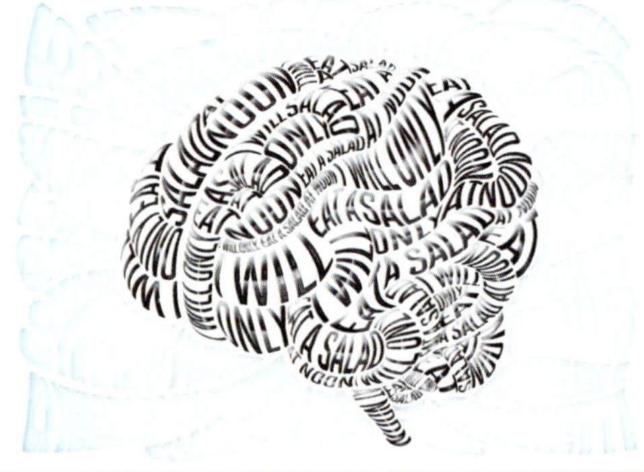

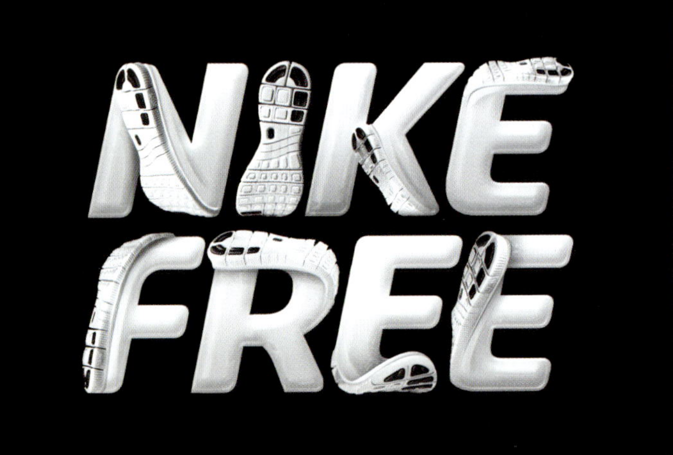
NIKE
FREE

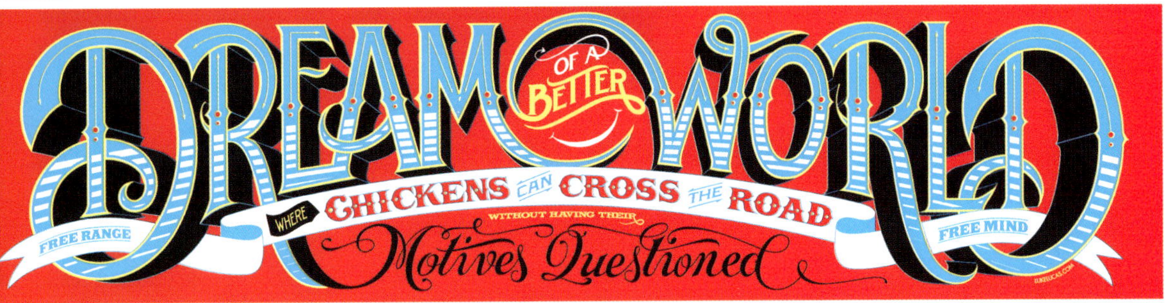
DREAM
OF A BETTER
WORLD
WHERE CHICKENS CAN CROSS THE ROAD
WITHOUT HAVING THEIR
Motives Questioned
FREE RANGE
FREE MIND

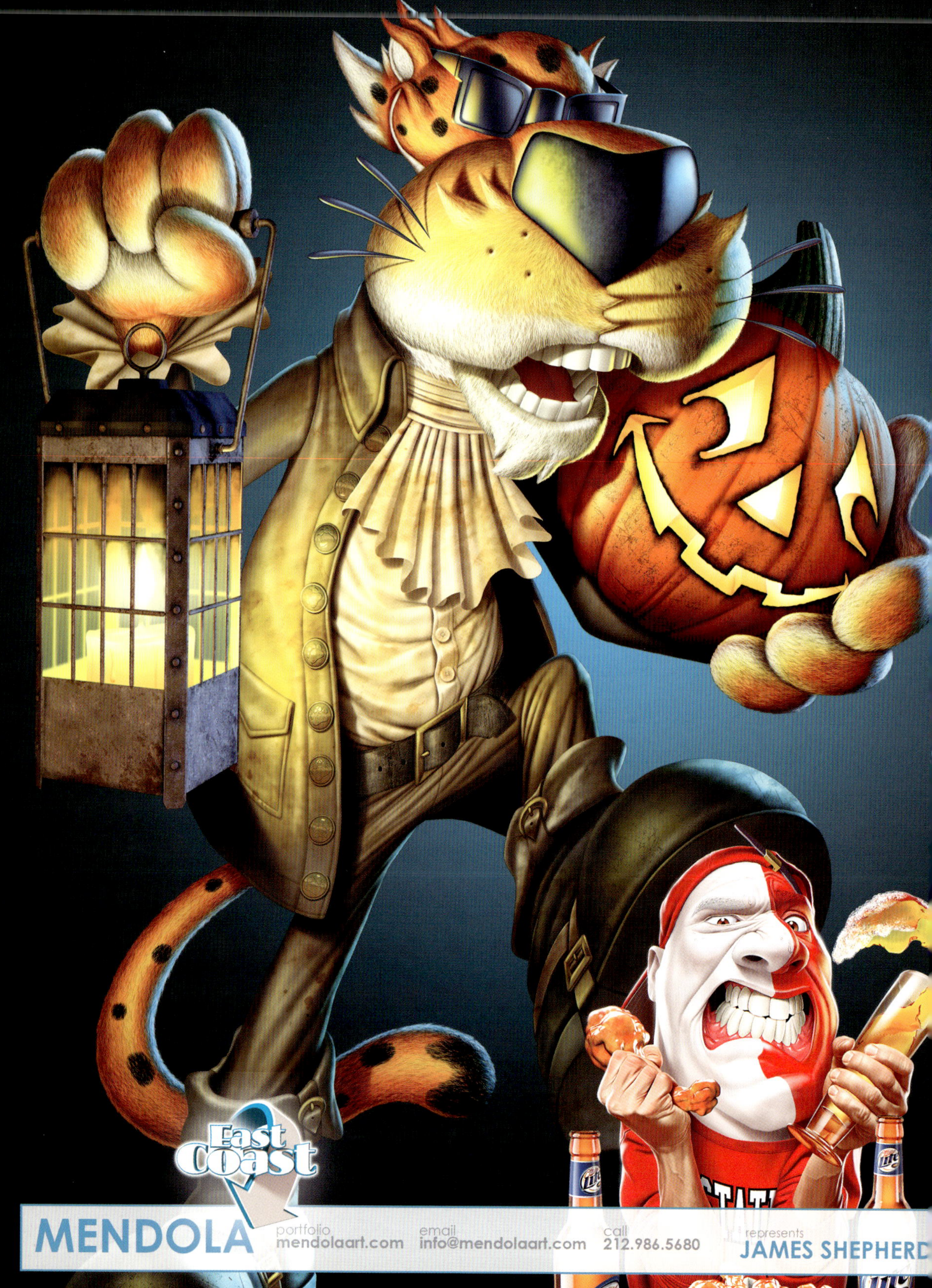
East Coast
MENDOLA
portfolio
mendolaart.com
email
info@mendolaart.com
call
212.986.5680
represents
JAMES SHEPHERD
Lite
STATE

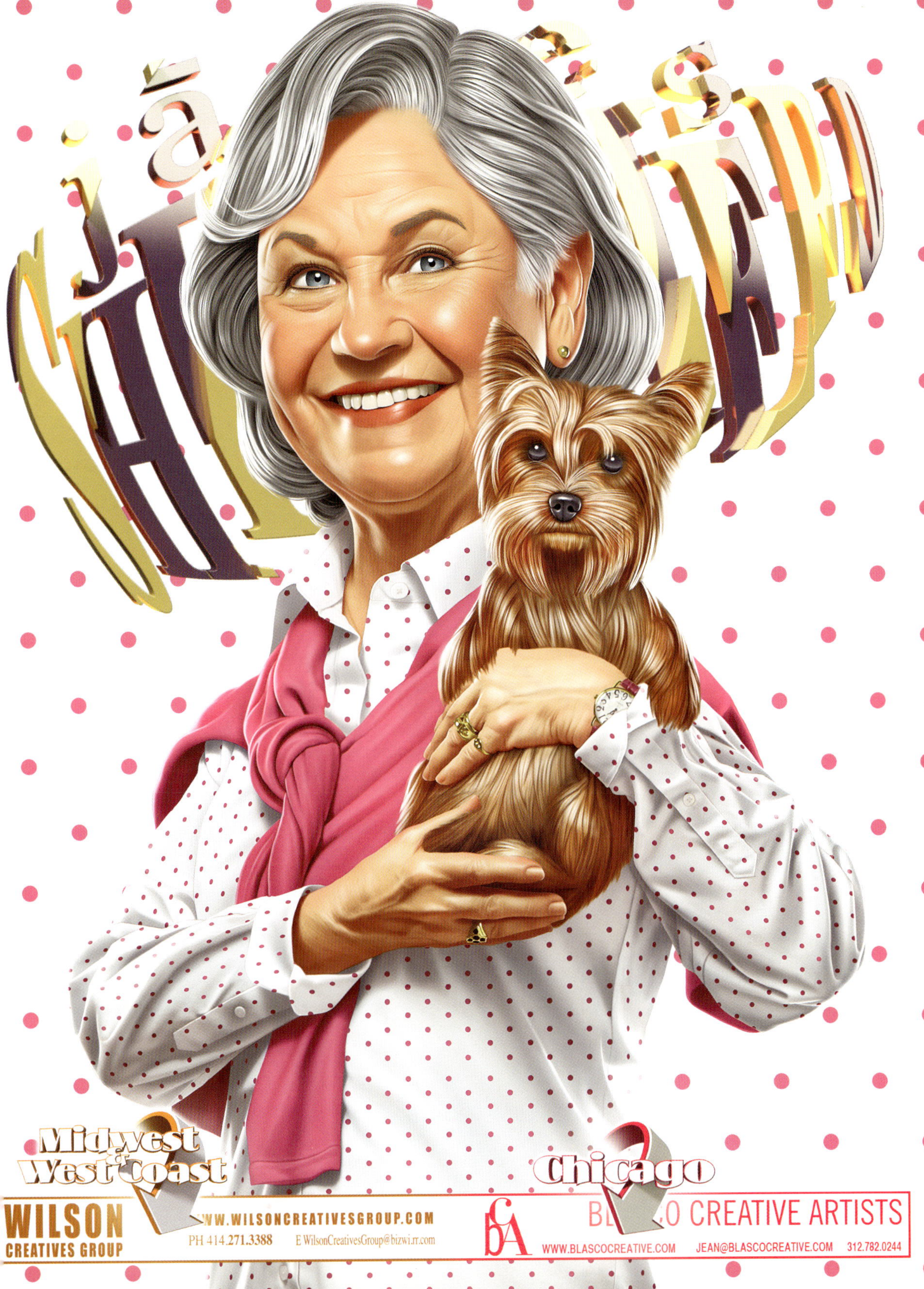

Midwest & West Coast
WILSON CREATIVES GROUP
WWW.WILSONCREATIVESGROUP.COM
PH 414.271.3388
E WilsonCreativesGroup@bizwi.rr.com
Chicago
BLASCO CREATIVE ARTISTS
WWW.BLASCOCREATIVE.COM
JEAN@BLASCOCREATIVE.COM
312.782.0244

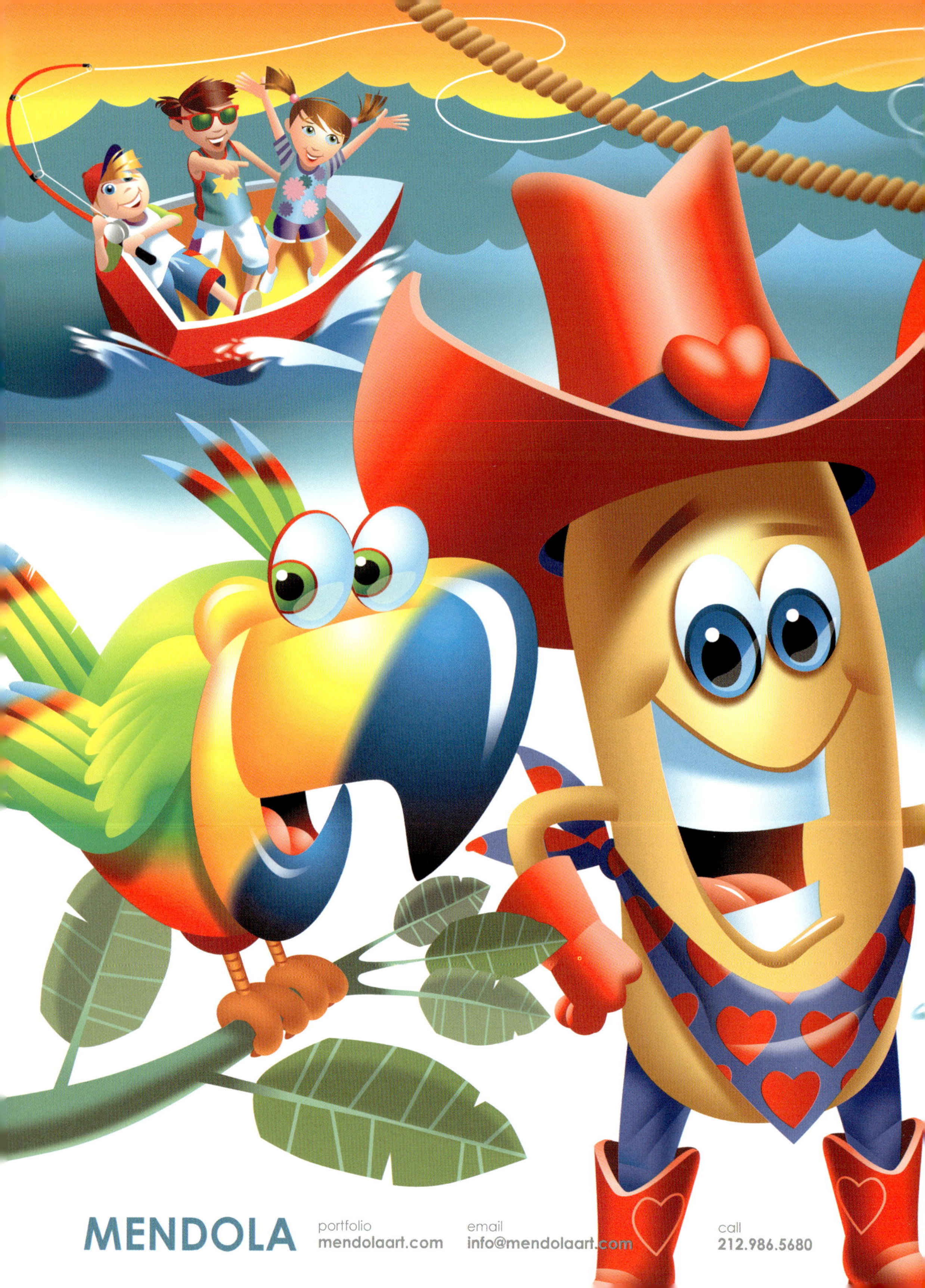

MENDOLA
portfolio
mendolaart.com
email
info@mendolaart.com
call
212.986.5680

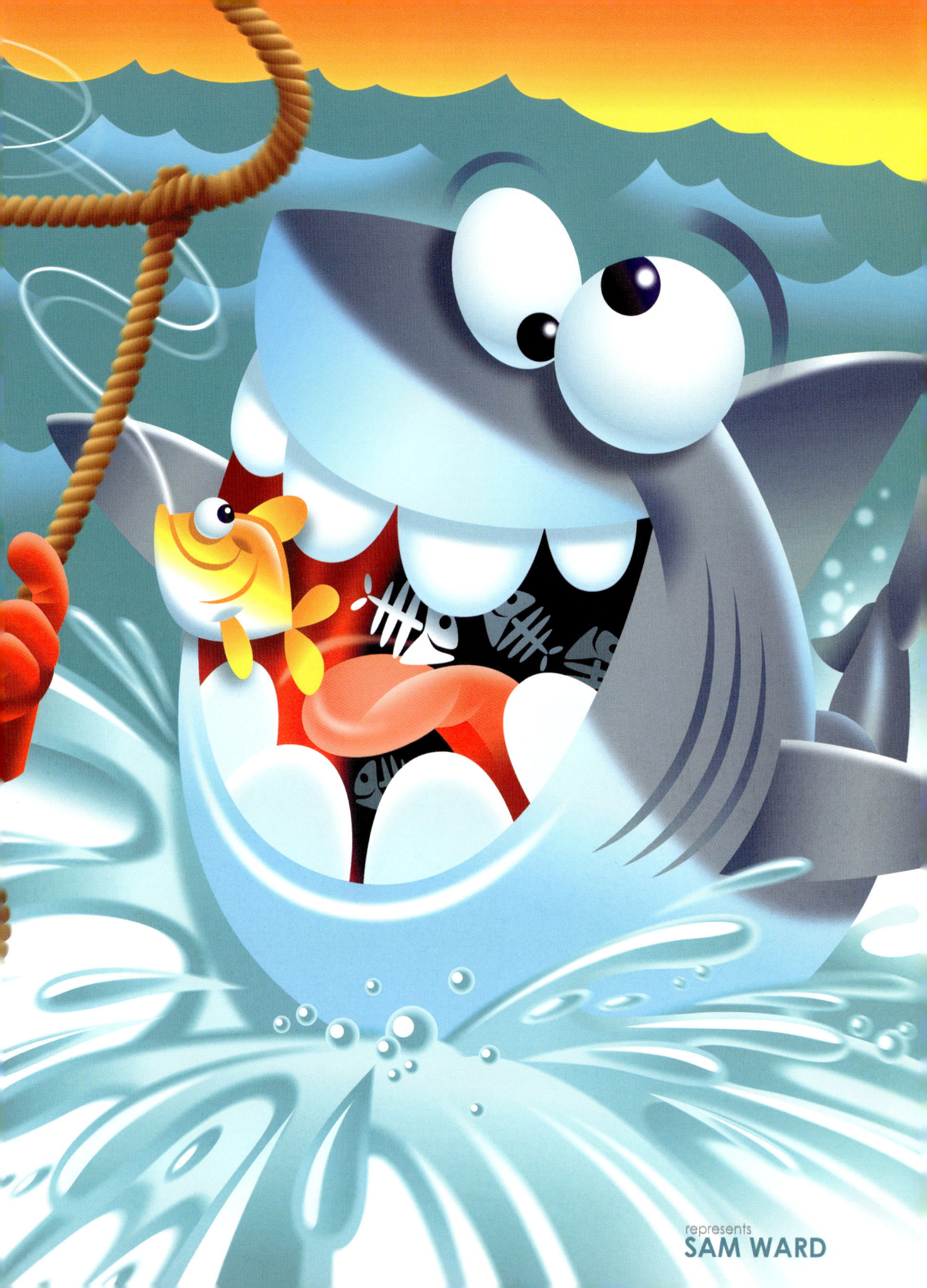
represents
SAM WARD

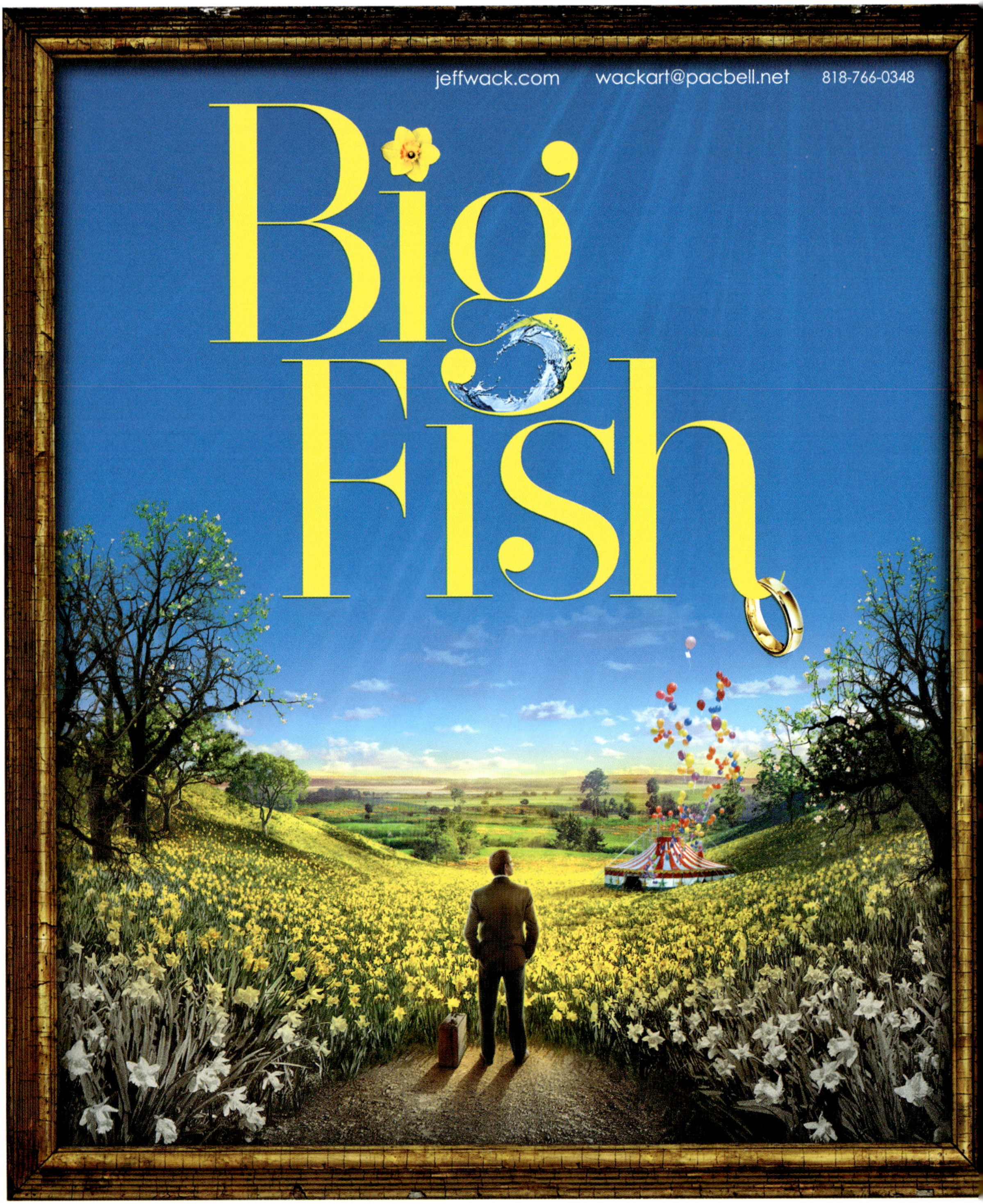

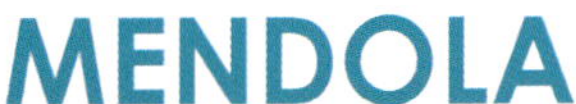

jeffwack.com
wackart@pacbell.net
818-766-0348
Big Fish

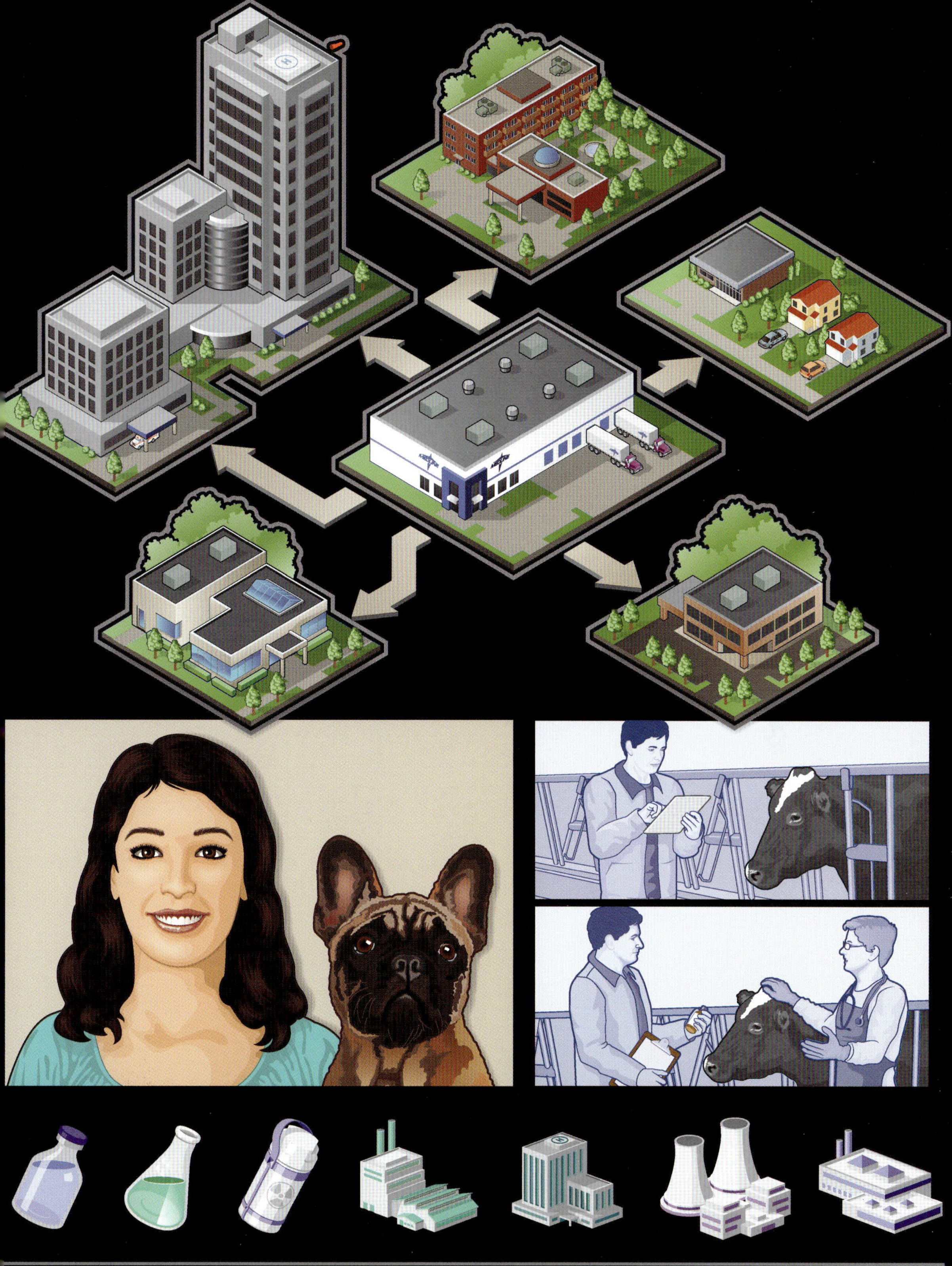
MENDOLA
portfolio
mendolaart.com
email
info@mendolaart.com
call
212.986.5680
represents
KOPP ILLUSTRATION

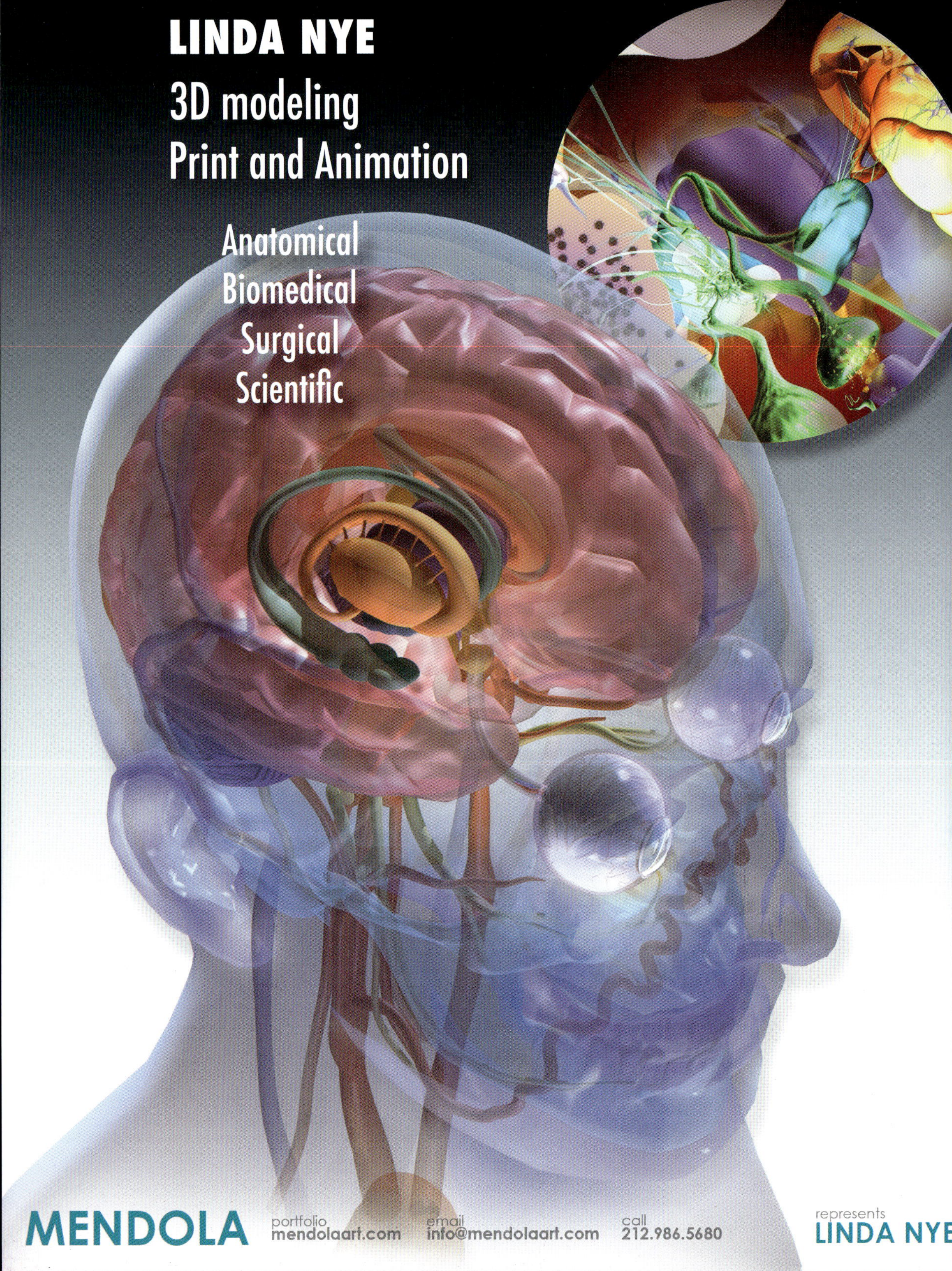
LINDA NYE
3D modeling
Print and Animation

Anatomical
Biomedical
Surgical
Scientific

MENDOLA
portfolio
mendolaart.com
email
info@mendolaart.com
call
212.986.5680
represents
LINDA NYE

MENDOLA
portfolio
mendolaart.com
email
info@mendolaart.com
call
212.986.5680
represents
HEIDI SCHMIDT
heidischmidt.com

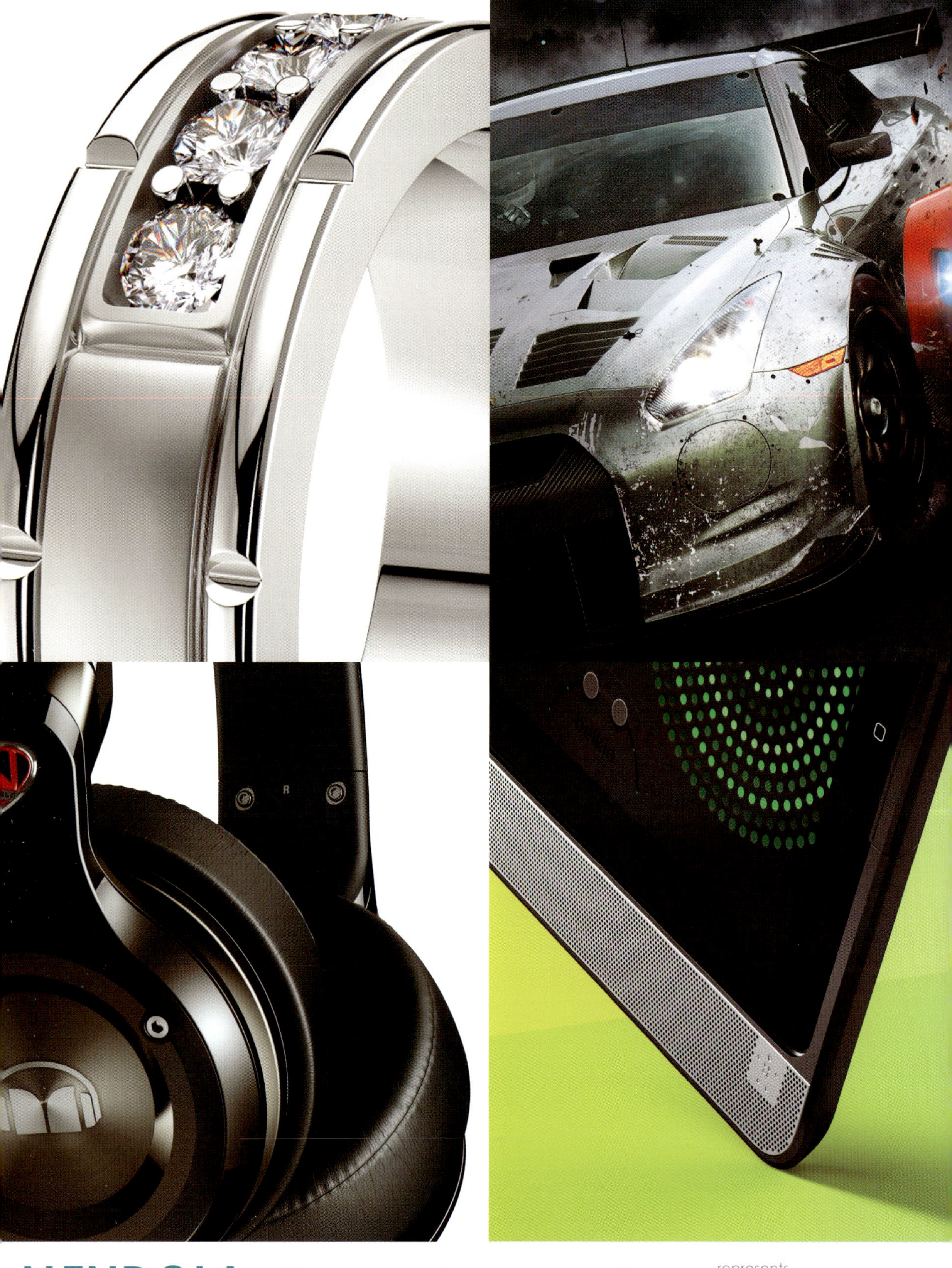
MENDOLA
portfolio
mendolaart.com
email
info@mendolaart.com
call
212.986.5680
represents
BRENDAN McCAFF

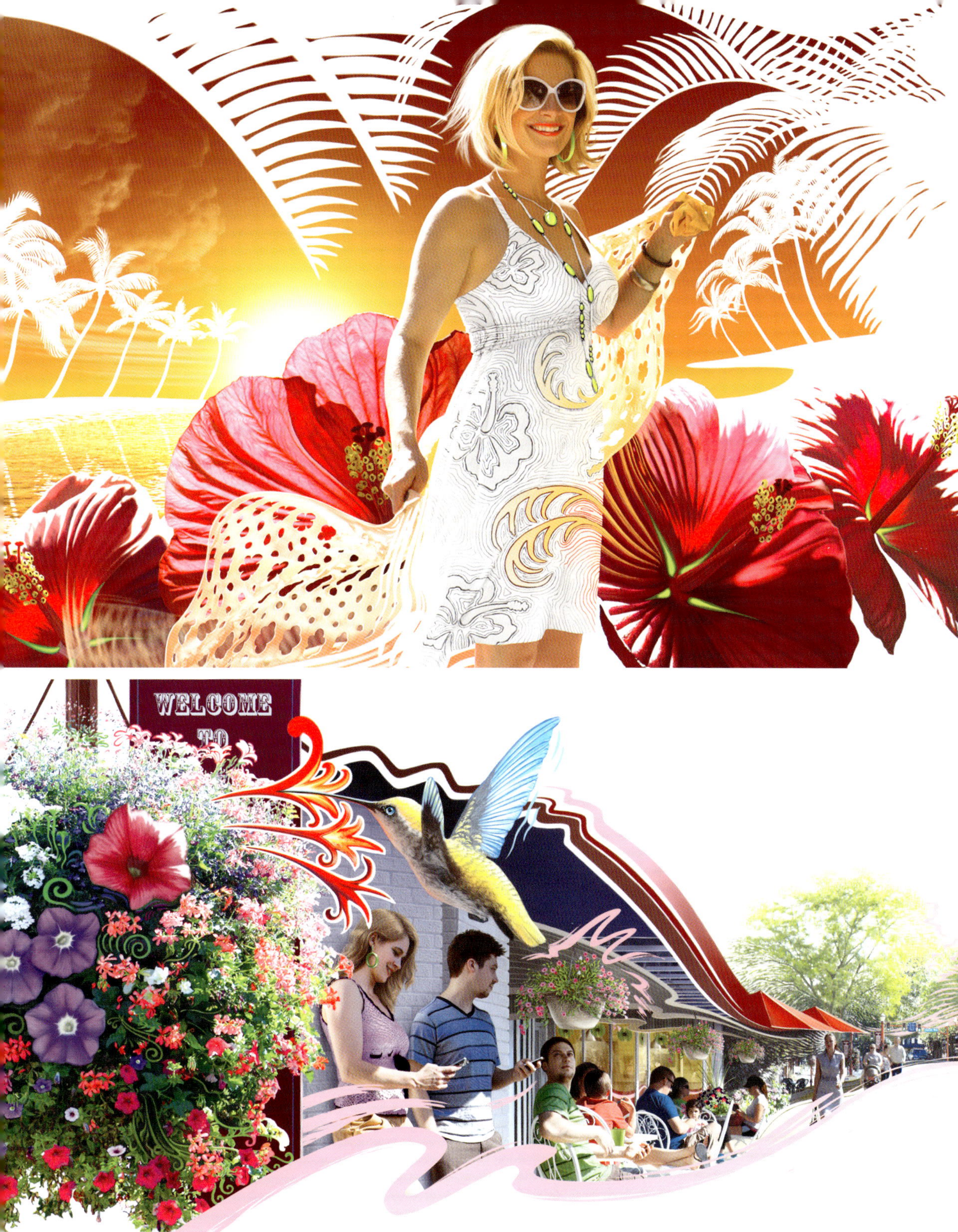

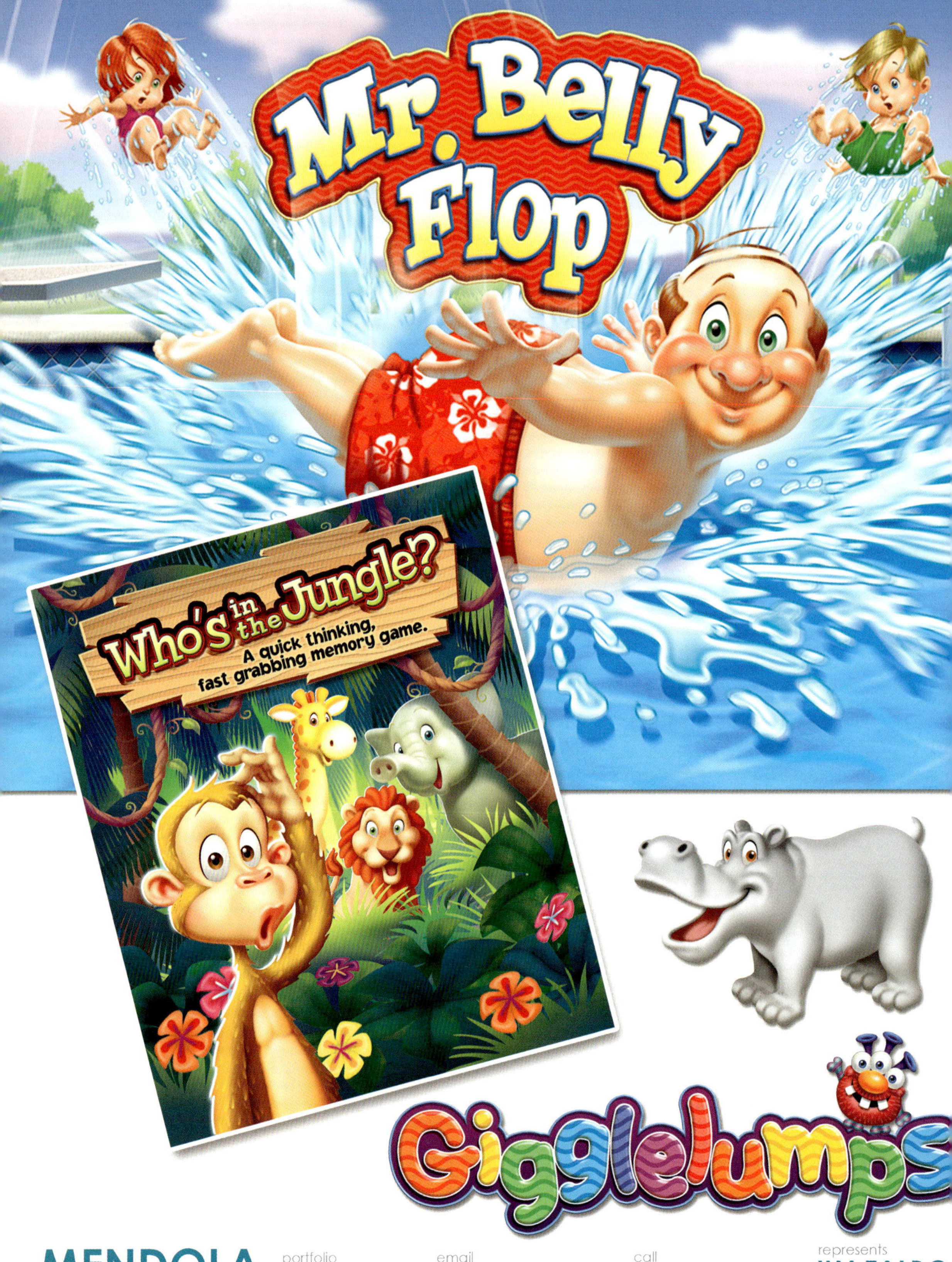

Mr. Belly Flop
Who's in the Jungle?
A quick thinking, fast grabbing memory game.
Gigglelumps
MENDOLA
portfolio
mendolaart.com
email
info@mendolaart.com
call
212.986.5680
represents
JIM TALBO

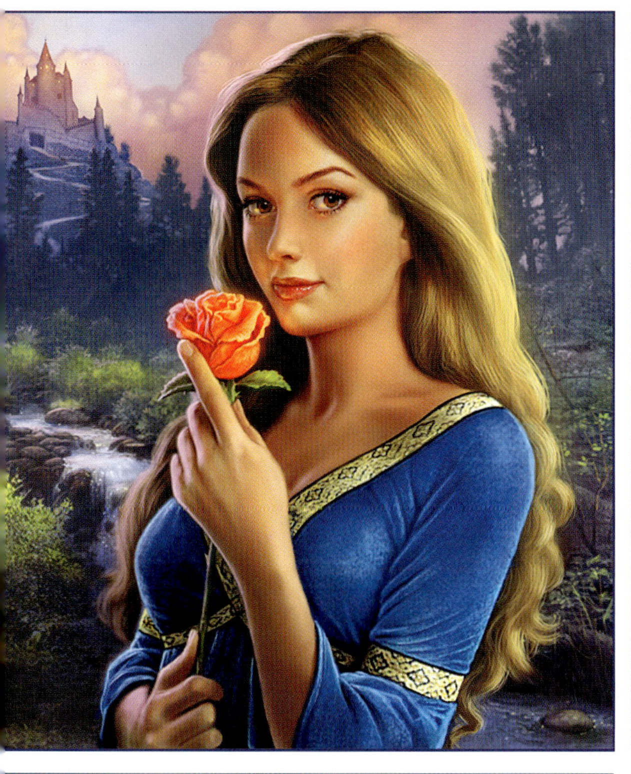

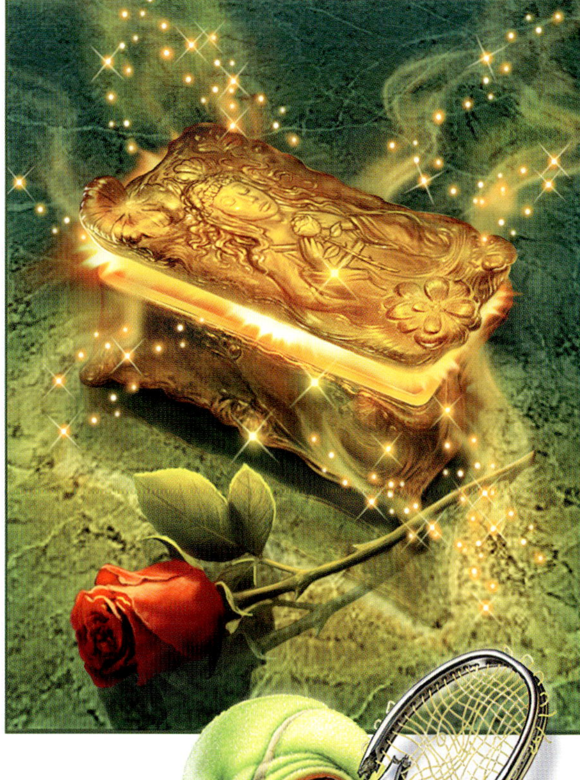

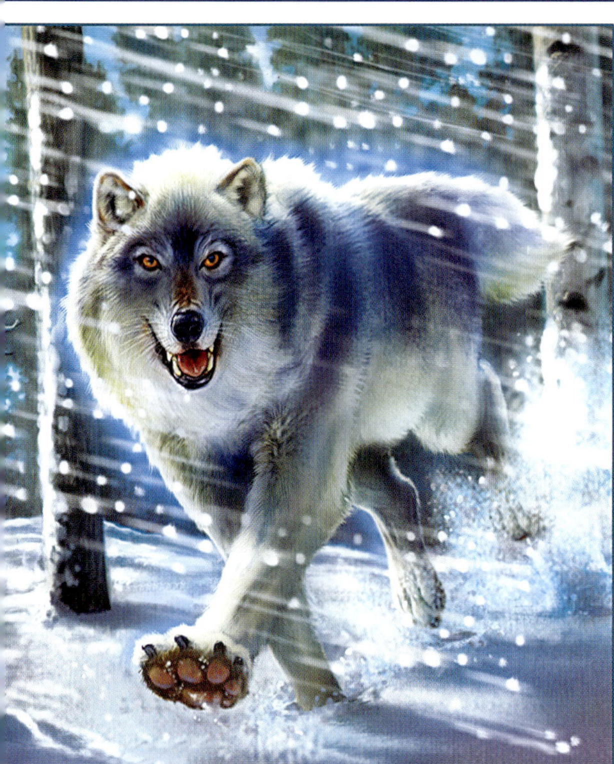

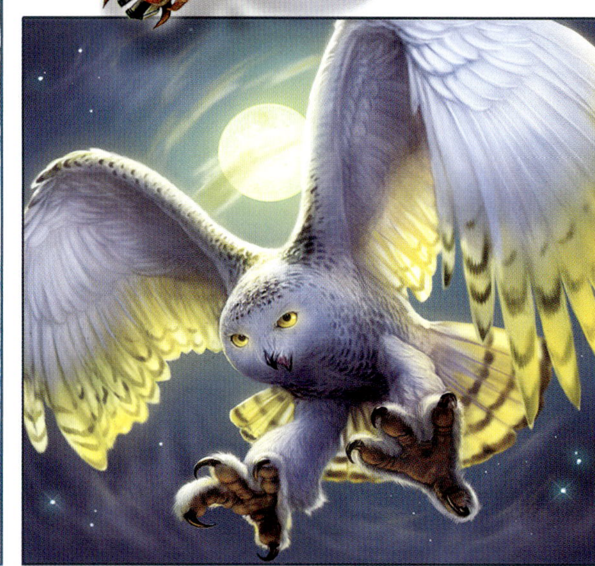

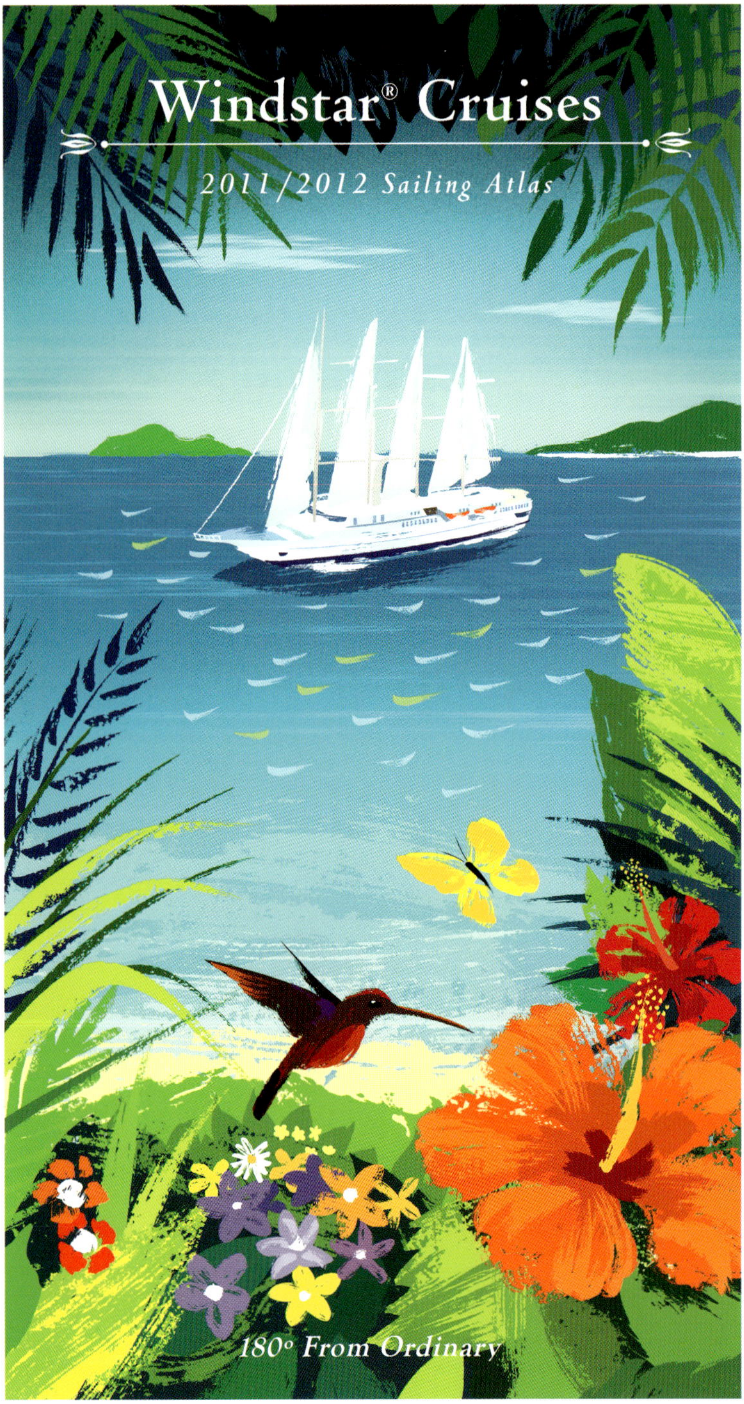

Windstar® Cruises
2011/2012 Sailing Atlas
180° From Ordinary

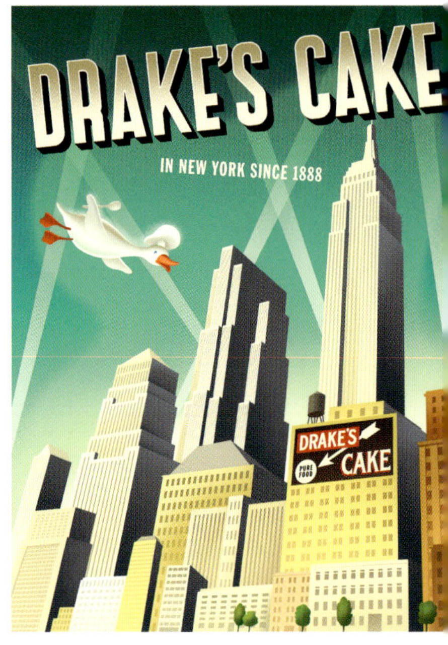

DRAKE'S CAKE
IN NEW YORK SINCE 1888
DRAKE'S
PURE FOOD
CAKE

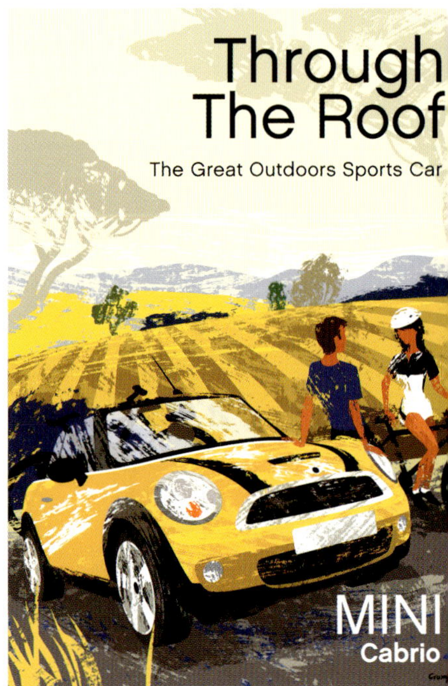

Through
The Roof
The Great Outdoors Sports Car
MINI
Cabrio

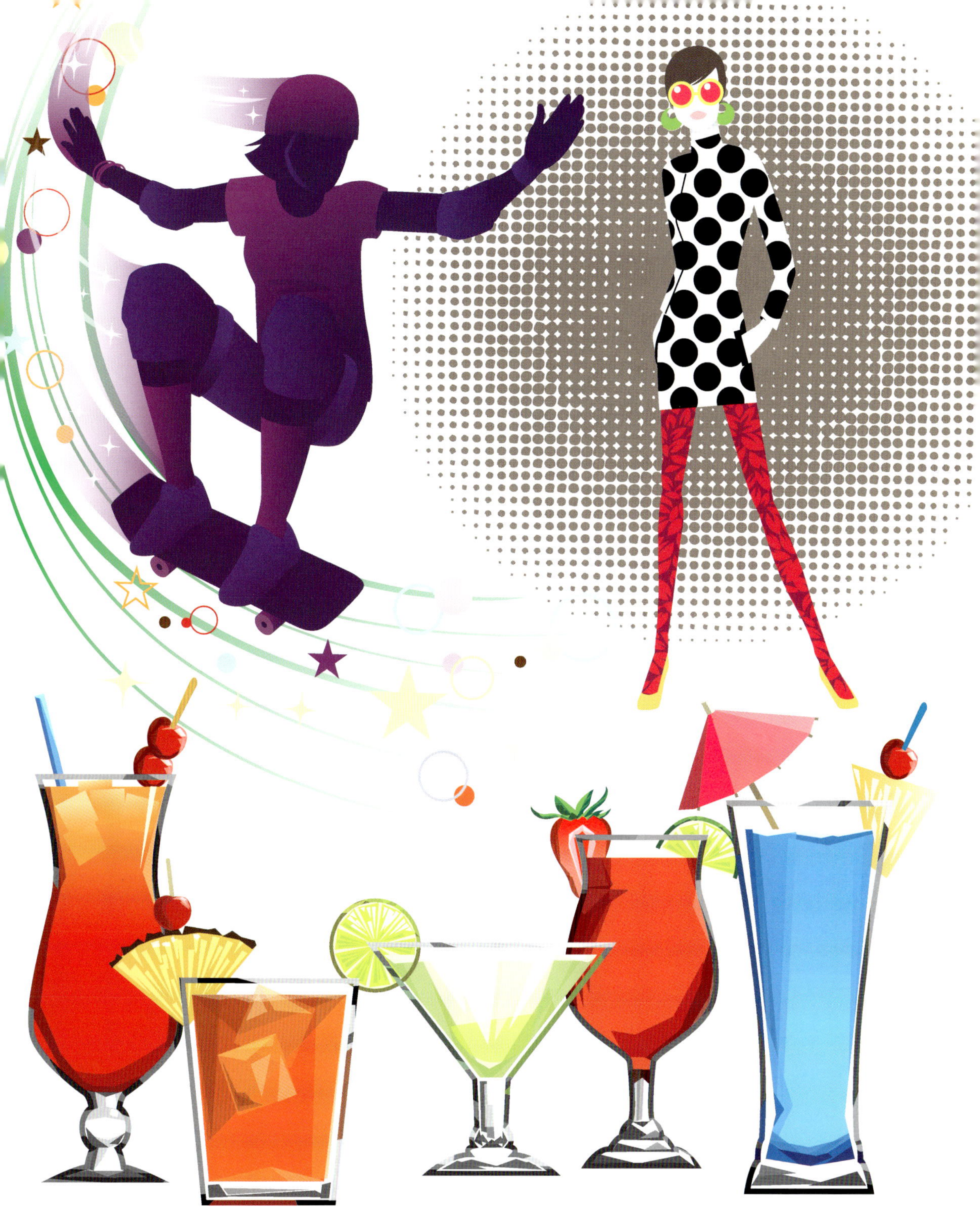

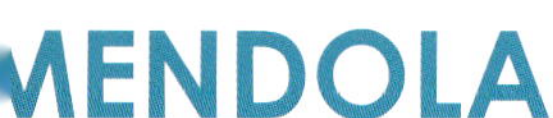
MENDOLA
portfolio
mendolaart.com
email
info@mendolaart.com
call
212.986.5680
represents
DAN SIPPLE

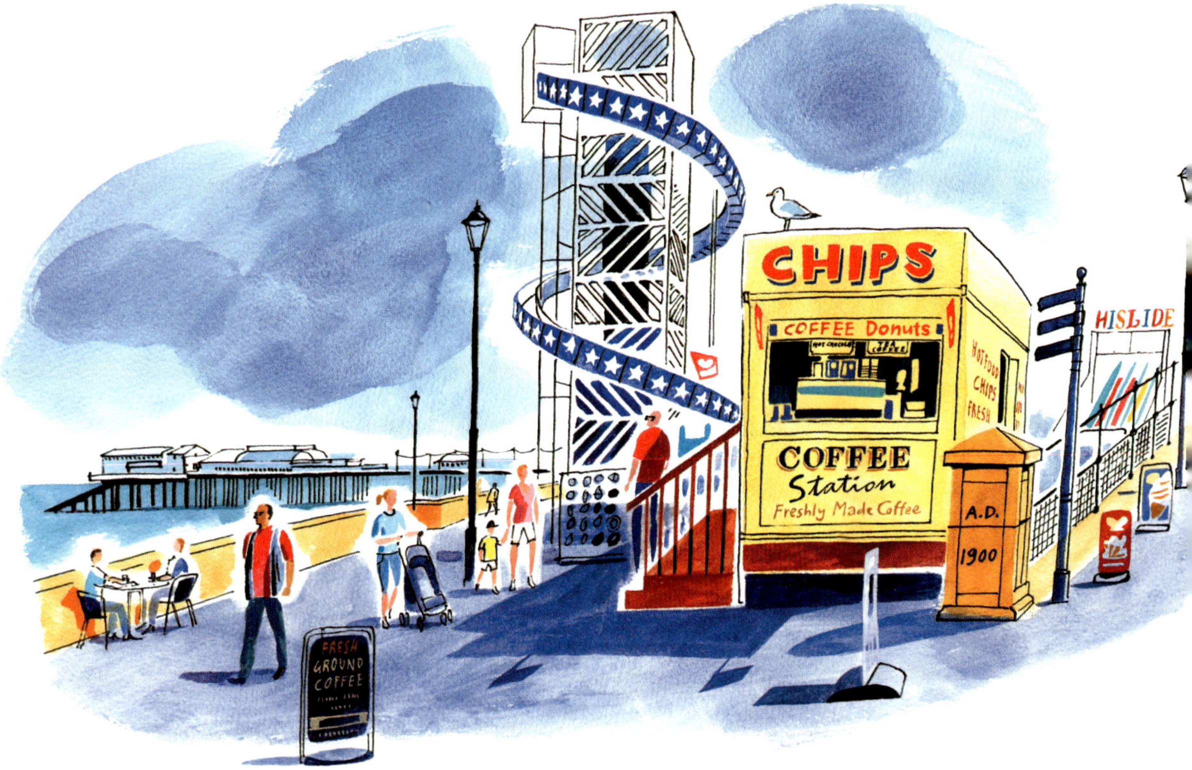

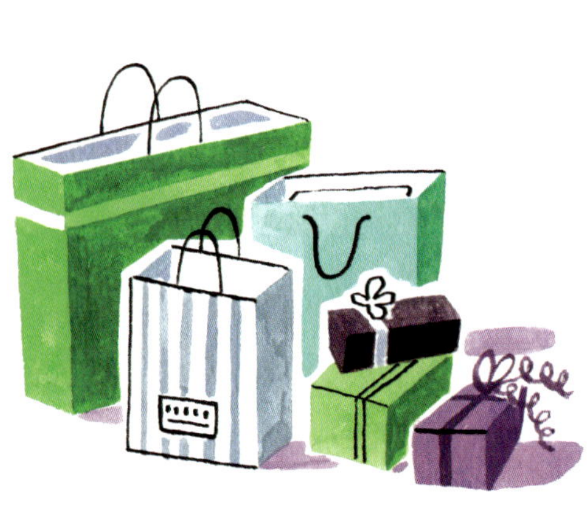

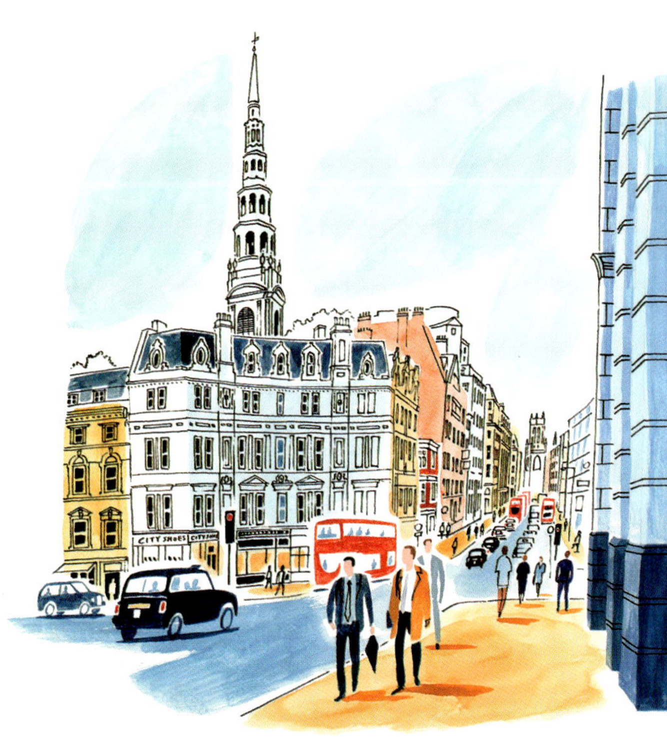
CHIPS
COFFEE Donuts
HOT FOOD CHIPS FRESH
COFFEE
Station
Freshly Made Coffee
A.D. 1900
HISLIDE
FRESH GROUND COFFEE
CITY SHOES CITY

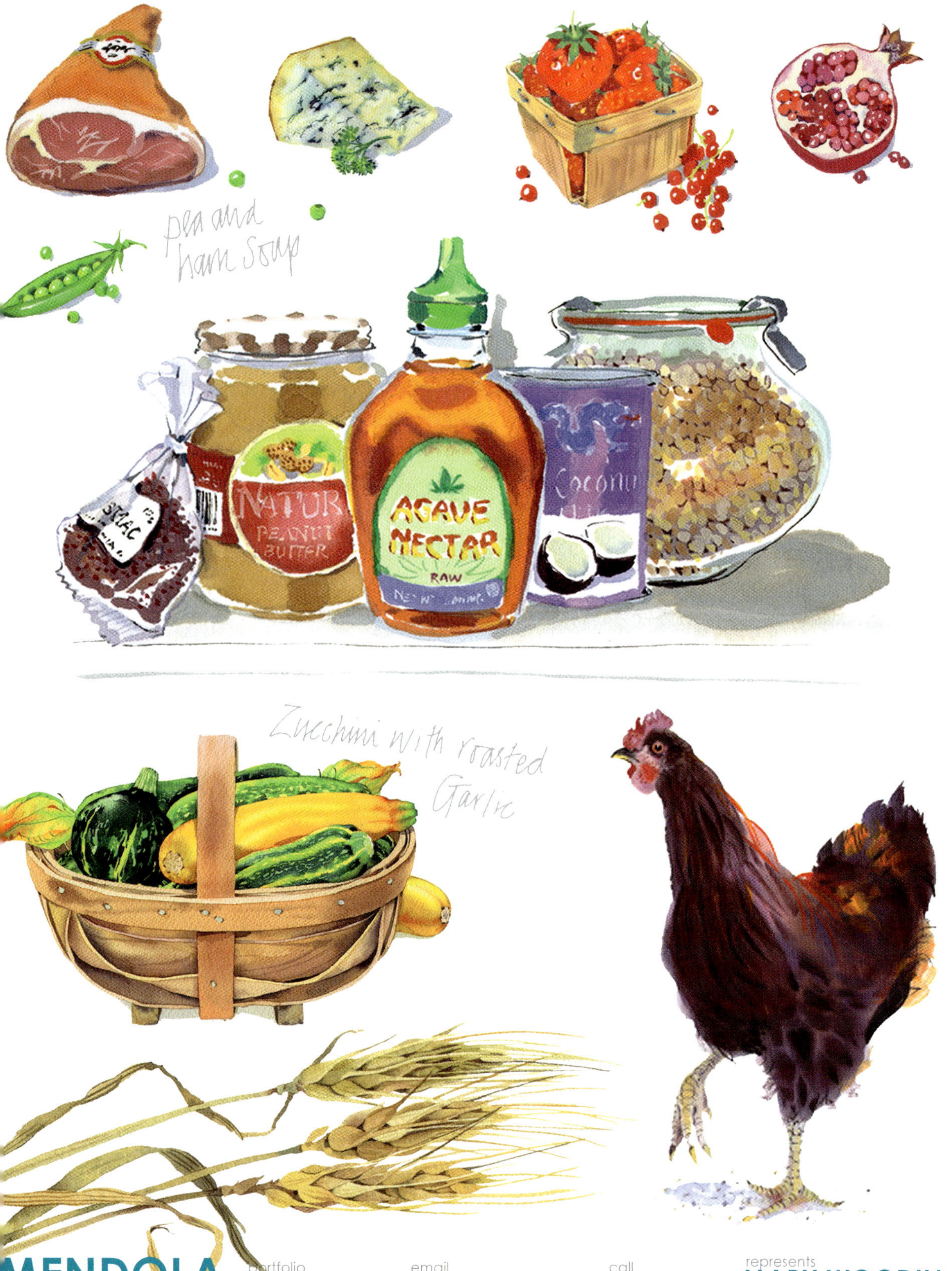

pea and ham soup
NATUR PEANUT BUTTER
AGAVE NECTAR RAW
Coconut
Zucchini with roasted Garlic

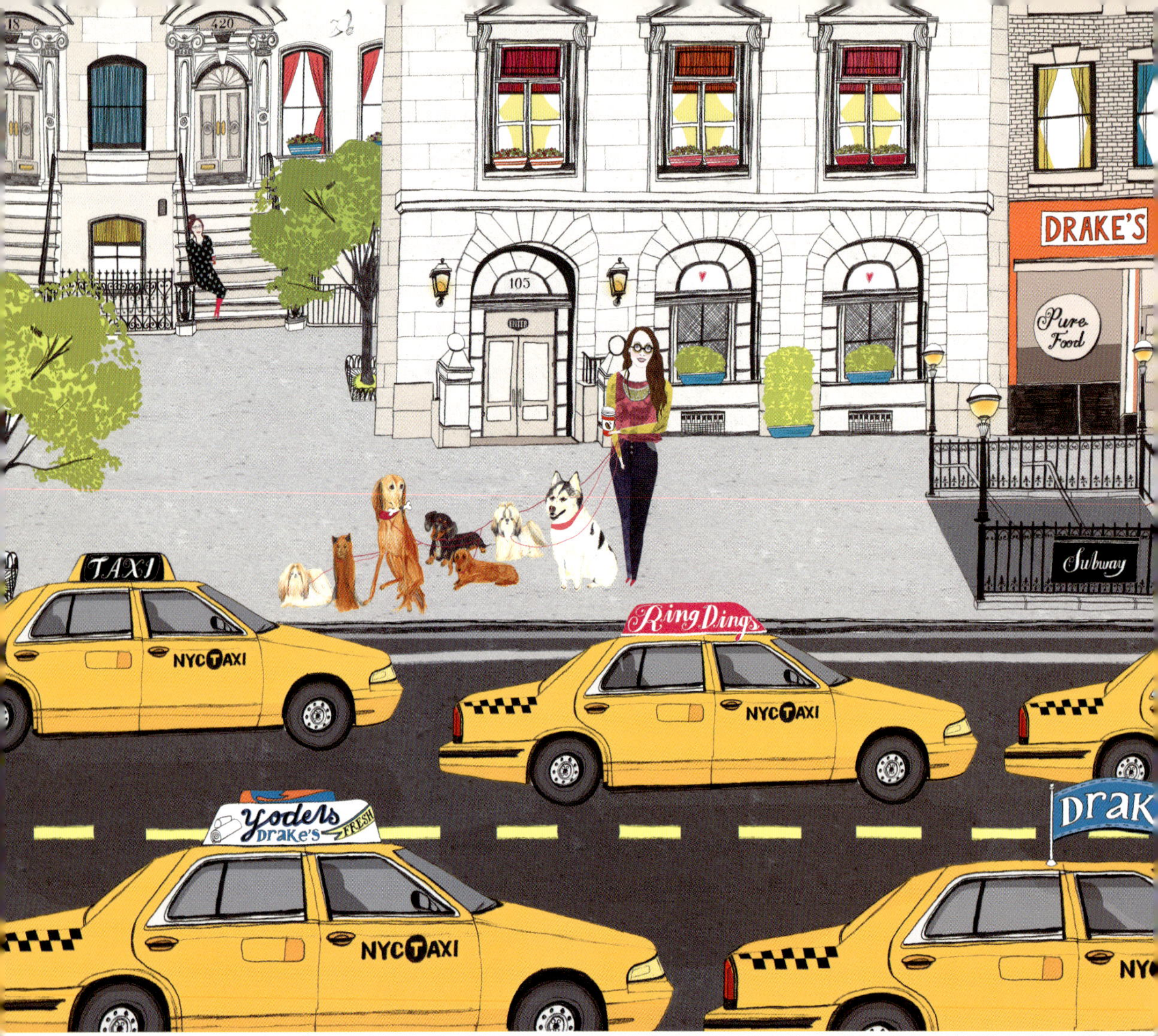

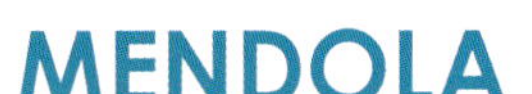

DRAKE'S
Pure Food
420
105
TAXI
NYC TAXI
Ring Dings
NYC TAXI
Yoders Drake's FRESH
NYC TAXI
DRAK 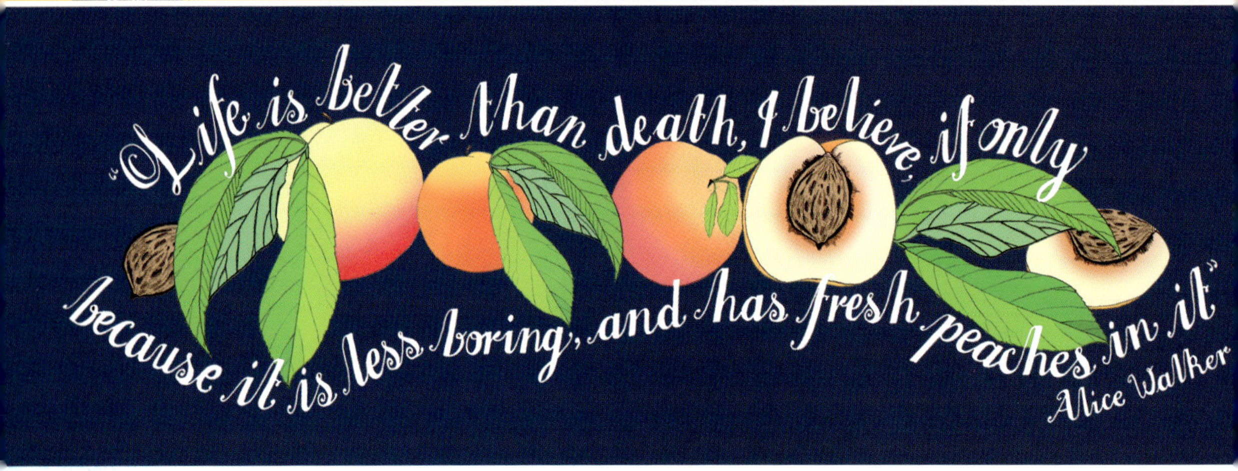
NYC
Subway
"Life is better than death, I believe, if only
because it is less boring, and has fresh peaches in it"
Alice Walker

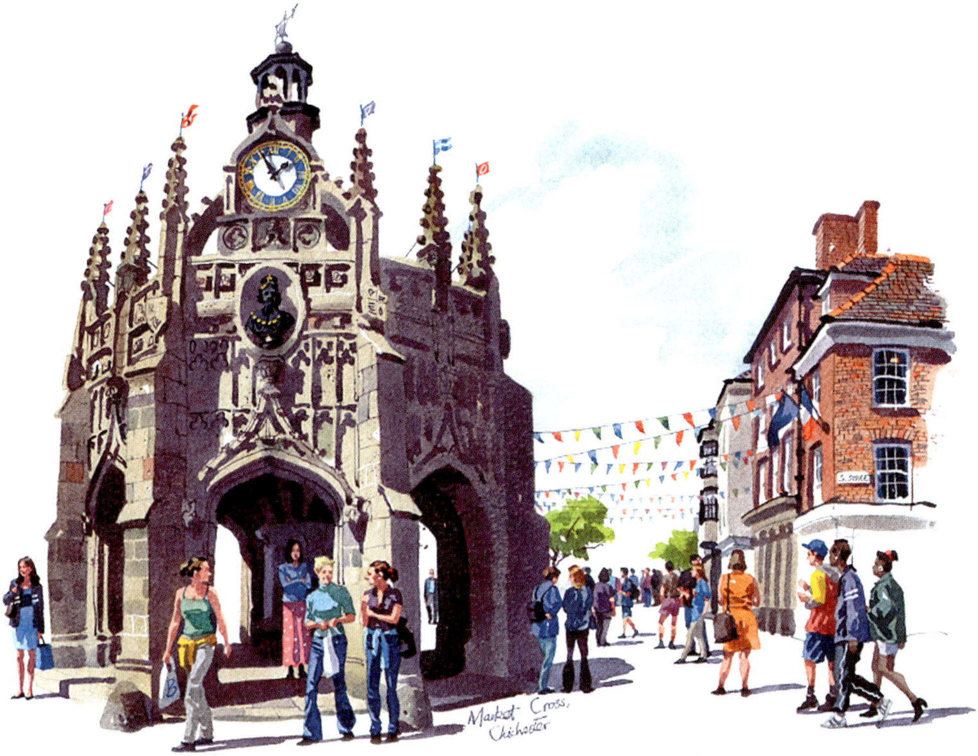

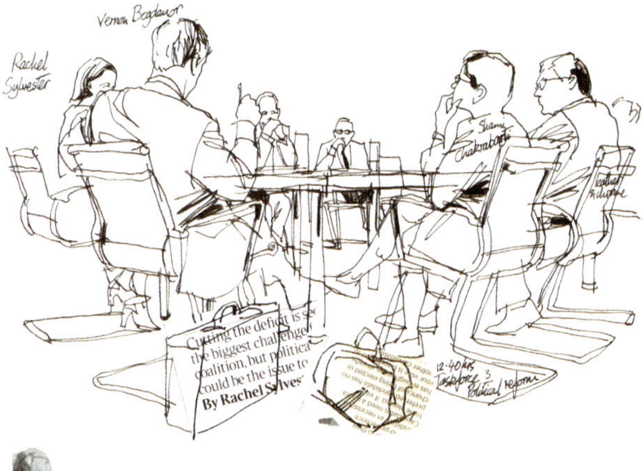

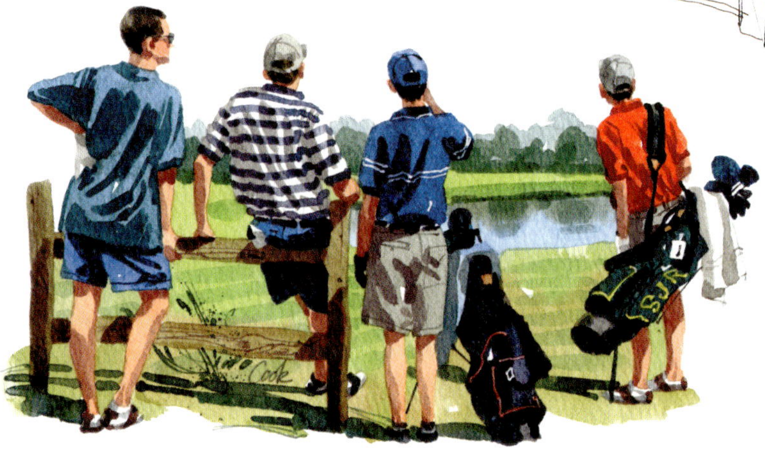

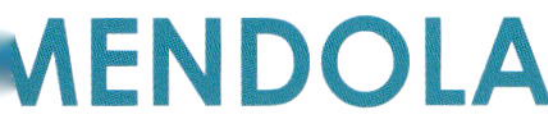

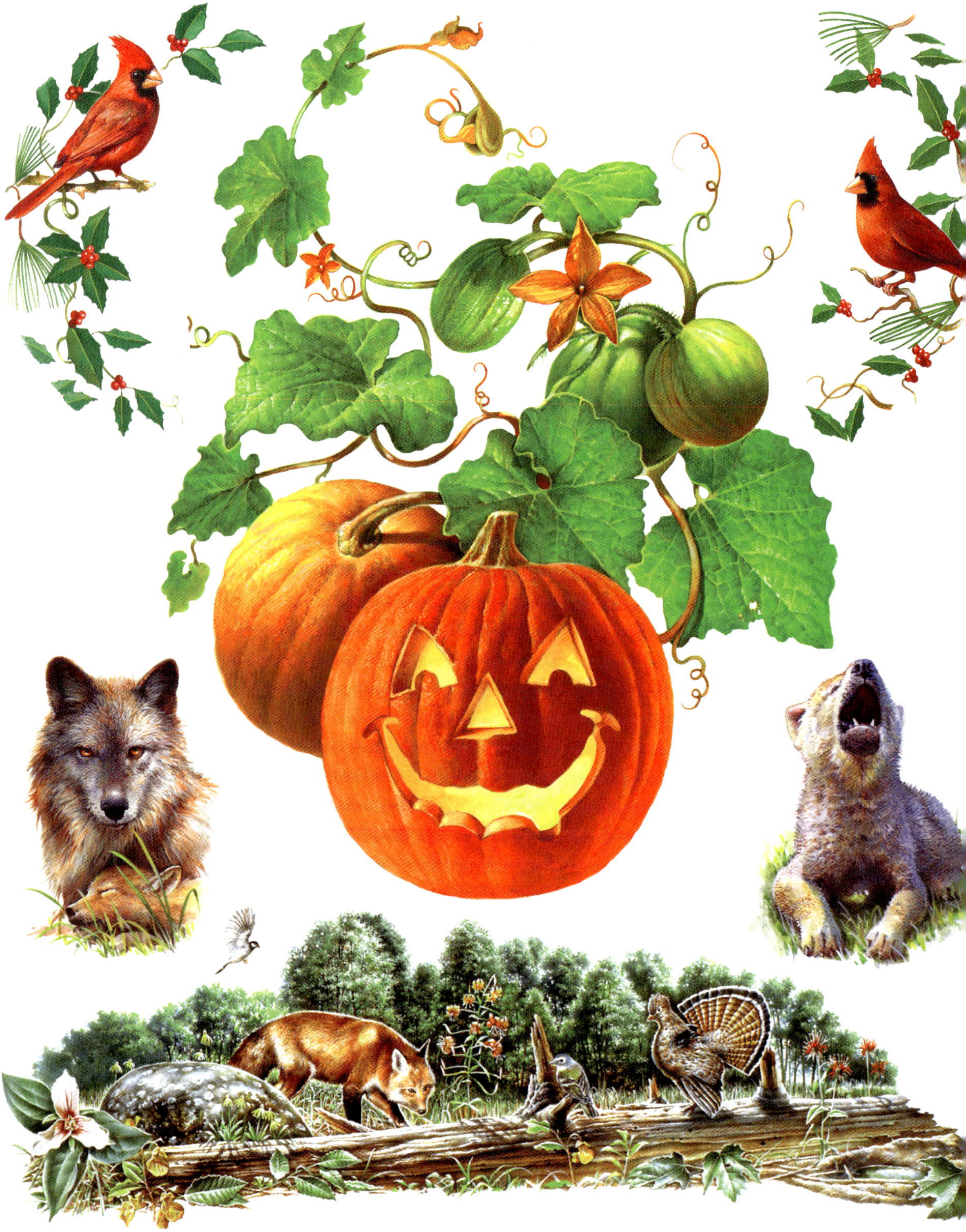

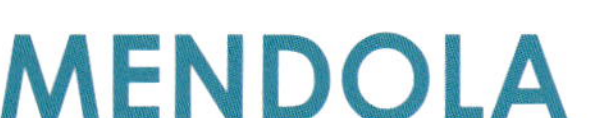

MENDOLA

portfolio
mendolaart.com

email
info@mendolaart.com

call
212.986.5680

represents
ROBERT HYNE
hynesstudio.com

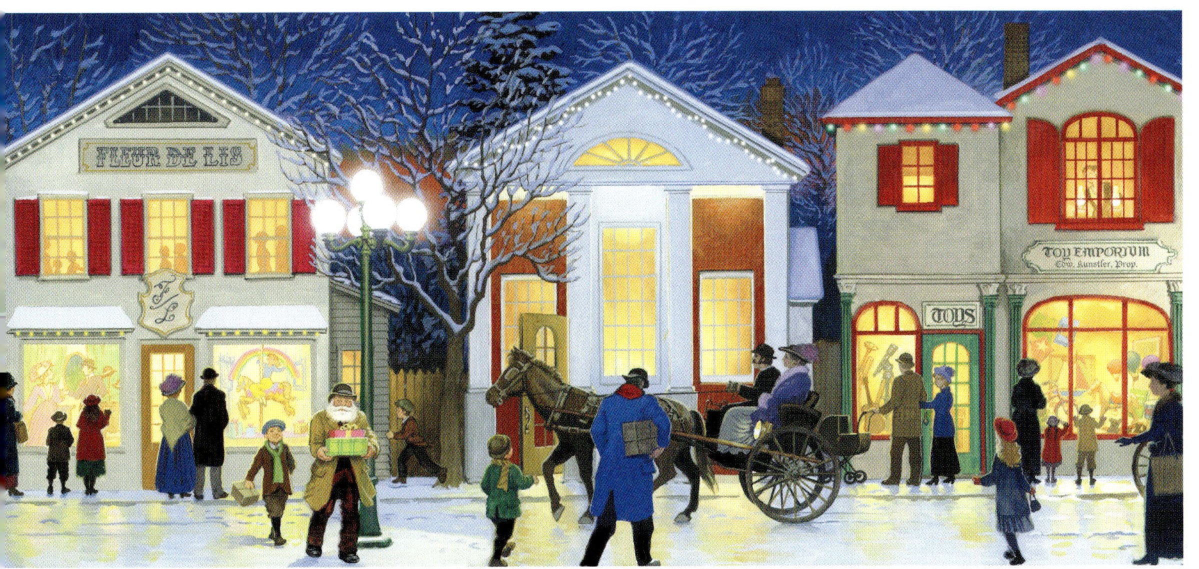

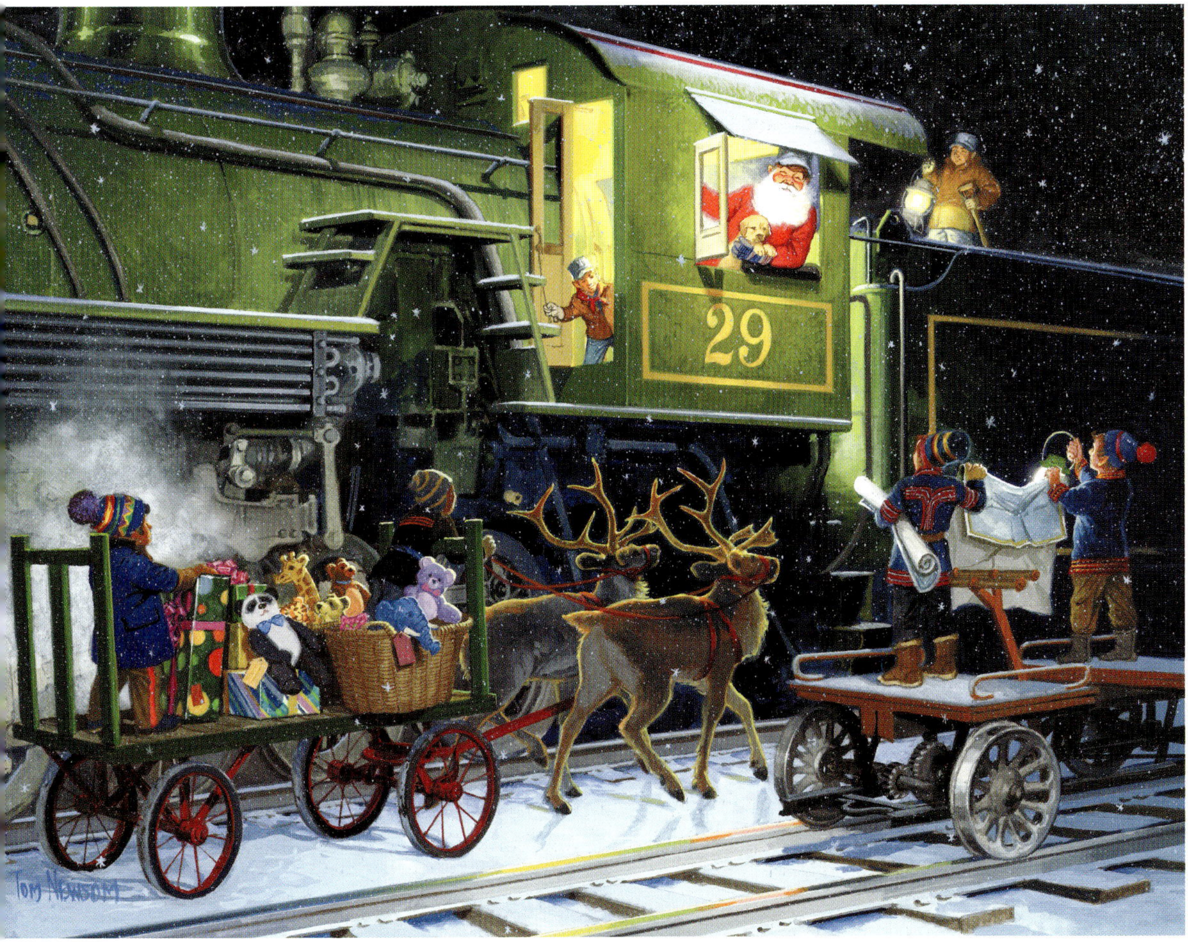

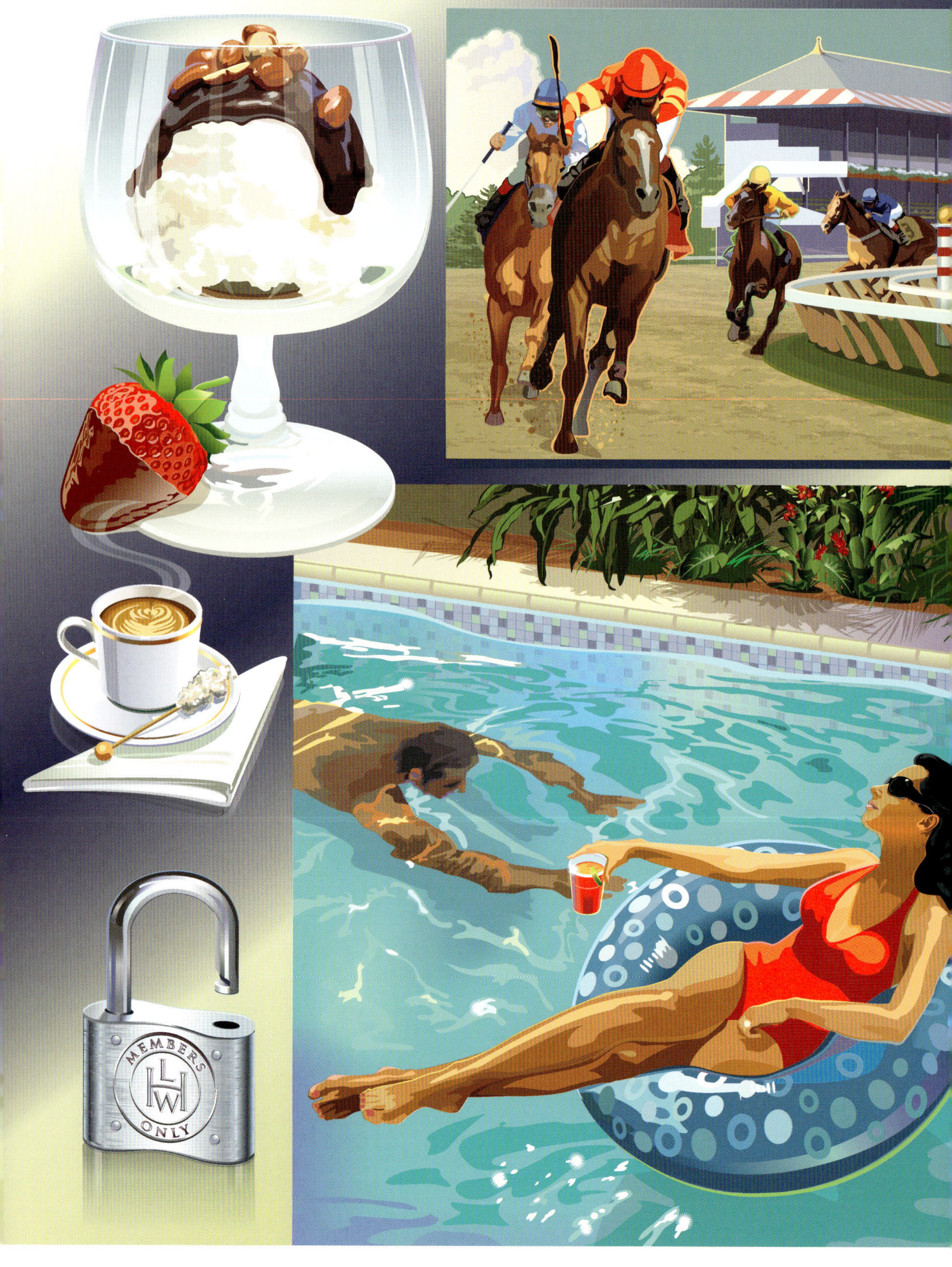

MEMBERS
LWL
ONLY

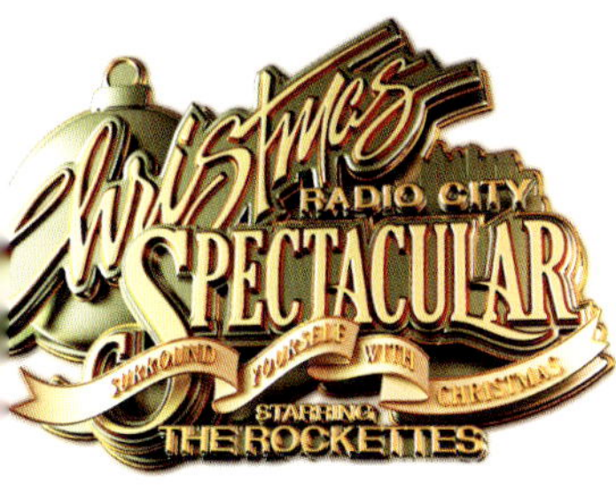

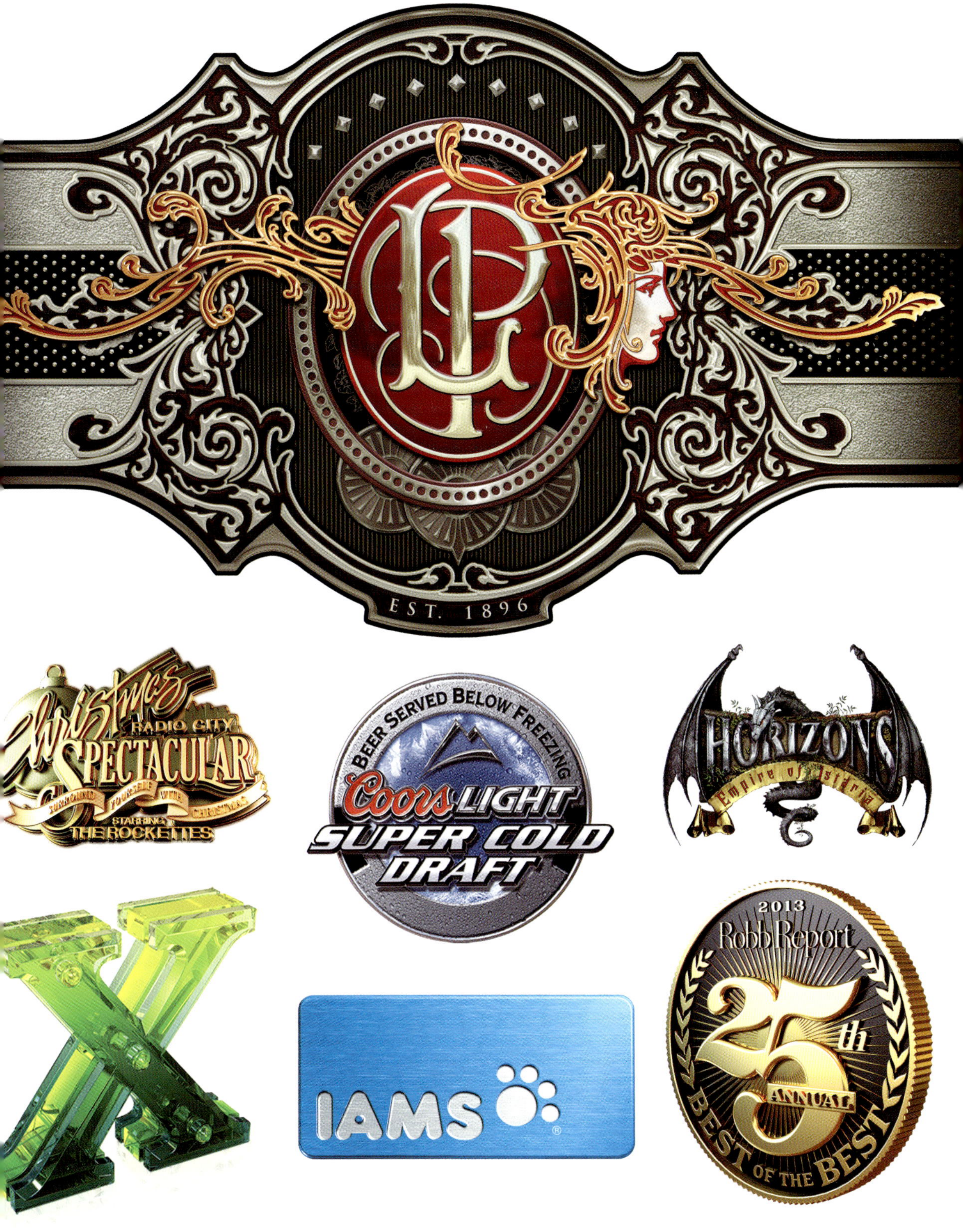

CHRISTMAS
RADIO CITY
SPECTACULAR
STARRING
THE ROCKETTES

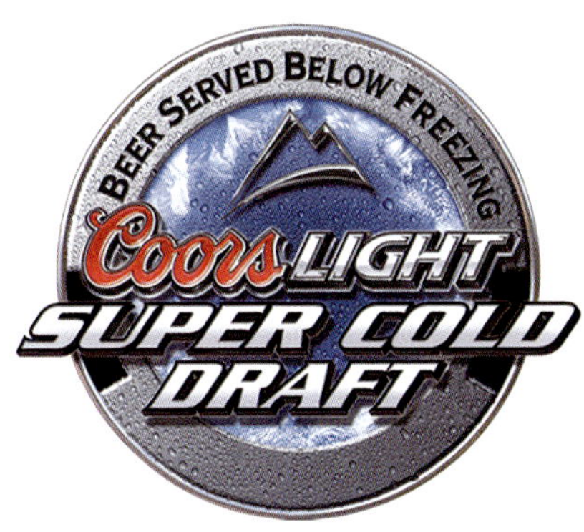

BEER SERVED BELOW FREEZING
Coors LIGHT
SUPER COLD
DRAFT

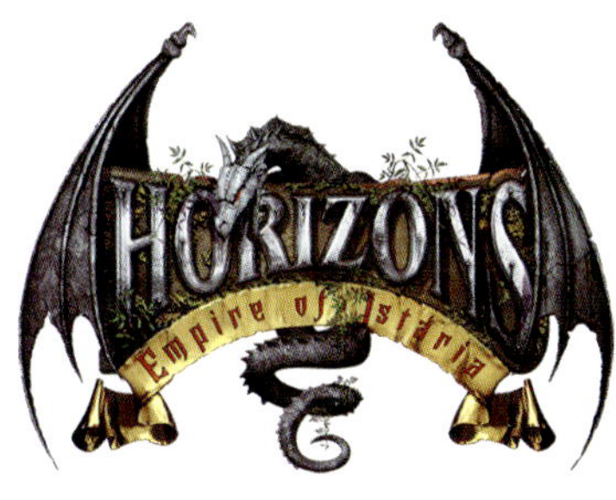

HORIZONS
Empire of Istaria

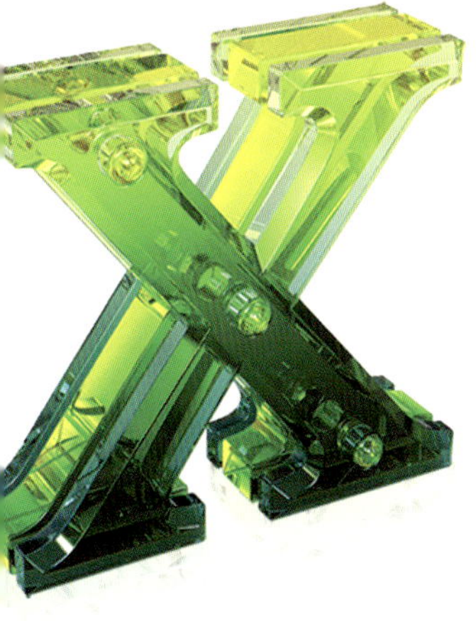

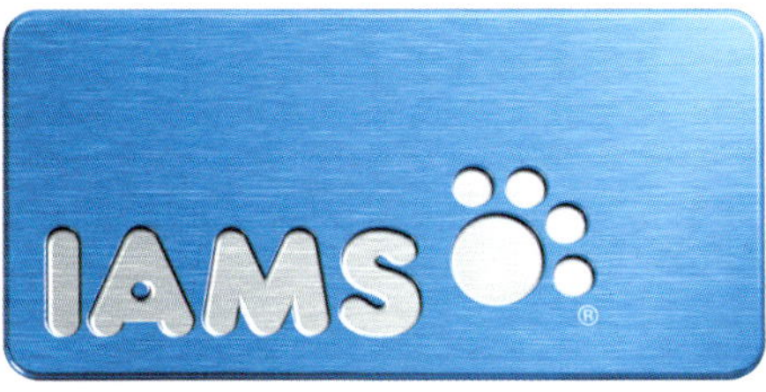

IAMS

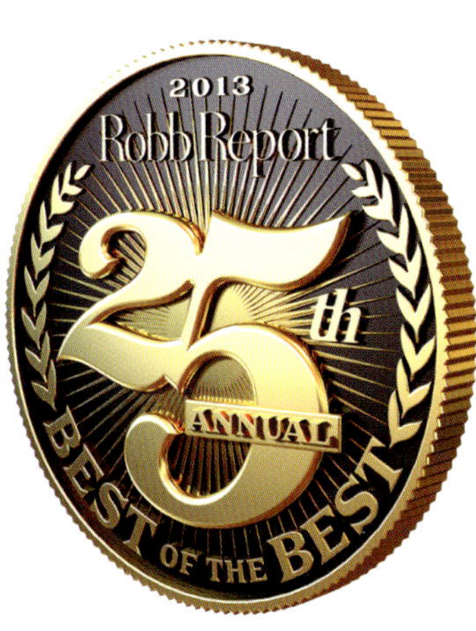

2013
RobbReport
25th
ANNUAL
BEST of the BEST

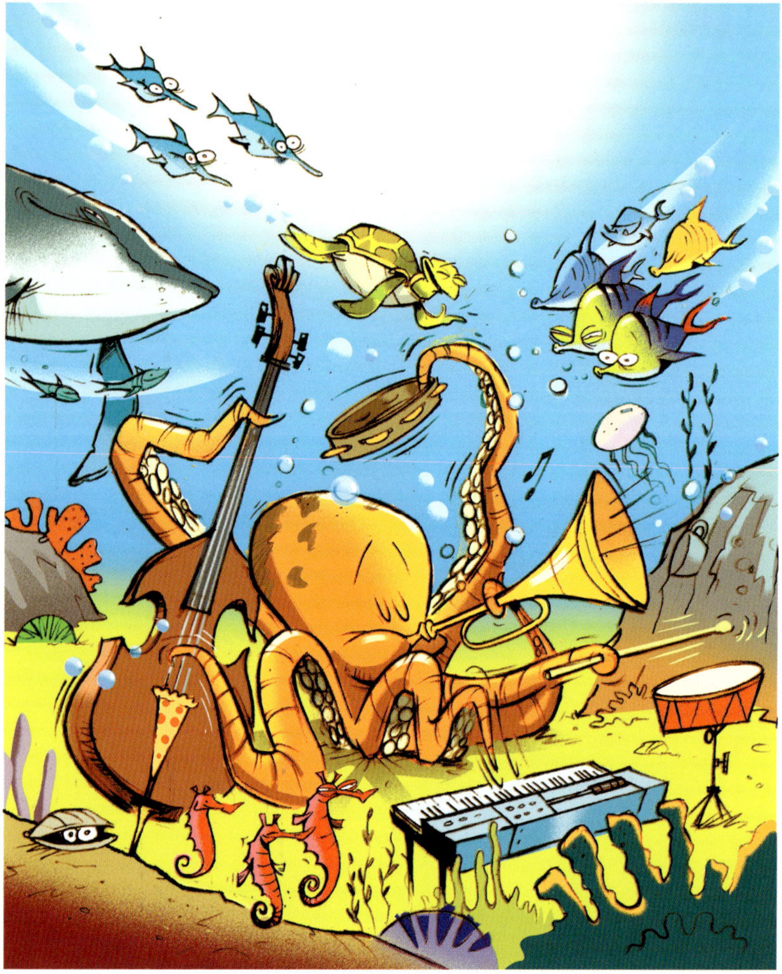

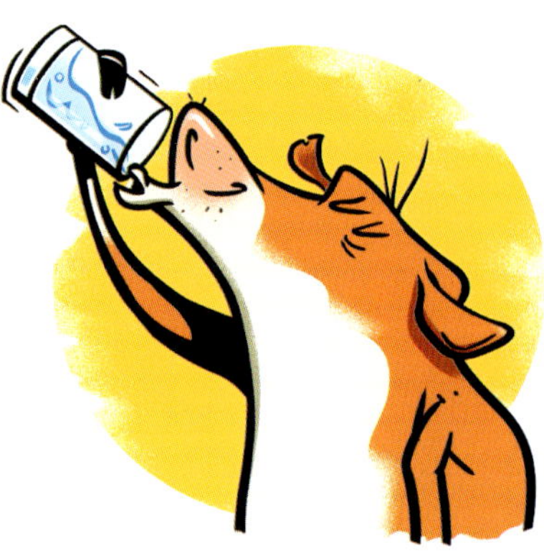

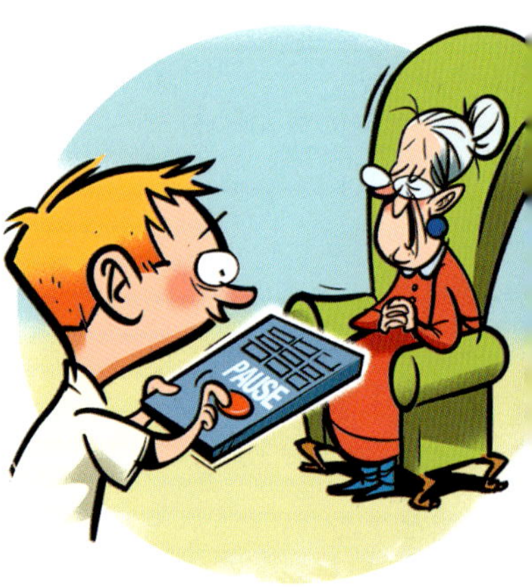

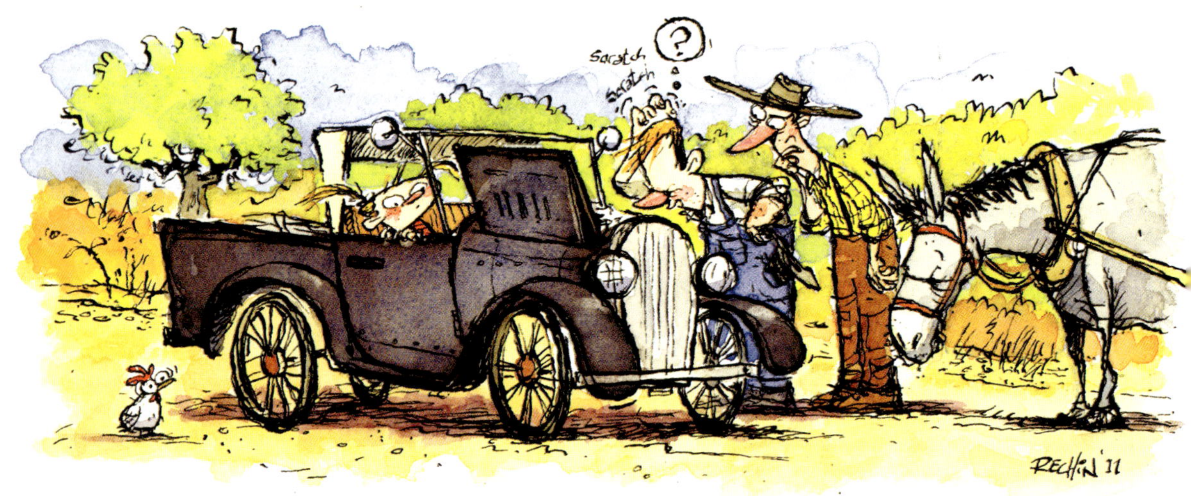
scratch
scratch
?
RECHiN '11

SEAN PARKES ILLUSTRATION
www.seanparkes.com

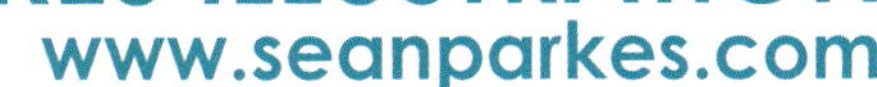

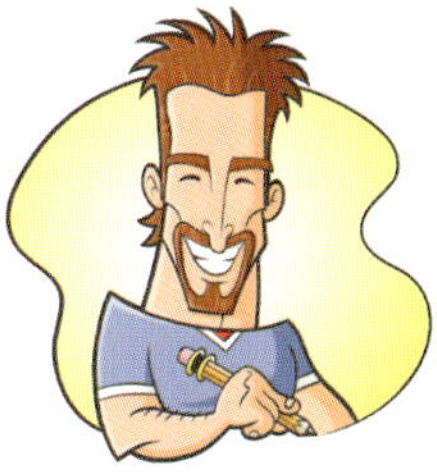

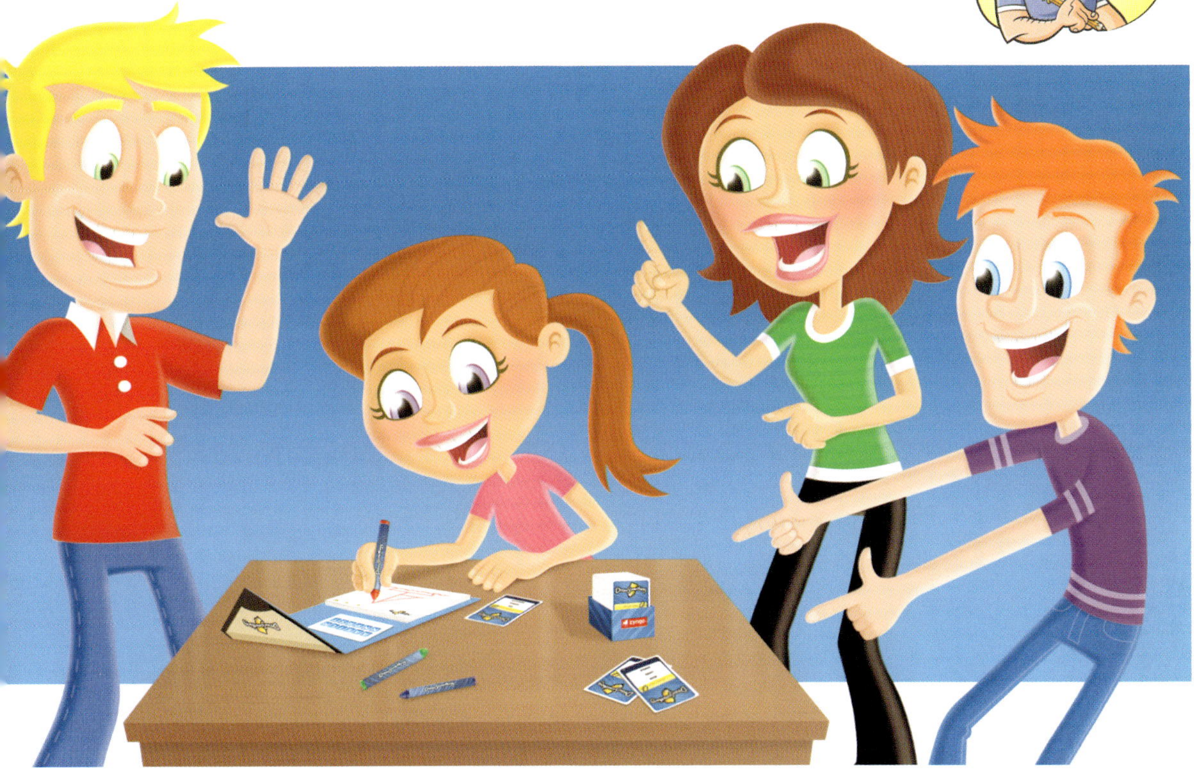

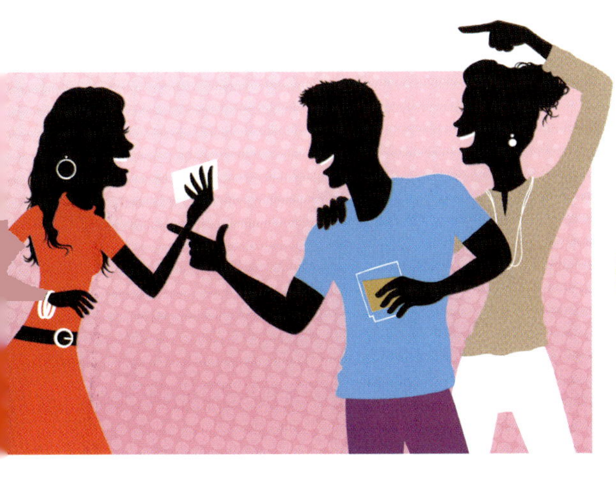

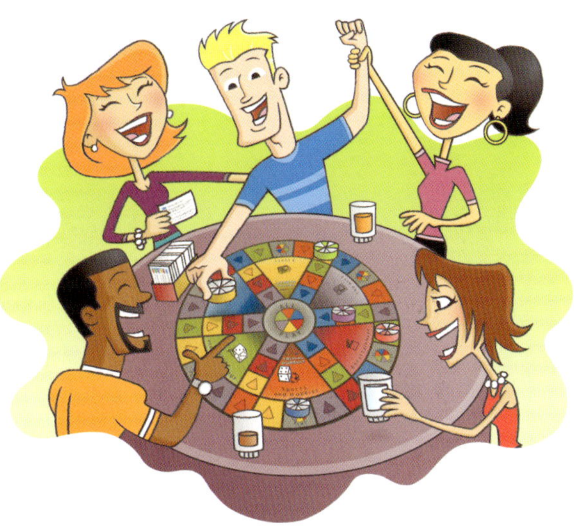

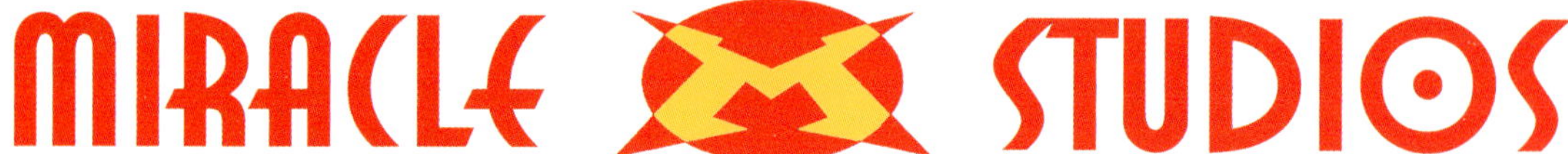

MIRACLE STUDIOS

APPS • COMIC BOOKS• CHARACTER DESIGN • CONCEPT ART • ANIMATION

www.miraclestudios.com

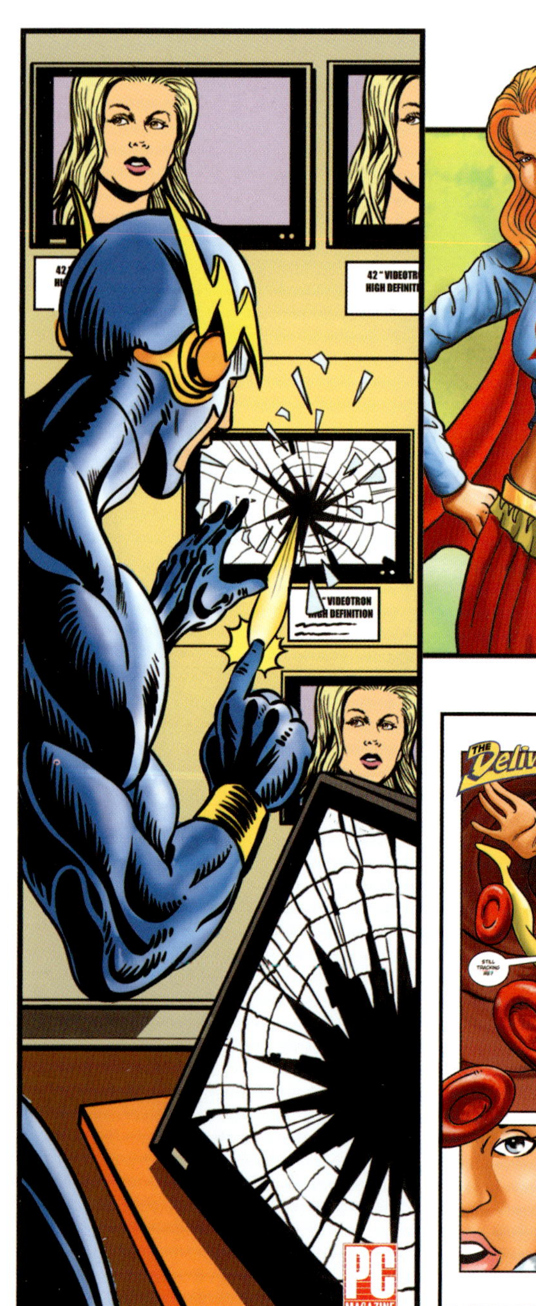

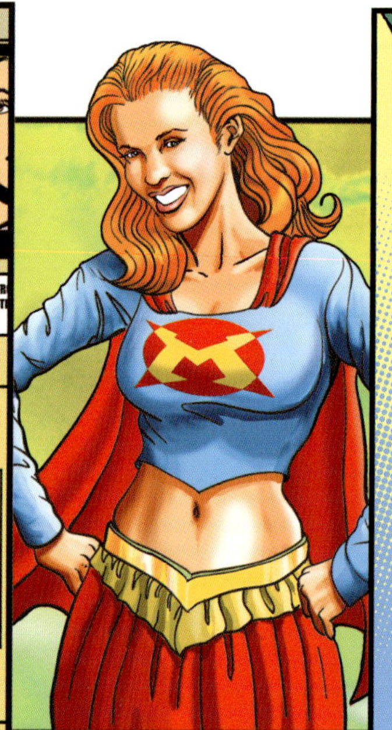

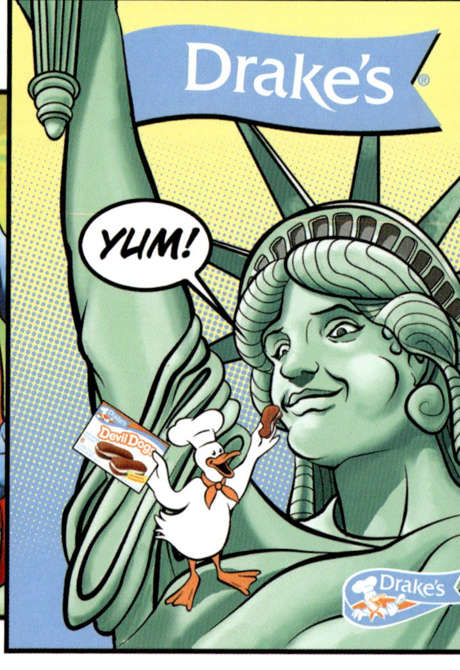

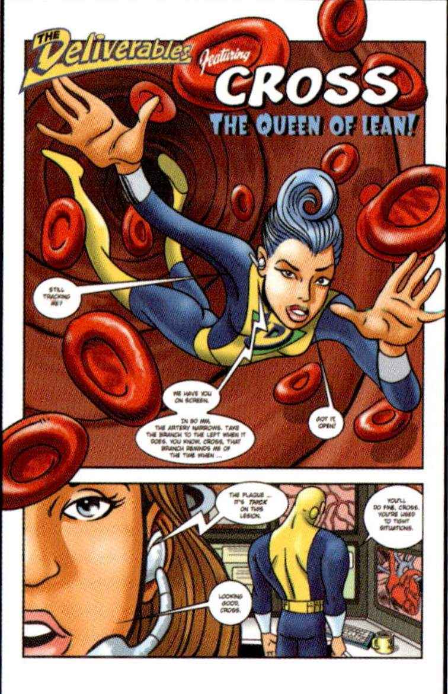

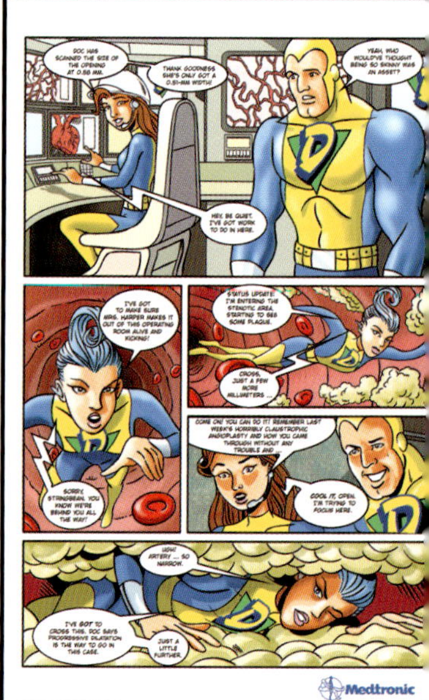

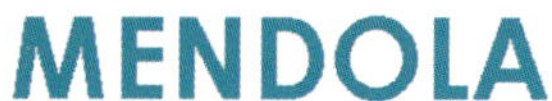

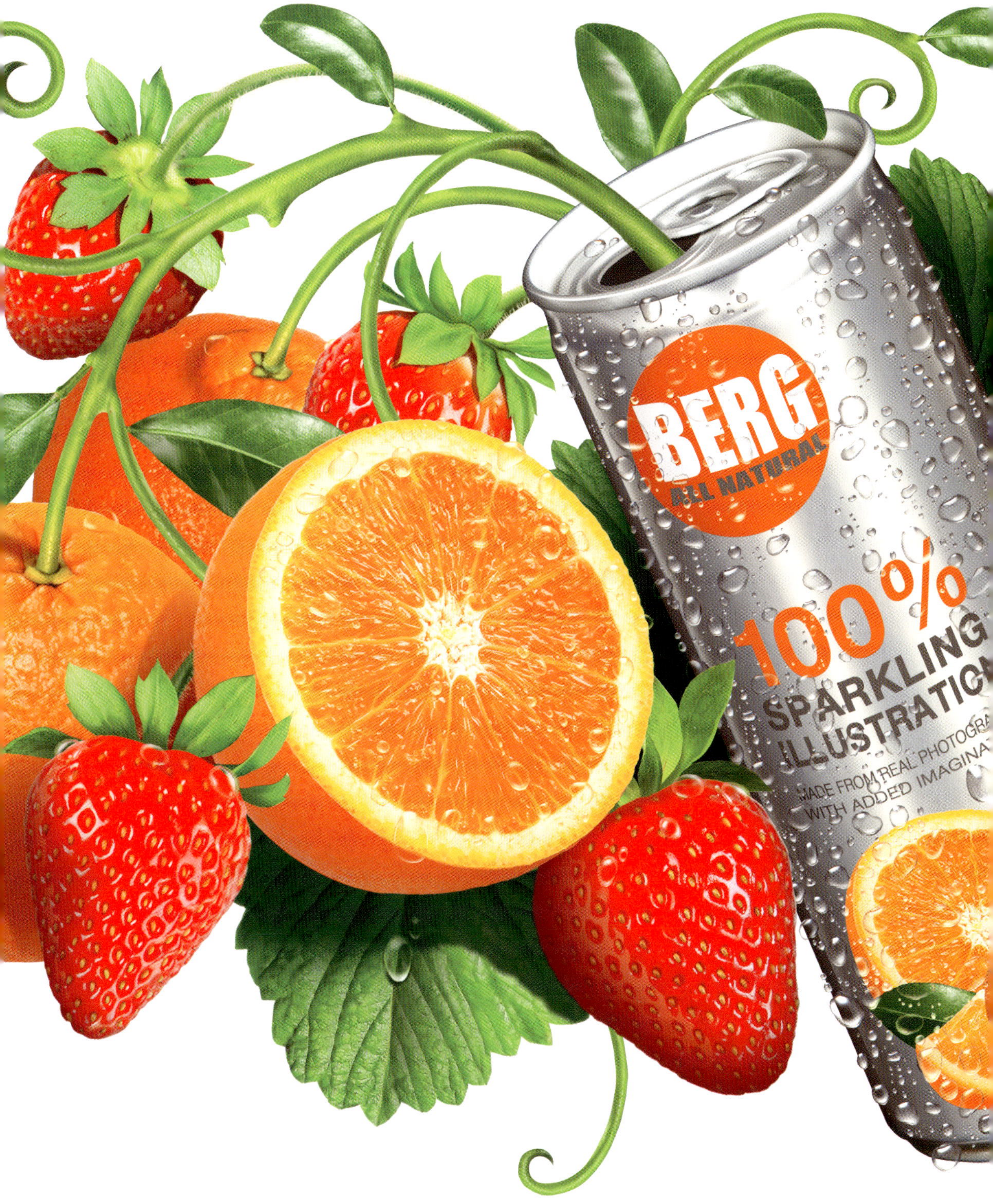

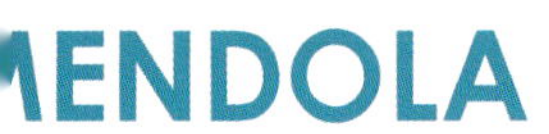

MENDOLA

portfolio
mendolaart.com

email
info@mendolaart.com

call
212.986.5680

represents
RON BERG

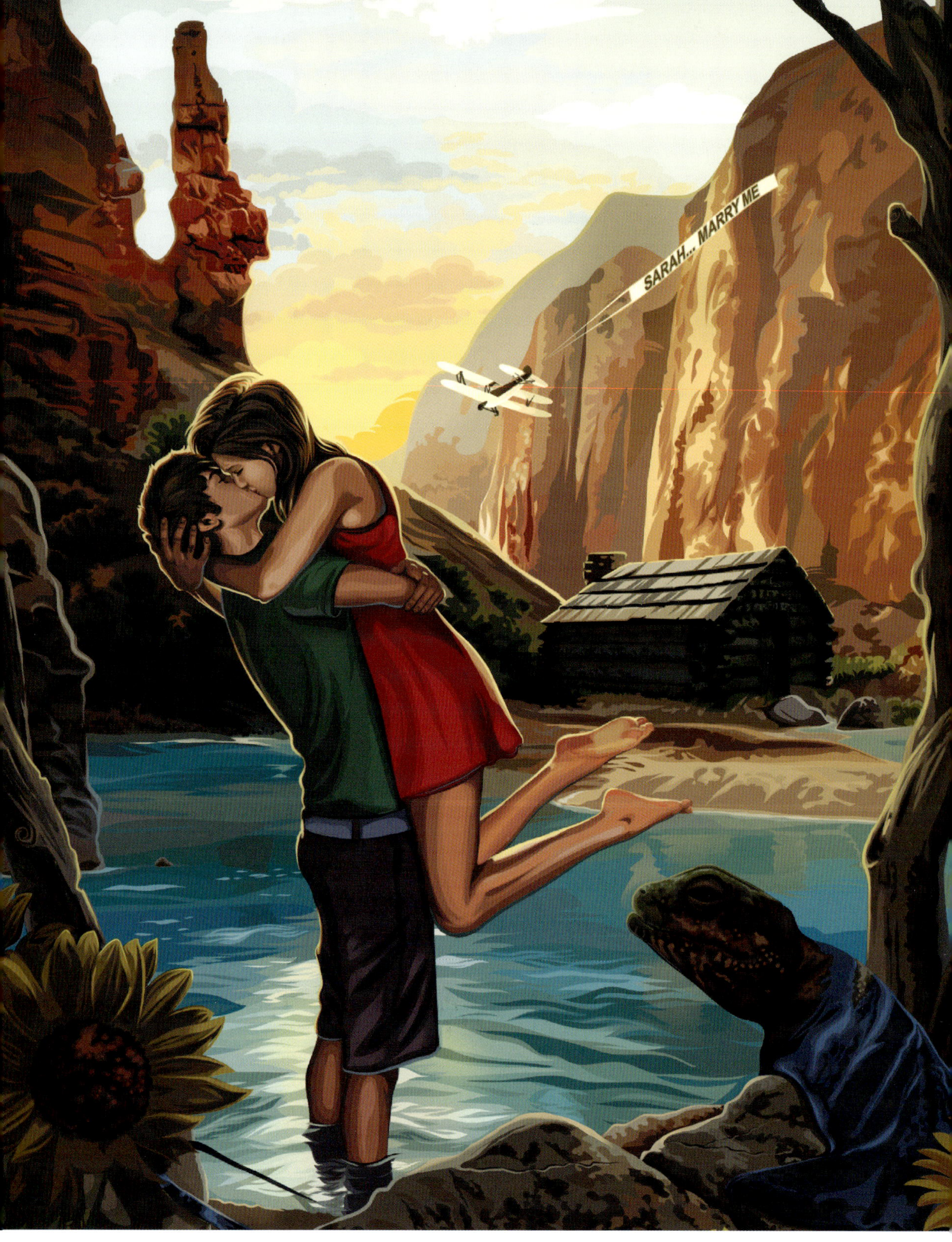

MENDOLA

portfolio
mendolaart.com

email
info@mendolaart.com

call
212.986.5680

represents
AARON SACCO

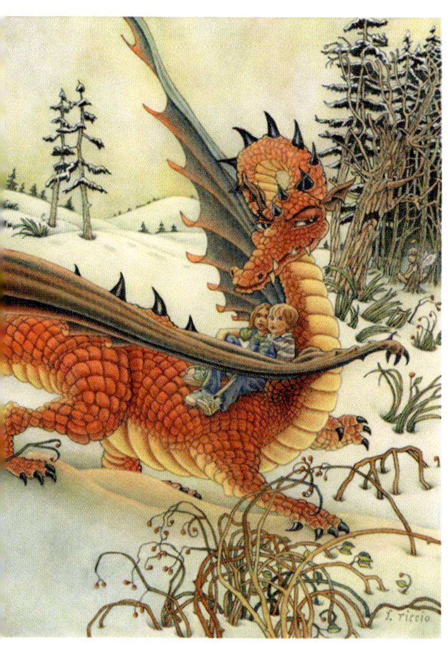

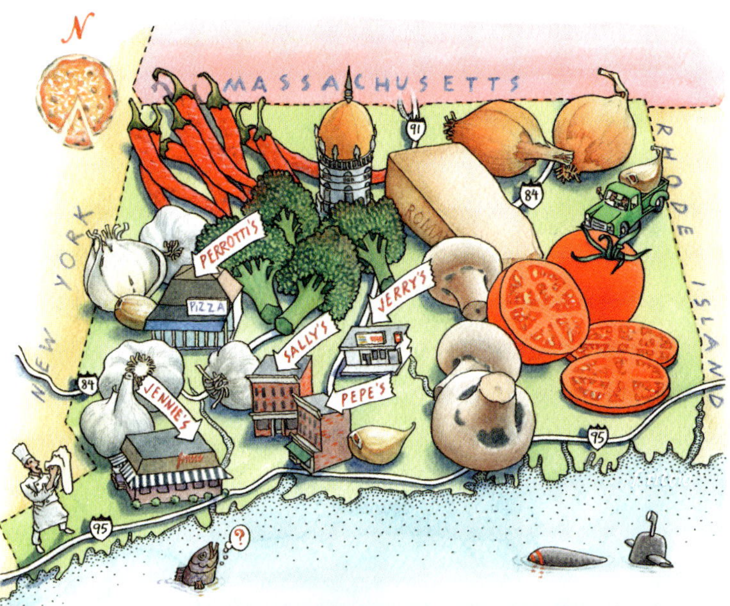

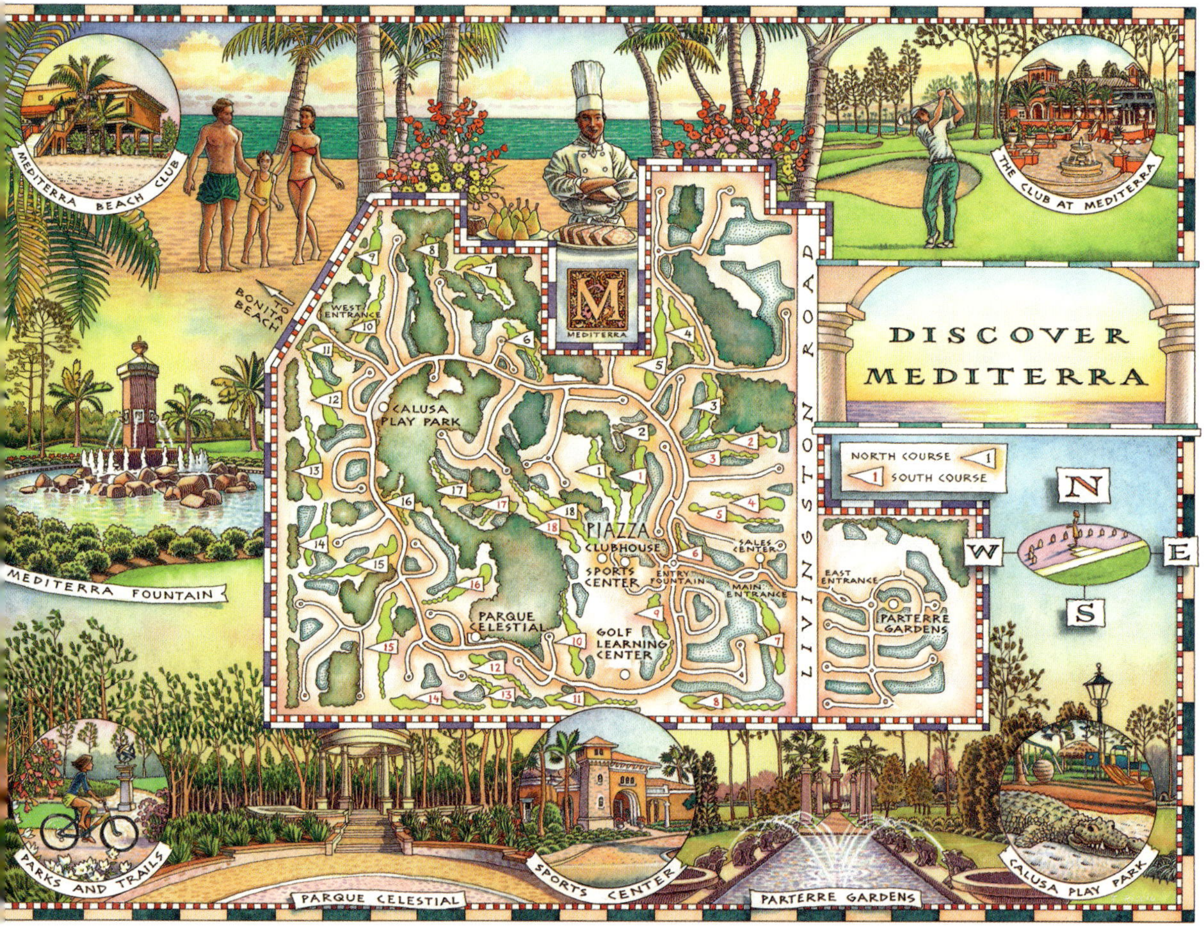

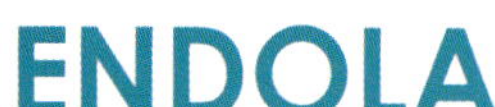

ENDOLA

portfolio
mendolaart.com

email
info@mendolaart.com

call
212.986.5680

represents
FRANK RICCIO

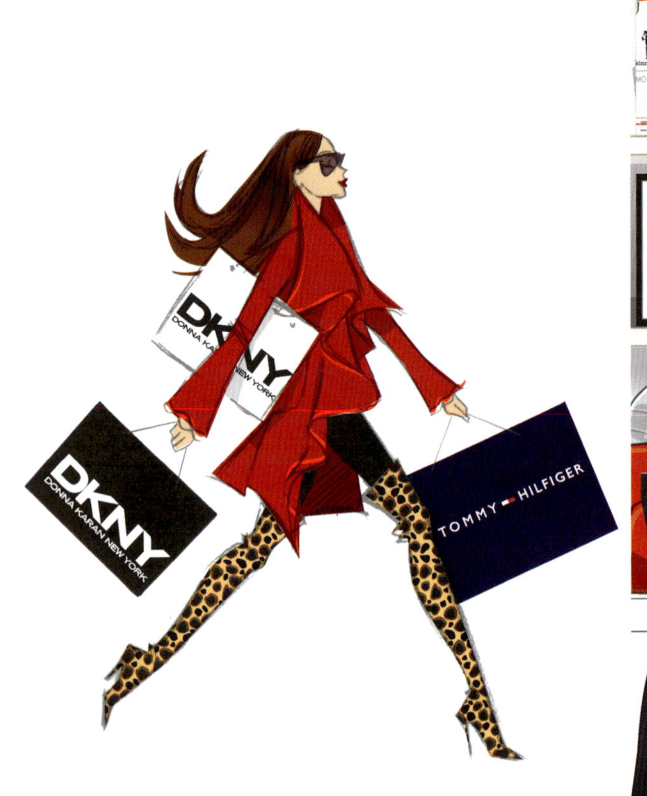

DKNY
DONNA KARAN NEW YORK
DKNY
DONNA KARAN NEW YORK
TOMMY HILFIGER

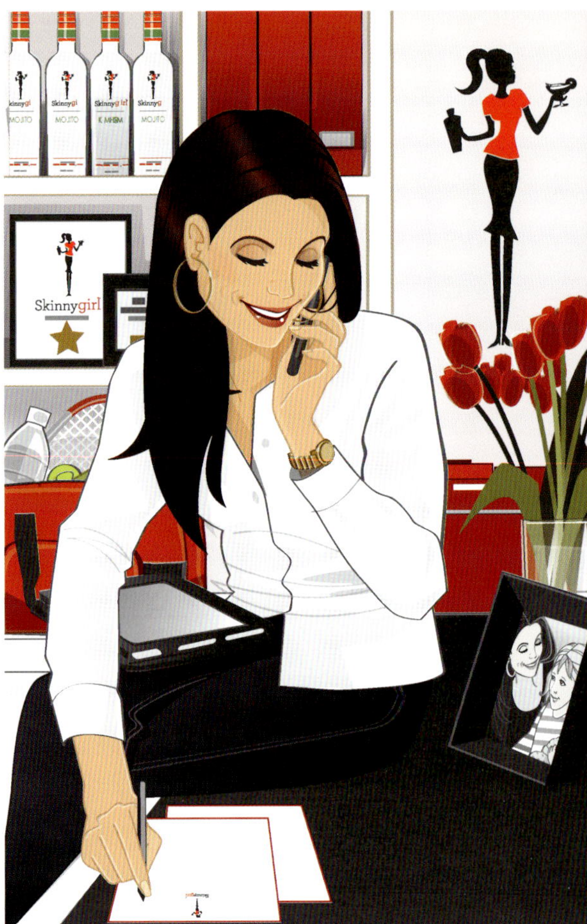

Skinnygirl

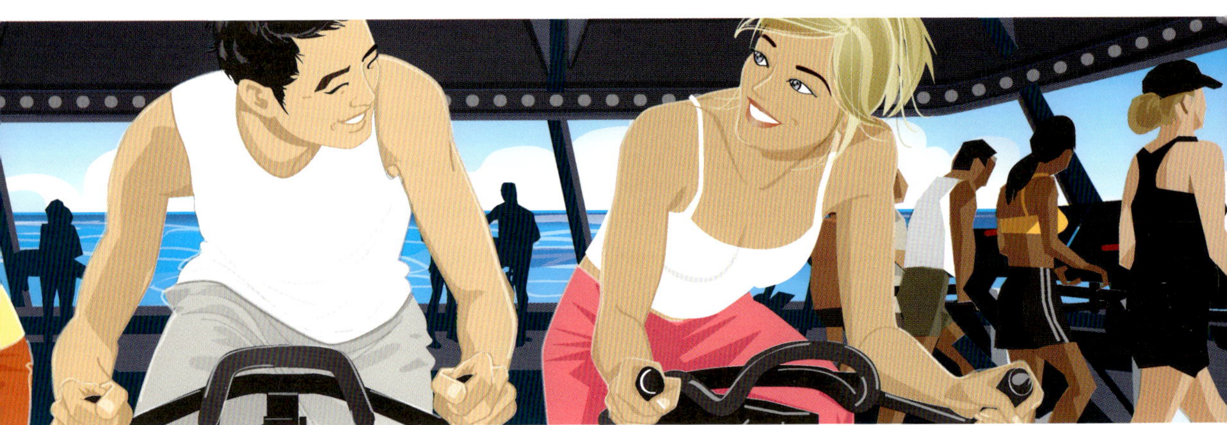

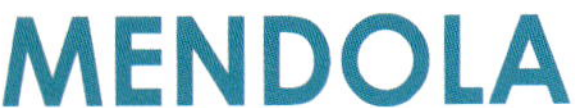

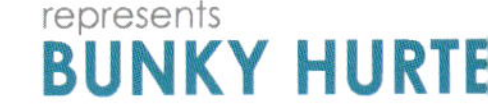

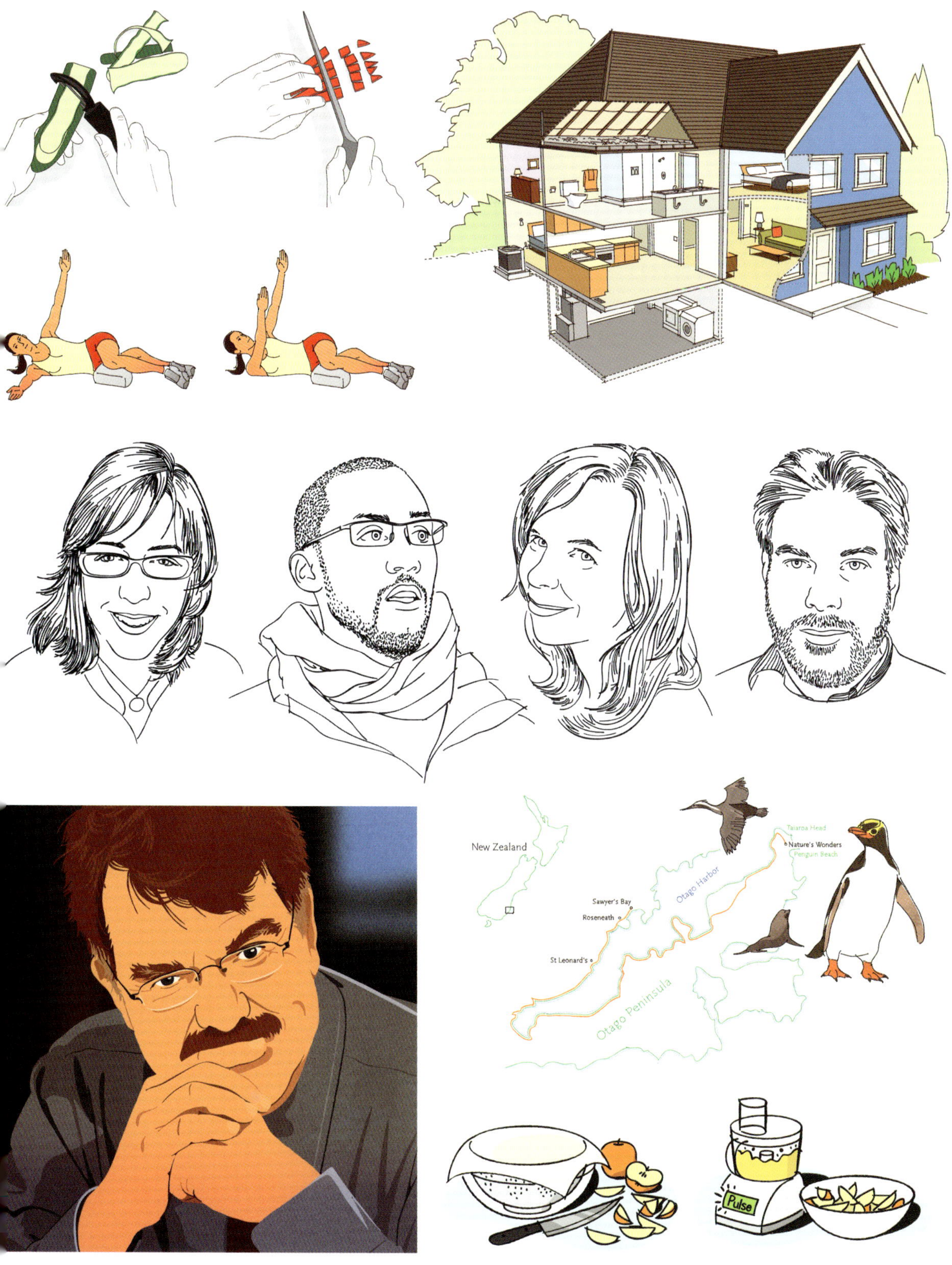

MENDOLA

portfolio
mendolaart.com

email
info@mendolaart.com

call
212.986.5680

represents
ARTHUR MOUNT

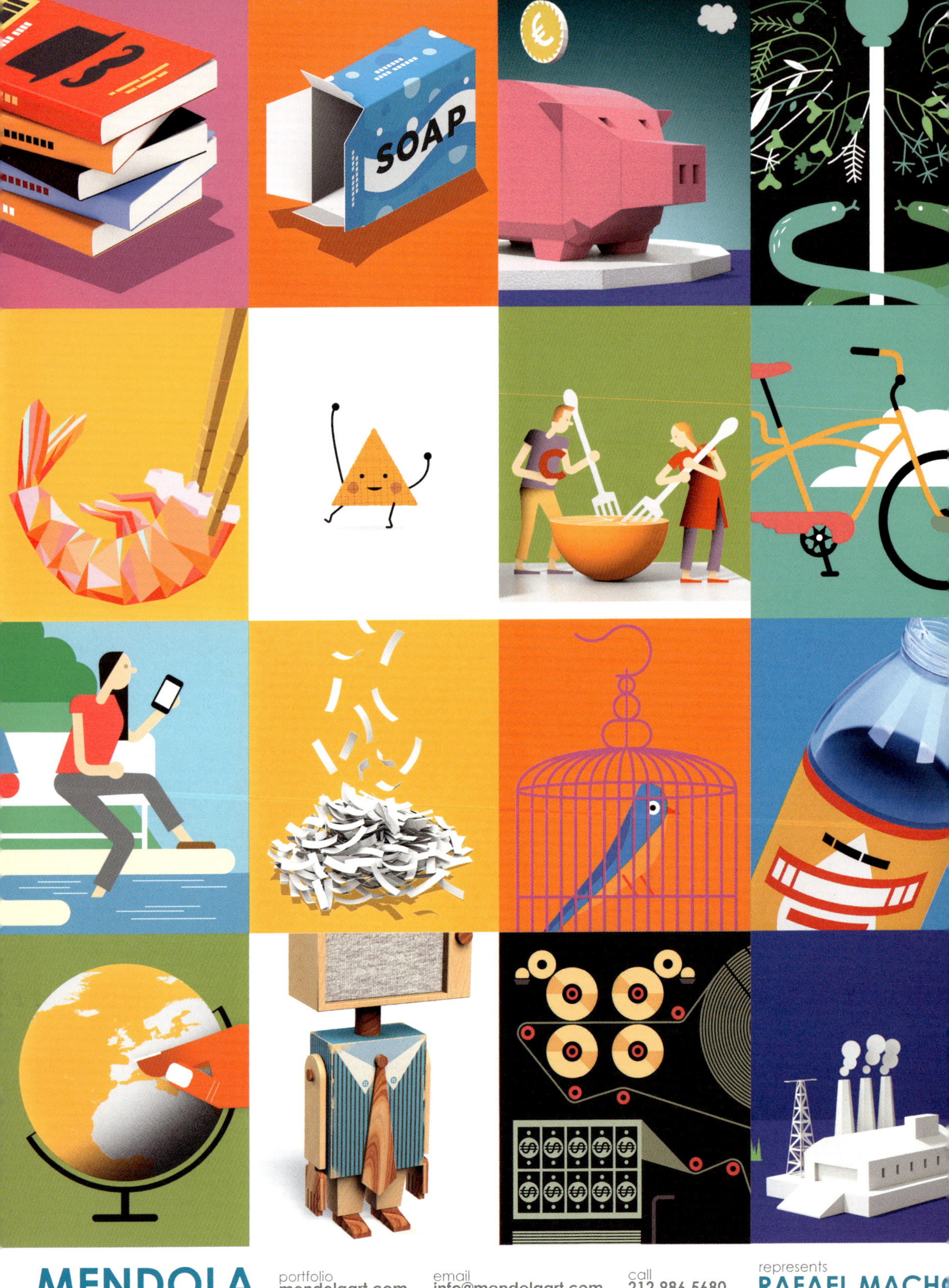

SOAP
€

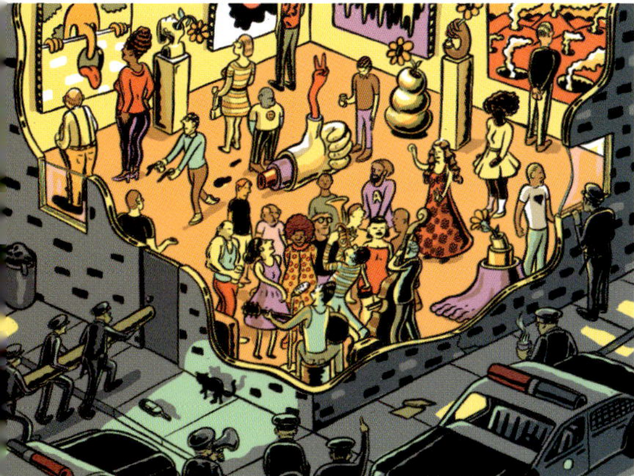

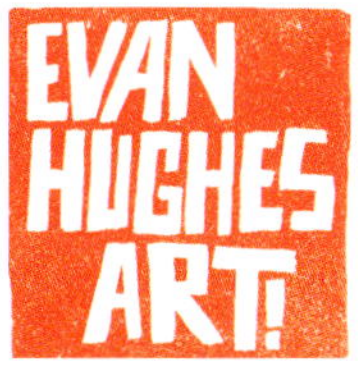

Evan Hughes • Illustrator
570.561.4006
evan.hughes.art@gmail.com
evanhughesart.com

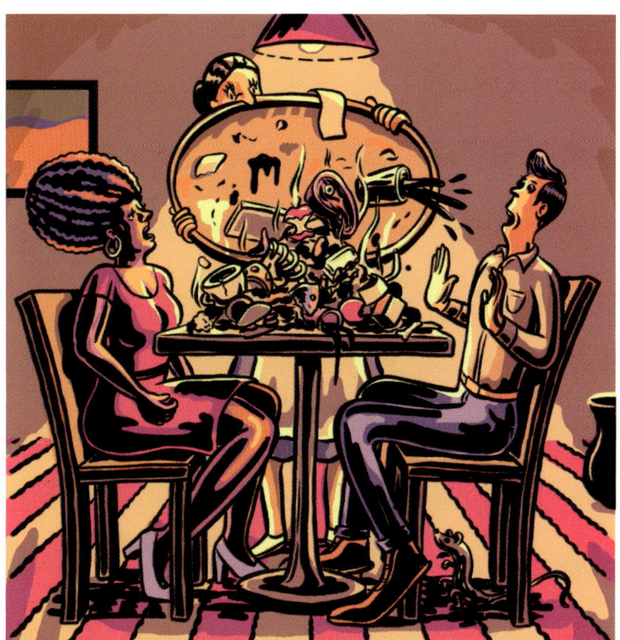

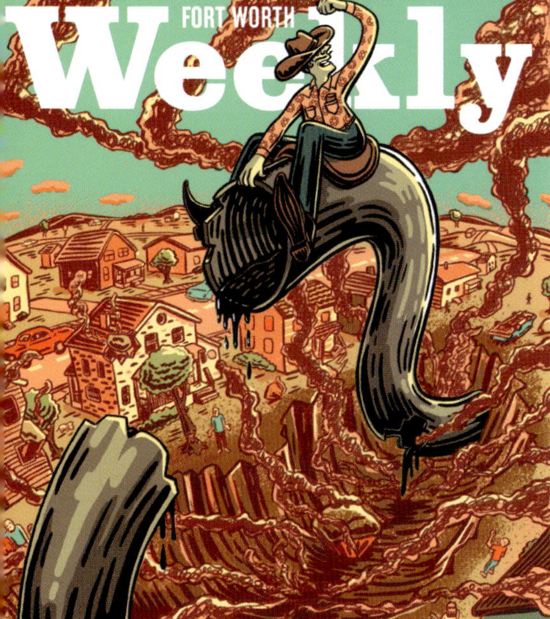

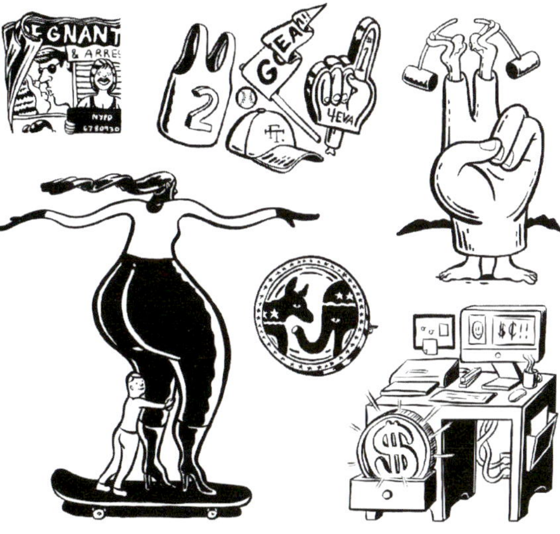

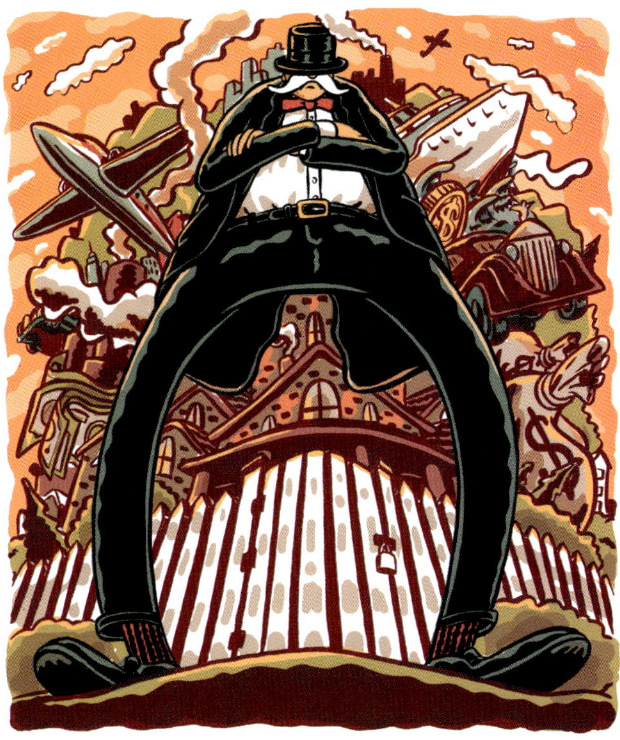

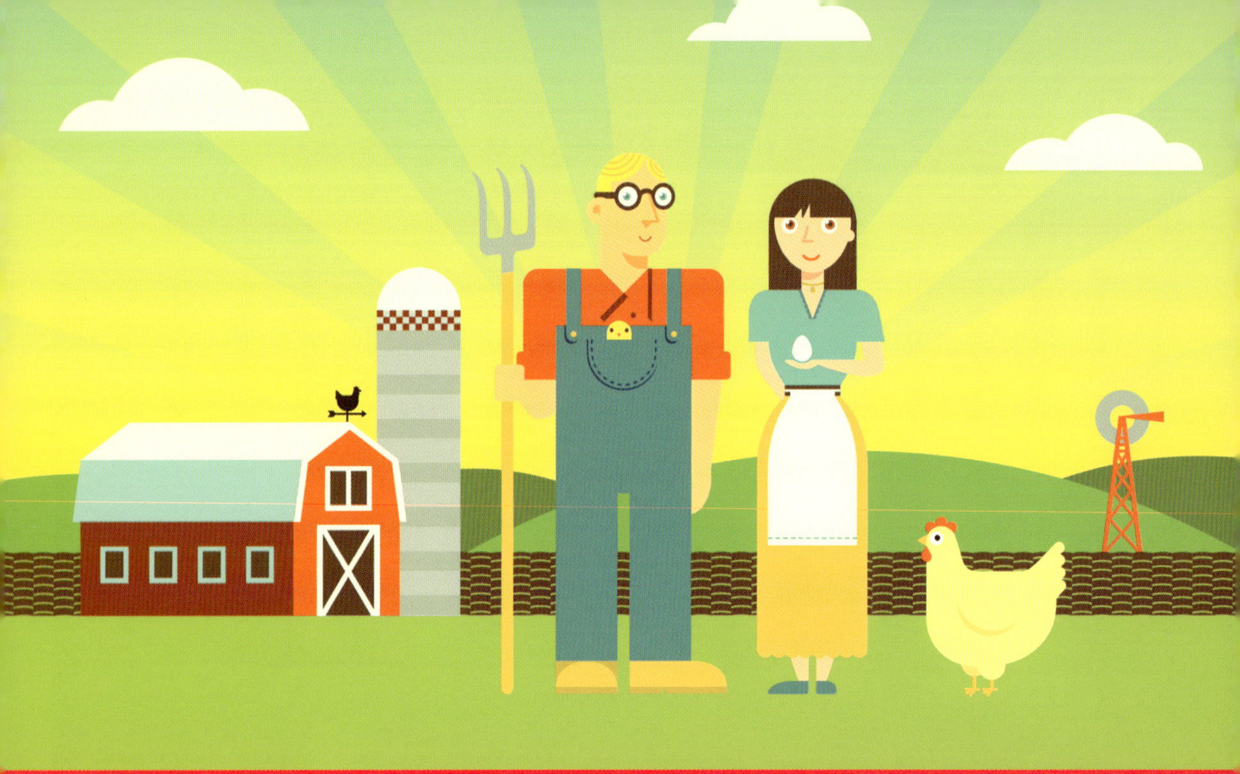

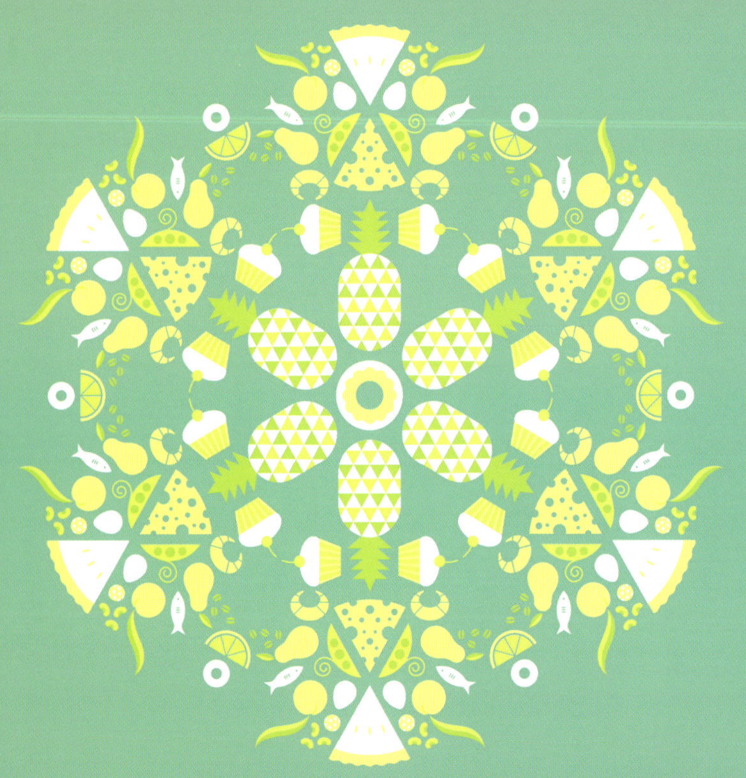

bee things 214.914.2786 | hello@bee-things.com | bee-things.com

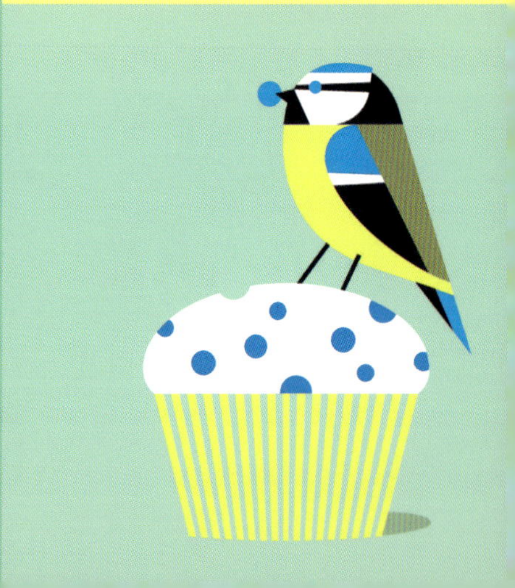

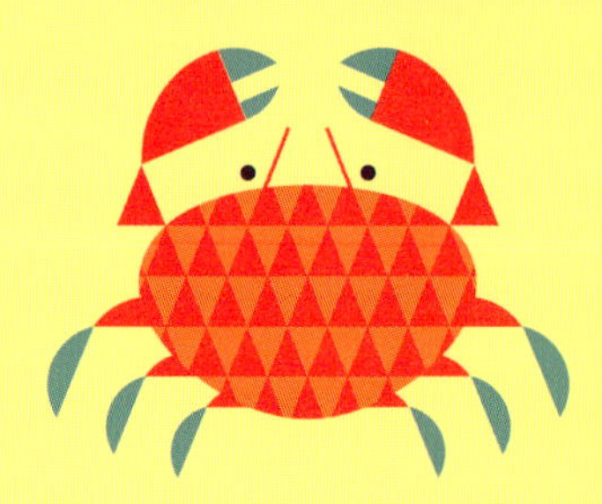

aterpella

Swaddled so soon, ah
From this defenseless cocoon
May come a monarch

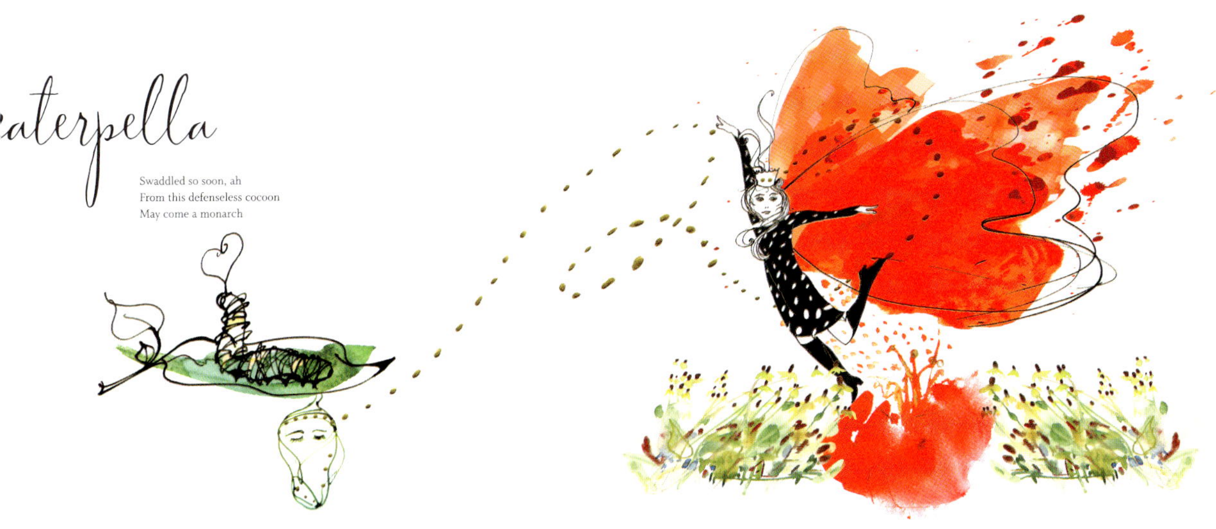

MARGARET HURST   margaret@studio1482.com   212-570-5187 ext. 15

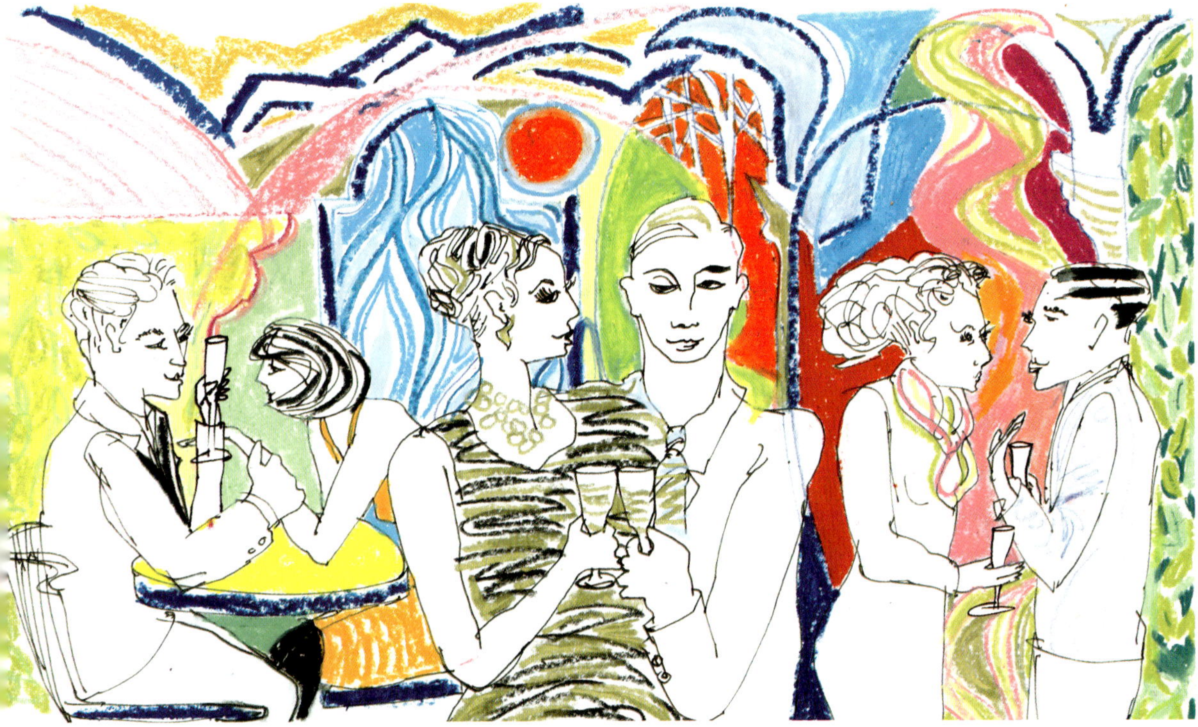

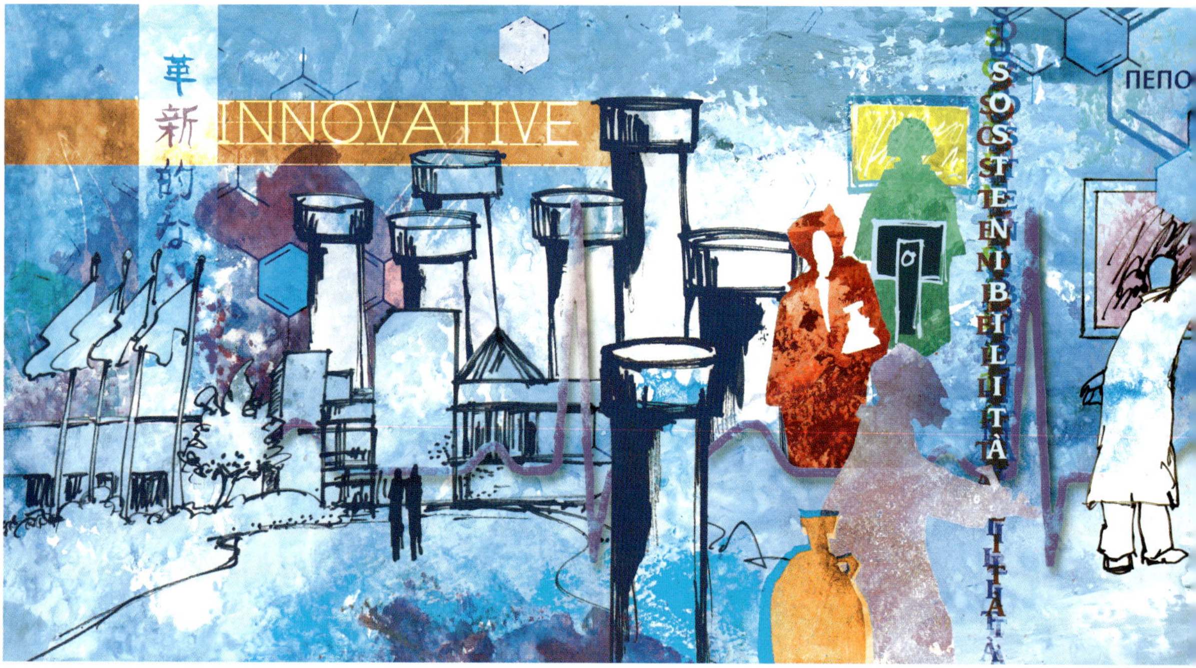

革新的な
INNOVATIVE
SOSTENIBILITÀ
ПЕПО

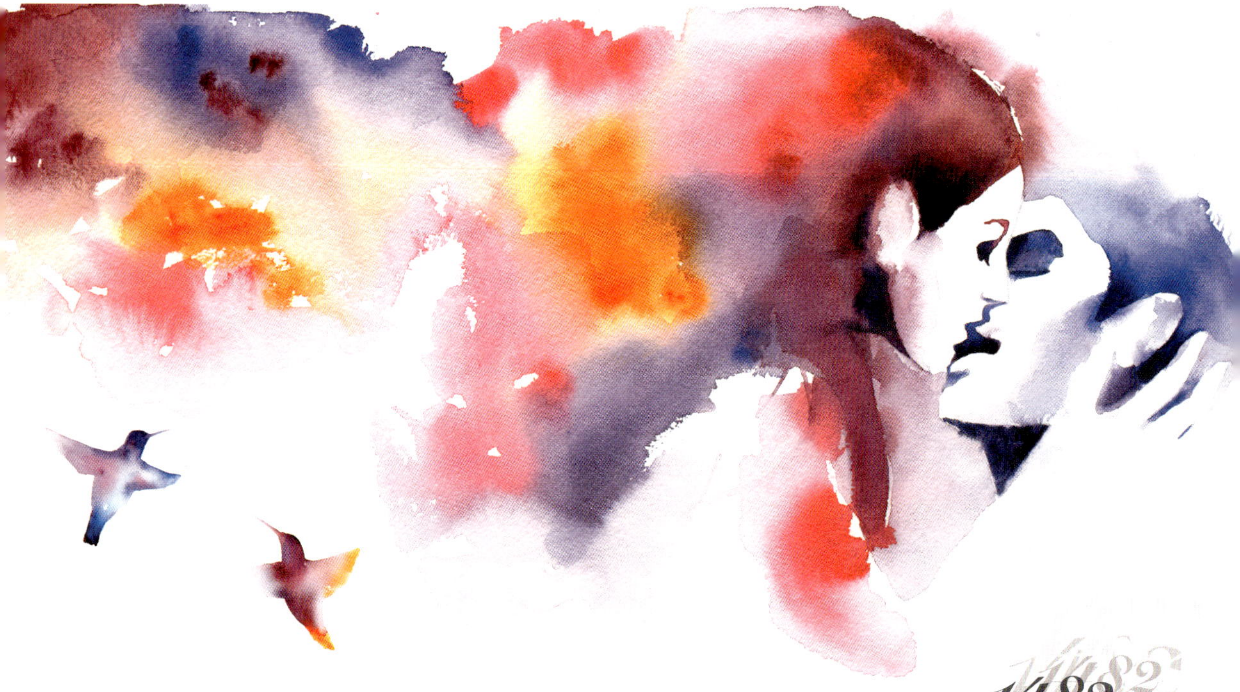

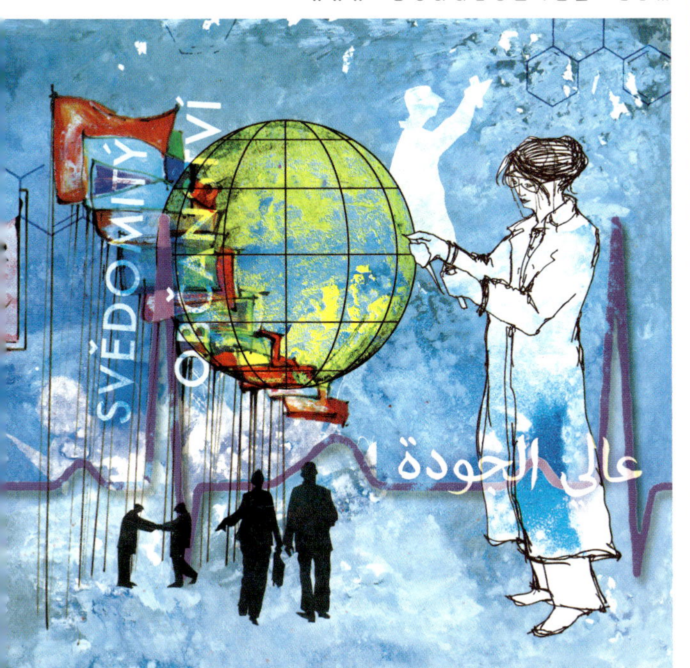

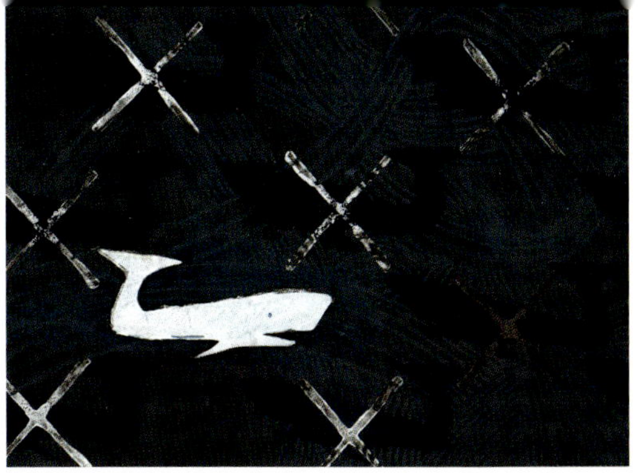

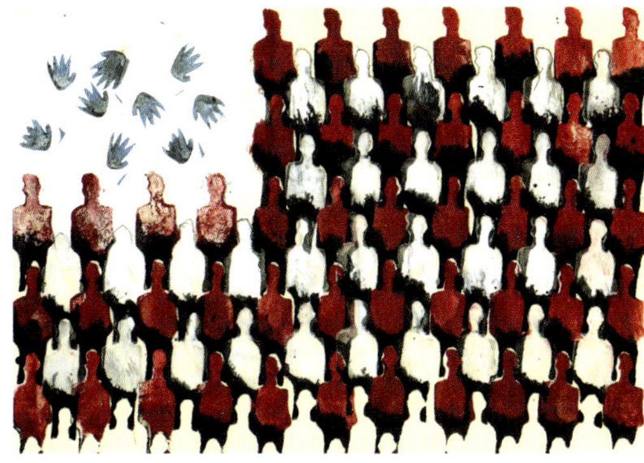

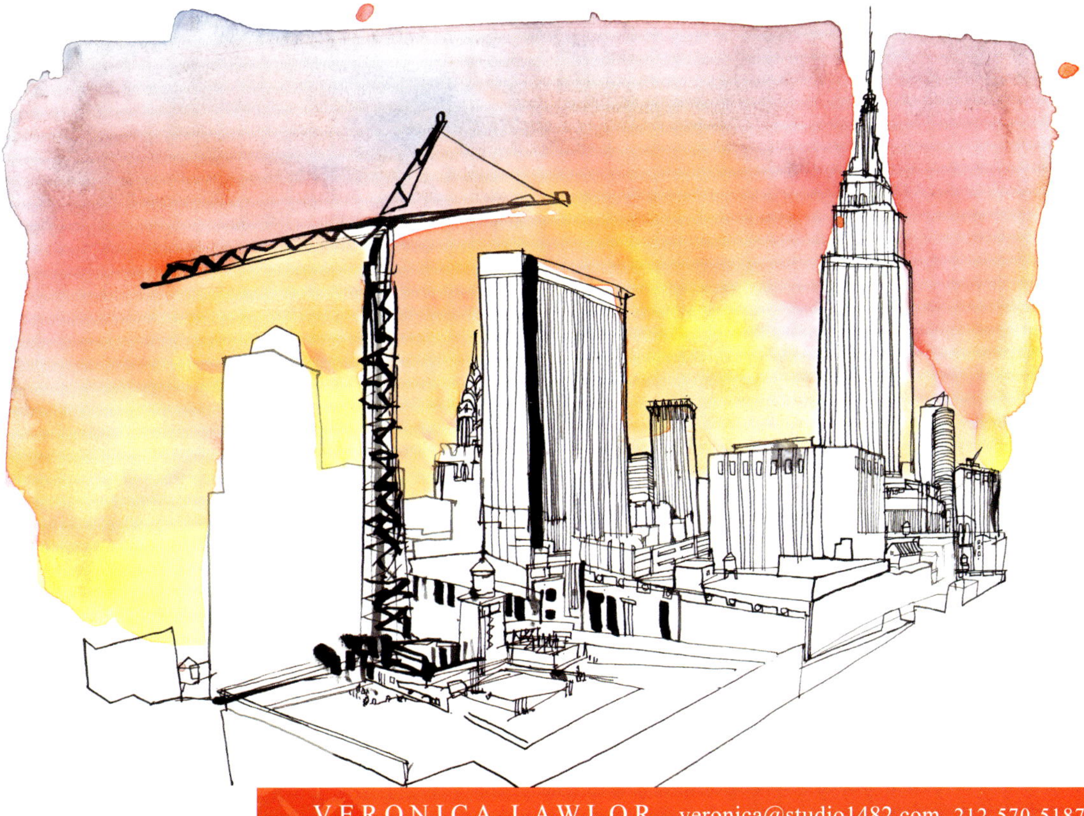

VERONICA LAWLOR   veronica@studio1482.com   212-570-5187 ext. 10

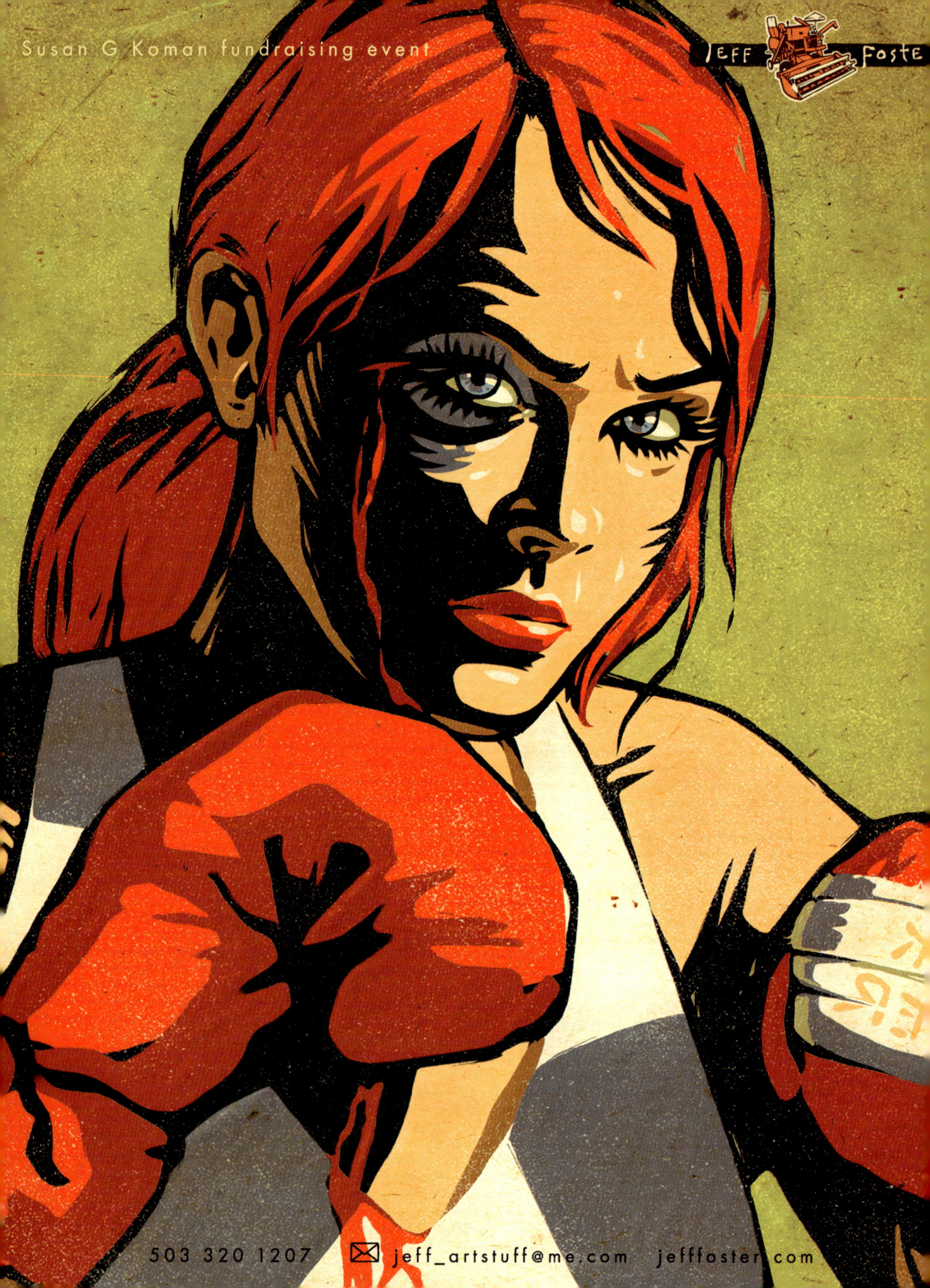

Susan G Koman fundraising event
JEFF FOSTE
503 320 1207   jeff_artstuff@me.com   jefffoster.com

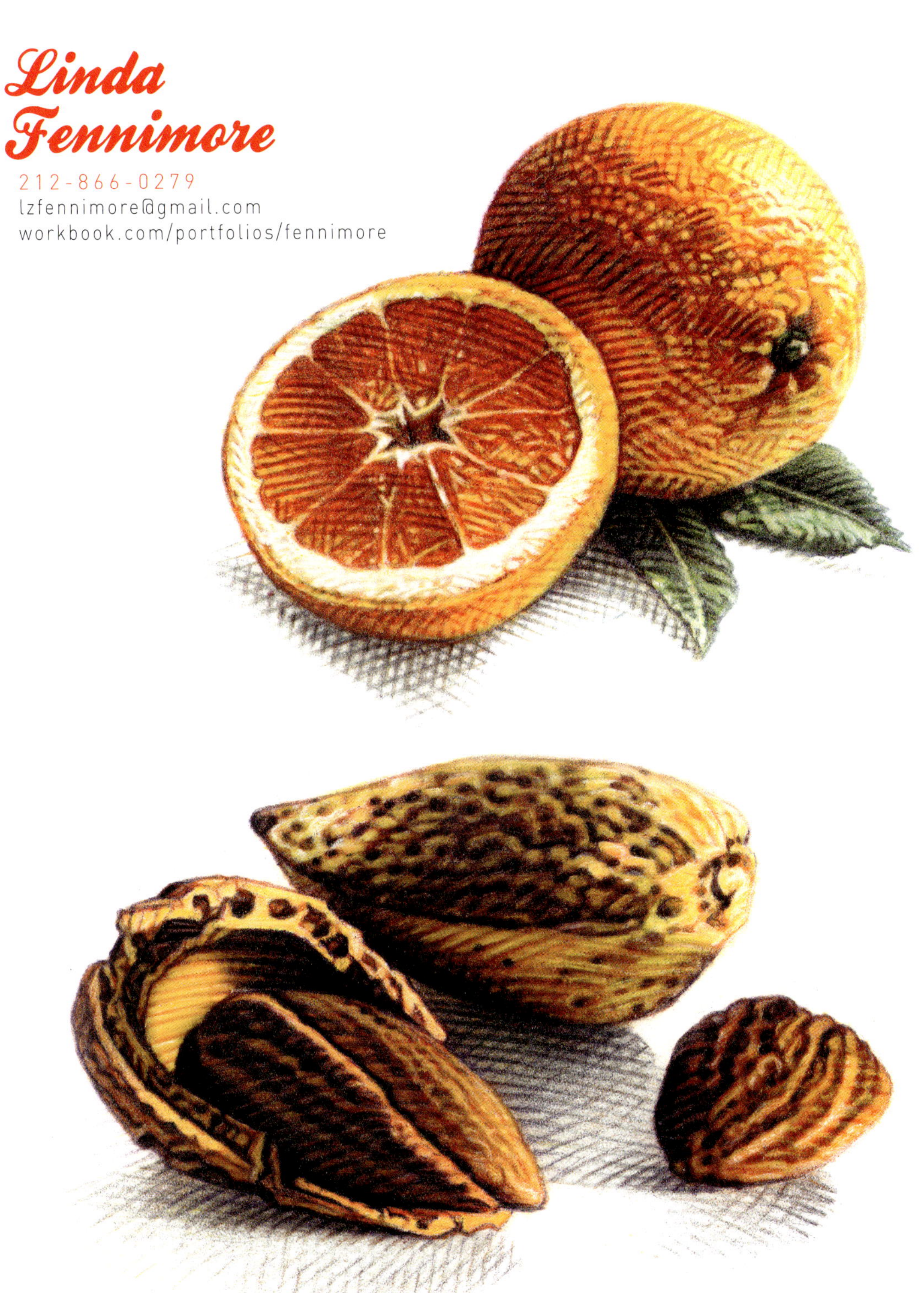

Linda Fennimore

212-866-0279
lzfennimore@gmail.com
workbook.com/portfolios/fennimore

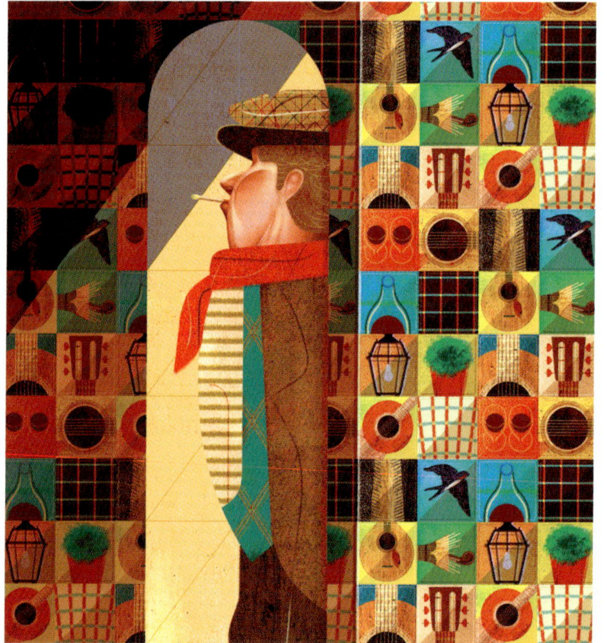

/ GONÇALO VIANA

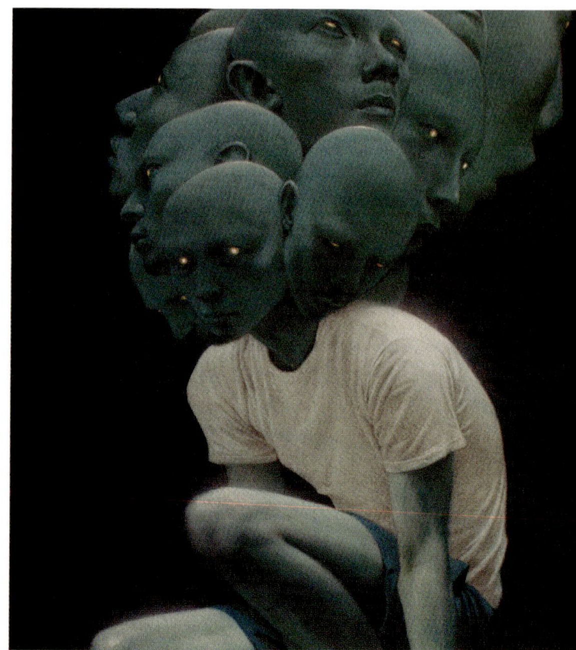

/ JEREMY ENECIO

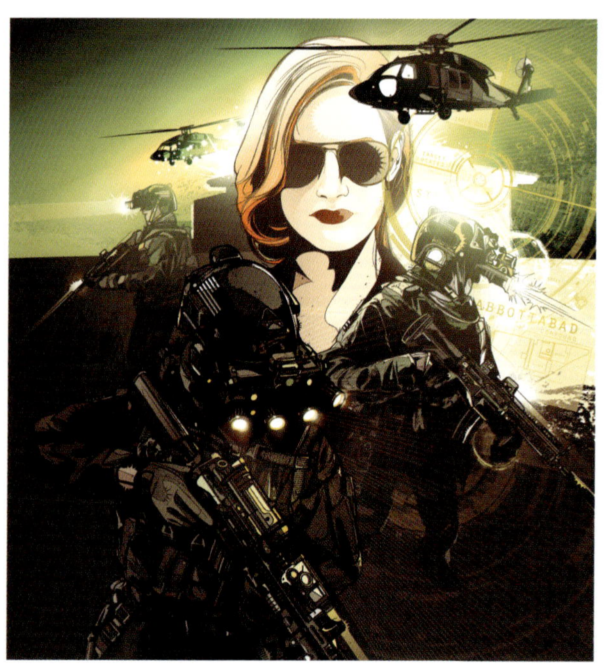

/ KAKO

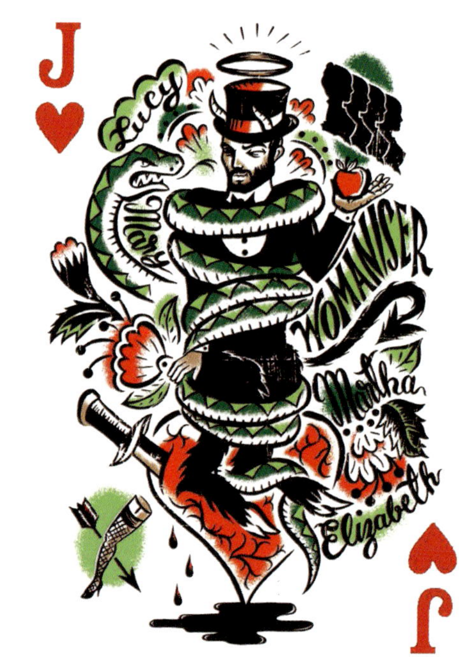

/ CHRISTOPHER NIELSEN

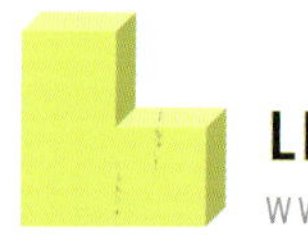

LEVY CREATIVE MANAGEMENT
www.levycreative.com   212.687.6463

316

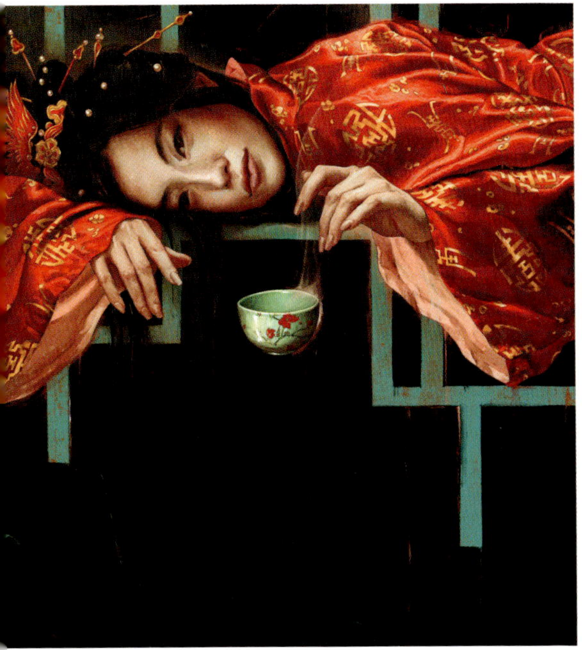

RORY KURTZ

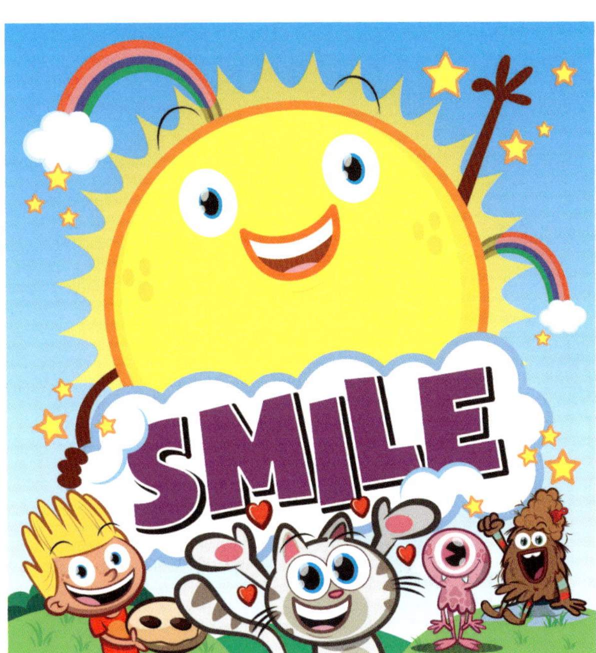

/ MICHAEL BYERS

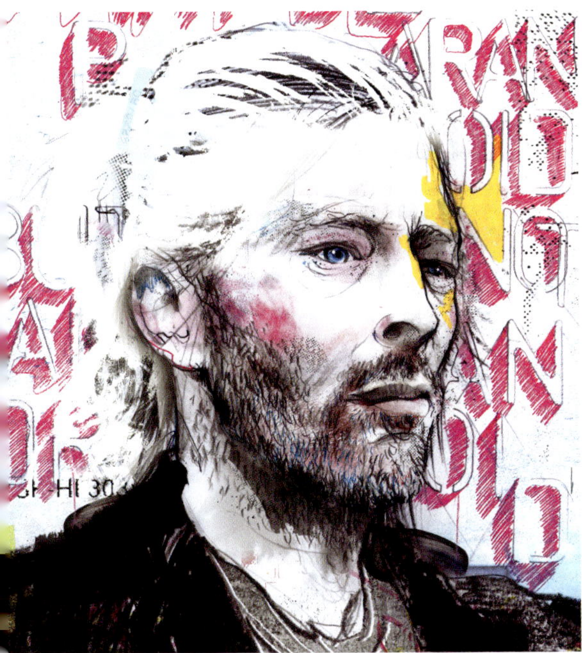

ZÉ OTAVIO

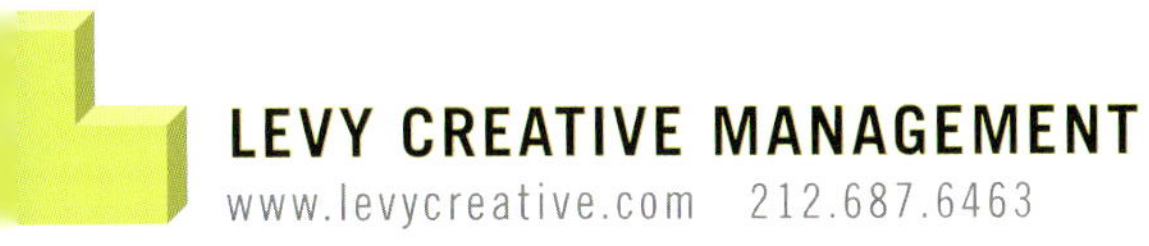

/ JASON THARP

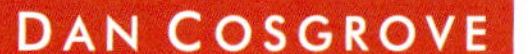
DAN COSGROVE cosgrovedesign.com | 312.765.8911

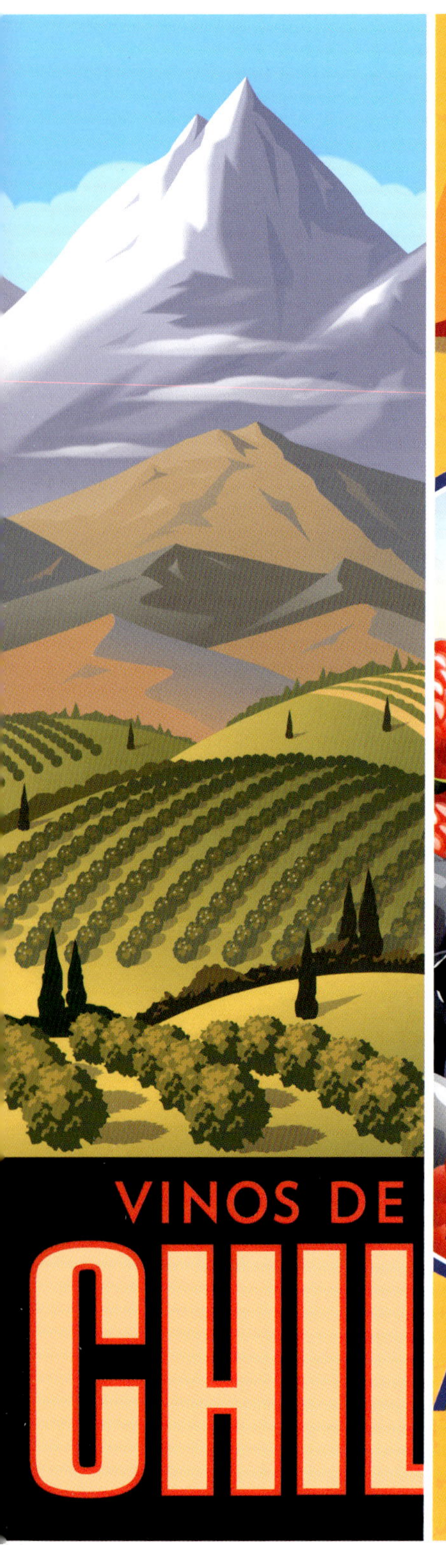
VINOS DE
CHIL

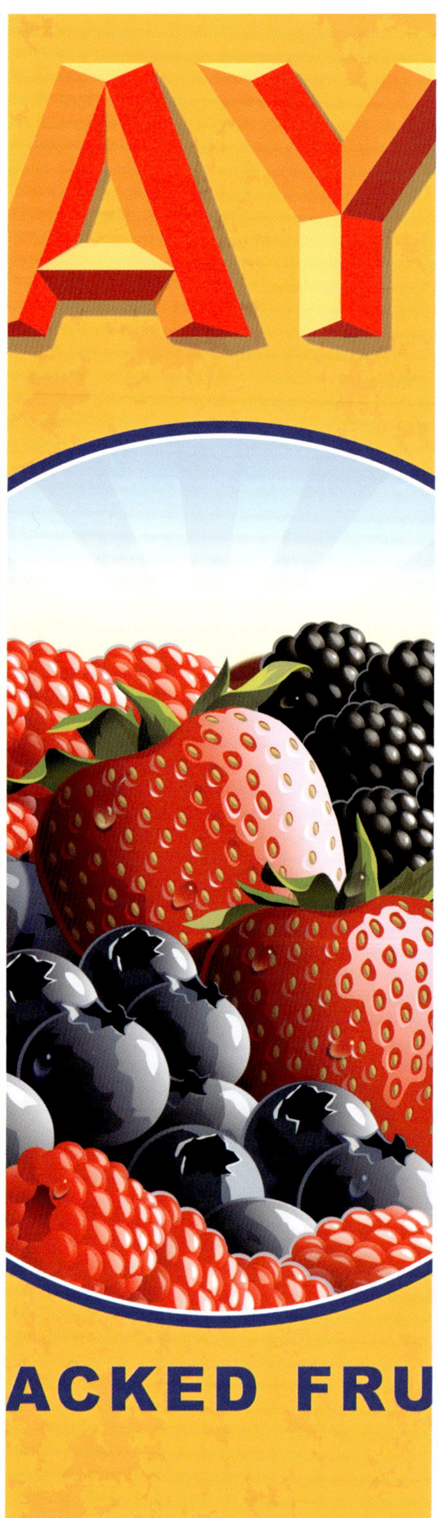
AY
ACKED FRU
COSGROVE

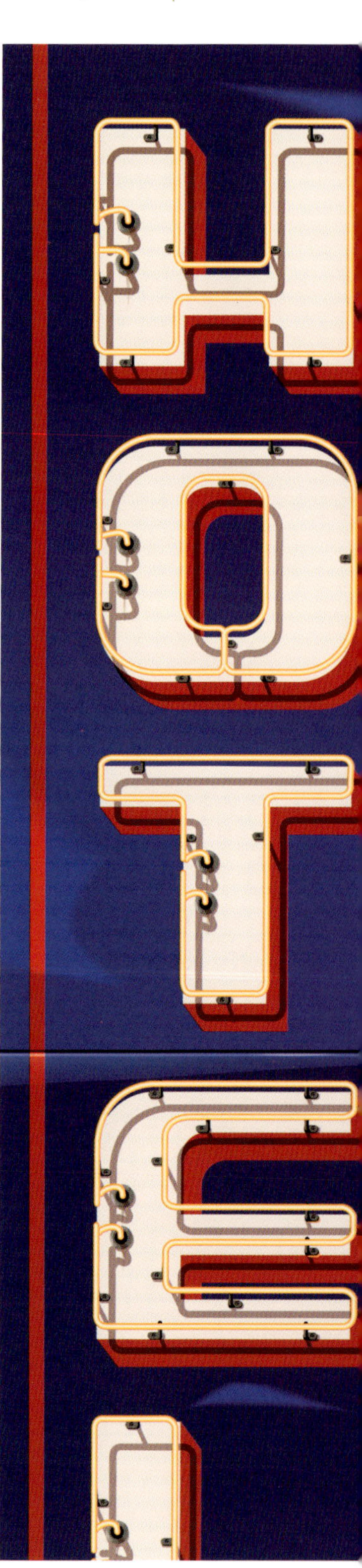
H
O
T
E

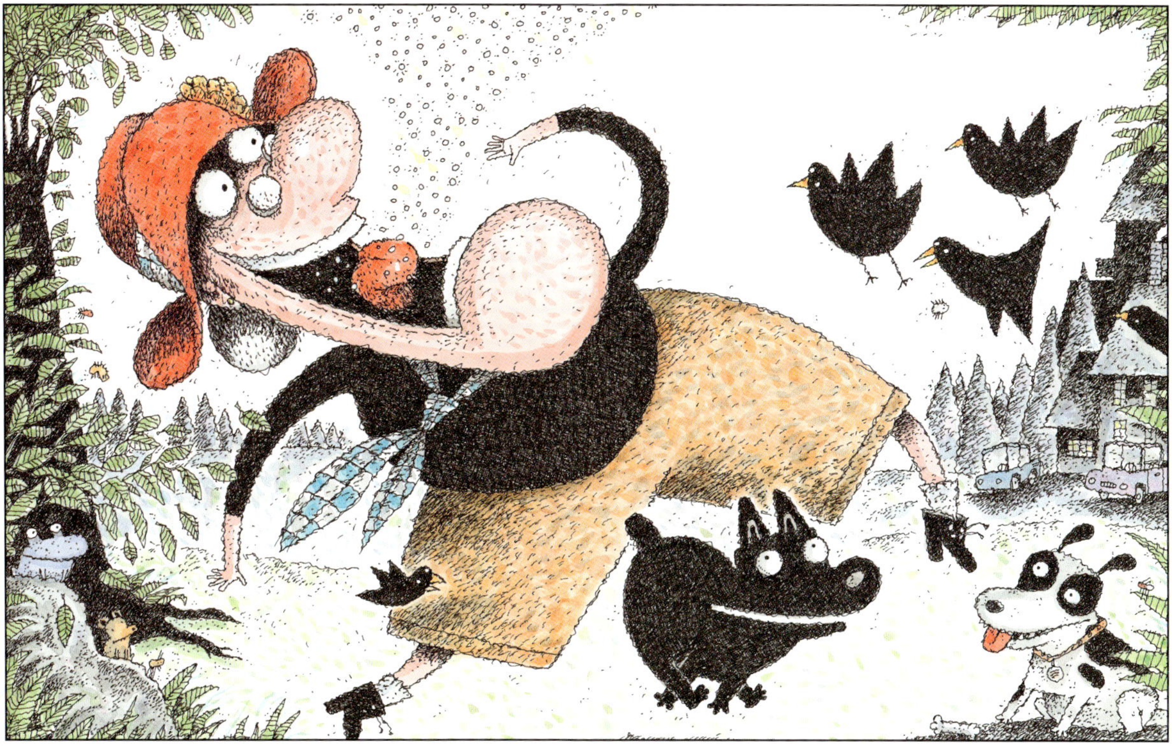

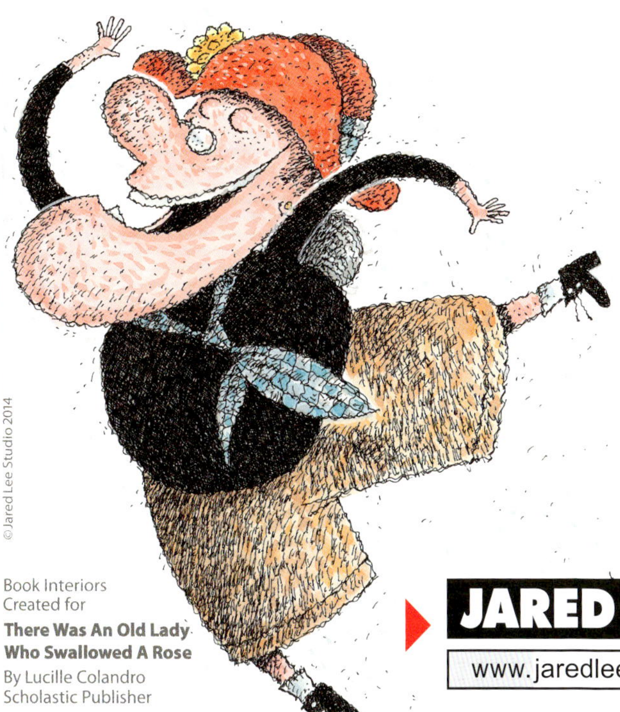

Book Interiors
Created for

**There Was An Old Lady
Who Swallowed A Rose**

By Lucille Colandro
Scholastic Publisher

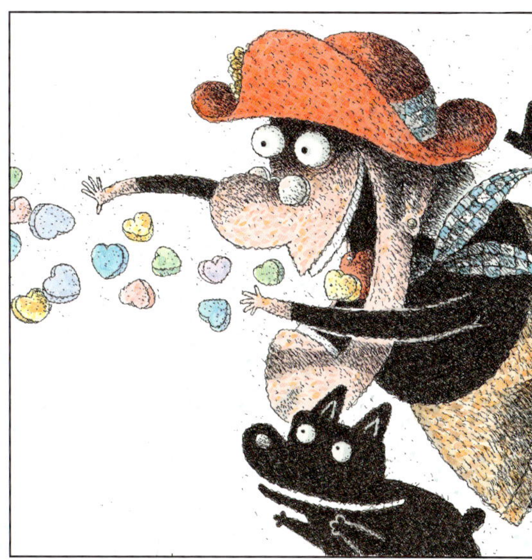

© Jared Lee Studio 2014

JARED LEE

www.jaredlee.com

Jared Lee started his
free-lance career in 1970
working with national
ad agencies, magazines,
and book publishers.
He has created over 100
children's books with
31,000,000 in print.

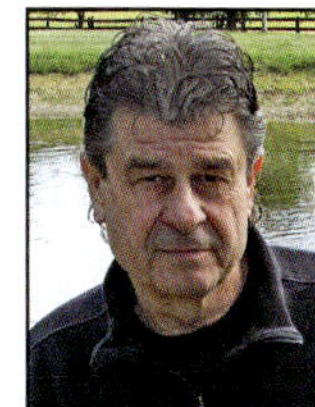

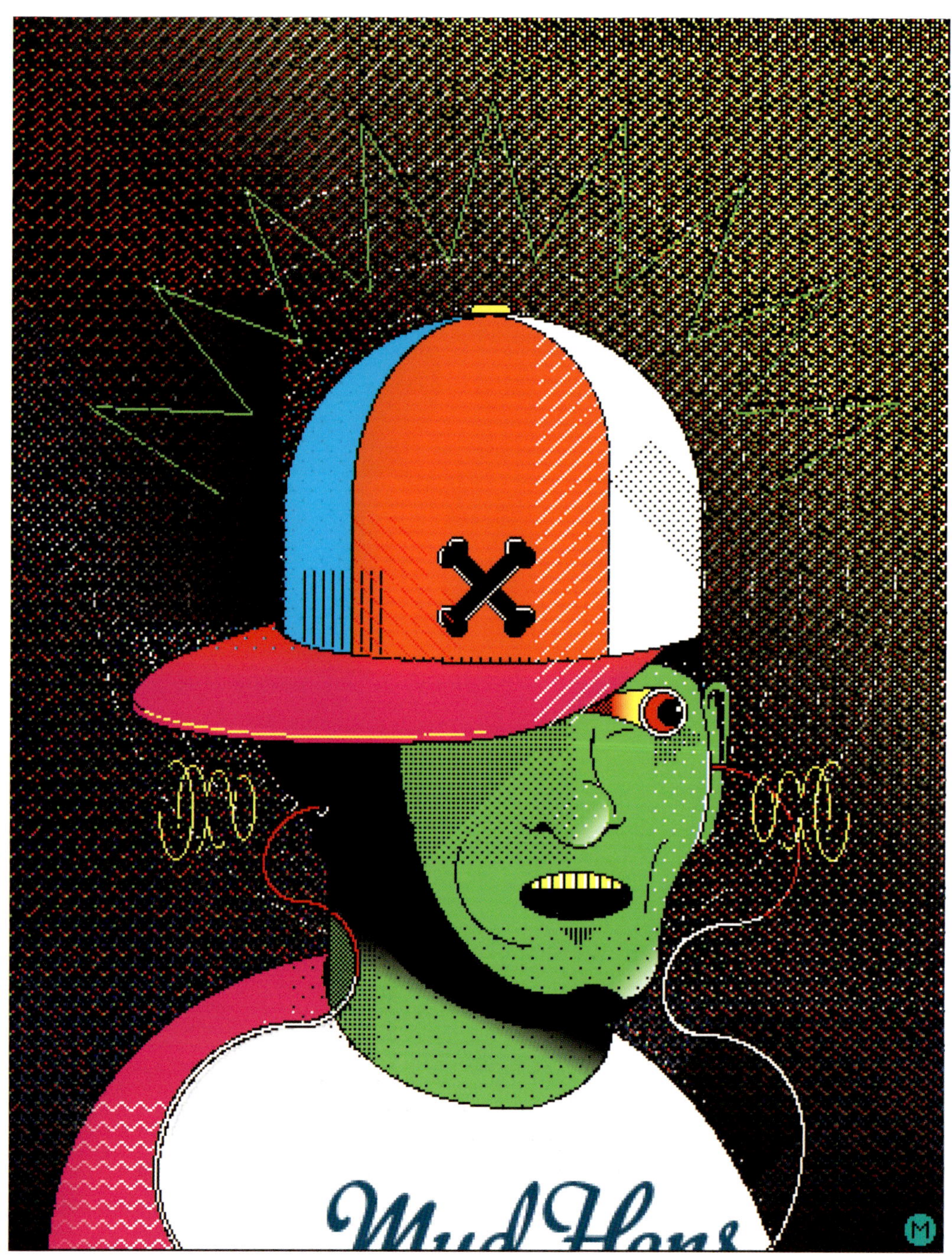
MudHens

RILEYILLUSTRATION.COM

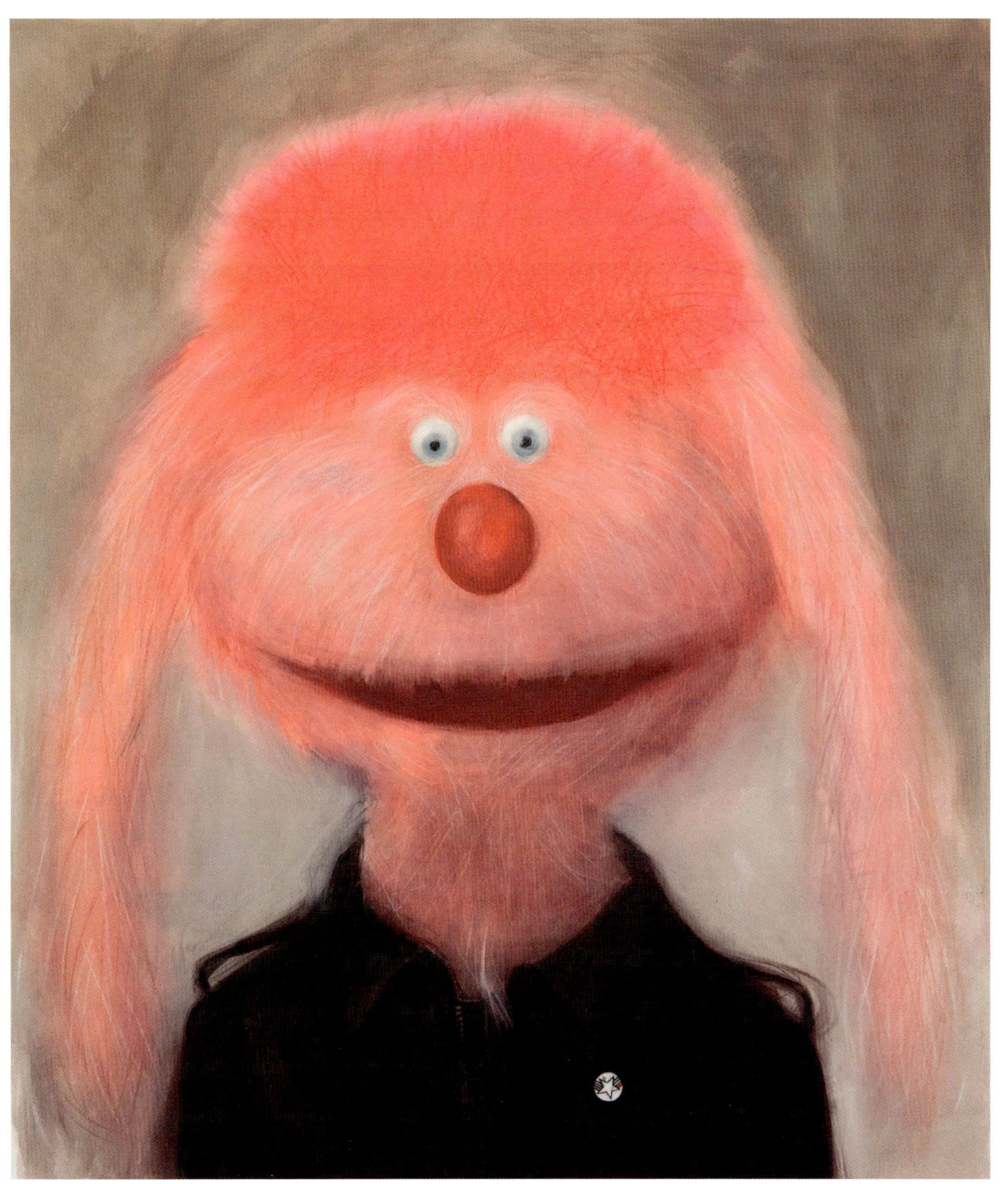

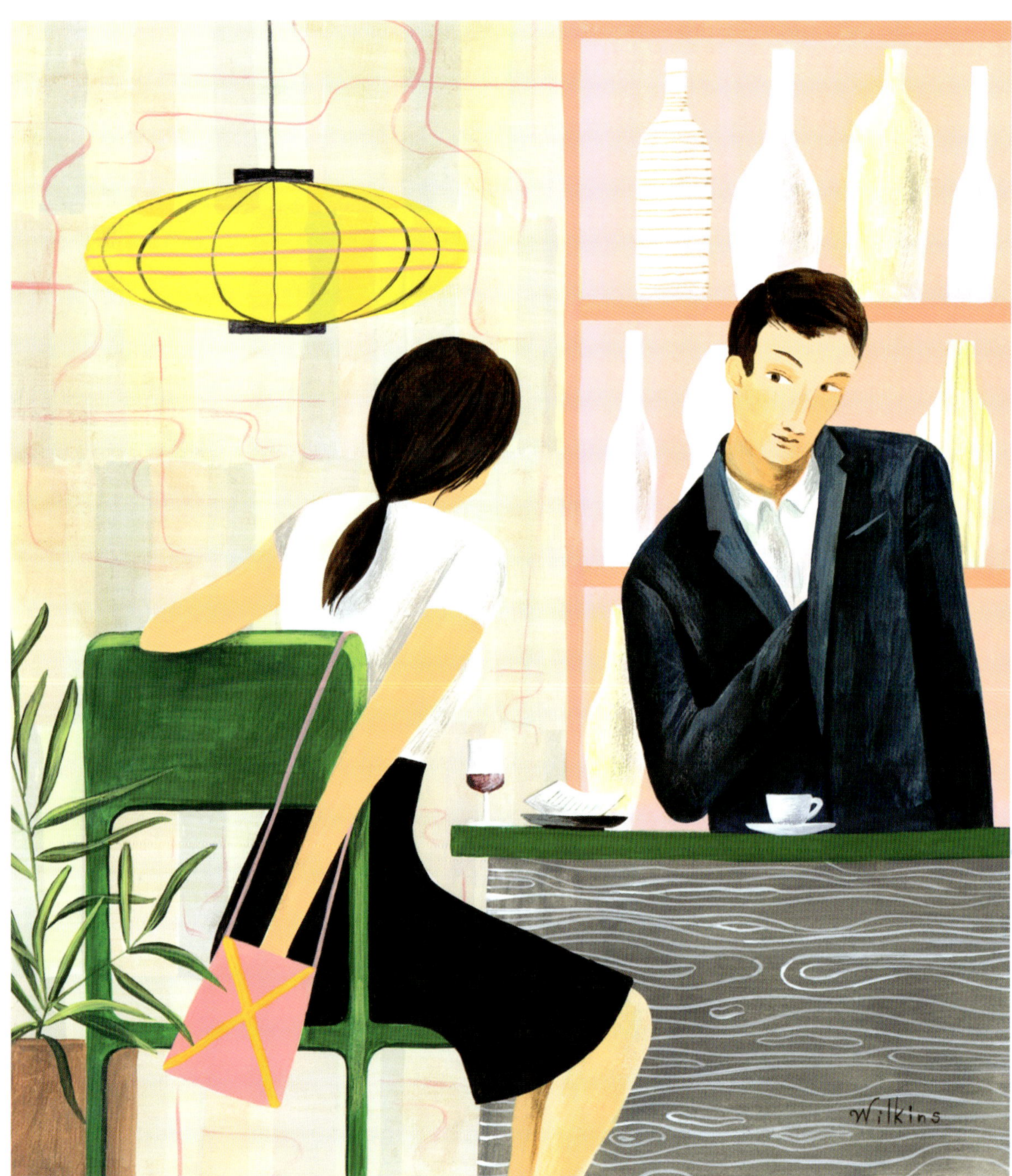

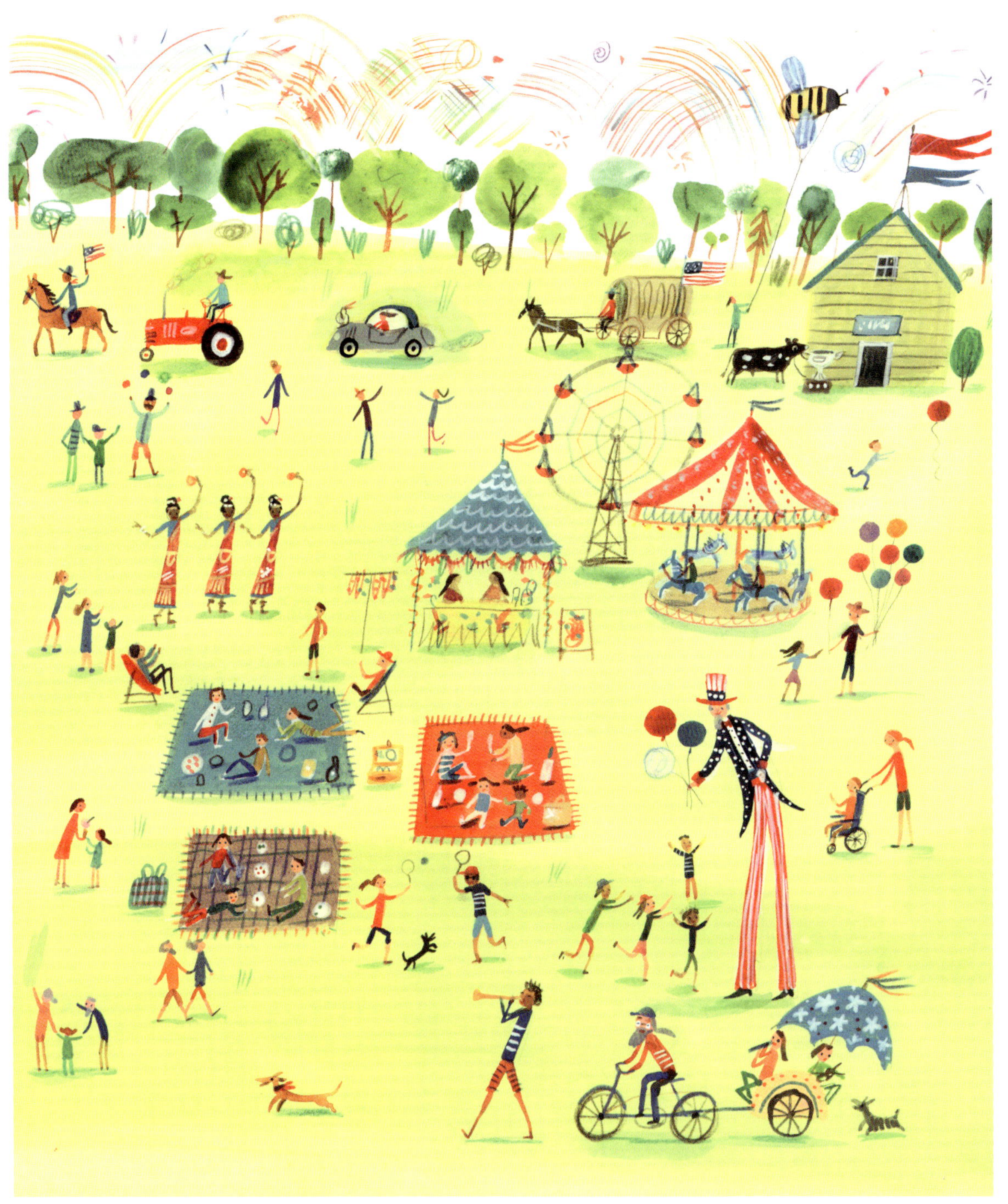

GISELLE POTTER

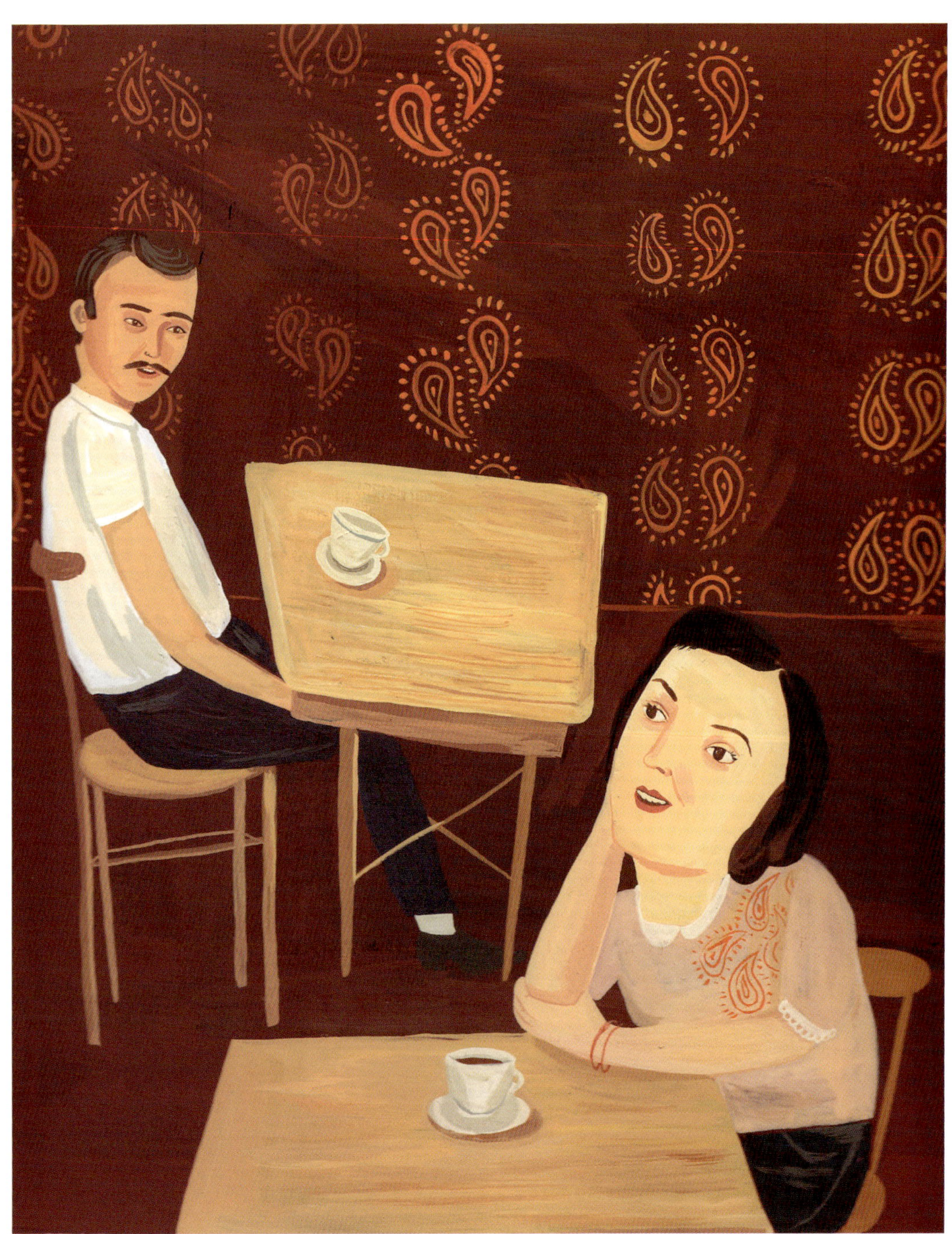

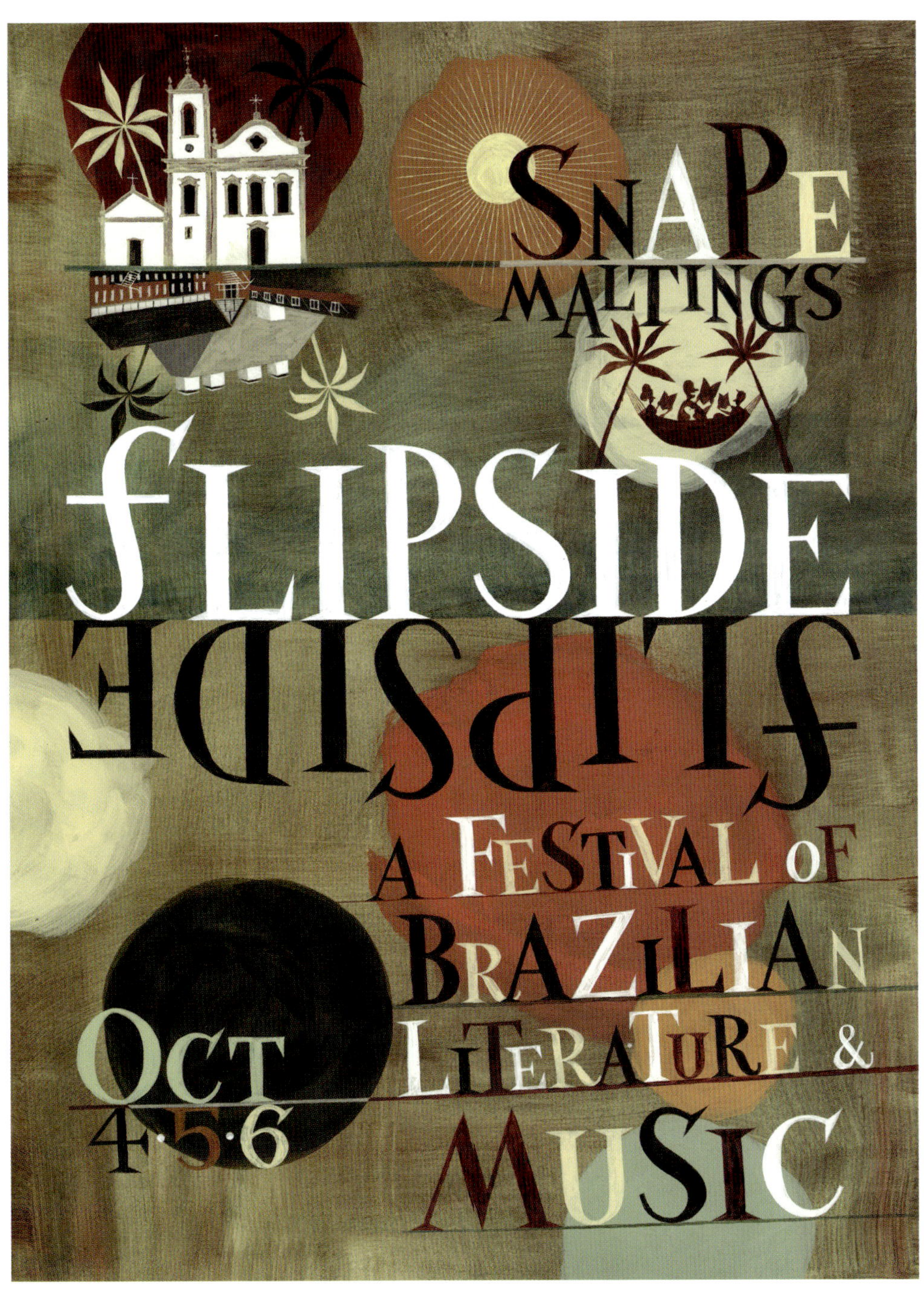
SNAPE
MALTINGS
FLIPSIDE
FLIPSIDE
A FESTIVAL OF
BRAZILIAN
LITERATURE &
MUSIC
OCT
4·5·6

NARDA LEBO
NARDALEBO.COM | THOSE3REPS.COM

www.**margaretberg**art.com 310.753.1595

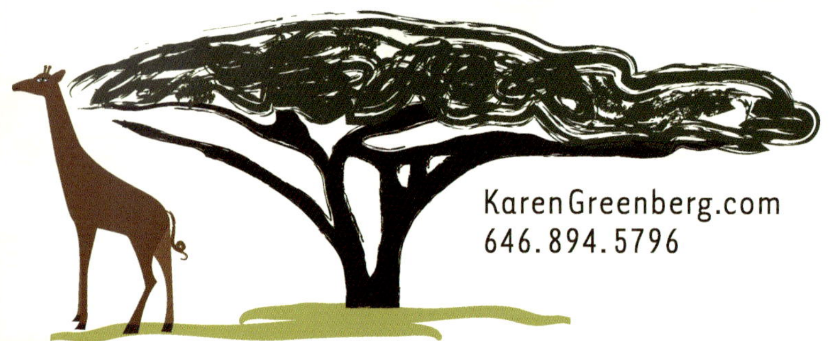

KarenGreenberg.com
646.894.5796

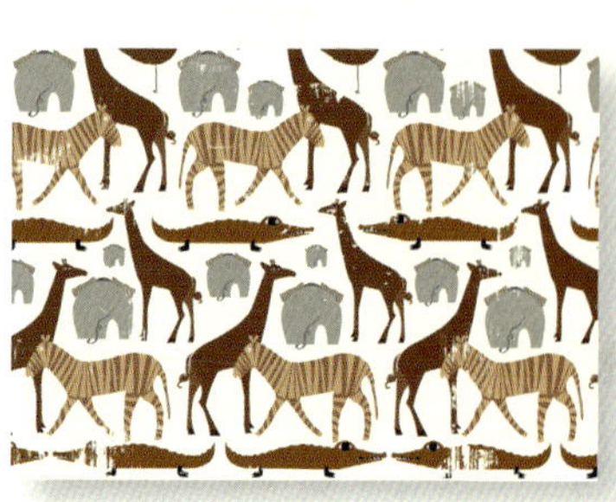

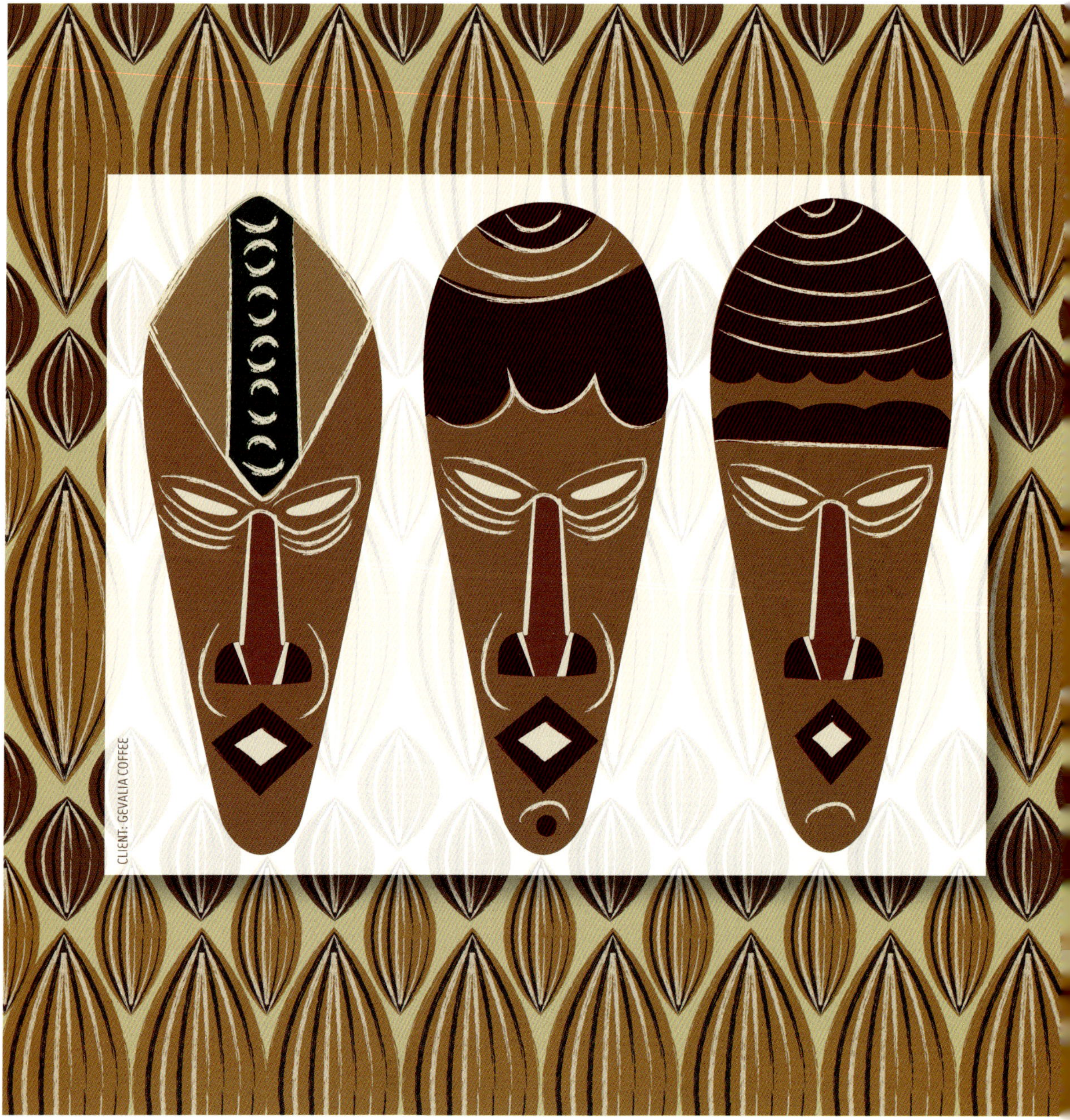

CLIENT: GEVALIA COFFEE

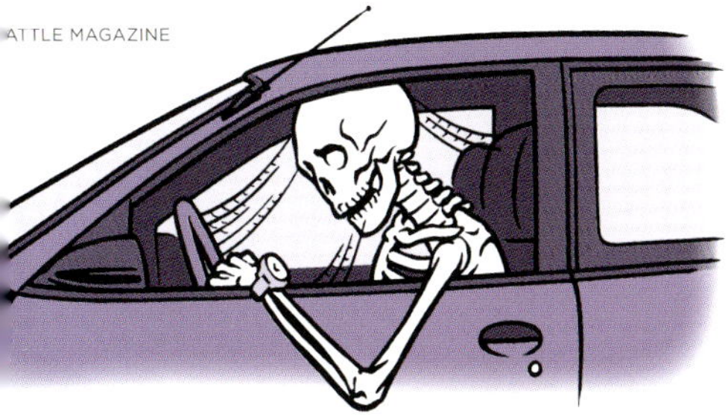

Larry Jost   www.larryjostillustration.com

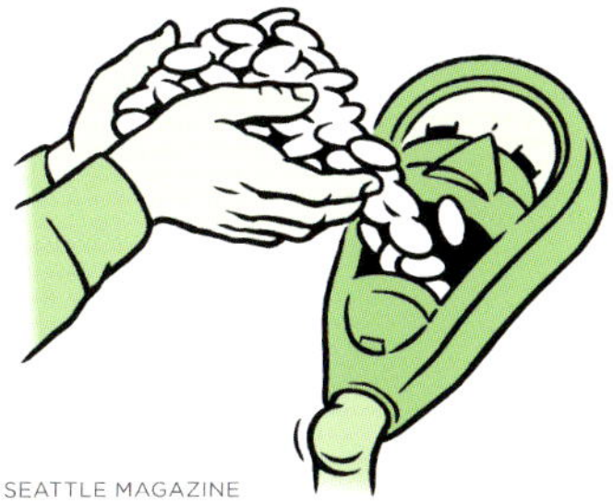

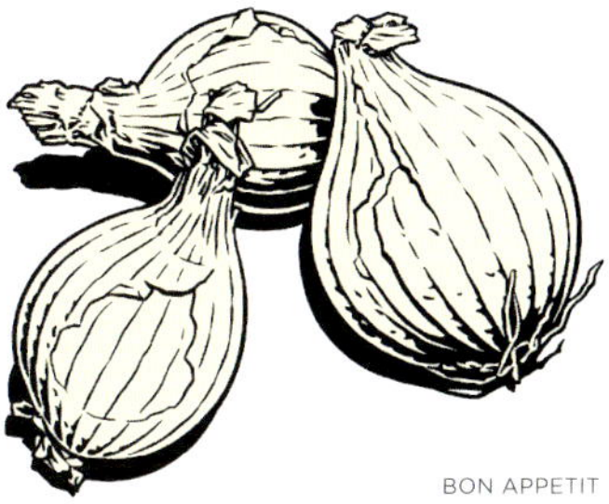

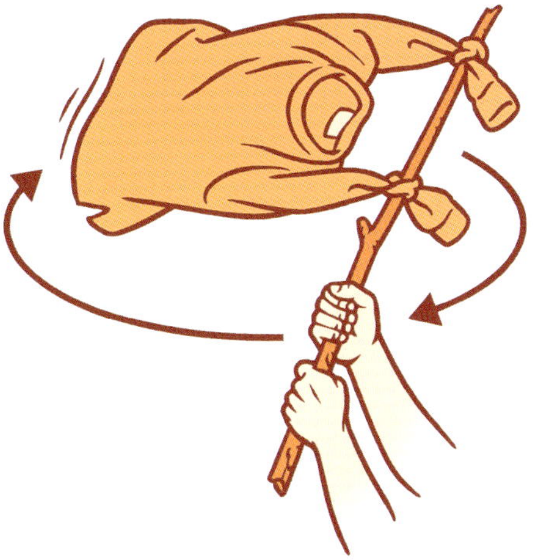

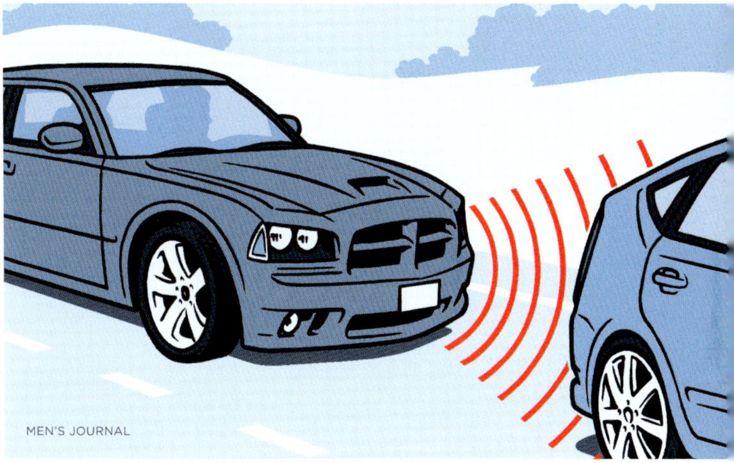

Represented by Susan and Co. • 206 232 7873 • www.susanandco.com

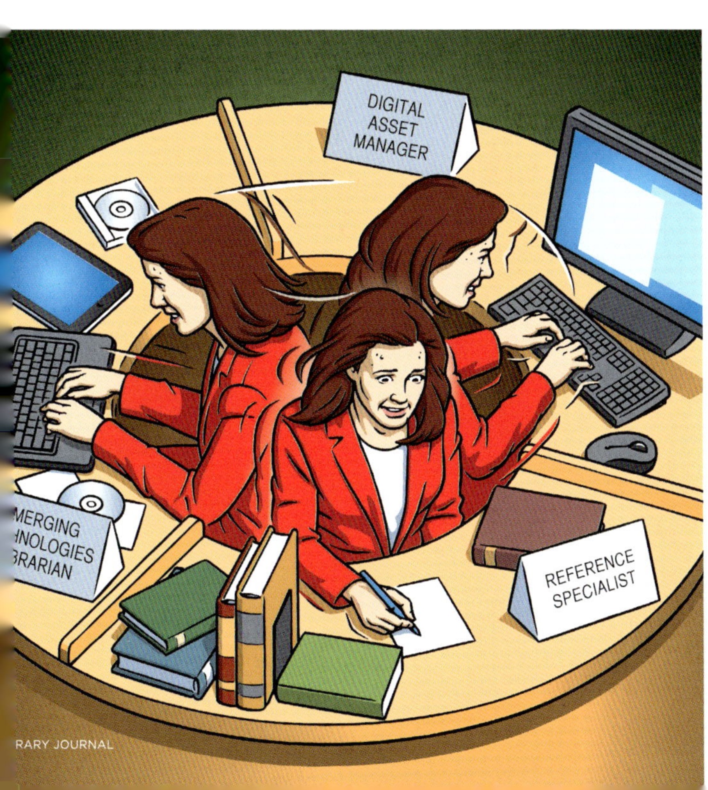

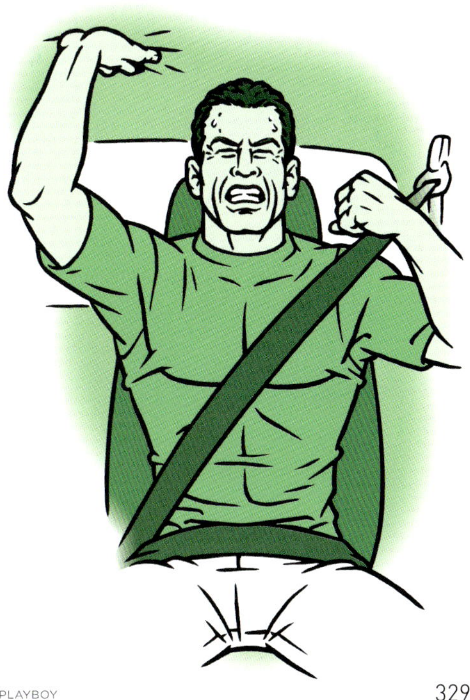

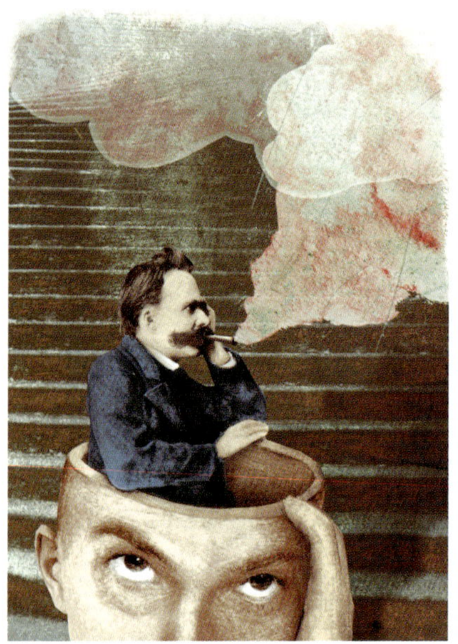

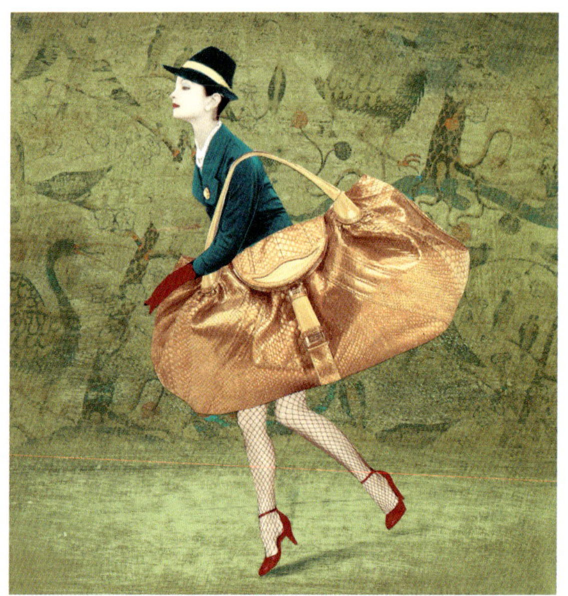

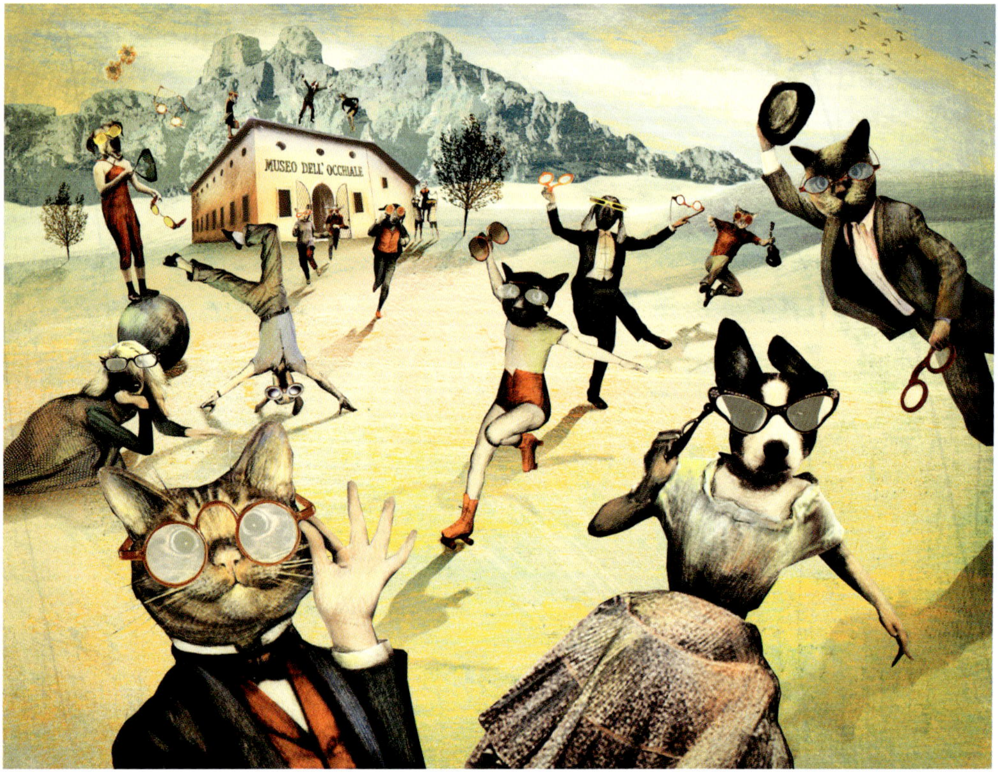

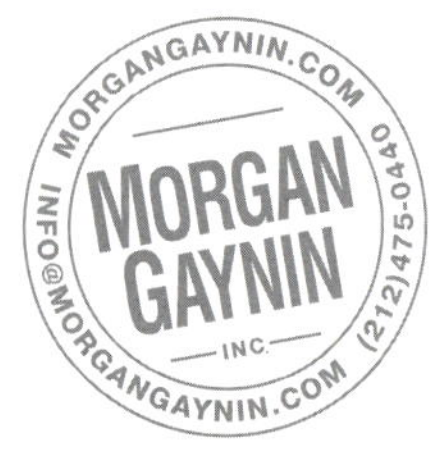

ALE + ALE

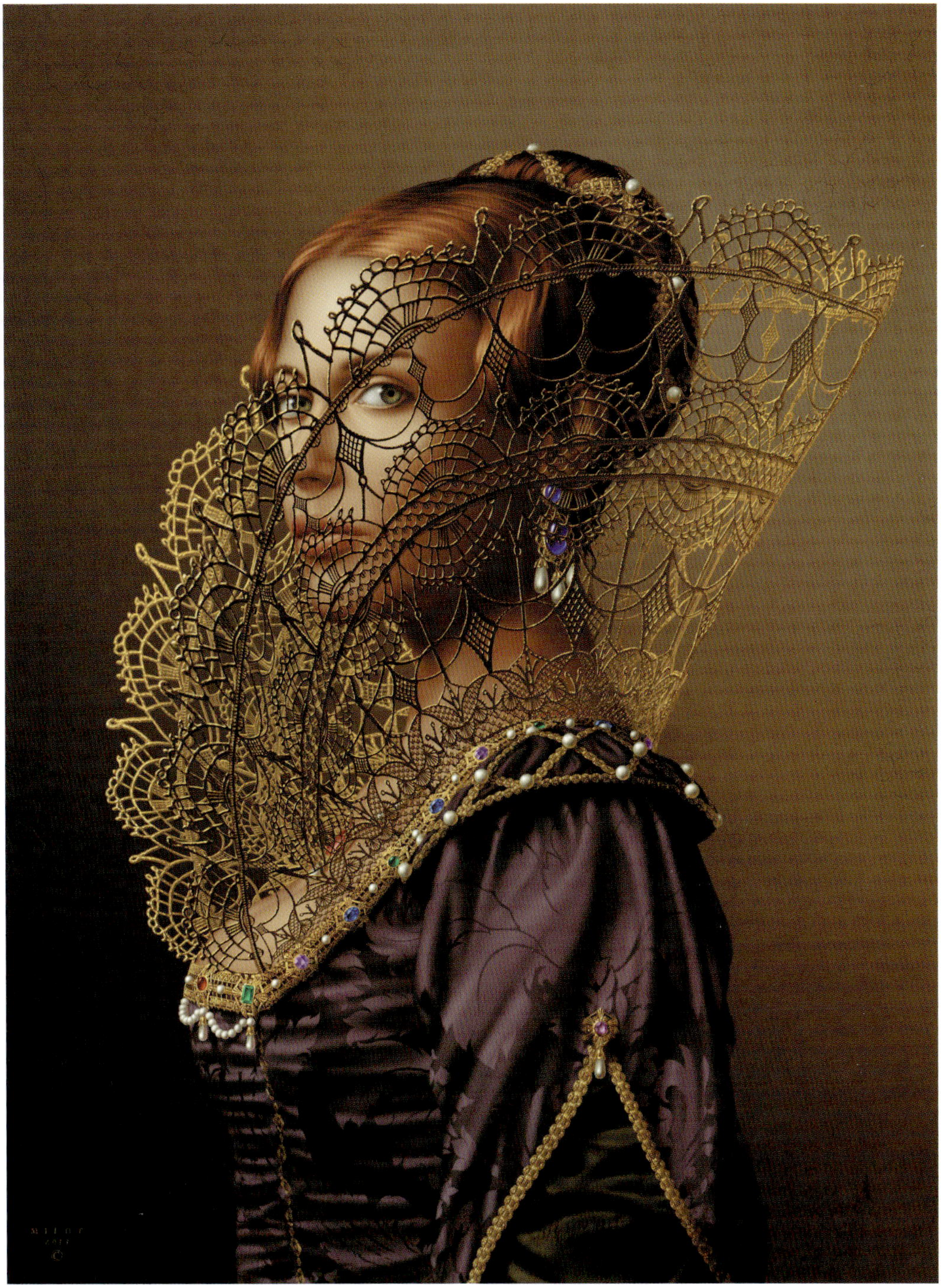

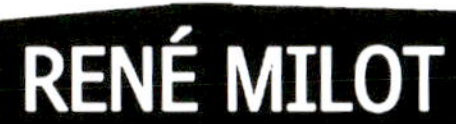
RENÉ MILOT

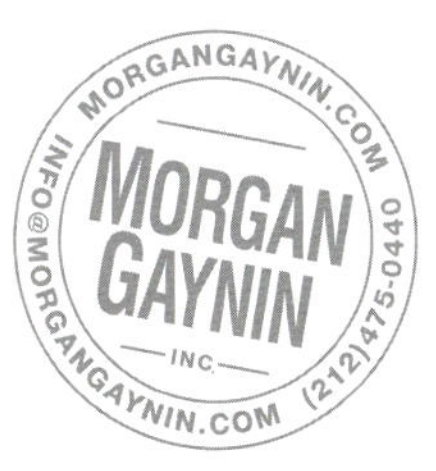
MORGANGAYNIN.COM
INFO@MORGANGAYNIN.COM
MORGAN GAYNIN INC.
(212) 475-0440

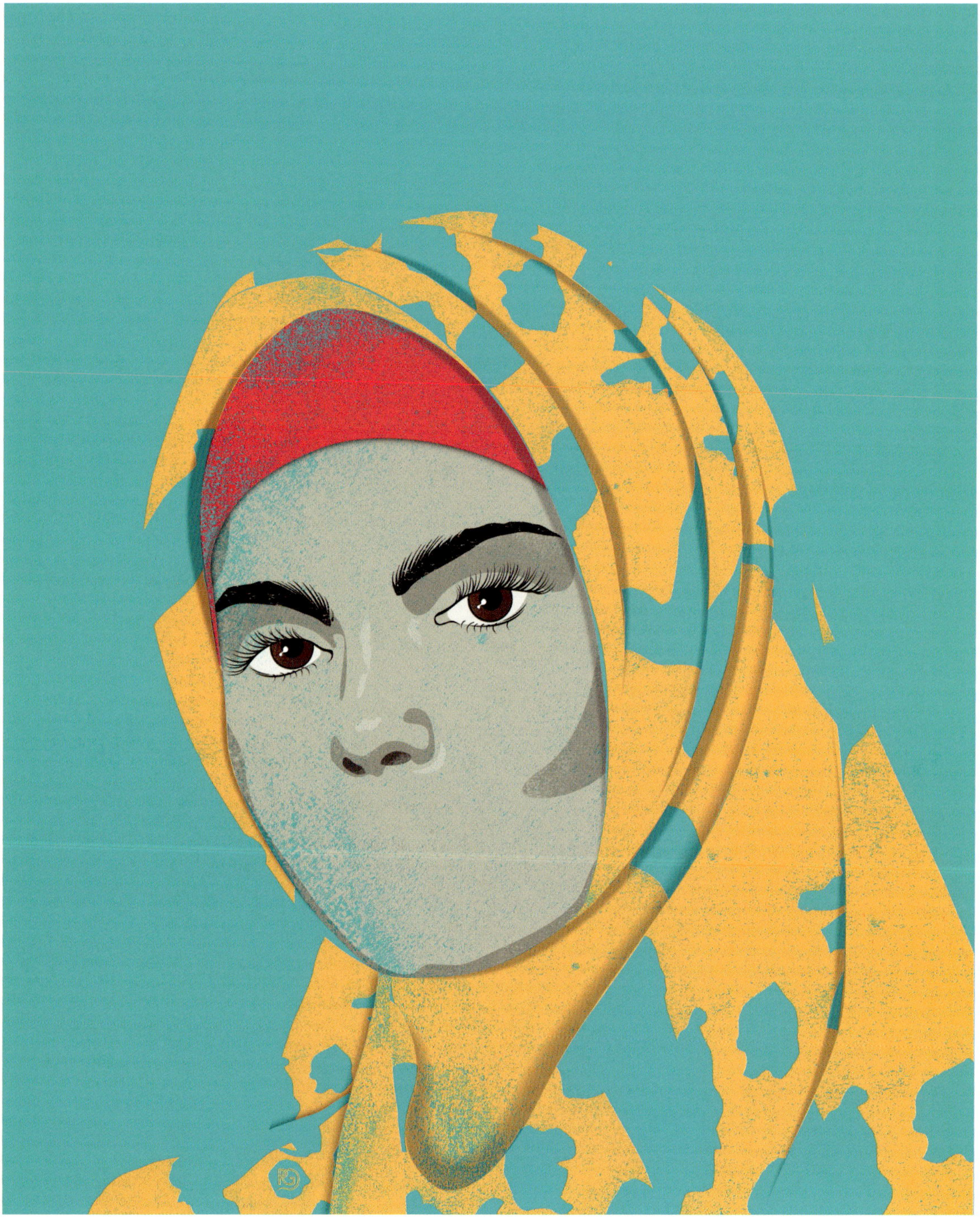

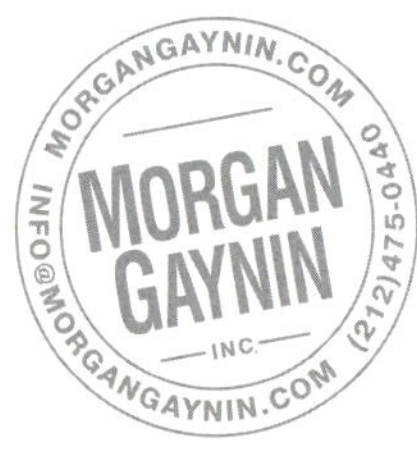

PAUL GARLAND

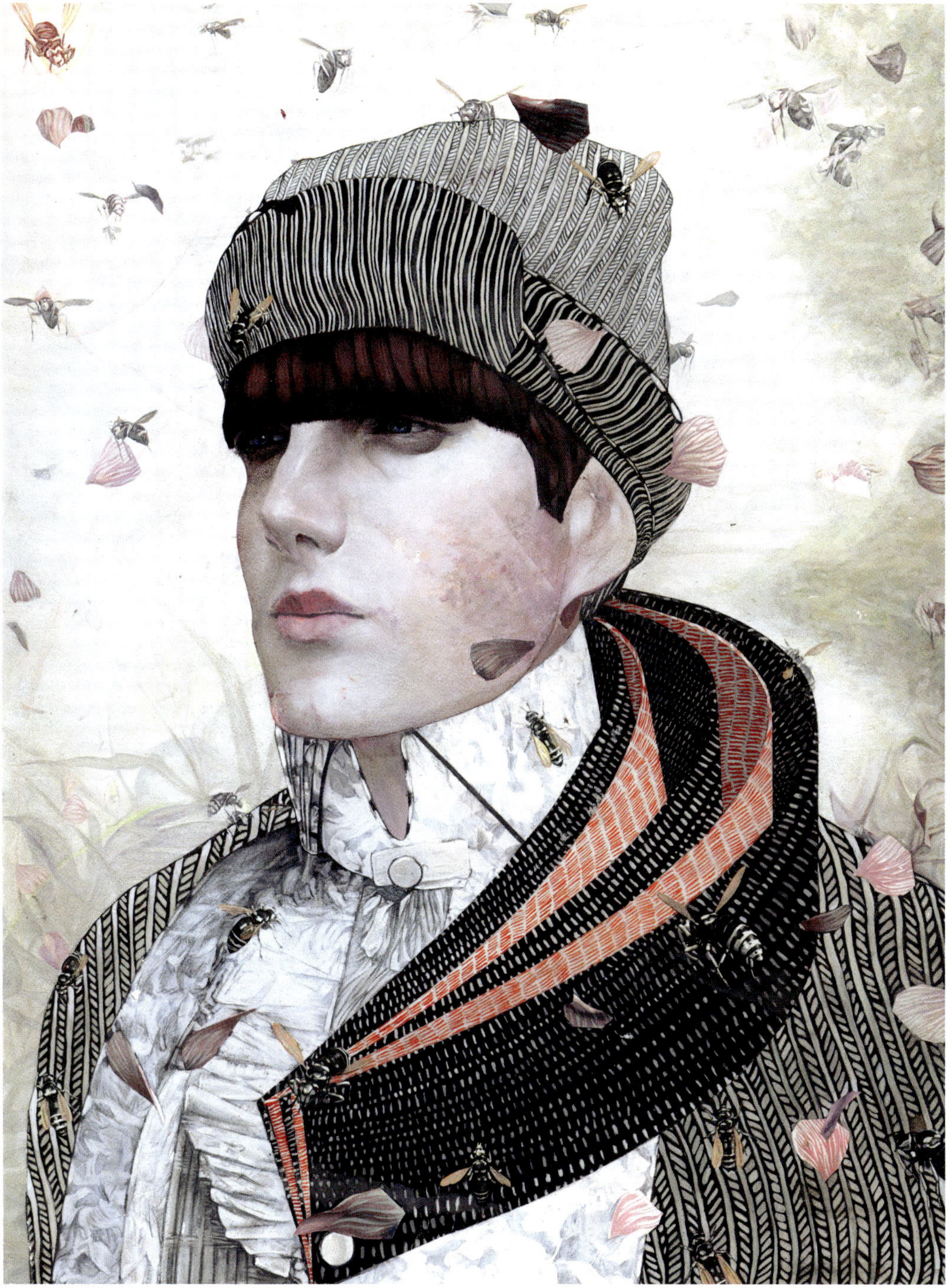

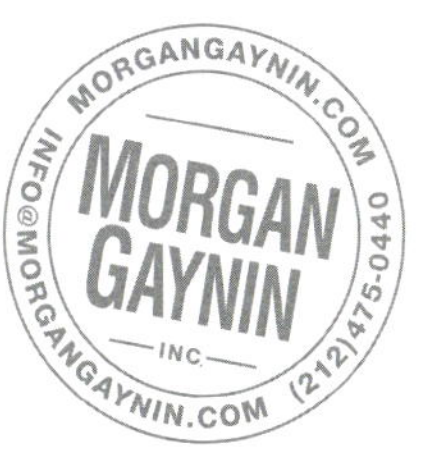

STEVEN TABBUTT

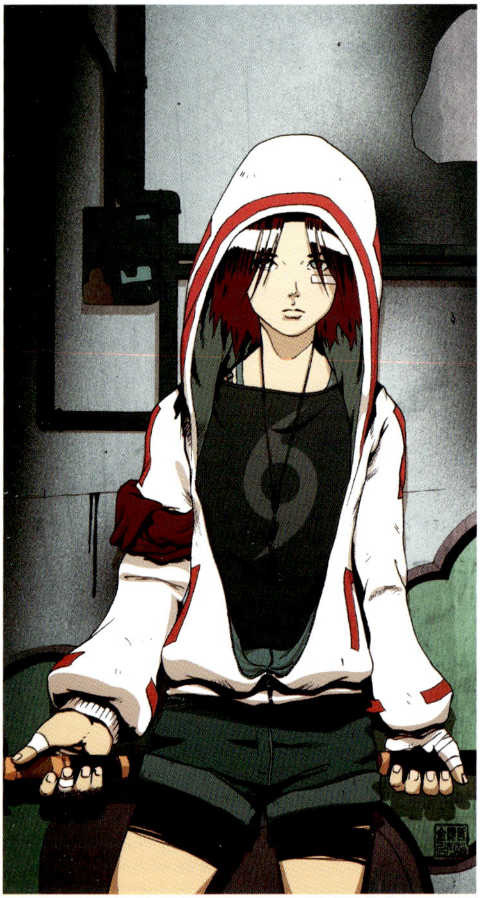

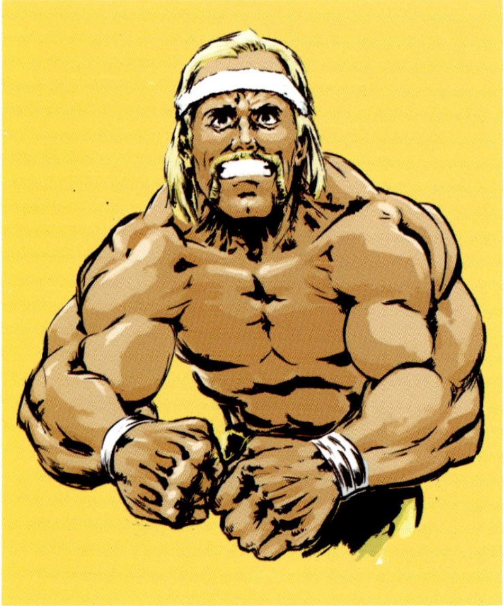

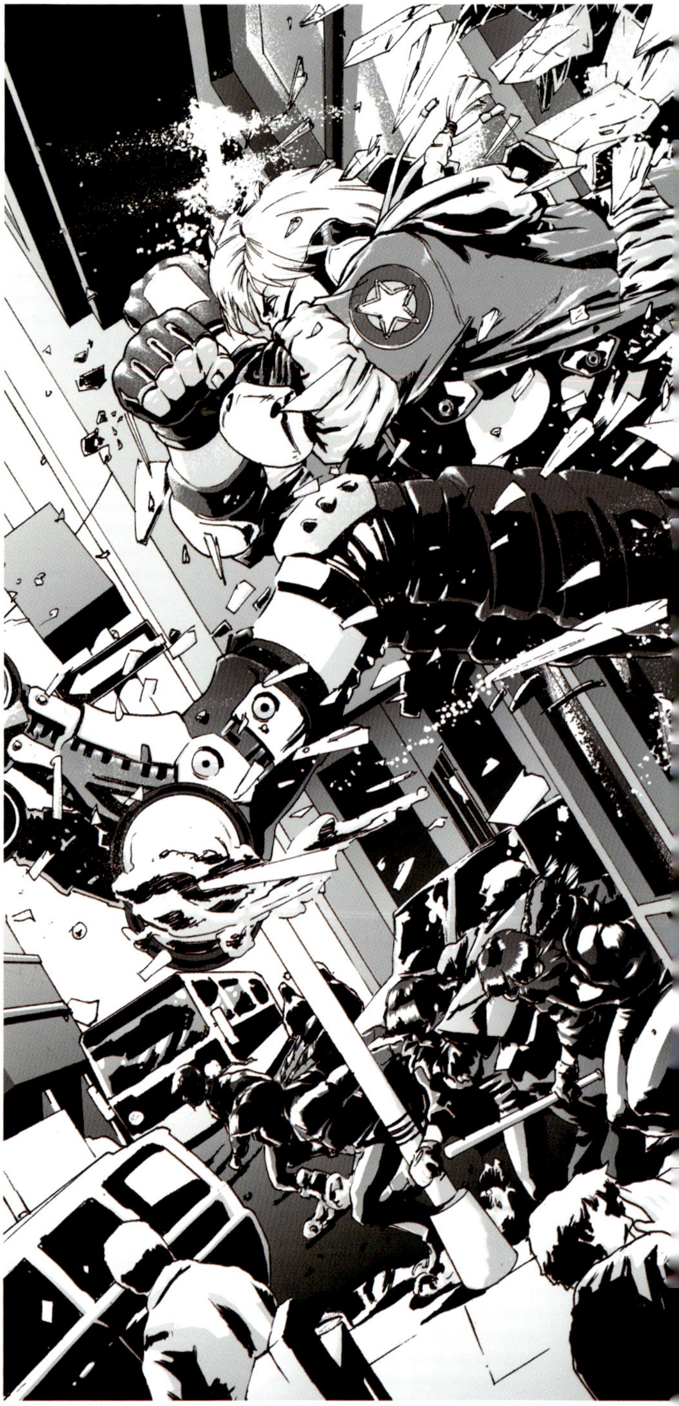

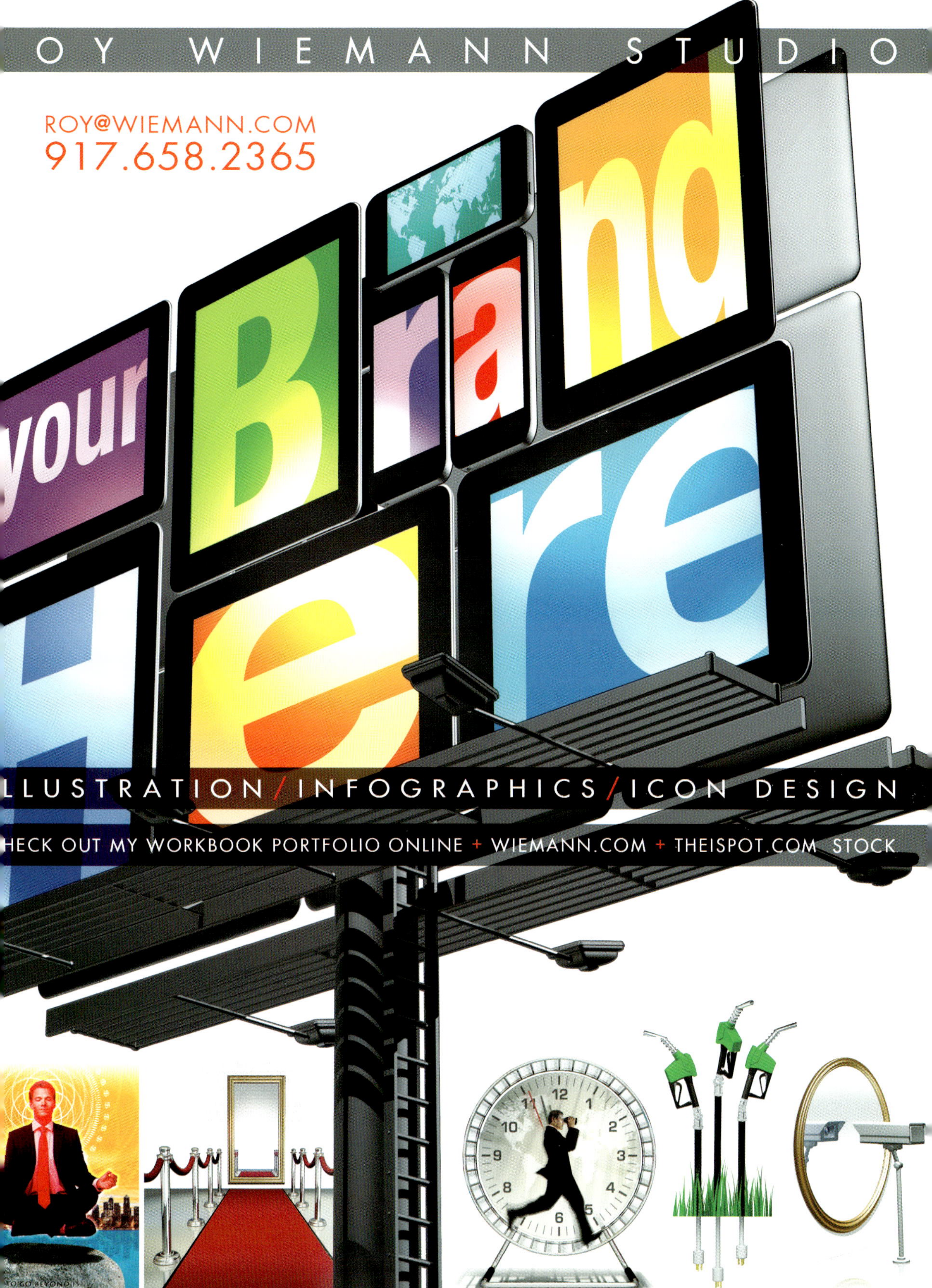
OY WIEMANN STUDIO
ROY@WIEMANN.COM
917.658.2365
your Brand Here
ILLUSTRATION / INFOGRAPHICS / ICON DESIGN
HECK OUT MY WORKBOOK PORTFOLIO ONLINE + WIEMANN.COM + THEISPOT.COM STOCK

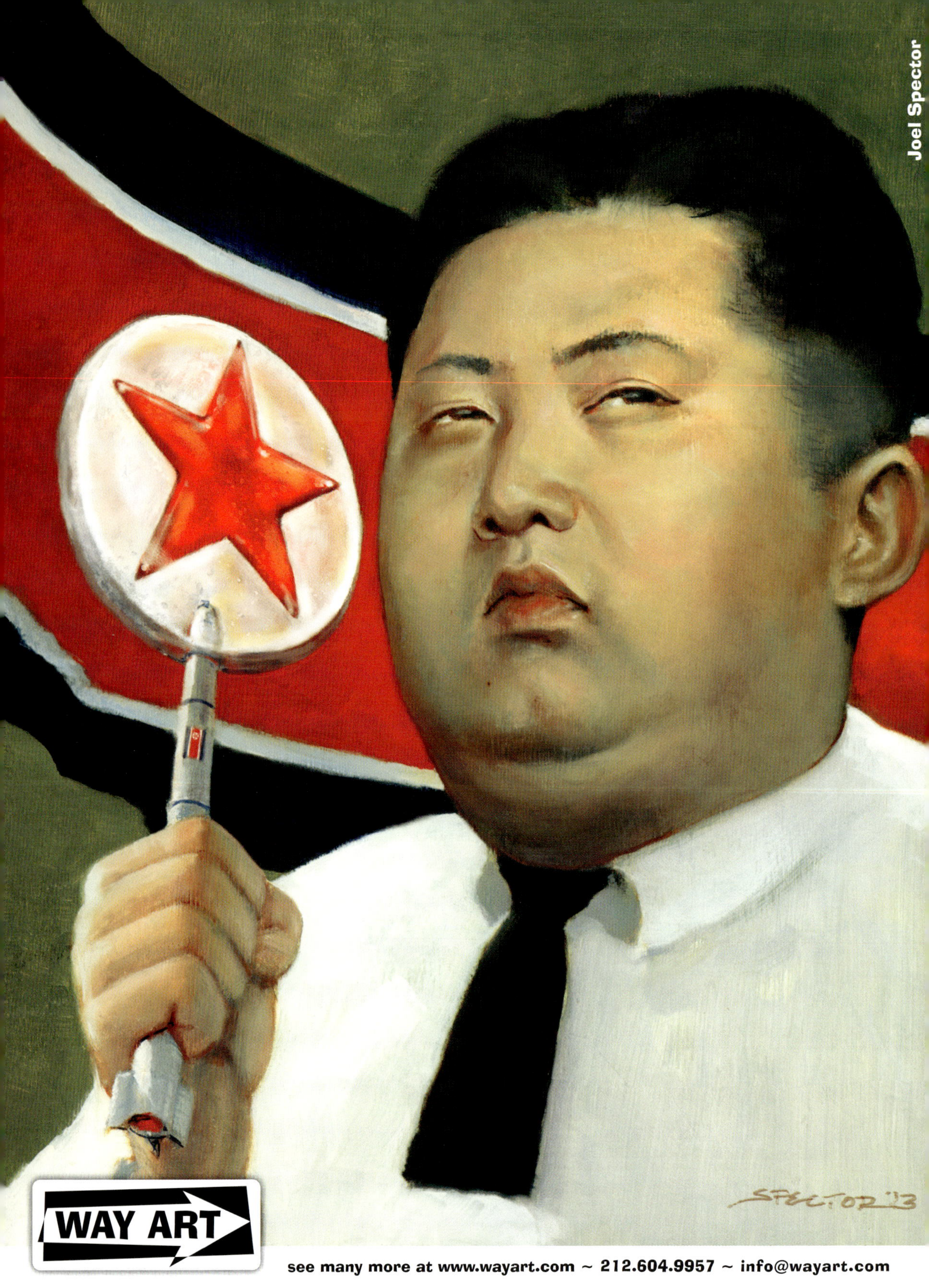
Joel Spector
WAY ART
SPECTOR '13

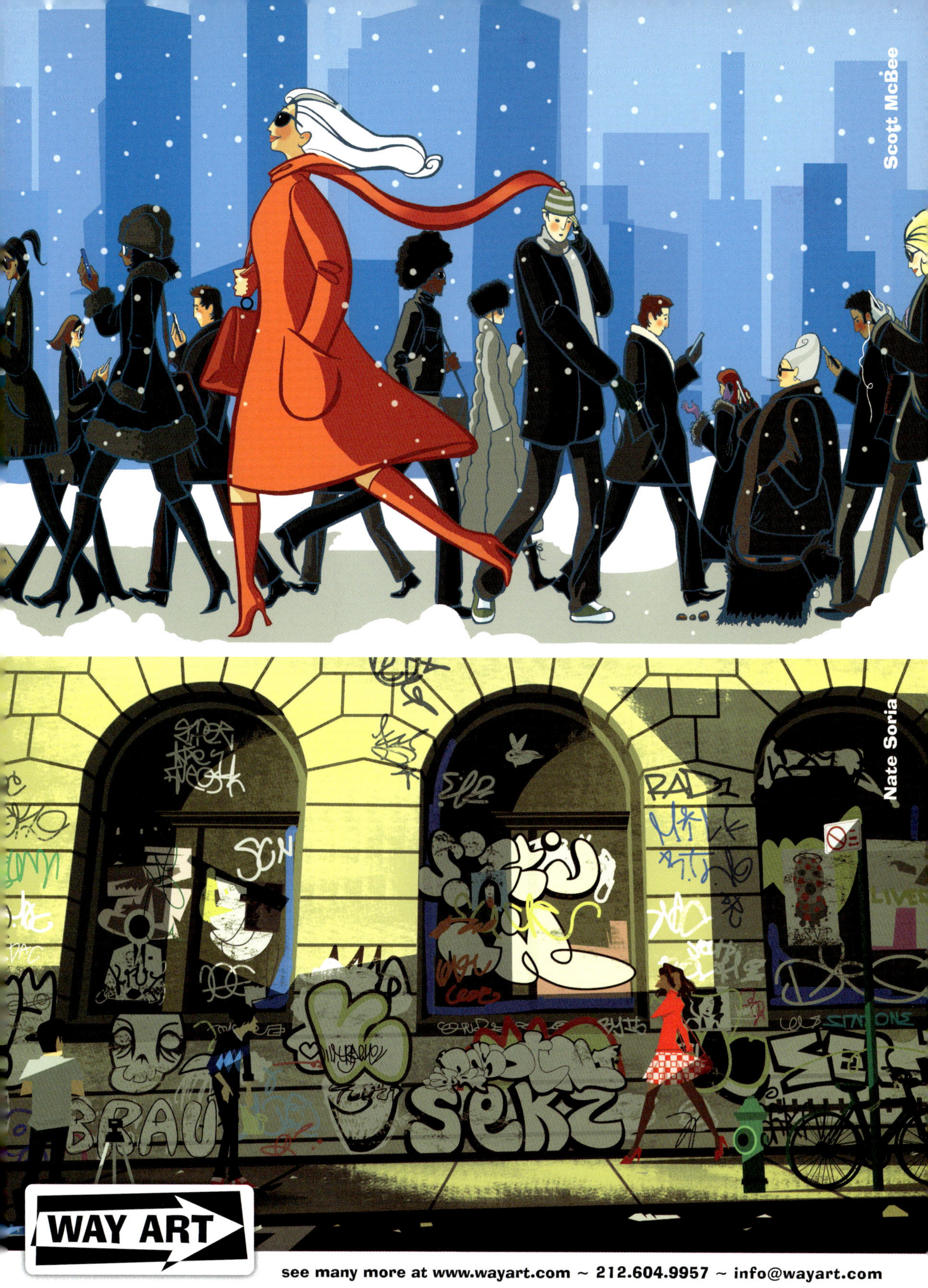

Scott McBee
Nate Soria
WAY ART
see many more at www.wayart.com ~ 212.604.9957 ~ info@wayart.com

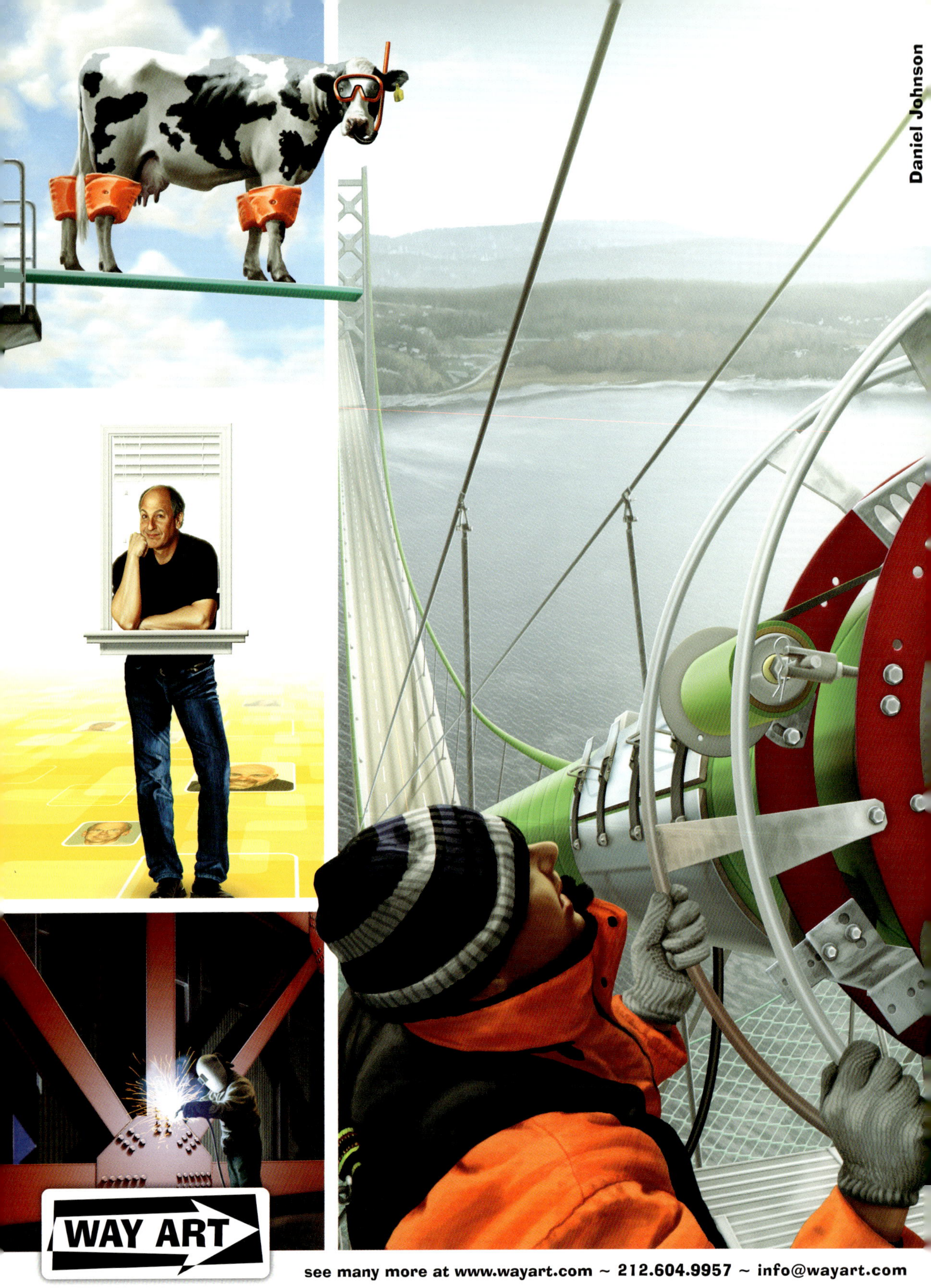
Daniel Johnson
WAY ART
see many more at www.wayart.com ~ 212.604.9957 ~ info@wayart.com

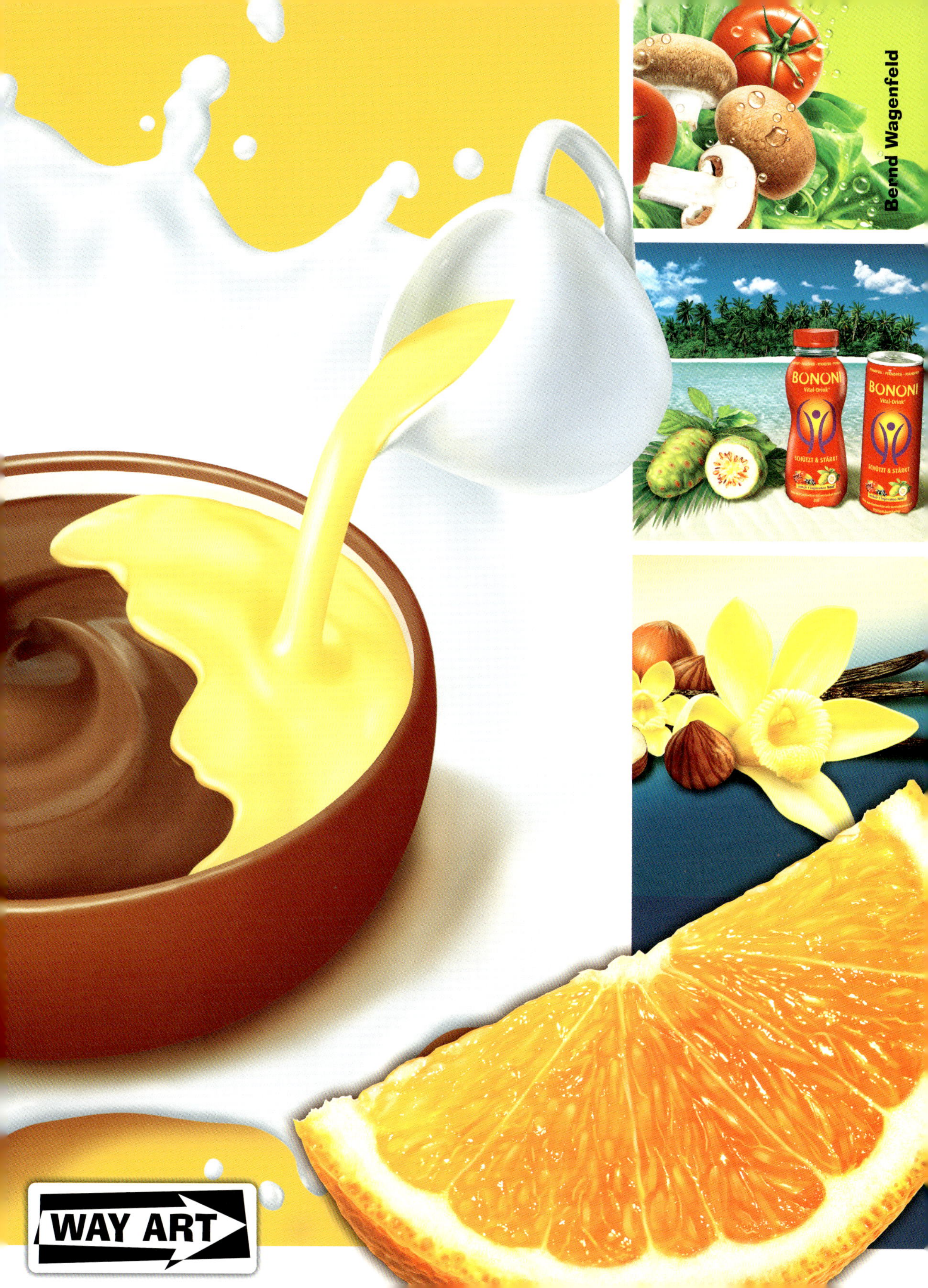

Bernd Wagenfeld
BONONI
BONONI
WAY ART

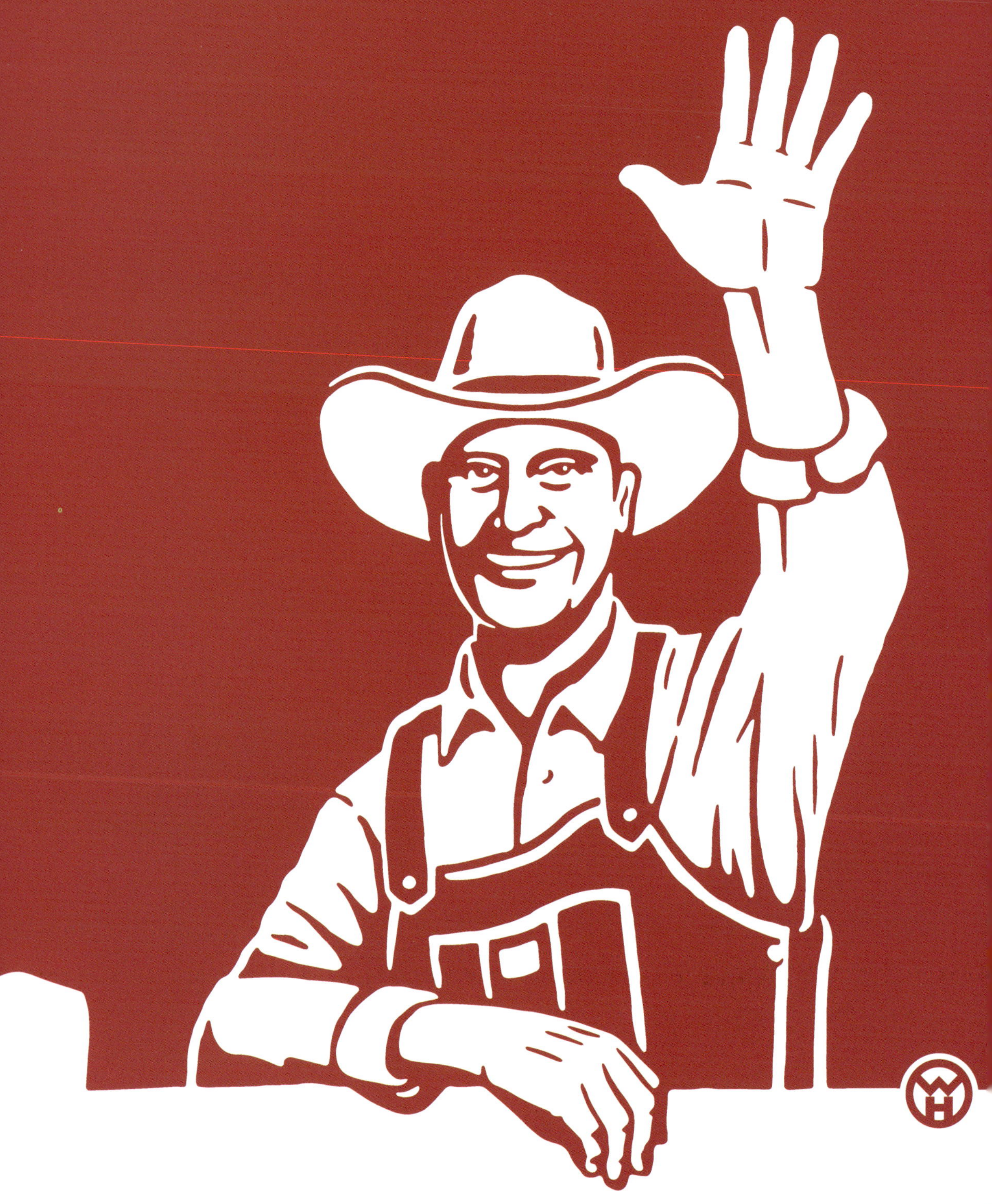

Chuck Gonzales

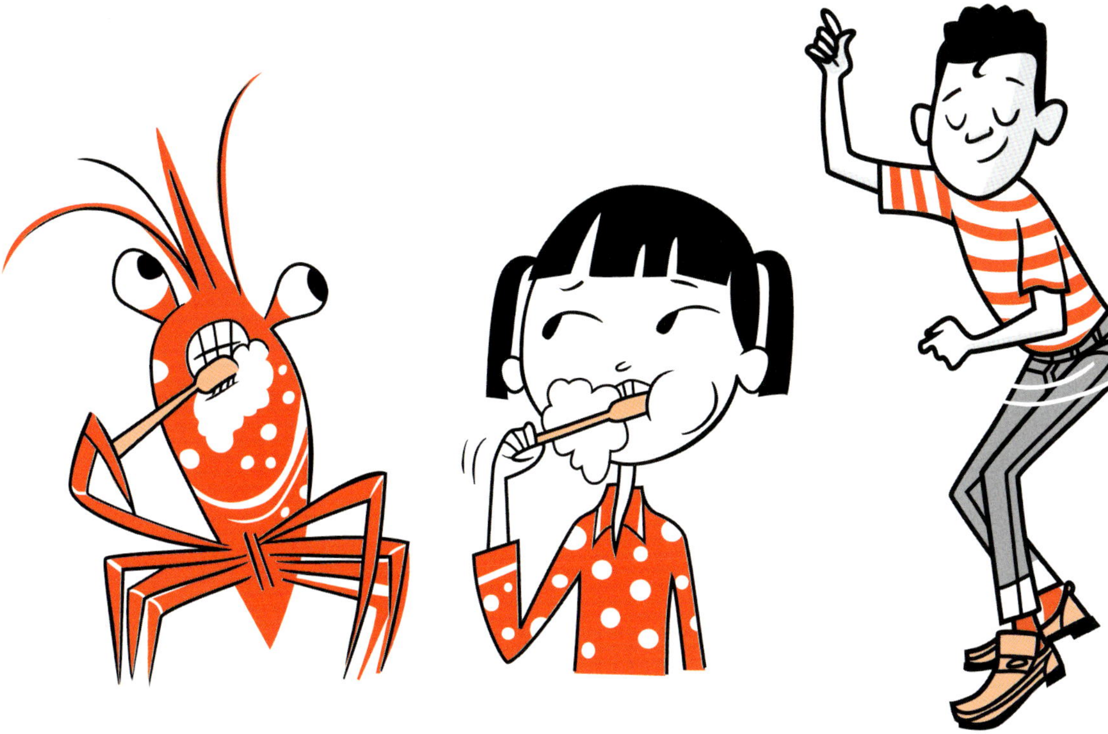

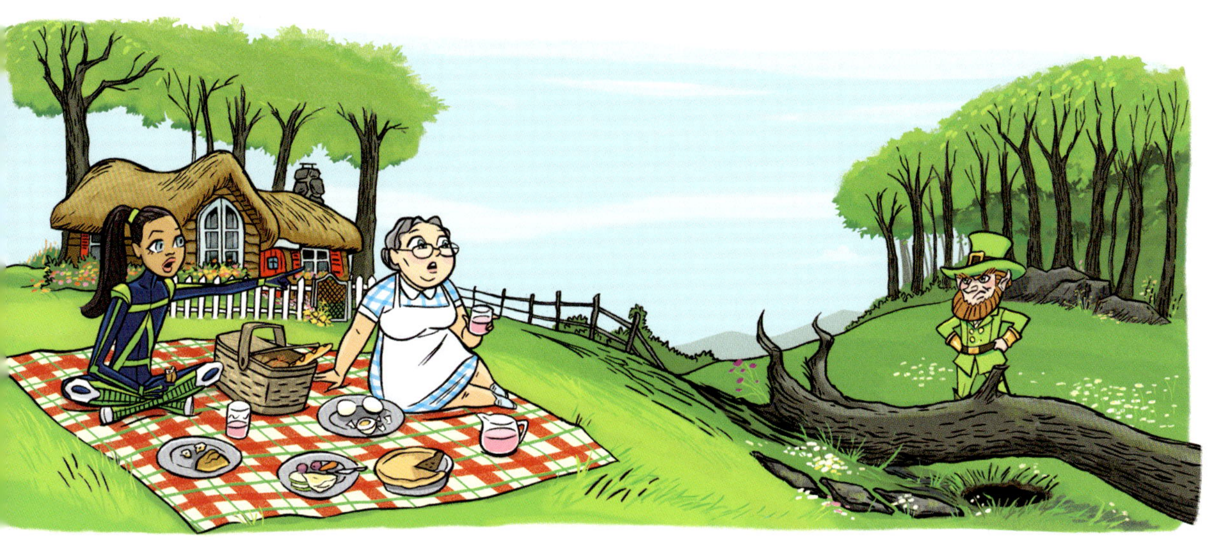

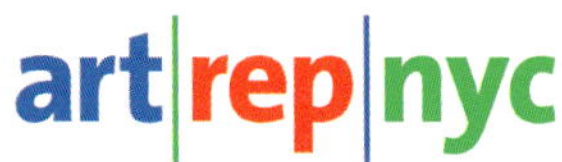

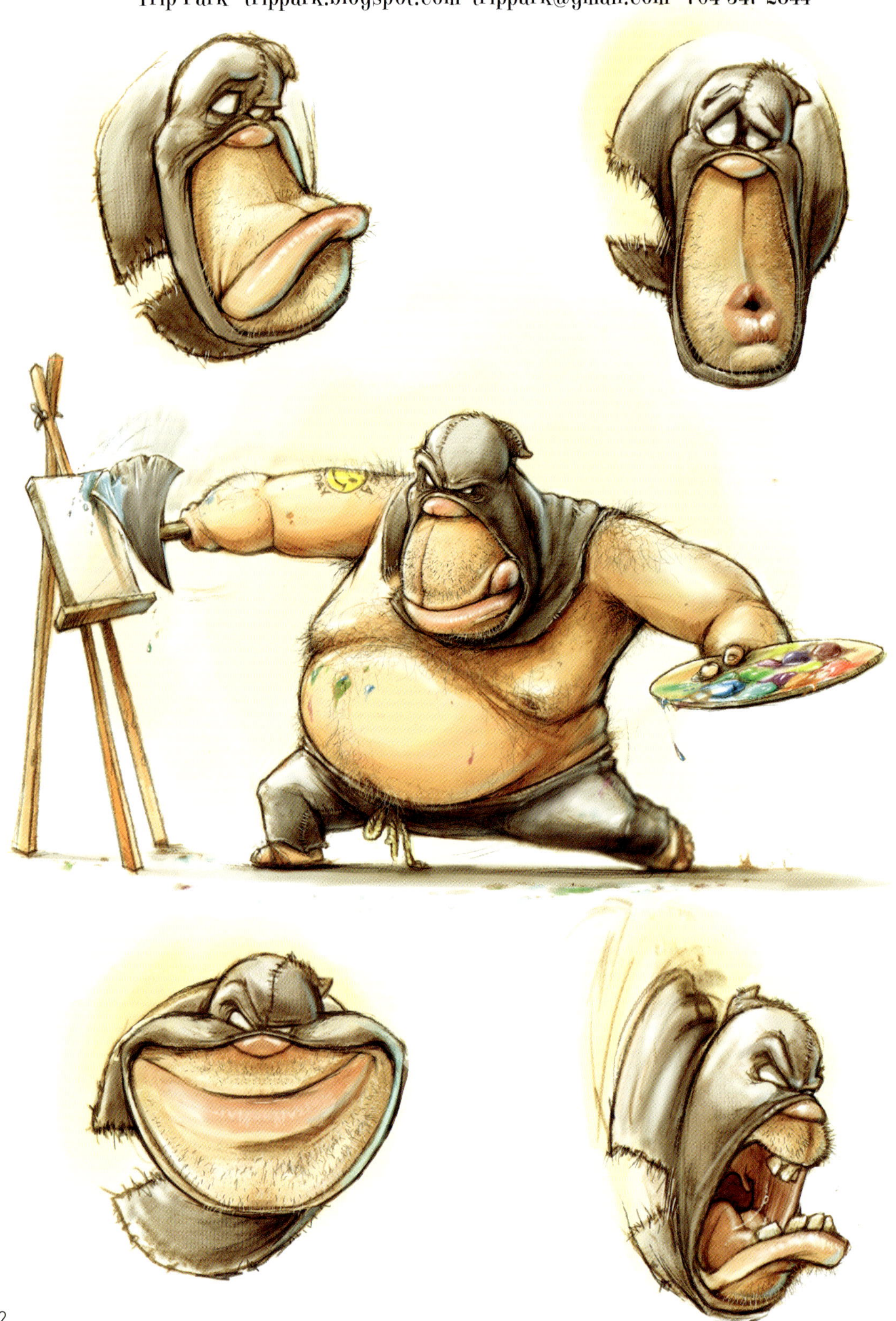

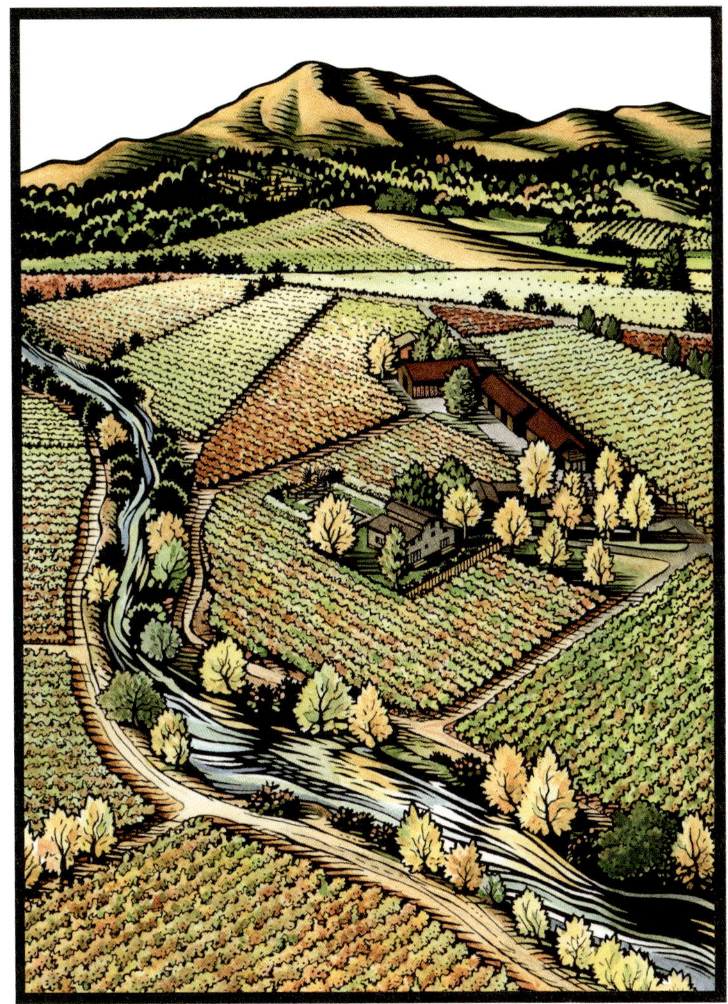

Honig Vineyard & Winery, Napa Valley

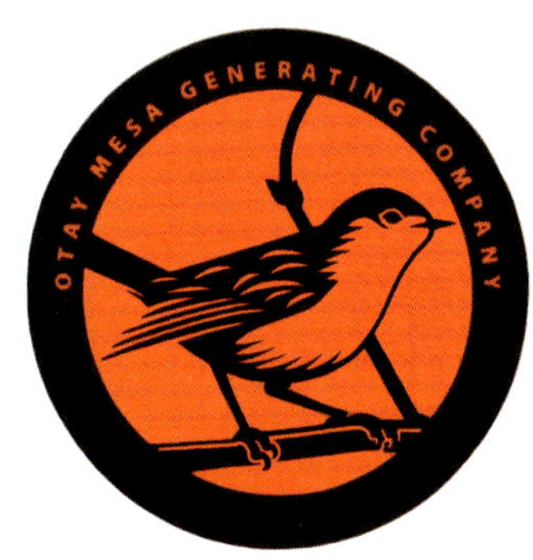

Solar Farm Mascot Decal

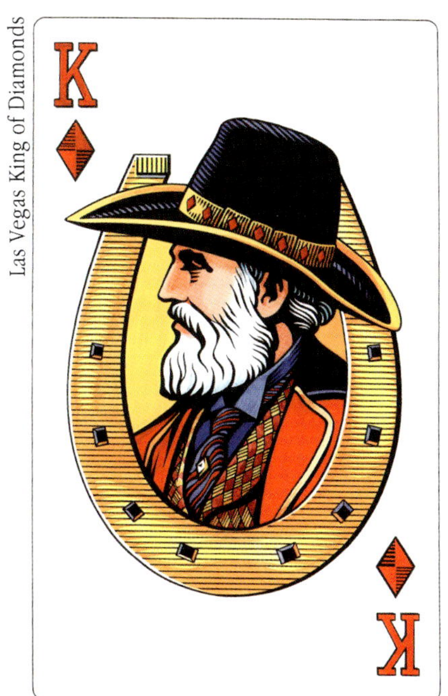

Las Vegas King of Diamonds

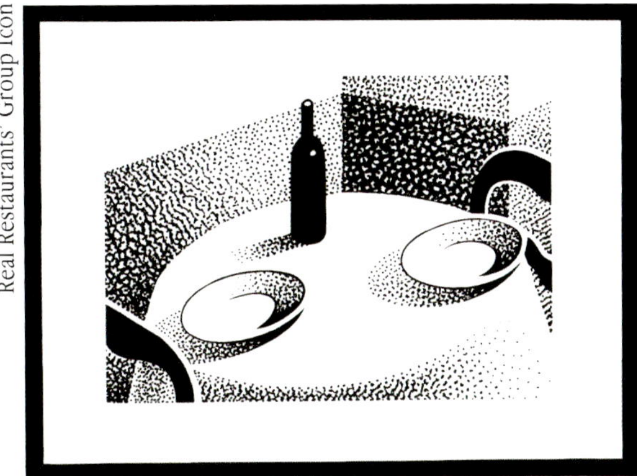

Real Restaurants' Group Icon

Yosemite National Park Souvenir Stamp

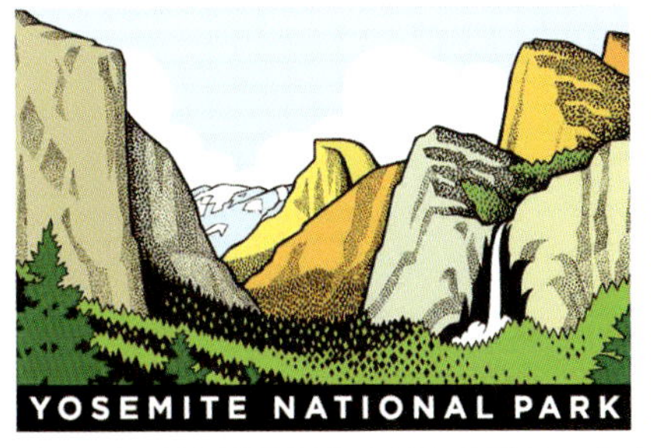

tom hennessy • www.hennessyart.com • tom@hennessyart.com • tel: 707 559 5341

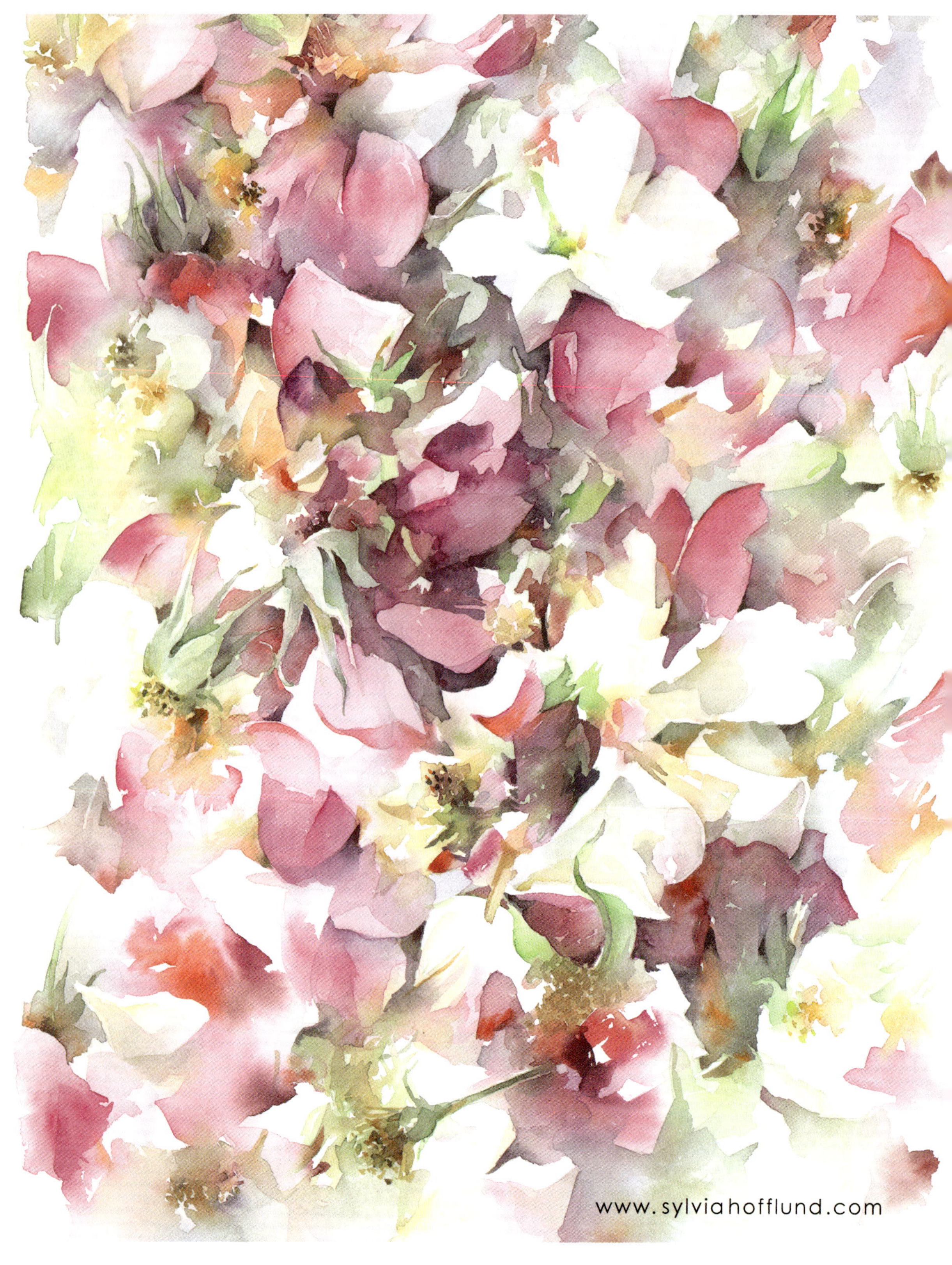

www.sylviahofflund.com

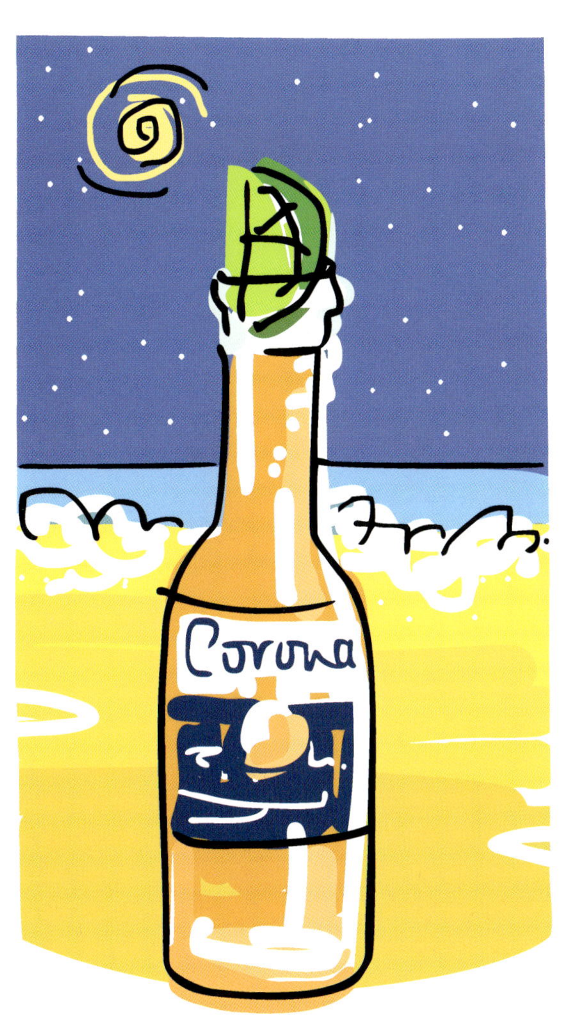
Corona

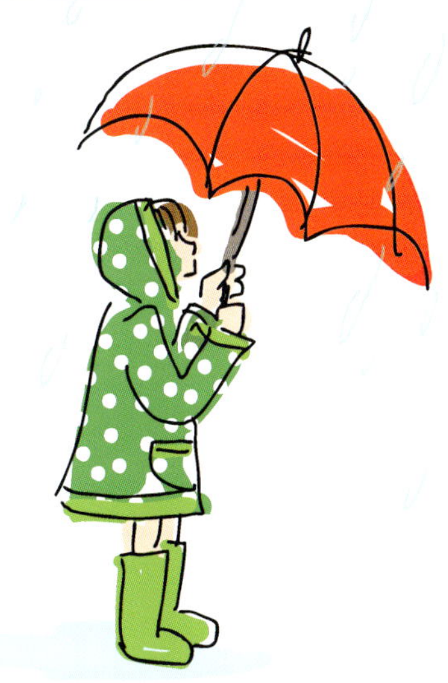

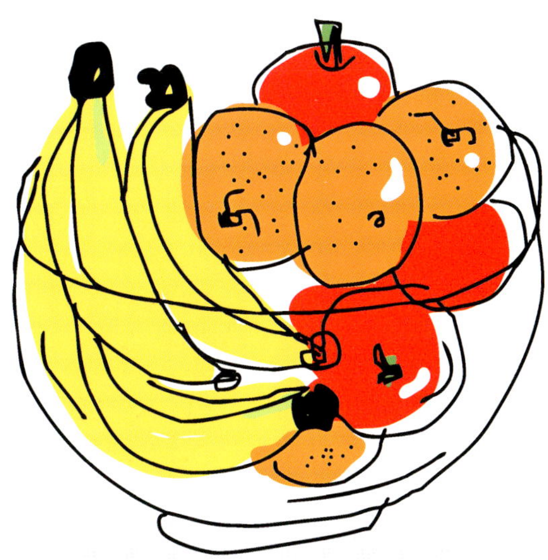

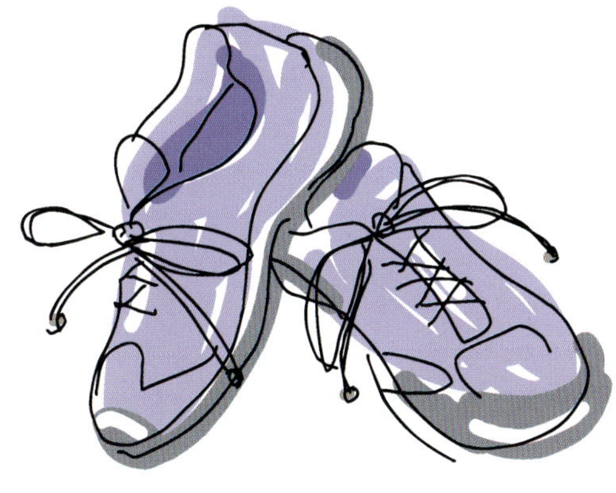

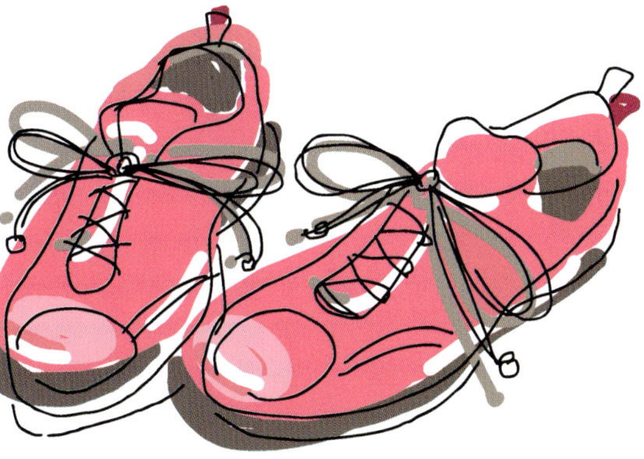

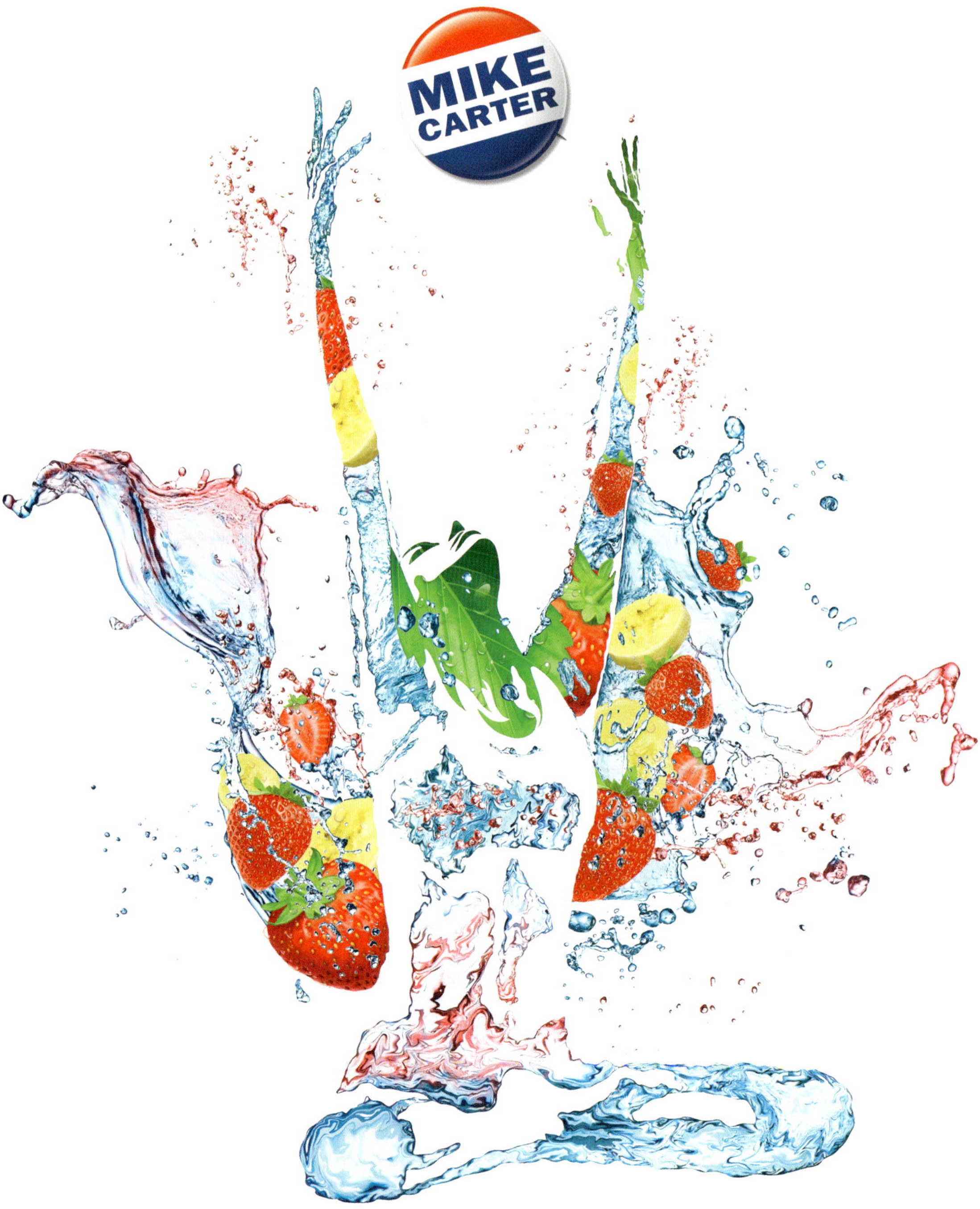

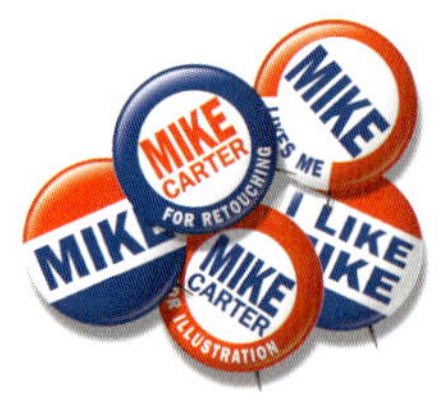

★ **MIKE CARTER STUDIO INC.** ★
416 425 2578 ★ ilikemike@mikecarterstudio.com
www.mikecarterstudio.com

346

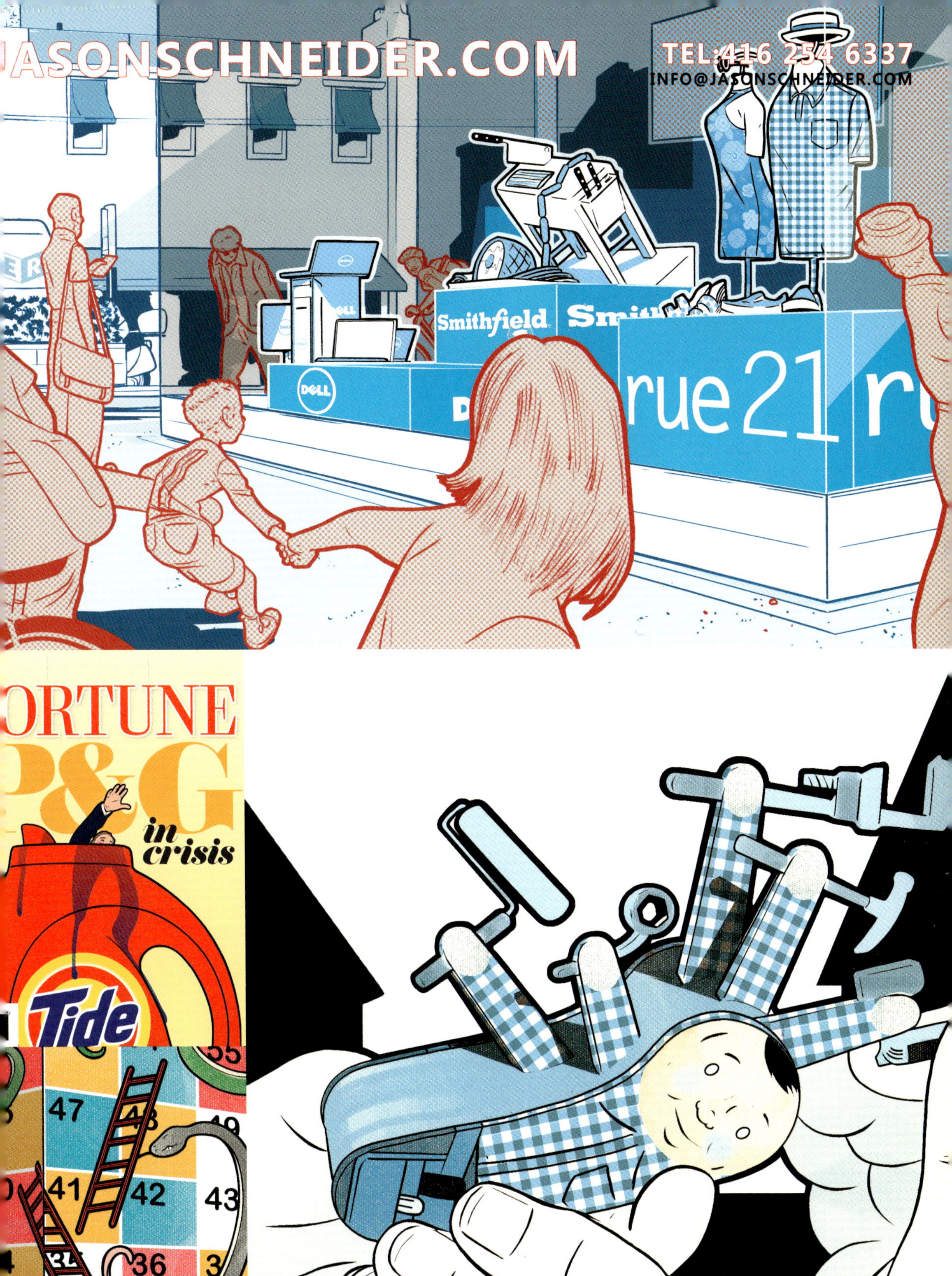
JASONSCHNEIDER.COM
TEL:416 254 6337
INFO@JASONSCHNEIDER.COM
Smithfield
Smith
rue21
ru
DELL
FORTUNE
P&G
in crisis
Tide
47
41
42
43
36
55

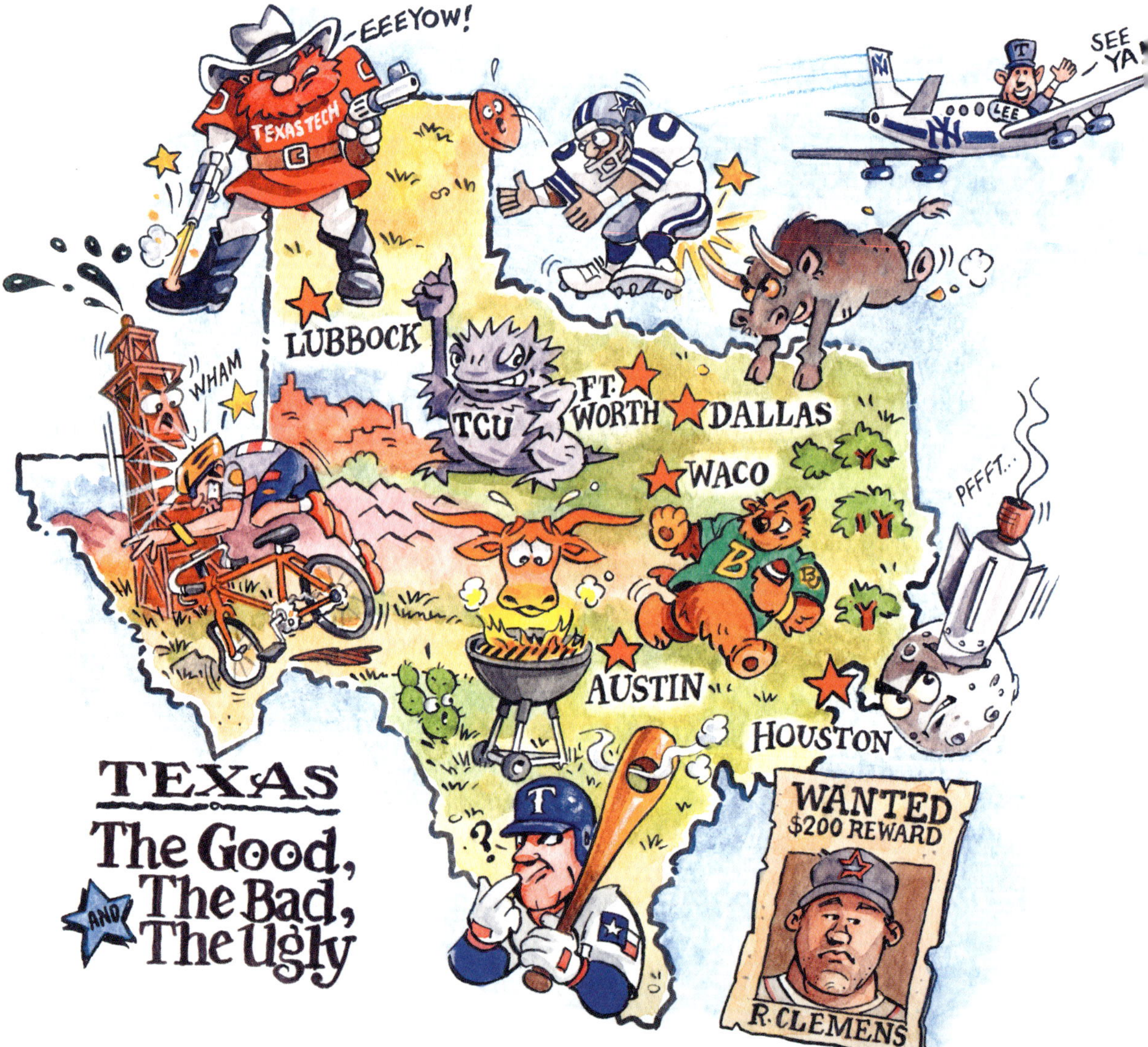

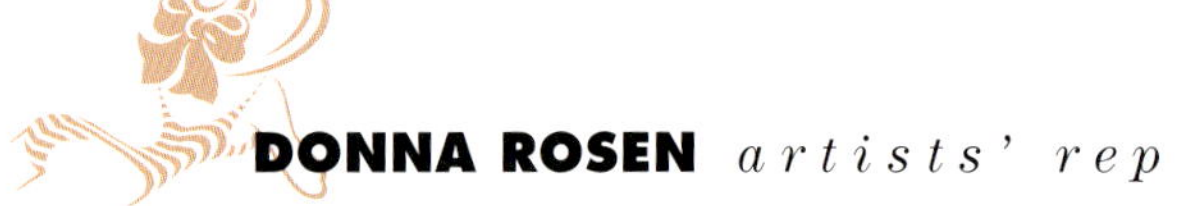

EEEYOW!
TEXAS TECH
SEE YA!
LEE
WHAM
LUBBOCK
TCU
FT. WORTH
DALLAS
WACO
PFFFT...
AUSTIN
HOUSTON
TEXAS
The Good,
The Bad,
The Ugly
AND
T
?
WANTED
$200 REWARD
R. CLEMENS

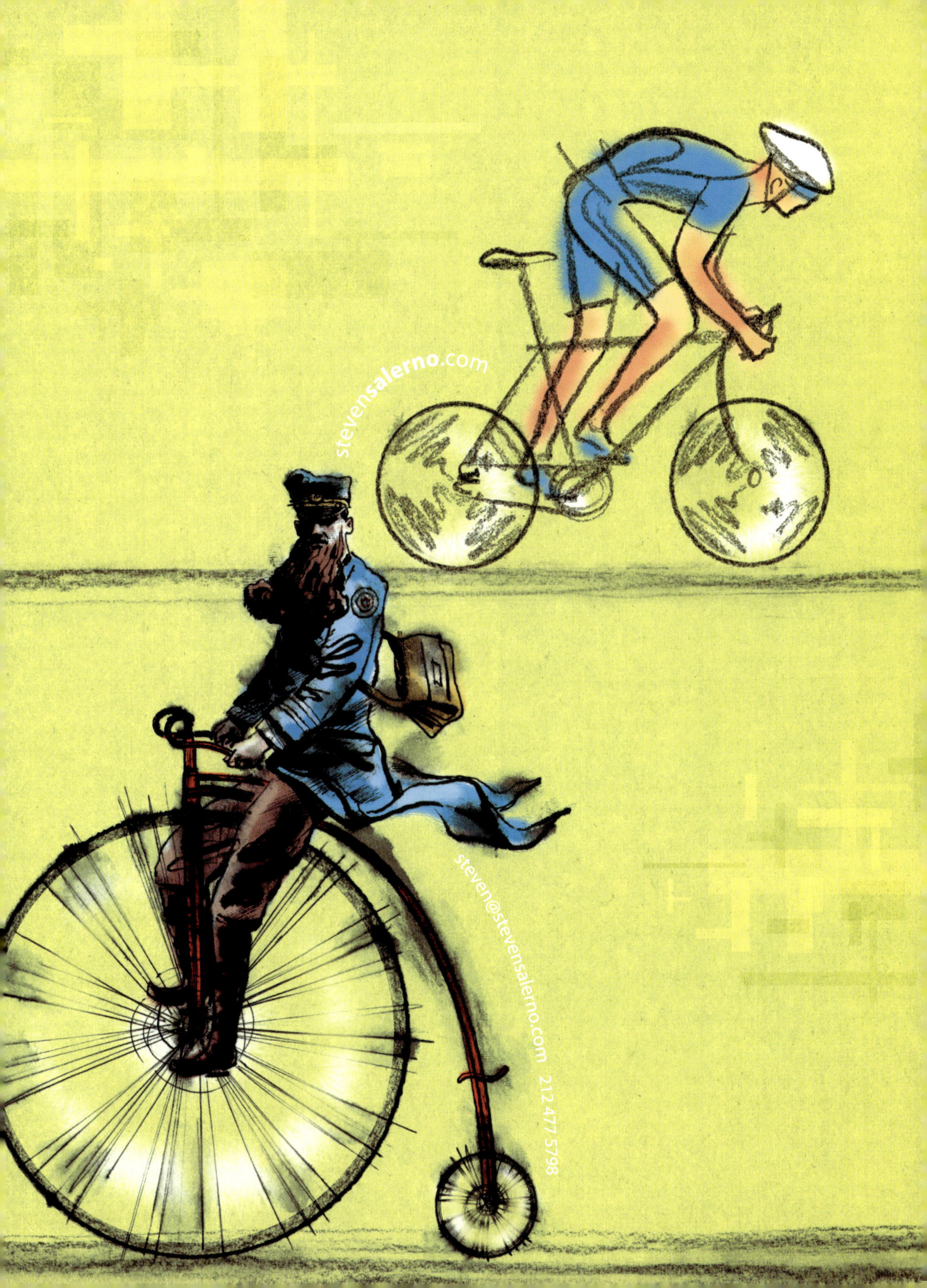
stevensalerno.com
steven@stevensalerno.com 212 477 5798

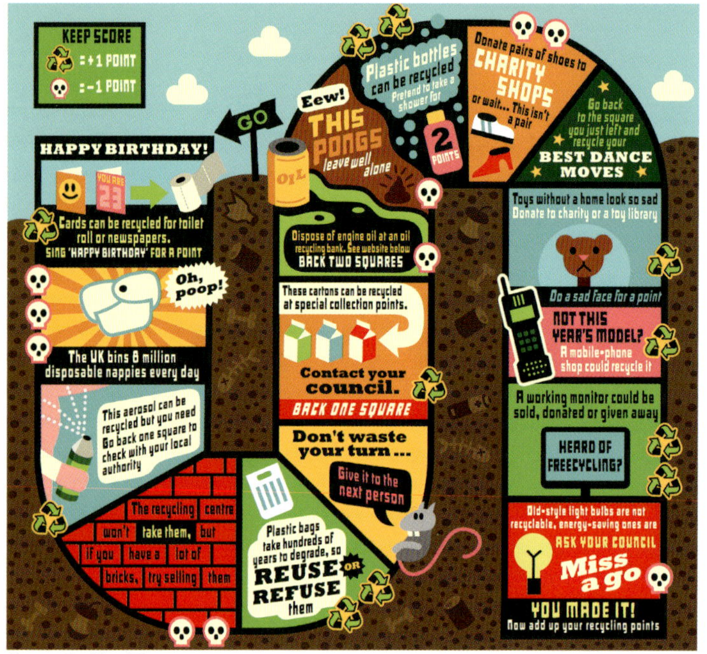
Comm. by The Observer.

Comm. by Runner's World Magazine.

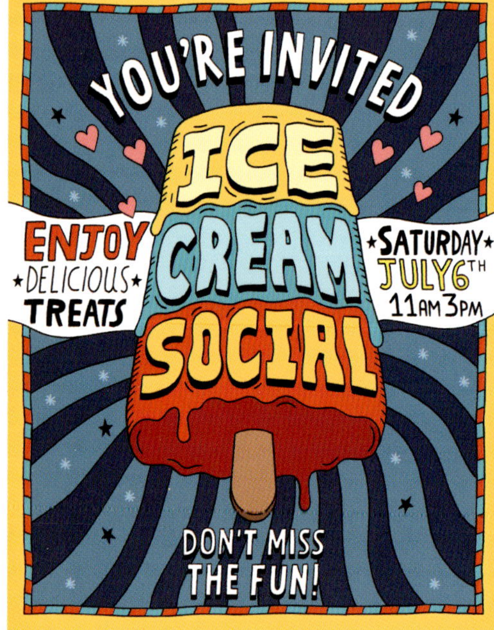
Comm. for Publix..

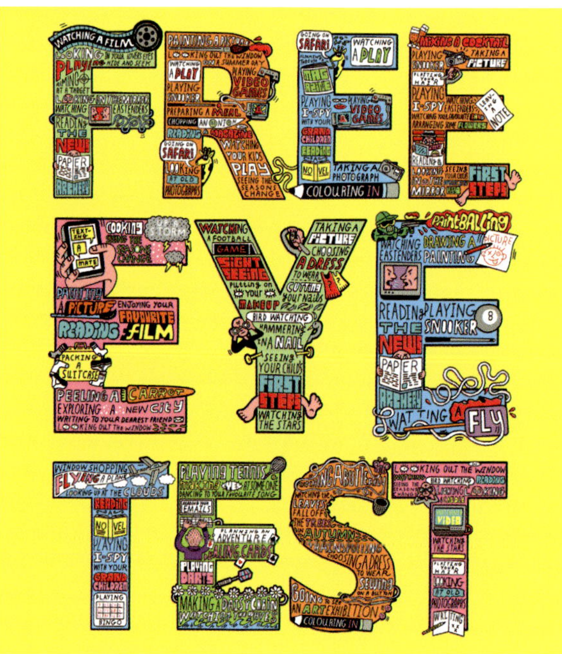
Comm. by Specsavers.

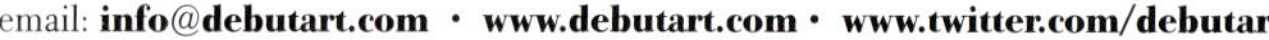

Serge Seidlitz

début **art** • Illustrators, Photographers and Fine Artists Agents. 30 Tottenham Street, London, W1T 4RJ. United Kingdom
Tel: 01144 20 7636 1064. Fax: 01144 20 7580 7017. **The Coningsby Gallery** • Tel: 01144 20 7636 7478

email: **info@debutart.com** • **www.debutart.com** • **www.twitter.com/debutart**

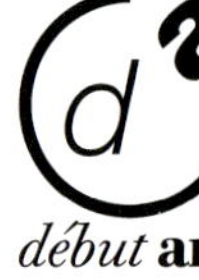
début **art**

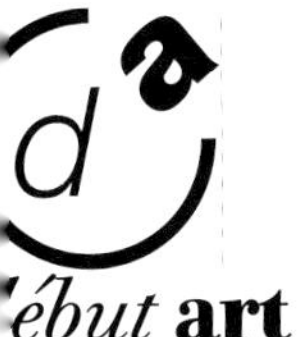

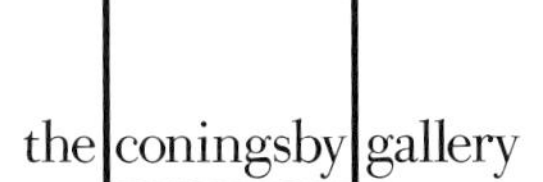

début **art** • Illustrators, Photographers and Fine Artists Agents
30 Tottenham Street, London, W1T 4RJ. United Kingdom
Tel: 01144 20 7636 1064. email: **info@debutart.com**

The Coningsby Gallery • Tel: 01144 20 7636 7478

www.debutart.com • **www.twitter.com/debutart**

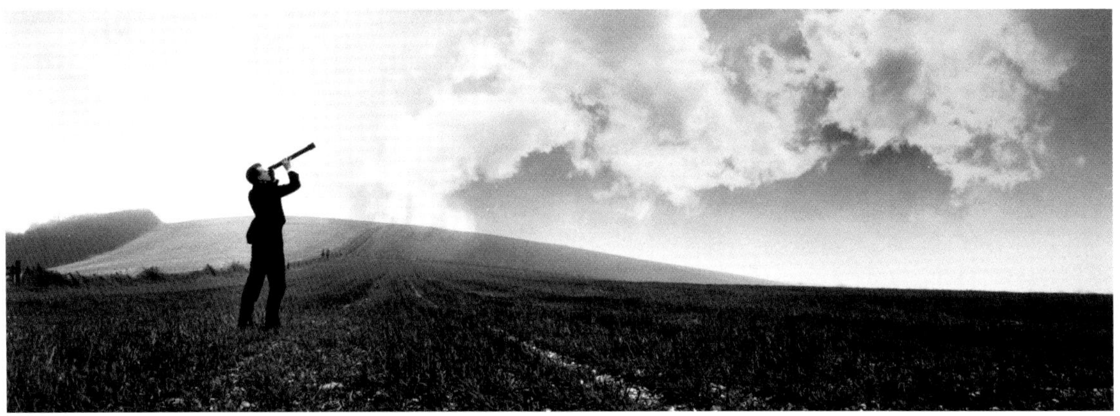

Since 1985, *début* **art** (based in London, England and now with offices in New York and Paris) has proactively sought out leading contemporary image-makers & clients who create original, progressive and commercially successful media material. Today, *début* **art** and the highly artistic illustrators it promotes, are widely regarded, both in the UK and around the world, as representing one of the finest and most contemporary talent groupings in the field of illustration.

début **art** and the illustrators it markets have successfully undertaken assignments worldwide for very many companies that are leaders in their fields including: Microsoft, Apple, Coca-Cola, Proctor and Gamble, Samsung, Levi's, Nokia, Rolls-Royce, BP, Shell, Nike, The Chicago Mercantile Exchange, The NYSE, The London Stock Exchange, Bloomberg, American Express, Barclaycard, HSBC, IBM, British Airways, Unilever, Harrods, Selfridges, Macy's (New York), McDonalds Topshop, Verizon, Lucas Inc, The Royal Opera House (London), Universal Music, Sony, Miller, Burton, Harper Collins, The Wall Street Journal, The New York Times, The Times (London), Le Monde, The Economist, The Financial Times, Vogue, Cosmopolitan and National Geographic Magazine.

Full portfolios for every artist can be reviewed and requested via our web site at **www.debutart.com**

The Coningsby Gallery stages some 30 exhibitions per year by selected leading illustrators, photographers and fine artists. Review of previous exhibitions, a look at upcoming shows and a photo tour of the gallery itself can be accessed at **www.coningsbygallery.com**

Contact: Andrew Coningsby, Jonathan Hedley, Rhiannon Lloyd, Mimi Rich and Robert Saxon

Alan Aldridge	Marta Cerda	Nanette Hoogslag	Yann Legendre	Pietari Posti	Sophie Toulouse
Arno	Matthew Dartford	Sarah Howell	Neil Leslie	Chris Price	Dominic Trevett
Andrew Baker	Paul Davis	Frazer Hudson	Andy Lovell	Paul Price	Triggerfish 21
Istvan Banyai	Carol del Angel	Drawn Ideas	Harry Malt	Peter Quinnell	Alex Trochut
Gary Bates	Pierre Doucin	ilovedust	Stephane Manel	Steve Rawlings	Jim Tsinganos
Kathrin Baxter	Barry Downard	Infomen	Sophie Marsham	Nick Reddyhoff	Vault49
Jon Berkeley	Katie Edwards	Jacey	Kim McGillivray	The Red Dress	Stephanie von Reiswitz
Chris Bianchi	El Señor	JaceyTec	Vince McIndoe	Redseal	Jeff Wack
Borja	Tim Ellis	Jackdaw	Wesley Merritt	Cath Riley	Kevin Waldron
Jacquie Boyd	Kilian Eng	Oliver Jeffers	Justin Metz	Craig Robinson	Stephan Walter
Norm Breyfogle	Sam Falconer	Ben Jennings	MinaLima	Kerry Roper	Neil Webb
Jon Burgerman	Helen Friel	Sarah Jones	Gabriel Moreno	Saeko	Jane Webster
Oliver Burston	Dan Funderburgh	Alan Kitching	Patrick Morgan	Serge Seidlitz	Louise Weir
Benedict Campbell	Peter Grundy	Ronald Kurniawan	Morten Morland	Craig Shuttlewood	Joe Wilson
Danny Capozzi	Sarah Hanson	Christina K	Huntley/Muir	Peter Strain	Oscar Wilson
James Carey	Jethro Haynes	Nik Keevil	Neasden Control Ctr	Michel Streich	Alex Williamson
Celyn	Sarah Haywood	Yuko Kondo	Chris Nurse	Sroop Sunar	Tina Zellmer
Russell Cobb	Matt Herring	Kolchoz	Alex Pang	Tado	Jurgen Ziewe
Matthew Cooper	Oliver Hibert	La Boca	Paper Work	James Taylor	Vasili Zorin
Peter Crowther	hitandrun	Chris Labrooy	Mac Premo	Yehrin Tong	

'Beauty is truth, truth beauty'
John Keats

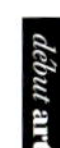

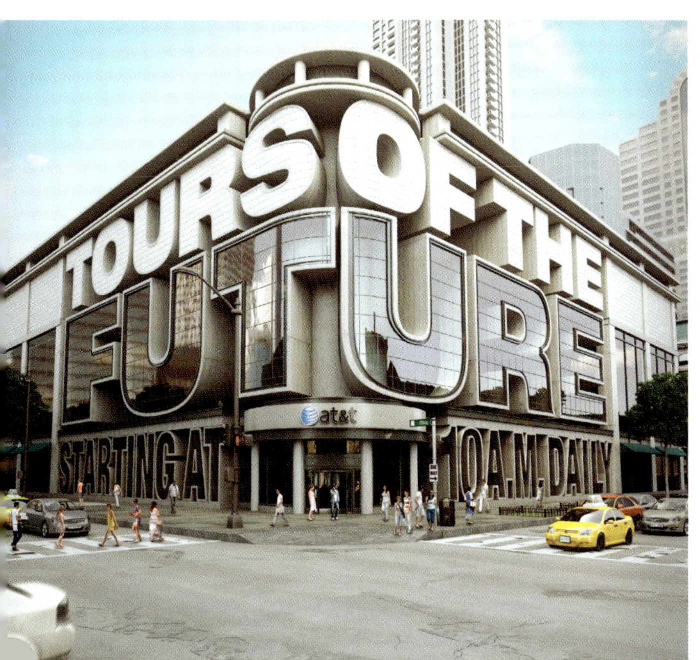

mm. for AT&T.

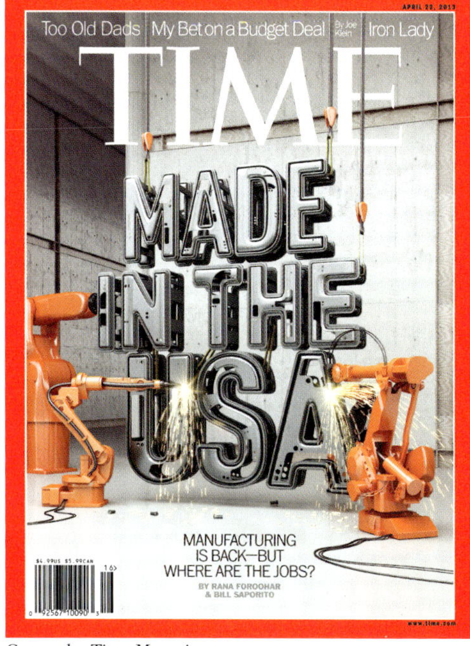

Comm. by Time Magazine.

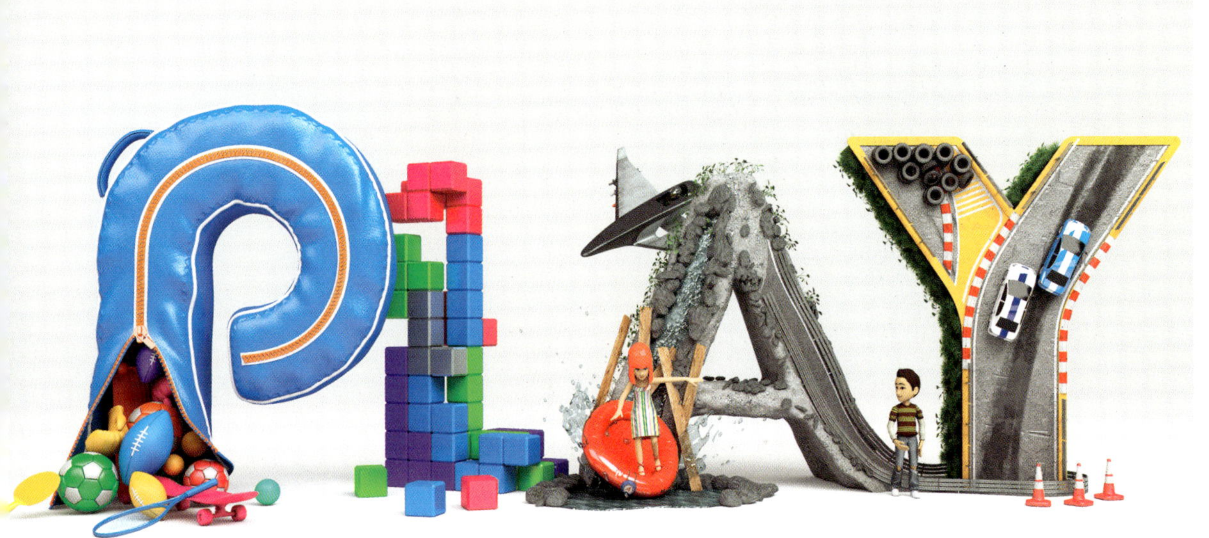

mm. by Microsoft.

Chris Labrooy

début art • Illustrators, Photographers and Fine Artists Agents. 30 Tottenham Street, London, W1T 4RJ. United Kingdom
Tel: 01144 20 7636 1064. Fax: 01144 20 7580 7017. **The Coningsby Gallery** • Tel: 01144 20 7636 7478

Email: **info@debutart.com** • **www.debutart.com** • **www.twitter.com/debutart**

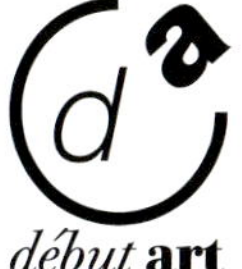

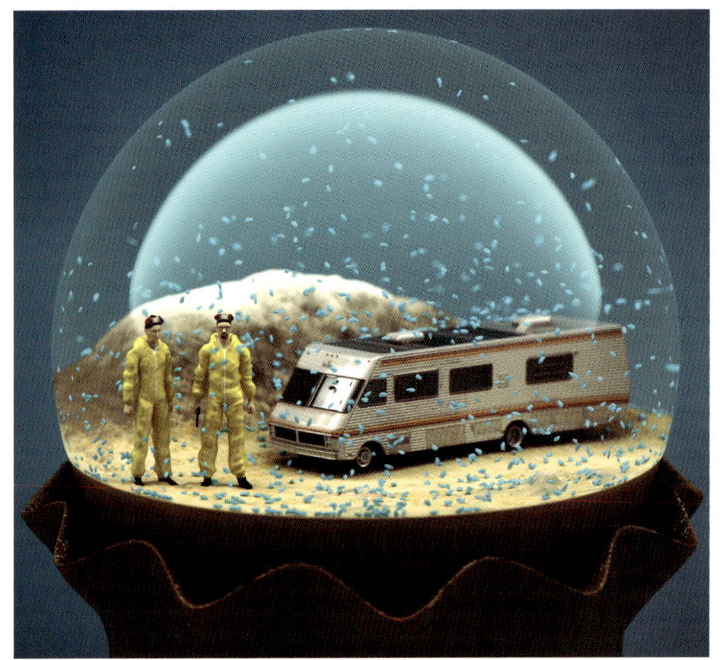

Comm. by Short List Magazine.

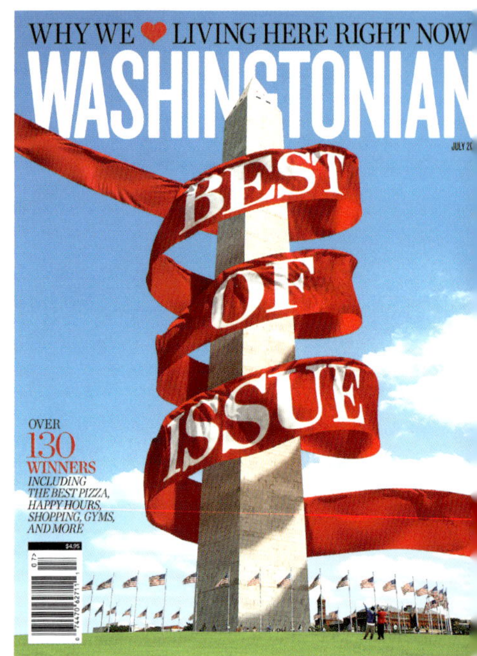

Comm. by Washintonian Magazine.

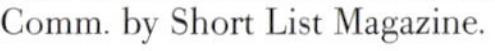

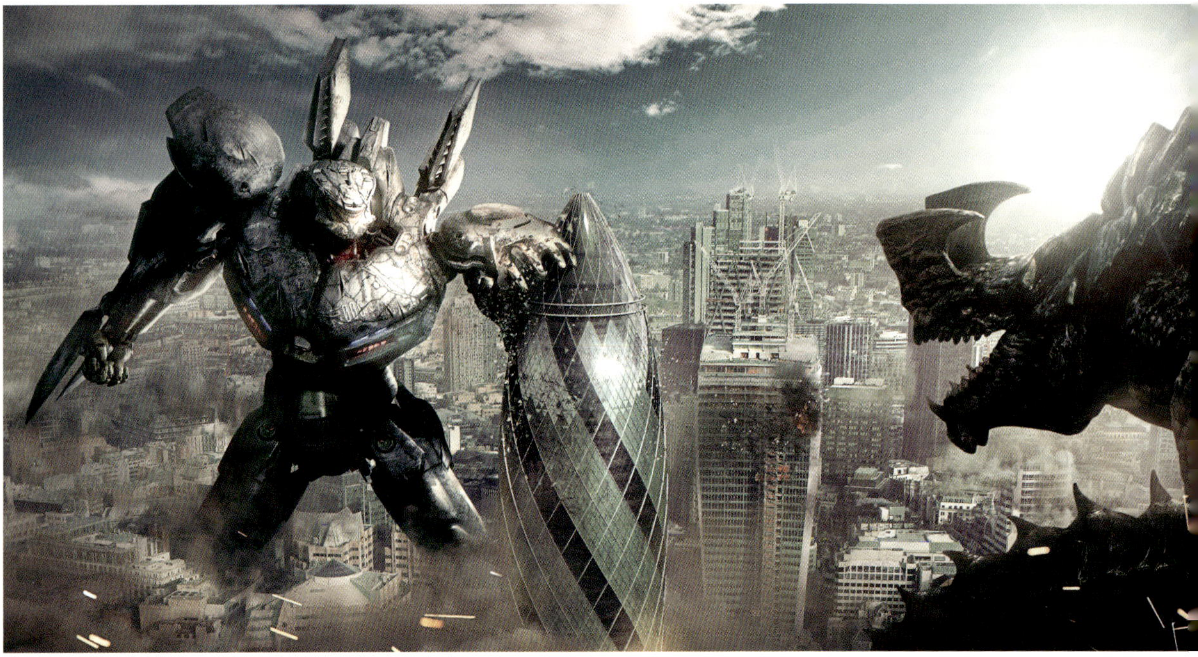

Comm. by Warner Brothers.

Justin Metz

début **art** • Illustrators, Photographers and Fine Artists Agents. 30 Tottenham Street, London, W1T 4RJ. United Kingdom
Tel: 01144 20 7636 1064. Fax: 01144 20 7580 7017. **The Coningsby Gallery** • Tel: 01144 20 7636 7478

email: **info@debutart.com** • **www.debutart.com** • **www.twitter.com/debutart**

354

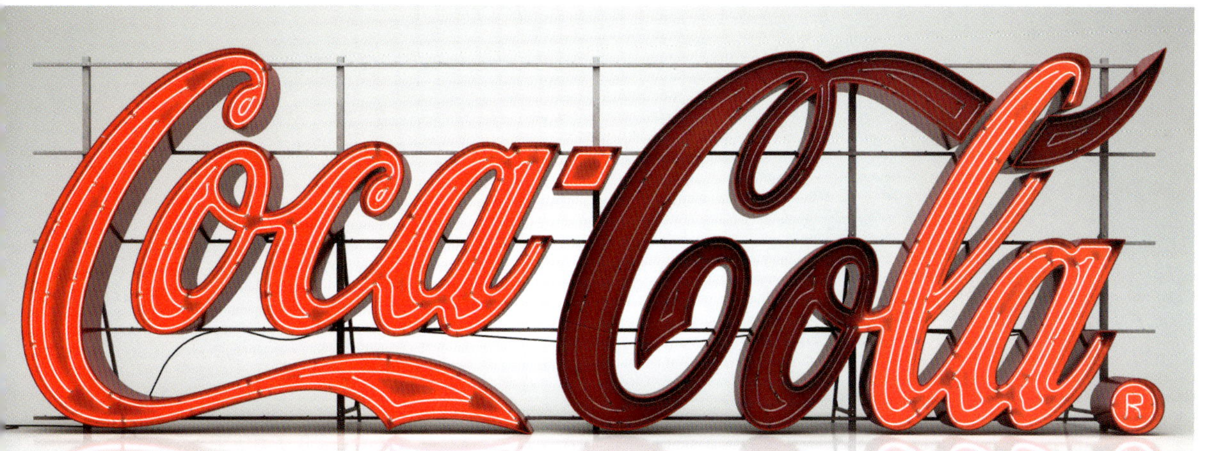

mm. for Coca-Cola.

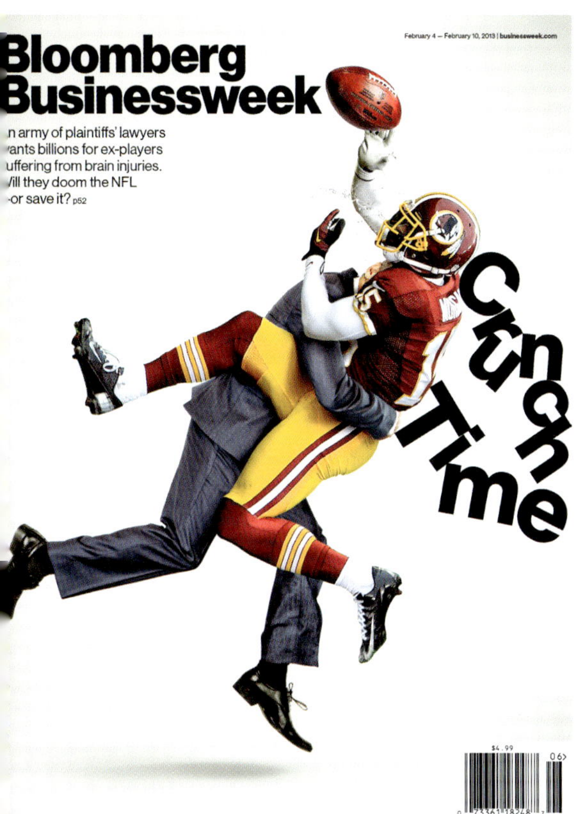

mm. by Bloomberg Businessweek.

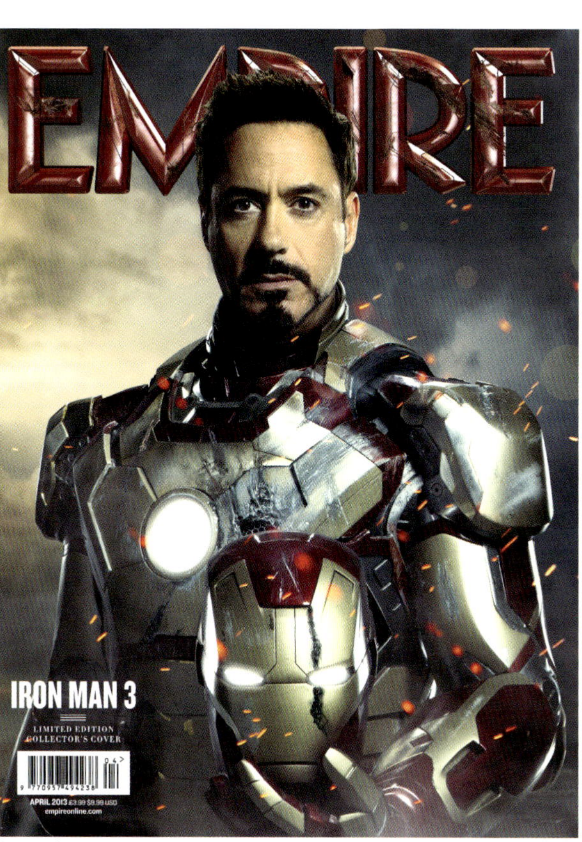

Comm. by Empire Magazine.

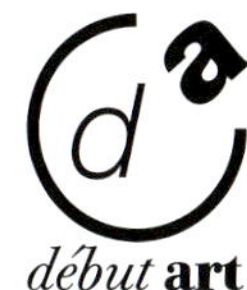

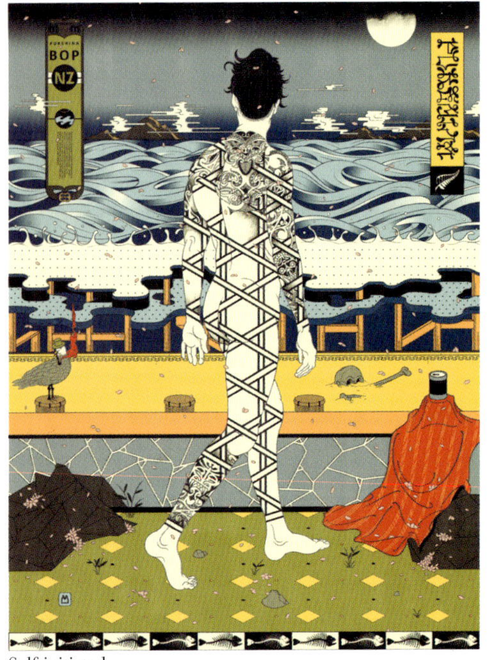
Self-initiated.

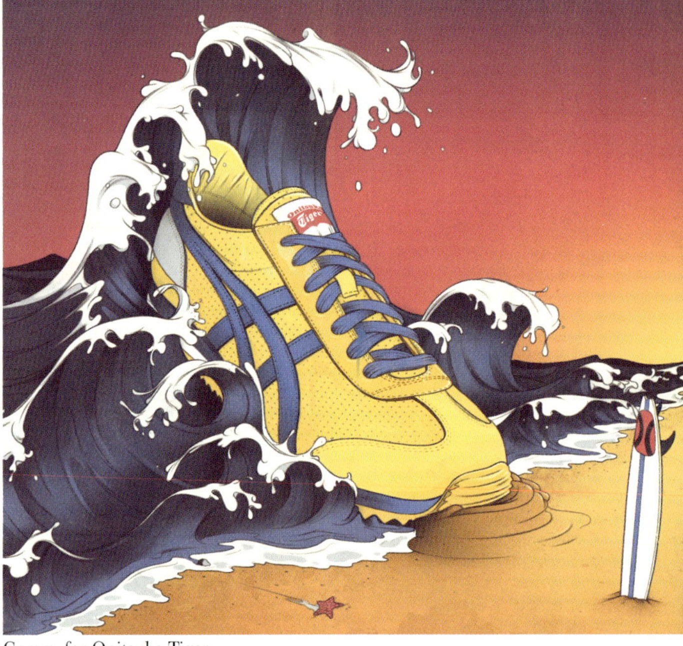
Comm. for Onitsuka Tiger.

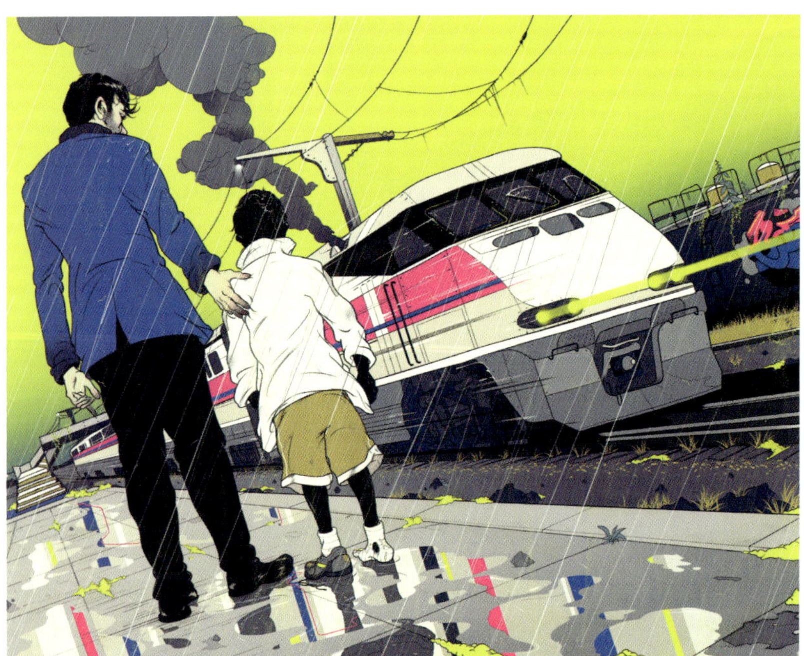
Comm. by Playboy Magazine.

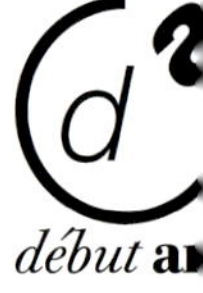
Comm. by Red Bull Racing.

Andrew Archer

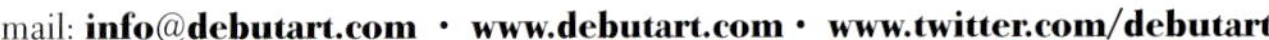

début **art** • Illustrators, Photographers and Fine Artists Agents. 30 Tottenham Street, London, W1T 4RJ. United Kingdom
Tel: 01144 20 7636 1064. Fax: 01144 20 7580 7017. **The Coningsby Gallery** • Tel: 01144 20 7636 7478

email: **info@debutart.com** • **www.debutart.com** • **www.twitter.com/debutart**

début art

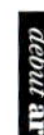

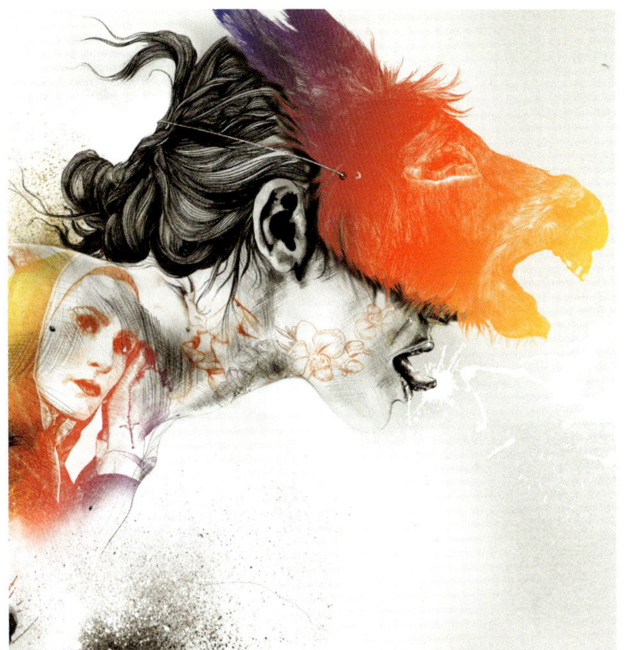
Comm. by El Pais Semanal.

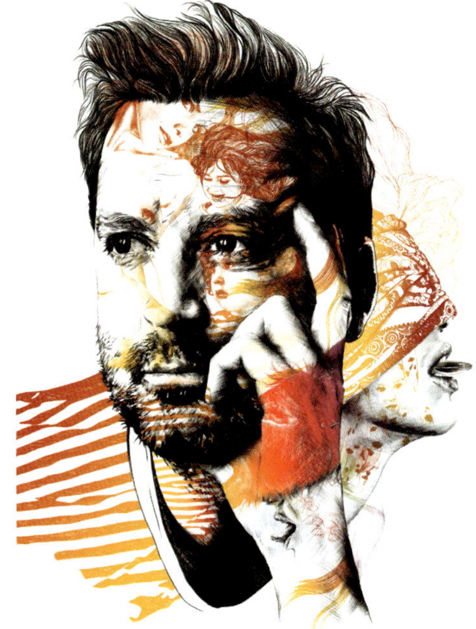
Self-initiated.

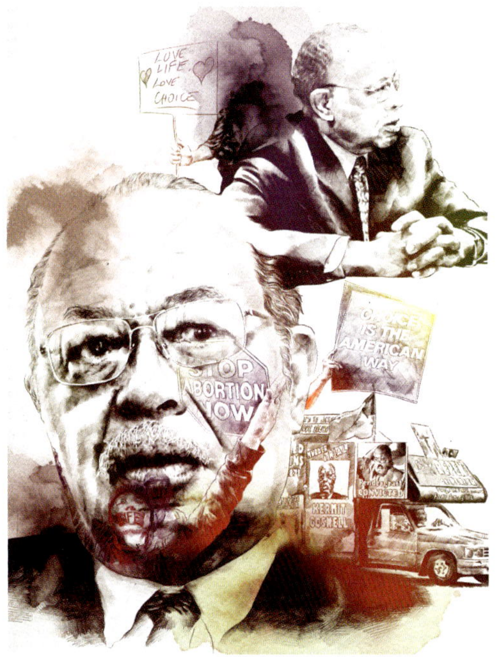

Comm. by Philadelphia Magazine.

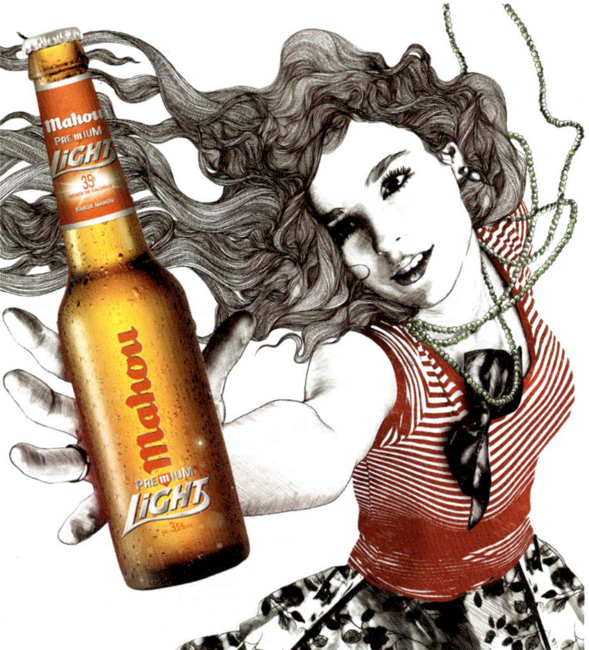

Comm. for Mahou Premium Light.

Gabriel Moreno

début **art** • Illustrators, Photographers and Fine Artists Agents. 30 Tottenham Street, London, W1T 4RJ. United Kingdom
l: 01144 20 7636 1064. Fax: 01144 20 7580 7017. **The Coningsby Gallery** • Tel: 01144 20 7636 7478

ail: **info@debutart.com** • **www.debutart.com** • **www.twitter.com/debutart**

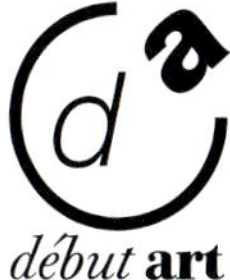

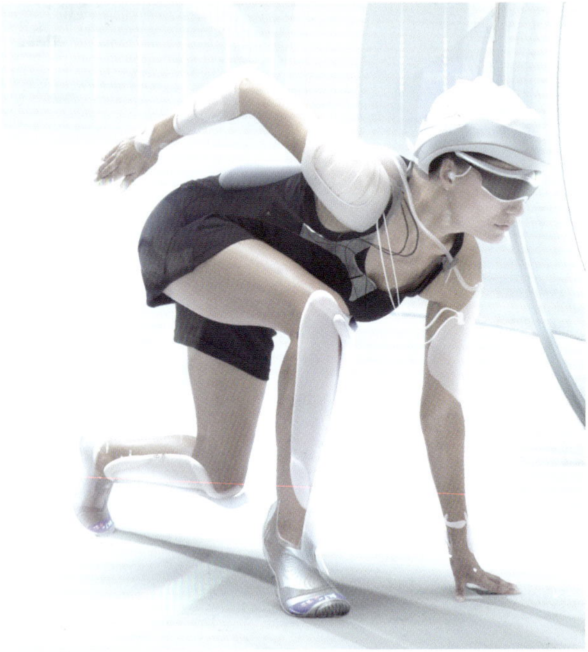

Comm. by Runners World Magazine.

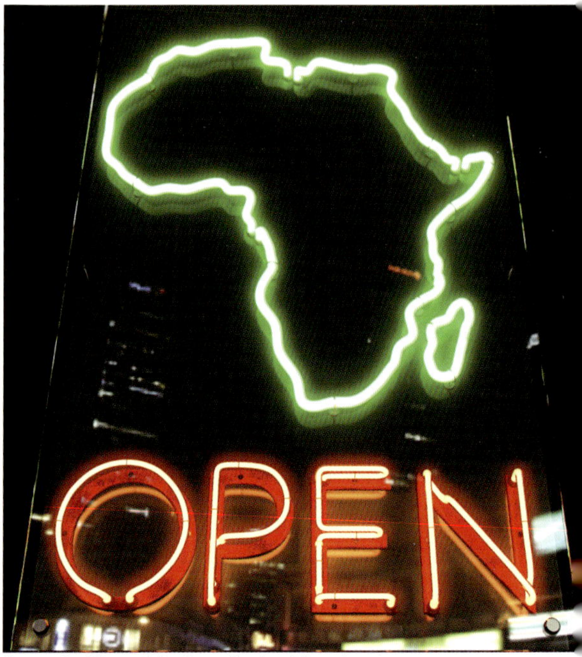

Comm. by Harvard Business Review Magazine.

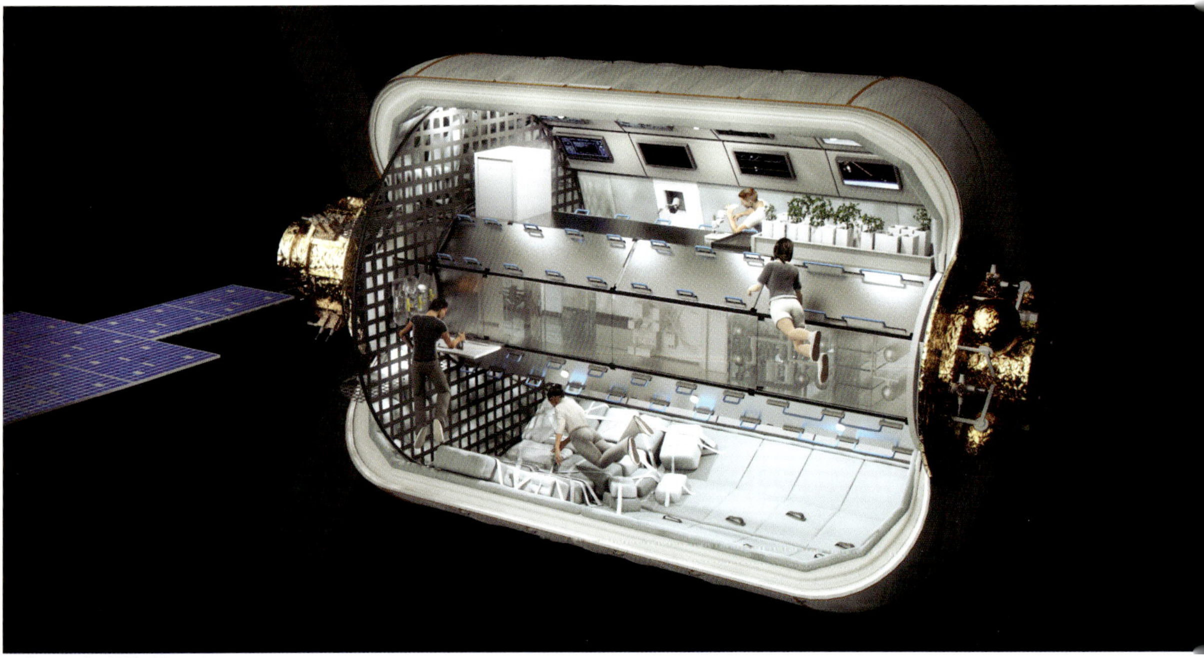

Comm. by INC. Magazine.

Peter Crowther Associates

début **art** • Illustrators, Photographers and Fine Artists Agents. 30 Tottenham Street, London, W1T 4RJ. United Kingdom
Tel: 01144 20 7636 1064. Fax: 01144 20 7580 7017. **The Coningsby Gallery** • Tel: 01144 20 7636 7478

email: **info@debutart.com** • **www.debutart.com** • **www.twitter.com/debutart**

CRUNCH TIME

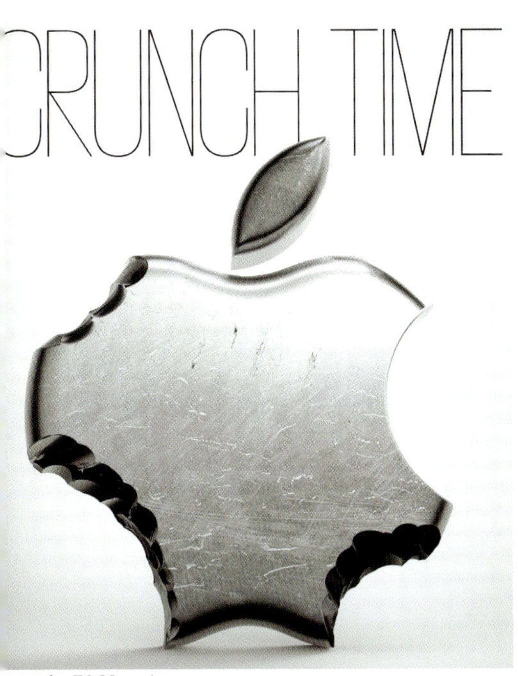

Comm. by ES Magazine.

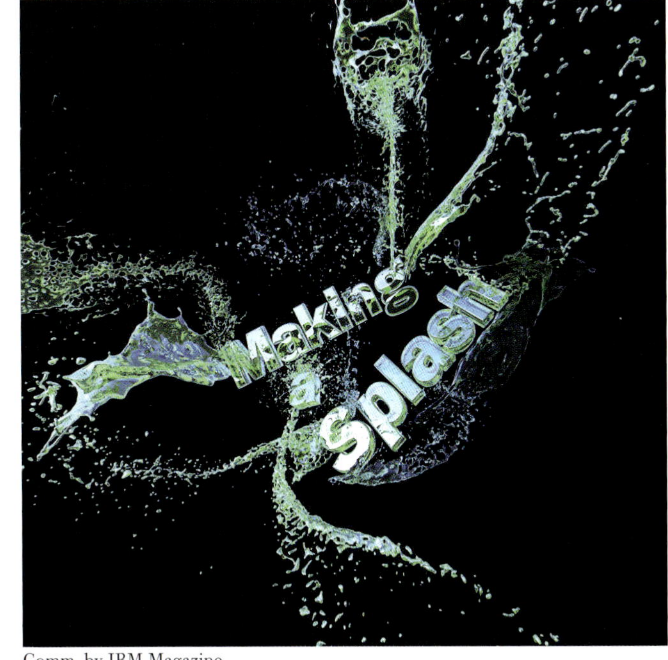

Comm. by IBM Magazine.

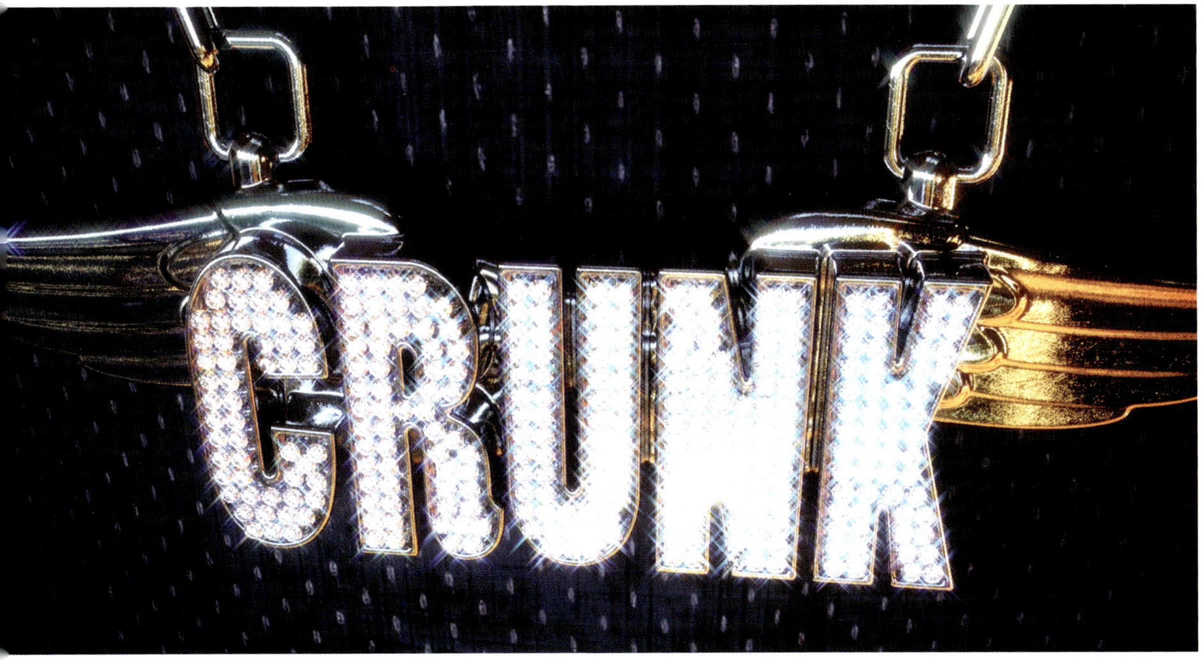

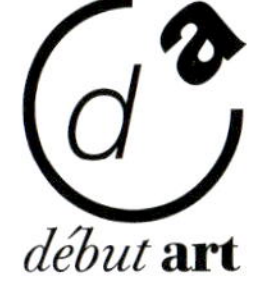

Comm. by EMI.

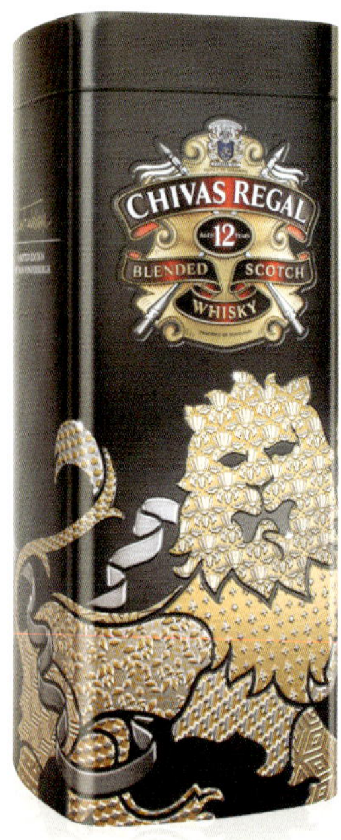
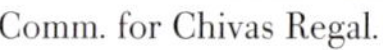
Comm. for Chivas Regal.

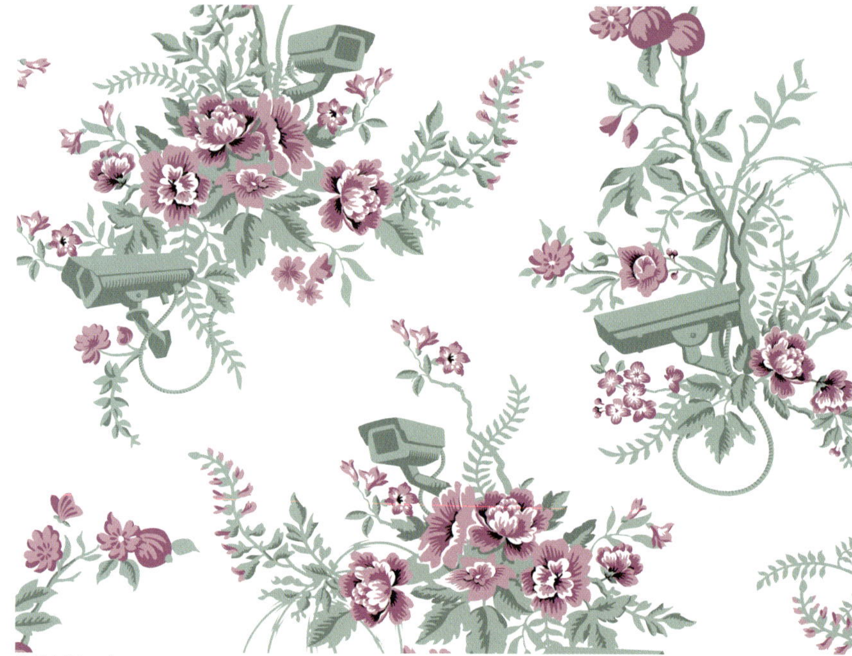
Self-initiated.

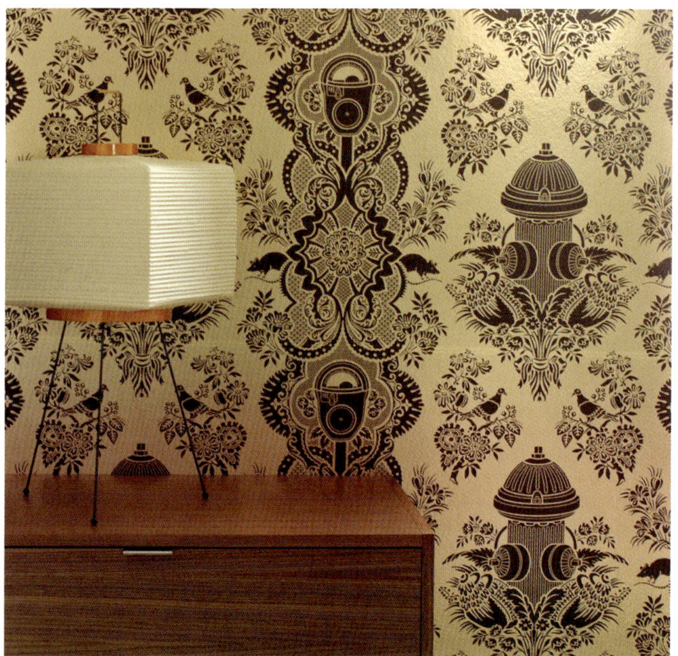
Self-initiated.

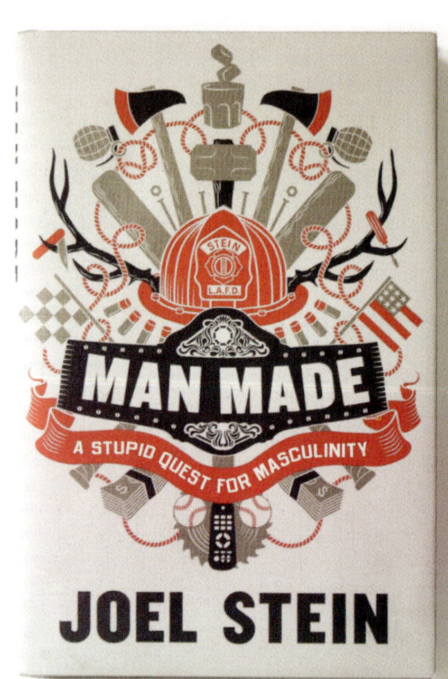

Comm. by Hachette Book Group.

Dan Funderburgh

début **art** • Illustrators, Photographers and Fine Artists Agents. 30 Tottenham Street, London, W1T 4RJ. United Kingdom
Tel: 01144 20 7636 1064. Fax: 01144 20 7580 7017. **The Coningsby Gallery** • Tel: 01144 20 7636 7478

email: **info@debutart.com** • **www.debutart.com** • **www.twitter.com/debutart**

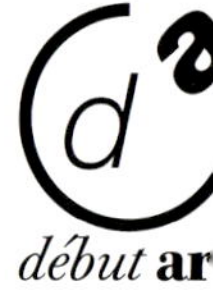
début art

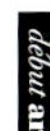

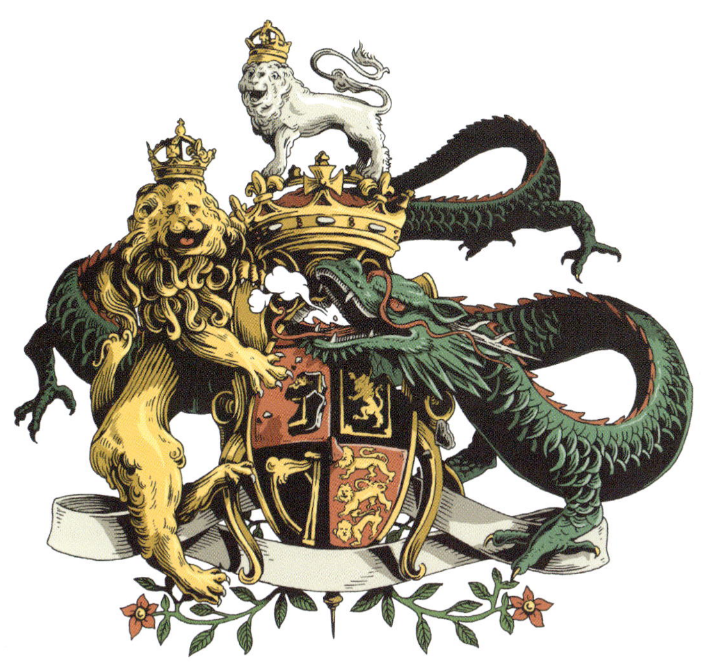

Comm. for Fashion Week Magazine.

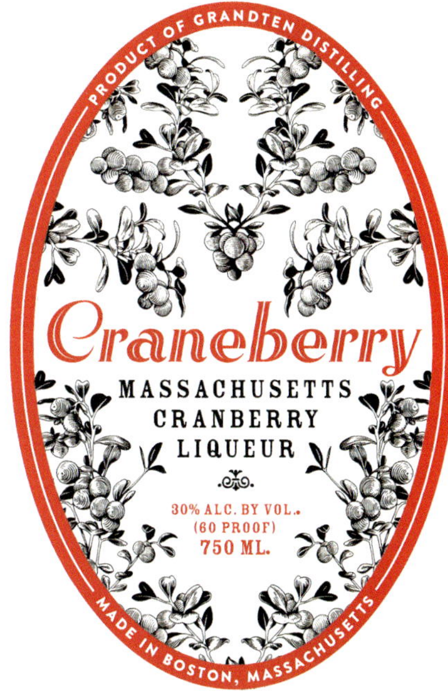

Comm. by Grandten Distilling.

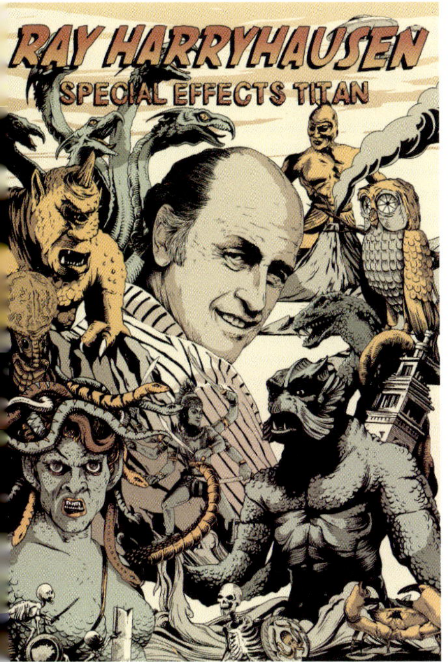

mm. by Arrow Films.

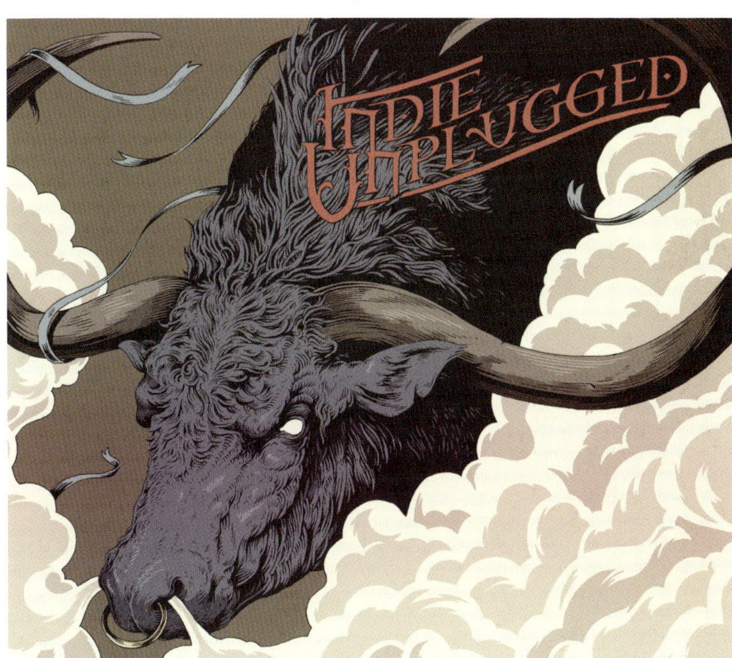

Comm. by EMI.

e Wilson

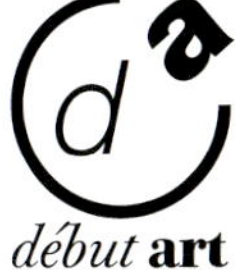

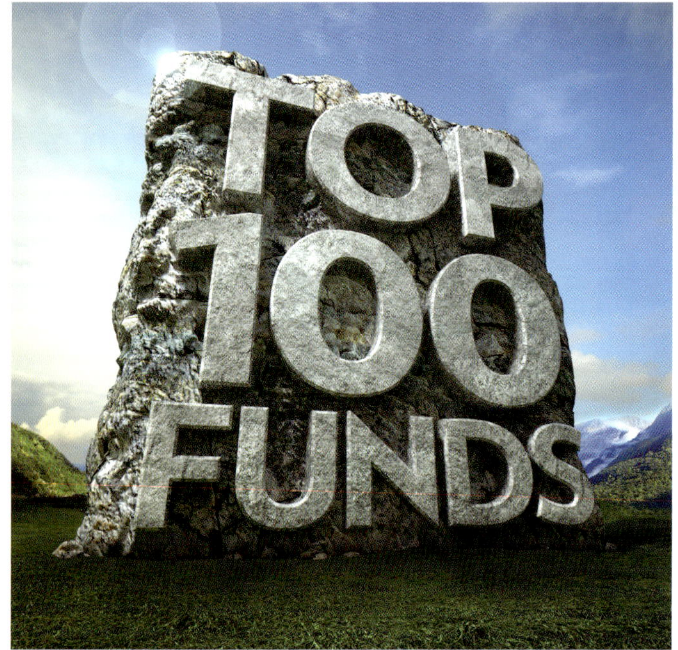

Comm. by Investor's Chronicle.

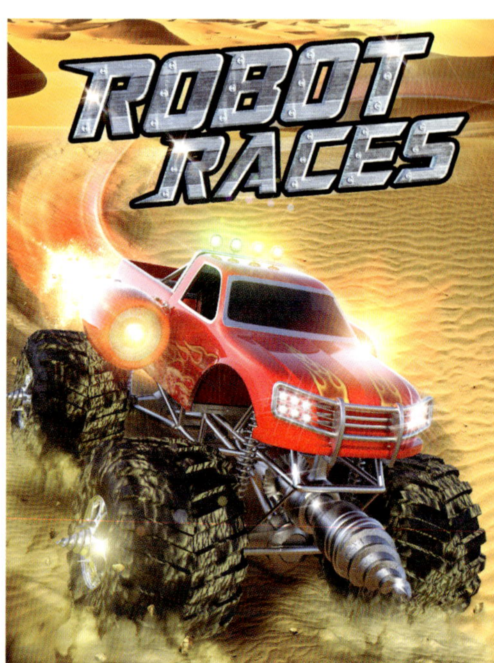

Comm. for Hothouse Fiction.

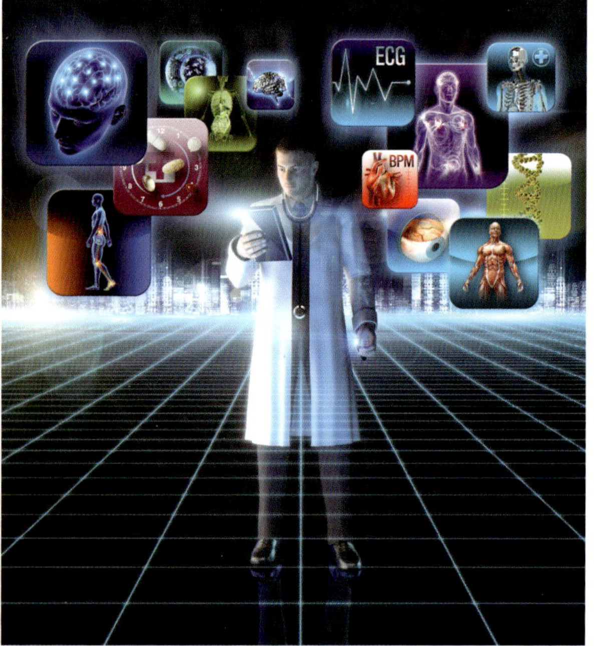

Comm. by New Electronics Magazine.

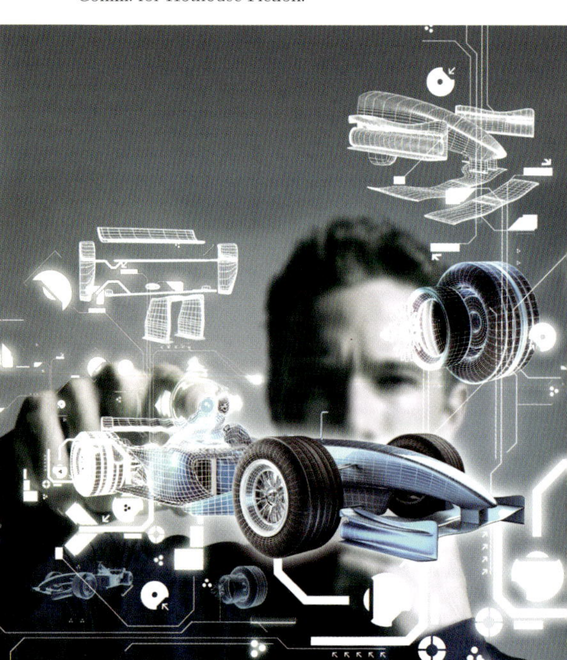

Comm. by Eureka Magazine.

Oliver Burston

début **art** • Illustrators, Photographers and Fine Artists Agents. 30 Tottenham Street, London, W1T 4RJ. United Kingdom
Tel: 01144 20 7636 1064. Fax: 01144 20 7580 7017. **The Coningsby Gallery** • Tel: 01144 20 7636 7478

email: **info@debutart.com** • **www.debutart.com** • **www.twitter.com/debutart**

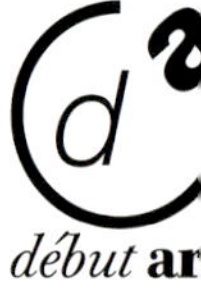

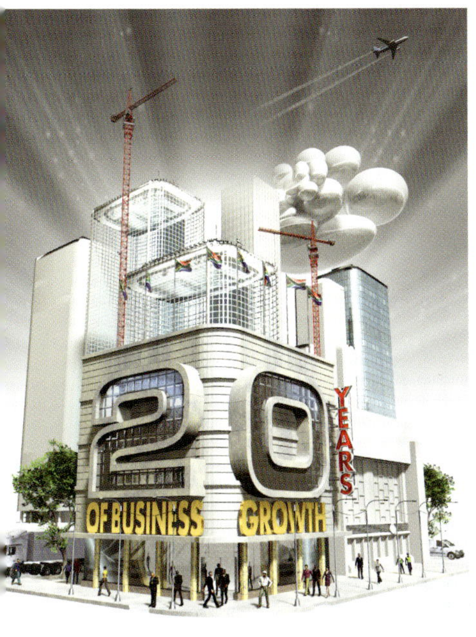

Comm. for a South African Business Development Group.

Comm. by EMI.

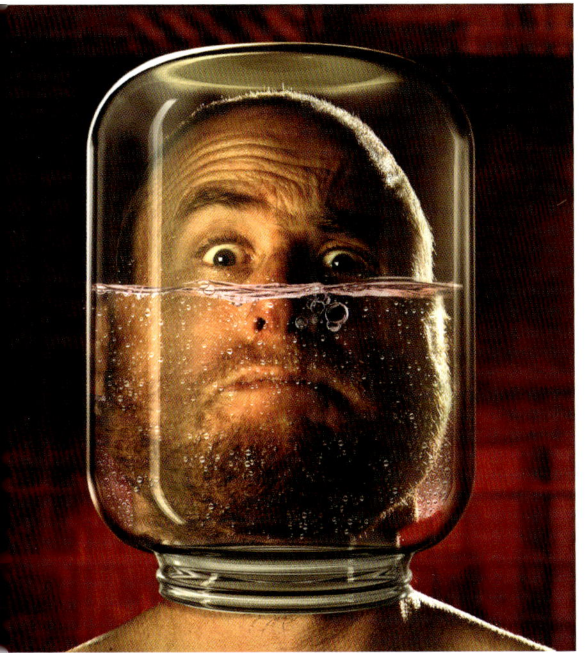

Comm. by ACM Magazine.

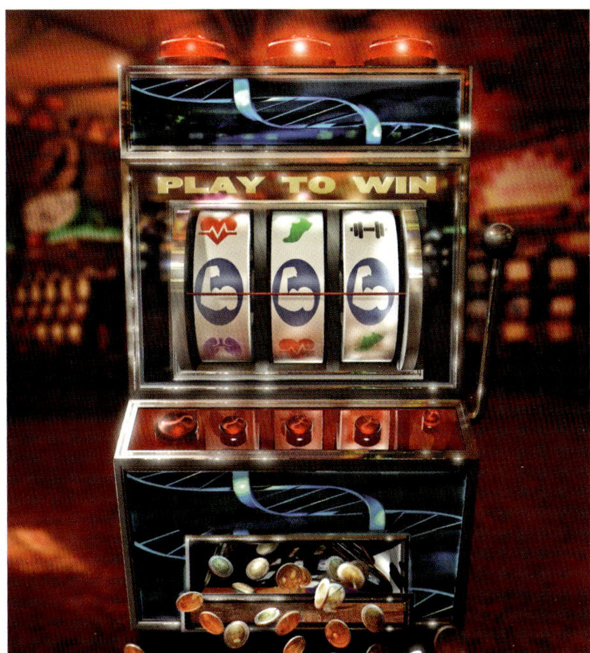

Comm. by Men's Fitness Magazine.

arry Downard

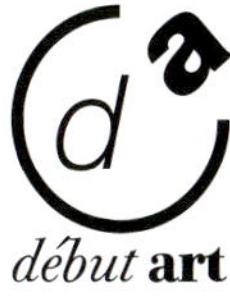

début art

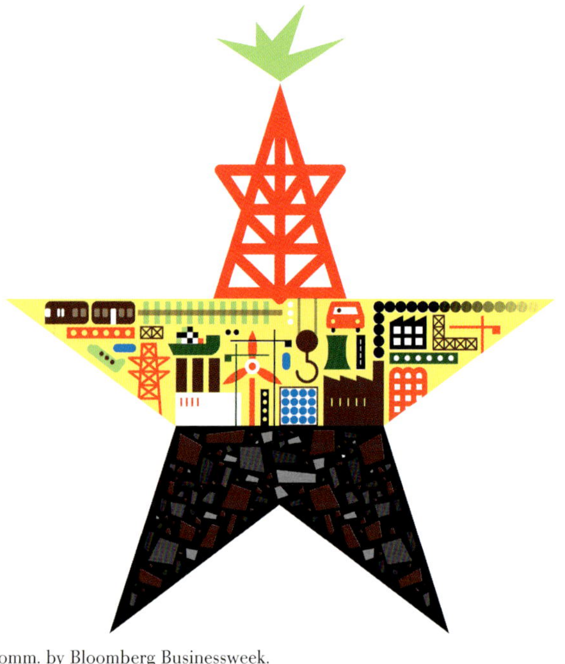

Comm. by Bloomberg Businessweek.

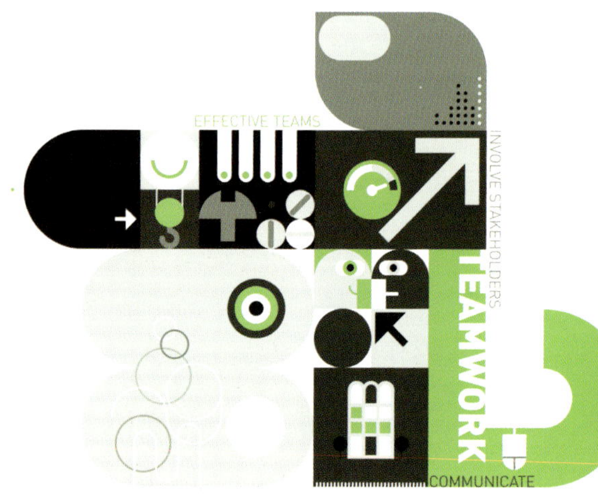

Comm. for Tronox.

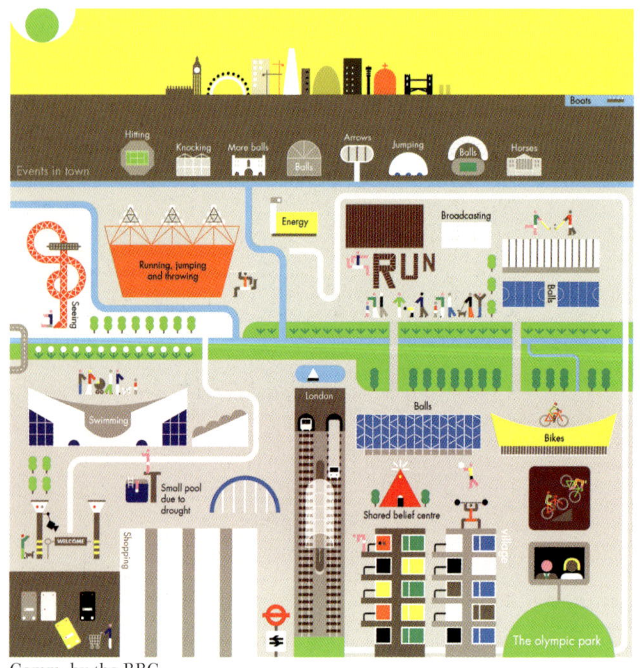

Comm. by the BBC.

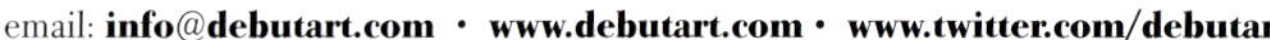

Self-initiated

Peter Grundy

début **art** • Illustrators, Photographers and Fine Artists Agents. 30 Tottenham Street, London, W1T 4RJ. United Kingdom
Tel: 01144 20 7636 1064. Fax: 01144 20 7580 7017. **The Coningsby Gallery** • Tel: 01144 20 7636 7478

email: **info@debutart.com** • **www.debutart.com** • **www.twitter.com/debutart**

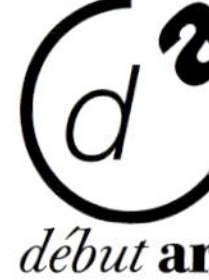

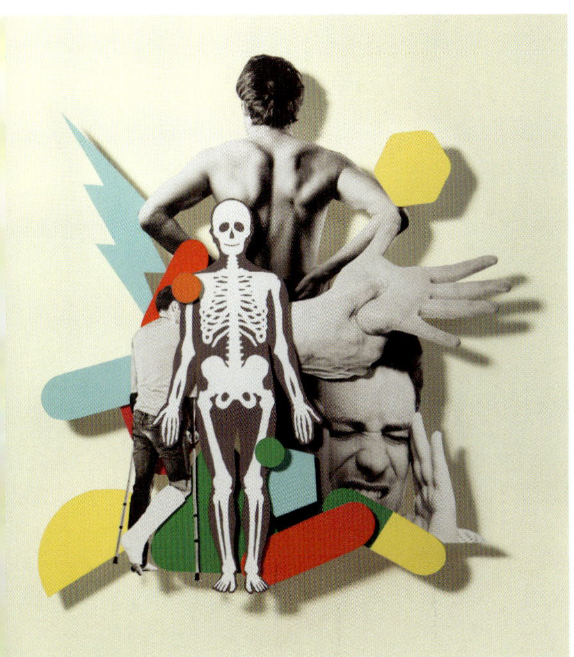

mm. by Men's Health Magazine.

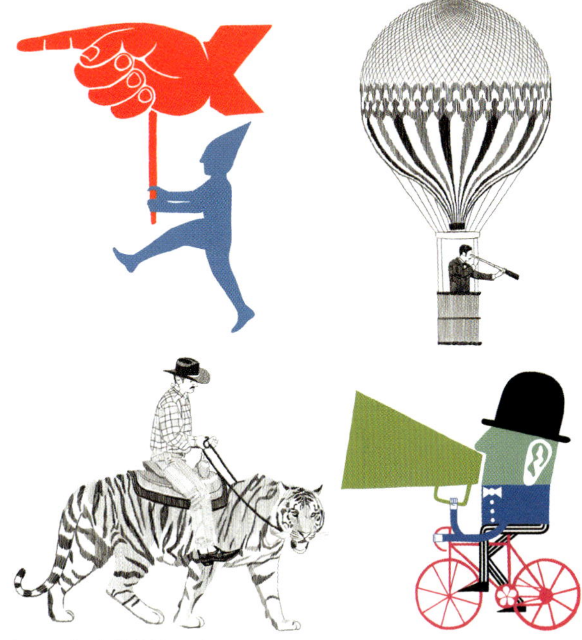

Comm. for AARP Magazine.

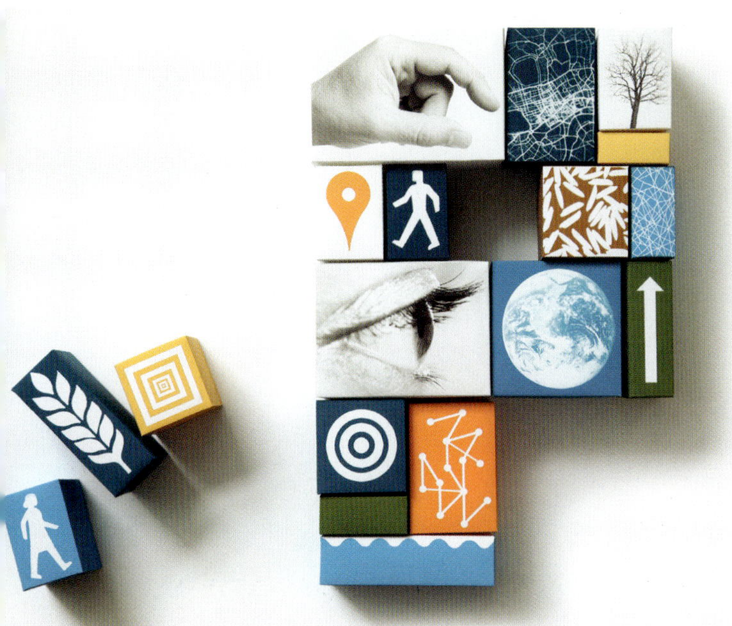

mm. for IFC.

Comm. by Men's Health Magazine.

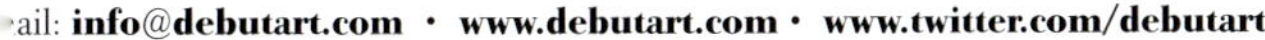

mes Taylor

but **art** • Illustrators, Photographers and Fine Artists Agents. 30 Tottenham Street, London, W1T 4RJ. United Kingdom
: 01144 20 7636 1064.   Fax: 01144 20 7580 7017.   **The Coningsby Gallery**   •   Tel: 01144 20 7636 7478

ail: **info@debutart.com**   •   **www.debutart.com**   •   **www.twitter.com/debutart**

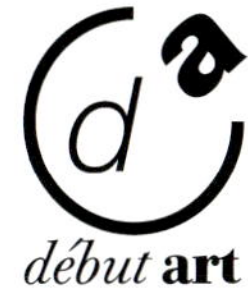

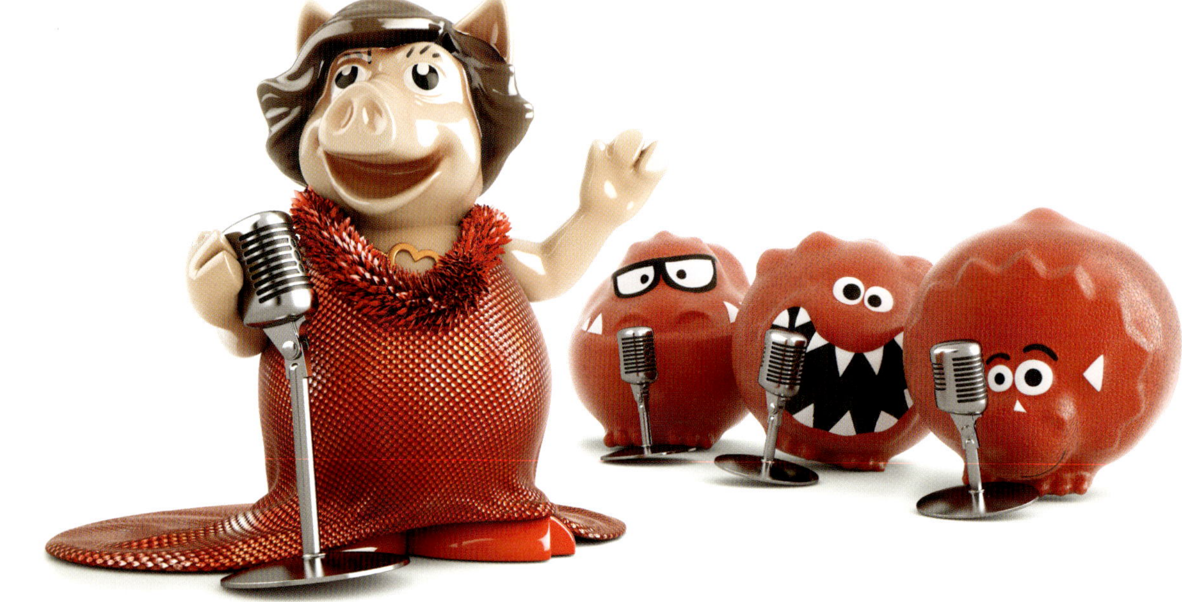

Comm. for NatWest Bank.

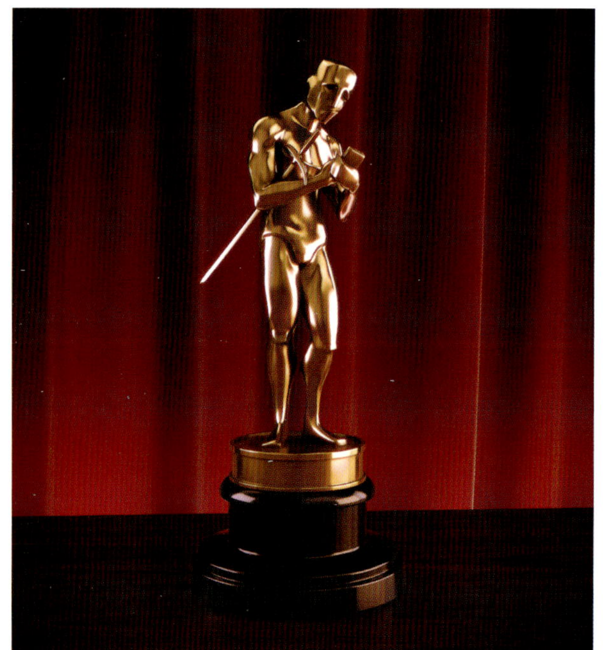

Comm. by Wall St Journal.

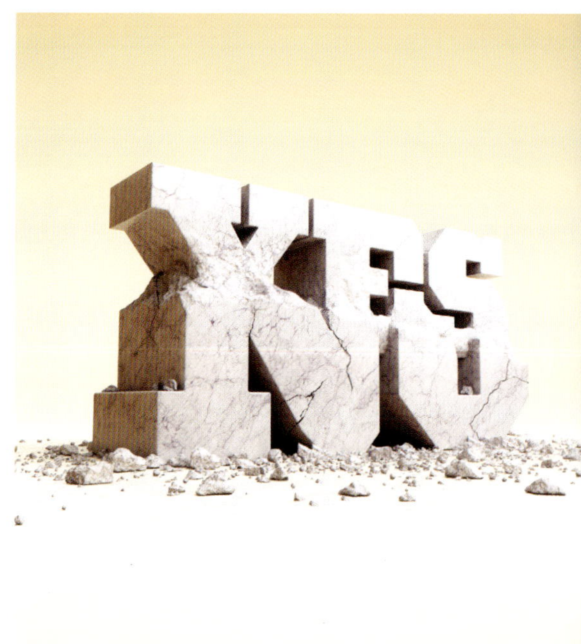

Comm. for New York Lottery.

Matt Dartford / Flip CG

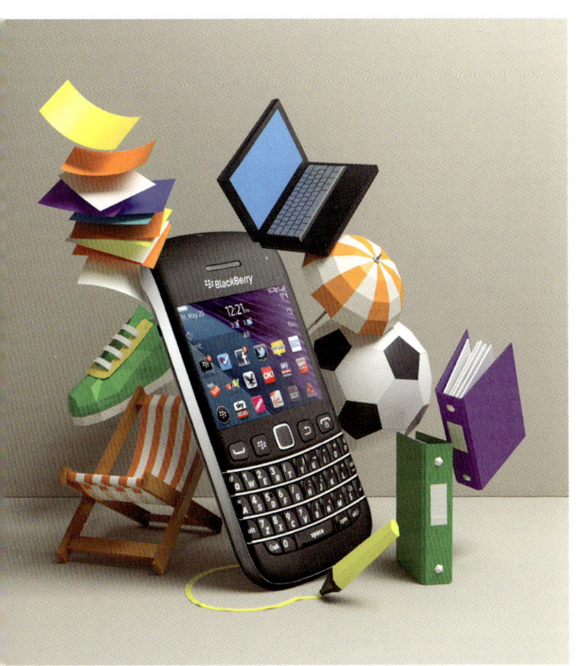

mm. by Orange Magazine.

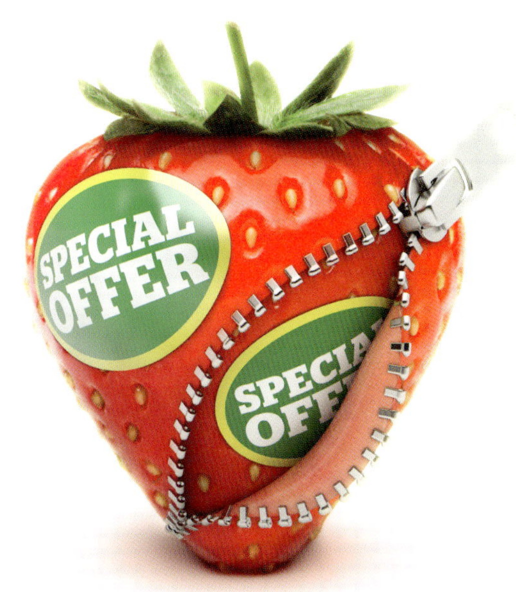

Comm. by Which? Magazine.

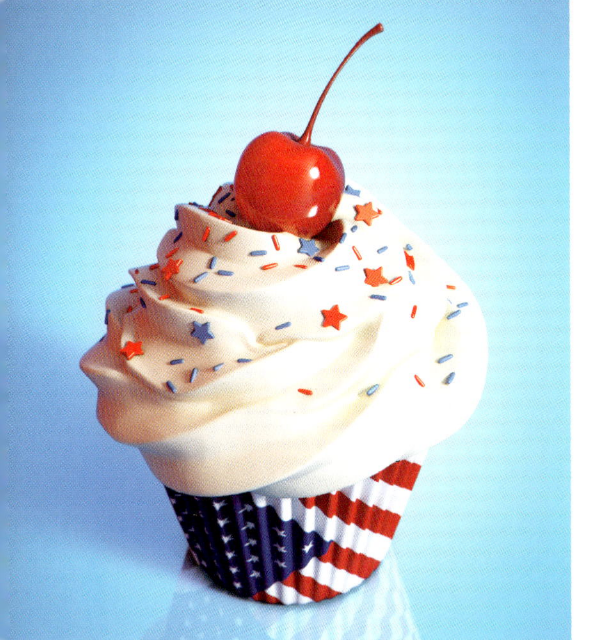

mm. by FDI Magazine.

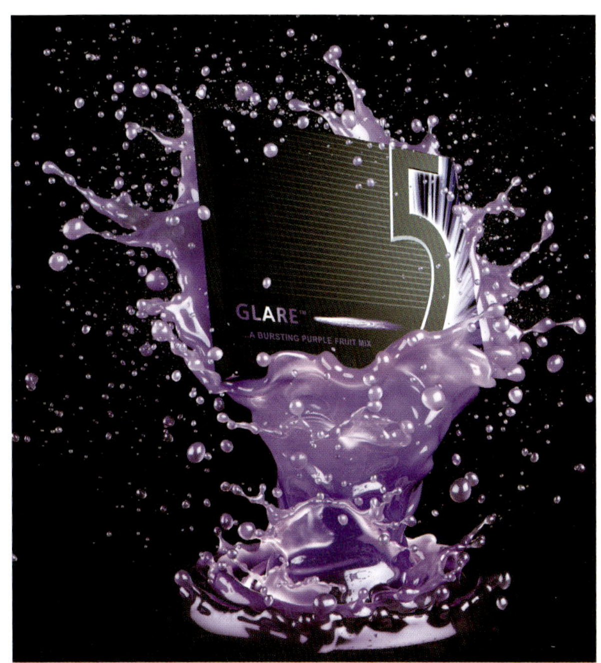

Comm. for Wrigley.

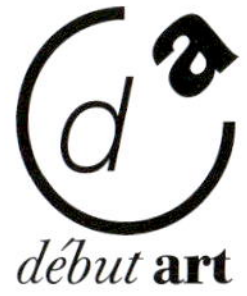

367

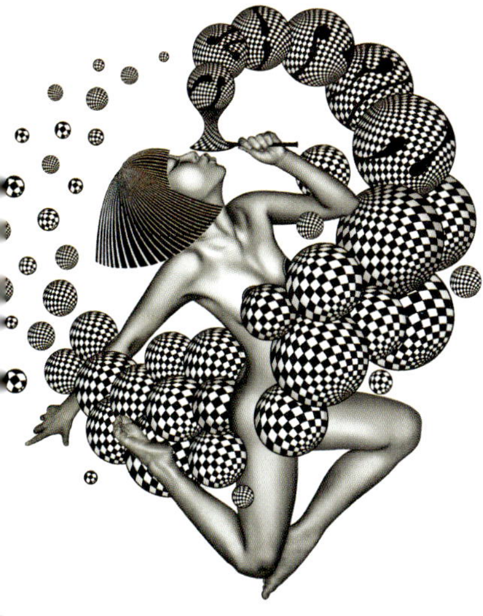

f-inititated.

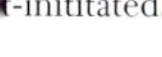

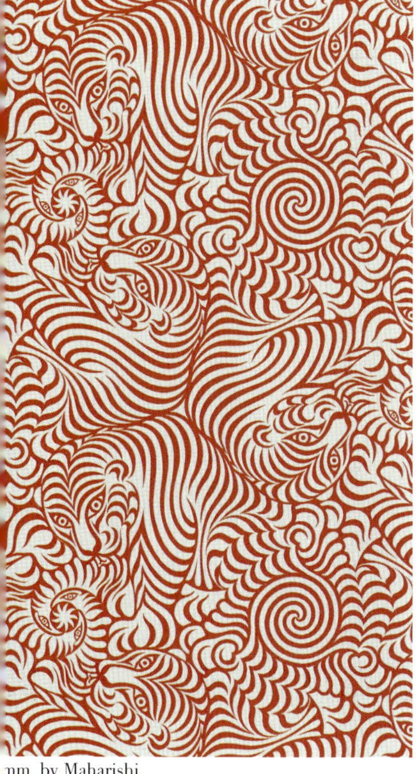

nm. by Maharishi.

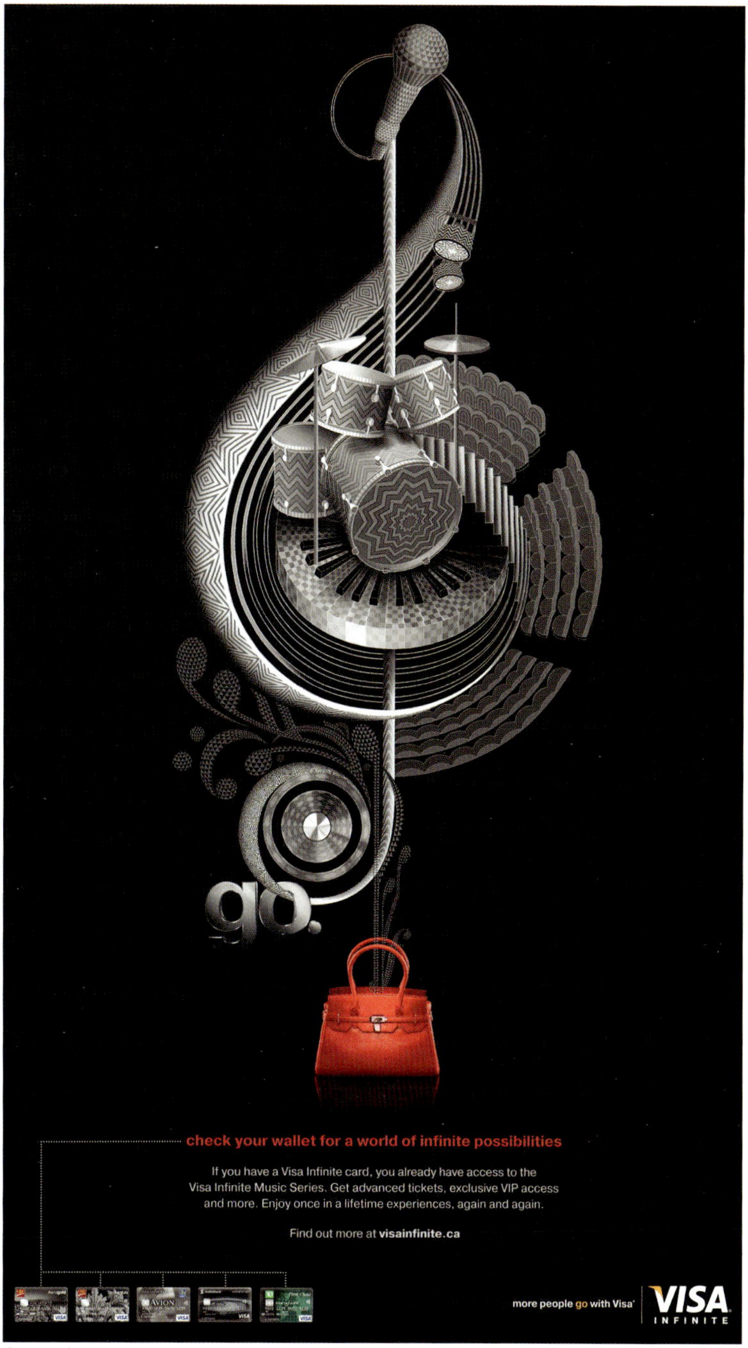

Comm. for Visa.

hrin Tong

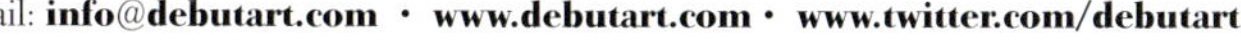

ut **art** • Illustrators, Photographers and Fine Artists Agents. 30 Tottenham Street, London, W1T 4RJ. United Kingdom
01144 20 7636 1064. Fax: 01144 20 7580 7017. **The Coningsby Gallery** • Tel: 01144 20 7636 7478

il: **info@debutart.com** • **www.debutart.com** • **www.twitter.com/debutart**

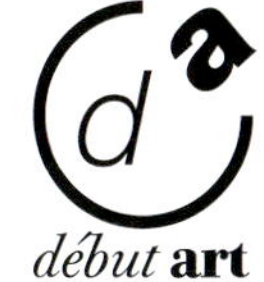

début art

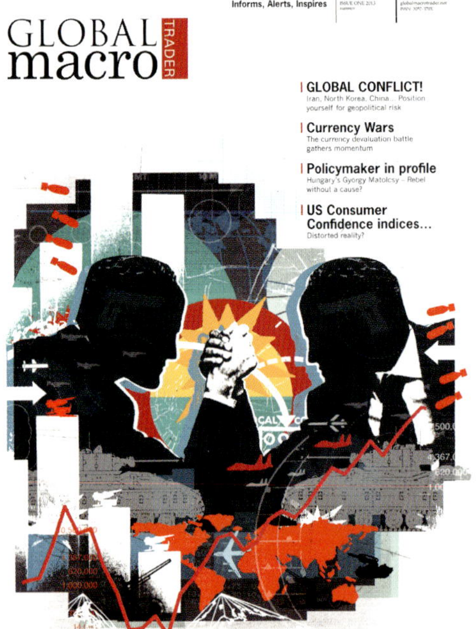

Comm. by Global Macro Trader Magazine.

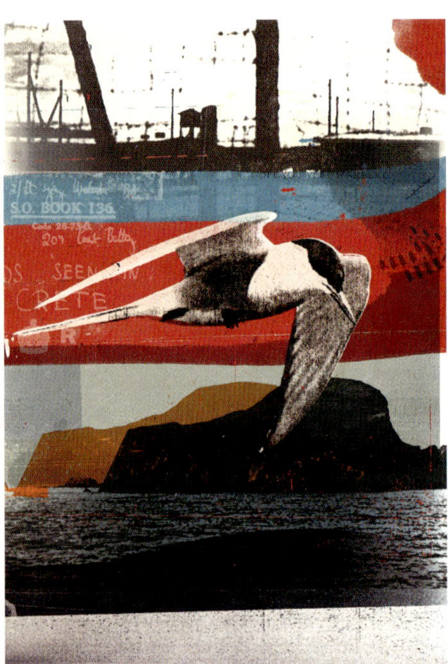

Comm. by National Trust.

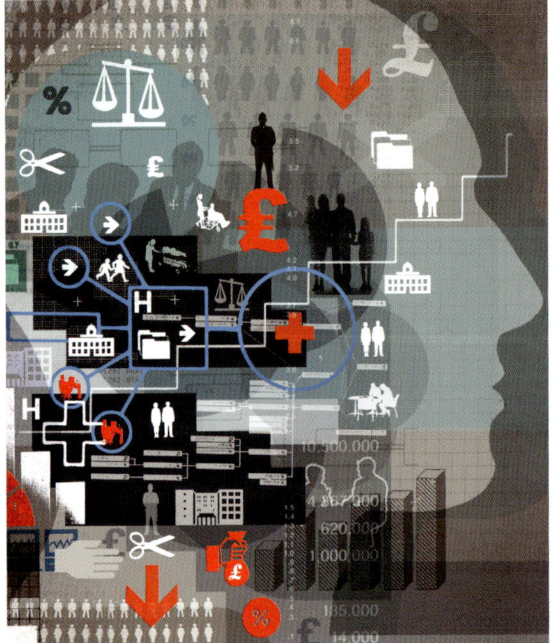

Comm. for Economia Magazine.

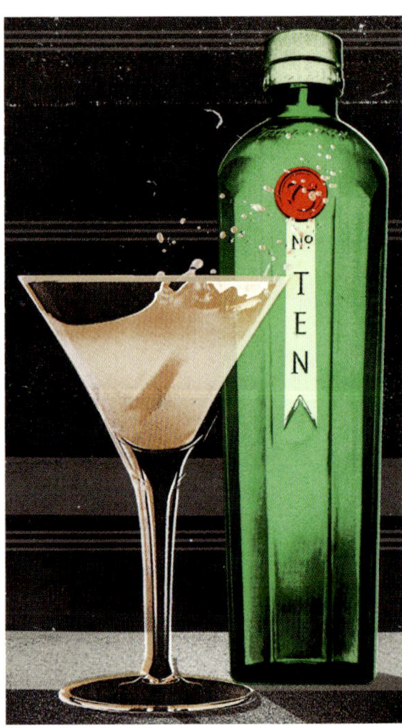

Comm. by Harrods.

Alex Williamson

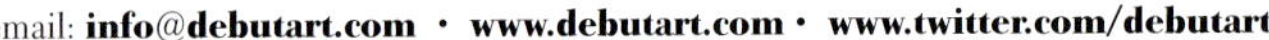

début **art** • Illustrators, Photographers and Fine Artists Agents. 30 Tottenham Street, London, W1T 4RJ. United Kingdom
Tel: 01144 20 7636 1064. Fax: 01144 20 7580 7017. **The Coningsby Gallery** • Tel: 01144 20 7636 7478

email: **info@debutart.com** • **www.debutart.com** • **www.twitter.com/debutart**

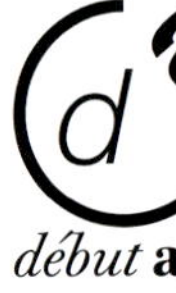

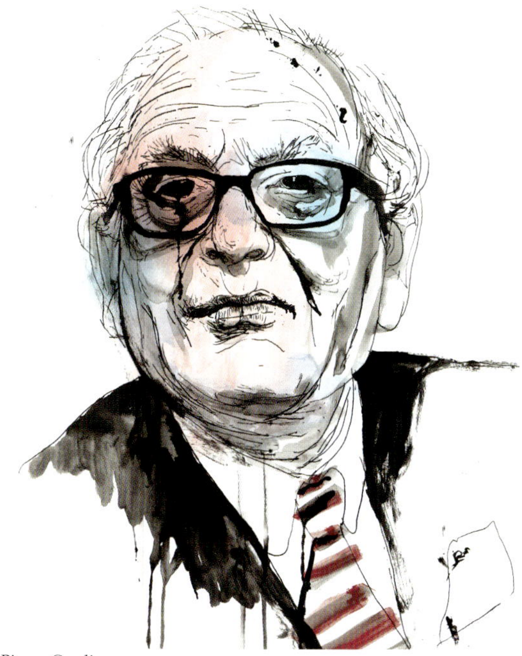

Pierre Cardin.

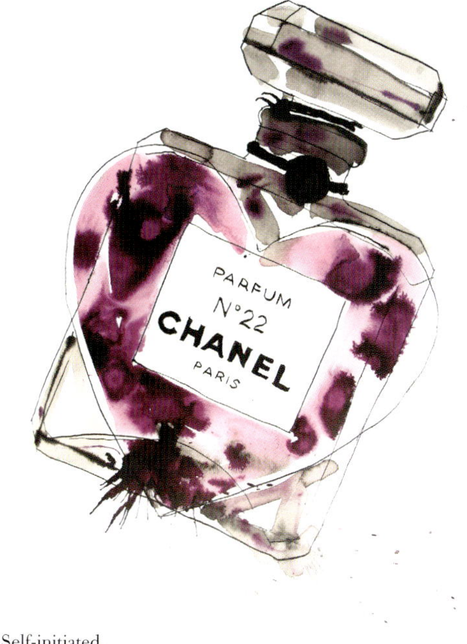

Self-initiated.

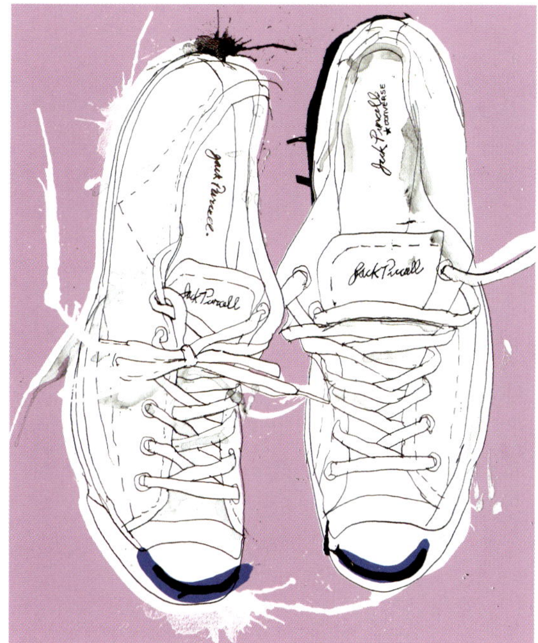

Comm. for Converse.

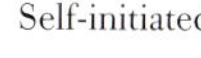

Comm. by The Observer.

trick Morgan

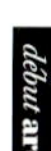

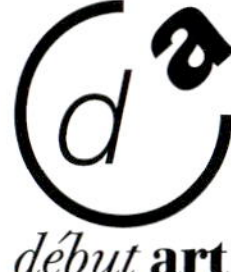

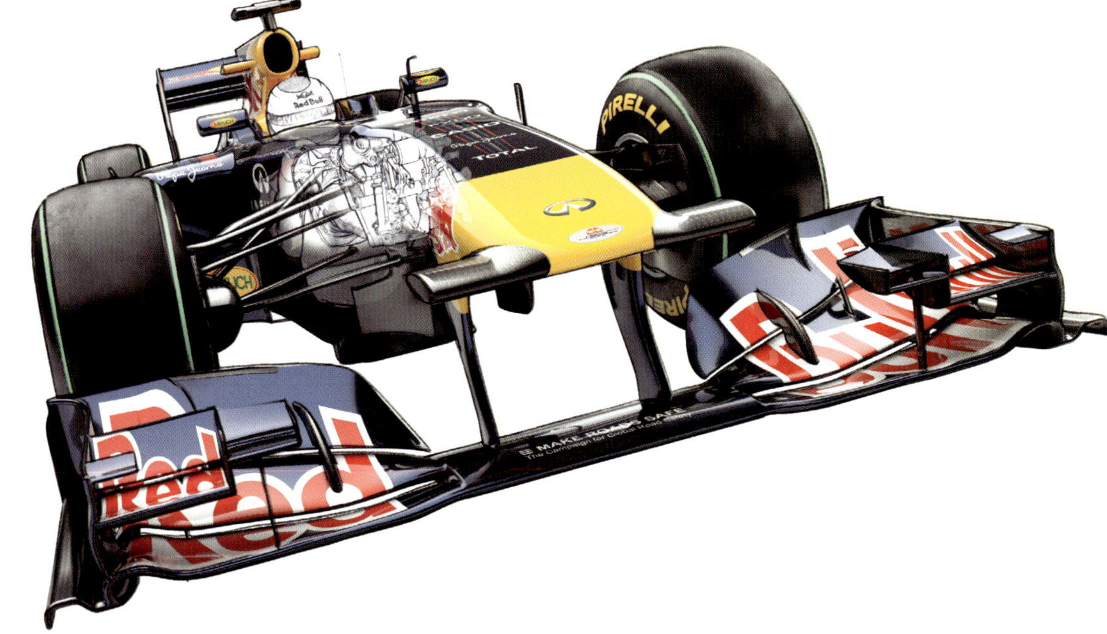

Comm. by Red Bull Racing.

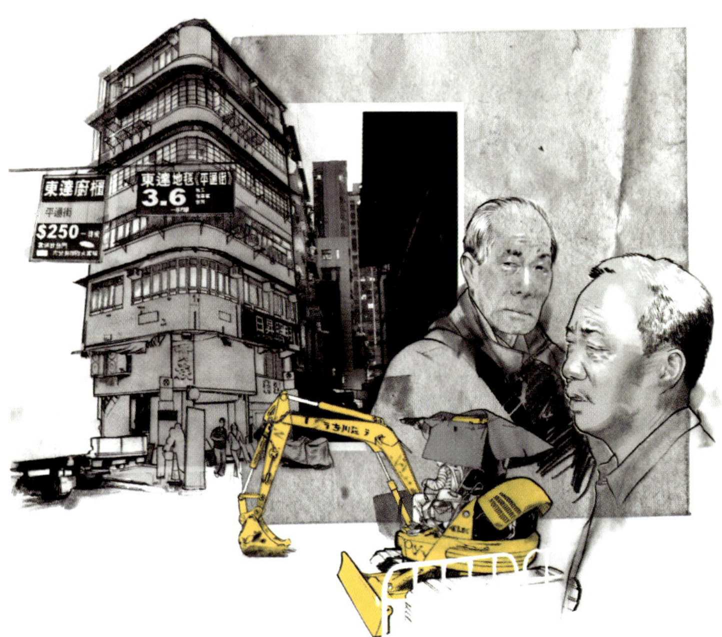

Self-initiated.

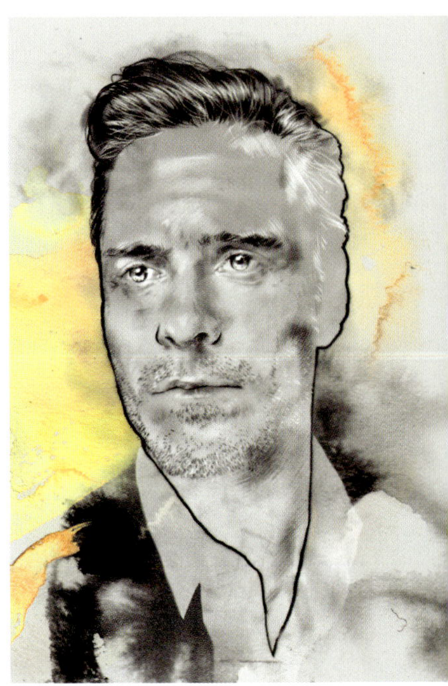

Self-initiated.

James Carey

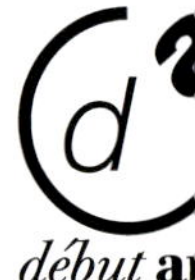

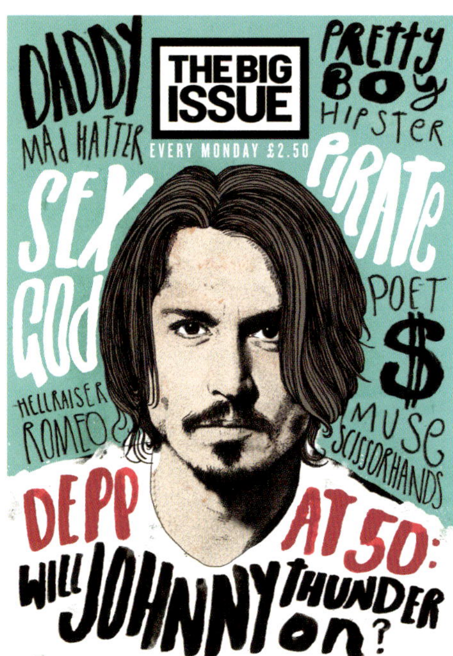

Comm. by The Big Issue.

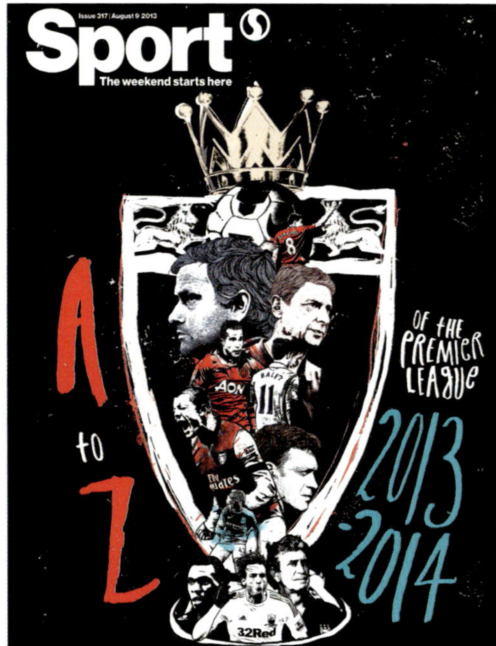

Comm. by Sport Magazine.

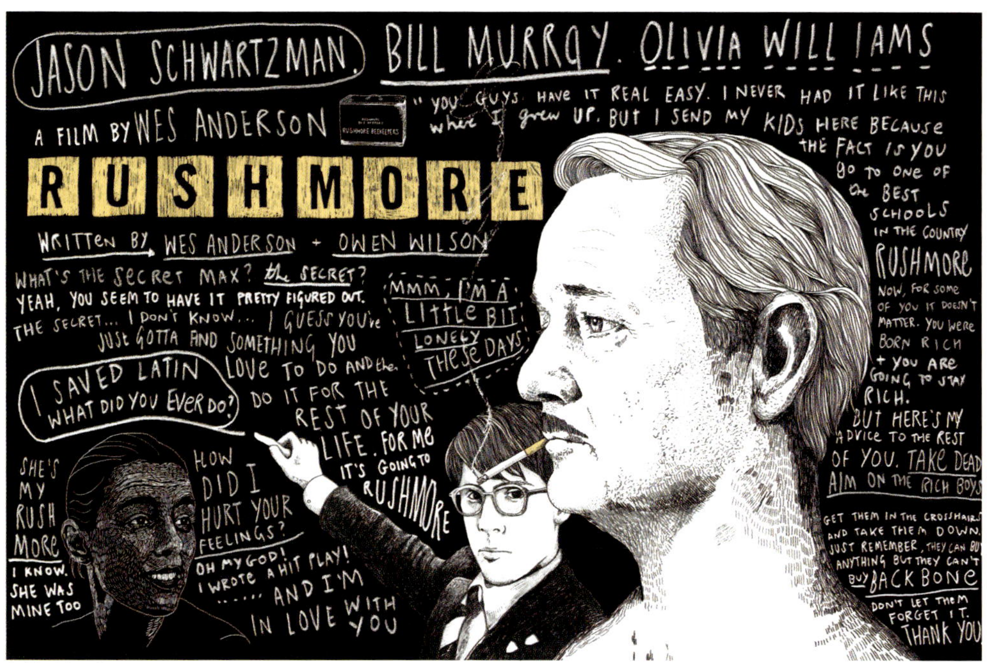

Self-initiated

...ter Strain

...but **art** • Illustrators, Photographers and Fine Artists Agents. 30 Tottenham Street, London, W1T 4RJ. United Kingdom
...: 01144 20 7636 1064. Fax: 01144 20 7580 7017. **The Coningsby Gallery** • Tel: 01144 20 7636 7478

...ail: **info@debutart.com** • **www.debutart.com** • **www.twitter.com/debutart**

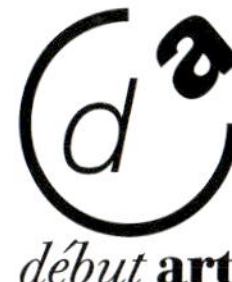

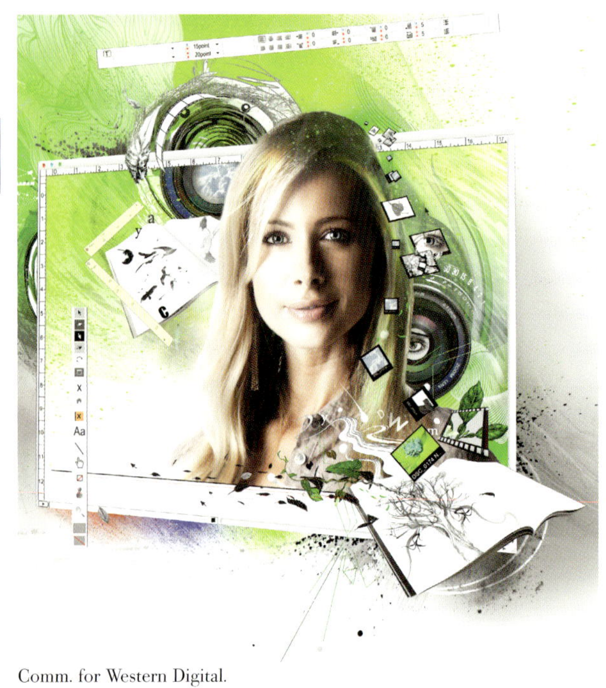

Comm. for Western Digital.

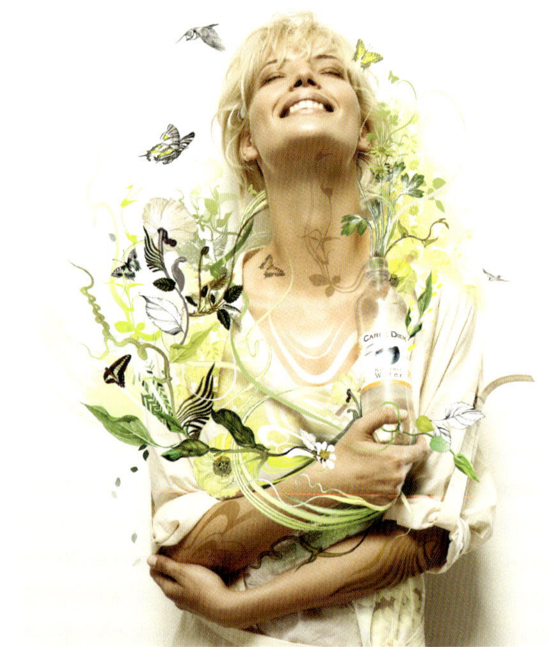

Comm. for Carpe Diem Water.

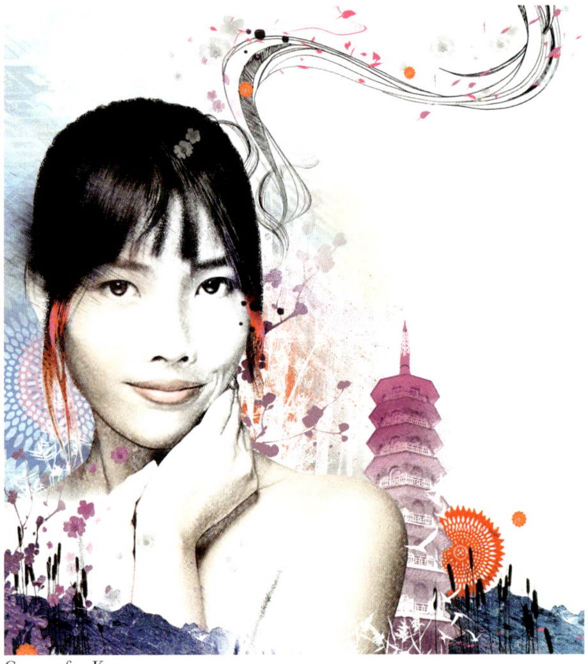

Comm. for Kyocera.

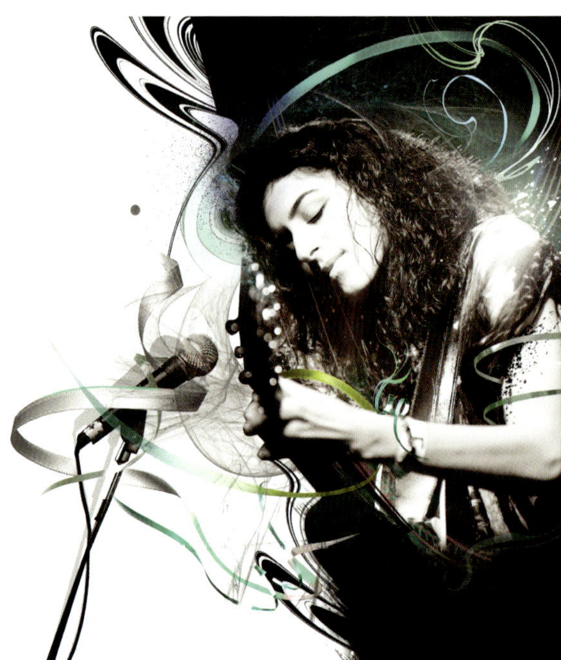

Comm. for The Institute of Contemporary Music Performance.

Sarah Howell

début **art** • Illustrators, Photographers and Fine Artists Agents. 30 Tottenham Street, London, W1T 4RJ. United Kingdom
Tel: 01144 20 7636 1064. Fax: 01144 20 7580 7017. **The Coningsby Gallery** • Tel: 01144 20 7636 7478

email: **info@debutart.com** • **www.debutart.com** • **www.twitter.com/debutart**

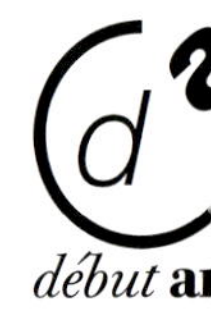

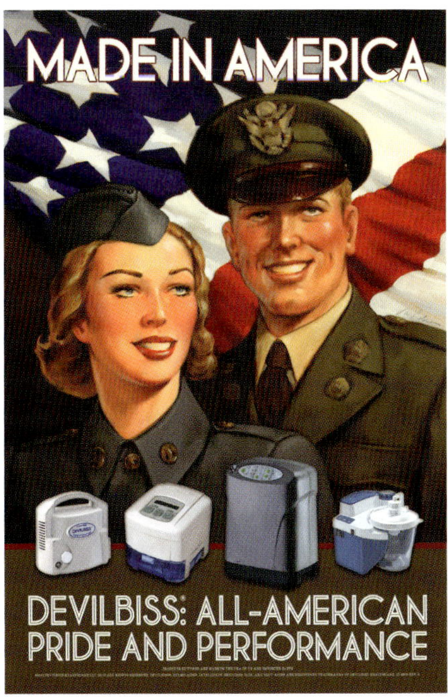

Comm. for DeVilbiss.

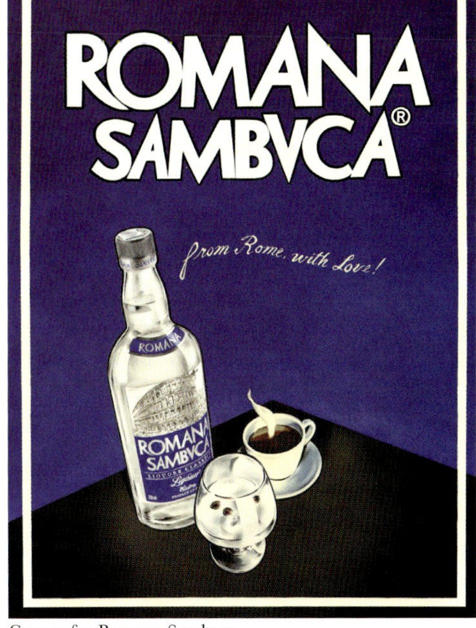

Comm. for Romana Sambvca.

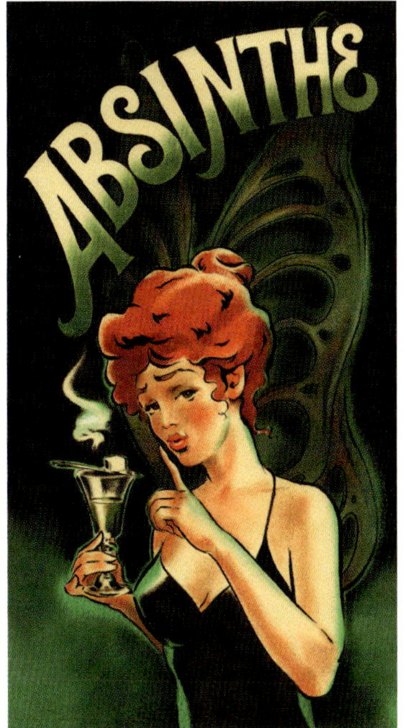

Comm. by The Radio Times.

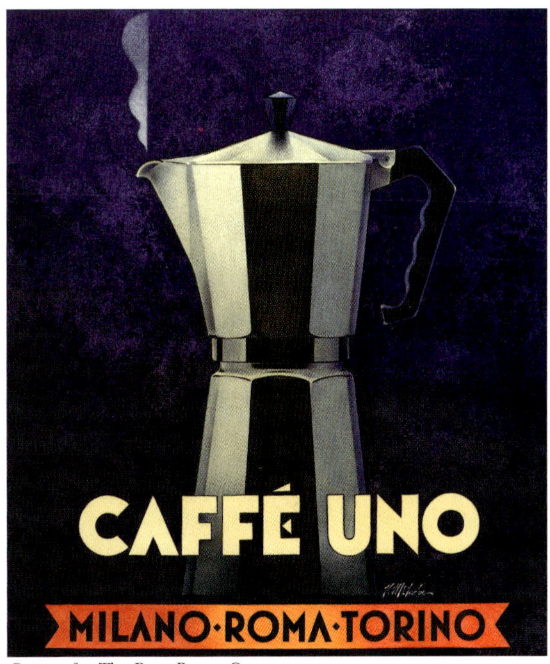

Comm. for The Ross Poster Group.

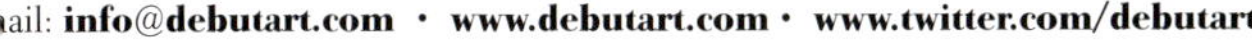

ince McIndoe

but **art** • Illustrators, Photographers and Fine Artists Agents. 30 Tottenham Street, London, W1T 4RJ. United Kingdom
: 01144 20 7636 1064. Fax: 01144 20 7580 7017. **The Coningsby Gallery** • Tel: 01144 20 7636 7478

ail: **info@debutart.com** • **www.debutart.com** • **www.twitter.com/debutart**

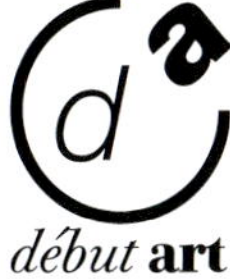

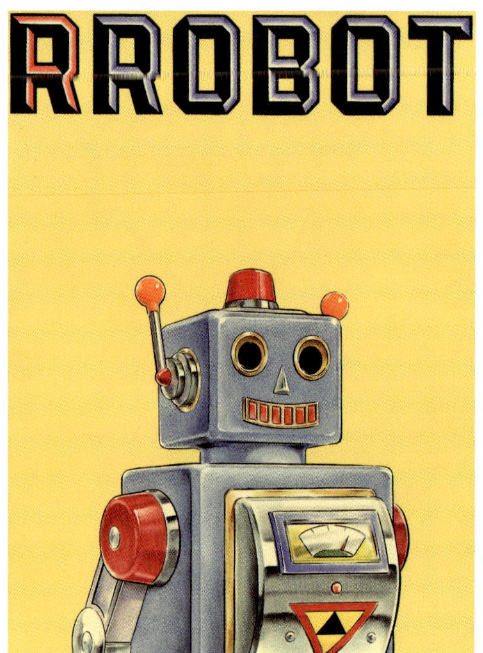

Self-initiated.

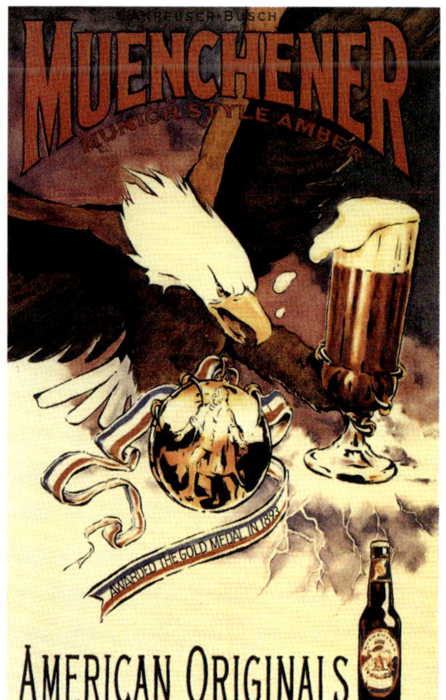

Comm. for Anheuser Busch.

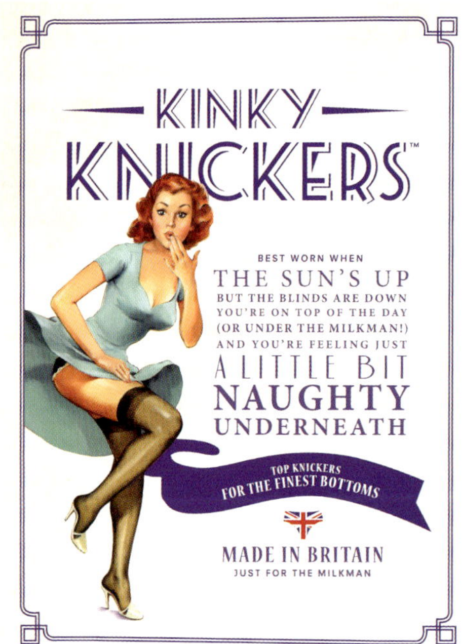

Comm. by Mary Portas.

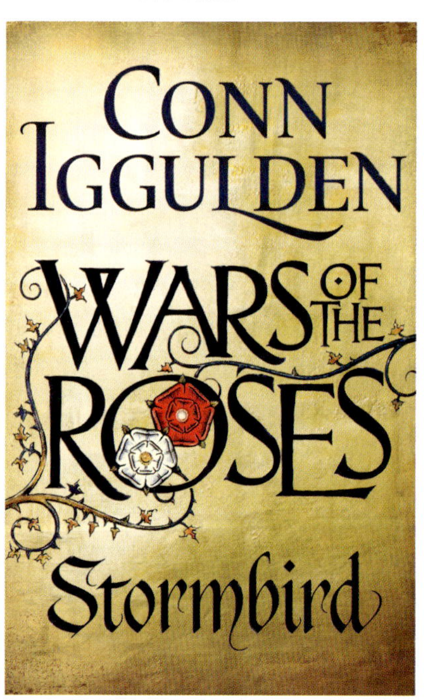

Comm. by Penguin Books.

Vince McIndoe

début **art** • Illustrators, Photographers and Fine Artists Agents. 30 Tottenham Street, London, W1T 4RJ. United Kingdom
Tel: 01144 20 7636 1064. Fax: 01144 20 7580 7017. **The Coningsby Gallery** • Tel: 01144 20 7636 7478

email: **info@debutart.com** • **www.debutart.com** • **www.twitter.com/debutart**

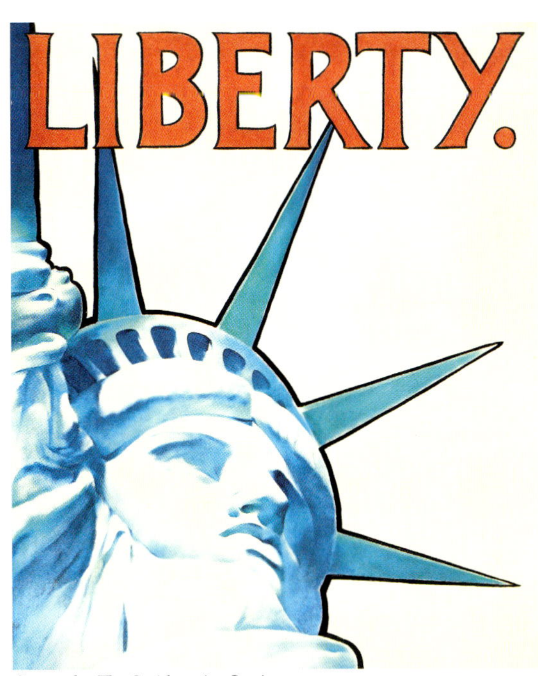

Comm. by The Smithsonian Institute.

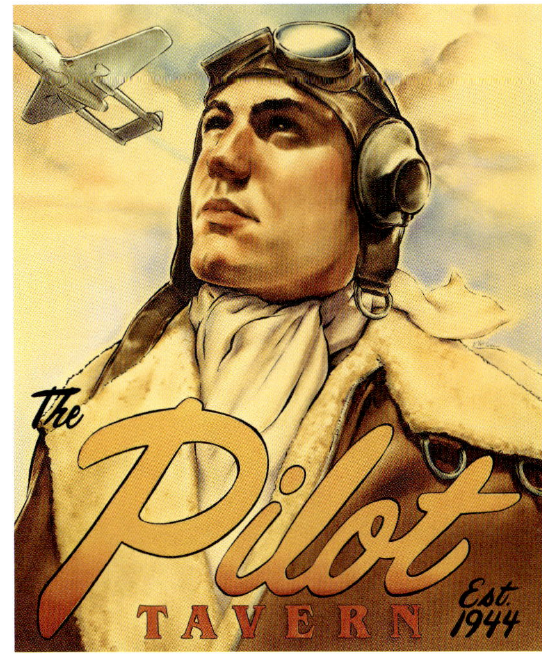

Comm. for The Pilot Tavern.

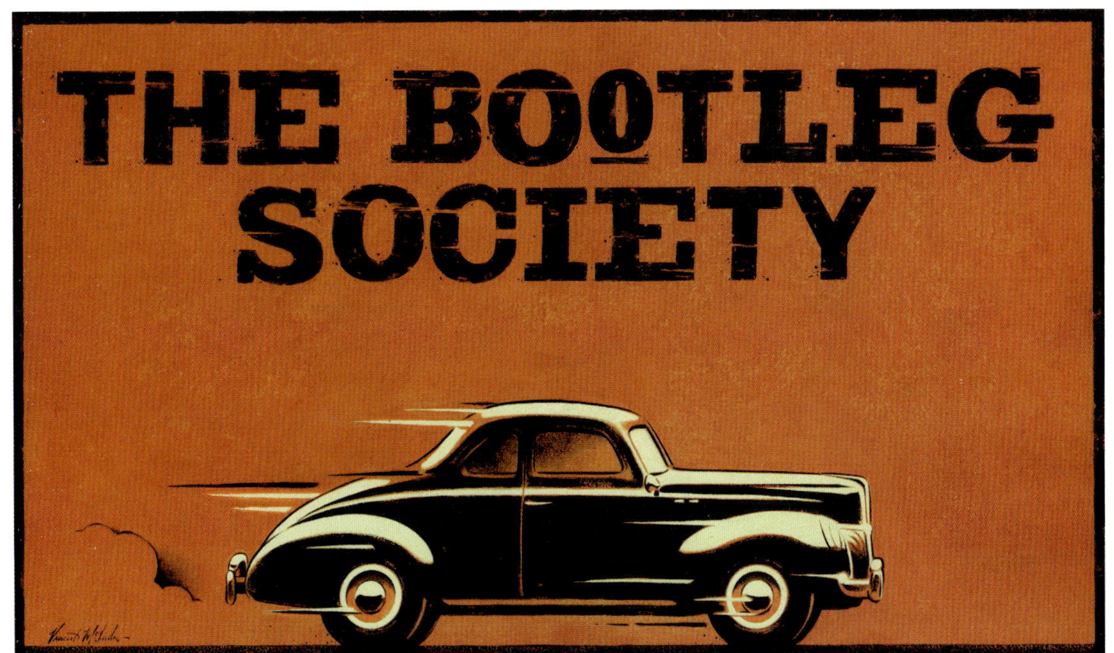

Comm. for St. Amant Winery.

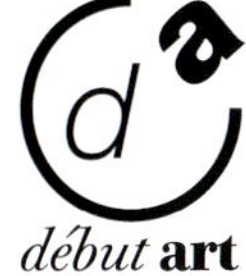

377

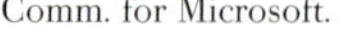

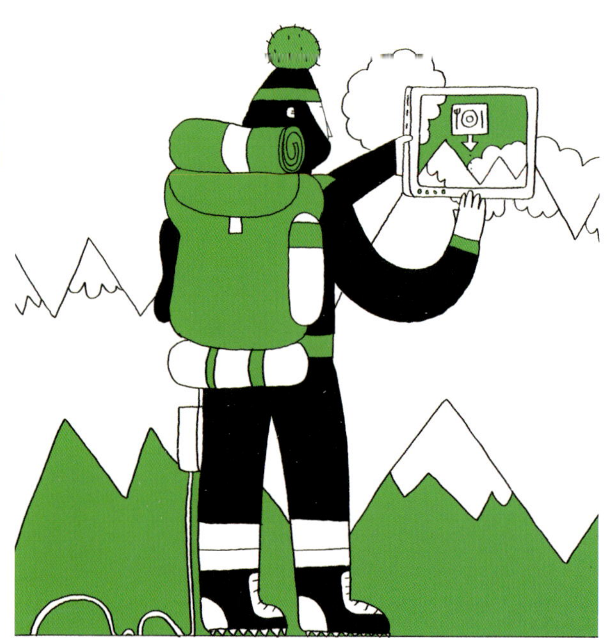

Comm. for Microsoft.

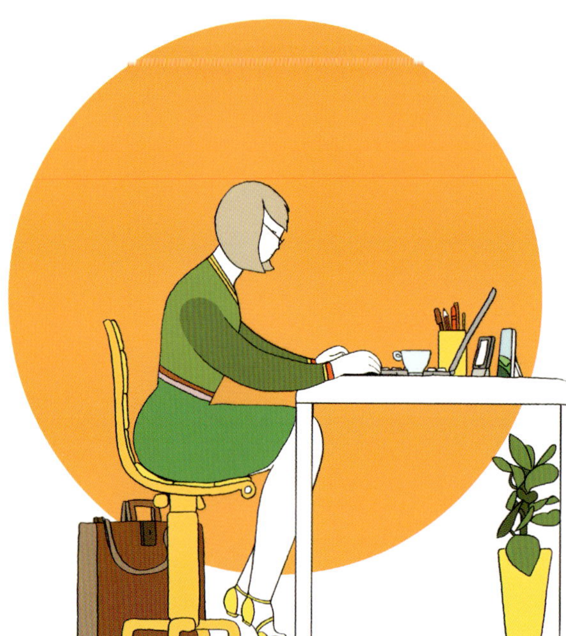

Comm. for Finers Stephens Innocent.

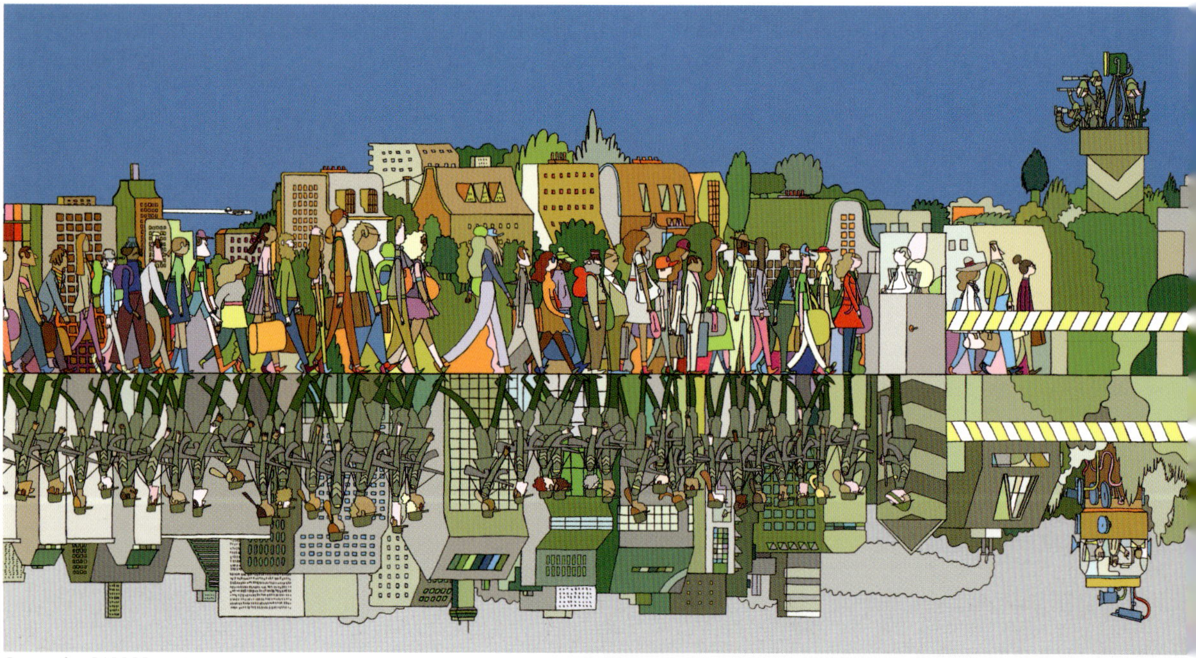

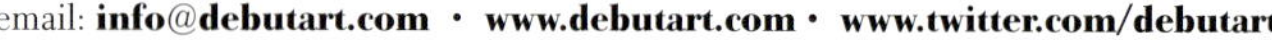

Comm. by CAM Magazine.

Celyn

début **art** • Illustrators, Photographers and Fine Artists Agents. 30 Tottenham Street, London, W1T 4RJ. United Kingdom
Tel: 01144 20 7636 1064. Fax: 01144 20 7580 7017. **The Coningsby Gallery** • Tel: 01144 20 7636 7478

email: **info@debutart.com** • **www.debutart.com** • **www.twitter.com/debutart**

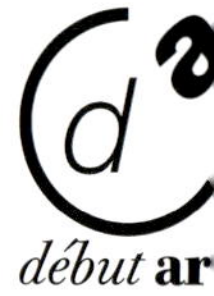

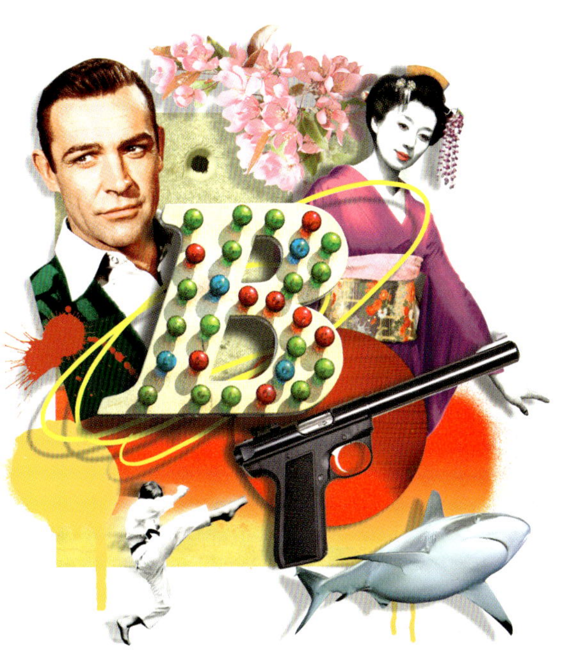

Comm. by The Mail On Sunday Magazine.

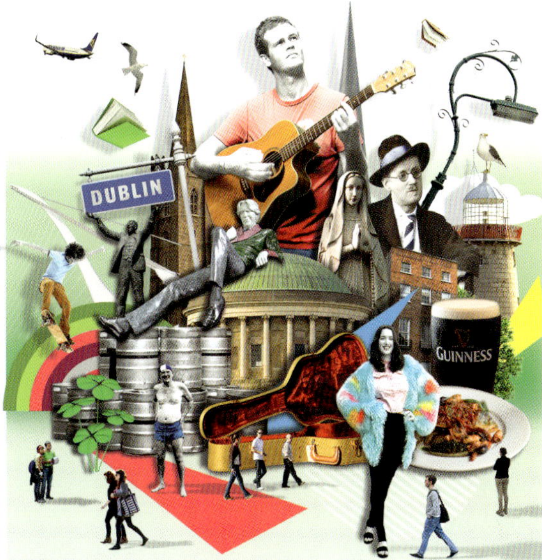

Comm. by The Mail On Sunday Magazine.

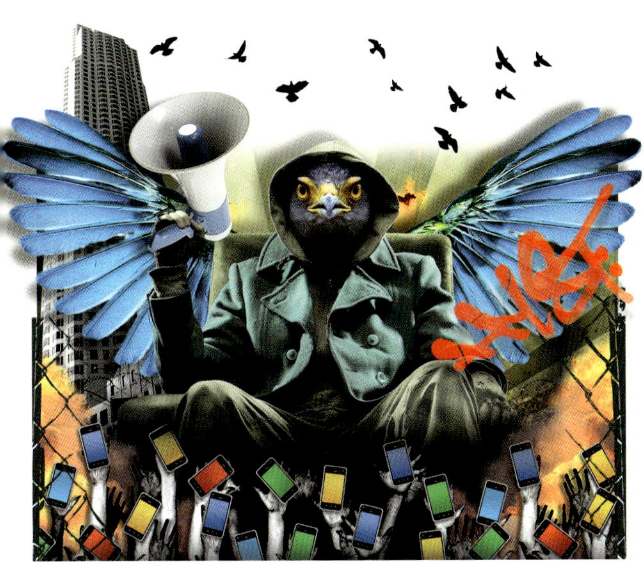

Comm. by The Economist Magazine.

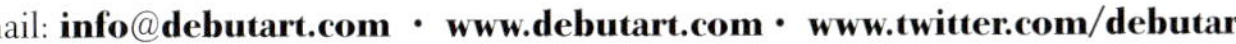

Comm. for Ryanair Let's Go Magazine.

Matt Herring

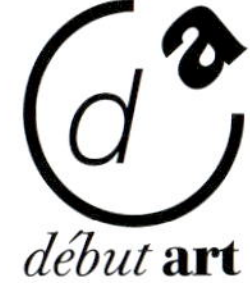

début art

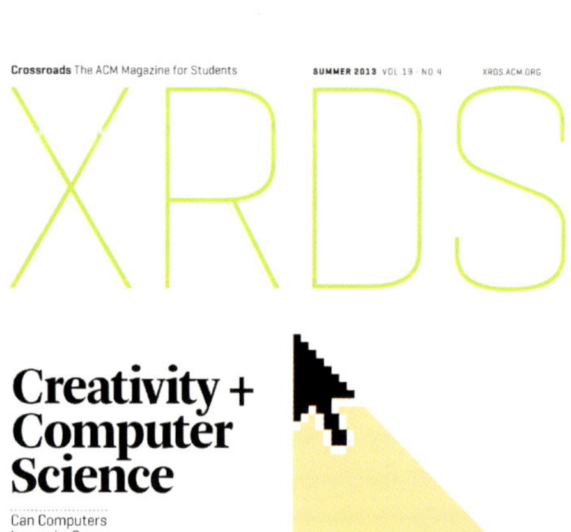

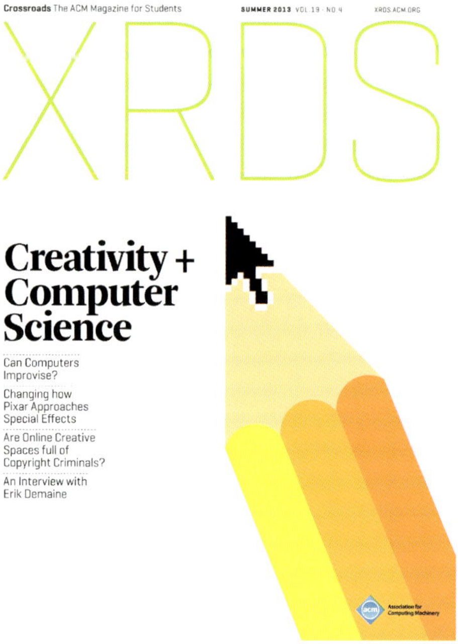

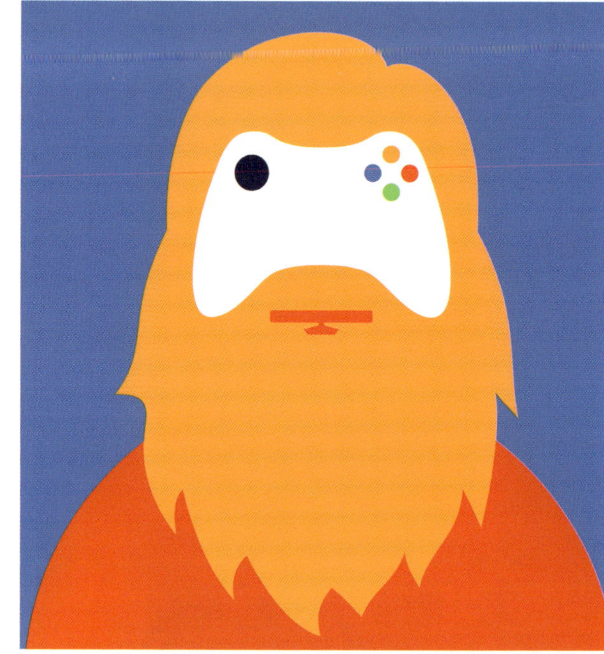

Comm. by XRDS Magazine.

Comm. for Microsoft.

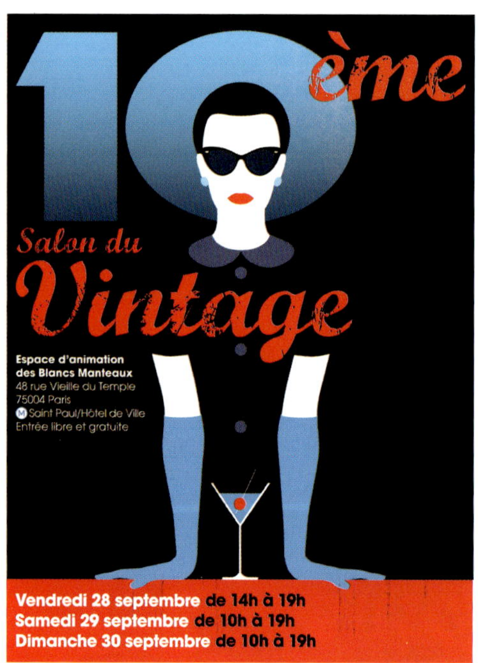

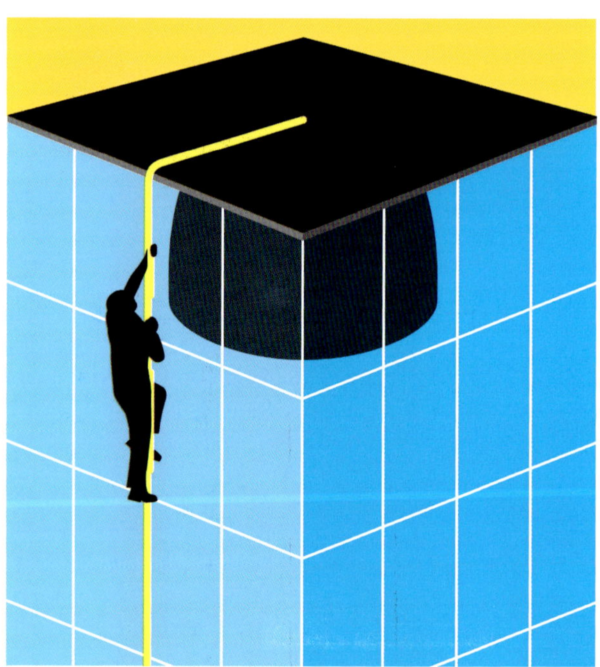

Comm. Salon du Vintage.

Comm. by Draper's Record Magazine.

Patrick George

début **art** • Illustrators, Photographers and Fine Artists Agents. 30 Tottenham Street, London, W1T 4RJ. United Kingdom
Tel: 01144 20 7636 1064.   Fax: 01144 20 7580 7017.   **The Coningsby Gallery**   •   Tel: 01144 20 7636 7478

email: **info@debutart.com**   •   **www.debutart.com**   •   **www.twitter.com/debutart**

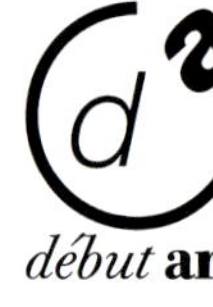

380

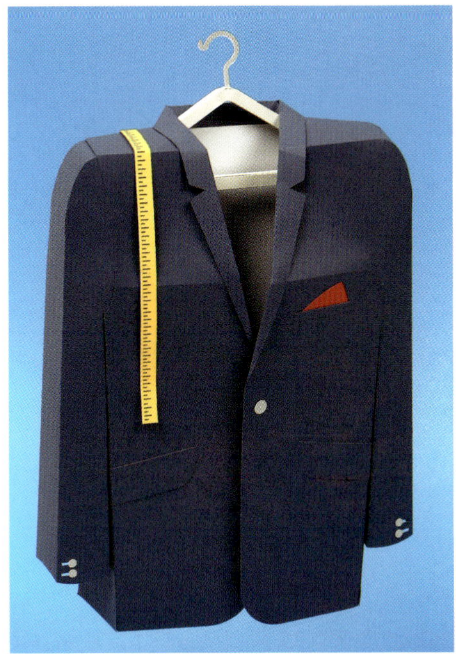

Comm. by Ted Baker Clothing C.o.

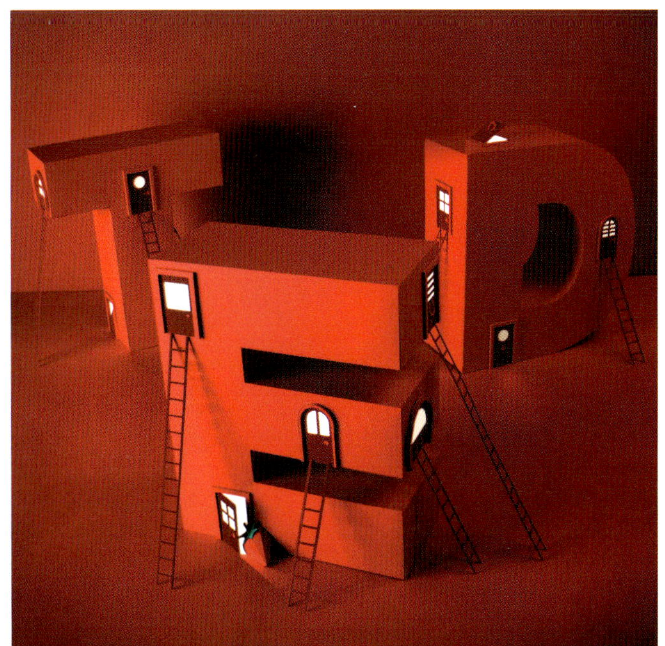

Comm. by Fast Company Magazine.

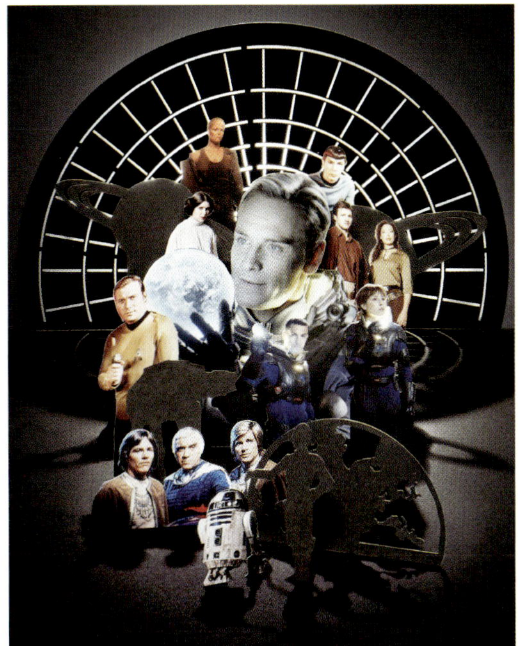

Comm. by Time Magazine.

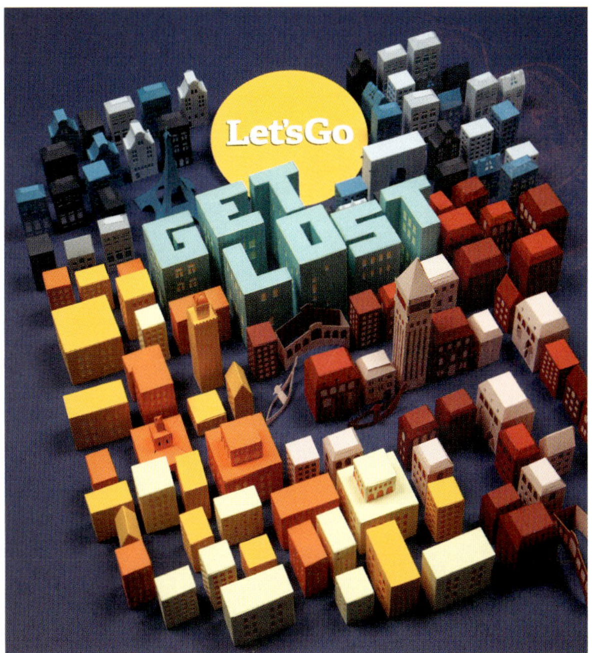

Comm. by Ryanair's Let's Go Magazine .

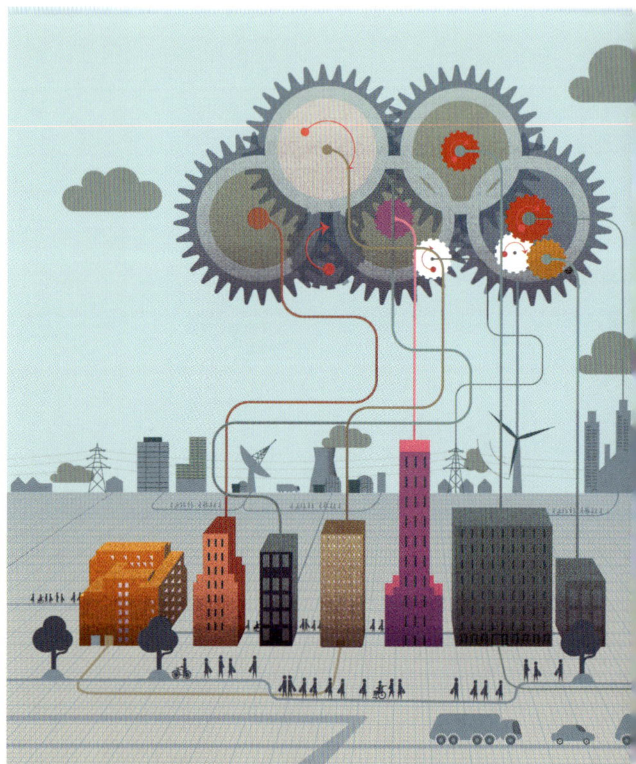

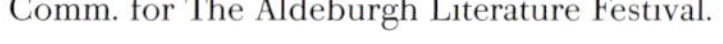

Comm. for The Aldeburgh Literature Festival.

Comm. by Computing In Science & Engineering Magazine.

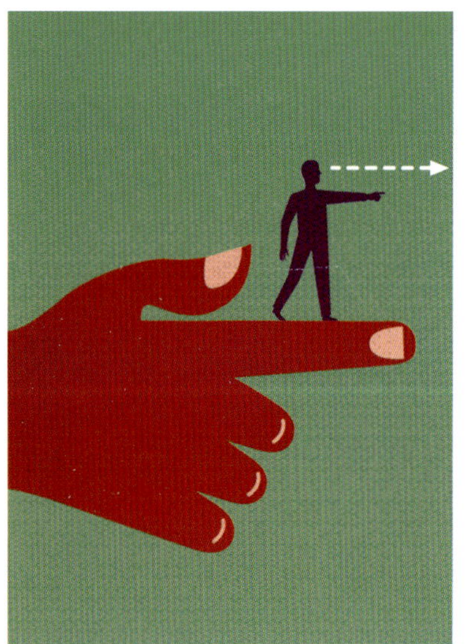

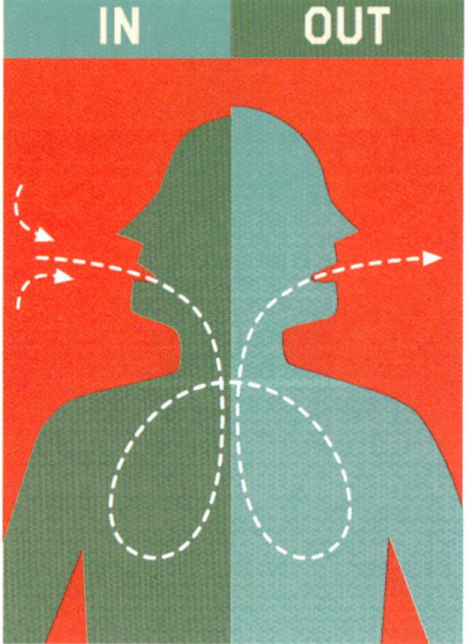

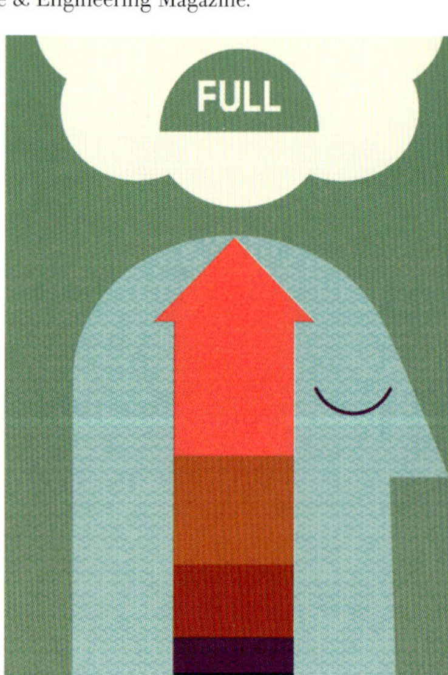

Comm. by The Guardian.

Andrew Baker

début **art** • Illustrators, Photographers and Fine Artists Agents. 30 Tottenham Street, London, W1T 4RJ. United Kingdom
Tel: 01144 20 7636 1064. Fax: 01144 20 7580 7017. **The Coningsby Gallery** • Tel: 01144 20 7636 7478

email: **info@debutart.com** • **www.debutart.com** • **www.twitter.com/debutart**

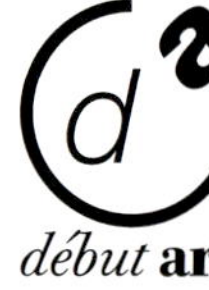

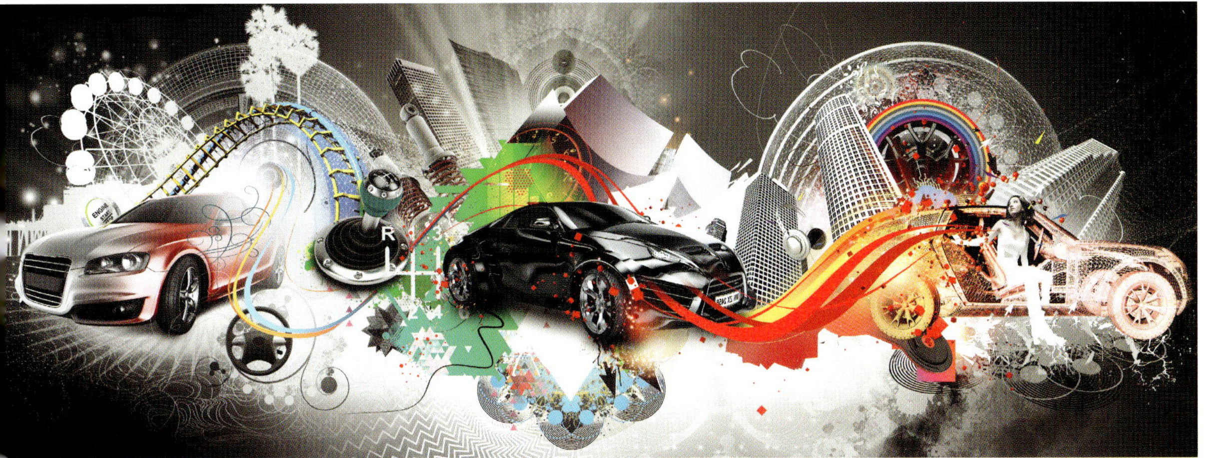

Comm. for LA Motorshow.

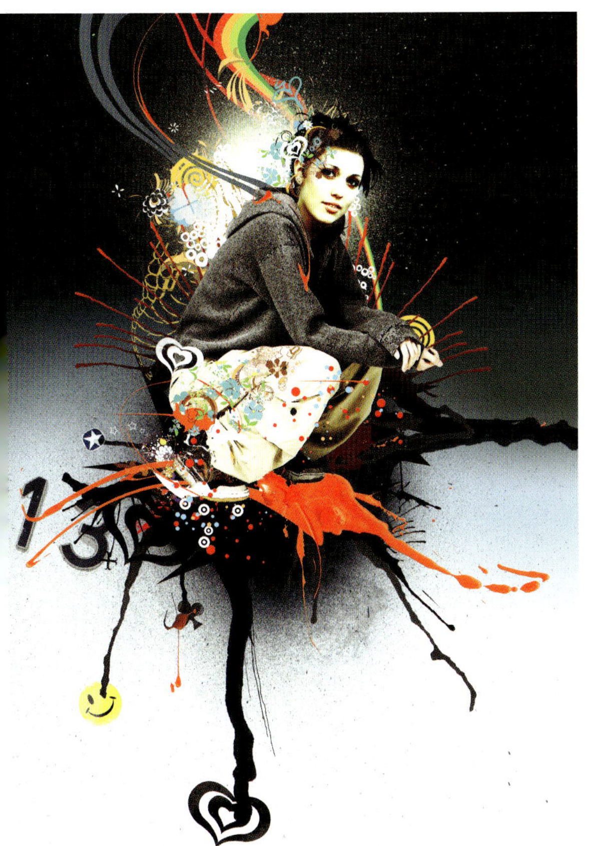

lf-initiated.

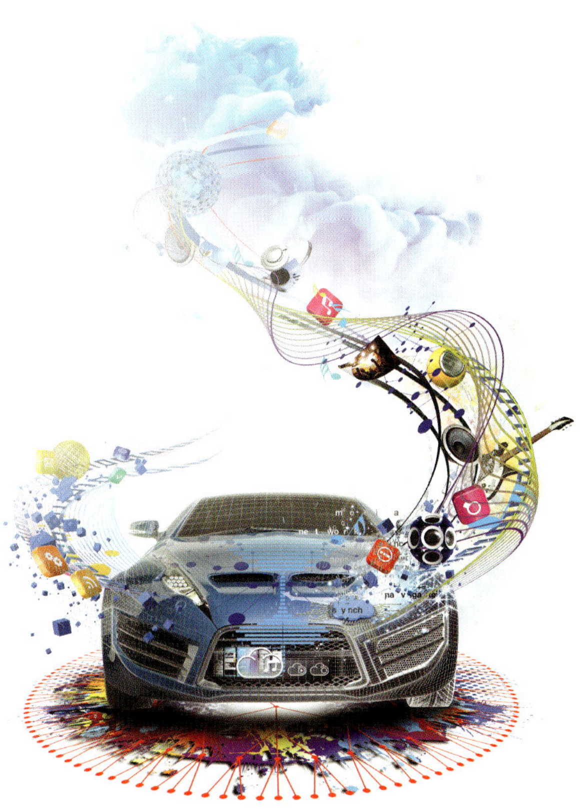

Comm. by i3 Magazine.

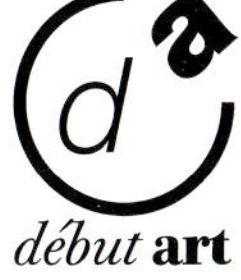

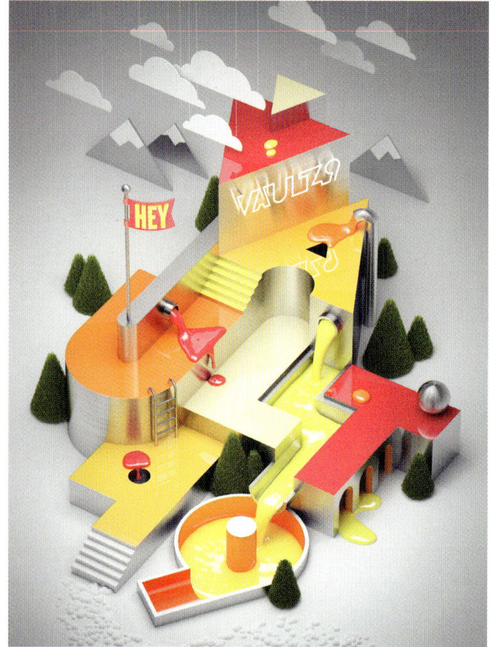

Self-initiated.

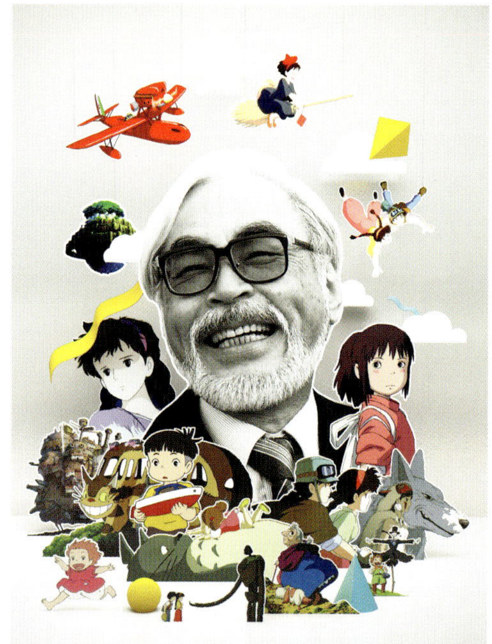

Comm. for Time Magazine.

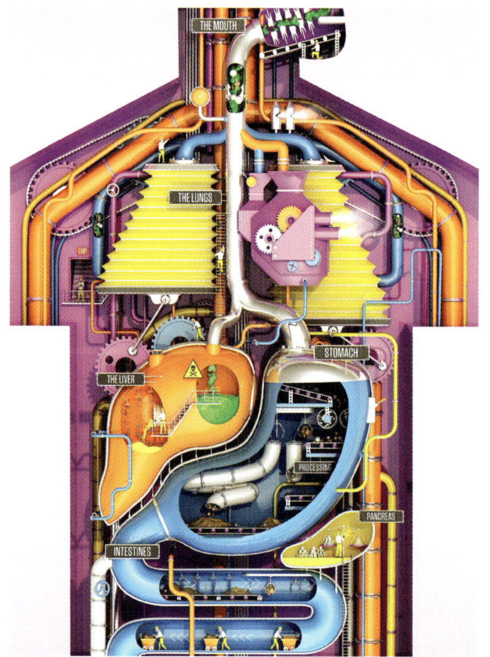

Comm. by Z-Life Magazine.

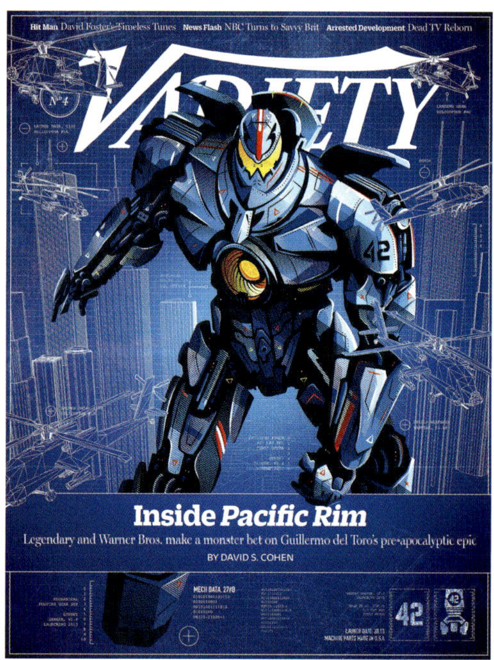

Comm. by Variety Magazine.

Vault49

début **art** • Illustrators, Photographers and Fine Artists Agents. 30 Tottenham Street, London, W1T 4RJ. United Kingdom
Tel: 01144 20 7636 1064. Fax: 01144 20 7580 7017. **The Coningsby Gallery** • Tel: 01144 20 7636 7478

email: **info@debutart.com** • **www.debutart.com** • **www.twitter.com/debutart**

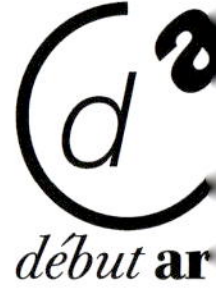

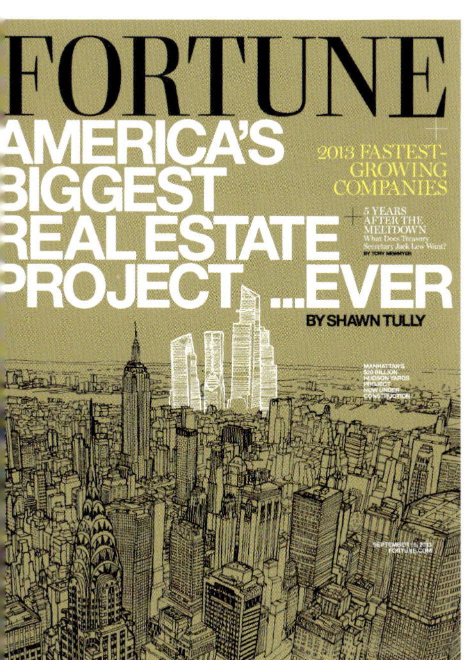

...mm. by Fortune Magazine.

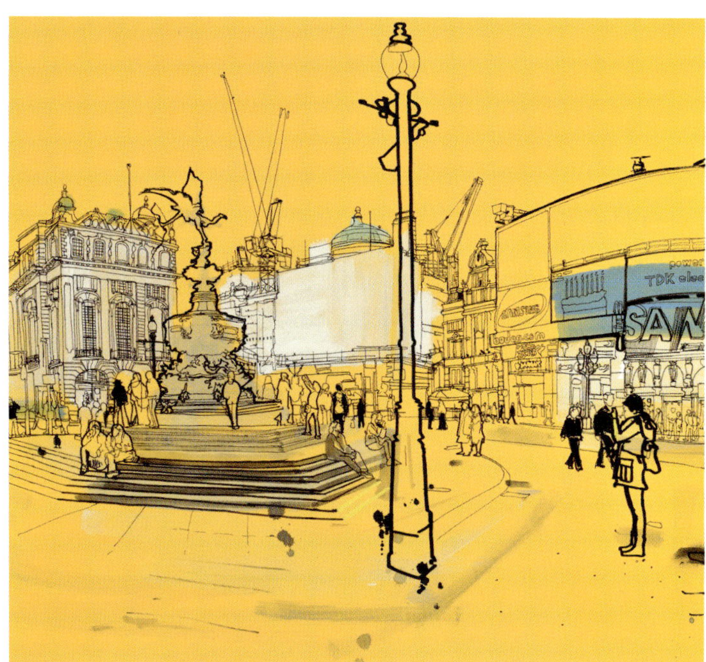

Self-initiated.

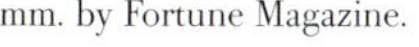

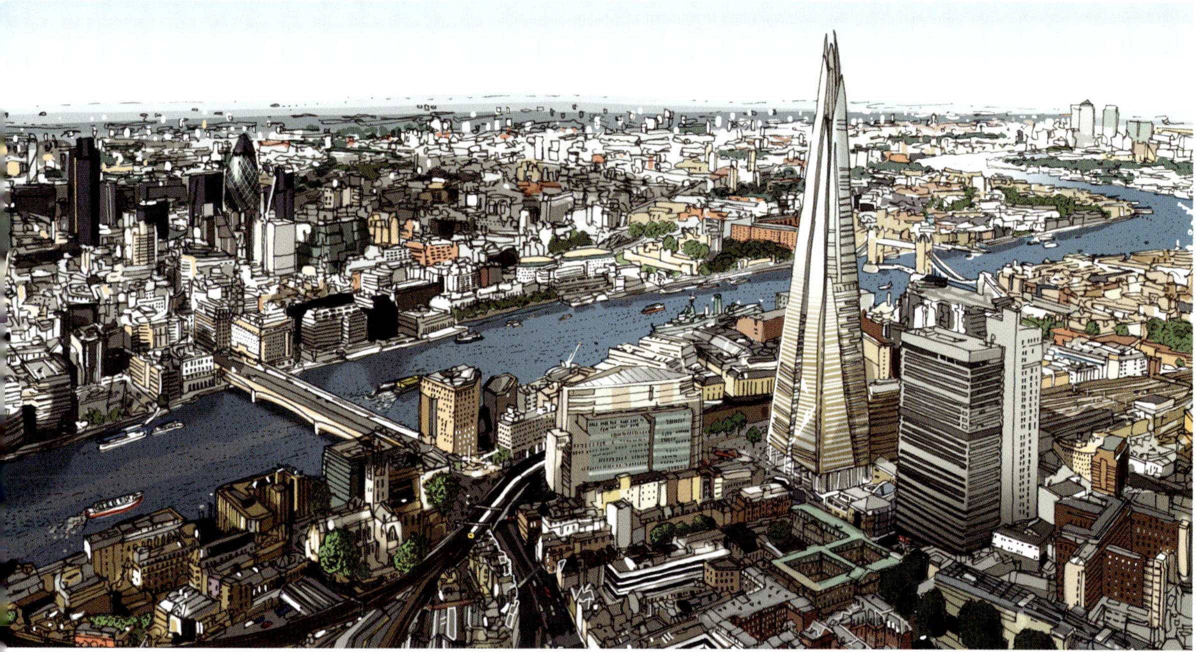

...f-initiated.

...trick Vale

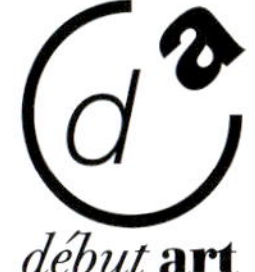

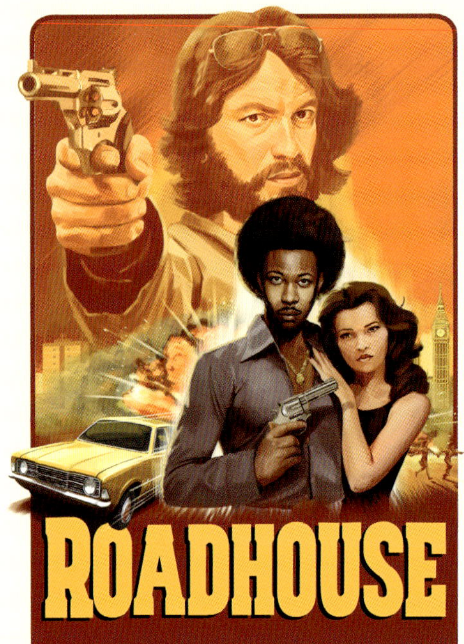

Comm. for Argonaut Pictures.

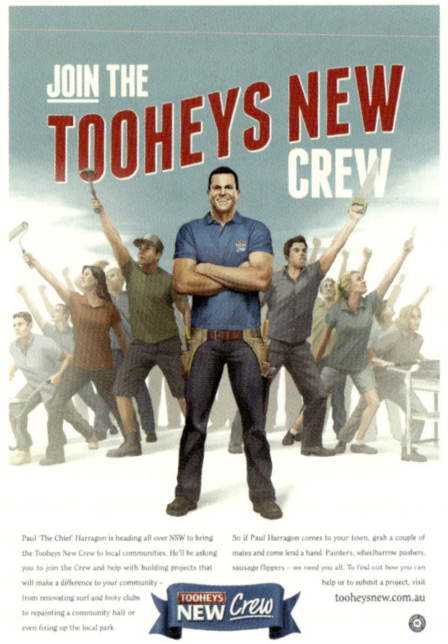

Comm. for Tooheys New.

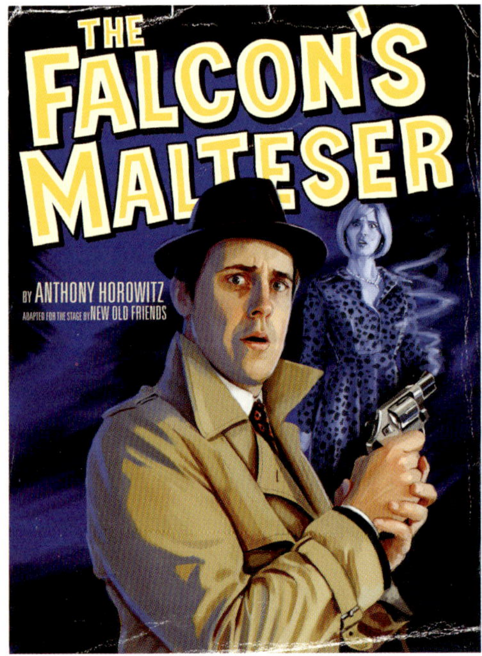

Comm. for New Old Friends

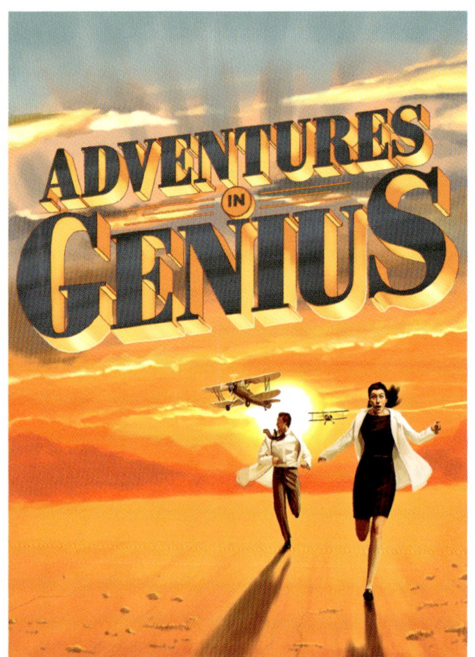

Comm. by Mental Floss Magazine.

The Red Dress

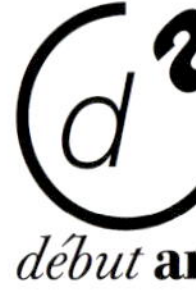

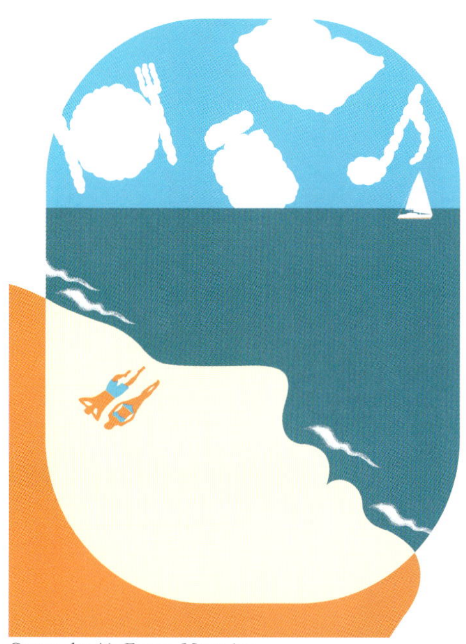

Comm. by Air France Magazine.

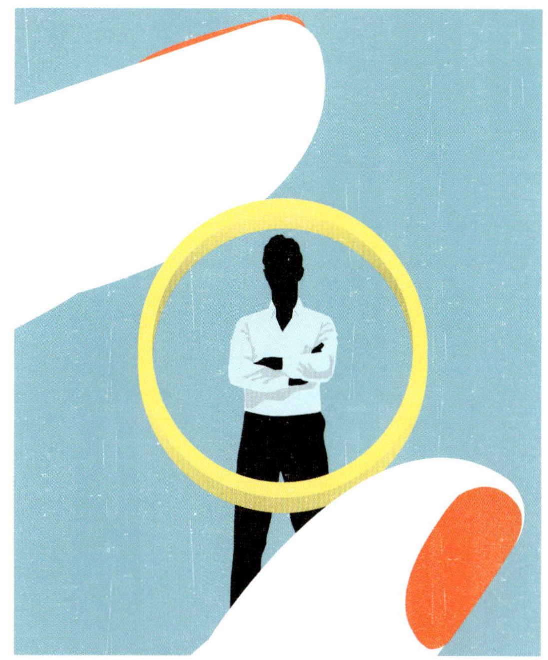

Comm. by The Mail on Sunday.

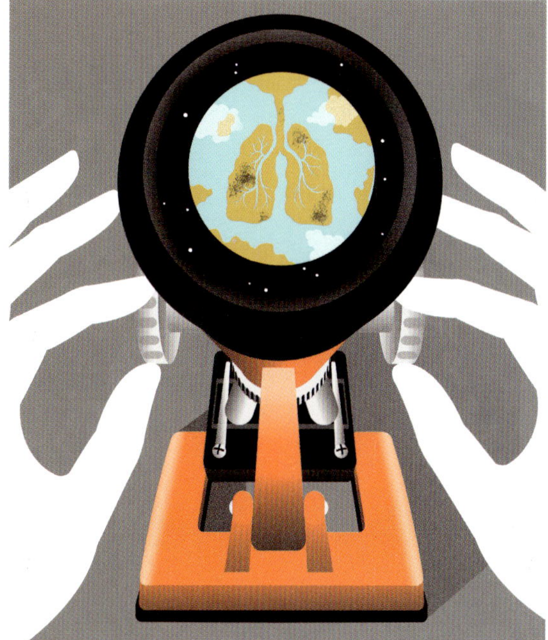

Comm. by Nature Magazine.

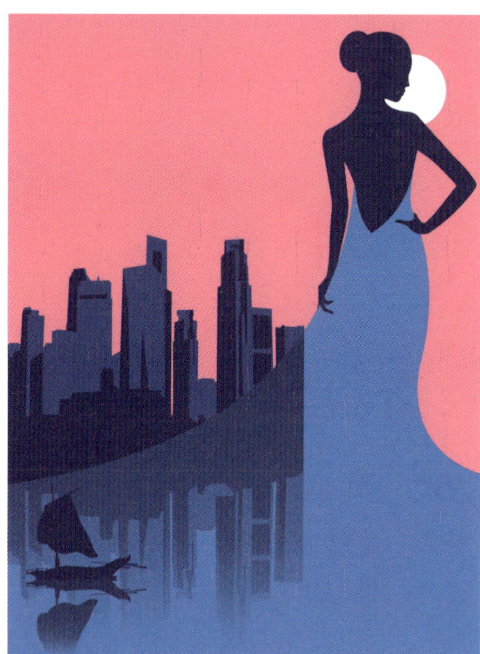

Comm. by SHOP Magazine.

Neil Webb

début **art** • Illustrators, Photographers and Fine Artists Agents. 30 Tottenham Street, London, W1T 4RJ. United Kingdom
Tel: 01144 20 7636 1064. Fax: 01144 20 7580 7017. **The Coningsby Gallery** • Tel: 01144 20 7636 7478

Email: **info@debutart.com** • **www.debutart.com** • **www.twitter.com/debutart**

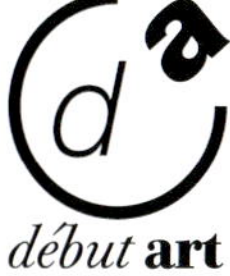

début **art**

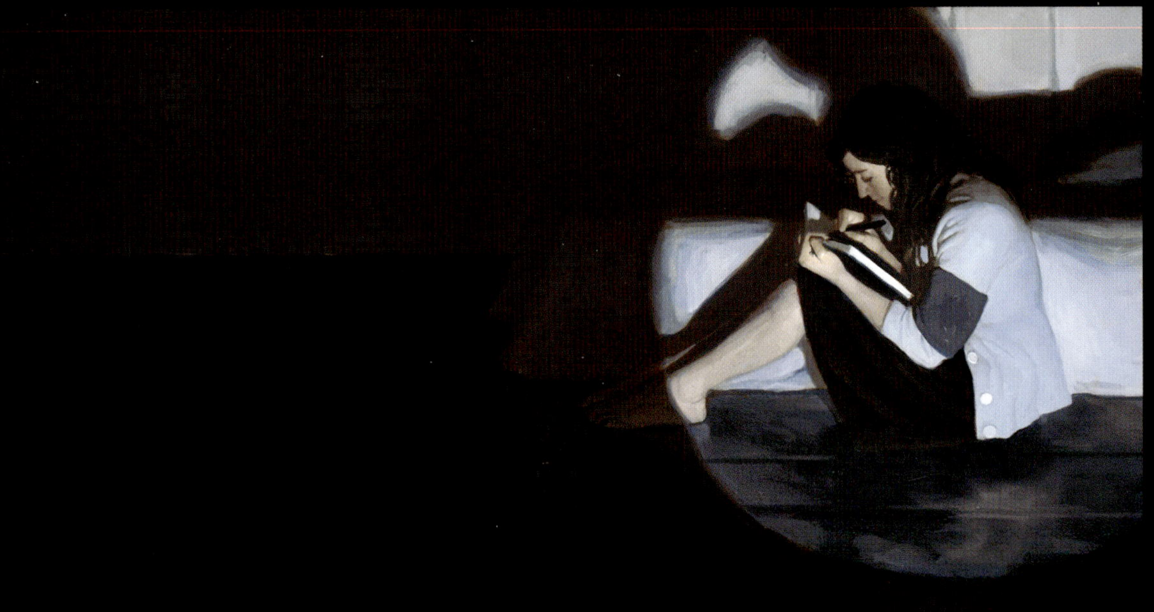

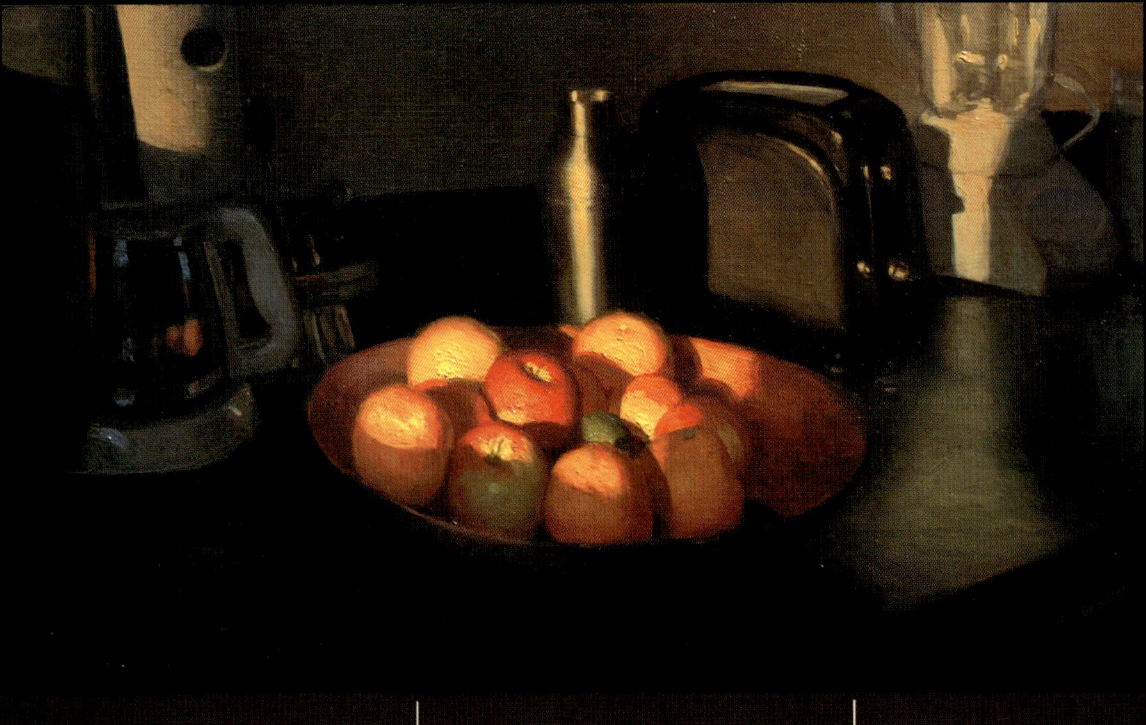

Raymond Bonilla | www.raymondbonilla.com | **718.781.8148**
ray@raymondbonilla.com

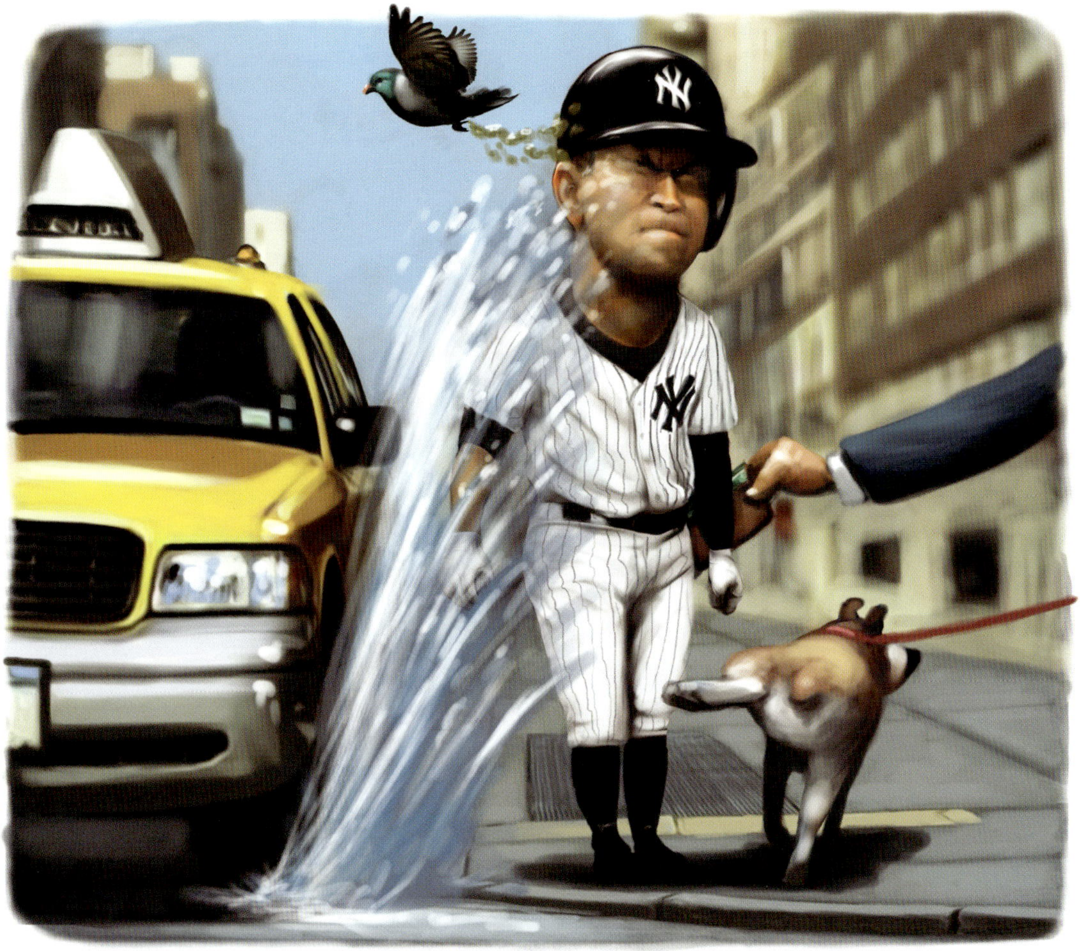

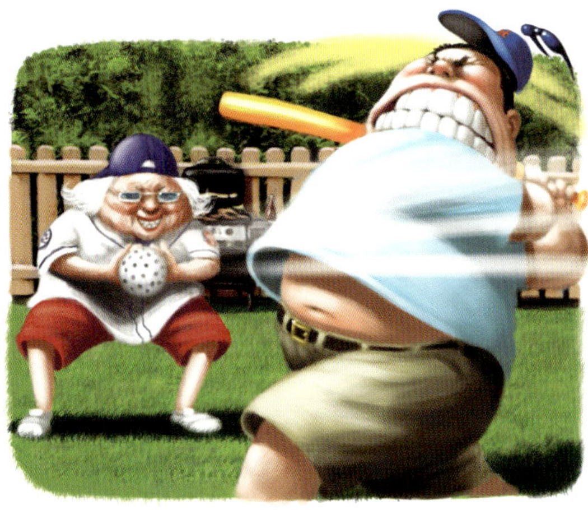

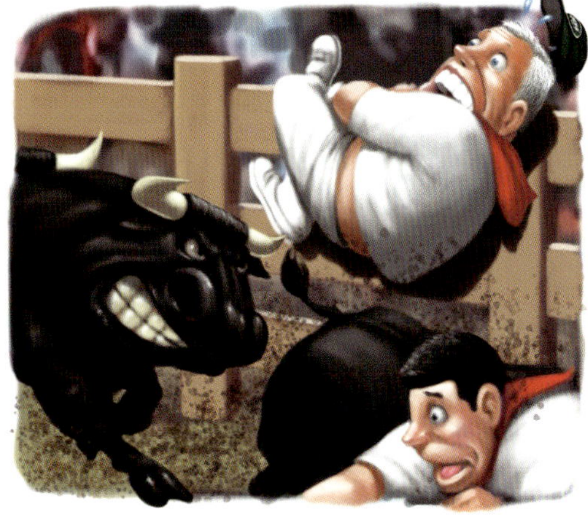

Scott Pollack   pollack@scottpollack.com   516-921-1908

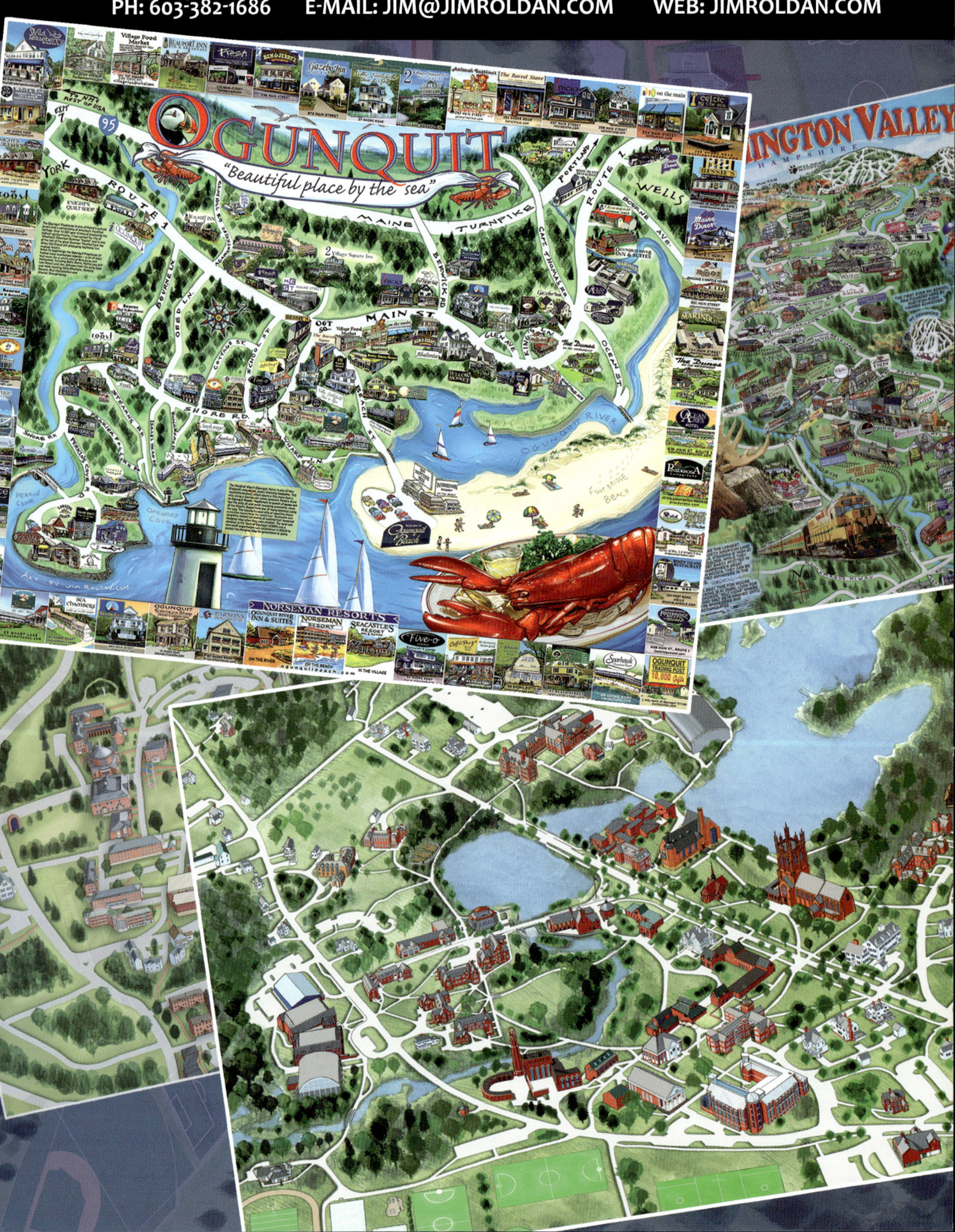

JIM ROLDAN/ILLUSTRATION
MAP ART OF DESTINATIONS, CAMPUSES & RESORTS FOR NAVIGATION, PROMOTION & LICENSING
PH: 603-382-1686   E-MAIL: JIM@JIMROLDAN.COM   WEB: JIMROLDAN.COM
OGUNQUIT
"Beautiful place by the sea"

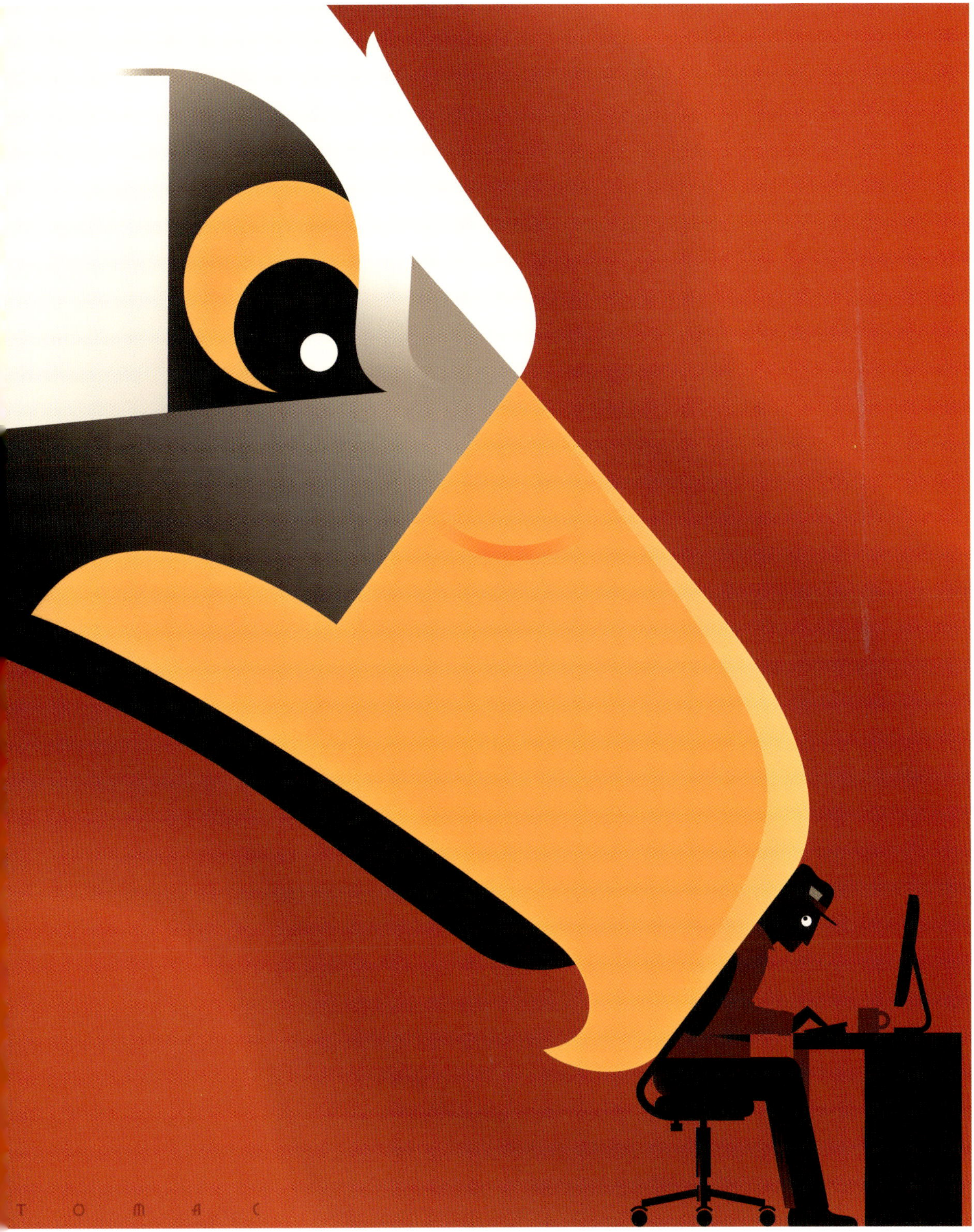

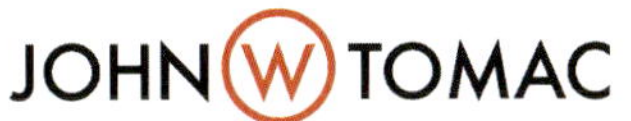

JOHN W TOMAC

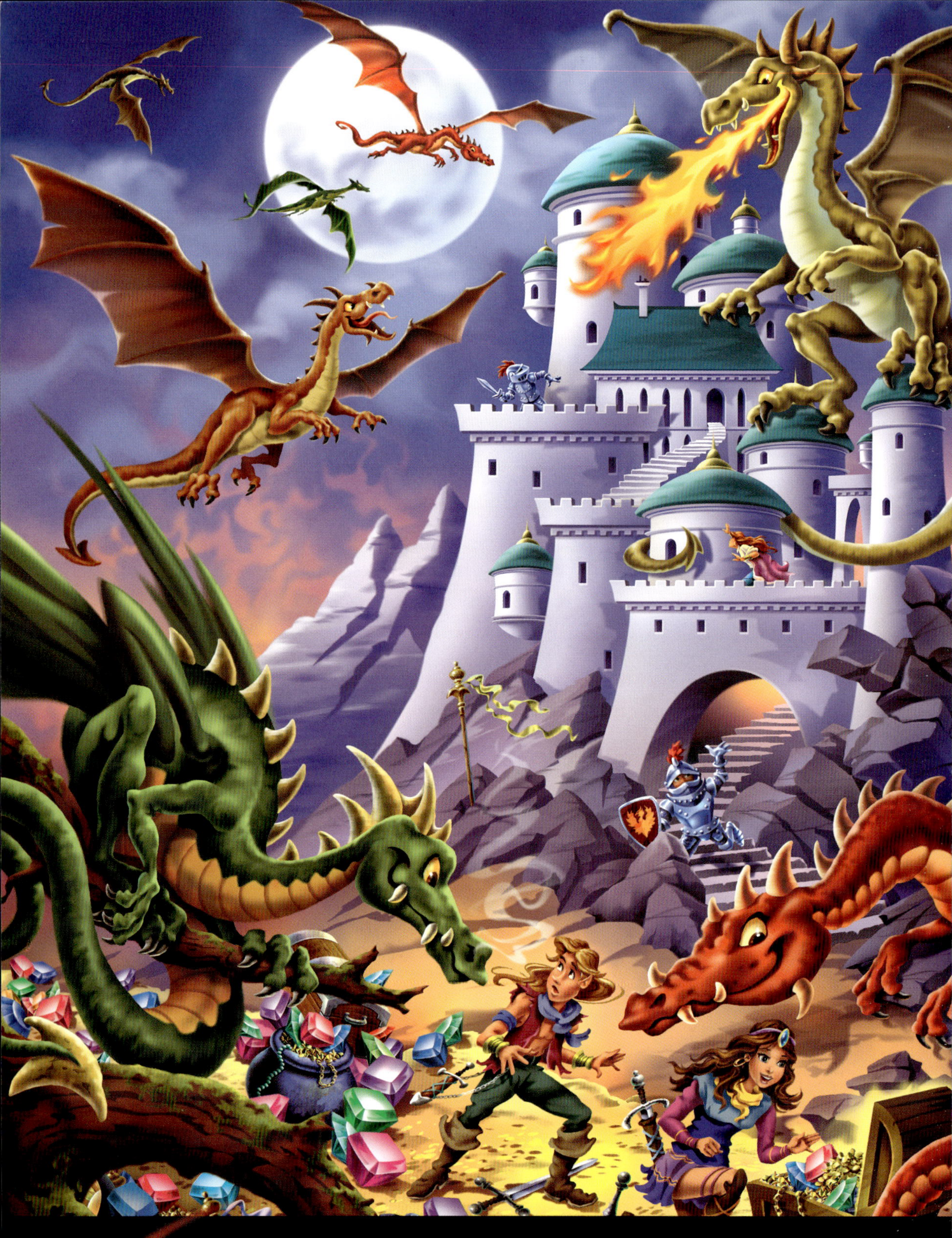
GRAYSON
S T U D I O S
508.898.3943
rick@rickgrayson.com
www.rickgrayson.com

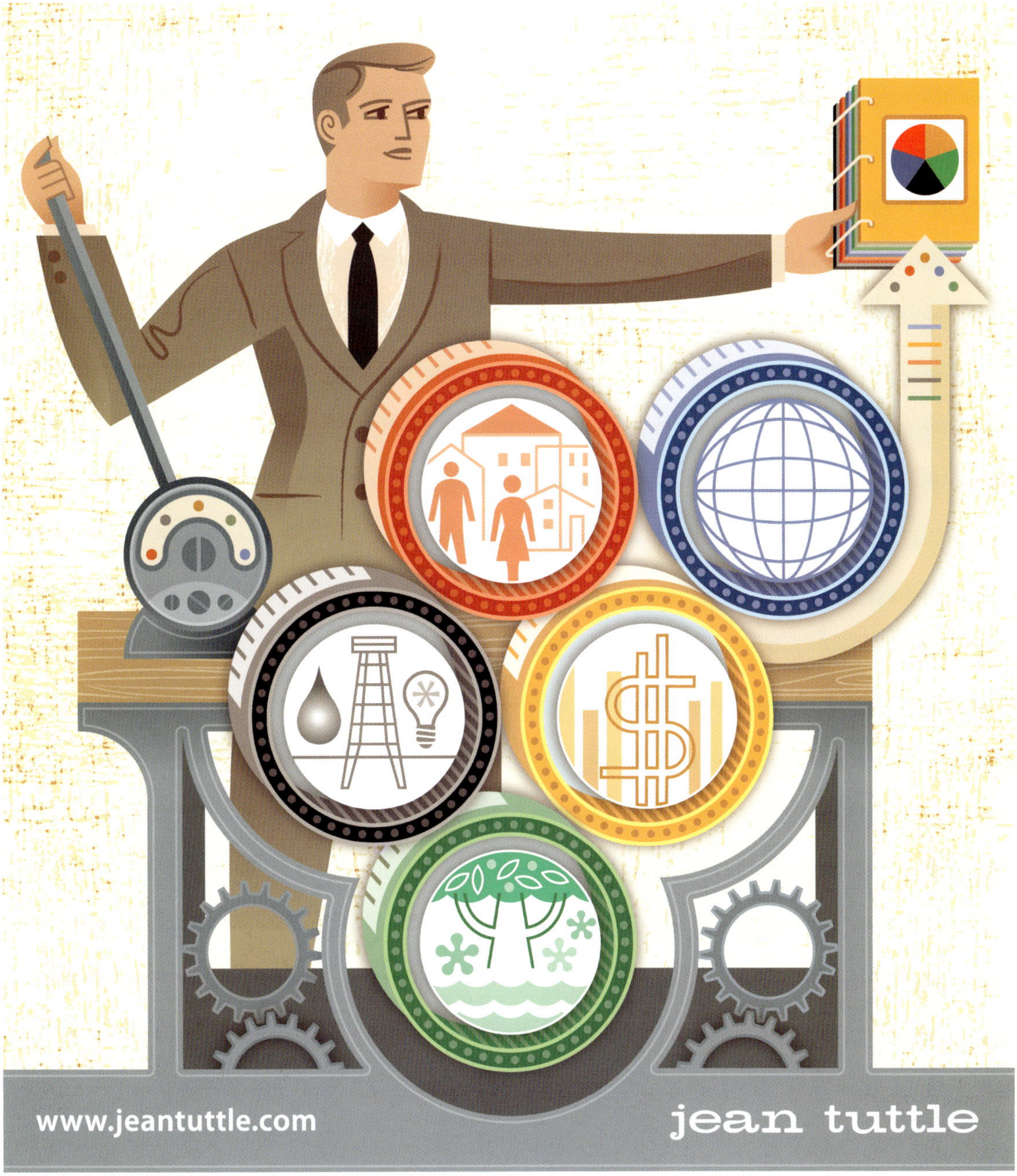

www.jeantuttle.com

jean tuttle

303-388-3333

jean@jeantuttle.com

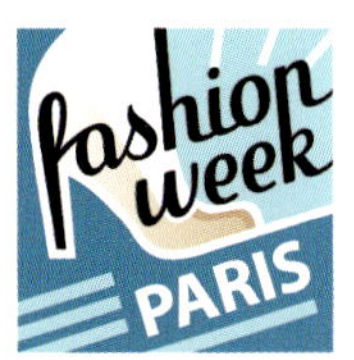

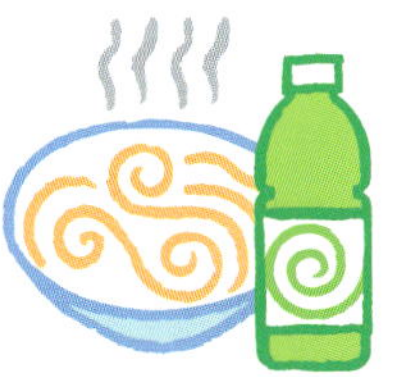

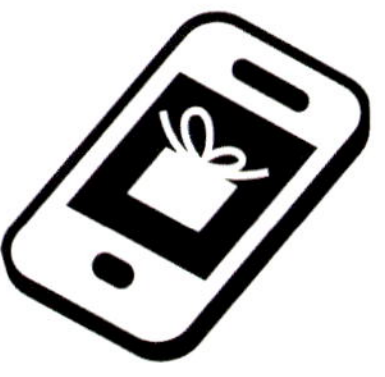
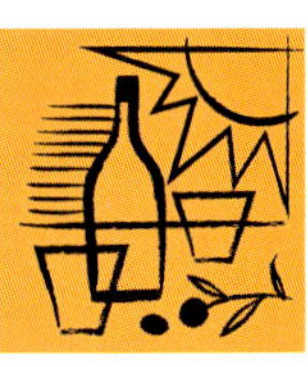

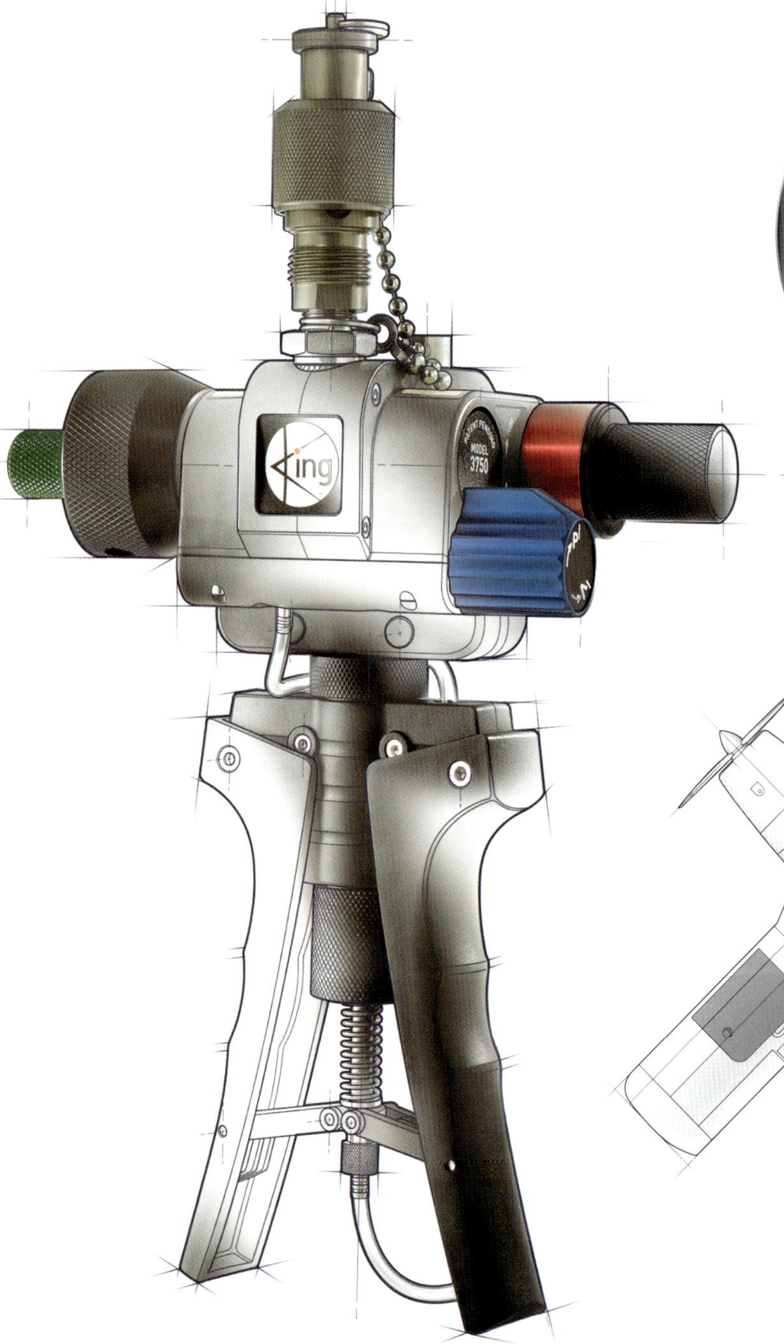

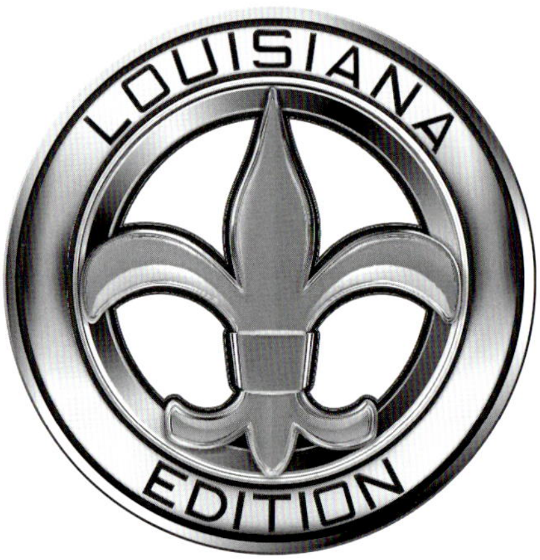

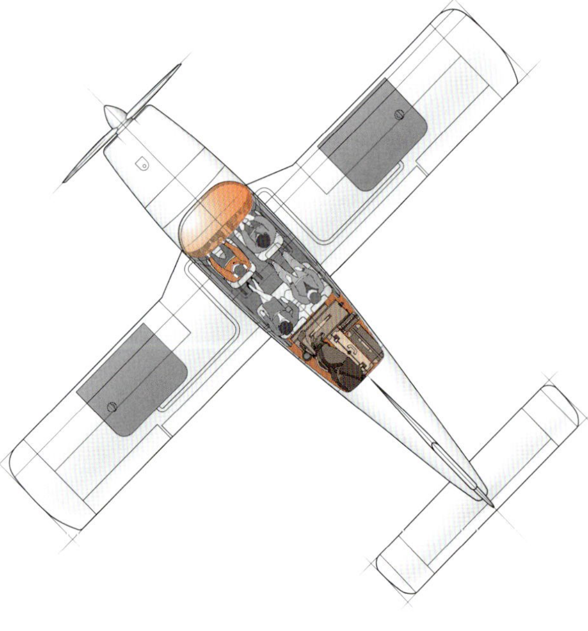

SAPUTO

Joe Saputo Technical Illustration • http://joesaputo.com • 541-746-9886

facebook.com/JoeSaputoIllustration

workbook.com/gallery/16588/view

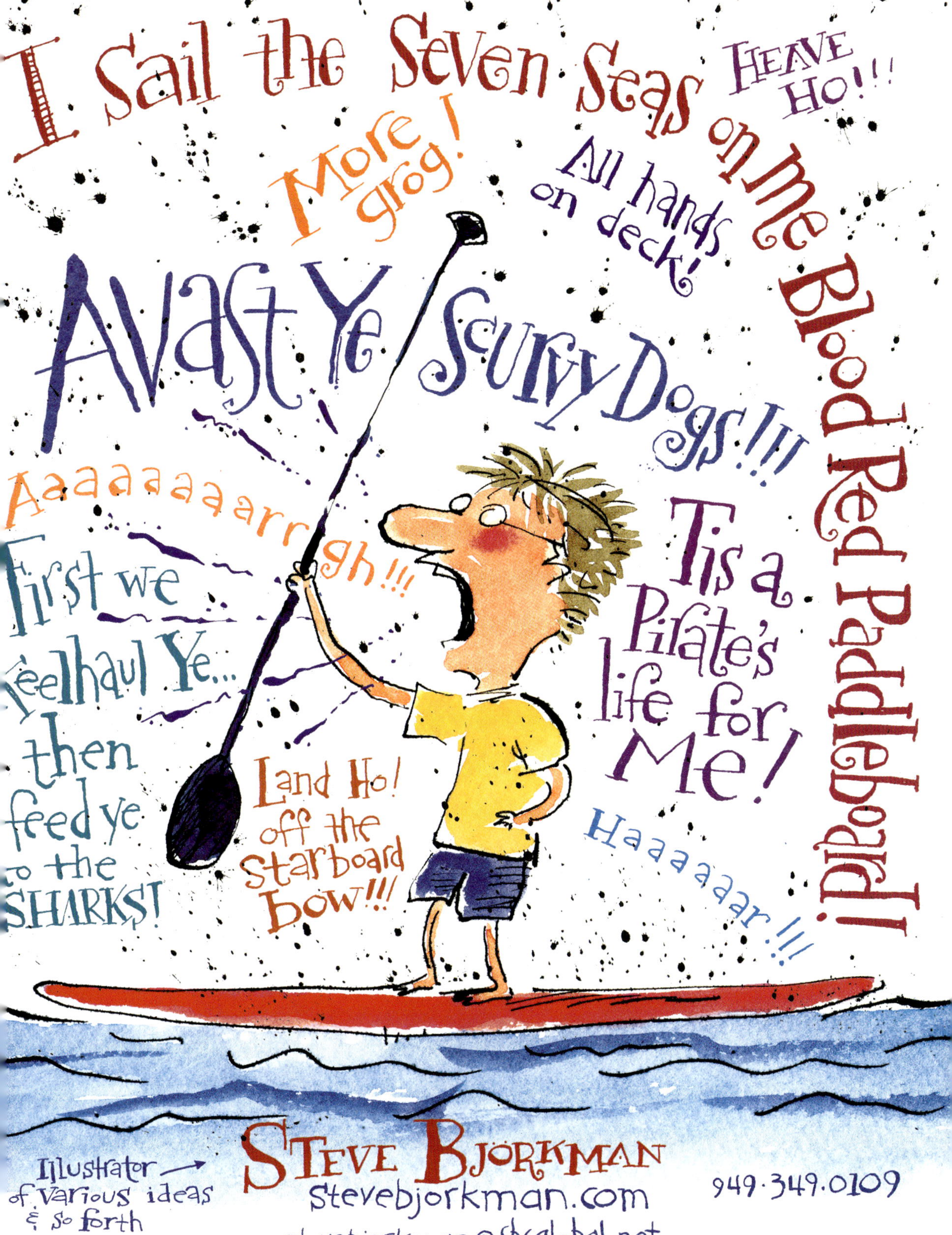

I Sail the Seven Seas on me Blood Red Paddleboard!
HEAVE HO!!!
More grog!
All hands on deck!
Avast Ye Scurvy Dogs!!!
Aaaaaaaarrgh!!!
First we keelhaul Ye... then feed ye to the SHARKS!
Land Ho! off the Starboard bow!!!
'Tis a Pirate's life for Me!
Haaaaaar!!!
Illustrator of various ideas & so forth
STEVE BJORKMAN
stevebjorkman.com
stevebjorkman@sbcglobal.net
949·349·0109

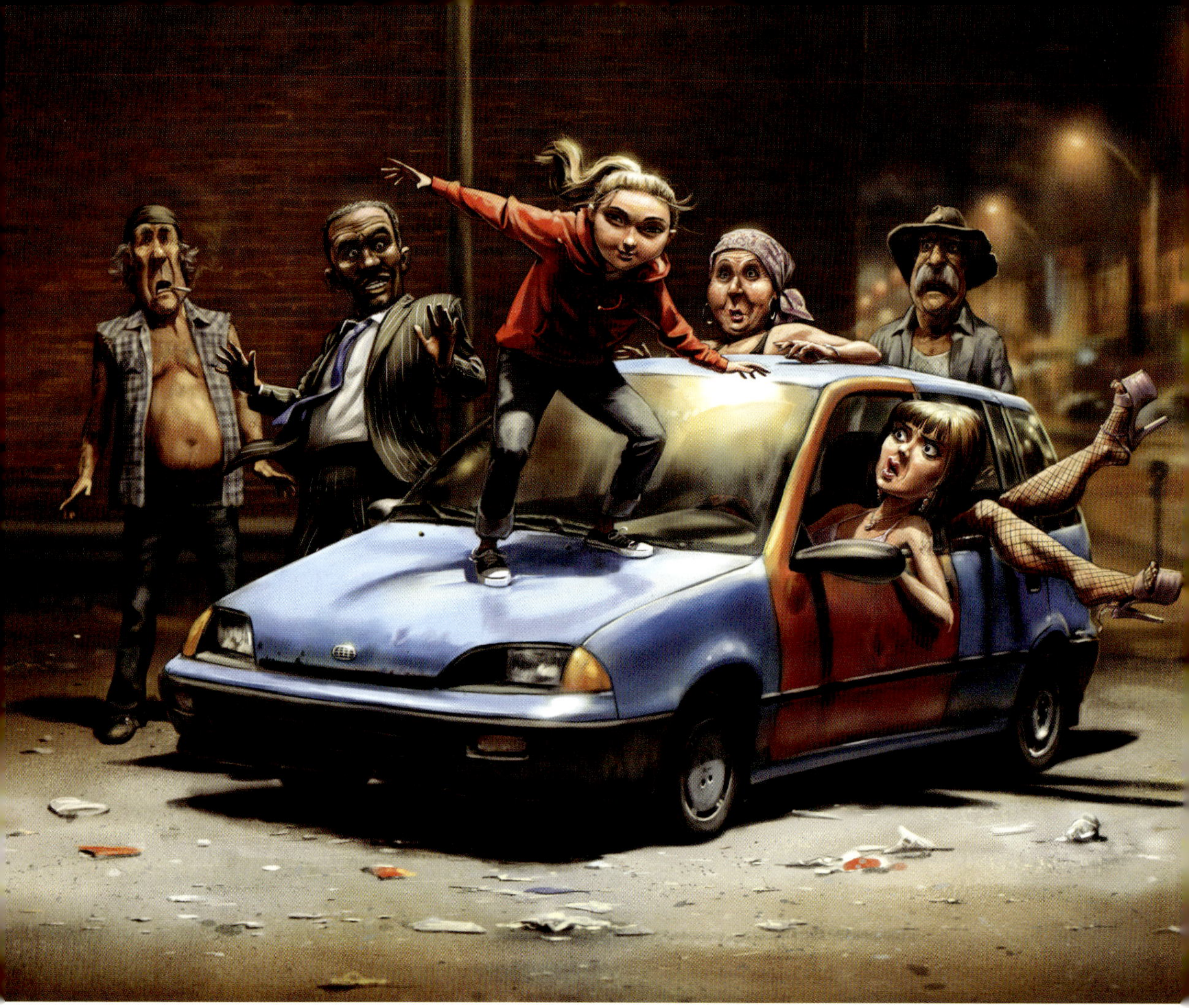

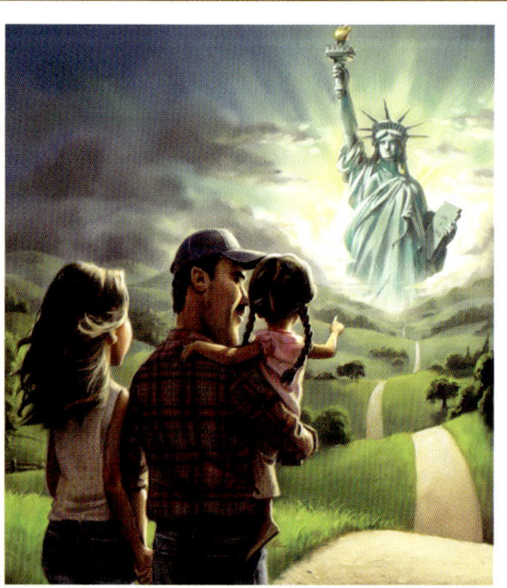
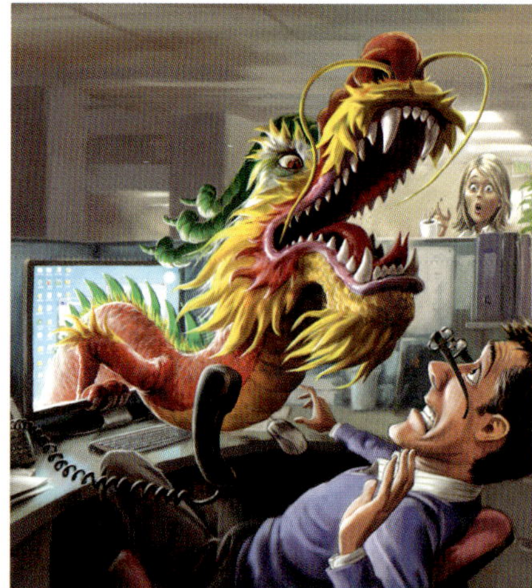
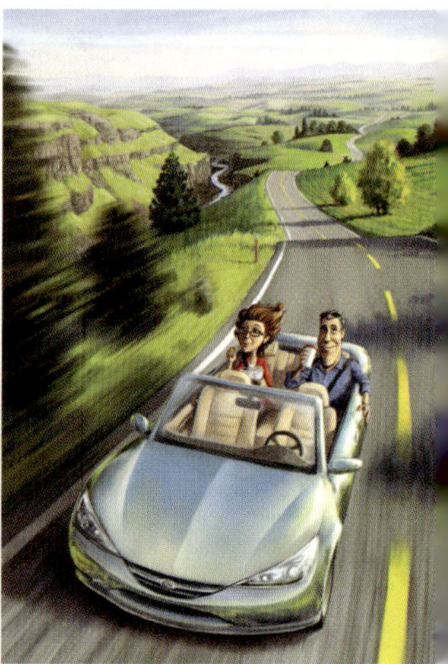

howard mcwilliam

blascocreative.com 312.782.0244

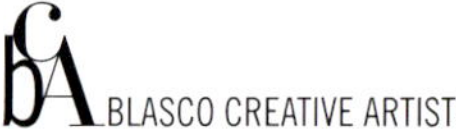

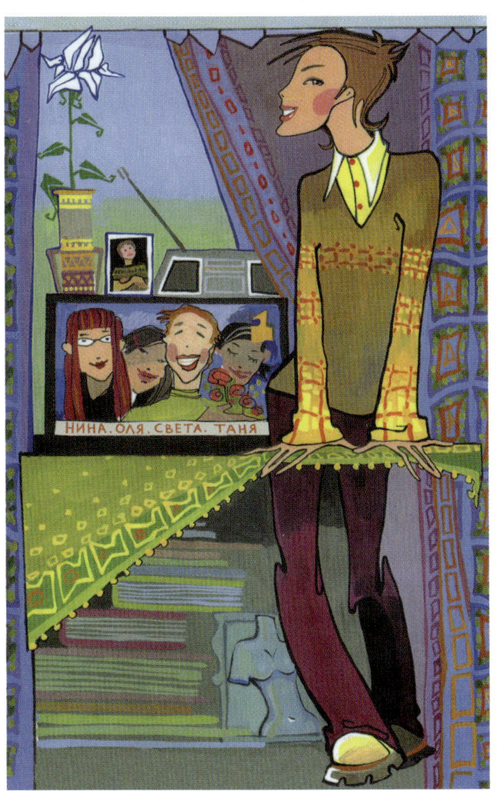

НИНА. ОЛЯ. СВЕТА. ТАНЯ

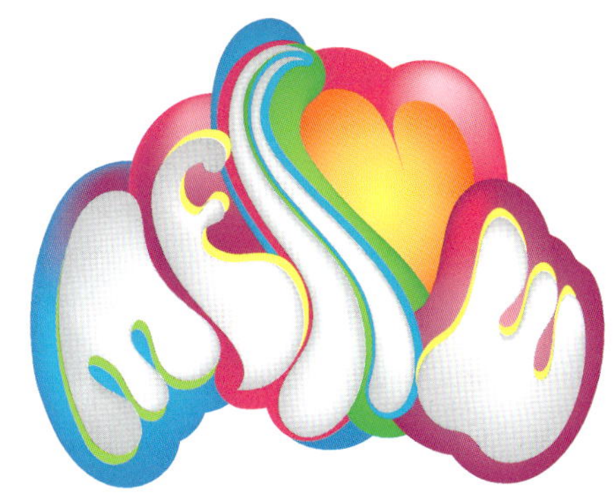

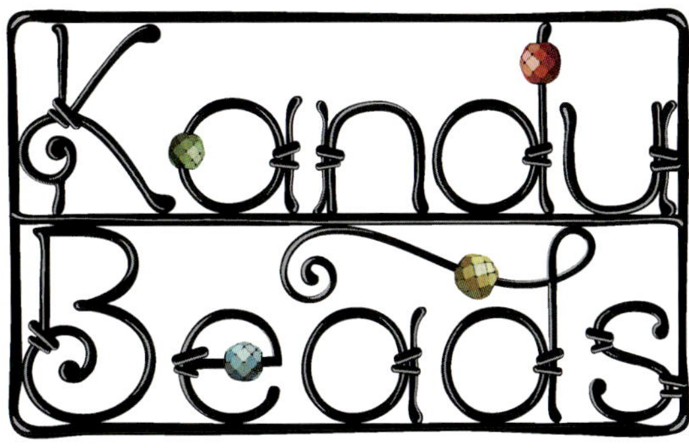

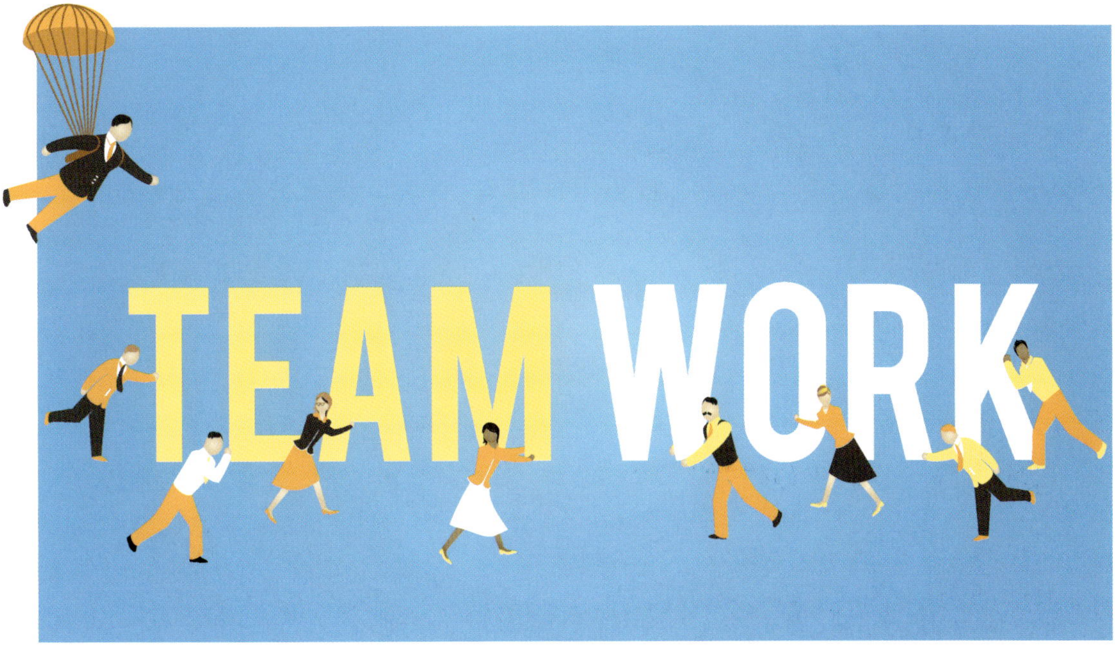

Kandu
Beads

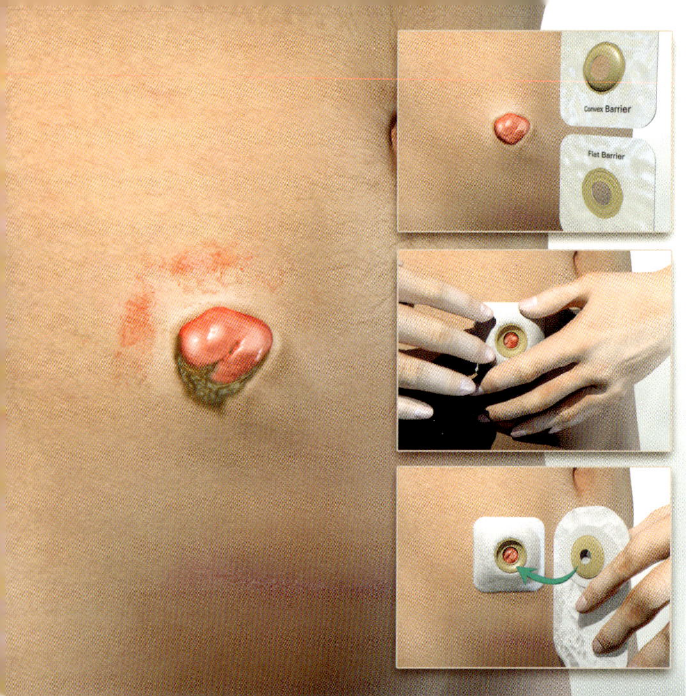

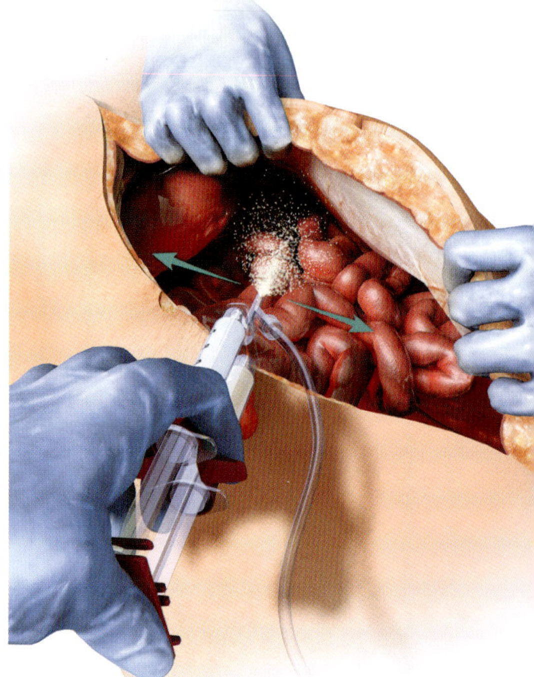

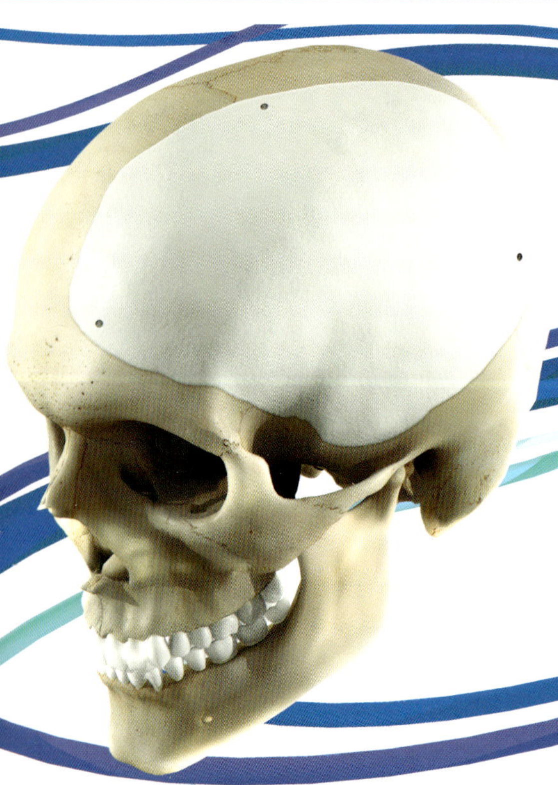

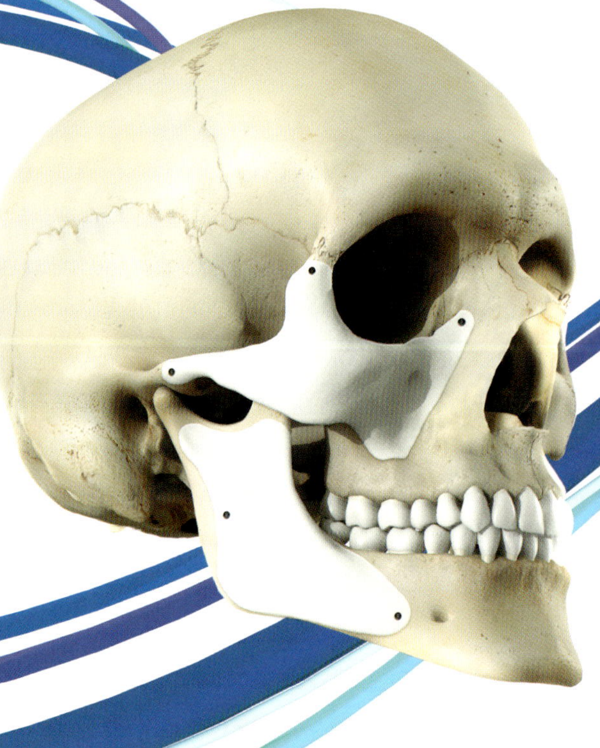

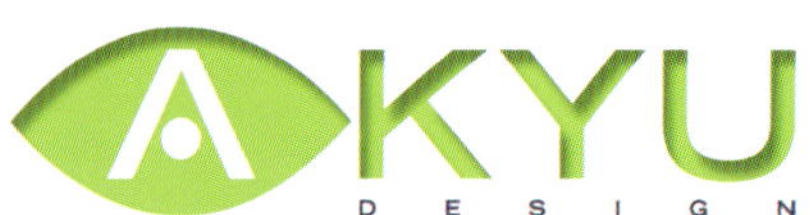

Adam Questell (questell@akyudesign.com)
9911 Vogue Lane Houston, TX 77080
713.468.9595 (tel) 713.392.3628 (cel)
w w w . a k y u d e s i g n . c o m

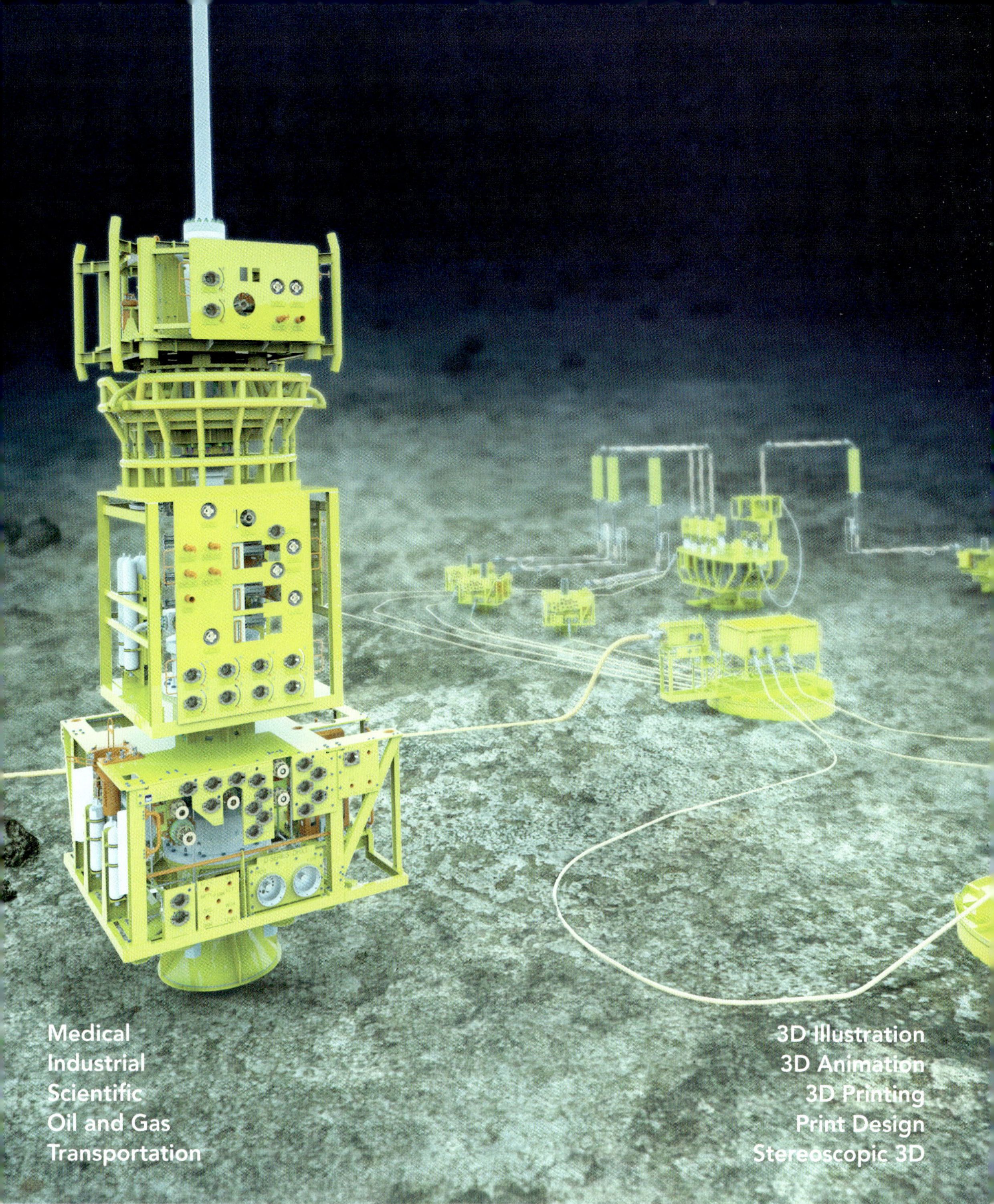
Medical
Industrial
Scientific
Oil and Gas
Transportation
3D Illustration
3D Animation
3D Printing
Print Design
Stereoscopic 3D
Do more than illustrate. Illuminate.

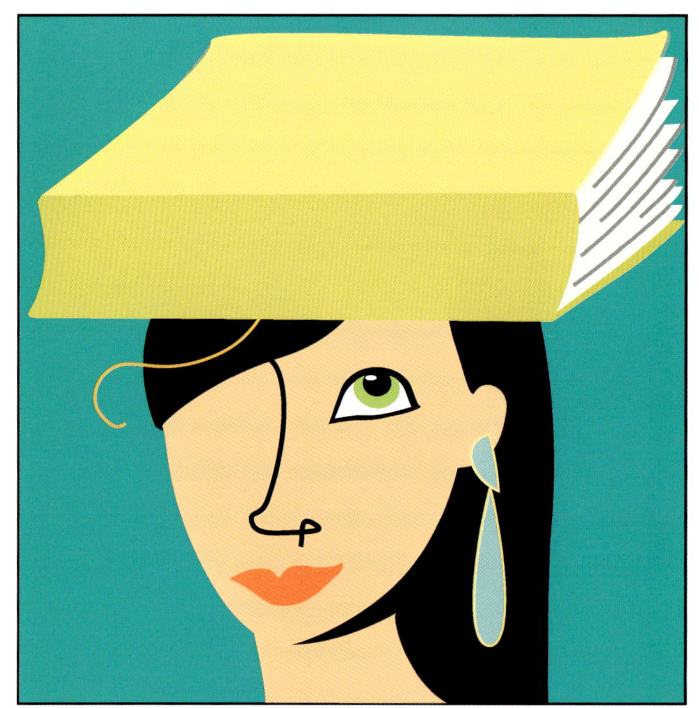

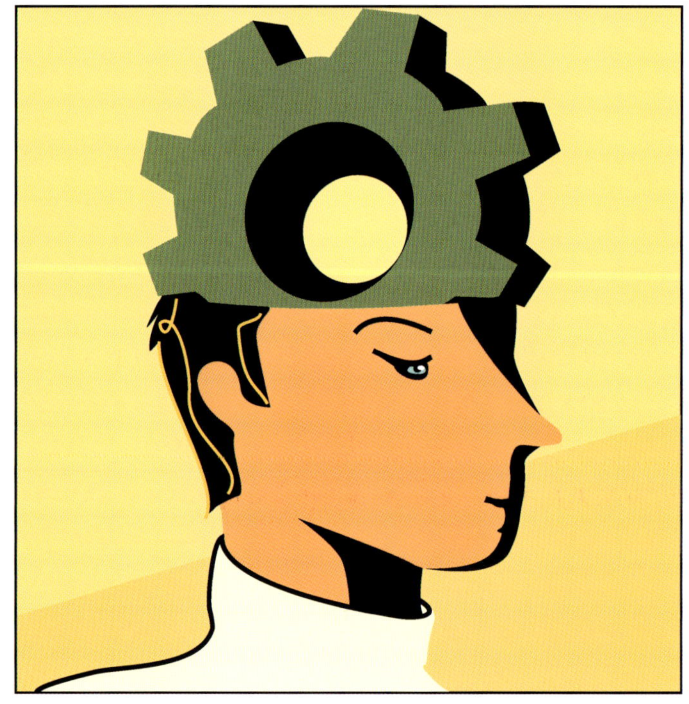

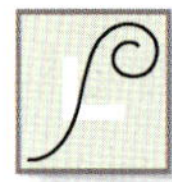
lindafountain.com
843.422.1732

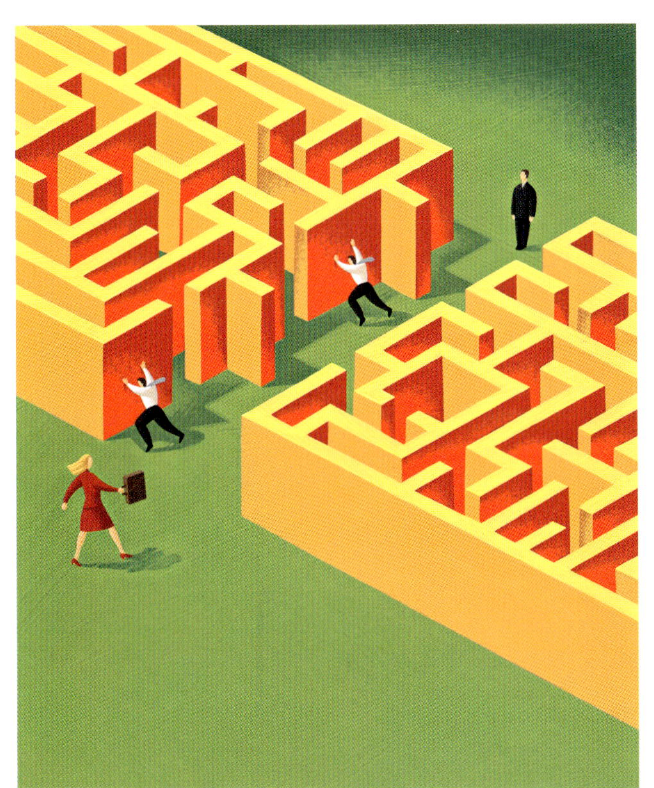

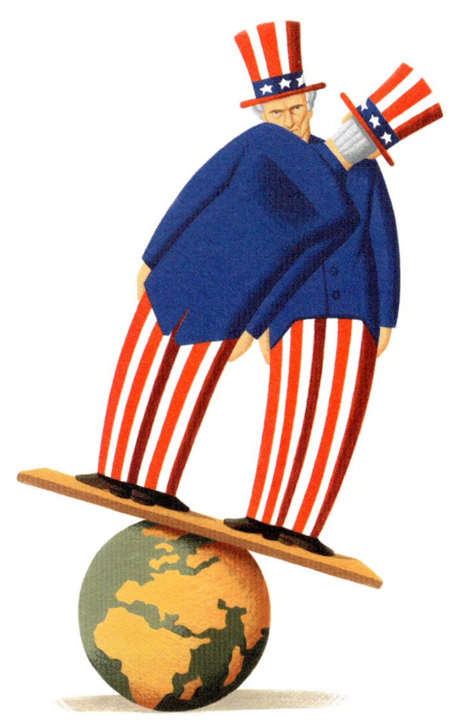

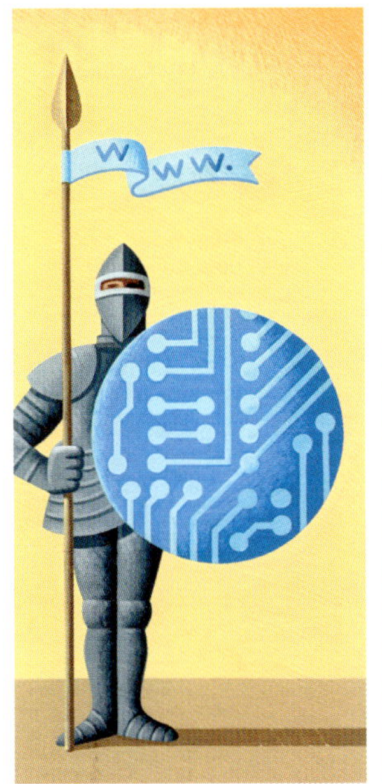

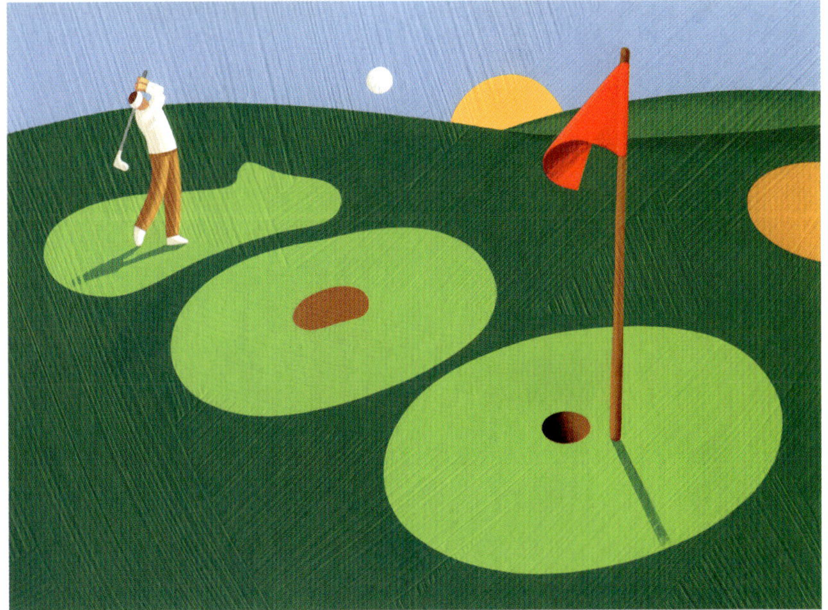

ADAM NIKLEWICZ

203.230.1024   www.illustratorUSA.com

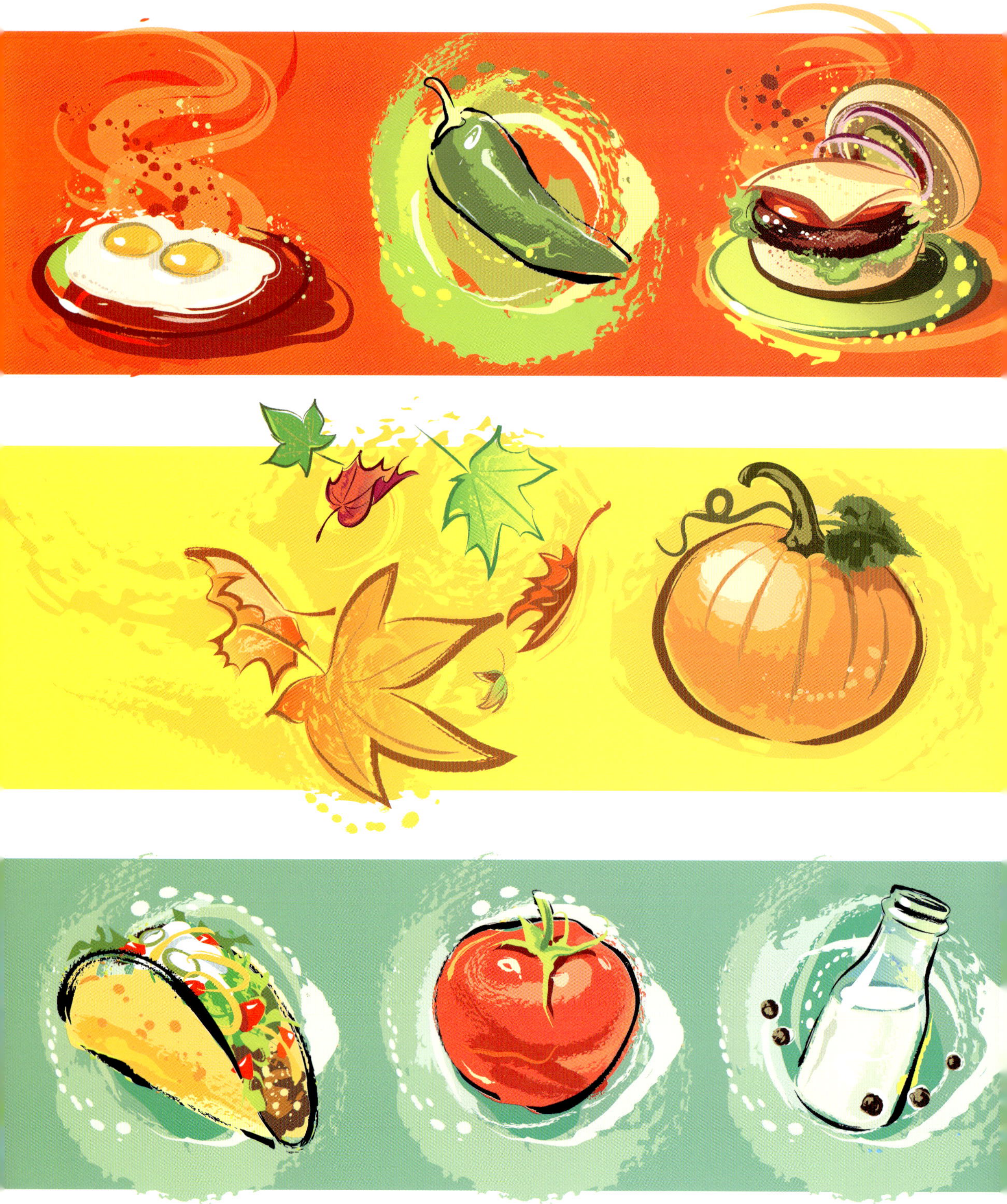

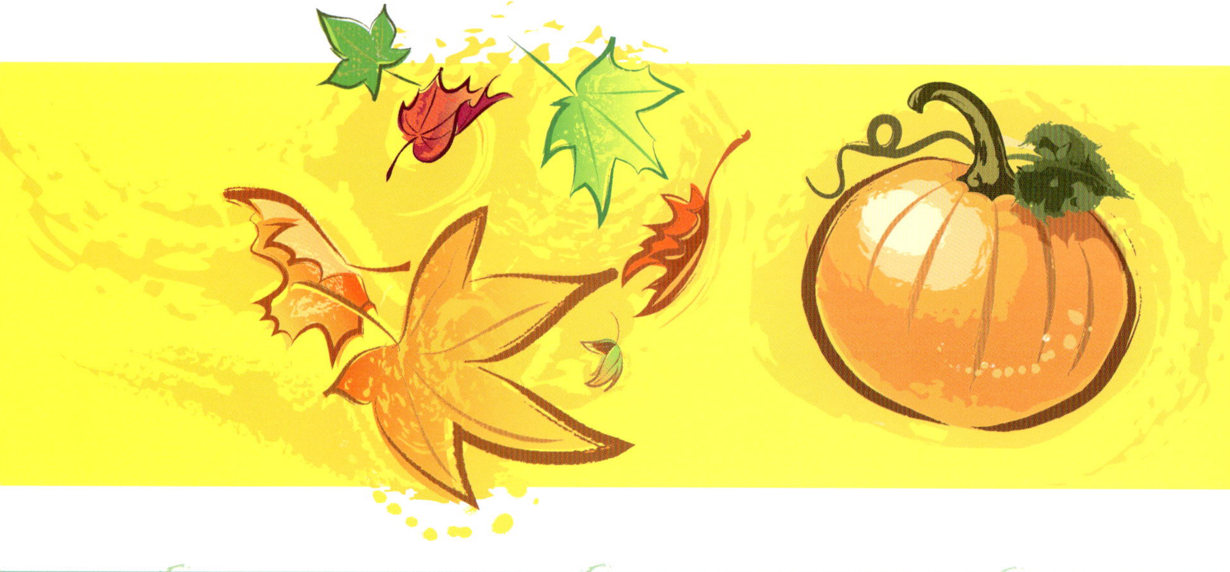

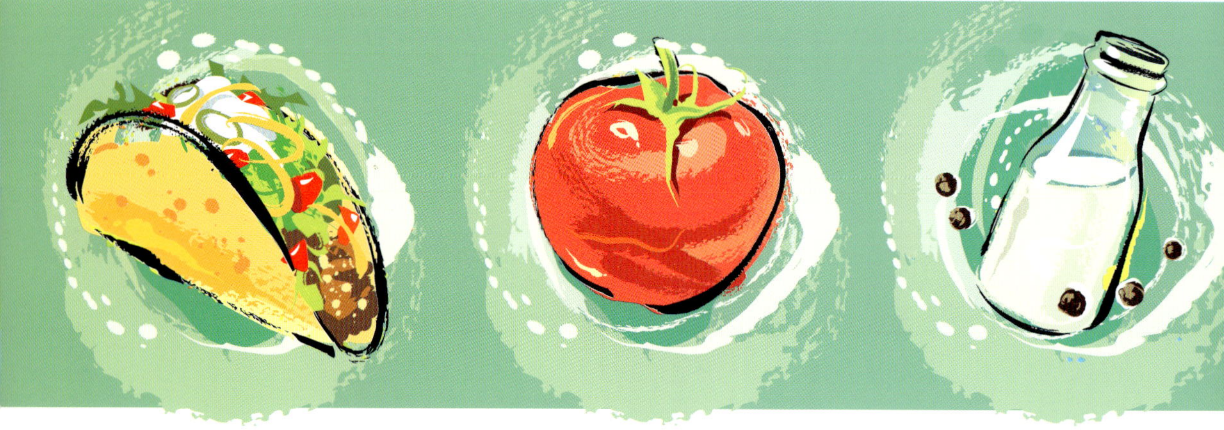

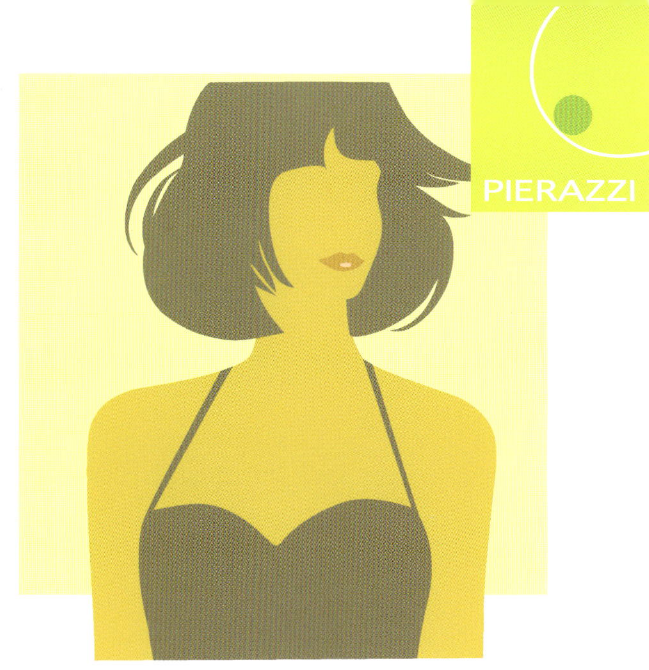

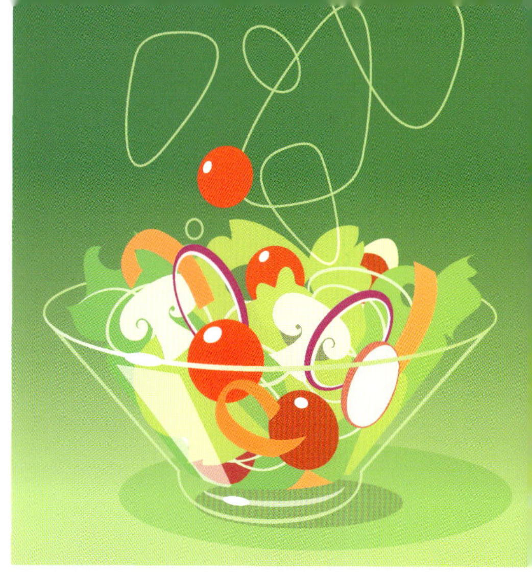

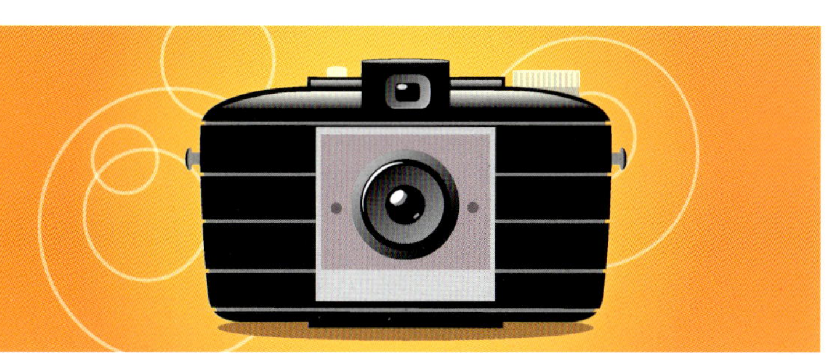

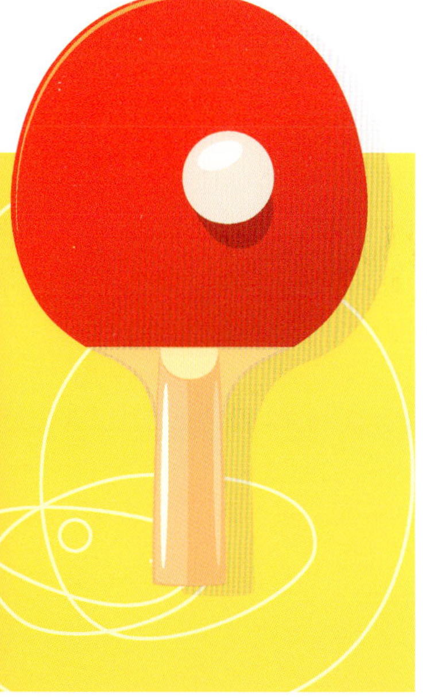

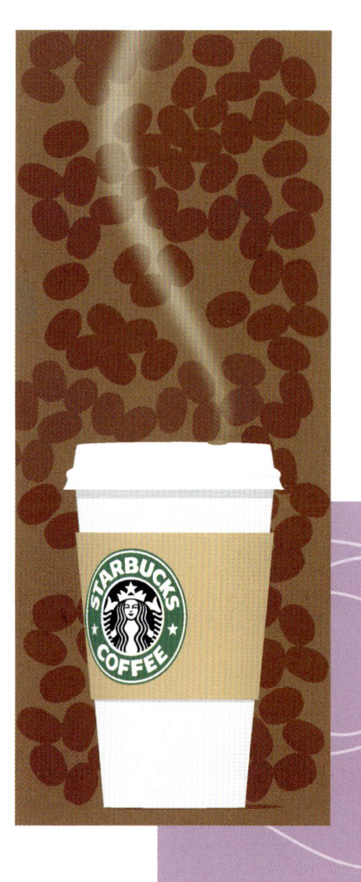

(530) 477-1950   see portfolio at garypierazzi.com

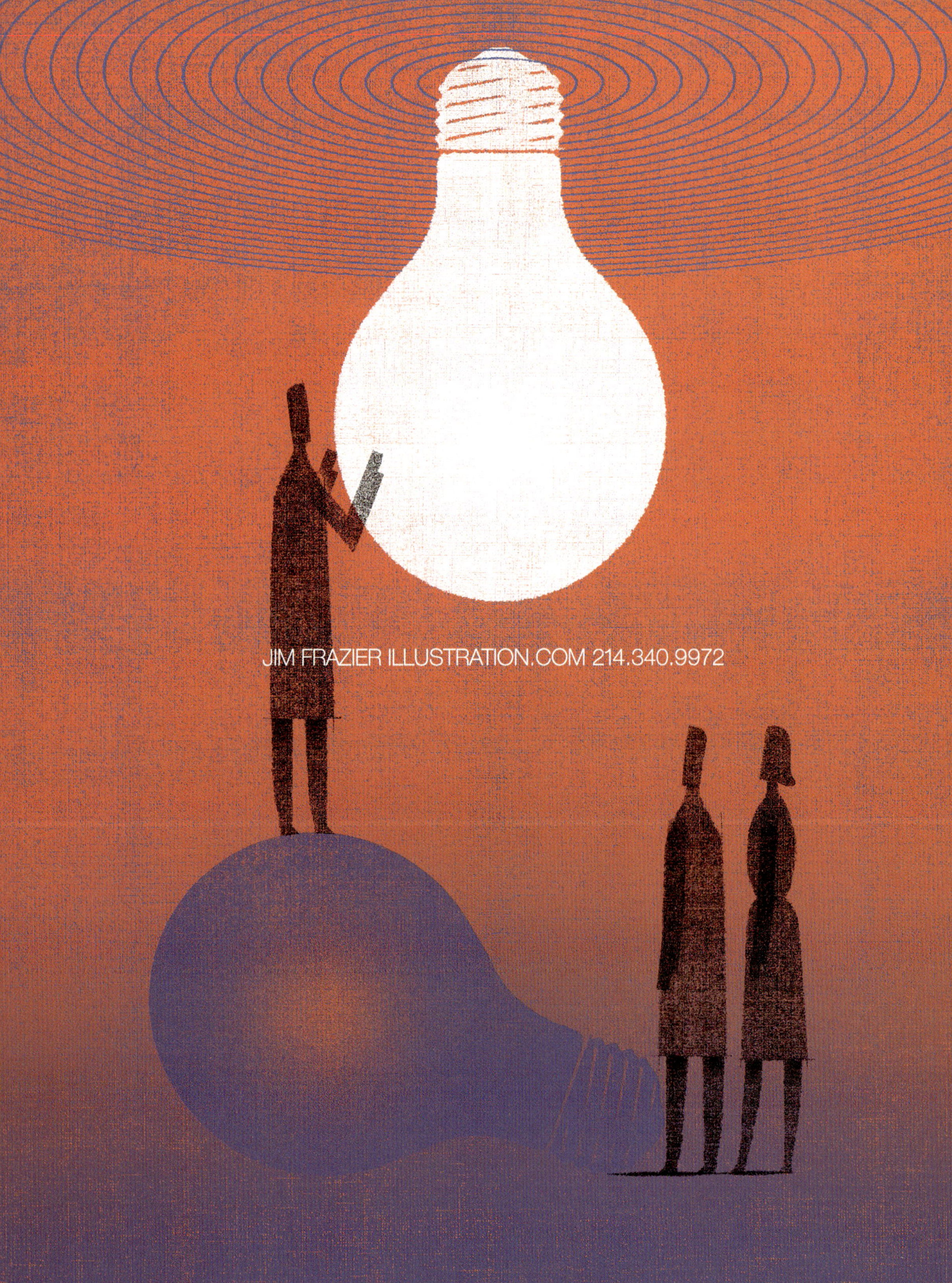
JIM FRAZIER ILLUSTRATION.COM 214.340.9972

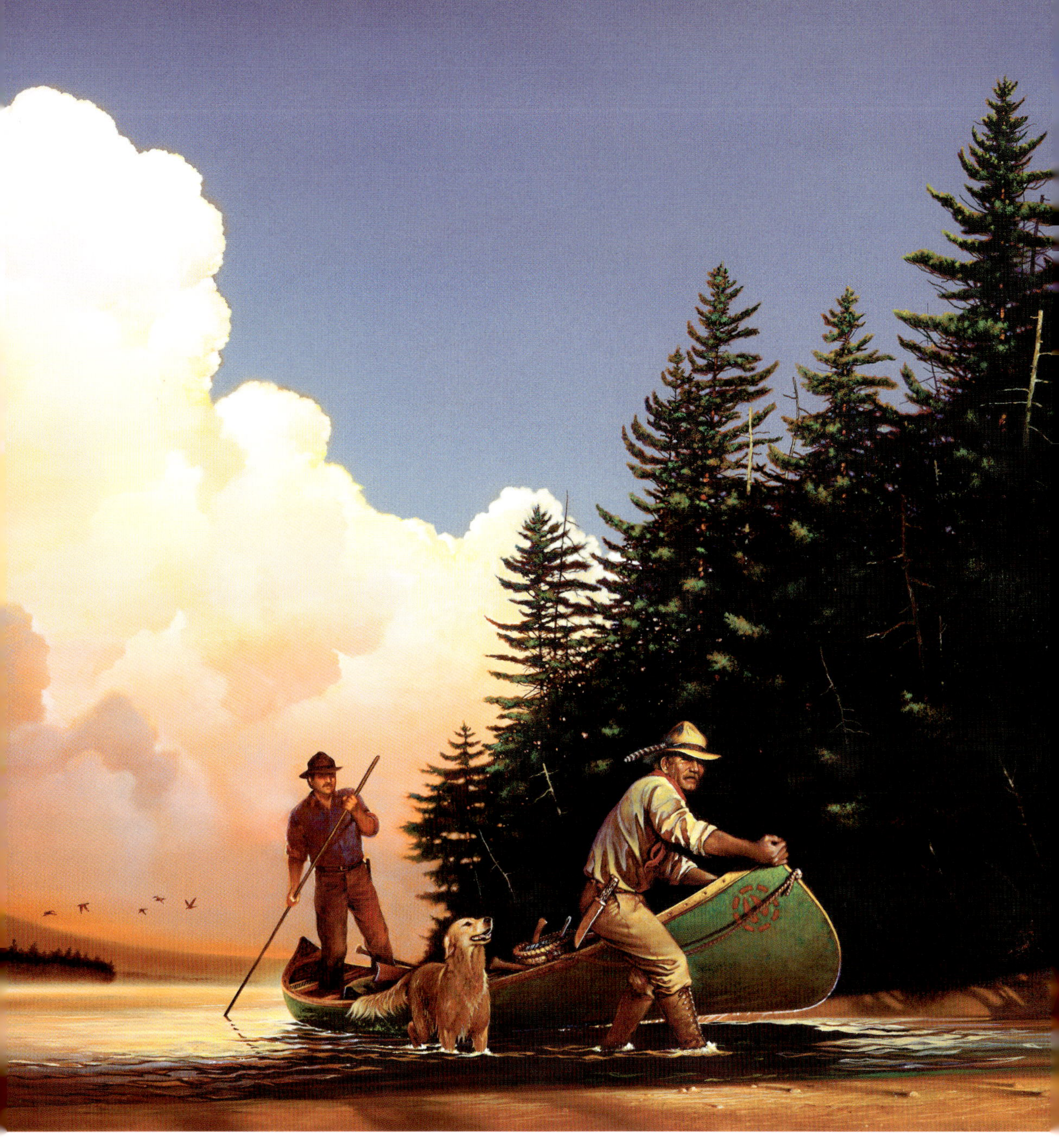

WAYNE McLOUGHLIN

waynemcloughlin.com • 603.445.2409

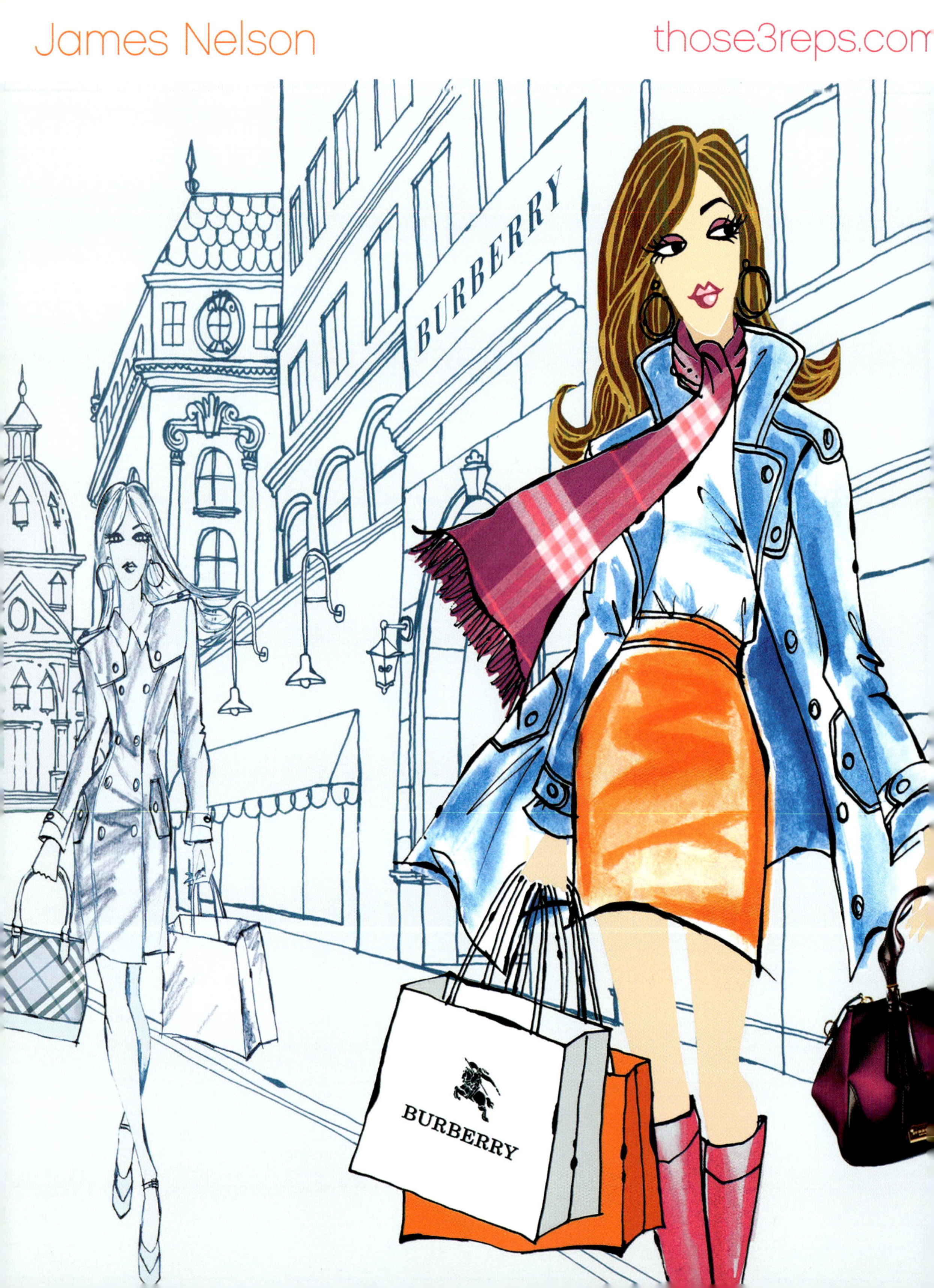

James Nelson
those3reps.com
BURBERRY
BURBERRY

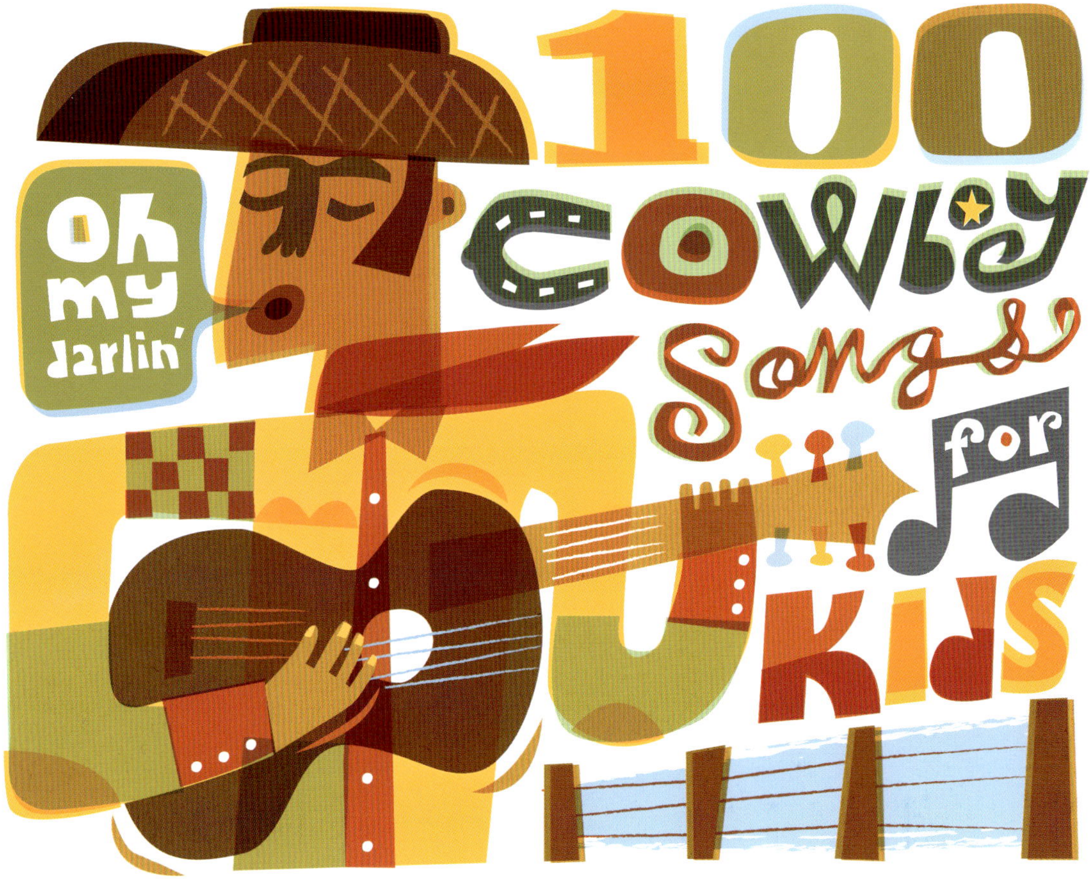

Oh my darlin'
100 COWBOY songs for KIDS

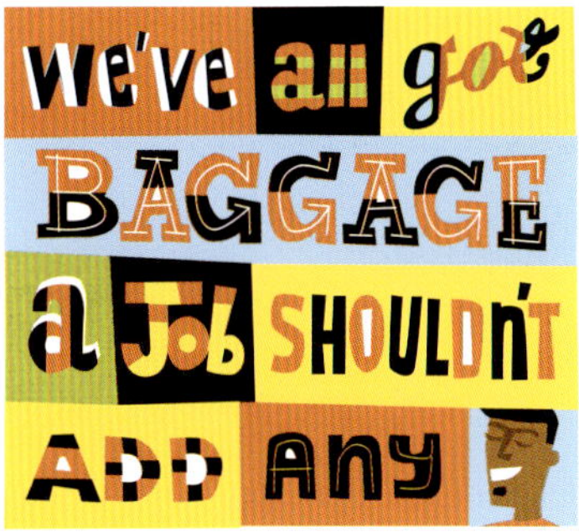

We've all got
BAGGAGE
a Job SHOULDN'T
ADD ANY

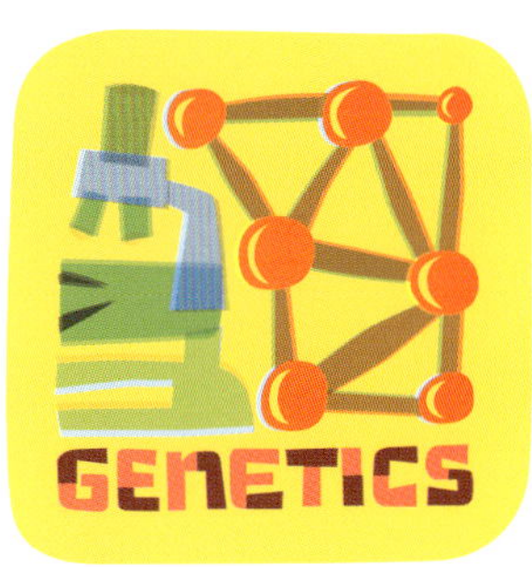

GENETICS

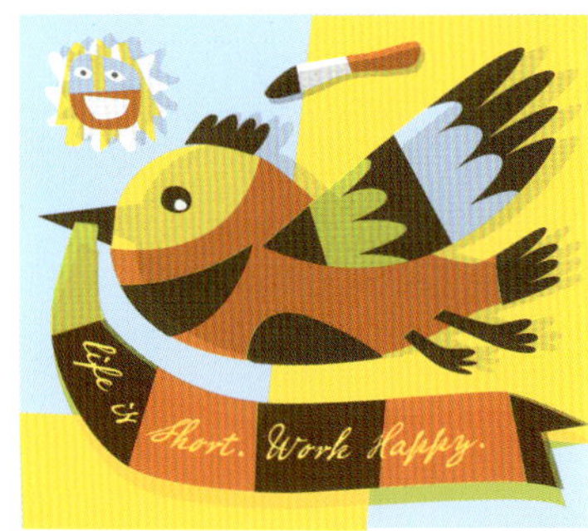

Life is Short. Work Happy.

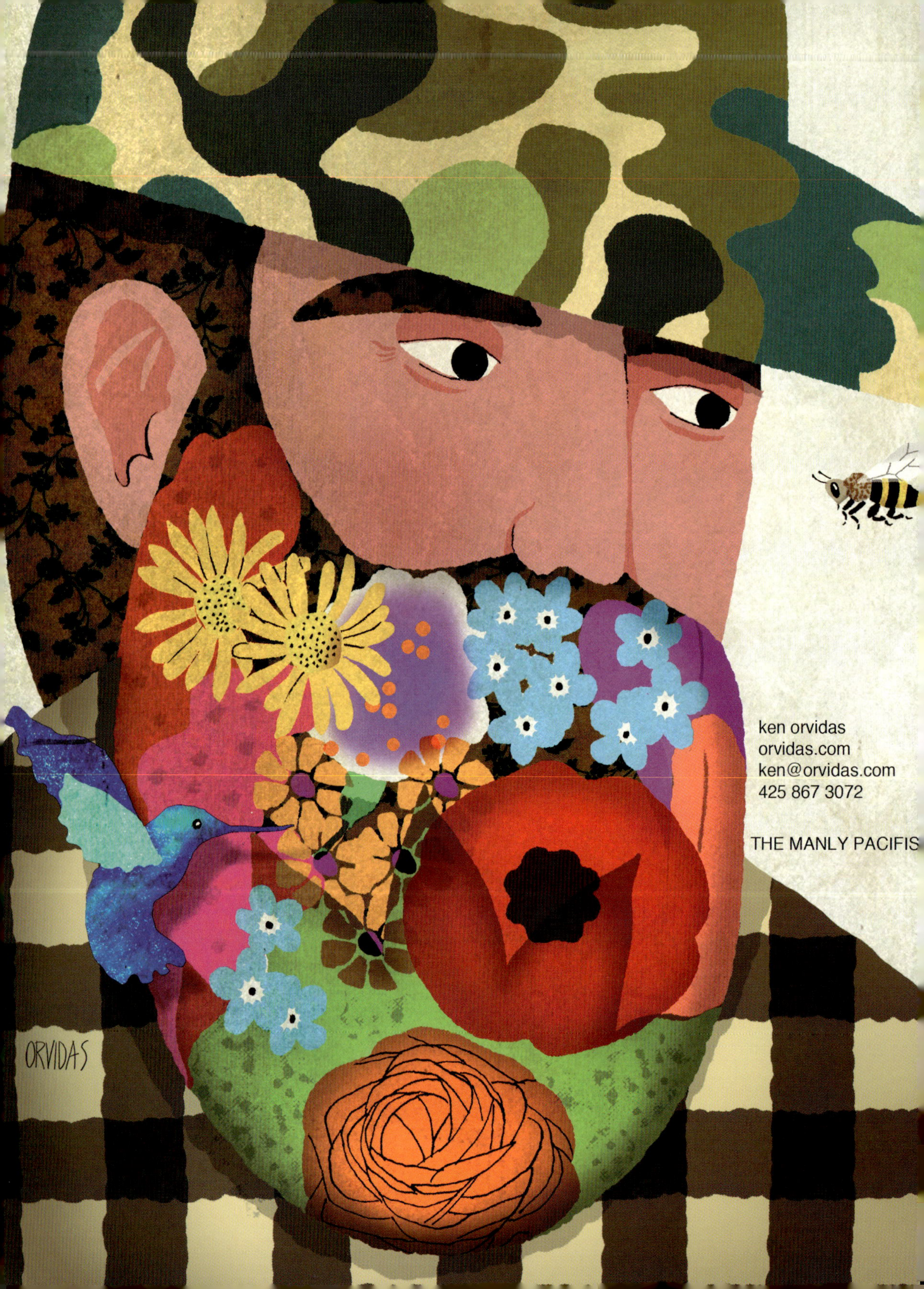
ORVIDAS
ken orvidas
orvidas.com
ken@orvidas.com
425 867 3072
THE MANLY PACIFIS

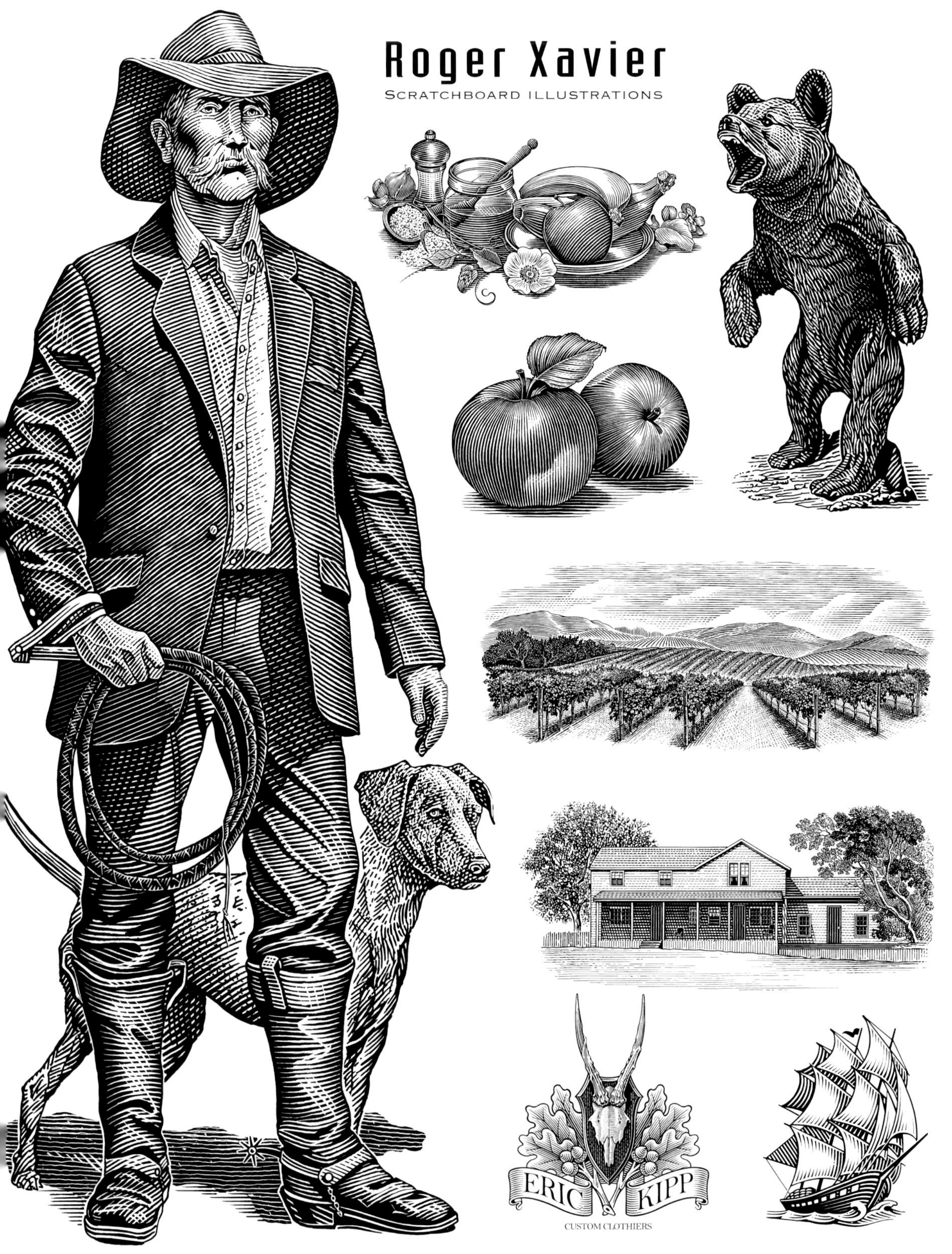
Roger Xavier
Scratchboard illustrations
ERIC KIPP
CUSTOM CLOTHIERS
(310) 722-3280 ~ WWW.ROGERXAVIER.COM ~ ROGER@ROGERXAVIER.COM

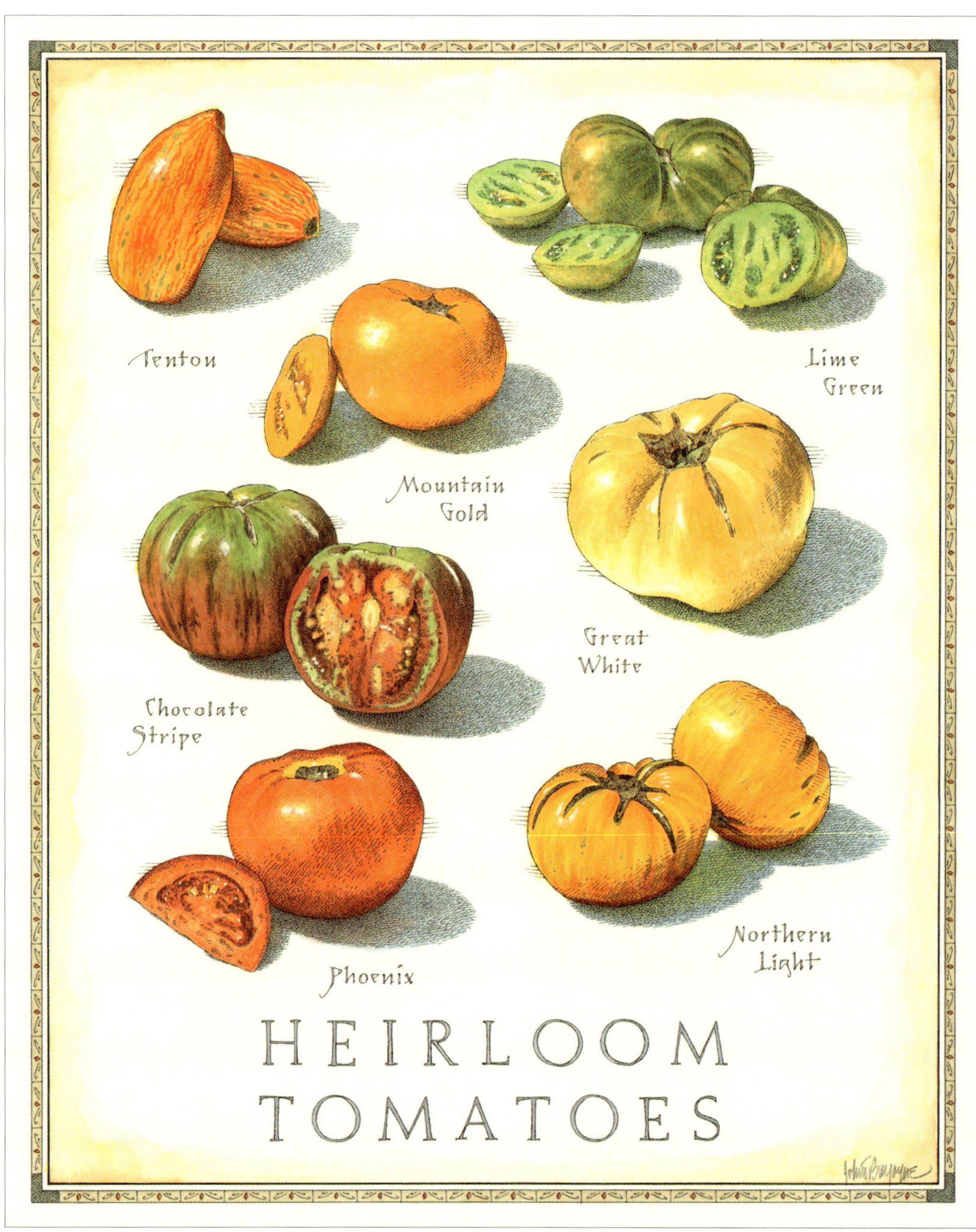

Tentou
Lime
Green
Mountain
Gold
Great
White
Chocolate
Stripe
Northern
Light
Phoenix
HEIRLOOM
TOMATOES

JOHN BURGOYNE

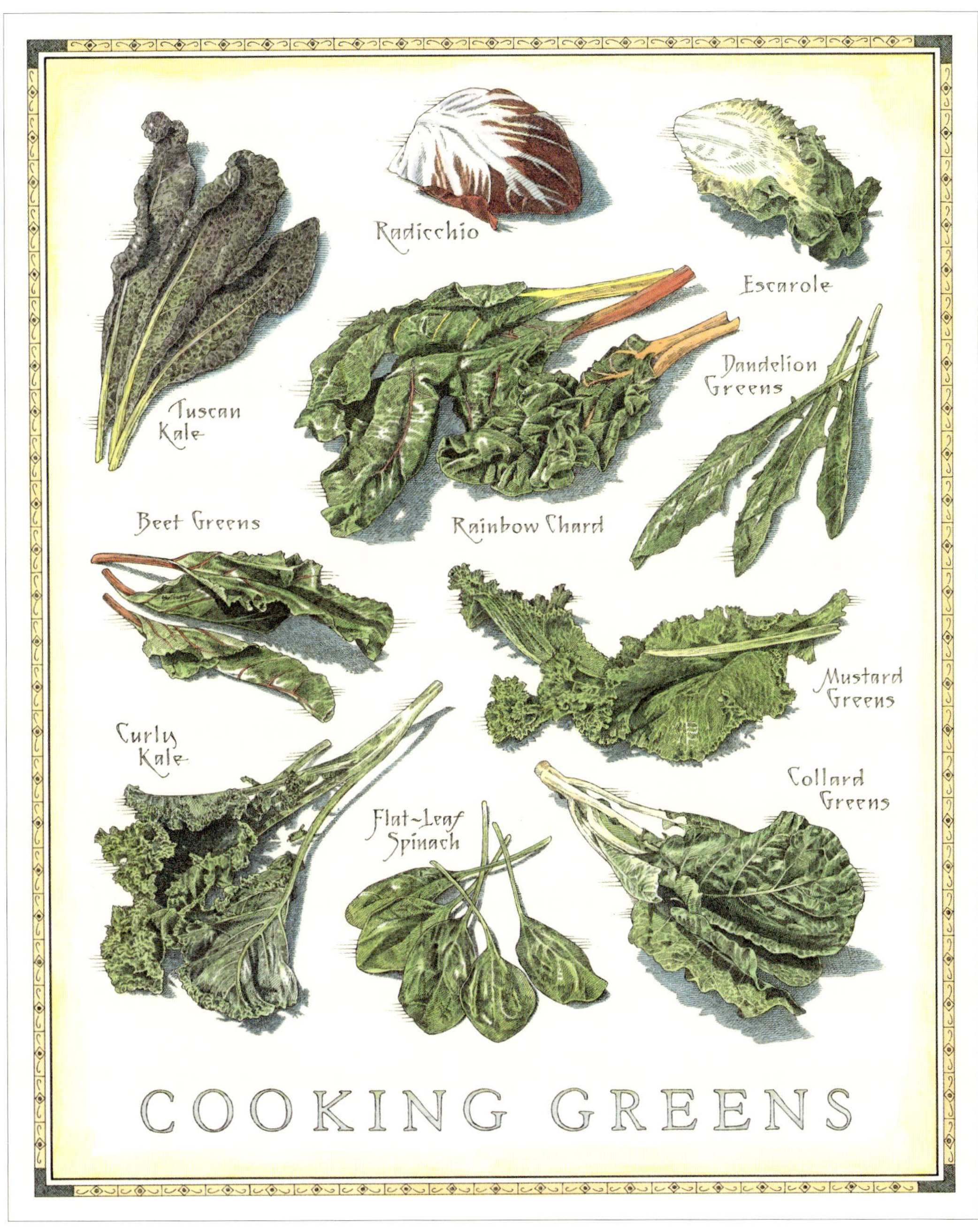

MAGNET REPS

[866] 390-5656   art@magnetreps.c

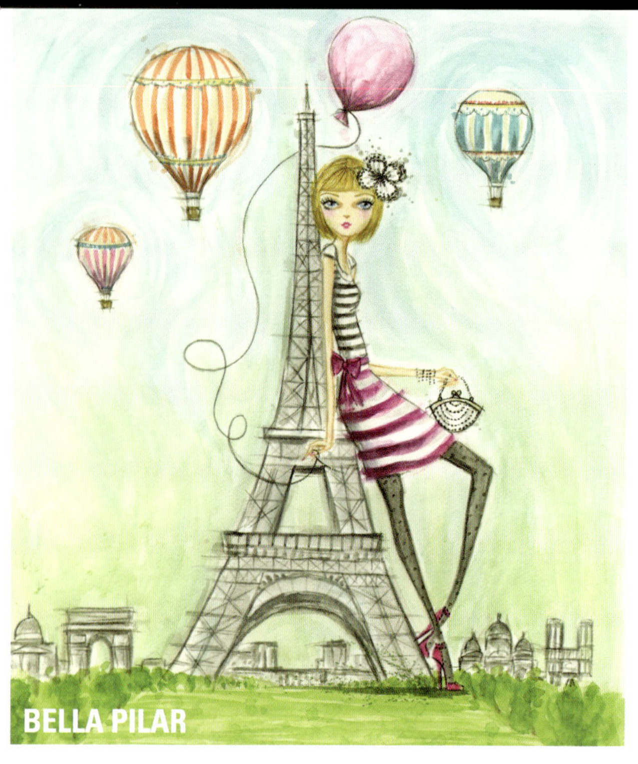

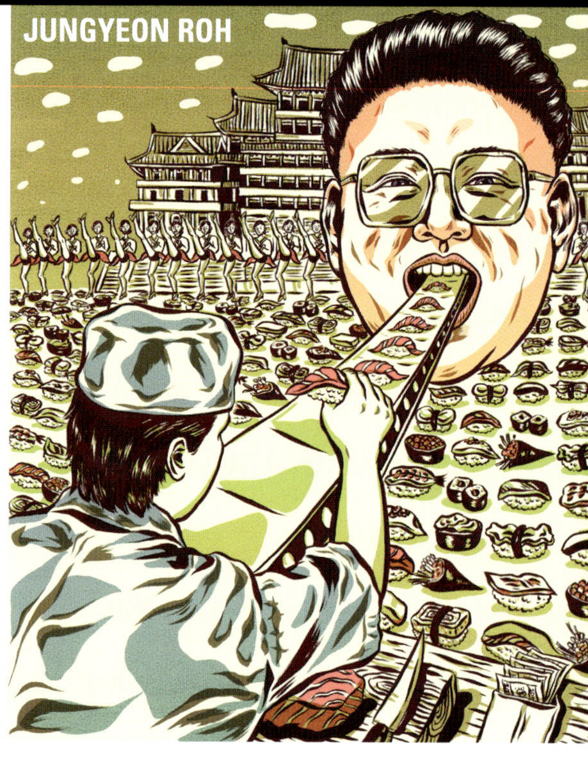

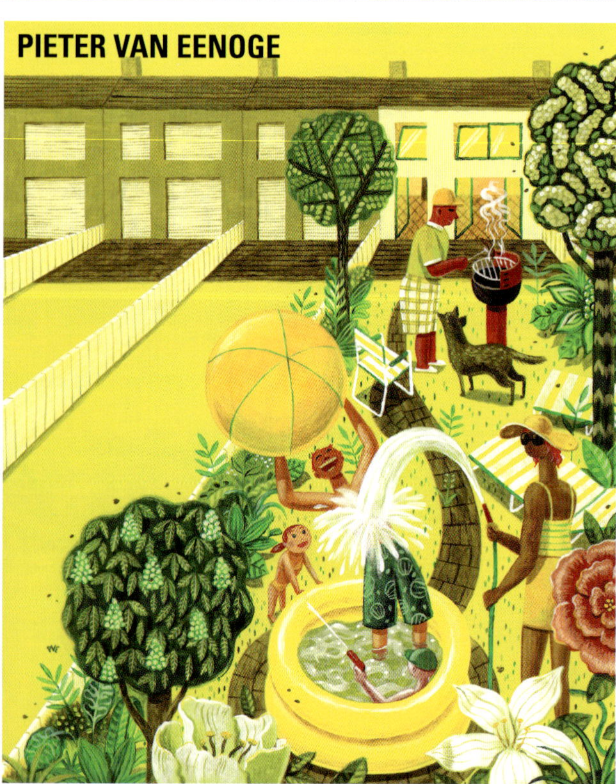

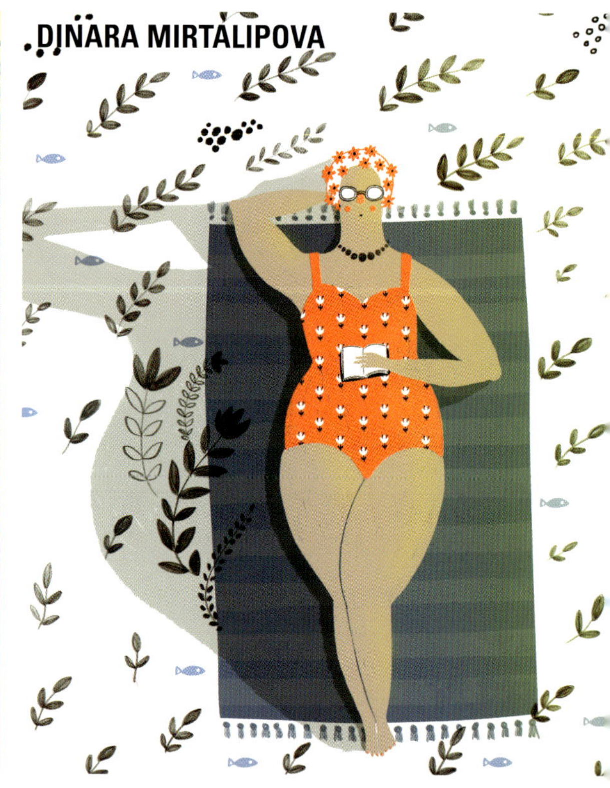

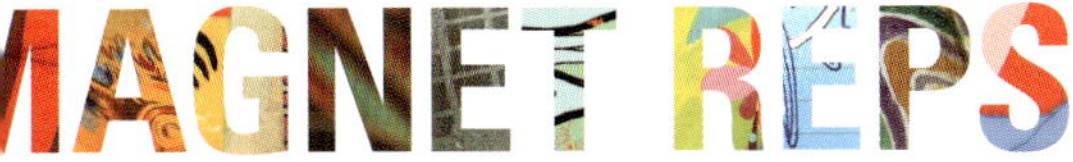

[866] 390-5656   art@magnetreps.com

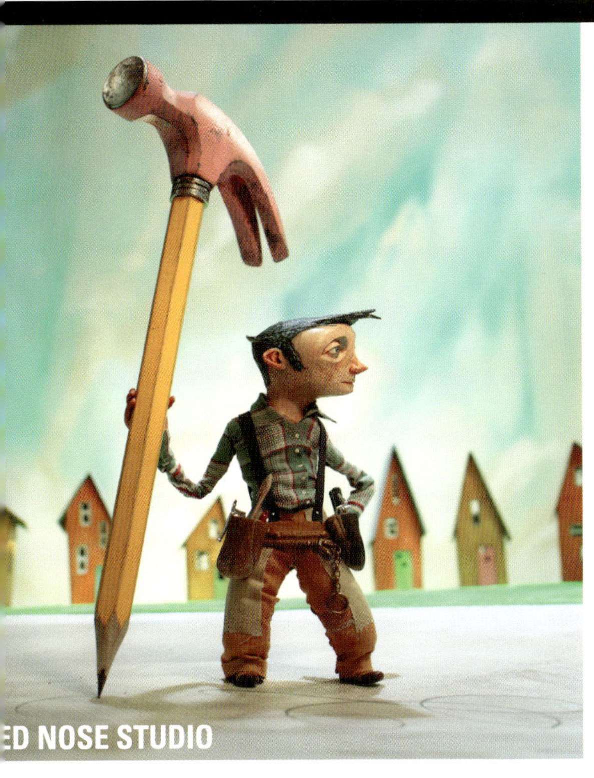

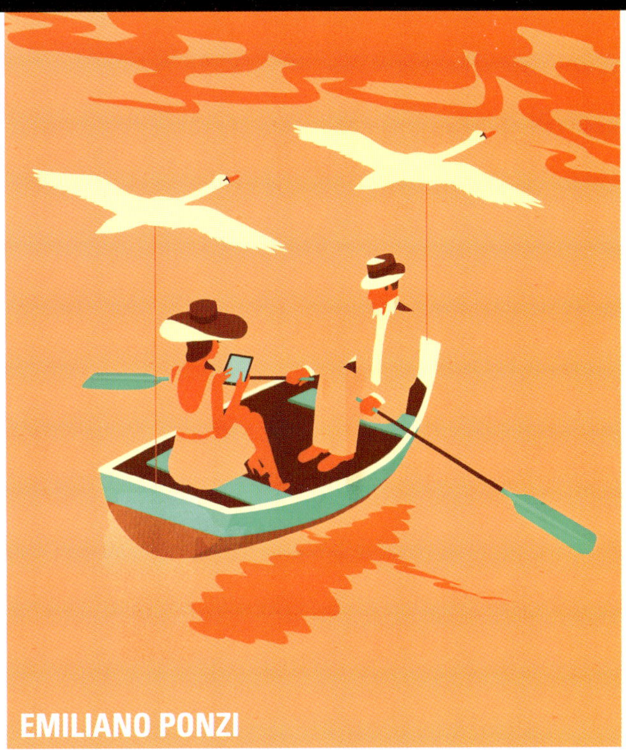

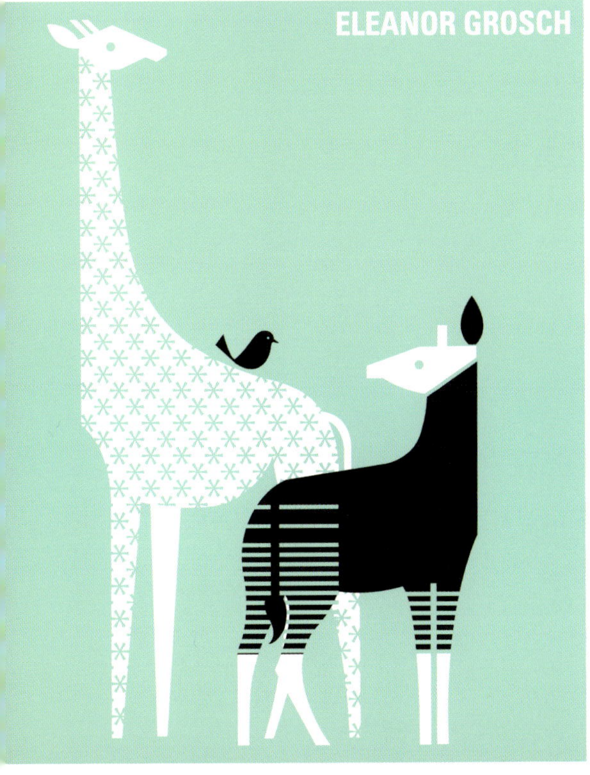

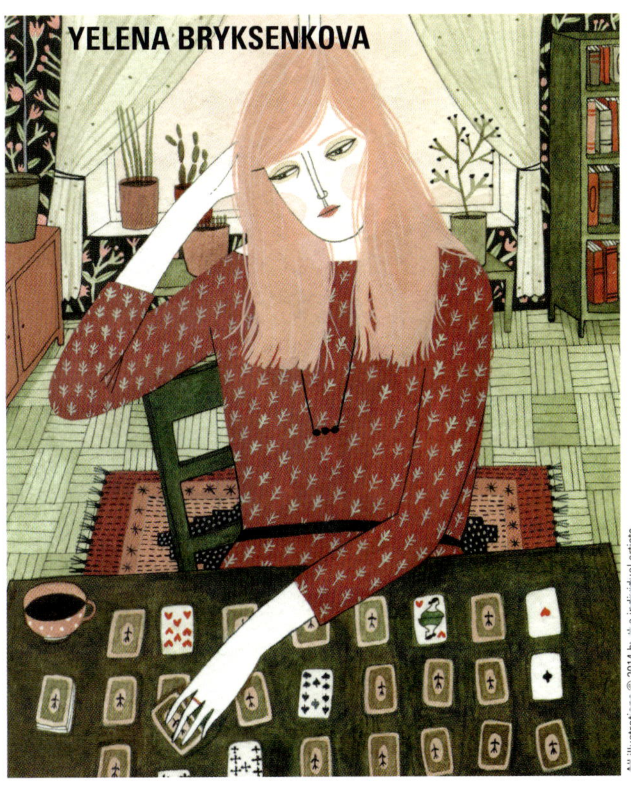

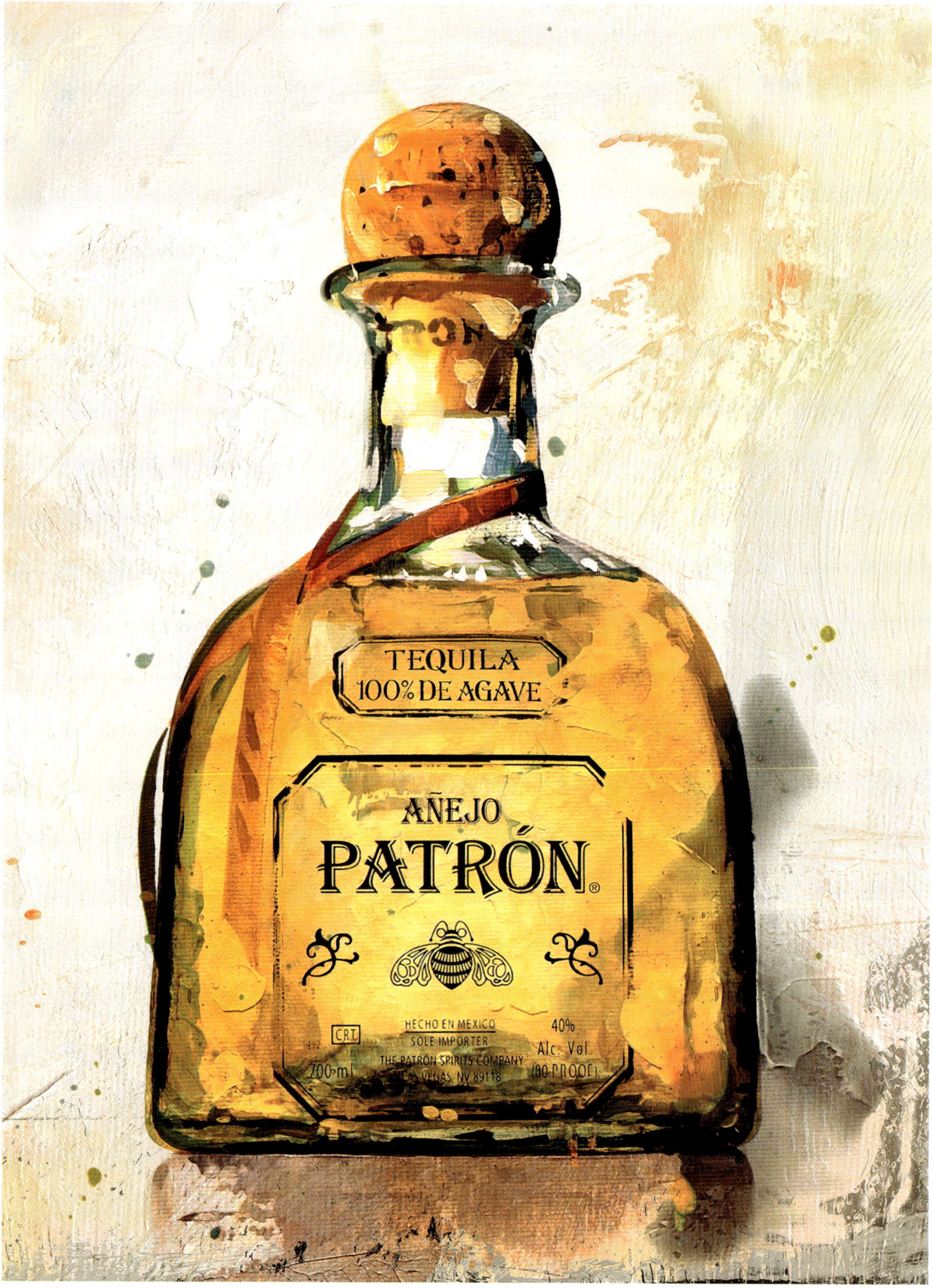

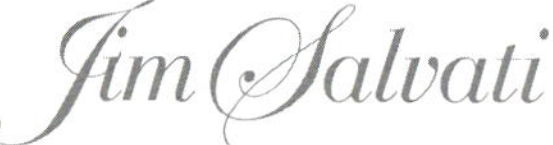

TEQUILA
100% DE AGAVE
AÑEJO
PATRÓN®
HECHO EN MEXICO
SOLE IMPORTER
THE PATRÓN SPIRITS COMPANY
LAS VEGAS, NV 89118
40%
Alc. Vol.
(80 PROOF)
700 ml
CRT

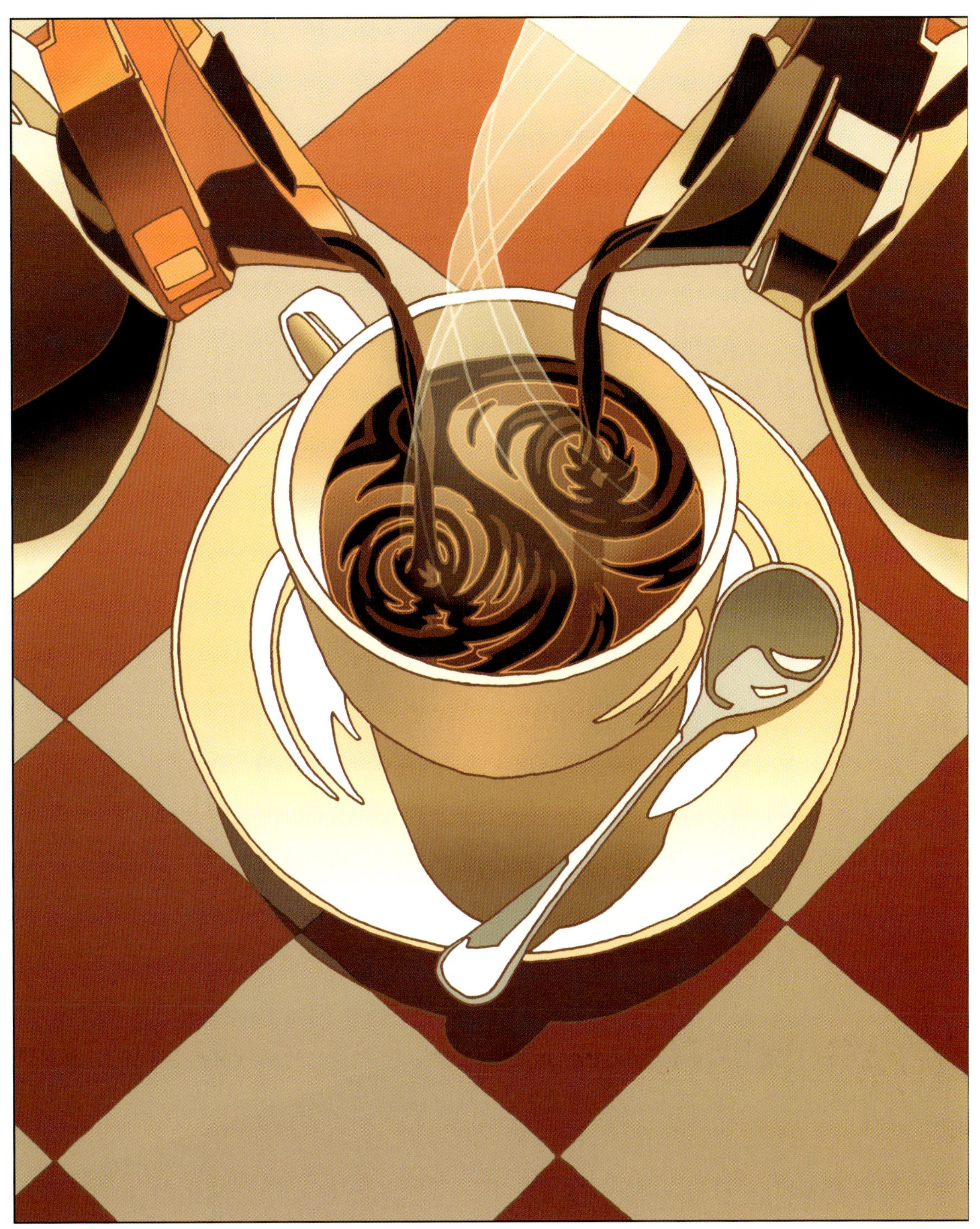

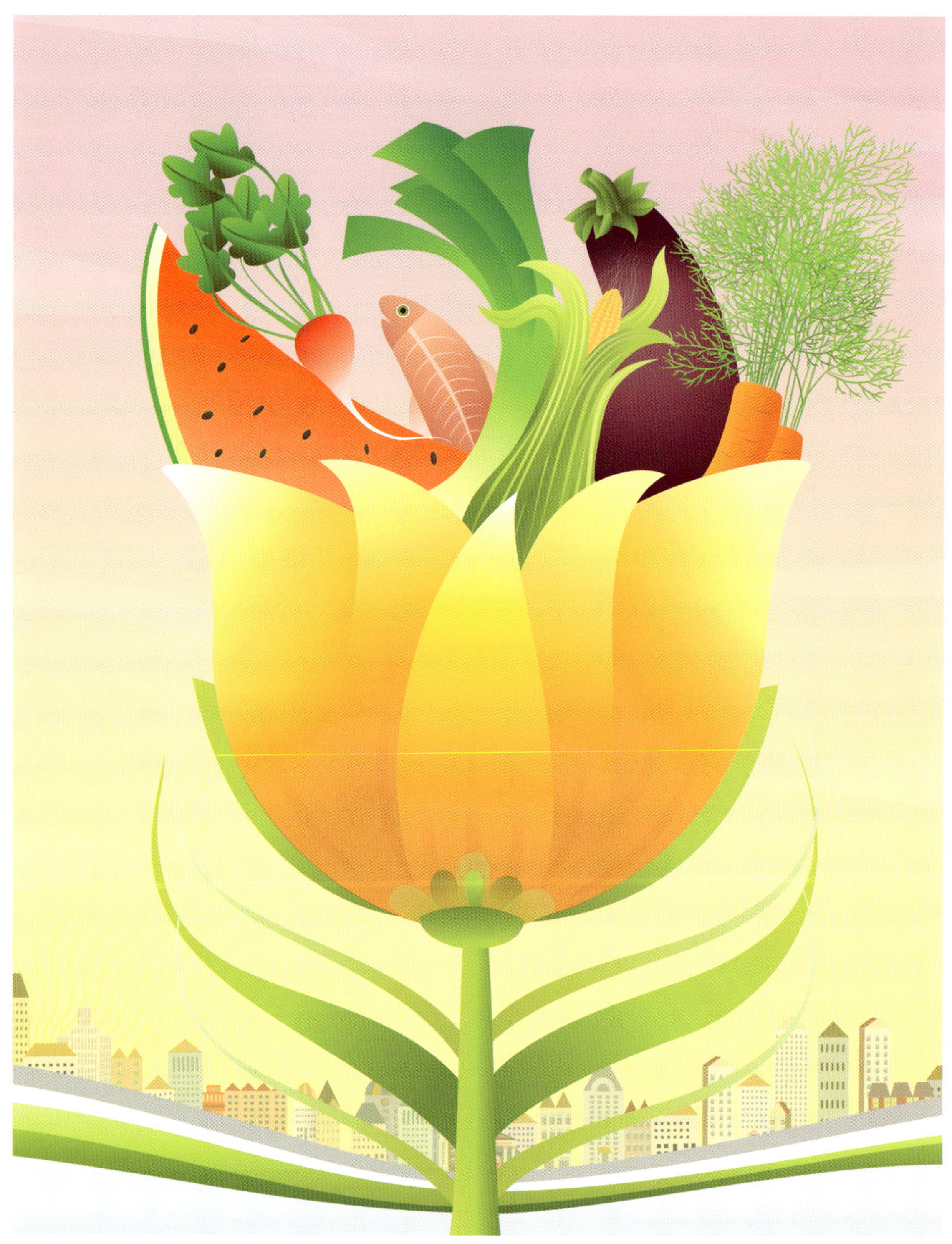

LINDGREN ■ SMITH
{212} 397-7330
Christiane Beauregard
LINDGRENSMITH.COM
INFO@LSILLUSTRATION.COM
416

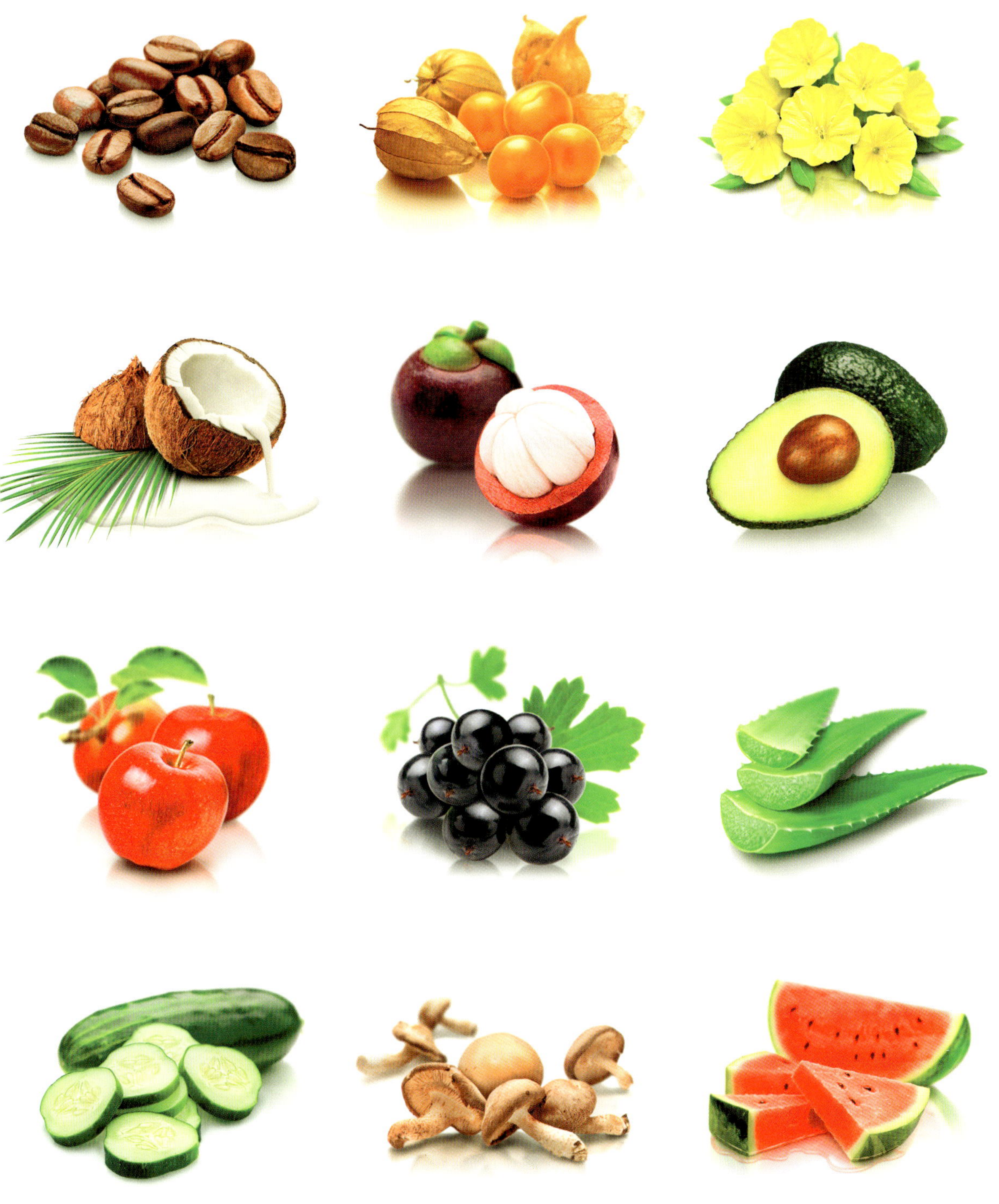

417

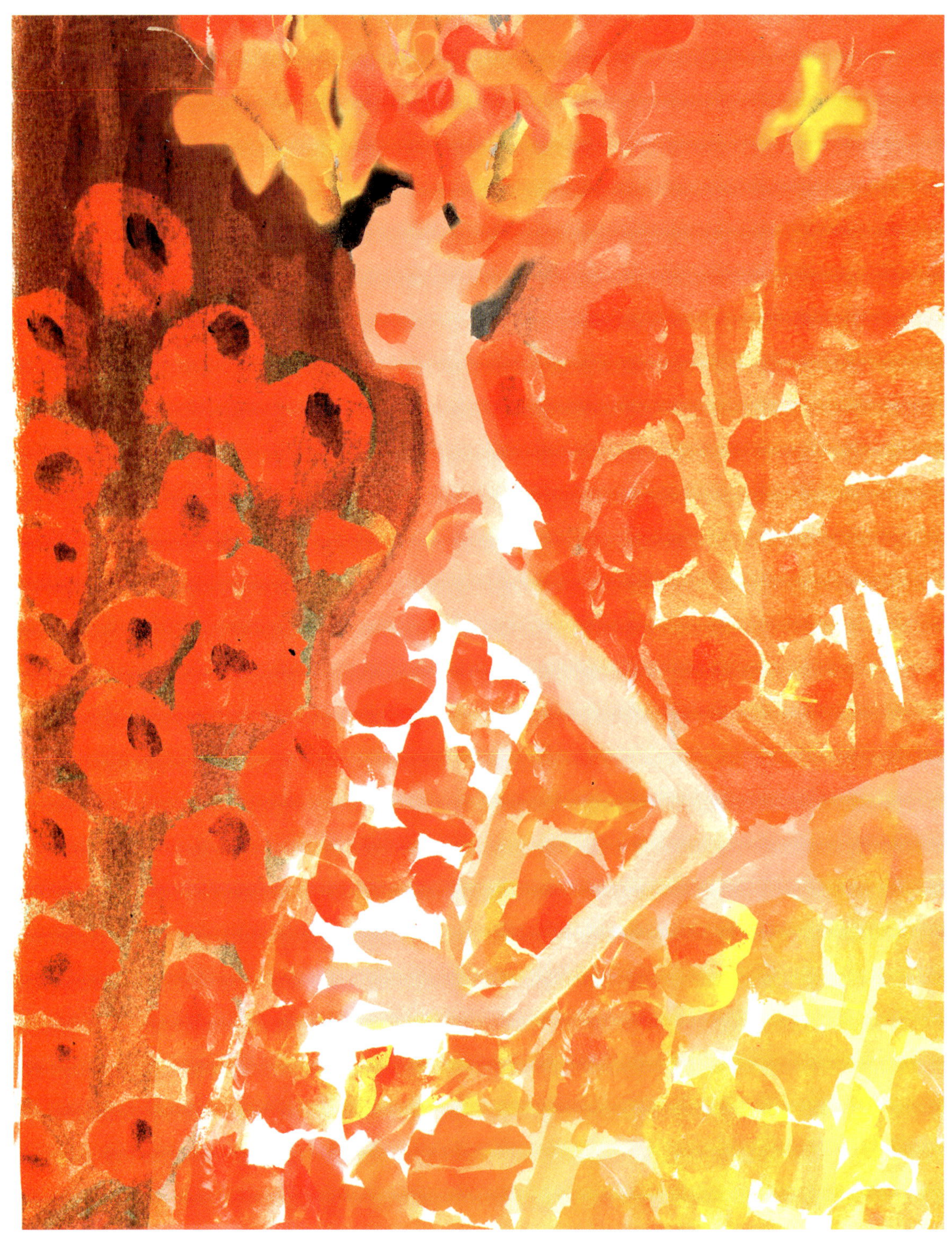

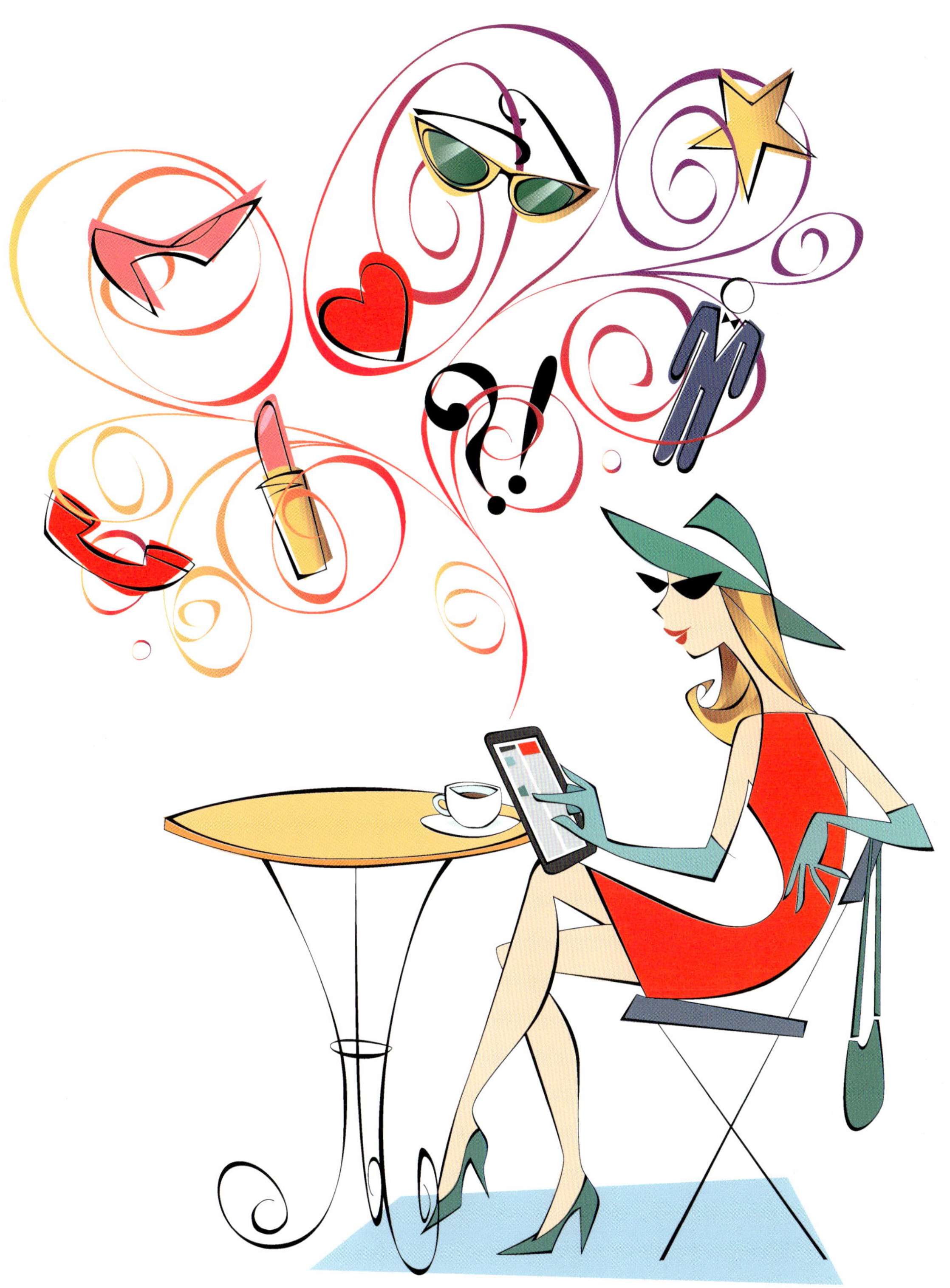

LINDGREN ◣ SMITH
{212} 397-7330
Kim Johnson
LINDGRENSMITH.COM
INFO@LSILLUSTRATION.COM

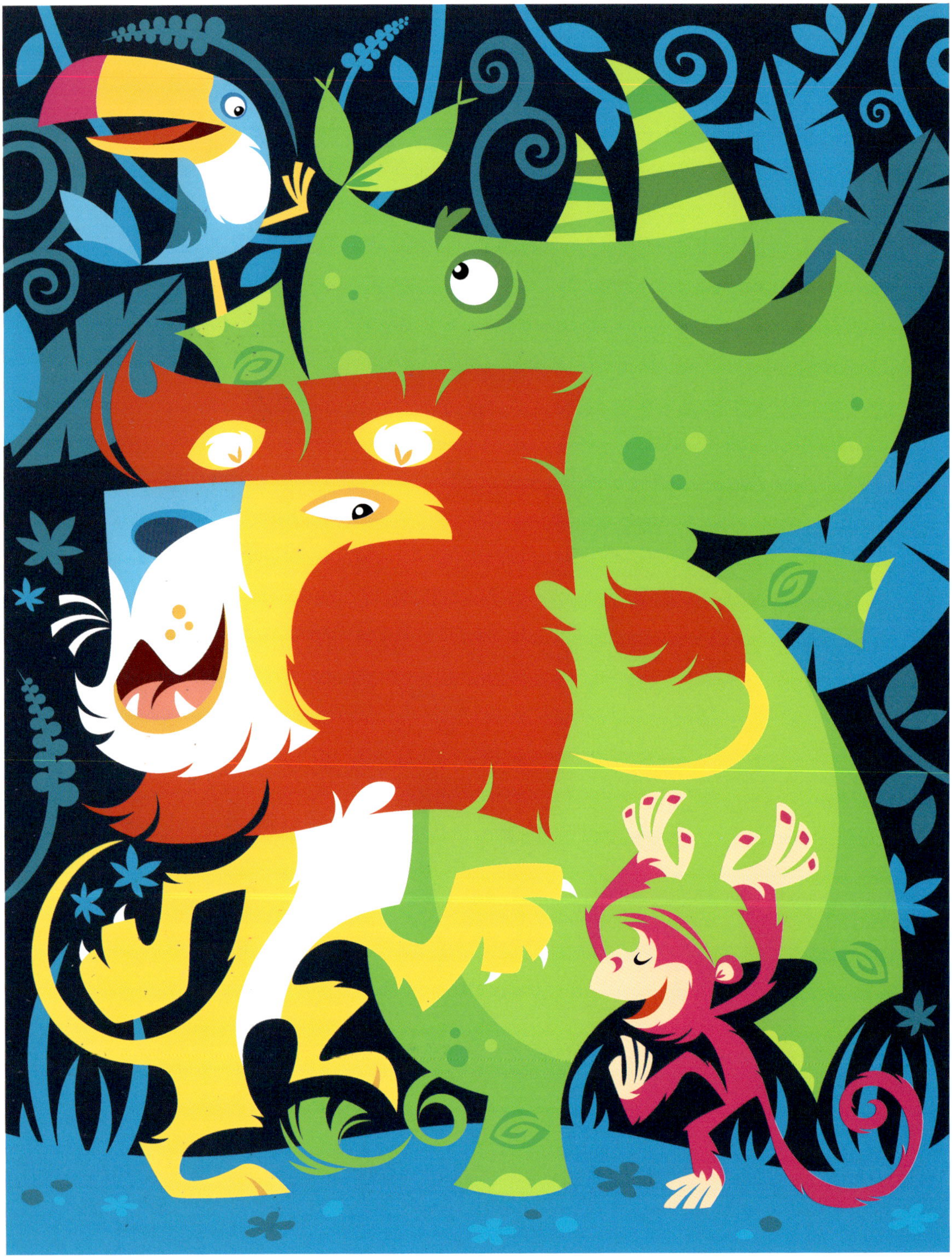

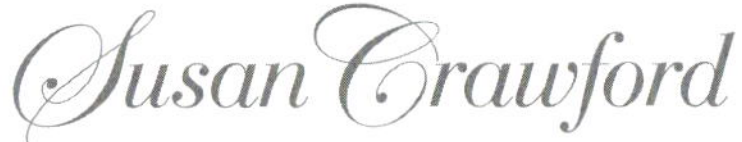

LINDGREN ◾ SMITH
{212} 397-7330
Susan Crawford
LINDGRENSMITH.COM
INFO@LSILLUSTRATION.COM

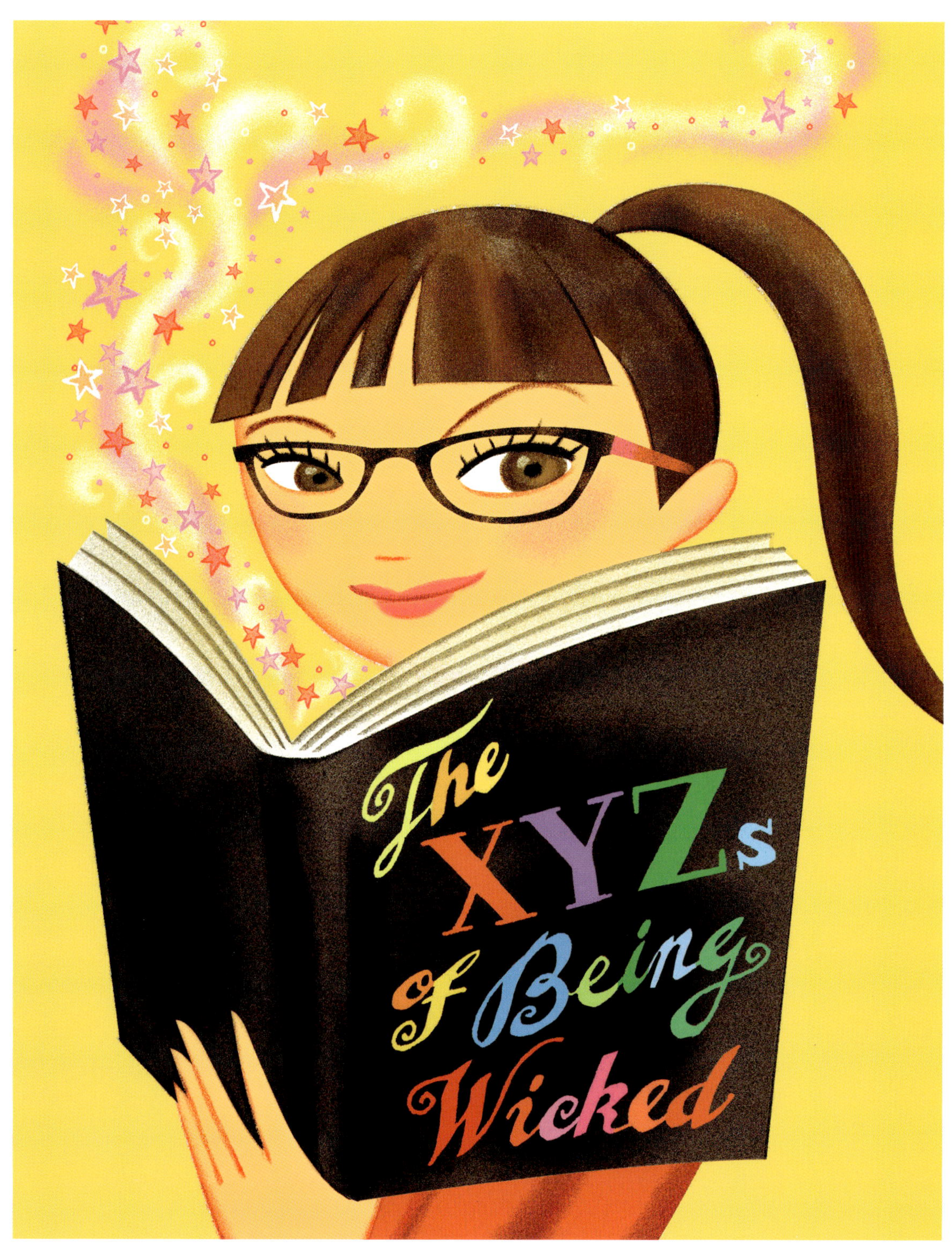

The XYZs of Being Wicked

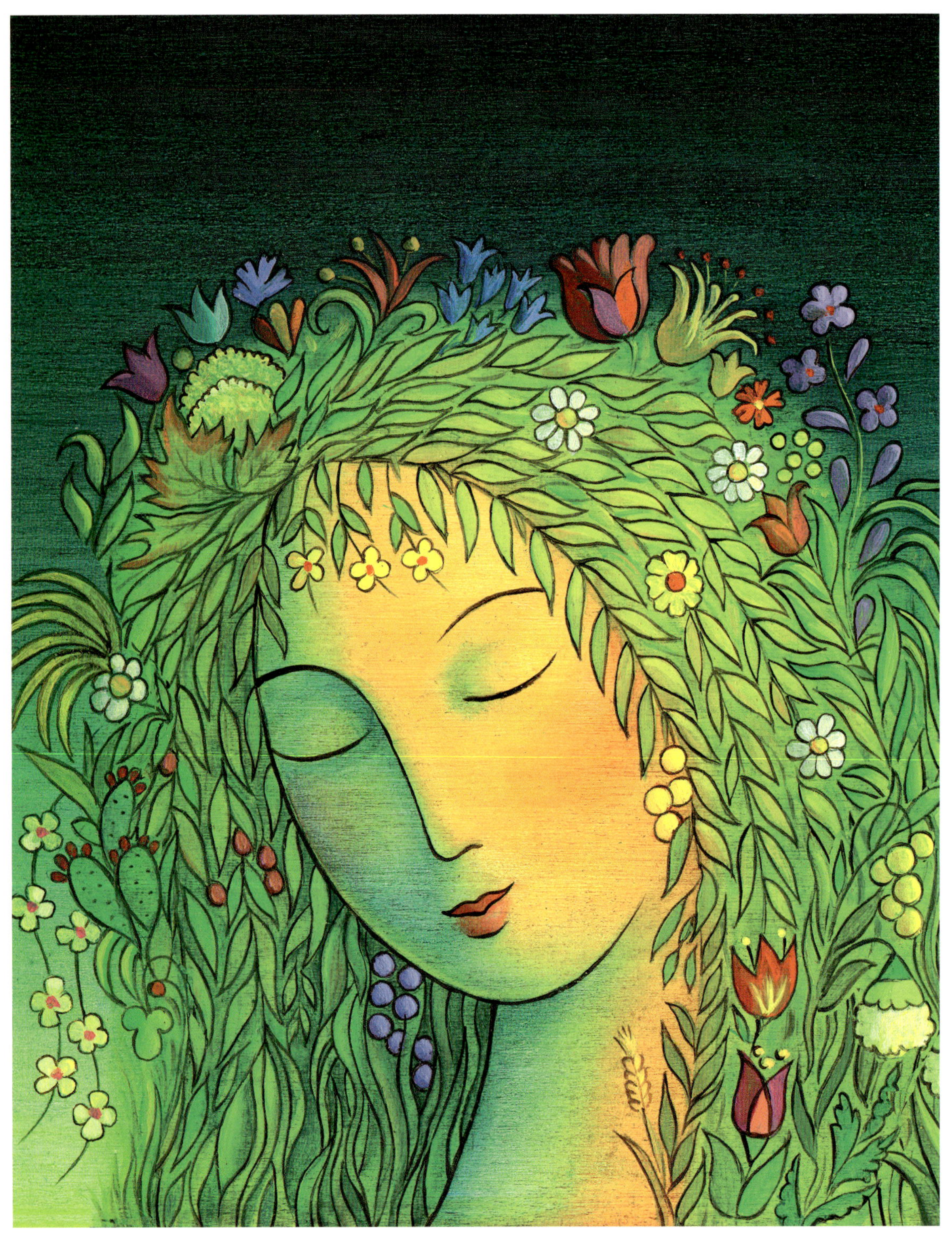

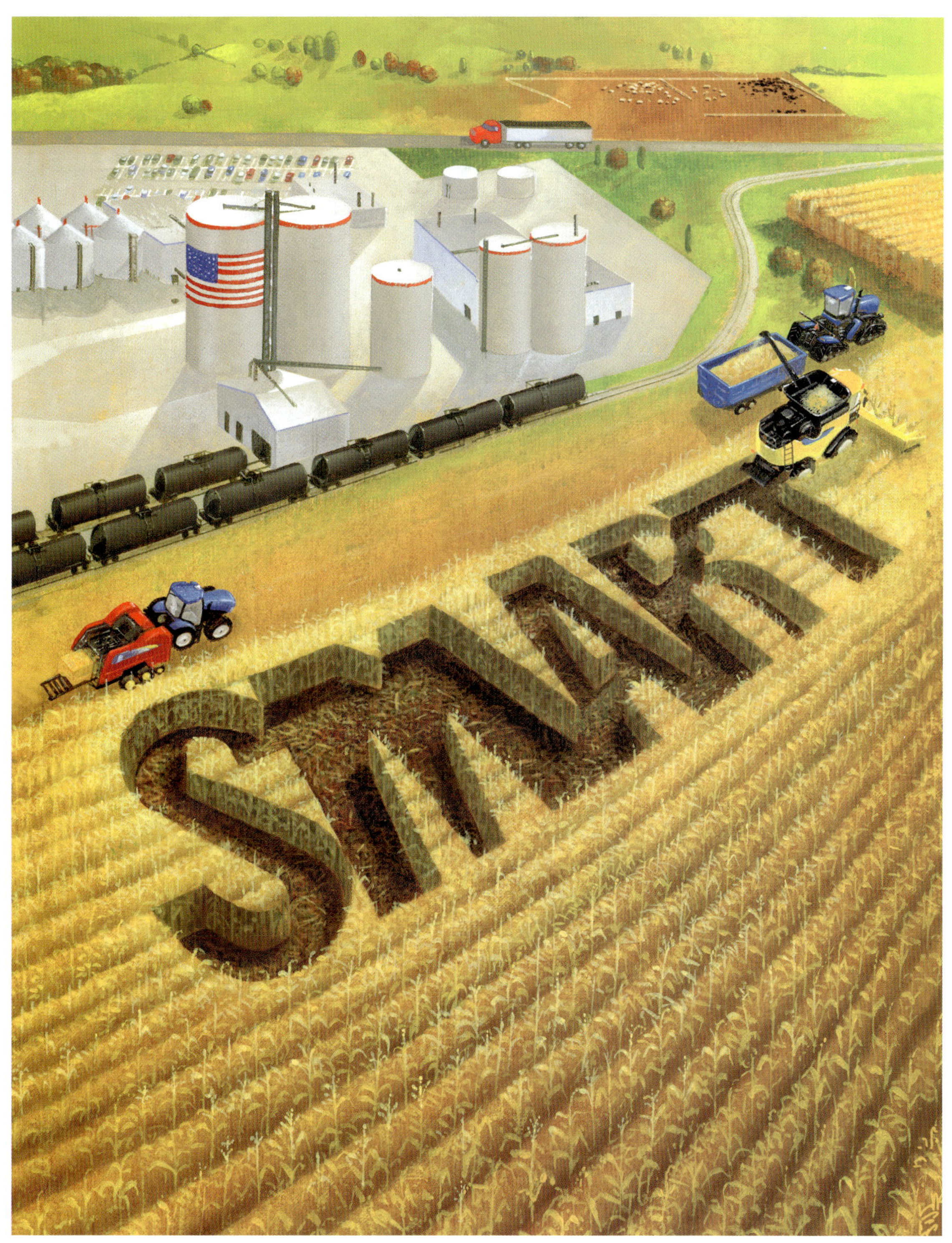

SMART

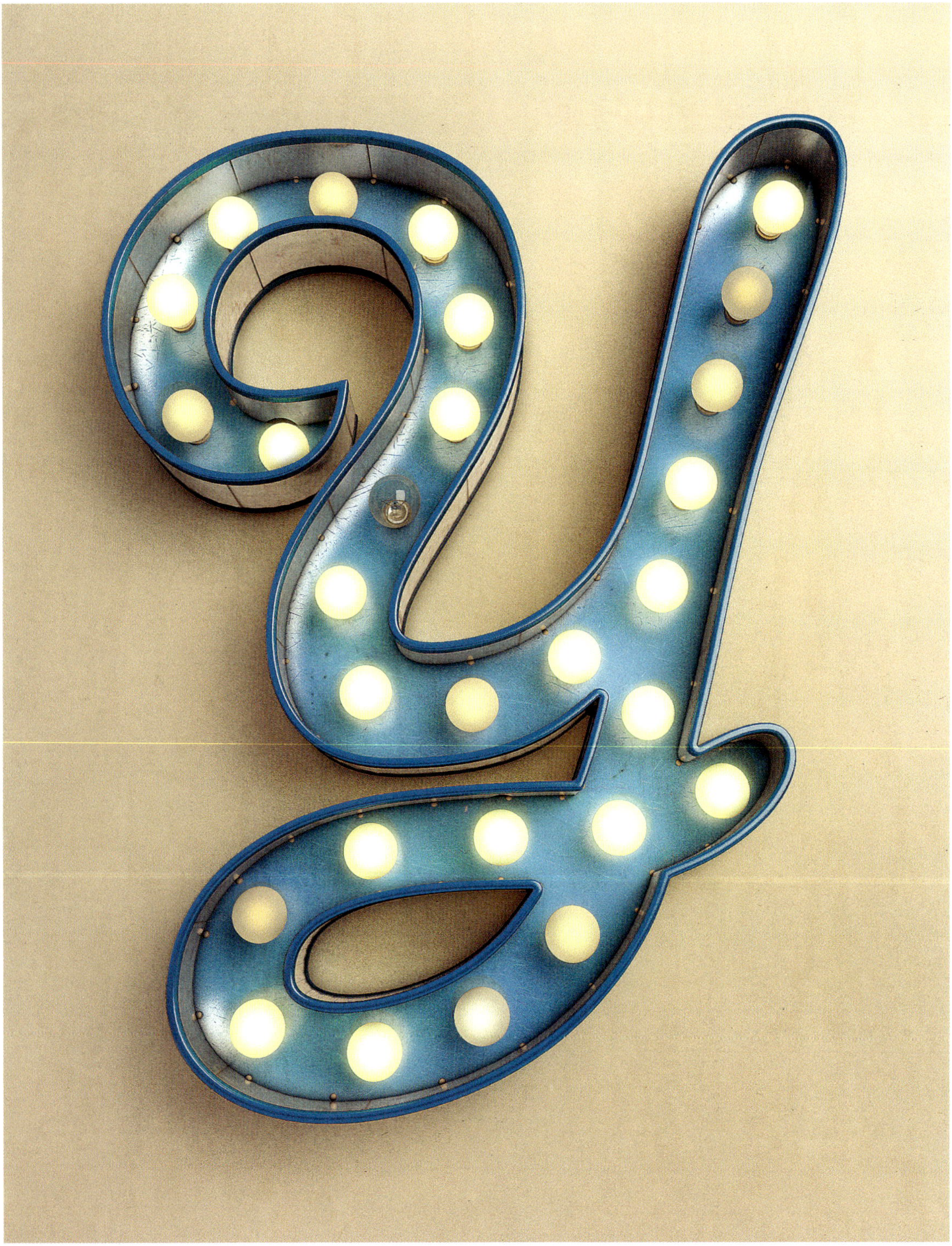

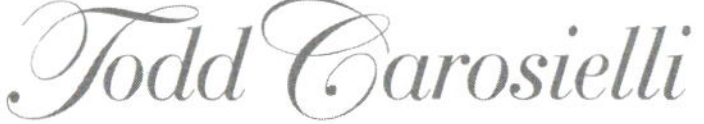
LINDGREN ■ SMITH
{212} 397-7330
Todd Carosielli
LINDGRENSMITH.COM
INFO@LSILLUSTRATION.COM

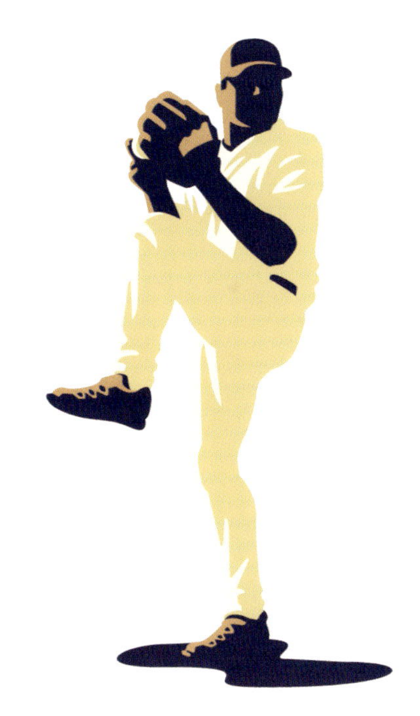

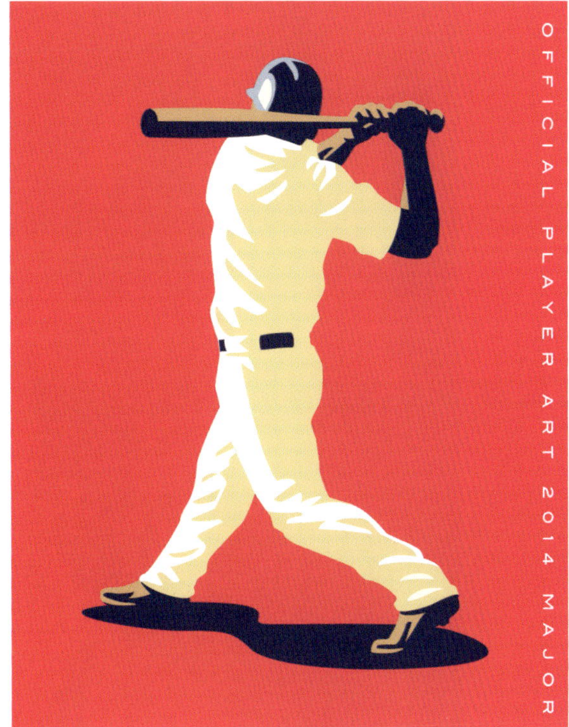

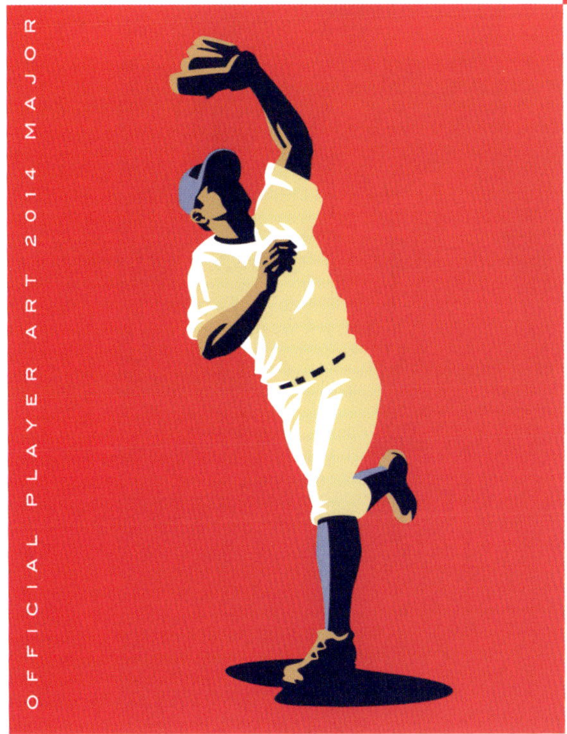

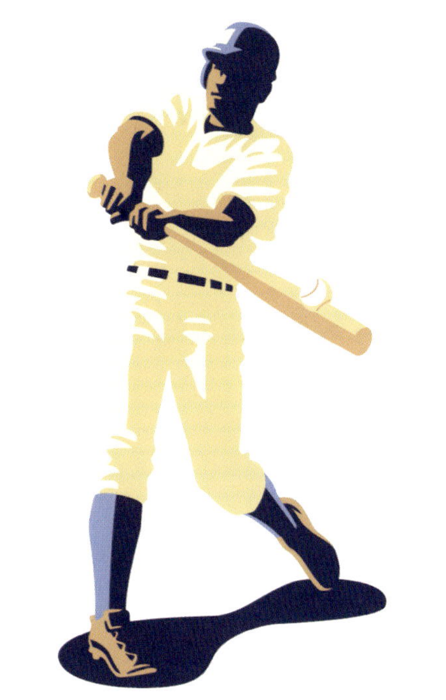

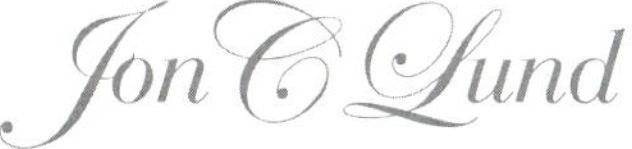

LINDGREN ◆ SMITH
{212} 397-7330

Jon C Lund

LINDGRENSMITH.COM
INFO@LSILLUSTRATION.COM

JULY 17-21
HIRSCH
CURAÇAO CURAÇAO
VERMOUTH DRY
tales of the
COCKTAIL
NEW ORLEANS
DRINK IT IN!

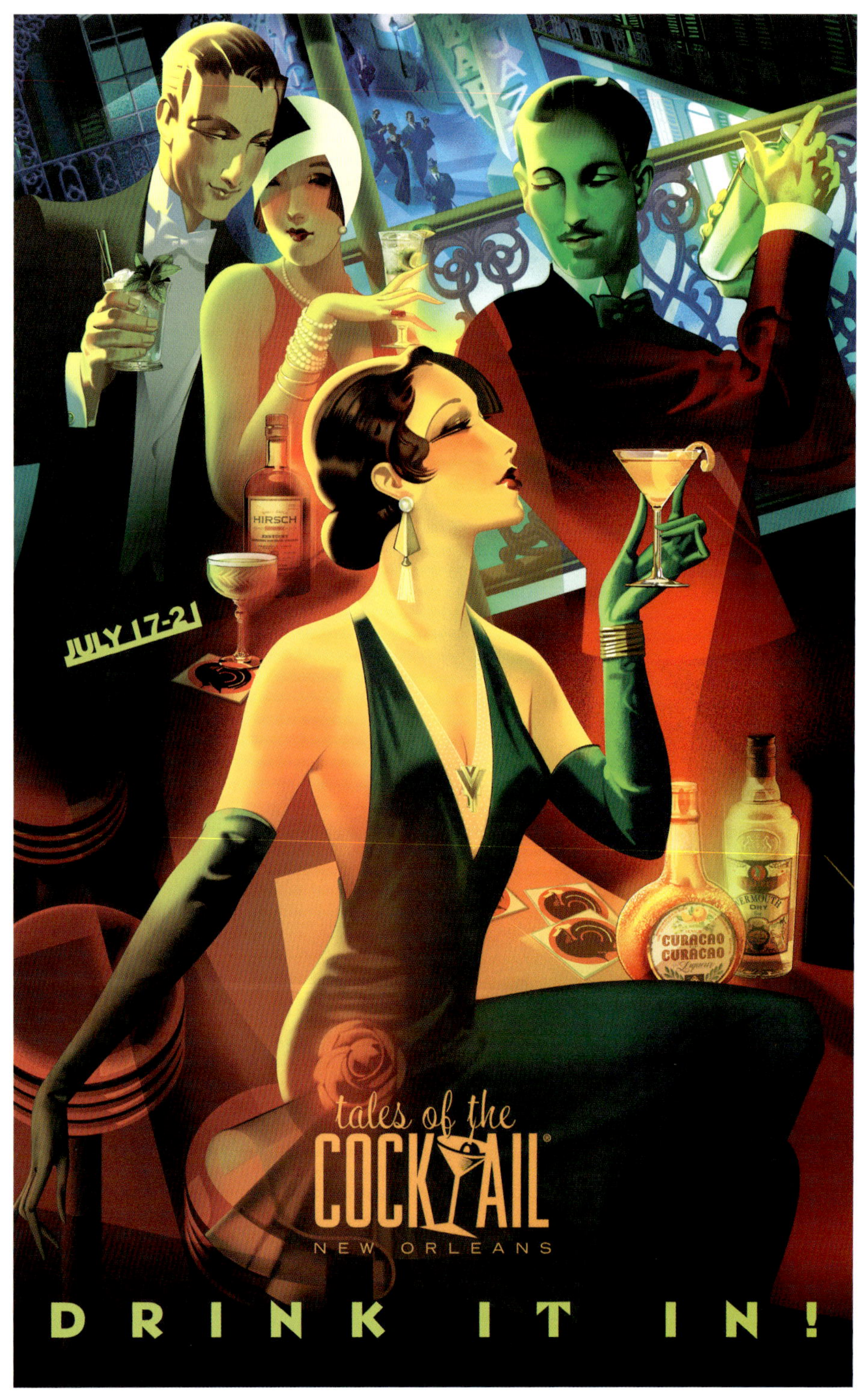

426

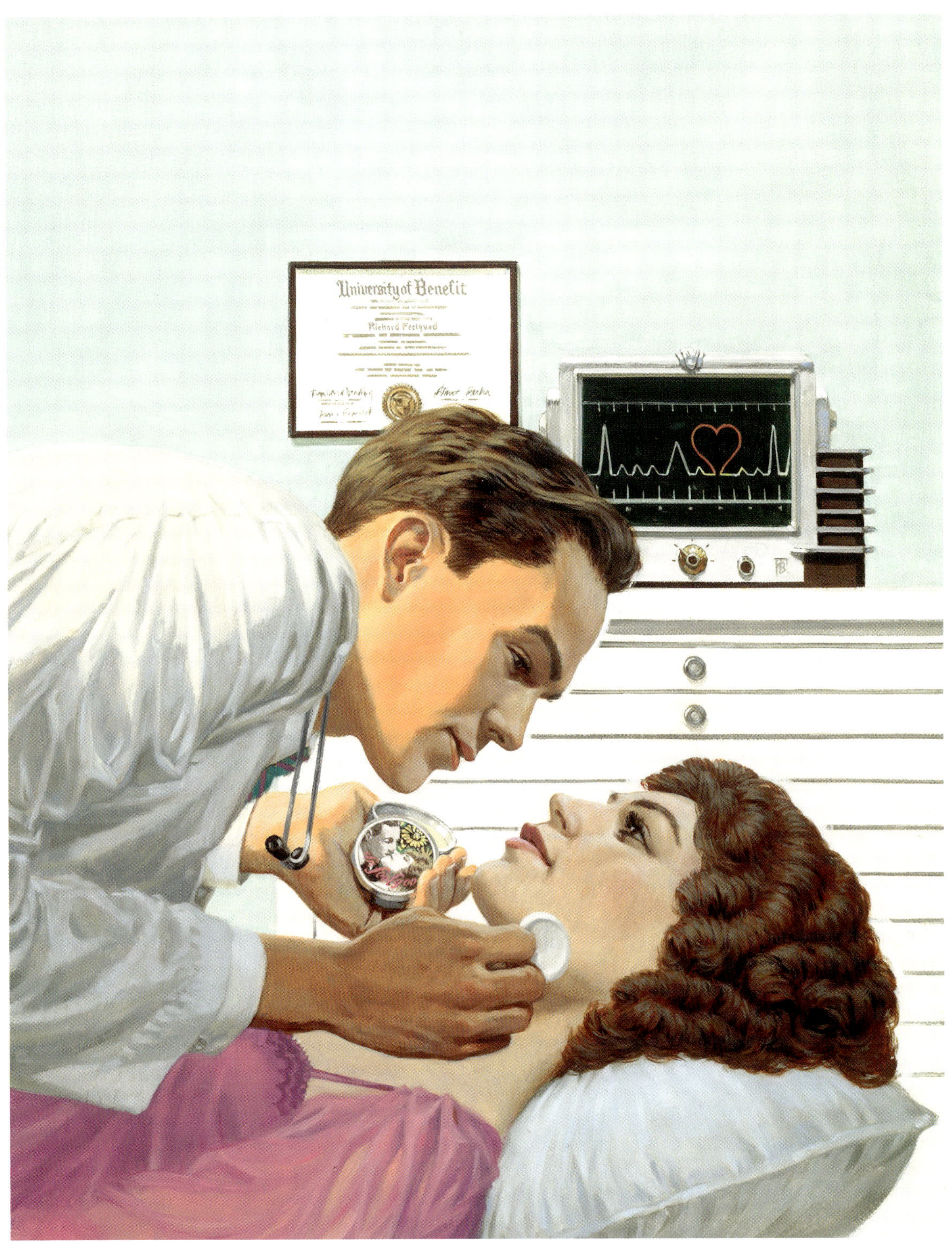

LINDGREN ■ SMITH
{212} 397-7330

Chuck Pyle

LINDGRENSMITH.COM
INFO@LSILLUSTRATION.COM

427

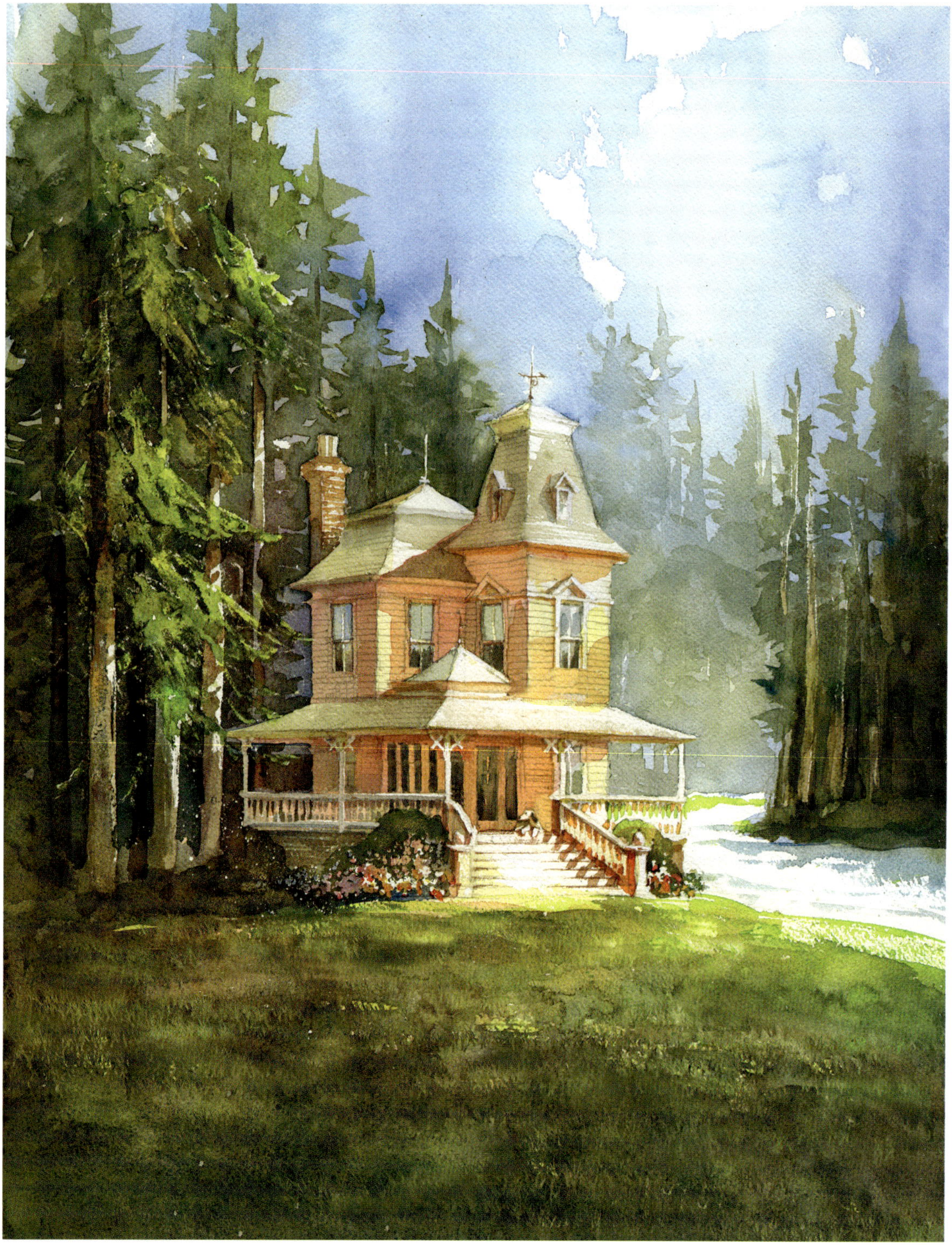

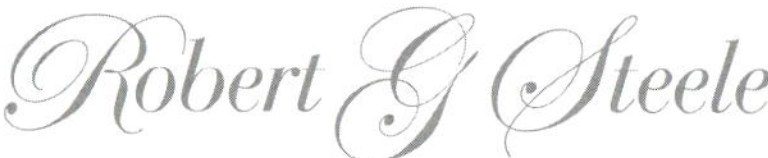

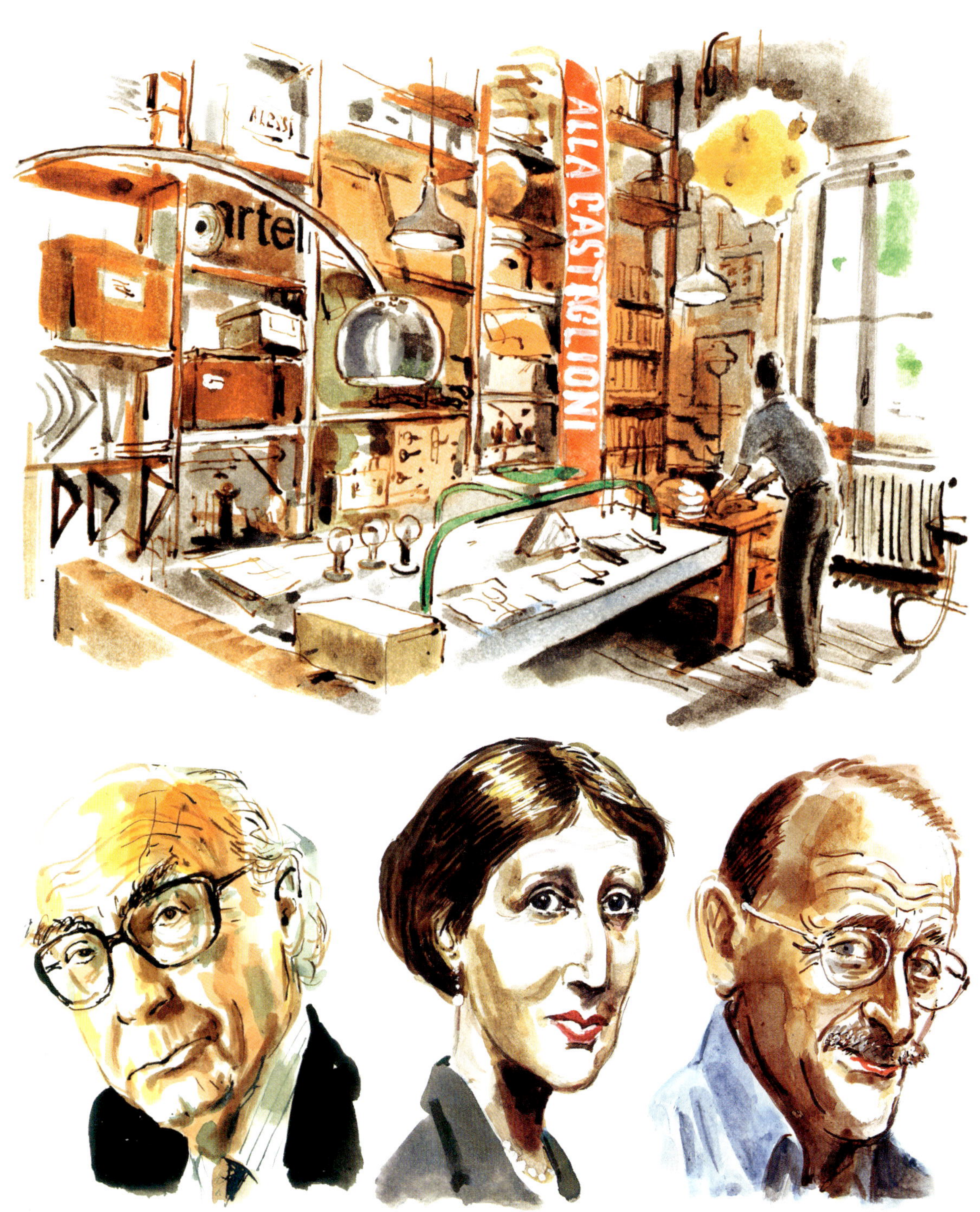

ALESSI
artell
ALLA CASTIGLIONI

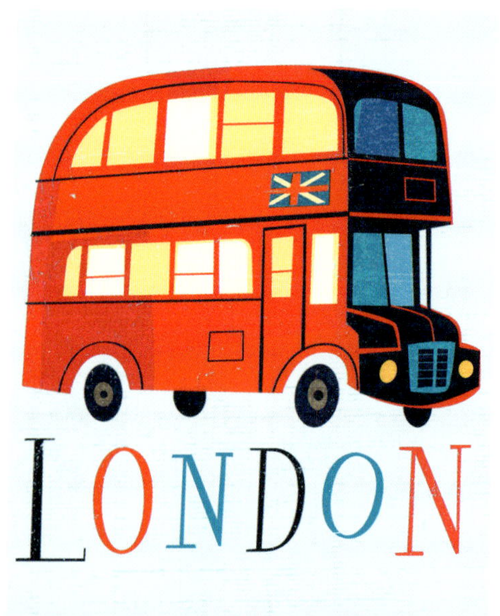

LONDON

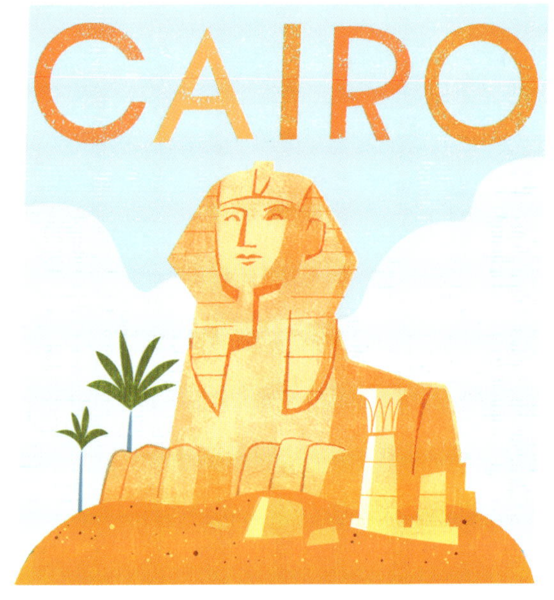

CAIRO

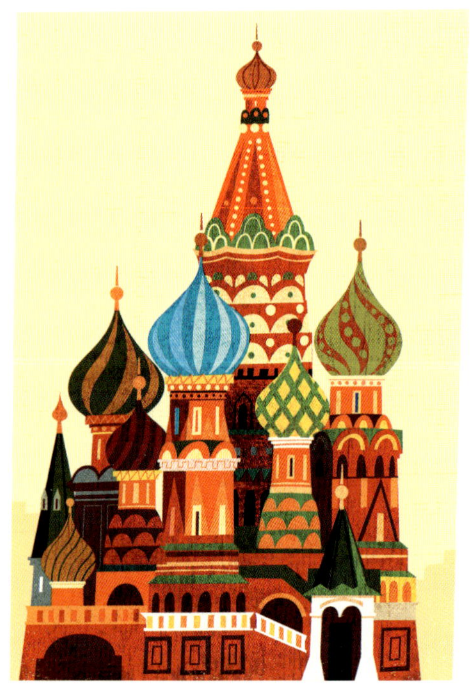

+ MOSCOW +

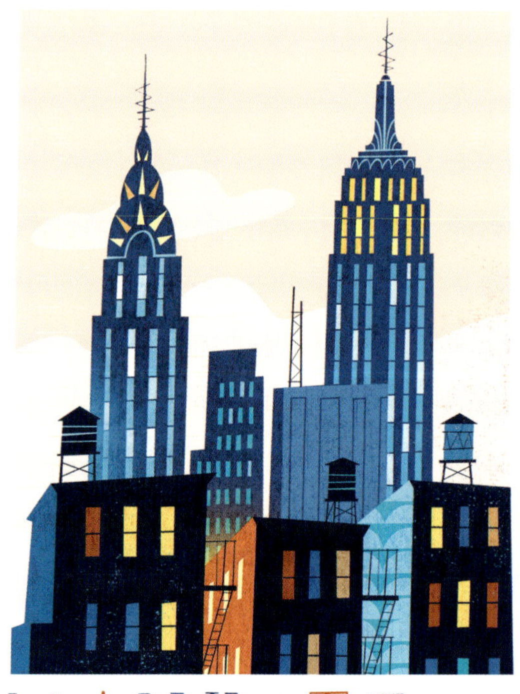

MANHATTAN

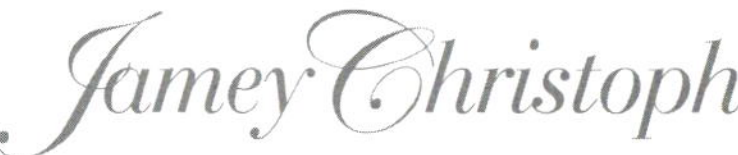

LINDGREN SMITH
{212} 397-7330
Jamey Christoph
LINDGRENSMITH.COM
INFO@LSILLUSTRATION.COM

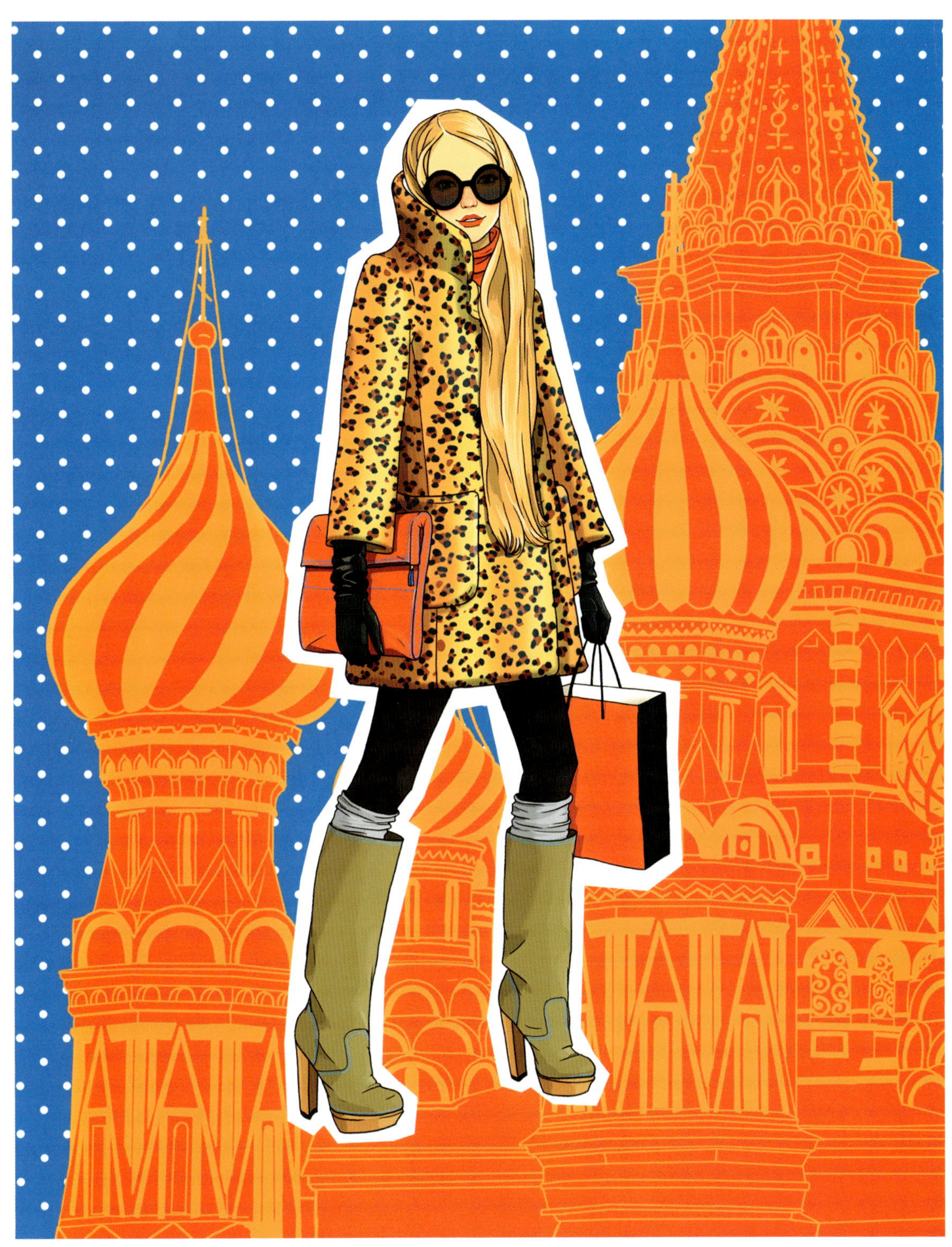

LINDGREN ◼ SMITH
{212} 397-7330
Anna Lazareva
LINDGRENSMITH.COM
INFO@LSILLUSTRATION.COM

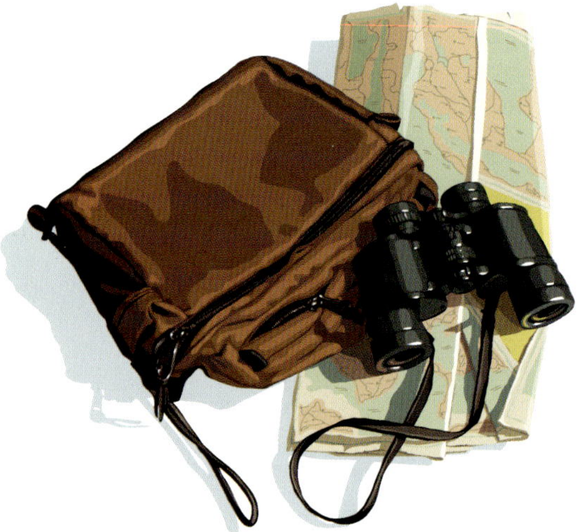

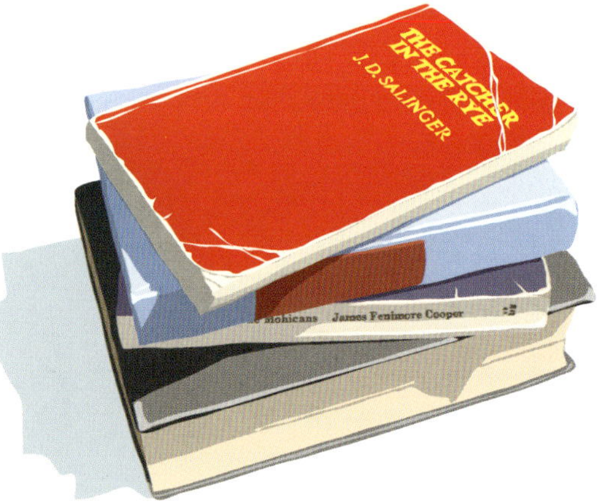

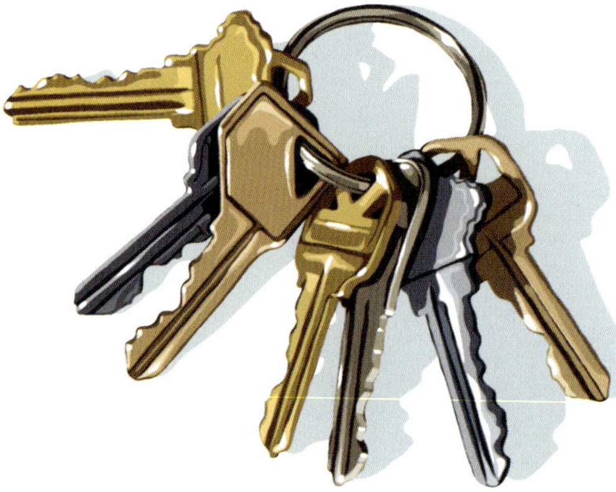

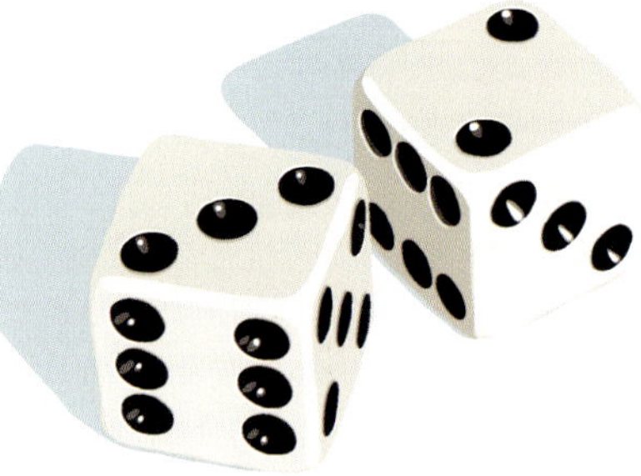

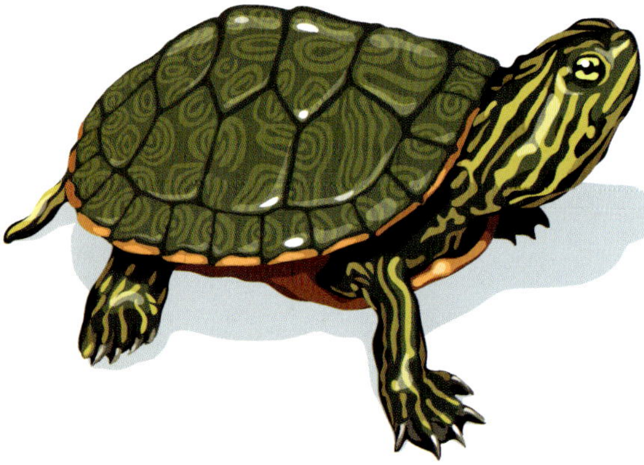

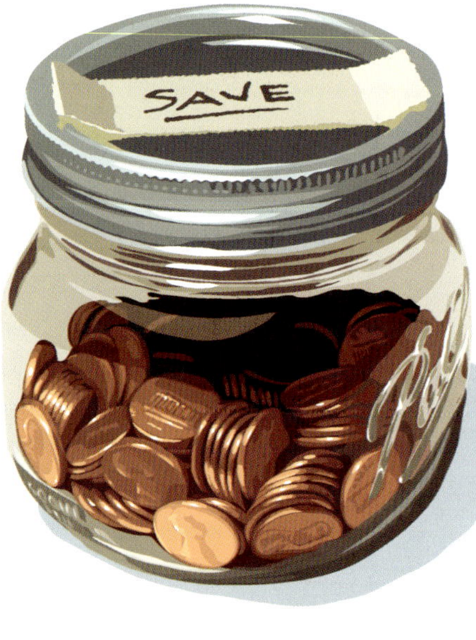

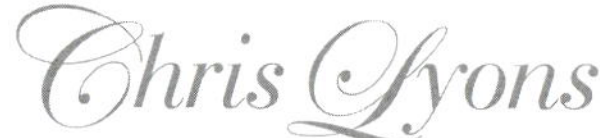

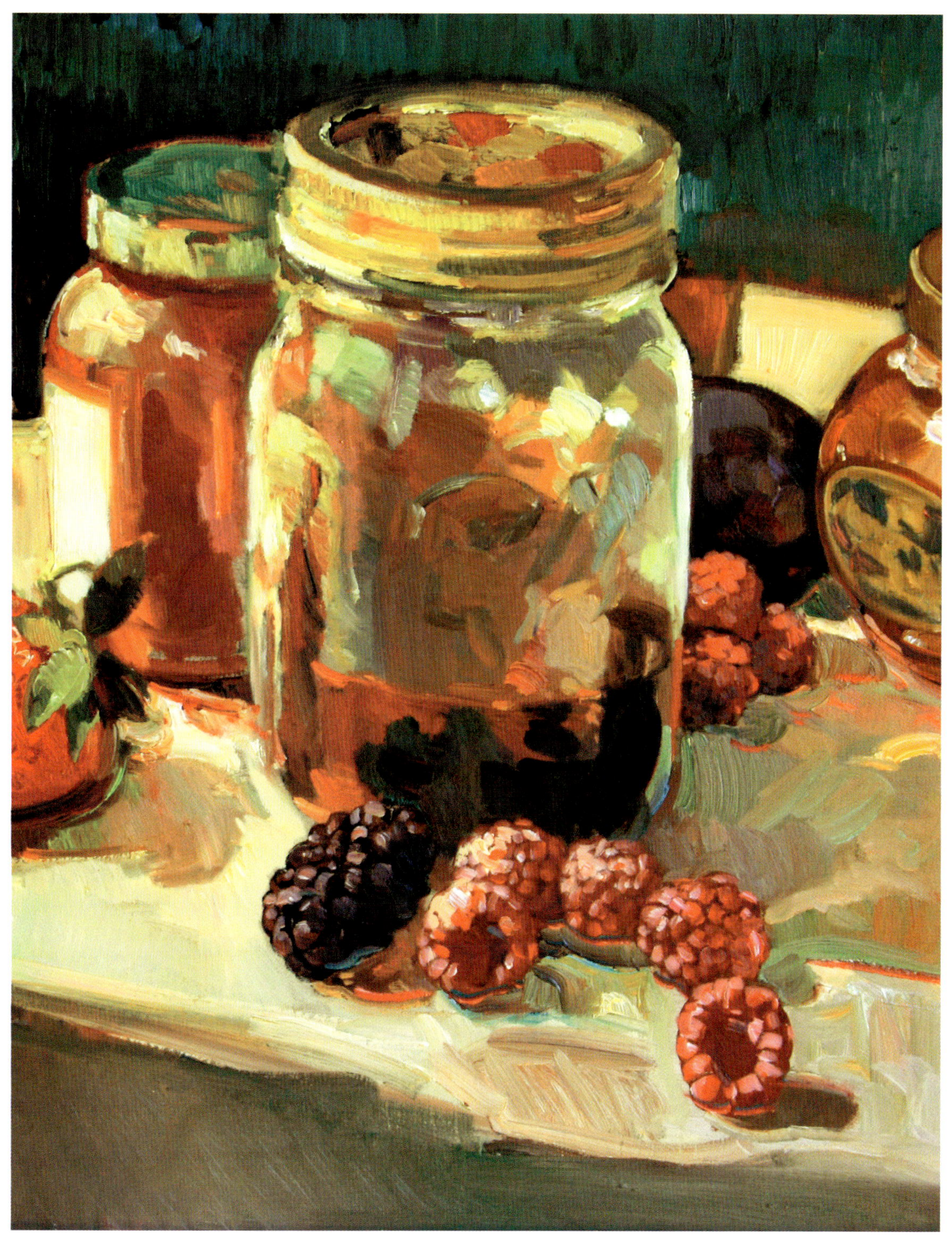

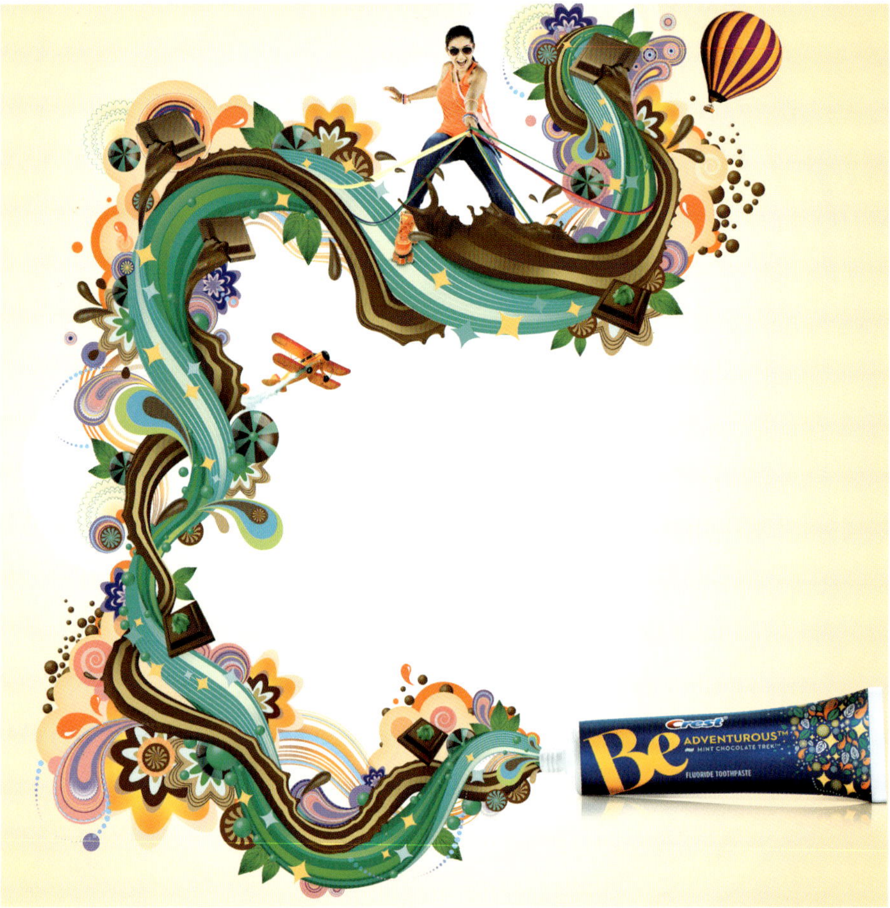

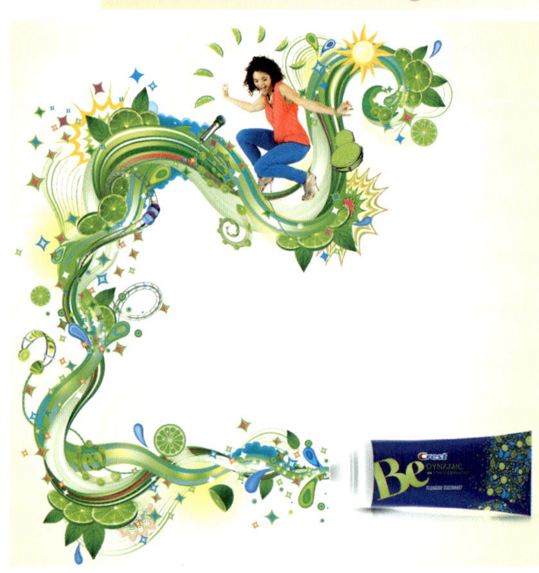

Crest
Be
DYNAMIC
FLUORIDE TOOTHPASTE

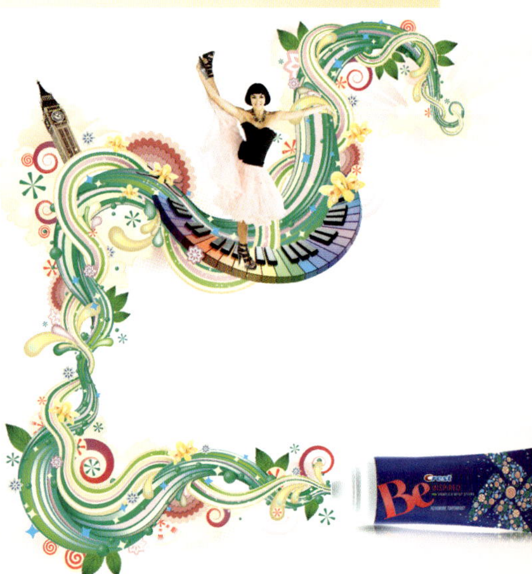

Crest
Be
INSPIRED
FLUORIDE TOOTHPASTE

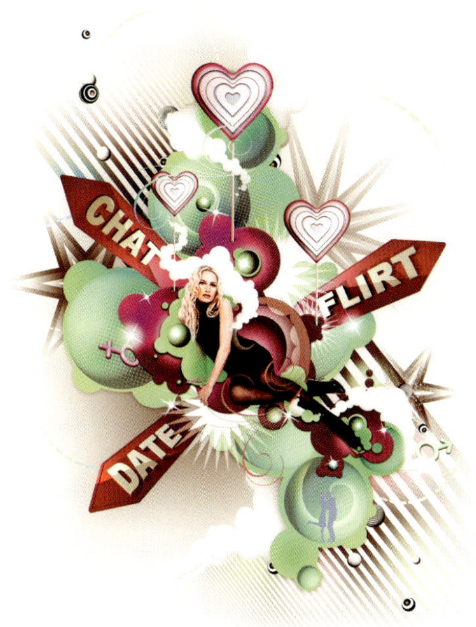
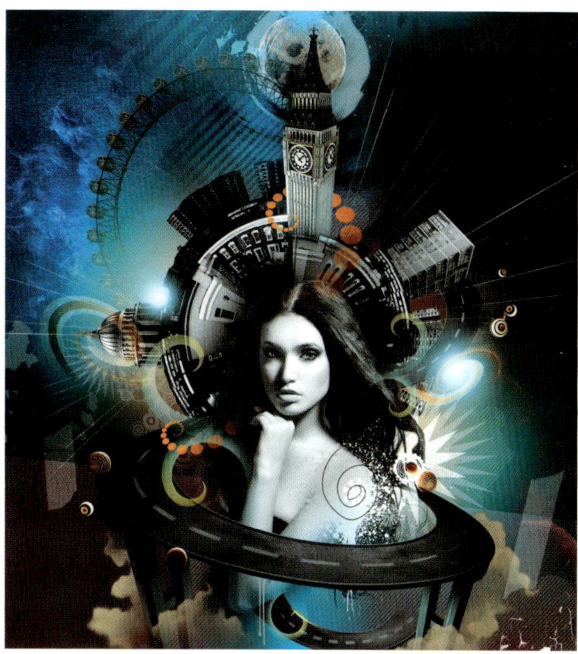

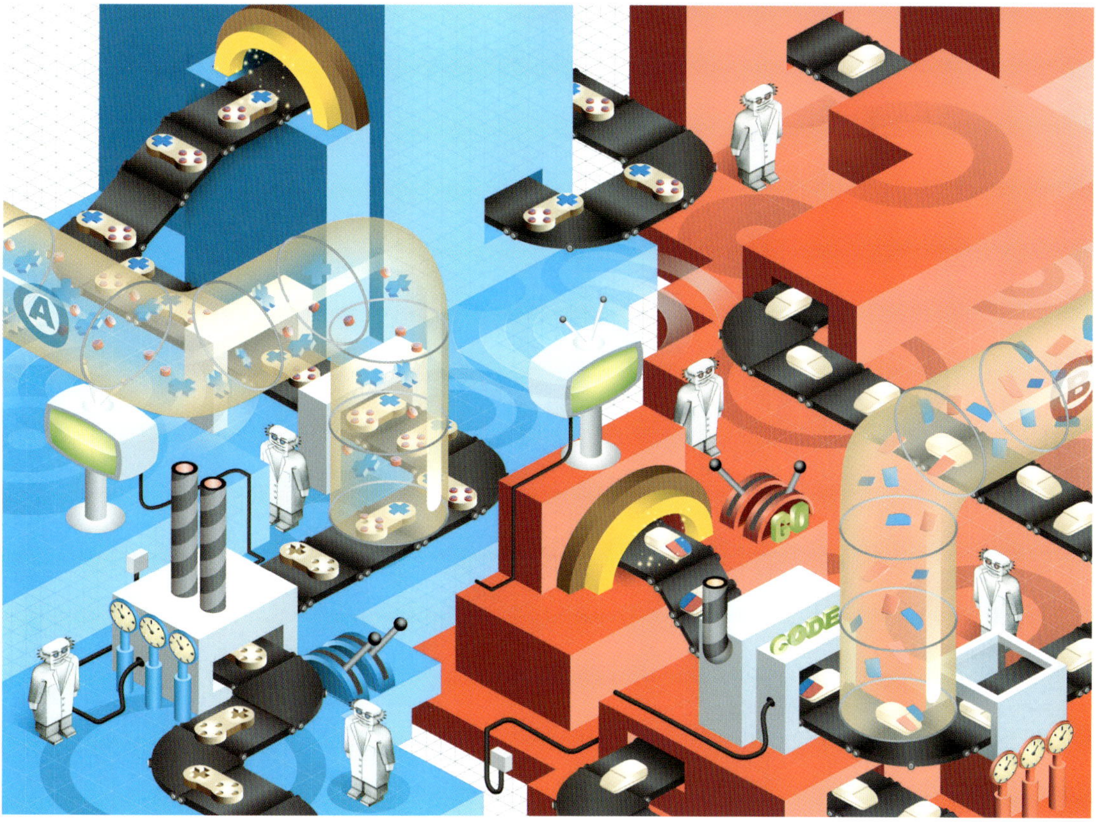

435